A DICTIONARY OF ARTISTS.

A

DICTIONARY OF ARTISTS

WHO HAVE EXHIBITED WORKS IN THE

PRINCIPAL LONDON EXHIBITIONS

FROM 1760 TO 1893

COMPILED BY

ALGERNON GRAVES, F.S.A.

AUTHOR OF

"A CATALOGUE OF THE WORKS OF SIR EDWIN LANDSEER, R.A.," "WORKS OF SAMUEL COUSINS, R.A.," "CATALOGUE OF THE WORKS OF SIR THOMAS LAWRENCE, P.R.A.," AND JOINT AUTHOR OF "HISTORY OF THE WORKS OF SIR JOSHUA REYNOLDS, P.R.A."

THIRD EDITION, WITH ADDITIONS AND CORRECTIONS

KINGSMEAD REPRINTS, BATH

Third Edition 1901
Facsimile Edition 1969
Reprinted 1970, 1973

KINGSMEAD REPRINTS
ROSEWELL HOUSE
KINGSMEAD SQUARE
BATH

SBN 901571 13 X

Reproduced and printed by photolithography and bound in Great Britain at The Pitman Press, Bath

PREFACE TO THE THIRD EDITION.

WHEN issuing the second edition of this work in 1895, it was in the hope that at some future time I might still further extend its scope. The calls on my own time subsequently rendering this utterly impossible, the task was voluntarily undertaken by my youngest son, Herbert Seymour, who displayed special aptitude and capability for the work, in which he had already made some progress in its continuation on the same lines, when unhappily a sudden illness and premature death in May, 1898, put an end to his labour of love.

The second edition being now exhausted, and the demand for the book continuing to increase, I have decided to reissue it without further alteration so far as the body of the work is concerned. The new edition, however, will I hope be of value to lovers of art, as it includes a large number of corrections which have been collected during the last seven years, as well as a list of those artists whose names have already appeared in the book, but who have since become members of one or other of the four principal art societies.

I take this opportunity of thanking all those friends and patrons of art who by their kind support made the two previous editions so successful, and trust they will take an equal interest in the present one, which is the last I intend to publish.

ALGERNON GRAVES.

6, Pall Mall.
March, 1901.

PREFACE TO THE FIRST EDITION.

THE object in publishing this "Dictionary of Artists" was to supply, if possible, a want long felt by myself, which may also be common to other students of the history of art. It was a desire to gain further information concerning the less known artists of England that prompted me to commence the series of manuscript lists, alphabetically arranged, of the works of those artists who had contributed to the five principal places of exhibition in London. The series completed down to the year 1880, which included nearly 16,000 names, has already been found of great use not only by myself but also by such critics and students of art as have consulted it.

As the cost of printing the whole series would have been too great, I have extracted such particulars as could be compressed into one line, with the endeavour, so far as I was able, during limited leisure time, to ascertain the full Christian names of the artists mentioned. Strange though it may seem, the catalogues of the different exhibitions have been of little use for this purpose, as from the first the compilers have either not been supplied with a full name with the pictures, or else they have neglected to print it. This defect has of late been corrected to a great extent, but there still remains much to be done, and I trust that for the future those gentlemen who may be responsible for the accuracy of catalogues of the various exhibitions will be more careful both to print those names supplied to them, and to request that all artists will clearly write their names in full. This may not at first seem necessary, but I am sure that all those who may refer to this Dictionary will, on finding a number of identical initials, be convinced that it will be of great service to future students of art to have the names in full. In the earliest catalogues extant the authors simply printed "Mr." (without the Christian name or initials), and this is the reason why so many names have no initial at all in this Dictionary. In the Royal Academy catalogues only are the full Christian names of members and associates printed, while at the Society of British Artists, Suffolk Street, even the secretaries do not know the Christian names of many of their own members. In the books themselves containing the signatures of membership, a scrutiny has shown that even in them, in a majority of cases, only initials have been used.

I shall be very grateful to anyone who will kindly forward me any Christian names of Artists still wanting, as also the maiden names of any of the married lady artists. Lack of information on this point has been a source of great difficulty to me, and I at one time contemplated deferring the publication of this Dictionary until the names were obtained, but it would have taken too long a time, and I hoped that its publication would enable me to get information from sources not at present available. The names of married ladies have in all cases been inserted under two headings, hence those works exhibited after their marriage have been kept distinct from those (if any) executed previously, consequently my entries will be correct even where I have failed to note cases in which two names indicate only one lady artist.

The type having been distributed as the work proceeded, many Christian names have been ascertained too late for insertion, but I shall always be pleased to give such additional information.

The names contained in this Dictionary include those of painters in oil and water-colour, also those of Architects, Engravers, Medallists, Sculptors, &c.; in fact, of everyone who has contributed to the exhibitions quoted for the last hundred and twenty years.

It will be found on referring to this work that one of its chief uses is the distinction between different members of one family, and it is by mistakes in this respect that so many dealers in works of art become confused. I have often been assured that there was only one "Glover" or two "Nasmyths," whereas there have been several artists of these names in both families, the authorship of whose works is often wrongly described. This also applies to some other artistic families. The name of the place from which the first exhibit was sent will enable an inquirer to determine the names of the followers of any particular school, such as that of "Norwich," and it is astonishing to note how few are able from memory to give more than the names of the principal artists belonging to any local school. If the numbers in only one series of exhibition catalogues were given it would form no criterion as to the relative number of works executed by each artist, but from a consideration of the numbers in five distinct series, we can form, in most cases, a very accurate idea. With respect to miniature painters, where five or six works have been exhibited in one frame, these have been treated as only one exhibit.

The fact that the Grosvenor Gallery has not been included in the list of principal exhibitions, seems to demand some explanation. Until 1880 there had been only four exhibitions, from which the number of works exhibited up to that date was not so large as to make it worth while to add another column to this Dictionary. A second edition, however, should I ever be able to complete one, would include both the Grosvenor and the two Water-Colour Societies.

The authorities from which many Christian names of artists have been taken are Redgrave's "Dictionary of Artists of the English School," and "Artists of the Nineteenth Century and their Works," by Clement and Hutton.

ALGERNON GRAVES.

6, PALL MALL.
February 24th, 1884.

PREFACE TO THE SECOND EDITION.

WHEN I began to compile a "Dictionary of Artists," my intention was to issue a new edition every ten years; but the responsibilities of the publishing house of Henry Graves and Co., which had been managed by my father nearly until his death in 1892, compelled me to abandon that idea, and decide to bring the work, in its present more copious and enlarged form, down to 1893, including the Winter as well as the Summer Exhibitions of every important London gallery. Besides adding all the new exhibitors of the last thirteen years, I have, through the whole range of the present work, made many improvements which were suggested by the use of the first version. By the introduction of the two great water-colour societies, the record of artists in that medium is now complete; the Portland Gallery brings Rossetti into view, and the "Associated Artists" includes many early English water-colour painters who did not join the Old Society. The Dudley "Black and White" introduces many engravers and etchers who are celebrated in those interesting branches of design. In the column describing Various Exhibitions (incorporated to save space) it will be possible by the dates which are given in the "List of Exhibitions" to recognize the different Societies.

In the 1880 edition instances occurred where two artists of the same name, not being members of any society, were placed as one; but, by means of reference to the addresses, and—where practicable—of communications made to the artists themselves, the exact numbers have now been allotted to each person.

In cases where a painter has worked in two or more modes, that in which he has the largest number of exhibits governs his designation.

In the section of miniatures more accuracy has been arrived at than before, by regarding each example as an exhibit, whereas, in the 1880 version of the Dictionary, a frame containing several miniatures was counted as one only.

More precision has been attained in the architectural section, where exhibits appear in the names of firms comprising two or more partners, by giving cross references to the individual members. This portion of the work has been carried out by my son Herbert.

The slips from which the present volume has been printed, preparing which cost me many years of unremitting care, shall be preserved, in order that they may be available for a further continuation, should a compiler of the future determine to undertake the labour.

To Collectors of Pictures, as well as to Fine Art Dealers, this Dictionary will be particularly useful, giving, as it does, the Artists' names and places of exhibition. To enter into further detail, by describing each exhibit, would necessitate such an enlargement of the work as to make its cost almost prohibitive; but it should be understood that the owner of any particular picture, painted by any of the artists herein scheduled, can, on application to Henry Graves and Co., ascertain whether such picture was an exhibited picture or not.

In conclusion, I may remark that any possessor of this Dictionary will be welcome to apply to me for information which could not be compressed into it, such as the titles of the works or the names of sitters for portraits, which, together with other valuable information, are contained in my manuscript volumes. These books are so arranged that reference can at once be made to the detailed list of the productions of any artist.

ALGERNON GRAVES.

6, PALL MALL.
May, 1895.

ABBREVIATIONS USED IN THIS WORK.

A.G.B.I. Artists' General Benevolent Institution.
A.I.B.A. Associate of the Institute of British Architects.
A.R.A. Associate of the Royal Academy.
A.R.C.A. Associate of the Royal Cambrian Academy.
A.R.H.A. Associate of the Royal Hibernian Academy.
A.R.I.B.A. Associate of the Royal Institute of British Architects.
A.R.P.E. Associate of the Royal Society of Painter-Etchers.
A.R.S.A. Associate of the Royal Scottish Academy.
A.R.W.S. Associate of the Royal Water-Colour Society.

Bart. Baronet.

C.B. Companion of the Bath.
C.E. Civil Engineer.
C.M.G. Companion of the Order of St. Michael and St. George.

D.C.L. Doctor of Civil Law.
D.D. Doctor of Divinity.

F.G.S. Fellow of the Geological Society.
F.I.B.A. Fellow of the Institute of British Architects.
F.R.A.S. Fellow of the Royal Astronomical Society.
F.R.C.S. Fellow of the Royal College of Surgeons.
F.R.G.S. Fellow of the Royal Geographical Society.
F.R.I.A. Fellow of the Royal Institute of Architects.
F.R.I.B.A. Fellow of the Royal Institute of British Architects.
F.R.S. Fellow of the Royal Society.
F.R.S.L. Fellow of the Royal Society of Literature.
F.S.A. Fellow of the Society of Artists (before 1791).
F.S.A. Fellow of the Society of Antiquaries.
F.S.B.A. Fellow of the Society of British Architects.
F.S.C.E. Fellow of the Society of Civil Engineers.

H.F.R.A. Honorary Foreign Royal Academician.
H.F.R.P.E. Honorary Fellow of Royal Society of Painter-Etchers.
H.P.R.I. Honorary President of Royal Institute of Painters in Water-Colours.
H.R.C.A. Honorary Royal Cambrian Academician.
H.R.I. Honorary Member of Royal Institute of Painters in Water-Colours.
H.R.S.A. Honorary Royal Scottish Academician.
H.R.S.W. Honorary Member of Royal Scottish Water-Colour Society.
H.R.W.S. Honorary Member of the Royal Water-Colour Society.

K.C.B. Knight Commander of the Order of the Bath.
K.L. } K.S.L. } Knight of St. Luke's Academy, Rome.
K.T. Knight of the Order of the Thistle.

LL.D. Doctor of Laws.

M.A. Master of Arts.
M.A.F. Member of the Academy of Florence.
M.D. Doctor of Medicine.
M.I.B.A. Member of Institute of British Architects.
M.P. Member of Parliament.
M.R.I.A. Member of the Royal Institute of Architects.
M.R.I.B.A. Member of the Royal Institute of British Architects.
M.V.O. Member of the Royal Victorian Order.

N.A. Member of National Academy of America.

P.N.W.S. President of the New Water-Colour Society.
P.O.W.S. President of the Old Water-Colour Society.
P.R.A. President of the Royal Academy.
P.R.B.A. President of the Royal Society of British Artists.
P.R.C.A. President of the Royal Cambrian Academy.
P.R.H.A. President of the Royal Hibernian Academy.
P.R.I.B.A. President of the Royal Institute of British Architects.
P.R.P.E. President of the Royal Society of Painter-Etchers.
P.R.S.A. President of the Royal Scottish Academy.
P.R.S.W. President of the Royal Scottish Water-Colour Society.
P.R.W.S. President of the Royal Water-Colour Society.
P.S.B.A. President of the Society of British Artists.

R.A. Royal Academician.
R.A. Royal Artillery.
R.B.A. Member of the Royal Society of British Artists.
R.C.A. Royal Cambrian Academician.
R.E. Royal Engineers.
R.H.A. Royal Hibernian Academician.
R.I. Royal Institute of Painters in Water-Colours.
R.N. Royal Navy.
R.P.E. Member of the Royal Society of Painter-Etchers.
R.S.A. Royal Scottish Academician.
R.S.W. Member of the Royal Scottish Water-Colour Society.
R.W.S. Member of the Royal Water-Colour Society.

V.P.I.O. Vice-President Institute of Painters in Oil.
V.P.N.W.S. Vice-President of the New Water-Colour Society.
V.P.R.C.A. Vice-President of the Royal Cambrian Academy.
V.P.R.I. Vice-President of the Royal Institute of Painters in Water-Colours.
V.P.R.I.B.A. Vice-President of the Royal Institute of British Architects.

LIST OF EXHIBITIONS INCLUDED IN THE DICTIONARY, WITH THE DATES OF THEIR FOUNDATIONS AND (WHEN EXTINCT) THEIR BEING CLOSED.

	FOUNDED.	CEASED.	EXISTING.
Society of Artists	1760	1791	——
Free Society of Artists	1761	1783	——
Royal Academy	1769	——	1893
British Institution	1806	1867	——
Society of British Artists	1824	——	1893
Royal Water-colour Society	1805	——	1893
Royal Institute, previously the New Water-colour Society	1832	——	1893
Grosvenor Gallery	1878	1890	——
New Gallery	1888	——	1893
Various Exhibitions.			
Associated Artists (Water-colour)	1808	1815	——
Portland Gallery	1848	1861	——
Dudley Gallery (Water-colour)	1865	1882	——
Dudley Gallery (Oil-colour)	1867	1882	——
Dudley Gallery (Black and White)	1872	1882	——
Institute of Oil Painters	1883	——	1893
Society of Portrait Painters	1891	——	1893

By comparing the dates of those artists who have numbers in the "Various Exhibitions" column with the above list, it will be possible to recognize to which Exhibition he contributed.

ADDITIONS AND CORRECTIONS.

Abbey, Edwin Austin, R.A., R.I., A.R.W.S. † ‡
Aborn, John, R.B.A. §
Adam, Patrick W., R.S.A.
Adams, Colonel George Gammon, F.S.A.
Adams, John Talbot.
Aitchison, George, R.A.
Aldham, Miss Harriet Kate.
Alken, Henry. *For* "Southampton" *read* "London."
Allan, Mrs. Archibald. *See* Miss Eliza Mann.
Allan, Robert Weir, R.W.S., R.S.W. † φ
Allbon, Charles Frederick, A.R.P.E.
Allen, C. Bruce.
Allen, Miss Margaret, H.R.H.A.
Alma-Tadema, Sir Lawrence, R.A., &c., *add* H.F.R.P.E.
Almond, W. Douglas, R.I., R.B.A. ‡ §
Alpenny, James S.
Alsop, J. J., R.B.A. §
Ambrose, Edward.
Amendola, Giovanni B.
Anderson, John F.
Archer, Edward, *not* Edwin.
Argyle, H.R.H. Louise, Duchess of. *See* Louise.
Armstrong, Miss Elizabeth A. *See* Mrs. S. A. Forbes.
Armstrong, Robert W.
Armitage, Edward, R.A. *For* "1840" *read* "1848."
Atkins, James.
Atkinson, George Mounsey.

Baker, Oliver, R.P.E.
Baker, Samuel H., R.P.E.
Ball, Wilfred Williams, R.P.E.
Ball-Hughes, Miss Georgina. *For* "Portraits" *read* "Miniatures."
Barker, Wright, R.B.A. §
Barlow, John Noble, R.B.A. §
Barratt, Reginald R., A.R.W.S. †
Barrett, Thomas, A.R.P.E.
Barter, Richard.
Barton, Miss Rose M., A.R.W.S. †
Baskett, Charles E., A.R.P.E.
Battersby, Edward.
Bayes, Alfred Walter, A.R.P.E.
Bayes, Walter J., A.R.W.S. †
Bayliss, Sir Wyke, P.R.B A., F.S.A. §
Baynes, Frederick T. Grandson of James Baynes.
Baynes, Thomas Man. Son of James Baynes.
Beechey, Admiral Richard Brydges, R.H.A.
Beetham, Miss J. *See* Mrs. Read. London, 1794-1797. Portraits R.A. 15, all the rest are Miss Betham.
Belcher, John, A.R.A.
Bell, Robert Anning, A.R.W.S. †
Bell, John. *For* "1831" *read* "1832."
Bentley, Joseph H., R.B.A. §
Berkeley, Mrs. Stanley. *See* Miss Edith Savill.
Betham, Miss. London 1804-1816. Miniatures:—R.A. 41, B.I. 3. O.W. 10, V.E. 9—Total 63.
Biffin, Miss Sarah. *See* Beffin. (She died in 1850)
Black, Francis, R.B.A. §
Blake, William. *For* "1812" *read* "1808."
Bloor, Daniel E. Smith.
Blore, Edward, D.C.L., F.R.S., F.S.A.
Bolinbroke, Miss Minna, *afterwards* Mrs. Charles James Watson.
Boot, William Henry James, V.P.R.B.A. §
Boughton, George Henry, R.A., R.I. ‡
Bouquet, Michael Emile.
Bouvier, Gustavus Arthur.
Bouvier, Urban James.
Boyce, George Price, R.W.S. † *For* "1861" *read* "1890."
Brade, Daniel Frank.
Breun, John Ernest, R.B.A. §
Brockman, Charles Drake. / Brockman, C. H. } *Should be* Charles Henry Drake Brockman — Witley 1871-1892, R.A. 11, S.S. 32, N.W. 1, V.E. 26 —Total 64.
Brown, Miss Alice G. *See* Mrs. Grinling.
Brown, Annesby, R.B.A. §
Brown, Miss Gertrude. *See* Mrs. Robert Dale.
Browne, Gordon Frederick, R.I., R.B.A. §
Brownlow, George Washington.
Brownsword, Harry A., R.B.A. §
Bruce, Martin B., R.B.A. §
Brühl, Burleigh L., R.B.A. § ("Romford" *not* "Ranford.")
Bryant, Joshua.
Buckley, William.
Bull, Richard.
Bulleid, George Laurence, A.R.W.S. †
Bunney, Rupert C., R.B.A. §
Burbank, Miss Leonora.
Burke, Harold Arthur, R.B.A. §
Burns, Cecil Leonard, R.B.A. §
Burrington, Arthur A., R.I. ‡
Burroughs, A., Leicester, R.B.A. §
Butler, Miss Mildred A., A.R.W.S. †
Buttery, Thomas Charles.
Byam, Miss Louisa Anne.
Byron, Frederick George.

Cafe, Thomas Smith.
Cafe, Thomas Watt, R.B.A. §
Cahill, Richard Staunton.
Calvert, Edward. *For* "Claremont" *read* "London."
Carrick, John Mulcaster.
Capper, James Henry. *Read* "1822-1831. B.I. 3, S.S. 2—Total 5."
Capper, Jasper John. *Add* 2 to S.S.—Total 8.
Cash, George.
Cathelineau, Christopher.
Chattock, Richard Samuel, R.P.E.
Christie, Archibald H., R.B.A. §
Christie, Robert, R.B.A. §
Clarke, Alfred Alexander.
Clausen, George, A.R.A., R.W.S., R.I. † ‡ φ
Clayton, John R.
Clifford, Edward C., R.I. ‡
Cobbe, H. Bernard.
Cole, Reginald (Rex) Vicat, R.B.A. §
Collier, William H., R.H.A.
Collins, Charles, R.B.A. §
Collins, Mrs. Charles Allston, &c.
Collins, William Wiehe, R.I. ‡
Collings, Albert H., R.B.A. §
Coombs, Joseph Epenetus.
Cooke, Isaac, R.B.A. §
Cope, Arthur Stockdale, A.R.A.
Corbet, Matthew Ridley. *For* "Portraits" *read* "Landscape."
Corbet, Mrs. M. Ridley. *See* Mrs. Arthur Murch *and* Miss Edith Edenborough.
Cotman, Miles Edmund.
Craft, Percy R., R.B.A. §
Crofts, Ernest, R.A.
Crompton, James Shaw, R.I. ‡
Crawley, Nicholas J.

Danby, G. *Should be* Francis Danby.
Daniel, P. A.
Daniel, Mrs. P. A. } *Should be all* P. A. Daniel.
Daniell, Rev. Edward Thomas. (Norwich.)
Darley, J. F., R.B.A. §
Darley, William Henry.
Davies, Edward, R.I. ‡
Davis, Fred W., R.I., R.B.A. ‡ §
Davis, Samuel.
Dean, H. (1860-1864) *is* Sir F. Seymour Haden.
Dean, Thomas Anthony.
De Breanski, Alfred, R.B.A. §
Del Hardinge, J. (1831-1832), R.A. 1, S.S. 2—Total 3.
Denham, John Charles.
Dicksee, Miss Margaret Isabel.
Dickson, Frank, R.B.A. §
Dixon, Charles, R.I. ‡
Donnelly, Major-General Sir John Fretchfield Dykes, K.C.B., R.E.
Doyle, Henry Edward, R.H.A.
Draper, Miss Mary. *See* Mrs. Albert Stevens.
Drury, E. Alfred B., A.R.A.
Dubois, Paul, H.F.R.A.

East, Alfred, A.R.A., R.I., R.B.A., R.P.E. ‡ § φ
Eastlake, Charles H., R.B.A. §
Edinborough (*read* Edenborough), Miss Edith. *See* Mrs. W. Ridley Corbet *and* Mrs. Arthur Murch.
Edward, Alfred S., R.B.A. §
Elliot, William (1761-1766).
Elmore, Miss Frances Mary.
Elsam, Richard.
Emmerson, Henry Hetherington.
Epps, Miss Emily. *See* Mrs. Williams.
Evans, Samuel T. G., R.W.S. †
Evershed, Dr. Arthur, R.P.E.
Evershed, Miss Ada, *afterwards* Mrs. Freeman Gell.
Eyre, John, R.B.A. §

Farquharson, Joseph, A.R.A. φ
Farrell, Sir Thomas, P.R.H.A.
Ferrier, George Straton, R.I., R.S.W. ‡
Fielding, A. C. V., *should be* A. V. C. Fielding.
Finnemore, Joseph, R.I., R.B.A. ‡ §
Fischer, T. Paul, *should be* Johann George Paul Fischer.
Fisher, William Mark.
Fitz-Cook, Henry.
Foley, Edward Arlington.
Folingsby, George Frederick.
Forbes, Mrs. Stanhope Alexander (Elizabeth), A.R.W.S. †
Ford, Edward Onslow, R.A.
Fowler, Trevor Thomas.
Fowler, Walter, R.B.A. §
Frampton, George Glanfield, *should be* George James Frampton, A.R.A.
Fraser, James Baillie. §
Frazer, Hugh.
Freeman, William P. Barnes.
Fripp, George Arthur, R.W.S. †
Friswell, Harry P. Hain-, R.B.A. §

Gagahan, Luke.
Garland, T. Valentine,
Garland, Tom William,
Garland, Valentine Thomas, } *are all* Valentine Thomas Garland.
Geary, Stephen.
Gell, Mrs. Freeman, *late* Miss Ada Evershed.
Gemmell, Miss Mary R. } Two Artists: Miss Marion Gemmell (Portraits). Miss Mary Gemmell (Flowers).
Georges, Charles E., R.B.A. §
Gilbert, Alfred, M.V.O., R.A., H.R.I. ‡
Gilbert, Horace Walter, *formerly* Williams.
Gilbert, Miss Kate Elizabeth Ellen, *afterwards* Mrs. Hughes.
Gilbert, Miss Oriana Pond.
Goodall, Edward Angelo, R.W.S. †
Goodall, Mrs. Frederick. *See* Miss Alice Tarry.
Gotch, Mrs. T. C. *See* Miss Caroline Burland Yates.
Gouldsmith, Edmund, R.B.A. §
Gower, Lord Ronald Leveson-, F.S.A.
Gowers, David.
Grace, Mrs., *formerly* Miss Mary Hodgkins.
Grant, Carleton, R.B.A. §
Grass, Andrew.
Gray, Mrs. Curwen, *late* Miss Kate Newenham, *should be* 1864-1875. Domestic. R.A. 1, B.I. 1, S.S. 8—Total 10.
Gray, Miss Kate. (Woodford.) Total 4 is the same as the above.
Gray, Henry Peters, N.A.
Green, Benjamin Richard. ‡
Green, David, R.I. ‡
Greenhead, Miss Mary. *See* Mrs. Stewart (1803).
Gregory, Edward John, R.A., P.R.I. ‡ φ
Grierson, C. MacIver, R.I. ‡
Grinling, Mrs. *See* Miss Alice G. Brown.
Griswold, C. C., N.A.
Groom, Alfred Henry.
Groome, William Henry Charles.
Guy, Seymour Joseph, N.A.

Haag, Carl, R.W.S. § † *For* "1888" *read* "1893."
Haddon, Arthur Trevor, R.B.A. §
Haden, Sir Francis Seymour, &c. *See* H. Dean.
Hague, Joseph Edward Homerville, *should read* "Cookham, 1884-1893, sculpture and figures, R.A. 6, S.S. 1, N.G. 7, V.E. 1—Total 15."
Hahnisch, Anton.
Hall, George Henry, N.A.
Hamilton, Henry Thomas.
Hamilton, Mrs. Vereker, *formerly* Miss Lilian Swainson.
Hamlyn, Janet T. (1819), *late* Miss Blanchard.
Hammond, Miss Gertrude P. Demain, R.I. ‡
Hankey, William Lee, R.I., R.B.A. ‡ §
Harcourt, George, R.B.A. §
Harding, Chester T.
Harding, James (Deptford), *father of* J. D. Harding.
Harding, James Duffield, †, *should be* 15 at S.S—Total 206.
Hardy, Dudley, R.I. ‡
Hare, Thomas.
Harpignies, Henri.
Harraden, Richard Parkes.
Harris, Sir James C., H.R.I. ‡
Harrison, Thomas Erat.
Hartley, Edward.
Hatton, Miss Helen Howard, *afterwards* Mrs. W. H. Margetson.
Haverty, Joseph Patrick, R.H.A.
Hay, Mrs. Jane Eleanor Benham. *See* Miss Jane Benham.
Hayes, William B.
Haynes, John William.
Healy, George Peter Alexander.
Hedgeland, John Pyke.
Hedley, Ralph, R.B.A. §
Helcké, Arnold, R.B.A. §
Hemy, Charles Napier, A.R.A., R.W.S., R.I. † ‡ φ
Hemy, M. W. *or* W. M., *should be* W. M. Henry.
Henry, William. *See* Hemy.
Henshall, John Henry, R.W.S.
Herbert, James Dowling.
Herkomer, Professor Hubert von, R.A., D.P.R.W.S., R.I., R.P.E. † ‡ φ
Hetherington, Ivystan, R.B.A. §
Hill, James S., R.I. ‡
Hobden, Frank, R.B.A. §
Hodgkins, Miss Mary. *See* Mrs. Grace.
Hopkins, Arthur, R.W.S. †
Hopwood, H. S., A.R.W.S. †
Hughes, Edward Robert, R.W.S. †
Hume, Robert, R.B.A. §

HUNT, ALFRED WILLIAM, R.W.S. †, *should be* R.A. 37, S.S. 5, O.W. 334, G.G. 2, N.G. 5, V.E. 11—Total 394.
HUNT, ANDREW, *should be* 1846-1856. R.A. 2, S.S. 2, V.E. 4—Total 8.
HUNT, MRS. EDWIN, *late* MISS EMMA CHARLOTTE WESLEY NEWENHAM.
HUNT, WILLIAM, R.B.A. §
HUTCHISON, R. GEMMELL, R.B.A. §
HUXLEY, MISS NETTIE. *See* Mrs. George R. Roller.

INSKIPP, JOHN HENRY, R.B.A. §
IRELAND, THOMAS, R.B.A. §
IZARD, MISS EDITH ANNE.

JACKSON, MULGRAVE PHIPPS B. The "B" is an error.
JACKSON, THOMAS GRAHAM, R.A., M.A., F.S.A.
JACOBS, JOHN E., R.B.A. §
JAMES, CHARLES STANFIELD. (Pupil of Beverley and godson of C. Stanfield, R.A.)
J'ANSON, EDWARD. *See* I'Anson.
JEAKES, JOSEPH.
JEAN, PHILIP.
JENNINGS, WILLIAM GEORGE. §
JOHN, WILLIAM GOSCOMBE, A.R.A.
JOHNSON, E. BOROUGH, R.B.A. §
JONES, ARTHUR BERTRAM LOUD. *See* Loud.
JONES, HENRY THADDEUS.
JONES, JOHN EDWARD.
JONES, RICHARD (1818-1820).
JONES, SAMUEL JOHN EGBERT.
JONES, WILLIAM EDWARD.
JOY, ARTHUR, R.H.A.
JUNCK, FERDINAND. *See* Tunck.
JUSTYNE, PERCY WILLIAM.

KEENAN, JOHN.
KING, YEEND, V.P R.I., R.B.A. § ‡ φ
KINSLEY, ALBERT, R.I., R.B.A., H.R.C.A. ‡ §
KIRCHHOFFER, HENRY, R.H.A.
KIRK, JOSEPH ROBINSON, R.H.A.
KIRK, WILLIAM BAYTON, R.H.A.
KIRKUP, SEYMOUR.
KNEEN, WILLIAM, R.B.A. §

LA THANGUE, HERBERT HENRY, A.R.A. φ
LAURENCE, SYDNEY M., R.B.A. §
LEADER, BENJAMIN WILLIAMS, R.A.
LEAR, CHARLES H.
LEE, THOMAS, JUNR.
LE FANU, G. BRINSLEY.
LEGGE, ARTHUR, R.B.A. §
LEIGHTON, FREDERIC, LORD, OF STRETTON, P.R.A., &c.
LEJEUNE, MISS ELIZABETH.
LEJEUNE, HENRY L., A.R.A. *The "L" is an error.*
LIMNER, LUKE, *was* JOHN LEIGHTON, F.S.A.
LINTON, SIR JAMES DROMGOLE, R.I., H.R.S.W. ‡ §
LITTLE, ROBERT, R.W.S., R.S.W. †
LIVENS, HORACE MANN, R.B.A. §
LONGFIELD, THOMAS HENRY.
LOUD, ARTHUR BERTRAM, R.C.A., *is* JONES.
LOUISE, H.R.H. PRINCESS (DUCHESS OF ARGYLE), H.R.W.S., H.R.S.W. †
LOW, CHARLES, R.B.A. §
LOWCOCK, CHARLES FREDERICK, R.B.A. §
LUCAS, JOHN SEYMOUR, R.A., R.I., F.S.A. ‡
LUCY, MRS. CHARLES, *formerly* MISS ANNIE BISHOP.
LUCY, HUBERT A.
LUND, NIELS M., R.B.A. §
LUKER, WILLIAM, JUNR., R.B.A. §
LUMLEY, LORD. *See* SIR JOHN SAVILE, K.C.B.
LUSCOMBE, HENRY ANDREWS.
LYSTER, RICHARD.
LYTTELTON, LADY (second wife of the 3rd Lord).

MACALLUM, HAMILTON, R.I., R.S.W. ‡ φ, and MCCALLUM, ANDREW, are brothers. *The name should be* MCCULLUM.
MACBRIDE, ALEXANDER, R.W.S., R.I. † ‡
MCCORMICK, ARTHUR D., R.B.A. §
MACBETH, ROBERT WALKER, A.R.A., A.R.W.S., R.I., R.P.E. † ‡ φ
MCGUINNESS, WILLIAM BINGHAM, R.H.A.
MACHELL, REGINALD, R.B.A. §
MACLEAN, ALEXANDER, R.B.A. §
MACKLIN, THOMAS EYRE, R.B.A. §
MCILWAINE, JOHN B. S., R.H.A.
MCWHIRTER, JOHN, R.A.
MAHON, ROBERT.
MANNING, WILLIAM WESTLEY, R.B.A. §
MANTON, G. GRENVILLE, R.B.A. §
MARGETSON, MRS. W. H. *See* Miss Helen Howard Hatton.
MARSHALL, HERBERT M., V.P.R.W.S. †
MARSHALL, J. FITZ, R.B.A. §
MARQUIS, JAMES ROBERT, R.H.A.
MARTIN, DAVID, should have 2 in Suffolk Street, erroneously placed to David Martin, F.S.A.
MEADE, ARTHUR, R.B.A. §
MELVILLE, ARTHUR, R.W.S., H.R.S.A., R.S.W. †
MELVILLE, HARDEN SIDNEY.
MELVILLE, MISS PATTIE, *afterwards* MRS. E. A. PETTITT.
MENPES, MORTIMER L., F.R.G.S., R.I., R.B.A., R.P.E. ‡ §
MENZEL, PROFESSOR ADOLPH FREDERICK ERDMAN, H.F.R.A., H.R.W.S. †
MEYERHEIM, ROBERT G., R.I. ‡
MILLAIS, SIR JOHN EVERETT, BART., P.R.A., H.R.I., H.R.C.A. ‡
MILLARD, FRED, R.B.A. §
MILNER, FRED, R.B.A. §
MONTEFIORE, EDWARD BRICE STANLEY.
MOORE, HENRY, R.A., R.W.S. § † φ
MORRIS, CHARLES GREVILLE, R.B.A. §
MOSTYN, TOM E., R.B.A. §
MULLER, ROBERT (1789-1800).
MULRENIN, BERNARD, R.H.A.
MURCH, MRS. ARTHUR, } Same Lady. *See* Miss Edith Edenborough
MURCH, EDITH, } *and* Mrs. Ridley Corbet.
MURPHY, DENIS BROWNALL.
MUSCHAMP, F. SYDNEY, R.B.A. §

NEWENHAM, MISS EMMA CHARLOTTE WESLEY. *See* Mrs. Edwin Hunt.
NEWMAN, PHILIP HARRY, R.B.A. §
NIEMANN, EDWARD JOHN, *misprinted* NIETNANN.
NIETNANN, EDWARD JOHN, *should be* NIEMANN.
NOBLETT, H. JOHN. ‡ *For* "1832" *read* "1831."
NORBURY, EDWIN ARTHUR, R.C.A.
NORTH, JOHN WILLIAM, A.R.A., R.W.S. †

O'DOHERTY, WILLIAM J.
OFFORD, JOHN JAMES.
OLIVER, WILLIAM. *See* William Oliver Williams.
OLIVIER, HERBERT A., R.B.A. §
OTTEWELL, B. J., R.I. ‡

PACK, FAITHFUL CHRISTOPHER.
PAIN, GEORGE RICHARD.
PANORMO, CONSTANTINE, A.R.H.A.
PARKE, ROBERT.
PARSONS, ALFRED, A.R.A., A.R.S.W., R.I. † ‡ φ
PASSEY, CHARLES HENRY.
PATERSON, JAMES, A.R.W.S., R.S.W. †
PEACOCK, JOSEPH, R.H.A.
PEDDER, JOHN, R.I. ‡
PEPPERCORN, ARTHUR D., R.I. ‡
PERCY, JOHN F.
PERCY, SAMUEL.
PETTITT, MRS. E. A., *formerly* MISS PATTIE MELVILLE.
PHILLIP, COLIN BENT, R.W.S., R.S.W. †
PILSBURY, WILMOT, R.W.S. †
POCOCK, H. CHILDE, R.B.A. §
PORTAELS, JEAN FRANÇOIS.
PORTER, SIR ROBERT KER.
POYNER, WILLIAM HENRY.

Poynter, Sir Edward James, P.R.A., R.W.S., H.F.R.P.E. †
Price, Frank Corbyn, R.B.A. §
Prynne, Edward A. Fellowes, R.B.A. §

Queen Alexandra, Her Majesty, H.R.W.S. †

Raimbach, David Wilkie.
Read, Edward H., R.B.A. §
Read, Mrs. *See* Miss J. Beetham.
Reeves, Edmond B.
Reid, John R., R.I § ‡ φ
Richardson, Daniel.
Richardson, Frederick Stuart, R.I., R.S.W. ‡
Richardson, Thomas Miles. ‡ *For* "1818" *read* "1814."
Richmond, Sir William Blake, K.C.B., R.A., F.S.A., M.A.
Riley, William.
Roberts, Henry.
Roberts, Henry Larpent.
Roberts, Thomas Edward, R.B.A. §
Robertson, Tom, R.B.A. §
Robertson, Walter Graham, R.B.A. §
Robinson, Mrs. Maria D. Webb.
Robotham, Miss Frances C., *should be* Mrs. Robotham.
Roe, Fred, R.B.A. §
Rogers, William P.
Roller, Mrs. George R. *See* Miss Nettie Huxley.
Ronner, Madame Henrietta, R.I. ‡
Rothwell, Thomas.
Rowe, Mrs. Jopling. *See* Mrs. Jopling *and* Mrs. Romer.
Rowe, Sidney Grant, R.B.A. §
Royal, Miss Elizabeth. *See* Mrs. Surtees.
Russell, James John, R.H.A.
Ryland, Henry, R.I. ‡

St. Gaudens, Augustine.
Sainton, Charles P., R.I. ‡
Sanders, George. 1834. R.A. 5—Total 5. These are put under Saunders, George L.
Sandys, Francis.
Sargent, John Singer, R.A.
Saunders, George Lethbridge, *should be* R.A. 25, S.S. 11—Total 36.
Savill, Miss Edith. *See* Mrs. Stanley Berkeley.
Settle, William F.
Shannon, James Jebusa, A.R.A., R.B.A. § φ
Shaw, Arthur Winter-, R.I. ‡
Shaw, J. Byam, R.I. ‡
Sheard, Thomas F. M., R.B.A. §
Shepherd, Miss Julianna Charlotte.
Shiel, Edward, R.H.A.
Shields, Harry G., R.B.A. §
Sims, Frrderick, } are one Artist
Sims, Frederick Thomas, } (Figures).
Skelton, William Percival.
Smith, Reginald, R.B.A. §
Smyth, T., *should be* Smythe, Thomas.
Smyth, Walter Montague, R.B.A. §
Smythe, Lionel Percy, A.R.A., R.W.S., R.I. † ‡ φ
Solomon, Soloman J., A.R.A.
Sparks, Herbert Blande.
Spenlove, Frank Spenlove, R.B.A. §
Stannard, Harry, R.B.A. §
Stannard, Harry J.
Stanton, Horace Hughes-, } *should be* H. Hughes-Stanton, 1889-1893. N.W. 2, G.G. 3, N.G. 1, V.E. 8—Total 14. Horace Hale Stanton, 1873-1882. R.A. 5, G.G. 1, V.E. 1—Total 7.

Staples, Robert Ponsonby, R.B.A. §
Stevens, Mrs. Albert. *See* Miss Mary Draper.
Stewart, Mrs. (1803). *See* Miss Mary Greenhead.
Stopford, William Henry.
Sullivan, James Francis, R.B.A. §
Surtees, Mrs. *See* Miss Elizabeth Royal.
Swainson, Miss Lilian. *See* Mrs. Vereker Hamilton.
Swan, John Macallan, A.R.A., A.R.W.S. †
Swanwick, Harold, R.I., A.R.C.A. ‡

Tayler, Norman Edward, A.R.W.S. † Son of J. Frederick Tayler, P.R.W.S. †
Teniswood, George F.
Tidey, Alfred, }
Tidey, Arthur, } *should all be* Alfred Tidey, London 1831-1887. Miniatures, R.A. 119, B.I. 1, S.S. 17, N.W. 1, V.E. 6—Total 144.
Tidey, A. W. }
Tidey, Henry Fryer. ‡ *Should be* "Historical."
Townshend, James, R.B.A. §
Tringham, Holland, R.B.A. §
Tucker, Arthur, R.B.A. §
Tuke, Henry Scott, A.R.A. §
Tupper, John Lucas.
Tuthill, Captain Jackson V.

Uvedale, Samuel.

Van Bartels, Professor Hans, H.R.I. ‡
Van Bever, Anthony *or* Antoine.

Walker, William Eyre, R.W.S. †
Wall, William G.
Ward, George Raphael, }
Ward, Henry, } all sons of James Ward, R.A.
Ward, James, }
Warrener, William T., R.B.A. §
Warrington, William.
Waterhouse, John William, R.A., R.I. ‡
Waterlow, Ernest Albert, A.R.A., P.R.W.S. † φ
Watkins, Bartholomew Colles, R.H.A.
Watt, Leonard, R.B.A. §
Weaver, John.
Webb, Aston, A.R.A.
Weguelin, John Reinhard, R.W.S. † φ
Wells, J. Sanderson, R.B.A. §
West, Joseph Walter, A.R.W.S. †
Weston, Lambert.
Whitehead, Frederick, R.B.A. §
Whistler, J. M., *was* P.R.B.A. *from* 1886 *to* 1889.
Wild, F. Percy, R.B.A. §
Wilkins, William Noy.
Wills, William German.
Williams, Alfred Mayhew.
Williams, Horace Walter Gilbert. *See* Gilbert.
Williams, Terrick, R.B.A. §
Williams, William Oliver. *See* Oliver.
Willink, *printed* Willinck *in error*.
Wimperis, Edward Monson, V.P.R.I. ‡ § φ
Windsor-Fry, Harry, R.B.A. §
Winter, W. Tatten, R.B.A. §
Wood, Miss Eleanor Stuart, *should be* 1876-1887, R.A. 7, N.W. 1—Total 8.
Wood, Miss Emmie Stewart, *should be* 1885-1893, R.A. 10, S.S. 3, N.W. 9, G.G. 11, N.G. 10, V.E. 12—Total 55.
Woods, Henry, R.A. φ

Yard, Charles.

A DICTIONARY OF ARTISTS.

S.A. Society of Artists, F.S. Free Society of Artists, R.A. Royal Academy, B.I. British Institution, S.S. Suffolk Street, O.W. Old Water-Colour Society, N.W. New Water-Colour Society, afterwards Royal Institute, G.G. Grosvenor Gallery, N.G. New Gallery, V.E. Various Exhibitions.

The letters F.S.A. after the name signify (before 1800) Fellow of the Society of Artists; a § after the name, Member of the Society of British Artists, Suffolk Street; † Member or Associate of Old Water-Colour Society; ‡ Member of New Water-Colour Society; φ Member of Institute of Painters in Oil-Colours; ‖ Member or Associate of the Society of Lady Artists; an * in any of the exhibition columns, that, owing to some oversight, the name appears in the index, but not in the body of the catalogue of that year.

Name.	Town.	First and Last Year of Ex.	Speciality.	S. A.	F. S.	R. A.	B. I.	S. S.	O. W.	N. W.	G. G.	N. G.	V. E.	Total.
ABBAYNE, C.	London	1857-1858	Landscape	—	—	1	—	1	—	—	—	—	—	2
ABBEY, EDWIN AUSTIN, R.I. ‡	London	1879-1890	Landscape	—	—	2	—	—	—	5	1	—	1	9
ABBEYSON, M.	London	1828	Sea Pieces	—	—	—	—	2	—	—	—	—	—	2
ABBOT, J.	London	1770	Still Life	1	—	—	—	—	—	—	—	—	—	1
ABBOTT, MISS D.	London	1886-1888	Sculpture	—	—	2	—	—	—	—	—	—	—	2
ABBOTT, EDWIN	Bradford	1886	Portraits	—	—	1	—	—	—	—	—	—	—	1
ABBOTT, GEORGE	London	1829-1867	Sculpture	—	—	26	11	12	—	—	—	—	—	49
ABBOTT, JOHN WHITE	Exeter	1793-1822	Landscape	—	—	16	—	—	—	—	—	—	—	16
ABBOTT, LEMUEL FRANCIS	London	1788-1800	Portraits	—	—	15	—	—	—	—	—	—	—	15
ABBOTT, RICHMOND	Liverpool	1861-1866	Animals	—	—	—	3	4	—	—	—	—	—	7
ABERCROMBIE, MISS M. C.	London	1891-1892	Portraits	—	—	—	—	—	—	3	—	1	1	5
ABERCROMBY, J. B.	Edinburgh	1873	Figures	—	—	2	—	—	—	—	—	—	—	2
ABERLI, SIGNOR	Rome	1790	Landscape	6	—	—	—	—	—	—	—	—	—	6
ABLETT, T. ROBERT	Bradford	1880-1893	Landscape	—	—	3	—	—	—	3	1	—	1	8
ABORN, JOHN	Milford	1885-1893	Landscape	—	—	10	—	19	—	—	—	1	7	37
ABRAHAM, FRANK	Stoke-on-Trent	1887	Landscape	—	—	—	—	—	—	1	—	—	—	1
ABRAHAM, F. H.	Doncaster	1833-1834	Churches	—	—	2	—	—	—	—	—	—	—	2
ABRAHAM, HENRY ROBERT	London	1827-1840	Architecture	—	—	2	—	2	—	—	—	—	—	4
ABRAHAM, MISS LILIAN	London	1880-1886	Flowers	—	—	—	—	2	—	3	—	—	—	5
ABRAHAM, ROBERT	London	1819-1832	Architecture	—	—	4	—	—	—	—	—	—	—	4
ABRAHAM MRS. R.	London	1814-1832	Flowers	—	—	1	—	3	—	—	—	—	—	4
ABRAHAM, R. F.	London	1846-1853	Historical	—	—	11	6	—	—	—	—	—	—	17
ABRAHAM, R. J.	Stoke-on-Trent	1877-1892	Rustic	—	—	10	—	—	—	4	—	1	3	18
ABRAHAM, VAN DEN. *See* V.	—	—	—	—	—	—	—	—	—	—	—	—	—	—
ABSOLON, HUGH WOLFGANG	London	1855	Figures	—	—	1	—	—	—	—	—	—	—	1
ABSOLON, JOHN, R.I. ‡ φ	London	1832-1889	Domestic	—	—	16	7	22	—	660	—	—	3	708
ABSOLON, JOHN DE MANSFIELD	London	1862-1868	Still Life	—	—	—	—	4	—	—	—	—	—	4
ABSOLON, LOUIS φ	London	1873-1888	Domestic	—	—	—	—	21	—	5	—	—	17	43
ACHENBACH, OSWALD	Düsseldorf	1860	Landscape	—	—	1	—	—	—	—	—	—	—	1
ACKERMANN, GERALD	London	1892-1893	Landscape	—	—	1	—	6	—	3	—	—	—	10
ACKERMANN, R.	Brighton	1854	Sculpture	—	—	—	—	1	—	—	—	—	—	1
ACLAND, MISS A.	Oxford	1875	Domestic	—	—	1	—	—	—	—	—	—	—	1
ACOCK, W. W.	Croydon	1870-1871	Fruit	—	—	—	—	2	—	—	—	—	—	2
ACRAMAN, MISS EDITH	London	1847-1852	Landscape	—	—	5	—	—	—	—	—	—	—	5
ACRAMAN, W. H.	Hastings	1856-1868	Landscape	—	—	1	—	5	—	—	—	—	5	11
ACRES, E.	London	1797-1823	Miniatures	—	—	20	—	—	—	—	—	—	—	20
ACRES, J.	London	1802-1813	Miniatures	—	—	7	—	—	—	—	—	—	—	7
ACRET, JOHN F.	London	1884-1893	Figures	—	—	2	—	2	—	—	—	—	—	4
ACTON, S.	London	1791-1802	Architecture	—	—	9	—	—	—	—	—	—	—	9
ACTON, MRS.	—	1806	Portraits	—	—	1	—	—	—	—	—	—	—	1
ADAM, JOSEPH	London	1857-1880	Landscape	—	—	17	10	13	—	—	—	—	15	55
ADAM, JOSEPH DENOVAN, R.S.A., R.S.W.	London	1859-1892	Fruit	—	—	25	6	6	—	1	—	4	11	53
ADAM, PATRICK W., A.R.S.A.	Edinburgh	1878-1892	Domestic	—	—	12	—	—	—	—	—	—	—	12
ADAM, STEPHEN	Glasgow	1892	Architecture	—	—	1	—	—	—	—	—	—	—	1
ADAMS. *See* SALTER AND ADAMS	—	—	Architecture	—	—	—	—	—	—	—	—	—	—	—
ADAMS —	London	1780	Allegorical	—	1	—	—	—	—	—	—	—	—	1
ADAMS, A.	—	1815	Portraits	—	—	1	—	—	—	—	—	—	—	1
ADAMS, ALBERT G.	London	1854-1887	Landscape	—	—	18	15	38	—	—	—	—	17	88
ADAMS, A. J.	London	1874-1879	Architecture	—	—	3	—	—	—	—	—	—	—	3
ADAMS, MISS CAROLINE	Billericay	1830-1837	Landscape	—	—	—	—	16	—	1	—	—	—	17
ADAMS, MISS CHARLOTTE	London	1829-1843	Landscape	—	—	10	—	8	—	—	—	—	—	18
ADAMS, COLE A.	London	1873-1883	Architecture	—	—	6	—	—	—	—	—	—	—	6
ADAMS, CHARLES J.	Leicester	1882-1893	Landscape	—	—	9	—	7	—	19	—	—	3	38
ADAMS, MISS CLARISSA M.	London	1870-1875	Sculpture	—	—	8	—	—	—	—	—	—	2	10
ADAMS, DACRES	Bushey	1892	Portraits	—	—	1	—	—	—	—	—	—	—	1

Name.	Town.	First and Last Year of Ex.	Speciality.	S. A.	F. S.	R. A.	B. I.	S. S.	O. W.	N. W.	G. G.	N. G.	V. E.	Total.
Adams, Douglas	London	1880-1893	Landscape	—	—	8	—	6	—	—	2	5	3	24
Adams, Miss E.	London	1828-1833	Landscape	—	—	—	—	2	—	—	—	—	—	2
Adams, Eliott Ashfield	Liverpool	1870	Landscape	—	—	—	—	—	—	—	—	—	1	1
Adams, George Gammon	London	1841-1885	Sculpture	—	—	119	4	—	—	—	—	—	—	123
Adams, Harry P.	Ipswich	1888	Architecture	—	—	1	—	—	—	—	—	—	—	1
Adams, James	London	1808-1819	Architecture	—	—	5	—	—	—	—	—	—	—	5
Adams, Miss Jane	London	1821-1851	Domestic	—	—	5	7	4	—	—	—	—	—	16
Adams, Miss Joan	Guildford	1890-1893	Rustic	—	—	1	—	—	—	—	—	—	2	3
Adams, John. *See* Adams-Acton	London	1854-1868	Sculpture	—	—	55	—	—	—	—	—	—	—	55
Adams-Acton, John, R.B.A. §	London	1869-1892	Sculpture	—	—	83	—	5	—	—	2	—	2	92
Adams, John	London	1869	Landscape	—	—	1	—	—	—	—	—	—	—	1
Adams, John Clayton	Edmonton	1863-1893	Landscape	—	—	75	—	25	—	5	3	3	32	143
Adams, James L.	Leeds	1877-1880	Figures	—	—	1	—	—	—	—	—	—	1	2
Adams, J. Seymour	London	1884-1885	Landscape	—	—	1	—	2	—	—	—	—	—	3
Adams, John T.	London	1861-1877	Landscape	—	—	1	7	10	—	—	—	—	—	18
Adams, L.	London	1833-1834	Portraits	—	—	—	—	9	—	—	—	—	—	9
Adams, Miss Lucy	Billericay	1815-1843	Domestic	—	—	13	—	39	—	1	—	—	3	56
Adams, L. B.	London	1828-1844	Rural subjects	—	—	5	6	23	—	—	—	—	—	34
Adams, Maurice B.	London	1876-1893	Architecture	—	—	14	—	—	—	—	—	—	—	14
Adams, R.	London	1820-1824	Landscape	—	—	5	1	—	—	—	—	—	—	6
Adams, Thomas	London	1865-1879	Fruit	—	—	—	1	4	—	—	—	—	6	11
Adams, William	London	1822-1823	Landscape	—	—	1	1	—	—	—	—	—	—	2
Adams, W. D.	Lechlade	1889-1891	Landscape	—	—	—	—	—	—	—	—	—	2	2
Adams, W. J.	London	1830-1831	Sculpture	—	—	1	—	1	—	—	—	—	—	2
Adams, Mrs.	London	1806-1832	Flowers	—	—	9	—	—	—	—	—	—	—	9
Adamson, David Comba	Glasgow	1887-1893	Domestic	—	—	2	—	—	—	—	—	—	1	3
Adamson, John	Hornsey	1890-1892	Domestic	—	—	2	—	—	—	—	—	—	1	3
Adamson, Miss	London	1845-1869	Flowers, &c.	—	—	7	—	19	—	—	—	—	—	26
Adan, F.	London	1878	Flowers	—	—	—	—	2	—	—	—	—	—	2
Adcock —	—	1845	—	—	—	*	—	—	—	—	—	—	—	—
Adcock, George H.	London	1827	Engraving	—	—	—	—	1	—	—	—	—	—	1
Addenbrooke, Miss Rosa	Salisbury	1891-1892	Fish	—	—	1	—	1	—	—	—	—	—	2
Adderley, Miss	—	1842	Landscape	—	—	—	1	—	—	—	—	—	—	1
Adderton, C. W.	Derby	1890-1892	Landscape	—	—	—	—	3	—	1	—	—	—	4
Addington, Sarah	London	1778	Miniatures	—	—	1	—	—	—	—	—	—	—	1
Addis, Miss E.	London	1775	Portraits	1	—	1	—	—	—	—	—	—	—	2
Addison, G. H. M.	Adelaide	1883	Architecture	—	—	1	—	—	—	—	—	—	—	1
Addison, William Grylls	London	1875-1893	Landscape	—	—	9	—	11	—	10	5	—	38	73
Addison, Mrs.	Ickenham	1831-1843	Landscape	—	—	3	—	4	—	—	—	—	—	7
Aders, Mrs. C.	London	1839	Figures	—	—	2	—	—	—	—	—	—	—	2
Aders, Mrs. Eliza (late Miss Smith)	London	1841	Miniatures	—	—	1	—	—	—	—	—	—	—	1
Adey, Virginia	Lyndhurst	1879-1881	Figures	—	—	—	—	2	—	—	—	—	5	7
Adie, Miss Edith Helena	London	1892-1893	Buildings	—	—	1	—	3	—	1	—	—	—	5
Adlington, Miss E. C.	London	1893	Still Life	—	—	1	—	—	—	—	—	—	—	1
Adloff, C.	London	1849-1850	Landscape	—	—	2	—	—	—	—	—	—	—	2
Adron, H.	London	1852-1857	Sculpture	—	—	9	—	—	—	—	—	—	—	9
Adshead, Joseph	Manchester	1863-1877	Landscape	—	—	3	—	2	—	—	—	—	6	11
Adye, General Sir John	London	1888	Fortresses	—	—	—	—	—	—	2	—	—	—	2
Affleck, William	London	1890-1893	Landscape	—	—	2	—	3	—	5	—	—	1	11
Agar, John Samuel	London	1796-1851	Portraits	—	—	28	7	—	—	—	—	—	—	35
Agasse, James Laurent	London	1801-1845	Sporting	—	—	29	7	5	2	—	—	—	—	43
Aglio, Agostino	London	1807-1850	Landscape	—	—	13	22	8	1	—	—	—	10	54
Aglio, Augustine	London	1836-1875	Landscape	—	—	2	5	23	—	—	—	—	2	32
Aglio, Miss Mary Elizabeth	London	1851	Historical	—	—	1	—	1	—	—	—	—	—	2
Agneni, Eugène	London	1859-1862	Historical	—	—	5	—	—	—	—	—	—	—	5
Agnetta, Miss	York	1774	Domestic	1	—	—	—	—	—	—	—	—	—	1
Agnew, Miss Caroline M.	Manchester	1874-1875	Landscape	—	—	2	—	—	—	—	—	—	1	3
Agnew, Vans. *See* V.	—	—	—	—	—	—	—	—	—	—	—	—	—	—
Agujari, G.	London	1869-1877	Figures	—	—	—	—	3	—	—	—	—	2	5
Aickin and Capes	London	1852-1853	Architecture	—	—	2	—	—	—	—	—	—	—	2
Aidé, Hamilton	London	1880-1881	Landscape	—	—	—	—	—	—	—	3	—	—	3
Aikin, Edmund	London	1801-1814	Architecture	—	—	12	—	—	—	—	—	—	—	12
Aikman, George, A.R.S.A.	Edinburgh	1874-1893	Landscape	—	—	6	—	3	—	—	—	—	—	9
Aikman, William	London	1893	Stained Glass	—	—	1	—	—	—	—	—	—	—	1
Ailesbury, Susanna, Countess of	—	1768	Needlework	1	—	—	—	—	—	—	—	—	—	1
Ainger, A.	London	1815-1834	Architecture	—	—	5	—	—	—	—	—	—	—	5
Ainsley, J.	Mansfield	1840	Figures	—	—	1	—	—	—	—	—	—	—	1
Ainsley, P.	London	1868-1871	Landscape	—	—	—	—	3	—	—	—	—	—	3
Ainsley, Samuel James	Leyton	1836-1855	Landscape	—	—	2	4	1	—	—	—	—	—	7
Ainslie, G.	—	1799-1819	Landscape	—	—	12	—	—	—	—	—	—	—	12
Ainslie, John	London	1827-1834	Domestic	—	—	—	2	5	—	2	—	—	—	9
Ainslie, W. *See* Woodd and Ainslie	—	—	Architecture	—	—	—	—	—	—	—	—	—	—	—

Name.	Town.	First and Last Year of Ex.	Speciality.	S. A.	F. S.	R. A.	B. I.	S. S.	O.W.	N.W.	G. G.	N. G.	V. E.	Total.
Ainslie, Miss	—	1823-1831	Game	—	—	11	—	—	—	—	—	—	—	11
Ainsworth —	London	1823	Landscape	—	—	3	—	—	—	—	—	—	—	3
Aitcherson, Miss S.	Strood	1839	Flowers	—	—	—	—	1	—	—	—	—	—	1
Aitchison, Alfred	London	1879	Churches	—	—	1	—	—	—	—	—	—	—	1
Aitchison, G.	London	1815-1849	Architecture	—	—	21	—	—	—	—	—	—	—	21
Aitchison, George, A.R.A.	London	1852-1893	Architecture	—	—	62	—	—	—	—	—	—	—	62
Aitken, James	Colwyn Bay	1889	Landscape	—	—	1	—	—	—	—	—	—	—	1
Aitken, James Alfred, A.R.H.A., R.S.W.	Glasgow	1874-1890	Figures	—	—	1	—	—	—	—	3	—	—	4
Aitkin, E. V.	Putney	1886	Domestic	—	—	—	—	1	—	—	—	—	—	1
Aitkins, J. M.	London	1824	Architecture	—	—	1	—	—	—	—	—	—	—	1
Akers, John	Oxford	1826-1844	Landscape	—	—	2	7	1	—	—	—	—	—	10
Akers, W. S.	London	1821	Portraits	—	—	2	—	—	—	—	—	—	—	2
Alabaster, H.	London	1871-1874	—	—	—	—	—	4	—	—	—	—	—	4
Alabaster, Mrs. Henry. *See* Miss Palacia	—	—	—	—	—	—	—	—	—	—	—	—	—	—
Emma Fahey	—	1887-1888	Siam	—	—	—	—	—	—	4	—	—	—	4
Alabaster, Miss Mary Ann. *See* Mrs. Criddle	London	1830-1836	Domestic	—	—	—	7	2	—	—	—	—	—	9
Alais, Alfred Clarence	London	1881	Engraving	—	—	1	—	—	—	—	—	—	—	1
Alais, William Wolfe	London	1829-1833	Portraits	—	—	3	—	—	—	—	—	—	—	3
Alasonière, F.	Paris	1881-1882	Etching	—	—	6	—	—	—	—	—	—	2	8
Alaux, Jean	Rome	1848	Historical	—	—	1	—	—	—	—	—	—	—	1
Albanesi, Angelo	London	1772	Figures	1	—	—	—	—	—	—	—	—	—	1
Albano, Salvatore	Florence	1881-1888	Sculpture	—	—	6	—	—	—	—	—	—	—	6
Albers, A.	London	1819	Landscape	—	—	2	—	—	—	—	—	—	—	2
Albert, Miss B.	London	1874	Sea Pieces	—	—	—	—	1	—	—	—	—	—	1
Albert, Ernest	London	1891	Rivers	—	—	1	—	—	—	—	—	—	—	1
Albert, Mrs. M.	—	1761	Needlework	—	1	—	—	—	—	—	—	—	—	1
Albertin, Louis	London	1832-1833	Figures	—	—	—	—	6	—	4	—	—	—	10
Albon, W.	London	1817-1852	Architecture	—	—	13	—	—	—	—	—	—	—	13
Alcobier, H. D.	London	1845	Figures	—	—	1	—	—	—	—	—	—	—	1
Alcock —	London	1778	Figures	—	6	1	—	—	—	—	—	—	—	7
Alcock, Miss Harriet. *See* Mrs. Easthed	Dulwich	1832-1835	Portraits	—	—	2	—	—	—	—	—	—	—	2
Alcock, J.	London	1821	Architecture	—	—	1	—	—	—	—	—	—	—	1
Alcott, Mary	London	1877	Birds	—	—	—	—	—	—	—	—	—	1	1
Alderson, M. A.	London	1838	Architecture	—	—	1	—	—	—	—	—	—	—	1
Aldham, Miss Kate	London	1867-1876	Figures	—	—	5	—	2	—	—	—	—	3	10
Aldin, Alfred	London	1862-1870	Landscape	—	—	1	—	10	—	—	—	—	—	11
Aldis, C. M.	London	1835-1842	Landscape	—	—	9	4	8	—	—	—	—	—	21
Aldous, W.	London	1824	Portraits	—	—	1	—	—	—	—	—	—	—	1
Aldrich, W.	London	1819-1828	Figures	—	—	3	—	1	—	—	—	—	—	4
Aldridge, Miss Emily. ‖ *See* Mrs. Crawford.	—	—	—	—	—	—	—	—	—	—	—	—	—	—
Aldridge, E. W.	London	1775-1778	Portraits	—	—	3	—	—	—	—	—	—	—	3
Aldridge, Frederick James	Worthing	1880-1892	Landscape	—	—	—	—	12	—	7	—	—	7	26
Aldwinckle, Thomas W. *See also* Wilson,	—	—	—	—	—	—	—	—	—	—	—	—	—	—
Son, and Aldwinckle	London	1890	Architecture	—	—	1	—	—	—	—	—	—	—	1
Alefounder, John	London	1777-1793	Miniatures	—	—	40	—	—	—	—	—	—	—	40
Alexander, Antonio	London	1776	Landscape	—	—	1	—	—	—	—	—	—	—	1
Alexander, C.	London	1874	Landscape	—	—	—	—	—	—	—	—	—	1	1
Alexander, Charles	Wooton-under-Edge	1893	Portraits	—	—	1	—	—	—	—	—	—	—	1
Alexander, Cosmus	Edinburgh	1765	Portraits	1	—	—	—	—	—	—	—	—	—	1
Alexander, Daniel Asher	London	1788-1818	Architecture	—	—	12	—	—	—	—	—	—	—	12
Alexander, G. *See also* Stevens & Alexander	London	1830-1849	Architecture	—	—	17	—	1	—	—	—	—	—	18
Alexander, George	Greenwich	1843-1857	Figures	—	—	3	—	—	—	—	—	—	4	7
Alexander, John	Balham	1878	Fruit	—	—	—	—	1	—	—	—	—	—	1
Alexander, Miss J.	London	1851-1859	Domestic	—	—	3	1	4	—	—	—	—	—	8
Alexander, Miss Marion	Farnborough	1887-1893	Domestic	—	—	—	—	—	—	—	1	1	2	4
Alexander, Robert, R.S.A., R.S.W.	Edinburgh	1878-1888	Animals	—	—	4	—	—	—	—	—	—	—	4
Alexander, William	London	1795-1804	Chinese L'pe	—	—	16	—	—	—	—	—	—	—	16
Alexander, William	Salisbury	1878-1889	Domestic	—	—	1	—	—	—	—	—	—	2	3
Alexander, Miss	—	1820	Flowers	—	—	1	—	—	—	—	—	—	—	1
Alexander, Miss	London	1861	Landscape	—	—	—	—	1	—	—	—	—	—	1
Alexander and Henman (C.)	Leeds	1877	Architecture	—	—	1	—	—	—	—	—	—	—	1
Alford, Agnes	London	1881	Flowers	—	—	—	—	1	—	—	—	—	—	1
Alford, Leonard, C.	Southampton	1885-1888	Sea Pieces	—	—	2	—	—	—	—	—	—	—	2
Alfred, C. Garnier	Paris	1878	Etching	—	—	—	—	—	—	—	—	—	1	1
Alfred, Henry Jervis	London	1855	Fish	—	—	—	—	2	—	—	—	—	—	2
Alger, Vivian C.	London	1882-1889	Landscape	—	—	8	—	—	—	—	—	—	—	8
Aliamet, Francis Germain	London	1762-1765	Engraving	—	5	—	—	—	—	—	—	—	—	5
Alison, Miss M.	Acton	1868-1874	Landscape	—	—	3	—	7	—	—	—	—	—	10
Alken, Henry	Southampton	1801-1802	Portraits	—	—	2	—	—	—	—	—	—	—	2
Alken, Samuel	London	1780	Architecture	—	—	1	—	—	—	—	—	—	—	1
Alkinson, Miss E.	Boston	1877	Churches	—	—	—	—	1	—	—	—	—	—	1
Allan, Mrs. A. F.	London	1866-1870	Fruit	—	—	2	—	11	—	—	—	—	—	13

Name.	Town.	First and Last Year of Ex.	Speciality.	S. A.	F. S.	R. A.	B. I.	S. S.	O.W.	N.W.	G. G.	N. G.	V. E.	Total.
Allan, C.	Hillhead	1880	Domestic	—	—	—	—	—	—	—	—	—	1	1
Allan, Miss Christina	London	1884-1885	Sea Pieces	—	—	—	—	—	—	—	2	—	—	2
Allan, David	Rome	1771-1799	Historical	3	4	12	—	—	—	—	—	—	—	19
Allan, Miss E.	London	1863-1865	Fruit	—	—	—	1	4	—	—	—	—	—	5
Allan, J. McGregor	London	1854-1856	Portraits	—	—	5	—	—	—	—	—	—	—	5
Allan, Patrick	Paris	1840-1841	Historical	—	—	1	2	—	—	—	—	—	—	3
Allan, Robert Weir, A.R.W.S., R.S.W. † φ	Glasgow	1874-1893	Landscape	—	—	26	—	4	94	13	8	7	37	189
Allan, Sir William, R.A., P.R.S.A.	Edinburgh	1803-1849	Historical	—	—	48	2	1	—	—	—	—	—	51
Allan-Schmidt, E. *See* S.	—	—	—	—	—	—	—	—	—	—	—	—	—	—
Allardyce, Miss Mary R.	London	1891	Domestic	—	—	1	—	—	—	—	—	—	—	1
Allason, Thomas	London	1805-1825	Architecture	—	—	16	—	—	—	—	—	—	—	16
Allbon, Charles Frederick	Croydon	1874-1892	Landscape	—	—	6	—	6	—	—	—	—	—	12
Allchin, Harry	London	1885	Landscape	—	—	1	—	—	—	—	—	—	—	1
Allchin, J. Herbert	Southall	1877-1881	Still Life	—	—	6	—	1	—	—	—	—	3	10
Allcock, S. A.	London	1821-1822	Portraits	—	—	2	—	—	—	—	—	—	—	2
Alldred, J.	London	1830-1832	Architecture	—	—	3	—	—	—	—	—	—	—	3
Alldridge, Miss Emily	Old Charlton	1865-1879	Domestic	—	—	—	—	12	—	—	—	—	13	25
Alldridge, Miss F. Maude	Old Charlton	1868-1875	Figures	—	—	—	—	5	—	—	—	—	4	9
Alldridge, R. L.	Old Charlton	1866-1882	Domestic	—	—	6	—	2	—	—	—	—	5	13
Allen —	Greenwich	1767-1772	Sea Pieces	—	14	—	—	—	—	—	—	—	—	14
Allen —	London	1771-1772	Sculpture	3	—	—	—	—	—	—	—	—	—	3
Allen —	London	1771	Portraits	2	—	—	—	—	—	—	—	—	—	2
Allen, Master	—	1773	Drawing	—	1	—	—	—	—	—	—	—	—	1
Allen, Miss Annie C.	London	1881-1883	Flowers	—	—	—	—	2	—	—	—	—	—	2
Allen, Arthur W.	London	1886	Domestic	—	—	—	—	1	—	—	—	—	—	1
Allen, C. B.	London	1854-1857	Architecture	—	—	3	—	—	—	—	—	—	—	3
Allen, C. J.	London	1854-1860	Architecture	—	—	3	—	—	—	—	—	—	—	3
Allen, Charles J.	London	1890-1893	Sculpture	—	—	5	—	—	—	—	—	—	—	5
Allen, C. W.	London	1891	Landscape	—	—	—	—	1	—	—	—	—	—	1
Allen, Mrs. Eliza	Greenwich	1860-1864	Figures	—	—	—	—	5	—	—	—	—	—	5
Allen, E. J. Milner. *See also* Simpson & Allen	London	1884	Architecture	—	—	1	—	—	—	—	—	—	—	1
Allen, F.	London	1878	Architecture	—	—	1	—	—	—	—	—	—	—	1
Allen, Miss Fanny	London	1833	Historical	—	—	—	—	1	—	—	—	—	—	1
Allen, G.	—	1830	Portraits	—	—	1	—	—	—	—	—	—	—	1
Allen, George	London	1820-1840	Architecture	—	—	9	—	1	—	—	—	—	—	10
Allen, George Maule	Putney	1880	Buildings	—	—	—	—	1	—	—	—	—	—	1
Allen, Geraldine Whitacre	London	1890-1893	Moonlight	—	—	—	—	1	—	—	—	—	1	2
Allen, H.	London	1784	Architecture	—	—	1	—	—	—	—	—	—	—	1
Allen, H.	London	1840	Architecture	—	—	1	—	—	—	—	—	—	—	1
Allen, Mrs. Hugh	Highgate	1893	Flowers	—	—	—	—	—	—	1	—	—	—	1
Allen, H. W.	London	1873	Landscape	—	—	—	—	1	—	—	—	—	—	1
Allen, Joseph	Birmingham	1792-1822	Portraits	—	—	50	2	—	—	—	—	—	—	52
Allen, James Baylis	Birmingham	1833-1859	Engraving	—	—	3	—	2	—	—	—	—	—	5
Allen, James C.	London	1824-1830	Engraving	—	—	—	—	5	—	—	—	—	—	5
Allen, John M.	London	1839-1885	Architecture	—	—	8	—	—	—	—	—	—	—	8
Allen, John Whitacre	Bath	1859-1886	Landscape	—	—	2	—	6	—	2	—	—	5	15
Allen, Joseph William §	London	1826-1853	Landscape	—	—	11	17	329	—	2	—	—	—	359
Allen, Lewis	London	1832	Churches	—	—	—	—	1	—	—	—	—	—	1
Allen, L. Barbara M.	London	1872-1877	Domestic	—	—	—	—	3	—	—	—	—	3	6
Allen, L. Jessie	London	1881-1886	Flowers	—	—	—	—	7	—	—	—	—	—	7
Allen, Marcus	London	1864	Figures	—	—	—	—	1	—	—	—	—	—	1
Allen, Marie	Taunton	1889	Landscape	—	—	—	—	1	—	—	—	—	—	1
Allen, Meadows	London	1864	Figures	—	—	—	—	2	—	—	—	—	—	2
Allen, Miss M.	London	1807-1813	Miniatures	—	—	9	—	—	—	—	—	—	—	9
Allen, Mrs. O.	Grasmere	1873	Figures	—	—	—	—	1	—	—	—	—	—	1
Allen, R. J.	Durham	1835	Architecture	—	—	1	—	—	—	—	—	—	—	1
Allen, Samuel	London	1869-1879	Sculpture	—	—	1	—	1	—	—	—	—	—	2
Allen, T.	London	1854	Enamels	—	—	1	—	—	—	—	—	—	—	1
Allen, Theophilus	London	1875-1892	Architecture	—	—	2	—	—	—	—	—	—	—	2
Allen, T. B.	London	1841-1843	Architecture	—	—	3	—	—	—	—	—	—	—	3
Allen, Thomas William	London	1881-1893	Landscape	—	—	10	—	14	—	—	1	—	7	32
Allen, Captain W., R.N.	London	1828-1847	Landscape	—	—	5	—	1	—	—	—	—	—	6
Allen, William	London	1828	Landscape	—	—	1	—	1	—	—	—	—	—	2
Allen, W. H.	London	1865-1874	Landscape	—	—	3	—	7	—	1	—	—	—	11
Allen, Walter James	London	1859-1861	Figures	—	—	1	—	—	—	—	—	—	2	3
Allen, Snooke (W.), and Stock (Henry)	London	1853	Architecture	—	—	1	—	—	—	—	—	—	—	1
Alleyne, Francis	London	1774-1790	Portraits	1	1	1	—	—	—	—	—	—	—	3
Allfrey, Henry W.	Stratford-on-Avon	1842-1861	Landscape	—	—	2	1	1	—	—	—	—	7	11
Allfrey, W.	—	1865	Landscape	—	—	—	2	—	—	—	—	—	—	2
Allies, Mary H.	London	1874	Etching	—	—	—	—	—	—	—	—	—	1	1
Allin, J. S. W.	London	1870-1874	Figures	—	—	—	—	5	—	—	—	—	—	5
Allinger, F. J.	—	1864	Landscape	—	—	—	—	1	—	—	—	—	—	1

Name.	Town.	First and Last Year of Ex.	Speciality.	S. A.	F. S.	R. A.	B. I.	S. S.	O. W.	N. W.	G. G.	N. G.	V. E.	Total.
Allingham, Miss A.	London	1853	Figures	—	—	—	—	1	—	—	—	—	—	1
Allingham, Charles	London	1802-1812	Domestic	—	—	15	2	—	—	—	—	—	—	17
Allingham, Mrs., R.W.S.† *See* Miss Paterson	London	1875-1893	Domestic	—	—	2	—	—	221	—	—	—	9	232
Allingham, W.	London	1849	Architecture	—	—	1	—	—	—	—	—	—	—	1
Allison, F.	London	1790-1799	Miniatures	1	—	9	—	—	—	—	—	—	—	10
Allison, W.	Southampton	1817	Portraits	—	—	1	—	—	—	—	—	—	—	1
Allnutt, Miss Mabel	Windsor	1891	Landscape	—	—	—	—	1	—	—	—	—	—	1
Allom, A.	London	1850	Architecture	—	—	1	—	—	—	—	—	—	—	1
Allom, A.	London	1859-1860	Landscape	—	—	—	—	3	—	—	—	—	—	3
Allom, Thomas, M.I.B.A.	London	1824-1871	Landscape	—	—	43	1	16	—	—	—	—	—	60
Allom and Cross	London	1848	Architecture	—	—	2	—	—	—	—	—	—	—	2
Allongé —.	Paris	1876-1878	Crayons	—	—	—	—	—	—	—	—	—	5	5
Allport, Harvey	London	1888-1890	Landscape	—	—	1	—	3	—	—	—	—	—	4
Allport, Henry C.†	Birmingham	1811-1823	Landscape	—	—	3	—	—	31	—	—	—	—	34
Allport, John	London	1831-1850	Figures	—	—	—	5	4	—	—	—	—	—	9
Allport, Miss Lily	London	1891-1892	Buildings	—	—	1	—	—	—	—	—	—	2	3
Allport, S.	Padstow	1865	Figures	—	—	—	—	1	—	—	—	—	—	1
Allsop, C.	London	1864-1865	Fruit	—	—	—	4	—	—	—	—	—	—	4
Allsop, J.	Birmingham	1857	Landscape	—	—	—	—	1	—	—	—	—	—	1
Allston, Washington, A.R.A.	Massachusetts	1802-1819	Scriptural	—	—	9	8	—	—	—	—	—	—	17
Allsworth, W.	London	1836-1856	Domestic	—	—	10	2	—	—	—	—	—	—	12
Allwood —	London	1776	Sea Pieces	1	—	—	—	—	—	—	—	—	—	1
Allwood, Thomas, F.S.A.	London	1770-1772	Sculpture	4	—	—	—	—	—	—	—	—	—	4
Alma-Tadema, Miss Anna	London	1885-1893	Landscape	—	—	4	—	—	—	2	4	8	—	18
Alma-Tadema, Lawrence, R.A., R.W.S., H.R.S.W., H.R.C.A.†	Brussels	1869-1893	Historical	—	—	57	—	—	22	—	43	22	11	155
Alma-Tadema, Mrs. *See* Miss Laura T. Epps ‖	London	1873-1893	Domestic	—	—	13	—	—	—	—	8	8	5	34
Almande, Charles	London	1777	Sea Pieces	1	—	1	—	—	—	—	—	—	—	2
Almgill, G. T.	London	1877	Domestic	—	—	—	—	—	—	—	—	—	1	1
Almond, W. Douglas, R.B.A. §	London	1886-1893	Domestic	—	—	1	—	20	—	—	—	—	—	21
Alpenny, J. S.	Kew	1825-1853	Portraits	—	—	9	—	4	—	—	—	—	—	13
Alport, Lily	London	1890	Buildings	—	—	—	—	1	—	—	—	—	—	1
Alsop, Frederick	Glasgow	1881-1883	Landscape	—	—	1	—	—	—	—	—	—	2	3
Alsop, J. J.	London	1892-1893	Landscape	—	—	—	—	5	—	—	—	—	1	6
Alsop, William	London	1774-1780	Portraits	—	8	—	—	—	—	—	—	—	—	8
Alston, Miss Charlotte M.	Brockley	1886-1893	Churches	—	—	2	—	3	—	2	—	—	7	14
Alston, Edward Constable	London	1886-1890	Rustic	—	—	1	—	1	—	—	—	—	—	2
Altamura —	Florence	1860	Figures	—	—	1	—	—	—	—	—	—	—	1
Althaus, Fritz B.	London	1881-1893	Sea Pieces	—	—	6	—	16	—	14	1	—	7	44
Altini, Professor, Francisco Fabri-	Rome	1880	Sculpture	—	—	—	—	—	—	—	1	—	—	1
Alvarez, L.	—	1885	Domestic	—	—	—	—	—	—	—	1	—	—	1
Alves, James	London	1775-1779	Miniatures	—	—	14	—	—	—	—	—	—	—	14
Ambler, Miss Esther	Handsworth	1891	Fruit	—	—	—	—	—	—	1	—	—	—	1
Ambler, Louis	London	1890-1892	Architecture	—	—	2	—	—	—	—	—	—	—	2
Ambrose, C.	London	1824-1848	Portraits	—	—	30	2	49	—	—	—	—	—	81
Ambrose, E.	London	1851-1864	Sculpture	—	—	2	—	—	—	—	—	—	—	2
Ambrosini, T.	London	1878	Figures	—	—	—	—	1	—	—	—	—	—	1
Ambucchi, Torello	London	1851-1864	Sculpture	—	—	8	9	1	—	—	—	—	—	18
Amendola, G. B.	London	1879-1886	Sculpture	—	—	7	—	—	—	—	8	—	1	16
Ames, J.	Bristol	1809	Landscape	—	—	1	—	—	—	—	—	—	—	1
Amiconi, Pupil of	—	1780	Sea Pieces	—	3	—	—	—	—	—	—	—	—	3
Amiconi, Berardo	London	1859-1875	Figures	—	—	22	2	3	—	—	—	—	—	27
Amor, Miss E.	London	1870	Flowers	—	—	1	—	—	—	—	—	—	—	1
Amphlett, Miss Kate	London	1878-1890	Landscape	—	—	4	—	37	—	—	—	—	1	42
Amyot, Mrs. *Late* Miss Catherine Engelhart	Diss	1879-1890	Scriptural	—	—	9	—	2	—	—	—	—	1	12
Ancona, Kate	London	1873	Domestic	—	—	—	—	2	—	—	—	—	—	2
Ancona, J. S.	London	1846-1856	Architecture	—	—	3	—	—	—	—	—	—	—	3
Ancrum, M.	Edinburgh	1891	Landscape	—	—	1	—	—	—	—	—	—	—	1
Anderegg, Melchior	London	1873-1877	Sculpture	—	—	—	—	—	—	—	—	—	3	3
Anderson —	—	1761	Architecture	—	1	—	—	—	—	—	—	—	—	1
Anderson, A.	Bedford	1882-1885	Landscape	—	—	—	—	5	—	2	—	—	—	7
Anderson, C.	London	1875-1881	Sculpture	—	—	3	—	—	—	—	—	—	—	3
Anderson, Charles Goldsborough	London	1887-1888	Portraits	—	—	3	—	—	—	—	—	—	1	4
Anderson, Sir Charles H. J. A., Bart.	—	1864-1870	Sea Pieces	—	—	—	—	4	—	—	—	—	—	4
Anderson, David	London	1880-1881	Fishermen	—	—	—	—	2	—	—	—	—	—	2
Anderson, D. J.	London	1872-1874	Woodcuts	—	—	—	—	—	—	—	—	—	3	3
Anderson, Edgar	London	1884-1886	Figures	—	—	3	—	—	—	—	—	—	—	3
Anderson, Miss Ellen	York	1890	Sculpture	—	—	1	—	—	—	—	—	—	—	1
Anderson, F.	London	1859-1860	Cameos	—	—	2	—	—	—	—	—	—	—	2
Anderson, F. C.	London	1855	Architecture	—	—	1	—	—	—	—	—	—	—	1
Anderson, George L.	Coventry	1893	Domestic	—	—	1	—	—	—	—	—	—	—	1
Anderson, G. W.	London	1826-1852	Landscape	—	—	7	3	3	—	—	—	—	—	13

Name.	Town.	First and Last Year of Ex.	Speciality.	S. A.	F. S.	R. A.	B. I.	S. S.	O. W.	N.W.	G. G.	N.G.	V.E.	Total.
Anderson, John	Coventry	1858-1884	Landscape	—	—	5	3	18	—	—	—	—	4	30
Anderson, John	London	1827-1839	Landscape	—	—	4		2	—	—	—	—	—	7
Anderson, J. F.	London	1879-1882	Sea Pieces	—	—	—	—	4	—	—	—	—	—	4
Anderson, J. H.	London	1892	Landscape	—	—	—	—	—	—	—	—	—	1	1
Anderson, John Macvicar	London	1856-1872	Architecture	—	—	5	—	—	—	—	—	—	—	5
Anderson, John Silvy	Dorking	1886-1890	Figures	—	—	1	—	1	—	4	—	—	—	6
Anderson, Captain J. W.	London	1857-1865	Sea Pieces	—	—	—	4	2	—	—	—	—	5	11
Anderson, Percy	London	1886	Figures	—	—	—	—	—	—	1	—	—	—	1
Anderson, Robert, A.R.S.A., R.S.W.	Edinburgh	1880-1884	Figures	—	—	1	—	—	—	3	—	—	—	4
Anderson, Robert Rowand, A.R.S.A.	Edinburgh	1884	Architecture	—	—	3	—	—	—	—	—	—	—	3
Anderson, S.	London	1855-1865	Domestic	—	—	3	3	8	—	—	—	—	—	14
Anderson, Miss S.	London	1863-1870	Still Life	—	—	2	—	—	—	—	—	—	—	2
Anderson, T. W.	London	1839	Landscape	—	—	1	—	—	—	—	—	—	—	1
Anderson, Walter	London	1856-1886	Domestic	—	—	2	2	13	—	—	—	—	—	17
Anderson, Mrs. Walter (Sophie)	London	1858-1890	Domestic	—	—	19	3	6	—	—	9	—	3	40
Anderson, W., Junr.	—	1799	Sea Pieces	—	—	1	—	—	—	—	—	—	—	1
Anderson, William	Horsleydown	1787-1834	Sea Pieces	5	—	45	9	4	—	—	—	—	—	63
Anderson, William	London	1856-1893	Landscape	—	—	10	—	33	—	2	—	—	14	59
Anderson, Will	London	1880-1889	Domestic	—	—	5	—	—	—	—	—	—	—	5
Andrade, Miss Ellen	London	1850-1857	Domestic	—	—	1	1	7	—	—	—	—	—	9
Andrade, Miss J.	London	1849-1858	Fruit	—	—	—	1	8	—	—	—	—	—	9
Andrade, Kate L.	London	1893	Flowers	—	—	—	—	1	—	—	—	—	—	1
Andras, Miss Catherine	London	1799-1824	Wax Models	—	—	31	8	—	—	—	—	—	—	39
André, James P., Junr.	London	1823-1867	Landscape	—	—	55	55	66	—	—	—	—	—	176
Andree, Miss	London	1825-1833	Miniatures	—	—	8	—	—	—	—	—	—	—	8
Andreotti, Frederigo	London	1879-1883	Domestic	—	—	8	—	—	—	—	—	—	—	8
Andreuve, J.	London	1841	Fruit	—	—	1	—	—	—	—	—	—	—	1
Andrew, C.	London	1849	Historical	—	—	—	1	—	—	—	—	—	—	1
Andrew, F. W.	London	1826-1827	Game	—	—	—	—	3	—	—	—	—	—	3
Andrew, F. W., Junr.	London	1842	Fruit	—	—	—	—	1	—	—	—	—	—	1
Andrews, A.	Buffalo	1859	Landscape	—	—	1	—	—	—	—	—	—	—	1
Andrews, C. W.	Dorchester	1865	Philippines	—	—	—	—	—	—	—	—	—	2	2
Andrews, D. R.	London	1820	Miniatures	—	—	1	—	—	—	—	—	—	—	1
Andrews, E. J.	London	1840	Architecture	—	—	1	—	—	—	—	—	—	—	1
Andrews, Edward William	London	1860-1892	Landscape	—	—	3	1	3	—	1	—	—	3	11
Andrews, George H., R.W.S., F.R.G.S.†	London	1840-1893	Landscape	—	—	5	1	3	368	—	—	—	1	378
Andrews, G. T.	York	1847-1848	Architecture	—	—	4	—	—	—	—	—	—	—	4
Andrews, H.	London	1827-1863	Historical	—	—	8	17	14	—	—	—	—	—	39
Andrews, H.	London	1795	Landscape	—	—	1	—	—	—	—	—	—	—	1
Andrews, James	Maidenhead	1868	Portraits	—	—	1	—	—	—	—	—	—	—	1
Andrews, John	London	1824-1870	Portraits	—	—	36	12	2	—	—	—	—	—	50
Andrews, John	Wimbledon	1865-1888	Landscape	—	—	1	—	—	—	1	—	—	13	15
Andrews, James Pettit	—	1767-1770	Sea Pieces	5	3	—	—	—	—	—	—	—	—	8
Andrews, R.	London	1793-1794	Landscape	—	—	3	—	—	—	—	—	—	—	3
Andrews, R. C.	London	1798	Landscape	—	—	1	—	—	—	—	—	—	—	1
Andrews, R. H.	London	1854-1860	L'sc'pes & Fruit	—	—	1	5	—	—	—	—	—	—	6
Andrews, S. H.	—	1844	Architecture	—	—	1	—	—	—	—	—	—	—	1
Andrews, Thomas	London	1832-1834	Landscape	—	—	—	2	—	—	—	—	—	—	2
Andrews, T. H.	London	1850	Landscape	—	—	—	2	—	—	—	—	—	—	2
Andrews, Mrs.	—	1768-1771	Landscape	5	—	—	—	—	—	—	—	—	—	5
Andy, N.	—	1839	Landscape	—	—	1	—	—	—	—	—	—	—	1
Anelay, H.	London	1845	Historical	—	—	1	—	—	—	—	—	—	—	1
Anelay, Henry	Blackheath	1858-1882	Historical	—	—	5	—	16	—	—	—	—	15	36
Angas, George French	London	1843-1874	Architecture	—	—	1	—	1	—	—	—	—	—	2
Angeli, Baron Heinrich von	Berlin	1874-1880	Portraits	—	—	6	—	—	—	—	3	—	—	9
Angelini —	London	1775	Sculpture	1	—	—	—	—	—	—	—	—	—	1
Angell, E. Frank	Bexley	1873-1876	Landscape	—	—	—	—	3	—	—	—	—	1	4
Angell, Frank	London	1889-1891	Landscape	—	—	—	—	2	—	1	—	—	—	3
Angell, Mrs. John.†‡ *See* Miss Helen Cordelia Coleman	—	—	—	—	—	—	—	—	—	—	—	—	—	—
	London	1875-1882	Flowers	—	—	6	—	—	58	25	4	—	18	111
Angell, Miss Maude	Hendon	1888-1893	Flowers	—	—	6	—	7	—	5	—	—	—	18
Angell, Samuel	London	1817-1839	Architecture	—	—	15	—	—	—	—	—	—	—	15
Angell, T. W.	London	1848-1852	Landscape	—	—	3	1	1	—	—	—	—	—	5
Angelletti, Signor	Rome	1790	Copies	5	—	—	—	—	—	—	—	—	—	5
Angelo, G. F.	—	1798-1803	Landscape	—	—	3	—	—	—	—	—	—	—	3
Angle, Miss Beatrice	London	1885-1893	Sculpture	—	—	15	—	—	—	—	—	—	—	15
Angley, H. J. P.	Catford Bridge	1880-1887	Landscape	—	—	6	—	9	—	1	—	—	3	19
Angus, Miss Maria L.	London	1887-1893	Domestic	—	—	1	—	4	—	4	—	—	3	12
Ankcorn, J.	London	1864-1868	Still Life	—	—	4	8	5	—	—	—	—	1	18
Anker, Albert	Paris	1879	Domestic	—	—	—	—	—	—	—	—	—	1	1
Anne, Marie	—	1851	Flowers	—	—	1	—	—	—	—	—	—	—	1
Anning, Miss	London	1761-1776	Flowers	5	1	—	—	—	—	—	—	—	—	6

Name.	Town.	First and Last Year of Ex.	Speciality.	S. A.	F. S.	R. A.	B. I.	S. S.	O. W.	N. W.	G. G.	N. G.	V. E.	Total.
Anning, Mrs. F. M.	—	1792	Flowers	—	—	1	—	—	—	—	—	—	—	1
Annis, J.	London	1796-1800	Landscape	—	—	5	—	—	—	—	—	—	—	5
Annis, W. T.	London	1798-1811	Landscape	—	—	10	—	—	—	—	—	—	4	14
Anonymous, with Initials	—	1761-1880	—	19	6	378	24	120	—	8	—	—	36	591
Anonymous, without Initials	—	1761-1890	—	238	380	631	26	84	—	6	—	—	5	1370
Ansdell, H.	—	1849	Landscape	—	—	1	—	—	—	—	—	—	—	1
Ansdell, Richard, R.A.	Liverpool	1840-1885	Animals	—	—	149	30	—	—	—	—	—	2	181
Ansel, M.	—	1776-1780	Needlework	5	—	—	—	—	—	—	—	—	—	5
Ansell, Miss Alice M.	Wimbledon	1892	Landscape	—	—	—	—	1	—	—	—	—	—	1
Ansell, Charles	—	1780-1781	Animals	—	—	4	—	—	—	—	—	—	—	1
Ansell, George	London	1879	Landscape	—	—	—	—	—	—	—	—	—	1	1
Ansell, Robert	London	1834	Figures	—	—	—	—	1	—	—	—	—	—	1
Ansley, Mrs. (formerly Miss Mary Anne Gandon)	London	1812-1834	Mythological	—	—	22	21	5	—	—	—	—	—	48
Anson, E. J.	London	1792-1793	Architecture	—	—	2	—	—	—	—	—	—	—	2
Anson, F. J.	London	1834-1835	Portraits	—	—	—	1	1	—	—	—	—	—	2
Anson, Mrs.	—	1799	Portraits	—	—	1	—	—	—	—	—	—	—	1
Anson, I'. *See* I.	—	—	—	—	—	—	—	—	—	—	—	—	—	—
Anson, J'. *See* J.	—	—	—	—	—	—	—	—	—	—	—	—	—	—
Ansted, H.	London	1826	Churches	—	—	1	—	—	—	—	—	—	—	1
Ansted, William Alexander	Chiswick	1888-1893	Etching	—	—	4	—	—	—	—	—	—	—	4
Anstie, S.	—	1803-1810	Landscape	—	—	3	—	—	—	—	—	—	—	3
Anthony, George Wilfred	Manchester	1831-1834	Landscape	—	—	4	3	3	—	—	—	—	—	10
Anthony, Henry Mark §	London	1837-1884	Landscape	—	—	37	7	84	—	—	1	—	—	129
Antigna, Madame	Paris	1873	Interiors	—	—	—	—	—	—	—	—	—	1	1
Antonin-Carles, Jean	Paris	1886	Sculpture	—	—	2	—	—	—	—	—	—	—	2
Antrobus, A. Lizzie	New Oscott	1882	Flowers	—	—	—	—	1	—	—	—	—	—	1
Antrobus, Edmund G.	London	1876-1877	Landscape	—	—	—	—	—	—	—	—	—	2	2
Appelbee, Horace R.	London	1889	Architecture	—	—	1	—	—	—	—	—	—	—	1
Appelius, Jean	Rome	1779	Portraits	—	1	—	—	—	—	—	—	—	—	1
Appian, Adolphe	London	1874-1881	Sea Pieces	—	—	—	—	—	—	—	—	—	13	13
Appleby, Ernest	London	1885-1893	Domestic	—	—	10	—	11	—	—	2	—	7	30
Appleby, Y. S.	London	1828	Landscape	—	—	—	—	1	—	—	—	—	—	1
Appleton, Herbert D.	London	1883-1890	Architecture	—	—	3	—	—	—	—	—	—	—	3
Appleton (H. D.), and Mountford (E. W.)	London	1890	Architecture	—	—	1	—	—	—	—	—	—	—	1
Appleton, Miss M.	London	1810	Figures	—	—	1	—	—	—	—	—	—	—	1
Appleton, Thomas G.	London	1877-1893	Engraving	—	—	13	—	—	—	—	—	—	—	13
Appleyard, C.	—	1810	Landscape	—	—	1	—	—	—	—	—	—	—	1
Apprentice, S. C.	London	1823	Medals	—	—	1	—	—	—	—	—	—	—	1
Aranda, José Jimenez Y.	Paris	1880-1881	Domestic	—	—	—	—	—	—	—	—	—	11	11
Arber. *See* Wimperis and Arber	—	—	Architecture	—	—	—	—	—	—	—	—	—	—	—
Arbouin, S.	—	1875-1877	Landscape	—	—	2	—	—	—	—	—	—	—	2
Arbringen, J. H.	—	1838	Portraits	—	—	1	—	—	—	—	—	—	—	1
Arbuthnot, George	London	1829-1854	Landscape	—	—	2	18	—	—	—	—	—	—	20
Archer, Archibald	London	1810-1845	Scriptural	—	—	16	6	1	—	—	—	—	—	23
Archer, C.	Birmingham	1873	Flowers	—	—	—	—	1	—	—	—	—	—	1
Archer, E.	—	1815	Architecture	—	—	—	—	—	—	—	—	—	1	1
Archer, Edwin or Edward	Great Malvern	1884-1891	Landscape	—	—	1	—	—	—	—	3	5	5	14
Archer, F. S.	London	1836-1851	Sculpture	—	—	22	—	—	—	—	—	—	—	22
Archer, J.	London	1779-1791	Portraits	3	11	—	—	—	—	—	—	—	—	14
Archer, James, R.S.A.	Edinburgh	1850-1893	Figures	—	—	108	1	4	—	—	—	—	1	114
Archer, Miss Janet	London	1873-1893	Figures	—	—	7	—	2	—	2	—	—	4	15
Archer, J. S.	London	1808-1827	Architecture	—	—	5	—	—	—	—	—	—	—	5
Archer, J. S.	—	1850	Sporting	—	—	1	—	—	—	—	—	—	—	1
Archer, J. Wykeham ‡	London	1842-1864	Landscape	—	—	—	—	—	—	63	—	—	—	63
Ardel, Mc. *See* M.	—	—	—	—	—	—	—	—	—	—	—	—	—	—
Arden, Edward	Ambleside	1881-1889	Landscape	—	—	—	—	—	—	5	1	—	4	10
Arding, J.	—	1811	Architecture	—	—	1	—	—	—	—	—	—	—	1
Arendrup, Madame. *See* Miss Edith Courtauld	Wimbledon	1873-1878	Eastern	—	—	2	—	3	—	—	—	—	2	7
Arendzen, Petrus J.	London	1890	Etching	—	—	1	—	—	—	—	—	—	—	1
Argent —	London	1782-1783	Animals	—	3	—	—	—	—	—	—	—	—	3
Argent, W.	London	1837	Landscape	—	—	—	—	1	—	—	—	—	—	1
Argenta, C.	London	1881	Sculpture	—	—	1	—	—	—	—	—	—	—	1
Argles, Alice	Stamford	1880	Flowers	—	—	—	—	—	—	—	—	—	1	1
Argles, T.	London	1809	Landscape	—	—	1	—	—	—	—	—	—	—	1
Argyll, George, 8th Duke of, K.T.	—	1882	Landscape	—	—	—	—	—	—	—	1	—	—	1
Arichall, F.	London	1797	Landscape	—	—	3	—	—	—	—	—	—	—	3
Arkell, Laura	Swindon	1887	Heads	—	—	—	—	1	—	—	—	—	—	1
Arkwright, Miss Edith	Brighton	1884	Miniatures	—	—	1	—	—	—	—	—	—	—	1
Arkwright, Emily	London	1878-1881	Pencil	—	—	—	—	—	—	—	—	—	4	4
Arlaud, Bernard	London	1793-1800	Miniatures	—	—	41	—	—	—	—	—	—	—	41
Arlaud, L. R.	London	1792	Miniatures	—	—	1	—	—	—	—	—	—	—	1

Name.	Town.	First and Last Year of Ex.	Speciality.	S. A.	F. S.	R. A.	B. I.	S. S.	O. W.	N.W.	G. G.	N. G.	V. E.	Total.
Armfield, George (Smith)	London	1840-1875	Animals	—	—	32	30	42	—	—	—	—	9	113
Armitage, Alfred	Shipley	1889-1892	Flowers	—	—	1	—	2	—	—	—	1	—	4
Armitage, C.	London	1870-1872	Rustic	—	—	2	—	—	—	—	—	—	—	2
Armitage, C. Liddall	London	1891	Sea Pieces	—	—	—	—	1	—	—	—	—	—	1
Armitage, Edward, R.A.	London	1840-1893	Scriptural	—	—	83	—	—	—	—	—	—	15	98
Armitage, Miss E.	London	1858	Figures	—	—	1	—	—	—	—	—	—	—	1
Armitage, Thomas Liddall	London	1885-1891	Domestic	—	—	1	—	—	—	—	—	—	1	2
Armitage, William	London	1848-1853	Scriptural	—	—	—	2	—	—	—	—	—	2	4
Armitage, William J.	London	1889	Landscape	—	—	1	—	—	—	—	—	—	—	1
Armour, G. Denholm	Edinburgh	1884-1893	Moorish	—	—	7	—	—	—	—	—	4	—	11
Armstead, Miss Charlotte W.	London	1886-1889	Flowers	—	—	2	—	—	—	—	—	—	—	2
Armstead, Henry Hugh, R.A.	London	1851-1892	Sculpture	—	—	72	—	—	—	—	—	—	—	72
Armstead, Miss Lottie	London	1885	Flowers	—	—	2	—	—	—	—	—	—	—	2
Armstrong, Miss Caroline	London	1885-1893	Miniatures	—	—	3	—	—	—	—	—	—	1	4
Armstrong, Miss Elizbeth A.	Penzance	1883-1889	Domestic	—	—	14	—	16	—	13	4	2	14	63
Armstrong, Miss Emily S.	London	1865-1872	Flowers	—	—	—	—	—	—	—	—	—	10	10
Armstrong, Miss Fanny	Oxford	1883-1890	Landscape	—	—	—	—	1	—	1	—	—	—	2
Armstrong, J.	—	1802	Figures	—	—	1	—	—	—	—	—	—	—	1
Armstrong, John	Conway	1879-1882	Landscape	—	—	3	—	—	—	—	—	—	—	3
Armstrong, R.	London	1872-1873	Architecture	—	—	2	—	—	—	—	—	—	—	2
Armstrong, R. W.	Dublin	1848-1857	Architecture	—	—	7	—	—	—	—	—	—	—	7
Armstrong, Thomas	Manchester	1860-1882	Figures	—	—	15	2	—	—	—	13	—	5	35
Armstrong, W.	—	1834	Sculpture	—	—	—	—	1	—	—	—	—	—	1
Armytage, Charles	London	1863-1874	Domestic	—	—	—	—	17	—	—	—	—	12	29
Arnald, Miss A. M.	London	1823-1831	Landscape	—	—	9	5	1	—	—	—	—	—	15
Arnald, George, A R.A.	London	1788-1842	Landscape	—	—	176	63	—	—	2	—	—	—	241
Arnald, Sebastian Wyndham	London	1823-1846	Sculpture	—	—	32	3	1	—	1	—	—	—	37
Arnald, W.	London	1797	Architecture	—	—	1	—	—	—	—	—	—	—	1
Arndt, F.	London	1885	Figures	—	—	1	—	—	—	—	—	—	—	1
Arnold, Edward	—	1773	Still Life	3	—	—	—	—	—	—	—	—	—	3
Arnold, Mrs. Edwin	London	1874-1885	Domestic	—	—	—	—	1	—	1	—	—	2	4
Arnold, George	Oxford	1770-1791	Still Life	17	—	—	—	—	—	—	—	—	—	17
Arnold, Harry	Putney	1877-1890	Domestic	—	—	2	—	6	—	8	—	—	5	21
Arnold, John	London	1829	Domestic	—	—	—	—	1	—	—	—	—	—	1
Arnold, J. J.	—	1799	Portraits	—	—	1	—	—	—	—	—	—	—	1
Arnold, R.	London	1791	Miniatures	1	—	1	—	—	—	—	—	—	—	2
Arnold, Reginald Ernest	Dorking	1876-1893	Sculpture	—	—	23	—	4	—	—	—	—	16	43
Arnold, Samuel James	London	1800-1808	Portraits	—	—	10	—	—	—	—	—	—	—	10
Arnold, V. *See also* Spurr and Arnold	Clapham	1849	Architecture	—	—	1	—	—	—	—	—	—	—	1
Arnold, Mrs. *See* Miss Harriet Gouldsmith	London	1840-1855	Landscape	—	—	15	15	—	—	—	—	—	—	30
Arnott, McLellan	Dumfries	1892	Figures	—	—	1	—	—	—	—	—	—	—	1
Aronson, Miss Meta	London	1883	Domestic	—	—	1	—	—	—	—	—	—	—	1
Arpin. *See* Lewen, Sharp and Arpin	—	—	Architecture	—	—	—	—	—	—	—	—	—	—	—
Arran, E.	London	1849	—	—	—	—	—	1	—	—	—	—	—	1
Arrobine, G.	London	1783	Rustic	—	—	1	—	—	—	—	—	—	—	1
Arrowsmith, C.	London	1830-1833	Churches	—	—	1	7	5	—	—	—	—	—	13
Arrowsmith, H.	London	1855	Domestic	—	—	—	—	1	—	—	—	—	—	1
Arrowsmith, Hannah F.	London	1867	Landscape	—	—	—	—	—	—	—	—	—	1	1
Arrowsmith, H. J.	London	1864-1865	Landscape	—	—	—	—	3	—	—	—	—	—	3
Arrowsmith, Thomas	London	1792-1829	Miniatures	—	—	26	—	—	—	—	—	—	—	26
Artaud, William	London	1780-1822	Portraits	—	—	85	—	—	—	—	—	—	—	85
Arthur, J.	London	1816-1824	Portraits	—	—	7	—	—	—	—	—	—	—	7
Arthur, Reginald	London	1881-1893	Historical	—	—	6	—	2	—	—	—	—	2	10
Arthur, Robert	London	1879	Domestic	—	—	—	—	—	—	—	—	—	1	1
Arthur, Miss Winifred	London	1889	Landscape	—	—	2	—	—	—	—	—	—	1	3
Artz, A.	—	1880	Domestic	—	—	—	—	—	—	—	2	—	—	2
Arundale, Francis	Rome	1830-1853	Landscape	—	—	43	2	—	—	—	—	—	—	45
Arundale, Mrs. F.	London	1839-1862	Miniatures	—	—	19	—	—	—	—	—	—	—	19
Arundle, Miss Kate	London	1866	Landscape	—	—	—	1	—	—	—	—	—	—	1
Asbonin, Sidney	Paris	1874	Landscape	—	—	—	—	—	—	—	—	—	1	1
Ascroft, William	London	1858-1886	Landscape	—	—	19	4	14	—	—	—	—	14	51
Ash, Albert Edward	Birmingham	1880-1882	Landscape	—	—	1	—	3	—	—	—	—	—	4
Ash, Miss Chrissie	London	1889-1892	Domestic	—	—	1	—	3	—	—	—	—	—	4
Ash, H.	London	1851-1858	Landscape	—	—	3	2	2	—	—	—	—	—	7
Ash, J. W.	London	1822-1833	Landscape	—	—	2	1	2	—	—	—	—	—	5
Ash, M.	London	1819-1820	Landscape	—	—	—	3	—	—	—	—	—	—	3
Ash, Thomas Morris	Birmingham	1881-1885	Landscape	—	—	—	—	4	—	—	—	—	2	6
Ashbee, Miss Agnes	London	1892	Flowers	—	—	—	—	—	—	1	—	—	—	1
Ashbee, Charles B.	London	1892	Architecture	—	—	1	—	—	—	—	—	—	—	1
Ashburner, G.	London	1881	Landscape	—	—	—	—	—	—	—	—	—	1	1
Ashby, H.	London	1794-1855	Portraits	—	—	69	8	1	—	—	—	—	—	78
Ashby, H. P.	Mitcham	1835-1865	Landscape	—	—	20	—	—	—	—	—	—	—	20

Name.	Town.	First and Last Year of Ex.	Speciality.	S. A.	F. S.	R. A.	B. I.	S. S.	O. W.	N.W.	G. G.	N. G.	V. E.	Total.
Ashby, Robert	Brentford	1855-1856	Domestic	—	—	—	—	—	—	—	—	—	4	4
Ashby, Miss	—	1856	Flowers	—	—	—	—	1	—	—	—	—	—	1
Ashby-Sterry, J. *See* S.	—	—	—	—	—	—	—	—	—	—	—	—	—	—
Ashe, J. W. L.	London	1866-1884	Sea Pieces	—	—	8	—	2	—	—	—	—	4	14
Ashford, Edith M.	Bramgrove	1889	Landscape	—	—	—	—	1	—	—	—	—	—	1
Ashford, William, P.R.H.A., F.S.A.	Dublin	1775-1811	Landscape	23	—	25	14	—	—	—	—	—	—	62
Ashley, Alfred	London	1850-1853	Landscape	—	—	—	—	—	—	—	—	—	7	7
Ashley, F. M.	London	1870-1877	Figures	—	—	3	—	—	—	—	—	—	8	11
Ashley, J.	London	1822-1839	Landscape	—	—	10	—	—	—	—	—	—	—	10
Ashley, Mrs.	London	1768-1772	Portraits	1	16	—	—	—	—	—	—	—	—	17
Ashlin, George C., R.H.A.	Dublin	1878	Architecture	—	—	1	—	—	—	—	—	—	—	1
Ashmore, Charles	Birmingham	1858-1870	Domestic	—	—	1	1	3	—	—	—	—	—	5
Ashpital, W. H.	London	1800-1806	Architecture	—	—	4	—	—	—	—	—	—	—	4
Ashpitel, Arthur, F.S.A.	London	1845-1864	Architecture	—	—	18	—	—	—	—	—	—	—	18
Ashton, A. F.	London	1837-1845	Architecture	—	—	5	—	—	—	—	—	—	—	5
Ashton, Miss E.	London	1839-1840	Flowers	—	—	3	—	—	—	—	—	—	—	3
Ashton, G. A.	London	1868	Landscape	—	—	1	—	—	—	—	—	—	—	1
Ashton, G. F.	London	1861-1871	Landscape	—	—	4	5	4	—	—	—	—	—	13
Ashton, G. R.	London	1874-1877	Animals	—	—	—	—	4	—	—	—	—	5	9
Ashton, Henry	London	1816-1856	Architecture	—	—	13	—	1	—	—	—	—	—	14
Ashton, H.	Prestwich	1867-1870	Figures	—	—	2	—	—	—	—	—	—	—	2
Ashton, Julian R.	London	1871-1879	Figures	—	—	4	—	30	—	—	—	—	17	51
Ashwell, Ellen	London	1877	Figures	—	—	—	—	—	—	—	—	—	2	2
Ashwell, Lawrence Tom	London	1883-1893	Landscape	—	—	4	—	10	—	—	—	—	2	16
Ashwell, Mrs.	Bath	1873	Landscape	—	—	—	—	1	—	—	—	—	—	1
Ashwell, Miss	Dieppe	1866	Figures	—	—	—	—	4	—	—	—	—	—	4
Ashworth, Miss Susan A.	London	1874-1880	Landscape	—	—	—	—	2	—	—	—	—	2	4
Askew, J. F.	Leicester	1836	Landscape	—	—	—	2	—	—	—	—	—	—	2
Askew, Richard J.	Shere	1885-1887	Landscape	—	—	—	—	1	—	3	—	—	—	4
Aspa, Signor Rosario	London	1874-1884	Landscape	—	—	1	—	1	—	—	—	—	—	2
Aspinal, George S.	Dorking	1881-1885	Landscape	—	—	2	—	7	—	1	—	—	5	15
Aspinwall, Reginald, A.R.C.A.	Lancaster	1883-1892	Landscape	—	—	5	—	1	—	5	—	—	1	12
Aspney, Amelia	Merton	1885	Figures	—	—	1	—	—	—	—	—	—	—	1
Assen, Francis	London	1779-1780	Portraits	—	3	—	—	—	—	—	—	—	—	3
Assen, Van. *See* V.	—	—	—	—	—	—	—	—	—	—	—	—	—	—
Asser, James	Brentwood	1780	Architecture	—	2	—	—	—	—	—	—	—	—	2
Astles, S.	Worcester	1827	Enamels	—	—	1	—	—	—	—	—	—	—	1
Astlett, G.	London	1807	Portraits	—	—	1	—	—	—	—	—	—	—	1
Aston, Charles Reginald, R.I.‡	Birmingham	1855-1893	Landscape	—	—	18	4	13	—	85	—	—	127	247
Aston, J.	London	1878	Figures	—	—	—	—	—	—	—	—	—	1	1
Aston, Miss Lilias	Birmingham	1865	Flowers	—	—	—	—	—	—	—	—	—	1	1
Athow, T.	London	1806-1822	Landscape	—	—	7	—	—	—	—	—	—	—	7
Atkey, W.	London	1821	Architecture	—	—	1	—	—	—	—	—	—	—	1
Atkins	—	1761	Sculpture	—	1	—	—	—	—	—	—	—	—	1
Atkins, Miss Catherine J.	London	1871-1893	Figures	—	—	10	—	21	—	6	3	2	25	67
Atkins, Miss Emmeline	London	1878-1885	Still Life	—	—	1	—	2	—	1	—	—	3	7
Atkins, Miss G.	London	1849-1850	Miniatures	—	—	—	—	8	—	—	—	—	—	8
Atkins, J.	Rome	1831-1833	Portraits	—	—	2	—	—	—	—	—	—	—	2
Atkins, S.	London	1787-1808	Sea Pieces	—	—	18	—	—	—	—	—	—	—	18
Atkins, S. E.	London	1794	Architecture	—	—	1	—	—	—	—	—	—	—	1
Atkinson, Miss Amy B.	London	1890-1893	Domestic	—	—	1	—	1	—	—	—	—	1	3
Atkinson, Arthur G.	London	1879-1891	Sculpture	—	—	13	—	1	—	—	—	—	—	14
Atkinson, Miss Alice Louisa Maria. *See* Mrs.	—	—	—	—	—	—	—	—	—	—	—	—	—	—
Val Bromley.	—	—	—	—	—	—	—	—	—	—	—	—	—	—
Atkinson, B. T.	London	1856	Landscape	—	—	—	2	—	—	—	—	—	—	2
Atkinson, B. W.	Egremont	1888	River Scene	—	—	1	—	—	—	—	—	—	—	1
Atkinson, Charles	Datchet	1879-1881	Portraits	—	—	—	—	—	—	—	3	—	2	5
Atkinson, E.	London	1793-1797	Game	—	—	3	—	—	—	—	—	—	—	3
Atkinson, Francis E.	Teddington	1891-1893	Engraving	—	—	2	—	—	—	—	—	—	—	2
Atkinson, G.	—	1800-1801	Architecture	—	—	3	—	—	—	—	—	—	—	3
Atkinson, G.	Cork	1850	Sea Piece	—	—	—	—	1	—	—	—	—	—	1
Atkinson, George M.	London	1859-1877	Landscape	—	—	1	5	9	—	—	—	—	3	18
Atkinson, Herbert D.	Beckenham	1889	Domestic	—	—	—	—	1	—	—	—	—	1	2
Atkinson, J.	—	1796	Animals	—	—	1	—	—	—	—	—	—	—	1
Atkinson, J.	London	1801-1802	Architecture	—	—	2	—	—	—	—	—	—	—	2
Atkinson, J.	Norwood	1836-1842	Architecture	—	—	2	—	—	—	—	—	—	—	2
Atkinson, James	London	1832-1833	Figures	—	—	—	4	1	—	—	—	—	—	5
Atkinson, John	London	1770-1775	Landscape	1	34	—	—	—	—	—	—	—	—	35
Atkinson, John Augustus	London	1803-1833	Battle Pieces	—	—	60	45	24	68	—	—	—	—	197
Atkinson, J. B.	York	1839	Architecture	—	—	1	—	—	—	—	—	—	—	1
Atkinson, John Gunson	London	1849-1879	Landscape	—	—	12	27	108	—	—	—	—	12	159
Atkinson, J. M.	London	1858	Domestic	—	—	—	1	—	—	—	—	—	—	1

Name.	Town.	First and Last Year of Ex.	Speciality.	S. A.	F. S.	R. A.	B. I.	S. S.	O. W.	N. W.	G. G.	N. G.	V. E.	Total.
Atkinson, Miss Kate E.	London	1871	Landscape	—	—	—	—	4	—	—	—	—	—	4
Atkinson, Miss Mary ‖	—	1833-1839	Birds	—	—	1	—	1	—	—	—	—	—	2
Atkinson, Peter	—	1801	Architecture	—	—	1	—	—	—	—	—	—	—	1
Atkinson, Richard	London	1772-1775	Portraits	1	—	4	—	—	—	—	—	—	—	5
Atkinson, Robert	Leeds	1891	Figures	—	—	2	—	—	—	—	—	—	—	2
Atkinson, Thomas Lewis	London	1857-1889	Engraving	—	—	41	—	—	—	—	—	—	—	41
Atkinson, Thomas Witlam	London	1830-1842	Architecture	—	—	8	—	—	—	—	—	—	—	8
Atkinson, William	London	1796-1811	Architecture	—	—	25	—	—	—	—	—	—	—	25
Atkinson, W. A.	London	1849-1867	Domestic	—	—	9	5	5	—	—	—	—	2	21
Atkinson, W. E.	Kew	1877-1878	Engraving	—	—	—	—	—	—	—	—	—	2	2
Attlee, Miss Della	London	1886-1893	Flowers	—	—	5	—	2	—	—	—	—	6	13
Attlee, Miss Kathleen Mabel *or* Mary	London	1886-1892	Flowers	—	—	6	—	2	—	—	—	—	5	13
Atwood, Miss	—	1773-1774	Copies	2	—	—	—	—	—	—	—	—	—	2
Atwood, Thomas	—	1761-1764	Flowers	8	—	—	—	—	—	—	—	—	—	8
Auber, H. Van den. *See* V.	—	—	—	—	—	—	—	—	—	—	—	—	—	—
Aubin, St. *See* S.	—	—	—	—	—	—	—	—	—	—	—	—	—	—
Aubiniere, De l'. *See* D.	—	—	—	—	—	—	—	—	—	—	—	—	—	—
Aublet, Albert	Neuilly	1884-1890	Domestic	—	—	7	—	—	—	—	—	—	—	7
Aubrey, C.	London	1836	Architecture	—	—	—	—	1	—	—	—	—	—	1
Aubrey, H.	London	1879	Landscape	—	—	—	—	1	—	—	—	—	—	1
Aubyn, St. *See* S.	—	—	—	—	—	—	—	—	—	—	—	—	—	—
Audinet, Philippe §	London	1826-1829	Engraving	—	—	—	—	7	—	—	—	—	—	7
Audubon, John James	Philadelphia	1829-1838	Sporting	—	—	—	—	7	—	—	—	—	—	7
Audubon, V. G.	London	1835-1838	Landscape	—	—	1	3	6	—	—	—	—	—	10
Aufray, J.	Paris	1876	Domestic	—	—	—	—	—	—	—	—	—	1	1
Auld, John	Blackheath	1869-1891	Figures	—	—	2	—	6	—	—	—	—	5	13
Auld, P.	London	1874-1877	Architecture	—	—	4	—	—	—	—	—	—	—	4
Auld, P. C.	London	1850-1865	Landscape	—	—	4	4	15	—	—	—	—	—	23
Aumonier, James, R.I. ‡ φ	Hornsey	1864-1893	Landscape	—	—	36	5	52	—	100	5	2	49	249
Aumonier, Miss Louisa	London	1868-1893	Flowers	—	—	3	—	17	—	13	1	—	19	53
Aumonier, W.	London	1889-1890	Architecture	—	—	2	—	—	—	—	—	—	—	2
Ausiter, T.	Southall	1783-1786	Still Life	—	—	5	—	—	—	—	—	—	—	5
Austen, George	Canterbury	1853	Windows	—	—	3	—	—	—	—	—	—	—	3
Austin, A. E.	London	1870-1871	Landscape	—	—	—	—	2	—	—	—	—	2	4
Austin, Miss Christina	London	1783-1797	Miniatures	4	—	5	—	—	—	—	—	—	—	9
Austin, Miss Emily	London	1879-1887	Flowers	—	—	1	—	—	—	—	—	—	2	3
Austin, F.	London	1780	Heads	1	—	—	—	—	—	—	—	—	—	1
Austin, F. *See also* Paley and Austin	London	1854	Architecture	—	—	2	—	—	—	—	—	—	—	2
Austin, Miss F. Roberts. (?) Austen	London	1886	Portraits	—	—	—	—	—	—	—	1	—	—	1
Austin, H.	London	1833	Cathedrals	—	—	1	—	—	—	—	—	—	—	1
Austin, Hubert J.	Lancaster	1887	Landscape	—	—	—	—	—	—	1	—	—	—	1
Austin, Richard T.	London	1803-1818	Landscape	—	—	3	—	—	—	—	—	—	—	3
Austin, Samuel † §	Liverpool	1820-1834	Landscape	—	—	1	—	9	62	—	—	—	—	72
Austin, T.	London	1767	Sculpture	3	—	—	—	—	—	—	—	—	—	3
Austin, Thomas, Jun.	London	1779	Enamels	—	1	—	—	—	—	—	—	—	—	1
Austin, William	London	1776-1786	Landscape	—	—	5	—	—	—	—	—	—	—	5
Austin, William	London	1848	Historical	—	—	—	—	1	—	—	—	—	—	1
Austin, Mrs.	Liverpool	1835-1838	Portraits	—	—	5	—	1	—	—	—	—	—	6
Autran, Eugène	—	1881	Enamels	—	—	2	—	—	—	—	—	—	—	2
Auty, Charles	London	1881-1887	Domestic	—	—	—	—	4	—	3	—	—	—	7
Avarne, C.	London	1793	Miniatures	—	—	3	—	—	—	—	—	—	—	3
Aveling, H. J.	London	1839-1842	Portraits	—	—	—	—	5	—	—	—	—	—	5
Averne, C.	—	1818-1829	Medals	—	—	7	—	—	—	—	—	—	—	7
Axenfeld, Henry	Paris	1874-1877	Domestic	—	—	—	—	—	—	—	—	—	5	5
Ayers, C. R.	London	1827-1829	Architecture	—	—	4	—	—	—	—	—	—	—	4
Ayers, R.	London	1823	Animals	—	—	1	—	—	—	—	—	—	—	1
Ayles, Mrs. Ellen	Tilbury	1893	Miniatures	—	—	1	—	—	—	—	—	—	—	1
Aylesford, Heneage, 4th Earl of	London	1786-1790	Landscape	—	—	7	—	—	—	—	—	—	—	7
Ayliffe, E.	London	1874	Engraving	—	—	—	—	—	—	—	—	—	1	1
Ayling, Albert W., R.C.A.	Guernsey	1843-1892	Domestic	—	—	18	—	40	—	3	—	—	—	61
Ayling, F.	London	1887	Domestic	—	—	—	—	1	—	—	—	—	—	1
Ayling, J.	London	1823-1842	Portraits	—	—	31	1	2	—	—	—	—	—	34
Aylmer, T. B.	London	1834-1856	Landscape	—	—	18	9	35	—	1	—	—	—	63
Ayre, Miss Minnie	London	1886	Flowers	—	—	—	—	1	—	1	—	—	—	2
Ayres, H. M. E.	London	1873	Flowers	—	—	—	—	1	—	—	—	—	—	1
Ayrton, Madame Annie	London	1878-1886	Flowers	—	—	8	—	—	—	—	—	—	1	9
Ayrton, Oliver	Paris	1888-1889	Figures	—	—	1	—	—	—	—	1	—	—	2
Ayrton, W. J.	London	1833-1834	Landscape	—	—	—	1	6	—	—	—	—	—	7
Ayvazofsky, John. (?) Ayvasowsky	London	1876	Landscape	—	—	1	—	—	—	—	—	—	—	1
Azile, B.	Ventnor	1861	Landscape	—	—	—	—	—	—	—	—	—	4	4

Name.	Town.	First and Last Year of Ex.	Speciality.	S. A.	F. S.	R. A.	B. I.	S. S.	O. W.	N.W.	G. G.	N. G.	V. E.	Total.
Babb, Miss Charlotte E.	London	1862-1885	Figures	—	—	—	2	9	—	—	—	—	6	17
Babb, J. Staines	London	1870-1892	Landscape	—	—	3	—	2	—	—	—	—	5	10
Babcock, W. P.	—	1855	Figures	—	—	1	—	—	—	—	—	—	—	1
Baber, J.	London	1806-1812	Architecture	—	—	15	—	—	—	—	—	—	—	15
Babington, P.	London	1870-1871	Figures	—	—	—	—	1	—	—	—	—	1	2
Babu —	London	1765-1775	Miniatures	3	4	—	—	—	—	—	—	—	—	7
Baccani, Attilio	London	1859-1890	Portraits	—	—	34	—	2	—	—	1	—	1	38
Baccani, Miss Italia	London	1885	Portraits	—	—	—	—	—	—	—	1	—	—	1
Baccuni, E.	London	1857	Figures	—	—	1	—	—	—	—	—	—	—	1
Bach, Edward	London	1874-1893	Figures	—	—	13	—	16	—	—	—	—	3	32
Bach, Franz	London	1880	Sea Pieces	—	—	—	—	1	—	—	—	—	—	1
Bach, Guido R., R.I.‡φ	London	1866-1891	Figures	—	—	2	—	—	—	137	3	—	13	155
Bach, W. H.	London	1829-1859	Landscape	—	—	24	2	7	—	1	—	—	2	36
Bacher, Otto H.	Venice	1882	Venice	—	—	1	—	—	—	—	—	—	—	1
Back, W. M.	London	1836	Portraits	—	—	1	—	—	—	—	—	—	—	1
Backhoffner, Charles	London	1827-1831	Architecture	—	—	2	—	—	—	—	—	—	—	2
Backhoffner, Mrs. *See* Miss Caroline Derby	London	1835	Miniatures	—	—	1	—	2	—	—	—	—	—	3
Backhouse, Henry	London	1856	Landscape	—	—	—	1	—	—	—	—	—	—	1
Backhouse, J.	London	1855	Landscape	—	—	—	1	—	—	—	—	—	—	1
Backhouse, James E.	Darlington	1886-1891	Landscape	—	—	—	—	—	—	5	—	—	—	5
Backhouse, Miss Mary. *See* Mrs. W. E. Miller‖	London	1866-1880	Figures	—	—	9	—	27	—	—	—	—	1	37
Backhouse, Mrs. *See* Miss Margaret Holden‖	London	1846-1882	Figures	—	—	15	—	26	—	—	—	—	4	45
Backhouse, R. W.	London	1783-1818	Architecture	2	—	4	—	—	—	—	—	—	—	6
Backhouse, R. W.	London	1827	Landscape	—	—	—	—	1	—	—	—	—	—	1
Backshell, W.	London	1848	Domestic	—	—	—	—	2	—	—	—	—	—	2
Bacon, C.	London	1800-1812	Architecture	—	—	9	—	—	—	—	—	—	—	9
Bacon, Charles	London	1842-1884	Sculpture	—	—	37	4	1	—	—	—	—	—	42
Bacon, D'Arcy	London	1855-1874	Animals	—	—	1	3	10	—	—	—	—	6	20
Bacon, Frederick	London	1830-1855	Engraving	—	—	1	—	2	—	—	—	—	—	3
Bacon, G.	London	1846-1848	Sculpture	—	—	3	—	—	—	—	—	—	—	3
Bacon, H. D.	London	1861	Sporting	—	—	—	—	—	—	—	—	—	1	1
Bacon (H. F.), and Bell (E. Ingress)	London	1879	Architecture	—	—	1	—	—	—	—	—	—	—	1
Bacon, Miss H. M.	London	1862	Fruit	—	—	—	2	—	—	—	—	—	—	2
Bacon, H. M.	London	1864	Historical	—	—	—	1	—	—	—	—	—	—	1
Bacon, John, R.A.	London	1762-1807	Sculpture	1	4	32	2	—	—	—	—	—	—	39
Bacon, John, Junr.	London	1792-1824	Sculpture	—	—	64	—	—	—	—	—	—	—	64
Bacon, J.	—	1813	Portraits	—	—	1	—	—	—	—	—	—	—	1
Bacon, John Henry F.	London	1889-1893	Domestic	—	—	8	—	—	—	—	—	—	2	10
Bacon, J. P.	Stoke-on-Trent	1865-1867	Landscape	—	—	—	3	—	—	—	—	—	—	3
Bacon, Percy C. H.	London	1885-1890	Stained Glass	—	—	3	—	—	—	—	—	—	—	3
Bacon (Percy) and Bros.	London	1892	Stained Glass	—	—	2	—	—	—	—	—	—	—	2
Bacon, T.	London	1793-1795	Sculpture	—	—	3	—	—	—	—	—	—	—	3
Bacon, T., F.S.A., F.R.A.S.	Florence	1844-1845	Landscape	—	—	1	—	1	—	—	—	—	—	2
Bacon, W.	London	1809-1823	Landscape	—	—	7	—	—	—	—	—	—	—	7
Bacon, W. E.	Bettws-y-Coed	1883	Landscape	—	—	1	—	—	—	—	—	—	—	1
Badcock, Miss Isabel B.	Ripon	1886-1889	Buildings	—	—	—	—	1	—	1	—	—	—	2
Badcock, Miss K. S.	Ripon	1889	Animals	—	—	—	—	1	—	—	—	—	—	1
Badcock, Miss Leigh	Norwood	1887-1893	Landscape	—	—	—	—	5	—	1	—	—	—	6
Baden-Powell, Frank, M.A.	London	1880-1893	Landscape	—	—	7	—	—	—	—	1	—	1	9
Badger, J.	London	1793	Architecture	—	—	1	—	—	—	—	—	—	—	1
Badger, Miss	London	1815	Flowers	—	—	—	—	—	1	—	—	—	—	1
Baertsoen, Albert	London	1890	Landscape	—	—	—	—	1	—	—	—	—	—	1
Bager, Johann Daniel	Amsterdam	1780	Domestic	2	—	—	—	—	—	—	—	—	—	2
Bagg, William	London	1827-1829	Portraits	—	—	8	2	—	—	—	—	—	—	10
Baggallay, Frank T.	Beckenham	1880-1891	Architecture	—	—	3	—	—	—	—	—	—	—	3
Bagnold, E. S. H.	—	1851	Sculpture	—	—	1	—	—	—	—	—	—	—	1
Bagot, R.	—	1796	—	—	—	*	—	—	—	—	—	—	—	—
Bagster, H.	London	1846-1849	Architecture	—	—	4	—	—	—	—	—	—	—	4
Bagster, T.	—	1833	Fruit, etc.	—	—	—	—	2	—	—	—	—	—	2
Baher, Professor	Dresden	1850	Historical	—	—	—	—	—	—	—	—	—	1	1
Baigent, R.	Winchester	1843-1846	Landscape	—	—	—	—	11	—	—	—	—	—	11
Baildon, W. A.	London	1824-1841	Landscape	—	—	2	6	18	—	—	—	—	—	26
Bailes, H. (?) H. Bailis	London	1830-1832	Sculpture	—	—	—	—	2	—	—	—	—	—	2
Bailey, Albert E.	Northampton	1890-1893	Landscape	—	—	5	—	3	—	—	—	—	—	8
Bailey, Arthur	London	1884-1885	Landscape	—	—	—	—	1	—	—	—	—	—	1
Bailey, E.	London	1796	Portraits	—	—	1	—	—	—	—	—	—	—	1
Bailey, Miss Elizabeth S.	London	1862-1873	Figures	—	—	—	—	4	—	—	—	—	1	5
Bailey, G.	London	1785-1797	Miniatures	—	—	17	—	—	—	—	—	—	—	17
Bailey, G.	London	1811-1823	Architecture	—	—	3	—	—	—	—	—	—	—	3
Bailey, H.	London	1835	Landscape	—	—	1	—	—	—	—	—	—	—	1
Bailey, Henry	London	1879-1893	Landscape	—	—	4	—	20	—	8	2	—	9	43
Bailey, J.	London	1803-1820	Architecture	—	—	7	—	—	—	—	—	—	—	7

Name.	Town.	First and Last Year of Ex.	Speciality.	S. A.	F. S.	R. A.	B. I.	S. S.	O. W.	N. W.	G. G.	N. G.	V. E.	Total.
BAILEY, JOHN	London	1851-1861	Sculpture	—	—	18	—	9	—	—	—	—	—	27
BAILEY, J. W.	London	1859-1889	Enamels	—	—	9	—	9	—	—	—	—	—	18
BAILEY, M. S.	London	1887	Architecture	—	—	1	—	—	—	—	—	—	—	1
BAILEY, R. H.	London	1848-1876	Landscape	—	—	—	—	3	—	—	—	—	—	3
BAILEY, THOMAS J.	London	1886-1891	Architecture	—	—	6	—	—	—	—	—	—	—	6
BAILEY, W.	Dulwich	1831-1834	Battle Pieces	—	—	4	1	—	—	—	—	—	—	5
BAILEY, WILLIAM G.	London	1889	Stained Glass	—	—	1	—	—	—	—	—	—	—	1
BAILEY, WILLIAM H.	Cookham	1879-1881	Landscape	—	—	—	—	1	—	—	—	—	3	4
BAILLIE, ALEXANDER	Edinburgh	1765	Engraving	1	—	—	—	—	—	—	—	—	—	1
BAILLIE, CAROLINE	Brighton	1872	Flowers	—	—	—	—	—	—	—	—	—	2	2
BAILLIE, CAPTAIN WILLIAM, F.S.A.	London	1762-1776	Engraving	29	—	—	—	—	—	—	—	—	—	29
BAILWARD, MISS M. B.	London	1889-1891	Landscape	—	—	1	—	1	—	2	1	4	—	9
BAILY, C.	London	1840	Architecture	—	—	1	—	—	—	—	—	—	—	1
BAILY, EDWARD HODGES, R.A.	London	1810-1862	Sculpture	—	—	187	12	10	—	—	—	—	—	209
BAILY, HENRY J.	Brimyard	1880	Sculpture	—	—	1	—	—	—	—	—	—	—	1
BAILY, R.	London	1843-1847	Fruit	—	—	4	—	—	—	—	—	—	—	4
BAILY, R. M.	—	1874	Landscape	—	—	—	—	—	—	—	—	—	1	1
BAILY, W. H.	London	1848	Architecture	—	—	1	—	—	—	—	—	—	—	1
BAIN, W.	London	1823-1847	Medals	—	—	23	—	—	—	—	—	—	—	23
BAINBRIGGE, ARTHUR	Torquay	1884	Landscape	—	—	—	—	—	—	2	—	—	—	2
BAINES, B. COOPER	London	1881	Flowers	—	—	—	—	—	—	—	—	—	1	1
BAINES, MISS CATHERINE	London	1857-1860	Enamels	—	—	3	—	4	—	—	—	—	—	7
BAINES, H.	London	1851	Landscape	—	—	—	1	—	—	—	—	—	—	1
BAINES, W.	London	1831	Architecture	—	—	—	—	1	—	—	—	—	—	1
BAIN-SMITH, HENRY	London	1885-1893	Sculpture	—	—	4	—	3	—	—	—	—	—	7
BAIRD, JOHN FOSTER	Teddington	1866-1874	Landscape	—	—	—	—	—	—	—	—	—	5	5
BAIRD, NATHANIEL HUGHES T.	Dawlish	1883-1892	Portraits	—	—	5	—	2	—	—	—	—	—	7
BAIRD, WILLIAM B.	London	1877-1891	Domestic	—	—	16	—	—	—	—	—	—	4	20
BAKALOWICZ, STEPHEN	Rome	1892	Figures	—	—	2	—	—	—	—	—	—	—	2
BAKER —	London	1777-1783	Landscape	1	1	—	—	—	—	—	—	—	—	2
BAKER —	London	1762-1768	Flowers	6	—	—	—	—	—	—	—	—	—	6
BAKER —	—	1858	—	—	—	—	—	—	—	—	—	—	2	2
BAKER, A.	Sydenham	1828	Engraving	—	—	—	—	1	—	—	—	—	—	1
BAKER, ALFRED	London	1870-1873	Rustic	—	—	—	—	4	—	—	—	—	1	5
BAKER, MISS ANNETTE	London	1890-1893	Flowers	—	—	1	—	7	—	—	—	—	5	13
BAKER, ARTHUR	London	1864-1889	Sporting	—	—	2	3	2	—	—	—	—	4	11
BAKER, ARTHUR, A.R.C.A., F.R.I.B.A.	London	1870-1884	Architecture	—	—	8	—	—	—	—	—	—	—	8
BAKER, MISS ALICE E. J.	London	1876-1882	Portraits	—	—	3	—	—	—	—	—	—	1	4
BAKER, A. J.	London	1852	Architecture	—	—	1	—	—	—	—	—	—	—	1
BAKER, ALFRED R.	Southampton	1885-1891	Harbours	—	—	2	—	1	—	—	—	—	—	3
BAKER, MISS BLANCHE ‖	Bristol	1869-1893	Landscape	—	—	13	—	1	—	8	—	9	1	32
BAKER, E.	Sudbury	1857-1858	Landscape	—	—	1	2	—	—	—	—	—	—	3
BAKER, E.	—	1832	Portraits	—	—	—	—	1	—	—	—	—	—	1
BAKER, MISS EVANGELINE	London	1889-1893	Domestic	—	—	—	—	6	—	—	—	—	—	6
BAKER, MISS F.	Southampton	1840-1841	Fruit	—	—	—	—	8	—	—	—	—	—	8
BAKER, FREDERICK W.	London	1850-1874	Landscape	—	—	9	10	6	—	—	—	—	18	43
BAKER, F. W., JUNR.	London	1873-1893	Landscape	—	—	19	—	8	—	4	—	—	9	40
BAKER, GEORGE ARNALD	London	1861-1867	Scriptural	—	—	—	1	1	—	—	—	—	—	2
BAKER, G. H. MASSY-. *See* M.	—	—	—	—	—	—	—	—	—	—	—	—	—	—
BAKER, H.	London	1822-1830	Architecture	—	—	4	—	—	—	—	—	—	—	4
BAKER, HARRY	Birmingham	1868-1874	Landscape	—	—	—	—	9	—	—	—	—	8	17
BAKER, HERBERT	Cobham	1892	Architecture	—	—	1	—	—	—	—	—	—	—	1
BAKER, JOHN, R.A.	London	1769-1771	Flowers	—	—	4	—	—	—	—	—	—	—	4
BAKER, J.	Sydenham	1828-1838	—	—	—	1	—	1	—	—	—	—	—	2
BAKER, J.	Woolwich	1840-1851	Landscape	—	—	—	—	6	—	—	—	—	—	6
BAKER, JOHN H.	London	1861-1865	Engraving	—	—	5	—	—	—	—	—	—	—	5
BAKER, MISS L. H.	—	1843	Fruit	—	—	1	—	—	—	—	—	—	—	1
BAKER, MISS MARY	London	1842-1860	Portraits	—	—	10	—	2	—	—	—	—	—	12
BAKER, OLIVER	Birmingham	1875-1893	Landscape	—	—	5	—	2	—	1	—	1	3	12
BAKER, S.	Lewes	1788	Landscape	—	—	1	—	—	—	—	—	—	—	1
BAKER, SIDNEY	London	1881-1883	Landscape	—	—	—	—	6	—	—	—	—	1	7
BAKER, SAMUEL H.	Birmingham	1856-1892	Landscape	—	—	3	1	24	—	7	—	3	21	59
BAKER, S. J.	Birmingham	1855	Landscape	—	—	2	—	—	—	—	—	—	—	2
BAKER, THOMAS.	Leamington	1831-1860	Landscape	—	—	4	19	—	—	—	—	—	—	23
BAKER, THOMAS	London	1872-1882	Fruit	—	—	1	—	2	—	—	—	—	3	6
BAKER, W.	—	1812	Portraits	—	—	1	—	—	—	—	—	—	—	1
BAKER, W.	Perth	1823-1832	Architecture	—	—	3	—	—	—	—	—	—	—	3
BAKER, W.	London	1859-1866	Figures	—	—	2	—	1	—	—	—	—	—	3
BAKER, W.	London	1839-1848	Historical	—	—	1	—	7	—	—	—	—	—	8
BAKER, WILLIAM §	London	1825-1847	Still Life	—	—	—	9	16	—	—	—	—	—	25
BAKER, W. J.	London	1840-1855	Landscape	—	—	2	2	21	—	—	—	—	—	25
BAKER, W. M.	London	1826-1843	Still Life	—	—	8	7	24	—	—	—	—	—	39

Name.	Town.	First and Last Year of Ex.	Speciality.	S. A.	F. S.	R. A.	B. I.	S. S.	O. W.	N.W.	G. G.	N. G.	V. E.	Total.
Baker, Miss	Cheltenham	1810-1820	Game	—	—	4	—	—	2	—	—	—	—	6
Baker and Turner	Liverpool	1783	Stained Glass	1	—	—	—	—	—	—	—	—	—	1
Bakewell, Miss Esther M.	London	1888-1891	Landscape	—	—	2	—	3	—	—	—	—	—	5
Bakewell, Miss H.	London	1877-1893	Flowers	—	—	—	—	—	—	1	—	—	2	3
Bakewell, W.	Leeds	1872-1878	Architecture	—	—	2	—	—	—	—	—	—	—	2
Bakhuysen, J. Van de Sande	—	1880	Landscape	—	—	—	—	—	—	—	2	—	—	2
Bakhuysen, Mdlle. G. J. Van de Sande	—	1880	Flowers	—	—	—	—	—	—	—	2	—	—	2
Bakkerkoff, A. N.	London	1877	Domestic	—	—	—	—	—	—	—	—	—	2	2
Balaam, S.	London	1817	Sculpture	—	—	1	—	—	—	—	—	—	—	1
Balaire, Charles	Paris	1872	Engraving	—	—	—	—	—	—	—	—	—	1	1
Baldery, John K. (?) Baldrey	London	1793-1794	Portraits	—	—	3	—	—	—	—	—	—	—	3
Balding, Alfred	Wisbech	1887	Buildings	—	—	—	—	—	—	—	—	—	1	1
Baldini, T.	—	1871	Figures	—	—	1	—	—	—	—	—	—	—	1
Baldock, James Walsham	Worksop	1867-1887	Cattle	—	—	—	—	16	—	6	—	—	2	24
Baldrey, S.	London	1780	Drawing	2	—	—	—	—	—	—	—	—	—	2
Baldry, Alfred Lys	London	1885-1887	Landscape	—	—	—	—	3	—	—	—	—	1	4
Baldry, Harry	London	1887-1890	Portraits	—	—	6	—	—	—	1	1	—	—	8
Balducci, Gregorio	London	1777	Mythological	1	—	—	—	—	—	—	—	—	—	1
Baldwin, B.	London	1842-1845	Portraits	—	—	3	—	—	—	—	—	—	—	3
Baldwin, Robert	London	1762-1783	Architecture	12	16	—	—	—	—	—	—	—	—	28
Baldwin, Samuel	Halifax	1843-1858	Domestic	—	—	—	—	8	—	—	—	—	—	8
Baldwin, William Wallis	Enfield	1884-1887	Architecture	—	—	2	—	—	—	—	—	—	—	2
Baldwyn, Charles H. C.	Worcester	1887-1893	Still Life	—	—	7	—	2	—	3	—	—	—	12
Bale, C. T.	London	1868-1875	Fruit	—	—	1	—	15	—	—	—	—	8	24
Bale, Edwin, R.I. ‡ φ	London	1867-1893	Domestic	—	—	16	—	—	—	80	3	—	39	138
Bale, J. E.	Tunb'dge Wells	1856-1859	Architecture	—	—	3	2	2	—	—	—	—	—	7
Bale, T. C.	London	1868-1873	Domestic	—	—	—	—	3	—	—	—	—	—	3
Balfour, J. Lawson	London	1892-1893	Domestic	—	—	—	—	2	—	1	—	—	—	3
Ball, Arthur E.	Putney	1878-1885	Landscape	—	—	5	—	4	—	—	—	—	8	17
Ball, A. J. F.	London	1872	Domestic	—	—	—	—	2	—	—	—	—	—	2
Ball, Isaac	London	1836-1837	Domestic	—	—	—	—	2	—	—	—	—	—	2
Ball, James	London	1817-1835	Scriptural	—	—	1	3	—	—	—	—	—	—	4
Ball, J. L. *See also* Ball and Goddard, and	—	—		—	—	—	—	—	—	—	—	—	—	—
Ball, Lee, and Pattinson	Birmingham	1885	Architecture	—	—	1	—	—	—	—	—	—	—	1
Ball, Percival	London	1865-1882	Sculpture	—	—	24	—	4	—	—	—	—	—	28
Ball, T.	London	1829	Landscape	—	—	—	—	1	—	—	—	—	—	1
Ball, Wilfred Williams	Putney	1876-1892	Landscape	—	—	34	—	22	—	12	11	5	17	101
Ball-Hughes, Miss Georgina	London	1889	Portraits	—	—	1	—	—	—	—	—	—	—	1
Ball (J. L.), and Goddard (R. W. K.)	Birmingham	1881	Architecture	—	—	1	—	—	—	—	—	—	—	1
Ball (J. L.), Lee (J. T.), and Pattinson	Manchester	1891	Architecture	—	—	1	—	—	—	—	—	—	—	1
Ballantyne, Miss Edith	London	1866-1883	Domestic	—	—	11	—	2	—	—	—	—	1	14
Ballantyne, John, R.S.A.	London	1834-1883	Figures	—	—	49	1	5	—	—	—	—	—	55
Ballard, Ph.	London	1823-1825	Landscape	—	—	1	1	1	—	—	—	—	—	3
Ballard, Thomas	London	1865-1877	Domestic	—	—	9	1	11	—	—	—	—	1	22
Ballin, Auguste	London	1872-1891	L'pe & Etchs.	—	—	9	—	12	—	—	—	—	49	70
Ballin, John	London	1871-1881	Engraving	—	—	12	—	—	—	—	—	—	1	13
Ballingall, A.	Edinburgh	1883	Domestic	—	—	—	—	—	—	1	—	—	—	1
Ballot, Madame Adelaide	Paris	1871-1872	Historical	—	—	—	—	—	—	—	—	—	3	3
Balmer, George	North Shields	1830-1841	Landscape	—	—	—	5	42	—	—	—	—	—	47
Balston, A.	London	1840	Buildings	—	—	1	—	—	—	—	—	—	—	1
Bambridge, Arthur L.	London	1891-1893	Portraits	—	—	4	—	—	—	—	—	—	1	5
Bamford, Alfred Bennett	Romford	1880-1893	Churches	—	—	5	—	2	—	7	—	—	3	17
Bamford, E.	London	1802	Figures	—	—	1	—	—	—	—	—	—	—	1
Bamfylde, Coplestone Warre	Hestercombe	1763-1783	Landscape	2	1	6	—	—	—	—	—	—	—	9
Bampiani, R.	Tenby	1879	Figures	—	—	1	—	—	—	—	—	—	—	1
Bancroft, Elias Mollineaux	Manchester	1869-1893	Landscape	—	—	14	—	16	—	5	—	—	21	56
Bancroft, H.	London	1836	Fruit	—	—	1	—	—	—	—	—	—	—	1
Bandel, E.	London	1852-1853	Sculpture	—	—	4	—	—	—	—	—	—	—	4
Bandel, H.	London	1853-1861	Sculpture	—	—	10	—	—	—	—	—	—	—	10
Banes, Frederick Matthias	London	1881	Figures	—	—	1	—	—	—	—	—	—	—	1
Banister, Frederick	London	1890	Architecture	—	—	1	—	—	—	—	—	—	—	1
Banks, Miss Catherine	London	1869-1873	Flowers	—	—	—	—	2	—	—	—	—	—	2
Banks, Charles. (?) Bancks	London	1775-1792	Sculpture	—	—	5	—	—	—	—	—	—	—	5
Banks, Edmund G.	London	1889-1890	Landscape	—	—	1	—	—	—	2	—	—	—	3
Banks, J. J.	York	1860-1874	Landscape	—	—	—	2	24	—	—	—	—	—	26
Banks, J. O.	London	1856-1873	Figures	—	—	4	1	1	—	—	—	—	2	8
Banks, Mary	—	1822	Landscape	—	—	1	—	—	—	—	—	—	—	1
Banks, R.	London	1816-1822	Architecture	—	—	3	—	—	—	—	—	—	—	3
Banks, Thos., R.A.	London	1767-1806	Sculpture	—	3	49	1	—	—	—	—	—	—	53
Banks, T.	London	1864	Landscape	—	—	—	—	3	—	—	—	—	—	3
Banks, Thos. J.	York	1860-1880	Landscape	—	—	4	—	3	—	—	—	—	4	11
Banks (T. L.), and Townsend	London	1884	Architecture	—	—	1	—	—	—	—	—	—	—	1

Name.	Town.	First and Last Year of Ex.	Speciality.	S. A.	F. S.	R. A.	B. I.	S. S.	O. W.	N. W.	G. G.	N. G.	V. E.	Total.
Banks, William	London	1877-1879	Landscape	—	—	—	—	5	—	—	—	—	—	5
Banks, William Lawrence, R.C.A., F.S.A.	Llanfairpwllgwngyl	1856-1880	Landscape	—	—	—	—	4	—	—	—	—	4	8
Banks, Miss	—	1796	Figures	—	—	2	—	—	—	—	—	—	—	2
Banks, Miss	London	1865-1869	Figures	—	—	4	—	—	—	—	—	—	—	4
Banks and Barry (Charles)	London	1852-1872	Architecture	—	—	15	—	—	—	—	—	—	—	15
Bannatyne, J. J., R.S.W.	London	1866-1891	Landscape	—	—	22	—	43	—	11	—	—	85	161
Banner, Joseph	Birmingham	1860-1871	Fruit	—	—	—	4	15	—	—	—	—	8	27
Bannerman, Alexander, F.S.A.	London	1761-1774	Engraving	14	—	—	—	—	—	—	—	—	—	14
Bannerman, Mrs. Frances	Great Marlow	1888-1891	Domestic	—	—	3	—	3	—	—	—	—	—	6
Bannerman, Hamlet	London	1879-1891	Domestic	—	—	9	—	20	—	—	—	—	2	31
Bannin, Miss Kate	London	1889-1890	Sculpture	—	—	3	—	3	—	—	—	—	—	6
Bannister, C. E.	London	1864	Landscape	—	—	—	1	—	—	—	—	—	—	1
Baquet —	London	1773	Sculpture	2	—	—	—	—	—	—	—	—	—	2
Barbason, M.	London	1888	Figures	—	—	—	—	1	—	—	—	—	—	1
Barbella, C.	London	1878	Figures	—	—	1	—	—	—	—	—	—	1	2
Barber —	London	1775-1777	Landscape	2	—	—	—	—	—	—	—	—	—	2
Barber —	London	1763-1769	Portraits	3	9	—	—	—	—	—	—	—	—	12
Barber, Alfred R.	Colchester	1879-1893	Game	—	—	—	—	7	—	—	—	—	11	18
Barber, Christopher	London	1770-1808	Portraits	—	—	22	—	—	—	—	—	—	—	22
Barber, Charles Burton	London	1866-1893	Sporting	—	—	32	—	2	—	—	1	—	15	50
Barber, Charles Vincent	Birmingham	1810-1850	Landscape	—	—	3	—	9	8	—	—	—	36	56
Barber, D.	Brighton	1828-1837	Portraits	—	—	4	1	8	—	—	—	—	—	13
Barber, Miss E.	Birmingham	1816	Flowers	—	—	—	—	—	2	—	—	—	—	2
Barber, J.	London	1823-1838	Medals	—	—	6	—	—	—	—	—	—	—	6
Barber, Joseph Moseley	Leicester	1858-1889	Landscape	—	—	12	5	42	—	2	—	—	23	84
Barber, J. S.	—	1840-1857	Historical	—	—	1	—	—	—	—	—	—	1	2
Barber, John Thomas (Beaumont)	London	1794-1806	Miniatures	—	—	53	—	—	—	—	—	—	—	53
Barber, Joseph Vincent	Birmingham	1810-1830	Landscape	—	—	5	11	—	1	—	—	—	—	17
Barber, Lucius. (?) Barbor	London	1763-1766	Enamels	4	—	—	—	—	—	—	—	—	—	4
Barber, Reginald	Manchester	1885-1893	Domestic	—	—	10	—	2	—	2	—	—	—	14
Barber, Thomas	Nottingham	1810-1829	Portraits	—	—	13	—	—	—	—	—	—	—	13
Barber, V.	—	1812	Cattle	—	—	1	—	—	—	—	—	—	—	1
Barber, W.	London	1833-1835	Medals	—	—	3	—	—	—	—	—	—	—	3
Barber, W. Swinden	London	1860-1890	Architecture	—	—	7	—	—	—	—	—	—	—	7
Barber, William Thompson	Bristol	1876-1885	Miniatures	—	—	14	—	—	—	—	—	—	—	14
Barber, W. T. Scott	Clifton	1893	Miniatures	—	—	4	—	—	—	—	—	—	—	4
Barber and Giles	—	1762	Enamels	5	—	—	—	—	—	—	—	—	—	5
Barbier, G. P.	London	1792-1795	Portraits	—	—	22	—	—	—	—	—	—	—	22
Barbor, Mrs. G. D.	London	1862-1864	Figures	—	—	—	2	1	—	—	—	—	—	3
Barbor, H.	Nottingham	1815	Portraits	—	—	1	—	—	—	—	—	—	—	1
Barbot, Miss Eliz.	—	1777	Needlework	1	—	—	—	—	—	—	—	—	—	1
Barbut, James	London	1777-1786	Still Life	—	—	17	—	—	—	—	—	—	—	17
Barclay, A.	London	1873	Flowers	—	—	—	—	1	—	—	—	—	1	2
Barclay, A. P.	Kilburn	1880	Landscape	—	—	—	—	—	—	—	—	—	1	1
Barclay, Edgar ϕ	London	1868-1893	Landscape	—	—	33	—	—	—	—	64	13	47	157
Barclay, G.	London	1826-1830	Intaglios	—	—	2	—	—	—	—	—	—	—	2
Barclay, G.	—	1876	Figures	—	—	1	—	—	—	—	—	—	—	1
Barclay J. Edward	London	1868-1888	Landscape	—	—	—	—	5	—	—	—	—	6	11
Barclay, J. M., R.S.A.	Perth	1850-1875	Portraits	—	—	13	—	2	—	—	—	—	—	15
Barclay, J. W.	London	1875	Sea Pieces	—	—	—	—	—	1	—	—	—	—	1
Barclay, W.	Edinburgh	1873-1876	Sea Pieces	—	—	3	—	—	—	—	—	—	—	3
Barclay, William	Tottenham	1763-1769	Miniatures	—	14	—	—	—	—	—	—	—	—	14
Barclay, William	London	1831-1856	Portraits	—	—	44	—	32	—	—	—	—	—	76
Bard —	Acton	1848	Portraits	—	—	—	—	—	—	—	—	—	1	1
Bard, De. *See* D.	—	—	—	—	—	—	—	—	—	—	—	—	—	—
Bardelle, W. E.	London	1876	Medals	—	—	1	—	—	—	—	—	—	—	1
Bardswell, Emily	Wimbledon	1880-1881	Landscape	—	—	—	—	—	—	—	—	—	2	2
Bardwell, William	London	1829-1845	Architecture	—	—	13	—	4	—	—	—	—	—	17
Bare, Henry B.	Liverpool	1888	Architecture	—	—	1	—	—	—	—	—	—	—	1
Barenger, James	London	1793-1799	Insects	—	—	8	—	—	—	—	—	—	—	8
Barenger, James, Junr	—	1807-1831	Sporting	—	—	40	8	3	—	—	—	—	—	51
Barenger, J. R.	London	1853-1855	Landscape	—	—	2	—	1	—	—	—	—	—	3
Barenger, M. S.	London	1828	Engraving	—	—	—	—	2	—	—	—	—	—	2
Barfoot, J. R.	London	1830-1857	Miniatures	—	—	7	—	—	—	—	—	—	—	7
Barfoot, S. R.	London	1820	Portraits	—	—	1	—	—	—	—	—	—	—	1
Barford, Richard	Birmingham	1879-1880	Landscape	—	—	—	—	—	—	—	—	—	2	2
Bargue —	Paris	1879	Soldiers	—	—	—	—	—	—	—	—	—	1	1
Baring, Lady Emma	London	1888	Landscape	—	—	—	—	—	—	1	—	—	—	1
Baring, Col. F.	London	1868-1881	Sculpture	—	—	2	—	—	—	—	1	—	—	3
Baringer —	London	1773	Still Life	1	—	—	—	—	—	—	—	—	—	1
Barkentin, George Slater. *See* Slater, Geo.	London	1876	Sculpture	—	—	2	—	—	—	—	—	—	—	2
Barker, A.	—	1834	Sporting	—	—	—	—	1	—	—	—	—	—	1

Name.	Town.	First and Last Year of Ex.	Speciality.	S. A.	F. S.	R. A.	B. I.	S. S.	O. W.	N. W.	G. G.	N. G.	V. E.	Total.
Barker, Miss A. E.	London	1858-1870	Figures	—	—	2	—	1	—	—	—	—	1	4
Barker, Benjamin	Bath	1800-1838	Landscape	—	—	18	145	40	38	1	—	—	4	246
Barker, B.	London	1841	Portraits	—	—	2	—	—	—	—	—	—	—	2
Barker, Clarissa	Dolgelly	1885-1886	Flowers	—	—	—	—	4	—	—	—	—	—	4
Barker, C. F.	London	1845	Figures	—	—	—	—	1	—	—	—	—	—	1
Barker, Joseph	Bath	1808-1809	Landscape	—	—	2	6	—	—	—	—	—	—	8
Barker, John Joseph	Bath	1835-1866	Historical	—	—	4	1	—	—	—	—	—	—	5
Barker, Joseph	York	1843-1848	Rustic	—	—	2	—	—	—	—	—	—	—	2
Barker, J. S.	London	1841-1858	Portraits	—	—	4	—	—	—	—	—	—	—	4
Barker, Miss Lucette E.	Thirsk	1853-1874	Domestic	—	—	4	1	—	—	—	—	—	16	21
Barker, Miss Marion	Manchester	1889	Figures	—	—	1	—	—	—	—	—	—	—	1
Barker, Miss M. A.	Bath	1820-1848	Landscape	—	—	1	4	—	—	—	—	—	9	14
Barker, Miss May H.	London	1891-1893	Medals	—	—	3	—	—	—	—	—	—	—	3
Barker, Thomas	Bath	1791-1847	Landscape	—	—	18	97	3	—	—	—	—	—	118
Barker, T. C.	London	1827	Architecture	—	—	1	—	—	—	—	—	—	—	1
Barker, Thomas Edward	London	1800-1801	Sea Pieces	—	—	2	—	—	—	—	—	—	—	2
Barker, Thomas Jones	London	1844-1876	Historical	—	—	29	34	15	—	—	—	—	—	78
Barker, W.	London	1859	Figures	—	—	—	—	1	—	—	—	—	—	1
Barker, Wright	Mansfield	1891-1893	Domestic	—	—	2	—	1	—	—	—	—	—	3
Barker, W. Bligh	Greenwich	1835-1850	Flowers	—	—	6	3	10	—	—	—	—	—	19
Barker, Mrs. W. Bligh	Greenwich	1834-1843	Fruit	—	—	1	—	2	—	—	—	—	—	3
Barker, W. D.	Trefrew	1870-1880	Landscape	—	—	—	—	4	—	—	—	—	19	23
Barkley, C. W.	London	1852	Landscape	—	—	1	—	—	—	—	—	—	—	1
Barkworth, Miss Emma L.	Tunb'dge Wells	1891	Landscape	—	—	—	—	—	—	1	—	—	—	1
Barkworth, Walter T.	Dorking	1884-1893	Landscape	—	—	—	—	—	—	—	—	—	5	5
Barland, Adam	London	1843-1875	Landscape	—	—	32	42	85	—	—	—	—	8	167
Barlin, F. B.	London	1802-1807	Portraits	—	—	3	—	—	—	—	—	—	—	3
Barlow, B. J.	London	1885	Landscape	—	—	—	—	1	—	—	—	—	—	1
Barlow, Emily S.	Old Charlton	1870-1876	Landscape	—	—	—	—	—	—	—	—	—	5	5
Barlow, Miss Florence E.	London	1878-1888	Figures	—	—	2	—	6	—	—	—	—	4	12
Barlow, H.	London	1835	Landscape	—	—	—	1	—	—	—	—	—	—	1
Barlow, Miss Hannah Bolton	London	1880-1889	Sculpture	—	—	11	—	9	—	—	—	—	9	29
Barlow, John Noble	St. Ives	1893	Sea-shores	—	—	2	—	—	—	—	—	—	2	4
Barlow, Thomas Oldham, R.A.	London	1849-1890	Engraving	—	—	46	—	1	—	—	—	—	—	47
Barlow, Miss	Clapton	1852-1855	Domestic	—	—	1	2	—	—	—	—	—	—	3
Barnard, Frank	London	1871-1883	Landscape	—	—	1	—	1	—	—	—	—	10	12
Barnard, Frederick § φ	Cullercoats	1858-1887	Domestic	—	—	18	—	25	—	—	—	—	14	57
Barnard, Geoffrey	Dorking	1888-1889	Domestic	—	—	—	—	—	—	—	—	1	2	3
Barnard, George	London	1832-1884	Landscape	—	—	19	7	52	—	8	—	—	9	95
Barnard, Gertrude	Putney	1892	Flowers	—	—	—	—	1	—	—	—	—	1	2
Barnard, Mrs. H. G. (Elizabeth)	London	1884-1886	Landscape	—	—	3	—	2	—	—	—	—	1	6
Barnard, J.	—	1835	Fruit	—	—	—	—	1	—	—	—	—	—	1
Barnard, J. Langton	London	1876-1893	Domestic	—	—	16	—	21	—	—	—	1	17	55
Barnard, Mrs. J. L. (late Miss Emily Cummins)	Virginia Water	1881-1886	Domestic	—	—	—	—	4	—	1	—	—	—	5
Barnard, J. P.	London	1840-1850	Intaglios	—	—	4	—	—	—	—	—	—	—	4
Barnard, Mrs. Kate L.	Chertsey	1885-1888	Flowers	—	—	1	—	—	—	1	—	—	—	2
Barnard, Louisa	Highbury	1871-1873	Landscape	—	—	—	—	—	—	—	—	—	2	2
Barnard, P.	—	1762	Sculpture	—	3	—	—	—	—	—	—	—	—	3
Barnard, Philip Augustus	London	1840-1884	Miniatures	—	—	16	—	—	—	—	—	—	—	16
Barnard, Mrs. Philip Augustus, late Miss Hebe Saunders	London	1852-1857	Miniatures	—	—	2	—	—	—	—	—	—	—	2
Barnard, Walter	London	1876-1891	Miniatures	—	—	10	—	—	—	—	—	—	—	10
Barnard, Mrs. William	Lewisham	1880-1881	Domestic	—	—	—	—	2	—	—	—	—	—	2
Barnes, A. W.	London	1837	Landscape	—	—	—	—	1	—	—	—	—	—	1
Barnes, D.	Hendon	1812	Architecture	—	—	1	—	—	—	—	—	—	—	1
Barnes, E. C. §	London	1856-1882	Domestic	—	—	10	17	38	—	—	—	—	1	66
Barnes, F.	Ipswich	1848-1854	Architecture	—	—	3	—	—	—	—	—	—	—	3
Barnes, G. E.	London	1866	Churches	—	—	—	—	1	—	—	—	—	—	1
Barnes, Isabella	London	1890	Still Life	—	—	—	—	1	—	—	—	—	—	1
Barnes, J.	London	1834	Landscape	—	—	—	—	—	—	1	—	—	—	1
Barnes, James	Liverpool	1870-1885	Figures	—	—	7	—	1	—	—	—	—	—	8
Barnes, Joseph H.	London	1867-1887	Domestic	—	—	9	—	22	—	5	—	—	9	45
Barnes, J. W.	Durham	1855	Landscape	—	—	—	—	—	—	—	—	—	2	2
Barnes, Miss Marian L.	Lewisham	1890-1893	Flowers	—	—	7	—	9	—	4	—	—	—	20
Barnes, Robert A.R.W.S. †	Berkhampstead	1873-1893	Domestic	—	—	14	—	—	62	—	—	—	—	76
Barnes, Samuel J.	Birmingham	1884-1886	Landscape	—	—	2	—	—	—	—	—	—	—	2
Barnes, T.	London	1831	Architecture	—	—	1	—	—	—	—	—	—	—	1
Barnes, W. *See* Smith and Barnes	London	1829-1837	Architecture	—	—	10	—	—	—	—	—	—	—	10
Barnes, W.	London	1860	Sculpture	—	—	1	—	—	—	—	—	—	—	1
Barnes, W. J.	London	1834	Landscape	—	—	1	—	—	—	—	—	—	—	1
Barnes, W. Rodway	Worcester	1886	Landscape	—	—	—	—	—	—	—	—	—	1	1
Barnett, John	London	1849-1860	Architecture	—	—	3	—	—	—	—	—	—	—	3

Name.	Town.	First and Last Year of Ex.	Speciality.	S. A.	F. S.	R. A.	B. I.	S. S.	O. W.	N. W.	G. G.	N. G.	V. E.	Total.
Barnett (J.), and Birch	London	1855-1856	Architecture	—	—	5	—	—	—	—	—	—	—	5
Barnett, James D.	Crouch End	1855-1892	Landscape	—	—	9	22	73	—	—	—	—	20	124
Barnett, R. C.	London	1798-1821	Landscape	—	—	3	3	—	—	—	—	—	—	6
Barnett, Capt. T.	—	1804-1805	Landscape	—	—	2	—	—	—	—	—	—	—	2
Barnett, W.	London	1786-1824	Medals	—	—	11	—	—	—	—	—	—	—	11
Barnett, W.	London	1848	India	—	—	—	—	—	—	—	—	—	3	3
Barnett, Miss	—	1814	Flowers	—	—	2	—	—	—	—	—	—	—	2
Barney, Joseph	Wolverhampton	1777-1829	Scriptural	3	2	75	49	13	1	—	—	—	—	143
Barney, Joseph W.	Greenwich	1815-1851	Fruit	—	—	2	10	6	4	—	—	—	—	22
Barney, Sophia	—	1819	Figures	—	—	1	—	—	—	—	—	—	—	1
Barney, W.	—	1834	Fruit	—	—	—	1	—	—	—	—	—	—	1
Barnicle, James	London	1821-1845	Landscape	—	—	18	52	53	—	—	—	—	—	123
Barns, G.	London	1872-1874	Domestic	—	—	1	—	12	—	—	—	—	—	13
Barnsley, Sydney H.	London	1891	Ruins	—	—	1	—	—	—	—	—	—	—	1
Barou, Mrs.	London	1797-1801	Miniatures	—	—	22	—	—	—	—	—	—	—	22
Barr, E.	Putney	1847-1865	Architecture	—	—	2	—	—	—	—	—	—	—	2
Barr, J.	London	1830-1846	Architecture	—	—	4	—	1	—	—	—	—	—	5
Barrable, George Hamilton	London	1873-1887	Domestic	—	—	13	—	16	—	—	1	—	9	39
Barrable, Mrs. T. J. (Amelia)	London	1847-1880	Miniatures	—	—	24	—	—	—	—	—	—	—	24
Barrable, Miss Millie	London	1883-1886	Miniatures	—	—	3	—	—	—	—	—	—	—	3
Barradale, Isaac	Leicester	1878-1888	Architecture	—	—	5	—	—	—	—	—	—	—	5
Barraghi, F.	London	1872	Sculpture	—	—	2	—	—	—	—	—	—	—	2
Barralet, James	London	1770-1779	Landscape	—	7	12	—	—	—	—	—	—	—	19
Barralet, John James, F.S.A.	—	1773-1780	Landscape	19	8	1	—	—	—	—	—	—	—	28
Barralet, John Melchor	London	1775-1787	Landscape	9	—	9	—	—	—	—	—	—	—	18
Barratt, Reginald R.	London	1885-1893	Venice, &c.	—	—	19	—	—	—	7	—	1	—	27
Barratt, Thomas	Stockbridge	1852-1893	Sporting	—	—	17	6	11	—	—	—	—	4	38
Barraud, Allan F.	Watford	1872-1893	Landscape	—	—	43	—	12	—	—	—	—	57	112
Barraud, Charles James	London	1871-1893	Landscape	—	—	6	—	16	—	3	—	—	34	59
Barraud, Francis	London	1878-1890	Domestic	—	—	3	—	15	—	2	—	—	9	29
Barraud, Francis P.	London	1877-1891	Churches	—	—	1	—	11	—	4	—	—	—	16
Barraud, Henry	London	1831-1868	Sporting	—	—	33	48	19	—	—	—	—	86	186
Barraud, Philip	London	1763-1783	Engraving	1	3	—	—	—	—	—	—	—	—	4
Barraud, William	London	1828-1850	Sporting	—	—	58	36	38	—	—	—	—	43	175
Barré, A.	London	1875	Figures	—	—	1	—	—	—	—	—	—	—	1
Barrell, H.	London	1785-1788	Landscape	—	—	5	—	—	—	—	—	—	—	5
Barrère, Emile	Neuilly	1878	River Scenes	—	—	—	—	—	—	—	—	—	2	2
Barret, George, R.A.	London	1764-1786	Landscape	13	7	32	—	—	—	—	—	—	—	52
Barret, George †	London	1800-1843	Landscape	—	—	5	19	8	581	—	—	—	1	614
Barret, James	London	1785-1819	Landscape	—	—	37	—	—	—	—	—	—	—	37
Barret, J. V.	London	1843	Landscape	—	—	2	—	—	—	—	—	—	—	2
Barret, Miss M. (Pupil of G. Romney)	London	1797-1835	Still Life	—	—	8	—	—	36	—	—	—	—	44
Barrett, C. P.	London	1836-1844	Landscape	—	—	3	—	3	—	—	—	—	—	6
Barrett, Mrs. Elizabeth	London	1875-1879	Miniatures	—	—	3	—	2	—	—	—	—	—	5
Barrett, G. *See* Hudson and Barrett	—	—	Architecture	—	—	—	—	—	—	—	—	—	—	—
Barrett, G.	London	1846-1849	Sculpture	—	—	2	—	—	—	—	—	—	—	2
Barrett, H.	London	1866	Historical	—	—	1	—	—	—	—	—	—	—	1
Barrett, Harry	Nottingham	1881-1883	Sculpture	—	—	—	—	9	—	—	—	—	—	9
Barrett, Jerry	Brighton	1851-1885	Figures	—	—	17	1	20	—	—	—	—	22	60
Barrett, John	Plymouth	1883	Landscape	—	—	1	—	—	—	—	—	—	—	1
Barrett, M.	London	1876-1880	Rustic	—	—	—	—	1	—	—	—	—	2	3
Barrett, Mrs., late Miss Marianne Foster	Rome	1872	Portraits	—	—	1	—	—	—	—	—	—	—	1
Barrett, T.	London	1807	Landscape	—	—	1	—	—	—	—	—	—	—	1
Barrett, Thomas	Nottingham	1883-1888	Domestic	—	—	5	1	—	—	—	—	—	—	6
Barrett, William	London	1837-1847	Buildings	—	—	1	—	4	—	—	—	—	—	5
Barrett, W.	London	1872	Sculpture	—	—	1	—	—	—	—	—	—	—	1
Barrilli, Signor	—	1783	Battle Pieces	—	2	—	—	—	—	—	—	—	—	2
Barrington, Arthur	Port Arthur	1882	Landscape	—	—	—	—	—	—	—	—	—	2	2
Barrington, W.	Kingston Hill	1874	Still Life	—	—	—	—	1	—	—	—	—	—	1
Barron, Hugh, F.S.A.	London	1766-1786	Portraits	20	—	4	—	—	—	—	—	—	—	24
Barron, William Augustus	London	1774-1777	Landscape	—	—	8	—	—	—	—	—	—	—	8
Barrow —	—	1785	Historical	—	—	1	—	—	—	—	—	—	—	1
Barrow, Master	—	1802	Landscape	—	—	1	—	—	—	—	—	—	—	1
Barrow, C.	London	1789-1802	Landscape	—	—	21	—	—	—	—	—	—	—	21
Barrow, Mrs. E.	—	1829	Copy	—	—	1	—	1	—	—	—	—	—	2
Barrow, Miss Edith Isabel	Dulwich	1887-1893	Flowers	—	—	9	—	10	—	2	—	—	—	21
Barrow, J. §	London	1797-1836	Enamels	—	—	21	—	4	—	—	—	—	—	25
Barrow, J., Junr.	London	1826-1837	Portraits	—	—	—	—	4	—	—	—	—	—	4
Barrow, Miss Jane	London	1891-1893	Domestic	—	—	—	—	1	—	—	—	—	1	2
Barrow, John	London	1812-1816	Portraits	—	—	8	—	—	—	—	—	—	—	8
Barrow, Jos. Charles	—	1790-1791	Landscape	14	—	—	—	—	—	—	—	—	—	14
Barrow, R. J.	Liverpool	1829-1834	Architecture	—	—	3	—	1	—	—	—	—	—	4

Name.	Town.	First and Last Year of Ex.	Speciality.	S. A.	F. S.	R. A.	B. I.	S. S.	O. W.	N. W.	G. G.	N. G.	V. E.	Total.
Barrow, Thomas	London	1769-1819	Portraits	11	1	13	—	—	—	—	—	—	—	25
Barrow, W. H.	Hastings	1887	Sea Pieces	—	—	—	—	—	—	—	—	—	3	3
Barry, Sir Charles, R.A.	London	1812-1859	Architecture	—	—	31	—	—	—	—	—	—	—	31
Barry, Charles, Junr. *See also* Banks and Barry.	London	1850-1884	Architecture	—	—	13	—	—	—	—	—	—	—	13
Barry, Desmond	London	1888-1889	Landscape	—	—	—	—	2	—	—	—	—	—	2
Barry, Dick	London	1883	Landscape	—	—	—	—	3	—	—	—	—	—	3
Barry, Edward Middleton, R.A.	London	1850-1876	Architecture	—	—	48	—	—	—	—	—	—	—	48
Barry, Miss E. M.	Bushey	1893	Portraits	—	—	1	—	—	—	—	—	—	—	1
Barry, Frederick	London	1826-1860	Sea Pieces	—	—	3	8	43	—	—	—	—	—	54
Barry, G.	London	1793-1800	Miniatures	—	—	3	—	—	—	—	—	—	—	3
Barry, James, R.A.	London	1771-1776	Historical	—	—	15	—	—	—	—	—	—	—	15
Barry, James	London	1813	Sporting	—	—	—	—	—	1	—	—	—	—	1
Barry, John	London	1784-1826	Miniatures	—	—	160	2	—	—	—	—	—	—	162
Barry, W.	—	1828	Landscape	—	—	—	—	1	—	—	—	—	—	1
Barry, W. Gerard	Ballyadam	1888	Domestic	—	—	1	—	—	—	—	—	—	—	1
Barstow, Montagu	London	1891-1892	Domestic	—	—	—	—	—	—	2	—	—	—	2
Barstowe, H.	Birmingham	1865-1869	Domestic	—	—	2	—	5	—	—	—	—	—	7
Bart, T.	Liverpool	1816	Portraits	—	—	1	—	—	—	—	—	—	—	1
Bartajago, E.	London	1881	Figures	—	—	—	—	—	—	—	—	—	1	1
Bartells, T.	London	1804	Architecture	—	—	1	—	—	—	—	—	—	—	1
Bartels, Professor Hans Von. *See* V.	—	—	—	—	—	—	—	—	—	—	—	—	—	—
Barter, Gertrude Mary	Watford	1889	Flowers	—	—	—	—	1	—	—	—	—	—	1
Barter, R.	Blarney	1864-1874	Sculpture	—	—	8	—	—	—	—	—	—	—	8
Barth, C. W.	London	1890	Sea Coast	—	—	—	—	—	—	—	1	—	—	1
Barth, J. S.	London	1808	Landscape	—	—	1	—	—	—	—	—	—	—	1
Barth, S.	London	1797-1809	Landscape	—	—	4	—	—	—	—	—	—	—	4
Barth, Wilhelm	London	1889	Domestic	—	—	1	—	—	—	—	—	—	—	1
Barthelmess, N.	London	1879	Engraving	—	—	1	—	—	—	—	—	—	—	1
Bartholomew, Alfred	London	1834	Architecture	—	—	1	—	—	—	—	—	—	—	1
Bartholomew, Harry	London	1889-1890	Domestic	—	—	—	—	—	—	—	—	—	2	2
Bartholomew, Valentine † ‡	London	1826-1876	Flowers, etc.	—	—	20	—	27	173	7	—	—	—	227
Bartholomew, Mrs. Valentine. *See* Mrs. Turnbull, and Miss Anne Charlotte Fayermann	London	1841-1862	Domestic	—	—	29	—	39	—	—	—	—	2	70
Bartholomew, W.	—	1832	Flowers	—	—	1	—	—	—	—	—	—	—	1
Bartlet, W.	London	1809-1827	Architecture	—	—	5	—	—	—	—	—	—	—	5
Bartlett, Miss Annie S.	London	1864-1870	Fruit	—	—	3	—	7	—	—	—	—	—	10
Bartlett, Arthur E.	Wimbledon	1890-1892	Architecture	—	—	4	—	—	—	—	—	—	—	4
Bartlett, Charles William	London	1884-1893	Historical	—	—	7	—	3	—	—	2	—	4	16
Bartlett, D.	—	1828	Landscape	—	—	1	—	—	—	—	—	—	—	1
Bartlett, William Henry	London	1831-1833	Landscape	—	—	4	—	—	—	2	—	—	—	6
Bartlett, William H. § φ	London	1874-1893	Domestic	—	—	19	—	40	—	—	15	8	19	101
Bartlette, Miss C. A.	London	1850	Copies	—	—	—	—	—	—	—	—	—	4	4
Bartoli, F.	London	1783	Figures	—	—	1	—	—	—	—	—	—	—	1
Bartoli, F., Junr.	London	1793	Portraits	—	—	3	—	—	—	—	—	—	—	3
Bartolini, Lorenzo	Carrara	1814	Sculpture	—	—	1	—	—	—	—	—	—	—	1
Bartolozzi, Francesco, R.A.	London	1765-1798	Engraving	8	2	18	—	—	—	—	—	—	—	28
Barton, Miss C. A.	Wincanton	1883	Flowers	—	—	—	—	—	—	—	1	—	—	1
Barton, J.	—	1854	Portraits	—	—	1	—	—	—	—	—	—	—	1
Barton, Miss Rose M. †	London	1880-1892	Landscape	—	—	6	—	1	4	16	2	—	1	30
Barton, T.	London	1807-1829	Architecture	—	—	6	—	—	—	—	—	—	—	6
Barton, T. L.	—	1823	Landscape	—	—	2	—	—	—	—	—	—	—	2
Barton, W.	Derby	1831	Portraits	—	—	1	—	—	—	—	—	—	—	1
Barton, Mrs. W. (Matilda M.)	London	1888-1889	Miniatures	—	—	2	—	—	—	—	—	—	—	2
Bartram, Miss	London	1833	Figures	—	—	—	—	1	—	—	—	—	—	1
Bartsch, E.	London	1891	Landscape	—	—	—	—	1	—	—	—	—	—	1
Barucco, F.	London	1865-1866	Portraits	—	—	3	—	—	—	—	—	—	—	3
Barwell, Frederick Bacon	London	1855-1887	Domestic	—	—	44	2	1	—	—	—	—	13	60
Barwell, Henry George	Norwich	1878-1891	Landscape	—	—	—	—	2	—	6	3	—	6	17
Barwell, John	Norwich	1835	Portraits	—	—	1	—	—	—	—	—	—	—	1
Barwick, J.	London	1844-1849	Portraits	—	—	2	—	—	—	—	—	—	—	2
Barwise, W.	—	1825	Figures	—	—	—	—	2	—	—	—	—	—	2
Barzaghi, A.	—	1889	Flowers	—	—	—	—	—	—	—	1	—	—	1
Barzaghi, Francesco	London	1875	Sculpture	—	—	2	—	—	—	—	—	—	—	2
Bas, Le. *See* L.	—	—	—	—	—	—	—	—	—	—	—	—	—	—
Basebé, Athelstane	London	1882	Miniatures	—	—	1	—	—	—	—	—	—	—	1
Basébé, C.	London	1835-1879	Miniatures	—	—	32	—	3	—	—	—	—	—	35
Basébé, C. E.	London	1878-1881	Miniatures	—	—	5	—	—	—	—	—	—	—	5
Basébé, Ernest	London	1886	Enamels	—	—	1	—	—	—	—	—	—	—	1
Basébé, Harold E.	London	1876-1881	Miniatures	—	—	4	—	—	—	—	—	—	—	4

Name.	Town.	First and Last Year of Ex.	Speciality.	S. A.	F. S.	R. A.	B. I.	S. S.	O. W.	N. W.	G. G.	N. G.	V. E.	Total.
Basevi, George G.	London	1820-1837	Architecture	—	—	6	—	—	—	—	—	—	—	6
Basire, James	London	1761-1783	Engraving	2	85	—	—	—	—	—	—	—	—	87
Baskett, Chas. E.	Colchester	1872-1893	Fruit, etc.	—	—	12	—	14	—	—	—	—	2	28
Baskett, Miss F. B.	London	1867-1868	Sculpture	—	—	2	—	—	—	—	—	—	—	2
Basnett, C. H.	London	1804-1821	Architecture	—	—	9	—	—	—	—	—	—	—	9
Bass, W.	London	1807-1818	Portraits	—	—	8	—	—	—	—	—	—	—	8
Basse, Mdlle. M. Van. *See* V.	—	—	—	—	—	—	—	—	—	—	—	—	—	—
Bassett, George	London	1829-1875	Landscape	—	—	2	1	3	—	—	—	—	—	6
Bassett, Henry	London	1826-1839	Architecture	—	—	4	—	—	—	—	—	—	—	4
Bassett, Miss R.	London	1862	Landscape	—	—	—	—	1	—	—	—	—	—	1
Bassett-Smith, William. *See* S.	—	—	—	—	—	—	—	—	—	—	—	—	—	—
Bastable, H.	Witley	1877	Landscape	—	—	—	—	2	—	—	—	—	—	2
Bastien-Lepage, Jules. *See* L.	—	—	—	—	—	—	—	—	—	—	—	—	—	—
Bastin, A. D.	London	1871-1892	Figures	—	—	—	—	11	—	—	—	—	1	12
Batchelor, Miss Kate	Bristol	1884	Flowers	—	—	—	—	—	—	—	—	—	3	3
Bate —	London	1810	Enamels	—	—	—	1	—	—	—	—	—	—	1
Bate, C.	—	1809-1810	Landscape	—	—	1	1	—	—	—	—	—	—	2
Bate, F.	London	1804-1832	Landscape	—	—	14	5	—	—	—	—	—	—	19
Bate, Francis	London	1885-1886	Domestic	—	—	—	—	4	—	—	—	—	—	4
Bate, H.	—	1833	Landscape	—	—	—	2	—	—	—	—	—	—	2
Bate, H. Francis	London	1883-1885	Flowers	—	—	—	—	—	—	—	4	—	—	4
Bate, M. N.	London	1821	Portraits	—	—	1	—	—	—	—	—	—	—	1
Bate, S.	—	1809-1810	Portraits	—	—	2	—	—	—	—	—	—	—	2
Bate, W.	London	1799-1827	Miniatures	—	—	8	—	—	—	—	—	—	—	8
Bate, W. H.	London	1808-1817	Landscape	—	—	3	2	—	—	—	—	—	—	5
Bate, W. J.	London	1808	Enamels	—	—	1	—	—	—	—	—	—	—	1
Bateman, B. Arthur	Reigate	1885-1888	Portraits	—	—	2	—	3	—	—	—	—	3	8
Bateman, James	London	1840-1850	Sporting	—	—	19	29	34	—	—	—	—	—	82
Bateman, L.	—	1775	Portraits	3	—	—	—	—	—	—	—	—	—	3
Bateman, Robert	London	1866-1889	Figures	—	—	6	—	—	—	—	14	—	17	37
Bateman and Bateman	Birmingham	1892	Architecture	—	—	1	—	—	—	—	—	—	—	1
Bateman and Keates (H. T.)	London	1883-1884	Architecture	—	—	2	—	—	—	—	—	—	—	2
Bates, David	Worcester	1868-1893	Landscape	—	—	26	—	3	—	—	5	5	12	51
Bates, Dewey	Streatham	1875-1891	Figures	—	—	3	—	6	—	3	1	—	12	25
Bates, Edwin	London	1836-1840	Landscape	—	—	—	4	2	—	—	—	—	—	6
Bates, Harry, A.R.A.	Paris	1884-1892	Sculpture	—	—	24	—	—	—	—	4	5	—	33
Bates, Henry W.	Leicester	1882-1888	Rustic	—	—	1	—	3	—	1	—	—	1	6
Bates, W. E.	London	1847-1872	Sea Pieces	—	—	31	25	90	—	—	—	—	78	224
Bateson, Miss Edith	London	1891-1893	Sculpture	—	—	2	—	1	—	—	—	1	—	4
Bath, W.	London	1840-1851	Landscape	—	—	2	7	3	—	—	—	—	—	12
Bathe, J.	London	1872-1874	Landscape	—	—	2	—	6	—	—	—	—	2	10
Bathgate, Miss Ellen	Edinburgh	1888	Landscape	—	—	1	—	—	—	—	—	—	—	1
Bathgate, George	Edinburgh	1885-1887	Figures	—	—	4	—	1	—	—	—	—	—	5
Batley, Henry William	London	1873-1893	Architecture	—	—	19	—	—	—	—	—	—	—	19
Batley, Walter D.	London	1875-1893	Landscape	—	—	16	—	4	—	—	—	—	8	28
Batoni, Baron Pompeo G.	Rome	1778	Portraits	1	—	—	—	—	—	—	—	—	—	1
Batsche, Julius	London	1882-1883	Military	—	—	2	—	—	—	—	—	—	—	2
Batson, A.	London	1843-1849	Architecture	—	—	4	—	—	—	—	—	—	—	4
Batson, Rev. A. Wellesley	London	1890	Landscape	—	—	—	—	—	—	—	1	—	—	1
Batson, Frank	Ramsbury	1890-1892	Landscape	—	—	1	—	—	—	1	—	—	—	2
Batson, H. M.	Ramsbury	1874-1875	Landscape	—	—	—	—	1	—	—	—	—	1	2
Batt, Arthur	Romsey	1879-1892	Domestic	—	—	4	—	14	—	—	4	—	6	28
Battam, T.	London	1833-1840	Enamels	—	—	3	—	—	—	—	—	—	—	3
Batten, John D.	London	1886-1893	Mythological	—	—	3	—	—	—	—	2	9	—	14
Batterby and Huxley	London	1876-1886	Architecture	—	—	6	—	—	—	—	—	—	—	6
Battersby. (?) Bettersby	London	1775-1783	Flowers	8	2	—	—	—	—	—	—	—	—	10
Battersby, E.	Rome	1879	Sculpture	—	—	1	—	—	—	—	—	—	—	1
Battersby, W., Junr.	—	1782-1783	Landscape	1	1	—	—	—	—	—	—	—	—	2
Battersby, Mrs.	Tenby	1833-1839	Figures	—	—	3	—	5	—	—	—	—	—	8
Battershall, John R.	London	1872-1875	Woodcuts	—	—	—	—	—	—	—	—	—	3	3
Battley, J. V.	London	1825-1827	Portraits	—	—	4	—	—	—	—	—	—	—	4
Batty, Edward	London	1864-1867	Domestic	—	—	—	—	5	—	—	—	—	—	5
Batty, John	York	1772-1788	Landscape	3	—	5	—	—	—	—	—	—	—	8
Batty, Colonel Robert	London	1813-1848	Landscape	—	—	10	—	—	—	—	—	—	—	10
Batty, R.	London	1848	Waterfalls	—	—	—	2	—	—	—	—	—	—	2
Batty, R. M.	—	1788-1797	Landscape	—	—	16	—	—	—	—	—	—	—	16
Batty, Miss	—	1809-1816	Landscape	—	—	9	—	—	—	—	—	—	—	9
Baud, Benjamin	London	1826-1851	Landscape	—	—	14	5	10	—	—	—	—	—	29
Baudenbach, John	London	1772-1777	Animals	1	—	4	—	—	—	—	—	—	—	5
Baudiot, Madame S.	Paris	1817	Landscape	—	—	1	—	—	—	—	—	—	—	1
Baudry, Paul Jacques Aimé	Paris	1890	Landscape	—	—	—	—	—	—	—	—	2	—	2
Bauer, Francis, F.R.S. (?) Ferdinand L. Bauer	London	1794-1814	Flowers	—	—	5	3	—	—	—	—	—	—	8

Name.	Town.	First and Last Year of Ex.	Speciality.	S. A.	F. S.	R. A.	B. I.	S. S.	O. W.	N. W.	G. G.	N. G.	V. E.	Total.
Bauerle, Carl	London	1870-1892	Portraits	—	—	35	—	40	—	—	1	—	15	91
Baugniet, Charles	London	1847-1870	Lithographs	—	—	9	1	—	—	—	—	—	—	10
Baumann, Mrs. Jerichau-. *See* J.	—	—	—	—	—	—	—	—	—	—	—	—	—	—
Baumann, Miss Elizabeth Maria Anna. *See*	—	—	—	—	—	—	—	—	—	—	—	—	—	—
Madame Jerichau-.	—	—	—	—	—	—	—	—	—	—	—	—	—	—
Baumann, Miss A. Hilda	London	1890	Domestic	—	—	—	—	—	—	—	—	—	1	1
Baumann, Miss Ida	London	1892	Portraits	—	—	2	—	—	—	—	—	—	1	3
Baumer, Lewis C. E.	London	1892-1893	Domestic	—	—	1	—	1	—	—	—	—	2	4
Bautebarne, C.	London	1849	Portraits	—	—	1	—	—	—	—	—	—	—	1
Baverts, G. V.	London	1800	Medals	—	—	1	—	—	—	—	—	—	—	1
Baxter, Charles §	London	1834-1879	Heads	—	—	45	3	154	—	—	—	—	—	202
Baxter, C. J.	London	1870-1875	Domestic	—	—	—	—	5	—	—	—	—	—	5
Baxter, George	London	1845	Historical	—	—	1	—	—	—	—	—	—	—	1
Baxter, Thomas	London	1802-1821	Enamels	—	—	16	—	—	—	—	—	—	1	17
Baxter, Mrs.	—	1791	Portraits	—	—	1	—	—	—	—	—	—	—	1
Bay, De. *See* D.	—	—	—	—	—	—	—	—	—	—	—	—	—	—
Bayes, Alfred Walter	London	1858-1893	Domestic	—	—	49	9	91	—	21	—	—	83	253
Bayes, Gilbert W.	London	1888-1893	Wax Models	—	—	16	—	1	—	2	—	—	2	21
Bayes, Walter J.	London	1890-1893	Rustic	—	—	5	—	17	—	7	—	—	10	39
Bayfield, Miss Fanny Jane	Norwich	1872-1889	Flowers	—	—	1	—	4	—	—	—	—	—	5
Bayley, Chapman	London	1818-1832	Landscape	—	—	15	15	7	—	—	—	—	—	37
Bayley, J.	—	1829	Interiors	—	—	—	—	1	—	—	—	—	—	1
Bayley, P.	London	1802	Allegorical	—	—	3	—	—	—	—	—	—	—	3
Bayley, S.	London	1838	Architecture	—	—	1	—	—	—	—	—	—	—	1
Bayley, W. P.	London	1832-1833	Landscape	—	—	1	—	2	—	—	—	—	—	3
Baylis, J. C.	London	1866-1867	Landscape	—	—	—	—	4	—	—	—	—	—	4
Baylis, William H.	Richmond	1890	Sculpture	—	—	1	—	—	—	—	—	—	—	1
Bayliss, J. B.	London	1854-1855	Landscape	—	—	—	—	2	—	—	—	—	—	2
Bayliss, Wyke, P.R.B.A., F.S.A. §	London	1855-1893	Churches	—	—	3	—	193	—	1	—	—	1	198
Bayly, M.	Brighton	1868	Historical	—	—	1	—	—	—	—	—	—	—	1
Bayne. *See* Heaton, Butler, and Bayne	—	—	Architecture	—	—	—	—	—	—	—	—	—	—	—
Bayne, J.	—	1807	Scriptural	—	—	1	—	—	—	—	—	—	—	1
Bayne, W.	London	1832	Landscape	—	—	—	—	1	—	—	—	—	—	1
Bayne, Walter McPherson	London	1833-1858	Landscape	—	—	—	7	6	—	—	—	—	1	14
Bayne, W. P.	London	1834	Landscape	—	—	—	—	1	—	—	—	—	—	1
Baynes, A. H.	Oxford	1879	Landscape	—	—	—	—	—	—	—	—	—	1	1
Baynes, Frederick T.	London	1833-1864	Fruit	—	—	21	1	12	—	—	—	—	—	34
Baynes, James	London	1796-1837	Landscape	—	—	52	—	14	7	—	—	—	39	112
Baynes, Robert	Windsor	1853	Landscape	—	—	—	2	—	—	—	—	—	—	2
Baynes, Thomas Mann	London	1811-1852	Landscape	—	—	41	—	5	—	5	—	—	—	51
Baynes, W. T.	London	1820	Landscape	—	—	—	—	—	7	—	—	—	—	7
Baynham, T.	London	1842	Landscape	—	—	—	—	1	—	—	—	—	—	1
Bazalgette, Sir Joseph W., C.B.	London	1863-1867	Architecture	—	—	10	—	—	—	—	—	—	—	10
Bazzani, Signor	London	1883	Fountains	—	—	—	—	—	—	1	—	—	—	1
Beacall, J.	London	1864-1868	Landscape	—	—	2	—	2	—	—	—	—	—	4
Beach, Ernest G.	London	1888-1891	Landscape	—	—	1	—	1	—	—	1	—	—	3
Beach, Thomas, F.S.A.	Bath	1772-1797	Portraits	49	—	27	—	—	—	—	—	—	—	76
Beachcroft, C.	London	1833	Architecture	—	—	1	—	—	—	—	—	—	—	1
Beachcroft, S.	London	1818-1822	Architecture	—	—	4	—	—	—	—	—	—	—	4
Beachcroft, T. S.	Putney	1880	Architecture	—	—	—	—	1	—	—	—	—	—	1
Beachey —	Norwich	1783	Portraits	3	—	—	—	—	—	—	—	—	—	3
Beadell, F.	London	1855	Landscape	—	—	2	—	—	—	—	—	—	—	2
Beadle, James Prinsep	London	1879-1893	Figures	—	—	7	—	—	—	—	12	6	3	28
Beadnell, G.	London	1801	Architecture	—	—	1	—	—	—	—	—	—	—	1
Beal, Miss Annie L.	London	1876-1888	Figures	—	—	6	—	2	—	—	—	—	6	14
Bealby, J.	London	1821-1838	Landscape	—	—	1	7	4	—	—	—	—	—	12
Beale, Ellen	London	1865	Landscape	—	—	—	—	1	—	—	—	—	—	1
Beale, Miss Sarah Sophia	London	1860-1889	Sea Pieces	—	—	8	1	30	—	—	—	—	34	73
Beamish, F. H.	London	1837	Architecture	—	—	—	—	1	—	—	—	—	—	1
Bean, Ainslie H.	London	1870-1886	Buildings	—	—	—	—	11	—	3	—	—	1	15
Beard, Miss Ada	London	1885-1892	Flowers	—	—	6	—	—	—	—	—	—	—	6
Beard, Miss Katherine L.	London	1885-1890	Flowers	—	—	—	—	3	—	—	—	—	5	8
Beardmore, William	Southampton	1822-1826	Fruit	—	—	—	1	4	—	—	—	—	—	5
Bearelle, Charles	London	1771	Architecture	2	—	—	—	—	—	—	—	—	—	2
Bearne, Edward H.	London	1868-1892	Domestic	—	—	30	—	5	—	9	—	—	8	52
Bearne, Mrs. Edward. *See* Miss Catherine	—	—	—	—	—	—	—	—	—	—	—	—	—	—
Charlton	London	1889-1890	Landscape	—	—	4	—	—	—	—	—	—	—	4
Beatherd —	—	1782	Miniatures	—	1	—	—	—	—	—	—	—	—	1
Beatrice, H.R.H. Princess, H.R.I. ‡	London	1883-1885	Landscape	—	—	—	—	—	—	3	—	—	—	3
Beatson, Miss (niece of Miss Catherine Read)	—	—	—	—	—	—	—	—	—	—	—	—	—	—
afterwards Mrs. Oakley	—	1774-1775	Domestic	6	—	2	—	—	—	—	—	—	—	8
Beatson, W.	London	1832-1841	Architecture	—	—	2	—	—	—	—	—	—	—	2

Name.	Town.	First and Last Year of Ex.	Speciality.	S. A.	F. S.	R. A.	B. I.	S. S.	O. W.	N. W.	G. G.	N. G.	V. E.	Total.
Beattie, W.	London	1829-1864	Sculpture	—	—	11	2	2	—	—	—	—	—	15
Beattie-Brown, W. *See* Brown.	—	—	—	—	—	—	—	—	—	—	—	—	—	—
Beauchamp, Mary Catherine, Countess	London	1872	Portraits	—	—	1	—	—	—	—	—	—	—	1
Beauchamp, Miss M.	London	1878	Buildings	—	—	—	—	1	—	—	—	—	—	1
Beauchi, Mosé	London	1880	Etching	—	—	—	—	—	—	—	—	—	1	1
Beauclerc, G.	London	1848	Sculpture	—	—	1	—	—	—	—	—	—	—	1
Beaufort, J. P.	New York	1843	Landscape	—	—	1	—	—	—	—	—	—	—	1
Beaumont, A.	Sardinia	1788	Waterfalls	—	—	4	—	—	—	—	—	—	—	4
Beaumont, Alfred	London	1832-1841	Buildings	—	—	5	—	2	—	—	—	—	—	7
Beaumont, Miss Anne. *See* Mrs. W. Pierce	London	1820-1833	Portraits	—	—	17	20	19	—	—	—	—	—	56
Beaumont, Miss A.	Liverpool	1873	Game	—	—	—	—	1	—	—	—	—	—	1
Beaumont, Frederick S.	London	1884-1893	Portraits	—	—	12	—	1	—	—	—	—	4	17
Beaumont, Sir George Howland, Bart.	Coleorton	1779-1825	Landscape	—	—	36	—	—	—	—	—	—	—	36
Beaumont, Jerold	London	1893	Domestic	—	—	—	—	—	—	—	—	—	1	1
Beaumont, John Thomas Barber. *See* Barber.	—	—	—	—	—	—	—	—	—	—	—	—	—	—
Beaumont, J. W. and R. F.	London	1890	Architecture	—	—	1	—	—	—	—	—	—	—	1
Beaumont, W.	Rochester	1832-1854	Cattle	—	—	—	1	3	—	1	—	—	1	6
Beaupre —	London	1764-1767	Sculpture	4	1	—	—	—	—	—	—	—	—	5
Beaurepaire, De. *See* D.	—	—	—	—	—	—	—	—	—	—	—	—	—	—
Beauvais, Simon, F.S.A.	—	1761-1778	Miniatures	30	3	—	—	—	—	—	—	—	—	33
Beauverie, Ch.	London	1880	Etching	—	—	—	—	—	—	—	—	—	1	1
Beavis, C.	London	1840	Domestic	—	—	—	1	—	—	—	—	—	—	1
Beavis, Maud	London	1881	Geese	—	—	—	—	1	—	—	—	—	—	1
Beavis, Richard, R.W.S. † ‡	London	1851-1893	Landscape	—	—	43	21	16	100	83	14	7	47	331
Beavoir, Richard	—	1763	Landscape	1	—	—	—	—	—	—	—	—	—	1
Beazley —	—	1846	Portraits	—	—	1	—	—	—	—	—	—	—	1
Beazley, Charles	London	1787-1806	Architecture	—	—	14	—	—	—	—	—	—	—	14
Beazley, Charles Nightingale	London	1875-1883	Architecture	—	—	2	—	—	—	—	—	—	—	2
Beazley, G.	—	1832	Landscape	—	—	1	—	—	—	—	—	—	—	1
Beazley, Samuel	London	1811-1848	Architecture	—	—	20	—	—	—	—	—	—	—	20
Becci, Luigi	London	1879	Domestic	—	—	—	—	1	—	—	—	—	—	1
Beck, Angelo	London	1884-1889	Sculpture	—	—	3	—	—	—	—	—	—	—	3
Beck, G.	London	1790-1793	Landscape	6	—	8	—	—	—	—	—	—	—	14
Beck, J. W.	Merton	1879-1892	Landscape	—	—	—	—	—	—	—	17	14	—	31
Beck, Mrs. Mary	London	1790-1793	Landscape	—	—	4	—	—	—	—	—	—	—	4
Beck, W.	London	1848	Architecture	—	—	2	—	—	—	—	—	—	—	2
Becker, E.	Bath	1793-1810	Landscape	—	—	2	2	—	—	—	—	—	—	4
Becker, E. A.	London	1849-1859	Figures	—	—	11	4	6	—	—	—	—	—	21
Becker, Harry	Colchester	1885-1893	Rustic	—	—	9	—	5	—	6	—	—	—	20
Beckett, J.	Dorking	1846-1847	Landscape	—	—	—	2	2	—	—	—	—	—	4
Beckingham, Arthur	London	1881-1893	Historical	—	—	7	—	1	—	—	—	—	4	12
Beckwith, H.	—	1832	Engraving	—	—	—	—	3	—	—	—	—	—	3
Beckwith, J. Carroll	New York	1892	Portraits	—	—	1	—	—	—	—	—	—	—	1
Becquet, S.	—	1847	Landscape	—	—	1	—	—	—	—	—	—	—	1
Bedder, J.	London	1824	Architecture	—	—	1	—	—	—	—	—	—	—	1
Bede, Cuthbert	Oakham	1876	Churches	—	—	—	—	—	—	—	—	—	1	1
Bederman, W. Clive	—	1838	Snow Pieces	—	—	1	—	—	—	—	—	—	—	1
Bedford —	Birmingham	1764	Coach Panels	—	3	—	—	—	—	—	—	—	—	3
Bedford, B.	London	1848	Scriptural	—	—	—	—	1	—	—	—	—	—	1
Bedford, Miss Ella M.	London	1882-1893	Figures	—	—	12	—	9	—	1	—	—	3	25
Bedford, F.	London	1814-1832	Architecture	—	—	6	—	—	—	—	—	—	—	6
Bedford, F., Junr.	London	1833-1849	Architecture	—	—	9	—	—	—	—	—	—	—	9
Bedford, Francis D.	London	1892	Landscape	—	—	1	—	—	—	—	—	—	—	1
Bedford, Francis W.	Leeds	1890-1892	Churches	—	—	10	—	—	—	—	—	—	—	10
Bedford, Henry E.	Richmond	1892-1893	Landscape	—	—	—	—	3	—	—	—	—	—	3
Bedford, J.	Acton	1793	Architecture	—	—	3	—	—	—	—	—	—	—	3
Bedford, John Bates	London	1848-1886	Portraits	—	—	41	5	3	—	—	—	—	19	68
Bedingfeld, Richard T.	London	1889	Figures	—	—	1	—	—	—	—	—	—	—	1
Bedingfield, J.	London	1890	Figures	—	—	1	—	—	—	—	—	—	—	1
Bednon, A.	Boulogne S/M	1893	Fishing	—	—	—	—	1	—	—	—	—	—	1
Bedsborough, A.	London	1875-1876	Architecture	—	—	4	—	—	—	—	—	—	—	4
Bedwell, E. P.	London	1828-1829	Portraits	—	—	1	1	4	—	—	—	—	—	6
Bedwell, Emily P.	Richmond	1877	Still Life	—	—	—	—	—	—	—	—	—	1	1
Beebe, Miss Annie A.	London	1888-1890	Figures	—	—	2	—	—	—	—	—	—	—	2
Beeby, Mrs. Elizabeth K.	Croydon	1868-1872	Landscape	—	—	—	—	4	—	—	—	—	1	5
Beech, A. J.	London	1888-1889	Flowers	—	—	2	—	1	—	1	—	—	—	4
Beech, Herbert J. G.	Cardiff	1893	Portraits	—	—	1	—	—	—	—	—	—	—	1
Beech, J.	Leicester	1830-1839	Portraits	—	—	6	—	—	—	—	—	—	—	6
Beecham, John	Cirencester	1835-1857	Historical	—	—	—	6	—	—	—	—	—	*	6
Beecham, W. R.	London	1824-1833	Figures	—	—	—	12	—	—	—	—	—	—	12
Beechey, Miss Augusta	London	1870-1872	Still Life	—	—	—	—	3	—	—	—	—	3	6
Beechey, Miss Frances. *See* Mrs. Edw. Hopkins	—	—	—	—	—	—	—	—	—	—	—	—	—	—

Name.	Town.	First and Last Year of Ex.	Speciality.	S. A.	F. S.	R. A.	B. I.	S. S.	O. W.	N. W.	G. G.	N. G.	V. E.	Total.
Beechey, Miss Frederika	London	1870-1874	Landscape	—	—	—	—	5	—	—	—	—	7	12
Beechey, George D.	London	1817-1832	Portraits	—	—	24	1	—	—	—	—	—	—	25
Beechey, H.	London	1829-1838	Sea Pieces	—	—	1	1	—	—	—	—	—	—	2
Beechey, Captain Richard B.	London	1832-1877	Sea Pieces	—	—	19	13	7	—	—	—	—	1	40
Beechey, S. R.	London	1859	Portraits	—	—	1	—	—	—	—	—	—	—	1
Beechey, Sir William, R.A.	London	1776-1839	Portraits	—	—	372	32	13	—	—	—	—	—	417
Beechey, Mrs. *See* Lady Beechey	London	1795-1798	Miniatures	—	—	12	—	—	—	—	—	—	—	12
Beechey, Lady. *See* Mrs. Beechey	London	1799-1805	Miniatures	—	—	8	—	—	—	—	—	—	—	8
Beek, W. G.	Cambr'dge H'th	1829	Indian	—	—	1	—	—	—	—	—	—	—	1
Beensen, H. P. and Co.	London	1853	Architecture	—	—	1	—	—	—	—	—	—	—	1
Beenson and Kuckuth	London	1854-1855	Architecture	—	—	3	—	—	—	—	—	—	—	3
Beer, T.	—	1833	Landscape	—	—	—	—	1	—	—	—	—	—	1
Beere, Alfred	Gravesend	1880-1887	Sculpture	—	—	4	—	—	—	—	—	—	—	4
Beernaert and Shÿffers	London	1845	Carvings	—	—	—	—	1	—	—	—	—	—	1
Beers, Jan Van. *See* V.	—	—	—	—	—	—	—	—	—	—	—	—	—	—
Beesley, John	London	1775-1779	Fruit	—	8	—	—	—	—	—	—	—	—	8
Beesley, Robert	London	1767-1783	Fruit	—	55	—	—	—	—	—	—	—	—	55
Beesley, Mrs. Ann	London	1774-1783	Flowers	—	10	—	—	—	—	—	—	—	—	10
Beeston, Arthur	London	1880-1883	Landscape	—	—	—	—	1	—	—	—	—	1	2
Beeston and Burmester	London	1893	Architecture	—	—	4	—	—	—	—	—	—	—	4
Beetham, Miss J. (?) Betham	London	1794-1816	Miniatures	—	—	56	3	—	10	—	—	—	9	78
Beetham, Miss M.	—	1807-1808	Rustic	—	—	2	—	—	—	—	—	—	—	2
Beetham, William	London	1834-1853	Portraits	—	—	16	—	2	—	—	—	—	—	18
Beetholme, George Law	London	1847-1878	Landscape	—	—	8	2	13	—	—	—	—	1	24
Beetholme, G. L. F., Junr.	London	1879-1880	Fruit	—	—	—	—	6	—	—	—	—	—	6
Beffin, Miss S. (She had no arms.)	London	1821	Miniatures	—	—	4	—	—	—	—	—	—	—	4
Begg, John	London	1890-1893	Architecture	—	—	3	—	—	—	—	—	—	—	3
Begg, Samuel	London	1886-1891	Sculpture	—	—	3	—	—	—	—	—	—	—	3
Behnes, William	London	1815-1863	Sculpture	—	—	216	—	—	—	—	—	—	—	216
Behr, Miss Julia	London	1870-1885	Figures	—	—	3	—	1	—	—	1	—	—	5
Beiderman, J. C.	Tedbury	1794-1796	Domestic	—	—	2	—	—	—	—	—	—	—	2
Beilby, W.	London	1780-1791	Landscape	4	—	3	—	—	—	—	—	—	—	7
Belanger, L.	London	1790-1797	Landscape	—	—	3	—	—	—	—	—	—	—	3
Belcher, Arthur H.	London	1887-1889	Architecture	—	—	3	—	—	—	—	—	—	—	3
Belcher, Miss E. Beatrice	London	1885	Landscape	—	—	1	—	—	—	—	—	—	—	1
Belcher, F.	London	1874-1879	Domestic	—	—	—	—	—	—	—	—	—	1	1
Belcher, John	London	1854-1885	Architecture	—	—	12	—	—	—	—	—	—	—	12
Belcher, John, Junr.	London	1882-1893	Architecture	—	—	36	—	—	—	—	—	—	—	36
Belford, Miss Kate A.	Tunbr'ge Wells	1871-1887	Domestic	—	—	—	—	5	—	4	—	—	27	36
Belgrave, Dacres T. C.	London	1880-1885	Landscape	—	—	1	—	1	—	3	—	—	1	6
Belgrave, Percy	London	1880-1893	Landscape	—	—	30	—	24	—	3	1	2	3	63
Belgrave, William	London	1890-1893	Landscape	—	—	3	—	—	—	—	—	—	1	4
Belisario, J. M.	London	1815-1831	Landscape	—	—	4	—	—	4	—	—	—	—	8
Belk, E.	London	1762-1786	Architecture	4	1	5	—	—	—	—	—	—	—	10
Bell, Lady. *See* Miss Maria Hamilton, also	—	—	—	—	—	—	—	—	—	—	—	—	—	—
Mrs. Bell (Pupil of Reynolds.)	London	1819-1824	Portraits	—	—	6	—	4	—	—	—	—	—	10
Bell, A.	London	1852-1857	Architecture	—	—	7	—	—	—	—	—	—	—	7
Bell, A. *See* Clayton and Bell	—	—	Stained Glass	—	—	—	—	—	—	—	—	—	—	—
Bell, Miss Ada	London	1878-1891	Landscape	—	—	15	—	21	—	14	10	1	21	82
Bell, Alfred	London	1890	Churches	—	—	1	—	—	—	—	—	—	—	1
Bell, Alexander Carlyle	London	1866-1891	Landscape	—	—	3	—	7	—	16	—	—	26	52
Bell, Arthur George	London	1875-1893	Domestic	—	—	21	—	45	—	9	1	—	20	96
Bell, Asahel P.	Manchester	1881-1882	Architecture	—	—	2	—	—	—	—	—	—	—	2
Bell, A. R.	London	1851-1853	Portraits	—	—	—	—	4	—	—	—	—	—	4
Bell, Catherine	London	1783-1806	Portraits	—	—	37	—	—	—	—	—	—	—	37
Bell, Charles	London	1881-1890	Architecture	—	—	4	—	—	—	—	—	—	—	4
Bell, Edward	Worcester	1811-1847	Still Life	—	—	22	24	22	—	—	—	—	—	68
Bell, Edward H.	Kew	1873-1881	Mythological	—	—	—	—	2	—	—	1	—	1	4
Bell, Edward Ingress. *See also* Bacon and Bell,	—	—	—	—	—	—	—	—	—	—	—	—	—	—
Clarke and Bell, and Webb and Bell	London	1879-1883	Architecture	—	—	8	—	—	—	—	—	—	—	8
Bell, Miss Eleanor	Munich	1874-1885	Domestic	—	—	4	—	5	—	—	—	—	1	10
Bell, Hesketh	London	1852-1872	Landscape	—	—	—	1	—	—	—	—	—	1	2
Bell, H.	Manchester	1872	Landscape	—	—	1	—	—	—	—	—	—	—	1
Bell, Henry A.	Highbury	1889	Sea Pieces	—	—	—	—	1	—	—	—	—	1	2
Bell, H. D.	London	1849	Landscape	—	—	—	1	—	—	—	—	—	—	1
Bell, Miss H. E.	London	1877	Fruit	—	—	—	—	—	—	—	—	—	1	1
Bell, Rev. J.	London	1863	Figures	—	—	1	—	—	—	—	—	—	—	1
Bell, James	London	1838-1857	Architecture	—	—	15	—	2	—	—	—	—	—	17
Bell, John	Bettws-y-Coed	1852-1861	Landscape	—	—	2	3	4	—	—	—	—	19	28
Bell, John	London	1831-1879	Sculpture	—	—	66	6	17	—	—	—	—	—	89
Bell, J. A.	Edinburgh	1845	Architecture	—	—	1	—	—	—	—	—	—	—	1
Bell, J. C.	Scarborough	1858-1868	Sporting	—	—	—	—	6	—	—	—	—	—	6

Name.	Town.	First and Last Year of Ex.	Speciality.	S. A.	F. S.	R. A.	B. I.	S. S.	O. W.	N.W.	G. G.	N. G.	V. E.	Total.
Bell, John Clement	London	1878-1892	Landscape	—	—	1	—	—	—	1	—	—	1	3
Bell, Miss Jane Campbell	London	1850-1863	Figures	—	—	10	—	12	—	—	—	—	—	22
Bell, John Zephaniah	Edinburgh	1824-1865	Domestic	—	—	28	11	15	—	—	—	—	19	73
Bell, Miss Lucy Hilda	London	1889-1892	Fruit	—	—	1	—	1	—	2	—	—	—	4
Bell, Percy F. H.	Hounslow	1887-1892	Figures	—	—	1	—	3	—	—	—	—	2	6
Bell, Robert Anning	Chiswick	1880-1893	Figures	—	—	4	—	5	—	—	—	—	8	17
Bell, Robert Clifton	East Moulsey	1882-1883	Landscape	—	—	—	—	3	—	—	—	—	—	3
Bell, R. P., A.R.S.A.	Edinburgh	1876	Oriental	—	—	—	—	—	—	—	—	—	1	1
Bell, William	Newcastle	1775-1776	Scriptural	—	1	1	—	—	—	—	—	—	—	2
Bell, William C.	London	1870-1891	Miniatures	—	—	6	—	—	—	—	—	—	—	6
Bell, Mrs. *See* Lady Bell and Miss Maria	—	—	—	—	—	—	—	—	—	—	—	—	—	—
Hamilton	London	1809-1816	Figures	—	—	2	3	—	—	—	—	—	—	5
Bell, Mrs.	Mansfield	1859	Flowers	—	—	—	—	1	—	—	—	—	—	1
Bell, Miss	—	1851	Study	—	—	—	—	—	—	—	—	—	1	1
Bell and Corbet	London	1853	Architecture	—	—	1	—	—	—	—	—	—	—	1
Bell and Roper	Manchester	1878	Architecture	—	—	2	—	—	—	—	—	—	—	2
Bell-Smith, F. M. *See* S.	—	—	—	—	—	—	—	—	—	—	—	—	—	—
Bellamy, A. S.	London	1868-1874	Fruit, &c.	—	—	1	—	13	—	—	—	—	—	14
Bellamy, J.	London	1802	Flowers	—	—	2	—	—	—	—	—	—	—	2
Bellamy, Thomas, F.I.B A.	London	1816-1837	Architecture	—	—	7	—	—	—	—	—	—	—	7
Bellandi, F.	London	1880	Domestic	—	—	—	—	—	—	—	—	—	1	1
Bellanger, G.	London	1869	Domestic	—	—	1	—	—	—	—	—	—	—	1
Bellay, Charles R.	Rome	1871-1879	Figures	—	—	—	—	—	—	—	—	—	7	7
Bellecour, Etienne Prosper Berne-. *See* Berne.	—	—	—	—	—	—	—	—	—	—	—	—	—	—
Bellei, Gaetano	London	1882	Figures	—	—	1	—	—	—	—	—	—	—	1
Bellel, Jean Joseph	Paris	1868-1869	Landscape	—	—	7	—	—	—	—	—	—	—	7
Bellenger, Albert	Paris	1875-1881	Woodcuts	—	—	1	—	—	—	—	—	—	7	8
Bellenger, Georges	Paris	1875-1879	Figures	—	—	—	—	—	—	—	—	—	2	2
Bellers, William	London	1761-1773	Landscape	—	65	—	—	—	—	—	—	—	—	65
Bellew, Capt.	—	1764-1767	Landscape	3	—	—	—	—	—	—	—	—	—	3
Bellhouse, F. T.	London	1862	Architecture	—	—	1	—	—	—	—	—	—	—	1
Bellhouse, Richard Taylor	Bruges	1880-1884	Buildings	—	—	—	—	6	—	1	—	—	4	11
Belli, Enrico	London	1862-1884	Portraits	—	—	3	—	8	—	—	—	—	—	11
Bellin, Arthur	London	1877-1888	Sea Pieces	—	—	6	—	3	—	—	1	—	2	12
Bellin, Miss J.	—	1839	Religious	—	—	—	—	2	—	—	—	—	—	2
Bellin, Samuel	London	1835-1867	Engraving	—	—	3	—	1	—	—	—	—	—	4
Bellinger —	London	1803	Sporting	—	—	3	—	—	—	—	—	—	—	3
Bellingham —	London	1766-1767	Miniatures	2	—	—	—	—	—	—	—	—	—	2
Bellis, Frank	Mold	1888	Architecture	—	—	1	—	—	—	—	—	—	—	1
Bellot, Mrs. Julia Cecilia	London	1884	Figures	—	—	1	—	—	—	—	—	—	1	2
Bellott, Herbert M.	London	1874-1884	Figures	—	—	1	—	2	—	1	—	—	—	4
Bellotti —	London	1765	Ruins	1	—	—	—	—	—	—	—	—	—	1
Bellows, Albert F.	London	1869	Landscape	—	—	—	—	—	—	—	—	—	2	2
Belshaw, Frank	Nottingham	1881-1882	Fish	—	—	1	—	2	—	—	—	—	—	3
Belson, Miss	London	1880-1802	Landscape	—	—	2	—	—	—	—	—	—	—	2
Belt, Richard C.	London	1873-1885	Sculpture	—	—	20	—	—	—	—	2	—	—	22
Bemfleet, G.	London	1772-1790	Enamels	1	—	7	—	—	—	—	—	—	—	8
Benazech, Charles	London	1761-1791	Portraits	3	—	6	—	—	—	—	—	—	—	9
Benbridge, Henry	London	1770	Portraits	—	—	2	—	—	—	—	—	—	—	2
Bencraft —	—	1783	Dramatic	—	1	—	—	—	—	—	—	—	—	1
Bendixen, S.	London	1833-1864	Historical	—	—	18	61	42	—	1	—	—	1	123
Benecke, Miss Amy M.	London	1885	Landscape	—	—	—	—	—	—	1	—	—	—	1
Benedict, R.	London	1856-1862	Domestic	—	—	—	—	4	—	—	—	—	—	4
Benefiati, Chevalier, a disciple of	—	1779-1780	Figures	—	9	—	—	—	—	—	—	—	—	9
Benett, Newton	Lyndhurst	1875-1893	Landscape	—	—	5	—	5	—	11	8	9	7	45
Benger, Berenger	Liverpool	1884-1893	Landscape	—	—	1	—	—	—	4	—	—	—	5
Benger, W. Edmund	Llandudno	1890-1892	Landscape	—	—	1	—	1	—	1	—	—	—	3
Bengo, John	Edinburgh	1830	Historical	—	—	—	1	—	—	—	—	—	—	1
Bengough, R. W.	London	1830-1836	Sea Pieces	—	—	—	3	14	—	—	—	—	—	17
Benham, Miss Jane. *See* Mrs. Benham Hay	London	1848-1849	Historical	—	—	2	—	—	—	—	—	—	—	2
Benham, Miss Jessie	London	1887-1893	Sea Pieces	—	—	2	—	—	—	—	—	—	1	3
Benham, Thomas C. S.	London	1878-1893	Landscape	—	—	23	—	—	—	2	2	—	17	44
Benjamin, J.	London	1825	Engraving	—	—	—	—	1	—	—	—	—	—	1
Benjamin, R.	London	1858	Figures	—	—	1	—	—	—	—	—	—	—	1
Benner, Jean	Paris	1887	Animals	—	—	1	—	—	—	—	—	—	—	1
Bennet, George Montagu, Lord	London	1885-1891	Miniatures	—	—	30	—	—	—	—	—	—	—	30
Bennet, M.	Maidstone	1796-1801	Historical	—	—	4	—	—	—	—	—	—	—	4
Bennet, R. S.	London	1845-1889	Miniatures	—	—	3	—	—	—	—	—	—	—	3
Bennet, T.	Woodstock	1796-1799	Sporting	—	—	7	—	—	—	—	—	—	—	7
Bennett —	London	1783	Animals	—	1	—	—	—	—	—	—	—	—	1
Bennett, Alfred	London	1861-1880	Landscape	—	—	4	2	17	—	—	—	—	—	23
Bennett, Ebenezer	London	1857-1872	Sculpture	—	—	15	4	1	—	—	—	—	3	23

Name.	Town.	First and Last Year of Ex.	Speciality.	S. A.	F. S.	R. A.	B. I.	S. S.	O. W.	N.W.	G. G.	N. G.	V. E.	Total.
Bennett, Edmund J.	Gravesend	1893	Architecture	—	—	1	—	—	—	—	—	—	—	1
Bennett, G. F.	London	1841-1845	Medals	—	—	4	—	—	—	—	—	—	—	4
Bennett, G. R.	London	1877	Portraits	—	—	1	—	—	—	—	—	—	—	1
Bennett, H.	Forest Hill	1879-1880	Domestic	—	—	—	—	4	—	—	—	—	—	4
Bennett, Miss Harriet M.	London	1877-1892	Domestic	—	—	3	—	—	—	2	—	—	16	21
Bennett, Miss Isabel	London	1870-1876	Landscape	—	—	1	—	28	—	—	—	—	—	29
Bennett, J.	London	1801-1803	Landscape	—	—	4	—	—	—	—	—	—	—	4
Bennett, J. A.	Manchester	1882	Figures	—	—	1	—	—	—	—	—	—	—	1
Bennett, J. Lovett	Parson Town	1885	Domestic	—	—	—	—	1	—	—	—	—	—	1
Bennett, John M.	Sheffield	1827-1838	Domestic	—	—	7	3	7	—	—	—	—	—	17
Bennett, Miss Kate	Forest Hill	1888	Domestic	—	—	—	—	—	—	1	—	—	—	1
Bennett, Miss Mary	London	1871-1876	Landscape	—	—	—	—	1	—	—	—	—	2	3
Bennett, Miss Mary Louisa	Plymouth	1877-1878	Sculpture	—	—	2	—	—	—	—	—	—	—	2
Bennett, S. E.	Forest Hill	1880	Figures	—	—	—	—	—	—	—	—	—	1	1
Bennett, Thomas	Woodstock	1816-1819	Animals	—	—	—	—	—	6	—	—	—	—	6
Bennett, William ‡	London	1842-1871	Landscape	—	—	18	3	8	—	378	—	—	—	407
Bennett, William	London	1878-1887	Landscape	—	—	—	—	6	—	2	—	—	2	10
Bennett, William James †	London	1808-1825	Landscape	—	—	—	—	—	7	—	—	—	42	49
Bennett, William Mineard	Exeter	1812-1816	Portraits	—	—	15	—	—	—	—	—	—	—	15
Bennett, W. T.	London	1807	Buildings	—	—	1	—	—	—	—	—	—	—	1
Bensa, Francesco	Florence	1875-1880	Domestic	—	—	1	—	1	—	—	—	—	—	2
Benson, Eugene	Venice	1872-1892	Figures	—	—	10	—	—	—	—	41	7	8	66
Benson, Eleanor B.	—	1870	Historical	—	—	—	—	1	—	—	—	—	—	1
Benson, Frank W.	London	1885	Sea Pieces	—	—	1	—	—	—	—	—	—	—	1
Benson, G.	London	1800	Architecture	—	—	1	—	—	—	—	—	—	—	1
Benson, Miss H.	London	1875	Flowers	—	—	—	—	1	—	—	—	—	—	1
Benson, Miss Henrietta	Hertford	1885	Domestic	—	—	—	—	—	—	1	—	—	—	1
Benson, Miss Mary K.	Hertford	1879-1890	Domestic	—	—	2	—	6	—	—	—	—	3	11
Benson, J.	London	1805-1811	Sporting	—	—	5	—	—	—	—	—	—	—	5
Benson, Sir John	London	1815-1843	Architecture	—	—	3	—	—	—	—	—	—	—	3
Benson, W.	London	1844	Architecture	—	—	2	—	—	—	—	—	—	—	2
Bensted, Hubert	Maidstone	1886	Architecture	—	—	1	—	—	—	—	—	—	—	1
Bensted, J.	Maidstone	1828-1847	Game	—	—	7	—	4	—	—	—	—	—	11
Bentham, A. W.	—	1893	River	—	—	—	—	—	—	—	—	1	—	1
Bentham, R. H.	Guernsey	1871-1874	Landscape	—	—	—	—	8	—	—	—	—	—	8
Bentley, Charles †	London	1832-1854	Sea Pieces	—	—	—	11	3	209	10	—	—	—	233
Bentley, Edward	Bexley Heath	1866-1883	Fruit, &c.	—	—	1	—	38	—	—	—	—	—	39
Bentley, J.	London	1861	Architecture	—	—	1	—	—	—	—	—	—	—	1
Bentley, Joseph Clayton	London	1833-1853	Landscape	—	—	10	11	21	—	—	—	—	20	62
Bentley, Joseph H.	Lincoln	1885-1892	Figures	—	—	9	—	—	—	—	—	—	2	11
Bentley, Mrs. *See* Miss Lucy B. Smith.	—	—	—	—	—	—	—	—	—	—	—	—	—	—
Benton, Mrs. Julia I.	London	1883-1885	Domestic	—	—	2	—	3	—	—	—	—	—	5
Bentz, Frederick	Edinburgh	1877-1885	Landscape	—	—	5	—	1	—	—	—	—	4	10
Benuzzi, Edwin	London	1888-1889	Venice	—	—	—	—	6	—	—	—	—	—	6
Benwell, J.	—	1808	Landscape	—	—	1	—	—	—	—	—	—	—	1
Benwell, Joseph Austin	London	1865-1886	East'rn Subj'cts	—	—	5	—	43	—	2	—	—	5	55
Benwell, John Hodges	London	1784	Mythological	—	—	1	—	—	—	—	—	—	—	1
Benwell, Miss Mary (afterwards Mrs. Code)	London	1762-1782	Miniatures	61	—	22	—	—	—	—	—	—	—	83
Benwell, S.	London	1803-1817	Architecture	—	—	13	—	—	—	—	—	—	—	13
Benwell, Mrs.	—	1807	Churches	—	—	1	—	—	—	—	—	—	—	1
Benwell, Mrs.	London	1870-1871	Landscape	—	—	—	—	3	—	—	—	—	—	3
Béraud, Jean	London	1882	Figures	—	—	1	—	—	—	—	—	—	—	1
Berchère, N.	Paris	1881	Egyptian	—	—	—	—	—	—	—	4	—	—	4
Berckhardt —	London	1795	Domestic	—	—	2	—	—	—	—	—	—	—	2
Berczy —	Florence	1790	Miniatures	—	—	1	—	—	—	—	—	—	—	1
Berczy, Mrs.	Florence	1790	Interiors	—	—	2	—	—	—	—	—	—	—	2
Berdienruth, Adolph	London	1883	Landscape	—	—	—	—	—	—	—	—	—	1	1
Berend, Edward	Paris	1881	Engraving	—	—	—	—	—	—	—	—	—	3	3
Berens, A. H.	London	1888	Figures	—	—	1	—	—	—	—	—	—	—	1
Beresford, Miss E. M. (?) C. M.	London	1865-1885	Figures	—	—	—	—	6	—	1	—	—	25	32
Beresford, Miss P.	London	1871-1880	Figures	—	—	—	—	6	—	—	1	—	—	7
Berg, Furmack M.	London	1865	Landscape	—	—	—	—	—	—	—	—	—	2	2
Berg, Oscar	London	1883	Sculpture	—	—	1	—	—	—	—	—	—	—	1
Berger, C.	London	1837	Landscape	—	—	—	1	—	—	—	—	—	—	1
Berger, Johan	London	1839	Sea Pieces	—	—	—	2	—	—	—	—	—	—	2
Berger, P. P.	London	1825	Portraits	—	—	4	—	—	—	—	—	—	—	4
Bergh, Professor E.	Stockholm	1865-1871	Landscape	—	—	3	—	—	—	—	—	—	—	3
Berghe, Van der. *See* V.	—	—	—	—	—	—	—	—	—	—	—	—	—	—
Bergson, Miss Mina	London	1885-1889	Historical	—	—	3	—	—	—	—	—	—	—	3
Berick, Samuel	London	1774	Copies	1	—	—	—	—	—	—	—	—	—	1
Beringen, E.	Munich	1882	Cairo	—	—	1	—	—	—	—	—	—	—	1
Beringer Beringer	Birkenhead	1890	Domestic	—	—	—	—	—	—	1	—	—	—	1

Name.	Town.	First and Last Year of Ex.	Speciality.	S. A.	F. S.	R. A.	B. I.	S. S.	O. W.	N. W.	G. G.	N. G.	V. E.	Total.
Berkeley, Harriet	London	1854	Figures	—	—	1	—	—	—	—	—	—	—	1
Berkeley, Colonel	—	1802	Gibraltar	—	—	1	—	—	—	—	—	—	—	1
Berkeley, Stanley	London	1878-1892	Animals	—	—	15	—	14	—	9	1	—	18	57
Berkeley, Mrs. Stanley (Edith)	London	1883-1893	Figures	—	—	9	—	4	—	11	1	—	5	30
Berkham, C.	London	1816	Sea Pieces	—	—	1	—	—	—	—	—	—	—	1
Berkley, Miss M.	London	1854	Figures	—	—	—	1	—	—	—	—	—	—	1
Bermingham —	London	1774	Portraits	5	—	—	—	—	—	—	—	—	—	5
Bernan, Miss Charlotte A.	—	1884	Flowers	—	—	—	—	—	—	1	—	—	—	1
Bernard, Miss Margaret	Bath	1883-1893	Landscape	—	—	4	—	—	—	8	—	—	—	12
Bernard, Miss	—	1800	Landscape	—	—	1	—	—	—	—	—	—	—	1
Bernasconi, G. H.	London	1861-1866	Domestic	—	—	3	5	6	—	—	—	—	—	14
Bernasconi, P.	Milan	1875	Sculpture	—	—	1	—	—	—	—	—	—	—	1
Bernau, Miss Charlotte	London	1887-1892	Sculpture	—	—	3	—	—	—	—	—	—	—	3
Berne-Bellecour, Etienne Prosper	London	1881	Etching	—	—	—	—	—	—	—	—	—	1	1
Berne, H.	—	1800	Miniatures	—	—	5	—	—	—	—	—	—	—	5
Bernede —	London	1797	Miniatures	—	—	1	—	—	—	—	—	—	—	1
Bernet, Mrs.	London	1774	Needlework	1	2	—	—	—	—	—	—	—	—	3
Bernhardt, Carl W. W.	London	1882	Architecture	—	—	1	—	—	—	—	—	—	—	1
Berrac, G.	London	1797	Miniatures	—	—	2	—	—	—	—	—	—	—	2
Berrecloth, R.	London	1826-1827	Architecture	—	—	2	—	—	—	—	—	—	—	2
Berridge, John, F.S.A., Pupil of Reynolds	London	1766-1792	Portraits	28	—	9	—	—	—	—	—	—	—	37
Berringer —	London	1774-1775	Still Life	5	—	—	—	—	—	—	—	—	—	5
Berry. *See* Kidner and Berry	—	—	Architecture	—	—	—	—	—	—	—	—	—	—	—
Berry, Berry Francis	London	1874-1893	Domestic	—	—	3	—	13	—	6	—	1	5	28
Berry, Miss Maude	London	1880-1885	Portraits	—	—	1	—	—	—	—	—	—	3	4
Berry, T. T.	—	1830-1838	Landscape	—	—	2	—	—	—	—	—	—	—	2
Berry, William H. Atkins	London	1884-1893	Landscape	—	—	4	—	—	—	—	—	—	—	4
Berrydew, W.	Derby	1817-1818	Landscape	—	—	2	—	—	—	—	—	—	—	2
Berryman, J.	London	1802-1809	Landscape	—	—	4	—	—	—	—	—	—	—	4
Berryman, J.	London	1824	Woodcuts	—	—	—	—	1	—	—	—	—	—	1
Berryman, W.	London	1802	Portraits	—	—	1	—	—	—	—	—	—	—	1
Bertaux, Madame L.	—	1874	Sculpture	—	—	1	—	—	—	—	—	—	—	1
Bertha, Julia	Cookham	1881	Landscape	—	—	—	—	2	—	—	—	—	—	2
Bertham, W.	London	1834	Portraits	—	—	—	—	1	—	—	—	—	—	1
Berthon, G. T.	London	1835-1838	Portraits	—	—	5	2	—	—	—	—	—	—	7
Berthoud, H.	London	1846	Game	—	—	—	—	2	—	—	—	—	—	2
Berti, G.	London	1835-1839	Figures	—	—	3	—	3	—	—	—	—	—	6
Bertie, Marion A.	London	1886-1888	Landscape	—	—	1	—	1	—	—	—	—	—	2
Bertier, C. A.	London	1886	Domestic	—	—	1	—	—	—	—	—	—	—	1
Bertin, E. F.	—	1872	Landscape	—	—	—	—	1	—	—	—	—	—	1
Bertinot, G.	Paris	1886	Engraving	—	—	1	—	—	—	—	—	—	—	1
Bertioli, Frank	London	1871-1889	Domestic	—	—	3	—	6	—	11	—	—	—	20
Berton, E.	Putney	1880-1881	Domestic	—	—	—	—	2	—	—	—	—	1	3
Bertram, Miss	London	1867	Game	—	—	—	—	1	—	—	—	—	—	1
Bertram, Miss Marion	London	1884	Figures	—	—	—	—	—	—	—	1	—	—	1
Bertrand, G.	Paris	1878-1881	Figures	—	—	—	—	—	—	—	—	—	3	3
Bertrand, Miss Mary	London	1772-1800	Portraits	—	—	10	—	—	—	—	—	—	—	10
Bertraud —	London	1764	Portraits	—	4	—	—	—	—	—	—	—	—	4
Berwick, C. F.	London	1850-1851	Architecture	—	—	2	—	—	—	—	—	—	—	2
Berwick, C. M.	London	1880	Figures	—	—	—	—	—	—	—	—	—	1	1
Besch, Miss L.	London	1889	Domestic	—	—	—	—	—	—	1	—	—	—	1
Besché, Lucien	Stoke	1883-1885	Miniatures	—	—	2	—	—	—	—	—	—	—	2
Besnard, Albert	London	1881-1882	Portraits	—	—	4	—	—	—	—	—	—	—	4
Besnard, Miss Charlotte	London	1881	Sculpture	—	—	1	—	—	—	—	—	—	—	1
Bessemer, Miss	London	1832	Churches	—	—	1	—	—	—	—	—	—	—	1
Besset, Mrs. Jane M.	London	1846-1856	Domestic	—	—	1	—	10	—	—	—	—	4	15
Besson, M.	Manchester	1853	Mythological	—	—	—	—	—	—	—	—	—	2	2
Best, Miss F. G. S.	Andover	1878-1879	Venice	—	—	—	—	2	—	—	—	—	—	2
Best, G.	London	1812	Architecture	—	—	1	—	—	—	—	—	—	—	1
Best, George Hollings	Streatham	1873-1890	Landscape	—	—	8	—	—	—	—	—	—	3	11
Best, J.	London	1772-1787	Sporting	7	—	2	—	—	—	—	—	—	—	9
Best, R. H.	London	1827	Architecture	—	—	1	—	—	—	—	—	—	—	1
Best, Thomas	London	1834-1839	Domestic	—	—	1	—	3	—	—	—	—	—	4
Best, W. R.	London	1827	Intaglios	—	—	1	—	—	—	—	—	—	—	1
Best, Miss	London	1773	Drawing	—	1	—	—	—	—	—	—	—	—	1
Bestland, Charles	London	1783-1837	Historical	—	—	71	37	7	—	—	—	—	—	115
Bestoesmith, W.	Sudbury	1836-1837	Fish	—	—	2	—	—	—	—	—	—	—	2
Beswick, Frank	Chester	1881-1883	Landscape	—	—	1	—	—	—	1	—	—	—	2
Bethell, James	London	1826-1835	Scriptural	—	—	7	9	3	—	—	—	—	—	19
Bethell, Miss V. S.	—	1884	Landscape	—	—	—	—	—	—	—	1	—	—	1
Bethell, W. Wood	London	1882	Architecture	—	—	1	—	—	—	—	—	—	—	1
Betsellere, Pierre Émile	London	1877	Landscape	—	—	—	—	1	—	—	—	—	—	1

Name.	Town.	First and Last Year of Ex.	Speciality.	S. A.	F. S.	R. A.	B. I.	S. S.	O.W.	N.W.	G. G.	N. G.	V. E.	Total.
Bettelini, P.	London	1786	Scriptural	—	—	2	—	—	—	—	—	—	—	2
Betts, B.	London	1831	Sculpture	—	—	—	—	1	—	—	—	—	—	1
Betts, B. W.	London	1854	Architecture	—	—	1	—	—	—	—	—	—	—	1
Bettwes, D.	Plaistow	1836	Landscape	—	—	—	1	—	—	—	—	—	—	1
Beurden, Alphonse Van	Antwerp	1887-1892	Sculpture	—	—	6	—	—	—	—	—	—	—	6
Bevan, J.	London	1846	Portraits	—	—	1	—	—	—	—	—	—	—	1
Bevan, R. and J.	London	1835	Architecture	—	—	1	—	—	—	—	—	—	—	1
Bevan, W.	York	1857	Architecture	—	—	1	—	—	—	—	—	—	—	1
Bevans, J.	London	1818	Architecture	—	—	1	—	—	—	—	—	—	—	1
Bever, Van. *See* V.	—	—	—	—	—	—	—	—	—	—	—	—	—	—
Beverley, J.	—	1838	Portraits	—	—	1	—	—	—	—	—	—	—	1
Beverly, William Roxby	London	1865-1880	Sea Pieces	—	—	28	—	—	—	—	—	—	28	56
Bewick, William (pupil of B. R. Haydon)	London	1820-1848	Historical	—	—	4	8	9	1	—	—	—	—	22
Beyerhans, E.	London	1857	Portraits	—	—	1	—	—	—	—	—	—	—	1
Beyle, P. M.	Paris	1881	Figures	—	—	—	—	—	—	—	2	—	—	2
Beynon, Mary	London	1889	Landscape	—	—	—	—	1	—	—	—	—	—	1
Bezzi, A.	London	1850-1853	Sculpture	—	—	4	—	—	—	—	—	—	—	4
Bezzüoli, Professor Chevalier Guiseppe	Florence	1848-1849	Historical	—	—	1	1	—	—	—	—	—	—	2
Biago —	London	1768	Architecture	—	1	—	—	—	—	—	—	—	—	1
Biard, Auguste François	Paris	1840-1847	Historical	—	—	6	—	—	—	—	—	—	—	6
Biard, J.	London	1824-1825	Portraits	—	—	6	—	3	—	—	—	—	—	9
Biard, M.	London	1824	Copies	—	—	—	—	4	—	—	—	—	—	4
Biarelle, C.	London	1770	Architecture	1	—	—	—	—	—	—	—	—	—	1
Bibb, Charles	Paris	1764-1765	Engraving	2	—	—	—	—	—	—	—	—	—	2
Bibbs, Louisa H.	Worcester	1864	Fruit	—	—	—	—	1	—	—	—	—	—	1
Bibron-Belloc, Madame Jenny	Paris	1871	Landscape	—	—	—	—	—	—	—	—	—	1	1
Bichard, A. Géry	London	1877	Engraving	—	—	—	—	—	—	—	—	—	1	1
Bickerdike, A. *See also* Paull & Bickerdike	London	1874-1877	Architecture	—	—	3	—	—	—	—	—	—	—	3
Bickers, George	London	1837	Still Life	—	—	—	—	2	—	—	—	—	—	2
Bickerton, T. A.	London	1870-1879	Sculpture	—	—	6	—	—	—	—	—	—	—	6
Bickham, George	London	1761-1765	Engraving	—	8	—	—	—	—	—	—	—	—	8
Bickley, H. M.	Woking	1883	Landscape	—	—	—	—	1	—	—	—	—	—	1
Bicknell, Mrs. *See* Miss Emily Desvignes.	—	—	—	—	—	—	—	—	—	—	—	—	—	—
Bida —	Paris	1875-1876	Illustrations	—	—	—	—	—	—	—	—	—	8	8
Bidden, R. O.	London	1833	Game	—	—	—	—	—	—	2	—	—	—	2
Biddle, R. J.	London	1877-1882	Sea Pieces	—	—	1	—	12	—	—	—	—	—	13
Biddlecombe, Walter	Southampton	1883-1886	Rustic	—	—	1	—	2	—	—	—	—	—	3
Biddulph, Miss Edith	London	1892-1893	Flowers	—	—	1	—	—	—	1	—	—	—	2
Biddulph, General Sir Michael A.	London	1889-1890	Landscape	—	—	—	—	3	—	—	—	—	—	3
Bidlake, G.	Wolverhampt'n	1852-1862	Architecture	—	—	7	—	—	—	—	—	—	—	7
Bidlake, William H.	Birmingham	1888-1892	Architecture	—	—	5	—	—	—	—	—	—	—	5
Bidouz, J.	London	1861-1862	Portraits	—	—	—	—	2	—	—	—	—	—	2
Biedermann, J. C.	London	1799-1831	Domestic	—	—	16	19	—	—	—	—	—	—	35
Bielefield, C. F.	London	1832	Sculpture	—	—	1	—	—	—	—	—	—	—	1
Bielfeld, H.	Near Exeter	1825-1856	Mythological	—	—	15	18	28	—	—	—	—	—	61
Bienaime, A.	London	1829-1850	Sculpture	—	—	7	—	—	—	—	—	—	—	7
Biers, H.	London	1816	Architecture	—	—	1	—	—	—	—	—	—	—	1
Bierstadt, Albert	New York	1869-1879	Landscape	—	—	6	—	—	—	—	—	—	—	6
Biffin, Miss Sarah	Liverpool	1850	Miniatures	—	—	1	—	—	—	—	—	—	—	1
Bigg, Charles O.	London	1869-1876	Landscape	—	—	—	—	3	—	—	—	—	3	6
Bigg, William Redmore, R.A.	London	1780-1828	Domestic	—	1	129	30	—	—	—	—	—	—	160
Biggs, C. F.	London	1819	Architecture	—	—	1	—	—	—	—	—	—	—	1
Bighosche, J.	London	1865	Portraits	—	—	1	—	—	—	—	—	—	—	1
Bigland, Mary B.	Birkenhead	1869-1887	Landscape	—	—	—	—	—	—	1	—	—	22	23
Bigland, Percy	Liverpool	1882-1893	Portraits	—	—	11	—	4	—	—	3	8	17	43
Bigland, W.	London	1802-1804	Landscape	—	—	3	—	—	—	—	—	—	—	3
Bihan, D. L.	London	1852	Landscape	—	—	1	—	—	—	—	—	—	—	1
Bilbie, James L.	Nottingham	1884	Landscape	—	—	2	—	—	—	—	—	—	—	2
Bilinska, Miss Anna	London	1888-1892	Portraits	—	—	2	—	—	—	—	—	—	—	2
Bilioski, J.	London	1869	Sculpture	—	—	1	—	—	—	—	—	—	—	1
Biller, A.	Bickley	1871	Landscape	—	—	1	—	—	—	—	—	—	—	1
Biller, C.	—	1873	Domestic	—	—	—	—	2	—	—	—	—	—	2
Billing, Arthur. *See also* Gabriel & Billing	London	1848-1886	Architecture	—	—	4	—	—	—	—	—	—	—	4
Billing, J.	Reading	1807	Architecture	—	—	1	—	—	—	—	—	—	—	1
Billing, J.	London	1855	Architecture	—	—	2	—	—	—	—	—	—	—	2
Billing, R.	London	1806	Architecture	—	—	1	—	—	—	—	—	—	—	1
Billings, R. W.	London	1845-1872	Landscape	—	—	22	—	—	—	—	—	—	—	22
Billington, Horace W.	London	1802	Landscape	—	—	1	—	—	—	—	—	—	—	1
Billoin, C.	Brussels	1848	Lithograph	—	—	—	—	—	—	—	—	—	1	1
Billop, W.	Greenwich	1794-1800	Architecture	—	—	2	—	—	—	—	—	—	—	2
Billyeald, Arthur	Catford Bridge	1882-1887	River Scenes	—	—	1	—	2	—	—	—	—	—	3
Bilson. *See* Botterill, Son and Bilson	—	—	Architecture	—	—	—	—	—	—	—	—	—	—	—

Name.	Town.	First and Last Year of Ex.	Speciality.	S. A.	F. S.	R. A.	B. I.	S. S.	O. W.	N. W.	G. G.	N. G.	V. E.	Total.
Bilton, A.	Gunnersbury	1893	Figures	—	—	—	—	—	—	1	—	—	—	1
Binckes, Henry Ashby	London	1846	Domestic	—	—	1	—	—	—	—	—	—	—	1
Bindley, Frank	London	1878-1883	Sea Pieces	—	—	1	—	8	—	—	—	—	—	9
Bindon, George	London	1886-1893	Sculpture	—	—	4	—	—	—	—	—	—	—	4
Binet, V.	London	1886	Landscape	—	—	1	—	—	—	—	—	—	—	1
Binfield, E. H. *or* W.	London	1869-1877	Granada	—	—	1	—	—	—	—	—	—	6	7
Binfield, Miss F. D.	London	1873	Domestic	—	—	—	—	1	—	—	—	—	—	1
Binfield, W.	London	1826	Wax	—	—	1	—	—	—	—	—	—	—	1
Bingham, Hon. A. Y.	London	1878	Landscape	—	—	2	—	—	—	—	—	—	—	2
Bingham, W. R.	London	1844	Landscape	—	—	1	—	—	—	—	—	—	—	1
Bingley, James George	Godalming	1871-1891	Landscape	—	—	27	—	1	—	3	—	—	26	57
Bings —	—	1782	Shipping	—	1	—	—	—	—	—	—	—	—	1
Binney, Hibbert C.	Snaresbrook	1893	Sculpture	—	—	1	—	—	—	—	—	—	—	1
Binns, Miss Elizabeth J.	Worcester	1882-1893	Flowers	—	—	4	—	4	—	—	—	—	1	9
Binns, Miss Frances Rachael	Streatham	1880-1886	Landscape	—	—	5	—	4	—	—	—	—	—	9
Binstead, J.	London	1809-1814	Flowers	—	—	4	—	—	—	—	—	—	—	4
Binyon, Brightwen	Ipswich	1887-1893	Architecture	—	—	3	—	—	—	—	—	—	—	3
Binyon, Edward	London	1857-1876	Landscape	—	—	9	—	1	—	—	—	—	29	39
Biondi, N.	London	1780	Scriptural	—	—	1	—	—	—	—	—	—	—	1
Birch. *See* Barnett and Birch	—	—	Architecture	—	—	—	—	—	—	—	—	—	—	—
Birch, Miss Annie	London	1892	Landscape	—	—	—	—	1	—	—	—	—	—	1
Birch, Charles Bell, R.A.	Berlin	1852-1893	Sculpture	—	—	82	1	—	—	1	3	—	5	92
Birch, C. B.	London	1871-1877	Domestic	—	—	—	—	4	—	—	—	—	—	4
Birch, Downward	London	1857-1892	Landscape	—	—	5	3	—	—	—	—	—	2	10
Birch, George H.	London	1886	Buildings	—	—	2	—	—	—	—	—	—	—	2
Birch, J.	London	1826-1827	Architecture	—	—	—	—	3	—	—	—	—	—	3
Birch, John	Sheffield	1842-1856	Landscape	—	—	—	4	7	—	—	—	—	—	11
Birch, John	London	1877-1886	Architecture	—	—	6	—	—	—	—	—	—	—	6
Birch, J. R.	London	1830	Architecture	—	—	1	—	—	—	—	—	—	—	1
Birch, S.	London	1773-1775	Hair Work	5	—	—	—	—	—	—	—	—	—	5
Birch, Miss Sarah	Croydon	1884-1893	Figures	—	—	9	—	3	—	—	1	1	1	15
Birch, Samuel J.	Manchester	1893	Landscape	—	—	1	—	—	—	—	—	—	—	1
Birch, William	London	1775-1794	Enamels	2	—	41	—	—	—	—	—	—	—	43
Bircham, J. B.	London	1837-1838	Dramatic	—	—	—	2	—	—	—	—	—	—	2
Bird, Edward, R.A.	Bristol	1809-1822	Historical	—	—	18	13	—	—	—	—	—	—	31
Bird, Miss E.	—	1793-1803	Miniatures	—	—	13	—	—	—	—	—	—	—	13
Bird, Harrington	London	1870-1893	Sporting	—	—	5	—	3	—	—	—	—	3	11
Bird, H. D.	London	1846	Portraits	—	—	1	—	—	—	—	—	—	—	1
Bird, Miss H. M.	Bristol	1875	Figures	—	—	—	—	1	—	—	—	—	—	1
Bird, Isaac F.	Exeter	1826-1861	Portraits	—	—	15	12	4	—	—	—	—	—	31
Bird, Miss Margaret	Haywards Heath	1891-1892	Domestic	—	—	3	—	2	—	—	—	—	—	5
Bird, Samuel C.	London	1865-1893	Domestic	—	—	12	3	7	—	—	—	8	1	31
Bird, W. D.	London	1840	Portraits	—	—	—	—	1	—	—	—	—	—	1
Bird, W. S.	London	1834-1835	Architecture	—	—	2	—	—	—	—	—	—	—	2
Bird, Mrs. *See* Miss Hannah Essex.	—	—	—	—	—	—	—	—	—	—	—	—	—	—
Birdwood, J.	—	1796	Landscape	—	—	1	—	—	—	—	—	—	—	1
Birkenruth, Adolph	London	1883-1893	Pastoral	—	—	7	—	12	—	1	1	—	14	35
Birket, Miss	—	1791	Needlework	3	—	—	—	—	—	—	—	—	—	3
Birkett, B.	London	1865	Figures	—	—	—	—	1	—	—	—	—	—	1
Birkett, P.	London	1847-1848	Portraits	—	—	—	—	2	—	—	—	—	—	2
Birkhead, B.	London	1805-1808	Architecture	—	—	2	—	—	—	—	—	—	—	2
Birkmyer, James B.	Exeter	1868-1892	Landscape	—	—	13	—	3	—	—	—	—	—	16
Birnie, A. D.	London	1828-1834	Domestic	—	—	1	—	4	—	—	—	—	—	5
Birnie, F.	London	1791	Engraving	3	—	—	—	—	—	—	—	—	—	3
Birnie, Rix	London	1885-1887	Domestic	—	—	—	—	6	—	—	—	—	—	6
Birt, Herbert W.	London	1891-1892	Sculpture	—	—	3	—	—	—	—	—	—	—	3
Birtles, Henry	Birmingham	1859-1892	Landscape	—	—	7	2	27	—	10	—	—	40	86
Bischoff, C. F.	London	1848	Sea Pieces	—	—	—	—	1	—	—	—	—	—	1
Bischoff, F. H.	London	1823-1849	Portraits	—	—	37	2	5	—	—	—	—	—	44
Biseau, De. *See* D.	—	—	—	—	—	—	—	—	—	—	—	—	—	—
Bishop —	—	1816	Arctic	—	—	2	—	—	—	—	—	—	—	2
Bishop, E. W.	London	1823	Architecture	—	—	2	—	—	—	—	—	—	—	2
Bishop, Harry	London	1890-1893	Portraits	—	—	1	—	1	—	—	—	—	1	3
Bishop, J.	Charlton	1825	Landscape	—	—	2	—	2	—	—	—	—	—	4
Bishop, J. W.	London	1829	Architecture	—	—	2	—	—	—	—	—	—	—	2
Bishop, Miss P. E.	Ashford	1891	Domestic	—	—	—	—	1	—	—	—	—	—	1
Bishop, S.	London	1833	Figures	—	—	—	—	1	—	—	—	—	—	1
Bishop, T.	London	1787-1798	Enamels	—	—	5	—	—	—	—	—	—	—	5
Bishop, W. Follen, R.B.A. §	Liverpool	1880-1893	Landscape	—	—	14	—	40	—	12	—	—	—	66
Bishopp, George	Horsham	1880-1885	Still Life	—	—	—	—	1	—	—	—	—	2	3
Bispham, Henry C.	Philadelphia	1880	Animals	—	—	1	—	—	—	—	—	—	—	1
Bisschop, Christophe	London	1876	Domestic	—	—	1	—	—	—	—	—	—	—	1

Name.	Town.	First and Last Year of Ex.	Speciality.	S. A.	F. S.	R. A.	B. I.	S. S.	O. W.	N. W.	G. G.	N. G.	V. E.	Total.
Bisschop, Mrs. Christopher. *See* Miss K. Swift	London	1872-1880	Domestic	—	—	2	—	—	—	—	2	—	3	7
Bissen, Vilhelm	Copenhagen	1890	Sculpture	—	—	2	—	—	—	—	—	—	—	2
Bizo, John	London	1839-1879	Domestic	—	—	17	8	4	—	—	—	—	3	32
Blaas, Professor Eugene de. *See* D.	—	—	—	—	—	—	—	—	—	—	—	—	—	—
Black, Alexander	—	1779-1797	Landscape	—	—	2	—	—	—	—	—	—	—	2
Black, Andrew	Glasgow	1883-1890	Sea Shores	—	—	8	—	—	—	1	—	—	—	9
Black, A. E.	London	1868	Figures	—	—	1	—	—	—	—	—	—	—	1
Black, Arthur J.	Nottingham	1882-1893	Landscape	—	—	4	—	—	—	—	—	6	—	10
Black, E. *See* Clayton and Black.	—	—	Architecture	—	—	—	—	—	—	—	—	—	—	—
Black, Edwin	London	1875-1889	Figures	—	—	3	—	2	—	3	—	—	9	17
Black, Miss Emma L. (Mrs. J. D. K. Mahomed)	London	1879-1891	Portraits	—	—	7	—	4	—	—	—	—	—	11
Black, Francis	London	1891-1893	Coast Scenes	—	—	1	—	2	—	—	—	—	—	3
Black, G. B.	London	1855	Portraits	—	—	1	—	—	—	—	—	—	—	1
Black, J.	—	1844	—	—	—	—	—	*	—	—	—	—	—	—
Black, Miss Margaret L.	London	1893	Landscape	—	—	1	—	—	—	—	—	—	—	1
Black, Miss Mary	London	1768	Portraits	3	—	—	—	—	—	—	—	—	—	3
Black, N.	London	1783-1803	Landscape	—	2	4	—	—	—	—	—	—	—	6
Black, Thomas	London	1764	Portraits	—	1	—	—	—	—	—	—	—	—	1
Blackall. *See* Brown and Blackall	—	—	Architecture	—	—	—	—	—	—	—	—	—	—	—
Blackall, J.	London	1862	Still Life	—	—	—	1	—	—	—	—	—	—	1
Blackbeard, C.	London	1784-1810	Portraits	—	—	6	—	—	—	—	—	—	—	6
Blackbourne, J. F.	Rome	1876-1881	Domestic	—	—	2	—	—	—	—	—	—	2	4
Blackburn, Arthur	Leeds	1890-1891	Landscape	—	—	2	—	—	—	—	—	—	—	2
Blackburn, C.	London	1836	Architecture	—	—	1	—	—	—	—	—	—	—	1
Blackburn, Mrs. Hugh. *See* Miss J. Wedderburn	Glasgow	1863-1875	Animals	—	—	1	—	—	—	—	—	—	1	2
Blackburn, John	London	1769-1775	Mythological	—	3	5	—	—	—	—	—	—	—	8
Blackburn, Samuel	Edinburgh	1842-1857	Historical	—	—	3	—	3	—	—	—	—	—	6
Blackburn, William	London	1775	Architecture	—	—	2	—	—	—	—	—	—	—	2
Blackburne, Edward Lushington	London	1831-1872	Architecture	—	—	9	—	—	—	—	—	—	—	9
Blackburne, E. R. Ireland	Newlyn	1891-1892	Sea Shores	—	—	3	—	—	—	—	—	—	—	3
Blackburne, Miss Helena	London	1880-1892	Domestic	—	—	2	—	5	—	7	—	—	3	17
Blackburne, Lilian G.	London	1875	Figures	—	—	—	—	—	—	—	—	—	2	2
Blackden, M. W.	London	1890	Scriptural	—	—	1	—	—	—	—	—	—	—	1
Blackesly, Anna	London	1772	Portraits	—	—	1	—	—	—	—	—	—	—	1
Blackett, Walter	London	1854-1860	Architecture	—	—	3	—	—	—	—	—	—	—	3
Blackham, J.	Birmingham	1867-1874	Flowers	—	—	1	—	17	—	—	—	—	—	18
Blacklock, C.	Manchester	1885-1886	Landscape	—	—	2	—	—	—	—	—	—	—	2
Blacklock, W. J.	London	1836-1855	Landscape	—	—	36	4	11	—	—	—	—	—	51
Blackman, Walter	London	1878-1890	Domestic	—	—	5	—	3	—	—	1	—	5	14
Blackmore, Miss Isabel	London	1836-1853	Miniatures	—	—	36	—	7	—	—	—	—	—	43
Blackmore, J.	London	1833-1841	Portraits	—	—	3	—	2	—	—	—	—	—	5
Blackmore, Thomas	London	1769-1773	Engraving	1	1	—	—	—	—	—	—	—	—	2
Blackwell, Miss Elizabeth	—	1819	Birds	—	—	1	—	—	—	—	—	—	—	1
Blackwood, Lady A.	Boxwood	1878-1880	Landscape	—	—	—	—	2	—	—	—	—	—	2
Bladen, Thomas W.	London	1887	Stained Glass	—	—	1	—	—	—	—	—	—	—	1
Blades, Miss Daisy	Folkestone	1889-1891	Miniatures	—	—	2	—	—	—	—	—	1	—	3
Blaikley, Alexander	London	1842-1867	Portraits	—	—	27	8	17	—	—	—	—	28	80
Blaikley, Edith S.	London	1880	Flowers	—	—	—	—	1	—	—	—	—	—	1
Blaikley, Miss Ruth	London	1865-1874	Domestic	—	—	—	—	2	—	—	—	—	—	2
Blaine, Mrs. Robertson	London	1867	Caravan	—	—	—	1	—	—	—	—	—	—	1
Blair, Andrew	Dunfermline	1847-1885	Domestic	—	—	—	1	1	—	1	—	—	—	3
Blair, C. E. A.	London	1833-1847	Landscape	—	—	4	—	2	—	—	—	—	—	6
Blair, John	Edinburgh	1885-1888	Domestic	—	—	—	—	—	—	3	—	—	—	3
Blaisel, Du. *See* D.	—	—	—	—	—	—	—	—	—	—	—	—	—	—
Blake, Benjamin §	London	1807-1832	Still Life	—	—	13	17	19	3	—	—	—	—	52
Blake, C.	London	1845	Portraits	—	—	—	—	1	—	—	—	—	—	1
Blake, E. C. H.	London	1876-1884	Architecture	—	—	4	—	—	—	—	—	—	—	4
Blake, Miss E. Jex-	Düsseldorf	1886	Figures	—	—	—	—	—	—	—	—	—	1	1
Blake, Master Fasham	London	1776	Still Life	—	3	—	—	—	—	—	—	—	—	3
Blake, T.	London	1831	Portraits	—	—	—	—	1	—	—	—	—	—	1
Blake, Leonard	London	1876-1885	Figures	—	—	8	—	—	—	2	—	—	3	13
Blake, William	London	1780-1812	Scriptural	—	—	12	—	—	—	—	—	—	4	16
Blakeley, S.	London	1840	Sea Shores	—	—	1	—	—	—	—	—	—	—	1
Blakeley, Miss	London	1848	Buildings	—	—	—	—	1	—	—	—	—	—	1
Blakemorn, W.	London	1800	Landscape	—	—	1	—	—	—	—	—	—	—	1
Blakesley, Miss Alicia	London	1893	Domestic	—	—	—	—	1	—	—	—	—	—	1
Blakesly, Miss	—	1770	Landscape	—	—	2	—	—	—	—	—	—	—	2
Blakewell, Miss Elizabeth	—	1819	Landscape	—	—	—	1	—	—	—	—	—	—	1
Blakiston, Douglas Y.	London	1853-1865	Portraits	—	—	18	6	2	—	—	—	—	4	30
Blakiston, Miss Evelyn	London	1889-1891	Portraits	—	—	2	—	—	—	—	—	—	—	2
Blaksley, Miss M. C.	London	1847-1848	Scriptural	—	—	2	—	1	—	—	—	—	—	3
Blamire, W.	London	1843-1844	Landscape	—	—	1	—	2	—	—	—	—	—	3

Name.	Town.	First and Last Year of Ex.	Speciality.	S. A.	F. S.	R. A.	B. I.	S. S.	O. W.	N. W.	G. G.	N. G.	V. E.	Total.
Blanc, E.	Paris	1876	Figures	—	—	—	—	—	—	—	—	—	1	1
Blanc, Hippolyte J., A.R.S.A.	Edinburgh	1892-1893	Architecture	—	—	3	—	—	—	—	—	—	—	3
Blanchard, Auguste Thomas Marie	Paris	1874-1893	Engraving	—	—	11	—	—	—	—	—	—	—	11
Blanchard, Miss A.	London	1816-1824	Portraits	—	—	4	—	—	—	—	—	—	—	4
Blanchard, J.	—	1818	Portraits	—	—	1	—	—	—	—	—	—	—	1
Blanche, Jacques E.	Paris	1882-1888	Domestic	—	—	—	—	5	—	—	—	—	1	6
Bland, Miss Emily B.	London	1890	Flowers	—	—	1	—	—	—	—	—	—	—	1
Bland, John H.	London	1860-1872	Landscape	—	—	4	1	1	—	—	—	—	10	16
Blanden, L.	London	1844	Portraits	—	—	1	—	—	—	—	—	—	—	1
Blandy, Miss L. V.	London	1879-1881	Flowers	—	—	—	—	—	—	—	5	—	—	5
Blane, L.	—	1850	Figures	—	—	2	—	—	—	—	—	—	—	2
Blankly, Mrs. E.	London	1843	Portraits	—	—	—	—	1	—	—	—	—	—	1
Blashfield, Edwin H.	Paris	1876-1886	Historical	—	—	4	—	—	—	—	—	—	1	5
Blatherwick, Dr. Charles, R.S.W.	Helensburgh	1874-1884	Landscape	—	—	5	—	—	—	—	2	—	12	19
Blatherwick, Miss Lily	Helensburgh	1877-1893	Flowers	—	—	5	—	—	—	5	2	2	9	23
Bleaden, Miss Mary	London	1853-1882	Domestic	—	—	3	8	16	—	—	—	—	8	35
Bleeck, Pieter Van	—	1761	Portraits	3	—	—	—	—	—	—	—	—	—	3
Blencowe, S. J.	London	1850-1854	Scriptural	—	—	—	—	14	—	—	—	—	—	14
Blenkarn, A. B.	London	1851	Architecture	—	—	1	—	—	—	—	—	—	—	1
Blenner, P.	London	1871	Domestic	—	—	—	—	1	—	—	—	—	—	1
Bles, David	London	1877	Figures	—	—	—	—	—	—	—	1	—	—	1
Blewitt, R.	London	1874-1878	Figures	—	—	2	—	1	—	—	—	—	—	3
Bligh, E. R.	Broadstairs	1872-1875	Landscape	—	—	—	—	1	—	—	—	—	1	2
Bligh, Jabez	Worcester	1863-1889	Fruit, etc.	—	—	17	—	16	—	6	—	—	1	40
Blind, Rudolf	London	1876-1887	Figures	—	—	1	—	—	—	—	—	—	6	7
Blinks, Thomas	London	1881-1893	Sporting	—	—	9	—	4	—	—	—	—	8	21
Bliss, M.	Sandwich	1880	Landscape	—	—	—	—	—	—	—	—	—	1	1
Block, L.	London	1879-1893	Fruit	—	—	1	—	2	—	5	—	—	1	9
Block, De. *See* D.	—	—	—	—	—	—	—	—	—	—	—	—	—	—
Blockley, E.	London	1870	Rustic	—	—	—	—	1	—	—	—	—	—	1
Bloeme, De. *See* D.	—	—	—	—	—	—	—	—	—	—	—	—	—	—
Blofeld, Mrs.	London	1834	Landscape	—	—	—	—	—	—	5	—	—	—	5
Blofield, L.	London	1849-1851	Sea Pieces	—	—	—	—	3	—	—	—	—	—	3
Blogg, W.	London	1793-1798	Architecture	—	—	4	—	—	—	—	—	—	—	4
Blois, D. *See* D.	—	—	—	—	—	—	—	—	—	—	—	—	—	—
Blomefield, Eardley W.	London	1880-1893	Landscape	—	—	4	—	1	—	—	—	—	6	11
Blomfield, Arthur C.	London	1889-1893	Buildings	—	—	7	—	—	—	—	—	—	—	7
Blomfield, Sir Arthur William, A.R.A., M.A.	London	1856-1893	Architecture	—	—	33	—	—	—	—	—	—	—	33
Blomfield, Reginald T.	London	1884-1892	Architecture	—	—	12	—	—	—	—	—	—	—	12
Blommers, Bernaudes J.	London	1880-1893	Domestic	—	—	2	—	—	—	—	3	—	—	5
Blondel, Jean Francois	London	1765-1774	Engraving	2	9	—	—	—	—	—	—	—	—	11
Bloomer, H. Reynolds	New York	1879-1890	Landscape	—	—	7	—	8	—	—	4	3	3	25
Bloor, D. E. Smith	London	1880-1882	Sculpture	—	—	3	—	1	—	—	—	—	1	5
Blore, Burton	London	1885	Figures	—	—	—	—	1	—	—	—	—	—	1
Blore, Edward	London	1814-1836	Architecture	—	—	3	—	—	—	—	—	—	6	9
Blore, J.	London	1831-1856	Architecture	—	—	20	—	—	—	—	—	—	—	20
Blount, Juliane	London	1853	Portraits	—	—	1	—	—	—	—	—	—	—	1
Bloxham —	—	1782	Landscape	—	1	—	—	—	—	—	—	—	—	1
Bluck, J.	London	1791-1819	Landscape	—	—	14	—	—	—	—	—	—	—	14
Bluhm, H. Faber	Lee	1875-1881	Landscape	—	—	6	—	2	—	—	—	—	7	15
Blum, Robert H.	London	1888	Figures	—	—	1	—	—	—	—	—	—	—	1
Blundell, Mrs. Grace E. M.	London	1893	Portraits	—	—	1	—	—	—	—	—	—	—	1
Blunden, Miss Anna E. *See* Mrs. Martino	Exeter	1854-1877	Figures	—	—	11	1	34	—	—	—	—	25	71
Blunt, Lady Anne	London	1880	Egyptian	—	—	—	—	—	—	—	3	—	—	3
Blunt, Arthur Cadogan	London	1890	Domestic	—	—	—	—	—	—	1	—	—	1	2
Blyth, John	London	1832-1837	Architecture	—	—	3	—	—	—	—	—	—	—	3
Blyth, Robert	London	1780-1783	Engraving	5	—	—	—	—	—	—	—	—	—	5
Boaden, John	London	1810-1840	Figures	—	—	40	90	59	4	—	—	—	4	197
Boadle, William B.	London	1874-1893	Portraits	—	—	8	—	—	—	—	—	—	1	9
Boberg, Ferdinand, A.R.P.E.	London	1888	Etching	—	—	1	—	—	—	—	—	—	—	1
Bochmann, G.	Düsseldorf	1875	Figures	—	—	1	—	—	—	—	—	—	—	1
Bocquet, E.	London	1817-1849	Landscape	—	—	12	4	10	—	—	—	—	—	26
Boddington, Edwin H.	London	1853-1869	Landscape	—	—	11	25	45	—	—	—	—	25	106
Boddington, Henry John (Williams Family)§	London	1837-1869	Landscape	—	—	51	60	244	—	—	—	—	—	355
Boddington, Thomas F.	London	1828-1843	Figures	—	—	8	5	5	—	1	—	—	—	19
Boddy, William J.	York	1860-1890	Churches	—	—	11	—	7	—	4	—	—	7	29
Bode, Lewis	Egham	1772-1783	Miniatures	4	22	—	—	—	—	—	—	—	—	26
Bodeman, W.	Brussels	1847	Landscape	—	—	2	1	—	—	—	—	—	—	3
Boden, S. S.	London	1865-1873	Landscape	—	—	—	—	7	—	—	—	—	1	8
Bodger, J.	Stilton	1821	Sporting	—	—	1	—	—	—	—	—	—	—	1
Bodichon, Miss Barbara Leigh Smith	London	1869-1872	Sea Pieces	—	—	4	—	—	—	—	—	—	—	4
Bodichon, Mme. Eugène. *See* Miss B. L. Smith	London	1863-1881	Landscape	—	—	—	1	3	—	—	—	—	36	40

Name.	Town.	First and Last Year of Ex.	Speciality.	S. A.	F. S.	R. A.	B. I.	S. S.	O. W.	N. W.	G. G.	N. G.	V. E.	Total.
Bodilly, Frank	Penzance	1885-1886	Landscape	—	—	2	—	1	—	—	—	—	—	3
Bodilo —	—	1783	Landscape	—	1	—	—	—	—	—	—	—	—	1
Bodkin, Edwin	Highgate	1874	Rustic	—	—	—	—	—	—	—	—	—	2	2
Bodkin, Frederic E.	London	1872-1893	Game	—	—	19	—	14	—	2	—	—	36	71
Bodkin, R.	Highgate	1875	Landscape	—	—	—	—	—	—	—	—	—	1	1
Bodley, George Frederick, A.R.A.	Brighton	1854-1892	Architecture	—	—	15	—	—	—	—	—	—	—	15
Bodmer, Karl	Hereford	1876-1877	Landscape	—	—	1	—	—	—	—	—	—	6	7
Boeck, Van der. *See* V.	—	—	—	—	—	—	—	—	—	—	—	—	—	—
Boehm, A. William	London	1856-1857	Figures	—	—	—	3	—	—	—	—	—	—	3
Boehm, Sir Joseph Edgar, Bart., R.A.	London	1862-1891	Sculpture	—	—	130	—	—	—	—	29	5	—	164
Boehm, Wolfgang	London	1850-1869	Portraits	—	—	10	4	—	—	—	—	—	—	14
Boehmer and Gibbs (J. A.)	London	1891	Architecture	—	—	1	—	—	—	—	—	—	—	1
Boekbinder, James M.	London	1887-1890	Architecture	—	—	3	—	—	—	—	—	—	—	3
Bœrens, Mrs. M. M., R.A., of Copenhagen	Copenhagen	1790	Flowers	—	—	1	—	—	—	—	—	—	—	1
Boesch, August	Zurich	1888	Sculpture	—	—	1	—	—	—	—	—	—	—	1
Bogaert, Em.	London	1829	Sculpture	—	—	—	—	1	—	—	—	—	—	1
Bogardus, Mrs. J.	London	1839	Miniatures	—	—	4	—	—	—	—	—	—	—	4
Boggis, J. H. or M.	Cambridge	1832-1846	Landscape	—	—	—	—	8	—	—	—	—	—	8
Bogle, John	Edinburgh	1769-1794	Miniatures	2	—	44	—	—	—	—	—	—	—	46
Bogle, W. Lockhart	Bushey	1886-1893	Sculpture	—	—	18	—	1	—	—	—	6	4	29
Bohmfield, A.	London	1880	Landscape	—	—	1	—	—	—	—	—	—	—	1
Bohse —.	London	1773	Fruit	—	1	—	—	—	—	—	—	—	—	1
Boilvin, Emile	London	1879	Etching	—	—	—	—	—	—	—	—	—	1	1
Boimaison, J. J.	London	1847	Architecture	—	—	1	—	—	—	—	—	—	—	1
Boinville, De, C. A. C. *See* Morris & De Boinville	—	—	Architecture	—	—	—	—	—	—	—	—	—	—	—
Bois, Miss	London	1861-1867	Landscape	—	—	—	—	14	—	—	—	—	—	14
Bois, Du. *See* D.	—	—	—	—	—	—	—	—	—	—	—	—	—	—
Boisragon, T. S. G.	London	1879	Landscape	—	—	—	—	—	—	—	1	—	—	1
Boisserée, Frederick	Bettws-y-Coed	1876-1877	Landscape	—	—	—	—	6	—	—	—	—	4	10
Bokelmann, C. L.	Düsseldorf	1887	Fires	—	—	1	—	—	—	—	—	—	—	1
Boks, E. J.	Antwerp	1879	Figures	—	—	1	—	—	—	—	—	—	—	1
Boldini, Jean	Florence	1870-1893	Portraits	—	—	—	—	—	—	—	—	—	8	8
Bolingbroke, Miss Minna, A.R.P.E.	Norwich	1888-1892	Rustic	—	—	2	—	1	—	—	—	—	—	3
Bollard, P.	London	1825	—	—	—	—	—	*	—	—	—	—	—	—
Bolt, Miss Marion	Sunbury	1886	Flowers	—	—	—	—	—	—	1	—	—	—	1
Bolton, A.	Brighton	1875	Landscape	—	—	—	—	—	—	—	—	—	2	2
Bolton, Albert J.	London	1891-1892	Architecture	—	—	3	—	1	—	—	—	—	—	4
Bolton, Miss Alice	London	1874-1879	Portraits	—	—	1	—	1	—	—	—	—	1	3
Bolton, Miss Emily	London	1872-1879	Landscape	—	—	2	—	2	—	—	—	—	5	9
Bolton, R.	London	1834-1838	Historical	—	—	4	—	3	—	—	—	—	—	7
Bolton, Mrs. R. (Louisa)	Shepton Mallet	1881-1891	Miniatures	—	—	16	—	—	—	—	—	—	—	16
Bolton, William Treacher	London	1857-1881	Landscape	—	—	12	—	34	—	—	—	—	10	56
Bolton, Miss	London	1834	Copies	—	—	—	—	—	—	1	—	—	—	1
Bomford, L. G.	London	1871-1882	Landscape	—	—	1	—	23	—	—	—	—	6	30
Bompiani, R.	Rome	1879-1882	Figures	—	—	2	—	—	—	—	—	—	—	2
Bonavia, George	London	1851-1876	Domestic	—	—	27	5	16	—	—	—	—	1	49
Bond —	Bathford	1776-1777	Flowers	2	—	—	—	—	—	—	—	—	—	2
Bond, J.	Liverpool	1858	Landscape	—	—	—	1	—	—	—	—	—	—	1
Bond, Miss J.	Bettws-y-Coed	1875	Domestic	—	—	—	—	2	—	—	—	—	—	2
Bond, John Daniel	Birmingham	1761-1780	Landscape	1	36	—	—	—	—	—	—	—	—	37
Bond, John Lloyd	London	1868-1872	Landscape	—	—	—	—	11	—	—	—	—	—	11
Bond, John Sinnell	London	1782-1833	Architecture	—	—	46	—	3	—	—	—	—	—	49
Bond, L.	Bettws-y-Coed	1871	Landscape	—	—	2	—	—	—	—	—	—	—	2
Bond, Miss Mildred B.	British Museum	1884-1885	Domestic	—	—	—	—	—	—	—	—	—	3	3
Bond, Richard Sebastian	Bettws-y-Coed	1846-1872	Landscape	—	—	7	13	5	—	—	—	—	9	34
Bond, T.	Lancaster	1804-1805	Portraits	—	—	2	—	—	—	—	—	—	—	2
Bond, William	London	1828-1836	Portraits	—	—	5	—	4	—	—	—	—	—	9
Bond, William	—	1772-1776	Figures	—	9	—	—	—	—	—	—	—	—	9
Bond, William J. J. C.	Liverpool	1857-1881	Landscape	—	—	2	2	20	—	—	1	—	11	36
Bone, Charles	London	1815-1826	Sculpture	—	—	2	1	—	—	—	—	—	—	3
Bone, C. R.	London	1826-1848	Miniatures	—	—	67	7	27	—	—	—	—	—	101
Bone, Henry, R.A.	London	1781-1834	Enamels	—	2	242	7	4	—	—	—	—	—	255
Bone, Herbert	Windsor	1877-1892	Figures	—	—	4	—	2	—	—	—	—	—	6
Bone, Herbert Alfred	London	1874-1892	Domestic	—	—	9	—	1	—	1	—	—	1	12
Bone, Henry Pierce	London	1799-1855	Portraits	—	—	215	58	1	—	—	—	—	8	282
Bone, H. T.	London	1826-1827	Figures	—	—	2	2	—	—	—	—	—	—	4
Bone, Miss Louisa	London	1844	Portraits	—	—	1	—	—	—	—	—	—	—	1
Bone, P. J.	London	1801	Enamels	—	—	1	—	—	—	—	—	—	—	1
Bone, Robert Trewick	London	1813-1841	Historical	—	—	50	74	25	—	3	—	—	—	152
Bone, S. V.	London	1819-1824	Landscape	—	—	3	1	—	—	—	—	—	—	4
Bone, T. M., R.N.	London	1817	Boats	—	—	2	—	—	—	—	—	—	—	2
Bone, William	London	1815-1843	Landscape	—	—	47	1	4	—	—	—	—	—	52

Name.	Town.	First and Last Year of Ex.	Speciality.	S. A.	F. S.	R. A.	B. I.	S.	O. W.	N.W.	G. G.	N. G.	V. E.	Total.
Bone, W.	London	1827-1851	Still Life, Enamels	—	—	18	—	20	—	—	—	—	—	38
Bonella. *See* Paull and Bonella.	—	—	Architecture	—	—	—	—	—	—	—	—	—	—	—
Boney —	Cornwall, Linc.	1783	Architecture	1	—	—	—	—	—	—	—	—	—	1
Boney, William H.	London	1888	Architecture	—	—	1	—	—	—	—	—	—	—	1
Bonham, Miss A.	London	1871	Sculpture	—	—	1	—	—	—	—	—	—	—	1
Bonheur, François Auguste	Paris	1857-1874	Landscape	—	—	3	—	—	—	—	—	—	—	3
Bonheur, Jules Isidore	Paris	1875-1876	Sculpture	—	—	3	—	—	—	—	—	—	—	3
Bonheur, Madame Peyrol (Juliette)	Paris	1876	Animals	—	—	1	—	—	—	—	—	—	—	1
Bonheur, Mdlle. Marie Rosa, H.R.I.‡	Thomeres	1867-1884	Animals	—	—	2	—	—	—	3	—	—	4	9
Bonifazi, A.	Rome	1876	Figures	—	—	—	—	1	—	—	—	—	—	1
Bonington, R.	Nottingham	1797-1808	Portraits	—	—	2	—	—	—	—	—	—	—	2
Bonington, Richard Parkes	London	1826-1829	Landscape	—	—	4	5	—	—	—	—	—	—	9
Bonlian, Miss A.	London	1873-1874	Fruit	—	—	—	—	2	—	—	—	—	—	2
Bonnar, George William, R.S.A.	London	1828-1830	Landscape	—	—	—	—	4	—	—	—	—	—	4
Bonnat, Leon Joseph Florentin	Paris	1876-1893	Portraits	—	—	—	—	—	—	—	—	—	4	4
Bonneau, Miss Florence M.	London	1871-1884	Flowers	—	—	1	—	14	—	—	—	—	5	20
Bonneau, Jacob, F.S.A.	London	1765-1784	Landscape	12	—	7	—	—	—	—	—	—	—	19
Bonnemaison, J.	London	1794-1795	Portraits	—	—	7	—	—	—	—	—	—	—	7
Bonner, Horace T.	Lewisham	1886	Architecture	—	—	1	—	—	—	—	—	—	—	1
Bonner, Thomas	London	1773-1807	Engraving	4	—	3	—	—	—	—	—	—	—	7
Bonney, Charles Henry	Rugeley	1888-1892	Landscape	—	—	3	—	1	—	—	—	—	—	4
Bonnor, Miss A. S.	Hereford	1874-1878	Landscape	—	—	—	—	2	—	—	—	—	—	2
Bonnycastle, H.	London	1873-1875	Domestic	—	—	—	—	1	—	—	—	—	2	3
Bonomi, Joseph, A.R.A.	London	1783-1806	Architecture	—	—	38	—	—	—	—	—	—	—	38
Bonomi, Joseph, F.R.S.L., F.R.A.S.	London	1809-1838	Sculpture	—	—	12	1	1	—	—	—	—	—	14
Bonser, J.	London	1843-1857	Landscape	—	—	14	1	2	—	—	—	—	—	17
Booby, G.	—	1831	Sculpture	—	—	1	—	—	—	—	—	—	—	1
Boodle, Walter	Bath	1891	Landscape	—	—	1	—	—	—	—	—	—	—	1
Booker, A. E.	London	1871-1872	Historical	—	—	2	—	—	—	—	—	—	—	2
Bool, G.	London	1868	Sculpture	—	—	1	—	—	—	—	—	—	—	1
Bool, G. M.	London	1832-1836	Sculpture	—	—	9	2	4	—	—	—	—	—	15
Boom, A. S.	London	1857	Figures	—	—	1	—	—	—	—	—	—	—	1
Boorer, J.	London	1834	Architecture	—	—	1	—	—	—	—	—	—	—	1
Boosey, W.	London	1848-1872	Landscape	—	—	7	2	7	—	—	—	—	1	17
Boot, Miss Charlotte	London	1847-1850	Portraits	—	—	1	—	1	—	—	—	—	—	2
Boot, William Henry James, R.B.A.§	London	1872-1893	Landscape	—	—	15	—	46	—	4	—	—	8	73
Booth, Colonel	—	1803	Buildings	—	—	1	—	—	—	—	—	—	—	1
Booth, Charles	London	1882-1892	Figures	—	—	1	—	1	—	1	—	—	—	3
Booth, D.	—	1807	Sketch	—	—	1	—	—	—	—	—	—	—	1
Booth, Edward C.	Leeds	1856-1864	Landscape	—	—	6	—	—	—	—	—	—	2	8
Booth, George	London	1857-1878	Landscape	—	—	1	—	—	—	—	—	—	5	6
Booth, Mrs. H. Gore	Glasgow	1856-1884	Sculpture	—	—	11	—	—	—	—	—	—	—	11
Booth, Herbert W.	Halifax	1884	Architecture	—	—	1	—	—	—	—	—	—	—	1
Booth, M.	—	1802	Landscape	—	—	1	—	—	—	—	—	—	—	1
Booth, Miss R. E. R.	Folkestone	1893	Landscape	—	—	1	—	—	—	—	—	—	—	1
Booth, Rev. R. S.	—	1796-1807	Landscape	—	—	16	—	—	—	—	—	—	—	16
Booth, Miss Sclater-. *See* S.	London	—	—	—	—	—	—	—	—	—	—	—	—	—
Booth, William	London	1827-1845	Miniatures	—	—	123	—	15	—	—	—	—	—	138
Booth, W. J.	London	1816-1833	Architecture	—	—	9	—	—	—	—	—	—	—	9
Booth, Miss	—	1796-1809	Portraits	—	—	2	—	—	—	—	—	—	—	2
Booth, Miss Elizabeth	Florence	1879-1885	Flowers	—	—	2	—	—	—	—	—	—	4	6
Booty, Edward	Brighton	1846-1848	Landscape	—	—	4	—	4	—	—	—	—	—	8
Booty, Henry R.	London	1882-1883	Landscape	—	—	1	—	1	—	—	—	—	—	2
Boratynski, E.	London	1839	Portraits	—	—	2	—	—	—	—	—	—	—	2
Borckhardt, C.	London	1784-1825	Miniatures	—	—	20	1	—	—	—	—	—	—	21
Bordier, M.	London	1792	Sculpture	—	—	1	—	—	—	—	—	—	—	1
Borgia, E. C.	Florence	1869	Landscape	—	—	2	—	—	—	—	—	—	—	2
Borgnis —	London	1783	Portraits	—	2	—	—	—	—	—	—	—	—	2
Borop, Louis	London	1864-1873	Domestic	—	—	—	—	3	—	—	—	—	4	7
Borough, F. or T.	London	1836	Landscape	—	—	1	—	—	—	—	—	—	—	1
Borras —	London	1822	Landscape	—	—	2	—	—	—	—	—	—	—	2
Borrekens, Jan Pieter Frans	London	1797	Mythological	—	—	2	—	—	—	—	—	—	—	2
Borrow, J. A.	—	1800	Landscape	—	—	1	—	—	—	—	—	—	—	1
Borrow, William H.	London	1863-1893	Sea Pieces	—	—	28	1	28	—	—	—	—	34	91
Borrows, Henry	Huddersfield	1884-1889	Flowers	—	—	4	—	—	—	—	—	—	—	4
Borselen, J. W. Van. *See* V.	—	—	—	—	—	—	—	—	—	—	—	—	—	—
Borstone, H.	—	1868	Fruit	—	—	—	—	2	—	—	—	—	—	2
Borthwick, J. D.	London	1860-1870	Domestic	—	—	2	1	2	—	—	—	—	2	7
Bortignoni, G.	London	1883-1884	Domestic	—	—	2	—	—	—	—	—	—	—	2
Borwitz, Miss R. E. Von *See* V.	—	—	—	—	—	—	—	—	—	—	—	—	—	—
Borycreski, K.	London	1860	Sculpture	—	—	4	—	—	—	—	—	—	—	4
Bos, G Van den. *See* V.	—	—	—	—	—	—	—	—	—	—	—	—	—	—

Name.	Town.	First and Last Year of Ex.	Speciality.	S. A.	F. S.	R. A.	B. I.	S. S.	O. W.	N. W.	G. G.	N. G.	V. E.	Total.
Bosboom, Johannes	The Hague	1847-1880	Churches	—	—	—	1	—	—	—	3	—	—	4
Bosch, Van den. *See* V.	—	—	—	—	—	—	—	—	—	—	—	—	—	—
Bosch-Reitz, S. C.	Amsterdam	1889-1893	Fishing Boats	—	—	1	—	1	—	—	—	1	—	3
Bosdet, H. T.	London	1876-1885	Portraits	—	—	1	—	—	—	—	—	—	1	2
Bossé, E.	London	1855	Portraits	—	—	1	—	—	—	—	—	—	—	1
Bosset, J. B.	London	1778-1780	Miniatures	—	—	10	—	—	—	—	—	—	—	10
Bossoli, C.	Turin	1855-1859	Landscape	—	—	3	—	—	—	—	—	—	—	3
Bostock, Miss Edith	London	1863-1868	Fruit	—	—	2	—	—	—	—	—	—	1	3
Bostock, H.	London	1833-1841	Architecture	—	—	6	—	—	—	—	—	—	—	6
Bostock, John †	London	1826-1869	Portraits	—	—	48	3	8	4	—	—	—	3	66
Boswell, J.	—	1838	Sea Pieces	—	—	1	—	—	—	—	—	—	—	1
Boswood, J.	London	1832	Sculpture	—	—	1	—	—	—	—	—	—	—	1
Bosworth, John	London	1828-1839	Landscape	—	—	9	—	7	—	—	—	—	—	16
Bosworth, Philip A.	London	1867-1878	Landscape	—	—	5	—	24	—	—	—	—	13	42
Bosworth, R.	London	1791-1793	Portraits	—	—	4	—	—	—	—	—	—	—	4
Botham, W.	London	1807	Landscape	—	—	1	—	—	—	—	—	—	—	1
Bothams, Walter	London	1882-1891	Domestic	—	—	6	—	1	—	4	—	—	—	11
Bott, C.	London	1808-1809	Architecture	—	—	2	—	—	—	—	—	—	—	2
Bott, R. T.	London	1847-1862	Domestic	—	—	3	3	—	—	—	—	—	—	6
Bott, T.	London	1810	Architecture	—	—	1	—	—	—	—	—	—	—	1
Bott, Thomas	Worcester	1857-1860	Enamels	—	—	2	—	—	—	—	—	—	—	2
Botterill, Son, and Bilson	London	1888-1891	Architecture	—	—	2	—	—	—	—	—	—	—	2
Bottomley, John William	Rome	1845-1881	Sporting	—	—	37	16	3	—	—	—	—	61	117
Bottomley, Reginald	Paris	1875-1885	Figures	—	—	2	—	1	—	—	—	—	6	9
Bottomly, J.	London	1791-1795	Architecture	—	—	9	—	—	—	—	—	—	—	9
Boucher, A.	—	1888	Sculpture	—	—	—	—	—	—	—	—	2	—	2
Boucher, William Henry, A.R.P.E.	London	1888-1891	Etching	—	—	3	—	—	—	—	—	—	—	3
Bouchett, A.	London	1873-1888	Domestic	—	—	—	—	8	—	—	—	—	—	8
Boucneau, Victor E.	London	1888	Sculpture	—	—	2	—	1	—	—	—	—	—	3
Bough, Samuel, R.S.A.	Edinburgh	1856-1876	Landscape	—	—	15	—	—	—	—	—	—	—	15
Boughton, George Henry, A.R.A., R.I. ‡	London	1862-1893	Figures	—	—	59	4	1	—	7	30	11	5	117
Boughton, H.	London	1827-1872	Scriptural	—	—	28	10	5	—	—	—	—	—	43
Boughton, Miss R.	—	1806	Landscape	—	—	1	—	—	—	—	—	—	—	1
Boughton, T.	Guildford	1845-1847	Game	—	—	—	—	4	—	—	—	—	—	4
Bougron, L. V.	Paris	1844	Sculpture	—	—	1	—	—	—	—	—	—	—	1
Bouguereau, William Adolphe	Paris	1884-1892	Figures	—	—	2	—	—	—	—	—	—	—	2
Boulat P. or P. Bowlat	London	1849	Domestic	—	—	—	—	1	—	—	—	—	—	1
Boulderson, B.	London	1884	Landscape	—	—	—	—	—	—	—	—	—	1	1
Boullemier, Antonin	Stoke	1881-1882	Miniatures	—	—	3	—	—	—	—	—	—	—	3
Boulnois, W. Allen. *See also* Porter & Boulnois	London	1853-1880	Architecture	—	—	8	—	—	—	—	—	—	—	8
Boulogne, Miss M.	—	1815-1817	Landscape	—	—	2	—	—	—	—	—	—	—	2
Boult, A. S.	London	1815-1853	Sporting	—	—	10	4	3	—	—	—	—	—	17
Boult, Francis Cecil	London	1885	Sporting	—	—	—	—	1	—	—	—	—	—	1
Boultbee, John	London	1775-1788	Sporting	3	3	6	—	—	—	—	—	—	—	12
Boultbee, Thomas	London	1775-1783	Landscape	3	3	6	—	—	—	—	—	—	—	12
Boulton, Miss C. B.	Totteridge	1884	Landscape	—	—	—	—	—	—	1	—	—	—	1
Boulton, R. L.	Birmingham	1859	Sculpture	—	—	1	—	—	—	—	—	—	—	1
Bouquet, M. Emile	London	1848-1849	Landscape	—	—	4	—	—	—	—	—	—	—	4
Bouquet, W. V.	London	1782-1827	Wax Models	5	—	20	—	—	—	—	—	—	—	25
Bource, Hans Joseph	Antwerp	1870-1877	Sea Pieces	—	—	5	—	—	—	—	—	—	1	6
Bourchier, Edward H.	London	1884	Architecture	—	—	1	—	—	—	—	—	—	—	1
Bourcicault, W. S.	—	1866	Eastern	—	—	—	—	1	—	—	—	—	—	1
Bourdillon, Frank W.	London	1881-1892	Landscape	—	—	9	—	6	—	—	2	—	10	27
Bourg, Du. *See* D.	—	—	—	—	—	—	—	—	—	—	—	—	—	—
Bourgain, G.	London	1883	Engraving	—	—	1	—	—	—	—	—	—	—	1
Bourgeois, Sir Francis Peter, R.A.	London	1779-1810	Landscape	—	—	103	5	—	—	—	—	—	—	108
Bourges, Mdlle. L.	Paris	1878	Domestic	—	—	—	—	—	—	—	—	—	1	1
Bourgogne, Pierre	Sèvres	1888	Domestic	—	—	1	—	—	—	—	—	—	—	1
Bourgoin, J.	London	1869	Figures	—	—	1	—	—	—	—	—	—	—	1
Bourlier, Mdlle.	London	1800-1812	Portraits	—	—	3	—	—	—	—	—	—	5	8
Bournan, E. G.	London	1870	Landscape	—	—	—	—	—	—	—	—	—	1	1
Bourne, E.	London	1838-1844	Flowers	—	—	2	—	2	—	—	—	—	—	4
Bourne, Miss F.	London	1840-1846	Flowers	—	—	3	—	—	—	—	—	—	—	3
Bourne, Herbert	London	1831-1885	Engraving	—	—	9	—	1	—	—	—	—	—	10
Bourne, James	London	1800-1809	Landscape	—	—	13	—	—	—	—	—	—	—	13
Bourne, John C.	London	1863-1885	Landscape	—	—	1	—	2	—	1	—	—	—	4
Bourne, S.	London	1822-1823	Rustic	—	—	2	—	—	—	—	—	—	—	2
Bourne, S.	Nottingham	1880-1887	Landscape	—	—	—	—	1	—	4	—	—	—	5
Bousfield. *See* Taylor, Gordon, and Bousfield	—	—	Architecture	—	—	—	—	—	—	—	—	—	—	—
Bousfield, Miss H. Mary	Bedford	1893	Flowers	—	—	1	—	—	—	—	—	—	—	1
Bouterwek J. (?) Frederick	London	1840	Figures	—	—	1	—	—	—	—	—	—	—	1
Boutflower, C.	Harrogate	1871-1878	Landscape	—	—	—	—	3	—	—	—	—	—	3

Name.	Town.	First and Last Year of Ex.	Speciality.	S. A.	F. S.	R. A.	B. I.	S. S.	O. W.	N.W.	G. G.	N. G	V. E.	Total.
Boutibonne, E.	Paris	1856-1857	Portraits	—	—	4	—	—	—	—	—	—	—	4
Bouton, Le Chevalier Charles Marie	London	1840	Buildings	—	—	—	2	—	—	—	—	—	—	2
Bouton, J.	London	1816-1840	Portraits	—	—	17	—	—	—	—	—	—	—	17
Boutellier, Victor	London	1861	Domestic	—	—	—	—	—	—	—	—	—	3	3
Boutwood, Charles Edward	London	1881-1887	Landscape	—	—	4	—	1	—	—	—	—	2	7
Bouvier —	London	1774	Portraits	1	—	—	—	—	—	—	—	—	—	1
Bouvier, Arthur	London	1875	Landscape	—	—	1	—	—	—	—	—	—	—	1
Bouvier, Augustus Jules ‡	London	1845-1881	Figures	—	—	9	8	6	—	241	—	—	14	278
Bouvier, Miss Agnes Rose. *See* Mrs. S. J. Nicholl	London	1866-1874	Figures	—	—	3	—	28	—	—	—	—	1	32
Bouvier, Gustavus A.	London	1866-1884	Figures	—	—	12	—	39	—	—	—	—	22	73
Bouvier, Miss J.	London	1853-1873	Game	—	—	—	—	20	—	—	—	—	3	23
Bouvier, Joseph	London	1839-1888	Figures	—	—	26	17	81	—	—	—	—	2	126
Bouvier, Jules	London	1845-1865	Domestic	—	—	—	1	55	—	—	—	—	4	60
Bouvier, Urbain	London	1854-1856	Figures	—	—	4	3	8	—	—	—	—	—	15
Bouvin, F. (?) Bonvin	Paris	1876	Domestic	—	—	—	—	—	—	—	—	—	1	1
Bouwens, Mrs. T. (Amata)	—	1891-1893	Domestic	—	—	6	—	—	—	—	—	—	—	6
Bovie, F.	Brussels	1848	Landscape	—	—	—	—	—	—	—	—	—	1	1
Bovill, Percy C.	Chiswick	1883-1893	Landscape	—	—	5	—	8	—	—	—	—	3	16
Bowcher, Alfred W.	London	1886-1889	Sculpture	—	—	8	—	—	—	—	—	2	—	10
Bowcher, Frank	London	1889-1893	Sculpture	—	—	3	—	—	—	—	—	1	—	4
Bowden —	Gosport	1764	Engraving	—	1	—	—	—	—	—	—	—	—	1
Bowden, Mrs. Ambrose (Mary)	London	1871-1890	Flowers	—	—	6	—	8	—	—	—	—	7	21
Bowden, E. J.	Paris	1875	Landscape	—	—	—	—	1	—	—	—	—	—	1
Bowden, J.	—	1862	Landscape	—	—	—	—	1	—	—	—	—	—	1
Bowen, Eva	London	1882	Domestic	—	—	—	—	—	—	—	—	—	1	1
Bowen, Lola	London	1889-1891	Venice	—	—	—	—	2	—	—	—	—	—	2
Bowen, Owen	Leeds	1892	Coast Scene	—	—	1	—	—	—	—	—	—	—	1
Bowen, Ralph	Worcester	1887	Figures	—	—	1	—	—	—	—	—	—	—	1
Bower, G. J.	London	1827	Architecture	—	—	1	—	—	—	—	—	—	—	1
Bower, Lewis	London	1761-1775	Miniatures	2	2	1	—	—	—	—	—	—	—	5
Bowers, Albert Edward	Kew	1875-1893	Landscape	—	—	1	—	29	—	5	—	—	2	37
Bowers, Miss Georgina	St. Albans	1878-1880	Punch	—	—	—	—	—	—	—	—	—	3	3
Bowers, H.	London	1852	Buildings	—	—	—	—	1	—	—	—	—	—	1
Bowers, Stephen	Kew	1874-1891	Landscape	—	—	—	—	17	—	1	—	—	—	18
Bowes, Miss Constance	Paris	1890	Flowers	—	—	1	—	—	—	—	—	—	—	1
Bowes, Mrs.	—	1868	Landscape	—	—	1	—	—	—	—	—	—	—	1
Bowie, John	London	1886	Figures	—	—	1	—	—	—	—	—	—	—	1
Bowkett, Miss A.	London	1878	Landscape	—	—	—	—	1	—	—	—	—	—	1
Bowkett, Miss E. M.	London	1862-1867	Landscape	—	—	2	11	9	—	—	—	—	—	22
Bowkett, Miss Jessie	Acton	1880-1881	Domestic	—	—	—	—	2	—	—	—	—	1	3
Bowkett, Miss Jane Maria. *See* Mrs. Ch. Stuart	London	1860-1885	Domestic	—	—	4	9	33	—	—	—	—	4	50
Bowkett, Miss Kate	London	1866-1867	Landscape	—	—	—	1	1	—	—	—	—	—	2
Bowkett, Miss Leila (?) Lilly	Acton	1876-1881	Landscape	—	—	—	—	4	—	—	—	—	3	7
Bowlby, Mrs. A.	London	1884	Churches	—	—	—	—	—	—	1	—	—	—	1
Bowler, Miss Annie E.	London	1888-1891	Portraits	—	—	5	—	—	—	—	—	—	1	6
Bowler, Miss Ellen A.	London	1887-1891	Domestic	—	—	—	—	—	—	3	—	—	—	3
Bowler, Henry A.	London	1847-1887	Landscape	—	—	10	6	1	—	2	—	—	2	21
Bowler, Thomas William	Brighton	1857-1860	Buildings	—	—	2	—	1	—	—	—	—	—	3
Bowles, C. O.	London	1821-1824	Shipping	—	—	2	—	—	—	—	—	—	—	2
Bowles, Miss E.	London	1851	Still Life	—	—	—	1	—	—	—	—	—	—	1
Bowles, George	London	1857-1869	Still Life	—	—	2	—	5	—	—	—	—	3	10
Bowles, James	London	1852-1859	Figures	—	—	2	6	9	—	—	—	—	9	26
Bowles, J. G.	London	1856-1859	Landscape	—	—	—	—	7	—	—	—	—	—	7
Bowles, Oldfield, F.S.A.	—	1772-1795	Landscape	15	1	2	—	—	—	—	—	—	—	18
Bowley, C.	—	1857	No title	—	—	—	—	1	—	—	—	—	—	1
Bowley, Edward O.	Birmingham	1843-1870	Landscape	—	—	2	6	7	—	—	—	—	5	20
Bowley, Miss May	Lee	1890-1892	Decorative	—	—	3	—	—	—	—	—	—	—	3
Bowley, Miss S.	London	1828-1834	Flowers	—	—	—	—	8	—	5	—	—	—	13
Bowman, Master	London	1783	Figures	—	6	—	—	—	—	—	—	—	—	6
Bowman, Alfred George	Croydon	1880-1890	Landscape	—	—	4	—	1	—	1	—	—	—	6
Bowman, Ernest	London	1884-1885	Landscape	—	—	2	—	—	—	—	—	—	1	3
Bowman, H. E.	London	1881-1892	Landscape	—	—	—	—	—	—	2	—	—	7	9
Bowman, Miss Margaret H.	Leytonstone	1889-1892	Domestic	—	—	—	—	1	—	—	—	—	1	2
Bowman, Thomas G.	London	1866-1867	Domestic	—	—	—	1	—	—	—	—	—	4	5
Bowness, William	London	1836-1867	Figures	—	—	35	26	86	—	—	—	—	14	161
Bowness-Burton, W.	Preston	1883	—	—	—	—	—	*	—	—	—	—	—	—
Bowring, Benjamin	London	1773-1781	Miniatures	—	—	11	—	—	—	—	—	—	—	11
Bowring, J.	London	1787-1808	Miniatures	—	—	18	—	—	—	—	—	—	—	18
Bowring, J. R.	London	1809	Architecture	—	—	1	—	—	—	—	—	—	—	1
Bowser, Miss Rosa Maude	London	1886-1889	Flowers	—	—	1	—	—	—	2	—	—	—	3
Bowyer, Miss Ellen	London	1888-1893	Landscape	—	—	3	—	—	—	5	1	6	—	15
Bowyer, Robert	London	1782-1828	Miniatures	—	1	32	—	—	—	—	—	—	—	33

Name.	Town.	First and Last Year of Ex.	Speciality.	S. A.	F. S.	R. A.	B. I.	S. S.	O. W.	N.W.	G. G.	N. G.	V. E.	Total.
Boxall, A.	London	1845-1846	Architecture	—	—	3	—	—	—	—	—	—	—	3
Boxall, Sir William, R.A., F.R.S, D.C.L.	Oxford	1818-1880	Portraits	—	—	86	11	7	—	—	—	—	—	104
Boyce —.	—	1852	Sculpture	—	—	1	—	—	—	—	—	—	—	1
Boyce, A.	—	1817-1818	Landscape	—	—	2	—	—	—	—	—	—	—	2
Boyce, Miss Dorothea	Wimbledon	1892	Sculpture	—	—	1	—	—	—	—	—	—	—	1
Boyce, George Price, R.W.S.†	London	1853-1861	Landscape	—	—	12	—	3	218	—	—	—	14	247
Boyce, H.	London	1819-1848	Landscape	—	—	7	1	—	—	—	—	—	—	8
Boyce, Miss Joanna Mary. *See* Mrs. H. T. Wells	London	1853-1857	Figures	—	—	3	—	1	—	—	—	—	—	4
Boyce, P.	Cheltenham	1850-1857	Architecture	—	—	3	—	—	—	—	—	—	—	3
Boyd, Major	London	1879	Ruins	—	—	—	—	1	—	—	—	—	—	1
Boyd, Dr., D.D.	Oxford	1885	Churches	—	—	—	—	—	—	1	—	—	—	1
Boyd, A.	London	1848	Landscape	—	—	1	—	—	—	—	—	—	—	1
Boyd, A.	London	1880	Landscape	—	—	1	—	—	—	—	—	—	—	1
Boyd, Miss Alice	London	1874	Figures	—	—	—	—	—	—	—	—	—	1	1
Boyd, Arthur M.	London	1891	Australia	—	—	1	—	—	—	—	—	—	—	1
Boyd, Mrs. A. M. (Emma M.)	London	1891	Domestic	—	—	1	—	—	—	—	—	—	—	1
Boyd, Alexander S. or J.	Glasgow	1884-1887	Domestic	—	—	1	—	—	—	1	—	—	—	2
Boyd, G.	London	1805-1810	Architecture	—	—	3	—	—	—	—	—	—	—	3
Boyd, Henry N.	Silverton	1869-1871	Sea Pieces	—	—	—	—	1	—	—	—	—	4	5
Boyd, Walter Scott	Birmingham	1883-1886	Domestic	—	—	4	—	—	—	—	—	—	1	5
Boyd, Miss, (?) Agnes S.	London	1873	River Scenes	—	—	1	—	—	—	—	—	—	—	1
Boydell, Creswick, A.R.C.A.	Liverpool	1889-1893	Landscape	—	—	2	—	1	—	—	—	—	—	3
Boydell, Alderman John	London	1765-1769	Engraving	4	—	—	—	—	—	—	—	—	—	4
Boydell, Josiah	London	1772-1779	Portraits	2	—	10	—	—	—	—	—	—	—	12
Boyden, E.	London	1827	Portraits	—	—	1	—	—	—	—	—	—	—	1
Boyes, Miss M. L.	London	1866	Landscape	—	—	—	—	1	—	—	—	—	—	1
Boyeston, G. A.	London	1830-1832	Portraits	—	—	2	—	—	—	—	—	—	—	2
Boyle, George A.	Greenwich	1884-1889	Landscape	—	—	4	—	11	—	—	—	—	—	15
Boyle, J. M.	—	1855	Figures	—	—	1	—	—	—	—	—	—	—	1
Boyle, Lockhart	London	1891	Historical	—	—	—	—	—	—	—	—	—	1	1
Boyle, Hon. Mrs. Richard, late Miss Eleanor Vere Gordon. Exhibited also as E.V.B.	Maidenhead	1878-1881	Figures	—	—	—	—	—	—	—	3	—	1	4
Boyle, W.	London	1850-1851	Architecture	—	—	3	—	—	—	—	—	—	—	3
Boyne, John	London	1788-1809	Historical	—	—	18	—	—	—	—	—	—	—	18
Boyns, Bessie	St. Just	1891	Sea Pieces	—	—	—	—	1	—	—	—	—	—	1
Boys, Thomas Shotter ‡	London	1824-1873	Landscape	—	—	2	—	14	—	158	—	—	—	174
Bozzini, L.	—	1847	Sculpture	—	—	1	—	—	—	—	—	—	—	1
Brabazon, H. B.	London	1865-1870	Landscape	—	—	—	—	—	—	—	—	—	4	4
Brace, Miss Eleanor	Reigate	1882-1891	Churches	—	—	1	—	7	—	1	—	—	3	12
Brackeleer, De. *See* D.	—	—	—	—	—	—	—	—	—	—	—	—	—	—
Bracken, A.	Florence	1885	Figures	—	—	1	—	—	—	—	—	—	—	1
Brackenbury, Miss G. A.	London	1891-1893	Portraits	—	—	—	—	—	—	—	—	—	2	2
Braconnot, Augustin	London	1887-1888	Sculpture	—	—	2	—	—	—	—	—	—	—	2
Bracquemond, Joseph Auguste, called Felix, H.F.R.P.E.	Paris	1861-1891	Etchings	—	—	5	—	—	—	—	—	—	9	14
Bracquemond, Madame Marié	—	1881	Domestic	—	—	—	—	—	—	—	—	—	5	5
Bradberry, Thomas	London	1820	Architecture	—	—	1	—	—	—	—	—	—	—	1
Bradburne, Miss L.	Wennington	1872	Figures	—	—	—	—	2	—	—	—	—	—	2
Bradbury, A. A.	Hanley	1879	Landscape	—	—	—	—	—	—	—	—	—	2	2
Brade, Daniel	Kendal	1883-1889	Architecture	—	—	3	—	—	—	—	—	—	—	3
Braden, Karl	Lewes	1886-1891	Landscape	—	—	1	—	1	—	1	—	—	—	3
Bradford, C.	London	1829	Portraits	—	—	2	—	—	—	—	—	—	—	2
Bradford, Miss Harriette	London	1862-1867	Flowers	—	—	1	—	6	—	—	—	—	—	7
Bradford, Master John	London	1773	Drawing	—	1	—	—	—	—	—	—	—	—	1
Bradford, Louis King, A.R.H.A.	Dublin	1854	Landscape	—	—	—	—	1	—	—	—	—	—	1
Bradford, Samuel	London	1772	Landscape	—	1	—	—	—	—	—	—	—	—	1
Bradford, William	New York	1875	Sea Pieces	—	—	1	—	—	—	—	—	—	—	1
Bradford, Miss	London	1828	Copies	—	—	—	—	3	—	—	—	—	—	3
Bradley, Basil, R.W.S.†	Milford	1866-1893	Landscape	—	—	7	—	1	141	—	—	—	7	156
Bradley, Rev. E. *See* Cuthbert Bede.	—	—	—	—	—	—	—	—	—	—	—	—	—	—
Bradley, Edward	London	1824-1867	Landscape	—	—	12	53	77	—	1	—	—	—	143
Bradley, Mrs. E.	Putney	1865	Still Life	—	—	—	—	1	—	—	—	—	—	1
Bradley, Gordon ‡	London	1832-1839	Landscape	—	—	6	—	3	—	12	—	—	—	21
Bradley, J.	London	1783	Landscape	—	—	1	—	—	—	—	—	—	—	1
Bradley, J.	London	1817-1843	Portraits	—	—	32	—	19	2	—	—	—	—	53
Bradley, J.	London	1864	Landscape	—	—	1	—	—	—	—	—	—	—	1
Bradley, James	Worcester	1883	Landscape	—	—	—	—	—	—	—	—	—	1	1
Bradley, John Henry	Leamington	1854-1884	Landscape	—	—	26	1	19	—	—	—	—	59	105
Bradley, Miss Mary	Hornsey	1811	Flowers	—	—	3	—	—	—	—	—	—	—	3
Bradley, T. J.	London	1827	Portraits	—	—	—	—	1	—	—	—	—	—	1
Bradley, William	Manchester	1823-1846	Portraits	—	—	21	13	8	—	—	—	—	—	42
Bradley, William	London	1872-1889	Portraits	—	—	4	—	32	—	6	—	—	11	53

Name.	Town.	First and Last Year of Ex.	Speciality.	S. A.	F. S.	R. A.	B. I.	S. S.	O. W.	N. W.	G. G.	N. G	V. E.	Total.
Bradling, A.	—	1839	Figures	—	—	—	1	—	—	—	—	—	—	1
Bradshaw, Florence	London	1890	Seashore	—	—	—	—	1	—	—	—	—	—	1
Bradshaw, Captain G.	—	1791	Landscape	—	—	1	—	—	—	—	—	—	—	1
Bradshaw, Samuel	Cheltenham	1869	Landscape	—	—	—	—	1	—	—	—	—	—	1
Bradshaw, Thomas	—	1780	Copies	1	—	—	—	—	—	—	—	—	—	1
Bradshaw and Gass	Bolton	1893	Architecture	—	—	1	—	—	—	—	—	—	—	1
Bradstreet, Miss E.	London	1868	Fruit	—	—	—	—	1	—	—	—	—	—	1
Bradstreet, Miss S.	Winchester	1887	Sculpture	—	—	1	—	—	—	—	—	—	—	1
Braga, E.	Milan	1872-1883	Sculpture	—	—	3	—	—	—	—	—	—	—	3
Bragg, A.	London	1829	Figures	—	—	—	—	1	—	—	—	—	—	1
Bragg, A.	London	1862	Medals	—	—	1	—	—	—	—	—	—	—	1
Bragg, C. W.	Birmingham	1855-1857	Flowers	—	—	—	1	—	—	—	—	—	3	4
Bragger, Charles	London	1879-1880	Portraits	—	—	1	—	—	—	—	—	—	2	3
Braham, Miss Jane	London	1780	Needlework	3	—	2	—	—	—	—	—	—	—	5
Brain, Miss Constance	London	1891	Flowers	—	—	—	—	—	—	1	—	—	—	1
Brain, Miss F.	London	1864-1867	Flowers	—	—	—	3	2	—	—	—	—	—	5
Brain, H.	London	1865	Landscape	—	—	—	1	—	—	—	—	—	—	1
Brain, John	London	1832-1836	Landscape	—	—	5	—	1	—	—	—	—	—	6
Braine, F. E.	London	1822-1823	Architecture	—	—	2	—	—	—	—	—	—	—	2
Braine, T.	London	1791-1802	Miniatures	—	—	65	—	—	—	—	—	—	—	65
Braine, W.	London	1813	Architecture	—	—	1	—	—	—	—	—	—	—	1
Braine, Mrs.	London	1811-1855	Portraits	—	—	29	1	5	—	—	—	—	—	35
Brakel, Van. *See* V.	—	—	—	—	—	—	—	—	—	—	—	—	—	—
Brakspear, W. H.	London	1843-1859	Architecture	—	—	6	—	—	—	—	—	—	—	6
Bramhall, H.	London	1844-1859	Landscape	—	—	6	—	6	—	—	—	—	—	12
Bramley, Frank, A.R.A.	Lincoln	1877-1893	Churches	—	—	10	—	6	—	—	—	—	5	21
Brandard, Miss Annie Caroline	London	1867-1884	Domestic	—	—	4	—	1	—	—	—	—	—	5
Brandard, Edward Paxman	Birmingham	1849-1885	Landscape	—	—	10	5	23	—	2	—	—	2	42
Brandard, Robert	Birmingham	1831-1858	Landscape	—	—	3	21	32	—	5	—	—	5	66
Brandion, Charles	London	1768-1772	Landscape	2	—	3	—	—	—	—	—	—	—	5
Brandling, Henry †	London	1847-1856	Portraits	—	—	2	—	—	9	—	—	—	—	11
Brandling, Henry C.	London	1850-1881	Portraits	—	—	2	—	—	—	—	—	—	2	4
Brandling, Miss	—	1774	Needlework	1	—	—	—	—	—	—	—	—	—	1
Brandish, A.	London	1872-1873	Landscape	—	—	—	—	5	—	—	—	—	—	5
Brandon, A.	—	1801-1803	Landscape	—	—	2	—	—	—	—	—	—	—	2
Brandon, David, F.S.A.	London	1831-1878	Architecture	—	—	23	—	—	—	—	—	—	—	23
Brandon, Dolly	London	1891	Landscape	—	—	—	—	1	—	—	—	—	—	1
Brandon, E.	—	1870	Engraving	—	—	1	—	—	—	—	—	—	—	1
Brandon, Raphael. *See also* Wyatt & Brandon	London	1838-1874	Architecture	—	—	20	—	—	—	—	—	—	—	20
Brandon and Ritchie	London	1853-1856	Architecture	—	—	2	—	—	—	—	—	—	—	2
Brandon and Wyatt	London	1850	Architecture	—	—	3	—	—	—	—	—	—	—	3
Brandon, Mrs.	London	1864	Flowers	—	—	—	—	1	—	—	—	—	—	1
Brandt, Otto	Staplehurst	1867	Domestic	—	—	—	—	3	—	—	—	—	—	3
Branegan, J. F.	—	1871-1875	Sea-shores	—	—	3	—	1	—	—	—	—	—	4
Brangwin, Noah	Henley-on-Thames	1851-1856	Rural	—	—	4	10	8	—	—	—	—	—	22
Brangwyn, Frank, R.B.A. § φ	London	1885-1893	Domestic	—	—	16	—	26	—	1	3	1	5	52
Brangwyn (W. C.) and Withall (L. A.)	London	1875-1879	Architecture	—	—	5	—	—	—	—	—	—	—	5
Brannan, J.	London	1859	Figures	—	—	1	—	—	—	—	—	—	—	1
Branscombe, Charles H.	Bournemouth	1891	Landscape	—	—	—	—	—	—	—	—	—	1	1
Branson, Mrs. Juliet	London	1886-1889	Landscape	—	—	1	—	2	—	—	—	—	—	3
Branston, Miss Eva M.	Beckenham	1892	Landscape	—	—	1	—	—	—	—	—	—	1	2
Branston, F. W.	London	1833	Domestic	—	—	—	—	2	—	—	—	—	—	2
Branston and Wright	London	1832	Domestic	—	—	—	—	1	—	—	—	—	—	1
Branwhite, Charles †	Bristol	1843-1879	Landscape	—	—	9	25	2	265	—	—	—	—	301
Branwhite C. Brooke	Liverpool	1873-1890	Landscape	—	—	—	—	4	—	2	—	—	1	7
Branwhite, Nathan C.	Bristol	1802-1825	Miniatures	—	—	15	—	—	—	—	—	—	—	15
Brasier, B.	London	1788	Architecture	—	—	1	—	—	—	—	—	—	—	1
Brassington, John	London	1835-1837	Portraits	—	—	1	—	3	—	—	—	—	—	4
Brauer, O.	London	1872	Figures	—	—	—	—	—	—	—	—	—	1	1
Braund, J.	London	1834	Buildings	—	—	1	—	—	—	—	—	—	—	1
Bray, G.	—	1785	Animals	—	—	2	—	—	—	—	—	—	—	2
Bray, Lieut.	Deal	1774	Still Life	—	2	—	—	—	—	—	—	—	—	2
Bray, Miss	Sunderland	1821	Flowers	—	—	1	—	—	—	—	—	—	—	1
Brayshay, W. H.	Burley-on-Wharfedale	1867	Landscape	—	—	1	—	—	—	—	—	—	—	1
Breach, E. R.	London	1868-1886	Sporting	—	—	1	—	30	—	—	—	—	1	32
Breakell, Miss Mary Louise	Richmond	1879-1893	Figures	—	—	8	—	8	—	—	—	—	12	28
Breakspeare, W. A.	London	1883-1893	Domestic	—	—	3	—	11	—	—	6	—	3	23
Breamer, F. C.	London	1793	Sculpture	—	—	1	—	—	—	—	—	—	—	1
Breanski, De. *See* D.	—	—	—	—	—	—	—	—	—	—	—	—	—	—
Breast, Henry	London	1830-1833	Landscape	—	—	—	4	1	—	—	—	—	—	5
Brebant, Albert	Liverpool	1848-1852	Domestic	—	—	1	—	—	—	—	—	—	4	5
Breda, De. *See* D.	—	—	—	—	—	—	—	—	—	—	—	—	—	—

Name.	Town.	First and Last Year of Ex.	Speciality.	S. A.	F. S.	R. A.	B. I.	S. S.	O. W.	N.W.	G. G.	N. G.	V. E.	Total.
Bredburg, Madame Mina	London	1892	Portraits	—	—	—	—	—	—	—	—	1	—	1
Bredon, Albert C.	London	1887-1891	Architecture	—	—	4	—	—	—	—	—	—	—	4
Bree, Rev. W.	—	1803	Landscape	—	—	2	—	—	—	—	—	—	—	2
Bree, De. *See* D.	—	—	—	—	—	—	—	—	—	—	—	—	—	—
Brees, S. C.	Birmingham	1832-1837	Landscape	—	—	7	—	11	—	1	—	—	—	19
Bregazzi, D.	Derby	1811	Allegorical	—	—	1	—	—	—	—	—	—	—	1
Brely, A. de la	London	1883-1884	Domestic	—	—	—	—	4	—	—	—	—	1	5
Bremner, P.	Southampton	1856	Architecture	—	—	1	—	—	—	—	—	—	—	1
Brenan, James, R.H.A.	London	1836	Sunset	—	—	—	—	1	—	—	—	—	—	1
Brenchard, A.	London	1892	Landscape	—	—	—	—	—	—	—	—	2	—	2
Brendel, Heinrich Albert	London	1874	Landscape	—	—	1	—	—	—	—	—	—	—	1
Brennan, Fitzjohn	London	1885-1887	Landscape	—	—	4	—	—	—	—	—	—	—	4
Brennan, Michael G.	Rome	1865-1872	Italian Life	—	—	15	—	—	—	—	—	—	5	20
Brereton, Robert	London	1835-1847	Domestic	—	—	2	—	2	—	—	—	—	—	4
Breslau, Madame Louise	London	1882	Domestic	—	—	1	—	—	—	—	—	—	—	1
Bretherton, James	London	1771-1772	Engraving	4	—	—	—	—	—	—	—	—	—	4
Breton, Emile	Paris	1881	Etching	—	—	—	—	—	—	—	—	—	1	1
Brett, B.	London	1841-1845	Landscape	—	—	3	1	12	—	—	—	—	—	16
Brett, John, A.R.A.	London	1856-1893	Sea Pieces	—	—	78	—	—	—	—	—	—	—	78
Brett, J.	London	1858	Birds	—	—	—	—	2	—	—	—	—	—	2
Brett, Joseph William	London	1830	Copies	—	—	—	—	2	—	—	—	—	—	2
Brett, Miss Rosa. *See* Rosarius	Maidstone	1867-1881	Landscape	—	—	6	—	—	—	—	—	—	1	7
Brettingham, Robert Furze	London	1783-1800	Architecture	—	—	26	—	—	—	—	—	—	—	26
Breun, John Ernest	London	1879-1892	Portraits	—	—	9	—	1	—	2	—	—	9	21
Brewer, Miss Amy Cobham	Bushey	1893	Landscape	—	—	1	—	—	—	—	—	1	—	2
Brewer, H. C.	London	1888	Landscape	—	—	1	—	—	—	—	—	—	—	1
Brewer, Henry William	London	1858-1893	Churches	—	—	26	1	15	—	—	—	—	19	61
Brewer, John	London	1763-1779	Landscape	—	9	—	—	—	—	—	—	—	—	9
Brewer, Julian C.	Plymouth	1855-1876	Portraits	—	—	7	—	—	—	—	—	—	—	7
Brewer, John James	London	1779-1780	Still Life	1	1	—	—	—	—	—	—	—	—	2
Brewer, M.	London	1785	Balloons	—	—	1	—	—	—	—	—	—	—	1
Brewer, Miss Maude	Sevenoaks	1888-1890	Landscape	—	—	—	—	—	—	3	—	—	—	3
Brewer, R.	London	1796	Landscape	—	—	1	—	—	—	—	—	—	—	1
Brewer, Mrs.	London	1763-1780	Miniatures	27	5	—	—	—	—	—	—	—	—	32
Brewer, Mrs.	Worcester	1848-1853	Miniatures	—	—	6	—	—	—	—	—	—	—	6
Brewer, Miss	—	1776	Needlework	1	—	—	—	—	—	—	—	—	—	1
Brewers, R.	London	1797	Landscape	—	—	1	—	—	—	—	—	—	—	1
Brewill, Arthur W.	Nottingham	1891	Architecture	—	—	1	—	—	—	—	—	—	—	1
Brewster, E.	London	1802	Flowers	—	—	1	—	—	—	—	—	—	—	1
Brewster, H.	London	1823	Portraits	—	—	1	—	—	—	—	—	—	—	1
Brewster, W.	London	1845	Architecture	—	—	2	—	—	—	—	—	—	—	2
Brewtnall, Edward Fred., R.W.S., R.B.A. § † φ	Penge	1868-1893	Domestic	—	—	14	—	8	156	—	4	—	46	228
Breymann, A.	Brunswick	1872	Sculpture	—	—	2	—	—	—	—	—	—	—	2
Briand, G.	—	1847	Architecture	—	—	1	—	—	—	—	—	—	—	1
Briant, W. N.	Reading	1842-1843	Architecture	—	—	2	—	—	—	—	—	—	—	2
Brias —.	Brussels	1830	Interiors	—	—	1	—	—	—	—	—	—	—	1
Brice, E.	London	1780	Sculpture	—	—	1	—	—	—	—	—	—	—	1
Brice, E. Kington	Manchester	1893	Domestic	—	—	1	—	—	—	—	—	—	—	1
Brickdale, C. F.	Norwood	1887	Landscape	—	—	—	—	—	—	1	—	—	—	1
Bridel, W.	London	1795-1797	Architecture	—	—	5	—	—	—	—	—	—	—	5
Bridell, Miss E.	London	1861	Figures	—	—	—	1	—	—	—	—	—	—	1
Bridell, Frederick Lee	Helyford	1851-1863	Landscape	—	—	7	11	2	—	—	—	—	15	35
Bridell, Mrs. F. Lee. *See* Miss Eliza Florance	—	—	—	—	—	—	—	—	—	—	—	—	—	—
Fox, afterwards Mrs. George Edward Fox	London	1859-1881	Figures	—	—	11	2	—	—	—	—	—	7	20
Bridge, Annie	Highgate	1889-1891	Flowers	—	—	—	—	2	—	—	—	—	—	2
Bridge, J.	London	1866-1872	Figures	—	—	6	—	1	—	—	—	—	—	7
Bridgeford, Thomas, R.H.A.	London	1835-1844	Portraits	—	—	21	3	4	—	—	—	—	—	28
Bridgens, R.	London	1813-1826	Buildings	—	—	9	—	—	—	—	—	—	—	9
Bridges, Miss Fidelia	Philadelphia	1879-1880	Domestic	—	—	1	—	—	—	—	—	—	2	3
Bridges, James	Oxford	1819-1853	Landscape	—	—	23	4	9	—	4	—	—	—	40
Bridges, John	Oxford	1818-1854	Domestic	—	—	23	24	5	—	—	—	—	—	52
Bridgewater, Henry Scott	Bushey	1889-1893	Engraving	—	—	8	—	—	—	—	—	—	—	8
Bridgewater, Mrs. H. Scott	Bushey	1893	Domestic	—	—	1	—	—	—	—	—	—	—	1
Bridgman, —	London	1774	Sea Pieces	1	—	—	—	—	—	—	—	—	—	1
Bridgman, C. J.	Paris	1878	Landscape	—	—	—	—	—	—	—	—	—	1	1
Bridgman, Frederic Arthur	Paris	1871-1893	Historical	—	—	21	—	1	—	—	—	—	20	42
Bridgman, G.	London	1880	Landscape	—	—	—	—	—	—	—	—	—	1	1
Bridgman, T. B. or D.	London	1865	Still Life	—	—	—	—	1	—	—	—	—	—	1
Bridoux, François Eugène Augustin	Paris	1875	Charcoal	—	—	—	—	—	—	—	—	—	1	1
Bridport, G.	—	1806	Architecture	—	—	1	—	—	—	—	—	—	—	1
Bridport, H.	London	1813	Portraits	—	—	3	—	—	—	—	—	—	—	3
Brierley. *See* Demaine and Brierley	—	—	Architecture	—	—	—	—	—	—	—	—	—	—	—

Name.	Town.	First and Last Year of Ex.	Speciality.	S. A.	F. S.	R. A.	B. I.	S. S.	O. W.	N. W.	G. G.	N. G.	V. E.	Total.
Brierly, Sir Oswald Walter, R.W.S., F.R.G.S.†‡	London	1839-1893	Sea Pieces	—	—	11	—	—	192	2	—	—	3	208
Briesbroeck, Van. *See* V.	—	—	—	—	—	—	—	—	—	—	—	—	—	—
Briggs —	—	1785	Portraits	—	—	2	—	—	—	—	—	—	—	2
Briggs, Ernest E.	London	1889-1893	Landscape	—	—	9	—	8	—	4	—	—	—	21
Briggs, H.	Acton	1816-1831	Landscape	—	—	21	12	7	—	—	—	—	—	40
Briggs, Henry Perronet, R.A.	London	1814-1844	Portraits	—	—	132	21	—	—	—	—	—	—	153
Briggs, Miss Irlam	Parkstone	1892-1893	Portraits	—	—	3	—	—	—	—	—	—	—	3
Briggs, John	London	1889	Landscape	—	—	1	—	—	—	—	—	—	—	1
Briggs, R. A. *See also* Killmister and Briggs	London	1884-1893	Architecture	—	—	19	—	—	—	—	—	—	—	19
Briggs, W.	London	1844-1858	Portraits	—	—	14	—	1	—	—	—	—	—	15
Briggs, William Keighley	Leeds	1849-1860	Portraits	—	—	—	—	2	—	—	—	—	15	17
Bright, Henry ‡	London	1836-1876	Landscape	—	—	12	26	11	—	33	—	—	—	82
Bright, Henry	Giggs Hill	1884	Figures	—	—	—	—	—	—	1	—	—	—	1
Bright, Mary	London	1837-1846	Landscape	—	—	—	—	4	—	—	—	—	—	4
Bright, William	London	1828-1834	Landscape	—	—	2	5	6	—	—	—	—	—	13
Brightwell, G.	London	1877-1881	Landscape	—	—	—	—	1	—	—	—	—	4	5
Brighty, G. M.	London	1809-1827	Portraits	—	—	18	1	—	—	—	—	—	1	20
Brigstocke, Thomas	London	1842-1865	Portraits	—	—	16	2	—	—	—	—	—	—	18
Brimmer, Miss Anne	London	1846-1858	Portraits	—	—	5	—	13	—	—	—	—	—	18
Brinckman, Lady	London	1848	Scriptural	—	—	—	1	—	—	—	—	—	—	1
Brindley, Charles A.	Surbiton	1888-1893	Domestic	—	—	3	—	—	—	—	—	—	—	3
Brindley, John Angell J.	London	1884-1890	Domestic	—	—	2	—	6	—	5	—	—	—	13
Brindley, Sarah	London	1879	Rustic	—	—	—	—	1	—	—	—	—	—	1
Brindley, William	London	1881-1882	Figures	—	—	4	—	—	—	—	—	—	—	4
Brini, C.	Florence	1855	Scriptural	—	—	1	—	—	—	—	—	—	—	1
Brinton, Miss Edith D.	London	1885-1893	Domestic	—	—	3	—	1	—	—	—	—	2	6
Briscoe, Claude	London	1872-1873	Figures	—	—	—	—	4	—	—	—	—	—	4
Briscoe, C. J.	—	1800	Insects	—	—	1	—	—	—	—	—	—	—	1
Brissot, Frank	London	1879	Figures	—	—	1	—	—	—	—	—	—	—	1
Brissot de Warville F.	Paris	1880-1881	Etchings	—	—	—	—	—	—	—	2	—	2	4
Bristow, Edmund	Windsor	1809-1838	Sporting	—	—	7	11	8	—	—	—	—	—	26
Bristow, George L.	London	1883-1887	Landscape	—	—	—	—	—	—	8	—	—	—	8
Bristow, J.	London	1792-1793	Architecture	—	—	2	—	—	—	—	—	—	—	2
Bristow, J. J.	London	1793-1802	Architecture	—	—	4	—	—	—	—	—	—	—	4
Bristow, Miss Lily	London	1889-1892	Domestic	—	—	—	—	2	—	—	—	—	5	7
Bristow, W. H.	London	1834-1840	Figures	—	—	—	2	1	—	—	—	—	—	3
Bristowe, Miss Beatrice M.	London	1893	Portraits	—	—	1	—	—	—	—	—	—	—	1
Brittan, C. E.	Truro	1858	Animals	—	—	—	—	1	—	—	—	—	—	1
Britten, William Edward Frank	London	1873-1893	Domestic	—	—	8	—	5	—	—	18	15	23	69
Britton, John, F.S.A.	London	1799-1819	Ruins	—	—	25	—	—	—	—	—	—	—	25
Brix, R.	London	1803	Historical	—	—	1	—	—	—	—	—	—	—	1
Broad, John	London	1890-1891	Sculpture	—	—	2	—	—	—	—	—	—	—	2
Broadbent, Frank	Liverpool	1884	Architecture	—	—	1	—	—	—	—	—	—	—	1
Broadbridge, Miss Alma	London	1879-1891	Domestic	—	—	5	—	7	—	—	—	—	2	14
Broadhurst, John, Jun.	London	1776-1779	Miniatures	5	—	—	—	—	—	—	—	—	—	5
Brocas, C.	Dublin	1821	Portraits	—	—	1	—	—	—	—	—	—	—	1
Brock, Charles Edmund	Cambridge	1891	Domestic	—	—	—	—	—	—	—	—	—	1	1
Brock, Miss Ellen	Guernsey	1868-1884	Domestic	—	—	—	—	5	—	—	—	—	11	16
Brock, E. P.	London	1862	Architecture	—	—	1	—	—	—	—	—	—	—	1
Brock, Fannie	Brockley	1883	Flowers	—	—	—	—	1	—	—	—	—	—	1
Brock, G.	London	1830-1838	Architecture	—	—	2	—	—	—	—	—	—	—	2
Brock, J. S. or J. L. B.	London	1853-1862	Historical	—	—	—	1	1	—	—	—	—	—	2
Brock, Thomas, R.A.	London	1868-1893	Sculpture	—	—	59	—	—	—	—	—	—	—	59
Brockbank, Albert E., R.B.A. §	Liverpool	1886-1893	Landscape	—	—	7	—	29	—	10	—	—	—	46
Brockedon, William	Totnes	1812-1837	Historical	—	—	36	29	—	—	—	—	—	—	65
Brockedon, Mrs.	London	1827	—	—	—	—	*	—	—	—	—	—	—	—
Brockell, Miss Jeanie F.	London	1883	Animals	—	—	1	—	—	—	—	—	—	—	1
Brockman, Charles Drake	London	1870-1887	Landscape	—	—	2	—	32	—	1	—	—	17	52
Brockman, C. H.	Witley	1871-1892	Landscape	—	—	9	—	—	—	—	—	—	3	12
Brockman, Walter	London	1885	Figures	—	—	—	—	—	—	—	—	—	2	2
Brockmer —	London	1762-1776	Miniatures	46	—	—	—	—	—	—	—	—	—	46
Brocky, Charles ‡	London	1839-1855	Figures	—	—	43	16	—	—	3	—	—	—	62
Brodie, Alexander	Aberdeen	1864	Sculpture	—	—	2	—	—	—	—	—	—	—	2
Brodie, John Lamont	London	1848-1881	Historical	—	—	25	1	1	—	—	—	—	9	36
Brodie, Miss Margaret	London	1874-1875	Landscape	—	—	—	—	2	—	—	—	—	—	2
Brodie, William, R.S.A.	Edinburgh	1850-1881	Sculpture	—	—	32	—	—	—	—	—	—	—	32
Brodies, William	—	1770	Landscape	1	—	—	—	—	—	—	—	—	—	1
Brodrick, Cuthbert	Hull	1854-1867	Architecture	—	—	3	—	—	—	—	—	—	—	3
Brodrick, William	Chudleigh	1881	Domestic	—	—	1	—	—	—	—	—	—	—	1
Brome, Charles	London	1798-1801	Portraits	—	—	10	—	—	—	—	—	—	—	10
Bromet, William	London	1819-1843	Landscape	—	—	13	4	13	—	—	—	—	—	30
Bromfield, E. B.	London	1868	Sculpture	—	—	1	—	—	—	—	—	—	—	1

Name.	Town.	First and Last Year of Ex.	Speciality.	S. A.	F. S.	R. A.	B. I.	S. S.	O. W.	N. W.	G. G.	N. G.	V. E.	Total.
Bromilaw, John G.	London	1886	Stained Glass	—	—	1	—	—	—	—	—	—	—	1
Bromley, A.	London	1864-1865	Sculpture	—	—	4	—	—	—	—	—	—	—	4
Bromley, Albert N.	London	1874-1892	Architecture	—	—	3	—	—	—	—	—	—	—	3
Bromley, C. Shailor	London	1882-1886	Fruit	—	—	—	—	10	—	—	—	—	—	10
Bromley, Clough W.	London	1870-1892	Landscape	—	—	15	—	40	—	2	—	—	43	100
Bromley, E.	London	1828	Engraving	—	—	1	—	1	—	—	—	—	—	2
Bromley, Frederick	London	1833-1869	Engraving	—	—	4	—	12	—	—	—	—	—	16
Bromley, J., Senr.	London	1829-1832	Historical	—	—	2	—	—	—	1	—	—	—	3
Bromley, James	London	1829-1833	Engraving	—	—	—	—	12	—	—	—	—	—	12
Bromley, John Charles	London	1824-1833	Engraving	—	—	2	—	18	—	—	—	—	—	20
Bromley, John Mallard, R.B.A. §	London	1876-1892	Landscape	—	—	16	—	92	—	10	2	—	3	123
Bromley, Valentine Walter ‡ §	London	1865-1877	Historical	—	—	5	—	29	—	42	—	—	8	84
Bromley, Mrs. Val. *See* Miss Alice Louisa Maria Atkinson	—	1877-1890	Landscape	—	—	—	—	6	—	7	10	2	8	33
Bromley, William, A.R.A.	London	1786-1842	Engraving	3	—	51	—	2	—	1	—	—	—	57
Bromley, William §	London	1835-1888	Domestic	—	—	15	26	187	—	—	—	—	—	228
Bromley, Walter Lewis (?) Louis	London	1866-1882	Domestic	—	—	—	—	5	—	—	—	—	3	8
Brompton, Richard, F.S.A.	London	1767-1780	Portraits	22	6	2	—	—	—	—	—	—	—	30
Brondgeest, Albert	London	1831	Landscape	—	—	—	4	—	—	—	—	—	—	4
Brook, Mrs. Caroline W.	London	1877-1888	Figures	—	—	2	—	7	—	—	—	—	3	12
Brook, Miss Marian Burnham. (?) Brock	London	1872-1885	Domestic	—	—	7	—	10	—	—	—	—	5	22
Brook, Mrs. T.	Stoke Newington	1883	Domestic	—	—	—	—	1	—	—	—	—	—	1
Brookbank, W.	Brighton	1847	Flowers	—	—	—	—	1	—	—	—	—	—	1
Brookbank, W. H.	London	1864-1887	Landscape	—	—	—	2	6	—	1	—	—	—	9
Brookbank, Mrs. † *See* Miss M. Scott	Brighton	1834-1837	Fruit	—	—	—	—	—	3	—	—	—	—	3
Brooke, Edward	London	1846-1878	Landscape	—	—	4	—	—	—	—	—	—	—	4
Brooke, E. Adveno	London	1844-1864	Domestic	—	—	3	1	5	—	—	—	—	3	12
Brooke, Edmund W.	Paris	1890-1891	Portraits	—	—	2	—	—	—	—	—	—	—	2
Brooke, F. William	London	1886-1891	Landscape	—	—	—	—	2	—	1	—	—	—	3
Brooke, Henry	Dublin	1776	Mythological	1	—	—	—	—	—	—	—	—	—	1
Brooke, H.	Hastings	1849	Landscape	—	—	—	1	—	—	—	—	—	—	1
Brooke, J.	London	1840	Portraits	—	—	1	—	—	—	—	—	—	—	1
Brooke, J.	—	1870	Sculpture	—	—	1	—	—	—	—	—	—	—	1
Brooke, James, and Sons	London	1892-1893	Architecture	—	—	3	—	—	—	—	—	—	—	3
Brooke, John	Manchester	1889-1893	Architecture	—	—	6	—	—	—	—	—	—	—	6
Brooke, John	London	1883	Etching	—	—	1	—	—	—	—	—	—	—	1
Brooke, L. Leslie	London	1887-1892	Figures	—	—	6	—	—	—	1	—	—	—	7
Brooke, R.	London	1802-1822	Rustic	—	—	10	—	—	—	—	—	—	—	10
Brooke, William	London	1779-1783	Cattle	—	—	2	—	—	—	—	—	—	—	2
Brooke, William Henry	London	1808-1833	Historical	—	—	9	6	9	—	1	—	—	8	33
Brooker, Miss Catherine P.	London	1881-1893	Portraits	—	—	2	—	1	—	1	—	—	3	7
Brooker, E. W.	London	1870	Japanese	—	—	—	—	1	—	—	—	—	—	1
Brooker, Harry	London	1876-1880	Domestic	—	—	1	—	4	—	—	—	—	—	5
Brooker, J.	Bath	1857	Figures	—	—	—	1	—	—	—	—	—	—	1
Brooker, W. G.	Thames Ditton	1878	Sculpture	—	—	1	—	—	—	—	—	—	—	1
Brookes, R. W.	Balham	1884	Sculpture	—	—	1	—	—	—	—	—	—	—	1
Brookes, W. M.	London	1829-1838	Architecture	—	—	9	—	—	—	—	—	—	—	9
Brooks, Frank	Salisbury	1880-1892	Portraits	—	—	5	—	1	—	3	—	—	3	12
Brooks, Miss F. C.	—	1882	Figures	—	—	—	—	—	—	—	1	—	—	1
Brooks, G. E.	London	1836	Architecture	—	—	1	—	—	—	—	—	—	—	1
Brooks, H.	London	1816-1836	Architecture	—	—	4	—	—	—	—	—	—	—	4
Brooks, Henry	Salisbury	1876-1891	Domestic	—	—	2	—	1	—	1	—	—	—	4
Brooks, Henry Jamyn	London	1884-1891	Portraits	—	—	3	—	—	—	—	—	2	—	5
Brooks, James	London	1853-1891	Architecture	—	—	52	—	—	—	—	—	—	—	52
Brooks, J. G.	London	1832	Domestic	—	—	2	—	—	—	—	—	—	—	2
Brooks, J. Martin	London	1879-1887	Architecture	—	—	2	—	—	—	—	—	—	—	2
Brooks, Miss Maria	London	1869-1890	Portraits	—	—	33	—	29	—	—	3	—	11	76
Brooks, P. G.	London	1828	Portraits	—	—	2	—	—	—	—	—	—	—	2
Brooks, Samuel	London	1883	Figures	—	—	1	—	—	—	—	—	—	—	1
Brooks, T.	London	1782-1791	Landscape	—	9	1	—	—	—	—	—	—	—	10
Brooks, Thomas	Hull	1843-1882	Domestic	—	—	55	19	11	—	—	—	—	4	89
Brooks, T. J.	London	1829	Portraits	—	—	—	—	1	—	—	—	—	—	1
Brooks, T. W.	London	1808	Landscape	—	—	1	—	—	—	—	—	—	—	1
Brooks, W.	London	1780-1801	Landscape	—	—	17	—	—	—	—	—	—	—	17
Brooks, W.	London	1803-1815	Architecture	—	—	9	—	—	—	—	—	—	—	9
Brooks, W. A.	London	1821	Architecture	—	—	1	—	—	—	—	—	—	—	1
Brooks, W. W.	London	1869	Portraits	—	—	1	—	—	—	—	—	—	—	1
Brooksbank, Mrs. *See* Miss Scott.	—	—	—	—	—	—	—	—	—	—	—	—	—	—
Brookshaw, George	London	1780	Wood Work	—	6	—	—	—	—	—	—	—	—	6
Brookshaw, G.	—	1819	Flowers	—	—	1	—	—	—	—	—	—	—	1
Broom, J.	—	1831	Ruins	—	—	—	—	1	—	—	—	—	—	1
Broome, G. J.	London	1867-1873	Fruit	—	—	3	—	3	—	—	—	—	1	7

Name.	Town.	First and Last Year of Ex.	Speciality.	S. A.	F. S.	R. A.	B. I.	S. S.	O. W.	N. W.	G. G.	N. G.	V. E.	Total.
Broomfield, G. H.	London	1877	Fruit	—	—	—	—	1	—	—	—	—	—	1
Broomhead, T.	Birmingham	1846	Cattle	—	—	—	1	—	—	—	—	—	—	1
Brophy, A. F.	London	1876-1877	Figures	—	—	—	—	—	—	—	—	—	2	2
Bros, Miss A.	London	1868	Flowers	—	—	1	—	—	—	—	—	—	—	1
Bros, J.	London	1874	Landscape	—	—	—	—	—	—	—	—	—	2	2
Brotherton, A. H.	Rome	1846-1864	Landscape	—	—	1	4	—	—	—	—	—	—	5
Brough, William	London	1823-1852	Historical	—	—	14	11	4	—	—	—	—	—	29
Broughton, Rev. B.	—	1796-1798	Landscape	—	—	2	—	—	—	—	—	—	—	2
Broughton, Emily J.	London	1878-1882	Heads	—	—	2	—	1	—	—	—	—	1	4
Broughton, H.	London	1836	Portraits	—	—	—	—	1	—	—	—	—	—	1
Browing, T.	London	1804	Landscape	—	—	1	—	—	—	—	—	—	—	1
Brown, Miss A.	London	1805	Landscape	—	—	1	—	—	—	—	—	—	—	1
Brown, Alfred	London	1845-1855	Sculpture	—	—	14	1	—	—	—	—	—	—	15
Brown, Miss Alberta	London	1870-1871	Domestic	—	—	—	—	—	—	—	—	—	2	2
Brown, Arnesby	St. Ives, Cornw.	1890-1893	Landscape	—	—	6	—	1	—	—	—	—	1	8
Brown, Miss Alice G.	Harrow	1890-1892	Domestic	—	—	6	—	—	—	—	—	—	—	6
Brown, A. K., A.R.S.A.	Glasgow	1873-1893	Landscape	—	—	33	—	9	—	3	3	7	9	64
Brown, B.	London	1850	Domestic	—	—	—	—	1	—	—	—	—	—	1
Brown, Miss Beatrice A.	Beckenham	1888-1893	Sculpture	—	—	6	—	1	—	—	5	—	—	12
Brown, Miss Bessie	London	1885	Flowers	—	—	—	—	—	—	—	1	—	—	1
Brown, Charles	London	1771-1785	Gems	—	—	16	—	—	—	—	—	—	—	16
Brown, Miss Charlotte	London	1807-1816	Figures	—	—	2	4	—	—	—	—	—	—	6
Brown, C. J.	London	1868	Domestic	—	—	—	—	—	—	—	—	—	1	1
Brown, Miss Catherine Madox afterwards Mrs. Hueffer	London	1869-1872	Figures	—	—	3	—	—	—	—	—	—	1	4
Brown, D. *See* Gordon and Brown.	—	—	—	—	—	—	—	—	—	—	—	—	—	—
Brown, David	London	1792-1797	Landscape	—	—	10	—	—	—	—	—	—	—	10
Brown, Miss E.	Richmond	1798-1802	Flowers	—	—	21	—	—	—	—	—	—	—	21
Brown, E.	New Whitby	1873	Landscape	—	—	—	—	—	—	—	—	—	2	2
Brown, Edward	Bedford	1893	Landscape	—	—	—	—	1	—	—	—	—	—	1
Brown, Miss Ellinor	London	1857-1872	Landscape	—	—	—	1	2	—	—	—	—	—	3
Brown, Miss Ella G.	Lytham	1887-1888	Game	—	—	2	—	—	—	—	—	—	—	2
Brown, Frederick	London	1875-1891	Landscape	—	—	13	—	22	—	—	2	—	17	54
Brown, Miss F.	Richmond	1797	Flowers	—	—	3	—	—	—	—	—	—	—	3
Brown, Frank B.	Selkirk	1880	Landscape	—	—	—	—	—	—	—	—	—	1	1
Brown, Ford Madox	London	1841-1867	Figures	—	—	5	5	—	—	—	—	—	6	16
Brown, George	London	1773-1780	Landscape	—	—	6	—	—	—	—	—	—	—	6
Brown, George	London	1825-1837	Portraits	—	—	11	—	1	—	—	—	—	—	12
Brown, G. A.	London	1864	Flowers	—	—	1	—	—	—	—	—	—	—	1
Brown, G. Lunell	London	1884	Domestic	—	—	1	—	—	—	—	—	—	—	1
Brown, George Peploe	London	1876-1890	Sculpture	—	—	—	—	—	—	5	11	—	15	31
Brown, Colonel G. R., R.H.A.	London	1865-1877	Indian	—	—	1	—	1	—	—	—	—	—	2
Brown, G. W.	London	1877	Heads	—	—	—	—	—	—	—	—	—	1	1
Brown, H.	London	1799-1801	Architecture	—	—	6	—	—	—	—	—	—	—	6
Brown, H.	—	1830	Sea Pieces	—	—	—	1	—	—	—	—	—	—	1
Brown, Miss Helen	Forest Gate	1883-1887	Flowers	—	—	2	—	—	—	4	—	—	—	6
Brown, H. Harris	Northampton	1889-1893	Portraits	—	—	4	—	1	—	—	—	5	3	13
Brown, H. L.	London	1876-1877	Coast Scenes	—	—	—	—	2	—	—	—	—	—	2
Brown, J.	Edinburgh	1786	Miniatures	—	—	8	—	—	—	—	—	—	—	8
Brown, J.	Richmond	1803-1808	Portraits	—	—	2	—	—	—	—	—	—	—	2
Brown, J.	London	1839-1864	Sculpture	—	—	1	1	—	—	—	—	—	—	2
Brown, J.	London	1856-1858	Flowers	—	—	2	—	—	—	—	—	—	—	2
Brown, J.	London	1873-1874	Landscape	—	—	—	—	2	—	—	—	—	—	2
Brown, John	Rome	1774	Landscape	—	—	2	—	—	—	—	—	—	—	2
Brown, John	London	1819-1850	Landscape	—	—	1	2	6	—	—	—	—	—	9
Brown, John	London	1820-1842	Architecture	—	—	12	—	—	—	—	—	—	—	12
Brown, Joseph	London	1857-1886	Engraving	—	—	10	—	—	—	—	—	—	—	10
Brown, J. Alfred	Bushey	1890	Landscape	—	—	1	—	2	—	—	—	—	—	3
Brown, J. B.	London	1862	Domestic	—	—	—	—	1	—	—	—	—	—	1
Brown, John C., A.R.S.A.	London	1833	Landscape	—	—	1	1	1	—	1	—	—	—	4
Brown, J. G.	London	1880-1885	Domestic	—	—	2	—	—	—	—	—	—	—	2
Brown, Miss J. H.	London	1874	Figures	—	—	—	—	1	—	—	—	—	—	1
Brown, John Lewis	Paris	1875	Rustic	—	—	1	—	—	—	—	—	—	—	1
Brown, J. Michael	Edinburgh	1885-1893	Landscape	—	—	4	—	3	—	1	—	—	—	8
Brown, J. Osborn	London	1869	Interiors	—	—	—	—	—	—	—	—	—	1	1
Brown, J. W.	London	1876-1878	Domestic	—	—	—	—	—	—	—	—	—	3	3
Brown, Mrs. J. W. *See* Miss Eleanor Fairlam	London	1853-1876	Landscape	—	—	—	12	10	—	—	—	—	18	40
Brown, K.	London	1826	Portraits	—	—	1	—	—	—	—	—	—	—	1
Brown, Kellock	Glasgow	1887-1893	Sculpture	—	—	2	—	—	—	—	—	—	—	2
Brown, L.	London	1846-1848	Sculpture	—	—	2	—	—	—	—	—	—	—	2
Brown, Miss L.	London	1801-1804	Portraits	—	—	5	—	—	—	—	—	—	—	5
Brown, Miss L. Henrietta	London	1887	Sculpture	—	—	—	—	1	—	—	—	—	—	1
Brown, Miss Lucy Madox. *See* Mrs. W. M. Rossetti	London	1869-1872	Domestic	—	—	1	—	—	—	—	—	—	6	7

Name.	Town.	First and Last Year of Ex.	Speciality.	S. A.	F. S.	R. A.	B. I.	S. S.	O. W.	N. W.	G. G.	N. G.	V. E.	Total.
Brown, Margaret	London	1881	Flowers	—	—	—	—	—	—	—	—	—	1	1
Brown, Mather	London	1782-1831	Portraits	—	—	80	28	21	—	—	—	—	—	129
Brown, Miss Matilda	London	1822-1839	Flowers	—	—	4	3	—	—	—	—	—	—	7
Brown, Maynard	Nottingham	1878-1887	Historical	—	—	4	—	—	—	—	—	—	3	7
Brown, Miss M. C.	London	1800-1807	Portraits	—	—	21	—	—	—	—	—	—	—	21
Brown, Nathaniel	London	1765-1779	Portraits	—	54	—	—	—	—	—	—	—	—	54
Brown, Oliver Madox	London	1869-1870	Domestic	—	—	1	—	—	—	—	—	—	2	3
Brown, Peter	London	1766-1791	Flowers	5	3	21	—	—	—	—	—	—	—	29
Brown, Peter	Shrewsbury	1832-1833	Landscape	—	—	—	—	1	—	13	—	—	—	14
Brown, Richard	London	1804-1828	Architecture	—	—	27	—	—	—	—	—	—	—	27
Brown, Robert	London	1792-1834	Landscape	—	—	33	53	5	—	—	—	—	16	107
Brown, R.	Shrewsbury	1830	Portraits	—	—	1	—	—	—	—	—	—	—	1
Brown, Richard	—	1854	Architecture	—	—	3	—	—	—	—	—	—	—	3
Brown, R. G.	—	1844	Game	—	—	1	—	—	—	—	—	—	—	1
Brown, R. W.	London	1821-1822	Figures	—	—	2	—	—	—	—	—	—	—	2
Brown, S.	London	1808	Architecture	—	—	1	—	—	—	—	—	—	—	1
Brown, S.	—	1806	Portraits	—	—	1	—	—	—	—	—	—	—	1
Brown, Thomas	London	1842-1855	Sculpture	—	—	1	2	—	—	—	—	—	—	3
Brown, T. Austen, R.I., A.R.S.A. ‡	Edinburgh	1885-1893	Domestic	—	—	10	—	--	—	10	4	—	2	26
Brown, T. B.	London	1817-1819	Rural	—	—	3	1	—	—	—	—	—	—	4
Brown, T. H.	London	1830-1831	Sea Pieces	—	—	2	—	—	—	—	—	—	—	2
Brown, T. S.	London	1865-1874	Sculpture	—	—	4	—	—	—	—	—	—	—	4
Brown, Vandyke	London	1833-1835	Landscape	—	—	—	3	—	—	—	—	—	—	3
Brown, W., Junr.	London	1798-1808	Sporting	—	—	2	—	—	—	—	—	—	—	2
Brown, W.	London	1801-1809	Architecture	—	—	3	—	—	—	—	—	—	—	3
Brown, William	London	1825-1833	Domestic	—	—	—	—	3	—	—	—	—	—	3
Brown, William	London	1766-1830	Gems	4	—	90	3	—	—	—	—	—	—	97
Brown, W. B.	London	1799-1831	Portraits	—	—	16	2	1	—	—	—	—	—	19
Brown, William Beattie-, R.S.A.	Edinburgh	1863-1888	Landscape	—	—	22	—	—	—	4	—	—	3	29
Brown, W. E.	London	1879-1881	Landscape	—	—	—	—	4	—	—	—	—	3	7
Brown (W. Edward) and Brown (F.)	London	1891-1892	Architecture	—	—	3	—	—	—	—	—	—	—	3
Brown, W. G.	Leicester	1835	Domestic	—	—	1	—	—	—	—	—	—	—	1
Brown, W. M.	London	1813-1829	Portraits	—	—	2	—	—	—	—	—	—	—	2
Brown, W. M.	London	1849-1856	Animals	—	—	—	1	4	—	—	—	—	3	8
Brown, W. Talbot	Wellingbor'gh	1881	Architecture	—	—	2	—	—	—	—	—	—	—	2
Brown, Mrs.	London	1822-1824	Fruit	—	—	1	—	1	—	—	—	—	—	2
Brown, Mrs.	London	1810-1811	Landscape	—	—	—	4	—	—	—	—	—	—	4
Brown, Miss	Yarmouth	1771-1783	Miniatures	2	—	—	—	—	—	—	—	—	—	2
Brown, Van. *See* V.	—	—		—	—	—	—	—	—	—	—	—	—	—
Brown and Blackall	—	1855	Architecture	—	—	1	—	—	—	—	—	—	—	1
Browne, Alfred J. Warne	Ealing	1884-1893	Sea Pieces	—	—	3	—	—	—	5	—	—	3	11
Browne, Cecil	London	1887	Domestic	—	—	—	—	—	—	—	—	—	1	1
Browne, Charles Henry	Shrewsbury	1860-1875	Fruit	—	—	1	—	12	—	—	—	—	1	14
Browne, E.	London	1853-1860	Landscape	—	—	6	—	—	—	—	—	—	—	6
Browne, Mrs. E.	Horsham	1871	Still Life	—	—	1	—	—	—	—	—	—	—	1
Browne, Miss E.	Horsham	1877	Flowers	—	—	—	—	1	—	—	—	—	—	1
Browne, E. F.	Cullercoats	1873	Landscape	—	—	1	—	—	—	—	—	—	—	1
Browne, E. H.	London	1831-1843	Architecture	—	—	7	—	1	—	—	—	—	—	8
Browne, Miss Florence Crichton	London	1885-1889	Sculpture	—	—	—	—	3	—	—	1	—	—	4
Browne, Gordon Frederick, R.B.A. §	London	1886-1893	Landscape	—	—	8	—	4	—	13	1	—	2	28
Browne, G. H.	London	1836-1885	Landscape	—	—	11	5	62	—	—	—	—	61	139
Browne, Mrs. H.	London	1830-1841	Miniatures	—	—	9	—	9	—	—	—	—	—	18
Browne, Hamilton	Streatham	1886	Buildings	—	—	—	—	—	—	1	—	—	—	1
Browne, Mrs. Heitland	London	1885-1886	Domestic	—	—	—	—	3	—	—	—	—	—	3
Browne, Mme. Henriette, Hon. R.I. ‡ (Mme. Jules de Saux)	Paris	1867-1879	Domestic	—	—	5	—	—	—	1	—	—	—	6
Browne, Harry E. J.	Hethersett	1889-1893	Figures	—	—	1	—	1	—	—	—	—	2	4
Browne, Hablot Knight ("Phiz")	London	1834-1875	Comic	—	—	3	14	10	—	4	—	—	9	40
Browne, J.	Richmond	1816-1826	Rustic	—	—	4	—	—	—	—	—	—	—	4
Browne, John, A.R.A.	London	1767-1801	Engraving	2	—	13	—	—	—	—	—	—	—	15
Browne, J. B.	London	1861-1863	Game	—	—	1	—	1	—	—	—	—	—	2
Browne, J. Lennox	London	1868-1887	Landscape	—	—	—	—	17	—	4	—	—	6	27
Browne, James Loxham	Hethersett	1891-1893	Landscape	—	—	—	—	2	—	1	—	—	—	3
Browne, Philip	Shrewsbury	1824-1865	Fruit, &c.	—	—	70	—	13	—	—	—	—	—	83
Browne, Robert	—	1778-1798	Architecture	—	—	12	—	—	—	—	—	—	—	12
Browne, Rupert M.	Thornton Heath	1880	Landscape	—	—	—	—	—	—	—	—	—	1	1
Browne, Robert Palmer	Greenwich	1835-1871	Architecture	—	—	6	—	—	—	—	—	—	—	6
Browne, T. D. H.	London	1861-1867	Scriptural	—	—	2	6	3	—	—	—	—	—	11
Browne, Walter	London	1866	Domestic	—	—	—	—	1	—	—	—	—	—	1
Browne, William	London	1799-1801	Gems	—	—	2	—	—	—	—	—	—	—	2
Browning, E.	London	1867-1871	Portraits	—	—	3	—	—	—	—	—	—	—	3
Browning, George	London	1826-1858	Figures	—	—	8	11	5	—	—	—	—	4	28
Browning, G., Junr.	London	1848	Sea Coasts	—	—	—	—	—	—	—	—	—	1	1

Name.	Town.	First and Last Year of Ex.	Speciality.	S. A.	F. S.	R. A.	B. I.	S. S.	O. W.	N. W.	G. G.	N. G.	V. E.	Total.
Browning, G. F.	London	1854-1873	Portraits	—	—	9	—	—	—	—	—	—	—	9
Browning, G. W.	London	1827-1830	Architecture	—	—	3	—	1	—	—	—	—	—	4
Browning, Mrs. John. *See* Miss H. A. E. Jackson	—	1825-1834	Historical	—	—	6	7	—	—	—	—	—	—	13
Browning, L.	London	1811-1815	Architecture	—	—	5	—	—	—	—	—	—	—	5
Browning, Robert Barrett	London	1878-1889	Domestic	—	—	11	—	—	—	—	15	—	—	26
Brownlow, Charles V.	Tottenham	1892	Landscape	—	—	1	—	—	—	—	—	—	—	1
Brownlow, Miss Emma	London	1852-1869	Domestic	—	—	17	23	28	—	—	—	—	1	69
Brownlow, G. Washington	London	1858-1875	Domestic	—	—	8	13	23	—	—	—	—	—	44
Brownsword, Harry A.	Nottingham	1889-1892	Landscape	—	—	3	—	5	—	—	—	—	—	8
Bruce, Blair	Barbizon	1883-1885	Figures	—	—	2	—	—	—	—	—	—	—	2
Bruce, Mrs. Carmichael	London	1883	Flowers	—	—	—	—	2	—	—	—	—	—	2
Bruce, Miss Helen or Eleanor	London	1883	Flowers	—	—	—	—	—	—	3	4	—	—	7
Bruce, Miss Harriet C.	Edinburgh	1882-1891	Landscape	—	—	1	—	4	—	3	—	—	1	9
Bruce, Martin B.	London	1893	Landscape	—	—	—	—	2	—	—	—	—	—	2
Bruck-Lajos L.	London	1889-1891	Domestic	—	—	2	—	—	—	—	—	—	—	2
Bruggemann, Hans	London	1880	Landscape	—	—	1	—	—	—	—	—	—	—	1
Brühl, Burleigh L.	Ranford	1889-1893	Landscape	—	—	1	—	9	—	—	—	—	—	10
Brun, Alexandre	Paris	1881-1882	Figures	—	—	1	—	—	—	—	1	—	—	2
Brun, S. J.	—	1837	Sculpture	—	—	1	—	—	—	—	—	—	—	1
Brunais, Augustin	London	1763-1777	Landscape	2	2	1	—	—	—	—	—	—	—	5
Brunais, Austin	London	1779	Landscape	—	—	2	—	—	—	—	—	—	—	2
Brune, G. R. Prideaux	—	1878-1879	Sea Pieces	—	—	—	—	2	—	—	—	—	—	2
Brune, Miss Gertrude R. Prideaux-. *See* P.	—	—	—	—	—	—	—	—	—	—	—	—	—	—
Brunel, Isambard Kingdom	—	1837	Architecture	—	—	1	—	—	—	—	—	—	—	1
Brunet-Debaines, Alfred	London	1872-1886	Etchings	—	—	6	—	—	—	—	—	—	11	17
Brunner, H.	London	1861	Landscape	—	—	1	—	—	—	—	—	—	—	1
Brunner, H. or K. Lacoste	London	1858-1860	Trees	—	—	1	1	—	—	—	—	—	—	2
Brunning, William Allen §	London	1840-1850	Landscape	—	—	19	8	27	—	—	—	—	—	54
Brunton, E.	London	1857	Game	—	—	—	—	1	—	—	—	—	—	1
Brussell, J. G.	London	1784	Landscape	—	—	1	—	—	—	—	—	—	—	1
Brutey, Robert S.	Teignmouth	1888-1893	Landscape	—	—	2	—	—	—	—	—	—	—	2
Bruton, E. G.	Oxford	1853	Architecture	—	—	1	—	—	—	—	—	—	—	1
Bruyn, De. *See* D.	—	—	—	—	—	—	—	—	—	—	—	—	—	—
Bruzzi, Stefano J.	Florence	1879-1883	Landscape	—	—	3	—	—	—	—	—	—	2	5
Bryan, H.	London	1856	Landscape	—	—	—	1	—	—	—	—	—	—	1
Bryan, John	London	1786-1791	Sea Pieces	3	—	4	—	—	—	—	—	—	—	7
Bryans, H. W.	London	1891	Cairo	—	—	—	—	1	—	—	—	—	—	1
Bryant, H. C.	London	1860-1880	Landscape	—	—	1	2	35	—	—	—	—	—	38
Bryant, J.	London	1798-1809	Landscape	—	—	23	3	—	—	—	—	—	—	26
Bryant, W. N.	—	1843	Architecture	—	—	1	—	—	—	—	—	—	—	1
Brydall, Robert	Glasgow	1874	Landscape	—	—	—	—	2	—	—	—	—	—	2
Brydges, Mrs.	—	1807	Portraits	—	—	1	—	—	—	—	—	—	—	1
Brydon, John McK. *See also* Cubitt & Brydon	London	1869-1893	Architecture	—	—	27	—	—	—	—	—	—	—	27
Bryer, Henry	London	1765-1774	Engraving	3	—	—	—	—	—	—	—	—	—	3
Bryer, S.	London	1828	Portraits	—	—	1	—	—	—	—	—	—	—	1
Brymner, William	London	1884	Birds	—	—	—	—	—	—	—	—	—	1	1
Bryson, Robert M.	London	1863-1876	Landscape	—	—	1	—	10	—	—	—	—	4	15
Bryson, W.	London	1845	Architecture	—	—	1	—	—	—	—	—	—	—	1
Bubb, J. G.	London	1805-1831	Sculpture	—	—	10	—	1	—	—	—	—	—	11
Bucciarelli, Daniel	London	1874-1888	Figures	—	—	—	—	2	—	1	—	—	3	6
Buchanan, George F.	London	1848-1864	Landscape	—	—	27	17	8	—	—	—	—	—	52
Buchanan, Mrs. G. F.	London	1865	Landscape	—	—	1	—	—	—	—	—	—	—	1
Buchanan, James	Liverpool	1848	Figures	—	—	1	—	—	—	—	—	—	—	1
Buchanan, J.	London	1874-1876	Figures	—	—	1	—	3	—	—	—	—	—	4
Buchanan, J. A.	Glasgow	1851-1855	Landscape	—	—	—	5	3	—	—	—	—	—	8
Buchanan, J. P.	Malvern	1890-1891	Domestic	—	—	—	—	1	—	—	—	1	—	2
Buchanan, Mrs. Percy	—	1893	Landscape	—	—	—	—	—	—	—	—	1	—	1
Buchanan, Peter	Putney	1887-1888	Landscape	—	—	2	—	—	—	—	—	—	—	2
Büchel, Eduard	Dresden	1892	Etching	—	—	1	—	—	—	—	—	—	—	1
Buchser, E.	Scarborough	1854	Portraits	—	—	—	—	1	—	—	—	—	—	1
Buchser, Frank	Scarborough	1877	Figures	—	—	—	—	—	—	—	3	—	—	3
Buck, Adam	London	1795-1833	Portraits	—	—	172	6	8	—	1	—	—	—	187
Buck, John	London	1817-1833	Scriptural	—	—	3	3	—	—	—	—	—	—	6
Buck, Miss L. Margaret	Ipswich	1892-1893	Domestic	—	—	—	—	—	—	—	—	—	2	2
Buck, Samuel	London	1761-1775	Landscape	1	6	2	—	—	—	—	—	—	—	9
Buck, Sidney	London	1839-1849	Domestic	—	—	7	—	5	—	—	—	—	—	12
Buck, Miss T.	London	1821	Landscape	—	—	1	—	—	—	—	—	—	—	1
Buck, W.	London	1864	Still Life	—	—	—	—	1	—	—	—	—	—	1
Buck, Miss	London	1789	Landscape	—	—	1	—	—	—	—	—	—	—	1
Buckeridge, Charles E.	London	1882-1883	Landscape	—	—	1	—	1	—	—	—	—	—	2
Buckingham, Miss Ethel	Bushey	1893	Domestic	—	—	1	—	—	—	—	—	—	—	1
Buckle, S.	Peterborough	1849	Landscape	—	—	—	—	—	—	—	—	—	4	4

Name.	Town.	First and Last Year of Ex.	Speciality.	S. A.	F. S.	R. A.	B. I.	S. S.	O. W.	N.W.	G. G.	N. G.	V. E.	Total.
Buckler, C.	London	1841-1842	Churches	—	—	2	—	—	—	—	—	—	—	2
Buckler, E. H.	London	1879	Churches	—	—	—	—	—	—	—	—	—	1	1
Buckler, G.	London	1835-1853	Architecture	—	—	11	—	—	—	—	—	—	—	11
Buckler, John, F.S.A.	London	1796-1849	Cathedrals, etc.	—	—	143	—	—	—	—	—	—	—	143
Buckler, John Chessel	London	1810-1844	Landscape	—	—	39	—	2	15	—	—	—	—	56
Buckler, W.	London	1836-1856	Miniatures	—	—	62	2	—	—	—	—	—	—	64
Buckley, Arthur	Hampton Wick	1878-1881	Landscape	—	—	—	—	—	—	—	—	—	3	3
Buckley, C. F.	London	1841-1869	Landscape	—	—	—	2	31	—	—	—	—	—	33
Buckley, J.	London	1803	Landscape	—	—	2	—	—	—	—	—	—	—	2
Buckley, J. E.	London	1843-1861	Historical	—	—	—	—	9	—	—	—	—	—	9
Buckley, R. E.	London	1877	Landscape	—	—	—	—	1	—	—	—	—	—	1
Buckley, W.	London	1840-1845	Landscape	—	—	—	—	15	—	—	—	—	—	15
Buckman, Charles	Witley	1875	Landscape	—	—	—	—	—	—	—	—	—	1	1
Buckman, Edwin, A.R.W.S. †	London	1866-1893	Domestic	—	—	12	—	2	74	—	—	—	13	101
Buckman, Percy W. I.	London	1886-1893	Domestic	—	—	—	—	2	—	8	—	—	1	11
Buckmaster, Martin A.	London	1890-1893	Landscape	—	—	—	—	2	—	1	—	—	—	3
Bucknall, A. H.	London	1887	Domestic	—	—	—	—	—	—	—	—	—	1	1
Bucknall, Ernest P.	Reigate	1885-1893	Landscape	—	—	14	—	2	—	12	2	—	3	33
Bucknall, William	London	1885-1887	Architecture	—	—	3	—	—	—	—	—	—	—	3
Bucknall, (W.) and Comber (J. N.)	London	1889	Architecture	—	—	2	—	—	—	—	—	—	—	2
Buckner, Richard	Chichester	1840-1879	Portraits	—	—	77	32	44	—	—	3	—	1	157
Buckstone, Frederick	London	1857-1874	Landscape	—	—	1	3	18	—	—	—	—	—	22
Budd, H.	London	1819-1820	Architecture	—	—	2	—	—	—	—	—	—	—	2
Budd, Rev. R.	—	1800	Buildings	—	—	1	—	—	—	—	—	—	—	1
Budgen, Captain	—	1835	Figures	—	—	—	—	1	—	—	—	—	—	1
Budgett, Miss S. E.	Guildford	1883-1884	Flowers	—	—	—	—	—	—	—	—	—	3	3
Buhl, John	—	1772	Copies	—	1	—	—	—	—	—	—	—	—	1
Buhler, E.	London	1889	Mountains	—	—	1	—	—	—	—	—	—	—	1
Buhot, Felix	Paris	1878-1880	Etchings	—	—	—	—	—	—	—	—	—	26	26
Bührer, Conrad	London	1882-1893	Sculpture	—	—	1	—	—	—	—	—	1	—	2
Bukovac, B.	London	1890	Flowers	—	—	1	—	—	—	—	—	—	—	1
Bulewski, L.	London	1855-1860	Portraits	—	—	2	—	—	—	—	—	—	—	2
Bulgin, C. F.	—	1855	Sea Pieces	—	—	—	—	1	—	—	—	—	—	1
Bulkeley, C. F.	London	1833	Domestic	—	—	—	—	—	—	1	—	—	—	1
Bulkeley, J.	London	1825	Landscape	—	—	—	1	—	—	—	—	—	—	1
Bulkeley, W.	London	1827-1828	Scriptural	—	—	—	—	6	—	—	—	—	—	6
Bull, Miss Nora	Richmond	1885-1893	Portraits	—	—	5	—	—	—	—	—	—	—	5
Bull, R.	London	1794-1809	Miniatures	—	—	68	—	—	—	—	—	—	—	68
Bull, S.	London	1832	Engraving	—	—	—	—	1	—	—	—	—	—	1
Bull, S. T.	London	1809-1810	Architecture	—	—	2	—	—	—	—	—	—	—	2
Bull, William Cater	Streatham	1893	Landscape	—	—	—	—	1	—	—	—	—	—	1
Bullar, G. F.	London	1803-1808	Architecture	—	—	6	—	—	—	—	—	—	—	6
Bullar, Miss Mary	Southampton	1872	Buildings	—	—	—	—	1	—	—	—	—	—	1
Bulleid, George Lawrence, A.R.W.S. †	London	1884-1893	Mythological	—	—	3	—	—	19	3	—	—	2	27
Bullen, Miss Elizabeth	London	1873-1880	Landscape	—	—	—	—	9	—	—	—	—	—	9
Bulley, Ashburnham H.	London	1841-1851	Still Life	—	—	3	13	7	—	—	—	—	—	23
Bulley, Miss Georgina E.	London	1880-1893	Sculpture	—	—	9	—	—	—	1	—	1	—	11
Bullock, Edith	Manchester	1889-1891	Landscape	—	—	—	—	3	—	—	—	—	2	5
Bullock, E. E.	London	1848	Still Life	—	—	—	2	—	—	—	—	—	—	2
Bullock, G.	Liverpool	1804-1816	Sculpture	—	—	18	—	—	—	—	—	—	—	18
Bullock, G. G.	London	1827-1859	Still Life	—	—	54	37	24	—	—	—	—	10	125
Bullpit, H.	Leyton	1842-1843	Landscape	—	—	—	—	4	—	—	—	—	—	4
Bulmer. *See* Perkin and Bulmer	—	—	Architecture	—	—	—	—	—	—	—	—	—	—	—
Bumford, E.	London	1803	Sketch	—	—	1	—	—	—	—	—	—	—	1
Bunbury, Henry William	Mildenhall	1780-1808	Caricatures	—	—	20	—	—	—	—	—	—	—	20
Bunbury, T. H.	London	1881	Landscape	—	—	—	—	—	—	—	—	—	1	1
Bunce, Miss Kate E.	Birmingham	1880-1891	Domestic	—	—	3	—	—	—	—	—	—	1	4
Bunce, Miss Maria L. (?) Myra	Birmingham	1878-1893	Landscape	—	—	2	—	—	—	1	—	—	1	4
Bunce, S.	London	1786-1797	Architecture	—	—	11	—	—	—	—	—	—	—	11
Bunck, James H.	London	1766-1775	Candlelight	—	32	4	—	—	—	—	—	—	—	36
Bundy, Edgar, R.I., R.B.A. § ‡ φ	London	1881-1893	Domestic	—	—	10	—	11	—	8	—	—	13	42
Bundy, Miss Elizabeth E.	London	1851-1858	Rustic Figures	—	—	—	5	3	—	—	—	—	1	9
Bunkell, Miss Alice	London	1885	Domestic	—	—	1	—	—	—	—	—	—	—	1
Bunker, Joseph	Bath	1871-1890	Domestic	—	—	2	—	—	—	3	—	—	1	6
Bunney, John	London	1849-1881	Landscape	—	—	10	—	3	—	—	1	—	—	14
Bunney, John Wharlton	London	1856-1878	Figures	—	—	6	—	9	—	—	—	—	5	20
Bunney, Rupert C. W.	London	1887-1893	Figures	—	—	6	—	4	—	3	—	1	3	17
Bunney, W.	London	1853-1861	Figures	—	—	4	2	1	—	—	—	—	—	7
Bunney, William B.	Bexley	1870-1880	Domestic	—	—	3	—	18	—	—	—	—	1	22
Bunning, James Bunstone	London	1819-1848	Architecture	—	—	15	—	—	—	—	—	—	—	15
Buott, C.	London	1879	Landscape	—	—	—	—	—	—	—	—	—	1	1
Burbank, J., Senr.	London	1821-1849	Landscape	—	—	28	—	11	—	2	—	—	—	41

Name.	Town.	First and Last Year of Ex.	Speciality.	S. A.	F. S.	R. A.	B. I.	S. S.	O. W.	N. W.	G. G.	N. G.	V. E.	Total.
Burbank, J. M. ‡	London	1825-1872	Animals	—	—	12	6	19	—	21	—	—	—	58
Burbank, Miss L.	London	1826-1842	Fruit	—	—	10	—	2	—	2	—	—	—	14
Burbidge, John	London	1862-1880	Landscape	—	—	3	—	6	—	—	—	—	5	14
Burch, Edward, R.A.	London	1771-1808	Gems	—	—	107	—	—	—	—	—	—	—	107
Burch, E., Junr.	London	1790-1804	Gems	—	—	5	—	—	—	—	—	—	—	5
Burch, H.	London	1760-1769	P'rtr'its in Wax	16	—	—	—	—	—	—	—	—	—	16
Burch, H., Junr.	—	1787-1834	P'rtr'its in Wax	3	—	101	—	7	—	—	—	—	—	111
Burcham, R. P.	London	1852-1872	Fruit, etc.	—	—	18	—	12	—	—	—	—	12	42
Burchell, Miss Anna	—	1819	Flowers	—	—	1	—	—	—	—	—	—	—	1
Burchell, W. J.	—	1805-1820	Landscape	—	—	2	—	—	—	—	—	—	—	2
Burchell, Mrs.	—	1800	Flowers	—	—	2	—	—	—	—	—	—	—	2
Burchett, Arthur	London	1874-1885	Domestic	—	—	4	—	4	—	2	—	—	8	18
Burchett, J. P.	S. K. M.	1868	Figures	—	—	—	—	—	—	—	—	—	1	1
Burchett, Richard	London	1847-1873	Historical	—	—	5	1	—	—	—	—	—	3	9
Burden, J.	London	1796-1814	Landscape	—	—	16	14	—	—	—	—	—	7	37
Burder, A. W. N.	London	1872-1878	Architecture	—	—	5	—	—	—	—	—	—	—	5
Burder, W. C.	London	1859	Landscape	—	—	1	—	—	—	—	—	—	—	1
Burdett, Peter Perez	Liverpool	1770-1773	Engraving	6	—	—	—	—	—	—	—	—	—	6
Burdon, Miss. *See* Madame de Schobinger.	—	—	—	—	—	—	—	—	—	—	—	—	—	—
Burfield, James M.	London	1865-1883	Figures	—	—	6	2	6	—	—	—	—	9	23
Burford, John	London	1812-1829	Landscape	—	—	4	—	—	—	—	—	—	—	4
Burford, Robert	London	1812-1818	Landscape	—	—	4	—	—	—	—	—	—	—	4
Burford, R. W.	London	1852	Fruit	—	—	—	1	—	—	—	—	—	—	1
Burford, Thomas	London	1762-1774	Engraving	7	—	—	—	—	—	—	—	—	—	7
Burge, G. H.	London	1855	Landscape	—	—	—	—	1	—	—	—	—	—	1
Burges, William, A.R.A.	London	1860-1880	Architecture	—	—	24	—	—	—	—	—	—	—	24
Burgess —	London	1770-1775	Portraits	4	18	—	—	—	—	—	—	—	—	22
Burgess, A.	London	1866-1867	Engraving	—	—	3	—	—	—	—	—	—	—	3
Burgess, Miss Adelaide	Leamington	1857-1872	Domestic	—	—	11	—	—	—	—	—	—	—	11
Burgess, Arthur	London	1883-1884	Domestic	—	—	—	—	3	—	—	—	—	2	5
Burgess, Edward	London	1880-1888	Architecture	—	—	7	—	—	—	—	—	—	—	7
Burgess, Miss Emma	Wigston	1873-1882	Landscape	—	—	—	—	—	—	—	—	—	7	7
Burgess, Miss Florence	London	1885-1890	Domestic	—	—	3	—	1	—	2	—	—	—	6
Burgess, Frederick	London	1882-1892	Landscape	—	—	1	—	9	—	3	—	1	—	14
Burgess, F. L.	London	1778	Sporting	—	—	1	—	—	—	—	—	—	—	1
Burgess, G. H.	London	1871	Portraits	—	—	—	—	1	—	—	—	—	—	1
Burgess, Miss H.	London	1857-1865	Domestic	—	—	—	—	4	—	—	—	—	—	4
Burgess, H. H.	London	1843-1844	Landscape	—	—	—	—	3	—	—	—	—	—	3
Burgess, H. W.	London	1809-1844	Landscape	—	—	33	20	24	—	12	—	—	4	93
Burgess, J. (?) Thomas	London	1803-1811	Flowers	—	—	12	—	—	—	—	—	—	—	12
Burgess, John ‡	London	1816-1840	Portraits	—	—	25	3	8	2	9	—	—	—	47
Burgess, John, Junr. †	London	1834-1879	Landscape	—	—	4	—	2	263	—	—	—	6	275
Burgess, Miss Jane Amelia	London	1843-1848	Flowers	—	—	2	—	3	—	—	—	—	—	5
Burgess, John Bagnold, R.A.	London	1850-1893	Figures	—	—	66	15	4	—	—	—	—	33	118
Burgess, John Cart	London	1812-1837	Landscape	—	—	31	11	15	—	—	—	—	—	57
Burgess, Thomas	London	1778-1791	Historical	—	—	15	—	—	—	—	—	—	—	15
Burgess, Thomas	London	1802-1807	Landscape	—	—	12	—	—	—	—	—	—	—	12
Burgess, William	London	1762-1811	Portraits	24	16	49	—	—	—	—	—	—	—	89
Burgess, William	Dover	1838-1856	Landscape	—	—	2	—	9	—	—	—	—	—	11
Burgess, Walter William, R.P.E.	London	1874-1892	Etchings	—	—	20	—	—	—	—	—	—	4	24
Burgherst, Priscilla Anne, Lady. *See* Countess of Westmorland	—	1833-1841	Figures	—	—	—	6	—	—	—	—	—	—	6
Burke —	Bath	1772-1781	Portraits	1	—	2	—	—	—	—	—	—	—	3
Burke, Augustus, R.H.A.	Dublin	1863-1891	Landscape	—	—	12	—	1	—	—	—	—	13	26
Burke, Harold Arthur	London	1890-1891	Portraits	—	—	2	—	2	—	—	—	—	—	4
Burkett (J. R. E.) & Langham (J.)	Manchester	1891	Architecture	—	—	1	—	—	—	—	—	—	—	1
Burkett, Thomas	—	1776	Paper Work	1	—	—	—	—	—	—	—	—	—	1
Burkinshaw, Samuel	Liverpool	1865	Domestic	—	—	1	—	—	—	—	—	—	—	1
Burkly, Z.	—	1852	Portraits	—	—	—	—	1	—	—	—	—	—	1
Burlison, Clement	Durham	1846-1863	Landscape	—	—	10	15	—	—	—	—	—	—	25
Burlison, J.	London	1846	Landscape	—	—	2	—	—	—	—	—	—	—	2
Burlowe, Henry Behnes	London	1831-1833	Sculpture	—	—	12	—	2	—	—	—	—	—	14
Burman, John	Sutton	1886	Domestic	—	—	2	—	—	—	—	—	—	—	2
Burmester. *See* Beeston & Burmester	—	—	Architecture	—	—	—	—	—	—	—	—	—	—	—
Burn, George Adam	London	1835-1859	Architecture	—	—	4	—	—	—	—	—	—	—	4
Burn, Gerald M.	London	1881-1888	Shipping	—	—	3	—	4	—	—	—	—	1	8
Burn, H.	London	1830	Landscape	—	—	2	—	—	—	—	—	—	—	2
Burn, T. F.	London	1861-1867	Landscape	—	—	—	2	1	—	—	—	—	—	3
Burn-Murdoch, W. G. *See* M.	—	—	—											
Burnard, Arthur	London	1893	Portraits	—	—	1	—	—	—	—	—	—	—	1
Burnard, George	London	1858-1884	Figures	—	—	6	1	—	—	—	—	—	—	7
Burnard, Neville Northy	London	1848-1873	Sculpture	—	—	18	—	—	—	—	—	—	—	18
Burnard, Thomas	London	1868-1886	Sculpture	—	—	4	—	—	—	—	—	—	—	4

Name.	Town.	First and Last Year of Ex.	Speciality.	S. A.	F. S.	R. A.	B. I.	S. S.	O. W.	N.W.	G. G.	N. G.	V. E.	Total.
Burne-Jones, Sir Edward Coley, Bart., A.R.A., R.W.S., H.R.C.A. †	London	1872-1893	Mythological	—	—	1	—	—	112	—	123	98	12	346
Burne-Jones, Philip	London	1886-1893	Domestic	—	—	—	—	—	—	—	2	35	6	43
Burnell, Benjamin	London	1790-1828	Scriptural	—	—	105	18	—	—	—	—	—	—	123
Burnell, Henry Hockey	—	1845-1847	Architecture	—	—	6	—	—	—	—	—	—	—	6
Burnell, T.	London	1802-1806	Architecture	—	—	4	—	—	—	—	—	—	—	4
Burnet, James M.	Edinburgh	1783-1817	Cattle	—	1	6	24	—	—	—	—	—	—	31
Burnet, John, F.R.S.	London	1808-1862	Figures	—	—	4	30	6	—	—	—	—	—	40
Burnett, G. R.	London	1873-1887	Portraits	—	—	—	—	—	—	—	1	—	1	2
Burnett, John J.	Glasgow	1882-1885	Architecture	—	—	2	—	—	—	—	—	—	—	2
Burnett, Thomas Stuart, A.R.S.A.	Glasgow	1885-1887	Sculpture	—	—	6	—	—	—	—	—	—	—	6
Burnett, William H.	London	1844-1860	Landscape	—	—	2	10	—	—	—	—	—	12	24
Burnett, Son, and Campbell	Glasgow	1887-1893	Architecture	—	—	6	—	—	—	—	—	—	—	6
Burnett-Stuart, A. T. *See* S.	—	—	—	—	—	—	—	—	—	—	—	—	—	—
Burney, Edward Francis	London	1781-1803	Portraits	—	—	19	—	—	—	—	—	—	—	19
Burney, T. F.	London	1785	Portraits	—	—	1	—	—	—	—	—	—	—	1
Burnier, Richard	Düsseldorf	1880	Rustic	—	—	1	—	—	—	—	—	—	—	1
Burns, Balfour	Streatham	1884-1890	Landscape	—	—	6	—	—	—	—	—	—	—	6
Burns, Cecil Leonard	Bushey	1880-1892	Portraits	—	—	8	—	4	—	—	—	—	—	12
Burns, Clarence Laurence	Tooting	1885-1889	Domestic	—	—	1	—	—	—	—	—	—	8	9
Burnside, Miss H.	Bromley	1859	Fruit	—	—	1	—	—	—	—	—	—	—	1
Burnsie, A.	—	1796-1798	Landscape	—	—	2	—	—	—	—	—	—	—	2
Burr, Alexander Hohenlohe φ	London	1860-1893	Domestic	—	—	16	1	9	—	—	1	—	11	38
Burr, John, R.B.A., A.R.W.S. § †	London	1862-1892	Domestic	—	—	18	1	35	18	—	3	—	27	102
Burrell, J.	London	1817-1845	Architecture	—	—	6	—	—	—	—	—	—	—	6
Burrell, J.	London	1859-1865	Sea Pieces	—	—	1	—	4	—	—	—	—	—	5
Burrell, J. E.	London	1869-1870	Churches	—	—	—	—	2	—	—	—	—	—	2
Burrell, J. F.	London	1801-1854	Landscape	—	—	16	—	—	—	—	—	—	—	16
Burrington, Arthur A.	Wellington	1880-1893	Domestic	—	—	4	—	7	—	2	—	—	7	20
Burroughs, A. Leicester	London	1881-1892	Figures	—	—	5	—	3	—	1	—	—	3	12
Burroughs, Mrs. *See* Frances B. Warren.	—	—	—	—	—	—	—	—	—	—	—	—	—	—
Burrow, Harry John	London	1868-1876	Scriptural, etc.	—	—	10	—	—	—	—	—	—	—	10
Burrow, J.	—	1800	Portraits	—	—	1	—	—	—	—	—	—	—	1
Burrows, H.	London	1835	Landscape	—	—	—	—	1	—	—	—	—	—	1
Burrows, R.	Ipswich	1851-1855	Landscape	—	—	2	1	—	—	—	—	—	—	3
Burrows, Miss	London	1811	Portraits	—	—	—	1	—	—	—	—	—	—	1
Bursill, H.	London	1855-1870	Sculpture	—	—	19	—	—	—	—	—	—	—	19
Burt, A. R.	London	1807	Churches	—	—	1	—	—	—	—	—	—	—	1
Burt, Albin R.	London	1830	Historical	—	—	1	—	1	—	—	—	—	—	2
Burt, Charles Thomas	Birmingham	1846-1892	Landscape	—	—	18	6	6	—	—	1	—	12	43
Burt, H. A. B.	Wokingham	1878-1880	Flowers	—	—	—	—	—	—	—	—	—	3	3
Burt, Miss Maria E., afterwards Mrs. Simpson	London	1872-1880	Miniatures	—	—	21	—	—	—	—	—	—	—	21
Burton, A.	London	1827-1831	Architecture	—	—	3	—	—	—	—	—	—	—	3
Burton, A. F.	London	1874	Domestic	—	—	—	—	1	—	—	—	—	—	1
Burton, C.	London	1800-1802	Churches	—	—	3	—	—	—	—	—	—	—	3
Burton, C.	London	1845-1846	Architecture	—	—	3	—	—	—	—	—	—	—	3
Burton, Decimus, F.R.S.	London	1817-1838	Architecture	—	—	28	—	—	—	—	—	—	—	28
Burton, Edward	Edinburgh	1865	Engraving	—	—	1	—	—	—	—	—	—	—	1
Burton, Sir Frederick William, R.H.A., F.S.A., LL.D., H.R.W.S. †	London	1842-1882	Historical	—	—	8	—	—	68	—	2	—	7	85
Burton, F. W.	London	1855-1858	Landscape	—	—	—	—	3	—	—	—	—	—	3
Burton, Henry	London	1883-1884	Landscape	—	—	—	—	—	—	2	—	—	—	2
Burton, Henry Marley	London	1867	Architecture	—	—	1	—	—	—	—	—	—	—	1
Burton, J.	London	1855-1858	Portraits	—	—	2	—	—	—	—	—	—	—	2
Burton, James	London	1800-1830	Landscape	—	—	6	11	—	—	—	—	—	—	17
Burton, John, F.S.A.	London	1769-1784	Sea Pieces	25	—	4	—	—	—	—	—	—	—	29
Burton, J.	London	1826-1844	Landscape	—	—	—	14	4	—	—	—	—	—	18
Burton, Miss M. R. Hill	Edinburgh	1891-1893	Landscape	—	—	1	—	3	—	—	—	1	2	7
Burton, R.	Dorking	1859	Landscape	—	—	1	—	—	—	—	—	—	—	1
Burton, T.	London	1842-1843	Figures	—	—	—	2	3	—	—	—	—	—	5
Burton, T.	London	1838-1847	Portraits	—	—	6	—	1	—	—	—	—	—	7
Burton, William	London	1827-1831	Buildings	—	—	3	1	3	—	—	—	—	—	7
Burton, William	Barnes	1887	Domestic	—	—	2	—	—	—	—	—	—	—	2
Burton, W. Bowness-. *See* Bowness.	—	—	—	—	—	—	—	—	—	—	—	—	—	—
Burton, W. K.	London	1803-1804	Portraits	—	—	2	—	—	—	—	—	—	—	2
Burton, William P. §	Witley	1862-1883	Landscape	—	—	23	—	18	—	1	3	—	50	95
Burton, William Shakespere	London	1846-1876	Mythological	—	—	17	1	—	—	—	—	—	1	19
Burton, Mrs.	London	1874-1875	Landscape	—	—	—	—	—	—	—	—	—	3	3
Burton, Mrs.	Birkenhead	1890	Buildings	—	—	—	—	—	—	1	—	—	—	1
Burton, Master	—	1780	Landscape	1	—	—	—	—	—	—	—	—	—	1
Burton, Miss	—	1773-1778	Fruit	5	—	—	—	—	—	—	—	—	—	5
Bury, Viscount	—	1878	Nuremberg	—	—	—	—	—	—	—	—	—	1	1

Name.	Town.	First and Last Year of Ex.	Speciality.	S. A.	F. S.	R. A.	B. I.	S. S.	O. W.	N.W.	G. G.	N. G.	V. E.	Total.
Bury, Thomas Talbot	London	1838-1872	Architecture	—	—	18	—	—	—	—	—	—	—	18
Busby, Charles A.	London	1801-1830	Architecture	—	—	22	—	—	—	—	—	—	—	22
Busby, T. L.	London	1804-1837	Portraits	—	—	15	—	2	—	—	—	—	—	17
Busby and Wilds. *See* Wilds and Busby	Brighton	1825	Architecture	—	—	1	—	—	—	—	—	—	—	1
Busch, Mrs. H. M.	London	1892	Landscape	—	—	—	—	—	—	1	—	—	—	1
Bush, Van der. *See* V.	—	—	—	—	—	—	—	—	—	—	—	—	—	—
Bushman, J.	—	1820	Portraits	—	—	1	—	—	—	—	—	—	—	1
Busk, Miss E. M.	London	1873-1889	Portraits	—	—	13	—	—	—	—	—	—	—	13
Busk, William	Dorchester	1889-1892	Figures	—	—	2	—	—	—	—	—	—	—	2
Buss, Robert William ‡	London	1826-1859	Domestic	—	—	25	20	45	—	7	—	—	15	112
Buss, Rev. Septimus	London	1854-1859	Landscape	—	—	2	3	2	—	—	—	—	2	9
Busse, George	—	1854	Landscape	—	—	1	—	—	—	—	—	—	—	1
Busson, M.	Paris	1878	Landscape	—	—	—	—	—	—	—	—	—	1	1
Butin, U.	Paris	1881	Figures	—	—	—	—	—	—	—	2	—	—	2
Butland, G. W.	London	1831-1843	Sea Pieces	—	—	6	17	14	—	—	—	—	—	37
Butler. *See* Heaton, Butler, and Bayne,	—	—	—	—	—	—	—	—	—	—	—	—	—	—
and Mitchell and Butler	—	—	Architecture	—	—	—	—	—	—	—	—	—	—	—
Butler, Lady. *See* Miss Elizabeth Thompson	—	—	—	—	—	—	—	—	—	—	—	—	—	—
and Mrs. Butler	Cairo	1887-1893	Military	—	—	5	—	—	—	—	—	—	—	5
Butler, Miss Clehorow Caroline	London	1881-1883	Sculpture	—	—	3	—	—	—	—	—	—	—	3
Butler, Charles E.	London	1889-1893	Portraits	—	—	7	—	—	—	—	—	—	—	7
Butler, E. F.	Ramsgate	1856	Sea Pieces	—	—	—	—	2	—	—	—	—	—	2
Butler, F.	London	1871	Architecture	—	—	1	—	—	—	—	—	—	—	1
Butler, F. A.	London	1871	Architecture	—	—	1	—	—	—	—	—	—	—	1
Butler, Herbert E.	London	1881-1888	Sea Pieces	—	—	3	—	3	—	—	—	—	5	11
Butler, James	London	1763	Landscape	—	3	—	—	—	—	—	—	—	—	3
Butler, J. P. R.	London	1842	Architecture	—	—	1	—	—	—	—	—	—	—	1
Butler, (J. P. R) and Hodge (H.)	London	1848	Architecture	—	—	1	—	—	—	—	—	—	—	1
Butler, Miss Mildred A. ‖	Kilmurry	1888-1893	Landscape	—	—	7	—	2	—	12	1	6	—	28
Butler, Miss Mary E.	London	1867-1893	Flowers	—	—	12	—	1	—	17	—	—	14	44
Butler, Richard	Sevenoaks	1862-1886	Landscape	—	—	32	—	—	—	—	—	—	—	32
Butler, Samuel	London	1869-1875	Figures	—	—	6	—	—	—	—	—	—	5	11
Butler, Miss S. A.	Tetbury	1890	Figures	—	—	2	—	—	—	—	—	—	—	2
Butler, Mrs. Thomas (Nina H)	London	1884	Flowers	—	—	—	—	1	—	—	—	—	—	1
Butler, Timothy	London	1828-1879	Sculpture	—	—	106	—	—	—	—	—	—	—	106
Butler, T. W. G.	London	1874	Figures	—	—	1	—	2	—	—	—	—	—	3
Butler, William Deane	Dublin	1847	Architecture	—	—	1	—	—	—	—	—	—	—	1
Butler, Mrs. *See* Miss Elizabeth Thompson	—	—	—	—	—	—	—	—	—	—	—	—	—	—
and Lady Butler	London	1879-1885	Military	—	—	5	—	—	—	—	—	—	—	5
Butlin, W.	London	1828-1834	Sculpture	—	—	10	—	4	—	—	—	—	—	14
Butson, Miss Nora	Henley	1891-1892	Portraits	—	—	1	—	—	—	—	—	—	1	2
Butt, J. Acton	Birmingham	1884-1886	Landscape	—	—	—	—	—	—	—	—	—	3	3
Buttersworth, Thomas	London	1813-1827	Sea Pieces	—	—	1	1	1	—	—	—	—	—	3
Butterton, J.	London	1847	Heads	—	—	1	—	—	—	—	—	—	—	1
Butterton, Mary	London	1889	Landscape	—	—	—	—	1	—	—	—	—	—	1
Butterworth, Charles	London	1887-1888	Engraving	—	—	2	—	—	—	—	—	—	—	2
Butterworth, George	Thornt'n Heath	1865-1881	Landscape	—	—	1	—	6	—	—	1	—	15	23
Butterworth, J.	London	1839-1854	Historical	—	—	—	4	7	—	—	—	—	—	11
Buttery, T. C.	London	1825-1829	Portraits	—	—	6	—	—	—	—	—	—	—	6
Buttlar, Mrs.	London	1824	Portraits	—	—	1	—	—	—	—	—	—	—	1
Button, Kate	Clevedon	1881	Flowers	—	—	—	—	1	—	—	—	—	—	1
Butts, Miss Amy. *See* Madame Giampietri ‖	Winchester	1867	Figures	—	—	—	—	—	—	—	—	—	1	1
Buttura, M.	London	1878	Landscape	—	—	—	—	1	—	—	—	—	—	1
Buxton, A.	Jersey	1848	Portraits	—	—	1	—	—	—	—	—	—	—	1
Buxton, A. J.	London	1827-1844	Figures	—	—	—	—	3	—	—	—	—	—	3
Buxton, Miss Amy L.	Wimbledon	1893	Domestic	—	—	—	—	—	—	—	—	—	2	2
Buxton, J.	London	1818	Portraits	—	—	2	—	—	—	—	—	—	—	2
Buxton, R.	—	1804	Portraits	—	—	1	—	—	—	—	—	—	—	1
Buxton, William Graham-	London	1885-1892	Landscape	—	—	1	—	5	—	—	—	—	1	7
Buxton, William J.	London	1891	Landscape	—	—	1	—	—	—	—	—	—	—	1
Buzzanga, G.	London	1888	Figures	—	—	—	—	—	—	—	—	1	—	1
Buzzard, Thomas	London	1866-1881	Etchings	—	—	—	—	—	—	—	—	—	5	5
Buzzi, A.	—	1870	Figures	—	—	—	—	1	—	—	—	—	—	1
Byam, Miss	—	1817	Historical	—	—	1	—	—	—	—	—	—	—	1
Byard, Miss Florence	London	1890-1891	Flowers	—	—	1	—	—	—	—	—	—	1	2
Byard, Frederick	London	1878-1879	Domestic	—	—	—	—	3	—	—	—	—	—	3
Byck —	London	1771-1772	Shell Work	—	3	—	—	—	—	—	—	—	—	3
Byfield, C.	London	1801-1803	Landscape	—	—	3	—	—	—	—	—	—	—	3
Byfield, George	London	1780-1812	Architecture	—	—	34	—	—	—	—	—	—	—	34
Byfield, J.	London	1793-1800	Landscape	—	—	6	—	—	—	—	—	—	—	6
Bygate, Joseph E.	London	1890	Landscape	—	—	—	—	1	—	—	—	—	—	1
Bylandt, De. *See* D.	—	—	—	—	—	—	—	—	—	—	—	—	—	—

Name.	Town.	First and Last Year of Ex.	Speciality.	S. A.	F. S.	R. A.	B. I.	S. S.	O. W.	N. W.	G. G.	N. G.	V. E.	Total.
BYNON, MISS C. S.	London	1832-1833	Landscape	—	—	3	—	2	—	—	—	—	—	5
BYRNE, MISS ANNA FRANCES †	London	1796-1833	Fruit	—	—	6	1	10	60	—	—	—	—	77
BYRNE, C.	London	1800-1808	Portraits	—	—	4	—	—	—	—	—	—	—	4
BYRNE, DANIEL	London	1840-1880	Portraits	—	—	20	—	—	—	—	—	—	—	20
BYRNE, MISS ELIZABETH	London	1838-1849	Landscape	—	—	9	—	2	—	—	—	—	—	11
BYRNE, JOHN †	London	1822-1847	Landscape	—	—	15	5	23	100	—	—	—	—	143
BYRNE, J.	Manchester	1870	Domestic	—	—	—	—	1	—	—	—	—	—	1
BYRNE, MISS LETITIA	London	1799-1848	Landscape	—	—	21	—	—	—	—	—	—	—	21
BYRNE, MISS MARY. *See* MRS. JAMES GREEN	London	1795-1804	Miniatures	—	—	37	—	—	—	—	—	—	—	37
BYRNE, OSCAR	—	1828	Architecture	—	—	—	—	1	—	—	—	—	—	1
BYRNE, WILLIAM, F.S.A.	London	1766-1780	Engraving	17	—	—	—	—	—	—	—	—	—	17
BYRNE, WILLIAM S.	London	1879-1889	Landscape	—	—	5	—	1	—	—	1	—	1	8
BYRON, F. G.	—	1791	Figures	5	—	—	—	—	—	—	—	—	—	5
BYWATER, MISS ELIZABETH	London	1879-1891	Flowers	—	—	22	—	8	—	3	4	—	7	44
BYWATER, MISS KATHARINE D. M. ‖	London	1883-1890	Domestic	—	—	9	—	1	—	—	—	—	—	10
BYWATER, MRS.	London	1851	Domestic	—	—	—	—	1	—	—	—	—	—	1
CABBELL, R.	London	1805	Dramatic	—	—	1	—	—	—	—	—	—	—	1
CABIANCA, VINCENZO	Rome	1875-1890	Landscape	—	—	7	—	—	—	5	1	—	15	28
CADART, A.	Paris	1874	Etching	—	—	—	—	—	—	—	—	—	4	4
CADDICK, W.	Liverpool	1780	Portraits	—	—	1	—	—	—	—	—	—	—	1
CADENHEAD, JAMES, R.S.W.	Aberdeen	1876	Etching	—	—	—	—	—	—	—	—	—	1	1
CADMAN, WILLIAM E.	London	1854-1856	Landscape	—	—	—	—	1	—	—	—	—	2	3
CADOGAN, LADY H. (?) AUGUSTA	London	1869	Landscape	—	—	—	—	3	—	—	—	—	—	3
CADOGAN, SIDNEY RUSSELL	London	1877-1893	Landscape	—	—	11	—	—	—	—	5	9	5	30
CAFE, JAMES W.	London	1877-1893	Churches	—	—	7	—	4	—	9	—	—	1	21
CAFE, THOMAS, JUNR.	London	1844-1868	Landscape	—	—	9	—	22	—	—	—	—	1	32
CAFE, THOMAS S.	London	1816-1840	Sea Pieces	—	—	11	3	8	—	1	—	—	—	23
CAFE, THOMAS WATT	London	1876-1893	Landscape	—	—	18	—	5	—	—	—	—	2	25
CAFFIERI, HECTOR, R.I., R.B.A., ‡ §	Cheltenham	1869-1893	Landscape	—	—	31	—	84	—	45	2	—	41	203
CAFFIN, MISS MAUD C.	Broadway	1888-1889	Sculpture	—	—	—	—	2	—	—	—	—	—	2
CAFFYN, WALTER WALLOR	Dorking	1874-1893	Landscape	—	—	10	—	26	—	—	—	—	6	42
CAHILL, RICHARD S.	London	1853-1889	Figures	—	—	3	4	6	—	2	—	—	2	17
CAHUSAC, J. A., F.R.S., F.S.A. ‡	London	1827-1853	Figures	—	—	19	6	35	—	36	—	—	7	103
CAILLE, LÉON	Paris	1878	Domestic	—	—	—	—	—	—	—	—	—	3	3
CALAME, ALEXANDRE	Geneva	1840	Landscape	—	—	—	3	—	—	—	—	—	—	3
CALCAVELLA, SIGNIOR	—	1783	Seaport	—	1	—	—	—	—	—	—	—	—	1
CALCOTT, J.	Portsmouth	1861-1862	Landscape	—	—	—	—	2	—	—	—	—	—	2
CALCUTT. *See* WOODZELL AND CALCUTT	—	—	Architecture	—	—	—	—	—	—	—	—	—	—	—
CALDECOTT, RANDOLPH, R.I. ‡ φ	London	1872-1885	Illustrations	—	—	4	—	—	—	10	7	—	14	35
CALDERON, ABELARDO ALVAREZ	London	1880-1882	Figures	—	—	1	—	1	—	—	—	—	1	3
CALDERON, CHARLES	London	1886	Sculpture	—	—	1	—	—	—	—	—	—	—	1
CALDERON, PHILIP HERMOGENES, R.A.	London	1853-1893	Figures	—	—	100	6	9	—	—	6	1	12	134
CALDERON, W. FRANK φ	London	1882-1893	Landscape	—	—	18	—	3	—	—	1	—	7	29
CALDWALL, JAMES	London	1768-1780	Engraving	1	29	—	—	—	—	—	—	—	—	30
CALDWELL, EDMUND	London	1880-1893	Animals	—	—	6	—	4	—	11	—	—	10	31
CALKIN, LANCE §	London	1881-1893	Portraits	—	—	18	—	14	—	—	4	4	14	54
CALLANDER, ADAM	London	1780-1811	Landscape	—	—	51	10	—	—	—	—	—	—	61
CALLARD, J. PERCY	London	1882-1889	Landscape	—	—	1	—	3	—	—	1	—	3	8
CALLARD, MISS LOTTIE	London	1883-1892	Domestic	—	—	3	—	2	—	—	—	—	3	8
CALLARD, THOMAS	London	1767-1774	Landscape	6	6	4	—	—	—	—	—	—	—	16
CALLAWAY, WILLIAM FREDERICK	London	1855-1861	Dramatic	—	—	3	1	—	—	—	—	—	5	9
CALLCOTT, A.	London	1856-1864	Landscape	—	—	—	1	7	—	—	—	—	—	8
CALLCOTT, SIR AUGUSTUS WALL, R.A.	London	1799-1844	Landscape	—	—	129	13	—	—	—	—	—	—	142
CALLCOTT, C.	London	1873-1877	Domestic	—	—	3	—	17	—	—	—	—	—	20
CALLCOTT, FREDERICK T.	London	1877-1893	Sculpture	—	—	13	—	10	—	—	—	1	5	29
CALLCOTT, J. STUART	London	1862-1868	Historical	—	—	7	2	—	—	—	—	—	—	9
CALLCOTT, WILLIAM	London	1856-1865	Landscape	—	—	—	3	3	—	—	—	—	1	7
CALLCOTT, WILLIAM J.	London	1843-1890	Sea Pieces	—	—	11	2	17	—	2	—	—	4	36
CALLINGHAM, J.	Surbiton	1873-1879	Sea Pieces	—	—	—	—	3	—	—	—	—	—	3
CALLOW, GEORGE D.	London	1858-1873	Landscape	—	—	2	15	16	—	—	—	—	7	40
CALLOW, JOHN † ‡	London	1844-1878	Sea Pieces	—	—	7	9	2	352	38	—	—	—	408
CALLOW, WILLIAM, R.W.S., F.R.G.S. †	London	1838-1893	Landscape	—	—	29	36	1	1152	—	—	—	3	1221
CALLOW, JAMES W.	London	1860	Landscape	—	—	1	—	—	—	—	—	—	—	1
CALLWELL, MISS ANETTE	London	1880-1887	Figures	—	—	3	—	2	—	—	1	—	3	9
CALOMBO, A.	—	1874	Landscape	—	—	1	—	—	—	—	—	—	—	1
CALOSCI, ARTURO	London	1890	Figures	—	—	—	—	1	—	—	—	—	—	1
CALTHROP, CLAUDE	London	1864-1893	Historical	—	—	43	1	12	—	—	—	—	10	66
CALTHROP, MRS. M. A.	Uppingham	1877-1883	Flowers	—	—	3	—	1	—	—	—	—	—	4
CALVERT —	London	1767-1783	Portraits	6	1	—	—	—	—	—	—	—	—	7

Name.	Town.	First and Last Year of Ex.	Speciality.	S. A.	F. S.	R. A.	B. I.	S. S.	O. W.	N.W.	G. G.	N.G.	V.E.	Total.
Calvert, Charles	Manchester	1825-1837	Landscape	—	—	—	1	1	—	—	—	—	—	2
Calvert, Edward	Claremont	1825-1836	Landscape	—	—	5	—	1	—	—	—	—	—	6
Calvert, Edith L.	London	1893	Domestic	—	—	—	—	2	—	—	—	—	—	2
Calvert, Edwin Sherwood, R.S.W.	Glasgow	1878-1893	Landscape	—	—	14	—	1	—	1	—	5	—	21
Calvert, Frederick	London	1827-1844	Sea Pieces	—	—	—	2	4	—	—	—	—	—	6
Calvert, Henry	Manchester	1826-1854	Sporting	—	—	4	—	—	—	—	—	—	—	4
Calvert, L. Delepierre	London	1877-1890	Sculpture	—	—	2	—	—	—	1	—	—	—	3
Calvi, Pietro	Milan	1872-1883	Sculpture	—	—	6	—	—	—	—	—	—	—	6
Calvin —	Penrith	1773	Birds	—	—	1	—	—	—	—	—	—	—	1
Calza F. (Edward Francis Cunningham, called	—	—	—	—	—	—	—	—	—	—	—	—	—	—
Il Bolognese)	London	1777-1781	Crayons	—	—	6	—	—	—	—	—	—	—	6
Calze, Edward Francis	London	1770-1773	Crayons	—	—	8	—	—	—	—	—	—	—	8
Cambruzzi, De	London	1775-1777	Crayons	—	—	6	—	—	—	—	—	—	—	6
Camden, W.	—	1799	Sea Pieces	—	—	1	—	—	—	—	—	—	—	1
Came, Richard Adolphus	London	1878	Architecture	—	—	3	—	—	—	—	—	—	—	3
Cameron, Mrs. Campbell	London	1879-1882	Landscape	—	—	—	—	—	—	—	2	—	1	3
Cameron, Charles	London	1767-1772	Engraving	3	7	—	—	—	—	—	—	—	—	10
Cameron, Duncan	Stirling	1871-1890	Landscape	—	—	22	—	28	—	—	—	—	—	50
Cameron, Hugh, R.S.A., R.S.W. ϕ	Edinburgh	1871-1892	Domestic	—	—	25	—	1	—	—	9	—	6	41
Cameron, Miss Julia	London	1880-1891	Flowers	—	—	—	—	2	—	1	—	—	—	3
Camigi —	London	1876	Sculpture	—	—	—	—	1	—	—	—	—	—	1
Camm, Thomas W.	Birmingham	1888	Stained Glass	—	—	2	—	—	—	—	—	—	—	2
Cammell, Bernard E.	London	1883-1888	Figures	—	—	5	—	—	—	—	3	—	1	9
Camp, Isabella	Watford	1882	Figures	—	—	—	—	1	—	—	—	—	1	2
Campanella, Miss Catherine	London	1854-1862	Landscape	—	—	2	2	2	—	—	—	—	—	6
Campanile, Signior	London	1829	Churches	—	—	—	3	—	—	—	—	—	—	3
Campbell. *See* Burnett, Son, and Campbell	—	—	Architecture	—	—	—	—	—	—	—	—	—	—	—
Campbell, Archibald	London	1865-1868	Figures	—	—	—	4	4	—	—	—	—	—	8
Campbell, C.	London	1876-1877	Architecture	—	—	3	—	—	—	—	—	—	—	3
Campbell, Lady Colin	London	1886	Landscape	—	—	—	—	1	—	—	—	—	—	1
Campbell, Mrs. Corbett	London	1888	Landscape	—	—	—	—	—	—	—	1	—	—	1
Campbell, Charles William	Sevenoaks	1887	Engraving	—	—	1	—	—	—	—	—	—	—	1
Campbell, D.	London	1857	Sculpture	—	—	1	—	—	—	—	—	—	—	1
Campbell, Duvar	London	1865-1873	Fruit	—	—	1	1	3	—	—	—	—	—	5
Campbell, Hon. Mrs. E.	London	1879	Figures	—	—	—	—	1	—	—	—	—	—	1
Campbell, H.	London	1850	Figures	—	—	—	—	2	—	—	—	—	—	2
Campbell, Mrs. H.	Greenwich	1872	Domestic	—	—	—	—	2	—	—	—	—	—	2
Campbell, Hay	London	1892-1893	Buildings	—	—	—	—	1	—	—	—	—	1	2
Campbell, James	Liverpool	1855-1868	Domestic	—	—	2	—	13	—	—	—	—	1	16
Campbell, J. A. D.	London	1864	Fruit	—	—	—	—	1	—	—	—	—	—	1
Campbell, J. Hodgson	Newcastle	1884-1891	Domestic	—	—	3	—	—	—	3	—	—	—	6
Campbell, Oswald R.	London	1847-1852	Scriptural	—	—	2	—	—	—	—	—	—	24	26
Campbell, Peter	London	1776	Landscape	1	—	—	—	—	—	—	—	—	—	1
Campbell, Samuel	London	1854-1857	Landscape	—	—	1	5	3	—	—	—	—	4	13
Campbell, Thomas	Rome	1827-1857	Sculpture	—	—	38	—	—	—	—	—	—	—	38
Campbell, Captain T. H.	London	1847-1849	Scriptural	—	—	—	1	1	—	—	—	—	3	5
Campbell, W. H.	London	1842-1849	Architecture	—	—	4	—	—	—	—	—	—	—	4
Campbell and Smith	London	1885-1886	Architecture	—	—	3	—	—	—	—	—	—	—	3
Campiani —	London	1789	Figures	—	—	1	—	—	—	—	—	—	—	1
Campion, George B. ‡	London	1829-1869	Landscape	—	—	—	—	10	—	463	—	—	—	473
Campion, Howard T. S.	London	1876-1883	Landscape	—	—	3	—	15	—	—	2	—	5	25
Campion, Mrs. Howard	London	1880	Landscape	—	—	—	—	1	—	—	—	—	—	1
Campion, S. M.	London	1882	River Scenes	—	—	1	—	—	—	—	—	—	—	1
Campione, S.	London	1831-1833	Still Life	—	—	2	6	—	—	—	—	—	—	8
Campling —	London	1770-1774	Architecture	—	14	—	—	—	—	—	—	—	—	14
Campotosto, Henry	London	1871-1878	Domestic	—	—	6	—	1	—	—	—	—	—	7
Campo-Tosto, Mdlle. Octavia	London	1871-1874	Figures	—	—	4	—	—	—	—	—	—	—	4
Campoverde, G.	London	1878	Sculpture	—	—	1	—	—	—	—	—	—	—	1
Camroux, Sydney George	London	1858-1870	Sculpture	—	—	3	—	1	—	—	—	—	—	4
Canavari, G. B.	London	1853-1854	Portraits	—	—	2	—	—	—	—	—	—	—	2
Canavari, S.	Rome	1848-1871	Portraits	—	—	4	—	—	—	—	—	—	—	4
Canchois, Henri	London	1883-1890	Still Life	—	—	—	—	10	—	—	—	—	1	11
Cane, Herbert Collins	London	1883-1891	Animals	—	—	3	—	—	—	5	—	—	—	8
Cane, R.	London	1818	Sculpture	—	—	1	—	—	—	—	—	—	—	1
Cannicci, Niccolo	London	1883	Landscape	—	—	1	—	—	—	—	—	—	—	1
Canning, Miss Mary G.	Stortford	1853-1868	Landscape	—	—	1	—	1	—	—	—	—	—	2
Canning, Mrs. J. Cater (M. W.)	Bishop's Stortford	1850-1852	Landscape	—	—	3	—	—	—	—	—	—	2	5
Cannon, Miss Edith M.	Ealing	1892-1893	Domestic	—	—	—	—	—	—	—	—	—	3	3
Canon —	—	1878	Portraits	—	—	—	—	—	—	—	1	—	—	1
Canot, Peter Charles, A.R.A.	London	1760-1776	Engraving	15	1	5	—	—	—	—	—	—	—	21
Canova, Antonio (Marchese d'Ischia.)	Rome	1817-1818	Sculpture	—	—	4	—	—	—	—	—	—	—	4
Cantelo, Miss Ellen	London	1859	Landscape	—	—	—	—	1	—	—	—	—	2	3

Name.	Town.	First and Last Year of Ex.	Speciality.	S. A.	F. S.	R. A.	B. I.	S. S.	O. W.	N. W	G. G.	N. G.	V. E.	Total.
Canter, James	London	1771-1783	Landscape	2	20	2	—	—	—	—	—	—	—	24
Canton, C.	—	1819	Cattle	—	—	1	—	—	—	—	—	—	—	1
Canton, Miss Susan Ruth	London	1880-1892	Sculpture	—	—	14	—	8	—	—	—	—	2	24
Cantwell, R.	London	1809-1839	Landscape	—	—	5	—	—	—	—	—	—	—	5
Canziani, Madame. *See* Miss Louisa Starr ‖	London	1885-1893	Portraits	—	—	14	—	—	—	—	—	5	4	23
Capalti, Cavaliere A.	Rome	1851-1858	Portraits	—	—	4	—	—	—	—	—	—	—	4
Caparn, W. J.	Oundle	1882-1893	Landscape	—	—	—	—	1	—	2	—	—	—	3
Cape, E. J.	London	1879	Landscape	—	—	—	—	1	—	—	—	—	—	1
Cape, H.	London	1830-1838	Landscape	—	—	1	—	2	—	—	—	—	—	3
Capelain, Le. *See* L.	—	—	—	—	—	—	—	—	—	—	—	—	—	—
Capes, Miss Mary	London	1881	Landscape	—	—	—	—	—	—	—	—	—	1	1
Caplin, J.	London	1834	Landscape	—	—	—	—	1	—	—	—	—	—	1
Capon, William	London	1788-1827	Landscape	1	—	56	5	5	—	—	—	—	—	67
Caporn, J.	London	1843-1846	Architecture	—	—	2	—	—	—	—	—	—	—	2
Cappe, J.	London	1780	Portraits	—	—	1	—	—	—	—	—	—	—	1
Capper, Miss Edith	Southampton	1865-1884	Landscape	—	—	2	—	1	—	2	1	—	11	17
Capper, J. H.	Hailsham	1822-1850	Landscape	—	—	—	3	4	—	—	—	—	—	7
Capper, J. J.	London	1849-1859	Landscape	—	—	6	—	—	—	—	—	—	—	6
Caputi, J.	London	1815	Intaglios	—	—	1	—	—	—	—	—	—	—	1
Carbonnier, C.	London	1815-1836	Portraits	—	—	14	4	8	—	—	—	—	—	26
Card, Master John	London	1772	Heads	—	1	—	—	—	—	—	—	—	—	1
Cardelli, P.	London	1815-1816	Sculpture	—	—	4	1	—	—	—	—	—	—	5
Carden, *or* Corden, Victor	London	1888	Military	—	—	—	—	—	—	—	—	—	1	1
Carder, Frederick	Wordsley	1893	Sculpture	—	—	1	—	—	—	—	—	—	—	1
Cardon, Claude	London	1892-1893	Domestic	—	—	2	—	1	—	—	—	—	—	3
Cardwell, H.	London	1836-1856	Sculpture	—	—	7	1	2	—	—	—	—	—	10
Caree —	London	1783	Cattle	—	1	—	—	—	—	—	—	—	—	1
Carelli, Conrad H. R.	Sutton	1886-1893	Buildings	—	—	—	—	2	—	2	—	1	—	5
Carelli, Gabriel	Kenilworth	1866-1880	Buildings	—	—	4	—	—	—	—	—	—	16	20
Carew —	London	1783	Figures	—	1	—	—	—	—	—	—	—	—	1
Carew, F.	Brighton	1834	Sculpture	—	—	2	—	—	—	—	—	—	—	2
Carew, F., Junr.	London	1849	Sculpture	—	—	1	1	—	—	—	—	—	—	2
Carew, John Edward	London	1812-1845	Sculpture	—	—	19	7	3	—	—	—	—	—	29
Carey —	London	1830	Portraits	—	—	—	—	1	—	—	—	—	—	1
Carey, Miss A. S.	—	1881	Figures	—	—	—	—	—	—	—	1	—	—	1
Carey, Charles W.	London	1882	Domestic	—	—	—	—	1	—	—	—	—	—	1
Carey, Mrs. Charles	Guernsey	1869-1872	Landscape	—	—	—	—	—	—	—	—	—	7	7
Carey, P.	London	1795	Landscape	—	—	2	—	—	—	—	—	—	—	2
Carfrae, G.	London	1787	Historical	—	—	1	—	—	—	—	—	—	—	1
Carin, Miss Marie	Lille	1889	Miniatures	—	—	3	—	—	—	—	—	—	—	3
Carkeet, N.	London	1819	Buildings	—	—	1	—	—	—	—	—	—	—	1
Carl, C.	London	1857	Heads	—	—	—	1	—	—	—	—	—	—	1
Carlandi, Onorato	London	1879-1892	Landscape	—	—	11	—	1	—	7	—	1	3	23
Carlaw, John, R.S.W.	Glasgow	1883-1891	Landscape	—	—	8	—	—	—	1	—	—	—	9
Carles, Jean Antonin-. *See* A.	—	—	—	—	—	—	—	—	—	—	—	—	—	—
Carles, Antonin	Paris	1882	Sculpture	—	—	1	—	—	—	—	—	—	—	1
Carlill, Stephen B.	Hull	1888-1892	Portraits	—	—	3	—	—	—	1	—	3	—	7
Carline, George	Lincoln	1886-1893	Rustic	—	—	7	—	3	—	10	—	—	2	22
Carline, H.	—	1849	Scriptural	—	—	1	—	—	—	—	—	—	—	1
Carline, J.	Shrewsbury	1825	Sculpture	—	—	1	—	—	—	—	—	—	—	1
Carline, T.	Shrewsbury	1825-1828	Sculpture	—	—	3	—	—	—	—	—	—	—	3
Carling and Maberley	—	1853	Architecture	—	—	1	—	—	—	—	—	—	—	1
Carlini, Agostino, R.A.	London	1760-1786	Sculpture	5	—	11	—	—	—	—	—	—	—	16
Carlionary —	—	1782	Copies	—	2	—	—	—	—	—	—	—	—	2
Carlisle, George James, 9th Earl of, H.R.W.S.	London	1889-1893	Landscape	—	—	2	—	—	7	—	—	6	—	15
Carlisle, John	London	1866-1893	Landscape	—	—	3	—	38	—	9	—	—	42	92
Carlisle, Miss Mary H.	London	1891-1893	Domestic	—	—	4	—	—	—	—	—	—	—	4
Carlow, S.	London	1837	Architecture	—	—	2	—	—	—	—	—	—	—	2
Carlton. *See* MacCarthy and Carlton	—	—	Sculpture	—	—	—	—	—	—	—	—	—	—	—
Carlton, C.	London	1870	Landscape	—	—	—	—	3	—	—	—	—	1	4
Carman, H. A.	Crayford	1867-1873	Fruit, etc.	—	—	—	—	13	—	—	—	—	—	13
Carmichael, Duncan	London	1891	Architecture	—	—	1	—	—	—	—	—	—	—	1
Carmichael, Mrs. Elizabeth	London	1768-1811	Portraits	5	1	10	1	—	—	—	—	—	—	17
Carmichael, James	London	1767-1774	Miniatures	4	—	—	—	—	—	—	—	—	—	4
Carmichael, James Wilson	Newcastle	1835-1862	Sea Pieces	—	—	21	21	6	—	—	—	—	8	56
Carmichael, Miss M. D. T.	London	1857	Flowers	—	—	—	—	—	—	—	—	—	1	1
Carne, De. *See* D.	—	—	—	—	—	—	—	—	—	—	—	—	—	—
Carne, Richard A.	London	1880	Architecture	—	—	1	—	—	—	—	—	—	—	1
Carnevale, Giuseppe	Rome	1889	Sculpture	—	—	1	—	—	—	—	—	—	—	1
Caröe, William Douglas, M.A.	London	1882-1893	Architecture	—	—	25	—	—	—	—	—	—	—	25
Carolus-Duran, Emile A.	Paris	1883-1893	Portraits	—	—	7	—	—	—	—	—	—	4	11

Name.	Town.	First and Last Year of Ex.	Speciality.	S. A.	F. S.	R. A.	B. I.	S. S.	O. W.	N. W.	G. G.	N. G.	V. E.	Total
Caron, Miss L.	London	1854-1855	Portraits	—	—	2	—	—	—	—	—	—	—	2
Carpeaux, Jean Baptiste	London	1871-1874	Sculpture	—	—	10	—	—	—	—	—	—	—	10
Carpenter, Aaron	London	1762-1767	Seals	—	5	—	—	—	—	—	—	—	—	5
Carpenter, A. A. *See* Cooke and Carpenter	—	—	Drawings	—	—	—	—	—	—	—	—	—	—	—
Carpenter, Miss Dora	London	1880-1883	Domestic	—	—	1	—	2	—	—	—	—	—	3
Carpenter, G.	London	1831-1832	Figures	—	—	2	1	—	—	—	—	—	—	3
Carpenter, Miss Henrietta	London	1847-1857	Portraits	—	—	10	—	—	—	—	—	—	—	10
Carpenter, H. Barrett	Liverpool	1890	Still Life	—	—	—	—	—	—	—	—	—	1	1
Carpenter, J.	London	1837-1855	Portraits	—	—	11	—	—	—	—	—	—	—	11
Carpenter, J. Lant	Derby	1868-1892	Landscape	—	—	3	—	2	—	—	—	—	2	7
Carpenter, Percy	London	1841-1858	Churches	—	—	5	3	—	—	—	—	—	—	8
Carpenter, Richard Cromwell	London	1830-1849	Architecture	—	—	9	—	—	—	—	—	—	—	9
Carpenter, Richard Herbert. *See also* Slater	—	—	—	—	—	—	—	—	—	—	—	—	—	—
and Carpenter	London	1875-1876	Architecture	—	—	2	—	—	—	—	—	—	—	2
Carpenter (R. H.) and Ingelow (B.)	London	1877-1893	Architecture	—	—	14	—	—	—	—	—	—	—	14
Carpenter, William	London	1840-1885	Figures	—	—	25	9	3	—	—	1	—	2	40
Carpenter, Mrs. William. *See* Miss Mar-	—	—	—	—	—	—	—	—	—	—	—	—	—	—
garet Geddes	London	1818-1866	Portraits	—	—	147	50	19	1	—	—	—	—	217
Carpenter, William John	London	1885-1893	Architecture	—	—	1	—	8	—	4	—	—	1	14
Carpenter, Miss	London	1854	Portraits	—	—	1	—	—	—	—	—	—	—	1
Carpentier, Felix	London	1888	Flowers	—	—	—	—	1	—	—	—	—	—	1
Carpentiers, Adrien	—	1760-1774	Portraits	6	9	4	—	—	—	—	—	—	—	19
Carr, Miss Bessie	Worthing	1883-1890	Portraits	—	—	3	—	2	—	—	—	—	—	5
Carr, David	London	1875-1893	Figures	—	—	6	—	4	—	7	12	11	29	69
Carr, Ellis	London	1884	Landscape	—	—	—	—	—	—	—	—	—	1	1
Carr, J.	York	1818	Portraits	—	—	1	—	—	—	—	—	—	—	1
Carr, Miss Kate	London	1871-1877	Portraits	—	—	—	—	—	—	—	1	—	21	22
Carr, Lyell	New York	1890	Domestic	—	—	1	—	—	—	—	—	—	—	1
Carr, R.	London	1811-1817	Architecture	—	—	5	—	—	—	—	—	—	—	5
Carr, Rev. William Howell (?) Holwell	—	1804-1821	Landscape	—	—	12	—	—	—	—	—	—	—	12
Carrazzo —	—	1768	Landscape	—	2	—	—	—	—	—	—	—	—	2
Carrick, J. M.	London	1854-1878	Landscape	—	—	18	1	2	—	—	—	—	4	25
Carrick, Robert, R.I. ‡ φ	London	1847-1893	Domestic	—	—	17	—	1	—	66	—	—	16	100
Carrick, Thomas Heathfield	London	1841-1866	Miniatures	—	—	140	—	—	—	—	—	—	—	140
Carrier, A.	—	1873	Sculpture	—	—	1	—	—	—	—	—	—	—	1
Carrington, E. (?) Edith	London	1871-1873	Landscape	—	—	2	—	—	—	—	—	—	—	2
Carrington, Frances E.	Dunkeld	1869-1870	Landscape	—	—	—	—	—	—	—	—	—	4	4
Carrington, James Yates	London	1881-1891	Animals	—	—	11	—	8	—	—	3	—	12	34
Carrington, Louis	Forest Hill	1874-1888	Landscape	—	—	—	—	6	—	4	—	—	1	11
Carrington, Mrs. Patty	Worcester	1883-1887	Flowers	—	—	—	—	—	—	3	—	—	—	3
Carrole, W.	London	1790-1793	Landscape	—	—	7	—	—	—	—	—	—	—	7
Carroll, Colin R.	Liverpool	1893	Landscape	—	—	1	—	—	—	—	—	—	—	1
Carroll, Miss Jane De la Cour-. *See* De.	—	—	—	—	—	—	—	—	—	—	—	—	—	—
Carruthers, Richard	London	1816-1819	Portraits	—	—	12	1	—	—	—	—	—	—	13
Carse, Alexander	Edinburgh	1812-1820	Domestic	—	—	11	18	—	—	—	—	—	—	29
Carse, J. H.	London	1860-1862	Landscape	—	—	—	—	1	—	—	—	—	3	4
Carse, William	London	1820-1829	Domestic	—	—	4	7	7	—	—	—	—	—	18
Carsoe, W.	Bath	1849-1853	Scriptural	—	—	—	2	—	—	—	—	—	—	2
Carswell, J.	London	1842-1853	Landscape	—	—	—	4	2	—	—	—	—	—	6
Carte, M.	London	1867	Figures	—	—	—	1	—	—	—	—	—	—	1
Carte, Miss Rose	London	1873-1885	Landscape	—	—	—	—	2	—	—	1	—	—	3
Carte, Miss Viola	London	1874-1877	Figures	—	—	2	—	—	—	—	—	—	2	4
Carter, Miss Austin	Torquay	1862-1873	Dramatic	—	—	1	—	18	—	—	—	—	—	19
Carter, Miss B.	London	1856-1859	Portraits	—	—	3	—	—	—	—	—	—	—	3
Carter, C.	London	1801-1802	Landscape	—	—	3	—	—	—	—	—	—	—	3
Carter, C.	London	1850	Figures	—	—	—	—	1	—	—	—	—	—	1
Carter, Charles	London	1868-1873	Fruit	—	—	—	—	2	—	—	—	—	1	3
Carter, D.	—	1847	Architecture	—	—	1	—	—	—	—	—	—	—	1
Carter, E.	London	1877	Churches	—	—	—	—	1	—	—	—	—	—	1
Carter, Emily	Wallington	1880	Flowers	—	—	—	—	—	—	—	—	—	1	1
Carter, Mrs. E. S.	London	1861-1874	Fruit	—	—	—	—	28	—	—	—	—	10	38
Carter, Francis	London	1788-1803	Architecture	1	—	5	—	—	—	—	—	—	—	6
Carter, Frank P.	Newcastle	1892	Landscape	—	—	—	—	1	—	—	—	—	—	1
Carter, George	London	1769-1784	Portraits	22	—	16	—	—	—	—	—	—	—	38
Carter, G. A.	London	1870-1878	Sculpture	—	—	5	—	—	—	—	—	—	—	5
Carter, H.	Birmingham	1867	Landscape	—	—	—	—	1	—	—	—	—	—	1
Carter, Henry	London	1866	Animals	—	—	—	—	2	—	—	—	—	—	2
Carter, Hugh, R.I. ‡ φ	London	1859-1893	Domestic	—	—	14	—	—	—	133	—	—	52	199
Carter, H. B.	Plymouth	1827-1830	Landscape	—	—	4	1	5	—	—	—	—	—	10
Carter, Miss H. B.	London	1864	Sculpture	—	—	1	—	—	—	—	—	—	—	1
Carter, Henry William	London	1867-1893	Domestic	—	—	3	—	10	—	—	—	—	—	13
Carter, J.	London	1788-1814	Historical	—	—	2	—	—	—	—	—	—	—	2

Name.	Town.	First and Last Year of Ex.	Speciality.	S. A.	F. S.	R. A.	B. I.	S. S.	O. W.	N. W.	G. G.	N. G.	V. E.	Total.
Carter, John	London	1765-1794	Architecture	10	8	21	—	—	—	—	—	—	—	39
Carter, J., Junr.	London	1821-1839	Architecture	—	—	6	—	—	—	—	—	—	—	6
Carter, J.	London	1843-1844	Landscape	—	—	2	—	—	—	—	—	—	—	2
Carter, James	Bexley	1855	Flowers	—	—	1	—	—	—	—	—	—	—	1
Carter, J.	London	1868-1872	Figures	—	—	2	—	—	—	—	—	—	—	2
Carter, James	London	1855	Engraving	—	—	1	—	—	—	—	—	—	—	1
Carter, J. B.	Greenwich	1822	Churches	—	—	2	—	—	—	—	—	—	—	2
Carter, J. Coates. *See also* Seddon and Carter	Cardiff	1887-1890	Churches	—	—	3	—	—	—	—	—	—	—	3
Carter, J. H.	London	1839-1856	Portraits	—	—	8	—	—	—	—	—	—	—	8
Carter, Mrs. J. H.	London	1839-1869	Miniatures	—	—	47	—	1	—	—	—	—	—	48
Carter, J. M.	Gibraltar	1842-1865	Landscape	—	—	5	4	4	—	—	—	—	—	13
Carter, Joseph N.	Scarborough	1857-1860	Sea Pieces	—	—	—	—	—	—	—	—	—	6	6
Carter, J. T.	London	1869	Figures	—	—	1	—	—	—	—	—	—	—	1
Carter, M.	London	1839-1849	Miniatures	—	—	4	—	—	—	—	—	—	—	4
Carter, Miss Mabel	Bexley	1892	Figures	—	—	—	—	—	—	—	—	—	1	1
Carter, Miss M. Austin	London	1884-1893	Flowers	—	—	—	—	—	—	3	—	—	—	3
Carter, Miss Mary E.	London	1884	Flowers	—	—	—	—	1	—	—	—	—	—	1
Carter, Noel N.	London	1826-1833	Portraits	—	—	12	—	8	—	—	—	—	—	20
Carter, O.	Greenwich	1820	Churches	—	—	1	—	—	—	—	—	—	—	1
Carter, Owen Browne	Winchester	1847-1851	Architecture	—	—	4	—	—	—	—	—	—	—	4
Carter, Robert	Southampton	1874	Landscape	—	—	—	—	2	—	—	—	—	1	3
Carter, Miss Rosa	London	1889-1892	Domestic	—	—	2	—	1	—	—	—	—	1	4
Carter, Richard Harry	Truro	1864-1893	Landscape	—	—	11	—	3	—	18	2	—	6	40
Carter, Samuel, Junr.	London	1880-1888	Landscape	—	—	—	—	3	—	—	—	—	3	6
Carter, Samuel John ϕ	London	1855-1892	Animals	—	—	49	3	10	—	—	1	—	15	78
Carter, T.	London	1787	Architecture	—	—	1	—	—	—	—	—	—	—	1
Carter, T.	London	1815-1817	Landscape	—	—	4	—	—	—	—	—	—	—	4
Carter, Thomas	Cheltenham	1886-1889	Sculpture	—	—	2	—	—	—	—	—	—	—	2
Carter, T. A.	Leamington	1885	Canals	—	—	—	—	1	—	—	—	—	—	1
Carter, T. W.	London	1847	Churches	—	—	1	—	—	—	—	—	—	—	1
Carter, Vernet	London	1892	Engraving	—	—	1	—	—	—	—	—	—	—	1
Carter, W.	London	1849-1850	Landscape	—	—	1	—	1	—	—	—	—	—	2
Carter, William	London	1836-1876	Landscape	—	—	32	33	52	—	—	—	—	21	138
Carter, William §	London	1883-1893	Portraits	—	—	29	—	7	—	—	3	3	1	43
Carter, W. A.	London	1863-1869	Architecture	—	—	4	—	—	—	—	—	—	—	4
Carter, W. J. B.	London	1876-1880	Portraits	—	—	1	—	—	—	—	—	—	1	2
Carter, Miss	London	1764	Needlework	—	2	—	—	—	—	—	—	—	—	2
Carteret, C.	Stamford	1828-1829	Landscape	—	—	—	—	3	—	—	—	—	—	3
Carteux —	Paris	1776	Medals	—	—	2	—	—	—	—	—	—	—	2
Cartmill, E.	London	1858	Landscape	—	—	—	—	1	—	—	—	—	—	1
Cartwright, C. M.	London	1812	Sea Pieces	—	—	—	—	—	—	—	—	—	3	3
Cartwright, Frederick W.	London	1854-1893	Landscape	—	—	22	3	20	—	9	—	—	15	69
Cartwright, J.	London	1785-1786	Architecture	—	—	2	—	—	—	—	—	—	—	2
Cartwright, John	London	1767-1828	Landscape	—	1	25	—	—	—	—	—	—	—	26
Cartwright, Joseph §	Dawlish	1823-1829	Sea Pieces	—	—	—	10	6	—	—	—	—	—	16
Cartwright, Miss Rose	London	1883-1888	Landscape	—	—	—	—	—	—	—	5	1	—	6
Cartwright, T.	London	1801-1802	Landscape	—	—	2	—	—	—	—	—	—	—	2
Cartwright, Miss	—	1777	Needlework	1	—	—	—	—	—	—	—	—	—	1
Caruson, S.	—	1839	Miniatures	—	—	1	—	—	—	—	—	—	—	1
Carver, J.	London	1826	Portraits	—	—	1	—	1	—	—	—	—	—	2
Carver, Robert, F.S.A.	London	1765-1790	Landscape	29	2	4	—	—	—	—	—	—	—	35
Carver, R.	London	1811	Architecture	—	—	1	—	—	—	—	—	—	—	1
Carveth, J.	London	1828	Landscape	—	—	—	2	—	—	—	—	—	—	2
Carwardine —	London	1771-1772	Portraits	2	—	—	—	—	—	—	—	—	—	2
Carwardine, Miss Mary E.	London	1882-1888	Landscape	—	—	—	—	8	—	4	—	—	—	12
Carwardine, Mrs. Thomas (Anne)	—	1761-1762	Miniatures	4	—	—	—	—	—	—	—	—	—	4
Cary, Francis Stephen	London	1834-1876	Domestic	—	—	34	8	20	—	—	—	—	4	66
Cary, W. L.	London	1831	Landscape	—	—	—	—	1	—	—	—	—	—	1
Casali, Chevalier Andrea	Rome	1760-1783	Historical	7	72	—	—	—	—	—	—	—	—	79
Casanova, A.	London	1878-1880	Etching	—	—	—	—	—	—	—	—	—	2	2
Casanova, Francis	London	1767	Battle Pieces	—	2	—	—	—	—	—	—	—	—	2
Case, Bertha L.	Maidstone	1873	Flowers	—	—	—	—	—	—	—	—	—	2	2
Case, H.	London	1839-1845	Architecture	—	—	5	—	—	—	—	—	—	—	5
Casella, Miss Ella	London	1884-1893	Wax	—	—	23	—	—	—	—	10	7	—	40
Casella, Miss Julia	—	1885	Sculpture	—	—	—	—	—	—	—	2	—	—	2
Casella, Miss Nelia	London	1886-1893	Wax	—	—	25	—	—	—	—	4	8	—	37
Casey, John Archibald	London	1830-1859	Historical	—	—	9	6	2	—	—	—	—	—	17
Casey, W. S.	London	1863-1868	Landscape	—	—	1	2	8	—	—	—	—	—	11
Cash, G.	—	1807	Landscape	—	—	1	—	—	—	—	—	—	—	1
Cash, John	Harlesden	1885-1892	Architecture	—	—	4	—	—	—	1	—	—	—	5
Cashel, Miss Mary	London	1892	Interiors	—	—	—	—	—	—	1	—	—	—	1
Casley, William	The Lizard	1891	Seashores	—	—	—	—	—	—	1	—	—	—	1

Name.	Town.	First and Last Year of Ex.	Speciality.	S. A.	F. S.	R. A.	B. I.	S. S.	O. W.	N. W.	G. G.	N. G.	V. E.	Total.
Cass, Miss Margaret	London	1890	Flowers	—	—	—	—	—	—	—	—	—	1	1
Cassamaio, Signorina	London	1882	—	—	—	1	—	—	—	—	—	—	—	1
Cassatt, M. S.	Paris	1876	Figures	—	—	—	—	—	—	—	—	—	1	1
Cassels, William	Glasgow	1893	Landscape	—	—	1	—	—	—	—	—	—	—	1
Cassidy, John	Manchester	1893	Portraits	—	—	—	—	—	—	—	—	3	—	3
Cassie, James, R.S.A., R.S.W.	Aberdeen	1854-1879	Rustic	—	—	21	4	2	—	—	—	—	3	30
Castan, Louis	London	1865-1867	Sporting	—	—	2	—	—	—	—	—	—	—	2
Castel, J.	Oxford	1849	Sculpture	—	—	1	—	—	—	—	—	—	—	1
Castelli, Madame	London	1825	Portraits	—	—	1	—	—	—	—	—	—	—	1
Castiglione, Guiseppe	London	1869-1870	Domestic	—	—	3	—	2	—	—	—	—	2	7
Castle, Miss Florence	London	1891-1893	Figures	—	—	1	—	3	—	—	—	—	1	5
Castle, T. Charles H.	London	1890-1891	Portraits	—	—	1	—	1	—	—	—	—	—	2
Castro, De. *See* D.	—	—	—	—	—	—	—	—	—	—	—	—	—	—
Castruzzi —	London	1774	Portraits	3	—	—	—	—	—	—	—	—	—	3
Caswall, Miss A. M.	Binfield	1870-1874	Figures	—	—	1	—	3	—	—	—	—	—	4
Catchpool, H.	Crouch End	1881-1882	Domestic	—	—	—	—	1	—	—	—	—	—	1
Catel, Franz Ludwig	Rome	1828	Historical	—	—	1	—	—	—	—	—	—	—	1
Cathelinau —	London	1868	Figures	—	—	1	—	—	—	—	—	—	—	1
Catherwood, F.	London	1820-1831	Architecture	—	—	4	—	—	—	—	—	—	—	4
Catlin, George	London	1848	Figures	—	—	—	—	—	—	—	—	—	5	5
Catlow, George Spawton	Leicester	1884-1893	Landscape	—	—	6	—	—	—	2	—	—	—	8
Caton, Miss M.	—	1808	Portraits	—	—	1	—	—	—	—	—	—	—	1
Cattermole, Charles, R.I., R.B.A.§ ‡ φ	London	1858-1893	Figures	—	—	1	5	85	—	188	—	—	2	281
Cattermole, George †	London	1819-1850	Figures	—	—	6	2	—	97	—	—	—	—	105
Cattermole, Leonardo F. G.	London	1872-1886	Historical	—	—	—	—	8	—	—	8	—	3	19
Cattermole, Richard	London	1814-1818	Historical	—	—	—	—	—	6	—	—	—	—	6
Catton, Charles, R.A.	London	1760-1798	Animals	16	—	43	—	—	—	—	—	—	—	59
Catton, Charles, Junr.	—	1776-1800	Animals	—	—	37	—	—	—	—	—	—	—	37
Catty, A.	—	1854	Figures	—	—	1	—	—	—	—	—	—	—	1
Cauder, A.	London	1853	Flowers	—	—	—	—	—	—	—	—	—	1	1
Caudron, J.	Barnet	1864	Figures	—	—	1	—	—	—	—	—	—	—	1
Cauer, C.	Kreutznach	1869-1870	Sculpture	—	—	2	—	—	—	—	—	—	—	2
Cauer, Ludwig	London	1892-1893	Sculpture	—	—	6	—	—	—	—	—	2	—	8
Cauldwell, Leslie Giffen	Paris	1887-1893	Figures	—	—	2	—	3	—	—	—	—	—	5
Cauley, Miss	—	1768	Flowers	1	—	—	—	—	—	—	—	—	—	1
Caulfield, F. W.	Crowthorn	1878	Flowers	—	—	—	—	—	—	—	—	—	1	1
Caulfield, J.	London	1792	Miniatures	—	—	3	—	—	—	—	—	—	—	3
Caulton, J.	London	1800-1810	Insects	—	—	8	—	—	—	—	—	—	—	8
Caunter, R.	Edinburgh	1850	Boats	—	—	1	—	—	—	—	—	—	—	1
Cause, John D.	London	1815-1817	Domestic	—	—	—	2	—	—	—	—	—	—	2
Cauty, Horace Henry, R.B.A.§	London	1867-1893	Domestic	—	—	25	—	93	—	—	—	—	12	130
Cauty, Horace Robert	London	1870-1893	Landscape	—	—	—	—	74	—	2	—	—	3	79
Cave, H.	Newmarket	1871	Etching	—	—	—	—	—	—	—	—	—	1	1
Cave, Henry	York	1814-1825	Landscape	—	—	4	1	—	—	—	—	—	—	5
Cave, James	Winchester	1801-1817	Churches	—	—	7	—	—	—	—	—	—	—	7
Cave, Rev. R. H.	Clapton	1872-1874	Etching	—	—	—	—	—	—	—	—	—	3	3
Cave, Walter	London	1890	Architecture	—	—	1	—	—	—	—	—	—	—	1
Cave, Le. *See* L.	—	—	—	—	—	—	—	—	—	—	—	—	—	—
Caveler, W. C.	—	1844-1850	Architecture	—	—	2	—	—	—	—	—	—	—	2
Cavell, John Scott	London	1851-1863	Domestic	—	—	7	9	4	—	—	—	—	4	24
Cawker, L. G.	London	1857-1858	Flowers	—	—	—	—	2	—	—	—	—	—	2
Cawley, J. C.	London	1837	Churches	—	—	—	1	—	—	—	—	—	—	1
Cawley, Mrs.	—	1770-1771	Flowers	1	—	1	—	—	—	—	—	—	—	2
Cawse, Miss Clara	London	1841-1867	Historical	—	—	12	6	3	—	—	—	—	—	21
Cawse, John	London	1801-1845	Historical	—	—	24	41	17	15	—	—	—	1	98
Cawston, Arthur	London	1880-1884	Architecture	—	—	3	—	—	—	—	—	—	—	3
Cayley, Mrs. Emma	—	1838-1839	Sculpture	—	—	2	—	—	—	—	—	—	—	2
Cayley, W. E.	—	1833	Sculpture	—	—	1	—	—	—	—	—	—	—	1
Cazenave, De. *See* D.	—	—	—	—	—	—	—	—	—	—	—	—	—	—
Cazin, J.	Paris	1879-1881	Scriptural	—	—	—	—	—	—	—	1	—	1	2
Cazin, Madame M.	London	1872-1878	Landscape	—	—	2	—	—	—	—	—	—	13	15
Ceccarini, F. W.	Dulwich	1872	Sculpture	—	—	2	—	—	—	—	—	—	—	2
Ceccoli, R.	Athens	1855-1856	Figures	—	—	4	—	—	—	—	—	—	—	4
Celli, A.	London	1808-1812	Domestic	—	—	—	10	—	—	—	—	—	—	10
Cels, Cornelius	London	1836	Portraits	—	—	1	—	—	—	—	—	—	—	1
Cenni, Quinto	Milan	1876-1881	Military	—	—	—	—	—	—	—	—	—	4	4
Ceracchi, Guiseppe	London	1776-1779	Sculpture	—	—	12	—	—	—	—	—	—	—	12
Cerio, J.	Capri	1876-1878	Domestic	—	—	—	—	1	—	—	—	—	1	2
Cervan, John	Exeter	1776	Landscape	—	—	2	—	—	—	—	—	—	—	2
Cerveng, John	London	1771-1773	Sporting	5	—	2	—	—	—	—	—	—	—	7
Cervi, Giulio	London	1881	Domestic	—	—	—	—	—	—	—	—	—	1	1
Cesare, Cavaliere	Florence	1887	Sculpture	—	—	1	—	—	—	—	—	—	—	1

Name.	Town.	First and Last Year of Ex.	Speciality.	S. A.	F. S.	R. A.	B. I.	S. S.	O. W.	N.W.	G. G.	N. G.	V. E.	Total.
Chabot, A.	London	1841-1846	Landscape	—	—	1	—	6	—	—	—	—	—	7
Chadburn, G. H.	Sutton	1891	Still Life	—	—	—	—	1	—	—	—	—	—	1
Chadley, J.	High Wycombe	1819	Architecture	—	—	2	—	—	—	—	—	—	—	2
Chadwick, Miss Emma L.	Paris	1890	Domestic	—	—	—	—	—	—	—	—	—	2	2
Chadwick, Henry Daniel	Hornsey	1879-1890	Figures	—	—	9	—	2	—	—	—	—	—	11
Chaigneau, Ferdinand	London	1865-1881	Farmyards	—	—	—	2	—	—	—	—	—	1	3
Chair, De. *See* D.	—	—	—	—	—	—	—	—	—	—	—	—	—	—
Chaix, P.	London	1832	Interiors	—	—	2	—	—	—	—	—	—	—	2
Chalker, Miss Cissie	Bath	1890-1893	Miniatures	—	—	5	—	—	—	—	—	—	—	5
Chalker, Miss Sophia	Bath	1888-1889	Miniatures	—	—	1	—	3	—	—	—	—	—	4
Chalkley, C.	London	1800	Architecture	—	—	1	—	—	—	—	—	—	—	1
Chalkley, H. E.	London	1848	Landscape	—	—	—	—	2	—	—	—	—	—	2
Challenger, J.	Twickenham	1893	Landscape	—	—	—	—	1	—	—	—	—	—	1
Challice, Miss Annie Jane	London	1866-1884	Domestic	—	—	2	—	9	—	—	—	—	2	13
Challis, E.	London	1846-1863	Ruins	—	—	9	—	22	—	—	—	—	—	31
Chalmers, A.	London	1798	Monuments	—	—	3	—	—	—	—	—	—	—	3
Chalmers, Sir George, Bart.	Edinburgh	1775-1790	Portraits	—	—	24	—	—	—	—	—	—	—	24
Chalmers, George Paul, R.S.A., R.S.W.	Edinburgh	1863-1876	Figures	—	—	6	—	—	—	—	—	—	—	6
Chalmers, J.	—	1799	Architecture	—	—	1	—	—	—	—	—	—	—	1
Chalmers, Mary H.	London	1880	Domestic	—	—	—	—	2	—	—	—	—	—	2
Chalmers, Sir R., Bart.	—	1790-1799	Sea Pieces	—	—	10	—	—	—	—	—	—	—	10
Chalmers, W. A.	London	1790-1794	Churches	—	—	9	—	—	—	—	—	—	—	9
Chalon, Alfred Edward, R.A.	London	1801-1860	Portraits	—	—	396	21	—	—	—	—	—	15	432
Chalon, Henry Bernard	London	1792-1849	Sporting	—	—	198	28	21	1	—	—	—	2	250
Chalon, John James, R.A. †	London	1801-1854	Landscape	—	—	86	48	—	55	—	—	—	—	189
Chalon, Miss Maria A. *See* Mrs. H. Moseley	London	1819-1840	Miniatures	—	—	71	—	5	—	—	—	—	—	76
Chaloner, J.	London	1799	Architecture	—	—	1	—	—	—	—	—	—	—	1
Chambars, Thomas, A.R.A.	—	1761-1773	Engraving	6	—	1	—	—	—	—	—	—	—	7
Chamberlain, Miss C.	—	1816	Shells	—	—	1	—	—	—	—	—	—	—	1
Chamberlain, E.	London	1825	Landscape	—	—	1	—	—	—	—	—	—	—	1
Chamberlain, Miss E.	—	1816	Fish	—	—	1	—	—	—	—	—	—	—	1
Chamberlain, William (Pupil of J. Opie)	—	1794-1817	Animals	—	—	6	—	—	—	—	—	—	—	6
Chamberlain, W.B., R.S.W.	Brighton	1879-1889	Landscape	—	—	2	—	—	—	1	—	—	—	3
Chamberlin, Mason, R.A.	London	1760-1786	Portraits	22	2	50	—	—	—	—	—	—	—	74
Chamberlin, Mason, Junr.	London	1786-1827	Landscape	—	—	59	8	1	—	—	—	—	—	68
Chambers, Arthur J.	Norwich	1876	Etching	—	—	—	—	—	—	—	—	—	1	1
Chambers, Miss Alice May	London	1880-1893	Mythological	—	—	9	—	—	—	3	—	1	3	16
Chambers, Alfred P.	London	1859-1862	Historical	—	—	—	2	3	—	—	—	—	3	8
Chambers, Coutts L.	London	1883-1890	Landscape	—	—	—	—	—	—	—	10	—	—	10
Chambers, E.	London	1855	Sea Pieces	—	—	—	1	—	—	—	—	—	—	1
Chambers, Frederick	London	1886-1891	Landscape	—	—	1	—	1	—	—	—	—	1	3
Chambers, George ‡	London	1827-1840	Sea Pieces	—	—	3	15	28	41	3	—	—	—	90
Chambers, George, Junr.	London	1848-1862	Sea Pieces	—	—	11	15	30	—	—	—	—	—	56
Chambers, John	London	1886	Landscape	—	—	—	—	1	—	—	—	—	—	1
Chambers, Robert	London	1761-1783	Sculpture	57	19	—	—	—	—	—	—	—	—	76
Chambers, T.	Hereford	1834	Architecture	—	—	1	—	—	—	—	—	—	—	1
Chambers, T.	Scarborough	1852-1858	Sea Pieces	—	—	—	—	3	—	—	—	—	—	3
Chambers, Sir William, R.A.	London	1761-1777	Architecture	16	—	21	—	—	—	—	—	—	—	37
Chambers, William	London	1892-1893	Engraving	—	—	2	—	—	—	—	—	—	—	2
Chambers, Master	—	1782-1783	Portraits	—	4	—	—	—	—	—	—	—	—	4
Chambre, Mrs.	Putney	1869-1874	Figures	—	—	—	—	3	—	—	—	—	—	3
Chambrulard, De. *See* D.	—	—	—	—	—	—	—	—	—	—	—	—	—	—
Champante, T.	London	1801	Seashore	—	—	1	—	—	—	—	—	—	—	1
Champion, Edward C.	London	1870-1883	Domestic	—	—	4	—	10	—	—	—	—	—	14
Champion, Mrs. H.	London	1868-1885	Figures	—	—	6	—	33	—	4	—	—	42	85
Champion, H. E.	—	1874	Heads	—	—	—	—	2	—	—	—	—	—	2
Champion, William Scott	London	1871-1879	Architecture	—	—	12	—	—	—	—	—	—	—	12
Champneys, Basil	London	1874-1893	Architecture	—	—	36	—	—	—	—	—	—	—	36
Champollion, Eugène André	London	1879	Etching	—	—	—	—	—	—	—	—	—	1	1
Chance, Miss Jane	London	1888	Portraits	—	—	—	—	—	—	—	—	—	1	1
Chandepie de Boiviers	London	1819-1823	Portraits	—	—	11	—	—	—	—	—	—	—	11
Chandler, A.	—	1825	Flowers	—	—	1	—	—	—	—	—	—	—	1
Chandler, J. W.	London	1787-1791	Portraits	—	—	10	—	—	—	—	—	—	—	10
Chandler, Miss Rose M.	Haslemere	1882-1891	Domestic	—	—	—	—	4	—	7	—	—	1	12
Chandois —	London	1780	Portraits	—	1	—	—	—	—	—	—	—	—	1
Chanet, Henri	Paris	1883	Portraits	—	—	1	—	—	—	—	—	—	—	1
Channer, Miss C. Alfreda	Leytonstone	1876-1892	Crayons	—	—	4	—	6	—	5	—	—	6	21
Channon, Miss M. E.	London	1858-1865	Flowers	—	—	1	—	5	—	—	—	—	—	6
Chant, J.	London	1849	Fruit	—	—	—	—	—	—	—	—	—	1	1
Chant, James John	London	1861-1883	Engraving	—	—	17	—	—	—	—	—	—	—	17
Chantre, C.	Clapton	1863	Fruit	—	—	1	—	—	—	—	—	—	—	1
Chantrell, R. D.	London	1812-1814	Architecture	—	—	4	—	—	—	—	—	—	—	4

Name.	Town.	First and Last Year of Ex.	Speciality.	S. A.	F. S.	R. A.	B. I.	S. S.	O.W.	N.W.	G. G.	N. G.	V. E.	Total.
Chantry, Sir Francis Legatt, R.A., F.R.S., F.S.A.	London	1804-1842	Sculpture	—	—	124	1	—	1	—	—	—	—	126
Chantry, N.	London	1797-1838	Still Life	—	—	27	42	19	—	—	—	—	—	88
Chantry, R.	London	1793-1794	Architecture	—	—	2	—	—	—	—	—	—	—	2
Chaplin, Miss Alice M.	London	1877-1893	Sculpture	—	—	16	—	—	—	1	15	6	20	58
Chaplin, Miss Annie	London	1883	Figures	—	—	1	—	—	—	—	—	—	—	1
Chaplin, Charles	Paris	1849	Figures	—	—	1	—	—	—	—	—	—	—	1
Chaplin, Florence	London	1882	Figures	—	—	—	—	1	—	—	—	—	—	1
Chaplin, Frank	Worcester	1879	Fruit	—	—	—	—	1	—	—	—	—	—	1
Chaplin, Henry	Worcester	1855-1879	Still Life	—	—	10	14	18	—	—	—	—	10	52
Chapman, Charles	London	1776	Crayons	—	—	1	—	—	—	—	—	—	—	1
Chapman, C. W.	London	1829	Flowers	—	—	1	—	—	—	—	—	—	—	1
Chapman, Ernest J.	London	1892	Stained Glass	—	—	1	—	—	—	—	—	—	—	1
Chapman, George R.	London	1863-1874	Portraits	—	—	4	—	—	—	—	—	—	5	9
Chapman, H.	London	1823-1841	Landscape	—	—	—	1	2	—	—	—	—	—	3
Chapman, H. W.	London	1855-1856	Landscape	—	—	—	—	—	—	—	—	—	2	2
Chapman, John	London	1772-1778	Architecture	1	—	4	—	—	—	—	—	—	—	5
Chapman, J.	London	1819-1836	Scriptural	—	—	2	—	—	—	—	—	—	—	2
Chapman, John	London	1833	Sculpture	—	—	—	1	—	—	—	—	—	—	1
Chapman, J.	Slough	1855	Domestic	—	—	1	—	—	—	—	—	—	—	1
Chapman, John Watkins	London	1853-1890	Domestic	—	—	30	15	112	—	8	—	—	31	196
Chapman, R.	London	1825-1828	Architecture	—	—	1	—	2	—	—	—	—	—	3
Chapman, R. Hamilton	Leatherhead	1881-1891	Landscape	—	—	7	—	20	—	7	—	—	2	36
Chapman, R. W.	London	1855-1861	Domestic	—	—	2	—	14	—	—	—	—	—	16
Chapman, W.	London	1820	Historical	—	—	2	—	—	—	—	—	—	—	2
Chapman, William	York	1866-1869	Engraving	—	—	2	—	—	—	—	—	—	—	2
Chapman, Miss	—	1815-1826	Flowers	—	—	8	—	—	—	—	—	—	—	8
Chappel, Edouard	London	1892	Fruit	—	—	1	—	—	—	—	—	—	—	1
Chappell, G.	—	1804	Portraits	—	—	1	—	—	—	—	—	—	—	1
Chappell, William	London	1858-1882	Figures	—	—	1	4	34	—	—	—	—	11	50
Chappellsmith, J.	London	1842	Portraits	—	—	2	—	—	—	—	—	—	—	2
Chapu, Henri	Paris	1877	Sculpture	—	—	—	—	—	—	—	1	—	—	1
Chardini, P. J.	London	1842-1843	Sculpture	—	—	7	—	—	—	—	—	—	—	7
Charles, James	London	1865-1893	Domestic	—	—	19	—	2	—	—	8	13	6	48
Charles, John	London	1875-1888	Portraits	—	—	17	—	—	—	—	—	—	—	17
Charles, Mrs. R. C., afterwards Mrs. F. G. Stephens	London	1865	Figures	—	—	1	—	—	—	—	—	—	—	1
Charles, W.	London	1870-1871	Seashores	—	—	—	—	3	—	—	—	—	—	3
Charlet, Franz	London	1888	Figures	—	—	—	—	—	—	—	—	—	1	1
Charlet, Nicolas Toussaint	Paris	1834	Figures	—	—	1	—	—	—	—	—	—	—	1
Charlton, Miss Catherine. *See* Mrs. Edward Bearne	Stanton by Dale	1878-1886	Landscape	—	—	3	—	2	—	—	3	—	4	12
Charlton, Edward W., A.R.P.E.	Ringwood	1891-1892	Landscape	—	—	3	—	—	—	—	—	—	1	4
Charlton, John, R.B.A. § ϕ	London	1870-1893	Sporting	—	—	36	—	21	—	1	2	4	34	98
Charlton, W. H.	Newcastle	1889-1891	Landscape	—	—	2	—	—	—	—	—	—	—	2
Charnay, Armand	Marlotte, Fr'nce	1892	—	—	—	—	—	—	—	—	—	*	—	—
Charnock, Miss Ellen	London	1852-1861	Flowers	—	—	—	—	—	—	—	—	—	21	21
Charpentier, Eugene	Versailles	1874	Animals	—	—	—	—	—	—	—	—	—	1	1
Charpin —	London	1765	Landscape	—	1	—	—	—	—	—	—	—	—	1
Charpin, Miss	London	1761-1767	Miniatures	4	13	—	—	—	—	—	—	—	—	17
Charretie, Mrs. John, formerly Miss Anna Maria Kenwell	London	1842-1875	Figures	—	—	40	4	50	—	—	—	—	43	137
Charsley, Matilda	Beaconsfield	1867-1869	Sculpture	—	—	5	—	—	—	—	—	—	1	6
Charteau, A. de	London	1832	Landscape	—	—	—	1	—	—	—	—	—	—	1
Charteris, E. M.	London	1880	Crayons	—	—	—	—	—	—	—	—	—	1	1
Charteris, Hon. Captain F. W.	Quidenham	1876-1883	Landscape	—	—	—	—	—	—	1	13	—	4	18
Charteris, Lady Louisa	London	1876-1881	Landscape	—	—	—	—	—	—	—	13	—	1	14
Charteris, Miss	London	1888	Figures	—	—	—	—	—	—	—	1	—	—	1
Chartran, G.	—	1887	Portraits	—	—	—	—	—	—	—	1	—	—	1
Chartran, Theobald	Paris	1881-1892	Miniatures	—	—	5	—	—	—	—	4	—	1	10
Chase, Frank M.	London	1874-1890	Landscape	—	—	7	—	22	—	4	—	—	9	42
Chase, G.	London	1797-1811	Portraits	—	—	17	—	—	—	—	—	—	—	17
Chase, Miss Jessie ‖	Kilburn	1885-1886	Flowers	—	—	—	—	—	—	3	—	—	—	3
Chase, John ‡	London	1826-1879	Churches	—	—	11	—	8	—	465	—	—	—	484
Chase, Mrs. John ‡	London	1836-1839	Landscape	—	—	—	—	—	—	10	—	—	—	10
Chase, Miss Marian, R.I. ‡	London	1866-1893	Flowers	—	—	8	—	9	—	205	3	—	7	232
Chase, Powell	London	1893	Figures	—	—	1	—	2	—	—	—	—	—	3
Chasemore, Archibald	London	1874-1878	"Judy"	—	—	—	—	—	—	—	—	—	7	7
Chatelin, John Baptiste Claude	London	1761-1763	Engraving	—	3	—	—	—	—	—	—	—	—	3
Chatfield, Edward	London	1823-1838	Scriptural	—	—	14	6	8	—	—	—	—	—	28
Chatfield, Rev. H.	—	1798-1801	Game	—	—	2	—	—	—	—	—	—	—	2
Chatrousse, Emile	Paris	1887	Sculpture	—	—	1	—	—	—	—	—	—	—	1
Chattock, Richard S., R.P.E	Solihull	1865-1891	Etching	—	—	22	—	1	—	1	—	—	7	31
Chauncey, Miss M. S.	London	1835	Portraits	—	—	1	—	—	—	—	—	—	—	1

Name.	Town.	First and Last Year of Ex.	Speciality.	S. A.	F. S.	R. A.	B. I.	S. S.	O. W.	N. W.	G. G.	N. G.	V. E.	Total.
Chauncy, Auschar	London	1860-1861	Scriptural	—	—	—	2	—	—	—	—	—	—	2
Chauvel, Théophile Narcisse	Paris	1872-1893	Etching	—	—	4	—	—	—	—	—	—	15	19
Chauvin, A.	—	1851	Scriptural	—	—	3	—	—	—	—	—	—	—	3
Chavalliaud, Leon	London	1893	Sculpture	—	—	1	—	—	—	—	—	—	—	1
Chawner, T.	London	1791-1800	Architecture	—	—	12	—	—	—	—	—	—	—	12
Cheadle, Henry	Birmingham	1875-1878	London	—	—	—	—	7	—	—	—	—	—	7
Checkley, Mrs. C.	London	1828-1831	Flowers	—	—	1	2	1	—	—	—	—	—	4
Cheere, Sir Henry William, Bart.	—	1798	Landscape	—	—	1	—	—	—	—	—	—	—	1
Cheesman, J.	London	1798	Head	—	—	1	—	—	—	—	—	—	—	1
Cheesman, Thomas	London	1802-1834	Mythological	—	—	18	9	12	—	—	—	—	—	39
Cheesman, Thomas Gedge	London	1890-1891	Domestic	—	—	1	—	—	—	—	—	—	1	2
Cheesman, William	Esher	1890-1891	Landscape	—	—	2	—	—	—	—	—	—	—	2
Cheetham, Miss M. E.	—	1868-1870	Figures	—	—	1	—	1	—	—	—	—	—	2
Cheffins, C. F.	London	1839-1843	Architecture	—	—	4	—	—	—	—	—	—	—	4
Cheffins, G. A.	London	1827-1828	Architecture	—	—	2	—	—	—	—	—	—	—	2
Cheffins, Miss Mary	Hoddesdon	1830-1850	Landscape	—	—	1	5	7	—	—	—	—	—	13
Cheli, C.	London	1839	Sculpture	—	—	1	—	—	—	—	—	—	—	1
Chelius, A.	Munich	1892	Cattle	—	—	1	—	—	—	—	—	—	—	1
Chelminski, Jan Von	London	1890-1893	Military	—	—	3	—	—	—	—	—	5	7	15
Cheloni, M.	London	1882	Domestic	—	—	1	—	—	—	—	—	—	—	1
Chenu, D.	London	1794	Sculpture	—	—	2	—	—	—	—	—	—	—	2
Chenu, Peter Francis	London	1771-1833	Sculpture	—	3	16	6	1	—	—	—	—	—	26
Cherveng —	—	1775	Landscape	1	—	—	—	—	—	—	—	—	—	1
Chesham, Francis	London	1777-1780	Engraving	4	—	—	—	—	—	—	—	—	—	4
Chesneau, A.	London	1863-1875	Sculpture	—	—	14	—	4	—	—	—	—	—	18
Chester, F.	London	1833	Figures	—	—	—	—	—	—	1	—	—	—	1
Chester, George	London	1846-1892	Landscape	—	—	37	22	20	—	—	—	3	9	91
Chester, George Frederick	London	1861-1889	Figures	—	—	9	3	2	—	—	—	—	3	17
Chester, J.	London	1783	Portraits	—	—	1	—	—	—	—	—	—	—	1
Chesters, S.	London	1849-1885	Enamels	—	—	12	—	—	—	—	—	—	1	13
Cheston (Horace), and Perkin (J. C.)	London	1887-1893	Architecture	—	—	3	—	—	—	—	—	—	—	3
Chettle, Miss Elizabeth M.	London	1880-1889	Figures	—	—	1	—	1	—	—	—	1	2	5
Chetwynd, Ida	London	1892	Domestic	—	—	—	—	1	—	—	—	—	—	1
Chetwynd, Kate F.	London	1892	Figures	—	—	—	—	1	—	—	—	—	—	1
Chevalier, Nicholas	London	1852-1887	Eastern	—	—	25	—	2	—	3	—	—	—	30
Chevalier, Robert Magnus	London	1876-1893	Egypt	—	—	3	—	26	—	3	1	1	11	45
Chevalier-Tayler, A. *See* T.	—	—		—	—	—	—	—	—	—	—	—	—	—
Cheverton, Benjamin	London	1835-1849	Sculpture	—	—	—	—	3	—	—	—	—	—	3
Cheyney, Miss Lucy M.	London	1837-1868	Flowers	—	—	10	—	10	—	—	—	—	—	20
Cheyney, Miss S. Emma	Redhill	1891-1892	Flowers	—	—	—	—	1	—	1	—	—	2	4
Chialiva, L.	Ecouen	1886	Rustic	—	—	—	—	—	—	1	—	—	—	1
Chiappini —	London	1800	Scriptural	—	—	1	—	—	—	—	—	—	—	1
Chierici, A.	London	1856	Figures	—	—	2	—	—	—	—	—	—	—	2
Chierici, Gaetano Reggio Emilia	Birmingham	1877-1881	Domestic	—	—	6	—	—	—	—	—	—	—	6
Chifflart, François	London	1874-1881	Etching	—	—	—	—	—	—	—	—	—	3	3
Chilcott, Mrs. J. W.	London	1844	Still Life	—	—	—	—	1	—	—	—	—	—	1
Child. *See* Goldie, Child, and Goldie	—	—	Architecture	—	—	—	—	—	—	—	—	—	—	—
Child, Master	London	1775	Figures	—	1	—	—	—	—	—	—	—	—	1
Child, Miss H.	London	1802-1803	Landscape	—	—	2	—	—	—	—	—	—	—	2
Child, J.	London	1798-1810	Landscape	—	—	12	—	—	—	—	—	—	—	12
Child, J.	—	1838	Portraits	—	—	1	—	—	—	—	—	—	—	1
Child, J. M.	Dudley	1827	Flowers, etc.	—	—	1	—	2	—	—	—	—	—	3
Child, W. *or* R.	Eltham	1783-1788	Game	—	—	4	—	—	—	—	—	—	—	4
Child, W.	London	1847-1851	Domestic	—	—	2	4	5	—	—	—	—	—	11
Child, Mrs.	—	1848	—	—	—	—	—	1	—	—	—	—	—	1
Childe, Elias §	London	1798-1848	Landscape	—	—	59	114	314	5	3	—	—	—	495
Childe, Miss Ellen E.	London	1878	Figures	—	—	1	—	—	—	—	—	—	—	1
Childe, H. S.	London	1810	Landscape	—	—	1	—	—	—	—	—	—	—	1
Childe, James Warren	London	1815-1853	Miniatures	—	—	67	—	16	—	—	—	—	—	83
Childe, Maria	London	1839-1841	Portraits	—	—	3	—	—	—	—	—	—	—	3
Childers, Miss Louise	London	1885	Buildings	—	—	—	—	—	—	2	—	—	—	2
Childers, Miss Milly	London	1890-1893	Portraits	—	—	—	—	3	—	—	—	1	—	4
Childes, D. T.	London	1850	Architecture	—	—	1	—	—	—	—	—	—	—	1
Childs, Alfred Edward	London	1867-1875	Birds	—	—	—	—	4	—	—	—	—	—	4
Childs, Miss Agnes	London	1852-1871	Flowers, etc.	—	—	—	—	11	—	—	—	—	—	11
Childs, George	London	1826-1873	Landscape	—	—	17	1	23	—	1	—	—	—	42
Childs, Miss Julia	London	1851-1864	Fruit, etc.	—	—	4	—	24	—	—	—	—	—	28
Childs, J. M.	Dudley	1828	Fish	—	—	—	—	1	—	—	—	—	—	1
Childs-Clarke, Miss Sophia	Thorverton	1889	Still Life	—	—	1	—	—	—	—	—	—	—	1
Chilman, Miss Lizzie	London	1856-1864	Flowers	—	—	1	—	24	—	—	—	—	16	41
Chilton, E.	London	1869	Flowers	—	—	—	—	1	—	—	—	—	—	1
Chinn, S. (?) Thomas	London	1833-1845	Portraits	—	—	12	—	1	—	—	—	—	—	13

Name.	Town.	First and Last Year of Ex.	Speciality.	S. A.	F. S.	R. A.	B. I.	S. S.	O. W.	N.W.	G. G.	N. G.	V. E.	Tota
Chinnery —	London	1764-1766	Portraits	—	2	—	—	—	—	—	—	—	—	2
Chinnery, George, R.H.A.	London	1791-1846	Miniatures	—	—	39	—	—	—	—	—	—	—	39
Chipchase-Smith, R. *See* S.	—	—	—	—	—	—	—	—	—	—	—	—	—	—
Chipp, Herbert	London	1877-1885	Landscape	—	—	—	—	1	—	2	—	—	—	3
Chippendale, Thomas	London	1784-1801	Rustic	—	—	5	—	—	—	—	—	—	—	5
Chisholm, Alexander, F.S.A.†	London	1820-1847	Historical	—	—	15	15	11	40	—	—	—	—	81
Chisholm, Miss Annie	London	1890-1893	Miniatures	—	—	3	—	—	—	2	—	—	—	5
Chisholm, Miss Helen	Haslemere	1887	Domestic	—	—	—	—	—	—	1	—	—	—	1
Chisholme, Alex. C.	London	1841-1856	Domestic	—	—	10	5	—	—	—	—	—	—	15
Chisholme, J.	London	1803-1808	Architecture	—	—	6	—	—	—	—	—	—	—	6
Chisholme, R.	London	1876-1892	Buildings	—	—	8	—	—	—	—	—	—	—	8
Chisholme, R. F.	London	1858-1859	Sea Pieces	—	—	1	1	—	—	—	—	—	—	2
Chitqua —	London	1770	Sculpture	—	—	1	—	—	—	—	—	—	—	1
Chittenden, T.	London	1845-1864	Figures	—	—	4	4	—	—	—	—	—	—	8
Cholmney, Mrs. Isabel	Rome	1864-1869	Sculpture	—	—	6	—	1	—	—	—	—	—	7
Cholmondley, R.	London	1856-1867	Portraits	—	—	11	—	—	—	—	—	—	—	11
Chorley and Connor	Leeds	1888-1891	Architecture	—	—	6	—	—	—	—	—	—	—	6
Choveeaux, L. N.	London	1817	Buildings	—	—	1	—	—	—	—	—	—	—	1
Christian, B.	—	1780	Buildings	—	—	2	—	—	—	—	—	—	—	2
Christian, Mrs. Edward (Eleanor E.)	London	1843-1854	Portraits	—	—	10	—	—	—	—	—	—	—	10
Christian, Ewan	London	1833-1879	Architecture	—	—	19	—	—	—	—	—	—	—	19
Christian, Miss Gertrude	Penzance	1888	Flowers	—	—	—	—	—	—	1	—	—	—	1
Christian, John Christopher	London	1776-1780	Still Life	3	1	—	—	—	—	—	—	—	—	4
Christie, Alexander, A.R.S.A.	Edinburgh	1848-1853	Historical	—	—	1	—	—	—	—	—	—	3	4
Christie, Alex.	London	1838-1840	Historical	—	—	1	3	—	—	—	—	—	—	4
Christie, Archibald H.	London	1888-1893	Still Life	—	—	—	—	—	—	—	—	—	3	3
Christie, Ernest	Redhill	1886-1893	Landscape	—	—	2	—	7	—	—	—	—	1	10
Christie, F.	London	1874	Landscape	—	—	—	—	1	—	—	—	—	—	1
Christie, F. H.	Blackheath	1874-1878	Landscape	—	—	2	—	2	—	—	—	—	1	5
Christie, Henry C.	London	1881-1893	Sculpture	—	—	11	—	1	—	—	—	—	—	12
Christie, James Elder	London	1876-1893	Domestic	—	—	19	—	7	—	—	10	6	8	50
Christie, Robert	London	1891-1893	Figures	—	—	1	—	1	—	—	—	—	3	5
Christie, Miss Vera	—	1893	Portraits	—	—	—	—	—	—	—	—	1	1	2
Christman, J.	London	1783	Birds	—	—	1	—	—	—	—	—	—	—	1
Christmas, Thomas C.	London	1819-1825	Sporting	—	—	2	11	6	5	—	—	—	—	24
Christopher, John Thomas	London	1854	Architecture	—	—	1	—	—	—	—	—	—	—	1
Christopher and White	London	1882-1889	Architecture	—	—	6	—	—	—	—	—	—	—	6
Christophers, J. M.	Exeter	1871	Landscape	—	—	—	—	1	—	—	—	—	—	1
Christy, Miss Josephine	Chelmsford	1889	Fruit	—	—	—	—	2	—	—	—	—	—	2
Chrone, Robert	London	1768	Landscape	1	—	—	—	—	—	—	—	—	—	1
Chubard —	—	1763	Miniatures	1	—	—	—	—	—	—	—	—	—	1
Chubbard —	Liverpool	1771-1773	Landscape	4	2	—	—	—	—	—	—	—	—	6
Church —	Rotherhithe	1801	Sea Pieces	—	—	1	—	—	—	—	—	—	—	1
Church, A. H.	London	1854-1870	Landscape	—	—	5	3	—	—	—	—	—	—	8
Church, Frederick Edwin	New York	1852	Landscape	—	—	1	—	—	—	—	—	—	—	1
Churcher, G. P.	Oxford	1886	Buildings	—	—	—	—	1	—	—	—	—	—	1
Churchill, H.	London	1872	Algiers	—	—	—	—	1	—	—	—	—	—	1
Churchyard, Thomas	Woodbridge	1830-1833	Landscape	—	—	2	—	8	—	1	—	—	—	11
Chuysenaar, Alfred	—	1891	Portraits	—	—	—	—	—	—	—	—	—	1	1
Ciapelli, G.	Florence	1888-1889	Landscape	—	—	—	—	—	—	—	—	—	4	4
Ciardiello, Michele	London	1873-1889	Domestic	—	—	—	—	6	—	—	—	—	—	6
Ciceri, Eugene	London	1871	Landscape	—	—	—	—	1	—	—	—	—	—	1
Cipriani, Captain Sir Henry	London	1781	Portraits	—	—	1	—	—	—	—	—	—	—	1
Cipriani, John Baptist, R.A.	London	1769-1783	Mythological	—	1	14	—	—	—	—	—	—	—	15
Cipriani, Nazareno	Rome	1877-1891	Venice	—	—	3	—	—	—	4	—	—	3	10
Ciseri, A.	London	1870	Scriptural	—	—	1	—	—	—	—	—	—	—	1
Civiletti, B.	Palermo	1876	Sculpture	—	—	1	—	—	—	—	—	—	—	1
Clabburn, Arthur E.	Norwich	1875-1879	Portraits	—	—	3	—	—	—	—	—	—	—	3
Clack, Richard Augustus	London	1827-1875	Portraits	—	—	27	5	14	—	—	—	—	—	46
Clack, Thomas	Coventry	1851-1891	Domestic	—	—	13	—	—	—	—	—	—	3	16
Clacy, Miss Ellen	London	1870-1893	Domestic	—	—	23	—	25	—	—	1	—	4	53
Clair, St. *See* S.	—	—	—	—	—	—	—	—	—	—	—	—	—	—
Clapham, Master	London	1768-1771	Flowers	—	4	—	—	—	—	—	—	—	—	4
Clapham, James T.	Crayford	1862-1868	Fruit	—	—	—	—	2	—	—	—	—	1	3
Clapham, Miss Mary	London	1885	Moonlight	—	—	—	—	—	—	—	—	—	1	1
Clare, George	Birmingham	1864-1873	Flowers	—	—	3	7	32	—	—	—	—	2	44
Clare, Oliver	London	1873-1883	Fruit	—	—	1	—	2	—	—	—	—	—	3
Clare, T.	St. Albans	1831	Landscape	—	—	1	—	—	—	—	—	—	—	1
Clare, Miss	London	1858	Flowers	—	—	1	—	—	—	—	—	—	—	1
Claris, F. G.	London	1884	Landscape	—	—	—	—	1	—	—	—	—	—	1
Clark —	—	1777-1778	Landscape	—	—	2	—	—	—	—	—	—	—	2
Clark —	—	1814	Animals	—	—	—	—	—	—	—	—	—	1	1

Name.	Town.	First and Last Year of Ex.	Speciality.	S. A.	F. S.	R. A.	B. I.	S. S.	O. W.	N. W.	G. G.	N. G.	V. E.	Total.
Clark, Junr. *See* Hartshorne and Clark	—	—	Architecture	—	—	—	—	—	—	—	—	—	—	—
Clark, B.	London	1875	Animals	—	—	—	—	1	—	—	—	—	—	1
Clark, C. Macdonald	Bournemouth	1879-1881	Figures	—	—	1	—	—	—	—	—	—	1	2
Clark, C. W.	London	1839-1843	Portraits	—	—	8	—	—	—	—	—	—	—	8
Clark, Dixon	Blaydon	1890-1891	Cattle	—	—	4	—	—	—	—	—	—	—	4
Clark, Falconer	Dorking	1888-1889	Domestic	—	—	—	—	1	—	2	—	—	—	3
Clark, Francis	London	1853-1865	Figures	—	—	6	3	5	—	—	—	—	—	14
Clark, G.	London	1806	Flowers	—	—	1	—	—	—	—	—	—	—	1
Clark, James φ	Hartlepool	1881-1893	Scriptural	—	—	16	—	11	—	1	—	—	17	45
Clark, John Heaviside	London	1801-1804	Landscape	—	—	4	—	—	—	—	—	—	—	4
Clark, John	Bury	1848	Architecture	—	—	1	—	—	—	—	—	—	—	1
Clark, Joseph § φ	London	1857-1893	Domestic	—	—	83	7	3	—	1	—	—	48	142
Clark, Joseph Benwell	London	1876-1893	Rustic	—	—	7	—	6	—	—	7	—	13	33
Clark, John Heaviside	London	1812-1832	Figures	—	—	8	—	—	—	—	—	—	—	8
Clark, J. M.	London	1829-1847	Architecture	—	—	3	—	—	—	—	—	—	—	3
Clark, J. W.	London	1824	Enamels	—	—	1	—	—	—	—	—	—	—	1
Clark, Miss Louisa Campbell	London	1887-1891	Miniatures	—	—	3	—	—	—	—	—	—	—	3
Clark, M.	London	1831	Architecture	—	—	1	—	—	—	—	—	—	—	1
Clark, Miss Mary	London	1844-1848	Figures	—	—	6	—	1	—	—	—	—	—	7
Clark, Miss Mary Brodie	Brentford	1889	Fruit	—	—	—	—	1	—	—	—	—	—	1
Clark, R.	London	1825-1846	River Scenes	—	—	16	—	—	—	—	—	—	—	16
Clark, R.	London	1860	Figures	—	—	—	—	—	—	—	—	—	2	2
Clark, S. H.	London	1830-1831	Architecture	—	—	3	—	—	—	—	—	—	—	3
Clark, Thomas, A.R.S.A.	London	1827-1870	Landscape	—	—	12	15	6	—	—	—	—	14	47
Clark, William	Worcester	1860	Landscape	—	—	—	—	3	—	—	—	—	—	3
Clark, W. B.	London	1830	Pompeii	—	—	—	—	1	—	—	—	—	—	1
Clark, W. F. C.	London	1884-1890	Landscape	—	—	—	—	2	—	7	—	—	—	9
Clark, W. T.	London	1826-1845	Architecture	—	—	11	—	—	—	—	—	—	—	11
Clark, Mrs.	London	1763	Flowers	—	1	—	—	—	—	—	—	—	—	1
Clark, Miss	London	1765	Needlework	—	1	—	—	—	—	—	—	—	—	1
Clark-Hardy, Miss Ida. *See* H.	—	—	—	—	—	—	—	—	—	—	—	—	—	—
Clarke —. *See* Dawkes and Clarke	—	—	Architecture	—	—	—	—	—	—	—	—	—	—	—
Clarke, A.	London	1817	Landscape	—	—	1	—	—	—	—	—	—	—	1
Clarke, A.	Blackheath	1892	Flowers	—	—	—	—	1	—	—	—	—	—	1
Clarke, A. A.	Taunton	1851	Landscape	—	—	1	—	—	—	—	—	—	—	1
Clarke (Sir Andrew) and Bell (E. Ingress)	London	1885	Architecture	—	—	2	—	—	—	—	—	—	—	2
Clarke, A. F. Graham	Rhayadr	1883	Landscape	—	—	—	—	—	—	—	—	—	1	1
Clarke, A. T.	London	1890-1891	Domestic	—	—	—	—	—	—	1	—	—	—	1
Clarke, Miss Bethia	Eastbourne	1892-1893	Domestic	—	—	—	—	4	—	—	—	—	—	4
Clarke, Caspar	Colwich, Rugeley	1856-1871	Landscape	—	—	2	—	4	—	—	—	—	1	7
Clarke, C. A.	London	1818-1840	Landscape	—	—	3	4	1	—	—	—	—	—	8
Clarke, C. J.	London	1852	Architecture	—	—	2	—	—	—	—	—	—	—	2
Clarke, E.	London	1842	Fruit	—	—	1	—	—	—	—	—	—	—	1
Clarke, Edward	London	1878-1880	Architecture	—	—	3	—	—	—	—	—	—	—	3
Clarke, Miss E.	London	1799	Miniatures	—	—	5	—	—	—	—	—	—	—	5
Clarke, Edward Francis C.	London	1872-1887	Architecture	—	—	12	—	8	—	6	—	—	5	31
Clarke, F.	London	1819	Buildings	—	—	1	—	—	—	—	—	—	—	1
Clarke, Frederick	Leicester	1834-1870	Game	—	—	10	—	—	—	—	—	—	—	10
Clarke, George	Birmingham	1821-1839	Sculpture	—	—	15	—	—	—	—	—	—	—	15
Clarke, George Frederick	London	1868-1872	Figures	—	—	2	—	1	—	—	—	—	—	3
Clarke, G. R.	London	1856-1883	Architecture	—	—	5	—	—	—	—	—	—	—	5
Clarke, George Row	London	1858-1888	Landscape	—	—	3	7	37	—	—	—	—	7	54
Clarke, George Somers, F.R.I.B.A.	London	1842-1881	Architecture	—	—	20	—	—	—	—	—	—	—	20
Clarke, H.	London	1834	Portraits	—	—	1	—	—	—	—	—	—	—	1
Clarke, Mrs. H. Savile ‖	London	1882-1890	Landscape	—	—	—	—	—	—	1	11	5	—	17
Clarke, Miss Ida Wilson	London	1884-1889	Sculpture	—	—	3	—	—	—	—	1	3	—	7
Clarke, J.	London	1824-1825	Figures	—	—	—	—	5	—	—	—	—	—	5
Clarke, J.	London	1841	Fruit	—	—	1	—	—	—	—	—	—	—	1
Clarke, Jane	London	1833-1842	Landscape	—	—	3	—	—	—	—	—	—	—	3
Clarke, John	Liverpool	1893	Architecture	—	—	1	—	—	—	—	—	—	—	1
Clarke, Joseph, F.S.A., V.P.R.I.B.A.	London	1845-1878	Architecture	—	—	24	—	—	—	—	—	—	—	24
Clarke, J. R.	London	1861	Landscape	—	—	—	—	1	—	—	—	—	—	1
Clarke, J. S.	London	1874	Architecture	—	—	4	—	—	—	—	—	—	—	4
Clarke (J. W.) and Norton (J.)	—	1850	Architecture	—	—	1	—	—	—	—	—	—	—	1
Clarke, Miss Kate	London	1863-1884	Flowers	—	—	—	1	1	—	—	—	—	4	6
Clarke, L. J. Graham-, R.C.A.	Rhayadr	1879-1887	Landscape	—	—	9	—	1	—	—	—	—	2	12
Clarke, Miss Mary C.	Bromley	1873	Churches	—	—	—	—	1	—	—	—	—	—	1
Clarke, Miss Minnie E.	Bedford Park	1892	Figures	—	—	—	—	—	—	—	—	—	1	1
Clarke, Miss Polly	Bushey	1893	Flowers	—	—	1	—	—	—	—	—	—	—	1
Clarke, R. E.	London	1825-1848	Sea Pieces	—	—	1	17	25	—	—	—	—	—	43
Clarke, S.	London	1873	Cattle	—	—	—	—	1	—	—	—	—	—	1
Clarke, Somers, F.S.A. *See also* Micklethwaite and Clarke	London	1871-1893	Architecture	—	—	11	—	—	—	—	—	—	—	11

Name.	Town.	First and Last Year of Ex.	Speciality.	S. A.	F. S.	R. A.	B. I.	S. S.	O. W.	N.W.	G. G.	N. G.	V. E.	Total.
Clarke, Samuel Barling	London	1852-1878	Domestic	—	—	15	9	31	—	—	—	—	7	62
Clarke, Miss Sophia Childs-. *See* Childs.	—	—	—	—	—	—	—	—	—	—	—	—	—	—
Clarke, Theophilus, A.R.A.	London	1795-1810	Portraits	—	—	67	2	—	—	—	—	—	—	69
Clarke, Thomas (Pupil of Reynolds)	London	1769-1775	Portraits	—	—	4	—	—	—	—	—	—	—	4
Clarke, Thomas Chatfield	London	1874-1878	Architecture	—	—	3	—	—	—	—	—	—	—	3
Clarke, T. C. and Son	London	1891	Architecture	—	—	1	—	—	—	—	—	—	—	1
Clarke, T. H.	London	1833	Architecture	—	—	2	—	—	—	—	—	—	—	2
Clarke, William	London	1774	Architecture	—	1	—	—	—	—	—	—	—	—	1
Clarke, William. *See* Eddington	Worcester	1860	Landscape	—	—	1	—	—	—	—	—	—	—	1
Clarke, W. B.	London	1832-1835	Architecture	—	—	2	—	—	—	—	—	—	—	2
Clarke, W. D.	London	1858-1862	Landscape	—	—	—	—	2	—	—	—	—	—	2
Clarke, Miss	Bromley	1872	Landscape	—	—	1	—	—	—	—	—	—	—	1
Clarkson, A.	London	1835-1836	Portraits	—	—	3	—	—	—	—	—	—	—	3
Clarkson, Jane	London	1840	Landscape	—	—	1	—	—	—	—	—	—	—	1
Clarkson, John, and Samuel Flint	London	1877	Architecture	—	—	1	—	—	—	—	—	—	—	1
Clarkson, Miss Marion	London	1891	Domestic	—	—	1	—	—	—	—	—	—	—	1
Clarkson, Nathaniel	London	1762-1767	Portraits	4	—	—	—	—	—	—	—	—	—	4
Clarkson, Robert	Parklington	1880-1891	Landscape	—	—	3	—	1	—	—	—	—	—	4
Clarkson, W. H.	Highgate	1893	Landscape	—	—	—	—	1	—	—	—	—	—	1
Classon, W. B.	Boston, U.S.A.	1881	Woodcuts	—	—	—	—	—	—	—	—	—	1	1
Clater, F. R.	London	1848-1854	Sea Pieces	—	—	2	2	7	—	—	—	—	—	11
Clater, Thomas §	London	1819-1859	Domestic	—	—	43	91	194	—	1	—	—	—	329
Clater, T. B.	London	1842	Domestic	—	—	—	—	1	—	—	—	—	—	1
Clater, Miss, afterwards Mrs. T. C. Collingwood	London	1843-1846	Figures	—	—	—	1	7	—	—	—	—	—	8
Claudel, Camille	Paris	1886	Sculpture	—	—	1	—	—	—	—	—	—	—	1
Claudet, Mrs. M. H.	London	1877	Landscape	—	—	—	—	1	—	—	—	—	—	1
Clausen, Miss Eleanor M.	London	1886-1890	Flowers	—	—	—	—	1	—	—	1	—	—	2
Clausen, George, A.R.W.S., R.I., † ‡ φ	London	1874-1893	Figures	—	—	16	—	4	18	39	12	4	27	120
Clausen, Mrs. George (Agnes M.)	—	1882-1884	Domestic	—	—	—	—	2	—	2	—	—	—	4
Clausen, William	London	1876-1882	Architecture	—	—	4	—	—	—	—	—	—	—	4
Clave, P.	Rome	1846	Historical	—	—	1	—	—	—	—	—	—	—	1
Claxton, Miss Adelaide, afterwards Mrs.	—	—	—	—	—	—	—	—	—	—	—	—	—	—
George Gordon Turner	London	1860-1876	Domestic	—	—	4	—	20	—	—	—	—	9	33
Claxton, Miss Florence A.	London	1859-1879	Historical	—	—	5	—	5	—	—	—	—	9	19
Claxton, Marshall	London	1832-1875	Scriptural	—	—	32	31	27	—	—	—	—	17	107
Clay, Lady	—	1888	Medals	—	—	—	—	—	—	—	—	1	—	1
Clay, Sir Arthur, Bart.	Shere	1872-1893	Domestic	—	—	19	—	6	—	1	5	11	31	73
Clay, Alfred Barron	London	1852-1870	Figures	—	—	19	1	2	—	—	—	—	7	29
Clay, G.	London	1846-1860	Landscape	—	—	8	9	3	—	—	—	—	—	20
Clay, John	Ramsgate	1837-1856	Sea Pieces	—	—	1	1	4	—	—	—	—	—	6
Clay, Julia M.	London	1880-1881	Figures	—	—	—	—	—	—	—	—	—	5	5
Clay, T.	London	1799	Landscape	—	—	1	—	—	—	—	—	—	—	1
Clays, Paul Jean	Paris	1884	Sea Pieces	—	—	—	—	—	—	—	1	—	—	1
Clayton, A. B.	London	1814-1837	Architecture	—	—	34	—	2	—	—	—	—	—	36
Clayton, C.	London	1762-1778	Fruit	9	2	—	—	—	—	—	—	—	—	11
Clayton (C. E.), and Black (E.)	Brighton	1890	Architecture	—	—	1	—	—	—	—	—	—	—	1
Clayton, C. J.	—	1849	Architecture	—	—	1	—	—	—	—	—	—	—	1
Clayton, H.	London	1847	Domestic	—	—	1	—	—	—	—	—	—	—	1
Clayton, H. B.	—	1830	Domestic	—	—	1	—	—	—	—	—	—	—	1
Clayton, John	London	1763	Fruit	—	2	—	—	—	—	—	—	—	—	2
Clayton, Joseph	London	1839-1856	Architecture	—	—	7	—	—	—	—	—	—	—	7
Clayton (J. B.), and Bell (A.)	London	1861	Stained Glass	—	—	1	—	—	—	—	—	—	—	1
Clayton, J. Essex	London	1871-1885	Domestic	—	—	5	—	1	—	—	—	—	2	8
Clayton, Captain J. W.	London	1872	Landscape	—	—	—	—	—	—	—	—	—	1	1
Clayton, Miss Mary Anna	Brighton	1884-1885	Flowers	—	—	—	—	—	—	—	—	—	3	3
Clayton, W.	London	1857	Landscape	—	—	1	—	—	—	—	—	—	—	1
Clayton, W. H.	London	1846-1847	Architecture	—	—	2	—	—	—	—	—	—	—	2
Clear, Le. *See* L.	—	—	—	—	—	—	—	—	—	—	—	—	—	—
Cleave, W.	London	1819-1820	Architecture	—	—	2	—	—	—	—	—	—	—	2
Cleaver, W.	London	1813	Architecture	—	—	1	—	—	—	—	—	—	—	1
Cleaver, Miss	Streatham	1848	Landscape	—	—	—	—	—	—	—	—	—	5	5
Clefan, J.	London	1827	Architecture	—	—	—	—	1	—	—	—	—	—	1
Cleavesmith, Edmund	Sheffield	1880-1884	Landscape	—	—	—	—	8	—	5	—	—	—	13
Clegg, S.	—	1852-1853	Landscape	—	—	2	—	—	—	—	—	—	—	2
Cleghorn, J.	London	1824-1828	Buildings	—	—	—	—	5	—	—	—	—	—	5
Cleghorn, John	London	1840-1881	Figures	—	—	5	2	7	—	—	—	—	3	17
Cleland, A.	Edinburgh	1818-1819	Figures	—	—	2	1	—	—	—	—	—	—	3
Cleland, William H.	London	1892	Sculpture	—	—	—	—	—	—	—	—	1	—	1
Clemence, J.	London	1815	Architecture	—	—	1	—	—	—	—	—	—	—	1
Clements, C. V.	Clapham	1841	Domestic	—	—	1	—	—	—	—	—	—	—	1
Clements, G. H.	London	1886	Domestic	—	—	—	—	1	—	—	—	—	—	1
Clements, John	Worcester	1818-1831	Portraits	—	—	13	—	1	—	—	—	—	—	14

Name.	Town.	First and Last Year of Ex.	Speciality.	S. A.	F. S.	R. A.	B. I.	S. S.	O. W.	N. W.	G. G.	N. G.	V. E.	Total.
Cleminshaw, M. T.	London	1891	Sea Pieces	—	—	—	—	2	—	—	—	—	—	2
Cleminson, Robert	London	1865-1868	Sporting	—	—	—	10	5	—	—	—	—	—	15
Clemmes, Miss	London	1764	Needlework	—	1	—	—	—	—	—	—	—	—	1
Clennell, Luke	London	1810-1818	Figures	—	—	6	15	—	18	—	—	—	31	70
Clerihew, W.	London	1840-1841	Architecture	—	—	2	—	—	—	—	—	—	—	2
Clerisseau, Charles Louis, F.S.A.	Paris	1772-1790	Ruins	14	—	4	—	—	—	—	—	—	—	18
Cleveley, John	Deptford	1764-1786	Shipping	—	55	31	—	—	—	—	—	—	—	86
Cleveley, Robert	Deptford	1767-1806	Sea Pieces	—	15	57	1	—	—	—	—	—	—	73
Cleverly, Charles F.	London	1893	Figures	—	—	1	—	—	—	—	—	—	—	1
Cleynheus, T.	Antwerp	1870	Churches	—	—	1	—	—	—	—	—	—	—	1
Clifford, Edward	London	1866-1893	Portraits	—	—	25	—	3	—	3	15	10	40	96
Clifford, Edward C.	London	1891-1893	Figures	—	—	2	—	1	—	1	—	—	3	7
Clifford, Henry	Blackheath	1866-1884	Landscape	—	—	—	—	—	—	1	—	—	1	2
Clifford, Henry Charles	London	1890-1893	Landscape	—	—	4	—	3	—	—	—	—	2	9
Clifford, J.	—	1842	Cameos	—	—	1	—	—	—	—	—	—	—	1
Clifford, Maurice	London	1890-1892	Domestic	—	—	1	—	—	—	—	—	—	4	5
Clift, A.	London	1879	Landscape	—	—	—	—	2	—	—	—	—	—	2
Clift, Stephen	Croydon	1868-1886	Landscape	—	—	1	—	7	—	—	—	—	2	10
Clifton, Edward Norton	London	1836-1838	Architecture	—	—	3	—	1	—	—	—	—	—	4
Clifton, J.	—	1849-1850	Figures	—	—	2	—	—	—	—	—	—	—	2
Clifton, John S.	Oxford	1852-1869	Dramatic	—	—	3	2	—	—	—	—	—	1	6
Clifton, William	London	1849-1885	Landscape	—	—	2	3	—	—	2	—	—	2	9
Clink, Miss Matilda J.	London	1891	Flowers	—	—	1	—	—	—	—	—	—	—	1
Clint, Alfred § ‡	London	1828-1881	Sea Pieces	—	—	24	35	406	—	3	—	—	—	468
Clint, F. R.	London	1825	Intaglios	—	—	1	—	—	—	—	—	—	—	1
Clint, George, A.R.A.	London	1802-1847	Dramatic	—	—	99	9	15	2	—	—	—	—	125
Clint, Leonidas	London	1811-1817	Domestic	—	—	2	—	—	—	—	—	—	—	2
Clint, R.	London	1817-1828	Intaglios	—	—	6	—	—	—	—	—	—	—	6
Clint, Raphael	London	1857-1858	Landscape	—	—	—	—	2	—	—	—	—	—	2
Clint, Scipio	London	1825-1838	Medals	—	—	16	—	18	—	—	—	—	—	34
Clive, T.	Hampton Court	1856-1857	Portraits	—	—	3	—	—	—	—	—	—	—	3
Clode, Miss	—	1832	Figures	—	—	—	—	1	—	—	—	—	—	1
Clothier, Robert	London	1842-1873	Domestic	—	—	19	15	19	—	—	—	—	—	53
Cloud, Mrs. J. Lizzie	Galway	1873-1878	Domestic	—	—	1	—	4	—	—	—	—	2	7
Clouston, Robert S.	Bushey	1887-1892	Engraving	—	—	6	—	—	—	—	—	—	1	7
Clover, Joseph	London	1804-1836	Mythological	—	—	58	12	—	—	—	—	—	—	70
Clow, Miss Florence	London	1882-1884	Portraits	—	—	1	—	4	—	—	—	—	1	6
Clowes, Butler	London	1768-1773	Engraving	—	16	—	—	—	—	—	—	—	—	16
Clowes, Miss C.	London	1878	Flowers	—	—	1	—	—	—	—	—	—	—	1
Cluff, Elsie M.	Walthamstow	1891	Churches	—	—	—	—	1	—	—	—	—	—	1
Clutterbuck, C.	London	1826-1842	Historical	—	—	9	—	4	—	—	—	—	—	13
Clutton, Miss	Acton	1802-1803	Landscape	—	—	3	—	—	—	—	—	—	—	3
Clutton, Miss B.	—	1803	Landscape	—	—	3	—	—	—	—	—	—	—	3
Clutton, Miss D.	Acton	1802-1803	Landscape	—	—	2	—	—	—	—	—	—	—	2
Clutton, Miss E.	—	1806	Landscape	—	—	2	—	—	—	—	—	—	—	2
Clutton, H.	London	1845-1861	Architecture	—	—	10	—	—	—	—	—	—	—	10
Coad, Richard	London	1885-1887	Architecture	—	—	5	—	—	—	—	—	—	—	5
Coad (Richard) and Maclaren (J. M.)	London	1886	Architecture	—	—	1	—	—	—	—	—	—	—	1
Coade, Miss Eleanor	—	1773-1791	Sculpture	33	6	—	—	—	—	—	—	—	—	39
Coate, S.	London	1812	Drawings	—	—	1	—	—	—	—	—	—	—	1
Coates —	London	1775	Globes	1	—	—	—	—	—	—	—	—	—	1
Coates, Miss Kate Belford	Streatham	1890	Landscape	—	—	—	—	—	—	1	—	—	—	1
Coates, Miss	London	1833	Landscape	—	—	—	—	—	—	1	—	—	—	1
Cobb, Alfred F.	London	1878-1889	Landscape	—	—	—	—	11	—	—	—	—	6	17
Cobb, Edward F.	London	1872	Landscape	—	—	—	—	—	—	—	—	—	2	2
Cobb, Mrs. Emily J.	London	1890	Miniature	—	—	1	—	—	—	—	—	—	—	1
Cobb, T. P.	London	1865	Landscape	—	—	—	—	—	—	—	—	—	1	1
Cobbe, Bernard	London	1868-1883	Domestic	—	—	5	—	6	—	—	—	—	—	11
Cobbett, Edward John, R.B.A. §	London	1833-1880	Landscape	—	—	50	49	343	—	—	—	—	36	478
Cobbett, Miss Phoebe M.	London	1875-1882	Domestic	—	—	—	—	12	—	—	—	—	—	12
Cobbett, William V. H.	Richmond	1888-1890	Venice	—	—	—	—	8	—	—	—	—	—	8
Cobden, T.	London	1813	Architecture	—	—	1	—	—	—	—	—	—	—	1
Cobden, T. A.	London	1835-1839	Architecture	—	—	3	—	—	—	—	—	—	—	3
Coblenz —	London	1809	Portraits	—	—	1	—	—	—	—	—	—	—	1
Cobley, Miss Florence	London	1888-1889	Flowers	—	—	—	—	—	—	—	—	—	2	2
Cochran, John	London	1821-1827	Miniatures	—	—	2	—	16	—	—	—	—	—	18
Cock, De. *See* D.	—	—	—	—	—	—	—	—	—	—	—	—	—	—
Cockaine, J.	London	1817-1818	Sculpture	—	—	3	—	—	—	—	—	—	—	3
Cockburn, Miss C.	Dulwich	1825	Figures	—	—	1	—	—	—	—	—	—	—	1
Cockburn, Edwin	London	1837-1868	Domestic	—	—	15	16	34	—	—	—	—	1	66
Cockburn, Miss Madeline. *See* Mrs. Marrable	—	—	—	—	—	—	—	—	—	—	—	—	—	—
Cockburn, Ralph	London	1802-1812	Portraits	—	—	2	—	—	—	—	—	—	3	5

Name.	Town.	First and Last Year of Ex.	Speciality.	S. A.	F. S.	R. A.	B. I.	S. S.	O. W.	N. W.	G. G.	N. G.	V. E.	Total.
Cockburn, William	—	1866	Buildings	—	—	—	—	—	—	—	—	—	1	1
Cockburn, W. A.	London	1850-1852	Landscape	—	—	2	1	—	—	—	—	—	—	3
Cockerell, Charles Robert, R.A.	London	1818-1858	Architecture	—	—	17	—	—	—	—	—	—	—	17
Cockerell, Miss Christabel A.	London	1884-1893	Domestic	—	—	7	—	—	—	—	—	—	1	8
Cockerell, Edward A.	London	1883	Landscape	—	—	—	—	1	—	—	—	—	—	1
Cockerell, Frederick Pepys	London	1854-1877	Architecture	—	—	24	—	—	—	—	—	—	—	24
Cockerell, Samuel Pepys	London	1785-1803	Architecture	—	—	18	—	—	—	—	—	—	—	18
Cockerell, Samuel Pepys	London	1874-1893	Domestic	—	—	19	—	3	—	—	1	—	9	32
Cockerill, Miss Alice M.	London	1893	Flowers	—	—	1	—	—	—	—	—	—	—	1
Cocking, Edward	London	1830-1848	Still Life	—	—	1	2	8	—	—	—	—	—	11
Cocking, R.	—	1839	Figures	—	—	1	—	—	—	—	—	—	—	1
Cockram, George, R.C.A.	Liverpool	1883-1893	Landscape	—	—	19	—	3	—	13	—	—	—	35
Cockran, Henrietta	London	1871	Landscape	—	—	—	—	—	—	—	—	—	1	1
Cockrell, Louis	Birmingham	1891-1892	Domestic	—	—	2	—	—	—	—	—	—	—	2
Codd, John	London	1876-1885	Architecture	—	—	3	—	—	—	—	—	—	—	3
Code, Mrs., formerly Miss Mary Benwell	London	1783-1791	Miniatures	—	—	22	—	—	—	—	—	—	—	22
Codina, Victoriano. *See* Langlin	London	1879-1880	Domestic	—	—	6	—	2	—	—	—	—	—	8
Codman, W. C.	London	1884	Architecture	—	—	1	—	—	—	—	—	—	—	1
Coe, E. O.	London	1833-1851	Churches	—	—	10	—	2	—	—	—	—	—	12
Coe, Henry Edward	Lewisham	1849-1863	Architecture	—	—	4	—	—	—	—	—	—	—	4
Coe (H. E.) and Goodwin (E.)	Lewisham	1848-1855	Architecture	—	—	7	—	—	—	—	—	—	—	7
Coe and Robinson	London	1878	Architecture	—	—	2	—	—	—	—	—	—	—	2
Coffee, H.	London	1819-1845	Sculpture	—	—	14	1	7	—	—	—	—	—	22
Coffee, J. T.	London	1816	Sculpture	—	—	1	—	—	—	—	—	—	—	1
Coffee, W. J.	London	1801-1816	Sculpture	—	—	8	—	—	—	—	—	—	—	8
Coffin, E.	London	1787-1803	Sculpture	—	—	25	—	—	—	—	—	—	—	25
Cogghe, Remy	Roubaix	1887-1889	Figures	—	—	2	—	—	—	—	—	—	—	2
Coggin, Clarence	London	1892	Streets	—	—	1	—	—	—	—	—	—	—	1
Coggin, Mrs. Jeannie	London	1892	Buildings	—	—	1	—	—	—	—	—	—	—	1
Cohen, Miss A.	London	1833	Miniatures	—	—	—	—	1	—	—	—	—	—	1
Cohen, Miss Ellen Gertrude	London	1881-1893	Sculpture	—	—	6	—	3	—	5	—	—	4	18
Cohen, Miss Minnie	Manchester	1891	Domestic	—	—	2	—	—	—	—	—	—	—	2
Coignet, Jules Louis Philippe	Paris	1841-1850	Landscape	—	—	3	—	—	—	—	—	—	—	3
Coilers, L. B.	London	1784	Domestic	—	—	1	—	—	—	—	—	—	—	1
Coindet, J.	London	1831	Landscape	—	—	—	1	—	—	—	—	—	—	1
Coke, Alfred Sacheverel-	London	1869-1892	Historical	—	—	7	—	1	—	—	—	—	15	23
Coker, G.	London	1858-1860	Sculpture	—	—	2	—	—	—	—	—	—	—	2
Colarossi, Philippo	Paris	1884-1889	Sculpture	—	—	3	—	—	—	—	1	—	—	4
Colby, Joseph	London	1851-1886	Domestic	—	—	25	31	6	—	—	—	—	—	62
Cole, Miss A.	London	1855-1856	Portraits	—	—	2	—	—	—	—	—	—	—	2
Cole, Miss Augusta. *See* Mrs. Samwell	London	1831-1860	Miniatures	—	—	71	—	8	—	—	—	—	—	79
Cole, Alfred Benjamin	London	1867-1883	Landscape	—	—	2	—	33	—	—	—	—	5	40
Cole, Miss Blanche Vicat	London	1890-1893	Domestic	—	—	—	—	—	—	—	—	—	3	3
Cole, Chisholm, A.R.C.A.	Llanbedr	1890-1892	Landscape	—	—	2	—	—	—	—	—	—	—	2
Cole, Miss Ellen	London	1841-1858	Domestic	—	—	9	—	5	—	—	—	—	—	14
Cole, E. S.	London	1837-1868	Churches	—	—	6	—	2	—	—	—	—	5	13
Cole, George §	Portsmouth	1838-1883	Landscape	—	—	19	35	223	—	—	—	—	—	277
Cole, George Vicat, R.A.§	Portsmouth	1852-1892	Landscape	—	—	76	10	48	—	—	—	—	5	139
Cole, Sir Henry, K.C.B.	London	1827-1866	Landscape	—	—	6	—	—	—	—	—	—	—	6
Cole, Miss H.	London	1877	Still Life	—	—	—	—	1	—	—	—	—	—	1
Cole, James	London	1856-1885	Figures	—	—	8	9	72	—	1	—	—	2	92
Cole, Joseph	London	1770-1782	Flowers	1	—	9	—	—	—	—	—	—	—	10
Cole, J. Foxcroft	London	1875-1877	Landscape	—	—	4	—	1	—	—	—	—	1	6
Cole, John H., R.C.A.	Llanwrst	1869-1892	Landscape	—	—	6	—	5	—	—	—	—	6	17
Cole, John Jenkins, F.R.A.S.	London	1841-1850	Architecture	—	—	6	—	—	—	—	—	—	—	6
Cole, James William	London	1849-1882	Domestic	—	—	11	24	28	—	—	—	—	—	63
Cole, Miss Mary Ann	London	1841-1872	Domestic	—	—	29	3	8	—	—	—	—	—	40
Cole, M. E.	London	1832	Figures	—	—	1	—	—	—	—	—	—	—	1
Cole, Miss M. M.	London	1871	Figures	—	—	—	—	1	—	—	—	—	—	1
Cole, Philip Tennyson	London	1878-1889	Domestic	—	—	2	—	13	—	1	—	—	—	16
Cole, Reginald Vicat	London	1892-1893	Landscape	—	—	—	—	—	—	—	—	—	3	3
Cole, Solomon	Worcester	1845-1859	Portraits	—	—	16	—	—	—	—	—	—	—	16
Cole, Thomas	London	1830-1831	Landscape	—	—	3	5	1	—	—	—	—	—	9
Cole, Thomas W.	London	1886-1892	Flowers	—	—	2	—	4	—	—	—	—	2	8
Cole, William	Chester	1831-1832	Architecture	—	—	2	—	—	—	—	—	—	—	2
Cole, Mrs.	London	1824-1840	Fruit, etc.	—	—	7	—	3	—	—	—	—	—	10
Cole, Miss	—	1866	Mosaic	—	—	1	—	—	—	—	—	—	—	1
Colebatch, G.	London	1805-1809	Architecture	—	—	3	—	—	—	—	—	—	—	3
Colekin, Miss H.	London	1828	Fruit	—	—	—	—	1	—	—	—	—	—	1
Colelough, W.	Burslem	1847	Enamels	—	—	—	1	—	—	—	—	—	—	1
Coleman —	Woolwich	1768	Shipping	1	—	—	—	—	—	—	—	—	—	1
Coleman, Miss A. G.	London	1877	Flowers	—	—	—	—	1	—	—	—	—	—	1

Name.	Town.	First and Last Year of Ex.	Speciality.	S. A.	F. S.	R. A.	B. I.	S. S.	O. W.	N. W.	G. G.	N. G.	V. E.	Total.
COLEMAN, CHARLES	Rome	1839-1869	Figures	—	—	4	—	—	—	—	—	—	1	5
COLEMAN, CHARLES CARYL	Rome	1878-1891	Landscape	—	—	1	—	—	—	—	4	3	2	10
COLEMAN, EDWARD	Birmingham	1813-1848	Game	—	—	16	—	—	—	—	—	—	—	16
COLEMAN, EDWARD THOMAS	London	1849-1877	Landscape	—	—	4	3	12	—	—	—	—	1	20
COLEMAN, FRANK	Bradford	1885-1892	Domestic	—	—	5	—	11	—	—	—	—	—	16
COLEMAN, MRS. GERTRUDE	London	1881	Flowers	—	—	—	—	1	—	—	—	—	—	1
COLEMAN, MISS HELEN CORDELIA. *See* Mrs. John Angell	Henley	1865-1874	Still Life	—	—	—	—	2	—	—	—	—	45	47
COLEMAN, HENRY	Rome	1882-1889	Landscape	—	—	1	—	—	—	—	—	—	2	3
COLEMAN, H. S.	London	1845	Architecture	—	—	1	—	—	—	—	—	—	—	1
COLEMAN, R.	London	1831-1833	Intaglios	—	—	2	—	—	—	—	—	—	—	2
COLEMAN, MISS REBECCA ‖	London	1867-1879	Domestic	—	—	1	—	1	—	—	—	—	21	23
COLEMAN, WILLIAM STEPHEN	London	1865-1879	Figures	—	—	—	—	1	—	—	—	—	30	31
COLEPEPER, H.	London	1874	Landscape	—	—	—	—	1	—	—	—	—	—	1
COLERIDGE, LADY, FORMERLY MRS. JOHN DUKE COLERIDGE	London	1864-1878	Portraits	—	—	15	—	—	—	—	—	—	—	15
COLERIDGE, F. G.	Mapledurham	1866-1891	Landscape	—	—	2	—	16	—	1	—	—	20	39
COLERIDGE, MISS MAUD	—	1893	Portraits	—	—	—	—	—	—	—	—	—	1	1
COLERIDGE, HON. STEPHEN	London	1886-1893	Landscape	—	—	—	—	11	—	—	—	—	—	11
COLES, H.	London	1819-1820	Portraits	—	—	2	—	—	—	—	—	—	—	2
COLES, MISS MARY	Cheltenham	1873-1877	Fruit	—	—	—	—	1	—	—	—	—	1	2
COLES, WILLIAM C.	—	1881-1890	Landscape	—	—	1	—	1	—	—	—	—	1	3
COLIBERT, JULIEN	London	1777	Sculpture	—	—	1	—	—	—	—	—	—	—	1
COLIBERT, NICOLAS	London	1785	Landscape	—	—	1	—	—	—	—	—	—	—	1
COLIN, ALEXANDRE MARIE	Paris	1829-1853	Figures	—	—	5	—	—	—	—	—	—	—	5
COLIN, A.	London	1830-1853	Historical	—	—	5	8	3	—	—	—	—	—	16
COLIN-LIBOUR, MADAME	London	1883	Domestic	—	—	1	—	—	—	—	—	—	—	1
COLKETT, S. D.	Norwich	1825-1862	Landscape	—	—	2	30	33	—	—	—	—	—	65
COLKETT, MISS VICTORIA S. *See* Mrs. Hine	Cambridge	1859-1874	Landscape	—	—	1	9	10	—	—	—	—	9	29
COLLCUTT, THOMAS EDWARD	London	1873-1893	Architecture	—	—	32	—	—	—	—	—	—	—	32
COLLEN, HENRY	London	1820-1872	Miniatures	—	—	100	—	86	1	—	—	—	1	188
COLLET, JOHN	London	1761-1783	Domestic	—	47	—	—	—	—	—	—	—	—	47
COLLETT, MISS SOPHIA E.	Bury St. Edm'ds	1889-1893	Miniatures	—	—	7	—	—	—	—	—	—	—	7
COLLEY, ANDREW	Newcastle	1893	Figures	—	—	1	—	—	—	—	—	—	—	1
COLLEY, JOHN L.	Plymouth	1836-1838	Figures	—	—	—	—	5	—	—	—	—	—	5
COLLIER, ALEXANDER	Southampton	1870-1882	Landscape	—	—	—	—	8	—	—	—	—	4	12
COLLIER, ALEXANDER	London	1889-1892	Miniatures	—	—	5	—	—	—	—	—	—	—	5
COLLIER, MISS AMY	Callington	1874	Still Life	—	—	—	—	1	—	—	—	—	—	1
COLLIER, ARTHUR BEVAN	London	1855-1890	Landscape	—	—	20	7	53	—	—	—	—	12	92
COLLIER, BERNARD C.	Canterbury	1878-1887	Seashores	—	—	1	—	3	—	—	—	—	2	6
COLLIER, MISS EMILY E.	Short'ands	1879-1890	Domestic	—	—	—	—	1	—	2	—	—	2	5
COLLIER, HON. JOHN φ	London	1874-1893	Portraits	—	—	53	—	—	—	1	34	14	37	139
COLLIER, MRS JOHN (MARIAN HUXLEY)	London	1880-1884	Figures	—	—	3	—	1	—	—	6	—	—	10
COLLIER, MISS K. WINIFRED	Leicester	1892	Miniatures	—	—	—	—	—	—	3	—	—	—	3
COLLIER, MRS. MARY J.	London	1878-1881	Flowers	—	—	—	—	—	—	—	—	—	5	5
COLLIER, MARIA LOUISA	Tottenham	1839-1841	Sculpture	—	—	3	—	—	—	—	—	—	—	3
COLLIER, RT. HON. SIR ROBERT PORRELT. § *See* Lord Monkswell	London	1864-1885	Landscape	—	—	23	—	11	—	—	4	—	—	38
COLLIER, ROBERT WILLIAM	Shortlands	1881	Architecture	—	—	1	—	—	—	—	—	—	—	1
COLLIER, THOMAS, R.I. ‡ φ	Manchester	1863-1892	Landscape	—	—	4	—	1	—	80	—	—	15	100
COLLIER, THOMAS F.	London	1856-1874	Landscape	—	—	2	—	9	—	—	—	—	—	11
COLLIER, W. H.	London	1826	Animals	—	—	1	—	—	—	—	—	—	—	1
COLLIGNON, J. L.	London	1831-1834	Domestic	—	—	—	—	6	—	3	—	—	—	9
COLLING, JAMES KELLAWAY	—	1844-1883	Architecture	—	—	10	—	—	—	—	—	—	—	10
COLLINGHAM, G.	London	1880	Figures	—	—	—	—	—	—	—	—	—	2	2
COLLINGRIDGE, MISS ELIZABETH CAMPBELL	Hampton	1866-1873	Figures	—	—	—	3	2	—	—	—	—	1	6
COLLINGRIDGE, MRS. JOHN	Winchmore Hill	1888	Landscape	—	—	—	—	—	—	—	—	—	1	1
COLLINGS, ALBERT H.	London	1893	Domestic	—	—	—	—	2	—	—	—	—	—	2
COLLINGS, ROBERT	London	1883	Portraits	—	—	—	—	1	—	—	—	—	—	1
COLLINGS, S.	London	1784-1789	Domestic	—	—	6	—	—	—	—	—	—	—	6
COLLINGS, W.	London	1790-1791	Portraits	2	—	1	—	—	—	—	—	—	—	3
COLLINGWOOD, A. J.	London	1864	Landscape	—	—	—	—	1	—	—	—	—	—	1
COLLINGWOOD, ELLEN	London	1880	Domestic	—	—	—	—	—	—	—	—	—	1	1
COLLINGWOOD, H.	London	1824	Sculpture	—	—	2	—	—	—	—	—	—	—	2
COLLINGWOOD, LILLY	London	1882	Flowers	—	—	—	—	—	—	—	—	—	1	1
COLLINGWOOD, MRS. T. C. *See* Miss Clater.	—	—	—	—	—	—	—	—	—	—	—	—	—	—
COLLINGWOOD, WILLIAM, R.W.S. † ‡	Greenwich	1838-1893	Landscape	—	—	26	4	7	732	108	2	—	—	879
COLLINGWOOD, W. GERSHAM	Windermere	1880-1891	Landscape	—	—	6	—	3	—	6	1	—	4	20
COLLINGWOOD, W. J.	Liverpool	1875	Lake Scenes	—	—	—	—	—	—	—	—	—	1	1
COLLINS, ALFRED	London	1851-1882	Landscape	—	—	12	10	17	—	—	—	—	1	40
COLLINS, ARCHIBALD	London	1877-1893	Figures	—	—	—	—	17	—	—	—	—	6	23
COLLINS, CHARLES	Dorking	1867-1893	Figures	—	—	24	—	64	—	10	1	—	19	118
COLLINS, MRS. CHARLES. *See* Miss Kate Dickens and Mrs. C. E. Perugini.	—	—	—	—	—	—	—	—	—	—	—	—	—	—

Name.	Town.	First and Last Year of Ex.	Speciality.	S. A.	F. S.	R. A.	B. I.	S. S.	O. W.	N. W.	G. G.	N. G.	V. E.	Total.
Collins, Miss Charlotte	Winchester	1780	Mythological	2	—	—	—	—	—	—	—	—	—	2
Collins, Charles Allston	London	1847-1872	Figures	—	—	14	2	—	—	—	—	—	4	20
Collins, Charles J.	Chudleigh	1893	Landscape	—	—	1	—	—	—	—	—	—	—	1
Collins, D. Lincoln	London	1871-1882	Landscape	—	—	—	—	—	—	—	—	—	13	13
Collins, E.	Lewisham	1867-1880	Landscape	—	—	—	—	14	—	—	—	—	—	14
Collins, Miss Elizabeth L.	London	1866-1869	Still Life	—	—	—	—	4	—	—	—	—	—	4
Collins, Henry	London	1874	Rustic	—	—	—	—	—	—	—	—	—	1	1
Collins, Hugh	Edinburgh	1868-1891	Figures	—	—	3	—	4	—	—	—	—	—	7
Collins, Hyman Henry	London	1875	Architecture	—	—	2	—	—	—	—	—	—	—	2
Collins, Miss Jennett	Edinburgh	1892	Domestic	—	—	1	—	—	—	—	—	—	—	1
Collins, J.	London	1806	Sculpture	—	—	1	—	—	—	—	—	—	—	1
Collins, J.	Blackheath	1811	Landscape	—	—	2	—	—	—	—	—	—	—	2
Collins, James Edgell	London	1841-1875	Portraits	—	—	23	20	14	—	—	—	—	3	60
Collins, Mrs. M.	Gravesend	1874-1881	Figures	—	—	1	—	—	—	—	—	—	20	21
Collins, Miss Maria	Edinburgh	1889	Landscape	—	—	1	—	—	—	—	—	—	—	1
Collins, Richard	London	1777-1818	Miniatures	—	—	33	—	—	—	—	—	—	—	33
Collins, R.	London	1860	Fruit	—	—	—	—	2	—	—	—	—	—	2
Collins, S.	London	1829-1833	Portraits	—	—	2	—	5	—	—	—	—	—	7
Collins, Miss Sophia	London	1783	—	—	*	—	—	—	—	—	—	—	—	—
Collins, T.	Birmingham	1867-1873	Flowers	—	—	1	—	5	—	—	—	—	—	6
Collins, William	London	1760-1778	Sculpture	23	—	—	—	—	—	—	—	—	—	23
Collins, W.	—	1791	Portraits	2	—	—	—	—	—	—	—	—	—	2
Collins, W.	London	1816	Windows	—	—	5	—	—	—	—	—	—	—	5
Collins, W.	London	1822	Landscape	—	—	1	—	—	—	—	—	—	—	1
Collins, William, R.A.	London	1807-1846	Landscape	—	—	124	45	—	—	—	—	—	—	169
Collins, William	London	1885	Landscape	—	—	—	—	—	—	—	—	—	1	1
Collins, W. H.	London	1822-1859	Portraits	—	—	12	—	—	—	—	—	—	—	12
Collins, W. J.	London	1859	Figures	—	—	1	—	—	—	—	—	—	—	1
Collins, W. T., M.D.	London	1858-1859	Coast Scenes	—	—	—	—	—	—	—	—	—	2	2
Collins, W. W.	London	1849	Figures	—	—	1	—	—	—	—	—	—	—	1
Collins, William Wiehe	London	1886-1893	Landscape	—	—	1	—	14	—	10	—	1	3	29
Collins, Miss	London	1820-1825	Landscape	—	—	1	—	—	1	—	—	—	—	2
Collins and Merrin. (?) Collier and Merrin	—	1886	Architecture	—	—	1	—	—	—	—	—	—	—	1
Collinson, Frank G.	London	1893	Architecture	—	—	1	—	—	—	—	—	—	—	1
Collinson, James §	London	1846-1880	Domestic	—	—	17	7	27	—	—	—	—	8	59
Collinson, Robert	London	1854-1890	Domestic	—	—	31	10	13	—	—	—	—	17	71
Collinson, Mrs. Robert (Eliza)	London	1856-1868	Flowers	—	—	3	—	1	—	—	—	—	—	4
Collis, A. P.	Brethwaite	1852-1854	Landscape	—	—	—	—	2	—	—	—	—	—	2
Collis, J.	London	1836-1839	Architecture	—	—	3	—	—	—	—	—	—	—	3
Collmann, L. W.	London	1842-1849	Architecture	—	—	5	—	—	—	—	—	—	—	5
Collopy, Ty.	London	1786-1788	Scriptural	—	—	3	—	—	—	—	—	—	—	3
Colls, Ebenezer	London	1852-1854	Sea Pieces	—	—	—	7	—	—	—	—	—	—	7
Colls, Harry	Barnes	1878-1890	Sea Pieces	—	—	4	—	2	—	—	1	—	4	11
Colls, Richard	London	1831-1855	Fruit	—	—	21	6	6	—	—	—	—	3	36
Collucci, Z. *or* V.	London	1860-1861	Portraits	—	—	2	—	4	—	—	—	—	—	6
Collyer, Joseph, A.R.A.	London	1770-1822	Engraving	11	2	18	—	—	—	—	—	—	—	31
Collyer, W.	London	1820	Game	—	—	1	—	—	—	—	—	—	—	1
Collyer, Miss Winifred Kate	Leicester	1891-1892	Miniatures	—	—	12	—	—	—	—	—	—	—	12
Colman, F.	Bristol	1889	Domestic	—	—	—	—	2	—	—	—	—	—	2
Colman, S.	London	1839-1840	Figures	—	—	2	—	—	—	—	—	—	—	2
Colman, S. G.	London	1872	Landscape	—	—	1	—	—	—	—	—	—	—	1
Colman, W.	London	1843	Architecture	—	—	1	—	—	—	—	—	—	—	1
Colman, William Gooding	London	1834	Churches	—	—	—	—	1	—	—	—	—	—	1
Colmar, W. J.	London	1839	Architecture	—	—	1	—	—	—	—	—	—	—	1
Colnet. F.	London	1848	Architecture	—	—	1	—	—	—	—	—	—	—	1
Colomb, Wellington	London	1865-1870	Landscape	—	—	2	—	2	—	—	—	—	3	7
Colonna-Castiglione, Duchess of. *See* Marcello	Paris	1866-1867	Sculpture	—	—	2	—	—	—	—	—	—	—	2
Colquhon, Miss Annie T.	Londonderry	1893	Domestic	—	—	—	—	—	—	1	—	—	—	1
Colson, J.	London	1844	Architecture	—	—	2	—	—	—	—	—	—	—	2
Colson, Miss	London	1874	Landscape	—	—	—	—	2	—	—	—	—	—	2
Colton, William R.	London	1889-1893	Mythological	—	—	7	—	—	—	—	—	1	—	8
Columba, J. B. Innocente	London	1774	Landscape	—	—	4	—	—	—	—	—	—	—	4
Columbani, Placido	London	1775	Architecture	1	—	—	—	—	—	—	—	—	—	1
Colville, Charles John, Baron, K.T.	London	1876-1878	Landscape	—	—	—	—	—	—	—	—	—	2	2
Colville, Miss E.	London	1880-1884	Flowers	—	—	—	—	1	—	—	—	—	1	2
Coman, Mrs. Charlotte B.	Paris	1879	Landscape	—	—	—	—	2	—	—	—	—	—	2
Combe, Miss	—	1790	Domestic	—	—	1	—	—	—	—	—	—	—	1
Combe, Miss E.	London	1834-1840	Portraits	—	—	13	—	7	—	—	—	—	—	20
Comber, J. N. *See* Bucknall and Comber	—	—	Architecture	—	—	—	—	—	—	—	—	—	—	—
Comber, Miss Mary E.	Warrington	1887	Fish	—	—	1	—	—	—	—	—	—	—	1
Combes, Miss Alice H.	London	1885	Landscape	—	—	—	—	—	—	—	—	—	1	1
Combes, Hon. Edward, C.M.G., H.R.I. ‡	Sydney	1884-1892	Australia	—	—	1	—	—	—	12	—	—	3	16

Name.	Town.	First and Last Year of Ex.	Speciality.	S. A.	F. S.	R. A.	B. I.	S. S.	O.W.	N.W.	G. G.	N. G.	V. E.	Total.
Combes, Miss Emily	London	1879-1882	Flowers	—	—	—	—	6	—	—	—	—	—	6
Combes, Mrs. G. E.	London	1885-1887	Flowers	—	—	—	—	—	—	3	—	—	—	3
Comer, John	London	1763	Portraits	—	1	—	—	—	—	—	—	—	—	1
Comerford, John	Dublin	1804-1809	Portraits	—	—	3	—	—	—	—	—	—	—	3
Comerford, Mrs.	London	1801	Portraits	—	—	1	—	—	—	—	—	—	—	1
Comerre, Léon	—	1892	Portraits	—	—	—	—	—	—	—	—	—	2	2
Comfort, Arthur	London	1893	Engraving	—	—	1	—	—	—	—	—	—	—	1
Comolèra, Madame Melani de	London	1826-1854	Flowers	—	—	38	6	3	—	—	—	—	—	47
Compton —	—	1773	Heads	—	—	1	—	—	—	—	—	—	—	1
Compton, A.	Epsom	1878-1879	Landscape	—	—	—	—	2	—	—	—	—	—	2
Compton, Charles	London	1847-1867	Figures	—	—	11	4	9	—	—	—	—	—	24
Compton, Lady Elizabeth	—	1781	Flowers	—	—	1	—	—	—	—	—	—	—	1
Compton, E. H.	Weston-super-Mare	1873	Landscape	—	—	—	—	—	—	—	—	—	1	1
Compton, Edward T.	Bavaria	1879-1891	Landscape	—	—	10	—	1	—	9	2	—	8	30
Compton, John	London	1883	Domestic	—	—	—	—	1	—	—	—	—	—	1
Compton, T.	Woolwich	1812	Landscape	—	—	—	—	—	—	—	—	—	4	4
Compton, Theodore	London	1866-1874	Flowers	—	—	—	—	—	—	—	—	—	2	2
Conant, Amy L. E.	Oakham	1884	Landscape	—	—	—	—	1	—	—	—	—	—	1
Condamine, E. J. De la. *See* D.	—	—	—	—	—	—	—	—	—	—	—	—	—	—
Condé, P.	London	1806-1824	Portraits	—	—	27	—	—	—	—	—	—	2	29
Conder, E. Lauriston	London	1887	Architecture	—	—	1	—	—	—	—	—	—	—	1
Conder, Miss H. Louise	London	1890-1893	Landscape	—	—	—	—	3	—	2	—	—	—	5
Conder, Josiah	Tokio, Japan	1885	Japan	—	—	3	—	—	—	—	—	—	—	3
Conder, Roger T.	London	1883	Venice	—	—	1	—	—	—	—	—	—	—	1
Condy, Nicholas	Plymouth	1830-1845	Landscape	—	—	2	4	1	—	—	—	—	—	7
Condy, Nicholas Matthew	Plymouth	1842-1845	Sea Pieces	—	—	3	—	—	—	—	—	—	—	3
Coney, John	London	1805-1821	Churches	—	—	10	—	—	6	—	—	—	14	30
Coney, R. H.	London	1877	Figures	—	—	—	—	1	—	—	—	—	—	1
Connell, Miss M. Christine	Chiswick	1885-1890	Domestic	—	—	4	—	5	—	—	—	—	5	14
Connell, Miss Janet	London	1890-1892	Miniatures	—	—	4	—	—	—	—	—	—	—	4
Connell, William	London	1876-1877	Sea Pieces	—	—	—	—	—	—	—	—	—	2	2
Connelly, Pierce Francis	Florence	1871	Portraits	—	—	2	—	—	—	—	—	—	—	2
Conning, George J.	London	1890	Seashores	—	—	1	—	—	—	—	—	—	—	1
Connolly, Michael	London	1885-1893	Domestic	—	—	3	—	—	—	—	—	—	—	3
Connop, T. H.	London	1852	Figures	—	—	—	2	1	—	—	—	—	—	3
Connor —. *See* Chorley and Connor	—	—	Architecture	—	—	—	—	—	—	—	—	—	—	—
Conolly, Miss Ellen	London	1873-1885	Figures	—	—	10	—	10	—	—	—	—	5	25
Conolly, Francis	London	1849-1870	Sculpture	—	—	5	1	1	—	—	—	—	—	7
Conquest, Alfred	Woodford	1880-1890	Landscape	—	—	10	—	12	—	—	4	—	1	27
Conradi, Moritz	London	1865-1876	Domestic	—	—	8	—	—	—	—	—	—	—	8
Constable, A. A.	London	1847-1853	Landscape	—	—	8	—	—	—	—	—	—	—	8
Constable, E. P.	London	1879	Landscape	—	—	1	—	2	—	—	—	—	—	3
Constable, G., Junr.	Arundel	1862	Landscape	—	—	—	1	—	—	—	—	—	—	1
Constable, Miss Isabel ‖	London	1851-1852	Flowers	—	—	2	—	—	—	—	—	—	—	2
Constable, John, R.A.	London	1802-1837	Landscape	—	—	104	32	1	—	—	—	—	—	137
Constable, L. B.	London	1849-1855	Landscape	—	—	13	1	—	—	—	—	—	—	14
Constable, S. C.	London	1891	Landscape	—	—	—	—	1	—	—	—	—	—	1
Contencin, Peter	London	1777-1819	Portraits	2	—	5	—	—	—	—	—	—	—	7
Contencin, W.	London	1803	Portraits	—	—	2	—	—	—	—	—	—	—	2
Conti, Tito	Florence	1874-1884	Domestic	—	—	11	—	—	—	—	—	—	—	11
Conway, C. J.	—	1855	Figures	—	—	—	—	1	—	—	—	—	—	1
Conway, George	London	1854-1871	Landscape	—	—	2	6	28	—	—	—	—	—	36
Conybeare, H.	Kew	1856-1873	Architecture	—	—	10	—	—	—	—	—	—	—	10
Coode, Miss Helen Hoppner ‖	London	1859-1880	Figures	—	—	2	4	4	—	—	—	—	—	10
Cook, Ambrose B.	London	1886	Domestic	—	—	—	—	1	—	—	—	—	—	1
Cook, C.	London	1831-1832	Landscape	—	—	2	—	—	—	—	—	—	—	2
Cook, C.	London	1860	Still Life	—	—	—	—	1	—	—	—	—	—	1
Cook, C. A.	Blackheath	1877-1882	Landscape	—	—	—	—	1	—	—	—	—	5	6
Cook, Miss Emily Annie	London	1881-1889	Flowers	—	—	10	—	10	—	—	—	—	3	23
Cook, E. Wake	London	1874-1893	Landscape	—	—	13	—	18	—	9	4	—	7	51
Cook, Frederick	London	1878-1891	Landscape	—	—	—	—	7	—	1	—	—	—	8
Cook, F. B.	London	1877	Landscape	—	—	—	—	1	—	—	—	—	—	1
Cook, George Edward	London	1874-1893	Landscape	—	—	18	—	5	—	—	8	6	29	66
Cook, George Frederick	London	1879-1891	Still Life	—	—	4	—	14	—	—	—	—	1	19
Cook, Henry	Walthamstow	1840-1859	Figures	—	—	10	2	3	—	—	—	—	3	18
Cook, H.	London	1880-1883	Venice	—	—	1	—	—	—	—	5	—	—	6
Cook, H. Moxon	London	1868-1893	Landscape	—	—	3	—	10	—	6	—	—	10	29
Cook, Henry S.	London	1890	Domestic	—	—	1	—	—	—	—	—	—	—	1
Cook, J.	London	1800	Sculpture	—	—	1	—	—	—	—	—	—	—	1
Cook, J.	London	1808-1809	Game	—	—	2	—	—	—	—	—	—	—	2
Cook, Joshua	London	1838-1848	Still Life	—	—	8	14	5	—	—	—	—	—	27
Cook, Joshua, Junr.	London	1852-1854	Fruit	—	—	—	3	2	—	—	—	—	—	5

Name.	Town.	First and Last Year of Ex.	Speciality.	S. A.	F. S.	R. A.	B. I.	S. S.	O. W.	N. W.	G. G.	N. G.	V. E.	Total.
Cook, J. A.	—	1883	Portraits	—	—	—	—	—	—	—	2	—	—	2
Cook, J. B.	Leamington	1859	Landscape	—	—	—	1	—	—	—	—	—	—	1
Cook, John Thomas	Sheffield	1883	Landscape	—	—	1	—	—	—	—	—	—	—	1
Cook, Miss L. S.	Rochdale	1870-1881	Flowers	—	—	—	—	—	—	—	1	—	1	2
Cook, Miss Nelly E.	London	1887-1890	Flowers	—	—	2	—	1	—	1	—	—	—	4
Cook, Richard, R.A.	London	1785-1826	Scriptural	—	—	26	9	—	—	—	—	—	—	35
Cook, R.	London	1809-1814	Portraits	—	—	4	—	—	—	—	—	—	—	4
Cook, Samuel ‡	Plymouth	1843-1860	Rural	—	—	—	—	1	—	70	—	—	—	71
Cook, S. J.	London	1843	Animals	—	—	1	—	—	—	—	—	—	—	1
Cook, Theodore	London	1881-1890	Rustic	—	—	5	—	3	—	—	—	—	1	9
Cook, Thomas	London	1886	Domestic	—	—	—	—	—	—	—	—	—	1	1
Cook, T. M.	London	1799-1802	Architecture	—	—	6	—	—	—	—	—	—	—	6
Cook, W.	Plymouth	1877-1879	Landscape	—	—	—	—	4	—	—	—	—	—	4
Cook, Miss	London	1832-1833	Portraits	—	—	—	1	2	—	1	—	—	—	4
Cooke, Arthur C.	London	1890-1893	Domestic	—	—	2	—	2	—	—	—	—	—	4
Cooke, Arthur J.	London	1882	Architecture	—	—	1	—	—	—	—	—	—	—	1
Cooke, C. G.	—	1829	Interiors	—	—	—	—	1	—	—	—	—	—	1
Cooke, C. H.	London	1885	Domestic	—	—	—	—	1	—	—	—	—	—	1
Cooke, Charles Henry	London	1859-1877	Architecture	—	—	8	—	—	—	—	—	—	—	8
Cooke, Miss Ellen Miller	Balham	1886-1892	Flowers	—	—	5	—	2	—	—	—	—	3	10
Cooke, Ernest O.	London	1886	Birds	—	—	1	—	—	—	—	—	—	—	1
Cooke, Edward William, R.A.	Barnes	1835-1879	Sea Pieces	—	—	129	115	3	—	—	—	—	9	256
Cooke, George	London	1824-1825	Engraving	—	—	—	—	2	—	—	—	—	—	2
Cooke, George R.	Clovelly	1881-1884	Seashores	—	—	—	—	4	—	—	—	—	1	5
Cooke, Isaac	Liscard	1877-1893	Landscape	—	—	6	—	4	—	13	—	—	4	27
Cooke, J.	Birmingham	1830	Portraits	—	—	1	—	—	—	—	—	—	—	1
Cooke, John	Balham	1887-1893	Landscape	—	—	12	—	6	—	—	—	1	1	20
Cooke, Miss L.	Bath	1884	Flowers	—	—	—	—	—	—	1	—	—	—	1
Cooke, R.	London	1838-1841	Architecture	—	—	2	—	—	—	—	—	—	—	2
Cooke, T. A.	London	1838	Landscape	—	—	—	—	1	—	—	—	—	—	1
Cooke, T. B.	London	1850-1857	Landscape	—	—	—	2	4	—	—	—	—	—	6
Cooke, Thomas Etherington	Edinburgh	1865-1868	Landscape	—	—	—	3	1	—	—	—	—	2	6
Cooke, William C.	London	1890-1891	Buildings	—	—	—	—	2	—	—	—	—	—	2
Cooke (W. C.), and Carpenter (A. A.)	London	1893	Drawing	—	—	1	—	—	—	—	—	—	—	1
Cooke, William Edward	Loughborough	1872-1886	Landscape	—	—	8	—	9	—	—	—	—	4	21
Cooke, William John	London	1829-1830	—	—	—	—	—	2	—	—	—	—	—	2
Cooke, Miss	—	1804	Buildings	—	—	1	—	—	—	—	—	—	—	1
Cookes, Miss Laura	Warwick	1866	Portraits	—	—	—	—	1	—	—	—	—	—	1
Cooks —	London	1768	Architecture	1	—	—	—	—	—	—	—	—	—	1
Cooksey, Arthur W. *See also* Cox and Cooksey	London	1892	Architecture	—	—	1	—	—	—	—	—	—	—	1
Cooksley, Mrs. Margaret Murray-	London	1884-1893	Egypt	—	—	7	—	—	—	1	—	—	15	23
Cool, De. *See* D.		—		—	—	—	—	—	—	—	—	—	—	—
Cooley, Thomas	London	1765-1768	Architecture	—	6	—	—	—	—	—	—	—	—	6
Cooley, Thomas	London	1813-1845	Portraits	—	—	52	4	—	—	—	—	—	—	56
Cooling, John A.	London	1878-1880	Figures	—	—	1	—	—	—	—	—	—	1	2
Coombe, Arthur E.	Dorking	1882-1889	Etching	—	—	7	—	—	—	—	—	—	1	8
Coombe, Miss L. Ella	London	1887	Flowers	—	—	—	—	—	—	—	—	—	1	1
Coombes, Grace Emily	London	1879	Flowers	—	—	—	—	1	—	—	—	—	—	1
Coombs, J. E.	London	1832-1833	Engraving	—	—	—	—	3	—	—	—	—	—	3
Cooper, Abraham, R.A.	London	1812-1869	Battle Pieces	—	—	332	74	1	13	—	—	—	—	420
Cooper, Alfred	London	1854-1864	Landscape	—	—	20	9	14	—	—	—	—	19	62
Cooper, Alick	London	1873-1893	Rustic	—	—	5	—	13	—	1	—	—	18	37
Cooper, Alexander Davis	London	1837-1888	Landscape	—	—	67	27	23	—	—	—	—	20	137
Cooper, Mrs. A. Davis	London	1854-1875	Fruit	—	—	11	3	2	—	—	—	—	3	19
Cooper, Alfred Heaton	London	1885-1893	Domestic	—	—	4	—	2	—	3	—	—	1	10
Cooper, A. W.	London	1850-1890	Domestic	—	—	32	7	17	—	3	—	—	26	85
Cooper, B.	London	1795-1797	Architecture	—	—	3	—	—	—	—	—	—	—	3
Cooper, Byron	Manchester	1881-1893	Landscape	—	—	18	—	1	—	4	—	—	—	23
Cooper, Claude	Winkfield	1870	Fish	—	—	—	—	—	—	—	—	—	1	1
Cooper, Mrs. C. B., formerly Miss Emma Wren ‖	London	1881-1893	Miniatures	—	—	8	—	—	—	2	—	—	2	12
Cooper, E.	London	1803-1831	Horses	—	—	2	—	—	—	—	—	—	—	2
Corkling, Miss May	Manchester	1875-1880	Landscape	—	—	1	—	—	—	—	3	—	2	6
Cooper, Miss Emma	New Barnet	1872-1893	Domestic	—	—	1	—	3	—	12	—	—	15	31
Cooper, Miss Edith A.	London	1885-1889	Portraits	—	—	2	—	1	—	—	1	—	2	6
Cooper, Frederick Charles	London	1844-1868	Figures	—	—	4	9	11	—	—	—	—	—	24
Cooper, Miss Florence M.	London	1887-1889	Religious	—	—	1	—	—	—	—	—	—	1	2
Cooper, George	London	1792-1830	Architecture	—	—	17	—	—	—	—	—	—	4	21
Cooper, George	London	1820-1830	Landscape	—	—	2	3	8	4	—	—	—	—	17
Cooper, George	Putney	1875-1884	Landscape	—	—	2	—	10	—	—	—	—	2	14
Cooper, George Warren	London	1886	Architecture	—	—	1	—	—	—	—	—	—	—	1
Cooper, Henry M.	London	1842-1872	Historical	—	—	2	3	2	—	—	—	—	7	14
Cooper, J.	London	1813-1827	Architecture	—	—	12	—	—	—	—	—	—	2	14

Name.	Town.	First and Last Year of Ex.	Speciality.	S. A.	F. S.	R. A.	B. I.	S. S.	O. W.	N.W.	G. G.	N. G.	V. E.	Total.
Cooper, Miss Louisa	Maidenhead	1879	Portraits	—	—	1	—	—	—	—	—	—	—	1
Cooper, Miss Lydia	London	1891-1893	Portraits	—	—	1	—	2	—	—	—	—	—	3
Cooper, Mrs. Mary Cuthbert	Kilburn	1880-1884	Sculpture	—	—	8	—	—	—	—	—	—	—	8
Cooper, Richard	London	1761-1783	Engraving	18	7	7	—	—	—	—	—	—	—	32
Cooper, Richard	London	1787-1809	Landscape	—	—	24	—	—	—	—	—	—	—	24
Cooper, R.	London	1793-1799	Miniatures	—	—	11	—	—	—	—	—	—	—	11
Cooper, R.	Uckfield	1847	Domestic	—	—	—	—	1	—	—	—	—	—	1
Cooper, Robert	Brighton	1850-1874	Landscape	—	—	4	—	—	—	—	—	—	3	7
Cooper, T.	London	1818-1819	Architecture	—	—	2	—	—	—	—	—	—	—	2
Cooper, T.	London	1845	Portraits	—	—	1	—	—	—	—	—	—	—	1
Cooper, Thomas George	London	1861-1893	Rustic	—	—	30	3	—	—	13	—	—	25	71
Cooper, Thomas Sidney, R.A. ‡	London	1833-1893	Animals	—	—	230	48	14	—	2	—	—	18	312
Cooper, W.	—	1799	—	—	—	*	—	—	—	—	—	—	—	—
Cooper, W.	London	1846-1862	Portraits	—	—	30	4	9	—	—	—	—	—	43
Cooper, W. F. White	London	1886	Architecture	—	—	1	—	—	—	—	—	—	—	1
Cooper, W. J.	London	1874-1882	Etchings	—	—	2	—	6	—	—	—	—	7	15
Cooper, W. Savage	London	1882-1891	Scriptural	—	—	15	—	7	—	3	—	—	2	27
Cooper, W. Sidney	London	1871-1891	Landscape	—	—	12	—	36	—	2	—	—	13	63
Cooper, Mrs.	London	1863-1864	Sculpture	—	—	2	—	—	—	—	—	—	—	2
Coote, Miss Sarah	London	1777-1784	Miniatures	6	—	12	—	—	—	—	—	—	—	18
Cope, Arthur Stockdale	London	1875-1893	Portraits	—	—	56	—	—	—	1	1	1	11	70
Cope, Charles West, R.A.	London	1833-1882	Domestic	—	—	134	14	1	—	—	—	—	—	149
Cope, F. C.	London	1839-1845	Architecture	—	—	2	—	—	—	—	—	—	—	2
Cope (F. C.), Eales, and Elmslie	London	1843-1844	Architecture	—	—	4	—	—	—	—	—	—	—	4
Cope, J. J.	London	1824	Architecture	—	—	—	—	1	—	—	—	—	—	1
Cope, J. T.	London	1873	Figures	—	—	—	—	1	—	—	—	—	—	1
Cope, S.	London	1763-1766	Fruit	—	3	—	—	—	—	—	—	—	—	3
Cope, W. Henry	London	1848-1855	Landscape	—	—	1	—	8	—	—	—	—	11	20
Copeland, A. J.	Watford	1882	Landscape	—	—	—	—	1	—	—	—	—	—	1
Copeland, G.	—	1835	Portraits	—	—	1	—	—	—	—	—	—	—	1
Copland, Miss L.	London	1842	Portraits	—	—	1	—	—	—	—	—	—	—	1
Copley, John Singleton, R.A., F.S.A., &c.	Boston, U.S.A.	1768-1812	Historical	6	—	43	8	—	—	—	—	—	—	57
Copley, William	Boston, U.S.A.	1766-1767	Portraits	2	—	—	—	—	—	—	—	—	—	2
Coppard, C. Law	Brighton	1858-1880	Landscape	—	—	9	11	45	—	—	—	—	9	74
Coppin, Miss E.	Norwich	1823-1825	Flowers	—	—	—	2	1	—	—	—	—	—	3
Copping, Harold	London	1881-1891	Domestic	—	—	12	—	2	—	2	—	—	—	16
Coppinger, Miss. *See* Miss Frances Rayner.	—	—	—	—	—	—	—	—	—	—	—	—	—	—
Corah, William J.	Conway	1888	Landscape	—	—	1	—	—	—	—	—	—	—	1
Corbaux, Miss Fanny ‡	London	1828-1854	Figures	—	—	86	15	48	—	38	—	—	—	187
Corbaux, Miss Louisa ‡	London	1828-1881	Domestic	—	—	3	—	17	—	86	—	—	—	106
Corbet —. *See* Bell and Corbet	—	—	Architecture	—	—	—	—	—	—	—	—	—	—	—
Corbet, D.	—	1851	Landscape	—	—	—	1	—	—	—	—	—	—	1
Corbett, F.	London	1854	Cattle	—	—	1	—	—	—	—	—	—	—	1
Corbett, Matthew Ridley	London	1871-1893	Portraits	—	—	17	—	2	—	2	34	18	9	82
Corbett, Mrs. M. Ridley (Edith). *See* Mrs. Arthur Marsh	—	1891-1893	Portraits	—	—	3	—	—	—	—	—	5	—	8
Corbett, Philip	Shrewsbury	1823-1856	Dramatic	—	—	31	1	—	—	—	—	—	—	32
Corbett, S. Bertha	Stockport	1881	Landscape	—	—	—	—	—	—	—	—	—	1	1
Corbin, Miss Rosa H.	Southampton	1889	Landscape	—	—	1	—	—	—	—	—	—	—	1
Corbould, Alfred	London	1831-1875	Sporting	—	—	22	21	16	—	—	—	—	14	73
Corbould, Alfred Chantrey, R.B.A. §	London	1878-1893	Illustrations	—	—	5	—	3	—	2	—	—	17	27
Corbould, Alfred Hitchens	London	1844-1863	Portraits	—	—	20	—	—	—	—	—	—	—	20
Corbould, Aster R. C.	London	1842-1877	Cattle	—	—	35	32	59	—	—	—	—	12	138
Corbould, Edward Henry, R.I. ‡	London	1835-1880	Figures	—	—	17	1	13	—	241	3	—	18	293
Corbould, G.	London	1801-1806	Historical	—	—	4	—	—	—	—	—	—	—	4
Corbould, George James	London	1824	Engraving	—	—	—	—	5	—	—	—	—	—	5
Corbould, Henry	London	1802-1840	Historical	—	—	44	21	3	7	—	—	—	—	75
Corbould, Ph.	—	1824	Historical	—	—	—	1	—	—	—	—	—	—	1
Corbould, Richard	London	1776-1817	Landscape	—	4	100	27	—	—	—	—	—	—	131
Corbould, Walter Edward	London	1889-1890	Domestic	—	—	1	—	—	—	2	—	—	—	3
Corbould-Haywood, Miss Evelyn	London	1887	Landscape & History	—	—	—	—	—	—	—	—	—	1	1
Corbynprice, Frank	London	1882-1883	Landscape	—	—	—	—	1	—	—	—	—	—	1
Corden, William	Windsor	1836-1855	Figures	—	—	8	1	—	—	—	—	—	—	9
Corder, C. E.	Lee	1873	Theatrical	—	—	—	—	3	—	—	—	—	—	3
Corder, E.	London	1828	Enamels	—	—	1	—	—	—	—	—	—	—	1
Corder, Miss Rosa	London	1879-1882	Portraits	—	—	1	—	—	—	—	1	—	—	2
Corder, W.	London	1825-1829	Enamels	—	—	3	—	—	—	—	—	—	—	3
Cordier, Mdlle. A. Delville	Paris	1860-1882	Figures	—	—	8	—	2	—	—	—	—	—	10
Cordier, Henry Joseph Charles	London	1853	Sculpture	—	—	1	—	—	—	—	—	—	—	1
Cordiner, Rev. Charles	Banff	1790-1791	Landscape	8	—	—	—	—	—	—	—	—	—	8
Cordingley, Georges R.	London	1893	Sea Pieces	—	—	1	—	—	—	—	—	—	—	1
Corelli, A.	London	1881-1882	Figures	—	—	1	—	1	—	—	—	—	—	2

Name.	Town.	First and Last Year of Ex.	Speciality.	S. A.	F. S.	R. A.	B. I.	S. S.	O. W.	N. W.	G. G.	N. G.	V. E.	Total.
Corkran, Miss A.	—	1868	Landscape	—	—	—	—	1	—	—	—	—	—	1
Corkran, Miss Henriette L.	London	1872-1893	Figures	—	—	13	—	—	—	—	—	—	6	19
Cormack, Mrs., formerly Miss Minnie Everett	London	1892-1893	Engraving	—	—	2	—	—	—	—	—	—	—	2
Cormack, N.	London	1814-1816	Portraits	—	—	5	—	—	—	—	—	—	—	5
Cormon, Fernand	—	1891-1893	Portraits	—	—	—	—	—	—	—	—	—	3	3
Cornelissen, Miss Marie E. *See* Mrs. J. Seymour	—	—	—	—	—	—	—	—	—	—	—	—	—	—
Lucas	London	1873-1884	Figures	—	—	4	—	14	—	—	—	—	7	25
Corner, A.	London	1846-1847	Architecture	—	—	2	—	—	—	—	—	—	—	2
Corner, George E.	Blackheath	1886-1891	Domestic	—	—	—	—	9	—	—	—	—	—	9
Corner, S.	London	1838-1849	—	—	—	—	—	7	—	—	—	—	—	7
Cornicelius, G.	Munich	1852	Scriptural	—	—	1	—	—	—	—	—	—	—	1
Cornilliet, J.	London	1870	Figures	—	—	1	—	—	—	—	—	—	—	1
Cornish, Mrs. Mary	London	1869	Fishing Boats	—	—	—	—	—	—	—	—	—	1	1
Cornish, William Permeanus	London	1875-1892	Landscape	—	—	—	—	12	—	3	—	—	—	15
Cornman, H.	London	1782-1821	Sculpture	—	2	23	—	—	—	—	—	—	—	25
Cornman, P.	London	1788-1792	Sculpture	—	—	5	—	—	—	—	—	—	—	5
Cornuaud, Jean D.	Richmond	1875-1877	Flowers	—	—	—	—	—	—	—	—	—	2	2
Cornwall, W. H.	—	1821-1823	Landscape	—	—	2	—	—	—	—	—	—	—	2
Corot, Jean Baptiste Camille	Paris	1869	Landscape	—	—	2	—	—	—	—	—	—	—	2
Corrie, Miss E. J.	Exeter	1877	Game	—	—	1	—	—	—	—	—	—	—	1
Corrodi, H.	Rome	1879-1881	Landscape	—	—	1	—	4	—	—	1	—	—	6
Corser, Thomas	Bristol	1827-1829	Landscape	—	—	2	1	1	—	—	—	—	—	4
Corson, George	Leeds	1875-1879	Architecture	—	—	7	—	—	—	—	—	—	—	7
Corson, H.	Pontaven	1879	Figures	—	—	—	—	—	—	—	—	—	1	1
Cort, De. *See* D.	—	—	—	—	—	—	—	—	—	—	—	—	—	—
Cortissos, Charles	London	1872-1875	Fruit	—	—	—	—	1	—	—	—	—	3	4
Cosbie, S.	London	1864	Figures	—	—	1	—	—	—	—	—	—	—	1
Coslett, R. G.	London	1808-1827	Portraits	—	—	39	—	1	—	—	—	—	—	40
Cosse, Laurence J.	London	1784-1837	Domestic	—	—	113	49	8	—	—	—	—	—	170
Costa, A.	Rome	1884	—	—	—	—	—	—	—	—	*	—	—	—
Costa, Professor Giovanni da	London	1869-1893	Landscape	—	—	10	—	—	—	—	24	23	—	57
Costa, John da. *See* D.	—	—	—	—	—	—	—	—	—	—	—	—	—	—
Costa, De. *See* D.	—	—	—	—	—	—	—	—	—	—	—	—	—	—
Costeker, Miss Jane O.	Eccles	1886	Flowers	—	—	—	—	—	—	—	—	—	1	1
Costello, Henry	London	1880	Figures	—	—	—	—	—	—	—	—	—	1	1
Costello, Miss Louisa Stuart	London	1822-1838	Portraits	—	—	14	—	—	—	—	—	—	—	14
Costoli, Aristodème	Florence	1845	Sculpture	—	—	1	—	—	—	—	—	—	—	1
Cosway, Richard, R.A.	Tiverton	1760-1806	Miniatures	11	19	45	—	—	—	—	—	—	—	75
Cosway, Mrs. Richard, late Miss Maria	—	—	—	—	—	—	—	—	—	—	—	—	—	—
Cecilia Louisa Hadfield	London	1781-1801	Mythological	—	—	42	—	—	—	—	—	—	—	42
Cotchett, T.	London	1849	Flowers	—	—	1	—	—	—	—	—	—	—	1
Cotes, Francis, R.A.	London	1760-1770	Portraits	48	—	15	—	—	—	—	—	—	—	63
Cotes, P. B.	London	1798-1802	Architecture	—	—	6	—	—	—	—	—	—	—	6
Cotes, Samuel	London	1760-1789	Miniatures	28	—	58	—	—	—	—	—	—	—	86
Coteswortн, Miss Lillias E.	Winchester	1885-1888	Flowers	—	—	1	—	1	—	—	—	—	4	6
Cotman, Frederick George, R.I. ‡ φ	London	1870-1893	Figures	—	—	39	—	9	—	44	3	—	65	160
Cotman, John Joseph	Norwich	1852-1856	Landscape	—	—	1	8	—	—	—	—	—	—	9
Cotman, John Sell †	London	1800-1839	Sea Pieces	—	—	30	9	1	51	—	—	—	10	101
Cotman, Miles Edward (?) Edmund	London	1835-1856	Sea Pieces	—	—	4	10	19	—	—	—	—	—	33
Coton —	London	1782	Intaglios	—	—	1	—	—	—	—	—	—	—	1
Cotsworth, W. H.	London	1836-1839	Architecture	—	—	3	—	—	—	—	—	—	—	3
Cottam, Miss Ellen	London	1892	Flowers	—	—	—	—	1	—	—	—	—	—	1
Cotterill, Edmund	London	1822-1858	Sculpture	—	—	28	9	17	—	—	—	—	—	54
Cottin, Pierre	Paris	1876-1879	Domestic	—	—	—	—	—	—	—	—	—	6	6
Cottingham, Lewis Nockalls	London	1826-1846	Architecture	—	—	22	—	—	—	—	—	—	—	22
Cottingham, N. J.	London	1841-1853	Architecture	—	—	7	—	—	—	—	—	—	—	7
Cotton, Henry Robert	London	1871	Fruit	—	—	—	—	1	—	—	—	—	—	1
Cotton, J.	London	1809-1810	Flowers	—	—	2	—	—	—	—	—	—	—	2
Cotton, Mrs. Leslie (Mariette)	Munich	1891-1893	Portraits	—	—	3	—	—	—	—	—	—	1	4
Cotton, W.	—	1834-1843	Domestic	—	—	—	—	14	—	—	—	—	—	14
Cotton, Miss	Chicheley	1815-1822	Flowers	—	—	7	—	—	2	—	—	—	—	9
Cottrell, A.	Birmingham	1873-1876	Landscape	—	—	—	—	7	—	—	—	—	—	7
Cottrell, Wellesley	Birmingham	1889-1893	Landscape	—	—	4	—	—	—	—	—	12	—	16
Couchman, C.	London	1836-1841	Architecture	—	—	2	—	—	—	—	—	—	—	2
Couchman, Miss Florence A.	Tottenham	1883-1890	Buildings	—	—	1	—	5	—	2	—	—	—	8
Coughtrie, James B.	London	1863-1881	Domestic	—	—	1	—	1	—	—	—	—	—	2
Cougnard, Miss Augusta	London	1886-1892	Miniatures	—	—	3	—	1	—	—	—	—	—	4
Coulderey, W. E.	London	1805-1806	Architecture	—	—	4	—	—	—	—	—	—	—	4
Couldery, B. A.	London	1862-1877	Animals	—	—	—	5	5	—	—	—	—	1	11
Couldery, C. A.	Lewisham	1870-1872	Domestic	—	—	—	—	3	—	—	—	—	—	3
Couldery, Horatio Henry	London	1861-1893	Animals	—	—	20	13	62	—	—	—	—	49	144

Name.	Town.	First and Last Year of Ex.	Speciality.	S. A.	F. S.	R. A.	B. I.	S. S.	O. W.	N.W.	G. G.	N. G.	V. E.	Total.
Couldery, R., Junr.	Lewisham	1843-1861	Landscape	—	—	4	4	4	—	—	—	—	—	12
Couldery, Thomas W.	London	1883-1893	Domestic	—	—	3	—	4	—	7	—	—	—	14
Coulon, James	London	1892	Flowers	—	—	1	—	—	—	—	—	—	—	1
Coulon, John	London	1889	Figures	—	—	—	—	1	—	—	—	—	—	1
Coulson, J.	London	1864-1867	Landscape	—	—	—	4	—	—	—	—	—	—	4
Coulter, William	London	1869-1889	Still Life	—	—	2	—	4	—	—	1	—	3	10
Countze, F.	London	1795-1799	Landscape	—	—	10	—	—	—	—	—	—	—	10
Couper, William	Florence	1885-1892	Sculpture	—	—	3	—	—	—	1	—	—	—	4
Cour, De la. *See* D.	—	—	—	—	—	—	—	—	—	—	—	—	—	—
Courant, Maurice Auguste François	London	1878-1879	Sea Pieces	—	—	2	—	—	—	—	—	—	—	2
Courdonan, V.	Toulon	1854	Landscape	—	—	1	—	—	—	—	—	—	—	1
Courselles-Dumont, Henri	London	1889-1890	Fishing	—	—	—	—	1	—	2	—	—	—	3
Court, Miss Catherine Payn	London	1886-1891	Flowers	—	—	—	—	2	—	—	—	—	1	3
Court, W.	London	1785-1836	Miniatures	—	1	30	—	—	—	—	—	—	—	31
Court, William	Battle Bridge	1829	Still Life	—	—	—	—	2	—	—	—	—	—	2
Courtauld, Miss Edith. *See* Mrs. Arendrup	Braintree	1864-1873	Landscape	—	—	5	3	—	—	—	—	—	2	10
Courtney, F.	London	1835-1841	Portraits	—	—	7	—	—	—	—	—	—	—	7
Courtney, F. T.	London	1834-1839	Architecture	—	—	3	—	—	—	—	—	—	—	3
Courtney, J.	London	1836	Landscape	—	—	1	—	—	—	—	—	—	—	1
Courtois —	Paris	1879	Engraving	—	—	—	—	—	—	—	—	—	1	1
Courtois, Derring	—	1893	Portraits	—	—	—	—	—	—	—	—	—	1	1
Courtois, Gustave	—	1893	Portraits	—	—	—	—	—	—	—	—	—	1	1
Courtry, Charles Louis	Paris	1881-1884	Engraving	—	—	1	—	—	—	—	—	—	2	3
Cousen, Charles	Norwood	1848	Portraits	—	—	—	—	1	—	—	—	—	—	1
Cousen, John	Norwood	1863-1864	Landscape	—	—	2	—	—	—	—	—	—	—	2
Cousins, Charles	London	1877-1879	Portraits	—	—	—	—	—	—	—	5	—	—	5
Cousins, Samuel, R.A.	London	1837-1880	Engraving	—	—	35	—	—	—	—	—	—	—	35
Cousins, T. S.	London	1862-1873	Landscape	—	—	—	—	3	—	—	—	—	—	3
Coutts —	—	1838	Portraits	—	—	1	—	—	—	—	—	—	—	1
Coutts, Hubert (?) Herbert	Ambleside	1874-1893	Landscape	—	—	31	—	3	—	13	—	—	11	58
Coutts, William G.	Edinburgh	1867	Portraits	—	—	1	—	—	—	—	—	—	—	1
Coutts-Michie. *See* M.	—	—	—	—	—	—	—	—	—	—	—	—	—	—
Couture, Thomas	London	1840	Figures	—	—	1	—	—	—	—	—	—	—	1
Couzens, Charles	London	1838-1875	Portraits	—	—	61	1	12	—	—	—	—	5	79
Covell, Miss	London	1810	Portraits	—	—	1	—	—	—	—	—	—	—	1
Coventry, C. C.	London	1802-1819	Domestic	—	—	11	22	—	3	—	—	—	—	36
Coventry, James	London	1854-1861	Landscape	—	—	1	2	6	—	—	—	—	12	21
Coventry, Robert M. G., R.S.W.	Glasgow	1890-1893	Sea Pieces	—	—	5	—	—	—	—	—	—	—	5
Cowan, C. A.	Blackheath	1871-1874	Venice	—	—	—	—	—	—	—	—	—	3	3
Cowan, Miss Edith C.	London	1891	Figures	—	—	1	—	—	—	—	—	—	—	1
Cowan, Miss Janet D.	London	1882-1893	Domestic	—	—	—	—	3	—	—	—	—	4	7
Coward, Miss	Bath	1809	Landscape	—	—	—	3	—	—	—	—	—	—	3
Cowden, William	London	1798-1820	Sea Pieces	—	—	3	11	—	—	—	—	—	—	14
Cowderoy, William	London	1858-1885	Figures	—	—	1	4	16	—	—	—	—	1	22
Cowell, Miss Grace Charlotte (afterwards Mrs. F. Dixon)	London	1851	Miniatures	—	—	2	—	2	—	—	—	—	—	4
Cowell, Edwin, Junr.	London	1851-1865	Landscape	—	—	—	4	1	—	—	—	—	—	5
Cowell, Miss Emma	London	1849-1856	Landscape	—	—	5	8	12	—	—	—	—	1	26
Cowell, G. B.	London	1851	—	—	—	—	—	—	—	—	—	—	*	—
Cowell, G. H. Sydney	London	1890-1892	Domestic	—	—	1	—	2	—	—	—	—	2	5
Cowell, George J.	London	1886-1893	Sculpture	—	—	9	—	—	—	—	—	4	—	13
Cowell, H. B.	London	1851-1853	Landscape	—	—	1	2	—	—	—	—	—	—	3
Cowen, Lionel J., R.B.A. §	London	1869-1888	Figures	—	—	15	—	5	—	—	1	—	3	24
Cowen, William ‡	Rotherham	1811-1860	Landscape	—	—	16	32	13	—	15	—	—	15	91
Cowie, Frederick	London	1845-1870	Dramatic	—	—	11	8	30	—	—	—	—	2	51
Cowie, J.	—	1801-1803	Landscape	—	—	4	—	—	—	—	—	—	—	4
Cowley, T. C.	London	1835	Landscape	—	—	—	2	1	—	—	—	—	—	3
Cowlishaw, Thomas	Ashby-de-la-Zouch	1891	Architecture	—	—	1	—	—	—	—	—	—	—	1
Cowper, Anna	London	1871-1875	Flowers	—	—	—	—	—	—	—	—	—	3	3
Cowper, Douglas	London	1837-1839	Dramatic	—	—	6	3	8	—	—	—	—	—	17
Cowper, M. E.	—	1875	Flowers	—	—	—	—	—	—	—	—	—	1	1
Cowper, Richard	London	1882-1883	Landscape	—	—	—	—	—	—	1	—	—	2	3
Cowper, Thomas	Acton	1891-1893	Flowers	—	—	1	—	—	—	—	—	—	3	4
Cox, Arthur	Birkenhead	1876-1882	Domestic	—	—	—	—	—	—	—	—	—	9	9
Cox, A. H.	London	1842	Animals	—	—	—	—	1	—	—	—	—	—	1
Cox, Albert J.	London	1885-1887	Landscape	—	—	—	—	1	—	4	—	—	—	5
Cox, Alfred Wilson	Nottingham	1868-1885	Landscape	—	—	7	—	2	—	—	—	—	1	10
Cox, Bertram	Bedford Park	1893	Figures	—	—	—	—	1	—	—	—	—	—	1
Cox, C. Arthur	Manchester	1874-1887	Landscape	—	—	1	—	1	—	1	—	—	—	3
Cox, Charles Edward	London	1879-1893	Landscape	—	—	5	—	16	—	—	—	—	2	23
Cox, C. H.	Birkenhead	1866-1889	Landscape	—	—	—	—	1	—	1	1	—	48	51

Name.	Town.	First and Last Year of Ex.	Speciality.	S. A.	F. S.	R. A.	B. I.	S. S.	O. W.	N. W.	G. G.	N. G.	V. E.	Total.
Cox, David †	Birmingham	1805-1859	Landscape	—	—	13	3	4	849	—	—	—	104	973
Cox, David, Junr., R.W.S. † ‡	London	1827-1884	Landscape	—	—	3	—	1	579	87	—	—	—	670
Cox, Everard Morant	London	1878-1885	Domestic	—	—	2	—	—	—	—	—	—	2	4
Cox, Frank E.	London	1870-1892	Landscape	—	—	25	—	4	—	8	5	—	33	75
Cox, Rev. Sir George W., Bart.	York	1888-1889	Landscape	—	—	—	—	—	—	2	—	—	—	2
Cox, H.	London	1797	Architecture	—	—	1	—	—	—	—	—	—	—	1
Cox, H.	—	1873	Landscape	—	—	—	—	1	—	—	—	—	—	1
Cox, Miss Hilda	—	1888	Sculpture	—	—	—	—	—	—	—	—	1	—	1
Cox, J.	London	1793	Portraits	—	—	4	—	—	—	—	—	—	—	4
Cox, J., Junr.	Christchurch	1797-1800	Architecture	—	—	4	—	—	—	—	—	—	—	4
Cox, Miss Jane Wells	London	1880-1882	Landscape	—	—	—	—	6	—	—	—	—	3	9
Cox, Miss Louisa E.	Nottingham	1874-1888	Miniatures	—	—	8	—	—	—	—	—	—	—	8
Cox, Richard	London	1775	Architecture	—	—	1	—	—	—	—	—	—	—	1
Cox, Walter Alfred	London	1888-1893	Etching	—	—	—	—	1	—	—	—	—	2	3
Cox, Wilson	London	1881-1884	Landscape	—	—	—	—	3	—	—	—	—	—	3
Cox and Cooksey	London	1893	Architecture	—	—	1	—	—	—	—	—	—	—	1
Coxwell, A. F.	Bracknell	1869	Ducks	—	—	—	—	—	—	—	—	—	1	1
Cozens, Alexander	London	1760-1781	Landscape	18	7	8	—	—	—	—	—	—	—	33
Cozens, John Robert	London	1767-1776	Landscape	5	—	1	—	—	—	—	—	—	—	6
Cozens, William	Aveley	1820-1828	Sporting	—	—	6	1	—	—	—	—	—	—	7
Crabb, J.	London	1811-1841	Fruit & Flowers	—	—	2	7	5	—	—	—	—	—	14
Crabb, William	London	1848-1863	Domestic	—	—	9	4	9	—	—	—	—	8	30
Crabb, W. A.	London	1829-1859	Flowers	—	—	23	—	10	—	1	—	—	—	34
Crabb, Miss	Peckham	1833-1837	Flowers	—	—	4	—	—	—	—	—	—	—	4
Crabbe, Herbert G.	Beckenham	1885-1891	Landscape	—	—	4	—	8	—	2	—	—	—	14
Crabtree, Phillip	London	1786-1787	Flowers	—	—	3	—	—	—	—	—	—	—	3
Crace, J. D.	Dulwich	1870-1877	Egyptian Views	—	—	4	—	—	—	—	—	—	—	4
Crace, John Gregory, and Son	London	1877-1885	Architecture	—	—	7	—	—	—	—	—	—	—	7
Crace, Lewis Paxton	London	1877-1886	Architecture	—	—	4	—	—	—	—	—	—	—	4
Cracknell, Thomas C.	Birmingham	1865-1866	Landscape	—	—	—	—	3	—	—	—	—	—	3
Craft, Percy R.	London	1878-1893	Figures	—	—	15	—	10	—	—	—	—	11	36
Craft, William H.	London	1774-1795	Enamels	—	—	17	—	—	—	—	—	—	—	17
Crafton, Richard	London	1877-1882	Landscape	—	—	—	—	15	—	—	—	—	—	15
Craig, Alexander	London	1840-1857	Domestic	—	—	6	4	—	—	—	—	—	—	10
Craig, E.	—	1801-1803	Landscape	—	—	3	—	—	—	—	—	—	—	3
Craig, Miss E.	London	1812-1813	Flowers	—	—	3	—	—	—	—	—	—	—	3
Craig, E. W.	Leeds	1802	Landscape	—	—	1	—	—	—	—	—	—	—	1
Craig, F.	London	1892-1893	Domestic	—	—	—	—	2	—	—	—	—	—	2
Craig, H.	London	1815	Birds	—	—	1	—	—	—	—	—	—	—	1
Craig, H. D.	—	1816-1817	Domestic	—	—	2	—	—	—	—	—	—	—	2
Craig, J.	London	1811-1812	Landscape	—	—	—	—	—	—	—	—	—	7	7
Craig, J. K.	London	1819-1821	Portraits	—	—	5	—	—	—	—	—	—	—	5
Craig, James Stephenson	London	1854-1870	Domestic	—	—	3	7	12	—	—	—	—	—	22
Craig, Phillip	—	1887	Flowers	—	—	—	—	1	—	—	—	—	—	1
Craig, W., Junr.	London	1801-1806	Scriptural	—	—	5	—	—	—	—	—	—	—	5
Craig, W. H.	London	1802-1807	Rustic	—	—	5	—	—	—	—	—	—	—	5
Craig, William Marshall	Manchester	1788-1828	Landscape	—	—	152	10	12	—	—	—	—	85	259
Craister, Mrs. Walter	Chester	1870-1892	Flowers	—	—	—	—	3	—	2	—	—	5	10
Crake, Miss Ciceley	Wimbledon	1893	Sculpture	—	—	1	—	—	—	—	—	—	—	1
Crake, J.	London	1836-1841	Architecture	—	—	3	—	—	—	—	—	—	—	3
Crake, M.	London	1795-1802	Architecture	—	—	7	—	—	—	—	—	—	—	7
Crake, M. J.	London	1832	Sculpture	—	—	—	—	1	—	—	—	—	—	1
Crambrook, W.	Deal	1824-1862	Landscape	—	—	1	6	92	—	—	—	—	2	101
Cramer, R.	London	1797-1811	Portraits	—	—	27	—	—	—	—	—	—	—	27
Cramm, Baroness Helga von	London	1878-1879	Landscape	—	—	—	—	3	—	—	—	—	—	3
Cramp, Viola	London	1875	Landscape	—	—	—	—	—	—	—	—	—	1	1
Cramphorn, J.	London	1831	Figures	—	—	—	—	1	—	—	—	—	—	1
Cramphorn, W.	London	1772-1819	Sculpture	—	2	4	—	—	—	—	—	—	—	6
Cramphorn, W., Junr.	London	1809	Sculpture	—	—	1	—	—	—	—	—	—	—	1
Crampton, James S.	Bootle	1876	Landscape	—	—	—	—	—	—	—	—	—	1	1
Cranbrook —	—	1854	Landscape	—	—	—	1	—	—	—	—	—	—	1
Cranch, John	Kingsbridge	1791-1808	Poker Pictures	1	—	—	8	—	—	—	—	—	—	9
Crane, R.	—	1834	Domestic	—	—	—	—	1	—	—	—	—	—	1
Crane, Thomas	Liverpool	1842-1858	Historical	—	—	9	3	3	—	—	—	—	—	15
Crane, Thomas	London	1890	Landscape	—	—	1	—	—	—	—	—	—	—	1
Crane, Walter, A.R.W.S., R.I., † ‡ φ	London	1862-1893	Figures	—	—	2	—	—	67	13	105	10	71	268
Cranke, James	London	1775-1800	Portraits	—	—	12	—	—	—	—	—	—	—	12
Cranmer, Charles	London	1793-1839	Rustic	—	—	51	51	6	2	—	—	—	—	110
Cranmer, C., Junr.	London	1806-1815	Landscape	—	—	16	—	—	—	—	—	—	—	16
Cranston, W. A.	London	1878-1879	Domestic	—	—	—	—	—	—	—	—	—	2	2
Cranstone, L. J.	London	1845-1867	Figures	—	—	5	1	3	—	—	—	—	—	9

Name.	Town.	First and Last Year of Ex.	Speciality.	. .	F. S.	R. A.	B. I.	S. S.	O. W.	N.W.	G. G.	N. G.	V. E.	Total.
Crapp, C. F.	London	1855-1858	Architecture	—	—	2	—	—	—	—	—	—	—	2
Crashley —	London	1775-1777	Sculpture	9	—	—	—	—	—	—	—	—	—	9
Crauen, J., *or* Craven	London	1855	Landscape	—	—	—	—	1	—	—	—	—	—	1
Craven, Hawes	London	1867-1875	Sea Pieces	—	—	—	—	7	—	—	—	—	—	7
Crawford, A.	—	1800	Moonlight	—	—	1	—	—	—	—	—	—	—	1
Crawford, Edmund T., R.S.A.	Edinburgh	1836	Sea Pieces	—	—	1	—	—	—	—	—	—	—	1
Crawford, Ebenezer	London	1858-1873	Domestic	—	—	11	7	2	—	—	—	—	2	22
Crawford, G.	—	1770	Landscape	—	—	2	—	—	—	—	—	—	—	2
Crawford, J.	—	1797-1799	Moonlight	—	—	3	—	—	—	—	—	—	—	3
Crawford, James	London	1826-1827	Churches	—	—	—	2	3	—	—	—	—	—	5
Crawford, John	London	1828	Landscape	—	—	—	3	—	—	—	—	—	—	3
Crawford, Robert C.	Glasgow	1872-1893	Domestic	—	—	11	—	—	—	—	—	—	2	13
Crawford, Miss S.	—	1829	Landscape	—	—	—	—	1	—	—	—	—	—	1
Crawford, T. Hamilton, R.S.W.	Glasgow	1891	Figures	—	—	1	—	—	—	—	—	—	—	1
Crawford, William, A.R.S.A.	Edinburgh	1852-1868	Portraits	—	—	23	—	—	—	—	—	—	—	23
Crawford, Mrs. *See* Miss Emily Aldridge ‖	London	1869-1891	Figures	—	—	6	—	1	—	—	—	—	1	8
Crawhall, Joseph	Newcastle	1883	Landscape	—	—	1	—	—	—	—	—	—	—	1
Crawhall, W.	Newcastle	1860-1864	Sea Pieces	—	—	—	3	1	—	—	—	—	—	4
Crawley, Edmund	London	1772	Rustic	—	2	—	—	—	—	—	—	—	—	2
Crawley, F. S.	London	1836-1837	Cattle	—	—	2	—	2	—	—	—	—	—	4
Crawley, John	London	1878	Architecture	—	—	2	—	—	—	—	—	—	—	2
Crease, Harold	London	1812-1814	Portraits	—	—	1	—	—	—	—	—	—	3	4
Creasey, Miss Maria	London	1850	Portraits	—	—	1	—	—	—	—	—	—	—	1
Creasy, Mrs.	Tonbridge	1839-1841	Fruit	—	—	—	—	3	—	—	—	—	—	3
Creeke, C. C.	London	1846	Architecture	—	—	1	—	—	—	—	—	—	—	1
Cregan, Martin, P.R.H.A.	—	1812-1851	Portraits	—	—	37	6	—	—	—	—	—	—	43
Cregeen, Miss Nesey Isabel	London	1887-1893	Figures	—	—	3	—	—	—	—	—	—	—	3
Creighton, J.	Hackney	1815	Architecture	—	—	1	—	—	—	—	—	—	—	1
Creke, W.	London	1803-1824	Enamels	—	—	7	—	1	—	—	—	—	—	8
Crellin, H. N.	London	1825	Portraits	—	—	1	—	—	—	—	—	—	—	1
Crellin, H. P.	London	1832	Portraits	—	—	—	—	1	—	—	—	—	—	1
Crèpin, L. M.	Brussels	1865-1872	Landscape	—	—	2	—	2	—	—	—	—	—	4
Creswell, A. E. B.	Clifton	1861-1866	Landscape	—	—	—	—	3	—	—	—	—	1	4
Creswell, Miss Henrietta	London	1875-1892	Flowers	—	—	1	—	5	—	4	1	—	2	13
Creswell, Herbert Osborn	London	1888-1890	Architecture	—	—	2	—	—	—	—	—	—	—	2
Creswell, J.	—	1789-1790	Portraits	—	—	2	—	—	—	—	—	—	—	2
Creswell, J.	London	1857	Birds	—	—	1	—	—	—	—	—	—	—	1
Creswick, Benjamin	Manchester	1888-1891	Sculpture	—	—	2	—	—	—	—	—	—	—	2
Creswick, H. G.	—	1855	Portraits	—	—	1	—	—	—	—	—	—	—	1
Creswick, Mortimer	Liverpool	1889	Landscape	—	—	1	—	—	—	—	—	—	—	1
Creswick, Thomas, R.A.	Birmingham	1828-1870	Landscape	—	—	139	80	46	—	—	—	—	1	266
Creswick, Mrs.	—	1865-1867	Fruit	—	—	2	—	—	—	—	—	—	—	2
Cresy, E.	London	1821-1835	Architecture	—	—	6	—	—	—	—	—	—	—	6
Cretius, Professor	Berlin	1883	Historical	—	—	1	—	—	—	—	—	—	—	1
Creux, Du. *See* D.	—	—	—	—	—	—	—	—	—	—	—	—	—	—
Crew, J. T.	London	1833-1859	Architecture	—	—	19	—	—	—	—	—	—	—	19
Crew, Miss	London	1833	Portraits	—	—	1	—	—	—	—	—	—	—	1
Crichton, N. S.	Bradford	1880-1888	Churches	—	—	—	—	2	—	—	—	—	—	2
Crickitt, Miss	London	1769-1770	Flowers	—	2	—	—	—	—	—	—	—	—	2
Crickmay, George L.	London	1890	Architecture	—	—	1	—	—	—	—	—	—	—	1
Crickmay and Son	London	1884	Architecture	—	—	1	—	—	—	—	—	—	—	1
Criddle, Mrs. Harry.† *See* Miss Mary Ann Alabaster	London	1837-1879	Figures	—	—	11	18	14	149	—	—	—	2	194
Cridland, Miss Helen	Bushey	1886-1892	Domestic	—	—	2	—	1	—	—	—	1	3	7
Crighton, Hugh Ford	London	1865	Figures	—	—	1	—	1	—	—	—	—	—	2
Crighton, W.	—	1785	Ruins	—	—	1	—	—	—	—	—	—	—	1
Crisp —. *See* Godwin and Crisp	—	—	Architecture	—	—	—	—	—	—	—	—	—	—	—
Crisp, Anna E.	—	1819	Flowers	—	—	2	—	—	—	—	—	—	—	2
Crisp, D.	London	1816	Intaglios	—	—	1	—	—	—	—	—	—	—	1
Crisp, Miss H.	Torquay	1877	Landscape	—	—	—	—	2	—	—	—	—	—	2
Crispe, Miss Leila Constance	London	1885-1887	Flowers	—	—	—	—	1	—	—	—	—	2	3
Cristall, Miss Anna	London	1888	Miniatures	—	—	1	—	—	—	—	—	—	—	1
Cristall, Joshua †	London	1803-1847	Figures	—	—	3	3	—	376	—	—	—	—	382
Crittenden, Miss Dora E.	London	1884	Flowers	—	—	1	—	—	—	—	—	—	—	1
Crittenden, John D.	London	1853-1878	Sculpture	—	—	47	5	—	—	—	—	—	—	52
Crochez, T.	London	1850	Portraits	—	—	2	—	—	—	—	—	—	—	2
Crocker, A. C.	Cheshunt	1885-1886	Sea Pieces	—	—	—	—	—	—	3	—	—	—	3
Crockett, Edwin Arthur Brassey	London	1868	Architecture	—	—	1	—	—	—	—	—	—	—	1
Crockford, Miss F.	London	1839	Figures	—	—	1	—	—	—	—	—	—	—	1
Crockford, George §	London	1835-1865	Landscape	—	—	13	14	70	—	—	—	—	32	129
Crockford, Miss Gertrude	London	1877-1886	Sculpture	—	—	1	—	18	—	—	1	—	1	21
Crockford, Miss	London	1845	Landscape	—	—	—	—	1	—	—	—	—	—	1

Name.	Town.	First and Last Year of Ex.	Speciality.	S. A.	F. S.	R. A.	B. I.	S. S.	O. W.	N.W.	G. G.	N.	V. E.	Total.
Croft, Adolphus	London	1879	Architecture	—	—	1	—	—	—	—	—	—	—	1
Croft, Arthur	London	1865-1893	Landscape	—	—	36	—	3	—	3	—	—	29	71
Croft, John	London	1868-1875	Churches	—	—	—	—	—	—	—	—	—	2	2
Croft, J. B.	London	1829-1830	Sculpture	—	—	3	—	—	—	—	—	—	—	3
Croft, John Ernest	Tunb'dge Wells	1868-1873	Cattle	—	—	2	—	5	—	—	—	—	13	20
Croft, Miss Marian ‖	London	1869-1882	Landscape	—	—	—	—	6	—	—	—	—	16	22
Croft, Miss Mary Anne	London	1804-1814	Still Life	—	—	6	—	—	—	—	—	—	—	6
Crofts, Ernest, A.R.A.	Leeds	1867-1893	Historical	—	—	30	—	3	—	—	—	—	14	47
Croix, De la. *See* D.	—	—	—	—	—	—	—	—	—	—	—	—	—	—
Croizier —	London	1825	Portraits	—	—	6	—	—	—	—	—	—	—	6
Crola, Georg Heinrich	Düsseldorf	1874	Animals	—	—	1	—	—	—	—	—	—	—	1
Crombie, Miss E. E.	London	1890-1893	Flowers	—	—	1	—	—	—	1	—	—	—	2
Crome, Miss E.	Norwich	1825	Fruit	—	—	—	1	3	—	—	—	—	—	4
Crome, H. H.	Norwich	1830	Landscape	—	—	—	—	1	—	—	—	—	—	1
Crome, John	Norwich	1806-1824	Landscape	—	—	13	6	—	—	—	—	—	—	19
Crome, John Bernay	Norwich	1811-1843	Landscape	—	—	7	35	55	—	—	—	—	—	97
Crome, Vivian	London	1867	Flowers	—	—	1	2	—	—	—	—	—	—	3
Crome, William H.	Norwich	1826-1848	Landscape	—	—	—	1	4	—	—	—	—	5	10
Cromek, Thomas Hartley ‡	London	1835-1872	Grecian Landscape	—	—	6	—	4	—	60	—	—	—	70
Cromer, J. B.	—	1842	Sea Pieces	—	—	—	—	1	—	—	—	—	—	1
Crommelin, Miss M.	London	1870	Figures	—	—	1	—	—	—	—	—	—	—	1
Crompton, Edward	Southampton	1893	Sculpture	—	—	1	—	—	—	—	—	—	—	1
Crompton, John	London	1872-1886	Landscape	—	—	1	—	7	—	—	—	—	1	9
Crompton, James Shaw	London	1882-1893	Domestic	—	—	—	—	11	—	15	—	—	—	26
Crompton, Miss Mildred Roberts	London	1892-1893	Flowers	—	—	—	—	—	—	2	—	—	—	2
Crone, Robert	London	1770-1778	Landscape	—	—	26	—	—	—	—	—	—	—	26
Croneau, F.	—	1835	Domestic	—	—	—	1	—	—	—	—	—	—	1
Cronk, Edwyn Evans	London	1881	Architecture	—	—	1	—	—	—	—	—	—	—	1
Crook, A. W.	London	1884	Architecture	—	—	1	—	—	—	—	—	—	—	1
Crook, James	London	1778-1781	Portraits	—	—	5	—	—	—	—	—	—	—	5
Crook, W.	London	1845	Architecture	—	—	1	—	—	—	—	—	—	—	1
Crooke, John	Newlyn	1890-1892	Landscape	—	—	1	—	—	—	—	1	—	—	2
Crooke, W.	London	1878-1879	Churches	—	—	—	—	—	—	—	—	—	6	6
Crooke, W. P.	London	1879	Etchings	—	—	1	—	—	—	—	—	—	—	1
Croome, C. J.	London	1842-1845	Animals	—	—	—	—	5	—	—	—	—	—	5
Croome, J. D.	London	1839-1852	Figures	—	—	7	2	3	—	—	—	—	—	12
Cropley, Miss	London	1789-1811	Portraits	—	—	3	—	—	—	—	—	—	—	3
Cropsey, Jasper F.	New York	1845-1862	Landscape	—	—	13	1	—	—	—	—	—	—	14
Cros, J. B.	London	1836	Portraits	—	—	1	—	—	—	—	—	—	—	1
Crosby, William	Sunderland	1859-1873	Domestic	—	—	8	—	5	—	—	—	—	—	13
Croshaw, C. W.	London	1831	Architecture	—	—	1	—	—	—	—	—	—	—	1
Croshaw, T.	London	1846	Still Life	—	—	1	—	—	—	—	—	—	—	1
Crosland, Enoch	Whatstandwell	1883-1889	Sheep	—	—	2	—	1	—	—	—	—	—	3
Crosley, Miss Edith A.	London	1880-1884	Figures	—	—	1	—	6	—	—	—	—	1	8
Cross. *See* Allom and Cross	—	—	Architecture	—	—	—	—	—	—	—	—	—	—	—
Cross, Alfred W. *See also* Spalding and Cross	London	1881-1885	Architecture	—	—	2	—	—	—	—	—	—	—	2
Cross, F.	London	1845-1855	Architecture	—	—	5	—	—	—	—	—	—	—	5
Cross, John	Tiverton	1850-1858	Historical	—	—	6	—	—	—	—	—	—	—	6
Cross, Joseph	Preston	1890-1892	Landscape	—	—	2	—	—	—	—	—	—	—	2
Cross, William	London	1867	Landscape	—	—	—	—	—	—	—	—	—	1	1
Crosse, Edwin Reeve	Leeds	1888-1890	Domestic	—	—	2	—	—	—	—	—	—	—	2
Crosse, Richard	Cullompton	1760-1796	Miniatures	14	20	41	—	—	—	—	—	—	—	75
Crosse, S.	Herne Hill	1843	Architecture	—	—	1	—	—	—	—	—	—	—	1
Crossland, James H.	Belper	1885	Landscape	—	—	—	—	2	—	—	—	—	—	2
Crossland, J. M.	London	1832-1845	Portraits	—	—	5	—	1	—	—	—	—	—	6
Crossland, William Henry	London	1855-1884	Architecture	—	—	18	—	—	—	—	—	—	—	18
Crosswell, J.	—	1788	Sculpture	—	—	1	—	—	—	—	—	—	—	1
Crosthwaite, Daniel	London	1833-1845	Portraits	—	—	2	—	6	—	—	—	—	—	8
Crosthwaite, S.	London	1823	Landscape	—	—	2	—	—	—	—	—	—	—	2
Crotch, Dr. William	—	1799-1809	Landscape	—	—	3	—	—	—	—	—	—	—	3
Crouch, E. A.	London	1827-1834	Sea Pieces	—	—	—	4	7	—	2	—	—	—	13
Crouch, W.	London	1774-1776	Miniatures	—	4	—	—	—	—	—	—	—	—	4
Croudace, Mrs. E. H.	London	1852-1869	Domestic	—	—	4	—	20	—	—	—	—	1	25
Croughton, George	London	1874	Flowers	—	—	—	—	1	—	—	—	—	—	1
Crow, M. G.	London	1879	Heads	—	—	1	—	1	—	—	—	—	1	3
Crowdace, W. A. H.	London	1873	Figures	—	—	—	—	1	—	—	—	—	—	1
Crowdy, Miss Fanny	Reading	1859	Domestic	—	—	—	—	—	—	—	—	—	1	1
Crowe, Eyre, A.R.A.	London	1846-1893	Figures	—	—	84	2	1	—	—	—	—	8	95
Crowe, J.	London	1831	Architecture	—	—	2	—	—	—	—	—	—	—	2
Crowe, T.	London	1854-1855	Portraits	—	—	5	—	—	—	—	—	—	—	5
Crowley, Nicholas J., R.H.A.	Belfast	1835-1858	Domestic	—	—	47	17	1	—	—	—	—	—	65

Name.	Town.	First and Last Year of Ex.	Speciality.	S. A.	F. S.	R. A.	B. I.	S. S.	O. W.	N. W.	G. G.	N. G.	V. E.	Total.
Crowley, P. L.	London	1847-1859	Sculpture	—	—	5	1	—	—	—	—	—	—	6
Crowley, Walter	Manchester	1874-1875	Domestic	—	—	—	—	1	—	—	—	—	2	3
Crowquill, Alfred (Alfred Henry Forrester)	London	1845-1846	Domestic	—	—	4	—	—	—	—	—	—	—	4
Crowther, G.	London	1875-1876	Churches	—	—	3	—	—	—	—	—	—	—	3
Crowther, John	London	1876-1892	Architecture	—	—	5	—	2	—	3	—	—	2	12
Crowther, S.	Stockport	1826	Sea Pieces	—	—	—	1	—	—	—	—	—	—	1
Croxford, Miss Gertrude	London	1884	Sculpture	—	—	—	—	1	—	—	—	—	—	1
Croxford, Thomas Swainson	Brentford	1876-1884	Landscape	—	—	2	—	2	—	—	—	—	11	15
Croxford, William Edward	Brentford	1871-1892	Landscape	—	—	3	—	7	—	4	—	—	—	14
Croydon, W. J.	Windsor	1858-1864	Landscape	—	—	1	3	—	—	—	—	—	—	4
Crozier, Miss Anne Jane	Oxford	1868-1886	Domestic	—	—	4	—	—	—	4	—	—	8	16
Crozier, George, R.C.A.	Oxford	1865-1886	Landscape	—	—	7	—	—	—	1	—	—	9	17
Crozier, J.	London	1826	Portraits	—	—	—	—	2	—	—	—	—	—	2
Crozier, Robert	London	1836-1848	Sea Pieces	—	—	11	5	6	—	—	—	—	—	22
Crozier, Robert	Manchester	1854-1882	Domestic	—	—	5	—	6	—	—	—	—	—	11
Cruickshank, Miss Catherine Gertrude	London	1868-1889	Miniatures	—	—	9	—	—	—	—	—	—	2	11
Cruickshank, F.	London	1822-1860	Portraits	—	—	149	1	16	—	—	—	—	—	166
Cruickshank, Francis	Edinburgh	1852-1855	Portraits	—	—	2	—	—	—	—	—	—	—	2
Cruickshank, George	Manchester	1864	Still Life	—	—	—	—	1	—	—	—	—	—	1
Cruickshank, Miss Grace	London	1860-1892	Miniatures	—	—	15	—	5	—	2	—	—	4	26
Cruickshank, William	London	1866-1886	Game	—	—	7	—	22	—	—	—	—	—	29
Cruikshank, Miss Dora	London	1884	Landscape	—	—	—	—	—	—	1	—	—	—	1
Cruikshank, George	London	1830-1867	Humorous	—	—	8	15	—	—	—	—	—	—	23
Cruikshank, Isaac	London	1789-1792	Historical	—	—	3	—	—	—	—	—	—	—	3
Cruikshank, Robert Isaac	London	1811-1817	Portraits	—	—	8	—	—	—	—	—	—	—	8
Cruikshanks, J.	London	1802	Medals	—	—	1	—	—	—	—	—	—	—	1
Cruise, John	London	1832-1834	Dramatic	—	—	4	6	2	—	—	—	—	—	12
Crunden —	London	1766-1777	Architecture	7	—	—	—	—	—	—	—	—	—	7
Cruttwell, Miss Maud	London	1880-1893	Domestic	—	—	1	—	—	—	—	—	—	12	13
Cuadras, J.	Edinburgh	1872	Domestic	—	—	1	—	—	—	—	—	—	—	1
Cubitt, James	London	1883-1890	Architecture	—	—	5	—	—	—	—	—	—	—	5
Cubitt, L.	London	1842-1851	Architecture	—	—	3	—	—	—	—	—	—	—	3
Cubitt, Mrs. L. (Charlotte)	—	1873-1880	Sculpture	—	—	8	—	—	—	—	—	—	—	8
Cubitt, Thomas	London	1775-1778	Miniatures	2	—	1	—	—	—	—	—	—	—	3
Cubitt (James) and Brydon (J. M.)	London	1887	Architecture	—	—	1	—	—	—	—	—	—	—	1
Cubley, H. Hadfield	Wolverhampt'n	1884-1887	Landscape	—	—	2	—	3	—	—	—	—	3	8
Cubley, W. H.	Newark	1863-1878	Landscape	—	—	4	—	9	—	—	—	—	—	13
Cucinotta, Saro	London	1874	Engraving	—	—	—	—	—	—	—	—	—	1	1
Cudlip, S. B.	London	1828-1833	Fruit	—	—	8	10	5	—	—	—	—	—	23
Cuenot —	London	1771	Sculpture	1	—	—	—	—	—	—	—	—	—	1
Cuff, R. Parminter	London	1859-1876	Architecture	—	—	4	—	2	—	—	—	—	6	12
Cuisset, J. J.	London	1830-1839	Intaglios	—	—	8	—	—	—	—	—	—	—	8
Cuitt, George	London	1776-1818	Landscape	—	—	14	—	—	—	—	—	—	—	14
Cull, James Allanson	London	1872-1886	Figures	—	—	3	—	—	—	1	—	—	10	14
Cullen, D.	London	1819	Portraits	—	—	5	—	—	—	—	—	—	—	5
Cullin, Isaac	London	1881-1889	Domestic	—	—	4	—	—	—	—	—	—	—	4
Cullum, John	London	1833-1849	Domestic	—	—	6	7	8	—	—	—	—	6	27
Cullum, Mrs. J.	London	1834	Domestic	—	—	—	—	—	—	1	—	—	—	1
Culver, Fred	London	1889-1893	Landscape	—	—	1	—	12	—	1	—	—	—	14
Cumber, J.	London	1825	Architecture	—	—	1	—	—	—	—	—	—	—	1
Cumberland, C.	London	1861	Landscape	—	—	1	—	—	—	—	—	—	—	1
Cumberland, George	London	1773-1776	Miniatures	—	—	3	—	—	—	—	—	—	—	3
Cumberland, G.	—	1782-1783	Landscape	—	—	6	—	—	—	—	—	—	—	6
Cumberland, G., Junr.	London	1816-1818	Landscape	—	—	4	—	—	1	—	—	—	—	5
Cumberlege, C. N.	London	1827-1834	Architecture	—	—	2	—	—	—	—	—	—	—	2
Cumbo, E.	Florence	1874	Landscape	—	—	1	—	—	—	—	—	—	—	1
Cuming, J. B.	London	1793-1812	Landscape	—	—	18	—	—	—	—	—	—	—	18
Cuming, R.	London	1797-1803	Landscape	—	—	14	—	—	—	—	—	—	—	14
Cumming, Miss M.	London	1874	Flowers	—	—	1	—	—	—	—	—	—	—	1
Cummins, Miss Emily. *See* Mrs. J. L. Barnard	—	—	—	—	—	—	—	—	—	—	—	—	—	—
Cummins, E. L.	Darmstadt	1863	Miniatures	—	—	2	—	—	—	—	—	—	—	2
Cunard, Mrs. William	London	1890-1893	Landscape	—	—	—	—	8	—	—	—	—	—	8
Cunard, W. S.	London	1889-1893	Landscape	—	—	—	—	12	—	—	—	—	—	12
Cundall, H. M.	London	1881	—	—	—	—	—	—	—	—	—	—	*	—
Cundell, C. E.	London	1860-1869	Portraits	—	—	3	—	—	—	—	—	—	—	3
Cundell, H.	London	1838-1858	Landscape	—	—	14	—	—	—	—	—	—	—	14
Cundell, Naomi	Reading	1883	Fruit	—	—	—	—	2	—	—	—	—	—	2
Cundy, James	London	1817-1825	Mythological	—	—	*	4	1	—	—	—	—	—	5
Cundy, Thomas	London	1795-1816	Architecture	—	—	12	—	—	—	—	—	—	—	12
Cundy, Thomas, Junr.	London	1807-1817	Architecture	—	—	7	—	—	—	—	—	—	—	7
Cundy, Thomas	London	1864	Architecture	—	—	2	—	—	—	—	—	—	—	2

Name.	Town.	First and Last Year of Ex.	Speciality.	S. A.	F. S.	R. A.	B. I.	S. S.	O. W.	N. W.	G. G.	N. G.	V. E.	Total
Cunliffe — (aged 12)	—	1775	Portraits	1	—	—	—	—	—	—	—	—	—	1
Cunliffe, D.	London	1826-1855	Landscape	—	—	11	3	7	—	—	—	—	—	21
Cunliffe, E. S.	London	1855	Architecture	—	—	1	—	—	—	—	—	—	—	1
Cunliffe, Foster	—	1812-1828	Landscape	—	—	8	—	—	—	—	—	—	—	8
Cunningham —	London	1773	Sculpture	10	—	—	—	—	—	—	—	—	—	10
Cunningham, Edward Francis. *See* Calza.	—	—	—	—	—	—	—	—	—	—	—	—	—	—
Cunningham, Mrs. Georgina	Putney	1888	Domestic	—	—	1	—	—	—	—	—	—	—	1
Cunningham, H. F.	London	1846-1849	Miniatures	—	—	8	—	—	—	—	—	—	—	8
Cunynghame, H.	—	1888	Ruins	—	—	—	—	—	—	—	—	1	—	1
Curdie, John	Kilmarnock	1850	Landscape	—	—	—	—	1	—	—	—	—	—	1
Curnock, James	Bristol	1847-1862	Portraits	—	—	13	—	8	—	—	—	—	—	21
Curnock, James Jackson, R.C.A.	Bristol	1863-1891	Landscape	—	—	17	—	56	—	19	—	—	22	114
Currer, R. W.	London	1865	Domestic	—	—	—	1	—	—	—	—	—	—	1
Currey, Miss Ada	Weybridge	1878-1889	Domestic	—	—	—	—	3	—	2	—	—	—	5
Currey, Miss Fanny W.‖	Lismore	1880-1893	Landscape	—	—	17	—	3	—	18	13	6	14	71
Currey, Henry	London	1866	Architecture	—	—	1	—	—	—	—	—	—	—	1
Currie, A.	Melrose	1877	Portraits	—	—	1	—	—	—	—	—	—	—	1
Currie, James	London	1865-1887	Sculpture	—	—	8	—	—	—	—	—	—	—	8
Currie, Robert	Methven, N.B.	1880-1885	Birds	—	—	1	—	—	—	—	—	—	2	3
Currie, Captain R. W.	—	1835-1840	Still Life	—	—	—	2	6	—	—	—	—	—	8
Currie, Sydney	Birmingham	1892	Churches	—	—	—	—	1	—	—	—	—	—	1
Curtice, George M.	London	1885-1888	Sculpture	—	—	3	—	—	—	—	—	—	—	3
Curtis, Charles M.	London	1827-1832	Flowers	—	—	—	—	1	—	1	—	—	—	2
Curtis, Miss F. A. *See* Mrs. H. Toogood	Acton	1850-1852	Sculpture	—	—	2	—	—	—	—	—	—	—	2
Curtis, George D.	Manchester	1889-1893	Rustic	—	—	5	—	—	—	—	1	—	—	6
Curtis, Miss Isabel C.	London	1850-1856	Landscape	—	—	4	—	2	—	—	—	—	—	6
Curtis, John (Pupil of W. Marlow)	Twickenham	1790-1822	Landscape	—	—	9	—	—	1	—	—	—	—	10
Curtis, J. D.	Newark	1827	Landscape	—	—	—	—	1	—	—	—	—	—	1
Curtis, Miss R. F.	London	1887-1891	Flowers	—	—	—	—	2	—	1	—	—	—	3
Curtis, R. W.	Paris	1882-1890	Figures	—	—	1	—	—	—	—	1	—	—	2
Curtis, William	London	1775	Herbs	1	—	—	—	—	—	—	—	—	—	1
Curtis, Sir W., Bart.	—	1862	Landscape	—	—	—	1	1	—	—	—	—	—	2
Curtis, Mrs.	London	1848	Landscape	—	—	—	—	6	—	—	—	—	—	6
Curtois, Miss Dering. (?) Courtois	Lincoln	1887-1892	Domestic	—	—	6	—	—	—	—	—	1	—	7
Curtois, Miss Ella. (?) Courtois	Paris	1885-1893	Sculpture	—	—	2	—	—	—	—	—	—	—	2
Curtovich, Ovide	Smyrna	1892	Landscape	—	—	2	—	—	—	—	—	—	—	2
Cust —	—	1784-1785	Landscape	—	—	2	—	—	—	—	—	—	—	2
Custard, A. M.	Yeovil	1856-1860	Churches	—	—	—	—	—	—	—	—	—	7	7
Cutbush, L. F.	—	1819-1821	Landscape	—	—	2	—	—	—	—	—	—	—	2
Cutbush, T. C.	—	1807	Landscape	—	—	1	—	—	—	—	—	—	—	1
Cuthbert, Rev. G.	—	1802-1803	Landscape	—	—	2	—	—	—	—	—	—	—	2
Cuthbert, John Spreckley	London	1852-1877	Dramatic	—	—	18	2	2	—	—	1	—	—	23
Cutler, Cecil E. L.	Putney	1886	Domestic	—	—	—	—	1	—	—	—	—	1	2
Cutler, Ernest J. H.	London	1887	Landscape	—	—	—	—	2	—	—	—	—	—	2
Cutler, Thomas William	London	1873-1893	Architecture	—	—	6	—	—	—	—	—	—	—	6
Cutts, John T.	Liverpool	1885	Landscape	—	—	—	—	—	—	1	—	—	—	1
Dabis, Miss Anna	London	1888-1893	Sculpture	—	—	7	—	—	—	—	—	—	—	7
Da Costa, Professor G. *See* C.	—	—	—	—	—	—	—	—	—	—	—	—	—	—
Da Costa, John	Newlyn	1890-1892	Heads	—	—	2	—	—	—	—	1	—	—	3
Dacre, James	London	1829-1833	Landscape	—	—	—	2	2	—	—	—	—	—	4
Dacre, Miss Susan Isabel	Manchester	1876-1893	Figures	—	—	8	—	—	—	—	—	1	—	9
Dadd, Frank, R.I. ‡ φ	Lewisham	1872-1893	Figures	—	—	7	—	9	—	19	—	—	42	77
Dadd, R.	London	1837-1842	Dramatic	—	—	4	5	16	—	—	—	—	—	25
Dadd, Stephen T.	London	1879-1892	Domestic	—	—	—	—	1	—	10	—	—	7	18
Dade, Ernest	London	1887-1893	Seashores	—	—	8	—	7	—	—	—	—	—	15
Dadley, J.	London	1793-1797	Architecture	—	—	3	—	—	—	—	—	—	—	3
Dadson, W.	Rochester	1834	Landscape	—	—	—	—	3	—	—	—	—	—	3
Daffarn, Miss Alice	Haslemere	1886	Landscape	—	—	—	—	—	—	—	—	—	1	1
Daffarn, William George	London	1872-1893	Landscape	—	—	31	—	5	—	2	—	—	4	42
Dafforne, James	Clapton	1837-1845	Landscape	—	—	6	—	—	—	—	—	—	—	6
Dafforul, J.	London	1830	Rustic	—	—	1	—	—	—	—	—	—	—	1
Dagley, Miss E. F.	London	1817-1834	Domestic	—	—	2	—	7	—	—	—	—	—	9
Dagley, Richard	London	1785-1833	Figures	—	—	65	3	3	—	—	—	—	1	72
Dagnall, T. W.	London	1824-1836	Sea Pieces	—	—	9	15	27	—	1	—	—	—	52
Dagnan-Bouveret, Pascal A. J.	Paris	1884-1893	Domestic	—	—	1	—	—	—	—	—	—	1	2
Dagobert, F.	London	1880	Landscape	—	—	—	—	1	—	—	—	—	1	2
Daguerre, Louis Jacques Mandé	London	1838	Deluge	—	—	—	1	—	—	—	—	—	—	1
Daintrey, Alice S.	Petworth	1879	Still Life	—	—	—	—	—	—	—	—	—	1	1

Name.	Town.	First and Last Year of Ex.	Speciality.	S. A.	F. S.	R. A.	B. I.	S. S.	O. W.	N. W.	G. G.	N. G.	V. E.	Total.
Dakin, Joseph	London	1859-1888	Landscape	—	—	14	8	51	—	1	—	—	20	94
Dakin, Miss Sylvia C.	London	1893	Landscape	—	—	—	—	3	—	—	—	—	—	3
Daking, W.	London	1831	Portraits	—	—	1	—	—	—	—	—	—	—	1
Dalby, Edwin	London	1887	Architecture	—	—	1	—	—	—	—	—	—	—	1
Dale, Miss Annie	London	1867	Sea Pieces	—	—	—	1	—	—	—	—	—	—	1
Dale, E.	London	1873	Landscape	—	—	—	—	2	—	—	—	—	—	2
Dale, Mrs. Robert (late Miss Gertrude Brown)	London	1890-1893	Engraving	—	—	3	—	—	—	—	—	—	1	4
Dale, H.	London	1872	Landscape	—	—	—	—	1	—	—	—	—	—	1
Dale, Henry Sheppard	London	1878-1893	Landscape	—	—	5	—	1	—	1	—	—	6	13
Dalgliesh, Theodore Irving, R.P.E.	Nottingham	1878-1892	Etching	—	—	11	—	1	—	—	—	—	3	15
Dalglish, William	Glasgow	1891-1893	Landscape	—	—	—	—	—	—	2	—	—	—	2
Dall, Nicholas Thomas, A.R.A.	London	1761-1776	Landscape	37	—	18	—	—	—	—	—	—	—	55
Dallas, E. W.	Rome	1839-1853	Churches	—	—	5	5	3	—	—	—	—	—	13
D'Almaine, William Frederick	London	1846-1864	Figures	—	—	13	13	12	—	—	—	—	1	39
Dalmas, F. E. de Saint	Guernsey	1871-1872	Landscape	—	—	—	—	4	—	—	—	—	—	4
D'Almeida, W. B.	London	1885	Landscape	—	—	—	—	—	—	—	—	—	1	1
Dalou, Jules	London	1872-1879	Sculpture	—	—	22	—	—	—	—	—	—	6	28
Dalton, Miss Caroline	London	1879	Copies	—	—	1	—	—	—	—	—	—	—	1
Dalton, Edwin	London	1818-1844	Portraits	—	—	6	—	—	—	—	—	—	—	6
Dalton, Mrs. Edwin (late Miss Magdalene Ross)	London	1842-1856	Miniatures	—	—	16	—	—	—	—	—	—	—	16
Dalton, E. C.	London	1876-1879	Landscape	—	—	—	—	1	—	—	—	—	2	3
Dalton, F.	—	1847	Architecture	—	—	1	—	—	—	—	—	—	—	1
Dalton, Frank	Old Charlton	1877	Landscape	—	—	—	—	—	—	—	—	—	1	1
Dalton, Mrs. M.	London	1879	Birds	—	—	2	—	—	—	—	—	—	—	2
Dalton, Richard	London	1766	Figures	1	—	—	—	—	—	—	—	—	—	1
Dalton, Mrs.	—	1808-1809	Landscape	—	—	3	—	—	—	—	—	—	—	3
Dalton, Miss	London	1871	—	—	—	—	—	*	—	—	—	—	—	—
Dalziel, Brothers	London	1861-1877	Woodcuts	—	—	21	—	—	—	—	—	—	3	24
Dalziel, Edward	—	1841-1871	Figures	—	—	3	1	—	—	—	—	—	2	6
Dalziel, E. Gilbert	London	1866-1882	Domestic	—	—	—	—	—	—	—	—	—	5	5
Dalziel, Edward Gurdon	London	1865-1887	Domestic	—	—	16	—	4	—	2	—	—	16	38
Dalziel, Herbert	London	1877-1893	Figures	—	—	8	—	24	—	1	1	3	15	52
Dalziel, James B.	London	1848-1880	Landscape	—	—	7	3	7	—	—	—	—	1	18
Dalziel, Owen	London	1878-1893	Domestic	—	—	11	—	26	—	1	2	—	14	54
Dalziel, R.	London	1840-1842	Domestic	—	—	—	3	7	—	—	—	—	—	10
Dalziel, Thomas Bolton	London	1846-1874	Historical	—	—	6	1	3	—	—	—	—	9	19
Dalziels, Thomas J.	London	1884	Architecture	—	—	1	—	—	—	—	—	—	—	1
Damer, Hon. Mrs. Anne Seymour	—	1784-1818	Sculpture	—	—	32	—	—	—	—	—	—	—	32
Damis, J.	—	1879	Flowers	—	—	1	—	—	—	—	—	—	—	1
Damman, Benjamin Auguste Louis	Paris	1879-1881	Etchings	—	—	—	—	—	—	—	—	—	3	3
Dampier, Arthur	London	1866-1875	Landscape	—	—	—	—	41	—	—	—	—	25	66
Dampier, E.	—	1784-1786	Miniatures	—	—	4	—	—	—	—	—	—	—	4
Dana, William P. W.	Paris	1873-1877	Figures	—	—	2	—	—	—	—	—	—	1	3
Danby, Collinson	London	1866-1870	River Scenes	—	—	—	—	8	—	—	—	—	—	8
Danby, Francis, A.R.A.	Bristol	1820-1860	Landscape	—	—	48	17	2	—	—	—	—	—	67
Danby, Frederick	Exmouth	1849	Landscape	—	—	—	1	—	—	—	—	—	—	1
Danby, G.	Clifton	1817	Landscape	—	—	1	—	—	—	—	—	—	—	1
Danby, James Francis §	London	1842-1876	Landscape	—	—	35	42	67	—	—	—	—	10	154
Danby, Joseph	London	1854	Landscape	—	—	—	2	—	—	—	—	—	—	2
Danby, Jacob C.	London	1863-1882	Landscape	—	—	—	1	7	—	—	—	—	—	8
Danby, Thomas, R.W.S. †	London	1841-1885	Landscape	—	—	32	42	1	234	—	—	—	13	322
Dance, George, R.A.	London	1761-1800	Portraits	3	—	24	—	—	—	—	—	—	—	27
Dance, G.	London	1821-1827	Portraits	—	—	4	—	—	—	—	—	—	—	4
Dance, Nathaniel, R.A., F.S.A. (afterwards Sir Nathaniel Dance Holland)	Rome	1761-1800	Historical	5	1	22	—	—	—	—	—	—	—	28
Dance, W.	London	1780	Miniatures	—	2	—	—	—	—	—	—	—	—	2
Dance, W., Junr.	London	1819-1859	Portraits	—	—	42	—	—	—	—	—	—	—	42
D'Ancona, T. *or* V.	London	1869-1872	Domestic	—	—	4	—	—	—	—	—	—	1	5
Danford, Charles G.	Harpenden	1883-1885	Landscape	—	—	—	—	—	—	3	—	—	—	3
Dangerfield, J.	London	1808-1809	Architecture	—	—	3	—	—	—	—	—	—	—	3
Daniel —	London	1764-1767	Game	—	4	—	—	—	—	—	—	—	—	4
Daniel, Miss A. S. W.	London	1824-1853	Portraits	—	—	21	2	—	—	—	—	—	—	23
Daniel, C. G.	London	1837	Game	—	—	1	—	—	—	—	—	—	—	1
Daniel, Frank	London	1889	Portraits	—	—	1	—	—	—	—	—	—	—	1
Daniel, G.	—	1830	Landscape	—	—	—	1	—	—	—	—	—	—	1
Daniel, J.	Bristol	1783-1799	Miniatures	1	—	5	—	—	—	—	—	—	—	6
Daniel, P. A.	London	1853-1870	Figures	—	—	3	2	4	—	—	—	—	—	9
Daniel, Mrs. P. A.	London	1854	Figures	—	—	—	—	1	—	—	—	—	—	1
Daniell, Rev. E. T.	—	1836-1840	Landscape	—	—	4	4	—	—	—	—	—	—	8
Daniell, J. B.	London	1819	Portraits	—	—	1	—	—	—	—	—	—	—	1
Daniell, Samuel	London	1791-1812	Landscape	1	—	6	—	—	—	—	—	—	—	7
Daniell, Miss S. M.	—	1853	Heads	—	—	—	1	—	—	—	—	—	—	1

Name.	Town.	First and Last Year of Ex.	Speciality.	S. A.	F. S.	R. A.	B. I.	S. S.	O. W.	N. W.	G. G.	N. G.	V. E.	Total.
Daniell, Miss S. S. *See* Mrs. Gent	London	1826-1831	Portraits	—	—	16	1	5	—	—	—	—	—	22
Daniell, Thomas, R.A.	London	1772-1830	Landscape	—	—	125	10	—	—	—	—	—	—	135
Daniell, William, R.A.	London	1795-1838	Landscape	—	—	168	64	—	—	—	—	—	—	232
Daniels, Mrs. Amy	London	1889	Landscape	—	—	1	—	—	—	—	—	—	—	1
Daniels, George	London	1884-1893	Miniatures	—	—	7	—	—	—	—	—	—	—	7
Daniels, William	Liverpool	1840-1846	Figures	—	—	7	—	—	—	—	—	—	—	7
Danks, B.	London	1783-1790	Domestic	—	—	2	—	—	—	—	—	—	—	2
Danloux, G. P.	London	1795	Portraits	—	—	6	—	—	—	—	—	—	—	6
Danloux, Henri Pierre	London	1792-1800	Portraits	—	—	19	—	—	—	—	—	—	—	19
Dannat, W. T. F. §	Paris	1885-1890	Figures	—	—	1	—	9	—	—	—	—	—	10
Danner, J.	London	1830	Still Life	—	—	—	—	2	—	—	—	—	—	2
Danse, A.	Mons	1876	Etchings	—	—	—	—	—	—	—	—	—	7	7
Danson, George	London	1823-1848	Landscape	—	—	4	1	6	—	—	—	—	—	11
Danson, J.	London	1832	Landscape	—	—	—	—	4	—	—	—	—	—	4
Danson, R.	London	1862	Animals	—	—	—	1	—	—	—	—	—	—	1
Danson, Thomas	London	1846-1855	Landscape	—	—	1	—	4	—	—	—	—	—	5
Dantan, E.	Paris	1881	Atelier	—	—	—	—	—	—	—	1	—	—	1
Dantan, Antoine Laurent	London	1834	Sculpture	—	—	2	—	—	—	—	—	—	—	2
Dante, F.	London	1884	Sculpture	—	—	1	—	—	—	—	—	—	—	1
Danyell, Herbert (Berto)	Florence	1890-1893	Figures	—	—	—	—	—	—	1	1	—	—	2
Daplyn, A. J.	London	1875-1880	Landscape	—	—	—	—	1	—	—	—	—	2	3
Da Porzo, C.	London	1882	Venice	—	—	—	—	—	—	—	—	—	1	1
Da Pozzo, G.	London	1876-1892	Scriptural	—	—	2	—	2	—	1	—	—	—	5
Daragon, Laurent	Paris	1878	Sculpture	—	—	2	—	—	—	—	—	—	—	2
Darbishire, Henry Astley	London	1857-1870	Architecture	—	—	6	—	—	—	—	—	—	—	6
Darbon, William	Plymouth	1886	Ships	—	—	—	—	—	—	1	—	—	—	1
Darby, Miss A.	—	1813-1817	Flowers	—	—	2	—	—	—	—	—	—	—	2
Darbyshire, W.	London	1813	Dogs	—	—	1	—	—	—	—	—	—	—	1
D'Arce, Miss C.	—	1814	Portraits	—	—	1	—	—	—	—	—	—	—	1
D'Arcy, Colonel J.	—	1808-1830	Landscape	—	—	5	—	—	—	—	—	—	—	5
Darcy, Miss Laura	London	1881-1891	Domestic	—	—	7	—	4	—	3	—	—	—	14
D'Arcy, Mary C.	London	1879	Crayon	—	—	—	—	—	—	—	—	—	1	1
Dardoize, Emile	Paris	1874-1881	Landscape	—	—	—	—	—	—	—	—	—	18	18
Dare, J.	London	1783	Landscape	1	—	—	—	—	—	—	—	—	—	1
Da Rios, L.	London	1884-1888	Domestic	—	—	1	—	—	—	4	—	—	1	6
Darley, J. F.	London	1886-1893	Landscape	—	—	—	—	10	—	—	—	—	1	11
Darley, William H.	London	1836-1850	Scriptural	—	—	4	1	—	—	—	—	—	—	5
Darling. *See* Haines and Darling	—	—	Architecture	—	—	—	—	—	—	—	—	—	—	—
Darling —	—	1762	Miniatures	1	—	—	—	—	—	—	—	—	—	1
Darly —	London	1765-1771	Architecture	7	—	—	—	—	—	—	—	—	—	7
Darmesteter, Madame Arsène	Paris	1884-1893	Portraits	—	—	1	—	—	—	—	5	—	2	8
Darmesteter, Madame Helena	—	1893	Portraits	—	—	—	—	—	—	—	—	—	1	1
Darney, Miss (?) Mrs., Lilian D.	Kinghorn, N.B.	1891-1892	Miniatures	—	—	2	—	—	—	—	—	—	—	2
Dartiguenave, P.	London	1859	Domestic	—	—	1	—	—	—	—	—	—	—	1
Dartiguenave, Victor	London	1841-1854	Domestic	—	—	35	—	13	—	—	—	—	—	48
Darton, William	Plymouth	1887	Sea Pieces	—	—	—	—	—	—	1	—	—	—	1
Darvall, Charles G.	London	1855	Domestic	—	—	—	—	—	—	—	—	—	1	1
Darvall, Frank	London	1881	Venice	—	—	—	—	—	—	—	1	—	—	1
Darvall, Henry	London	1848-1889	Landscape	—	—	12	2	13	—	—	2	—	36	65
Dashwood, J.	Newp'rt, I. of W.	1790	Sea Pieces	1	—	—	—	—	—	—	—	—	—	1
Dashwood, R.	—	1789-1797	Landscape	—	—	3	—	—	—	—	—	—	—	3
Dasilva, H. C.	London	1852	Landscape	—	—	—	—	1	—	—	—	—	—	1
Dassy, Jean Joseph	Marseilles	1846	Mythological	—	—	—	1	—	—	—	—	—	—	1
Daubigny, Charles François	Paris	1866-1870	River Scenes	—	—	4	—	—	—	—	—	—	—	4
Daubrawa, De. *See* De.	—	—	—	—	—	—	—	—	—	—	—	—	—	—
Daugars, Madame	Sydenham	1852-1879	Figures	—	—	1	—	—	—	—	—	—	6	7
Daun, B.	London	1858	Figures	—	—	—	—	1	—	—	—	—	—	1
Davenport, C. Talbot	Hawkhurst	1892	Landscape	—	—	—	—	1	—	—	—	—	—	1
Davenport, H. P.	London	1845-1846	Domestic	—	—	—	—	2	—	—	—	—	—	2
Davey, Florence	Horsham	1881	Flowers	—	—	—	—	2	—	—	—	—	—	2
Davey, R.	London	1877	Architecture	—	—	1	—	—	—	—	—	—	—	1
Davey, William T.	London	1859-1884	Engraving	—	—	13	—	—	—	—	—	—	—	13
David, F. M.	Montreal	1891	Sculpture	—	—	1	—	—	—	—	—	—	—	1
David, Miss Mary R.	London	1866-1877	Churches	—	—	—	—	1	—	—	—	—	2	3
David, Pierre Jean	Paris	1829	Sculpture	—	—	1	—	—	—	—	—	—	—	1
David, R. B.	Bristol	1866	Landscape	—	—	—	—	1	—	—	—	—	—	1
Davidis, Miss A. E.	Tunb'dge Wells	1883	Landscape	—	—	—	—	—	—	—	1	—	1	2
Davidson, Alexander, R.S.W.	Glasgow	1873-1892	Domestic	—	—	3	—	7	—	—	—	—	2	12
Davidson, Andrew	Inverness	1878-1886	Sculpture	—	—	4	—	—	—	—	—	—	—	4
Davidson, Charles, R.W.S. † ‡	London	1844-1893	Landscape	—	—	4	6	24	800	114	—	—	16	964
Davidson, Charles Topham	Redhill	1870-1893	Landscape	—	—	12	—	52	—	22	2	—	14	102
Davidson, Mrs. C. D.	London	1879	Figures	—	—	—	—	1	—	—	—	—	—	1

Name.	Town.	First and Last Year of Ex.	Speciality.	S. A.	F. S.	R. A.	B. I.	S. S.	O.W.	N.W.	G. G.	N. G.	V. E.	Total.
Davidson, H.	Wimbledon	1873	Venice	—	—	—	—	1	—	—	—	—	—	1
Davidson, John	Edinburgh	1871	Landscape	—	—	—	—	—	—	—	—	—	1	1
Davidson, Miss Jessie Y.	Liverpool	1892	Landscape	—	—	1	—	—	—	—	—	—	—	1
Davidson, Thomas, Junr.	London	1863-1893	Figures	—	—	26	5	65	—	—	—	—	45	141
Davidson, W.	—	1831	Engraving	—	—	—	—	1	—	—	—	—	—	1
Davie, W. G.	London	1872-1879	Architecture	—	—	3	—	—	—	—	—	—	—	3
Daviel, Leon	London	1893	Portraits	—	—	1	—	—	—	—	—	—	—	1
Davies, Alfred	Leicester	1888-1889	Landscape	—	—	—	—	—	—	2	—	—	—	2
Davies, C.	—	1845	Animals	—	—	1	—	—	—	—	—	—	—	1
Davies, Edward	Leicester	1880-1893	Landscape	—	—	16	—	1	—	24	—	—	7	48
Davies, E. M.	—	1840	Portraits	—	—	4	—	—	—	—	—	—	—	4
Davies, Edgar W.	Manchester	1893	Architecture	—	—	1	—	—	—	—	—	—	—	1
Davies, G.	London	1827	Fruit	—	—	1	—	—	—	—	—	—	—	1
Davies, George E.	Leicester	1893	Landscape	—	—	—	—	2	—	8	—	—	—	10
Davies, G. S.	London	1885	Landscape	—	—	—	—	2	—	—	—	—	—	2
Davies, J.	Hackney	1819-1853	Architecture	—	—	15	—	—	—	—	—	—	—	15
Davies, J. A.	London	1842	Architecture	—	—	1	—	—	—	—	—	—	—	1
Davies, James Henry	Manchester	1872-1892	Landscape	—	—	14	—	3	—	—	—	—	—	17
Davies, J. Hey, R.C.A.	Manchester	1875-1891	Rustic	—	—	—	—	8	—	—	—	—	4	12
Davies, John Scarlett	London	1822-1844	Interiors	—	—	7	6	14	—	—	—	—	—	27
Davies, Miss M. I.	London	1893	Flowers	—	—	—	—	1	—	—	—	—	—	1
Davies, Miss Minnie M.	London	1884-1890	Miniatures	—	—	3	—	2	—	2	—	—	—	7
Davies, Norman Prescott, R.B.A., A.R.C.A. §	Isleworth	1880-1893	Domestic	—	—	11	—	13	—	3	1	—	6	34
Davies, Captain R.	—	1771-1806	Landscape	—	—	18	—	—	—	—	—	—	—	18
Davies, W.	Shrewsbury	1819	Game	—	—	4	—	—	—	—	—	—	—	4
Davies, William	Runcorn	1871	Pencil	—	—	—	—	—	—	—	—	—	1	1
Davies, William H.	London	1818-1838	Still Life	—	—	8	—	—	—	—	—	—	—	8
D'Avigdor, Miss Estelle	London	1890	Snakes	—	—	2	—	—	—	—	—	—	—	2
Da Vinci, L.	London	1839	Sporting	—	—	—	1	—	—	—	—	—	—	1
Davis —	London	1778	Landscape	1	—	—	—	—	—	—	—	—	—	1
Davis, Alfred	Pinner	1863-1879	Landscape	—	—	—	2	2	—	—	—	—	—	4
Davis, Annie	London	1879	Mountains	—	—	—	—	1	—	—	—	—	—	1
Davis, Arthur Alfred	London	1877-1884	Domestic	—	—	—	—	6	—	—	—	—	1	7
Davis, Arthur H.	London	1871-1893	Landscape	—	—	1	—	12	—	—	—	—	2	15
Davis, Miss C.	London	1860-1862	Domestic	—	—	2	—	—	—	—	—	—	—	2
Davis, Miss Celia	York	1889-1892	Fish	—	—	1	—	1	—	—	—	—	—	2
Davis, C. D.	Lee	1877	Landscape	—	—	—	—	1	—	—	—	—	—	1
Davis, Charles Edward, F.S.A.	Bath	1865	Architecture	—	—	1	—	—	—	—	—	—	—	1
Davis, Charles H.	London	1891	Landscape	—	—	4	—	—	—	—	—	—	—	4
Davis, Miss C. L.	London	1877	Landscape	—	—	—	—	1	—	—	—	—	1	2
Davis, D.	London	1809	Architecture	—	—	1	—	—	—	—	—	—	—	1
Davis, David	London	1863-1887	Sculpture	—	—	13	—	—	—	—	—	—	—	13
Davis, D. H.	London	1831	River Scenes	—	—	—	—	1	—	—	—	—	—	1
Davis, Edward	Bath	1828-1867	Domestic	—	—	25	16	1	—	—	—	—	—	42
Davis, Edward	London	1834-1877	Sculpture	—	—	115	2	1	—	—	—	—	—	118
Davis, Mrs. E.	Weymouth	1855-1856	Fruit	—	—	2	—	—	—	—	—	—	—	2
Davis, F.	Bournemouth	1872-1874	Landscape	—	—	—	—	—	—	—	—	—	3	3
Davis, Frederick	Colchester	1853-1892	Landscape	—	—	5	2	18	—	—	—	—	10	35
Davis, Miss F.	London	1875-1876	Fruit	—	—	—	—	3	—	—	—	—	—	3
Davis, Fred. W., R.B.A. §	Birmingham	1891-1893	Domestic	—	—	—	—	5	—	2	—	—	—	7
Davis, G. G. Markwell	London	1884	Figures	—	—	—	—	—	—	—	—	—	1	1
Davis, H.	London	1832-1846	Historical	—	—	2	—	3	—	—	—	—	—	5
Davis, Herbert	London	1859	Engraving	—	—	1	—	—	—	—	—	—	—	1
Davis, H. B.	London	1852	Sculpture	—	—	2	—	—	—	—	—	—	—	2
Davis, H. E.	London	1862	Historical	—	—	—	1	—	—	—	—	—	—	1
Davis, H. N.	London	1860	Landscape	—	—	—	—	1	—	—	—	—	—	1
Davis, Henry William Banks, R.A.	London	1853-1893	Landscape	—	—	100	5	17	—	—	—	5	14	141
Davis, J.	London	1799-1812	Miniatures	—	—	12	—	—	—	—	—	—	—	12
Davis, J. Barnard	London	1890-1893	Landscape	—	—	1	—	3	—	2	—	—	—	6
Davis, J. D.	—	1831	Architecture	—	—	—	—	1	—	—	—	—	—	1
Davis, John J.	London	1882-1884	Landscape	—	—	1	—	4	—	—	—	—	1	6
Davis, J. M.	London	1810-1839	Miniatures	—	—	63	—	—	—	—	—	—	—	63
Davis, J. Pain (Pope Davis), R.C.A.	Ashburton	1811-1875	Portraits	—	—	33	17	61	—	3	—	—	14	128
Davis, J. S.	Argenteuil	1877	Domestic	—	—	—	—	—	—	—	—	—	1	1
Davis, J. Valentine, R.B.A. §	London	1875-1893	Landscape	—	—	26	—	27	—	2	—	2	17	74
Davis, Miss Kathleen	Tulse Hill	1892-1893	Portraits	—	—	—	—	—	—	—	—	2	3	5
Davis, Lucien, R.I. ‡	London	1878-1893	Domestic	—	—	17	—	—	—	2	—	—	14	33
Davis, Miss Lena M.	London	1891-1892	Domestic	—	—	—	—	2	—	—	—	—	—	2
Davis, M.	—	1800	Landscape	—	—	1	—	—	—	—	—	—	—	1
Davis, Miss Miriam J.	London	1884-1893	Flowers	—	—	3	—	20	—	—	1	3	6	33
Davis, Owen William	London	1874-1884	Architecture	—	—	4	—	—	—	—	—	—	—	4
Davis Richard Barrett §	Windsor	1802-1853	Sporting	—	—	70	57	141	3	2	—	—	11	284

Name.	Town.	First and Last Year of Ex.	Speciality.	S. A.	F. S.	R. A.	B. I.	S. S.	O. W.	N.W.	G. G.	N. G.	V. E.	Total.
Davis, S.	—	1807-1809	Indian Lands'pe	—	—	6	—	—	—	—	—	—	—	6
Davis, Miss Sarah	London	1846-1855	Portraits	—	—	6	—	7	—	—	—	—	5	18
Davis, Stuart G.	London	1893	Figures	—	—	1	—	—	—	—	—	—	—	1
Davis, Miss S. J.	London	1870	Figures	—	—	—	—	1	—	—	—	—	—	1
Davis, T.	—	1852	Sporting	—	—	1	—	—	—	—	—	—	—	1
Davis, Thomas	Bromley	1877-1880	Landscape	—	—	—	—	3	—	—	—	—	—	3
Davis, T. C.	London	1806	Landscape	—	—	1	—	—	—	—	—	—	—	1
Davis, T. P.	Ightham	1886	Domestic	—	—	—	—	1	—	—	—	—	—	1
Davis, Tyddesley R. T.	Brighton	1831-1857	Sporting	—	—	—	7	—	—	—	—	—	—	7
Davis, V.	London	1801-1823	Architecture	—	—	17	—	—	—	—	—	—	—	17
Davis, William	London	1851-1878	Landscape	—	—	16	—	1	—	—	—	—	3	20
Davis, William	London	1851-1888	Sculpture	—	—	40	—	—	—	—	—	—	—	40
Davis, William A.	London	1890	Emblematical	—	—	1	—	—	—	—	—	—	—	1
Davis, W. H.	London	1803-1849	Sporting	—	—	30	7	8	—	—	—	—	—	45
Davis, W. H.	Southampton	1893	Domestic	—	—	—	—	1	—	—	—	—	—	1
Davis, Miss W. J.	London	1883	Landscape	—	—	—	—	1	—	—	—	—	—	1
Davis, W. Paul	London	1875-1893	Domestic	—	—	2	—	7	—	—	—	—	2	11
Davis, Miss	London	1771-1773	Hair Work	3	2	—	—	—	—	—	—	—	—	5
Davis, Miss	—	1817-1818	Flowers	—	—	2	—	—	—	—	—	—	—	2
Davis and Emanuel	London	1883	Architecture	—	—	1	—	—	—	—	—	—	—	1
Davison —	—	1783	Rustic	—	1	—	—	—	—	—	—	—	—	1
Davison, E. Eleanor	London	1880	Flowers	—	—	—	—	—	—	—	—	—	1	1
Davison, H.	London	1868-1877	Churches	—	—	—	—	13	—	—	—	—	—	13
Davison, Miss M. D.	London	1893	Domestic	—	—	1	—	—	—	—	—	—	—	1
Davison, Miss Nora	London	1881-1893	Landscape	—	—	—	—	20	—	2	5	10	1	38
Davison, Thomas	London	1892	Architecture	—	—	1	—	—	—	—	—	—	—	1
Davison, Thomas Raffles	Manchester	1877-1889	Architecture	—	—	13	—	—	—	—	—	—	—	13
Davison, W.	London	1797-1798	Architecture	—	—	6	—	—	—	—	—	—	—	6
Davison, William	London	1813-1843	Figures	—	—	22	16	10	—	—	—	—	—	48
Davy, C.	London	1833-1846	Architecture	—	—	9	—	—	—	—	—	—	—	9
Davy, Henry	Ipswich	1829	Landscape	—	—	—	—	3	—	—	—	—	—	3
Davy, Robert	London	1762-1782	Miniatures	17	—	21	—	—	—	—	—	—	—	38
Dawbarn, Mrs. A. G. *See* Miss M. Wilson	London	1879	Landscape	—	—	—	—	1	—	—	—	—	—	1
Dawber, Edward Guy	London	1885-1893	Architecture	—	—	6	—	—	—	—	—	—	—	6
Dawe, George, R.A.	London	1804-1832	Portraits	—	—	47	7	1	—	—	—	—	—	55
Dawe, Henry E.§	London	1824-1845	Engraving	—	—	1	4	72	—	—	—	—	—	77
Dawe, J. P.	London	1820-1828	Portraits	—	—	2	1	—	—	—	—	—	—	3
Dawe, Philip	London	1769-1782	Engraving	—	18	—	—	—	—	—	—	—	—	18
Dawe, Miss	London	1836	Domestic	—	—	—	—	1	—	—	—	—	—	1
Dawes, William	London	1760-1774	Historical	7	17	—	—	—	—	—	—	—	—	24
Dawkes and Clarke	London	1877	Architecture	—	—	1	—	—	—	—	—	—	—	1
Dawkes, Samuel Whitfield	Gloucester	1839-1856	Architecture	—	—	15	—	—	—	—	—	—	—	15
Daws, C.	Dorking	1877	Landscape	—	—	1	—	—	—	—	—	—	—	1
Daws, Philip	Dorking	1873-1879	Landscape	—	—	4	—	13	—	—	—	—	—	17
Dawson, Alfred	Chertsey	1860-1893	Landscape, etc.	—	—	8	7	15	—	—	—	—	2	32
Dawson, Amy	London	1889-1891	Fruit	—	—	—	—	3	—	—	—	—	—	3
Dawson, Mrs. B. *See* Miss Elizabeth Rumley	London	1859-1876	Fruit	—	—	10	6	11	—	—	—	—	—	27
Dawson, Chester	London	1881	Landscape	—	—	—	—	—	—	—	—	—	1	1
Dawson, George	London	1829	Landscape	—	—	—	1	—	—	—	—	—	—	1
Dawson, Henry §	Nottingham	1838-1875	Landscape	—	—	28	33	6	—	—	—	—	18	85
Dawson, H. Thomas §	Chertsey	1860-1878	Sea Pieces	—	—	5	6	19	—	—	—	—	1	31
Dawson, J. C.	Chiswick	1863	Sea Pieces	—	—	—	1	—	—	—	—	—	—	1
Dawson, Mabel	London	1880-1881	Flowers	—	—	—	—	—	—	—	—	—	2	2
Dawson, Nelson, R.B.A.§.	London	1885-1893	Landscape	—	—	14	—	56	—	8	5	—	—	83
Dawson, Russell	Eton	1868-1883	Landscape	—	—	—	—	—	—	—	1	—	1	2
Day, Barclay	London	1873-1879	Domestic	—	—	2	—	7	—	—	—	—	—	9
Day, C.	London	1821	Enamels	—	—	1	—	—	—	—	—	—	—	1
Day, C.	Worcester	1835-1838	Architecture	—	—	4	—	—	—	—	—	—	—	4
Day, C. H.	London	1826-1827	Architecture	—	—	2	—	—	—	—	—	—	—	2
Day, C. W.	Deal	1821-1859	Portraits	—	—	14	—	2	—	—	—	—	—	16
Day, Miss Frances S.	London	1838-1858	Miniatures	—	—	48	—	15	—	—	—	—	—	63
Day, G. F.	Leicester	1850-1869	Domestic	—	—	3	—	3	—	—	—	—	—	6
Day, Hannah	London	1849	Portraits	—	—	—	—	1	—	—	—	—	—	1
Day, H. H.	London	1837	Portraits	—	—	1	—	—	—	—	—	—	—	1
Day, H. S.	London	1837-1848	Figures	—	—	3	1	4	—	—	—	—	—	8
Day, J. C.	London	1835-1836	Sculpture	—	—	2	—	—	—	—	—	—	—	2
Day, Lewis F.	London	1880-1886	Architecture	—	—	4	—	—	—	—	—	—	—	4
Day, R.	London	1827-1841	Architecture	—	—	5	—	—	—	—	—	—	—	5
Day, R., Junr.	London	1843-1847	Architecture	—	—	6	—	1	—	—	—	—	—	7
Day, Thomas	London	1768-1788	Miniatures	6	4	51	—	—	—	—	—	—	—	61
Day, T.	Romford	1774-1785	Landscape	2	—	4	—	—	—	—	—	—	—	6
Day, William	—	1782-1801	Landscape	—	—	21	—	—	—	—	—	—	—	21

Name.	Town.	First and Last Year of Ex.	Speciality.	S. A.	F. S.	R. A.	B. I.	S. S.	O. W.	N.W.	G. G.	N. G.	V. E.	Total.
Day, William Cave	Dewsbury	1890-1893	Domestic	—	—	2	—	—	—	—	—	—	—	2
Day, Mrs. W. C.	London	1847	Portraits	—	—	1	—	—	—	—	—	—	—	1
Dayes, Edward	London	1786-1804	Landscape	5	—	64	—	—	—	—	—	—	—	69
Dayes, Mrs.	London	1797-1800	Miniatures	—	—	8	—	—	—	—	—	—	—	8
Dayman, Francis S.	Tiverton	1884	Landscape	—	—	—	—	—	—	1	—	—	—	1
Dayson, L. J.	London	1855	Ducks	—	—	—	—	1	—	—	—	—	—	1
Deacon, Augustus Oakley	London	1840-1862	Landscape	—	—	9	10	10	—	—	—	—	23	52
Deacon, G. S.	Southampton	1872-1879	Landscape	—	—	5	—	5	—	—	—	—	3	13
Deacon, Henry D.	Bristol	1880	Landscape	—	—	—	—	1	—	—	—	—	1	2
Deacon, Miss Virginia	Eastbourne	1885	Still Life	—	—	—	—	—	—	1	—	—	—	1
Deakin, Andrew	Birmingham	1856-1857	Landscape	—	—	—	3	2	—	—	—	—	—	5
Deakin, Miss Jane ‖	London	1861-1884	Landscape	—	—	1	—	19	—	1	—	—	8	29
Deakin, Peter	Birmingham	1855-1879	Landscape	—	—	20	13	59	—	—	—	—	18	110
Dealy, Miss Jane M., R.I. ‡	Blackheath	1879-1893	Domestic	—	—	20	—	8	—	21	—	—	4	53
Dean, Frankland	Leeds	1885-1890	Landscape	—	—	4	—	2	—	—	—	—	—	6
Dean, H.	London	1794	Sculpture	—	—	1	—	—	—	—	—	—	—	1
Dean, H.	London	1860-1864	Etching	—	—	13	—	—	—	—	—	—	—	13
Dean, Hugh Primrose	London	1765-1780	Landscape	13	3	3	—	—	—	—	—	—	—	19
Dean, John	London	1777-1791	Engraving	5	—	6	—	—	—	—	—	—	—	11
Dean, P.	London	1789-1790	Flowers	1	—	1	—	—	—	—	—	—	—	2
Dean, Richard	London	1777	Gems	—	—	1	—	—	—	—	—	—	—	1
Dean, T. A.	London	1773-1825	Engraving	2	—	3	—	3	—	—	—	—	—	8
Dean, W.	London	1810-1815	Architecture	—	—	2	—	—	—	—	—	—	3	5
Dean, W.	London	1826	Engraving	—	—	—	—	4	—	—	—	—	—	4
Dean, Miss	—	1778	Engraving	—	—	1	—	—	—	—	—	—	—	1
Dean, Miss	London	1890	Portraits	—	—	—	—	—	—	—	1	—	—	1
Deane, Charles	London	1815-1851	Landscape	—	—	42	103	9	20	—	—	—	—	174
Deane, D. W.	London	1841-1868	Figures	—	—	28	23	15	—	—	—	—	21	87
Deane, Miss Emmeline	Bath	1879-1892	Miniatures	—	—	5	—	—	—	—	—	—	—	5
Deane, E. E.	London	1876-1879	Architecture	—	—	3	—	—	—	—	—	—	—	3
Deane (E. E.) and Tiltman (A. H.)	London	1880	Architecture	—	—	1	—	—	—	—	—	—	—	1
Deane, J. Manly	Dublin	1893	Architecture	—	—	2	—	—	—	—	—	—	—	2
Deane, L.	Bath	1885	Landscape	—	—	—	—	—	—	1	—	—	—	1
Deane, Sir T. Newenham, R.H.A.	London	1853	Landscape	—	—	—	—	1	—	—	—	—	—	1
Deane (T. N.) and Son	Dublin	1886-1888	Architecture	—	—	2	—	—	—	—	—	—	—	2
Deane, William Wood † ‡	London	1844-1873	Venice, etc.	—	—	23	4	13	58	102	—	—	9	209
Deanes, Edward	London	1860-1893	Figures	—	—	7	8	17	—	—	—	—	2	34
Deanes, Mrs. H. Christabella	London	1887	Domestic	—	—	1	—	—	—	—	—	—	—	1
Deanes, Miss Mary	London	1870-1871	Fruit	—	—	—	—	2	—	—	—	—	—	2
Deans, D.	London	1871-1872	Domestic	—	—	—	—	6	—	—	—	—	—	6
Dear, Miss Mary E.	London	1848-1867	Domestic	—	—	7	—	5	—	—	—	—	—	12
Dearden, A.	Womaston	1866-1874	Portraits	—	—	2	—	1	—	—	—	—	2	5
Deare, John	Rome	1788	Sculpture	—	—	1	—	—	—	—	—	—	—	1
Deare, Joseph	London	1826-1832	Sculpture	—	—	10	—	—	—	—	—	—	—	10
Deare, Miss Margaret	Staines	1884-1887	Domestic	—	—	—	—	3	—	—	—	—	—	3
Dearle, John	Jersey	1852-1871	Landscape	—	—	20	—	—	—	—	—	—	—	20
Dearle, John H.	London	1853-1891	Landscape	—	—	15	12	12	—	10	1	—	35	85
Dearman, Miss Elizabeth J.	London	1828-1846	Landscape	—	—	6	4	12	—	1	—	—	—	23
Dearman, John	London	1824-1856	Landscape	—	—	45	74	47	—	1	—	—	—	167
Dearman, Miss M.	London	1834-1842	Fruit	—	—	—	1	8	—	—	—	—	—	9
Dearmer, Thomas	London	1840-1867	Landscape	—	—	21	14	23	—	—	—	—	2	60
Dearn, F. D. M.	London	1806-1808	Architecture	—	—	6	—	—	—	—	—	—	—	6
Dearn, T.	London	1798-1799	Architecture	—	—	3	—	—	—	—	—	—	—	3
Dearn, T. D. W.	Cranbrook	1828	Architecture	—	—	2	—	—	—	—	—	—	—	2
Deas, Kenneth	London	1890	Sea Pieces	—	—	—	—	—	—	—	1	—	2	3
Death, H.	London	1848	Figures	—	—	—	—	1	—	—	—	—	—	1
Debaines, Alfred Brunet-. *See* B.	—	—	—	—	—	—	—	—	—	—	—	—	—	—
De Bar, Alexander	London	1874	Woodcut	—	—	—	—	—	—	—	—	—	1	1
De Bard, Chevalier L. C.	London	1797-1814	Still Life	—	—	8	—	—	—	—	—	—	2	10
Debat-Ponsan, Edouard Bernard	Harrow	1891	Domestic	—	—	—	—	—	—	—	—	—	1	1
De Bay, Jean Baptiste Joseph	Nantes	1841	Landscape	—	—	1	—	—	—	—	—	—	—	1
De Beaupré, A. Bastien	Paris	1884	Figures	—	—	1	—	—	—	—	—	—	—	1
De Beaurepaire, Mdlle.	London	1804-1822	Miniatures	—	—	38	—	—	—	—	—	—	—	38
De Bengy, Puy Vallee Georges	Paris	1890	Sculpture	—	—	1	—	—	—	—	—	—	—	1
De Bernhardt, Mrs. *See* Miss Julia Bouvier.	—	—	—	—	—	—	—	—	—	—	—	—	—	—
De Biseau, A.	Brussels	1877-1880	Landscape	—	—	1	—	4	—	—	—	—	—	5
De Blaas, Eugene	Vienna	1875-1892	Figures	—	—	12	—	—	—	—	1	1	—	14
De Block, Eugene.	Brussels	1845-1867	Sporting	—	—	1	—	—	—	—	—	—	1	2
De Bloeme, H. A.	The Hague	1856	Figures	—	—	1	—	—	—	—	—	—	—	1
Deblois, Charles Theodore	London	1877-1888	Engraving	—	—	2	—	—	—	—	—	—	—	2
De Boinville, C.A.C. *See* Morris & De Boinville	—	—	Architecture	—	—	—	—	—	—	—	—	—	—	—
De Brackeleer, Ferdinandus	London	1831	Historical	—	—	—	—	1	—	—	—	—	—	1

Name.	Town.	First and Last Year of Ex.	Speciality.	S. A.	F. S.	R. A.	B. I.	S. S.	O. W.	N.W.	G. G.	N. G.	V. E.	Total.
De Brackeleer, J.	London	1874	Sculpture	—	—	2	—	—	—	—	—	—	—	2
De Breanski, Alfred, A.R.C.A. §	Greenwich	1869-1893	Landscape	—	—	43	—	65	—	6	1	—	36	151
De Breanski, Gustave	Lewisham	1877-1892	Landscape	—	—	8	—	51	—	—	—	—	12	71
De Breda, Charles Frederick, R.A. of Stockholm	London	1788-1796	Portraits	—	—	26	—	—	—	—	—	—	—	26
De Bree, Anthony	Greenwich	1876-1893	Interiors	—	—	—	—	8	—	—	—	—	1	9
De Brisay, Miss Marguerite	Oxford	1892-1893	Sculpture	—	—	2	—	—	—	—	—	—	—	2
De Bruyn, H.	London	1793-1797	Portraits	—	—	4	—	—	—	—	—	—	—	4
De Bruyn, John	London	1780	Copies	—	2	—	—	—	—	—	—	—	—	2
De Bruyn, Jos.	London	1871-1893	Sculpture	—	—	8	—	1	—	—	—	—	—	9
De Bruyn, Theodore	London	1769-1803	Sculpture	1	4	25	—	—	—	—	—	—	—	30
De Burgho, Alfred	London	1872	Woodcut	—	—	—	—	—	—	—	—	—	1	1
De Bylandt, A.	London	1853-1884	Landscape	—	—	8	6	21	—	—	—	—	7	42
Decaisne, Henri	Paris	1829	Theatrical	—	—	1	—	—	—	—	—	—	—	1
De Cambruzzi. *See* C.	—	—	—	—	—	—	—	—	—	—	—	—	—	—
Decamp, E. M.	Paris	1834	Animals	—	—	5	—	—	—	—	—	—	—	5
Decamps —	Paris	1874	Figures	—	—	—	—	—	—	—	—	—	2	2
De Carne, H.	London	1801-1821	Portraits	—	—	2	—	—	—	—	—	—	—	2
De Castro, Harry M.	London	1877-1886	Landscape	—	—	4	—	5	—	—	—	—	2	11
De Castro, Miss Mary B.	—	1892	Miniatures	—	—	1	—	—	—	—	—	—	—	1
De Castro, P. P.	Madrid	1872-1874	Landscape	—	—	3	—	—	—	—	—	—	2	5
De Castro, Mrs.	—	1777-1778	Flowers	—	—	2	—	—	—	—	—	—	—	2
De Cazenove, Simon	London	1856-1875	Portraits	—	—	3	—	—	—	—	—	—	2	5
De Chair, R. B.	—	1785	Miniatures	—	—	6	—	—	—	—	—	—	—	6
De Chambrulard, J.	London	1799-1802	Portraits	—	—	5	—	—	—	—	—	—	—	5
De Charteau. *See* C.	—	—	—	—	—	—	—	—	—	—	—	—	—	—
De Cock, Cesar	—	1867	Landscape	—	—	1	—	—	—	—	—	—	—	1
De Cool, Madame Delphine	Paris	1879-1881	Enamels	—	—	5	—	—	—	—	—	—	—	5
De Cort, Henry	Paris	1790-1806	Landscape	—	—	63	3	—	—	—	—	—	—	66
De Costa, S., *or* De Koster	London	1800-1801	Portraits	—	—	4	—	—	—	—	—	—	—	4
De Daubrawa, Henry	London	1842-1861	Figures	—	—	4	3	4	—	—	—	—	—	11
De Dominius, Achille	London	1882	Verona	—	—	—	—	—	—	—	—	—	1	1
De Dreux, Alfred	London	1850-1851	Portraits	—	—	2	—	—	—	—	—	—	—	2
Dedrick —	—	1813	Landscape	—	—	1	—	—	—	—	—	—	—	1
Deeble, W.	London	1814	Churches	—	—	2	—	—	—	—	—	—	—	2
Deer —	Rome	1791	Sculpture	1	—	—	—	—	—	—	—	—	—	1
Deering, John Peter, R.A. *See* J. P. Gandy, R.A.	London	1828-1833	Landscape	—	—	8	—	—	—	—	—	—	—	8
Deey, Rev. William	London	1829-1874	Figures	—	—	21	4	26	—	—	—	—	—	51
De Fabeck. *See* F.	—	—	—	—	—	—	—	—	—	—	—	—	—	—
De Fayll, Mdlle.	London	1872	Figures	—	—	—	—	3	—	—	—	—	—	3
De Feyl, Madame	London	1864-1866	Scriptural	—	—	1	2	3	—	—	—	—	—	6
Deffell, H.	—	1834	Figures	—	—	—	1	—	—	—	—	—	—	1
Deffell, Miss Justina ‖	London	1859-1871	Figures	—	—	—	11	6	—	—	—	—	11	28
De Fleury, J.	London	1799-1822	Landscape	—	—	60	1	—	—	—	—	—	—	61
De Fleury, J. V.	London	1847-1869	Landscape	—	—	16	12	36	—	—	—	—	17	81
De Fleury, W.	London	1865	Landscape	—	—	—	—	—	—	—	—	—	1	1
De Forestier, Mdlle. Alice	London	1872-1874	Landscape	—	—	—	—	—	—	—	—	—	6	6
De Forget, Mdlle.	London	1798	Flowers	—	—	1	—	—	—	—	—	—	—	1
De Fretag, Chevalier	—	1798	Portraits	—	—	1	—	—	—	—	—	—	—	1
Defries, Miss Lily	London	1886	Portraits	—	—	—	—	—	—	—	1	—	—	1
Defries, Miss Sara	—	1878-1879	Historical	—	—	—	—	—	—	—	2	—	—	2
De Gantes —	London	1804	Heads	—	—	4	—	—	—	—	—	—	—	4
De Giovanni, Cavaliere G.	London	1878- 188	Sculpture	—	—	2	—	—	—	—	—	—	—	2
De Girardy, J.	London	1784	Flowers	—	—	2	—	—	—	—	—	—	—	2
D'Egloffstein. *See* E.	—	—	—	—	—	—	—	—	—	—	—	—	—	—
Degrain, M.	London	1873	Granada	—	—	—	—	1	—	—	—	—	—	1
Degrave, P.	—	1877	Domestic	—	—	1	—	—	—	—	—	—	—	1
De Grimaldi. *See* G.	—	—	—	—	—	—	—	—	—	—	—	—	—	—
De Gronckel, Vital	London	1879	Portraits	—	—	2	—	—	—	—	—	—	—	2
De Groot, F. A. B.	—	1851	Domestic	—	—	1	—	—	—	—	—	—	—	1
De Guérard, E.	Melbourne	1865	Landscape	—	—	1	—	—	—	—	—	—	—	1
De Guérin, Mrs. A. L. *See* G.	—	—	—	—	—	—	—	—	—	—	—	—	—	—
D'Egville, J.	London	1826	Architecture	—	—	2	—	—	—	—	—	—	—	2
D'Egville, J. F. ‡	London	1837-1880	Landscape	—	—	3	1	—	—	256	—	—	—	260
D'Egville, J. Hervé	London	1868-1877	Venice	—	—	—	—	—	—	—	—	—	8	8
De Haas, J. H. L.	London	1869-1874	Landscape	—	—	6	—	—	—	—	—	—	—	6
Dehaussey, J.	London	1848-1851	Portraits	—	—	12	2	—	—	—	—	—	—	14
Dehaussy, Madame	London	1851	Birds	—	—	—	2	—	—	—	—	—	—	2
De Hoghton, Miss	London	1883-1887	Portraits	—	—	—	—	—	—	—	5	—	—	5
De Hormann, Theodore	Vienna	1890	Fishermen	—	—	2	—	—	—	—	—	—	—	2
De Janvry, H.	London	1798-1800	Miniatures	—	—	16	—	—	—	—	—	—	—	16
De Jong, P. de Josselin	—	1891	Portraits	—	—	—	—	—	—	—	—	—	2	2
De Jonghe, Gustave	Tulse Hill	1875	Domestic	—	—	1	—	—	—	—	—	—	—	1

Name.	Town.	First and Last Year of Ex.	Speciality.	S. A.	F. S.	R. A.	B. I.	S. S.	O. W.	N.W.	G. G.	N. G.	V. E.	Total.
De Katowy, P.	London	1872-1873	Battles	—	—	—	—	3	—	—	—	—	—	3
De Kerk, W.	Dort	1838	Landscape	—	—	1	—	—	—	—	—	—	—	1
De Keyser, J.	Brussels	1883	Sculpture	—	—	1	—	—	—	—	—	—	—	1
De Koningh, Leendert	London	1809-1812	Cattle	—	—	3	5	—	—	—	—	—	—	8
De la Brely, A. *See* B.	—	—	—	—	—	—	—	—	—	—	—	—	—	—
De la Condamine, E. J.	Ryde	1872-1874	Landscape	—	—	—	—	—	—	—	—	—	2	2
Delacour —	Edinburgh	1766	Landscape	1	—	—	—	—	—	—	—	—	—	1
De la Cour, B.	London	1818-1843	Portraits	—	—	23	—	—	—	—	—	—	—	23
De la Cour-Carroll, Miss Jane	London	1883	Sculpture	—	—	1	—	—	—	—	—	—	—	1
De la Croix, Ferdinand Victor Eugene	Paris	1828-1830	Historical	—	—	1	1	—	—	—	—	—	—	2
De la Croix, Madame	London	1874-1880	Portraits	—	—	7	—	—	—	—	—	—	—	7
De la Crouée, H.	London	1885	Landscape	—	—	—	—	—	—	1	—	—	—	1
De Lacy, Charles J.	London	1885-1893	Landscape	—	—	2	—	14	—	—	—	—	—	16
De Lafage, G. L.	Paris	1857	Landscape	—	—	2	—	—	—	—	—	—	—	2
De Lafollie, A.	London	1857-1862	Portraits	—	—	3	—	—	—	—	—	—	—	3
Delahante —	London	1798-1799	Portraits	—	—	2	—	—	—	—	—	—	—	2
De la Houliere, R.	London	1789	Portraits	—	—	2	—	—	—	—	—	—	—	2
De Lalaing, J.	Brussels	1883	Portraits	—	—	1	—	—	—	—	—	—	—	1
De la Mare, A.	London	1836-1839	Figures	—	—	1	—	1	—	—	—	—	—	2
De la Moriniere, F.	London	1850	Portraits	—	—	1	—	—	—	—	—	—	—	1
De la Motte, George O.	Great Marlow	1809	Landscape	—	—	1	—	—	—	—	—	—	—	1
Delamotte, Philip Henry, F.S.A.	London	1861-1876	Buildings	—	—	2	—	2	—	—	—	—	12	16
Delamotte, William	Oxford	1793-1850	Landscape	—	—	53	13	7	11	—	—	—	—	84
Delane, Solomon, F.S.A.	Rome	1763-1784	Landscape	4	—	8	—	—	—	—	—	—	—	12
Delany —	—	1782	Drawings	—	4	—	—	—	—	—	—	—	—	4
Delap, Mrs.	—	1820-1824	Flowers	—	—	1	—	2	—	—	—	—	—	3
Delaplanche, Eugene	Paris	1877	Sculpture	—	—	—	—	—	—	—	1	—	—	1
Delaroche, Paul Hippolyte	Paris	1844-1850	Historical	—	—	3	—	—	—	—	—	—	—	3
De Latre —	—	1838	Sporting	—	—	—	1	—	—	—	—	—	—	1
Delâtre, Auguste	London	1872-1875	Etching	—	—	2	—	1	—	—	—	—	8	11
Delattre, Jean Marie	London	1770	Engraving	1	—	—	—	—	—	—	—	—	—	1
De l'Aubinière, Madame C. A. (Georgina M.)	St. Quentin	1876-1891	Domestic	—	—	8	—	3	—	—	1	—	11	23
Delaunay, Jules-Elie	London	1882	Figures	—	—	2	—	—	—	—	—	—	—	2
De Laune, C. de L. Taunce. *See* T.	—	—	—	—	—	—	—	—	—	—	—	—	—	—
De Laune, C. D. F.	London	1872	Ruins	—	—	1	—	—	—	—	—	—	—	1
De la Vega, P. L.	Spain	1775	Portraits	3	—	—	—	—	—	—	—	—	—	3
Del Campo, Federico	London	1879	Figures	—	—	—	—	—	—	—	—	—	1	1
Del Don Martino. *See* M.	—	—	—	—	—	—	—	—	—	—	—	—	—	—
De Leeuw, Alexis	London	1863-1864	Domestic	—	—	1	2	2	—	—	—	—	—	5
Delfosse, E.	Brussels	1849-1861	Figures	—	—	5	—	—	—	—	—	—	—	5
Del Hardinge, J.	London	1832	Portraits	—	—	1	—	—	—	—	—	—	—	1
Delion, Mdlle.	Blackheath	1835-1836	Portraits	—	—	—	—	3	—	—	—	—	—	3
De Liphart, Ernest	Paris	1880	Portraits	—	—	—	—	—	—	—	—	—	1	1
De Lisle, Madame	London	1832	Figures	—	—	—	1	—	—	—	—	—	—	1
Delissa, Joseph. *See* Hemmings and Delissa.	—	—	—	—	—	—	—	—	—	—	—	—	—	—
Del Kop, L. W.	London	1869	Landscape	—	—	—	—	—	—	—	—	—	1	1
Dell, Miss Etheline E.	New Malden	1885-1891	Domestic	—	—	2	—	1	—	7	—	—	2	12
Dell, J.	London	1794-1797	Sculpture	—	—	7	—	—	—	—	—	—	—	7
Dell, John H	London	1851-1886	Landscape	—	—	31	31	29	—	—	—	—	19	110
Delmar, William §	Canterbury	1823-1856	Landscape	—	—	15	13	52	—	—	—	—	—	80
De Longastre, L.	London	1790-1798	Portraits	—	—	20	—	—	—	—	—	—	—	20
De Longastre, W.	London	1799	Portraits	—	—	1	—	—	—	—	—	—	—	1
Delort, Charles Edouard	Paris	1877	Figures	—	—	—	—	—	—	—	—	—	1	1
De Los Rios, R. *See* R.	—	—	—	—	—	—	—	—	—	—	—	—	—	—
Delotz, G. G.	London	1848-1864	Fruit	—	—	4	7	2	—	—	—	—	—	13
De Loutherbourg, A. C. H.	London	1793	Miniatures	—	—	9	—	—	—	—	—	—	—	9
De Loutherbourg, Philip James, R.A.	London	1772-1814	Landscape	—	5	147	3	—	—	—	—	—	—	155
Del Sarto, Antonio	—	1768	Scriptural	—	1	—	—	—	—	—	—	—	—	1
Delten —	—	1780	Drawings	—	4	—	—	—	—	—	—	—	—	4
De Lubersac. *See* L.	—	—	—	—	—	—	—	—	—	—	—	—	—	—
De Lyoncourt, Baron Hubard	London	1869-1883	Landscape	—	—	3	—	—	—	—	3	—	1	7
De Maine, Miss A.	Skipton	1884	Landscape	—	—	—	—	—	—	1	—	—	—	1
Demaine, G.	London	1887	Landscape	—	—	—	—	1	—	—	—	—	—	1
Demaine and Brierley	York	1892	Architecture	—	—	1	—	—	—	—	—	—	—	1
Demain-Hammond. *See* H.	—	—	—	—	—	—	—	—	—	—	—	—	—	—
Demana, H.	London	1852	Portraits	—	—	1	—	—	—	—	—	—	—	1
Demannez, Joseph	—	1878	Etching	—	—	—	—	—	—	—	—	—	1	1
De Marcilly, Millet	London	1889	Sculpture	—	—	1	—	—	—	—	—	—	—	1
D'Emarest, E.	Guildford	1875	Landscape	—	—	—	—	1	—	—	—	—	—	1
De Maria, S.	London	1802	Figures	—	—	1	—	—	—	—	—	—	—	1
De Martino. *See* M.	—	—	—	—	—	—	—	—	—	—	—	—	—	—

Name.	Town.	First and Last Year of Ex.	Speciality.	S. A.	F. S.	R. A.	B. I.	S. S.	O. W.	N.W.	G. G.	N. G.	V. E.	Total.
De Mattos, Henry T.	London	1891	Sculpture	—	—	1	—	—	—	—	—	—	—	1
De Meuron, Maximilien	Neuchatel	1830	Landscape	—	—	—	2	—	—	—	—	—	—	2
De Michele, Miss	London	1826-1827	Landscape	—	—	—	—	3	—	—	—	—	—	3
De Monge, C.	London	1840	Sculpture	—	—	1	—	—	—	—	—	—	—	1
De Montpezat, H.	London	1853	Animals	—	—	—	2	—	—	—	—	—	—	2
De Monvel, Boutet	Paris	1892-1893	Portraits	—	—	1	—	—	—	—	—	—	9	10
De Morgan, Mrs. Evelyn	London	1887-1892	Figures	—	—	—	—	—	—	1	2	4	—	7
De Morgan, William F.	London	1863-1867	Scriptural	—	—	1	1	2	—	—	—	—	3	7
Dempsey, Charles W.	London	1880	Domestic	—	—	—	—	1	—	—	—	—	—	1
Dempster, Miss Margaret	Edinburgh	1891-1893	Portraits	—	—	1	—	1	—	—	—	1	—	3
Denby, J. W.	—	1812-1818	Landscape	—	—	8	—	—	—	—	—	—	—	8
Denby, William	London	1850-1869	Scriptural	—	—	7	3	3	—	—	—	—	—	13
Dendy, G.	London	1870	Domestic	—	—	—	—	—	—	—	—	—	3	3
Dendy, Walter C.	London	1842-1850	Landscape	—	—	5	—	4	—	—	—	—	12	21
Denes, William	—	1778	Landscape	—	2	—	—	—	—	—	—	—	—	2
De Neuville, Alphonse Marie	Paris	1875-1877	Military	—	—	—	—	—	—	—	—	—	2	2
Denew, Richard	London	1827-1858	Figures	—	—	6	1	19	—	1	—	—	—	27
Denham, J.	London	1830	Sculpture	—	—	—	—	1	—	—	—	—	—	1
Denham, J. C.	London	1796-1858	Landscape	—	—	56	—	—	—	—	—	—	—	56
Denham, Mrs.	London	1767-1774	Miniatures	16	1	2	—	—	—	—	—	—	—	19
Denis, V.	—	1865	Landscape	—	—	—	—	2	—	—	—	—	—	2
Denison, J.	—	1882	Landscape	—	—	—	—	—	—	—	1	—	—	1
De Nittis, J.	Paris	1880	Figures	—	—	—	—	—	—	—	2	—	—	2
Denley, Miss Mary	Balham	1889	Stained Glass	—	—	1	—	—	—	—	—	—	—	1
Denman, John	London	1824	Sheep	—	—	—	1	—	—	—	—	—	—	1
Denman, J. F.	London	1839	Portraits	—	—	1	—	1	—	—	—	—	—	2
Denman, Miss Maria (Mrs. Maria Flaxman)	London	1812	Sculpture	—	—	—	1	—	—	—	—	—	—	1
Denman, Thomas	London	1815-1837	Sculpture	—	—	12	3	4	—	—	—	—	—	19
Denn, A.	London	1877	Domestic	—	—	—	—	1	—	—	—	—	—	1
Denning, Stephen Poyntz	Dulwich	1814-1852	Miniatures	—	—	48	2	2	—	—	—	—	—	52
Dennis, Miss Ada	London	1891-1893	Domestic	—	—	—	—	5	—	—	—	—	—	5
Dennis, F.	London	1828	Landscape	—	—	—	2	—	—	—	—	—	—	2
Dennis, John	London	1800-1832	Landscape	—	—	28	10	—	—	—	—	—	—	38
Dennis, William	London	1834-1849	Game	—	—	4	—	7	—	—	—	—	8	19
Dennis, W. T.	London	1841-1850	Figures	—	—	2	—	2	—	—	—	—	3	7
Dennis, Miss	London	1866	Animals	—	—	—	—	1	—	—	—	—	—	1
Dennistoun, William	Capri	1880-1884	Landscape	—	—	—	—	—	—	1	—	—	2	3
Dennys —	London	1764	Landscape	—	1	—	—	—	—	—	—	—	—	1
Dent, Miss J.	London	1869	Birds	—	—	—	—	1	—	—	—	—	—	1
Dent, Rupert Arthur	Wolverhampt'n	1884-1890	Animals	—	—	3	—	—	—	2	—	—	1	6
Denton, W.	London	1792-1795	Miniatures	—	—	8	—	—	—	—	—	—	—	8
Denton, W. F.	London	1876	Landscape	—	—	—	—	1	—	—	—	—	—	1
Denyer, Alfred	Bedford	1882-1893	Landscape	—	—	—	—	13	—	—	—	—	—	13
Denys, Simon Alexandre Clément	London	1779	Animals	—	—	1	—	—	—	—	—	—	—	1
De Parmentier, Marie	London	1879	Landscape	—	—	—	—	1	—	—	—	—	—	1
D'Epinay, Count Prosper	Rome	1865-1881	Sculpture	—	—	20	—	—	—	—	—	—	—	20
De Poix-Tydel, Edmond	London	1862-1874	Landscape	—	—	1	—	10	—	—	—	—	4	15
De Poncy, Alfred V. *See* P.	—	—	—	—	—	—	—	—	—	—	—	—	—	—
De Prades, A. F.	London	1862-1879	Sporting	—	—	2	6	4	—	—	—	—	—	12
De Prades, Frank	London	1857-1861	Animals	—	—	2	—	—	—	—	—	—	—	2
De Prades, M.	London	1858	Landscape	—	—	—	1	—	—	—	—	—	—	1
De Precorbin, Mrs. *See* P.	—	—	—	—	—	—	—	—	—	—	—	—	—	—
De Pury, Baron Esmond	Neuchatel	1891	Venice	—	—	1	—	—	—	—	—	—	—	1
De Quelen —	London	1801	Portraits	—	—	2	—	—	—	—	—	—	—	2
De Querangal. *See* Q.	—	—	—	—	—	—	—	—	—	—	—	—	—	—
Derby, Alfred Thomas	London	1839-1872	Figures	—	—	22	8	6	—	—	—	—	—	36
Derby, Miss Caroline. *See* Mrs. Bachhoffner.	London	1830-1834	Copies	—	—	4	—	10	—	2	—	—	—	16
Derby, Miss Emma M. (afterwards Mrs. Chatfield).	London	1838	Figures	—	—	—	—	1	—	—	—	—	—	1
Derby, William	London	1811-1842	Portraits	—	—	49	16	15	1	5	—	—	—	86
De Ribbing, Miss E.	London	1872	—	—	—	1	—	—	—	—	—	—	—	1
Derick, J. M.	Oxford	1843-1852	Architecture	—	—	10	—	—	—	—	—	—	—	10
De Rigny. *See* R.	—	—	—	—	—	—	—	—	—	—	—	—	—	—
Dering, Arthur R.	Ashford	1866-1889	Figures	—	—	1	1	—	—	—	—	—	1	3
Dermot —	London	1762-1767	Figures	—	7	—	—	—	—	—	—	—	—	7
De Roc-B'hian, Aufray	London	1874-1882	Etching	—	—	3	—	—	—	—	—	—	3	6
De Rockstro, J. Lambroke	London	1835-1852	Rustic	—	—	7	—	3	—	—	—	—	—	10
De Roveray, Miss M.	—	1799	Figures	—	—	1	—	—	—	—	—	—	—	1
De Rovray, Fanny Gallandat	London	1848-1850	Portraits	—	—	1	—	3	—	—	—	—	—	4
Derrick, C.	London	1844	Architecture	—	—	1	—	—	—	—	—	—	—	1
Derry, Miss E. K.	Malden	1886	Indians	—	—	1	—	—	—	—	—	—	—	1
De St. Aubin. *See* S.	—	—	—	—	—	—	—	—	—	—	—	—	—	—

Name.	Town.	First and Last Year of Ex.	Speciality.	S. A.	F. S.	R. A.	B. I.	S. S.	O. W.	N. W.	G. G.	N. G.	V. E.	Total.
De St. Dalmas, F. Emeric	Guernsey	1872-1880	—	—	—	2	—	1	—	—	—	—	6	9
De St. Martin. *See* S.	—	—	—	—	—	—	—	—	—	—	—	—	—	—
De St. Michel. *See* S.	—	—	—	—	—	—	—	—	—	—	—	—	—	—
De Salome, Antoine	London	1848-1868	Crayons	—	—	14	—	2	—	—	—	—	—	16
De Sanctis, Guglielmo	Rome	1881	Portraits	—	—	1	—	—	—	—	—	—	—	1
Desanges, Miss A. J.	London	1841-1843	Domestic	—	—	—	—	2	—	—	—	—	—	2
Desanges, Chevalier Louis W.	London	1846-1887	Portraits	—	—	49	19	9	—	—	—	—	30	107
Desanges, Miss Louisa §	London	1837	Sea Pieces	—	—	—	—	1	—	—	—	—	—	1
De Satur, Edmond Byrne	London	1878-1885	Domestic	—	—	10	—	—	—	—	—	—	6	16
De Satur, Mrs. Francis	London	1879-1884	Landscape	—	—	6	—	—	—	—	—	—	—	6
Desboutin, M.	Paris	1878	Etching	—	—	—	—	—	—	—	—	—	6	6
De Schampheleer, Edmond	London	1873	Landscape	—	—	1	—	—	—	—	—	—	—	1
De Schobinger. *See* S.	—	—	—	—	—	—	—	—	—	—	—	—	—	—
De Schwiter B.	Paris	1848	Portraits	—	—	1	—	—	—	—	—	—	—	1
Deshon, F. C.	London	1874-1877	Architecture	—	—	7	—	—	—	—	—	—	—	7
Desmedi, T.	—	1847	Historical	—	—	1	—	—	—	—	—	—	—	1
De Soutterant, F. A.	London	1797	Miniatures	—	—	2	—	—	—	—	—	—	—	2
Dessoulavy, J.	Rome	1829-1848	Landscape	—	—	5	2	—	—	—	—	—	—	7
Dessurne, Mark B. A.	London	1842-1873	Landscape	—	—	2	8	19	—	—	—	—	2	31
De Steiger, Madame Isabel	London	1879-1883	Historical	—	—	1	—	2	—	—	—	—	3	6
Destouches, Mons.	Paris	1832	Domestic	—	—	—	1	—	—	—	—	—	—	1
Destrem, C.	Paris	1881	Landscape	—	—	—	—	—	—	—	1	—	—	1
De Suchemont, Mdlle. A. A.	—	1816	Portraits	—	—	2	—	—	—	—	—	—	—	2
De Suffrein, Madame	London	1799	Landscape	—	—	3	—	—	—	—	—	—	—	3
Desvachez, David Joseph	Paris	1878	Engraving	—	—	—	—	—	—	—	—	—	1	1
Desvignes, Miss Emily E.	London	1855-1876	Cattle	—	—	6	6	28	—	—	—	—	—	40
Desvignes, Miss F. C.	Lewisham	1868	Churches	—	—	—	—	1	—	—	—	—	—	1
Desvignes, Herbert Clayton	London	1833-1863	Cattle	—	—	20	27	36	—	—	—	—	—	83
Desvignes, P. H.	London	1824-1832	Architecture	—	—	6	—	2	—	—	—	—	—	8
Detaille, Jean Baptiste Edouard	Paris	1874-1878	Military	—	—	—	—	—	—	—	—	—	3	3
De Teissier, H. P.	London	1881	Mountains	—	—	—	—	—	—	—	—	—	2	2
De Thannberg, L.	London	1850-1853	Portraits	—	—	2	—	—	—	—	—	—	—	2
De Tivoli, Serafino	London	1866-1869	Figures	—	—	7	1	4	—	—	—	—	5	17
Detmold, Henry Ed.	Paris	1879-1893	Figures	—	—	13	—	24	—	—	1	—	8	46
De Tott, Countess	London	1801-1804	Portraits	—	—	16	—	—	—	—	—	—	—	16
De Triqueti, Baron Henri	Paris	1840-1862	Sculpture	—	—	9	—	—	—	—	—	—	—	9
Detti, Cesare	London	1889	Sporting	—	—	1	—	—	—	—	—	—	—	1
Deuck, W.	London	1836-1837	Architecture	—	—	—	—	3	—	—	—	—	—	3
Deuent, J.	London	1808	Portraits	—	—	1	—	—	—	—	—	—	—	1
Deutmann, F.	Lewisham	1891	Landscape	—	—	—	—	1	—	—	—	—	1	2
De Vaere —	London	1797-1809	Sculpture	—	—	5	—	—	—	—	—	—	—	5
De Varroe, E.	—	1849	Animals	—	—	—	—	1	—	—	—	—	—	1
De Vasselot, Anatole Marquet	Paris	1875-1883	Sculpture	—	—	3	—	—	—	—	—	—	—	3
De Vaux, A. R. Grant	London	1847-1867	Landscape	—	—	2	—	7	—	—	—	—	—	9
De Vaux, J. J.	London	1834	Intaglios	—	—	1	—	—	—	—	—	—	—	1
De Veaux, J. S.	London	1832-1833	Gems	—	—	4	—	—	—	—	—	—	—	4
De Veck, L.	London	1878	Landscape	—	—	—	—	1	—	—	—	—	—	1
De Vega, Pedro	Cambridge	1879-1885	Churches	—	—	2	—	—	—	—	—	—	2	4
Dever, Alfred	London	1859-1876	Domestic	—	—	16	—	4	—	—	—	—	—	20
Deverell, Walter H.	Kew	1847-1853	Historical	—	—	4	1	2	—	—	—	—	2	9
Deveria, E.	Edinburgh	1851-1856	Historical	—	—	2	—	—	—	—	—	—	—	2
Devey, George	London	1841-1848	Architecture	—	—	6	—	—	—	—	—	—	—	6
Devigne, Felix	London	1833	Figures	—	—	—	3	—	—	—	—	—	—	3
De Villalobos, A.	London	1838-1839	Portraits	—	—	2	—	—	—	—	—	—	—	2
De Vigne, Paul	Cambridge	1884	Sculpture	—	—	2	—	—	—	—	—	—	—	2
De Ville, J. S.	London	1823-1826	Sculpture	—	—	7	—	7	—	—	—	—	—	14
De Ville, L. *See also* Green and De Ville	London	1854-1 69	Architecture	—	—	3	—	—	—	—	—	—	—	3
De Ville, Vickers	Wolverhampt'n	1887-1893	Domestic	—	—	10	—	—	—	—	—	—	1	11
De Villebrune. *See* V.	—	—	—	—	—	—	—	—	—	—	—	—	—	—
Devine, Miss Catherine	London	1892-1893	Miniatures	—	—	2	—	—	—	—	—	—	—	2
Devis, Arthur	London	1762-1780	Portraits	—	29	—	—	—	—	—	—	—	—	29
Devis, Anthony T.	London	1772-1781	Landscape	—	—	4	—	—	—	—	—	—	—	4
Devis, Arthur William	London	1779-1821	Historical	—	13	65	13	—	1	—	—	—	—	92
Devis, Thomas Anthony	London	1761-1807	Landscape	—	13	—	1	—	—	—	—	—	—	14
Devis, Thomas Anthony, Junr.	London	1776-1788	Portraits	3	8	4	—	—	—	—	—	—	—	15
Devoto, John	London	1776	Flowers	1	—	—	—	—	—	—	—	—	—	1
De Waldeck, Count Frederick	London	1853	Portraits	—	—	1	—	—	—	—	—	—	—	1
De Walton, J.	London	1856	Portraits	—	—	1	—	—	—	—	—	—	—	1
De War, J. S.	London	1857	Domestic	—	—	1	—	—	—	—	—	—	—	1
De Warville, F. Brissot	London	1882	Sheep	—	—	1	—	—	—	—	—	—	—	1
Dewe, Miss N.	London	1893	Domestic	—	—	—	—	—	—	—	—	—	1	1

Name.	Town.	First and Last Year of Ex.	Speciality.	S. A.	F. S.	R. A.	B. I.	S. S.	O. W.	N. W.	G. G.	N. G.	V. E.	Total.
Dewes, R.	London	1842	Architecture	—	—	1	—	—	—	—	—	—	—	1
De Wette, Aug.	London	1887	Theatrical	—	—	—	—	—	—	—	—	—	1	1
Dewick, W. G.	London	1849	Sculpture	—	—	1	—	—	—	—	—	—	—	1
Dewilde, G. J.	Northampton	1855-1856	Landscape	—	—	—	—	—	—	—	—	—	6	6
De Wilde, Samuel	London	1776-1832	Theatrical	9	—	103	3	5	—	—	—	—	—	120
De Wilde, Miss	London	1879	Domestic	—	—	—	—	1	—	—	—	—	—	1
Dewint, Peter †	London	1807-1849	Landscape	—	—	13	11	—	417	—	—	—	13	454
Dewling, A.	—	1874	Clouds	—	—	—	—	1	—	—	—	—	—	1
Dexter, W.	Boston, U.S.A.	1840-1855	Birds	—	—	3	1	3	—	—	—	—	—	7
Deykes, J.	London	1810-1815	Architecture	—	—	4	—	—	—	—	—	—	—	4
Diakoff, Filetre	—	1773	Portraits	—	—	2	—	—	—	—	—	—	—	2
Dibdin, Charles	—	1801	Landscape	—	—	2	—	—	—	—	—	—	—	2
Dibdin, J. H.	—	1838	Architecture	—	—	1	—	—	—	—	—	—	—	1
Dibdin, Thomas Colman	London	1831-1883	Landscape	—	—	15	15	79	—	1	—	—	93	203
Dicey, Frank ɸ	London	1865-1888	Figures	—	—	17	—	8	—	1	14	—	18	58
Dickens, Miss Kate. *See* Mrs. C. E. Perugini	—	—	—	—	—	—	—	—	—	—	—	—	—	—
and Mrs. Charles Collins.	—	—	—	—	—	—	—	—	—	—	—	—	—	—
Dicker, Miss Alice M.	London	1888-1889	Figures	—	—	2	—	1	—	—	—	—	1	4
Dickes, William	London	1843-1881	Scriptural	—	—	1	—	—	—	—	—	—	1	2
Dickins, Frank	Putney	1886	Fruit	—	—	—	—	1	—	—	—	—	—	1
Dickins, S. A.	London	1861-1868	Sea Pieces	—	—	1	1	1	—	—	—	—	—	3
Dickins, Mrs. T.	—	1812-1814	Sculpture	—	—	3	—	—	—	—	—	—	—	3
Dickinson, Arthur	London	1877-1882	Landscape	—	—	2	—	3	—	—	—	—	5	10
Dickinson, Miss A.	London	1796-1804	Flowers	—	—	17	—	—	—	—	—	—	—	17
Dickinson, Miss Annie J.	London	1890	Domestic	—	—	1	—	—	—	—	—	—	—	1
Dickinson, Miss Florence	London	1892	Landscape	—	—	—	—	2	—	—	—	—	—	2
Dickinson, Miss H.	—	1803	Birds	—	—	1	—	—	—	—	—	—	—	1
Dickinson, H. R.	London	1881	Landscape	—	—	1	—	—	—	—	—	—	1	2
Dickinson, John	London	1876-1880	Portraits	—	—	9	—	1	—	—	—	—	—	10
Dickinson, J. Reed	London	1867-1881	Domestic	—	—	8	—	44	—	—	—	—	22	74
Dickinson, K. *or* R.	London	1878	Landscape	—	—	—	—	—	—	—	—	—	1	1
Dickinson, Miss Lilian	London	1880-1883	Portraits	—	—	4	—	—	—	—	—	—	—	4
Dickinson, Lowes Cato	London	1848-1891	Portraits	—	—	109	—	—	—	—	—	—	3	112
Dickinson, S.	—	1825	Churches	—	—	2	—	—	—	—	—	—	—	2
Dickinson, William	London	1769-1776	Engraving	12	—	—	—	—	—	—	—	—	—	12
Dickinson, Walter C.	London	1854	Still Life	—	—	1	—	2	—	—	—	—	—	3
Dickinson, William Robert	Dinan	1836-1882	Domestic	—	—	5	—	10	—	—	1	—	12	28
Dickinson and Foster	London	1879-1887	Miniatures	—	—	15	—	—	—	—	—	—	—	15
Dicksee, Frank J., R.A.	London	1872-1893	Historical	—	—	30	—	2	—	—	1	—	5	38
Dicksee, Herbert Thomas, R.P.E.	London	1881-1893	Animals	—	—	25	—	1	—	—	—	—	—	26
Dicksee, John Robert	London	1850-1893	Figures	—	—	42	6	13	—	1	—	—	5	67
Dicksee, Miss Margaret J.	London	1881-1893	Domestic	—	—	12	—	2	—	—	—	—	—	14
Dicksee, Thomas Francis	London	1841-1893	Figures	—	—	65	29	21	—	—	1	—	13	129
Dickson —	London	1772-1774	Miniatures	8	—	—	—	—	—	—	—	—	—	8
Dickson, A.	—	1850	Portraits	—	—	1	—	—	—	—	—	—	—	1
Dickson, Miss Anna	London	1864	Figures	—	—	—	—	1	—	—	—	—	—	1
Dickson, Arthur	London	1878	Landscape	—	—	—	—	—	—	—	—	—	1	1
Dickson, Miss Frances	London	1772	Portraits	3	—	—	—	—	—	—	—	—	—	3
Dickson, Frank	London	1889-1892	Domestic	—	—	2	—	—	—	—	—	—	4	6
Dickson, J.	London	1842	Portraits	—	—	3	—	—	—	—	—	—	—	3
Dickson, J. H.	—	1850	Figures	—	—	1	—	—	—	—	—	—	—	1
Dickson, R.	—	1808	Rustic	—	—	1	—	—	—	—	—	—	—	1
Dickson, William	London	1881-1893	Landscape	—	—	5	—	1	—	—	—	—	—	6
Diday, François	Geneva	1842-1846	Landscape	—	—	1	1	—	—	—	—	—	—	2
Didier, Adrien	London	1879	Engraving	—	—	—	—	—	—	—	—	—	1	1
Didier, J.	Paris	1872	Cattle	—	—	1	—	—	—	—	—	—	—	1
Diehl, Arthur	London	1889	Harbours	—	—	1	—	—	—	—	—	—	—	1
Diemar —	London	1766-1769	Miniatures	7	—	—	—	—	—	—	—	—	—	7
Diemar, Benjamin	Cambridge	1772-1783	Mythological	2	—	8	—	—	—	—	—	—	—	10
Diemar, John M., F.S.A.	London	1761-1790	Sculpture	32	3	—	—	—	—	—	—	—	—	35
Dien, Achille	Paris	1875-1881	Landscape	—	—	—	—	—	—	—	—	—	24	24
Dies, C.	Rome	1869	Scriptural	—	—	1	—	—	—	—	—	—	—	1
Dietz, Amelia Mary	London	1782-1783	Miniatures	—	—	2	—	—	—	—	—	—	—	2
Dietz, Miss Diana	London	1775-1798	Miniatures	3	—	20	—	—	—	—	—	—	—	23
Diez, S.	London	1842	Portraits	—	—	8	—	—	—	—	—	—	—	8
Digby, George	London	1888-1889	Sea Pieces	—	—	6	—	2	—	—	—	—	1	9
Dighton, Denis	London	1811-1825	Battle Pieces	—	—	17	8	—	—	—	—	—	9	34
Dighton, Mrs. Denis. *See* Mrs. Macintyre	London	1820-1835	Flowers	—	—	16	—	7	—	3	—	—	—	26
Dighton, George	Barnet	1857-1871	Figures	—	—	3	1	—	—	—	—	—	6	10
Dighton, J.	London	1832	Architecture	—	—	1	—	—	—	—	—	—	—	1
Dighton, Robert	London	1769-1799	Portraits	—	14	6	—	—	—	—	—	—	—	20

Name.	Town.	First and Last Year of Ex.	Speciality.	S. A.	F. S.	R. A.	B. I.	S. S.	O. W.	N. W.	G. G.	N. G.	V. E.	Total.
DIGHTON, THOMAS D.	London	1847-1848	Architecture	—	—	2	—	—	—	—	—	—	—	2
DIGHTON, WILLIAM EDWARD	London	1843-1853	Landscape	—	—	10	6	1	—	—	—	—	10	27
DILLENS, ADOLF	London	1869-1870	Figures	—	—	3	—	—	—	—	—	—	—	3
DILLON, HON. MRS. A.	—	1845	Figures	—	—	—	1	—	—	—	—	—	—	1
DILLON, FRANK, R.I. ‡ φ	London	1850-1893	Landscape	—	—	40	34	1	—	48	3	8	87	221
DIMES, FREDERICK	London	1837-1866	Landscape	—	—	—	4	13	—	—	—	—	5	22
DIMMA, MISS ADA C. G.	Clapton	1891-1892	Domestic	—	—	—	—	—	—	—	—	—	2	2
DIMOCK, MRS. J.	—	1817	Landscape	—	—	1	—	—	—	—	—	—	—	1
DIMSDALE, JOHN	Darlington	1875-1876	Landscape	—	—	—	—	—	—	—	—	—	2	2
DIMSDALE, T.	London	1813	Landscape	—	—	1	—	—	—	—	—	—	—	1
DINGLE, THOMAS	London	1846-1888	Landscape	—	—	8	4	14	—	—	—	—	—	26
DINGLE, THOMAS, JUNR.	Newton Ferrers	1879-1889	Landscape	—	—	—	—	5	—	—	—	—	—	5
DINHAM, JOSEPH	London	1823-1852	Sculpture	—	—	22	4	4	—	—	—	—	—	30
DINKEL, J.	London	1840	Still Life	—	—	1	—	—	—	—	—	—	—	1
DINSDALE, GEORGE	London	1808-1829	Landscape	—	—	14	23	4	8	—	—	—	32	81
DINSDALE, JOHN	London	1884-1889	Landscape	—	—	—	—	—	—	2	—	—	—	2
DISMORE, J. S.	Gravesend	1893	Miniatures	—	—	—	—	—	—	1	—	—	—	1
DITCHFIELD, ARTHUR	London	1864-1886	Landscape	—	—	12	3	5	—	4	—	—	98	122
DITRICH —	—	1779	Landscape	—	2	—	—	—	—	—	—	—	—	2
DIX, CHARLES TEMPLE	London	1867	Landscape	—	—	1	—	—	—	—	—	—	—	1
DIX, MRS.	London	1855-1860	Flowers	—	—	—	—	5	—	—	—	—	—	5
DIXCEE, JOHN	London	1828	Landscape	—	—	—	1	—	—	—	—	—	—	1
DIXCEE, T.	Hounslow	1828-1865	Landscape	—	—	4	7	5	—	—	—	—	—	16
DIXEY, FREDERICK CHARLES	London	1877-1891	Sea Pieces	—	—	1	—	10	—	4	—	—	4	19
DIXON —	London	1771	Miniatures	1	—	—	—	—	—	—	—	—	—	1
DIXON, ALFRED	Goring	1864-1891	Domestic	—	—	18	—	18	—	—	—	—	8	44
DIXON, MISS ANNIE	London	1844-1893	Miniatures	—	—	222	—	—	—	—	—	—	—	222
DIXON, ARTHUR A.	London	1892-1893	Domestic	—	—	—	—	3	—	—	—	—	—	3
DIXON, CHARLES	London	1889-1893	River Scenes	—	—	8	—	—	—	1	—	—	1	10
DIXON, CHARLES THOMAS	London	1846-1857	Landscape	—	—	3	11	17	—	—	—	—	—	31
DIXON, E.	London	1835-1839	Portraits	—	—	6	1	5	—	—	—	—	—	12
DIXON, MISS EMILY	Hull	1885-1886	Flowers	—	—	2	—	2	—	—	—	—	—	4
DIXON, E. H.	London	1847-1859	Landscape	—	—	1	1	2	—	—	—	—	—	4
DIXON, MRS. ELLA HEPWORTH	Brighton	1856	Landscape	—	—	1	—	—	—	—	—	—	—	1
DIXON, MISS ELLA HEPWORTH	London	1877-1883	Figures	—	—	—	—	4	—	—	—	—	—	4
DIXON, MRS. F. *See* Miss Charlotte Grace Cowell	London	1852-1875	Miniatures	—	—	19	—	9	—	—	—	—	—	28
DIXON, F. A.	London	1833	Portraits	—	—	—	—	—	—	1	—	—	—	1
DIXON, F. H.	London	1836-1858	Figures	—	—	1	—	4	—	—	—	—	—	5
DIXON, F. M.	London	1832-1834	Portraits	—	—	—	—	3	—	—	—	—	—	3
DIXON, HARRY	London	1881-1893	Sculpture	—	—	13	—	2	—	—	—	3	1	19
DIXON, J.	London	1781-1803	Architecture	—	—	7	—	—	—	—	—	—	—	7
DIXON, J.	London	1784-1811	Landscape	—	—	10	—	—	—	—	—	—	3	13
DIXON, JOHN	London	1766-1775	Engraving	20	—	—	—	—	—	—	—	—	—	20
DIXON, JOHN	Surbiton	1879-1885	Sea Pieces	—	—	—	—	4	—	1	—	—	3	8
DIXON, PERCY	London	1886-1893	Landscape	—	—	1	—	12	—	18	—	—	—	31
DIXON, ROBERT	London	1798-1811	Architecture	—	—	1	—	—	—	—	—	—	4	5
DIXON, S. H.	London	1831-1842	Portraits	—	—	4	—	—	—	—	—	—	—	4
DIXON, WILLIAM	London	1796-1827	Figures	—	—	10	2	—	—	—	—	—	—	12
DIXON, WILLIAM FRANCIS	London	1884-1889	Stained Glass	—	—	6	—	—	—	—	—	—	—	6
DIXON, W. H.	Birmingham	1881	Landscape	—	—	1	—	—	—	—	—	—	—	1
DIXON, MISS	London	1771	Portraits	1	—	—	—	—	—	—	—	—	—	1
DIXON, MISS	—	1802	Flowers	—	—	2	—	—	—	—	—	—	—	2
DIXSEE, F. H.	London	1845	Portraits	—	—	1	—	—	—	—	—	—	—	1
DLOFI, K.	London	1849	Figures	—	—	—	1	—	—	—	—	—	—	1
DOANE, C.	London	1835-1851	Portraits	—	—	4	—	21	—	—	—	—	—	25
DOBBIN, JOHN	London	1842-1884	Landscape	—	—	38	4	102	—	—	—	—	2	146
DOBELL, MISS ALICE	Cheltenham	1867	Flowers	—	—	—	—	2	—	—	—	—	—	2
DOBELL, CLARENCE M.	London	1857-1866	Figures	—	—	4	4	13	—	—	—	—	—	21
DOBIE, JAMES	London	1885-1893	Etching	—	—	15	—	—	—	—	—	—	—	15
DOBIE, W.	London	1824	Architecture	—	—	—	—	1	—	—	—	—	—	1
DOBINSON, W.	Carlisle	1864-1865	Scriptural	—	—	—	—	2	—	—	—	—	—	2
DOBREE, EDWIN DE S.	Jersey	1889	Landscape	—	—	1	—	—	—	—	—	—	—	1
DOBSON, A. T.	London	1893	Domestic	—	—	—	—	1	—	—	—	—	—	1
DOBSON, E.	London	1842-1843	Architecture	—	—	2	—	—	—	—	—	—	—	2
DOBSON, EDMUND A.	Petworth	1883-1889	Domestic	—	—	5	—	5	—	—	—	—	—	10
DOBSON, HENRY J., R.S.W.	Edinburgh	1881-1892	Domestic	—	—	4	—	3	—	2	—	—	—	9
DOBSON, H. R.	—	1834	Sculpture	—	—	1	—	—	—	—	—	—	—	1
DOBSON, JOHN, F.R I.B.A.	Newcastle	1818-1850	Architecture	—	—	2	—	—	—	—	—	—	—	2
DOBSON, R.	Birkenhead	1881	Landscape	—	—	—	—	—	—	—	1	—	—	1
DOBSON, WILLIAM THOMAS CHARLES, R.A., R.W.S.†	London	1842-1892	Scriptural	—	—	117	—	9	53	—	—	—	—	179
DOCHARTY, A. BROWNLIE	Glasgow	1882-1891	Landscape	—	—	4	—	—	—	—	—	—	—	4
DOCHARTY, JAMES, A.R.S.A.	Glasgow	1865-1877	Landscape	—	—	13	—	—	—	—	—	—	—	13

Name.	Town.	First and Last Year of Ex.	Speciality.	S. A.	F. S.	R. A.	B. I.	S. S.	O. W.	N. W.	G. G.	N. G.	V. E.	Total
Docke —	London	1763-1767	Miniatures	7	—	—	—	—	—	—	—	—	—	7
Docker, C.	London	1829-1830	Landscape	—	—	2	—	—	—	—	—	—	—	2
Docker, Edward	Newlyn	1890-1892	Domestic	—	—	3	—	—	—	—	—	—	2	5
Dockree, Mark Edwin	London	1856-1890	Landscape	—	—	10	6	46	—	—	—	—	6	68
Dodd, Arthur C.	Tunb'dgeWells	1878-1890	Rustic	—	—	8	—	37	—	—	3	—	12	60
Dodd, Charles T.	Tonbridge	1832-1892	Landscape	—	—	11	26	1	—	—	—	—	—	38
Dodd, Daniel	London	1761-1780	Portraits	4	78	—	—	—	—	—	—	—	—	82
Dodd, D. P.	London	1768-1780	Figures	—	9	—	—	—	—	—	—	—	—	9
Dodd, F.	Lewisham	1876	Figures	—	—	1	—	—	—	—	—	—	—	1
Dodd, G.	London	1810	Architecture	—	—	1	—	—	—	—	—	—	—	1
Dodd, J. J.	Paris	1832-1839	Landscape	—	—	5	—	4	—	—	—	—	—	9
Dodd, Miss M.	Bristol	1830-1832	Portraits	—	—	5	—	5	—	—	—	—	—	10
Dodd, P. G.	London	1825-1836	Portraits	—	—	45	—	16	—	—	—	—	—	61
Dodd, R.	London	1787-1789	Portraits	—	—	5	—	—	—	—	—	—	—	5
Dodd, Ralph	London	1779-1809	Sea Pieces	9	3	50	—	—	—	—	—	—	—	62
Dodd, Robert	London	1780	Sea Pieces	3	—	—	—	—	—	—	—	—	—	3
Dodd, R.	London	1800-1817	Architecture	—	—	9	—	—	—	—	—	—	—	9
Dodd, S. T.	Lewisham	1880	—	—	—	*	—	—	—	—	—	—	—	—
Dodd, W.	London	1829-1840	Portraits	—	—	5	—	4	—	—	—	—	—	9
Dodd, Miss	—	1769	Flowers	—	1	—	—	—	—	—	—	—	—	1
Dodds, Annie	Newcastle	1866	Flowers	—	—	—	—	2	—	—	—	—	—	2
Dodds, John	London	1865-1866	Figures	—	—	—	1	2	—	—	—	—	—	3
Dodds, Will. G.	London	1879-1885	Landscape	—	—	—	—	1	—	—	—	—	8	9
Dodgshun and Unsworth	London	1877-1879	Architecture	—	—	4	—	—	—	—	—	—	—	4
Dodgson, G.	London	1880	Landscape	—	—	—	—	—	—	—	2	—	—	2
Dodgson, George Haydock, R.W.S.†‡	London	1835-1880	Landscape	—	—	3	1	9	353	48	—	—	—	414
Dodgson, George P.	London	1867-1868	Figures	—	—	—	—	1	—	—	—	—	3	4
Dodgson, Miss Jessie	London	1876-1879	Landscape	—	—	—	—	6	—	—	—	—	1	7
Dodsley, Anne M. J.	London	1872	Fruit	—	—	—	—	—	—	—	—	—	1	1
Dodson, George	London	1817-1839	Architecture	—	—	6	—	—	—	—	—	—	—	6
Dodson, George	Lewisham	1893	Shipping	—	—	—	—	1	—	—	—	—	—	1
Doe, Miss Catherine	Torrington	1848-1852	Domestic	—	—	—	—	4	—	—	—	—	—	4
Doe, E.	Worcester	1823-1848	Flowers	—	—	2	—	5	—	—	—	—	—	7
Doggett, T.	London	1853	Heads	—	—	—	—	1	—	—	—	—	—	1
Doherty, O'. *See* O.	—	—	—	—	—	—	—	—	—	—	—	—	—	—
Doidge, Miss Sarah A.	Richmond	1859-1885	Landscape	—	—	5	—	8	—	—	—	—	—	13
Dolan, Philip	London	1867-1877	Fruit	—	—	5	—	6	—	—	—	—	1	12
Dolby, E.	London	1863-1877	Churches	—	—	1	—	9	—	—	—	—	—	10
Dolby, Edwin Thomas	London	1849-1865	Churches	—	—	1	—	—	—	—	—	—	5	6
Dolby, Joshua E. A.	London	1840-1846	Ruins	—	—	2	—	2	—	—	—	—	—	4
Dolland, W. Anstey	London	1879-1889	Figures	—	—	5	—	4	—	—	—	—	—	9
Dollar, Peter	London	1885-1893	Architecture	—	—	4	—	—	—	—	—	—	—	4
Dollman, Francis Thomas	London	1840-1878	Architecture	—	—	7	—	—	—	—	—	—	—	7
Dollman, Herbert P.	London	1874-1892	Domestic	—	—	5	—	9	—	3	—	—	10	27
Dollman, John Charles, R.I.‡ φ	London	1871-1893	Domestic	—	—	25	—	16	—	12	—	—	43	96
Dolores, Madame	London	1848	Figures	—	—	1	—	—	—	—	—	—	—	1
Domett, A. N.	London	1879	Flowers	—	—	1	—	—	—	—	—	—	—	1
Domett, Miss Susan C.	London	1864-1877	Domestic	—	—	1	—	6	—	—	—	—	2	9
Domingo, F.	—	1892	Portraits	—	—	—	—	—	—	—	—	—	2	2
Dominicus, Mrs.	—	1789	Mythological	—	—	1	—	—	—	—	—	—	—	1
Dominques, J.	London	1874-1875	Domestic	—	—	—	—	10	—	—	—	—	2	12
Dominy, J. S.	Gt. Yarmouth	1865-1876	Rustic	—	—	5	—	5	—	—	—	—	—	10
Dommerson, P. C.	London	1865-1878	Landscape	—	—	1	2	2	—	—	—	—	1	6
Don, C. B.	London	1885-1886	River Scenes	—	—	—	—	6	—	—	—	—	—	6
Donald, Emily	London	1886	Still Life	—	—	—	—	1	—	—	—	—	—	1
Donald, John Milne	London	1844-1847	Landscape	—	—	2	1	—	—	—	—	—	—	3
Donald, Tom	London	1875	Landscape	—	—	—	—	1	—	—	—	—	—	1
Donald-Smith, Miss Helen ‖	London	1883-1893	Landscape	—	—	1	—	3	—	13	2	2	14	35
Donaldson, Andrew Benjamin (*or* Brown)§	London	1861-1893	Historical	—	—	26	5	97	—	15	9	16	93	261
Donaldson, James	London	1777-1793	Architecture	—	—	3	—	—	—	—	—	—	—	3
Donaldson, John, F.S.A.	London	1761-1791	Miniatures	14	8	4	—	—	—	—	—	—	—	26
Donaldson, James H.	Scarborough	1883-1892	Still Life	—	—	2	—	—	—	1	—	—	—	3
Donaldson, T.	London	1795	Portraits	—	—	1	—	—	—	—	—	—	—	1
Donaldson, Thomas Leverton	London	1816-1854	Architecture	—	—	27	—	—	—	—	—	—	—	27
Donders, Mrs.	Dorking	1890-1891	Portraits	—	—	—	—	—	—	—	—	2	—	2
Done, Miss A. E.	Worcester	1875-1878	Animals	—	—	—	—	5	—	—	—	—	—	5
Donkin, Miss Alice E.	Oxford	1871-1892	Domestic	—	—	12	—	2	—	3	1	1	1	20
Donkin, John	London	1880	Churches	—	—	—	—	1	—	—	—	—	—	1
Donlevy, J. S.	London	1889	Domestic	—	—	—	—	1	—	—	—	—	—	1
Donn, William	London	1770-1775	Architecture	—	4	2	—	—	—	—	—	—	—	6
Donne, B. J. M.	London	1872-1891	Landscape	—	—	—	—	1	—	11	16	2	—	30
Donne, J. M.	London	1865-1885	Landscape	—	—	4	—	9	—	—	6	—	8	27

Name.	Town.	First and Last Year of Ex.	Speciality.	S. A.	F. S.	R. A.	B. I.	S. S.	O. W.	N. W.	G. G.	N. G.	V. E.	Total.
Donne, Walter J.	Scarborough	1885-1893	Landscape	—	—	6	—	6	—	4	—	1	—	17
Donnelly, General J. F. D., C.B., R.E.	London	1884-1893	Landscape	—	—	1	—	—	—	—	—	13	—	14
Donnequin, Alfred	London	1875	Etching	—	—	—	—	—	—	—	—	—	1	1
Donner, Edgar P.	Streatham	1893	Etching	—	—	1	—	—	—	—	—	—	—	1
Donoghue, J. P.	London	1846	Domestic	—	—	1	—	—	—	—	—	—	—	1
Donoghue, John	London	1890	Sculpture	—	—	2	—	—	—	—	—	—	—	2
Donoghue, O'. *See* O.	—	—	—	—	—	—	—	—	—	—	—	—	—	—
Donowell, John	London	1761-1786	Architecture	9	2	5	—	—	—	—	—	—	—	16
Donthorn, W. J.	London	1817-1853	Architecture	—	—	24	—	—	—	—	—	—	—	24
Doo, George Thomas, R.A., F.R.S.	Stanmore	1830-1882	Engraving	—	—	24	—	4	—	—	—	—	—	28
Door —	London	1782	Landscape	—	1	—	—	—	—	—	—	—	—	1
Doré, Paul Gustave	Paris	1876	Figures	—	—	—	—	—	—	—	—	—	1	1
Dorman —	London	1768	Mythological	—	1	—	—	—	—	—	—	—	—	1
Dorman, J. J.	Reading	1855-1859	Figures	—	—	2	—	2	—	—	—	—	—	4
Dorman, S.	Reading	1857	Landscape	—	—	—	—	1	—	—	—	—	—	1
Dormer, Hon. Louise	London	1891	Landscape	—	—	—	—	—	—	—	—	—	1	1
Dorothea, Lucy	—	1856	Figures	—	—	1	—	—	—	—	—	—	—	1
Dorrell, Edmund †	London	1807-1836	Landscape	—	—	15	—	14	59	—	—	—	—	88
Dorrington, Master	—	1773	Copies	—	1	—	—	—	—	—	—	—	—	1
D'Orsay, Count Alfred	London	1843-1848	Scriptural	—	—	17	—	3	—	—	—	—	—	20
Dorschweller, H.	London	1837	Figures	—	—	2	—	—	—	—	—	—	—	2
Dotchen, John	London	1772-1810	Architecture	3	—	14	—	—	—	—	—	—	—	17
Doubleday, William	Birmingham	1886	Architecture	—	—	2	—	—	—	—	—	—	—	2
Doubting, James	Bristol	1868-1881	Cattle	—	—	—	—	4	—	—	—	—	2	6
Doucet, Lucien	—	1892	Portraits	—	—	—	—	—	—	—	—	—	1	1
Dougan, A.	—	1867-1868	Landscape	—	—	—	—	2	—	—	—	—	—	2
Doughty, Eleanor F. M.	London	1889-1893	Flowers	—	—	—	—	6	—	—	—	—	—	6
Doughty, Thomas	Philadelphia	1838-1846	Landscape	—	—	2	8	8	—	—	—	—	—	18
Doughty, William (Pupil of Reynolds)	London	1776-1779	Portraits	—	—	7	—	—	—	—	—	—	—	7
Douglas, Arthur	London	1878	Figures	—	—	—	—	—	—	—	—	—	1	1
Douglas (C.) and Sellers	Glasgow	1878	Architecture	—	—	1	—	—	—	—	—	—	—	1
Douglas, Edwin	Edinburgh	1869-1892	Animals	—	—	41	—	—	—	—	—	—	17	58
Douglas, Edward Algernon Stuart	Barnes	1880-1892	Sporting	—	—	10	—	—	—	—	—	—	1	11
Douglas, J.	Southampton	1821-1827	Landscape	—	—	6	—	—	—	—	—	—	—	6
Douglas, James	Edinburgh	1885	Landscape	—	—	—	—	—	—	2	—	—	—	2
Douglas, John, R.C.A., F.R.I.B.A.	Chester	1881-1884	Architecture	—	—	6	—	—	—	—	—	—	—	6
Douglas, William	Edinburgh	1818-1849	Miniatures	—	—	7	2	—	—	—	—	—	—	9
Douglas, Sir William Fettes, P.R.S.A.	Edinburgh	1862-1890	Historical	—	—	9	—	—	—	—	1	—	6	16
Douglas, Miss	Edinburgh	1834-1841	Portraits	—	—	4	—	—	—	—	—	—	—	4
Douglas and Fordham	Chester	1885-1893	Architecture	—	—	12	—	—	—	—	—	—	—	12
Douglas-Hamilton, R.	London	1888	Figures	—	—	—	—	—	—	—	—	—	1	1
Douglass, J.	London	1812	Landscape	—	—	—	—	—	—	—	—	—	1	1
Douglass, Richard	London	1875-1890	Landscape	—	—	—	—	10	—	6	1	—	—	17
Doull, A.	—	1851	Models	—	—	1	—	—	—	—	—	—	—	1
Doull, W.	London	1821	Architecture	—	—	1	—	—	—	—	—	—	—	1
D'Ouseley, Miss Sophia	London	1889	Landscape	—	—	—	—	—	—	1	—	—	—	1
Doust, W. H.	Greenwich	1859-1880	Sea Pieces	—	—	—	22	15	—	—	—	—	4	41
Dove, W.	London	1850-1857	Landscape	—	—	3	—	—	—	—	—	—	—	3
Dove, Miss	—	1769	Needlework	1	—	—	—	—	—	—	—	—	—	1
Dovers, Mrs. H. A.	London	1854	Flowers	—	—	1	—	—	—	—	—	—	—	1
Dovey, F. A.	Staplehurst	1849-1861	Architecture	—	—	3	—	—	—	—	—	—	—	3
Dow, Lumley	London	1893	Game	—	—	—	—	—	—	—	—	—	1	1
Dow, Thomas Millie, R.S.W.	Glasgow	1886-1890	Flowers	—	—	—	—	4	—	—	2	—	—	6
Dowbiggen, E.	London	1820-1824	Landscape	—	—	2	2	1	—	—	—	—	—	5
Dowding, Miss M. A.	London	1794-1825	Flowers	—	—	6	—	—	—	—	—	—	—	6
Dowglas, J.	London	1802-1819	Landscape	—	—	17	—	—	—	—	—	—	—	17
Dowie, Miss Sybil M.	Brighton	1893	Portraits	—	—	1	—	—	—	—	—	—	—	1
Dowley, C.	Dulwich	1833-1851	Domestic	—	—	1	—	3	—	—	—	—	—	4
Dowley, H.	London	1833	Landscape	—	—	1	—	—	—	—	—	—	—	1
Dowley, J.	London	1836	Sea Pieces	—	—	—	2	—	—	—	—	—	—	2
Dowling, J.	London	1839-1872	Portraits	—	—	16	—	—	—	—	—	—	—	16
Dowling, Miss Mary	London	1845-1846	Miniatures	—	—	2	—	—	—	—	—	—	—	2
Dowling, Robert	London	1859-1882	Scriptural	—	—	16	5	25	—	—	—	—	7	53
Dowling, R. B.	London	1868	Figures	—	—	1	—	—	—	—	—	—	—	1
Downard, Ebenezer Newman	London	1849-1889	Scriptural	—	—	32	4	24	—	—	—	—	25	85
Downer, Nathan	London	1771-1774	Portraits	—	—	6	—	—	—	—	—	—	—	6
Downes, Miss Annabel	London	1885-1890	Portraits	—	—	6	—	1	—	3	1	—	—	11
Downes, Ada E.	London	1893	Buildings	—	—	—	—	1	—	—	—	—	—	1
Downes, Bernard	London	1761-1775	Portraits	12	—	11	—	—	—	—	—	—	—	23
Downes, J. P.	London	1826-1827	Portraits	—	—	2	—	—	—	—	—	—	—	2
Downes, Thomas Price	London	1835-1887	Figures	—	—	41	—	2	—	—	—	—	1	44
Downie, Patrick	Greenock	1887-1893	Landscape	—	—	3	—	3	—	1	—	—	—	7

Name.	Town.	First and Last Year of Ex.	Speciality.	S. A.	F. S.	R. A.	B. I.	S. S.	O. W.	N. W.	G. G.	N. G.	V. E.	Total.
Downing, Charles Palmer	London	1870-1893	Portraits	—	—	23	—	1	—	—	—	—	11	35
Downing, Delapoer	London	1885-1891	Domestic	—	—	3	—	2	—	—	—	—	9	14
Downing, Miss Edith E.	London	1891-1893	Sculpture	—	—	2	—	—	—	—	—	—	—	2
Downing, H. E. ‡	London	1827-1833	Landscape	—	—	8	2	6	—	54	—	—	—	70
Downman, John, A.R.A.	London	1768-1819	Portraits	—	1	333	7	—	—	—	—	—	—	341
Downs, J.	London	1859	Figures	—	—	1	—	—	—	—	—	—	—	1
Dowson, Russell	Eton	1867-1893	Landscape	—	—	4	—	6	—	4	3	—	5	22
Dowthwaite, R. W.	London	1788-1796	Architecture	—	—	4	—	—	—	—	—	—	—	4
Dowton, C.	—	1849	—	—	—	—	—	1	—	—	—	—	—	1
Doyle, Henry E., C.B., R.H.A.	London	1858	Portraits	—	—	1	—	—	—	—	—	—	—	1
Doyle, John (HB.)	London	1825-1835	Caricatures	—	—	6	—	—	—	—	—	—	—	6
Doyle, J. Francis	Liverpool	1884-1886	Architecture	—	—	5	—	—	—	—	—	—	—	5
Doyle, Richard	London	1868-1883	Landscape	—	—	2	—	—	—	—	61	—	—	63
Doyle, W.	London	1826	Enamels	—	—	1	—	—	—	—	—	—	—	1
Doyley, C.	—	1815	Landscape	—	—	1	—	—	—	—	—	—	—	1
Doyley, W.	London	1835-1849	Architecture	—	—	4	—	—	—	—	—	—	—	4
Drabble, J. D.	London	1880	Shells	—	—	—	—	2	—	—	—	—	—	2
Drabble, R. R.	Bowden	1859-1885	Landscape	—	—	20	5	1	—	—	—	—	—	26
Drage, J. Henry	Croydon	1882-1893	Landscape	—	—	3	—	—	—	5	—	3	—	11
Drage, Miss Mildred Frances	Hatfield	1885-1892	Landscape	—	—	3	—	1	—	—	—	6	1	11
Drake, F.	London	1828	Landscape	—	—	1	—	—	—	—	—	—	—	1
Drake, J.	Chatham	1867-1871	Landscape	—	—	2	—	—	—	—	—	—	—	2
Drake, Nathan, F.S.A.	York	1771-1783	Figures	5	1	—	—	—	—	—	—	—	—	6
Drake, W.	Hornsey	1861-1877	Landscape	—	—	—	—	5	—	—	—	—	—	5
Drane, Herbert Cecil	Dorking	1890-1893	Landscape	—	—	—	—	3	—	—	—	1	7	11
Draper, Amy G.	Bromley	1890	Landscape	—	—	—	—	2	—	—	—	—	—	2
Draper, Charles F., *or* C. E.	Canichers	1871-1887	Landscape	—	—	—	—	13	—	3	—	—	—	16
Draper, G.	London	1811-1841	Architecture	—	—	7	—	—	—	—	—	—	—	7
Draper, Herbert James	Bromley	1887-1893	Domestic	—	—	6	—	—	—	—	—	—	3	9
Draw, Miss Florence	Windsor	1877	Figures	—	—	1	—	—	—	—	—	—	—	1
Draw, H.	London	1865	Domestic	—	—	3	—	—	—	—	—	—	—	3
Drayton, L.	London	1864-1868	Landscape	—	—	—	1	7	—	—	—	—	—	8
Dredge, Miss	—	1815-1818	Still Life	—	—	3	—	—	—	—	—	—	—	3
Dresch, Augusta M.	London	1854	Domestic	—	—	—	—	1	—	—	—	—	—	1
Dresser, Arthur	Bexley Heath	1890	Domestic	—	—	1	—	—	—	—	—	—	—	1
Dresser, Mrs. A. R. (?) J. R.	Bexley Heath	1889	Domestic	—	—	1	—	—	—	—	—	—	—	1
Dressler, Miss Ada	London	1892	Flowers	—	—	1	—	1	—	—	—	—	—	2
Dressler, Conrad	London	1883-1893	Sculpture	—	—	22	—	7	—	1	8	12	—	50
Dreux, De. *See* De.	—	—												—
Drew, J. P.	London	1835-1861	Domestic	—	—	18	45	26	—	—	—	—	—	89
Drew, Miss Mary	London	1880-1892	Domestic	—	—	19	—	13	—	—	—	—	9	41
Drew, Richard William, M. A.	London	1867-1868	Architecture	—	—	2	—	—	—	—	—	—	—	2
Drew, S. J.	Bexley	1865-1867	Flowers	—	—	—	—	2	—	—	—	—	—	2
Drew, Thomas, R.H.A.	Dublin	1892	Architecture	—	—	1	—	—	—	—	—	—	—	1
Drew, W.	London	1833-1852	Architecture	—	—	19	—	2	—	—	—	—	—	21
Drewe, A.	London	1887	Architecture	—	—	1	—	—	—	—	—	—	—	1
Dribholtz, C L. W.	Dort	1838	Landscape	—	—	1	—	—	—	—	—	—	—	1
Drinkwater, H. J. W.	Oxford	1877	Architecture	—	—	1	—	—	—	—	—	—	—	1
Drioli, F.	Dalmatia	1846	Scriptural	—	—	1	—	—	—	—	—	—	—	1
Driver, Charles Henry	London	1855-1857	Architecture	—	—	1	—	1	—	—	—	—	—	2
Driver, G. N.	London	1813-1820	Architecture	—	—	3	—	—	—	—	—	—	—	3
Driver and Rew	London	1875	Architecture	—	—	1	—	—	—	—	—	—	—	1
Droege, F.	Berlin	1851-1854	Portraits	—	—	2	—	—	—	—	—	—	—	2
Droflig, Miss J. J.	London	1843	Rustic	—	—	—	—	1	—	—	—	—	—	1
Drown, J.	London	1821	Architecture	—	—	1	—	—	—	—	—	—	—	1
Druce, Miss Helen	London	1885-1890	Landscape	—	—	—	—	1	—	3	—	—	—	4
Druce, R.	London	1853-1860	Landscape	—	—	2	—	1	—	—	—	—	—	3
Druery, Henry	London	1881-1888	Architecture	—	—	1	—	—	—	—	—	—	2	3
Druitt, Miss Emily	London	1883-1885	Domestic	—	—	—	—	1	—	—	—	—	2	3
Drummond —	London	1792	Portraits	—	—	2	—	—	—	—	—	—	—	2
Drummond, Arthur	London	1890-1893	Domestic	—	—	2	—	—	—	—	—	—	3	5
Drummond, E.	London	1869	Figures	—	—	—	—	—	—	—	—	—	1	1
Drummond, Miss Eliza A.	London	1822-1843	Portraits	—	—	9	2	18	—	1	—	—	—	30
Drummond, Miss F. Ellen	London	1833-1860	Heads	—	—	15	—	1	—	—	—	—	—	16
Drummond, G.	York	1863	Portraits	—	—	1	—	—	—	—	—	—	—	1
Drummond, H.	London	1831	Portraits	—	—	1	—	—	—	—	—	—	—	1
Drummond, H.	London	1875-1880	Sea Pieces	—	—	1	—	7	—	—	—	—	1	9
Drummond, James, R.S.A.	London	1839-1874	Historical	—	—	11	5	6	—	—	—	—	3	25
Drummond, Miss Jane	London	1819-1833	Portraits	—	—	12	—	11	—	—	—	—	—	23
Drummond, Julian	London	1892	Domestic	—	—	- -	—	1	—	—	—	—	—	1
Drummond, J. Nelson	London	1888-1893	Landscape	—	—	3	—	1	—	—	—	—	—	4
Drummond, Miss Rose Emma	London	1815-1837	Portraits	—	—	21	—	9	—	1	—	—	—	31

Name.	Town.	First and Last Year of Ex.	Speciality.	S. A.	F. S.	R. A.	B. I.	S. S	O. W.	N. W.	G. G.	N. G.	V. E.	Total.
Drummond, Miss Rose Myra	London	1832-1849	Figures	—	—	8	3	9	—	—	—	—	—	20
Drummond, Samuel, A.R.A.	London	1790-1844	Historical	8	—	303	84	9	—	5	—	—	—	409
Drummond, W.	London	1830-1843	Figures	—	—	2	5	7	—	—	—	—	—	14
Drury, Miss Ada	London	1891-1892	Flowers	—	—	—	—	—	—	—	—	4	—	4
Drury, Alfred	Richmond	1885-1893	Sculpture	—	—	14	—	4	—	—	4	9	5	36
Drury, A. T.	London	1829	Landscape	—	—	—	1	1	—	—	—	—	—	2
Drysdale, J. T.	London	1887-1889	Landscape	—	—	1	—	4	—	—	—	—	1	6
Drysdale, Miss Mary	Richmond	1859-1860	Landscape	—	—	—	—	2	—	—	—	—	—	2
Duassut, Curtius	London	1889-1893	Landscape	—	—	7	—	19	—	4	—	—	4	34
Dubasty, Ad. Henry	London	1853	Domestic	—	—	2	—	—	—	—	—	—	—	2
Dube, Madame Mathé	Paris	1891	Fish	—	—	1	—	—	—	—	—	—	—	1
Dubisson, W.	London	1878-1879	Miniatures	—	—	2	—	—	—	—	—	—	—	2
Dubisson, W. C.	London	1821	Portraits	—	—	2	—	—	—	—	—	—	—	2
Du Blaisel, Miss H.	—	1812-1813	Portraits	—	—	4	—	—	—	—	—	—	—	4
Duboc, M. A.	Greenwich	1828-1842	Domestic	—	—	2	3	6	—	—	—	—	—	11
Du Bois, Drahonet Alexander Jean	London	1832-1834	Portraits	—	—	2	—	—	—	—	—	—	—	2
Dubois, Francis	London	1819	Mythological	—	—	1	—	—	—	—	—	—	—	1
Dubois, Frederick	St. Petersburg	1818-1819	Portraits	—	—	6	—	—	—	—	—	—	—	6
Dubois, Jules C.	London	1849	Sculpture	—	—	1	1	—	—	—	—	—	—	2
Dubois, M.	London	1873	Medals	—	—	1	—	—	—	—	—	—	—	1
Dubois, Paul	Paris	1877	Sculpture	—	—	—	—	—	—	—	1	—	—	1
Dubos, Madame	London	1791	Figures	—	—	1	—	—	—	—	—	—	—	1
Dubost, Antoine	London	1806-1808	Historical	—	—	3	—	—	—	—	—	—	—	3
Du Bourg, M.	London	1786-1808	Miniatures	—	—	3	—	—	—	—	—	—	—	3
Dubourg, Madame Victoria	—	1882-1893	Flowers	—	—	6	—	5	—	24	2	—	3	40
Dubourgh —	London	1771-1775	Architecture	2	—	—	—	—	—	—	—	—	—	2
Dubourjal, T. S.	London	1838	Heads	—	—	1	—	—	—	—	—	—	—	1
Dubray, Miss Charlotte Gabrielle	London	1875-1878	Sculpture	—	—	9	—	—	—	—	—	—	—	9
Dubufe, Claude Marie	London	1828-1831	Scriptural	—	—	6	3	—	—	—	—	—	—	9
Dubufe, Guillaume	Paris	1881	Domestic	—	—	—	—	—	—	—	2	—	—	2
Dubufe, Louis Edouard	London	1838-1873	Portraits	—	—	8	1	—	—	—	—	—	—	9
Dubuisson, A.	Lyons	1847	Domestic	—	—	1	—	—	—	—	—	—	—	1
Dubuisson, Miss	London	1809-1840	Still Life	—	—	20	2	4	—	—	—	—	—	26
Ducane, Miss Ella	London	1893	Landscape	—	—	—	—	—	—	1	—	—	—	1
Du Chattel, F. J.	—	1880	Landscape	—	—	—	—	—	—	—	2	—	—	2
Duché, de Vancy	London	1784	Domestic	—	—	5	—	—	—	—	—	—	—	5
Ducker, D. D.	London	1859-1863	Sculpture	—	—	1	—	2	—	—	—	—	—	3
Duckett, Thomas	London	1861-1867	Sculpture	—	—	8	1	—	—	—	—	—	—	9
Ducreux, Joseph	Vienna	1791	Portraits	—	—	5	—	—	—	—	—	—	—	5
Dudding, E. B.	St. Albans	1876	Landscape	—	—	—	—	—	—	—	—	—	2	2
Dudgeon, Miss Dorothea	London	1893	Fruit	—	—	1	—	—	—	—	—	—	—	1
Dudgeon, Miss E.	Rosherville	1876	Figures	—	—	—	—	1	—	—	—	—	—	1
Dudgeon, Miss Louisa	Leicester	1861-1868	Still Life	—	—	—	—	2	—	—	—	—	4	6
Dudley, Ambrose	London	1890-1891	Portraits	—	—	3	—	—	—	—	—	—	—	3
Dudley, Arthur	London	1890-1893	Flowers	—	—	2	—	6	—	3	—	—	—	11
Dudley, G.	—	1827	Domestic	—	—	—	—	1	—	—	—	—	—	1
Dudley, Robert	London	1865-1891	Sea Pieces	—	—	24	—	5	—	6	—	—	12	47
Dudley, Robert Charles	London	1853	Domestic	—	—	1	—	—	—	—	—	—	—	1
Dudley-Rolls, Miss F. A.	Surbiton	1893	Sculpture	—	—	1	—	—	—	—	—	—	—	1
Dudman, R.	London	1797	Portraits	—	—	1	—	—	—	—	—	—	—	1
Duepur, Master	London	1780	Landscape	—	3	—	—	—	—	—	—	—	—	3
Duesbury, H.	London	1837-1850	Architecture	—	—	9	—	—	—	—	—	—	—	9
Duff, John	London	1892	Architecture	—	—	1	—	—	—	—	—	—	—	1
Duff, John R. K.	Hendon	1891-1893	Rustic	—	—	1	—	6	—	—	—	—	—	7
Duff, Miss Margery F.	London	1884	Landscape	—	—	1	—	—	—	—	—	—	—	1
Duffer, L. S. F.	Paris	1872	Portraits	—	—	2	—	—	—	—	—	—	—	2
Duffield, Miss C. M	London	1873-1874	Fruit	—	—	—	—	2	—	—	—	—	—	2
Duffield, William	Bath	1838-1865	Still Life	—	—	10	17	38	—	—	—	—	37	102
Duffield, Mrs. William, R.I. ‡ *See* Miss	—	—	—	—	—	—	—	—	—	—	—	—	—	—
Mary Ann Rosenberg	Bath	1850-1893	Fruit, etc.	—	—	12	—	28	—	341	3	—	9	393
Duffield, William L.	London	1873-1880	Figures	—	—	—	—	4	—	—	—	—	1	5
Duffin, F. M.	London	1831	Landscape	—	—	1	—	—	—	—	—	—	—	1
Duffin, Paul	London	1772-1775	Domestic	2	—	1	—	—	—	—	—	—	—	3
Duffy, Patrick Vincent, R.H.A.	Dublin	1876-1888	Landscape	—	—	1	—	2	—	—	—	—	—	3
Dufour, A	London	1799-1800	Architecture	—	—	2	—	—	—	—	—	—	—	2
Dufour, A.	London	1867	Figures	—	—	1	—	—	—	—	—	—	—	1
Dufour, Charles	London	1778	Landscape	—	1	—	—	—	—	—	—	—	—	1
Dufour, William	London	1765-1770	Portraits	—	3	1	—	—	—	—	—	—	—	4
Dufourcq, A.	London	1830-1844	Landscape	—	—	3	—	—	—	—	—	—	—	3
Dufourcq, Mons. B.	London	1830-1834	Landscape	—	—	8	5	2	—	—	—	—	—	15
Du Fresnoy, F.	London	1801-1806	Landscape	—	—	6	—	—	—	—	—	—	—	6
Dufretay, Le Chevalier	London	1797-1802	Portraits	—	—	3	—	—	—	—	—	—	—	3

Name.	Town.	First and Last Year of Ex.	Speciality.	S. A.	F. S.	R. A.	B. I.	S. S.	O. W.	N. W.	G. G.	N. G.	V. E.	Total.
Duggan, J. F.	London	1849	Scriptural	—	—	1	—	—	—	—	—	—	—	1
Du Gue, Madame	—	1870	Figures	—	—	—	—	1	—	—	—	—	—	1
Du Hamel, G.	London	1767-1783	Landscape	9	6	—	—	—	—	—	—	—	—	15
Du Hamel, W.	London	1780-1783	Landscape	—	—	6	—	—	—	—	—	—	—	6
Dujardin, Edouard	London	1884	Sculpture	—	—	1	—	—	—	—	—	—	—	1
Dujardin, John	London	1820-1863	Landscape	—	—	4	59	32	—	—	—	—	—	95
Dujardin, J., Junr.	London	1837-1858	Sea Pieces	—	—	5	6	3	—	—	—	—	—	14
Dujardin, Miss. *See* Mrs. Meers	London	1827-1861	Moonlight	—	—	—	4	9	—	—	—	—	—	13
Duke, W. Medleycott	London	1888	Venice	—	—	—	—	1	—	—	—	—	—	1
Dukenfield, Mrs.	London	1858	Figures	—	—	—	—	—	—	—	—	—	1	1
Dukes, Charles	London	1829-1865	Domestic	—	—	35	33	27	—	—	—	—	33	128
Dukesell, Mrs. Eleanor	London	1862	Fruit	—	—	—	—	4	—	—	—	—	—	4
Dumaresque, Armand	London	1880	Sea Pieces	—	—	—	—	—	—	—	—	—	1	1
Du Maurier, George Louis, A.R.W.S †	London	1870-1893	Illustrations	—	—	39	—	—	38	—	—	6	61	144
Dumont, Henri Courselles-. *See* C.	—	—	—	—	—	—	—	—	—	—	—	—	—	—
Dun, John	Edinburgh	1872-1884	Landscape	—	—	3	—	—	—	—	—	—	—	3
Dunage, Thomas ‡	—	1834	—	—	—	—	—	—	—	*	—	—	—	—
Dunbar —	Newcastle	1840	Dogs	—	—	1	—	—	—	—	—	—	—	1
Dunbar, D.	London	1815-1823	Sculpture	—	—	3	—	—	—	—	—	—	—	3
Dunbar, D., Junr.	London	1841-1859	Sculpture	—	—	8	1	—	—	—	—	—	—	9
Dunbar, P.	London	1869-1877	Landscape	—	—	1	—	7	—	—	—	—	—	8
Dunbar, W.	Andover	1834-1845	Churches	—	—	—	—	3	—	1	—	—	—	4
Dunbar, W. N.	Rome	1839	Scriptural	—	—	—	—	4	—	—	—	—	—	4
Duncan, Alexander	London	1853-1862	Figures	—	—	—	5	8	—	—	—	—	3	16
Duncan, Allan	London	1854-1887	Landscape	—	—	15	—	41	—	5	—	—	16	77
Duncan, Miss C.	—	1859	Landscape	—	—	1	—	—	—	—	—	—	—	1
Duncan, C. S.	London	1846-1847	Architecture	—	—	3	—	—	—	—	—	—	—	3
Duncan, Edward, R.W.S. † ‡	London	1830-1882	Sea Pieces	—	—	7	13	18	332	188	—	—	—	558
Duncan, Miss Emily	London	1880-1890	Flowers	—	—	5	—	3	—	—	—	—	—	8
Duncan, E. G.	London	1892	Figures	—	—	—	—	—	—	—	—	1	—	1
Duncan, Miss Fanny	Manchester	1876-1889	Domestic	—	—	6	—	—	—	—	—	—	4	10
Duncan, John	Edinburgh	1893	Dramatic	—	—	1	—	—	—	—	—	—	—	1
Duncan, J. E.	Southampton	1875	River Scenes	—	—	—	—	1	—	—	—	—	—	1
Duncan, Laurence	London	1860-1891	Landscape	—	—	17	—	2	—	—	—	—	9	28
Duncan, Thomas, A.R.A., R.S.A.	Edinburgh	1832-1845	Historical	—	—	8	—	1	—	—	—	—	—	9
Duncan, Walter, A.R.W.S. †	London	1869-1893	Historical	—	—	8	—	3	224	1	4	3	8	251
Duncker, C.	Berlin	1841-1842	Scriptural	—	—	7	—	—	—	—	—	—	—	7
Duncumb, Miss E.	West Ham	1829-1843	Flowers	—	—	6	—	4	—	2	—	—	—	12
Dundas, Miss Agnes	London	1863-1873	Still Life	—	—	18	17	10	—	—	—	—	10	55
Dundee, Captain	—	1818-1854	Landscape	—	—	5	—	—	—	—	—	—	—	5
Dunk, W.	London	1837	Architecture	—	—	1	—	—	—	—	—	—	—	1
Dunkarton, Robert	London	1768-1779	Engraving	4	—	20	—	—	—	—	—	—	—	24
Dunlop, Miss Wallace	London	1871	Domestic	—	—	—	—	—	—	—	—	—	1	1
Dunn, A.	London	1809-1818	Miniatures	—	—	23	1	—	—	—	—	—	—	24
Dunn, A. M.	Newcastle	1873-1882	Architecture	—	—	2	—	—	—	—	—	—	—	2
Dunn (A.) and Hansom (E. J.)	Newcastle	1873-1886	Architecture	—	—	12	—	—	—	—	—	—	—	12
Dunn, Miss Constance	London	1883-1884	Flowers	—	—	—	—	1	—	—	—	—	1	2
Dunn, Miss Edith. *See* Mrs. T. O. Hume	Worcester	1862-1867	Domestic	—	—	—	3	4	—	—	—	—	1	8
Dunn, H. Treffry	Truro	1867-1869	Interiors	—	—	—	—	1	—	—	—	—	2	3
Dunn, John	London	1886-1891	Architecture	—	—	3	—	—	—	—	—	—	—	3
Dunn, John	London	1872	Domestic	—	—	—	—	—	—	—	—	—	1	1
Dunn, William. *See also* Maclaren, Dunn, and	—	—	—	—	—	—	—	—	—	—	—	—	—	—
Watson	London	1890	Architecture	—	—	1	—	—	—	—	—	—	—	1
Dunn (W.) and Watson (R.)	London	1892	Architecture	—	—	1	—	—	—	—	—	—	—	1
Dunn, Hansom, and Dunn	Newcastle	1888-1893	Architecture	—	—	4	—	—	—	—	—	—	—	4
Dunne, Isaac	Birmingham	1881	Landscape	—	—	—	—	—	—	—	—	—	3	3
Dunning, Miss Agnes	Streatham	1890	Flowers	—	—	—	—	1	—	—	—	—	—	1
Dunning, John R.	London	1892-1893	Landscape	—	—	—	—	2	—	—	—	—	—	2
Du Noblet, Mrs. *See* Villebrune.	—	—	—	—	—	—	—	—	—	—	—	—	—	—
Dunsmore, John Ward	Blackheath	1884-1888	Domestic	—	—	—	—	5	—	—	—	—	2	7
Dunthorne, John, Senr.	Colchester	1784-1786	Miniatures	—	—	2	—	—	—	—	—	—	—	2
Dunthorne, John, Junr.	Colchester	1783-1792	Domestic	—	—	14	—	—	—	—	—	—	—	14
Dunthorne, John	London	1827-1838	Landscape	—	—	7	3	—	—	—	—	—	—	10
Du Parc —	London	1766	Portraits	3	—	—	—	—	—	—	—	—	—	3
Dupart, Mrs.	London	1763	Figures	—	3	—	—	—	—	—	—	—	—	3
Duperier, J. G.	Cheshunt	1821-1822	Landscape	—	—	3	—	—	—	—	—	—	—	3
Dupeux, Joseph	London	1835-1839	Ruins	—	—	3	—	4	—	—	—	—	—	7
Dupont, Gainsborough	London	1790-1798	Portraits	—	—	26	—	—	—	—	—	—	—	26
Duppa, Bryan Edward	London	1832-1853	Portraits	—	—	6	1	7	—	—	—	—	—	14
Dupré, Mrs. S.	London	1843	Mythological	—	—	—	1	—	—	—	—	—	—	1
Dupuis, Philippe Felix	London	1874-1882	Portraits	—	—	3	—	2	—	—	2	—	—	7
Dupuy, Miss L.	—	1847	Landscape	—	—	—	1	—	—	—	—	—	—	1

Name.	Town.	First and Last Year of Ex.	Speciality.	S. A.	F. S.	R. A.	B. I.	S. S.	O. W.	N. W.	G. G.	N. G.	V. E.	Total.
Durade, J. B.	—	1767	Landscape	1	—	—	—	—	—	—	—	—	—	1
Duran, Emile A. Carolus-. *See* C.	—	—	—	—	—	—	—	—	—	—	—	—	—	—
Durand, Asher B.	New York	1845	Landscape	—	—	1	—	—	—	—	—	—	—	1
Durand, Godfrey	London	1873-1877	Battles	—	—	—	—	1	—	—	—	—	4	5
Durand, John	London	1777-1778	Landscape	—	—	2	—	—	—	—	—	—	—	2
Durant, J.	London	1774-1797	Allegorical	1	—	2	—	—	—	—	—	—	—	3
Durant, Miss Susan D.	London	1847-1873	Sculpture	—	—	39	1	—	—	—	—	—	—	40
D'Urban, William	Bushey	1886-1888	Landscape	—	—	—	—	1	—	—	—	1	1	3
Durell, Miss Amy	London	1889-1890	Portraits	—	—	1	—	1	—	—	—	—	—	2
Durell, A. C.	London	1882	Fruit	—	—	—	—	—	—	—	—	—	1	1
Durham, Cornelius B.	London	1828-1858	Miniatures	—	—	157	—	46	—	—	—	—	—	203
Durham, Mrs. C. B.	Tottenham	1868-1870	Flowers	—	—	—	—	2	—	—	—	—	—	2
Durham, C. J.	London	1859-1880	Domestic	—	—	1	—	15	—	—	—	—	4	20
Durham, E.	London	1827	Intaglios	—	—	1	—	—	—	—	—	—	—	1
Durham, Joseph, A.R.A.	London	1835-1878	Sculpture	—	—	126	6	—	—	—	—	—	—	132
Durham, Miss Mary Edith	London	1891-1892	Portraits	—	—	1	—	—	—	1	—	—	—	2
Durham, W. H.	Sydenham	1890	Miniatures	—	—	1	—	—	—	—	—	—	—	1
Durnford, F. Andrew	London	1836-1886	Sea Pieces	—	—	11	8	20	—	—	—	—	14	53
Durnford, Miss Lucy	London	1858-1859	Flowers	—	—	—	—	2	—	—	—	—	—	2
Durno, James, F.S.A.	London	1767-1773	Historical	10	1	—	—	—	—	—	—	—	—	11
Durrand, Miss G.	Newbury	1866	Dogs	—	—	1	—	—	—	—	—	—	—	1
Durrani, B.	Streatham	1880	Portraits	—	—	1	—	—	—	—	—	—	—	1
Duseigneur, Georges	Lyons	1874	Figures	—	—	—	—	—	—	—	—	—	2	2
Duterrau, Benjamin	London	1817-1827	Domestic	—	—	6	3	2	—	—	—	—	—	11
Duthie, Arthur L.	London	1892	Stained Glass	—	—	1	—	—	—	—	—	—	—	1
Duthie, Spottiswoode	Udney	1892	Domestic	—	—	—	—	2	—	—	—	—	—	2
Duthoit, Miss Elizabeth Emma	London	1885	Landscape	—	—	—	—	—	—	1	—	—	—	1
Duthoit, J.	London	1874	Landscape	—	—	1	—	—	—	—	—	—	—	1
Du Thuillay —	London	1765-1774	Enamels	—	13	—	—	—	—	—	—	—	—	13
Dutton, John	London	1828-1837	Intaglios	—	—	5	—	—	—	—	—	—	—	5
Dutton, Miss Mary Martha. *See* Mrs. Charles Pearson	London	1830-1856	Portraits	—	—	22	—	12	—	1	—	—	—	35
Dutton, Thomas G.	London	1858-1879	Sea Pieces	—	—	—	—	15	—	—	—	—	—	15
Dutton, W.	London	1871	Architecture	—	—	1	—	—	—	—	—	—	—	1
Dutton, W. E.	London	1854-1857	Figures	—	—	1	2	—	—	—	—	—	—	3
Duturcq, T.	London	1872	Sea Pieces	—	—	—	—	1	—	—	—	—	—	1
Duturcq, Madame T.	London	1872	Flowers	—	—	—	—	1	—	—	—	—	—	1
Duval, A.	London	1873	Still Life	—	—	—	—	1	—	—	—	—	—	1
Du Val, Charles Allen	Manchester	1836-1872	Portraits	—	—	20	—	—	—	—	—	—	1	21
Duval, E.	London	1857-1869	Landscape	—	—	1	2	—	—	—	—	—	—	3
Duval, Edward J.	Manchester	1876-1893	Landscape	—	—	1	—	5	—	—	—	—	5	11
Duval, John	Ipswich	1851-1882	Domestic	—	—	18	10	49	—	—	—	—	—	77
Duval, J. C. A.	London	1826-1856	Sea Pieces	—	—	17	3	14	—	—	—	—	7	41
Duval, Thomas George	London	1840-1879	Landscape	—	—	11	—	9	—	—	—	—	2	22
Duval-le-Camus, Pierre	Paris	1837-1839	Portraits	—	—	2	—	—	—	—	—	—	—	2
Duvernoy, A.	London	1834	Landscape	—	—	—	—	—	—	1	—	—	—	1
Duvigneaud —	London	1797	Miniatures	—	—	1	—	—	—	—	—	—	—	1
Duvivier, Albert	Paris	1872	Figures	—	—	—	—	—	—	—	—	—	1	1
Dwyer, John	London	1846-1851	Architecture	—	—	4	—	1	—	—	—	—	—	5
Dyason, E. H.	Worthing	1885-1886	Landscape	—	—	—	—	3	—	—	—	—	—	3
Dyball, Sextus	London	1893	Architecture	—	—	1	—	—	—	—	—	—	—	1
Dyce, J. Stirling	Paris	1884-1891	Landscape	—	—	5	—	—	—	—	—	—	—	5
Dyce, William, R.A., H.R.S.A.	Rome	1827-1861	Mythological	—	—	41	4	—	—	—	—	—	—	45
Dyckmans, Joseph Laurens	Antwerp	1846-1869	Domestic	—	—	4	—	—	—	—	—	—	—	4
Dyer, Charles	London	1818-1847	Architecture	—	—	13	—	—	—	—	—	—	—	13
Dyer, Charles E. *See also* Wilson and Dyer	London	1882	Architecture	—	—	1	—	—	—	—	—	—	—	1
Dyer, Charles F.	Munich	1880	Figures	—	—	1	—	—	—	—	—	—	—	1
Dyer, G.	London	1821-1847	Portraits	—	—	4	—	—	—	—	—	—	—	4
Dyer, G. E. O.	London	1835	Portraits	—	—	3	—	—	—	—	—	—	—	3
Dyer, Miss Gertrude M.	Leatherhead	1891-1893	Flowers	—	—	—	—	—	—	2	—	—	—	2
Dyer, Lowell	St. Ives, C'nwall	1890	Interiors	—	—	—	—	—	—	—	1	—	—	1
Dyer, R. H.	London	1827-1828	Engraving	—	—	—	—	6	—	—	—	—	—	6
Dyer, Wilson	Manchester	1852-1855	Domestic	—	—	—	3	1	—	—	—	—	—	4
Dyer, Miss	London	1825	Copies	—	—	—	—	1	—	—	—	—	—	1
Dyke, Miss Eleanor Hart-	Eynsford	1867-1892	Landscape	—	—	—	—	—	—	3	—	—	1	4
Dyke, R. H.	London	1856-1867	Sea Pieces	—	—	—	3	2	—	—	—	—	—	5
Eadie, William	London	1871-1890	Domestic	—	—	11	—	—	—	—	2	—	—	13
Eagle, W.	London	1866	Domestic	—	—	—	1	—	—	—	—	—	—	1

Name.	Town.	First and Last Year of Ex.	Speciality.	S. A.	F. S.	R. A.	B. I.	S. S.	O. W.	N.W.	G. G.	N. G.	V. E.	Total.
Eagles, Edmund	Gt. Missenden	1851-1877	Domestic	—	—	18	1	16	—	—	—	—	2	37
Eagles, Rev. John	Bristol	1808-1852	Landscape	—	—	1	5	—	—	—	—	—	—	6
Eales, Christopher. *See also* Cope, Eales, and Elmslie	— London	— 1838-1852	— Architecture	— —	— —	— 4	— —	— —	— —	— —	— —	— —	— —	— 4
Eales (C.) and Son	London	1886-1888	Architecture	—	—	2	—	—	—	—	—	—	—	2
Eales, Miss M.	London	1877	Portraits	—	—	1	—	—	—	—	—	—	—	1
Eamonson, S.	Homerton	1852-1857	Landscape	—	—	2	1	—	—	—	—	—	—	3
Earl, F.	London	1849	Domestic	—	—	1	—	—	—	—	—	—	—	1
Earl, G.	London	1830	Landscape	—	—	1	—	—	—	—	—	—	—	1
Earl, George	London	1856-1883	Sporting	—	—	19	9	18	—	—	—	—	—	46
Earl, Miss Maud	London	1884-1889	Animals	—	—	3	—	1	—	—	—	—	—	4
Earl, Ralph	London	1783-1785	Portraits	—	—	5	—	—	—	—	—	—	—	5
Earl, T.	London	1824	Sea Pieces	—	—	2	—	—	—	—	—	—	—	2
Earl, Thomas	London	1836-1885	Sporting	—	—	47	62	108	—	—	—	—	21	238
Earl, William Robert	London	1823-1867	Landscape	—	—	19	52	43	—	—	—	—	—	114
Earle, Augustus	London	1806-1838	Historical	—	—	11	—	—	—	—	—	—	—	11
Earle, Charles, R.I. ‡ φ	London	1857-1893	Landscape	—	—	24	3	25	—	81	3	8	128	272
Earle, Mrs. C. W. (Maria Theresa)	London	1878-1880	Landscape	—	—	—	—	—	—	—	—	—	6	6
Earle, F.	London	1839	Dogs	—	—	2	—	—	—	—	—	—	—	2
Earle, James	London	1787-1796	Portraits	1	—	17	—	—	—	—	—	—	—	18
Earle, J. H.	London	1842-1845	Historical	—	—	—	1	5	—	—	—	—	—	6
Earle, Miss Kate	London	1887-1893	Domestic	—	—	1	—	7	—	—	1	—	5	14
Earle, Thomas	London	1834-1873	Sculpture	—	—	62	24	1	—	—	—	—	5	92
Earle, Miss	—	1821-1822	Portraits	—	—	2	—	—	—	—	—	—	—	2
Earles, Chester	London	1842-1863	Portraits	—	—	56	18	56	—	—	—	—	—	130
Earlom, Richard	London	1762-1767	Engraving	1	1	—	—	—	—	—	—	—	—	2
Earnshaw, Mrs. Mary Harriot	London	1888-1889	Pastels	—	—	—	—	3	—	—	—	—	—	3
Earnst —	London	1783	Landscape	—	1	—	—	—	—	—	—	—	—	1
Earp, Henry	Brighton	1871-1884	Cattle	—	—	—	—	4	—	2	—	—	—	6
Easling, J. C., *or* Easting	—	1825-1833	Engraving	—	—	—	—	4	—	—	—	—	—	4
East, Alfred, R.I., R.B.A., R.P.E. ‡ § φ	Glasgow	1883-1893	Landscape	—	—	22	—	30	—	25	11	11	17	116
East, F.	—	1839	Architecture	—	—	1	—	—	—	—	—	—	—	1
East, J. B.	London	1818-1830	Portraits	—	—	33	—	—	—	—	—	—	—	33
East, Mary	Newcastle	1873	Still Life	—	—	—	—	2	—	—	—	—	—	2
East, William H.	Dover	1891	Figures	—	—	1	—	—	—	—	—	—	—	1
Easthed, Mrs. *See* Miss Harriet Alcock	London	1836	Portraits	—	—	1	—	—	—	—	—	—	—	1
Easthorpe —	—	1838	Architecture	—	—	1	—	—	—	—	—	—	—	1
Eastlake, Caroline H.	Plymouth	1868-1873	Flowers	—	—	—	—	—	—	—	—	—	28	28
Eastlake, Charles H.	Balham	1889-1893	Domestic	—	—	2	—	5	—	—	—	—	—	7
Eastlake, Sir Charles Lock, P.R.A.	Plymouth	1813-1855	Scriptural	—	—	51	18	—	—	—	—	—	—	69
Eastlake, Charles Lock	London	1855-1866	Architecture	—	—	2	—	—	—	—	—	—	4	6
Eastlake, Miss Elizabeth R.	Plymouth	1874-1883	Domestic	—	—	1	—	—	—	—	—	—	6	7
Eastlake, W.	Plymouth	1870-1877	Landscape	—	—	2	—	—	—	—	—	—	2	4
Easton, Reginald	London	1835-1887	Miniatures	—	—	160	—	—	—	—	—	—	—	160
Eastwood, Francis H.	London	1875-1893	Landscape	—	—	5	—	16	—	11	—	—	12	44
Eastwood, J. H.	London	1889	Architecture	—	—	1	—	—	—	—	—	—	—	1
Eaton, Charles Warren	London	1890-1891	Landscape	—	—	7	—	5	—	2	1	—	—	15
Eaton, Miss E.	London	1817-1822	Landscape	—	—	5	—	—	—	—	—	—	—	5
Eaton, George	Norwich	1862-1870	Landscape	—	—	2	—	2	—	—	—	—	1	5
Eaton, J. B.	London	1810-1821	Domestic	—	—	9	1	—	—	—	—	—	—	10
Eaton, Stephen O.	London	1889	Landscape	—	—	3	—	—	—	—	—	—	—	3
Eaton, W. P.	Weymouth	1884	—	—	—	—	—	—	—	—	—	—	*	—
Ebden (F. C.) and Williams (J. L.)	London	1892	Architecture	—	—	1	—	—	—	—	—	—	—	1
Ebdon, Christopher, F.S.A.	London	1767-1783	Architecture	18	—	—	—	—	—	—	—	—	—	18
Ebel, William Augustus	London	1884	Architecture	—	—	1	—	—	—	—	—	—	—	1
Ebner, Lewis F. (?) Louis	London	1888-1890	Domestic	—	—	1	—	—	—	—	—	2	—	3
Eburne, Miss Emma. *See* Mrs. William Oliver *and* Mrs. John Sedgwick.	— —	— —	— —	— —	— —	— —	— —	— —	— —	— —	— —	— —	— —	— —
Eccardt, John Giles	London	1761-1768	Portraits	2	—	—	—	—	—	—	—	—	—	2
Eccles, Rev. Mr.	—	1777	Fruit	—	—	1	—	—	—	—	—	—	—	1
Eccles, J. Evans	London	1881-1883	Figures	—	—	1	—	2	—	—	—	—	—	3
Eckhart, Miss E.	—	1798	Landscape	—	—	1	—	—	—	—	—	—	—	1
Eckhout, J. J.	The Hague	1845-1850	Portraits	—	—	2	—	—	—	—	—	—	—	2
Eckstein, George Paul	London	1777-1802	Sculpture	—	—	11	—	—	—	—	—	—	—	11
Eckstein, John	London	1762-1802	Sculpture	1	1	19	—	—	—	—	—	—	—	21
Ecles, W.	London	1826	Engraving	—	—	—	—	1	—	—	—	—	—	1
Eddington, William Clarke. *See* Clarke	Worcester	1861-1885	Landscape	—	—	12	—	19	—	5	—	—	23	59
Eddis, Eden Upton	London	1834-1883	Portraits	—	—	130	16	11	—	—	—	—	—	157
Eddison, Sam.	Leeds	1891-1892	Portraits	—	—	2	—	—	—	—	—	—	—	2
Edelfelt, Albert E.	Paris	1881-1891	Portraits	—	—	1	—	—	—	—	1	—	—	2
Edelsten, Miss A. J.	London	1878	Landscape	—	—	—	—	1	—	—	—	—	—	1

Name.	Town.	First and Last Year of Ex.	Speciality.	S. A.	F. S.	R. A.	B. I.	S. S.	O. W.	N. W.	G. G.	N. G.	V. E.	Total.
EDEN, HON. MARY J.	—	1815	Cattle	—	—	2	—	—	—	—	—	—	—	2
EDEN, SIR WILLIAM, BART.	Ferry Hill	1891-1893	—	—	—	—	—	—	—	2	—	—	—	2
EDEN, WILLIAM	Liverpool	1866-1893	Landscape	—	—	13	—	5	—	8	2	—	37	65
EDGAR, JAMES H.	Liverpool	1860-1864	Figures	—	—	—	1	1	—	—	—	—	—	2
EDGE, JOHN	London	1832-1834	Sea Pieces	—	—	—	—	—	—	7	—	—	—	7
EDGE, MARGARITA C.	London	1834	Landscape	—	—	1	—	—	—	—	—	—	—	1
EDGELOW, ALICE MAUD	London	1889	Heads	—	—	—	—	1	—	—	—	—	—	1
EDGINGTON, E. W.	London	1887-1888	Landscape	—	—	1	—	2	—	—	—	—	—	3
EDGINGTON-WILLIAMS, MISS E. *See* W.	—	—	—	—	—	—	—	—	—	—	—	—	—	—
EDINBOROUGH, MISS EDITH	—	1871	Heads	—	—	—	—	1	—	—	—	—	—	1
EDINGER, W. H.	Wanstead	1892	Landscape	—	—	—	—	—	—	1	—	—	—	1
EDIS, COL. ROBERT WILLIAM, F.S.A., F.R.I.B.A.	London	1862-1893	Architecture	—	—	53	—	—	—	—	—	—	—	53
EDMESTON —	—	1810	Architecture	—	—	1	—	—	—	—	—	—	—	1
EDMESTON, JAMES	Coventry	1854-1859	Architecture	—	—	2	—	—	—	—	—	—	—	2
EDMONDS, MISS ANNA MARIA. *See* Mrs. William Collings Lukis Guérin	Rome	1867	Rustic	—	—	1	—	—	—	—	—	—	—	1
EDMONDS, C.	London	1795-1801	Architecture	—	—	5	—	—	—	—	—	—	—	5
EDMONDS, C. W. C.	London	1834-1849	Architecture	—	—	13	—	—	—	—	—	—	—	13
EDMONDS, E. M.	Kendal	1872-1893	Landscape	—	—	—	—	3	—	—	—	10	—	13
EDMONDS, F. W.	—	1845	Figures	—	—	1	—	—	—	—	—	—	—	1
EDMONDS, G.	London	1825-1836	Landscape	—	—	—	1	7	—	—	—	—	—	8
EDMONDSON, ROBERT HOLT. (?) EDMONSON	Manchester	1870-1885	Landscape	—	—	2	—	—	—	—	—	—	4	6
EDMONSON, J.	London	1790-1792	Sculpture	—	—	3	—	—	—	—	—	—	—	3
EDMONSTON, SAMUEL	Edinburgh	1862-1864	Domestic	—	—	2	—	—	—	—	—	—	—	2
EDMONSTONE, ROBERT	London	1818-1834	Portraits	—	—	23	19	16	—	—	—	—	—	58
EDMUNDS, W.	Margate	1831	Architecture	—	—	1	—	—	—	—	—	—	—	1
EDNEY, J. M.	London	1829-1831	Landscape	—	—	—	—	3	—	—	—	—	—	3
EDOUART, A.	London	1815-1816	Animals	—	—	5	—	—	—	—	—	—	—	5
EDRIDGE, HENRY, A.R.A.	London	1786-1821	Miniatures	—	—	260	—	—	—	—	—	—	—	260
EDSON, ALLAN	London	1886	Landscape	—	—	2	—	2	—	—	—	—	—	4
EDWARD, ALBERT	London	1885-1886	Venice	—	—	—	—	—	—	2	—	—	—	2
EDWARD, ALFRED S.	London	1876-1893	Landscape	—	—	7	—	28	—	—	—	—	3	38
EDWARD, C.	London	1884	Rustic	—	—	2	—	—	—	—	—	—	1	3
EDWARDS, A.	Putney	1874-1876	Landscape	—	—	—	—	2	—	—	—	—	—	2
EDWARDS, MISS AMELIA B.	London	1858-1863	Domestic	—	—	—	2	6	—	—	—	—	—	8
EDWARDS, MISS A. G.	London	1893	Fruit	—	—	—	—	—	—	1	—	—	—	1
EDWARDS, C.	London	1824-1826	Architecture	—	—	2	—	—	—	—	—	—	—	2
EDWARDS, C. A.	Horton, Bucks.	1792-1797	Flowers	—	—	4	—	—	—	—	—	—	—	4
EDWARDS, MISS CATHERINE ADELAIDE. *See* Mrs. J. Sparkes	London	1866-1868	Figures	—	—	2	—	—	—	—	—	—	3	5
EDWARDS, E.	London	1800	Drawings	—	—	2	—	—	—	—	—	—	—	2
EDWARDS, E.	—	1825-1826	Sculpture	—	—	3	—	—	—	—	—	—	—	3
EDWARDS, EDWARD, A.R.A.	London	1766-1806	Portraits	6	1	104	1	—	—	—	—	—	—	112
EDWARDS, EDWIN	Sunbury	1861-1880	Sea Pieces & Etching	—	—	54	3	1	—	—	—	—	101	159
EDWARDS, MISS E. E.	London	1868	Portraits	—	—	1	—	—	—	—	—	—	—	1
EDWARDS, ELLIN H.	London	1879	Still Life	—	—	—	—	1	—	—	—	—	—	1
EDWARDS, MRS. E. W. (M. A.)	London	1857	Sculpture	—	—	1	—	—	—	—	—	—	—	1
EDWARDS, FRANCIS	London	1809-1830	Architecture	—	—	11	—	—	—	—	—	—	—	11
EDWARDS, F.	London	1868-1869	Historical	—	—	—	—	2	—	—	—	—	—	2
EDWARDS, FRANCES	London	1813	Portraits	—	—	1	—	—	—	—	—	—	—	1
EDWARDS, G.	London	1811-1818	Landscape	—	—	3	—	—	—	—	—	—	—	3
EDWARDS, G. H.	London	1837-1847	Landscape	—	—	3	—	4	—	—	—	—	—	7
EDWARDS, GEORGE H.	London	1883-1893	Domestic	—	—	—	—	5	—	6	—	—	—	11
EDWARDS, J.	—	1797	Game	—	—	1	—	—	—	—	—	—	—	1
EDWARDS, JAMES	Nottingham	1868	Landscape	—	—	—	—	—	—	—	—	—	2	2
EDWARDS, JOHN, F.S.A.	Brentford	1763-1812	Flowers	53	4	4	1	—	—	—	—	—	3	65
EDWARDS, JOSEPH	London	1838-1878	Sculpture	—	—	70	—	—	—	—	—	—	—	70
EDWARDS, MISS JESSIE A.	London	1865-1878	Domestic	—	—	—	—	18	—	—	—	—	—	18
EDWARDS, J. C.	London	1821	Figures	—	—	1	—	—	—	—	—	—	—	1
EDWARDS, KATE J.	London	1879	Domestic	—	—	—	—	1	—	—	—	—	—	1
EDWARDS, MISS LOUISA	London	1884-1886	Flowers	—	—	—	—	4	—	—	—	—	—	4
EDWARDS, MISS MARIAN ‖	Leytonstone	1875-1877	Landscape	—	—	2	—	—	—	—	—	—	6	8
EDWARDS, MISS MIA	Abergavenny	1893	Domestic	—	—	1	—	—	—	—	—	—	—	1
EDWARDS, MORTON	London	1864-1870	Sculpture	—	—	5	—	1	—	—	—	—	—	6
EDWARDS, MISS MARY ELLEN. *See* Mrs. John Freer *and* Mrs. John C. Staples	London	1862-1893	Domestic	—	—	13	2	6	—	—	—	—	11	32
EDWARDS, R.	London	1820	Cattle	—	—	1	—	—	—	—	—	—	—	1
EDWARDS, R.	Leicester	1849-1851	Enamels	—	—	—	—	—	—	—	—	—	8	8
EDWARDS, SAM.	London	1768-1771	Portraits	4	—	—	—	—	—	—	—	—	—	4
EDWARDS, SYDENHAM	London	1792-1814	Portraits	—	—	12	—	—	—	—	—	—	—	12
EDWARDS, SAMUEL ARLENT	London	1887	Engraving	—	—	1	—	—	—	—	—	—	—	1
EDWARDS, S. R. W.	London	1818-1822	Landscape	—	—	3	—	—	—	—	—	—	—	3

Name.	Town.	First and Last Year of Ex.	Speciality.	S. A.	F. S.	R. A.	B. I.	S. S.	O. W.	N.W.	G. G.	N. G.	V. E.	Total.
Edwards, T.	London	1816	Portraits	—	—	1	—	—	—	—	—	—	—	1
Edwards, T. W.	London	1847	Churches	—	—	1	—	—	—	—	—	—	—	1
Edwards, W.	London	1825	Domestic	—	—	1	—	—	—	—	—	—	—	1
Edwards, W.	London	1860	Churches	—	—	—	1	—	—	—	—	—	—	1
Edwards, W. Croxford. *See* Croxford, W. E.	Brentford	1874-1878	Sea Pieces	—	—	1	—	5	—	—	—	—	—	6
Edwards, W. H.	London	1793-1850	Fruit	—	—	7	—	10	—	—	—	—	—	17
Edwards, Mrs. W. H.	London	1847	Fruit	—	—	1	—	1	—	—	—	—	—	2
Edwards, W. Joseph	London	1858	Engraving	—	—	1	—	—	—	—	—	—	—	1
Edwart —	London	1821	Landscape	—	—	3	—	—	—	—	—	—	—	3
Edwin, Horace	London	1874-1882	Domestic	—	—	2	—	1	—	—	—	—	—	3
Edwin, Mrs. Mary	Norwood	1891-1892	Fruit	—	—	—	—	—	—	—	—	—	2	2
Edwin, Richard	London	1770-1777	Architecture	1	—	3	—	—	—	—	—	—	—	4
Edye, J. W.	London	1785-1807	Landscape	—	—	4	3	—	—	—	—	—	—	7
Eedes, R,	Warwick	1852	Portraits	—	—	1	—	—	—	—	—	—	—	1
Egan, C.	London	1807-1813	Landscape	—	—	5	—	—	—	—	—	—	—	5
Egan, James	London	1892	Stained Glass	—	—	1	—	—	—	—	—	—	—	1
Egenolf, G.	London	1795-1797	Architecture	—	—	3	—	—	—	—	—	—	—	3
Egerton, Miss A.	—	1859	Portraits	—	—	1	—	—	—	—	—	—	—	1
Egerton, Daniel Thomas §	London	1824-1840	Landscape	—	—	—	1	65	—	—	—	—	—	66
Egerton, Miss Jane Sophia ‡	London	1844-1857	Portraits	—	—	3	—	3	—	25	—	—	—	31
Egerton, Will.	London	1880-1881	Landscape	—	—	—	—	2	—	—	—	—	1	3
Egerton, Hon. Miss	—	1779	Portraits	—	—	1	—	—	—	—	—	—	—	1
Egg, Augustus Leopold, R.A.	London	1837-1860	Historical	—	—	28	9	9	—	—	—	—	—	46
Eggar, Miss Catherine A.	London	1886	Domestic	—	—	—	—	—	—	1	—	—	—	1
Eggart, D.	—	1762	Sculpture	—	1	—	—	—	—	—	—	—	—	1
Eggbrecht, John E.	London	1826-1828	Still Life	—	—	—	—	3	—	—	—	—	—	3
Egley, William	London	1824-1869	Miniatures	—	—	169	2	6	—	—	—	—	1	178
Egley, William Maw	London	1843-1893	Historical	—	—	33	18	27	—	—	—	—	30	108
Egley, Mrs.	London	1869	Portraits	—	—	1	—	—	—	—	—	—	—	1
Eglington, James T.	Liverpool	1847-1859	Domestic	—	—	2	3	2	—	—	—	—	—	7
Eglington, Samuel	Liverpool	1833-1855	Landscape	—	—	2	13	4	—	5	—	—	—	24
Egloffstein, Countess Julie von D	London	1839	Portraits	—	—	2	—	—	—	—	—	—	—	2
Egner, Miss Maria	London	1888	Farmyards	—	—	1	—	—	—	—	—	—	—	1
Egusquiza, R. de	—	1880	Portraits	—	—	—	—	—	—	—	1	—	—	1
Egville, D'. *See* D.	—	—	—	—	—	—	—	—	—	—	—	—	—	—
Ehninger, John W.	London	1864	Domestic	—	—	1	2	—	—	—	—	—	—	3
Ehret, Georg Dionysius	Baden	1770	Flowers	1	—	—	—	—	—	—	—	—	—	1
Ehrke, Julius	Great Malvern	1889-1890	Landscape	—	—	2	—	—	—	—	—	—	—	2
Eichbaum, M. D.	London	1822	Architecture	—	—	1	—	—	—	—	—	—	—	1
Eichel —	London	1770-1771	Landscape	—	5	—	—	—	—	—	—	—	—	5
Eiloart, Miss E. G.	London	1859-1862	Flowers	—	—	1	4	5	—	—	—	—	—	10
Einslie, S.	London	1785-1808	Miniatures	—	—	10	—	—	—	—	—	—	—	10
Ekman, Robert Wilhelm	London	1858	Domestic	—	—	1	—	—	—	—	—	—	—	1
Elcock, George A.	London	1876-1892	Domestic	—	—	—	—	9	—	—	—	—	5	14
Elder, Charles	London	1844-1852	Scriptural	—	—	11	5	5	—	—	—	—	—	21
Eldridge, W.	London	1825	Landscape	—	—	2	—	—	—	—	—	—	—	2
Elen, Philip West	London	1838-1872	Landscape	—	—	64	57	46	—	—	—	—	75	242
Elex, F.	Paris	1850	Portraits	—	—	1	—	—	—	—	—	—	—	1
Eley, Miss Frances	London	1890	Miniatures	—	—	2	—	—	—	—	—	—	—	2
Eley, Miss Mary	London	1874-1890	Domestic	—	—	14	—	11	—	7	—	—	10	42
Elford, Miss Eliza	—	1815-1821	Flowers	—	—	4	—	—	—	—	—	—	—	4
Elford, Sir William, Bart.	Plympton	1774-1837	Landscape	—	—	40	—	—	—	—	—	—	—	40
Elgie, Howard	London	1875-1881	Landscape	—	—	—	—	11	—	—	—	—	2	13
Elgood, George S., R.I. ‡ φ	Leicester	1872-1893	Landscape	—	—	—	—	5	—	64	—	—	12	81
Elias, Alfred	Tunb'dge Wells	1885-1893	Landscape	—	—	8	—	1	—	—	—	2	6	17
Elias, Miss Annette ‖	London	1881-1893	Landscape	—	—	5	—	12	—	1	—	5	11	34
Elias, Mrs. Emily	Tonbridge	1892-1893	Still Life	—	—	—	—	2	—	—	—	—	3	5
Elias, Miss Emily	Paris	1884	Landscape	—	—	1	—	—	—	—	—	—	—	1
Eliot, Granville	Horsham	1891	Fishing	—	—	1	—	—	—	—	—	—	—	1
Elkins, J. H.	London	1868	Sculpture	—	—	1	—	—	—	—	—	—	—	1
Elland, R.	Liverpool	1809-1810	Architecture	—	—	2	—	—	—	—	—	—	—	2
Elleby, William A.	Ashbourne, Derby	1888-1892	Landscape	—	—	8	—	—	—	—	—	—	—	8
Ellenor, Laura K.	Tooting	1893	Flowers	—	—	—	—	2	—	—	—	—	—	2
Ellerby, Thos.	London	1821-1857	Figures	—	—	72	31	5	—	—	—	—	—	108
Ellerby, W. Alfred	Clifton, Derby	1886	Rustic	—	—	—	—	2	—	—	—	—	—	2
Elleson, G.	—	1857	Portraits	—	—	1	—	—	—	—	—	—	—	1
Ellicombe, Captain	—	1810	Landscape	—	—	2	—	—	—	—	—	—	—	2
Elliot —	London	1761-1766	Landscape	5	—	—	—	—	—	—	—	—	—	5
Elliot —	London	1774	Chinese	—	2	—	—	—	—	—	—	—	—	2
Elliot, C. T.	Blackheath	1830-1833	Landscape	—	—	—	—	2	—	—	—	—	—	2
Elliot, Edward	Wymondham	1879-1893	Landscape	—	—	24	—	31	—	1	1	—	9	66
Elliot, J.	London	1816	Architecture	—	—	1	—	—	—	—	—	—	—	1

Name.	Town.	First and Last Year of Ex.	Speciality.	S. A.	F. S.	R. A.	B. I.	S. S.	O. W.	N.W.	G. G.	N. G.	V. E.	Total.
Elliot, Miss Rebecca	London	1878	Flowers	—	—	—	—	1	—	—	—	—	—	1
Elliot, R. B.	—	1815	Still Life	—	—	1	—	—	—	—	—	—	—	1
Elliot, W.	London	1817-1821	Architecture	—	—	2	—	—	—	—	—	—	—	2
Elliot, W. F.	London	1829-1834	Landscape	—	—	4	—	1	—	—	—	—	—	5
Elliott, Archibald	London	1794-1806	Architecture	—	—	6	—	—	—	—	—	—	—	6
Elliott, A., Junr. (?) Elliot	London	1817-1820	Architecture	—	—	4	—	—	—	—	—	—	—	4
Elliott, Charles	London	1876	Domestic	—	—	—	—	—	—	—	—	—	2	2
Elliott, Charles Loring	London	1852	Portraits	—	—	2	—	—	—	—	—	—	—	2
Elliott, Frank	London	1884	Fairies	—	—	1	—	—	—	—	—	—	—	1
Elliott, James	London	1848-1873	Domestic	—	—	4	—	4	—	—	—	—	7	15
Elliott, James	Manchester	1882-1892	Landscape	—	—	9	—	1	—	—	—	—	2	12
Elliott, Robinson	Newcastle	1835-1884	Domestic	—	—	11	4	13	—	2	—	—	14	44
Elliott, Captain Robert, F.S.A.	London	1784-1791	Sea Pieces	13	—	7	—	—	—	—	—	—	—	20
Ellis, Arthur	London	1874-1892	Domestic	—	—	8	—	9	—	3	1	2	4	27
Ellis, Miss Alice Blanche	Hereford	1876-1883	Landscape	—	—	1	—	13	—	—	—	—	4	18
Ellis, Bert	London	1890-1892	Sea Pieces	—	—	—	—	6	—	—	—	—	—	6
Ellis, C. Wynn	London	1880-1893	Domestic	—	—	4	—	2	—	8	—	3	2	19
Ellis, Edwin, R.B.A. §	Nottingham	1865-1891	Landscape	—	—	25	—	99	—	—	—	—	21	145
Ellis, Edward Brookes	London	1838-1877	Architecture	—	—	7	—	—	—	—	—	—	—	7
Ellis, Miss E. G.	London	1875	Landscape	—	—	—	—	1	—	—	—	—	—	1
Ellis, Edwin John	London	1870-1888	Figures	—	—	1	—	1	—	—	—	—	5	7
Ellis, G.	London	1797	Architecture	—	—	1	—	—	—	—	—	—	—	1
Ellis, H.	London	1820-1823	Architecture	—	—	2	—	—	—	—	—	—	—	2
Ellis, H.	London	1851	Landscape	—	—	1	—	—	—	—	—	—	—	1
Ellis, Henry	Brighton	1835	Figures	—	—	—	—	1	—	—	—	—	—	1
Ellis, John	London	1865	Architecture	—	—	1	—	—	—	—	—	—	—	1
Ellis, John	Clovelly	1884	Landscape	—	—	—	—	1	—	—	—	—	—	1
Ellis, Joseph F.	London	1819-1834	Sea Pieces	—	—	2	9	4	—	—	—	—	—	15
Ellis, Paul H.	Handsworth	1883-1891	Thistles	—	—	1	—	7	—	2	—	—	5	15
Ellis, Thomas	London	1842-1856	Flowers	—	—	2	—	1	—	—	—	—	—	3
Ellis, Mrs. T. H.	Tulse Hill	1871	Flowers	—	—	—	—	2	—	—	—	—	—	2
Ellis, Tristram J., A.R.P.E.	London	1868-1893	Landscape	—	—	19	—	2	—	8	25	18	23	95
Ellis, T. J.	London	1872-1877	Rustic	—	—	4	—	25	—	—	—	—	—	29
Ellis, William	London	1780	Engraving	1	—	—	—	—	—	—	—	—	—	1
Ellis, William	Birmingham	1863-1864	Landscape	—	—	—	—	2	—	—	—	—	—	2
Ellison, Miss Edith	Windsor	1884-1890	Portraits	—	—	5	—	—	—	—	2	—	1	8
Ellson, John	London	1833-1852	Animals	—	—	—	1	2	—	—	—	—	—	3
Elmer, Stephen, A.R.A.	Farnham	1764-1811	Still Life	—	113	117	4	—	—	—	—	—	—	234
Elmer, William	Farnham	1778-1799	Still Life	19	—	6	—	—	—	—	—	—	—	25
Elmes, H. J.	London	1803-1805	Architecture	—	—	5	—	—	—	—	—	—	—	5
Elmes, Harvey Lonsdale	London	1837-1853	Architecture	—	—	8	—	—	—	—	—	—	—	8
Elmes, James, R.H.A., M.R.I.A.	—	1801-1842	Architecture	—	—	36	—	—	—	—	—	—	—	36
Elmes, W.	London	1797	Architecture	—	—	1	—	—	—	—	—	—	—	1
Elmore, Alfred W., R.A.	London	1834-1880	Historical	—	—	72	10	10	—	—	—	—	3	95
Elmore, Miss Edith	London	1877-1887	Flowers	—	—	11	—	4	—	—	—	—	7	22
Elmore, Miss Fanny	Tunb'dge Wells	1861	Fruit	—	—	—	—	1	—	—	—	—	—	1
Elmore, Frances Mary	London	1872	Fruit	—	—	—	—	—	—	—	—	—	1	1
Elmore, Richard	Croydon	1852-1885	Landscape	—	—	2	11	5	—	—	—	—	4	22
Elmore, T. J.	London	1848-1849	Landscape	—	—	2	—	—	—	—	—	—	—	2
Elmore, T. W.	Tunb'dge Wells	1863	Landscape	—	—	1	—	—	—	—	—	—	—	1
Elmslie, E. W. *See also* Cope, Eales, & Elmslie	London	1841-1862	Architecture	—	—	4	—	—	—	—	—	—	—	4
Elouis, H.	London	1785-1787	Miniatures	—	—	16	—	—	—	—	—	—	—	16
Elphinstone, Archibald H.	London	1893	Clouds	—	—	—	—	1	—	—	—	1	1	3
Elphinstone, D.	London	1833	Landscape	—	—	—	—	1	—	—	—	—	—	1
Elrington, H. H.	London	1848	Ruins	—	—	1	—	—	—	—	—	—	—	1
Elsam, R.	London	1794-1807	Architecture	—	—	20	—	—	—	—	—	—	—	20
Elsley, Arthur John	London	1878-1893	Animals	—	—	19	—	4	—	—	—	—	14	37
Elsley, J.	—	1845	Animals	—	—	—	1	—	—	—	—	—	—	1
Elson, Robert	London	1878-1884	Copies	—	—	—	—	—	—	2	—	—	1	3
Elton, A. H.	Bristol	1852	Landscape	—	—	1	—	—	—	—	—	—	—	1
Elton, E. E.	London	1810-1815	Scriptural	—	—	1	2	—	—	—	—	—	—	3
Elton, Miss K.	Clifton	1872	Figures	—	—	—	—	1	—	—	—	—	—	1
Elton, Samuel J.	Durham	1860-1884	Landscape	—	—	2	—	2	—	—	—	—	2	6
Elton, T. M.	London	1837	Architecture	—	—	1	—	—	—	—	—	—	—	1
Elven, J. P.	London	1788-1791	Domestic	—	—	4	—	—	—	—	—	—	—	4
Elven, Van. *See* V.	—	—	—	—	—	—	—	—	—	—	—	—	—	—
Elvery, J.	—	1762	Portraits	—	3	—	—	—	—	—	—	—	—	3
Elwell, Frank E.	Cambridge, U.S.A.	1885	Sculpture	—	—	1	—	—	—	—	—	—	—	1
Elwes, Alfred Thomas	London	1874-1877	Animals	—	—	—	—	—	—	—	—	—	5	5
Elwes, F. C.	London	1871	Landscape	—	—	—	—	1	—	—	—	—	—	1
Elwes, R.	Congham	1861-1871	Landscape	—	—	—	1	1	—	—	—	—	—	2
Elwin, Mrs. Emma	Staines	1879	Still Life	—	—	2	—	—	—	—	—	—	—	2

Name.	Town.	First and Last Year of Ex.	Speciality.	S. A.	F. S.	R. A.	B. I.	S. S.	O. W.	N.W.	G. G.	N. G.	V. E.	Total.
Elwin, Fountain	London	1887	Sculpture	—	—	1	—	—	—	—	—	—	—	1
Ely, John. *See also* Salomons and Ely	Manchester	1893	Architecture	—	—	1	—	—	—	—	—	—	—	1
Emanuel —. *See* Davis and Emanuel	—	—	Architecture	—	—	—	—	—	—	—	—	—	—	—
Emanuel, Frank Lewis	London	1888-1893	Domestic	—	—	5	—	2	—	—	—	—	3	10
Embe, Von der K. *See* V.	—	—	—	—	—	—	—	—	—	—	—	—	—	—
Emden, William	London	1875	Architecture	—	—	1	—	—	—	—	—	—	—	1
Emdin, G.	London	1817-1818	Portraits	—	—	2	—	—	—	—	—	—	—	2
Emeris, Miss Frances	Gloucester	1889	Figures	—	—	—	—	—	—	1	—	—	—	1
Emerson, C. E.	London	1866-1881	Landscape	—	—	4	—	1	—	—	—	—	10	15
Emerson, William	Blackheath	1817-1843	Figures	—	—	28	3	—	—	—	—	—	—	31
Emerson, William	London	1870-1893	Indian Landscape	—	—	21	—	—	—	—	—	—	—	21
Emery, J.	London	1801-1817	Sea Pieces	—	—	19	—	—	—	—	—	—	—	19
Emery, J.	London	1849-1865	Figures	—	—	5	—	—	—	—	—	—	—	5
Emery, R.	—	1834	Domestic	—	—	—	1	—	—	—	—	—	—	1
Emes, John	London	1790-1791	Landscape	—	—	8	—	—	—	—	—	—	—	8
Emlyn, Henry, F.S.A.	Windsor	1785-1800	Architecture	—	—	2	—	—	—	—	—	—	—	2
Emmaure, Miss J.	London	1873	Landscape	—	—	—	—	—	—	—	—	—	1	1
Emmerson, Henry H.	Chester-le-Str't	1851-1893	Domestic	—	—	54	—	—	—	—	—	—	4	58
Emmerson, W. H.	Leicester	1859-1863	Domestic	—	—	—	2	3	—	—	—	—	—	5
Emmett, Captain	—	1852	Sculpture	—	—	1	—	—	—	—	—	—	—	1
Emmett, John Thomas	London	1846	Architecture	—	—	1	—	—	—	—	—	—	—	1
Emms, John	London	1866-1889	Domestic	—	—	20	1	51	—	3	1	—	12	88
Empson, J. F.	—	1820	Medals	—	—	1	—	—	—	—	—	—	—	1
Emptmeyer, Clement, *or* Clemens	London	1883-1888	Sculpture	—	—	3	—	—	—	—	—	—	—	3
Emslie, Alfred Edward, A.R.W.S. †	London	1867-1893	Domestic	—	—	56	—	25	19	6	16	7	55	184
Emslie, Mrs. A. E. (Rosalie M.)	London	1888-1893	Domestic	—	—	6	—	—	—	2	1	4	1	14
Emslie, John Phillipps	London	1869-1885	Domestic	—	—	2	—	32	—	1	2	—	18	55
Encke, Professor Erdmann	—	1878	Portraits	—	—	—	—	—	—	—	1	—	—	1
Enderby, Sam. G.	London	1886-1891	Domestic	—	—	2	—	—	—	—	—	—	—	2
Enfield, Henry	Nottingham	1872-1893	Landscape	—	—	9	—	2	—	—	—	—	4	15
Enfield, Miss Mary P.	Nottingham	1892-1893	Miniatures	—	—	3	—	—	—	—	—	—	—	3
Engel, J.	London	1840-1847	Sculpture	—	—	8	—	—	—	—	—	—	—	8
Engel, Joseph	London	1888	Sculpture	—	—	3	—	—	—	—	—	—	—	3
Engelhart, Miss Catherine. *See* Mrs. Amyot.	—	—	—	—	—	—	—	—	—	—	—	—	—	—
England, J.	London	1790-1794	Architecture	—	—	6	—	—	—	—	—	—	—	6
England, J.	London	1831	Moonlight	—	—	—	1	—	—	—	—	—	—	1
England, W.	London	1874	Figures	—	—	—	—	1	—	—	—	—	—	1
Englefield, Arthur	St. Albans	1891-1893	Domestic	—	—	1	—	—	—	1	—	—	1	3
Englefield, Sir H., Bart.	—	1787-1789	Landscape	—	—	3	—	—	—	—	—	—	—	3
Engleheart, Francis §	London	1824-1828	Engraving	—	—	—	—	6	—	—	—	—	—	6
Engleheart, George	Kew	1773-1812	Miniatures	—	—	85	—	—	—	—	—	—	—	85
Engleheart, J.	Richmond	1783	Sculpture	—	—	1	—	—	—	—	—	—	—	1
Engleheart, J. D.	London	1801-1828	Miniatures	—	—	157	2	—	—	—	—	—	—	159
Engleheart, Thomas	London	1773-1786	Sculpture	—	—	21	—	—	—	—	—	—	—	21
Engleheart, William F. S.	London	1801	Portraits	—	—	1	—	—	—	—	—	—	—	1
Enoch, G.	London	1850-1852	Architecture	—	—	3	—	—	—	—	—	—	—	3
Enock, Arthur Henry	Birmingham	1882-1893	Landscape	—	—	—	—	—	—	5	—	—	1	6
Ensom, William	London	1825-1831	Engraving	—	—	—	—	6	—	—	—	—	—	6
Ensor, Mrs. Henry (Mary)	Birkenhead	1871-1874	Flowers	—	—	—	—	7	—	—	—	—	—	7
Enthoven, Miss Julia	Sydenham	1889	Flowers	—	—	1	—	—	—	—	—	—	—	1
Epinay, D'. *See* D.	—	—	—	—	—	—	—	—	—	—	—	—	—	—
Epinette, Mdlle.	London	1881	Miniatures	—	—	1	—	—	—	—	—	—	—	1
Epps, E.	London	1874-1880	Landscape	—	—	—	—	1	—	—	—	—	6	7
Epps, Miss Laura T. *See* Mrs. Alma-Tadema.	—	—	—	—	—	—	—	—	—	—	—	—	—	—
Epps, N.	Birkenhead	1872-1874	Domestic	—	—	2	—	—	—	—	—	—	1	3
Epps, Miss Nellie. *See* Mrs. Edmund Gosse.	—	—	—	—	—	—	—	—	—	—	—	—	—	—
Ercoli, Signor Alcide Carlo	London	1857-1866	Portraits	—	—	11	—	—	—	—	—	—	—	11
Eric, F.	London	1863-1864	Domestic	—	—	—	1	2	—	—	—	—	—	3
Erichsen, Miss Nelly	Tooting	1882-1893	Domestic	—	—	11	—	3	—	—	—	—	2	16
Erlam, J.	London	1825-1828	Architecture	—	—	2	—	—	—	—	—	—	—	2
Erlam, J. S.	London	1842	Architecture	—	—	1	—	—	—	—	—	—	—	1
Erlam, S. B.	London	1815-1817	Architecture	—	—	2	—	—	—	—	—	—	2	4
Errington, Miss J.	North Shields	1846	Domestic	—	—	—	—	2	—	—	—	—	—	2
Erskine, Miss Edith E.	London	1886-1887	Flowers	—	—	2	—	—	—	—	—	—	—	2
Erskine, W. C. C.	Edinburgh	1879	Landscape	—	—	1	—	—	—	—	—	—	—	1
Erwood, A.	London	1860-1869	Domestic	—	—	9	—	2	—	—	—	—	—	11
Escarzena, J. M.	London	1841-1848	Buildings	—	—	2	1	—	—	—	—	—	—	3
Eschke, H.	London	1869-1885	Landscape	—	—	1	—	1	—	—	—	—	—	2
Eschke, Professor Richard	Berlin	1884-1889	Landscape	—	—	2	—	1	—	—	—	—	1	4
Escombe, Miss Anne	Guildford	1869-1875	Landscape	—	—	3	—	—	—	—	—	—	3	6
Escombe, Miss Jane	Guildford	1869-1887	Domestic	—	—	3	—	—	—	—	—	—	13	16
Escosura, Leon Y.	Paris	1870-1882	Figures	—	—	2	—	—	—	—	—	—	—	2

Name.	Town.	First and Last Year of Ex.	Speciality.	S. A.	F. S.	R. A.	B. I.	S. S.	O. W.	N. W.	G. G.	N. G.	V. E.	Total.
Essex, Charles	London	1847-1853	Sculpture	—	—	9	—	—	—	—	—	—	—	9
Essex, Miss Hannah, afterwards Mrs. Bird	London	1854-1856	Enamels	—	—	2	2	—	—	—	—	—	—	4
Essex, James	Cambridge	1764	Architecture	1	—	—	—	—	—	—	—	—	—	1
Essex, Richard Hamilton †	London	1823-1853	Churches	—	—	12	—	2	71	—	—	—	—	85
Essex, R. N.	—	1832	Portraits	—	—	1	—	—	—	—	—	—	—	1
Essex, Thomas R.	London	1888-1893	Sculpture	—	—	7	—	—	—	—	—	—	—	7
Essex, William	London	1818-1864	Enamels	—	—	109	20	17	2	—	—	—	—	148
Essex, William B.	London	1845-1851	Miniatures	—	—	10	1	3	—	—	—	—	—	14
Estall, William Charles	Manchester	1874-1892	Landscape	—	—	3	—	12	—	1	2	—	11	29
Estcourt, Miss F. J.	Bushey	1892	Figures	—	—	—	—	—	—	—	—	—	1	1
Estridge, Rev. Loraine	—	1891	Landscape	—	—	—	—	—	—	—	—	3	—	3
Ethelson, Edmund	London	1890	Domestic	—	—	—	—	1	—	—	—	—	—	1
Etherington, Miss Lilian M.	London	1884-1892	Domestic	—	—	3	—	2	—	—	—	—	1	6
Ethofer, T.	London	1877	Rome	—	—	1	—	—	—	—	—	—	—	1
Ethridge, H. A.	London	1882	Landscape	—	—	—	—	1	—	—	—	—	—	1
Etty, William, R.A.	London	1811-1850	Mythological	—	—	138	78	1	—	—	—	—	1	218
Etwards —	London	1825	Landscape	—	—	—	—	5	—	—	—	—	—	5
Euseby, L.	London	1813	Scriptural	—	—	1	—	—	—	—	—	—	—	1
Evans —	Wales	1774	Game	—	1	—	—	—	—	—	—	—	—	1
Evans, Amy	Sydenham	1880	Flowers	—	—	—	—	1	—	—	—	—	—	1
Evans, Bernard, R.I., R.B.A. ‡ §	London	1871-1893	Landscape	—	—	13	—	68	—	10	—	—	3	94
Evans, Mrs. Bernard	London	1888-1889	Rustic	—	—	—	—	2	—	—	—	—	—	2
Evans, Edmund	Witley	1868-1880	Etching	—	—	3	—	—	—	—	—	—	5	8
Evans, Edward	London	1857-1872	Landscape	—	—	—	—	11	—	—	—	—	1	12
Evans, E. H.	Taunton	1838-1839	Still Life	—	—	2	—	—	—	—	—	—	—	2
Evans, Edmund William	London	1879-1893	Landscape	—	—	8	—	5	—	—	—	—	—	13
Evans, Fred. M.	London	1886-1893	Domestic	—	—	4	—	—	—	11	—	—	—	15
Evans, Mrs. F. M.	London	1870-1881	Fruit	—	—	—	—	1	—	—	—	—	7	8
Evans, G.	London	1795-1796	Landscape	—	—	2	—	—	—	—	—	—	—	2
Evans, George	London	1762-1764	Domestic	2	—	—	—	—	—	—	—	—	—	2
Evans, G.	London	1842	Portraits	—	—	1	—	—	—	—	—	—	—	1
Evans, G. H.	London	1840	Portraits	—	—	—	—	1	—	—	—	—	—	1
Evans, Herbert Davies	London	1883-1894	Flowers	—	—	—	—	3	—	—	—	—	—	3
Evans, Herbert E.	London	1893	Fruit	—	—	1	—	—	—	—	—	—	—	1
Evans, Helena M.	Carmarthen	1891-1893	Flowers	—	—	—	—	1	—	4	—	—	—	5
Evans, John	London	1849-1891	Landscape	—	—	1	—	18	—	16	—	—	20	55
Evans, J. W.	London	1874	Domestic	—	—	—	—	1	—	—	—	—	—	1
Evans, Miss Kate	Norwood	1884	Flowers	—	—	1	—	—	—	—	—	—	—	1
Evans, Miss Lena M.	London	1890	Flowers	—	—	—	—	1	—	—	—	—	—	1
Evans, Miss Marjorie, R.S.W.	Richmond	1892	Flowers	—	—	1	—	—	—	—	—	—	1	2
Evans, M. E.	Winchester	1885	Sea Pieces	—	—	—	—	1	—	—	—	—	—	1
Evans, Richard	London	1816-1856	Historical	—	—	42	6	—	—	—	—	—	—	48
Evans, Samuel, T. G., A.R.W.S. †	Eton	1854-1893	Landscape	—	—	7	—	—	228	—	—	—	—	235
Evans, Dr. Sebastian	Dulwich	1878-1881	Domestic	—	—	1	—	—	—	—	—	—	1	2
Evans, T.	London	1821-1824	Architecture	—	—	2	—	—	—	—	—	—	—	2
Evans, Wilfrid	Hornsey	1880-1890	Churches	—	—	—	—	9	—	—	—	—	3	12
Evans, William	London	1797-1808	Portraits	—	—	19	1	—	—	—	—	—	—	20
Evans, William, of Eton †	Eton	1828-1873	Landscape	—	—	—	—	—	264	—	—	—	—	264
Evans, William, of Bristol †	London	1844-1859	Landscape	—	—	—	—	2	47	—	—	—	—	49
Evans, William Charles	London	1886	Architecture	—	—	1	—	—	—	—	—	—	—	1
Evans, William E.	London	1889-1893	Domestic	—	—	2	—	1	—	—	—	—	—	3
Evans, Wilfrid Muir	Bushey	1888-1890	Portraits	—	—	3	—	—	—	—	—	1	—	4
Evans, W. R.	Kingsland, Hereford	1836	Landscape	—	—	2	—	—	—	—	—	—	—	2
Evans, Miss	—	1786-1787	Portraits	—	—	2	—	—	—	—	—	—	—	2
Evans, Miss	—	1822-1823	Figures	—	—	2	—	—	—	—	—	—	—	2
Evatt, Miss	Wandsworth	1830	Portraits	—	—	1	—	—	—	—	—	—	—	1
Eve, George W., A.R.P.E.	London	1892-1893	Book-plates	—	—	2	—	—	—	—	—	—	—	2
Evelyn, Miss Edith M. (Miss Evelyn Lucas)	London	1886-1893	Portraits	—	—	5	—	—	—	—	—	—	5	10
Eveque, L'. *See* L.	—	—	—	—	—	—	—	—	—	—	—	—	—	—
Everdingen —	—	1782	Landscape	—	1	—	—	—	—	—	—	—	—	1
Everdingen, A. Van. *See* V.	—	—	—	—	—	—	—	—	—	—	—	—	—	—
Everett, Edwin W.	Tatton	1880-1884	Rustic	—	—	—	—	6	—	1	—	—	—	7
Everett, Frederic	Erith	1882-1890	Landscape	—	—	2	—	1	—	—	—	—	—	3
Everett, Miss Minnie. *See* Mrs. Cormack	—	—	—	—	—	—	—	—	—	—	—	—	—	—
Everett, Miss	—	1802	Landscape	—	—	1	—	—	—	—	—	—	—	1
Everitt, Allan E.	Birmingham	1853-1858	Buildings	—	—	7	—	—	—	—	—	—	—	7
Everitt, Edward	Birmingham	1819-1865	Landscape	—	—	6	1	22	5	2	—	—	—	36
Evershed, Dr. Arthur, A.R.P.E.	Billinghurst	1855-1892	Landscape	—	—	35	1	19	—	2	—	—	40	97
Every, George H.	London	1864-1891	Engraving	—	—	11	—	—	—	—	—	—	—	11
Evey —	—	1863	Sculpture	—	—	1	—	—	—	—	—	—	—	1
Eyre, St. *See* S.	—	—	—	—	—	—	—	—	—	—	—	—	—	—
Ewart, W.	London	1846-1863	Portraits	—	—	4	5	—	—	—	—	—	—	9

Name.	Town.	First and Last Year of Ex.	Speciality.	S. A.	F. S.	R. A.	B. I.	S. S.	O. W.	N.W.	G. G.	N. G.	V. E.	Total.
Ewbank, John Wilson, R.S.A.	London	1832	Sea Pieces	—	—	2	—	—	—	—	—	—	—	2
Ewbank, T. John, R.S.A.	Edinburgh	1826-1862	Rustic	—	—	1	1	7	—	—	—	—	3	12
Ewin, C.	London	1827	Landscape	—	—	—	1	—	—	—	—	—	—	1
Ewing, George Edwin	Glasgow	1862-1877	Sculpture	—	—	45	—	—	—	—	—	—	—	45
Ewing, W.	London	1822	Ivory Carving	—	—	4	—	—	—	—	—	—	—	4
Exshaw, Charles	London	1764	Landscape	3	—	—	—	—	—	—	—	—	—	3
Eycken, Van. *See* V.	—	—	—	—	—	—	—	—	—	—	—	—	—	—
Eyles, Charles	London	1881-1891	Landscape	—	—	8	—	9	—	—	—	—	3	20
Eyre, Lady Alice	London	1886	Figures	—	—	—	—	—	—	—	2	—	—	2
Eyre, Edward	—	1771-1786	Landscape	—	—	15	—	—	—	—	—	—	—	15
Eyre, James	Derby	1835-1837	Landscape	—	—	—	5	4	—	—	—	—	—	9
Eyre, John	London	1877-1893	Domestic	—	—	8	—	14	—	5	—	—	—	27
Eyres, John W.	Walton-on-Thames	1887-1889	Landscape	—	—	5	—	—	—	—	—	—	—	5
Ezdorff, J. C.	London	1834-1835	Landscape	—	—	7	3	—	—	—	—	—	—	10
Ezekiel, M.	Rome	1889	Portraits	—	—	1	—	—	—	—	—	—	—	1
Fabbrucci, Aristide	London	1880-1885	Sculpture	—	—	8	—	—	—	—	—	—	—	8
Fabbrucci, L.	London	1872-1884	Sculpture	—	—	8	—	—	—	—	—	—	—	8
Fabeck, La Baronne de	London	1834-1835	Portraits	—	—	2	—	—	—	—	—	—	—	2
Fabian —	—	1762	Miniatures	2	—	—	—	—	—	—	—	—	—	2
Fabian, Ernest	London	1889	Sculpture	—	—	1	—	—	—	—	—	—	—	1
Fabj-Altini, Professor F.	Rome	1881	Sculpture	—	—	1	—	—	—	—	—	—	—	1
Fabri, Aloisia	Naples	1875	Figures	—	—	1	—	—	—	—	—	—	—	1
Fabri-Altini. *See* A.	—	—	—	—	—	—	—	—	—	—	—	—	—	—
Fabris —	Naples	1768-1772	Landscape	2	1	—	—	—	—	—	—	—	—	3
Fabruzzi, Signor	—	1880	Sculpture	—	—	—	—	—	—	—	1	—	—	1
Facius, George Sigmund	London	1785-1788	Miniatures	—	—	5	—	—	—	—	—	—	—	5
Facon, E.	London	1846	Landscape	—	—	1	—	—	—	—	—	—	—	1
Faed, H.	—	1875	Figures	—	—	1	—	—	—	—	—	—	—	1
Faed, James	Edinburgh	1855-1893	Engraving	—	—	29	—	—	—	—	—	—	—	29
Faed, James, Junr.	Edinburgh	1880-1893	Animals	—	—	6	—	—	—	—	—	—	—	6
Faed, John, R.S.A.	Edinburgh	1855-1893	Domestic	—	—	40	—	3	—	—	—	—	—	43
Faed, John Francis	London	1882-1892	Sea Pieces	—	—	8	—	3	—	—	—	—	—	11
Faed, Miss S.	Gatehouse	1866-1868	Figures	—	—	3	—	—	—	—	—	—	—	3
Faed, Thomas, R.A., H.R.S.A. §	London	1851-1893	Domestic	—	—	98	—	1	—	—	—	—	—	99
Faed, William C.	Edinburgh	1881-1889	Domestic	—	—	3	—	2	—	—	—	—	—	5
Fagan, Louis Alexander	London	1872-1887	Etching	—	—	4	—	—	—	—	—	—	2	6
Fagan, Robert	Rome	1793-1816	Portraits	—	—	4	—	—	—	—	—	—	—	4
Fagan, William B.	London	1887	Heads	—	—	1	—	—	—	—	—	—	—	1
Fagen, O'. *See* O.	—	—	—	—	—	—	—	—	—	—	—	—	—	—
Fagerlin, Ferdinand J.	Stockholm	1869-1882	Domestic	—	—	6	—	—	—	—	—	—	—	6
Fagnani, Miss Nina	Paris	1892	Miniatures	—	—	1	—	—	—	—	—	—	—	1
Fahey, Edward Henry, R.I. ‡ φ	London	1863-1893	Landscape	—	—	38	—	7	—	127	12	9	53	246
Fahey, James, R.I. ‡	London	1825-1886	Landscape	—	—	16	3	5	—	485	—	—	—	509
Fahey, Miss Palacia Emma, afterwards Mrs. Alabaster	London	1864	Landscape	—	—	—	—	1	—	—	—	—	3	4
Faija, Guglielmo	London	1838-1848	Portraits	—	—	17	—	1	—	—	—	—	—	18
Fairbairn, Miss Hilda	Henley	1893	Domestic	—	—	—	—	—	—	—	—	—	2	2
Fairbairn, Thomas, R.S.W.	Hamilton, N.B.	1865-1877	Landscape	—	—	—	—	7	—	—	—	—	3	10
Fairbone, J.	London	1794-1798	Figures	—	—	18	—	—	—	—	—	—	—	18
Fairer, Charles G.	London	1872-1876	Flowers	—	—	—	—	—	—	—	—	—	3	3
Fairfax, A.	Manchester	1881	Portraits	—	—	—	—	—	—	—	1	—	—	1
Fairlam, Miss Eleanor. *See* Mrs. J. W. Brown	—	—	—	—	—	—	—	—	—	—	—	—	—	—
Fairland, Thomas	—	1828-1833	Lithographs	—	—	—	—	6	—	—	—	—	—	6
Fairland, W.	London	1828	Engraving	—	—	—	—	2	—	—	—	—	—	2
Fairless, Thomas Kerr	London	1848-1853	Landscape	—	—	4	5	7	—	—	—	—	6	22
Fairlie, John	—	1845	Landscape	—	—	1	—	—	—	—	—	—	—	1
Fairlie, William J.	Carlisle	1853-1865	Landscape	—	—	4	—	—	—	—	—	—	—	4
Fairman, Miss Frances C. ‖	London	1865-1893	Animals	—	—	—	—	1	—	—	—	—	16	17
Falcon, Miss Maud	London	1888-1890	Flowers	—	—	—	—	—	—	—	2	—	—	2
Falconer, Pierre Etienne	London	1767-1773	Portraits	35	—	4	—	—	—	—	—	—	—	39
Falconet, Miss C.	London	1812	Study	—	—	—	1	—	—	—	—	—	—	1
Faldonburn, P.	London	1857	—	—	—	—	—	—	—	—	—	—	*	—
Falero, Luis	London	1888-1893	Figures	—	—	8	—	—	—	—	—	—	3	11
Falkener, Edward	London	1840-1873	Oriental B'ld'gs	—	—	36	—	—	—	—	—	—	—	36
Falkner, Miss Annie L.	Bedford	1893	Landscape	—	—	—	—	1	—	—	—	—	—	1
Fall, Miss E. M.	London	1855-1856	Landscape	—	—	—	1	2	—	—	—	—	—	3
Fallon, A. D.	—	1828	Portraits	—	—	2	—	—	—	—	—	—	—	2
Fallon, Robert T.	London	1882	Sculpture	—	—	1	—	—	—	—	—	—	—	1

Name.	Town.	First and Last Year of Ex.	Speciality.	S. A.	F. S.	R. A.	B. I.	S. S.	O.W.	N.W.	G. G.	N. G.	V. E.	Total.
Fallon, Sara W. M.	Croydon	1888-1893	Domestic	—	—	—	—	4	—	—	—	—	—	4
Fallon, W. A.	London	1839-1840	Portraits	—	—	2	—	—	—	—	—	—	—	2
Falls, R.	London	1893	Sea Pieces	—	—	—	—	1	—	—	—	1	—	2
Fancourt, E.	London	1820-1821	Portraits	—	—	2	—	—	—	—	—	—	—	2
Fane —	London	1776	Miniatures	—	—	1	—	—	—	—	—	—	—	1
Fane, General Walter, C.B.	London	1859-1884	Temples	—	—	—	—	3	—	2	—	—	1	6
Fanneaux, Mdlle. Felicie de	Florence	1838	Sculpture	—	—	1	—	—	—	—	—	—	—	1
Fanner, Henry George	London	1854-1884	Portraits	—	—	24	—	14	—	—	—	—	7	45
Fantacchiotti, Cesare	Florence	1879-1880	Sculpture	—	—	3	—	—	—	—	—	—	—	3
Fantelli, Domenice	Rome	1778	Venus	—	1	—	—	—	—	—	—	—	—	1
Fantin-Latour, Henri. φ *See* Latour	Paris	1862-1893	Flowers	—	—	65	—	3	—	—	15	—	86	169
Fargues, Mrs.	London	1845-1852	Landscape	—	—	1	—	4	—	—	—	—	—	5
Farhill, Miss Emma	—	1801-1804	Domestic	—	—	6	—	—	—	—	—	—	—	6
Farington, George	London	1773-1782	Portraits	—	—	4	—	—	—	—	—	—	—	4
Farington, Joseph, R.A., F.S.A.	London	1765-1813	Landscape	27	—	83	—	—	—	—	—	—	—	110
Farmer, Mrs. A.	Porchester	1855-1867	Fruit	—	—	11	2	9	—	—	—	—	—	22
Farmer, Corrall	New Billingh'm	1893	Landscape	—	—	—	—	—	—	—	—	—	1	1
Farmer, Miss Emily, R.I.‡	London	1847-1892	Domestic	—	—	3	—	—	—	83	—	—	—	86
Farmer, Miss Fanny	Porchester	1857	Landscape	—	—	—	—	1	—	—	—	—	—	1
Farmer, F. W.	London	1866	Portraits	—	—	—	—	2	—	—	—	—	—	2
Farmer, G. W.	London	1865-1878	Landscape	—	—	—	1	6	—	—	—	—	—	7
Farmer, Henry	London	1865	Figures	—	—	—	—	—	—	—	—	—	1	1
Farmer, Miss Mary	Poole	1886	Landscape	—	—	—	—	—	—	—	—	—	1	1
Farmer, P. J.	London	1826-1827	Sculpture	—	—	1	—	1	—	—	—	—	—	2
Farmiage, W.	London	1808	Architecture	—	—	1	—	—	—	—	—	—	—	1
Farmworth, I.	—	1797	Figures	—	—	1	—	—	—	—	—	—	—	1
Farn, J.	London	1790	Figures	1	—	—	—	—	—	—	—	—	—	1
Farnborough, Lady. *See* Mrs. Charles Long	—	—	—	—	—	—	—	—	—	—	—	—	—	—
and Miss Amelia Hume.	—	—	—	—	—	—	—	—	—	—	—	—	—	—
Farquhar, C.	London	1791-1799	Architecture	—	—	5	—	—	—	—	—	—	—	5
Farquhar, L.	London	1867-1871	Portraits	—	—	3	—	—	—	—	—	—	—	3
Farquhar, R. T.	Grasmere	1873-1874	Landscape	—	—	—	—	3	—	—	—	—	1	4
Farquharson, David, A.R.S.A., R.S.W.	Edinburgh	1877-1893	Rustic	—	—	18	—	1	—	—	—	—	3	22
Farquharson, Joseph φ	Edinburgh	1873-1893	Domestic	—	—	37	—	—	—	—	3	—	19	59
Farr, Miss Henrietta	Bickley	1877-1879	Figures	—	—	—	—	4	—	—	—	—	1	5
Farran, Miss Lulu	London	1887-1892	Portraits	—	—	1	—	—	—	4	—	—	—	5
Farran, Thomas	London	1881	Domestic	—	—	1	—	—	—	—	—	—	—	1
Farrell, James, A.R.H.A.	Dublin	1843-1869	Sculpture	—	—	5	—	—	—	—	—	—	—	5
Farrell, Thomas, P.R.H.A.	Dublin	1858-1888	Sculpture	—	—	3	—	—	—	—	—	—	—	3
Farren, Miss Jessie	Scarborough	1886-1893	Miniatures	—	—	2	—	—	—	—	—	—	—	2
Farren, Robert	Cambridge	1868-1880	Figures	—	—	15	—	4	—	—	—	—	9	28
Farren, Robert	Scarborough	1889	York	—	—	1	—	—	—	—	—	—	—	1
Farrer, T.	London	1805-1825	Portraits	—	—	8	—	—	—	—	—	—	—	8
Farrer, Thomas Charles	London	1872-1891	Landscape	—	—	9	—	9	—	—	25	8	22	73
Farrier, Miss Charlotte	London	1826-1875	Portraits	—	—	81	1	25	—	—	—	—	—	107
Farrier, Robert	London	1818-1872	Domestic	—	—	35	50	32	—	4	—	—	—	121
Farrow, William John	London	1890-1893	Domestic	—	—	—	—	3	—	—	—	—	6	9
Farwell, Miss B. A.	St. Martin	1856-1861	Domestic	—	—	4	1	—	—	—	—	—	—	5
Fattori, Giovanni	London	1879	Figures	—	—	—	—	—	—	—	—	—	1	1
Faucigny —	London	1797	Miniatures	—	—	5	—	—	—	—	—	—	—	5
Faulkner, Benjamin Rawlinson	London	1821-1862	Portraits	—	—	64	8	32	—	—	—	—	—	104
Faulkner, C.	Fareham	1874	Landscape	—	—	—	—	1	—	—	—	—	—	1
Faulkner, J.	Lincoln	1829-1833	Churches	—	—	—	1	3	—	—	—	—	—	4
Faulkner, John	London	1858	Sea Pieces	—	—	—	—	1	—	—	—	—	—	1
Faulkner, J., R.H.A.	Dublin	1865	Deer	—	—	1	—	—	—	—	—	—	—	1
Faulkner, John	London	1884-1890	Landscape	—	—	4	—	2	—	1	—	—	—	7
Faulkner, Joshua Wilson	Manchester	1809-1820	Portraits	—	—	20	—	—	—	—	—	—	—	20
Faulkner, Miss Mary	London	1838-1842	Figures	—	—	5	1	1	—	—	—	—	—	7
Faulkner, Miss Nina	London	1892	Miniatures	—	—	1	—	—	—	—	—	—	—	1
Faulkner, Robert	—	1847-1849	Portraits	—	—	1	—	2	—	—	—	—	—	3
Faulkner, T.	London	1825-1833	Architecture	—	—	3	—	—	—	—	—	—	—	3
Faunce, Mrs.	London	1870-1875	Landscape	—	—	—	—	1	—	—	—	—	2	3
Fauner, H.	London	1834	Game	—	—	—	—	1	—	—	—	—	—	1
Faunthorpe, Mrs.	Wandsworth	1874	Flowers	—	—	—	—	—	—	—	—	—	2	2
Fauntleroy, Miss C. S.	Northcombe	1881	Flowers	—	—	—	—	1	—	—	—	—	—	1
Fauvelle, H.	London	1877	Architecture	—	—	1	—	—	—	—	—	—	—	1
Favard, Ville	London	1794-1797	Miniatures	—	—	5	—	—	—	—	—	—	—	5
Favier —	London	1774	Drawings	—	1	—	—	—	—	—	—	—	—	1
Favre —	—	1783	Domestic	—	7	—	—	—	—	—	—	—	—	7
Favretto, G.	London	1886	Landscape	—	—	1	—	—	—	—	—	—	—	1
Fawcett, Miss Emily Addis	London	1883-1890	Sculpture	—	—	9	—	—	—	—	—	—	—	9
Fawcett, William M.	Cambridge	1870-1893	Architecture	—	—	7	—	—	—	—	—	—	—	7

Name.	Town.	First and Last Year of Ex.	Speciality.	S. A.	F. S.	R. A.	B. I.	S. S.	O. W.	N. W.	G. G.	N. G.	V. E.	Total.
FAWINKEL, MAGDALEN VON. *See* V.	—	—	—	—	—	—	—	—	—	—	—	—	—	—
FAYE, F.	—	1837	Landscape	—	—	1	—	—	—	—	—	—	—	1
FAYERMANN, MISS ANNE CHARLOTTE. *See* Mrs. Bartholomew *and* Mrs. Turnbull	London	1826-1827	Figures	—	—	—	3	—	—	—	—	—	—	3
FAYLL, DE. *See* D.	—	—	—	—	—	—	—	—	—	—	—	—	—	—
FEAD, H. J.	London	1862	Landscape	—	—	—	—	1	—	—	—	—	—	1
FEARNLEY, THOMAS	London	1837-1838	Landscape	—	—	2	5	4	—	—	—	—	—	11
FEARNSIDE, J.	—	1793	Landscape	—	—	2	—	—	—	—	—	—	—	2
FEARNSIDE, W.	London	1791-1801	Landscape	—	—	8	—	—	—	—	—	—	—	8
FEARNSMITH, GEORGE	London	1871	Landscape	—	—	—	—	—	—	—	—	—	1	1
FEARSON, J.	—	1786-1789	Scriptural	—	—	4	—	—	—	—	—	—	—	4
FEARY, JOHN	London	1770-1787	Landscape	—	4	25	—	—	—	—	—	—	—	29
FEARY, V.	London	1788	Landscape	—	—	1	—	—	—	—	—	—	—	1
FEENEY, PATRICK M.	London	1879-1889	Landscape	—	—	2	—	—	—	—	—	—	7	9
FEENEY, WILLIAM P.	London	1880-1893	Landscape	—	—	1	—	11	—	—	—	—	—	12
FEHR, HENRY C.	Leytonstone	1887-1893	Sculpture	—	—	8	—	—	—	—	—	—	—	8
FEILLET, MDLLE. H.	Bayonne	1853-1854	Portraits	—	—	3	—	—	—	—	—	—	—	3
FELL, C.	Ambleside	1872	Portraits	—	—	1	—	—	—	—	—	—	—	1
FELL, H. GRANVILLE	London	1892-1893	Domestic	—	—	2	—	—	—	—	—	—	—	2
FELL, W. H.	Sydenham	1878	Landscape	—	—	—	—	1	—	—	—	—	—	1
FELLER, FRANK	London	1878-1887	Military	—	—	2	—	2	—	—	—	—	6	10
FELLOWES, ARTHUR	London	1869	Landscape	—	—	—	—	—	—	—	—	—	1	1
FELLOWES, MISS C. A.	Wolverhampt'n	1867-1872	Sculpture	—	—	15	—	—	—	—	—	—	—	15
FELLOWES-PRYNNE. *See* P.	—	—	—	—	—	—	—	—	—	—	—	—	—	—
FELLOWS, W.	London	1792-1810	Architecture	—	—	4	—	—	—	—	—	—	—	4
FELTON —	London	1769	Flowers	—	1	—	—	—	—	—	—	—	—	1
FELTON, LYDIA M.	London	1890-1891	Domestic	—	—	—	—	4	—	—	—	—	—	4
FENDER, MISS MAGGIE F.	Ayton	1891	Landscape	—	—	2	—	—	—	—	—	—	—	2
FENN, MISS A. S. MANVILLE ‖	Chiswick	1883-1885	Domestic	—	—	—	—	4	—	—	—	—	—	4
FENN, G.	London	1839	Dogs	—	—	1	—	—	—	—	—	—	—	1
FENN, W. W.	London	1848-1880	Landscape	—	—	23	9	14	—	—	—	—	40	86
FENNELL, JOHN GREVILLE	Staines	1851-1874	Landscape	—	—	—	—	9	—	—	—	—	—	9
FENNELL, MISS LOUISA	Wakefield	1876-1882	Buildings	—	—	—	—	11	—	—	—	—	—	11
FENNER, CHARLES	Hampton Wick	1858-1866	Animals	—	—	1	7	—	—	—	—	—	3	11
FENNER, J.	London	1838	Landscape	—	—	1	—	—	—	—	—	—	—	1
FENNESSY, MRS. R. J. (EMILY)	London	1873-1883	Sculpture	—	—	3	—	—	—	—	—	—	2	5
FENOLLERA, J. M.	—	1877	Figures	—	—	—	—	1	—	—	—	—	—	1
FENOULET, W.	London	1836-1839	Landscape	—	—	3	—	—	—	—	—	—	—	3
FENTON, MISS ANNIE GRACE	London	1875-1885	Domestic	—	—	11	—	1	—	—	—	—	4	16
FENTON, ENOS	London	1832-1860	Landscape	—	—	1	1	5	—	—	—	—	—	7
FENTON, EVA R.	London	1876	Domestic	—	—	—	—	—	—	—	—	—	1	1
FENTON, F.	London	1802	Rustic	—	—	1	—	—	—	—	—	—	—	1
FENTON, F.	London	1859	Figures	—	—	—	—	2	—	—	—	—	—	2
FENTON, ROGER	London	1849-1851	Domestic	—	—	3	—	—	—	—	—	—	—	3
FENTON, MISS ROSE M.	London	1877-1885	Domestic	—	—	2	—	—	—	—	—	—	1	3
FERARESI, V.	Sicily	1780	Architecture	—	—	1	—	—	—	—	—	—	—	1
FERGUS, ROBERT	London	1882	Landscape	—	—	—	—	1	—	—	—	—	—	1
FERGUSON, MRS. A. *See* Miss E. Marrable ‖	Kircaldy	1881	Portraits	—	—	—	—	—	—	—	1	—	—	1
FERGUSON, CHARLES J., F.S.A.	Carlisle	1881-1887	Architecture	—	—	16	—	—	—	—	—	—	—	16
FERGUSON, ELEANOR	London	1884	Fruit	—	—	—	—	1	—	—	—	—	—	1
FERGUSON, JANE	London	1882	Domestic	—	—	—	—	—	—	—	—	—	1	1
FERGUSON, JAMES, D.C.L., F.R.S.	London	1850-1864	Architecture	—	—	2	—	—	—	—	—	—	—	2
FERGUSON, JAMES	Edinburgh	1817-1857	Landscape	—	—	10	5	5	—	—	—	—	—	20
FERGUSON, J. KNOX	Edinburgh	1886-1887	Historical	—	—	2	—	—	—	—	—	—	—	2
FERGUSON, JAMES M.	London	1867-1882	Landscape	—	—	7	—	9	—	—	—	—	1	17
FERGUSON, JOHN MANSFIELD	London	1876-1885	Architecture	—	—	6	—	—	—	—	—	—	—	6
FERGUSON, MISS MARION	London	1883-1887	Sculpture	—	—	3	—	—	—	—	—	—	—	3
FERGUSON, T.	—	1820	Landscape	—	—	—	—	—	1	—	—	—	—	1
FERGUSON, T. R.	London	1867	Fruit	—	—	—	—	—	—	—	—	—	1	1
FERGUSON, W.	Edinburgh	1892	Flowers	—	—	1	—	—	—	—	—	—	—	1
FERGUSON, WILLIAM J.	London	1849-1886	Landscape	—	—	21	8	46	—	2	—	—	25	102
FERINI, SIGNOR	Rome	1771	Sculpture	1	—	—	—	—	—	—	—	—	—	1
FERNELEY, C. L.	Melt'n Mowbr'y	1855-1868	Horses	—	—	1	—	—	—	—	—	—	3	4
FERNELEY, C. N.	Melt'n Mowbr'y	1851	Landscape	—	—	1	—	—	—	—	—	—	—	1
FERNELEY, JOHN E.	Melt'n Mowbr'y	1806-1855	Sporting	—	—	22	4	13	—	—	—	—	5	44
FERNELEY, MISS S.	Melt'n Mowbr'y	1829	Game	—	—	—	—	1	—	—	—	—	—	1
FERRARI, GIUSEPPE	Rome	1877-1883	Street Scenes	—	—	2	—	—	—	—	—	—	—	2
FERREIRA, GUSTAVUS ADOLPHUS	Exeter	1845-1856	Landscape	—	—	6	3	2	—	—	—	—	—	11
FERRER, V.	Valencia	1876	Buildings	—	—	—	—	1	—	—	—	—	—	1
FERRERS, WASHINGTON, 5TH EARL, R.N.	—	1775	Ships	—	—	3	—	—	—	—	—	—	—	3
FERRIER, C. A.	London	1869	Engraving	—	—	1	—	—	—	—	—	—	—	1
FERRIER, GEORGE STRATON, R.S.W.	—	1878-1893	Etching	—	—	4	—	—	—	1	—	—	2	7

Name.	Town.	First and Last Year of Ex.	Speciality.	S. A.	F. S.	R. A.	B. I.	S. S.	O. W.	N. W.	G. G.	N. G.	V. E.	Total.
Ferrier, James	Edinburgh	1873	Landscape	—	—	1	—	—	—	—	—	—	—	1
Ferriere, Francis	London	1800-1829	Portraits	—	—	43	3	—	—	—	—	—	—	46
Ferriere, J.	London	1792-1799	Miniatures	—	—	36	—	—	—	—	—	—	—	36
Ferriere, L.	London	1817-1828	Miniatures	—	—	8	—	—	—	—	—	—	—	8
Ferris, E.	London	1875-1889	Landscape	—	—	1	—	12	—	—	—	—	—	13
Ferry, Benjamin. (?) Ferrey	London	1834-1877	Architecture	—	—	23	—	—	—	—	—	—	—	23
Ferry, C. E.	London	1875	River Scenes	—	—	—	—	1	—	—	—	—	—	1
Ferry and Wallen	London	1811	Architecture	—	—	1	—	—	—	—	—	—	—	1
Ferte, M.	—	1810	Flowers	—	—	—	—	—	—	—	—	—	1	1
Few, Mrs. C.	—	1806	Flowers	—	—	1	—	—	—	—	—	—	—	1
Feyen-Perrin. *See* Perrin.	—	—	—	—	—	—	—	—	—	—	—	—	—	—
Feyl, De. *See* D.	—	—	—	—	—	—	—	—	—	—	—	—	—	—
Ffitch, G. S.	London	1839-1847	Figures	—	—	8	3	4	—	—	—	—	—	15
Fichard, Baron de	Baden Baden	1877	Venice	—	—	—	—	—	—	—	—	—	1	1
Ficker —	London	1765	Sculpture	—	1	—	—	—	—	—	—	—	—	1
Ficklin, Alfred	Kingston-on-Thames	1865-1889	Landscape	—	—	—	2	4	—	3	—	—	—	9
Ficklin, George	London	1865-1885	Landscape	—	—	—	1	7	—	1	—	—	—	9
Ficklin, R.	London	1863	Fruit	—	—	—	1	—	—	—	—	—	—	1
Fidler, Gideon M.	Salisbury	1881-1893	Domestic	—	—	1	—	1	—	9	—	—	2	13
Fidler, Harry	Salisbury	1891	Domestic	—	—	5	—	—	—	—	—	—	—	5
Fidler, J.	London	1784-1803	Architecture	—	—	11	—	—	—	—	—	—	—	11
Field, B. C.	—	1820	Dogs	—	—	1	—	—	—	—	—	—	—	1
Field, Edwin	London	1865	Boats	—	—	—	—	—	—	—	—	—	1	1
Field, Miss E. W.	—	1827-1836	Fruit	—	—	4	—	—	—	—	—	—	—	4
Field, Miss Frances A.	Oxford	1882-1889	Flowers	—	—	2	—	3	—	6	—	—	—	11
Field, Freke	Ham	1890-1892	Domestic	—	—	2	—	—	—	—	—	—	—	2
Field, Horace	London	1854-1892	Architecture	—	—	10	—	—	—	—	—	—	—	10
Field, H. C.	London	1811-1836	Sculpture	—	—	11	—	6	—	—	—	—	—	17
Field, Henry William (Last Queen's Assay Master)	—	1822-1827	Medals	—	—	8	—	—	—	—	—	—	—	8
Field, J.	London	1819-1836	Architecture	—	—	9	—	—	—	—	—	—	—	9
Field, John	London	1815-1832	Landscape	—	—	—	—	3	—	1	—	—	1	5
Field, J. M.	London	1800-1856	Landscape	—	—	43	—	—	—	—	—	—	—	43
Field, M.	London	1832	Architecture	—	—	1	—	—	—	—	—	—	—	1
Field, Mrs. Mary F.	London	1869-1893	Domestic	—	—	2	—	1	—	—	—	—	1	4
Field, Miss Nora	London	1889	Landscape	—	—	—	—	—	—	—	—	—	1	1
Field, R.	Halifax, N.S.	1810	Portraits	—	—	1	—	—	—	—	—	—	—	1
Field, Rosa	Leamington	1874-1879	Domestic	—	—	—	—	—	—	—	—	—	3	3
Field, S.	—	1803	Portraits	—	—	1	—	—	—	—	—	—	—	1
Field, Samuel	London	1845	Architecture	—	—	1	—	—	—	—	—	—	—	1
Field, T.	London	1783-1785	Architecture	—	—	3	—	—	—	—	—	—	—	3
Field, W.	—	1838	Architecture	—	—	1	—	—	—	—	—	—	—	1
Field, Walter, A.R.W.S. †	London	1856-1893	Landscape	—	—	41	9	2	149	—	1	—	73	275
Field, Hon. Mrs. §	—	1825-1831	Landscape	—	—	3	—	3	—	—	—	—	—	6
Fielder —	—	1817	Still Life	—	—	1	—	—	—	—	—	—	—	1
Fielder, Henry	Dorking	1872-1885	Landscape	—	—	—	—	29	—	—	—	—	—	29
Fielder, Mrs. J. N.	Boulogne	1857	Domestic	—	—	1	—	—	—	—	—	—	—	1
Fielder, R. W.	Dorking	1877	Buildings	—	—	—	—	1	—	—	—	—	—	1
Fielding, Anthony Copley Vandyke †	London	1810-1855	Landscape	—	—	17	100	1	1671	—	—	—	—	1789
Fielding, Edward	London	1859	Landscape	—	—	—	—	1	—	—	—	—	—	1
Fielding, Miss Eliza M.	London	1848-1856	Figures	—	—	1	2	1	—	—	—	—	—	4
Fielding, F.	London	1826	Cattle	—	—	1	3	—	—	—	—	—	—	4
Fielding, F. F.	London	1808-1810	Landscape	—	—	2	—	—	—	—	—	—	—	2
Fielding, N.	London	1851	Sporting	—	—	—	—	—	—	—	—	—	12	12
Fielding, Nathan Theodore	London	1775-1818	Landscape	4	1	—	3	—	3	—	—	—	—	11
Fielding, Thales Henry Adolphus †	London	1799-1837	Landscape	—	—	19	21	27	88	—	—	—	—	155
Fielding, Mrs. Theodore Henry, late Miss Mary Ann Walton †	—	—	—	—	—	—	—	—	—	—	—	—	—	—
	London	1820-1834	Fruit	—	—	—	1	—	31	—	—	—	—	32
Figgins, Vincent	London	1838-1843	Landscape	—	—	5	1	6	—	—	—	—	—	12
Figgis, T. Phillips	London	1887-1890	Architecture	—	—	4	—	—	—	—	—	—	—	4
Figgis and Wilson	London	1890	Architecture	—	—	1	—	—	—	—	—	—	—	1
Filby, S. H.	London	1864-1865	Sea Pieces	—	—	—	3	—	—	—	—	—	—	3
Fildes, Luke, R.A.	London	1867-1893	Domestic	—	—	41	—	—	—	—	—	—	7	48
Fildes, Mrs. Luke, formerly Miss Fanny Woods	London	1875-1884	Domestic	—	—	3	—	—	—	—	—	—	7	10
Filidei, A.	Eldershaw	1863	Landscape	—	—	1	—	—	—	—	—	—	—	1
Fill, W.	—	1853	Landscape	—	—	—	—	1	—	—	—	—	—	1
Fillans, G.	London	1838-1840	Historical	—	—	2	2	—	—	—	—	—	—	4
Fillans, James	London	1837-1850	Sculpture	—	—	25	1	2	—	—	—	—	—	28
Filliette —	London	1770-1772	Domestic	—	2	—	—	—	—	—	—	—	—	2
Fillonniere, Miss	London	1766-1776	Flowers	—	13	—	—	—	—	—	—	—	—	13
Finberg, Alexander Joseph	Clapton	1888	Historical	—	—	—	—	—	—	1	—	—	—	1
Finch, A. W.	Ostend	1886-1887	Landscape	—	—	—	—	4	—	—	—	—	—	4
Finch, Christopher	London	1764-1766	Portraits	—	2	—	—	—	—	—	—	—	—	2

o

Name.	Town.	First and Last Year of Ex.	Speciality.	S. A.	F. S.	R. A.	B. I.	S. S.	O. W.	N. W.	G. G.	N. G.	V. E.	Total
FINCH, FRANCIS OLIVER †	London	1817-1863	Landscape	—	—	14	—	—	272	—	—	—	—	286
FINCH, R.	London	1795	Portraits	—	—	1	—	—	—	—	—	—	—	1
FINDEN, F.	—	1833	Buildings	—	—	—	—	—	—	1	—	—	—	1
FINDEN, GEORGE C.	London	1871-1880	Engraving	—	—	4	—	—	—	—	—	—	—	4
FINDEN, H.	London	1833	Architecture	—	—	1	—	—	—	—	—	—	—	1
FINDEN, J.	London	1800-1838	Architecture	—	—	5	—	—	—	—	—	—	—	5
FINDEN (T.) AND LEWIS (T. H.)	London	1845	Architecture	—	—	3	—	—	—	—	—	—	—	3
FINDEN, WILLIAM	—	1825-1829	Engraving	—	—	—	—	2	—	—	—	—	—	2
FINDEN AND GREEN	London	1841	Architecture	—	—	1	—	—	—	—	—	—	—	1
FINDLATER, WILLIAM	London	1800-1821	BattlePieces,&c	—	—	25	8	—	1	—	—	—	—	34
FINDLAY, MRS. EDITH A.	London	1885-1890	Landscape	—	—	1	—	3	—	—	—	—	—	4
FINDLAY, J.	London	1827-1838	Buildings	—	—	—	3	5	—	—	—	—	—	8
FINDLER, F.	—	1834	Interiors	—	—	1	—	—	—	—	—	—	—	1
FINELLI, C.	Rome	1840	Sculpture	—	—	1	—	—	—	—	—	—	—	1
FINES, C.	London	1833-1846	Wax	—	—	7	—	—	—	—	—	—	—	7
FINK, PHILIP	London	1862-1867	Domestic	—	—	1	6	1	—	—	—	—	—	8
FINLAY, A.	London	1840-1848	Landscape	—	—	4	—	1	—	—	—	—	—	5
FINLAY, ALEXANDER	Glasgow	1877-1881	Sea Pieces	—	—	2	—	—	—	—	—	—	3	5
FINLAY, K. J.	London	1855-1873	Landscape	—	—	4	—	—	—	—	—	—	—	4
FINLAYSON, ALFRED	London	1857-1876	Fruit	—	—	5	1	36	—	—	—	—	15	57
FINLAYSON, JOHN	London	1762-1770	Engraving	5	6	—	—	—	—	—	—	—	—	11
FINLAYSON, MRS.	London	1762-1768	Birds	1	1	—	—	—	—	—	—	—	—	2
FINLEY, R.	London	1866	Landscape	—	—	—	1	—	—	—	—	—	—	1
FINLEY, W.	Birmingham	1820-1839	Architecture	—	—	4	—	—	—	—	—	—	—	4
FINN, HERBERT J.	Deal	1886-1893	Domestic	—	—	—	—	3	—	—	—	—	—	3
FINNEMORE, JOSEPH, R.B.A.§	London	1885-1893	Domestic	—	—	1	—	9	—	4	—	—	—	14
FINNEY, SAMUEL	London	1761-1766	Miniatures	6	4	—	—	—	—	—	—	—	—	10
FINNEY, MRS. VIRGINIA	London	1887-1893	Domestic	—	—	2	—	—	—	—	—	1	1	4
FINNIE, JOHN, A.R.P.E. §	Liverpool	1861-1893	Landscape	—	—	36	6	44	—	3	1	—	17	107
FIRMIN, R. S.	Birmingham	1819-1836	Medals	—	—	4	—	—	—	—	—	—	—	4
FIRMINGER, REV. T. A. C.‡	Edmonton	1834-1871	Ruins	—	—	2	1	—	—	68	—	—	—	71
FISCHER, C.	Bushey	1890	Landscape	—	—	—	—	—	—	—	—	—	1	1
FISCHER, HENRY	London	1881	Black Paper	—	—	—	—	—	—	—	—	—	1	1
FISCHER, L.	London	1854	Miniatures	—	—	5	—	—	—	—	—	—	—	5
FISCHER, P.	—	1836	Portraits	—	—	1	—	—	—	—	—	—	—	1
FISCHER, P.	London	1871	Landscape	—	—	1	—	—	—	—	—	—	—	1
FISCHER, T. PAUL	London	1817-1852	Miniatures	—	—	80	—	17	—	—	—	—	—	97
FISH, W. C.	London	1825	Gems	—	—	1	—	—	—	—	—	—	—	1
FISHER —	—	1761	Sculpture	—	2	—	—	—	—	—	—	—	—	2
FISHER, ALEXANDER	London	1886	Mythological	—	—	—	—	—	—	—	—	—	1	1
FISHER, MISS AMY E.	London	1866-1890	Domestic	—	—	13	—	10	—	5	—	—	21	49
FISHER, ARTHUR E.	London	1891	Domestic	—	—	2	—	—	—	—	—	—	—	2
FISHER, A. HUGH	London	1887-1893	Landscape	—	—	4	—	5	—	2	—	—	—	11
FISHER, MISS BEATRICE	London	1889-1893	Portraits	—	—	—	—	6	—	—	—	1	1	8
FISHER, BEN., R.C.A	Conway	1886	Landscape	—	—	1	—	—	—	—	—	—	—	1
FISHER, CHARLES	London	1881-1890	Landscape	—	—	1	—	3	—	—	—	—	5	9
FISHER, DANIEL	London	1875-1890	Landscape	—	—	5	—	24	—	—	1	1	16	47
FISHER, EDWARD	London	1761-1776	Engraving	14	—	—	—	—	—	—	—	—	—	14
FISHER, MISS ELLEN	London	1865-1866	Still Life	—	—	—	—	—	—	—	—	—	2	2
FISHER, MISS ELIZABETH A.	Addlestone	1886-1893	Flowers	—	—	1	—	1	—	1	—	—	4	7
FISHER, E. J.	London	1836-1853	Portraits	—	—	5	1	9	—	—	—	—	—	15
FISHER, FRANK	Addlestone	1885-1891	Sculpture	—	—	2	—	2	—	—	—	—	—	4
FISHER, FREDERICK	Addlestone	1875	Portraits	—	—	1	—	—	—	—	—	—	—	1
FISHER, G.	—	1780-1781	Landscape	—	—	2	—	—	—	—	—	—	—	2
FISHER, G.	London	1849	Portraits	—	—	1	—	—	—	—	—	—	—	1
FISHER, HARLAND	Herne Hill	1884-1892	Domestic	—	—	—	—	10	—	—	—	—	—	10
FISHER, MISS HELENA	Addlestone	1891-1893	Animals	—	—	2	—	1	—	—	—	—	4	7
FISHER, HORACE	London	1882-1893	Domestic	—	—	16	—	7	—	—	—	—	10	33
FISHER, H. M.	London	1883	Landscape	—	—	—	—	1	—	—	—	—	—	1
FISHER, J.	—	1791-1792	Churches	—	—	3	—	—	—	—	—	—	—	3
FISHER, J.	Bristol	1849-1858	Miniatures	—	—	6	—	—	—	—	—	—	—	6
FISHER, J.	Wargrave	1856	Sea Pieces	—	—	—	—	1	—	—	—	—	—	1
FISHER, JAMES	London	1892	Stained Glass	—	—	3	—	—	—	—	—	—	—	3
FISHER, JOHN	Bristol	1887-1888	Sculpture	—	—	2	—	—	—	—	—	—	—	2
FISHER, J. E.	London	1836	Animals	—	—	2	—	—	—	—	—	—	—	2
FISHER, J. H. VIGNOLES	London	1884-1893	Landscape	—	—	4	—	4	—	6	—	—	2	16
FISHER, J. K.	London	1830-1832	Scriptural	—	—	3	1	3	—	—	—	—	—	7
FISHER, LOUISA	Penge	1870	Landscape	—	—	—	—	1	—	—	—	—	—	1
FISHER, MARK, R.I.‡	London	1872-1893	Landscape	—	—	27	—	16	—	4	33	13	37	13
FISHER, MAUD HORMAN-. *See* H.	—	—	—	—	—	—	—	—	—	—	—	—	—	—
FISHER, MISS M. J.	Wargrave	1858-1866	Landscape	—	—	4	—	5	—	—	—	—	—	9
FISHER, P. HARLAND	London	1886-1893	Domestic	—	—	7	—	—	—	—	—	—	8	15

Name.	Town.	First and Last Year of Ex.	Speciality.	S. A.	F. S.	R. A.	B. I.	S. S.	O. W.	N.W.	G. G.	N. G.	V. E.	Total.
Fisher, S. Melton φ	Herne Hill	1878-1893	Portraits	—	—	24	—	3	—	—	6	3	24	60
Fisher, Thomas	London	1804-1807	Churches	—	—	3	—	—	—	—	—	—	—	3
Fisher, W.	York	1800-1811	Sculpture	—	—	11	—	—	—	—	—	—	—	11
Fisher, William	London	1840-1886	Portraits	—	—	48	29	—	—	2	6	—	6	91
Fisher, W. M.	London	1868-1875	Landscape	—	—	4	—	11	—	—	—	—	1	16
Fisher, Major	—	1780-1808	Landscape	—	—	4	—	—	—	—	—	—	—	4
Fisher, Mrs.	London	1859	Rustic	—	—	—	—	1	—	—	—	—	—	1
Fisk, William	London	1818-1848	Historical	—	—	25	17	45	—	—	—	—	—	87
Fisk, William Henry	London	1846-1873	Landscape	—	—	11	7	5	—	—	—	—	13	36
Fitch, Walter	—	1848	Landscape	—	—	—	—	—	—	—	—	—	1	1
Fittler, James, A.R.A.	London	1776-1824	Engraving	—	2	30	—	—	—	—	—	—	—	32
Fitz, William	London	1880-1891	Landscape	—	—	2	—	3	—	—	—	—	2	7
Fitzadam, A.	London	1853	Domestic	—	—	—	—	1	—	—	—	—	—	1
Fitz-Cook, A.	London	1853	Figures	—	—	—	1	—	—	—	—	—	—	1
Fitz-Cook, H.	London	1846-1871	Scriptural	—	—	3	1	9	—	—	—	—	12	25
Fitzgerald, Lady	—	1893	Study	—	—	—	—	—	—	—	—	1	—	1
Fitzgerald, Mrs. Annie	Old Charlton	1888	Miniatures	—	—	1	—	—	—	—	—	—	—	1
Fitzgerald, Claude J.	Chiswick	1893	Still Life	—	—	—	—	—	—	—	—	—	1	1
Fitzgerald, Edith	London	1869	Domestic	—	—	—	—	—	—	—	—	—	1	1
Fitzgerald, F.	London	1848-1858	Figures	—	—	1	1	—	—	—	—	—	—	2
Fitzgerald, Miss Florence	London	1887-1893	Sculpture	—	—	10	—	21	—	—	—	—	4	35
Fitzgerald, H.	Newington	1846	Domestic	—	—	—	—	1	—	—	—	—	—	1
Fitzgerald, H. Jane	London	1851	Domestic	—	—	1	—	—	—	—	—	—	—	1
Fitz Gerald, John Anster	Newington	1845-1893	Domestic	—	—	33	27	62	—	12	—	—	59	193
Fitzgerald, Miss K.	London	1864-1866	Flowers	—	—	—	—	3	—	—	—	—	—	3
Fitzgerald, Michael	London	1875-1885	Figures	—	—	2	—	1	—	—	—	—	—	3
Fitzhenry, S.	London	1840	Coaches	—	—	—	—	1	—	—	—	—	—	1
Fitzhugh, William	—	1799-1809	Landscape	—	—	1	1	—	—	—	—	—	—	2
Fitzjames, Miss Anna Maria ‖	Bath	1852-1876	Flowers	—	—	4	—	9	—	—	—	—	2	15
Fitzjohn, E.	London	1884	Domestic	—	—	—	—	1	—	—	—	—	1	2
Fitz-Marshall. *See* Marshall.	—	—	—	—	—	—	—	—	—	—	—	—	—	—
Fitz Patrick, Arthur	London	1862-1868	Domestic	—	—	1	7	10	—	—	—	—	—	18
Fitzpatrick, Edmond, A.R.H.A.	London	1848-1870	Domestic	—	—	—	1	15	—	—	—	—	1	17
Fitzroy, Cyril D.	London	1885-1889	Architecture	—	—	5	—	—	—	—	—	—	—	5
Fitzwalter, Miss	—	1803	Heads	—	—	1	—	—	—	—	—	—	—	1
Flack, Charles	Bushey	1891-1892	Figures	—	—	3	—	1	—	—	—	—	—	4
Flack, Miss Edith Mary	London	1887-1889	Churches	—	—	1	—	1	—	—	—	—	—	2
Flamank, R.	London	1854	Sculpture	—	—	1	—	—	—	—	—	—	—	1
Flameng, Leopold Joseph	Paris	1872-1892	Etching	—	—	8	—	—	—	—	—	—	7	15
Flanders, French	London	1856-1857	Landscape	—	—	—	1	—	—	—	—	—	1	2
Flattely, T.	London	1852	Sculpture	—	—	1	—	—	—	—	—	—	—	1
Flatters —	London	1842	Sculpture	—	—	2	—	—	—	—	—	—	—	2
Flaxman, John, R.A.	London	1767-1838	Sculpture	—	6	90	2	—	—	—	—	—	—	98
Flaxman, Miss Mary Ann	London	1786-1819	Mythological	3	—	27	1	—	—	—	—	—	—	31
Flaxman, Miss Maria Denman. *See* Miss Maria Denman.	—	—	—	—	—	—	—	—	—	—	—	—	—	—
Flaxman, William	London	1768-1792	Sculpture	—	1	11	—	—	—	—	—	—	—	12
Fleckney —	—	1783	Horses	—	1	—	—	—	—	—	—	—	—	1
Fleetwood, J.	—	1799-1800	Landscape	—	—	2	—	—	—	—	—	—	—	2
Fleetwood, S.	London	1862	Landscape	—	—	—	—	1	—	—	—	—	—	1
Fleetwood, W.	London	1800-1802	Landscape	—	—	2	—	—	—	—	—	—	—	2
Fleischmann, Adolph	London	1851	Portraits	—	—	1	—	—	—	—	—	—	—	1
Fleming, Miss M. Le. *See* L.	—	—	—	—	—	—	—	—	—	—	—	—	—	—
Fleming, W.	Leyden	1842	Domestic	—	—	1	—	—	—	—	—	—	—	1
Fleming, W. B.	Croydon	1873-1874	Still Life	—	—	—	—	3	—	—	—	—	—	3
Fleming, William J.	Leeds	1887	Miniatures	—	—	2	—	—	—	—	—	—	—	2
Flemming, J.	London	1805	Architecture	—	—	1	—	—	—	—	—	—	—	1
Flemwell, George	Antwerp	1892-1893	Domestic	—	—	2	—	—	—	—	—	—	—	2
Flère, Herbert H.	London	1893	Domestic	—	—	—	—	—	—	—	—	—	1	1
Fletcher, A.	London	1831-1839	Sculpture	—	—	6	—	—	—	—	—	—	—	6
Fletcher, Arthur	Hornsey	1859	Landscape	—	—	1	—	—	—	—	—	—	—	1
Fletcher, Blandford	London	1879-1892	Domestic	—	—	11	—	12	—	1	—	—	4	28
Fletcher, C. J.	London	1836-1837	Figures	—	—	1	—	2	—	—	—	—	—	3
Fletcher, Clelia Lega	London	1862	Landscape	—	—	—	—	2	—	—	—	—	—	2
Fletcher, Evelyn	London	1880	Street Scene	—	—	—	—	1	—	—	—	—	—	1
Fletcher, Edith Croft	Windermere	1876	Landscape	—	—	—	—	—	—	—	—	—	1	1
Fletcher, Flitcroft	Croydon	1882-1886	Landscape	—	—	5	—	1	—	—	—	—	—	6
Fletcher, F. Morley	London	1888-1893	Portraits	—	—	2	—	—	—	—	—	—	1	3
Fletcher, Mrs. Grace	Paris	1888	Fruit	—	—	1	—	—	—	—	—	—	—	1
Fletcher, H. Murray	London	1883-1889	Landscape	—	—	—	—	3	—	1	—	—	—	4
Fletcher, J. H.	Nottingham	1889	Domestic	—	—	1	—	—	—	—	—	—	—	1
Fletcher, Miss Margaret	Oxford	1886	Figures	—	—	1	—	—	—	—	—	—	—	1

Name.	Town.	First and Last Year of Ex.	Speciality.	S. A.	F. S.	R. A.	B. I.	S. S.	O. W.	N.W.	G. G.	N. G.	V. E.	Total.
FLETCHER, MISS	—	1838	Landscape	—	—	1	—	—	—	—	—	—	—	1
FLEURY, R.	—	1841-1846	Domestic	—	—	2	—	—	—	—	—	—	—	2
FLEURY, DE. *See* D.	—	—	—	—	—	—	—	—	—	—	—	—	—	—
FLEUSS, HENRY	Marlbro' Coll'ge	1847-1874	Domestic	—	—	9	—	—	—	—	—	—	—	9
FLEUSS, OSWALD	London	1890	Stained Glass	—	—	1	—	—	—	—	—	—	—	1
FLICK, J.	London	1836	Domestic	—	—	—	1	—	—	—	—	—	—	1
FLICK, R.	London	1842	Figures	—	—	—	1	—	—	—	—	—	—	1
FLIGHT, J.	London	1802-1806	Miniatures	—	—	8	—	—	—	—	—	—	—	8
FLINT, SAVILE LUMLEY WILLIAM	London	1880-1893	Landscape	—	—	7	—	16	—	—	2	1	2	28
FLOCKHART, WILLIAM	London	1885-1893	Architecture	—	—	9	—	—	—	—	—	—	—	9
FLOCKTON, F.	Pangbourne	1866-1876	Still Life	—	—	2	—	4	—	—	—	—	—	6
FLOCKTON, T. J.	Sheffield	1848	Architecture	—	—	1	—	—	—	—	—	—	—	1
FLOCKTON AND GIBBS	Sheffield	1890	Architecture	—	—	1	—	—	—	—	—	—	—	1
FLOCKTON (T. J.) AND ROBSON (E. R.)	Sheffield	1878	Architecture	—	—	1	—	—	—	—	—	—	—	1
FLOOD, A. J.	London	1859-1862	Landscape	—	—	2	—	5	—	—	—	—	—	7
FLOR, F.	—	1831	Figures	—	—	1	—	—	—	—	—	—	—	1
FLORENCE, HENRY LOUIS. *See* Isaacs & Florence	London	1871-1891	Architecture	—	—	9	—	—	—	—	—	—	2	11
FLOUD, MISS M. C. F.	Exeter	1860	Landscape	—	—	—	—	—	—	—	—	—	2	2
FLOWER, ARTHUR SMYTH, M.A.	London	1893	Architecture	—	—	1	—	—	—	—	—	—	—	1
FLOWER, EDGAR	Stratford-on-Avon	1890	Landscape	—	—	—	—	1	—	—	—	—	—	1
FLOWER, MRS. E. WICKHAM	Croydon	1872-1873	Flowers	—	—	—	—	—	—	—	—	—	2	2
FLOWER, H. *See* Lindsay and Flower	—	1837	Architecture	—	—	1	—	—	—	—	—	—	—	1
FLOWER, MARMADUKE C. W.	Leeds	1878-1893	Domestic	—	—	18	—	—	—	—	—	—	1	19
FLOYD —	London	1783	Figures	—	3	—	—	—	—	—	—	—	—	3
FLOYD, HARRY	Eastbourne	1884-1890	Domestic	—	—	3	—	—	—	—	—	—	—	3
FLYNN, MRS.	London	1807-1809	Flowers	—	—	2	—	—	—	—	—	—	—	2
FOCADI, R.	Thornton Heath	1881	Etching	—	—	2	—	—	—	—	—	—	—	2
FOCARDI, GIOVANNI	Florence	1875-1888	Sculpture	—	—	4	—	—	—	1	7	—	1	13
FOGG, A.	Reading	1811-1812	Landscape	—	—	1	—	—	—	—	—	—	2	3
FOGGO, GEORGE	London	1816-1864	Scriptural	—	—	7	14	37	—	—	—	—	—	58
FOGGO, JAMES	London	1816-1858	Scriptural	—	—	5	8	22	—	—	—	—	—	35
FOLDSONE, JOHN	London	1769-1783	Portraits	5	—	18	—	—	—	—	—	—	—	23
FOLDSTONE, MISS ANNE. *See* Mrs. Mee.	—	—	—	—	—	—	—	—	—	—	—	—	—	—
FOLEY, CHARLES V.	London	1852-1860	Figures	—	—	2	2	—	—	—	—	—	—	4
FOLEY, EDWARD A.	London	1834-1873	Sculpture	—	—	37	—	1	—	—	—	—	—	38
FOLEY, G. C. E.	London	1869-1873	Rustic	—	—	—	—	2	—	—	—	—	—	2
FOLEY, H. W.	London	1872	Military	—	—	—	—	1	—	—	—	—	—	1
FOLEY, J. B.	London	1863-1877	Sea Pieces	—	—	—	2	15	—	—	—	—	—	17
FOLEY, JOHN HENRY, R.A.	London	1839-1875	Sculpture	—	—	49	8	—	—	—	—	—	—	57
FOLEY, MISS MARGARET F. (?) E.	London	1870-1877	Sculpture	—	—	3	—	—	—	—	—	—	—	3
FOLI, MADAME ROSITA	London	1885	Domestic	—	—	—	—	—	—	—	—	—	1	1
FOLINGSBY, G. F.	Munich	1869-1871	Historical	—	—	2	—	—	—	—	—	—	—	2
FOLKARD, MISS A.	London	1878	Domestic	—	—	—	—	1	—	—	—	—	—	1
FOLKARD, MISS ELIZABETH F.,	London	1876-1884	Domestic	—	—	5	—	5	—	2	—	—	6	18
FOLKARD, MISS JULIA B. ‖	London	1872-1893	Figures	—	—	24	—	8	—	—	1	—	15	48
FOLKS, F. C.	London	1852	Sea Pieces	—	—	—	1	3	—	—	—	—	—	4
FONDEVILA, A. MAS- Y.	Rome	1879	Landscape	—	—	1	—	—	—	—	—	—	1	2
FONTANA, ARISTIDE	London	1880-1884	Sculpture	—	—	6	—	5	—	—	—	—	—	11
FONTANA, A. F.	London	1881	Sculpture	—	—	—	—	1	—	—	—	—	—	1
FONTANA, GIOVANNI	London	1852-1886	Sculpture	—	—	22	—	13	—	1	—	—	1	37
FONTANA, V.	London	1877	Figures	—	—	—	—	—	—	—	—	—	1	1
FONTANELLA, C.	London	1779-1780	Portraits	—	1	1	—	—	—	—	—	—	—	2
FONTANESSI, A.	London	1866-1872	Domestic	—	—	4	—	1	—	—	—	—	2	7
FONTVILLE, A.	London	1893	Landscape	—	—	—	—	1	—	—	—	—	—	1
FOOT, F.	Ashburton	1857-1867	Landscape	—	—	6	7	7	—	—	—	—	—	20
FOOT, JOHN TAYLER	London	1882-1886	Medals	—	—	6	—	—	—	—	—	—	—	6
FOOT, WILLIAM YATES	Wallingford	1880	Landscape	—	—	—	—	1	—	—	—	—	—	1
FOOTE, D.	—	1825	Sculpture	—	—	2	—	—	—	—	—	—	—	2
FOOTTIT, F.	London	1873	Figures	—	—	1	—	—	—	—	—	—	—	1
FOOTTIT, HARRISON	London	1772-1774	Miniatures	—	—	6	—	—	—	—	—	—	—	6
FORBES, MISS C.	—	1827	Flowers	—	—	—	—	1	—	—	—	—	—	1
FORBES, H.	—	1862	Landscape	—	—	—	—	1	—	—	—	—	—	1
FORBES, JAMES G.	London	1853-1857	Historical	—	—	1	3	—	—	—	—	—	2	6
FORBES, PATRICK LEWIS	London	1893	Landscape	—	—	—	—	—	—	1	—	—	—	1
FORBES, STANHOPE ALEXANDER, A.R.A.	London	1874-1893	Domestic	—	—	26	—	5	—	—	5	1	5	42
FORBES, MRS. S. A. *See* Miss Eliz. Armstrong	London	1890-1893	Domestic	—	—	4	—	—	—	—	1	2	1	8
FORBES, MISS	London	1772	Portraits	—	—	4	—	—	—	—	—	—	—	4
FORBES-ROBERTSON. *See* Robertson.	—	—	—	—	—	—	—	—	—	—	—	—	—	—
FORBIN, M. LE COMTE DE	Paris	1833	Historical	—	—	1	—	—	—	—	—	—	—	1
FORD, B.	London	1887-1888	Buildings	—	—	—	—	2	—	—	—	—	—	2
FORD, C.	Bath	1830-1856	Portraits	—	—	21	—	—	—	—	—	—	—	21
FORD, EDWARD ONSLOW, A.R.A.	Blackheath	1875-1893	Sculpture	—	—	47	—	8	—	—	17	8	—	80

Name.	Town.	First and Last Year of Ex.	Speciality.	S. A.	F. S.	R. A.	B. I.	S. S.	O. W.	N.W.	G. G.	N. G.	V. E.	Total.
Ford, Miss Emily S.	Leeds	1889	Figures	—	—	—	—	—	—	—	1	—	3	4
Ford, F.	London	1852-1860	Landscape	—	—	10	—	1	—	—	—	—	—	11
Ford, F. J.	London	1845-1853	Landscape	—	—	5	—	10	—	—	—	—	—	15
Ford, Miss Harriet	St. Ives	1890-1892	Portraits	—	—	—	—	1	—	—	—	—	2	3
Ford, Henry Justice	London	1886-1893	Landscape	—	—	3	—	—	—	—	1	2	1	7
Ford, John	Bath	1764-1797	Sculpture, Enamels	—	7	6	—	—	—	—	—	—	—	13
Ford, J. A.	Edinburgh	1893	Portraits	—	—	1	—	—	—	—	—	—	—	1
Ford, Max Onslow	—	1888	Medals	—	—	—	—	—	—	—	—	1	—	1
Ford, W.	London	1810-1821	Architecture	—	—	4	—	—	—	—	—	—	—	4
Ford, William	London	1846-1858	Enamels	—	—	11	—	2	—	—	—	—	—	13
Ford, William B.	London	1859-1892	Enamels	—	—	24	—	13	—	—	—	—	—	37
Ford, Miss	—	1771-1783	Landscape	—	—	10	—	—	—	—	—	—	—	10
Fordham. *See* Douglas and Fordham	—	—	Architecture	—	—	—	—	—	—	—	—	—	—	—
Fores, Miss Mary H.	London	1888	Figures	—	—	1	—	—	—	—	—	—	—	1
Forestier, Mdlle. Alice De. *See* D.	—	—	—	—	—	—	—	—	—	—	—	—	—	—
Forestier, A.	Penge	1882	Domestic	—	—	—	—	1	—	—	—	—	—	1
Forget, De. *See* D.	—	—	—	—	—	—	—	—	—	—	—	—	—	—
Former, J. W.	London	1819	Portraits	—	—	1	—	—	—	—	—	—	—	1
Formilli, C.	Rome	1887	Landscape	—	—	—	—	—	—	—	2	—	—	2
Forrest, A.	Greenhithe	1858	Rustic	—	—	—	—	1	—	—	—	—	—	1
Forrest, A. S.	London	1893	Landscape	—	—	—	—	1	—	—	—	—	—	1
Forrest, Miss B.	—	1855	Portraits	—	—	1	—	—	—	—	—	—	—	1
Forrest, Charles	London	1776	Portraits	7	—	—	—	—	—	—	—	—	—	7
Forrest, Thomas Theodosius	—	1762-1781	Landscape	8	—	7	—	—	—	—	—	—	—	15
Forrest, W. S.	Greenhithe	1840-1866	Sporting	—	—	3	2	17	—	—	—	—	—	22
Forrester, Alfred Henry. *See* Crowquill.	—	—	—	—	—	—	—	—	—	—	—	—	—	—
Forrester, James	Rome	1771	Landscape	—	—	1	—	—	—	—	—	—	—	1
Forshall, Francis S. H.	London	1893	Portraits	—	—	1	—	—	—	—	—	—	—	1
Forster, C.	London	1828-1847	Portraits	—	—	8	—	—	—	—	—	—	—	8
Forster, Charles, Junr.	London	1835-1876	Rustic	—	—	4	1	47	—	—	—	—	6	58
Forster, C. F., Senr.	London	1846	Figures	—	—	—	—	1	—	—	—	—	—	1
Forster, Miss Emily	London	1840	Flowers	—	—	1	—	—	—	—	—	—	—	1
Forster, F. V.	London	1847	Figures	—	—	—	—	1	—	—	—	—	—	1
Forster, George	—	1772	Birds	—	—	1	—	—	—	—	—	—	—	1
Forster, G.	London	1816-1830	Domestic	—	—	16	6	2	—	—	—	—	—	24
Forster, Miss J.	Trowbridge	1862	Landscape	—	—	1	—	—	—	—	—	—	—	1
Forster, Joseph Wilson	London	1889-1893	Portraits	—	—	4	—	—	—	1	—	—	3	8
Forster, Miss Mary, A.R.W.S.,†‖ afterwards Mrs. Lofthouse	Trowbridge	1873-1884	Landscape	—	—	6	—	—	11	1	—	—	17	35
Forster, P.	Coldstream	1845-1858	Sporting	—	—	1	2	1	—	—	—	—	—	4
Forster, Robert E.	London	1838-1855	Portraits	—	—	9	—	—	—	—	—	—	—	9
Forster, R. T.	London	1828	Landscape	—	—	—	—	1	—	—	—	—	—	1
Forster, Miss Selina	London	1857-1858	Domestic	—	—	3	2	—	—	—	—	—	—	5
Forster, T. B. W.	Chippenham	1859-1886	Landscape	—	—	17	—	8	—	—	—	—	11	36
Forster, Mrs.	—	1800-1814	Portraits	—	—	4	—	—	—	—	—	—	—	4
Forsyth, Adam	Harlesden	1889-1892	Landscape	—	—	1	—	—	—	2	—	—	—	3
Forsyth, James	London	1864-1889	Sculpture	—	—	21	—	—	—	—	—	—	—	21
Forsyth, James Nesfield	London	1885-1892	Sculpture	—	—	10	—	—	—	—	1	—	—	11
Forsyth, W.	London	1834-1838	Flowers	—	—	1	—	1	—	—	—	—	—	2
Fortescue, William B.	Southport	1880-1893	Domestic	—	—	12	—	12	—	—	—	—	9	33
Fortie, John	Edinburgh	1847	Figures	—	—	1	—	—	—	—	—	—	—	1
Fortin, R.	—	1790-1794	Miniatures	—	—	19	—	—	—	—	—	—	—	19
Fortinelli —	—	1783	Landscape	—	2	—	—	—	—	—	—	—	—	2
Fortt, Frederick §	Bath	1848-1861	Buildings	—	—	1	4	8	—	—	—	—	—	13
Fortuny, A. Mariano	Barcelona	1869-1879	Figures	—	—	1	—	—	—	—	—	—	4	5
Fortye, W. H.	London	1875-1886	Landscape	—	—	—	—	—	—	5	—	—	3	8
Fosbrooke, Leonard	Ashby-de-la-Zouch	1884-1892	Landscape	—	—	5	—	1	—	9	—	—	—	15
Foster, Miss Amy H. *See* Mrs. R. K. Leather	Teignmouth	1886-1892	Landscape	—	—	—	—	1	—	5	—	1	—	7
Foster, Arthur J.	London	1880-1893	Portraits	—	—	8	—	3	—	—	—	—	1	12
Foster, B.	London	1812-1813	Architecture	—	—	3	—	—	—	—	—	—	—	3
Foster, Birket, R.W.S.†	London	1859-1893	Landscape	—	—	16	—	2	332	—	—	—	3	353
Foster, Miss C. E.	Hitchin	1871-1876	Landscape	—	—	—	—	2	—	—	—	—	—	2
Foster, Mrs. Elizabeth	London	1770-1772	Shell Work	—	2	—	—	—	—	—	—	—	—	2
Foster, E. W.	—	1812-1828	Landscape	—	—	22	—	—	—	—	—	—	—	22
Foster, Frederick	London	1867-1876	Landscape	—	—	—	—	16	—	—	—	—	—	16
Foster, Miss F. E.	Hitchin	1871-1879	Fruit	—	—	—	—	21	—	—	—	—	—	21
Foster, Helen	London	1879-1880	Landscape	—	—	—	—	3	—	—	—	—	—	3
Foster, Herbert Wilson	London	1870-1893	Figures	—	—	14	—	1	—	6	—	—	1	22
Foster, J.	London	1804-1806	Architecture	—	—	3	—	—	—	—	—	—	—	3
Foster, Miss Marianne. *See* Mrs. Barrett.	—	—	—	—	—	—	—	—	—	—	—	—	—	—
Foster, R.	London	1849-1878	Architecture	—	—	3	—	—	—	—	—	—	—	3
Foster, Sybilla C.	London	1881	Domestic	—	—	—	—	1	—	—	—	—	—	1

Name.	Town.	First and Last Year of Ex.	Speciality.	S. A.	F. S.	R. A.	B. I.	S. S.	O. W.	N.W.	G. G.	N. G.	V. E.	Total.
Foster, Sarah F.	Burton Overy	1876	Flowers	—	—	—	—	—	—	—	—	—	1	1
Foster, Thomas	London	1818-1826	Portraits	—	—	18	5	—	—	—	—	—	—	23
Foster, William	London	1772-1812	Portraits	8	—	28	4	—	—	—	—	—	12	52
Foster, William	Witley	1870-1893	Domestic	—	—	26	—	11	—	9	—	—	36	82
Foster, William Gilbert, R.B.A. §	Leeds	1876-1893	Domestic	—	—	22	—	10	—	—	—	—	1	33
Foster, Walter H. W.	Kingsland	1861-1888	Landscape	—	—	3	—	69	—	—	—	—	2	74
Foster, Mrs. Walter H. (Kate E.)	London	1882-1889	Landscape	—	—	—	—	2	—	—	—	—	—	2
Foster, Wallis H. W.	Haslemere	1870-1881	Landscape	—	—	10	—	4	—	—	—	—	—	14
Foster, William John	London	1885	Birds	—	—	—	—	—	—	—	1	—	—	1
Fothergill, Charles	Stoorington	1880-1883	Sea Pieces	—	—	—	—	3	—	—	—	—	2	5
Fothergill, S.	Darlington	1853	Landscape	—	—	—	—	1	—	—	—	—	—	1
Fougeron —	London	1764-1768	Engraving	1	2	—	—	—	—	—	—	—	—	3
Foulger, Howson Rutherford	London	1890	Domestic	—	—	1	—	—	—	—	—	—	—	1
Foulon, John	London	1828-1834	Landscape	—	—	2	1	—	—	—	—	—	—	3
Foulon, Madame V.	London	1837	Portraits	—	—	1	—	—	—	—	—	—	—	1
Foulston, John	London	1794-1813	Architecture	—	—	5	—	—	—	—	—	—	—	5
Fouquet, L.	—	1836	Interiors	—	—	1	—	—	—	—	—	—	—	1
Fourmois, F.	Brussels	1848	Landscape	—	—	—	—	—	—	—	—	—	1	1
Fournier, Charles	Paris	1828-1839	Historical	—	—	1	1	1	—	—	—	—	—	3
Fournier, John	London	1828	Landscape	—	—	—	2	—	—	—	—	—	—	2
Fowell, M.	London	1873-1874	Figures	—	—	—	—	2	—	—	—	—	—	2
Fowinkel, Von. *See* V.	—	—	—	—	—	—	—	—	—	—	—	—	—	—
Fowke, Capt. Francis, R.E.	London	1860-1863	Architecture	—	—	5	—	—	—	—	—	—	—	5
Fowke, F. R.	London	1884	Landscape	—	—	—	—	—	—	1	—	—	—	1
Fowke, Thomas	London	1851-1877	Sculpture	—	—	36	1	—	—	—	—	—	—	37
Fowler. *See* Kempson and Fowler	—	—	Architecture	—	—	—	—	—	—	—	—	—	—	—
Fowler —	London	1782-1783	Copies	—	3	—	—	—	—	—	—	—	—	3
Fowler, B., R.C.A.	Trefrew	1892	Landscape	—	—	1	—	—	—	—	—	—	—	1
Fowler, Charles, F.R.I.B.A.	London	1825-1849	Architecture	—	—	28	—	—	—	—	—	—	—	28
Fowler, Charles	London	1878	Architecture	—	—	1	—	—	—	—	—	—	—	1
Fowler, C. Hodgson	London	1862-1889	Street Scenes	—	—	4	—	—	—	—	—	—	—	4
Fowler, Daniel	London	1834-1842	Landscape	—	—	1	—	16	—	1	—	—	—	18
Fowler, F. E. H.	London	1843-1849	Architecture	—	—	10	—	—	—	—	—	—	—	10
Fowler, F. H. §	London	1860-1876	Architecture	—	—	1	—	*	—	—	—	—	—	1
Fowler, Howard	Norwich	1880-1891	Domestic	—	—	1	—	7	—	2	—	—	4	14
Fowler, J.	London	1812	Architecture	—	—	1	—	—	—	—	—	—	—	1
Fowler, J.	London	1872	Landscape	—	—	1	—	—	—	—	—	—	—	1
Fowler, J. T.	—	1833	Portraits	—	—	—	—	1	—	—	—	—	—	1
Fowler, James W.	Louth	1875-1884	Architecture	—	—	2	—	—	—	—	—	—	—	2
Fowler, Miss Martha	Southampton	1866-1880	Landscape	—	—	—	—	—	—	—	—	—	9	9
Fowler, Munro	Southampton	1884-1888	Landscape	—	—	—	—	4	—	3	—	—	—	7
Fowler, Miss Mary L. *See* Mrs. S. E. Waller	Gloucester	1871	Domestic	—	—	—	—	—	—	—	—	—	1	1
Fowler, Robert, R.I., A.R.C.A. ‡	Liverpool	1876-1893	Figures	—	—	13	—	13	—	20	1	2	9	58
Fowler, Miss R. J.	Woodford	1881	Flowers	—	—	—	—	1	—	—	—	—	—	1
Fowler, T. T.	London	1829	Portraits	—	—	1	—	—	—	—	—	—	—	1
Fowler, Walter	Richmond	1887-1893	Landscape	—	—	5	—	8	—	—	—	—	5	18
Fowler, William	—	1827	Portraits	—	—	—	—	2	—	—	—	—	—	2
Fowler, William §	London	1825-1867	Landscape	—	—	23	72	72	—	7	—	—	23	197
Fowler, Mrs.	London	1845-1852	Miniatures	—	—	3	—	—	—	—	—	—	—	3
Fowlkes, Clater	London	1852	Domestic	—	—	—	—	—	—	—	—	—	1	1
Fownes, H.	Battersea	1816-1818	Cameos	—	—	6	—	—	—	—	—	—	—	6
Fox, Augustus H.	London	1841-1849	Figures	—	—	3	—	1	—	—	—	—	—	4
Fox, A. W. T.	Edgeley	1850	Flowers	—	—	—	—	1	—	—	—	—	—	1
Fox, B.	London	1807-1808	Architecture	—	—	4	—	—	—	—	—	—	—	4
Fox, Bridell	Milden Hill	1867-1874	Portraits	—	—	3	—	—	—	—	—	—	—	3
Fox, Mrs. Bridell	London	1883	Domestic	—	—	1	—	—	—	—	—	—	—	1
Fox, Mrs. Caroline	St. Leonards	1892	Landscape	—	—	—	—	1	—	—	—	—	—	1
Fox, Charles	London	1836-1837	Portraits	—	—	4	—	—	—	—	—	—	—	4
Fox, Charles	London	1827	Landscape	—	—	—	1	—	—	—	—	—	—	1
Fox, Charles	Brighton	1850-1852	Sculpture	—	—	—	—	2	—	—	—	—	—	2
Fox, C. J.	London	1808	Architecture	—	—	2	—	—	—	—	—	—	—	2
Fox, Charles James	London	1883-1890	Landscape	—	—	5	—	3	—	2	—	—	1	11
Fox, Edward	London	1813-1854	Landscape	—	—	28	11	2	11	—	—	—	—	52
Fox, Edward	London	1880	Landscape	—	—	—	—	2	—	—	—	—	—	2
Fox, Miss Eliza Florance. *See* Mrs. F. L.	—	—	—	—	—	—	—	—	—	—	—	—	—	—
Bridell, afterwards Mrs. George Edward Fox	London	1846-1858	Portraits	—	—	8	—	14	—	—	—	—	—	22
Fox, Emanuel P.	St. Ives, Cornw'l	1890	Domestic	—	—	—	—	—	—	—	—	—	1	1
Fox, Ernest R.	Strood	1886-1893	Landscape	—	—	7	—	2	—	—	2	—	—	11
Fox, Miss Florence	London	1887-1892	Miniatures	—	—	2	—	—	—	—	—	—	—	2
Fox, G.	London	1792-1819	Landscape	—	—	1	2	—	—	—	—	—	—	3
Fox, George	London	1873-1889	Domestic	—	—	1	—	19	—	—	—	—	9	29
Fox, George E.	London	1878-1884	Decoration	—	—	8	—	—	—	—	—	—	—	8

Name.	Town.	First and Last Year of Ex.	Speciality.	S. A.	F. S.	R. A.	B. I.	S. S.	O.W.	N.W.	G. G.	N. G.	V. E.	Total.
Fox, Henry Charles, R.B.A. §	London	1879-1893	Domestic	—	—	8	—	92	—	6	—	—	17	123
Fox, J.	London	1830-1846	Miniatures	—	—	13	—	—	—	—	—	—	—	13
Fox, M.	London	1815	Landscape	—	—	1	—	—	—	—	—	—	—	1
Fox, Nicholas Percy	London	1892-1893	Landscape	—	—	1	—	—	—	1	—	—	—	2
Fox, Robert	London	1846-1868	Domestic	—	—	25	21	34	—	—	—	—	—	80
Fox, R.	London	1867	Fruit	—	—	1	—	—	—	—	—	—	—	1
Fox, Shirley	Norwood	1890-1893	Portraits	—	—	1	—	1	—	—	—	1	1	4
Fox, Miss S.	—	1796-1834	Churches	—	—	5	—	—	—	1	—	—	—	6
Fox, Samuel M.	London	1887	Sculpture	—	—	2	—	—	—	—	—	—	—	2
Fox, T.	London	1834	Portraits	—	—	1	—	—	—	—	—	—	—	1
Fox, T. M.	London	1843-1846	Miniatures	—	—	4	—	—	—	—	—	—	—	4
Fox, W.	London	1828	Architecture	—	—	1	—	—	—	—	—	—	—	1
Fox, W.	London	1864	Landscape	—	—	1	—	—	—	—	—	—	—	1
Fox, W. A. §	Penn	1828	Landscape	—	—	—	—	1	—	—	—	—	—	1
Fox, W. T.	London	1862-1867	Landscape	—	—	—	4	—	—	—	—	—	—	4
Foxhall, E. M.	London	1821	Sculpture	—	—	1	—	—	—	—	—	—	—	1
Foy —	Rome	1777	Sculpture	1	—	—	—	—	—	—	—	—	—	1
Foy, William	London	1828-1861	Portraits	—	—	14	10	7	—	—	—	—	—	31
Foyster, H. S.	London	1808-1809	Architecture	—	—	2	—	—	—	—	—	—	—	2
Fradelle, Henry Joseph	London	1817-1854	Historical	—	—	11	36	2	4	—	—	—	—	53
Fraikin, Charles Auguste	Brussels	1874	Domestic	—	—	1	—	—	—	—	—	—	—	1
Frampton, Alfred	London	1881-1882	Architecture	—	—	2	—	—	—	—	—	—	—	2
Frampton, Edward Reg.	London	1877-1893	Windows	—	—	17	—	1	—	—	—	—	—	18
Frampton, George Glanfield	London	1884-1893	Sculpture	—	—	18	—	3	—	—	—	5	—	26
Français, F.	Paris	1877	Etching	—	—	—	—	—	—	—	—	—	3	3
France, Charles	Skipton	1881-1889	Landscape	—	—	2	—	—	—	—	—	—	2	4
France, W. F., *or* J.	London	1839-1840	Architecture	—	—	2	—	—	—	—	—	—	—	2
Frances, Miss E.	London	1857-1859	Fruit	—	—	1	1	—	—	—	—	—	—	2
Frances, H. E.	London	1851-1875	Domestic	—	—	2	10	9	—	—	—	—	—	21
Frances, Miss S.	London	1859	Figures	—	—	1	—	—	—	—	—	—	—	1
Franceschi, B.	London	1842	Sculpture	—	—	1	—	—	—	—	—	—	—	1
Francessini, Signora	—	1762	Heads	1	—	—	—	—	—	—	—	—	—	1
Francia, Count Alexendi T.	Brussels	1841-1867	Sea Pieces	—	—	4	2	7	—	—	—	—	2	15
Francia, François Louis Thomas	London	1795-1821	Landscape	—	—	85	—	—	—	—	—	—	116	201
Francia, Mrs.	London	1801-1803	Landscape	—	—	2	—	—	—	—	—	—	—	2
Franoillon, Miss E. F.	London	1800-1824	Flowers	—	—	7	—	2	—	—	—	—	—	9
Francis —	London	1797	Miniatures	—	—	1	—	—	—	—	—	—	—	1
Francis, A.	Brussels	1873	Landscape	—	—	—	—	1	—	—	—	—	—	1
Francis, C. W.	London	1837-1845	Sculpture	—	—	2	—	—	—	—	—	—	—	2
Francis, Miss Eleanor	London	1889	Flowers	—	—	2	—	—	—	—	—	—	—	2
Francis, Miss Eva	Southsea	1891-1893	Flowers	—	—	—	—	—	—	3	—	—	—	3
Francis, Frederick and Horace	London	1860-1863	Architecture	—	—	3	—	—	—	—	—	—	—	3
Francis, Frederick John	London	1835-1838	Architecture	—	—	3	—	—	—	—	—	—	—	3
Francis, John	London	1820-1857	Sculpture	—	—	71	1	2	—	—	—	—	—	74
Francis, John Deffett	London	1837-1860	Domestic	—	—	1	1	6	—	—	—	—	—	8
Francis, M.	—	1834	Sculpture	—	—	1	—	—	—	—	—	—	—	1
Francis, Miss Mary. *See* Mrs. Thornycroft	—	1835-1840	Sculpture	—	—	6	1	—	—	—	—	—	—	7
Francis, Miss M.	London	1852	Game	—	—	—	—	1	—	—	—	—	—	1
Francis, Miss M.	London	1884-1886	Landscape	—	—	—	—	—	—	—	—	—	2	2
Francis, S. D.	London	1867	Domestic	—	—	—	1	—	—	—	—	—	—	1
Francis, W.	London	1822-1824	Animals	—	—	—	2	—	—	—	—	—	—	2
Francis, W. T. *See* W. Francis Tiffin	London	1844	Landscape	—	—	2	—	—	—	—	—	—	—	2
Francis and Saunders	London	1878	Architecture	—	—	1	—	—	—	—	—	—	—	1
Francis, Mrs.	London	1768-1776	Flowers	—	23	—	—	—	—	—	—	—	—	23
Francis, Miss	—	1799	Portraits	—	—	1	—	—	—	—	—	—	—	1
Franck, Joseph	Paris	1872	Engraving	—	—	—	—	—	—	—	—	—	1	1
Franck, Mrs. G. A. (E. A.)	London	1892-1893	Landscape	—	—	—	—	7	—	1	—	—	—	8
Franck, Miss Helene	London	1883-1893	Domestic	—	—	8	—	13	—	1	—	—	8	30
Francois, J.	Antwerp	1788	Mythological	—	—	1	—	—	—	—	—	—	—	1
Frank, Mrs. Alberta. *See* Miss Alberta Brown	—	1877	Street Scene	—	—	—	—	1	—	—	—	—	—	1
Frankland, Miss Harriet	—	1769-1772	Needlework	2	—	—	—	—	—	—	—	—	—	2
Franklin, George	London	1825-1847	Scriptural	—	—	9	8	3	—	—	—	—	—	20
Franklin, J.	London	1830-1868	Historical	—	—	9	10	9	—	—	—	—	3	31
Franklin, Matilda	Harlington	1883	Landscape	—	—	—	—	1	—	—	—	—	—	1
Franklin, W.	Brentford	1800-1818	Landscape	—	—	5	—	—	—	—	—	—	—	5
Franks, B.	London	1876-1877	Landscape	—	—	—	—	2	—	—	—	—	—	2
Franks, J. J.	London	1830-1831	Architecture	—	—	2	—	—	—	—	—	—	—	2
Franks, William	London	1776	Hair Work	1	—	—	—	—	—	—	—	—	—	1
Franquinet, William	London	1831-1836	Historical	—	—	1	7	10	—	—	—	—	—	18
Franz, Ettore Roesler. (?) Uttore	Rome	1875-1889	Landscape	—	—	4	—	—	—	6	—	—	12	22
Frascheri, G.	London	1872	Domestic	—	—	—	—	1	—	—	—	—	—	1
Fraser, A.	London	1857	Landscape	—	—	—	1	—	—	—	—	—	—	1

Name.	Town.	First and Last Year of Ex.	Speciality.	S. A.	F. S.	R. A.	B. I.	S. S.	O. W.	N.W.	G. G.	N. G.	V. E.	Total.
Fraser, Miss Agnes	London	1881-1887	Domestic	—	—	—	—	—	—	2	—	—	1	3
Fraser, Alexander, A.R.S.A.	Edinburgh	1810-1859	Domestic	—	—	32	97	37	—	—	—	—	10	176
Fraser, Alexander, R.S.A.	Hamilton	1866-1889	Landscape	—	—	11	1	8	—	—	1	—	4	25
Fraser, Alice	Stevenage	1891	Study	—	—	—	—	1	—	—	—	—	—	1
Fraser, Miss Annie	London	1866-1867	Portraits	—	—	2	—	—	—	—	—	—	—	2
Fraser, A. Anderson	London	1884-1885	Landscape	—	—	—	—	3	—	—	—	—	—	3
Fraser, F.	Sutton	1876	Domestic	—	—	—	—	2	—	—	—	—	—	2
Fraser, Miss Florence	London	1880-1883	Domestic	—	—	—	—	2	—	—	2	—	—	4
Fraser, Francis Arthur	London	1867-1883	Figures	—	—	4	—	11	—	—	—	—	13	28
Fraser, George Gordon	London	1880-1893	Landscape	—	—	8	—	—	—	—	1	—	1	10
Fraser, G. W.	Bedford	1876	Landscape	—	—	—	—	1	—	—	—	—	—	1
Fraser, John, R.B.A. §	London	1879-1893	Sea Pieces	—	—	35	—	72	—	13	1	—	9	130
Fraser, John A.	London	1889	Landscape	—	—	1	—	—	—	—	—	—	—	1
Frasèr, James B. §	London	1827-1831	Landscape	—	—	—	2	8	—	—	—	—	—	10
Fraser, James P. (?) John	London	1864-1884	Figures	—	—	11	4	7	—	—	—	—	—	22
Fraser, J. S.	Edinburgh	1883	Domestic	—	—	—	—	—	—	1	—	—	—	1
Fraser, P. Allan	Arbrook	1852-1878	Figures	—	—	4	—	—	—	—	—	—	—	4
Fraser, R.	Deptford	1798	Ships	—	—	1	—	—	—	—	—	—	—	1
Fraser, Robert W.	Bedford	1874-1893	Landscape	—	—	29	—	18	—	14	—	—	26	87
Fraser, William	London	1806-1811	Historical	—	—	7	1	—	—	—	—	—	—	8
Frasi, Horace C.	London	1892	Architecture	—	—	1	—	—	—	—	—	—	—	1
Fratelli, T.	London	1876	Cattle	—	—	—	—	—	—	—	—	—	1	1
Frazer, Charles E.	London	1881	Figures	—	—	1	—	—	—	—	—	—	—	1
Frazer, H., R.H.A.	London	1832-1841	Figures	—	—	—	2	2	—	—	—	—	—	4
Frazer, W. M.	Bridge of Erne	1892	Landscape	—	—	1	—	1	—	—	—	—	1	3
Frazer, Miss	Lynmouth	1866	Portraits	—	—	—	—	—	—	—	—	—	1	1
Freake, Mrs.	London	1879-1881	Sea Pieces	—	—	—	—	—	—	—	—	—	2	2
Frearson, John	London	1797-1831	Scriptural	—	—	28	12	—	—	—	—	—	—	40
Frederick, J.	London	1800-1801	Figures	—	—	2	—	—	—	—	—	—	—	2
Fredericks, J.	London	1856	Landscape	—	—	—	—	—	—	—	—	—	4	4
Frederics, A.	London	1877	Heads	—	—	—	—	1	—	—	—	—	—	1
Freebairn —	—	1830	Portraits	—	—	—	—	1	—	—	—	—	—	1
Freebairn, Robert	London	1782-1813	Landscape	—	—	54	22	—	8	—	—	—	—	84
Freebairn, R. G.	London	1818-1825	Sculpture	—	—	8	1	—	—	—	—	—	—	9
Freeling, K. J.	—	1857	Figures	—	—	1	—	—	—	—	—	—	—	1
Freeman, Lieut.	—	1783	Portraits	—	—	1	—	—	—	—	—	—	—	1
Freeman, C.	London	1844	Architecture	—	—	1	—	—	—	—	—	—	—	1
Freeman, Flower	London	1775-1776	Portraits	—	3	—	—	—	—	—	—	—	—	3
Freeman, G.	Bath	1828-1830	Portraits	—	—	11	—	—	—	—	—	—	—	11
Freeman, Henry	Liverpool	1874	Landscape	—	—	—	—	—	—	—	—	—	1	1
Freeman, Joseph	London	1775-1788	Still Life	1	2	1	—	—	—	—	—	—	—	4
Freeman, Miss M. Winifride	London	1886-1893	Domestic	—	—	—	—	—	—	11	—	3	—	14
Freeman, Miss Pauline	London	1869	Flowers	—	—	—	—	1	—	—	—	—	—	1
Freeman, R. Knill	Bolton-le-Moor	1882-1893	Architecture	—	—	8	—	—	—	—	—	—	—	8
Freeman, T.	Windsor	1780-1784	Scriptural	—	—	4	—	—	—	—	—	—	—	4
Freeman, Thomas	London	1774-1782	Architecture	—	—	7	—	—	—	—	—	—	—	7
Freeman, W.	Norwich	1808	Landscape	—	—	1	—	—	—	—	—	—	—	1
Freeman, William, Junr.	Norwich	1860	Landscape	—	—	1	—	—	—	—	—	—	—	1
Freeman, W. H.	London	1840	Figures	—	—	1	—	—	—	—	—	—	—	1
Freeman, William P. B.	Norwich	1862	Sea Pieces	—	—	—	—	1	—	—	—	—	—	1
Freer, Mrs. John. *See* Miss M. Ellen Edwards	—	—	—	—	—	—	—	—	—	—	—	—	—	—
and Mrs. Staples	London	1868-1871	Domestic	—	—	6	—	—	—	—	—	—	2	8
Freese, J.	London	1811	Portraits	—	—	1	—	—	—	—	—	—	—	1
Freese, N.	London	1794-1814	Portraits	—	—	14	—	—	—	—	—	—	—	14
Freezor, George Augustus	London	1861-1879	Figures	—	—	5	1	1	—	—	—	—	—	7
Freezor, Mrs.	London	1866	Fruit	—	—	—	1	—	—	—	—	—	—	1
Fremiet, E.	London	1891	Sculpture	—	—	—	—	—	—	—	—	—	1	1
French, Miss Annie	London	1863-1866	Landscape	—	—	—	2	5	—	—	—	—	2	9
French, G. R.	Wanstead	1821-1832	Architecture	—	—	3	—	—	—	—	—	—	—	3
French, Henry	London	1872-1875	Domestic	—	—	—	—	3	—	—	—	—	—	3
French, P. C.	Dublin	1885	Sporting	—	—	—	—	1	—	—	—	—	—	1
French, Thomas	London	1774	Landscape	—	4	—	—	—	—	—	—	—	—	4
Frend, Alfred Blackburne	London	1846-1860	Architecture	—	—	2	—	—	—	—	—	—	—	2
Frere, Augusta	London	1871	Landscape	—	—	—	—	—	—	—	—	—	1	1
Frére, Pierre Edouard	Ecouen	1868-1885	Domestic	—	—	28	—	—	—	—	—	—	1	29
Fresnoy, Du. *See* D.	—	—	—	—	—	—	—	—	—	—	—	—	—	—
Fretag, De. *See* D.	—	—	—	—	—	—	—	—	—	—	—	—	—	—
Frew, Alexander	Glasgow	1890	Landscape	—	—	2	—	—	—	—	—	—	—	2
Frewer, Mrs.	Norwich	1805	Feathers	—	—	2	—	—	—	—	—	—	—	2
Freyburg, Frank P.	Hassock	1893	Domestic	—	—	1	—	—	—	—	—	—	—	1
Friedenson, Arthur A.	Leeds	1889-1892	Landscape	—	—	4	—	—	—	—	—	—	—	4
Friedlander, N.	Stockholm	1844	Historical	—	—	1	—	—	—	—	—	—	—	1

Name.	Town.	First and Last Year of Ex.	Speciality.	S. A.	F. S.	R. A.	B. I.	S. S.	O. W.	N. W.	G. G.	N. G.	V. E.	Total.
Frieman, J.	London	1799	Portraits	—	—	1	—	—	—	—	—	—	—	1
Friend, J. S.	London	1839-1841	Figures	—	—	5	—	—	—	—	—	—	—	5
Friese, R.	Berlin	1879	Animals	—	—	—	—	—	—	—	—	—	3	3
Frigout, Mrs. Julie	London	1885-1889	Landscape	—	—	1	—	8	—	—	—	—	—	9
Frimt —.	London	1783	Fans	—	1	—	—	—	—	—	—	—	—	1
Fripp, Alfred Downing, R.W.S. †	London	1842-1893	Domestic	—	—	1	2	5	265	—	—	—	—	273
Fripp, Charles Edwin, A.R.W.S. †	London	1880-1893	Figures	—	—	2	—	—	23	—	—	—	4	29
Fripp, Miss Constance L. ‖	Southampton	1869-1892	Landscape	—	—	1	—	7	—	3	—	—	6	17
Fripp, George Arthur, R.W.S. † (?) Alfred	Bristol	1837-1893	Landscape	—	—	4	7	4	581	—	—	—	1	597
Fripp, Innes	London	1893	Stained Glass	—	—	1	—	—	—	—	—	—	—	1
Fripp, J. W.	—	1893	Landscape	—	—	—	—	—	—	—	—	1	—	1
Fripp, S. G.	London	1838-1854	Architecture	—	—	5	—	—	—	—	—	—	—	5
Fripp, Tom	London	1890-1892	Landscape	—	—	—	—	6	—	—	—	1	—	7
Friston, David Henry	London	1853-1869	Figures	—	—	14	6	1	—	—	—	—	—	21
Friswell, Harry P. Hain-	Conway	1882-1892	Landscape	—	—	5	—	7	—	—	—	—	4	16
Friswell, Mrs. J. (Emma)	London	1852-1862	Figures	—	—	3	4	7	—	—	—	—	—	14
Frith, Rev. Mr.	London	1788-1793	Figures	—	—	2	—	—	—	—	—	—	—	2
Frith, E.	—	1790-1791	Rustic	—	—	2	—	—	—	—	—	—	—	2
Frith, J.	Croydon	1819	Portraits	—	—	2	—	—	—	—	—	—	—	2
Frith, William Powell, R.A.	London	1838-1893	Figures	—	—	136	13	13	—	—	1	—	9	172
Frith, William S.	Herne Hill	1884-1892	Sculpture	—	—	5	—	—	—	—	—	—	—	5
Fritz, W.	London	1880	Heads	—	—	—	—	—	—	—	—	—	1	1
Froggatt, T.	London	1838-1850	Landscape	—	—	1	—	10	—	—	—	—	—	11
Frolich, F.	London	1890	Domestic	—	—	1	—	—	—	—	—	—	—	1
Frölich, L.	—	1875	Illustrations	—	—	—	—	—	—	—	—	—	1	1
Frome, W.	—	1831	Architecture	—	—	2	—	—	—	—	—	—	—	2
Fromont —.	—	1783	Landscape	—	1	—	—	—	—	—	—	—	—	1
Frost, Miss H.	Porchester	1858-1861	Still Life	—	—	—	—	6	—	—	—	—	—	6
Frost, James	London	1766-1783	Landscape	—	37	—	—	—	—	—	—	—	—	37
Frost, Miss Louisa A.	London	1853-1856	Figures	—	—	2	—	—	—	—	—	—	—	2
Frost, Miss Minnie P.	Willesden	1892	Domestic	—	—	—	—	1	—	—	—	—	—	1
Frost, R.	London	1882	Figures	—	—	1	—	—	—	—	—	—	—	1
Frost, W.	—	1803-1806	Sea Pieces	—	—	2	—	—	—	—	—	—	—	2
Frost, William Edward, R.A.	London	1836-1878	Allegorical	—	—	77	33	2	—	—	—	—	—	112
Frowd, Thomas T. J.	Windsor	1847-1864	Landscape	—	—	9	12	30	—	—	—	—	40	91
Frumaire, J. A.	Paris	1876	Engraving	—	—	—	—	—	—	—	—	—	1	1
Fry, H. Windsor-. *See* W.	—	—	—	—	—	—	—	—	—	—	—	—	—	—
Fry, Miss L. A.	Eltham	1855-1856	Flowers	—	—	2	—	3	—	—	—	—	—	5
Fry, Samuel	London	1877-1890	Sculpture	—	—	18	—	—	—	—	—	—	—	18
Fry, Mrs. Samuel. *See* Miss Caroline Nottidge	London	1880-1883	Figures	—	—	4	—	—	—	—	1	—	1	6
Fry, W. T.	London	1807-1811	Rustic	—	—	4	—	—	—	—	—	—	—	4
Fry, William Thomas	London	1824-1830	Engraving	—	—	—	—	13	—	—	—	—	—	13
Frye, Thomas	London	1760-1761	Engraving	6	—	—	—	—	—	—	—	—	—	6
Fryer, Edward H.	London	1834-1843	Landscape	—	—	9	6	3	—	—	—	—	—	18
Fryer, E. L.	London	1866	Landscape	—	—	—	2	1	—	—	—	—	—	3
Fryer, H.	London	1874-1875	Landscape	—	—	—	—	1	—	—	—	—	1	2
Fryer, Rose	London	1882	Venice	—	—	—	—	—	—	—	—	—	1	1
Fucigna, C. E.	London	1863-1879	Sculpture	—	—	10	—	—	—	—	—	—	—	10
Fudge, E.	Fareham	1845	Architecture	—	—	1	—	—	—	—	—	—	—	1
Fudge, J.	London	1815-1846	Landscape	—	—	25	—	—	—	—	—	—	—	25
Fuge, James	London	1832-1838	Landscape	—	—	—	2	3	—	3	—	—	—	8
Fuge, W. H.	Bocking	1849-1866	Figures	—	—	6	1	3	—	—	—	—	1	11
Fuhrlagh —. (?) Fuhrlogh	London	1773-1774	Sculpture	3	—	—	—	—	—	—	—	—	—	3
Fuidge, Edwin	Fareham	1854	Landscape	—	—	—	—	—	—	—	—	—	2	2
Fullagar, Miss H.	London	1839	Copies	—	—	—	—	3	—	—	—	—	—	3
Fuller. *See* Wilson and Fuller	—	—	Architecture	—	—	—	—	—	—	—	—	—	—	—
Fuller, Charles Francis	Florence	1859-1875	Sculpture	—	—	28	—	—	—	—	—	—	—	28
Fuller, Miss Edith	Croydon	1893	Domestic	—	—	—	—	—	—	—	—	1	—	1
Fuller, E. G.	St. Ives, Cornw'l	1893	Landscape	—	—	—	—	1	—	—	—	—	—	1
Fuller, Horace	London	1874-1884	Landscape	—	—	3	—	9	—	1	—	—	—	13
Fuller, J. A.	—	1831	Landscape	—	—	—	1	—	—	—	—	—	—	1
Fuller, S. P.	London	1863-1867	Landscape	—	—	—	—	3	—	—	—	—	—	3
Fullerton, Miss Jane	Paisley	1886	Sculpture	—	—	1	—	—	—	—	—	—	—	1
Fullerton, Mrs. (Elizabeth S.)	Paisley	1890-1893	Flowers	—	—	2	—	—	—	4	—	—	—	6
Fulleylove, John, R I. ‡ φ	Leicester	1871-1893	Landscape	—	—	10	—	16	—	100	5	—	36	167
Fullwood, Charles	Brandish	1888	Landscape	—	—	—	—	1	—	—	—	—	—	1
Fullwood, John, R.B.A. §	Twickenham	1881-1890	Landscape	—	—	12	—	16	—	2	—	2	1	33
Fulton, David, R.S.W.	Glasgow	1884	Landscape	—	—	1	—	—	—	—	—	—	—	1
Fulton, R.	London	1791-1793	Portraits	4	—	3	—	—	—	—	—	—	—	7
Funajoli, L. A.	London	1860	Sculpture	—	—	2	—	—	—	—	—	—	—	2
Furken, H.	Brussels	1838	Domestic	—	—	2	—	—	—	—	—	—	—	2
Furlong, Miss Marianne M.	Woolwich	1891-1893	Flowers	—	—	—	—	2	—	3	—	—	—	5

Name.	Town.	First and Last Year of Ex.	Speciality.	S. A.	F. S.	R. A.	B. I.	S. S.	O. W.	N. W.	G. G.	N. G.	V. E.	Total.
Furly, Miss	—	1783	Portraits	—	1	—	—	—	—	—	—	—	—	1
Furnell, Miss C.	Norwood	1843	Miniatures	—	—	3	—	—	—	—	—	—	—	3
Furness, Algerton	London	1856-1858	Landscape	—	—	1	2	—	—	—	—	—	—	3
Furniss, B. C.	London	1829-1833	Sculpture	—	—	3	—	—	—	—	—	—	—	3
Furniss, Harry	London	1875-1888	"Punch"	—	—	6	—	—	—	—	—	—	1	7
Furrell, C. J.	—	1872	Architecture	—	—	1	—	—	—	—	—	—	—	1
Furse, Charles A.	—	1891	Portraits	—	—	—	—	—	—	—	—	—	4	4
Furse, Charles W.	London	1885-1892	Portraits	—	—	9	—	1	—	—	1	4	2	17
Furse, J. H. Monsell	London	1891-1893	Sculpture	—	—	3	—	—	—	—	—	3	—	6
Furse, J. W.	London	1830	Figures	—	—	1	—	—	—	—	—	—	—	1
Furse, W. H.	Rome	1831-1850	Figures	—	—	6	4	—	—	—	—	—	—	10
Fuseli, Henry, R.A. (Fuessly)	Rome	1774-1825	Historical	3	—	69	3	—	—	—	—	—	—	75
Fussell, Alexander	London	1838-1881	Historical	—	—	5	4	6	—	—	2	—	21	38
Fussell, Frederick Ralph	London	1843-1858	Portraits	—	—	1	2	—	—	—	—	—	2	5
Fussell, Joseph	London	1821-1845	Landscape and Cattle	—	—	24	17	8	—	1	—	—	—	50
Füssli, W.	Munich	1874	Portraits	—	—	2	—	—	—	—	—	—	—	2
Fyfe, William B. C.	London	1865-1882	Domestic	—	—	26	2	4	—	—	—	—	6	38
Gaab —	London	1783	Sculpture	—	3	—	—	—	—	—	—	—	—	3
Gabriel (C.) and Billing (A.)	London	1848	Architecture	—	—	2	—	—	—	—	—	—	—	2
Gabriel, C. H.	London	1847-1850	Architecture	—	—	3	—	—	—	—	—	—	—	3
Gabriel, C. Wallis	Bath	1882	Domestic	—	—	1	—	—	—	—	—	—	—	1
Gabriel, Paul Jos. Constantine	London	1875-1880	Landscape	—	—	1	—	—	—	—	1	—	—	2
Gabrielli, G.	Dublin	1811-1819	Landscape	—	—	10	—	—	—	—	—	—	—	10
Gabrielli, Giuseppe	London	1863-1880	Sculpture	—	—	10	—	—	—	—	—	—	—	10
Gabrielli, M.	London	1814	Mythological	—	—	—	1	—	—	—	—	—	—	1
Gade, William R.	London	1878	Domestic	—	—	2	—	—	—	—	—	—	—	2
Gadsby, James	London	1872-1874	Flowers	—	—	—	—	1	—	—	—	—	1	2
Gadsby, William H., R.B.A. §	London	1869-1893	Domestic	—	—	5	—	73	—	—	—	—	1	79
Gahagan, C.	London	1824-1836	Sculpture	—	—	3	—	1	—	—	—	—	—	4
Gahagan, Edwin	London	1830-1857	Sculpture	—	—	4	5	4	—	—	—	—	—	13
Gahagan, L.	London	1798-1817	Sculpture	—	—	19	1	—	—	—	—	—	—	20
Gahagan, L., Junr.	London	1817	Sculpture	—	—	1	—	—	—	—	—	—	—	1
Gahagan, Sebastian	London	1817-1855	Sculpture	—	—	22	5	1	—	—	—	—	—	28
Gahagan, Sally	London	1802-1817	Sculpture	—	—	9	—	—	—	—	—	—	—	9
Gahagan, V.	London	1804-1823	Sculpture	—	—	8	—	—	—	—	—	—	—	8
Gaillard, J. F.	Paris	1876-1877	Etching	—	—	—	—	—	—	—	—	—	3	3
Gaines, G.	London	1770-1787	Landscape	—	7	9	—	—	—	—	—	—	—	16
Gainsborough, Thomas, R.A.	Bath	1761-1783	Portraits	18	3	96	—	—	—	—	—	—	—	117
Gainsford, F. G.	London	1805-1816	Portraits	—	—	6	—	—	—	—	—	—	—	6
Gair, Gillies	London	1872-1874	Portraits	—	—	3	—	1	—	—	—	—	1	5
Galbraith, W. C.	Whitley	1866-1870	Landscape	—	—	—	—	9	—	—	—	—	8	17
Gale —	London	1769-1770	Furniture	—	2	—	—	—	—	—	—	—	—	2
Gale, Arthur J. *See* Smith (T.) and Gale	—	—	Architecture	—	—	—	—	—	—	—	—	—	—	—
Gale, Frances	London	1877-1885	Thistles	—	—	1	—	—	—	—	—	—	1	2
Gale, J.	Orford	1820	Scriptural	—	—	1	—	—	—	—	—	—	—	1
Gale, Miss M.	London	1828	Still Life	—	—	—	—	—	—	—	—	—	1	1
Gale, R. L. §	Liverpool	1832-1841	Landscape	—	—	3	—	10	—	1	—	—	—	14
Gale, William	London	1844-1892	Scriptural	—	—	101	42	33	—	2	—	—	26	204
Gallagher, J.	London	1832-1844	Sculpture	—	—	4	—	—	—	—	—	—	—	4
Gallait, Louis, H.F.R.A., H.R.I. ‡	Brussels	1836-1872	Historical	—	—	3	—	—	—	4	—	—	—	7
Gallandat de Rovray, Miss Fanny. *See* De.	—	—	—	—	—	—	—	—	—	—	—	—	—	—
Gallaud, J. R.	London	1818	Portraits	—	—	3	—	—	—	—	—	—	—	3
Galli, F.	London	1866	Architecture	—	—	1	—	—	—	—	—	—	—	1
Gallimore, Samuel	Huddersfield	1861-1893	Domestic	—	—	5	—	1	—	1	—	—	—	7
Gallon, Robert	London	1868-1893	Landscape	—	—	21	—	27	—	—	—	—	7	55
Gallon, Robert Samuel Ennis	Greenwich	1830-1868	Figures	—	—	28	8	19	—	—	—	—	—	55
Gallori, E.	London	1875-1878	Sculpture	—	—	5	—	—	—	—	—	—	—	5
Galloway, E.	London	1847	Sea Pieces	—	—	1	—	—	—	—	—	—	—	1
Galloway, Samuel	London	1827-1835	Flowers	—	—	3	—	2	—	1	—	—	—	6
Galloway, S., Junr.	London	1832-1833	Portraits	—	—	—	—	5	—	—	—	—	—	5
Galofre, Baldomero	Paris	1881-1882	Landscape	—	—	2	—	—	—	—	2	—	—	4
Galpin, William Dixon	Roehampton	1883-1887	Domestic	—	—	3	—	1	—	—	—	—	—	4
Galsworthy, C. G.	London	1893	Domestic	—	—	—	—	2	—	—	—	—	—	2
Galsworthy, W. H.	London	1847-1856	Landscape	—	—	2	8	5	—	—	—	—	7	22
Gambardella, S.	London	1842-1852	Domestic	—	—	4	8	—	—	—	—	—	—	12
Gambel —	—	1773	Miniatures	—	2	—	—	—	—	—	—	—	—	2
Gamble —	—	1770	Hair Work	1	—	—	—	—	—	—	—	—	—	1
Gamble, James	London	1875-1892	Portraits	—	—	4	—	—	—	—	—	—	—	4

Name.	Town.	First and Last Year of Ex.	Speciality.	S. A.	F. S.	R. A.	B. I.	S. S.	O. W.	N. W.	G. G.	N. G.	V. E.	Total.
Gamble, Miss Louisa	London	1842	Portraits	—	—	1	—	—	—	—	—	—	—	1
Gammage, Miss Emma	Liverpool	1865-1868	Figures	—	—	—	3	3	—	—	—	—	—	6
Gandon, James, F.S.A.	London	1762-1780	Architecture	10	3	10	—	—	—	—	—	—	—	23
Gandy —	Liverpool	1778	Sea Pieces	—	2	—	—	—	—	—	—	—	—	2
Gandy, Miss Celia. *See* Mrs. Spencer	London	1826-1829	Flowers	—	—	5	—	—	—	—	—	—	—	5
Gandy, F.	London	1848-1859	Portraits	—	—	7	—	—	—	—	—	—	—	7
Gandy, Miss Hannah	London	1829-1833	Flowers	—	—	2	—	—	—	—	—	—	—	2
Gandy, Herbert	London	1879-1892	Landscape	—	—	11	—	3	—	1	—	—	8	23
Gandy, Joseph M., A.R.A.	London	1789-1838	Architecture	—	—	112	14	—	—	—	—	—	—	126
Gandy, John Peter, R.A. *See* Deering	London	1805-1827	Architecture	—	—	13	—	—	—	—	—	—	—	13
Gandy, Michael	London	1812	Conflagration	—	—	1	—	—	—	—	—	—	—	1
Gandy, T.	London	1824-1831	Architecture	—	—	4	—	1	—	—	—	—	—	5
Gandy, Walton	London	1893	Landscape	—	—	—	—	1	—	—	—	—	—	1
Gangalen, Van. *See* V.	—	—	—	—	—	—	—	—	—	—	—	—	—	—
Gant, James Y.	London	1827-1841	Landscape	—	—	13	13	—	—	—	—	—	—	26
Gantes, De. *See* D.	—	—	—	—	—	—	—	—	—	—	—	—	—	—
Ganthoney, R.	Richmond	1872	Landscape	—	—	—	—	1	—	—	—	—	—	1
Ganz, Henry F. W.	London	1888-1892	Portraits	—	—	1	—	—	—	—	1	—	2	4
Gapper, E.	London	1819	Landscape	—	—	—	1	—	—	—	—	—	—	1
Garbrand, Caleb J.	London	1773-1780	Portraits	6	10	8	—	—	—	—	—	—	—	24
Garden, J.	London	1834	Portraits	—	—	2	—	—	—	—	—	—	—	2
Garden, Miss Louisa E. (?) S.	London	1879	Landscape	—	—	—	—	1	—	—	—	—	1	2
Garden, W. F.	Bedford	1882-1890	Landscape	—	—	11	—	—	—	2	—	—	—	13
Gardener, R. B.	Tunbridge	1847	Architecture	—	—	2	—	—	—	—	—	—	—	2
Gardie, A. N.	London	1828	Portraits	—	—	1	—	—	—	—	—	—	—	1
Gardie, L.	London	1850-1854	Sculpture	—	—	6	—	—	—	—	—	—	—	6
Gardie, Mrs.	—	1828	Portraits	—	—	1	—	—	—	—	—	—	—	1
Gardiner, E.	—	1813	Architecture	—	—	1	—	—	—	—	—	—	—	1
Gardiner, Miss E.	—	1841	Landscape	—	—	—	—	2	—	—	—	—	—	2
Gardiner, J. B.	London	1803-1813	Architecture	—	—	9	—	—	—	—	—	—	—	9
Gardiner, Sarah	London	1815	Flowers	—	—	1	—	—	—	—	—	—	—	1
Gardiner, William Nelson	London	1787-1793	Figures	—	—	12	—	—	—	—	—	—	—	12
Gardiner, Miss	—	1762-1770	Figures	14	—	—	—	—	—	—	—	—	—	14
Gardner, Lord	Dorking	1887-1890	Landscape	—	—	—	—	—	—	5	—	—	—	5
Gardner, C.	London	1853-1856	Sea Pieces	—	—	1	3	—	—	—	—	—	—	4
Gardner, Daniel	London	1771	Figures	—	—	1	—	—	—	—	—	—	—	1
Gardner, Edwin C.	London	1867-1888	Domestic	—	—	3	—	11	—	3	—	—	1	18
Gardner, Emma E.	London	1875	Landscape	—	—	—	—	—	—	—	—	—	1	1
Gardner, G.	London	1884-1885	Fruit	—	—	—	—	2	—	—	—	—	—	2
Gardner, H.	London	1819	Bridges	—	—	1	—	—	—	—	—	—	—	1
Gardner, J. L.	London	1880-1888	Domestic	—	—	5	—	2	—	—	—	—	—	7
Gardner, Mabel	Cheltenham	1878-1879	Flowers	—	—	—	—	—	—	—	—	—	1	1
Gardner, W. Biscombe	London	1874-1893	Landscape & Etching	—	—	32	—	1	—	10	25	13	24	105
Gardner, Miss	—	1783	Landscape	—	—	2	—	—	—	—	—	—	—	2
Gardnor, Rev. John (?) James	London	1763-1796	Landscape	27	—	61	—	—	—	—	—	—	—	88
Gardnor, Richard	London	1765-1793	Landscape	—	7	8	—	—	—	—	—	—	—	15
Gare, G.	London	1802-1818	Miniatures	—	—	13	—	—	—	—	—	—	—	13
Garland, Charles Trevor	London	1874-1893	Landscape	—	—	19	—	19	—	1	—	—	27	66
Garland, H.	London	1867-1878	Sculpture	—	—	5	—	—	—	—	—	—	—	5
Garland, Henry	Winchester	1854-1890	Domestic	—	—	30	12	67	—	1	—	—	13	123
Garland, R.	London	1826-1831	Architecture	—	—	4	—	—	—	—	—	—	—	4
Garland, T. Valentine	Winchester	1871-1893	Domestic	—	—	7	—	40	—	—	—	—	14	61
Garland, T. W.	Winchester	1867-1871	Domestic	—	—	2	—	5	—	—	—	—	—	7
Garland, Valentine Thomas	Winchester	1884-1893	Domestic	—	—	4	—	—	—	8	—	—	—	12
Garland, William	Winchester	1857-1874	Domestic	—	—	4	—	10	—	—	—	—	—	14
Garlick, Park, and Sykes	London	1878	Architecture	—	—	1	—	—	—	—	—	—	—	1
Garling, H.	London	1820-1847	Architecture	—	—	4	—	—	—	—	—	—	—	4
Garling, Henry Bayly	London	1842-1875	Architecture	—	—	8	—	—	—	—	—	—	—	8
Garner, Thomas	London	1887-1892	Churches	—	—	3	—	—	—	—	—	—	—	3
Garnery —	London	1785	Portraits	—	—	3	—	—	—	—	—	—	—	3
Garnett, R.	London	1808-1811	Architecture	—	—	4	—	—	—	—	—	—	—	4
Garnett, Miss Ruth	London	1893	Domestic	—	—	2	—	—	—	—	—	1	1	4
Garnett, W.	London	1828-1834	Landscape	—	—	—	—	2	—	—	—	—	—	2
Garnham, G. R.	London	1878	Landscape	—	—	2	—	—	—	—	—	—	—	2
Garnier, A. *See* Alfred.	—	—	—	—	—	—	—	—	—	—	—	—	—	—
Garrard, Charles	London	1816-1829	Sculpture	—	—	19	2	5	—	—	—	—	—	26
Garrard, E.	London	1793	Landscape	—	—	7	—	—	—	—	—	—	—	7
Garrard, George, A.R.A.	London	1781-1826	Animals & Sculpture	—	—	215	14	9	—	—	—	—	—	238
Garrard, R. H.	London	1814	Horses	—	—	1	—	—	—	—	—	—	—	1
Garrard, T.	London	1809	Interiors	—	—	1	—	—	—	—	—	—	—	1
Garratt, Agnes M.	Walthamstow	1891	Domestic	—	—	—	—	1	—	—	—	—	—	1
Garratt, Eliza	Putney	1872	Still Life	—	—	—	—	—	—	—	—	—	1	1

Name.	Town.	First and Last Year of Ex.	Speciality.	S. A.	F. S.	R. A.	B. I.	S. S.	O. W.	N.W.	G. G.	N. G.	V. E.	Total.
Garratt, Thomas	London	1889-1892	Architecture	—	—	3	—	—	—	—	—	—	—	3
Garratt, William	London	1827-1831	Landscape	—	—	2	6	2	—	—	—	—	—	10
Garraway, Edward	London	1875-1878	Domestic	—	—	—	—	2	—	—	—	—	8	10
Garraway, G. Hervey	Liverpool	1870-1891	Figures	—	—	4	—	4	—	2	1	—	7	18
Garrer, J.	London	1876	Buildings	—	—	—	—	1	—	—	—	—	—	1
Garrett, W.	London	1844	Architecture	—	—	1	—	—	—	—	—	—	—	1
Garrie, R.	London	1865	Landscape	—	—	1	—	—	—	—	—	—	—	1
Garrod, Edith	London	1878-1880	Figures	—	—	—	—	—	—	—	—	—	2	2
Garstin, Norman	Paris	1882-1893	Domestic	—	—	9	—	12	—	—	3	—	4	28
Garth, B.	London	1796-1800	Landscape	—	—	8	—	—	—	—	—	—	—	8
Gartside, Miss	London	1781-1808	Flowers	—	—	3	—	—	—	—	—	—	6	9
Garvey, Miss Clara	Dulwich	1887-1892	Flowers	—	—	2	—	—	—	—	—	—	2	4
Garvey, Edmund, R.A.	Bath	1767-1809	Landscape	—	6	125	6	—	—	—	—	—	—	137
Garvie, T. Bowman	Morpeth	1886-1893	Domestic	—	—	5	—	2	—	—	—	—	—	7
Gascoigne, Mrs. G.	London	1871	Domestic	—	—	1	—	—	—	—	—	—	—	1
Gascoyne, George, R.P.E.	London	1882-1893	Domestic	—	—	8	—	—	—	—	—	1	7	16
Gaskell, George A.	London	1871-1879	Figures	—	—	6	—	4	—	—	—	—	4	14
Gaskell, J.	London	1774-1778	Miniatures	1	—	7	—	—	—	—	—	—	—	8
Gaskin, Arthur J.	Small Heath	1889-1891	Domestic	—	—	2	—	—	—	—	—	—	—	2
Gaspare, Gabrielli	London	1812	Landscape	—	—	—	1	—	—	—	—	—	—	1
Gass, John B.	Bolton	1880-1891	Architecture	—	—	3	—	—	—	—	—	—	—	3
Gassiot, H.	London	1877-1878	Domestic	—	—	—	—	—	—	—	—	—	3	3
Gast, Bertram	London	1888-1892	Rustic	—	—	4	—	6	—	1	—	—	—	11
Gast, Frank	London	1891-1892	Rustic	—	—	2	—	1	—	—	—	—	—	3
Gastineau, Henry G. †	London	1812-1875	Landscape	—	—	26	3	—	1310	—	—	—	2	1341
Gastineau, J. C.	—	1826	Landscape	—	—	1	—	—	—	—	—	—	—	1
Gastineau, Miss Maria ‖	London	1865-1867	Landscape	—	—	—	—	1	—	—	—	—	3	4
Gastrell —	—	1761	Metal Work	1	—	—	—	—	—	—	—	—	—	1
Gates, William H.	Wolverhampt'n	1888-1889	Sculpture	—	—	1	—	2	—	—	—	—	—	3
Gatley, Alfred	London	1841-1852	Sculpture	—	—	30	—	—	—	—	—	—	—	30
Gaubert, George Frederick	London	1829-1861	Sea Pieces	—	—	28	—	5	—	—	—	—	—	33
Gaucherel, Leon	Paris	1872-1881	Etching	—	—	—	—	—	—	—	1	—	9	10
Gauci, G.	London	1810-1827	Lithograph	—	—	9	—	6	—	—	—	—	4	19
Gauci, Paul	London	1834-1863	Landscape	—	—	4	1	2	—	1	—	—	—	8
Gaudens, A. St. *See* S.	—	—	—	—	—	—	—	—	—	—	—	—	—	—
Gaudez, A.	London	1879-1892	Sculpture	—	—	—	—	2	—	1	—	—	—	3
Gaugain, Mrs. Anne	London	1838-1847	Fruit	—	—	1	5	—	—	—	—	—	—	6
Gaugain, Ph. A.	London	1783-1847	Domestic	—	4	12	8	1	—	—	—	—	—	25
Gaugain, Thomas	London	1778-1782	Domestic	—	—	7	—	—	—	—	—	—	—	7
Gaujean, Edouard Henri	Paris	1888	Etching	—	—	2	—	—	—	—	—	—	—	2
Gault, Mdlle. Asile	—	1831	Portraits	—	—	—	1	—	—	—	—	—	—	1
Gaultier, A. T., *or* M.	London	1860-1861	Fruit	—	—	—	1	—	—	—	—	—	2	3
Gaunt, Thomas Edward	Tottenham	1876-1883	Figures	—	—	3	—	11	—	—	—	—	—	14
Gauntlett, Miss Gertrude E.	London	1866-1880	Domestic	—	—	1	—	13	—	—	—	—	4	18
Gaupp, Gustave	London	1884	Portraits	—	—	1	—	—	—	—	—	—	—	1
Gautier —	London	1792	Landscape	—	—	3	—	—	—	—	—	—	—	3
Gauthier, A.	London	1881	Landscape	—	—	—	—	—	—	—	—	—	1	1
Gautier, St. Elme, *or* St. Elène	London	1877	Engraving	—	—	—	—	—	—	—	—	—	1	1
Gautrey, J.	London	1819	Architecture	—	—	2	—	—	—	—	—	—	—	2
Gavarni, Mons.	Paris	1850	Figures	—	—	—	—	—	—	—	—	—	1	1
Gavey, R. E.	London	1828-1839	Figures	—	—	—	4	4	—	—	—	—	—	8
Gavin Robert, R.S.A.	Edinburgh	1855-1871	Domestic	—	—	5	—	—	—	—	—	—	—	5
Gawen, Joseph	London	1850-1882	Sculpture	—	—	7	—	—	—	—	—	—	—	7
Gay, B.	London	1807-1811	Portraits	—	—	2	—	—	—	—	—	—	—	2
Gay, Mdlle. Bertha	London	1883	Flowers	—	—	—	—	1	—	—	—	—	—	1
Gay, G.	London	1877-1880	Sculpture	—	—	2	—	—	—	—	—	—	—	2
Gay, Miss Lydia	London	1887-1893	Medallions	—	—	13	—	—	—	—	—	—	—	13
Gay, Miss Susan Elizabeth	Croydon	1874-1876	Landscape	—	—	2	—	—	—	—	—	—	—	2
Gay, Walter	Paris	1877-1891	Domestic	—	—	3	—	—	—	—	—	—	3	6
Gay, W. H.	London	1810	Landscape	—	—	—	—	1	—	—	—	—	—	1
Gaye, Howard	London	1880-1891	Architecture	—	—	2	—	—	—	—	—	—	—	2
Gayfere, Thomas	—	1777-1780	Landscape	1	—	3	—	—	—	—	—	—	—	4
Gayleard, Miss Sophia	London	1839-1846	Portraits	—	—	9	—	1	—	—	—	—	—	10
Gayler, Mrs. Ellen	Bristol	1891	Domestic	—	—	1	—	—	—	—	—	—	—	1
Gayler, J.	London	1830	Portraits	—	—	—	—	1	—	—	—	—	—	1
Gayton, Miss Anna M.	Much Hadham	1874-1893	Portraits	—	—	4	—	2	—	—	—	2	1	9
Gazzerini, Tommaso	—	1842	Scriptural	—	—	—	1	—	—	—	—	—	—	1
Gear, A. Händel	London	1877-1879	Sea Pieces	—	—	—	—	1	—	—	—	—	2	3
Gear, H. H.	—	1836	Portraits	—	—	—	—	2	—	—	—	—	—	2
Gear, J.	London	1815-1821	Sea Pieces	—	—	4	—	—	—	—	—	—	—	4
Gear, J. W.	London	1821-1852	Portraits	—	—	29	—	7	—	—	—	—	—	36
Geary, S.	London	1814-1838	Architecture	—	—	8	—	—	—	—	—	—	—	8

Name.	Town.	First and Last Year of Ex.	Speciality.	S. A.	F. S.	R. A.	B. I.	S. S.	O. W.	N.W.	G. G.	N. G.	V. E.	Total.
Geaussent, Mrs. George F.	London	1890	Flowers	—	—	—	—	—	—	—	—	—	1	1
Gebsattel, Baroness S.	Munich	1893	Domestic	—	—	1	—	—	—	—	—	—	—	1
Geddes, Andrew, A.R.A.	London	1806-1845	Portraits	—	—	100	28	—	—	—	—	—	—	128
Geddes, Ewan	Blairgowrie	1891-1892	Landscape	—	—	2	—	—	—	—	—	—	—	2
Geddes, Miss Margaret Sarah. *See* Mrs.	—	—	—	—	—	—	—	—	—	—	—	—	—	—
William Carpenter	London	1814-1817	Domestic	—	—	9	11	—	—	—	—	—	—	20
Geefs, C.	London	1858	Sculpture	—	—	1	—	—	—	—	—	—	—	1
Geefs, Madame G. (Fanny)	Brussels	1847-1849	Portraits	—	—	3	—	—	—	—	—	—	—	3
Geefs, Joseph	London	1855-1864	Sculpture	—	—	9	1	—	—	—	—	—	—	10
Geefs, William	Brussels	1843-1853	Sculpture	—	—	5	—	—	—	—	—	—	—	5
Geens, J. J.	Amsterdam	1828	Portraits	—	—	3	—	—	—	—	—	—	—	3
Geere, J.	London	1858-1867	Landscape	—	—	—	6	—	—	—	—	—	—	6
Geets, Willem	London	1884	Historical	—	—	1	—	—	—	—	—	—	—	1
Geflowski, E. Edward	London	1867-1888	Sculpture	—	—	4	—	4	—	—	3	—	4	15
Gegan, J. J.	Maidstone	1844-1860	Landscape	—	—	1	—	8	—	—	—	—	—	9
Gehrts, Carl	Düsseldorf	1889	Domestic	—	—	1	—	—	—	—	—	—	—	1
Geikie, Walter, R.S.A.	Edinburgh	1818-1835	Landscape	—	—	2	—	—	—	—	—	—	—	2
Geisler, C., *or* Giesler	London	1858	Landscape	—	—	—	—	1	—	—	—	—	—	1
Gelder, J.	Bradford	1865	Landscape	—	—	1	—	—	—	—	—	—	—	1
Gelder, Van. *See* V.	—	—	—	—	—	—	—	—	—	—	—	—	—	—
Gelissin, Maximilien Lambert	London	1833-1852	Landscape	—	—	1	2	—	—	—	—	—	—	3
Gell, Mrs. Freeman, formerly Miss Ada Evershed	Brighton	1887-1893	Sculpture	—	—	7	—	1	—	—	3	—	—	11
Geller, Miss Angelina	London	1865-1886	Fruit	—	—	—	—	2	—	1	—	—	—	3
Geller, S. B.	—	1848	Engraving	—	—	—	—	—	—	—	—	—	1	1
Geller, W. Henry	London	1848-1849	Flowers	—	—	1	—	—	—	—	—	—	1	2
Geller, William Overend	London	1834-1848	Engraving	—	—	—	5	—	—	—	—	—	1	6
Gelling, C.	London	1815	Landscape	—	—	—	—	—	—	—	—	—	5	5
Gemmell, Miss Mary R. (?) Marion	Anerley	1876-1893	Flowers	—	—	4	—	3	—	—	—	—	4	11
Gendall, John	Exeter	1818-1863	Landscape	—	—	25	1	—	—	—	—	—	—	26
Génisson, Julius Victor	Louvain	1851	Churches	—	—	—	1	—	—	—	—	—	—	1
Gennadios, C.	Pisa	1873	Figures	—	—	1	—	—	—	—	—	—	—	1
Genotin, Frederick	Edinburgh	1866	Domestic	—	—	1	—	1	—	—	—	—	—	2
Gent, G. W.	—	1804-1822	Landscape	—	—	9	—	—	—	—	—	—	—	9
Gent, Mrs. *See* Miss S. S. Daniell	—	1832-1845	Portraits	—	—	28	—	10	—	—	—	—	—	38
Geoffroi, Harry	Penzance	1884	Landscape	—	—	—	—	1	—	1	—	—	—	2
Geoffroy, Jean	London	1890	Domestic	—	—	1	—	—	—	—	—	—	—	1
Geoghegan, Charles	London	1849	Architecture	—	—	1	—	—	—	—	—	—	—	1
George, E.	London	1824-1826	Landscape	—	—	—	2	1	—	—	—	—	—	3
George, Ernest, R.B.A., R.P.E. §	London	1859-1893	Etching	—	—	45	—	33	—	2	—	—	31	111
George (Ernest) and Peto	London	1886-1893	Architecture	—	—	36	—	—	—	—	—	—	—	36
George, F. W. (G. F. Watts, R.A.)	London	1858	Portraits	—	—	3	—	—	—	—	—	—	—	3
George, John	London	1763-1771	Portraits	—	14	—	—	—	—	—	—	—	—	14
George, J.	London	1825-1838	Figures	—	—	12	1	7	—	—	—	—	—	20
George, S. G.	London	1874	Churches	—	—	—	—	—	—	—	—	—	1	1
George, W.	London	1847-1848	Landscape	—	—	1	1	3	—	—	—	—	—	5
George, W. Pettitt	Brethwaite	1852-1854	Landscape	—	—	—	1	8	—	—	—	—	—	9
George, St. *See* S.	—	—	—	—	—	—	—	—	—	—	—	—	—	—
Georges, Charles E.	London	1893	Rustic	—	—	—	—	1	—	—	—	—	—	1
Gerard, Baron Francis Pascal Simon	Paris	1824-1830	Portraits	—	—	2	—	—	—	—	—	—	—	2
Gerardin, D. De la Place	London	1868-1879	Landscape	—	—	—	—	6	—	—	—	—	—	6
Gere, Charles M.	Leamington	1890-1893	Figures	—	—	1	—	—	—	—	—	6	—	7
Germany, H.I.M. Empress Frederick of. *See*	—	—	—	—	—	—	—	—	—	—	—	—	—	—
Royal.	—	—	—	—	—	—	—	—	—	—	—	—	—	—
Gernion, E. D.	—	1853	Cattle	—	—	1	—	—	—	—	—	—	—	1
Gérôme, Jean Léon, H.F.R.A.	Paris	1870-1893	Historical	—	—	6	—	—	—	—	—	—	2	8
Gerrard, E.	London	1813	Domestic	—	—	1	—	—	—	—	—	—	—	1
Gerry, W.	London	1844	Architecture	—	—	1	—	—	—	—	—	—	—	1
Gerth, Fritz	Rome	1888-1892	Sculpture	—	—	4	—	—	—	—	—	—	—	4
Gervex, Henri	—	1893	Portraits	—	—	—	—	—	—	—	—	—	1	1
Gessner, Conrad	London	1799-1803	Landscape	—	—	24	—	—	—	—	—	—	—	24
Gewers, D.	London	1799-1800	Portraits	—	—	2	—	—	—	—	—	—	—	2
Ghent, Peter, R.C.A.	Birkenhead	1879-1892	Landscape	—	—	21	—	3	—	9	1	—	5	39
Gheys, James	London	1774-1778	Sculpture	—	—	3	—	—	—	—	—	—	—	3
Giachi (*or* Giacpi), F.	London	1888-1889	Domestic	—	—	—	—	—	—	—	—	—	2	2
Giachosa, F.	London	1842-1848	Portraits	—	—	2	—	—	—	—	—	—	1	3
Giampietri, Chevalier Settino	London	1893	Buildings	—	—	—	—	—	—	—	—	1	—	1
Giampietri, Madame.‖ *See* Miss Amy Butts	Rome	1883	Figures	—	—	—	—	—	—	—	—	—	1	1
Gianelli —	London	1777	Portraits	1	—	—	—	—	—	—	—	—	—	1
Giannelli, D.	London	1809-1820	Sculpture	—	—	7	—	—	—	—	—	—	—	7
Gianetti, Raffaele	Liverpool	1881-1887	Domestic	—	—	4	—	—	—	—	—	—	—	4
Gibb, J.	Edinburgh	1827	Architecture	—	—	1	—	—	—	—	—	—	—	1
Gibb, Robert, R.S.A.	Edinburgh	1882-1893	Historical	—	—	5	—	—	—	—	—	—	—	5

Name.	Town.	First and Last Year of Ex.	Speciality.	S. A.	F. S.	R. A.	B. I.	S. S.	O. W.	N. W.	G. G.	N. G.	V. E.	Total.
GIBBINS, H. J.	Dulwich	1871-1872	Landscape	—	—	1	—	1	—	—	—	—	—	2
GIBBON, BENJAMIN PHELPS	London	1828	Engraving	—	—	—	—	1	—	—	—	—	—	1
GIBBON, G.	London	1818-1821	Portraits	—	—	2	—	—	—	—	—	—	—	2
GIBBONS, A.	London	1869	Heads	—	—	1	—	—	—	—	—	—	—	1
GIBBONS, J. T.	London	1832	Heads	—	—	1	—	—	—	—	—	—	—	1
GIBBS, MISS BEATRICE	London	1888-1893	Domestic	—	—	4	—	1	—	—	—	—	5	10
GIBBS, CHARLES	Dorking	1877-1893	Landscape	—	—	9	—	22	—	—	—	—	5	36
GIBBS, E. M. *See also* Flockton and Gibbs. .	Sheffield	1874	Architecture	—	—	1	—	—	—	—	—	—	—	1
GIBBS, F. J.	London	1854	Domestic	—	—	1	—	—	—	—	—	—	—	1
GIBBS, HENRY	London	1850-1858	Sculpture	—	—	5	—	—	—	—	—	—	—	5
GIBBS, HENRY	London	1865-1893	Figures	—	—	26	—	5	—	—	—	—	2	33
GIBBS, H. F.	London	1833	Portraits	—	—	1	—	—	—	—	—	—	—	1
GIBBS, ISAAC A. *See also* Boehmer and Gibbs .	London	1881-1888	Architecture	—	—	2	—	—	—	—	—	—	2	4
GIBBS, JAMES	London	1840-1841	Architecture	—	—	2	—	—	—	—	—	—	—	2
GIBBS, J. F.	London	1854-1858	Sporting	—	—	—	4	—	—	—	—	—	—	4
GIBBS, J. W.	London	1874	Churches	—	—	—	—	2	—	—	—	—	—	2
GIBBS, MISS MARY	Brentford	1860-1878	Figures	—	—	—	2	5	—	—	—	—	3	10
GIBBS, REGINALD	Topsham	1889	Landscape	—	—	—	—	1	—	—	—	—	—	1
GIBBS, S. H.	London	1849	Domestic	—	—	—	1	—	—	—	—	—	—	1
GIBBS, MISS	London	1845	Portraits	—	—	1	—	—	—	—	—	—	—	1
GIBERNE, EDGAR	Epsom	1872-1888	Domestic	—	—	4	—	3	—	4	—	—	22	33
GIBLETT, J.	London	1846	Portraits	—	—	1	—	—	—	—	—	—	—	1
GIBSON. *See* Russell and Gibson.	—	—	Landscape	—	—	—	—	—	—	—	—	—	—	—
GIBSON, D.	London	1790-1795	Miniatures	—	—	15	—	—	—	—	—	—	—	15
GIBSON, DAVID COOKE	London	1855-1857	Domestic	—	—	5	—	—	—	—	—	—	—	5
GIBSON, EDWARD	London	1875-1876	Sculpture, etc.	—	—	3	—	—	—	—	—	—	4	7
GIBSON, MISS EDITH ‖.	New Barnet	1882-1886	Domestic	—	—	1	—	2	—	—	—	—	—	3
GIBSON, MISS EDITH M.	London	1884-1893	Domestic	—	—	1	—	2	—	—	—	—	2	5
GIBSON, F.	Saffron Walden	1786-1834	Buildings	—	—	2	—	1	—	7	—	—	—	10
GIBSON, G.	London	1837-1838	Landscape	—	—	3	—	3	—	—	—	—	—	6
GIBSON, G. M.	London	1876	Portraits	—	—	—	—	—	—	—	—	—	1	1
GIBSON, JOHN, R.A.	Liverpool	1816-1864	Sculpture	—	—	33	—	—	—	—	—	—	—	33
GIBSON, JOHN	London	1858-1878	Architecture	—	—	15	—	—	—	—	—	—	—	15
GIBSON, J. D.	London	1827	Portraits	—	—	2	—	—	—	—	—	—	—	2
GIBSON, JOSEPH J.	Cork	1877-1887	Domestic	—	—	1	—	3	—	—	—	—	—	4
GIBSON, JAMES S.	London	1889	Architecture	—	—	1	—	—	—	—	—	—	—	1
GIBSON, JOSEPH VINCENT	London	1861-1888	Domestic	—	—	6	1	1	—	—	—	—	6	14
GIBSON, MISS MARY JOSEPHINE	London	1885-1893	Miniatures	—	—	39	—	—	—	—	—	—	—	39
GIBSON, PETER	London	1805-1811	Landscape	—	—	8	1	—	—	—	—	—	—	9
GIBSON, ROBERT W	London	1880	Architecture	—	—	1	—	—	—	—	—	—	—	1
GIBSON, SOLOMON	Liverpool	1816-1822	Sculpture	—	—	2	—	—	—	—	—	—	—	2
GIBSON, THOMAS	London	1841	Landscape	—	—	—	—	4	—	—	—	—	—	4
GIDDENS, GEORGE	London	1879-1885	Landscape	—	—	—	—	8	—	—	—	—	1	9
GIESWELL, MISS	London	1830-1832	Flowers	—	—	—	—	4	—	—	—	—	—	4
GIFFORD, GEORGE, EARL OF	—	1854	Sculpture	—	—	1	—	—	—	—	—	—	—	1
GIFFORD, A. E.	Bath	1870	Portraits	—	—	1	—	—	—	—	—	—	—	1
GIFFORD, E.	London	1801	Architecture	—	—	3	—	—	—	—	—	—	—	3
GIFFORD, E. A.	London	1833-1841	Architecture	—	—	7	—	—	—	—	—	—	—	7
GIFFORD, E. A.	London	1837-1876	Figures	—	—	6	6	16	—	—	—	—	5	33
GIFFORD, HON. EDWARD SCOTT	London	1865	Coast Scenes	—	—	—	—	—	—	—	—	—	1	1
GIFFORD, F.	Exmouth	1854	Figures	—	—	1	—	—	—	—	—	—	—	1
GIFFORD, J.	London	1841-1847	Sculpture	—	—	5	—	—	—	—	—	—	—	5
GIFFORD, R. S., N.A.	New York	1881	Coast Scenes	—	—	1	—	—	—	—	—	—	—	1
GILARDI, P. C.	Venice	1884	Domestic	—	—	—	—	—	—	—	—	—	3	3
GILBERT, ALFRED, R.A., H.R.I. ‡	Rome	1882-1892	Sculpture	—	—	22	—	—	—	*	3	1	—	26
GILBERT, ARTHUR (WILLIAMS FAMILY) . . .	London	1838-1885	Landscape	—	—	48	51	111	—	—	—	—	50	260
GILBERT, ACHILLE-ISIDORE	Paris	1877-1884	Etching	—	—	4	—	—	—	—	—	—	4	8
GILBERT, MRS. E.	London	1843	Portraits	—	—	1	—	—	—	—	—	—	—	1
GILBERT, MISS ELLEN	Blackheath	1863-1891	Domestic	—	—	1	—	55	—	—	—	—	11	67
GILBERT, FREDERICK	Blackheath	1862-1877	Domestic	—	—	—	—	12	—	—	—	—	5	17
GILBERT, MRS. G. M.	—	1856	Landscape	—	—	1	—	—	—	—	—	—	—	1
GILBERT, HORACE W.	Redhill	1873-1885	Landscape	—	—	5	—	3	—	—	—	—	4	12
GILBERT, SIR JOHN, R.A., P.R.W.S., H.R.C.A., H.R.S.W. † §	Blackheath	1836-1893	Historical	—	—	51	40	20	260	—	—	—	4	375
GILBERT, JOSIAH	London	1837-1865	Portraits	—	—	37	1	15	—	—	—	—	—	53
GILBERT, JOSEPH FRANCIS	Portsmouth	1813-1853	Landscape	—	—	6	5	12	—	—	—	—	5	28
GILBERT, JOHN GRAHAM, R.S.A.	Glasgow	1844-1864	Landscape	—	—	9	1	—	—	—	—	—	—	10
GILBERT, J. M.	London	1825-1855	Sea Pieces	—	—	2	2	2	—	—	—	—	—	6
GILBERT, MISS KATE, AFTERWARDS MRS. HUGHES	Croydon	1885	Landscape	—	—	—	—	1	—	—	—	—	—	1
GILBERT, MISS MINNIE F. W.	Exeter	1889	Fruit	—	—	1	—	—	—	—	—	—	—	1
GILBERT, MISS O. P.	Blackheath	1862-1891	Domestic	—	—	—	—	58	—	—	—	—	15	73
GILBERT VARNEE	London	1888	Portraits	—	—	—	—	1	—	—	—	—	—	1

Name.	Town.	First and Last Year of Ex.	Speciality.	S. A.	F. S.	R. A.	B. I.	S. S.	O. W.	N. W.	G. G.	N. G.	V. E.	Total.
Gilbert, William H.	London	1888	Portraits	—	—	—	—	1	—	—	—	—	—	1
Gilbert, W. J.	Halsworth	1851	Figures	—	—	—	—	—	—	—	—	—	1	1
Gilbert, Mrs.	Worcester	1865	Landscape	—	—	1	—	—	—	—	—	—	1	2
Gilchrist, Herbert H.	London	1876-1888	Domestic	—	—	4	—	—	—	—	3	—	3	10
Gilchrist, Miss J. A.	Sidmouth	1885-1888	Landscape	—	—	—	—	—	—	3	—	—	—	3
Gilchrist, Mrs.	London	1774-1775	Portraits	5	—	—	—	—	—	—	—	—	—	5
Gildawie, James	London	1836	Figures	—	—	1	—	—	—	—	—	—	—	1
Gilder, Henry	Windsor	1773-1778	Landscape	—	—	5	—	—	—	—	—	—	—	5
Giles. *See* Barber and Giles	—	—	Enamels	—	—	—	—	—	—	—	—	—	—	—
Giles, C. E.	London	1864	Architecture	—	—	1	—	—	—	—	—	—	—	1
Giles, Edith	London	1891	Landscape	—	—	—	—	1	—	—	—	—	—	1
Giles, Major Godfrey Douglas	London	1882-1890	Military	—	—	5	—	1	—	—	2	—	1	9
Giles, John	London	1861-1866	Architecture	—	—	5	—	—	—	—	—	—	—	5
Giles (John) and Gough	London	1874-1882	Architecture	—	—	4	—	—	—	—	—	—	—	4
Giles, Gough, and Trollope	London	1890	Architecture	—	—	1	—	—	—	—	—	—	—	1
Giles, John Alfred	London	1849-1862	Domestic	—	—	5	—	—	—	—	—	—	—	5
Giles, John West	Aberdeen	1830-1864	Landscape	—	—	6	5	9	—	—	—	—	—	20
Giles, James William, R.S.A.	Aberdeen	1830-1868	Landscape	—	—	2	80	13	—	—	—	—	—	95
Giles, Margaret	—	1893	Buildings	—	—	—	—	1	—	—	—	—	—	1
Giles, Mary	London	1870	Figures	—	—	—	—	1	—	—	—	—	—	1
Giles, R. H.	Gravesend	1826-1876	Portraits	—	—	48	—	22	—	3	—	—	1	74
Gilks, Thomas	London	1859-1875	Landscape	—	—	—	—	1	—	—	—	—	10	11
Gill, Charles (Pupil of Sir J. Reynolds)	London	1772-1819	Portraits	—	—	14	—	—	—	—	—	—	—	14
Gill, Christopher	London	1879-1886	Architecture	—	—	3	—	—	—	—	—	—	—	3
Gill, E.	London	1810	Rustic	—	—	1	—	—	—	—	—	—	—	1
Gill, Edmund	Sutton	1868-1886	Waterfalls	—	—	11	—	6	—	—	—	—	7	24
Gill, Edw.	London	1842-1872	Waterfalls	—	—	50	32	36	—	—	—	—	—	118
Gill, E. W.	Hereford	1843-1868	Still Life	—	—	16	3	1	—	—	—	—	—	20
Gill, F. H.	London	1838-1842	Landscape	—	—	—	1	14	—	—	—	—	—	15
Gill, F. T.	London	1847	Sporting	—	—	—	1	—	—	—	—	—	—	1
Gill, Harry P.	London	1881-1889	Landscape	—	—	—	—	4	—	—	—	—	1	5
Gill, J.	London	1809	Landscape	—	—	1	1	—	—	—	—	—	—	2
Gill, J. S.	Reading	1847-1862	Landscape	—	—	1	1	2	—	—	—	—	—	4
Gill, R.	London	1807-1825	Portraits	—	—	3	—	—	—	—	—	—	—	3
Gill, R. A.	London	1872-1885	Landscape	—	—	2	—	7	—	1	—	—	5	15
Gill, T. W.	Ludlow	1860	Landscape	—	—	—	1	—	—	—	—	—	—	1
Gill, William §	London	1826-1869	Domestic	—	—	18	22	46	—	—	—	—	—	86
Gill, W. H.	Eltham	1871-1872	Landscape	—	—	—	—	1	—	—	—	—	1	2
Gill, W. W.	Ludlow	1854-1867	Landscape	—	—	—	5	4	—	—	—	—	—	9
Gill, Captain	—	1834-1840	Figures	—	—	3	—	—	—	—	—	—	—	3
Gillard, William	Liverpool	1856	Landscape	—	—	1	—	—	—	—	—	—	—	1
Giller, William	London	1825-1856	Engraving	—	—	3	—	22	—	—	—	—	—	25
Gillet, Miss C.	Biddeston	1859	Fruit	—	—	1	—	—	—	—	—	—	—	1
Gillet, John	London	1886-1892	Miniatures	—	—	5	—	—	—	—	—	—	—	5
Gillett, G.	M'lt'n Mowbray	1862-1871	Sporting	—	—	—	7	1	—	—	—	—	—	8
Gillett, William J.	London	1878-1884	Landscape	—	—	—	—	2	—	—	—	—	5	7
Gilli, Alberto Masso	Rome	1875-1887	Domestic	—	—	1	—	—	—	—	—	—	2	3
Gillies, Miss Margaret †	London	1832-1887	Portraits	—	—	101	2	8	258	—	8	—	7	384
Gillman, Gustave	Lee	1878-1881	Buildings	—	—	—	—	—	—	—	—	—	6	6
Gilmour, Miss	London	1869	Heads	—	—	—	—	1	—	—	—	—	—	1
Gilossi, G.	Slough	1882-1883	Landscape	—	—	—	—	2	—	—	—	—	—	2
Gilpin, H. S.	London	1797-1801	Landscape	—	—	3	—	—	—	—	—	—	—	3
Gilpin, Sawrey, F.S.A., R.A.	London	1762-1808	Sporting	83	—	36	1	—	—	—	—	—	—	120
Gilpin, William Sawrey †.	London	1800-1815	Landscape	—	—	1	—	—	85	—	—	—	—	86
Gimber, Stephen H.	London	1825-1828	Engraving	—	—	—	—	3	—	—	—	—	—	3
Gingell, Mrs. A. E.	Isle of Wight	1851	Flowers	—	—	—	—	1	—	—	—	—	—	1
Ginn, John	London	1832-1833	Sculpture	—	—	3	—	1	—	—	—	—	—	4
Gioli, Professor Francesco	London	1880-1887	Sea Pieces	—	—	2	—	1	—	—	1	—	—	4
Giovanni, De. *See* D.	—	—	—	—	—	—	—	—	—	—	—	—	—	—
Giradet, Edouard Henri	Paris	1879	Engraving	—	—	1	—	—	—	—	—	—	—	1
Giradin, Madame P.	London	1851	Flowers	—	—	1	—	—	—	—	—	—	—	1
Giradot, Alfred C.	London	1877	Landscape	—	—	—	—	1	—	—	—	—	—	1
Giradot, C. E.	London	1874	Domestic	—	—	—	—	1	—	—	—	—	—	1
Giradot, Ernest Gustave §	London	1860-1893	Domestic	—	—	18	11	76	—	—	—	—	5	110
Giradot, Jean Edine	London	1841	—	—	—	*	—	—	—	—	—	—	—	—
Giraldon (*or* Geraldon), Adolphe	Paris	1880	Landscape	—	—	—	—	—	—	—	—	—	1	1
Girardy, De. *See* D.	—	—	—	—	—	—	—	—	—	—	—	—	—	—
Giraudat, Edgard	Paris	1887	Streets	—	—	1	—	—	—	—	—	—	—	1
Girdlestone, Lucy	Sunningdale	1886	Flowers	—	—	—	—	2	—	—	—	—	—	2
Girling, Richard	London	1858	Landscape	—	—	1	—	—	—	—	—	—	—	1
Girtin, Thomas	London	1794-1801	Landscape	—	—	33	—	—	—	—	—	—	—	33
Girvin, Charles W.	Birkenhead	1873-1874	Landscape	—	—	—	—	5	—	—	—	—	5	10

Name.	Town.	First and Last Year of Ex.	Speciality.	S. A.	F. S.	R. A.	B. I.	S. S.	O. W.	N. W.	G. G.	N. G.	V. E.	Total.
Gittens, E.	London	1868	Architecture	—	—	1	—	—	—	—	—	—	—	1
Gittens, Miss Edith	Leicester	1869-1887	Landscape	—	—	2	—	—	—	4	—	—	4	10
Gittos, J. B.	London	1786-1787	Architecture	—	—	2	—	—	—	—	—	—	—	2
Giuliani, Don Andrea	Grenada	1853	Portraits	—	—	2	—	—	—	—	—	—	—	2
Giuntini, L.	London	1874	Portraits	—	—	1	—	—	—	—	—	—	—	1
Gladstone, J. G.	London	1834-1836	Sea Pieces	—	—	2	—	—	—	—	—	—	—	2
Gladstone, Miss Mary S.	Laurencekirk	1879	Portraits	—	—	1	—	—	—	—	—	—	—	1
Gladwell, Miss Ann	—	1776	Heads	—	1	—	—	—	—	—	—	—	—	1
Gladwin, G.	London	1828	Churches	—	—	—	—	1	—	—	—	—	—	1
Glaize, L.	—	1883	Portraits	—	—	—	—	—	—	—	1	—	—	1
Glanville —	London	1780	Portraits	1	—	—	—	—	—	—	—	—	—	1
Glardon, C. L.	Geneva	1872-1876	Enamels	—	—	11	—	—	—	—	—	—	—	11
Glascott, S.	Brighton	1833-1852	Sporting	—	—	1	1	16	—	—	—	—	1	19
Glasgow, Alexander	London	1859-1884	Domestic	—	—	15	6	16	—	—	—	—	—	37
Glasier, Annie	Teddington	1872	Domestic	—	—	—	—	—	—	—	—	—	1	1
Glasier, Miss Florence E.	Hampton Wick	1866-1873	Figures	—	—	—	1	5	—	—	—	—	2	8
Glaskett, S.	London	1864	Domestic	—	—	—	1	—	—	—	—	—	—	1
Glass, A.	London	1890	Sculpture	—	—	—	—	—	—	—	—	1	—	1
Glass, James W., A.R.S.A.	Edinburgh	1847-1859	Military	—	—	10	16	5	—	—	—	—	10	41
Glassby, Robert Edward	London	1865-1893	Sculpture	—	—	16	—	—	—	—	6	3	—	25
Glazebrook, Hugh de Twenebrokes	London	1885-1893	Portraits	—	—	11	—	—	—	—	4	—	15	30
Gleadall, W. C.	London	1851-1865	Figures	—	—	5	1	—	—	—	—	—	—	6
Glegg, T.	London	1829-1838	Architecture	—	—	5	—	1	—	—	—	—	—	6
Glehn, Von. *See* V.	—	—	—	—	—	—	—	—	—	—	—	—	—	—
Gleichen, H.S.H., Count, H.R.I.‡ *See* Hohenlohe	London	1868-1890	Sculpture	—	—	50	—	—	—	7	28	—	—	85
Gleichen, Feodora, Countess, H.F.R.P.E.	London	1879-1893	Sculpture	—	—	1	—	—	—	1	10	9	—	21
Glen, J.	London	1828	Portraits	—	—	—	—	1	—	—	—	—	—	1
Glendening, Alfred A.	Greenwich	1861-1892	Landscape	—	—	41	4	77	—	—	—	—	8	130
Glendening, Alfred, Jun., R.B.A. §	London	1880-1893	Domestic	—	—	24	—	47	—	2	—	—	13	86
Glennie, Arthur, R.W.S. †	London	1837-1890	Landscape	—	—	—	—	—	410	—	—	—	—	410
Glennie, George F.	London	1861-1882	Landscape	—	—	6	—	10	—	—	—	—	75	91
Glennie, J. D.	—	1810-1819	Landscape	—	—	8	—	—	—	—	—	—	—	8
Glenny, William J.	Wandsworth	1868-1874	Landscape	—	—	—	—	—	—	—	—	—	7	7
Glindon, Paul	London	1879	Rustic	—	—	—	—	—	—	—	—	—	1	1
Glindoni, Henry Gillard, R.B.A., A.R.W.S. § †	London	1872-1893	Figures	—	—	29	—	71	51	—	—	—	23	174
Glisenti, A. Achille	London	1882	Rustic	—	—	1	—	—	—	—	—	—	—	1
Gloag, H.	—	1893	Portraits	—	—	—	—	—	—	—	—	—	1	1
Gloag, J. L.	London	1890-1893	Domestic	—	—	1	—	2	—	—	—	—	2	5
Gloag, Miss T. L.	London	1889-1893	Domestic	—	—	—	—	1	—	3	—	—	—	4
Glossop, G. P. P.	Isleworth	1850	Landscape	—	—	1	—	—	—	—	—	—	—	1
Glover, Miss Emily	Derby	1871-1876	—	—	—	—	—	—	—	—	—	—	10	10
Glover, G. A.	—	1826-1834	Historical	—	—	2	1	—	—	—	—	—	—	3
Glover, Miss Hannah	Croydon	1884	Domestic	—	—	—	—	—	—	—	—	—	1	1
Glover, John § †	London	1795-1832	Landscape	—	—	20	22	113	290	—	—	—	—	445
Glover, J., Jun.	London	1808-1829	Landscape	—	—	26	—	—	—	—	—	—	—	26
Glover, William	London	1813-1833	Landscape	—	—	1	7	10	24	—	—	—	—	42
Gnoloby —	—	1778	Figures	—	2	—	—	—	—	—	—	—	—	2
Goatley, John	London	1831-1839	Landscape	—	—	7	—	1	—	—	—	—	—	8
Goble, Warwick	London	1893	Algiers	—	—	1	—	—	—	—	—	—	—	1
Goblet, H. F.	London	1822-1836	Figures	—	—	9	1	5	—	—	—	—	—	15
Goblet, L. A.	London	1799-1826	Sculpture	—	—	31	4	1	—	—	—	—	—	36
Godard, E. H.	London	1880	Domestic	—	—	—	—	—	—	—	—	—	2	2
Godart, Thomas	London	1852-1861	Landscape	—	—	—	1	1	—	—	—	—	1	1
Godbold, Samuel Berry	London	1842-1875	Miniatures	—	—	66	13	45	—	—	—	—	—	124
Goddard, A. G.	London	1843-1850	Landscape	—	—	3	—	—	—	—	—	—	—	3
Goddard, Charles	Hastings	1853	Domestic	—	—	—	—	2	—	—	—	—	—	2
Goddard, George Bouverie	Salisbury	1856-1886	Sporting	—	—	24	—	3	—	—	1	—	6	34
Goddard, G. H.	London	1837-1844	Flowers	—	—	1	—	3	—	—	—	—	—	4
Goddard, Miss H.	London	1823	Flowers	—	—	1	—	—	—	—	—	—	—	1
Goddard, James	London	1771-1783	Portraits	1	10	—	—	—	—	—	—	—	—	11
Goddard, J.	London	1811-1842	Portraits	—	—	49	—	—	—	—	—	—	2	51
Goddard, James	London	1800-1855	Flowers	—	—	19	5	4	—	—	—	—	6	34
Goddard, J. Bedloe	Christchurch	1875-1893	Landscape	—	—	—	—	4	—	2	—	—	2	8
Goddard, Miss K.	London	1860	Flowers	—	—	—	—	1	—	—	—	—	—	1
Goddard, Rainald W. K. *See also* Ball and	—	—	—	—	—	—	—	—	—	—	—	—	—	—
Goddard	London	1892	Architecture	—	—	1	—	—	—	—	—	—	—	1
Goddard, Thomas	London	1779-1788	Miniatures	—	—	20	—	—	—	—	—	—	—	20
Goddard, William Charles	London	1885	Landscape	—	—	—	—	—	—	1	—	—	—	1
Goddard and Sons	—	1868	Architecture	—	—	1	—	—	—	—	—	—	—	1
Goddard and Paget	Leicester	1880-1891	Architecture	—	—	4	—	—	—	—	—	—	—	4
Godefroy, P. M. F.	Pennsylvania	1820-1824	Landscape	—	—	9	—	—	—	—	—	—	—	9
Godelet, F.	London	1818-1819	Portraits	—	—	2	—	—	—	—	—	—	—	2

Name.	Town.	First and Last Year of Ex.	Speciality.	S. A.	F. S.	R. A.	B. I.	S. S.	O. W.	N.W.	G. G.	N. G.	V. E.	Total.
Godet, Julius	London	1844-1884	Landscape	—	—	16	40	51	—	1	—	—	36	144
Godfrey, Miss Adelaide A.	—	1848	Landscape	—	—	1	—	—	—	—	—	—	—	1
Godfrey, Louis	London	1885-1892	Engraving	—	—	3	—	—	—	—	—	—	—	3
Godfrey, Miss L. M. (?) Ellen	Cambridge	1882	Portraits	—	—	1	—	—	—	—	—	—	—	1
Godfrey, Miss M. A.	London	1855	Domestic	—	—	1	—	—	—	—	—	—	—	1
Godfrey, Richard B.	London	1765-1770	Engraving	5	—	—	—	—	—	—	—	—	—	5
Godon, Louis	London	1888-1890	Sculpture	—	—	—	—	1	—	—	2	—	—	3
Godsall, Miss Mary	London	1872-1892	Figures	—	—	2	—	13	—	—	—	—	13	28
Godsell, Miss Mary E.	Stroud	1884-1893	Domestic	—	—	3	—	—	—	2	—	—	—	5
Godward, John William, R.B.A. §	Wimbledon	1887-1893	Domestic	—	—	10	—	4	—	—	—	—	3	17
Godwin, Mrs. C. G.	London	1829-1832	Domestic	—	—	1	—	3	—	—	—	—	—	4
Godwin, E.	London	1801-1816	Portraits	—	—	13	—	—	—	—	—	—	—	13
Godwin, Edward William	London	1869-1872	Architecture	—	—	3	—	—	—	—	—	—	—	3
Godwin, G.	London	1811	Architecture	—	—	1	—	—	—	—	—	—	—	1
Godwin, George, F.R.S.	London	1832-1862	Architecture	—	—	2	—	—	—	—	—	—	—	2
Godwin, Gurth	London	1875-1877	Domestic	—	—	—	—	—	—	—	—	—	3	3
Godwin, James	London	1846-1851	Domestic	—	—	3	2	10	—	—	—	—	—	15
Godwin, J. Arthur	Bradford	1892-1893	Landscape	—	—	—	—	3	—	—	—	—	—	3
Godwin, S.	London	1851	Architecture	—	—	1	—	—	—	—	—	—	—	1
Godwin, Miss	—	1847	Domestic	—	—	1	—	—	—	—	—	—	—	1
Godwin and Crisp	London	1867-1868	Architecture	—	—	5	—	—	—	—	—	—	—	5
Goebel, C.	London	1870	Portraits	—	—	1	—	—	—	—	—	—	—	1
Goeghan, S.	London	1829	Seals	—	—	—	—	1	—	—	—	—	—	1
Goeneutte, N.	Paris	1881	Landscape	—	—	—	—	—	—	—	2	—	—	2
Goepel, James S.	London	1867	Landscape	—	—	—	—	1	—	—	—	—	—	1
Goetze, Sigismund	London	1888-1893	Domestic	—	—	8	—	—	—	—	1	—	4	13
Goff, E., Junr.	London	1792-1797	Architecture	—	—	2	—	—	—	—	—	—	—	2
Goff, F. E. J.	London	1891	Bridges	—	—	—	—	—	—	1	—	—	—	1
Goff, Colonel Robert, R.P.E.	London	1870-1892	Landscape	—	—	20	—	5	—	22	2	—	30	79
Gogin, Charles	London	1871-1893	Domestic	—	—	13	—	3	—	—	—	—	8	24
Gohli —	—	1773	Portraits	2	—	—	—	—	—	—	—	—	—	2
Gold —	London	1782	Sporting	—	2	—	—	—	—	—	—	—	—	2
Gold, F.	Bristol	1819-1820	Landscape	—	—	2	—	—	—	—	—	—	—	2
Goldar, John	London	1765-1772	Engraving	2	2	—	—	—	—	—	—	—	—	4
Golden, R.	Rome	1794-1796	Architecture	—	—	3	—	—	—	—	—	—	—	3
Goldicutt, John	London	1810-1842	Architecture	—	—	35	—	—	—	—	—	—	—	35
Goldie, Charles	London	1858-1879	Figures	—	—	22	6	11	—	—	—	—	3	42
Goldie, George, M.R.I.B.A. *See also* Hadfield and Goldie	London	1854-1872	Architecture	—	—	6	—	—	—	—	—	—	—	6
Goldie, Edward	London	1880	Architecture	—	—	1	—	—	—	—	—	—	—	1
Goldie, R. J.	London	1880	Charcoal	—	—	—	—	—	—	—	—	—	1	1
Goldie and Child	London	1874-1880	Architecture	—	—	5	—	—	—	—	—	—	—	5
Goldie, Child, and Goldie	London	1881-1892	Architecture	—	—	14	—	—	—	—	—	—	—	14
Goldingham, James A.	London	1870-1881	Domestic	—	—	6	—	2	—	—	—	—	1	9
Goldring, G.	London	1792-1802	Architecture	—	—	5	—	—	—	—	—	—	—	5
Goldsmid, C.	London	1884	Figures	—	—	—	—	1	—	—	—	—	—	1
Goldsmid, Miss Evelyn J.	London	1886	Sculpture	—	—	1	—	—	—	—	—	—	—	1
Goldsmith, Miss Georgina S.	Penge	1869-1870	Landscape	—	—	—	—	3	—	—	—	—	—	3
Goldsmith, Walter H.	Maidenhead	1880-1893	Landscape	—	—	15	—	24	—	5	—	—	9	53
Golf, Alfred	London	1861	Landscape	—	—	—	—	—	—	—	—	—	1	1
Gomme, Stephen	London	1835-1845	Architecture	—	—	3	—	3	—	—	—	—	—	6
Gomertz, E.	London	1836-1837	Figures	—	—	1	—	2	—	—	—	—	—	3
Gompertz, F. T.	London	1858-1860	Architecture	—	—	2	—	—	—	—	—	—	—	2
Gompertz, G.	London	1827-1843	Figures	—	—	7	1	10	—	2	—	—	—	20
Gompertz, M.	London	1833-1835	Ruins	—	—	—	—	2	—	—	—	—	—	2
Gompertz, S.	London	1836-1837	Architecture	—	—	2	—	—	—	—	—	—	—	2
Gonon, Eugene	London	1855	Sculpture	—	—	3	—	—	—	—	—	—	—	3
Gonsalvo-y-Perez, Paul	Madrid	1876	Venice	—	—	—	—	—	—	—	—	—	2	2
Gooch, James	Norwich	1819-1837	Landscape	—	—	—	5	6	—	—	—	—	—	11
Gooch, John	Norwich	1825-1831	Landscape	—	—	—	6	—	—	—	—	—	—	6
Gooch, Miss Mary Ann	Twickenham	1853-1877	Still Life	—	—	1	4	16	—	—	—	—	—	21
Gooch, Mrs. Matilda	Richmond	1860	Landscape	—	—	—	—	1	—	—	—	—	—	1
Gooch, R. A. C.	London	1845-1871	Domestic	—	—	2	4	8	—	—	—	—	—	14
Gooch, T.	London	1777-1802	Sporting	4	1	76	—	—	—	—	—	—	—	81
Good, Joseph Henry	London	1833-1840	Architecture	—	—	3	—	—	—	—	—	—	—	3
Good, John Willis	London	1870-1878	Sculpture	—	—	16	—	—	—	—	—	—	—	16
Good, M. R.	—	1826	Architecture	—	—	1	—	—	—	—	—	—	—	1
Good, Thomas Sword	Berwick	1820-1834	Domestic	—	—	19	43	2	—	—	—	—	—	64
Goodall, Edward	London	1822-1841	Landscape & Engraving	—	—	2	3	8	—	—	—	—	—	13
Goodall, Miss Eliza. *See* Mrs. Wild	London	1846-1854	Domestic	—	—	9	6	1	—	—	—	—	—	16
Goodall, Edward Alfred, R.W.S. †	London	1841-1893	Landscape	—	—	15	36	2	328	—	—	—	1	382
Goodall, Florence	Gunnersbury	1892	Domestic	—	—	—	—	1	—	—	—	—	—	1

Name.	Town.	First and Last Year of Ex.	Speciality.	S. A.	F. S.	R. A.	B. I.	S. S.	O. W.	N. W.	G. G.	N. G.	V. E.	Total.
Goodall, Frederick, R.A., H.R.I. ‡	London	1838-1893	Scriptural	—	—	179	33	6	—	5	3	1	13	240
Goodall, Frederick Trevelyan	London	1868-1871	Portraits	—	—	17	—	—	—	—	—	—	—	17
Goodall, Herbert	London	1890-1892	Domestic	—	—	—	—	6	—	—	—	—	—	6
Goodall, Howard	London	1870-1872	Historical	—	—	2	—	—	—	—	—	—	—	2
Goodall, J. Edward	London	1877-1891	Domestic	—	—	5	—	16	—	6	—	—	6	33
Goodall, Thomas F.	Dulwich	1875-1893	Domestic	—	—	12	—	45	—	—	4	6	23	90
Goodall, Walter, R.W.S. †	London	1852-1884	Figures	—	—	3	—	—	156	—	—	—	—	159
Goodchild, Miss Emily	London	1890-1893	Portraits	—	—	2	—	—	—	—	—	—	2	4
Goodchild, John E.	London	1855-1870	Architecture	—	—	2	—	—	—	—	—	—	—	2
Goode, John	Adderbury	1835	Sporting	—	—	—	—	2	—	—	—	—	—	2
Goode, Miss Louisa. *See* Mrs. L. Romer *and* Mrs. J. M. Jopling.	—	—	—	—	—	—	—	—	—	—	—	—	—	—
Goode, W.	London	1854	Domestic	—	—	—	—	—	—	—	—	—	1	1
Goode, W. E.	Adderbury	1845-1866	Sporting	—	—	—	4	4	—	—	—	—	—	8
Gooden, Master B.	London	1774	Heads	—	1	—	—	—	—	—	—	—	—	1
Gooden, James Chisholm	London	1835-1865	Sea Pieces	—	—	3	9	17	—	—	—	—	2	31
Gooderson, Emily	London	1860	—	—	—	—	—	*	—	—	—	—	—	—
Gooderson, Mrs. T.	London	1855	Domestic	—	—	1	—	—	—	—	—	—	—	1
Gooderson, Thomas Youngman	London	1846-1860	Scriptural	—	—	21	14	24	—	—	—	—	1	60
Goodhall, Miss M. C.	Twickenham	1887	Still Life	—	—	1	—	—	—	—	—	—	—	1
Goodier, Arthur	London	1870-1883	Landscape	—	—	—	—	13	—	—	—	—	—	13
Goodman, Mrs. L., late Miss Julia Salaman ‖	London	1836-1888	Domestic	—	—	7	2	15	—	—	—	—	—	24
Goodman, Miss Maude (Mrs. Scanes)	London	1874-1893	Domestic	—	—	40	—	6	—	12	8	—	8	74
Goodman, T.	London	1784-1812	Miniatures	—	—	12	—	—	—	—	—	—	4	16
Goodman, Thomas Warner	London	1854	Figures	—	—	1	—	—	—	—	—	—	—	1
Goodman, Walter	London	1859-1890	Domestic	—	—	3	2	1	—	—	—	—	12	18
Goodrich, Jerome	London	1829-1859	Historical	—	—	3	6	3	—	—	—	—	2	14
Goodrich, James B.	Topsham	1853-1858	Landscape	—	—	7	—	—	—	—	—	—	—	7
Goodridge, H. E., M.R.I.B.A.	Bath	1828-1848	Architecture	—	—	7	—	—	—	—	—	—	—	7
Goodridge and Son	London	1857	Architecture	—	—	2	—	—	—	—	—	—	—	2
Goodwin, Albert, R.W.S. † §	Arundel	1860-1893	Landscape	—	—	35	—	8	364	—	8	6	46	467
Goodwin, Edward	London	1801-1815	Landscape	—	—	13	—	—	9	—	—	—	20	42
Goodwin, E. *See* Coe and Goodwin	London	1853	Architecture	—	—	2	—	—	—	—	—	—	—	2
Goodwin, E. W.	London	1855	Architecture	—	—	1	—	—	—	—	—	—	—	1
Goodwin, Francis	Lynn	1806-1834	Architecture	—	—	24	—	—	—	—	—	—	—	24
Goodwin, Frank A.	London	1867-1873	Landscape	—	—	—	—	—	—	—	—	—	7	7
Goodwin, Miss F. W.	King's Lynn	1842-1843	Animals	—	—	—	—	3	—	—	—	—	—	3
Goodwin, G.	—	1800	Landscape	—	—	1	—	—	—	—	—	—	—	1
Goodwin, G.	London	1837-1854	Architecture	—	—	2	—	—	—	—	—	—	—	2
Goodwin, Harry	Maidstone	1867-1893	Domestic	—	—	15	—	27	—	17	—	—	75	134
Goodwin, Mrs. H. (Kate Malleson)	Croydon	1873-1893	Landscape	—	—	6	—	1	—	—	—	1	14	22
Goodwin, J. C.	—	1839	Sea Pieces	—	—	1	—	—	—	—	—	—	—	1
Goodwin, Mrs. L.	—	1837	Figures	—	—	1	—	—	—	—	—	—	—	1
Goodwin, T. A.	London	1867	Landscape	—	—	—	—	1	—	—	—	—	—	1
Goodwin, W. S.	Southampton	1870-1877	Landscape	—	—	—	—	11	—	—	—	—	15	26
Goody, Miss Florence	Lewisham	1888-1892	Domestic	—	—	1	—	3	—	3	—	—	—	7
Goodyear, E.	London	1827-1828	Landscape	—	—	2	—	—	—	—	—	—	—	2
Goodyear, Joseph	Birmingham	1830	Engraving	—	—	—	—	2	—	—	—	—	—	2
Gorden, G.	London	1836	Landscape	—	—	—	—	1	—	—	—	—	—	1
Gordigiani, Michele	Florence	1867-1886	Portraits	—	—	3	—	—	—	—	1	—	—	4
Gordon. *See* Taylor, Gordon, and Bousfield	—	—	Architecture	—	—	—	—	—	—	—	—	—	—	—
Gordon, Adam	—	1769	Figures	—	1	—	—	—	—	—	—	—	—	1
Gordon, Alexander	Largs, N.B.	1891-1892	Interiors	—	—	1	—	2	—	—	—	—	—	3
Gordon, A. J.	London	1887-1888	Architecture	—	—	2	—	—	—	—	—	—	—	2
Gordon (A. J.) and Brown (D.)	London	1890-1891	Architecture	—	—	5	—	—	—	—	—	—	—	5
Gordon, Miss Eleanor Vere. *See* Hon. Mrs. Richard Boyle.	—	—	—	—	—	—	—	—	—	—	—	—	—	—
Gordon, Mrs. Fred. J. *See* Miss Edith Tolhurst.	—	—	—	—	—	—	—	—	—	—	—	—	—	—
Gordon, G.	London	1821-1840	Portraits	—	—	2	—	—	—	—	—	—	—	2
Gordon, G.	Edinburgh	1836	Landscape	—	—	1	—	—	—	—	—	—	—	1
Gordon, G. C.	London	1856-1858	Landscape	—	—	—	—	4	—	—	—	—	—	4
Gordon, Herbert Huntley-. *See* H.	—	—	—	—	—	—	—	—	—	—	—	—	—	—
Gordon, H. P.	London	1874	Animals	—	—	—	—	—	—	—	—	—	1	1
Gordon, Sir John Watson, R.A., P.R.S.A. *See* John Watson	Edinburgh	1827-1864	Portraits	—	—	123	—	1	—	—	—	—	—	124
Gordon, R. G.	Canterbury	1890	Norway	—	—	—	—	—	—	1	—	—	—	1
Gordon, Robert James, R.B.A. §	London	1871-1893	Domestic	—	—	22	—	88	—	—	—	—	10	120
Gordon, Thomas	London	1884	Architecture	—	—	1	—	—	—	—	—	—	—	1
Gordon, Mrs. T.	—	1870	Landscape	—	—	—	—	3	—	—	—	—	—	3
Gordon, W.	London	1833-1858	Sea Pieces	—	—	2	1	8	—	—	—	—	—	11
Gore, Elizabeth M.	London	1875-1877	Domestic	—	—	—	—	—	—	—	—	—	5	5
Gore, William Henry, R.B.A. §	London	1880-1893	Domestic	—	—	18	—	21	—	12	3	—	12	66

Name.	Town.	First and Last Year of Ex.	Speciality.	S. A.	F. S.	R. A.	B. I.	S. S.	O. W.	N.W.	G. G.	N. G.	V. E.	Total.
Gore-Booth, Mrs. H. *See* B.	—	—	—	—	—	—	—	—	—	—	—	—	—	—
Gorst, Mrs. H. C.	Rock Ferry	1890-1892	Flowers	—	—	—	—	2	—	—	—	—	—	2
Gorstin, Miss A.	London	1856	Landscape	—	—	—	1	—	—	—	—	—	—	1
Gorton, C.	London	1848-1849	Fruit	—	—	—	2	—	—	—	—	—	—	2
Gos, Albert	Geneva	1883-1890	Mountains	—	—	2	—	1	—	—	—	—	—	3
Gosling, C.	London	1836-1845	Architecture	—	—	3	—	—	—	—	—	—	—	3
Gosling, William W., R.B.A.§	London	1849-1883	Landscape	—	—	13	23	176	—	—	—	—	5	217
Gosnell, D. H.	Brockham	1884-1885	Landscape	—	—	2	—	—	—	—	—	—	—	2
Gosse, Mrs. Edmund. *See* Miss Nellie Epps	London	1879-1890	Landscape	—	—	—	—	1	—	—	17	—	6	24
Gosse, W.	London	1814-1839	Portraits	—	—	2	—	—	—	—	—	—	—	2
Gosset, Isaac, F.S.A.	London	1760-1778	Sculpture	29	1	—	—	—	—	—	—	—	—	30
Gosset, M. C.	London	1876-1877	Domestic	—	—	—	—	—	—	—	—	—	3	3
Gotch, Thomas Cooper, R.B.A.§	London	1879-1893	Landscape	—	—	11	—	22	—	3	1	6	11	54
Gotch, Mrs. T. C. (Caroline)	Newlyn	1890-1893	Domestic	—	—	4	—	—	—	—	1	—	1	6
Gotch and Saunders	Kettering	1890	Architecture	—	—	1	—	—	—	—	—	—	—	1
Gott, Joseph	London	1820-1848	Sculpture	—	—	30	7	—	—	—	—	—	—	37
Gott, John William	London	1882-1891	Domestic	—	—	1	—	1	—	1	—	—	1	4
Gottefried, A.	London	1872	Domestic	—	—	—	—	1	—	—	—	—	—	1
Gotto, Basil	St. Albans	1889-1891	Sculpture	—	—	2	—	—	—	—	—	—	—	2
Gottschalk, Miss Blanche	London	1890-1893	Domestic	—	—	—	—	—	—	1	—	—	4	5
Gotzenberg, F.	London	1855-1857	Scriptural	—	—	2	2	1	—	—	—	—	—	5
Gough. *See* Giles and Gough, *and* Ponton and Gough	—	—	Architecture	—	—	—	—	—	—	—	—	—	—	—
Gough (Alexander D.) and Roumieu (R. L.)	London	1837-1849	Architecture	—	—	19	—	—	—	—	—	—	—	19
Gough, Hugh R.	London	1884-1887	Architecture	—	—	2	—	—	—	—	—	—	—	2
Gould, A. Carruthers	London	1892-1893	Landscape	—	—	—	—	2	—	—	—	—	—	2
Gould, Miss C.	London	1855-1856	Domestic	—	—	—	—	3	—	—	—	—	—	3
Gould, Charles Augustus	London	1851	Architecture	—	—	1	—	—	—	—	—	—	—	1
Gould, F. Carruthers	Buckhurst	1876-1877	Animals	—	—	—	—	—	—	—	—	—	2	2
Gould, H.	London	1877	Shipping	—	—	—	—	—	—	—	—	—	1	1
Gould, J. W.	London	1865	Sculpture	—	—	1	—	—	—	—	—	—	—	1
Gould, Walter	Florence	1857	Figures	—	—	1	—	—	—	—	—	—	—	1
Goulding, Frederick	London	1876-1881	Etching	—	—	1	—	—	—	—	—	—	8	9
Gouldsmith, Edmund	London	1877-1893	Landscape	—	—	2	—	6	—	1	—	—	4	13
Gouldsmith, Miss Harriett.† *See* Mrs. Arnold	London	1809-1839	Landscape	—	—	27	81	28	34	4	—	—	—	174
Goupy, Joseph	London	1765	Figures	2	—	—	—	—	—	—	—	—	—	2
Gourlie, Miss Edith	London	1883-1885	Domestic	—	—	1	—	—	—	—	—	—	2	3
Gouyn, Mrs. Anne	London	1763	Flowers	—	1	—	—	—	—	—	—	—	—	1
Gover, Miss Mary Edith	London	1886-1888	Flowers	—	—	1	—	1	—	2	—	—	—	4
Gover, S.	Winchester	1794	Monuments	—	—	2	—	—	—	—	—	—	—	2
Gow, Andrew Carrick, R.A., R.I.‡	London	1866-1893	Military	—	—	37	—	3	—	48	1	—	5	94
Gow, Charles	London	1844-1872	Portraits	—	—	7	—	1	—	—	—	—	—	8
Gow, David	London	1886-1888	Landscape	—	—	—	—	—	—	5	—	—	—	5
Gow, James §	London	1852-1885	Domestic	—	—	15	5	60	—	—	—	—	2	82
Gow, James F. Mackintosh	Edinburgh	1890-1893	Landscape	—	—	4	—	—	—	—	—	—	—	4
Gow, Miss Mary L., R.I.‡	London	1869-1893	Domestic	—	—	6	—	18	—	36	1	1	7	69
Gow, Robert F.	Wimbledon	1882	Etching	—	—	1	—	—	—	—	—	—	—	1
Gowans, George Russel, R.S.W.	Aberdeen	1877-1893	Landscape	—	—	4	—	1	—	1	—	—	—	6
Gower, Lord Ronald	London	1876-1881	Sculpture	—	—	6	—	—	—	—	1	—	—	7
Gowers, D.	London	1801-1808	Portraits	—	—	2	—	—	—	—	—	—	—	2
Gowers, W. R.	London	1888	Seashores	—	—	1	—	—	—	—	—	—	—	1
Grace, Alfred Fitzwalter, R.B.A.§	London	1865-1893	Landscape	—	—	48	6	81	—	10	5	3	55	208
Grace, Mrs. A. F. (Emily M.)	—	1874-1888	Enamels	—	—	10	—	—	—	—	—	—	1	11
Grace, Miss Anna M.	Brighton	1879-1889	Portraits	—	—	2	—	8	—	—	—	1	—	11
Grace, Miss Frances Lily	Brighton	1876-1889	Domestic	—	—	2	—	14	—	—	—	—	3	19
Grace, Miss Harriette Edith	Brighton	1877-1891	Domestic	—	—	8	—	15	—	—	—	—	3	26
Grace, James Edward, R.B.A.§	London	1871-1893	Landscape	—	—	32	—	158	—	14	16	16	47	283
Grace, Mrs. James E.	Milford	1881-1893	Landscape	—	—	—	—	1	—	—	—	3	—	4
Grace, Miss L. A.	London	1874	Figures	—	—	—	—	1	—	—	—	—	—	1
Grace, Mrs. (Miss Hodgkins)	London	1762-1769	Portraits	15	—	—	—	—	—	—	—	—	—	15
Grady, O'. *See* O.	—	—	—	—	—	—	—	—	—	—	—	—	—	—
Gräef, Professor Gustave	London	1880-1884	Portraits	—	—	5	—	—	—	—	2	—	—	7
Graeflé, A.	Paris	1851	Historical	—	—	1	—	—	—	—	—	—	—	1
Grafton —	London	1774	Flowers	—	—	1	—	—	—	—	—	—	—	1
Graglia, Alessandro	London	1777-1779	Miniatures	—	—	2	—	—	—	—	—	—	—	2
Graglia, Andrea	London	1777-1791	Miniatures	—	—	17	—	—	—	—	—	—	—	17
Graham-Clarke. *See* C.	—	—	—	—	—	—	—	—	—	—	—	—	—	—
Graham, Alexander	London	1875-1893	Architecture	—	—	10	—	—	—	—	—	—	5	15
Graham, C.	London	1841-1850	Portraits	—	—	2	—	5	—	—	—	—	—	7
Graham, Miss C.	—	1868	Figures	—	—	1	—	—	—	—	—	—	—	1
Graham, Dr. C. Honoria	London	1888-1891	Sculpture	—	—	3	—	2	—	—	—	—	—	5
Graham, Miss Florence E.‖	London	1882-1891	Figures	—	—	2	—	—	—	—	2	—	1	5

Name.	Town.	First and Last Year of Ex.	Speciality.	S. A.	F. S.	R. A.	B. I.	S. S.	O. W.	N. W.	G. G.	N. G.	V. E.	Total.
Graham, G.	—	1783	Dramatic	1	—	—	—	—	—	—	—	—	—	1
Graham, John	London	1780-1797	Historical	2	3	35	—	—	—	—	—	—	—	40
Graham, John	London	1820-1837	Scriptural	—	—	18	25	—	—	—	—	—	—	43
Graham, Miss J.	London	1883	Landscape	—	—	—	—	—	—	—	1	—	—	1
Graham, Miss J. Douglas	London	1890-1892	Figures	—	—	—	—	1	—	3	—	—	1	5
Graham, James Hunter-	Brighton	1889-1893	Landscape	—	—	3	—	1	—	—	—	—	—	4
Graham, Mrs. Lilias Jane	Bedford Park	1883-1885	Miniatures	—	—	1	—	1	—	—	—	—	—	2
Graham, Peter, R.A.	London	1866-1893	Landscape	—	—	59	—	—	—	—	—	—	—	59
Graham, T.	London	1820-1826	Landscape	—	—	—	—	2	3	—	—	—	—	5
Graham, Thomas A. F., H.R.S.A. φ	London	1863-1893	Figures	—	—	30	1	2	—	2	8	4	41	88
Graham, William	London	1845-1883	Sculpture	—	—	24	—	—	—	—	—	—	6	30
Graham, Mrs. W. J. (Josephine)	London	1883-1884	Flowers	—	—	—	—	—	—	3	—	—	—	3
Graham-Buxton, W. *See* B.	—	—	—	—	—	—	—	—	—	—	—	—	—	—
Graham-Clarke, L. J. *See* C.	—	—	—	—	—	—	—	—	—	—	—	—	—	—
Graham-Robertson, Walford. *See* R.	—	—	—	—	—	—	—	—	—	—	—	—	—	—
Graham-Yooll, Miss	Edinburgh	1887	Domestic	—	—	—	—	—	—	—	1	—	—	1
Grahame, A. B.	London	1871-1876	Domestic	—	—	3	—	11	—	—	—	—	2	16
Grahame, James B.	Edinburgh	1876-1879	Sheep	—	—	2	—	4	—	—	—	—	4	10
Grahame, John B.	London	1866-1876	Landscape	—	—	7	—	16	—	—	—	—	9	32
Grainger, Edward	Dudley	1889-1890	Landscape	—	—	2	—	—	—	—	—	—	—	2
Grainger, George A.	London	1782-1836	Landscape	—	3	3	14	—	—	—	—	—	—	20
Grallia, A. C.	London	1792	Miniatures	—	—	2	—	—	—	—	—	—	—	2
Gramlick, E. H.	London	1803	Landscape	—	—	2	—	—	—	—	—	—	—	2
Grampietri, Sellimo	London	1884-1888	Churches	—	—	—	—	4	—	—	—	—	—	4
Granby, Marchioness of. *See* Miss Violet	—	—	—	—	—	—	—	—	—	—	—	—	—	—
Lindsay *and* Mrs. Manners	—	1889-1893	Portraits	—	—	5	—	—	—	—	4	12	22	43
Granet, François Marius	Paris	1833	Convent Life	—	—	1	—	—	—	—	—	—	—	1
Granger, Miss Sophia	—	1776	Landscape	—	1	—	—	—	—	—	—	—	—	1
Grant, A.	London	1788-1789	Landscape	—	—	2	—	—	—	—	—	—	—	2
Grant, A.	London	1852	Portraits	—	—	1	—	—	—	—	—	—	—	1
Grant, Miss Alice ‖	London	1879-1893	Portraits	—	—	24	—	5	—	7	3	2	15	56
Grant, Aug. R.	London	1838-1840	Landscape	—	—	2	1	1	—	—	—	—	—	4
Grant, Carleton	Eton	1892-1893	Landscape	—	—	4	—	—	—	—	—	—	—	4
Grant, Charles	London	1825-1839	Portraits	—	—	12	1	—	—	—	—	—	—	13
Grant, Miss Emily	—	1854-1855	Landscape	—	—	—	—	2	—	—	—	—	—	2
Grant, Sir Francis, P.R.A.	Melton Mowbray	1834-1879	Portraits	—	—	253	7	9	—	—	3	—	—	272
Grant, F. J.	—	1833	Landscape	—	—	—	1	—	—	—	—	—	—	1
Grant, G. L.	—	1831	Landscape	—	—	—	3	—	—	—	—	—	—	3
Grant, G. P.	London	1850	Figures	—	—	—	1	—	—	—	—	—	—	1
Grant, Henry	London	1872-1888	Portraits	—	—	3	—	6	—	—	—	—	6	15
Grant, J.	London	1823-1824	Architecture	—	—	1	—	1	—	—	—	—	—	2
Grant, Miss Mary	Kilgraston	1866-1892	Sculpture	—	—	42	—	—	—	—	—	—	—	42
Grant, Miss Mary Isabella	Cullompton	1870-1893	Landscape	—	—	—	—	41	—	7	—	—	6	54
Grant, W.	Acton	1847-1854	Landscape	—	—	—	3	—	—	—	—	—	—	3
Grant, W. A.	London	1862-1864	Landscape	—	—	1	4	—	—	—	—	—	—	5
Grant, William James	London	1847-1866	Scriptural	—	—	39	5	—	—	—	—	—	—	44
Grantham, William	London	1773-1775	Architecture	—	—	2	—	—	—	—	—	—	—	2
Granville, Miss Evelyn	London	1883	Miniatures	—	—	1	—	1	—	—	—	—	—	2
Granville, R. C.	London	1879	Landscape	—	—	—	—	1	—	—	—	—	—	1
Granville, W. L. B.	London	1838-1859	Architecture	—	—	11	—	—	—	—	—	—	—	11
Grass, A.	London	1859-1867	Sculpture	—	—	12	—	—	—	—	—	—	—	12
Grassie, John	—	1776-1781	Portraits	—	—	2	—	—	—	—	—	—	—	2
Gratia, L.	London	1851-1862	Portraits	—	—	6	—	2	—	—	—	—	—	8
Gratitien, Sebastian	Cologne	1790-1795	Miniatures	1	—	10	—	—	—	—	—	—	—	11
Gratton, George	London	1812	Scriptural	—	—	3	2	—	—	—	—	—	—	5
Gravely, Percy	Lewes	1886-1892	Cattle	—	—	—	—	2	—	—	—	—	1	3
Graves, Charles A.	St. Leonards	1873-1884	Sea Pieces	—	—	1	—	1	—	—	—	—	—	2
Graves, C. R.	Hastings	1858	Landscape	—	—	—	—	1	—	—	—	—	—	1
Graves, Frederick Percy	London	1858-1872	Landscape	—	—	6	11	25	—	—	—	—	8	50
Graves, Hon. Henry Richard	London	1846-1881	Portraits	—	—	71	—	—	—	—	—	—	—	71
Graves, Robert, A.R.A. §	London	1824-1873	Engraving	—	—	25	—	13	—	—	—	—	—	38
Gravesande, Vans. *See* V.	—	—	—	—	—	—	—	—	—	—	—	—	—	—
Gravier, Alexandre Louis	London	1879-1891	Etching	—	—	9	—	—	—	—	—	—	3	12
Gravier, Florence	London	1879	Figures	—	—	—	—	—	—	—	—	—	1	1
Gray —	London	1783	Sporting	—	4	—	—	—	—	—	—	—	—	4
Gray, Miss Alice	Edinburgh	1891-1892	Domestic	—	—	2	—	1	—	—	—	—	—	3
Gray, C.	London	1845-1866	Architecture	—	—	7	—	—	—	—	—	—	—	7
Gray, Curwen	Woodford	1862-1871	Figures	—	—	—	2	7	—	—	—	—	—	9
Gray, Mrs. Curwen, late Miss Kate Newenham	Woodford	1864-1871	Domestic	—	—	—	1	5	—	—	—	—	—	6
Gray, D.	London	1854	Sculpture	—	—	2	—	—	—	—	—	—	—	2
Gray, F.	London	1852	Domestic	—	—	1	—	—	—	—	—	—	—	1
Gray, G.	London	1811	Fruit	—	—	1	—	—	—	—	—	—	—	1

Name.	Town.	First and Last Year of Ex.	Speciality.	S. A.	F. S.	R. A.	B. I.	S. S.	O. W.	N. W.	G. G.	N. G.	V. E.	Total.
Gray, George	London	1854-1873	Enamels	—	—	29	—	3	—	—	—	—	—	32
Gray, George	Kircaldy	1874-1879	Landscape	—	—	—	—	7	—	—	—	—	—	7
Gray, Henry	London	1849-1889	Miniatures	—	—	41	1	—	—	—	—	—	—	42
Gray, H. Barnard	London	1844-1871	Sporting	—	—	18	41	36	—	—	—	—	53	148
Gray, Henry Peters	New York	1852	Figures	—	—	—	2	—	—	—	—	—	—	2
Gray, J.	London	1833	Architecture	—	—	1	—	—	—	—	—	—	—	1
Gray, J.	London	1863-1872	Fruit	—	—	—	—	7	—	—	—	—	—	7
Gray, J., Junr.	London	1866-1867	Figures	—	—	—	—	2	—	—	—	—	—	2
Gray, John	London	1839-1842	Landscape	—	—	1	—	7	—	—	—	—	—	8
Gray, John	Bedford Park	1885-1893	Landscape	—	—	7	—	11	—	—	—	—	2	20
Gray, Miss Jessie D.	Edinburgh	1892	Domestic	—	—	1	—	—	—	—	—	—	—	1
Gray, John Hobday	London	1832-1837	Architecture	—	—	3	—	7	—	1	—	—	—	11
Gray, J. W.	London	1828	Portraits	—	—	1	—	—	—	—	—	—	—	1
Gray, Miss K.	Woodford	1873-1875	Birds	—	—	1	—	3	—	—	—	—	—	4
Gray, Miss L.	Tunb'dge Wells	1874-1875	Figures	—	—	—	—	3	—	—	—	—	—	3
Gray, Paul	London	1867	Figures	—	—	—	—	3	—	—	—	—	—	3
Gray, Ronald	—	1891-1892	Portraits	—	—	—	—	—	—	—	—	—	10	10
Gray, S.	London	1807-1830	Landscape	—	—	6	—	—	—	—	—	—	—	6
Gray, S.	London	1883	Domestic	—	—	—	—	1	—	—	—	—	—	1
Gray, Thomas	London	1859-1869	Domestic	—	—	6	2	10	—	—	—	—	—	18
Gray, Thomas	Turnham Green	1881-1893	Domestic	—	—	—	—	6	—	5	—	—	—	11
Gray, Tom	London	1866-1887	Religious	—	—	—	1	1	—	—	—	—	7	9
Gray, Thomas U.	London	1893	Sculpture	—	—	1	—	—	—	—	—	—	—	1
Gray, T. W.	Salisbury	1827-1851	Domestic	—	—	1	3	8	—	—	—	—	—	12
Gray, William	Ventnor	1835-1883	Landscape	—	—	—	5	4	—	1	—	—	45	55
Gray, William	London	1841-1857	Sculpture	—	—	12	—	—	—	—	—	—	—	12
Gray, Mrs.	London	1844-1857	Portraits	—	—	4	—	—	—	—	—	—	—	4
Grayfrere —, Junr.	—	1774	Landscape	1	—	—	—	—	—	—	—	—	—	1
Grayson, C.	London	1824	Churches	—	—	—	—	1	—	—	—	—	—	1
Grayson, Clifford P.	Finisterre	1883	Sea Pieces	—	—	—	—	1	—	—	—	—	—	1
Grayson, J.	London	1803	Architecture	—	—	2	—	—	—	—	—	—	—	2
Grayson, W.	London	1791-1801	Architecture	—	—	10	—	—	—	—	—	—	—	10
Grayson, W. T.	London	1868-1871	Landscape	—	—	—	—	3	—	—	—	—	—	3
Grayson and Ould	Chester	1886-1893	Architecture	—	—	11	—	—	—	—	—	—	—	11
Greata, Madame	London	1858-1860	Portraits	—	—	—	—	5	—	—	—	—	—	5
Greatbach, H.	London	1824	Engraving	—	—	—	—	1	—	—	—	—	—	1
Greatbach, William	London	1859	Engraving	—	—	1	—	—	—	—	—	—	—	1
Greathead, B.	—	1802-1803	Historical	—	—	2	—	—	—	—	—	—	—	2
Greaves, Henry	London	1873	Harmony	—	—	—	—	—	—	—	—	—	1	1
Greaves, Mabel	Leamington	1876	Domestic	—	—	—	—	—	—	—	—	—	1	1
Greaves, William	Leeds	1885-1888	Landscape	—	—	3	—	—	—	—	—	—	1	4
Greene. *See* Finden and Green	—	—	Architecture	—	—	—	—	—	—	—	—	—	—	—
Green, Amos	Birmingham	1760-1765	Fruit	5	—	—	—	—	—	—	—	—	—	5
Green, Arthur	London	1879	Domestic	—	—	—	—	—	—	—	—	—	1	1
Green, Alfred H.	Birmingham	1844-1862	Animals	—	—	1	3	4	—	—	—	—	—	8
Green, Benjamin	London	1765-1774	Engraving	8	—	—	—	—	—	—	—	—	—	8
Green, B.	Newcastle	1837	Sculpture	—	—	2	—	—	—	—	—	—	—	2
Green, Miss Blanche	London	1870	Domestic	—	—	—	—	4	—	—	—	—	—	4
Green, Benjamin Richard ‡ (?) Robert	London	1832-1876	Portraits	—	—	40	—	38	—	243	—	—	6	327
Green, C.	—	1804	Landscape	—	—	1	—	—	—	—	—	—	—	1
Green, Charles, R.I ‡ φ	London	1862-1893	Domestic	—	—	12	—	—	—	150	2	—	20	184
Green, Charles	Sheffield	1889	Sculpture	—	—	1	—	—	—	—	—	—	—	1
Green, C. B.	London	1853	Landscape	—	—	1	—	—	—	—	—	—	—	1
Green, David	London	1873-1893	Landscape	—	—	9	—	40	—	15	4	1	19	88
Green, E. F.	London	1824-1851	Portraits	—	—	14	21	20	—	—	—	—	5	60
Green, Mrs. E. Goodwin	Maidstone	1886	Flowers	—	—	—	—	—	—	—	—	—	1	1
Green, F. G.	London	1824-1831	Architecture	—	—	4	—	—	—	—	—	—	—	4
Green, George Pycock Everett	London	1841-1873	Figures	—	—	20	9	12	—	—	—	—	—	41
Green, Henry	London	1776	Landscape	—	2	—	—	—	—	—	—	—	—	2
Green, Herbert John	Norwich	1881-1885	Architecture	—	—	3	—	—	—	—	—	—	—	3
Green, H. Towneley, R.I. ‡ φ	London	1855-1893	Domestic	—	—	8	—	3	—	82	3	—	42	138
Green, H. Vaughan	Preston	1884-1886	Landscape	—	—	—	—	3	—	—	—	—	—	3
Green, Miss Isabella	Kimbford	1873-1875	Flowers	—	—	1	—	—	—	—	—	—	7	8
Green, J.	London	1790-1792	Still Life	—	—	4	—	—	—	—	—	—	—	4
Green, James	London	1792-1834	Miniatures	—	—	206	30	9	—	—	—	—	43	288
Green, Mrs. James. *See* Miss Mary Byrne	London	1805-1845	Miniatures	—	—	94	6	2	—	1	—	—	31	134
Green, J.	Richmond	1815	Portraits	—	—	1	—	—	—	—	—	—	—	1
Green, J.	Newcastle	1837	Architecture	—	—	2	—	—	—	—	—	—	—	2
Green, Josiah	London	1862-1868	Domestic	—	—	1	3	2	—	—	—	—	—	6
Green, J. G.	London	1835	Sculpture	—	—	1	—	—	—	—	—	—	—	1
Green, John Hippesley	London	1775-1820	Medals, etc.	—	—	33	—	—	—	—	—	—	—	33

Name.	Town.	First and Last Year of Ex.	Speciality.	S. A.	F. S.	R. A.	B. I.	S. S.	O. W.	N. W.	G. G.	N. G.	V. E.	Total.
GREEN, J. T.	London	1836	Figures	—	—	—	—	1	—	—	—	—	—	1
GREEN, MISS L. J.	London	1830-1845	Portraits	—	—	—	—	7	—	—	—	—	—	7
GREEN, MISS MABEL	Balham	1880-1893	Landscape	—	—	4	—	4	—	—	—	—	3	11
GREEN, MISS MARY C.	London	1890-1891	Churches	—	—	1	—	—	—	1	—	—	—	2
GREEN, MISS M. HELEN	London	1884-1887	Flowers	—	—	3	—	—	—	—	—	—	—	3
GREEN, NATHANIEL EVERETT	London	1854-1890	Landscape	—	—	18	1	24	—	12	—	—	33	88
GREEN, P.	Guernsey	1873	Landscape	—	—	—	—	2	—	—	—	—	—	2
GREEN, P. J.	London	1836	Figures	—	—	—	4	—	—	—	—	—	—	4
GREEN, R.	London	1781-1785	Domestic	—	—	6	—	—	—	—	—	—	—	6
GREEN, MRS. R.	Eltham	1846-1848	Copies	—	—	—	—	2	—	—	—	—	—	2
GREEN, RICHARD CROFTON	London	1869-1890	Domestic	—	—	1	—	27	—	—	—	—	1	29
GREEN, VALENTINE, A.R.A., F.S.A.	—	1766-1806	Engraving	15	—	29	—	—	—	—	—	—	—	44
GREEN, WILLIAM	London	1797-1811	Landscape	—	—	4	—	—	—	—	—	—	5	9
GREEN, W. A.	London	1841	Architecture	—	—	1	—	—	—	—	—	—	—	1
GREEN, WILLIAM JOHN	London	1860-1881	Architecture	—	—	10	—	—	—	—	—	—	—	10
GREEN, W. P.	Birmingham	1865	Landscape	—	—	—	—	1	—	—	—	—	—	1
GREEN, Y. Y. (?) GEENS	—	1831	Portraits	—	—	—	—	1	—	—	—	—	—	1
GREEN, MISS	—	1804	Landscape	—	—	2	—	—	—	—	—	—	—	2
GREEN AND DE VILLE	London	1861	Architecture	—	—	1	—	—	—	—	—	—	—	1
GREENAWAY, F. W.	Greenwich	1864	Landscape	—	—	—	—	1	—	—	—	—	—	1
GREENAWAY, JOHN	London	1872	Engraving	—	—	—	—	—	—	—	—	—	1	1
GREENAWAY, MISS KATE, R.I.‡	London	1868-1891	Children	—	—	6	—	11	—	6	1	—	29	53
GREENBANK, ARTHUR	London	1888-1893	Figures	—	—	5	—	4	—	8	—	—	5	22
GREENE, ALICE	Richmond	1883-1886	Landscape	—	—	—	—	4	—	—	—	—	2	6
GREENE, RICHARD MASSY	London	1875	Domestic	—	—	—	—	1	—	—	—	—	—	1
GREENER, E.	Twickenham	1812-1813	Flowers	—	—	2	—	—	—	—	—	—	—	2
GREENER, J.	London	1811-1838	Fruit, etc.	—	—	7	—	3	—	—	—	—	—	10
GREENER, MISS MARY ANN	London	1845-1853	Miniatures	—	—	11	—	5	—	—	—	—	—	16
GREENFIELD, E. LATHAM	London	1886	Landscape	—	—	—	—	1	—	—	—	—	—	1
GREENFIELD, MRS. LATHAM (C.)	Richmond	1883-1885	Landscape	—	—	—	—	2	—	—	1	—	3	6
GREENHEAD, MISS	London	1795-1800	Miniatures	—	—	9	—	—	—	—	—	—	—	9
GREENHILL, MISS CHARLOTTE A.	Bromley	1892	Shells	—	—	—	—	1	—	—	—	—	—	1
GREENHILL, MISS M. E.	London	1873-1885	Figures	—	—	2	—	4	—	—	—	—	—	6
GREENISH, MRS. FLORENCE E.	Leeds	1880-1886	Landscape	—	—	1	—	1	—	2	—	—	1	5
GREENLAND, MISS	—	1787	Portraits	—	—	1	—	—	—	—	—	—	—	1
GREENLEES, MISS GEORGINA MOSSMAN	Glasgow	1878-1880	Landscape	—	—	2	—	—	—	—	—	—	—	2
GREENLEES, ROBERT M., R.S.W.	Glasgow	1873-1877	Landscape	—	—	4	—	—	—	—	—	—	—	4
GREENLEY, MISS, *or* GREENBY	—	1795-1797	Landscape	—	—	4	—	—	—	—	—	—	—	4
GREENOUGH, G.	Rome	1879	Portraits	—	—	—	—	—	—	—	—	—	1	1
GREENOUGH, J.	London	1830-1838	Landscape	—	—	2	—	1	—	—	—	—	—	3
GREENOUGH, RICHARD S.	Paris	1865-1885	Sculpture	—	—	5	—	—	—	—	—	—	—	5
GREENSLADE, JAMES THOMAS	Walthamstow	1886-1887	Domestic	—	—	1	—	—	—	2	—	—	—	3
GREENSLADE, SIDNEY K.	London	1893	Architecture	—	—	2	—	—	—	—	—	—	—	2
GREENWOOD —	London	1790	Landscape	1	—	—	—	—	—	—	—	—	—	1
GREENWOOD, BEATRICE	Willesden	1892-1893	Domestic	—	—	—	—	2	—	—	—	—	—	2
GREENWOOD, COLIN H.	London	1869-1881	Landscape	—	—	8	—	28	—	—	—	—	—	36
GREENWOOD, F.	London	1840-1845	Sea Pieces	—	—	1	3	3	—	—	—	—	—	7
GREENWOOD, MISS ISABELLA	Cheltenham	1864-1874	Still Life	—	—	—	1	1	—	—	—	—	—	2
GREENWOOD, JOHN, F.S.A.	London	1764-1776	Engraving	12	—	—	—	—	—	—	—	—	—	12
GREESE, JOHN ALEXANDER	London	1763-1768	Miniatures	6	4	—	—	—	—	—	—	—	—	10
GREGG, J.	London	1796-1816	Flowers	—	—	11	—	—	—	—	—	—	—	11
GREGG, THOMAS HENRY	Cambridge	1824-1872	Domestic	—	—	17	3	6	—	—	—	—	—	26
GREGORY, CHARLES	Cowes	1848-1854	Landscape	—	—	—	—	2	—	—	—	—	7	9
GREGORY, CHARLES, R.W.S.†	London	1873-1893	Domestic	—	—	10	—	11	94	—	—	—	7	122
GREGORY, EDWARD JOHN, A.R.A., R.I.‡ φ	London	1870-1893	Portraits	—	—	18	—	—	—	55	14	—	19	106
GREGORY, MISS EDITH M.	London	1885-1893	Figures	—	—	2	—	—	—	—	2	—	8	12
GREGORY, MISS J.	London	1873	Flowers	—	—	—	—	—	—	—	—	—	1	1
GREGORY, J. G.	London	1845-1848	Architecture	—	—	2	—	—	—	—	—	—	—	2
GREGORY, MISS MARY F.	London	1870-1874	Landscape	—	—	1	—	5	—	—	—	—	5	11
GREIFFENHAGEN, MAURICE WILLIAM	London	1880-1893	Heads	—	—	6	—	4	—	—	—	—	3	13
GREIG, E. S.	Bristol	1866-1868	Domestic	—	—	1	1	2	—	—	—	—	—	4
GREIG, GEORGE M.	Edinburgh	1851-1866	Figures	—	—	3	—	—	—	—	—	—	5	8
GREIG, S. A.	Exeter	1839-1841	Architecture	—	—	3	—	—	—	—	—	—	—	3
GREIRSON —	—	1782	Sea Pieces	—	1	—	—	—	—	—	—	—	—	1
GRELLIER, WILLIAM	London	1828-1848	Architecture	—	—	19	—	—	—	—	—	—	—	19
GRENIER, F.	Paris	1856	Rustic	—	—	1	—	—	—	—	—	—	—	1
GREPPI, A.	London	1860-1861	Venice	—	—	1	3	2	—	—	—	—	1	7
GRESLEY, JAMES S.	Derby	1866-1883	Landscape	—	—	—	—	2	—	1	—	—	4	7
GRESLEY, MISS W. M.	Lichfield	1886	Domestic	—	—	—	—	—	—	1	—	—	—	1
GRESSELL, T.	London	1822	Architecture	—	—	1	—	—	—	—	—	—	—	1
GREVATT, W. M.	Woolwich	1789	Figures	—	—	1	—	—	—	—	—	—	—	1

Name.	Town.	First and Last Year of Ex.	Speciality.	S. A.	F. S.	R. A.	B. I.	S. S.	O. W.	N.W.	G. G.	N. G.	V. E.	Total.
Grevedon, H.	London	1814	Mythological	—	—	3	—	—	—	—	—	—	—	3
Greville, Lady Louisa Augusta	—	1762	Engraving	—	1	—	—	—	—	—	—	—	—	1
Greville, R. K., H.R.S.A.	Edinburgh	1844-1852	Landscape	—	—	3	—	2	—	—	—	—	—	5
Grew, J.	London	1788-1790	Miniatures	—	—	5	—	—	—	—	—	—	—	5
Grew, Thomas	London	1891-1892	Architecture	—	—	2	—	—	—	—	—	—	—	2
Grey, Alfred, R.H.A.	Dublin	1873-1887	Cattle	—	—	3	—	—	—	—	—	—	3	6
Grey, Miss Edith F.	Newcastle	1890-1892	Flowers	—	—	2	—	—	—	3	—	—	—	5
Grey, J.	London	1858	Domestic	—	—	1	2	—	—	—	—	—	—	3
Grey, James, R.H.A.	Dublin	1873-1875	Domestic	—	—	2	—	—	—	—	—	—	—	2
Grey, John	Thursley	1890-1892	Portraits	—	—	—	—	—	—	—	—	—	3	3
Grey, Mrs. Jane Willis	London	1877-1893	Domestic	—	—	4	—	18	—	7	—	—	6	35
Grey, Miss	—	1773	Landscape	—	—	1	—	—	—	—	—	—	—	1
Gribble, Bernard F.	London	1891-1893	Burning Ships	—	—	1	—	—	—	—	—	—	1	2
Gribble, C.	London	1855	Architecture	—	—	1	—	—	—	—	—	—	—	1
Gribble, Herbert Augustine Keate	London	1874-1882	Architecture	—	—	4	—	—	—	—	—	—	—	4
Gribble, Mrs. Nora	London	1883-1886	Domestic	—	—	—	—	—	—	2	—	—	—	2
Gribble, W.	London	1830	Portraits	—	—	1	—	—	—	—	—	—	—	1
Grieg, Mrs. M. A.	London	1852	Portraits	—	—	1	—	—	—	—	—	—	—	1
Grier, E. Wyly	St. Ives	1886-1892	Domestic	—	—	5	—	2	—	—	—	—	3	10
Grier, J. J.	Greenock	1877-1879	Landscape	—	—	—	—	—	—	—	—	—	6	6
Grier, Louis	St. Ives	1888-1893	River Scenes	—	—	1	—	3	—	—	1	—	3	8
Grierson, C.	London	1863-1871	Domestic	—	—	—	6	7	—	—	—	—	—	13
Grierson, Mrs. C.	London	1867-1875	Figures	—	—	—	—	12	—	—	—	—	1	13
Grierson, Miss C. G.	Dublin	1874	Game	—	—	—	—	1	—	—	—	—	—	1
Grierson, C. MacIvor, R.I ‡	London	1885-1893	Domestic	—	—	2	—	3	—	18	—	—	4	27
Griesbach, Charles Frederick William	London	1848-1856	Domestic	—	—	1	2	3	—	—	—	—	—	6
Griesbach, Mrs. Charles	London	1856-1868	Figures	—	—	2	—	3	—	—	—	—	1	6
Griesbach, G. A.	London	1833	Landscape	—	—	—	—	1	—	—	—	—	—	1
Griesbach, Miss Julia A.	London	1882-1883	Miniatures	—	—	2	—	—	—	—	—	—	—	2
Grieve, Alec	London	1891	Landscape	—	—	1	—	—	—	—	—	—	—	1
Grieve, F. J.	London	1877	Landscape	—	—	—	—	—	—	—	—	—	2	2
Grieve, Miss J. E.	London	1855-1873	Flowers	—	—	7	—	—	—	—	—	—	1	8
Grievé, J. G.	Paris	1877	Rotterdam	—	—	—	—	—	—	—	—	—	1	1
Grieve, Miss M. A.	London	1856-1859	Domestic	—	—	3	—	—	—	—	—	—	—	3
Grieve, R.	London	1838	Landscape	—	—	1	—	—	—	—	—	—	—	1
Grievé, Thomas	London	1825-1828	Landscape	—	—	5	—	—	—	—	—	—	—	5
Grieve, William	London	1826-1839	Landscape	—	—	11	2	1	—	—	—	—	—	14
Griffen, Anna	London	1888-1890	Portraits	—	—	—	—	1	—	1	—	—	—	2
Griffin, J. C. Heyness	London	1886	Landscape	—	—	—	—	—	—	1	—	—	—	1
Griffin, Miss J. L.	London	1885	Domestic	—	—	1	—	—	—	—	—	—	—	1
Griffin, William	London	1772-1776	Miniatures	5	—	5	—	—	—	—	—	—	—	10
Griffith, Agnes	Haslemere	1886	Flowers	—	—	—	—	1	—	—	—	—	—	1
Griffith, Mrs. Emily	London	1886-1892	Sculpture	—	—	4	—	—	—	—	—	—	—	4
Griffith, James Milo Ap	London	1863-1889	Sculpture	—	—	37	—	—	—	—	—	—	—	37
Griffith, J. W.	London	1807	Architecture	—	—	1	—	—	—	—	—	—	—	1
Griffith, Miss Kate	Winchfield	1879-1885	Still Life	—	—	4	—	6	—	—	—	—	—	10
Griffith, M.	London	1877	Mountains	—	—	—	—	1	—	—	—	—	—	1
Griffith, Mary F., *or* E.	London	1881-1892	Landscape	—	—	—	—	1	—	—	—	—	2	3
Griffith, William	Brentford	1875-1883	Flowers	—	—	2	—	3	—	—	—	—	—	5
Griffith, William Pettitt	London	1838-1842	Architecture	—	—	2	—	9	—	—	—	—	—	11
Griffith, Miss	—	1797	Flowers	—	—	1	—	—	—	—	—	—	—	1
Griffiths, Arthur Chatham	—	1872-1877	Landscape	—	—	7	—	1	—	—	—	—	7	15
Griffiths, Gwenny	Swansea	1892	Flowers	—	—	—	—	1	—	—	—	—	—	1
Griffiths, Henry	London	1835	Domestic	—	—	—	—	2	—	—	—	—	—	2
Griffiths, John	London	1764-1774	Still Life	—	21	—	—	—	—	—	—	—	—	21
Griffiths, John	Bombay	1869-1893	Indian figures	—	—	17	—	—	—	—	—	—	3	20
Griffiths, J.	London	1807-1811	Architecture	—	—	6	—	—	—	—	—	—	—	6
Griffiths, J.	London	1818-1821	Portraits	—	—	3	—	—	—	—	—	—	—	3
Griffiths, J. L.	London	1839-1844	Architecture	—	—	2	—	—	—	—	—	—	—	2
Griffiths, Mary E.	—	1893	Portraits	—	—	—	—	1	—	—	—	—	—	1
Griffiths, R.	Stafford	1867	Architecture	—	—	1	—	—	—	—	—	—	—	1
Griffiths, Richard William	London	1847	Architecture	—	—	1	—	—	—	—	—	—	—	1
Griffiths, T.	London	1811-1812	Rustic	—	—	2	—	—	—	—	—	—	—	2
Griffiths, Tom	Leeds	1871-1893	Landscape	—	—	17	—	22	—	2	—	1	16	58
Griffiths, W.	London	1799	Landscape	—	—	1	—	—	—	—	—	—	—	1
Griffiths, W. J. *See also* Taylor and Griffiths	London	1892	Architecture	—	—	1	—	—	—	—	—	—	—	1
Griffiths, W. T.	Ipswich	1878	Landscape	—	—	1	—	—	—	—	—	—	—	1
Griffiths, Miss	London	1774	Flowers	—	1	—	—	—	—	—	—	—	—	1
Grigg, F. R.	London	1890-1891	Domestic	—	—	—	—	3	—	—	—	—	—	3
Griggs, William	London	1830-1835	Sculpture	—	—	6	—	4	—	—	—	—	—	10
Grignion, Charles	London	1761-1781	Engraving	3	1	20	—	—	—	—	—	—	—	24

Name.	Town.	First and Last Year of Ex.	Speciality.	S. A.	F. S.	R. A.	B. I.	S. S.	O. W.	N. W.	G. G.	N. G.	V. E.	Total.
Grignion, C., Junr.	Rome	1784	Historical	—	—	1	—	—	—	—	—	—	—	1
Grimaldi, William de	London	1768-1830	Miniatures	1	4	89	—	—	1	—	—	—	—	95
Grimani, F.	London	1807-1831	Portraits	—	—	13	—	—	—	—	—	—	—	13
Grimbalston, William	London	1769-1778	Sculpture	—	11	—	—	—	—	—	—	—	—	11
Grimm, Samuel Hieronymus	London	1769-1793	Landscape	5	3	46	—	—	—	—	—	—	—	54
Grimmond, William	Glasgow	1887-1891	Domestic	—	—	3	—	—	—	—	—	—	—	3
Grimsby, T.	—	1834	Sculpture	—	—	—	1	—	—	—	—	—	—	1
Grimshaw, Atkinson	Leeds	1874-1886	Landscape	—	—	5	—	—	—	—	1	—	1	7
Grimshaw, Mrs. Eva M.	London	1888	Coast Scenes	—	—	1	—	—	—	—	—	—	—	1
Grimshaw, Thomas	Derby	1853-1864	Figures	—	—	—	3	—	—	—	—	—	5	8
Grimshaw, W. H. Murphy	London	1886-1893	Landscape	—	—	5	—	3	—	—	—	—	2	10
Grimsley, T.	London	1827-1840	Sculpture	—	—	5	—	1	—	—	—	—	—	6
Grimstone, E.	Ealing	1837-1879	Animals	—	—	15	3	13	—	—	—	—	—	31
Grimstone, Mary	London	1881	Flowers	—	—	—	—	—	—	—	—	—	1	1
Grindlay, Captain Robert Melville §	—	1828	Sketch	—	—	—	—	1	—	—	—	—	—	1
Grinling, Mrs. Alice G.	Stanmore	1893	Figures	—	—	1	—	—	—	—	—	—	—	1
Grinway, F.	London	1800-1802	Architecture	—	—	3	—	—	—	—	—	—	—	3
Grinway, T. H.	London	1803	Architecture	—	—	1	—	—	—	—	—	—	—	1
Grispini, Filippo	London	1863	Portraits	—	—	2	—	—	—	—	—	—	—	2
Griset, Ernest	London	1871	Animals	—	—	—	—	2	—	—	—	—	—	2
Griset, H. D.	London	1868-1874	Figures	—	—	—	—	4	—	—	—	—	1	5
Grissel, T.	London	1824	Architecture	—	—	—	—	1	—	—	—	—	—	1
Grissell, H.	London	1862	Architecture	—	—	2	—	—	—	—	—	—	—	2
Griswold, C. C.	London	1873-1880	Landscape	—	—	—	—	1	—	—	—	—	1	2
Gritten, Henry	London	1835-1849	Landscape	—	—	12	30	14	—	—	—	—	6	62
Gritton, T.	London	1807-1817	Flowers	—	—	4	—	—	—	—	—	—	—	4
Gritton, Miss	Keswick	1816	Landscape	—	—	2	—	—	—	—	—	—	—	2
Grivat —	—	1790	Dockyard	—	—	1	—	—	—	—	—	—	—	1
Grocock, George H.	Cardiff	1892	Architecture	—	—	1	—	—	—	—	—	—	—	1
Grogan, Nathaniel	London	1782	Landscape	—	4	—	—	—	—	—	—	—	—	4
Grolleron, P.	London	1883-1884	Military	—	—	—	—	—	—	—	—	—	4	4
Gronckel, De. *See* D.	—	—	—	—	—	—	—	—	—	—	—	—	—	—
Gröne, Ferdinand E.	Colchester	1888-1893	River Scenes	—	—	2	—	13	—	2	—	—	—	17
Grönland, Theude	Paris	1849-1867	Fruit	—	—	16	6	1	—	—	—	—	1	24
Groom, A. H.	London	1863-1872	Landscape	—	—	2	—	10	—	—	—	—	7	19
Groom, A. J.	London	1828	Architecture	—	—	1	—	—	—	—	—	—	—	1
Groom, Charles W.	Carshalton	1889-1893	Landscape	—	—	1	—	2	—	—	1	1	4	9
Groom, Edward	London	1858-1860	Domestic	—	—	—	—	3	—	—	—	—	—	3
Groom, J.	London	1851-1858	Landscape	—	—	8	—	—	—	—	—	—	—	8
Groom, Richard	London	1869-1874	Churches	—	—	4	—	—	—	—	—	—	—	4
Groombridge —	Goudhurst	1773-1776	Miniatures	8	11	—	—	—	—	—	—	—	—	19
Groombridge, William	London	1777-1790	Landscape	—	—	28	—	—	—	—	—	—	—	28
Groome, William H. C.	Ealing	1881-1892	Landscape	—	—	7	—	9	—	5	1	—	4	26
Groot, De. *See* D.	—	—	—	—	—	—	—	—	—	—	—	—	—	—
Grose, Miss Anne	London	1877	Houses	—	—	1	—	—	—	—	—	—	1	2
Grose, Capt. Daniel	—	1777	Tangiers	—	—	1	—	—	—	—	—	—	—	1
Grose, Miss Millicent S. ‖	Oxford	1879-1890	Flowers	—	—	1	—	14	—	3	—	—	4	22
Grosse, Captain Francis	—	1767-1777	Landscape	3	—	16	—	—	—	—	—	—	—	19
Grosse, Professor	Dresden	1886	Portraits	—	—	—	—	—	—	—	2	—	—	2
Grossmith, W. Weedon	London	1875-1890	Domestic	—	—	9	—	13	—	—	2	—	11	35
Grosvenor, E.	—	1817	Buildings	—	—	1	—	—	—	—	—	—	—	1
Grosvenor, Hon. Mrs. Norman (Caroline)	London	1889-1893	Miniatures	—	—	5	—	—	—	—	—	10	10	25
Grove, C.	London	1890-1893	Landscape	—	—	—	—	—	—	—	—	—	6	6
Grove, Miss Henrietta. *See* Mrs. James Hussey	—	—	—	—	—	—	—	—	—	—	—	—	—	—
Grove, J.	—	1789-1805	Landscape	—	—	23	—	—	—	—	—	—	—	23
Grove, J. A.	London	1838	Architecture	—	—	1	—	—	—	—	—	—	—	1
Grover, A. H.	London	1858	Landscape	—	—	—	—	1	—	—	—	—	—	1
Grover, Miss Jane Elizabeth	London	1841-1859	Domestic	—	—	4	—	—	—	—	—	—	—	4
Grover, Miss Louisa E.	Ghent	1840-1863	Historical	—	—	—	4	7	—	—	—	—	—	11
Grover, T.	London	1840	Figures	—	—	1	—	—	—	—	—	—	—	1
Groves, C.	London	1856-1864	Landscape	—	—	—	—	12	—	—	—	—	—	12
Groves, Frederick Humphrey	London	1847	Architecture	—	—	1	—	—	—	—	—	—	—	1
Groves, Mrs. J.	London	1814-1820	Portraits	—	—	11	—	—	5	—	—	—	—	16
Groves, John Thomas	London	1778-1807	Architecture	—	—	5	—	—	—	—	—	—	—	5
Groves, Miss L.	London	1882	River Scenes	—	—	—	—	—	—	—	—	—	1	1
Groves, Miss Mary	London	1884-1893	Domestic	—	—	4	—	6	—	1	—	—	5	16
Groves, Robert E.	London	1887-1893	Sea Pieces	—	—	1	—	2	—	8	—	—	—	11
Groves, Thomas	Leicester	1881-1889	Landscape	—	—	2	—	1	—	8	—	—	—	11
Groves, William.	London	1834-1861	Sculpture	—	—	12	—	—	—	—	—	—	—	12
Grubbe, Laurence Carrington	London	1893	Domestic	—	—	1	—	—	—	—	—	—	—	1
Grüder —	Dresden	1867	Portraits	—	—	1	—	—	—	—	—	—	—	1
Grundy, Cuthbert C., V.P.R.C.A., F.S.A.	Blackpool	1879-1893	Landscape	—	—	2	—	—	—	—	—	—	6	8

Name.	Town.	First and Last Year of Ex.	Speciality.	S. A.	F. S.	R. A.	B. I.	S. S.	O. W.	N. W.	G. G.	N. G.	V. E.	Total.
Grundy, J. R. G., R.C.A.	Bury	1880-1893	Landscape	—	—	2	—	—	—	—	—	—	1	3
Grützner, Edouard	Birmingham	1878	Religious	—	—	1	—	—	—	—	—	—	—	1
Gruyter, W.	Amsterdam	1851	Sea Pieces	—	—	2	—	—	—	—	—	—	—	2
Grylls, Thomas J.	London	1866-1882	Figures	—	—	3	—	—	—	—	—	—	6	9
Guarnerio, Pietro	Milan	1872	Figures	—	—	1	—	—	—	—	—	—	—	1
Gubbins, Miss H.	Leamington	1843-1849	Historical	—	—	6	—	—	—	—	—	—	—	6
Gucht, Vander. *See* V.	—	—	—	—	—	—	—	—	—	—	—	—	—	—
Gudin, Jean Antoine Theodore	Paris	1837-1873	Sea Pieces	—	—	16	2	—	—	—	—	—	—	18
Guenot —	—	1762	Sculpture	—	1	—	—	—	—	—	—	—	—	1
Guérand, Henry	Paris	1879-1881	Domestic	—	—	—	—	—	—	—	—	—	12	12
Guérard, De. *See* D.	—	—	—	—	—	—	—	—	—	—	—	—	—	—
Guérin, Mrs. William Collings Lukis. *See*	—	—	—	—	—	—	—	—	—	—	—	—	—	—
Mrs. Anna Maria Edmonds ‖	London	1873-1888	Flowers	—	—	12	—	11	—	1	—	—	21	45
Guest, Miss Agnes W.	London	1890-1893	Buildings	—	—	—	—	1	—	1	—	—	—	2
Guest, Douglas	London	1803-1839	Mythological	—	—	15	34	5	—	—	—	—	—	54
Guest, George	London	1806-1831	Sea Pieces	—	—	15	3	3	—	—	—	—	—	21
Guest, H.	London	1843-1853	Portraits	—	—	3	—	—	—	—	—	—	—	3
Guest, T., Junr.	London	1801	Miniatures	—	—	1	—	—	—	—	—	—	—	1
Guest, T. R.	Salisbury	1810-1814	Scriptural	—	—	—	6	—	—	—	—	—	—	6
Guglielmi, L.	Rome	1863-1870	Sculpture	—	—	3	—	—	—	—	—	—	—	3
Guidi, G.	London	1875	Pompeii	—	—	—	—	1	—	—	—	—	—	1
Guild, Mrs. Emma Cadwallader	London	1885-1893	Sculpture	—	—	9	—	—	—	—	1	—	—	10
Guillemard, Miss Mary F.	Cambridge	1882-1883	Miniatures	—	—	1	—	1	—	—	—	—	—	2
Guillod, Miss Bessie	London	1876-1893	Flowers	—	—	1	—	5	—	—	—	—	5	11
Guillod, Thomas Walker	London	1839-1860	Landscape	—	—	10	6	16	—	—	—	—	—	32
Guillon, Adolphe Irénée	Paris	1869-1879	Landscape	—	—	1	—	—	—	—	—	—	5	6
Guinness, Miss Elizabeth S.	London	1873-1890	Historical	—	—	8	—	11	—	—	1	—	25	45
Gülich, John P.	London	1890-1893	Etching	—	—	1	—	9	—	2	—	—	—	12
Gulland, Miss Elizabeth	Bushey	1886-1893	Domestic	—	—	5	—	—	—	—	—	1	3	9
Gullet, Miss	Exeter	1807	Flowers	—	—	1	—	—	—	—	—	—	—	1
Gullick, Thomas John	London	1851-1880	Miniatures	—	—	33	2	1	—	—	—	—	—	36
Gully, J.	—	1871	Landscape	—	—	1	—	—	—	—	—	—	—	1
Gulston, A. G.	—	1883	Landscape	—	—	—	—	—	—	—	1	—	—	1
Gulston, Miss Elizabeth	—	1795-1801	Figures	—	—	4	—	—	—	—	—	—	—	4
Gulston, Miss J.	London	1859	Figures	—	—	—	—	1	—	—	—	—	—	1
Gumbrage —	—	1778	Landscape	—	2	—	—	—	—	—	—	—	—	2
Gummery, H.	Worcester	1862-1878	Flowers	—	—	—	—	5	—	—	—	—	—	5
Gundry, Arthur	London	1866-1868	Domestic	—	—	4	—	2	—	—	—	—	1	7
Gundry, Thomas	London	1891	Domestic	—	—	1	—	—	—	—	—	—	—	1
Gunn, A.	London	1849-1871	Domestic	—	—	3	4	6	—	—	—	—	—	13
Gunn, Fred. G. T.	Edinburgh	1891-1892	Landscape	—	—	3	—	—	—	—	—	—	—	3
Gunning, Frank	London	1874	Portraits	—	—	—	—	—	—	—	—	—	1	1
Gunnis, J. W.	London	1889	Landscape	—	—	1	—	—	—	—	—	—	—	1
Gunnis, Louis J.	London	1887-1891	Domestic	—	—	3	—	—	—	—	—	—	—	3
Gunston, G. W.	London	1823-1833	Sea Pieces	—	—	3	—	—	—	—	—	—	—	3
Gunston, W.	London	1867-1874	Domestic	—	—	—	—	4	—	—	—	—	—	4
Gunthorp, Henry	Herne Hill	1884-1893	Sculpture	—	—	14	—	—	—	—	—	—	—	14
Gunton, W.	London	1829	Game	—	—	—	—	3	—	—	—	—	—	3
Gurden —	London	1783	Figures	—	1	—	—	—	—	—	—	—	—	1
Gurden, Lovel	London	1889	Domestic	—	—	—	—	1	—	—	1	—	—	2
Gurenstone, T.	London	1853	Portraits	—	—	—	—	2	—	—	—	—	—	2
Gush, Frederick	London	1847-1866	Portraits	—	—	9	1	6	—	—	—	—	—	16
Gush, Miss R.	London	1857-1879	Miniatures	—	—	21	—	—	—	—	—	—	—	21
Gush, William	London	1833-1874	Figures	—	—	53	4	2	—	—	—	—	—	59
Gussow, Charles	London	1878-1881	Figures	—	—	2	—	—	—	—	—	—	—	2
Gutch, G.	London	1810-1811	Landscape	—	—	4	—	—	—	—	—	—	—	4
Guthrie, D.	London	1837	Architecture	—	—	1	—	—	—	—	—	—	—	1
Guthrie, Miss E.	London	1849-1855	Portraits	—	—	—	—	3	—	—	—	—	—	3
Guthrie, James, R.S.A., R.S.W.	London	1882-1893	Landscape	—	—	2	—	—	—	—	2	—	5	9
Guthrie, John	Glasgow	1882	Flowers	—	—	1	—	—	—	—	—	—	—	1
Guthrie, W. D.	Witley	1881-1882	Study	—	—	1	—	3	—	—	—	—	2	6
Guttenbrunn —	Florence	1790-1795	Portraits	—	—	17	—	—	—	—	—	—	—	17
Guy, J. W.	London	1849	Sea Pieces	—	—	—	1	—	—	—	—	—	—	1
Guy, Seymour Joseph	London	1851	Mythological	—	—	—	1	—	—	—	—	—	—	1
Guyard, H.	Barmouth	1871	Portraits	—	—	—	—	—	—	—	—	—	1	1
Guyon, F. G.	Brussels	1834	Military	—	—	—	—	1	—	—	—	—	—	1
Guzzone, S.	Rome	1879-1890	Historical	—	—	1	—	1	—	—	—	—	—	2
Gwatkin, Arthur L.	Wallingham	1890-1893	Friezes	—	—	6	—	1	—	—	—	—	—	7
Gwatkin, Joshua Reynolds	London	1832-1851	Portraits	—	—	6	1	5	—	—	—	—	—	12
Gwatkin, Stewart Beauchamp	London	1888-1893	Domestic	—	—	—	—	9	—	6	—	—	—	15
Gwennap, Miss A.	London	1825-1826	Fruit	—	—	—	—	3	—	—	—	—	—	3
Gwennap, G.	London	1820	Historical	—	—	1	—	—	—	—	—	—	—	1

Name.	Town.	First and Last Year of Ex.	Speciality.	S. A.	F. S.	R. A.	B. I.	S. S.	O. W.	N. W.	G. G.	N. G.	V. E.	Total.
Gwennap, Thomas	London	1828	Fruit	—	—	1	2	1	—	—	—	—	—	4
Gwennap, Mrs. Thomas (L.)	London	1802-1832	Fruit	—	—	3	1	1	—	—	—	—	—	5
Gwilt, George, F.S.A.	London	1801-1827	Architecture	—	—	4	—	—	—	—	—	—	—	4
Gwilt, Joseph	London	1800-1830	Architecture	—	—	20	—	—	—	—	—	—	—	20
Gwilt, John Sebastian	London	1843-1845	Architecture	—	—	2	—	—	—	—	—	—	—	2
Gwynn, John, R.A.	London	1760-1772	Architecture	8	—	4	—	—	—	—	—	—	—	12
Gwynn, W.	London	1807-1817	Portraits	—	—	6	—	—	—	—	—	—	—	6
Gyfford, Edward	London	1791-1799	Architecture	—	—	5	—	—	—	—	—	—	—	5
Gyfford, S.	Fulham	1837	Landscape	—	—	1	—	—	—	—	—	—	—	1
Gyles, Rev. Mr.	Worcester	1765-1774	Landscape	3	1	3	—	—	—	—	—	—	—	7
Gyngell, Albert E.	Worcester	1874-1891	Landscape	—	—	8	—	—	—	—	—	—	2	10
Gyngell, Edmund	Bushey	1893	Portraits	—	—	2	—	—	—	—	—	—	—	2
Gyulas, B.	Munich	1874	Landscape	—	—	1	—	—	—	—	—	—	—	1
H. B. (HB.) *See* John Doyle.	—	—	—	—	—	—	—	—	—	—	—	—	—	—
Haag, Carl, R.W.S. § †	London	1849-1888	Portraits	—	—	11	—	3	343	—	7	—	8	372
Haager —	London	1773	Sculpture	3	—	—	—	—	—	—	—	—	—	3
Haanen, Miss Adriana	Oosterbeck	1883	Flowers	—	—	1	—	—	—	—	—	—	—	1
Haanen, Remi Van. *See* V.	—	—	—	—	—	—	—	—	—	—	—	—	—	—
Haaner, G. G.	Utrecht	1838	Churches	—	—	1	—	—	—	—	—	—	—	1
Haas, De. *See* D.	—	—	—	—	—	—	—	—	—	—	—	—	—	—
Habershon, Matthew	London	1807-1827	Architecture	—	—	13	—	—	—	—	—	—	—	13
Habershon, W. G.	London	1851-1871	Architecture	—	—	6	—	—	—	—	—	—	—	6
Haccou, J. C.	London	1836-1837	Dutch Landscape	—	—	1	—	2	—	—	—	—	—	3
Hacker, Arthur, A.R.A. φ	London	1878-1893	Domestic	—	—	30	—	3	—	—	5	4	26	68
Hacker, F.	London	1821	Landscape	—	—	1	—	—	—	—	—	—	—	1
Hacker, J.	London	1829-1839	Sculpture	—	—	3	—	—	—	—	—	—	—	3
Hackert, Johann Gottlieb	Rome	1771-1791	Landscape	40	—	9	—	—	—	—	—	—	—	49
Hacking, E.	Liverpool	1877	Landscape	—	—	—	—	—	—	—	—	—	1	1
Hacknisch, A.	—	1850	Miniatures	—	—	3	—	—	—	—	—	—	—	3
Hacon, Jessie	London	1886	Churches	—	—	—	—	1	—	—	—	—	—	1
Hadden, Miss Nellie	Sunningdale	1885-1893	Domestic	—	—	—	—	2	—	4	—	—	3	9
Haddo, George, Lord (afterwards 5th Earl of Aberdeen)	—	1845-1849	Landscape	—	—	2	—	—	—	—	—	—	—	2
Haddock, W.	Bath	1828-1832	Landscape	—	—	—	—	2	—	—	—	—	—	2
Haddon, Arthur Lumley	London	1866-1893	Domestic	—	—	2	—	13	—	—	—	—	21	36
Haddon, Arthur Trevor	London	1883-1893	Portraits	—	—	7	—	12	—	9	—	—	7	35
Haddon, G.	Liverpool	1874-1875	Buildings	—	—	2	—	—	—	—	—	—	—	2
Haddon, R.	Northampton	1866	Landscape	—	—	—	—	—	—	—	—	—	1	1
Haddon, Wilberforce	Wanstead	1880-1882	Landscape	—	—	1	—	2	—	—	—	—	1	4
Haden —	London	1774	Portraits	2	—	—	—	—	—	—	—	—	—	2
Haden, Sir Francis Seymour, F.R.C.S., P.R.P.E.	London	1865-1885	Etching	—	—	10	—	—	—	—	—	—	8	18
Hadfield, Charles A.	London	1881-1892	Arabs	—	—	1	—	2	—	1	—	—	—	4
Hadfield, George	London	1781-1795	Architecture	—	—	8	—	—	—	—	—	—	—	8
Hadfield, Miss Maria. *See* Mrs. Richard Cosway	—	—	—	—	—	—	—	—	—	—	—	—	—	—
Hadfield, Matthew Ellison	London	1861	Architecture	—	—	1	—	—	—	—	—	—	—	1
Hadfield (M. E.) and Son	Sheffield	1881-1885	Architecture	—	—	5	—	—	—	—	—	—	—	5
Hadfield, W.	London	1782-1783	Buildings	—	—	2	—	—	—	—	—	—	—	2
Hadfield and Goldie	London	1860	Architecture	—	—	2	—	—	—	—	—	—	—	2
Hadgie, A.	London	1851-1852	Oriental	—	—	—	1	1	—	—	—	—	—	2
Hadley, E.	—	1807	Buildings	—	—	1	—	—	—	—	—	—	—	1
Hadley, E. A.	London	1864	Landscape	—	—	1	—	—	—	—	—	—	—	1
Hadley, W. H.	Liverpool	1874-1876	Landscape	—	—	2	—	—	—	—	—	—	5	7
Haehnel, Julius	London	1854-1881	Sculpture	—	—	1	2	—	—	—	—	—	—	3
Haelin, A.	London	1855	Fruit	—	—	1	—	—	—	—	—	—	—	1
Hagan, O'. *See* O.	—	—	—	—	—	—	—	—	—	—	—	—	—	—
Hagarty, James	—	1767-1783	Sea Pieces	—	49	—	—	—	—	—	—	—	—	49
Hagarty —, Junr.	London	1772-1783	Scriptural	—	29	—	—	—	—	—	—	—	—	29
Hagarty, Miss Mary S.	Liverpool	1885-1892	Landscape	—	—	4	—	3	—	10	—	—	—	17
Hagarty, Parker, A.R.C.A.	Liverpool	1884-1893	Landscape	—	—	14	—	2	—	—	—	—	5	21
Hagbolt, T.	London	1826-1833	Sculpture	—	—	6	—	—	—	—	—	—	—	6
Hagelstein, Paul	London	1859	Domestic	—	—	—	1	—	—	—	—	—	—	1
Hagen, Vander. *See* V.	—	—	—	—	—	—	—	—	—	—	—	—	—	—
Haggart, Donald	Glasgow	1882	Sculpture	—	—	3	—	—	—	—	—	—	—	3
Haghe, Louis, H.P.R.I. ‡	London	1835-1884	Historical	—	—	—	8	—	—	217	—	—	—	225
Haghe, Mrs. L.	London	1880	Flowers	—	—	1	—	—	—	—	—	—	—	1
Hagreen, Henry B.	Ipswich	1853-1866	Domestic	—	—	1	—	2	—	—	—	—	1	4
Hagreen, H. W. Owen	London	1883-1885	Landscape	—	—	2	—	—	—	1	—	—	—	3
Hague, Anderson, R.I., R.B.A., R.C.A. ‡ § φ	Stockport	1873-1893	Landscape	—	—	31	—	14	—	18	8	5	6	82
Hague, Miss C. J.	London	1827-1831	Figures	—	—	2	3	9	—	—	—	—	—	14
Hague, E.	London	1790	Architecture	—	—	1	—	—	—	—	—	—	—	1

Name.	Town.	First and Last Year of Ex.	Speciality.	S. A.	F. S.	R. A.	B. I.	S. S.	O. W.	N.W.	G. G.	N. G.	V. E.	Total.
Hague, Homerville	London	1890-1893	Sculpture	—	—	1	—	1	—	—	—	7	—	9
Hague, J. Edward	Cookham	1884-1888	Sculpture	—	—	5	—	—	—	—	—	—	1	6
Hague, J. Houghton	Oldham	1874-1876	Domestic	—	—	4	—	—	—	—	—	—	—	4
Hague, L.	—	1828	Engraving	—	—	—	—	2	—	—	—	—	—	2
Hague, T.	Tottenham	1819	Architecture	—	—	1	—	—	—	—	—	—	—	1
Hahn, John Mellish Kay	London	1858	Architecture	—	—	1	—	—	—	—	—	—	—	1
Hahnel, A.	—	1870	Flowers	—	—	—	—	1	—	—	—	—	—	1
Hähnisch, A.	London	1851-1869	Portraits	—	—	18	—	—	—	—	—	—	—	18
Haig, Axel Herman, R.P.E.	London	1869-1892	Etching	—	—	25	—	11	—	10	—	—	26	72
Haig, E. Cotton	Edinburgh	1891	Domestic	—	—	1	—	—	—	—	—	—	—	1
Haig, Miss M. C.	London	1873	Fruit	—	—	—	—	1	—	—	—	—	—	1
Haigh-Wood, C. *See* W.	—	—	—	—	—	—	—	—	—	—	—	—	—	—
Hailes, D.	—	1771	Portraits	1	—	—	—	—	—	—	—	—	—	1
Hailey, George	London	1866	Landscape	—	—	—	—	—	—	—	—	—	2	2
Haines, Miss Agnes Eliza	London	1887	Fish	—	—	—	—	—	—	—	—	—	1	1
Haines, G.	—	1828	Still Life	—	—	1	—	—	—	—	—	—	—	1
Haines, Robert J.	Oxford	1888-1889	Landscape	—	—	2	—	—	—	—	—	—	—	2
Haines, William	London	1808-1840	Miniatures	—	—	57	19	7	3	—	—	—	—	86
Haines, W.	London	1854-1864	Portraits	—	—	1	4	1	—	—	—	—	—	6
Haines, William Henry	London	1843-1884	Domestic	—	—	30	40	108	—	—	—	—	45	223
Haines and Darling	Leeds	1877	Architecture	—	—	1	—	—	—	—	—	—	—	1
Hain-Friswell. *See* F.	—	—	—	—	—	—	—	—	—	—	—	—	—	—
Hains, Vincent	London	1881-1882	Domestic	—	—	—	—	2	—	—	—	—	—	2
Hainsselin, Henry	Exeter	1843-1853	Domestic	—	—	20	1	—	—	—	—	—	—	21
Hair, T. H.	London	1838-1849	Landscape	—	—	3	5	9	—	—	—	—	—	17
Haité, George C., R.B.A.§	Bedford Park	1883-1893	Landscape	—	—	10	—	19	—	7	—	—	8	44
Haite, W.	London	1849	Figures	—	—	—	—	1	—	—	—	—	—	1
Hake, Miss Mary Lily	London	1888-1889	Flowers	—	—	—	—	—	—	3	—	—	—	3
Hakewell, C.	London	1830	Scriptural	—	—	—	—	1	—	—	—	—	—	1
Hakewill, Arthur William	London	1826-1827	Architecture	—	—	2	—	—	—	—	—	—	—	2
Hakewill, Edward Charles	London	1840-1845	Architecture	—	—	7	—	—	—	—	—	—	—	7
Hakewill, F. C.	London	1827-1841	Domestic	—	—	1	3	2	—	—	—	—	—	6
Hakewill, G.	London	1806-1810	Architecture	—	—	5	—	—	—	—	—	—	—	5
Hakewill, Henry	London	1792-1809	Architecture	—	—	10	—	—	—	—	—	—	—	10
Hakewill, Henry James	—	1832-1834	Sculpture	—	—	5	—	3	—	—	—	—	—	8
Hakewill, James	London	1813-1834	Architecture	—	—	10	—	—	—	—	—	—	—	10
Hakewill, Mrs. James (Maria C.)	London	1808-1838	Domestic	—	—	37	45	16	—	—	—	—	—	98
Hakewill, John	London	1765-1773	Portraits	9	—	—	—	—	—	—	—	—	—	9
Hakewill, J. E.	London	1862	Architecture	—	—	2	—	—	—	—	—	—	—	2
Hakewill, John Henry	London	1828-1879	Architecture	—	—	9	—	—	—	—	—	—	—	9
Hakewill, S. H.	London	1843-1845	Architecture	—	—	2	—	—	—	—	—	—	—	2
Haldane, Miss Mary	Milford	1881-1892	Landscape	—	—	1	—	23	—	—	6	—	2	32
Hale, Bernard	Bridlingt'n Qu'y	1868	Landscape	—	—	—	—	—	—	—	—	—	2	2
Hale, E.	London	1809-1818	Architecture	—	—	3	—	—	—	—	—	—	—	3
Hale, Miss Ellen D.	London	1882	Domestic	—	—	1	—	—	—	—	—	—	1	2
Hale, Edward Matthew	London	1875-1893	Figures	—	—	8	—	2	—	—	14	8	27	59
Hale, Miss E. Thomas	London	1892-1893	Domestic	—	—	—	—	1	—	—	—	—	1	2
Hale, Fred	Newlyn	1886	Landscape	—	—	—	—	—	—	—	—	—	1	1
Hale, Lawrence	London	1861-1872	Sculpture	—	—	10	—	—	—	—	—	—	—	10
Hale, Miss M. A. *See* Mrs. Havell	London	1822-1825	Portraits	—	—	11	—	—	—	—	—	—	—	11
Hale, Miss M. B.	Bath	1878-1881	Flowers	—	—	1	—	1	—	—	—	—	5	7
Hale, Owen, R.B.A.§	London	1884-1889	Sculpture	—	—	4	—	3	—	3	—	—	5	15
Hale, William Matthew, R.W.S †	London	1865-1893	Sea Pieces	—	—	4	—	3	229	—	—	—	14	250
Hale, William Thomas	London	1868	Sculpture	—	—	1	—	—	—	—	—	—	—	1
Hale-Sanders, T. *See* S.	—	—	—	—	—	—	—	—	—	—	—	—	—	—
Hales, Miss	—	1815	Portraits	—	—	1	—	—	—	—	—	—	—	1
Hales, T.	Lowestoft	1864	Domestic	—	—	—	—	2	—	—	—	—	—	2
Haley, Herbert	Bradford	1893	Flowers	—	—	1	—	—	—	—	—	—	—	1
Halfnight, Richard William	Sunderland	1878-1892	Landscape	—	—	7	—	41	—	10	—	—	19	77
Halford, Miss Constance	London	1892	Landscape	—	—	1	—	1	—	—	—	—	—	2
Halford, F. W.	London	1831	Landscape	—	—	1	—	—	—	—	—	—	—	1
Halford, Master Robert	—	1776	Scriptural	—	1	—	—	—	—	—	—	—	—	1
Halfpenny, John C.	Liverpool	1885-1893	Landscape	—	—	3	—	4	—	2	—	—	1	10
Halfpenny, J. P.	London	1808	Domestic	—	—	—	1	—	—	—	—	—	—	1
Halfpenny, Joseph S. (?) Alpenny	London	1805-1808	Scriptural	—	—	8	—	—	—	—	—	—	—	8
Halhed, Miss Harriet	Canterbury	1890-1893	Domestic	—	—	3	—	4	—	—	—	—	—	7
Hall. *See* Young and Hall.	—	—	—	—	—	—	—	—	—	—	—	—	—	—
Hall, Amos	Leicester	1888	Architecture	—	—	1	—	—	—	—	—	—	—	1
Hall, Annie	Streatham	1884-1886	Buildings	—	—	—	—	2	—	—	—	—	—	2
Hall, Mrs. Ashley	London	1874	Fishing Boats	—	—	—	—	—	—	—	—	—	1	1
Hall, Arthur W.	London	1872	Fruit	—	—	—	—	—	—	—	—	—	1	1
Hall, C.	London	1812	Architecture	—	—	1	—	—	—	—	—	—	—	1

Name.	Town.	First and Last Year of Ex.	Speciality.	S. A.	F. S.	R. A.	B. I.	S. S.	O. W.	N. W.	G. G.	N. G.	V. E.	Total.
Hall, Charlotte	London	1856	Portraits	—	—	—	—	1	—	—	—	—	—	1
Hall, C. H.	Bisham	1867-1870	Landscape	—	—	—	—	5	—	—	—	—	1	6
Hall, Miss C. L.	Petworth	1878	Landscape	—	—	—	—	1	—	—	—	—	—	1
Hall, Edward, F.S.A.	London	1842-1845	Architecture	—	—	3	—	—	—	—	—	—	—	3
Hall, Edwin Thomas	London	1880-1893	Architecture	—	—	4	—	—	—	—	—	—	—	4
Hall, Frederick	Newlyn	1883-1893	Figures	—	—	12	—	7	—	—	2	4	2	27
Hall, Fanny R.	London	1830-1837	Figures	—	—	3	10	3	—	—	—	—	—	16
Hall, Gilbert	Handsworth	1858-1874	Landscape	—	—	2	3	5	—	—	—	—	—	10
Hall, George Henry	Paris	1889-1890	Flowers	—	—	—	—	—	—	—	2	—	—	2
Hall, George Henry A.	London	1867	Landscape	—	—	1	—	—	—	—	—	—	—	1
Hall, George Lowthian	London	1856-1878	Landscape	—	—	7	—	8	—	—	—	—	103	118
Hall, Harry	Newmarket	1838-1886	Sporting	—	—	11	17	26	—	—	—	—	1	55
Hall (Henry) and Young (K. D.)	London	1887	Architecture	—	—	2	—	—	—	—	—	—	—	2
Hall, H. B.	London	1840	Drawings	—	—	—	—	2	—	—	—	—	—	2
Hall, J.	Brighton	1890	Domestic	—	—	—	—	1	—	—	—	—	—	1
Hall, James	London	1835-1854	Landscape	—	—	8	7	—	—	—	—	—	—	15
Hall, Miss Jessie	Croydon	1893	Domestic	—	—	—	—	1	—	2	—	—	—	3
Hall, John, F.S.A.	London	1762-1776	Engraving	16	4	—	—	—	—	—	—	—	—	20
Hall, Joseph	Derby	1838-1843	Sculpture	—	—	2	—	—	—	—	—	—	—	2
Hall, J. E.	Newp'rt, I. of W.	1836	Landscape	—	—	—	—	2	—	—	—	—	—	2
Hall, J. R.	London	1830	Architecture	—	—	1	—	—	—	—	—	—	—	1
Hall, Lindsay Bernard	London	1882-1891	Portraits	—	—	7	—	5	—	—	—	—	5	17
Hall, Miss Mary B.	Lancing	1886	Flowers	—	—	1	—	—	—	—	—	—	—	1
Hall, North	London	1888-1889	Domestic	—	—	—	—	—	—	1	—	—	1	2
Hall, Oliver, A.R.P.E.	London	1890-1891	Seashores	—	—	1	—	3	—	2	—	—	—	6
Hall, Richard	London	1799-1837	Landscape	—	—	15	3	—	—	—	—	—	—	18
Hall, R. H.	Lee	1866	Landscape	—	—	—	1	—	—	—	—	—	—	1
Hall, Sydney Prior	London	1874-1893	Historical	—	—	7	—	—	—	1	14	4	21	47
Hall, T.	London	1796-1801	Buildings	—	—	3	—	—	—	—	—	—	—	3
Hall, Thomas	Edinburgh	1880-1887	Architecture	—	—	3	—	—	—	—	—	—	—	3
Hall, Thomas P.	London	1837-1867	Historical	—	—	7	29	11	—	—	—	—	2	49
Hall, William	Birmingham	1859-1885	Landscape	—	—	8	—	6	—	1	—	—	3	18
Hall, W. E.	London	1839	Architecture	—	—	1	—	—	—	—	—	—	—	1
Hall, W. E.	London	1866	Snowstorm	—	—	—	—	—	—	—	—	—	1	1
Hall, William Henry	Birmingham	1859-1884	Landscape	—	—	1	1	13	—	—	—	—	4	19
Hall, W. Honywell	Birmingham	1874-1890	Landscape	—	—	4	—	30	—	—	—	—	9	43
Hall, Mrs. W. Honnywill	London	1878-1884	Landscape	—	—	—	—	5	—	—	—	—	6	11
Hall, W. J.	—	1829	Landscape	—	—	1	—	—	—	—	—	—	—	1
Hall, W. T.	London	1823-1858	Landscape	—	—	17	—	1	—	—	—	—	—	18
Hall, Miss	London	1847	Flowers	—	—	1	—	—	—	—	—	—	—	1
Hallam, J.	—	1831	Landscape	—	—	—	—	2	—	—	—	—	—	2
Halland, J.	London	1827	Flowers	—	—	—	—	1	—	—	—	—	—	1
Hallé, Charles Edward	London	1866-1893	Portraits	—	—	28	—	—	—	—	57	31	6	122
Hallé, Miss Elinor	London	1881-1892	Sculpture	—	—	3	—	—	—	—	5	10	1	19
Hallé, Samuel Baruch	Frankfort	1847-1868	Domestic	—	—	22	32	15	—	—	—	—	—	69
Hallen, Maria	London	1829	Enamels	—	—	1	—	—	—	—	—	—	—	1
Hallett, J.	London	1827-1835	Architecture	—	—	6	—	—	—	—	—	—	—	6
Hallett, W. H.	Exmouth	1854	Landscape	—	—	—	1	—	—	—	—	—	—	1
Hallewell, Ben. Col.	Stroud	1865-1869	Battles	—	—	1	—	—	—	—	—	—	3	4
Hallewell, Gilling	Stroud	1850-1853	Landscape	—	—	1	1	3	—	—	—	—	—	5
Halliday, Miss C.§	London	1827	Landscape	—	—	—	—	2	—	—	—	—	—	2
Halliday, Michael Frederick	Merton	1853-1869	Domestic	—	—	8	—	1	—	—	—	—	5	14
Halling, G.	—	1834	Buildings	—	—	1	—	—	—	—	—	—	—	1
Halls, John J.	Colchester	1791-1828	Portraits	—	—	108	17	—	—	—	—	—	—	125
Halls, Robert	London	1892-1893	Miniatures	—	—	5	—	—	—	—	—	—	2	7
Hallward, Reginald F.	London	1880-1892	Domestic	—	—	—	—	1	—	—	1	2	3	7
Hallward, Mrs. Reginald	Hammersmith	1888-1890	Designs	—	—	5	—	—	—	—	—	—	—	5
Halpen, Francis H.	London	1868-1869	Sea Pieces	—	—	1	—	1	—	—	—	—	—	2
Halpen, M. Francis	London	1845-1866	Domestic	—	—	25	6	—	—	—	—	—	1	32
Halse, Miss Emmeline	London	1878-1892	Sculpture	—	—	19	—	—	—	—	—	—	—	19
Halse, George	London	1855-1888	Sculpture	—	—	47	15	21	—	—	—	—	—	83
Halswelle, Keeley, R.I., A.R.S.A.‡ ϕ	Edinburgh	1862-1891	Historical	—	—	36	—	5	—	34	17	4	27	123
Halton, E. W.	London	1848	Portraits	—	—	1	—	—	—	—	—	—	—	1
Ham, Miss Ada J.	London	1885-1887	Flowers	—	—	5	—	—	—	2	—	—	—	7
Hamacher, T.	London	1865	Portraits	—	—	1	—	—	—	—	—	—	—	1
Hamble, J. R.	London	1803-1824	Landscape	—	—	3	—	—	—	—	—	—	—	3
Hambleton —	London	1764	Figures	—	2	—	—	—	—	—	—	—	—	2
Hambly and Marriott	London	1841	Architecture	—	—	1	—	—	—	—	—	—	—	1
Hambridge, Charles	London	1858	Architecture	—	—	2	—	—	—	—	—	—	—	2
Hamburger, C.	London	1830-1834	Portraits	—	—	8	—	—	—	—	—	—	—	8
Hamel, Du. *See* D.	—	—	—	—	—	—	—	—	—	—	—	—	—	—
Hamer, J.	London	1861-1868	Landscape	—	—	4	—	15	—	—	—	—	—	19

Name.	Town.	First and Last Year of Ex.	Speciality.	S. A.	F. S.	R. A.	B. I.	S. S.	O. W.	N.W.	G. G.	N.G.	V.E.	Total.
Hamer, John	London	1890-1891	Buildings	—	—	—	—	2	—	—	—	—	—	2
Hamerton, Philip Gilbert, H.F.R.P.E.	Charinsy	1867-1869	Etching	—	—	8	—	—	—	—	—	—	1	9
Hamerton, Robert Jacob §	London	1831-1858	Domestic	—	—	7	11	48	—	—	—	—	—	66
Hames, Francis John	London	1874	Architecture	—	—	2	—	—	—	—	—	—	—	2
Hamill, E.	London	1842-1859	Landscape	—	—	—	—	3	—	—	—	—	—	3
Hamilton, Captain	—	1769	Landscape	—	—	1	—	—	—	—	—	—	—	1
Hamilton, Alexander	London	1871-1875	Coast Scenes	—	—	—	—	—	—	—	—	—	6	6
Hamilton, Andrew	London	1854-1875	Landscape	—	—	1	—	10	—	—	—	—	5	16
Hamilton, Miss Anne	London	1807	Mythological	—	—	1	—	—	—	—	—	—	—	1
Hamilton, Charles	Kensworth	1831-1867	Historical	—	—	12	22	12	—	—	—	—	1	47
Hamilton, E.	London	1841	Landscape	—	—	1	—	—	—	—	—	—	—	1
Hamilton, E. B.	—	1874	Flowers	—	—	—	—	1	—	—	—	—	—	1
Hamilton, Gavin, F.S.A.	Rome	1770-1788	Mythological	4	1	5	—	—	—	—	—	—	—	10
Hamilton, H.	Florence	1787-1791	Crayons	—	—	3	—	—	—	—	—	—	—	3
Hamilton, Hugh Douglas	Rome	1762-1775	Portraits	46	4	—	—	—	—	—	—	—	—	50
Hamilton, H. T.	London	1812-1813	Portraits	—	—	2	—	—	—	—	—	—	—	2
Hamilton, Rev. J.	London	1851	Landscape	—	—	—	—	—	—	—	—	—	1	1
Hamilton, James, A.R.S.A.	Edinburgh	1892	Domestic	—	—	1	—	—	—	—	—	—	—	1
Hamilton, John, F.S.A.	London	1767-1777	Landscape	12	—	—	—	—	—	—	—	—	—	12
Hamilton, John, Junr.	London	1778	Architecture	1	—	—	—	—	—	—	—	—	—	1
Hamilton, Miss J.	—	1799	Landscape	—	—	2	—	—	—	—	—	—	—	2
Hamilton, J. C.	Bushey	1887	Landscape	—	—	—	—	—	—	1	—	—	—	1
Hamilton, John McLure	Balham	1878-1893	Domestic	—	—	5	—	1	—	—	5	—	11	22
Hamilton, J. R.	Gloucester	1847	Architecture	—	—	3	—	—	—	—	—	—	—	3
Hamilton, J. Whitelaw	Helensburgh	1885-1892	River Scenes	—	—	1	—	—	—	—	—	—	1	2
Hamilton, Miss Kathleen	London	1885	Domestic	—	—	—	—	—	—	—	—	—	1	1
Hamilton, Miss Maria. *See* Mrs. Bell *and*	—	—	—	—	—	—	—	—	—	—	—	—	—	—
Lady Bell	London	1807	Miniatures	—	—	—	1	—	—	—	—	—	—	1
Hamilton, M.	—	1831-1839	Portraits	—	—	2	—	2	—	—	—	—	—	4
Hamilton, M. F.	London	1827	Fruit	—	—	—	—	2	—	—	—	—	—	2
Hamilton, Mrs. Mary F.	London	1807-1849	Miniatures	—	—	24	1	6	—	—	—	—	—	31
Hamilton, R. Douglas. *See* D.	—	—	—	—	—	—	—	—	—	—	—	—	—	—
Hamilton, Sydney D.	London	1834-1835	Dramatic	—	—	2	—	1	—	—	—	—	—	3
Hamilton, Thomas T.	London	1886	Landscape	—	—	1	—	—	—	—	—	—	—	1
Hamilton, Vereker Monteith, R.P.E.	London	1888-1893	Military	—	—	9	—	—	—	—	5	—	—	14
Hamilton, Mrs. Vereker (Lilian), A.R.P.E.	London	1889-1891	Medals	—	—	5	—	—	—	—	2	—	—	7
Hamilton, William, R.A.	London	1774-1801	Mythological	—	—	82	—	—	—	—	—	—	—	82
Hamilton, William E.	London	1874	Horses	—	—	—	—	—	—	—	—	—	1	1
Hamley, Miss Barbara	London	1881-1893	Miniatures	—	—	—	—	—	—	5	—	—	4	9
Hamlyn, Jane T.	London	1819	Game	—	—	1	—	—	—	—	—	—	—	1
Hammersley, J. A.	Newcastle	1842-1858	Landscape	—	—	3	3	10	—	—	—	—	13	29
Hammett, A. A.	London	1865	Landscape	—	—	—	—	—	—	—	—	—	2	2
Hammon —.	Colchester	1774	Landscape	1	—	—	—	—	—	—	—	—	—	1
Hammond, A.	—	1801-1803	Drawings	—	—	3	—	—	—	—	—	—	—	3
Hammond, Miss Christine M. Demain	London	1886-1893	Domestic	—	—	5	—	3	—	9	—	—	1	18
Hammond, Miss Gertrude E. Demain	London	1886-1893	Domestic	—	—	3	—	1	—	10	—	—	—	14
Hammond, H.	London	1850-1852	Sculpture	—	—	2	1	—	—	—	—	—	—	3
Hammond, J.	London	1800-1820	Landscape	—	—	25	13	—	—	—	—	—	—	38
Hammond, John (Royal Canadian Academician)	New Brunswick	1886-1890	Landscape	—	—	4	—	—	—	—	—	—	—	4
Hammond, T. W.	Nottingham	1890	Landscape	—	—	1	—	—	—	—	—	—	—	1
Hammond, Mrs.	London	1810-1826	Miniatures	—	—	18	—	—	—	—	—	—	—	18
Hammond, Miss	—	1782-1783	Landscape	—	—	2	—	—	—	—	—	—	—	2
Hamon, Jean Louis	Paris	1876	Figures	—	—	—	—	—	—	—	—	—	1	1
Hampton, E.	—	1880	Architecture	—	—	1	—	—	—	—	—	—	—	1
Hampton, Herbert	London	1886-1893	Sculpture	—	—	8	—	1	—	—	—	—	—	9
Hanbury, Miss Ada	London	1875-1887	Flowers	—	—	5	—	1	—	2	—	—	3	11
Hanbury, Miss Blanche	London	1876-1887	Flowers	—	—	2	—	11	—	2	—	—	13	28
Hance, J. W.	London	1830-1833	—	—	—	5	—	—	—	3	—	—	—	8
Hanchett, Captain	—	1791-1800	Buildings	—	—	10	—	—	—	—	—	—	—	10
Hancock, Charles	Marlborough	1819-1868	Sporting	—	—	23	55	47	—	9	—	—	12	146
Hancock, C.	London	1873-1874	Domestic	—	—	3	—	—	—	—	—	—	—	3
Hancock, C. S.	London	1869	Rustic	—	—	1	—	—	—	—	—	—	—	1
Hancock, Miss E. J.	London	1876	Flowers	—	—	—	—	1	—	—	—	—	—	1
Hancock, H. F.	London	1880-1881	Landscape	—	—	—	—	—	—	—	—	—	3	3
Hancock, John	London	1843-1864	Sculpture	—	—	34	3	—	—	—	—	—	—	37
Hancock, Miss Mildred L.	Harrow	1890-1893	Domestic	—	—	1	—	1	—	1	—	—	2	5
Hancock, Richard	Mortlake	1885	Stained Glass	—	—	1	—	—	—	—	—	—	—	1
Hancock, Robert	London	1805	Portraits	—	—	2	—	—	—	—	—	—	—	2
Hand, Richard	London	1803	Fruit	—	—	1	—	—	—	—	—	—	—	1
Hand, Thomas	London	1790-1804	Landscape	1	—	21	—	—	—	—	—	—	—	22
Handasyde, Charles	London	1760-1776	Enamels	10	4	1	—	—	—	—	—	—	—	15
Handfield, Captain G.	—	1775	Domestic	—	—	2	—	—	—	—	—	—	—	2

Name.	Town.	First and Last Year of Ex.	Speciality.	S. A.	F. S.	R. A.	B. I.	S. S.	O. W.	N. W.	G. G.	N. G.	V. E.	Total.
Handley, F. Montague	Rome	1873-1880	Sculpture	—	—	5	—	—	—	—	—	—	—	5
Handley, J. W. H.	London	1827-1846	Landscape	—	—	11	—	2	—	—	—	—	—	13
Hands, A. W.	London	1871	Venice	—	—	5	—	—	—	—	—	—	—	5
Hands, Miss Lydia	Wimbledon	1874-1875	Churches	—	—	—	—	2	—	—	—	—	—	2
Handsworth, W. T. M.	London	1888	Shipping	—	—	—	—	—	—	1	—	—	—	1
Handy, John	London	1787-1791	Landscape	2	—	6	—	—	—	—	—	—	—	8
Hanhart —	—	1848	Portraits	—	—	1	—	—	—	—	—	—	—	1
Hanhart, Henry A. F.	London	1875	Domestic	—	—	—	—	2	—	—	—	—	4	6
Hanhart, Michael	London	1870-1882	Landscape	—	—	4	—	13	—	—	—	—	15	32
Hankes, J. F.	London	1838-1859	Scriptural	—	—	19	5	9	—	—	—	—	—	33
Hankey, William L.	Chester	1893	Landscape	—	—	—	—	1	—	—	—	—	—	1
Hankins, Miss C.	—	1792	Fruit	—	—	1	—	—	—	—	—	—	—	1
Hankins, George	London	1879-1882	Landscape	—	—	—	—	9	—	—	—	—	—	9
Hanley, Edgar	London	1878-1883	Still Life	—	—	22	—	5	—	—	—	—	6	33
Hann, Walter	London	1859-1884	Landscape	—	—	2	—	7	—	—	—	—	—	9
Hannah, Robert	London	1842-1870	Domestic	—	—	22	1	2	—	—	—	—	—	25
Hannah, S. Crichton	London	1872-1890	Architecture	—	—	3	—	—	—	—	—	—	1	4
Hannam, Miss Florence	London	1890-1893	Historical	—	—	2	—	4	—	—	—	—	1	7
Hannan, William	High Wycombe	1769-1772	Landscape	8	—	—	—	—	—	—	—	—	—	8
Hannay, Mrs. Elliot (Alice M.)	Dorking	1877-1882	Domestic	—	—	—	—	—	—	—	—	—	6	6
Hannay, E. W. D.	Dorking	1874	Domestic	—	—	—	—	—	—	—	—	—	3	3
Hannay, Walter	London	1843-1851	Landscape	—	—	—	1	1	—	—	—	—	—	2
Hannon, Von. *See* V.	—	—	—	—	—	—	—	—	—	—	—	—	—	—
Hansard, Octavius	London	1871	Architecture	—	—	2	—	—	—	—	—	—	—	2
Hansell, T.	London	1880	Domestic	—	—	—	—	—	—	—	—	—	1	1
Hansen, Hans, R.S.W.	Copenhagen	1876-1893	Landscape	—	—	7	—	3	—	2	—	—	—	12
Hansen, Sigvard	London	1889-1890	Landscape	—	—	3	—	2	—	—	—	—	—	5
Hansom, E. J. *See* Dunn and Hansom, *and*	—	—	—	—	—	—	—	—	—	—	—	—	—	—
Dunn, Hansom, and Dunn	—	—	Architecture	—	—	—	—	—	—	—	—	—	—	—
Hansom (Joseph A.) and Son	London	1873-1884	Architecture	—	—	4	—	—	—	—	—	—	—	4
Hansom, J. T.	London	1869-1872	Landscape	—	—	—	—	2	—	—	—	—	—	2
Hanson. *See* Penny and Hanson	—	—	Architecture	—	—	—	—	—	—	—	—	—	—	—
Hanson, Albert J.	New S. Wales	1892-1893	Landscape	—	—	1	—	15	—	1	—	—	1	18
Hanson, J.	Newbury	1842	Architecture	—	—	1	—	—	—	—	—	—	—	1
Hanson, J.	London	1853-1856	Portraits	—	—	—	—	2	—	—	—	—	1	3
Hanwell, W.	London	1809	Portraits	—	—	1	—	—	—	—	—	—	—	1
Haquette, G.	Paris	1881	Figures	—	—	—	—	—	—	—	2	—	—	2
Harbutt, Mrs. B. Cambridge (Elizabeth)	Bath	1883-1893	Miniatures	—	—	13	—	1	—	—	—	—	—	14
Harbutt, W.	London	1873	Landscape	—	—	—	—	1	—	—	—	—	—	1
Harcourt, C. T.	London	1796	Architecture	—	—	2	—	—	—	—	—	—	—	2
Harcourt, George	Bushey	1893	Domestic	—	—	1	—	—	—	—	—	—	—	1
Harcourt, Hon. Mrs.	—	1785-1786	Landscape	—	—	4	—	—	—	—	—	—	—	4
Hardcastle, Miss Charlotte	London	1852-1866	Still Life	—	—	9	4	12	—	—	—	—	—	25
Harden, Edmund Harris (?) Edward	London	1851-1880	Figures	—	—	10	17	25	—	—	—	—	1	53
Harden, Silvester	London	1767-1783	Miniatures	1	2	—	—	—	—	—	—	—	—	3
Hardenberg, F.	London	1800	Mythological	—	—	1	—	—	—	—	—	—	—	1
Hardess, Miss Maria A.	London	1867-1869	Flowers	—	—	—	—	3	—	—	—	—	—	3
Hardgrave, Charles	London	1885-1893	Stained Glass	—	—	11	—	—	—	—	—	—	—	11
Hardie, Charles Martin, A.R.S.A.	Edinburgh	1880-1891	Domestic	—	—	8	—	—	—	1	—	—	1	10
Hardie, R.	London	1810-1829	Portraits	—	—	14	—	2	—	—	—	—	—	16
Harding, Charles	London	1822-1847	Domestic	—	—	9	3	13	—	—	—	—	—	25
Harding, Charles T. (?) Chester	London	1825-1826	Portraits	—	—	4	—	—	—	—	—	—	—	4
Harding, Edward	—	1792-1793	Domestic	—	—	2	—	—	—	—	—	—	—	2
Harding, Miss Emily J.	London	1877	Portraits	—	—	1	—	—	—	—	—	—	1	2
Harding, Frank	Clapton	1885-1890	Domestic	—	—	—	—	4	—	—	—	—	2	6
Harding, Frederick	London	1825-1857	Miniatures	—	—	38	—	10	—	—	—	—	—	48
Harding, George Perfect, F.S.A.	London	1802-1840	Miniatures	—	—	20	—	2	—	—	—	—	—	22
Harding, H. J.	London	1823-1825	Miniatures	—	—	9	—	2	—	—	—	—	—	11
Harding, J.	Deptford	1800-1807	Landscape	—	—	3	—	—	—	—	—	—	—	3
Harding, James Duffield †	London	1811-1864	Landscape	—	—	35	8	17	143	—	—	—	5	208
Harding, Miss Mary E.	Blackheath	1880-1893	Flowers	—	—	12	—	1	—	—	—	—	6	19
Harding, O.	London	1796	Portraits	—	—	1	—	—	—	—	—	—	—	1
Harding, Miss S.	London	1832	Flowers	—	—	—	—	1	—	—	—	—	—	1
Harding, Sylvester	London	1776-1802	Miniatures	—	3	23	—	—	—	—	—	—	—	26
Harding, T.	London	1796-1808	Landscape	—	—	5	—	—	—	—	—	—	—	5
Harding and Lepard	—	1831	Engraving	—	—	—	—	3	—	—	—	—	—	3
Hardinge, Hon. Charles S. *See* Viscount	—	—	—	—	—	—	—	—	—	—	—	—	—	—
Hardinge	—	1849-1856	Landscape	—	—	—	3	2	—	—	—	—	—	5
Hardinge, Viscount	London	1857-1880	Landscape	—	—	16	9	2	—	—	—	—	3	30
Hardinge, Del. *See* D.	—	—	—	—	—	—	—	—	—	—	—	—	—	—
Hardman, J.	London	1812	Horses	—	—	2	—	—	—	—	—	—	—	2

Name.	Town.	First and Last Year of Ex.	Speciality.	S. A.	F. S.	R. A.	B. I.	S. S.	O. W.	N. W.	G. G.	N. G.	V. E.	Total.
Hardman, Thomas Hawthorn	Potter's Bar	1885-1893	Domestic	—	—	3	—	11	—	1	—	—	1	16
Hardman, Mrs. Thomas (Emma L.)	Potter's Bar	1888-1893	Flowers	—	—	2	—	7	—	3	—	—	—	12
Hards, Charles G.	London	1883-1891	Domestic	—	—	6	—	3	—	4	—	—	2	15
Hardwick —	—	1773	Portraits	—	1	—	—	—	—	—	—	—	—	1
Hardwick, H.	—	1831	Landscape	—	—	3	—	—	—	—	—	—	—	3
Hardwick, J. Jessop, A.R.W.S. †	Chessington	1850-1893	Flowers, etc.	—	—	42	1	37	172	—	4	—	59	315
Hardwick, Philip, R.A.	London	1807-1844	Architecture	—	—	23	—	—	—	—	—	—	—	23
Hardwick, Philip Charles	London	1848-1869	Architecture	—	—	23	—	—	—	—	—	—	—	23
Hardwick, Thomas	London	1772-1805	Architecture	—	—	8	—	—	—	—	—	—	—	8
Hardwick, Thomas, Junr.	Brentford	1775-1800	Architecture	—	—	20	—	—	—	—	—	—	—	20
Hardwick, William N. ‡	London	1829-1864	Landscape	—	—	8	43	31	—	329	—	—	—	411
Hardy —	London	1790	Portraits	4	—	—	—	—	—	—	—	—	—	4
Hardy, Albert	London	1865-1888	Landscape	—	—	—	—	1	—	2	—	—	—	3
Hardy, Miss A.	London	1872	Portraits	—	—	2	—	—	—	—	—	—	—	2
Hardy, C.	London	1806-1810	Portraits	—	—	5	—	—	—	—	—	—	—	5
Hardy, David	Bath	1855-1870	Domestic	—	—	1	6	21	—	—	—	—	2	30
Hardy, Dorofield	London	1882-1892	Domestic	—	—	1	—	1	—	4	—	—	3	9
Hardy, Dudley, R.B.A. §	London	1884-1893	Domestic	—	—	11	—	31	—	5	2	—	4	53
Hardy, Edwin George	London	1881-1887	Architecture	—	—	14	—	—	—	—	—	—	—	14
Hardy, E. J. F.	London	1838-1844	Architecture	—	—	10	—	—	—	—	—	—	—	10
Hardy, F.	London	1875	Domestic	—	—	1	—	—	—	—	—	—	—	1
Hardy, Frederick Daniel	Windsor	1851-1889	Domestic	—	—	91	5	—	—	—	—	—	5	101
Hardy, George	Windsor	1846-1892	Domestic	—	—	41	4	4	—	—	—	—	—	49
Hardy, Heywood, A.R.W.S., R.P.E. † φ	Bristol	1861-1893	Animals	—	—	31	9	16	7	—	22	5	62	152
Hardy, Miss Ida Clark-	Bexley Heath	1890	Sculpture	—	—	1	—	—	—	—	—	—	—	1
Hardy, Mrs. Ida W.	Bexley Heath	1891	Sculpture	—	—	1	—	—	—	—	—	—	—	1
Hardy, J.	London	1809-1856	Landscape	—	—	9	—	—	—	—	—	—	—	9
Hardy, J.	London	1832-1856	Portraits	—	—	3	—	—	—	—	—	—	—	3
Hardy, James	London	1842-1867	Landscape	—	—	—	—	10	—	—	—	—	—	10
Hardy, James, Junr., R.I. ‡ φ	Bristol	1853-1888	Domestic	—	—	9	8	46	—	28	—	—	28	119
Hardy, J. C.	London	1816	Flowers	—	—	1	—	—	—	—	—	—	—	1
Hardy, John Forbes	London	1847-1874	Landscape	—	—	19	10	9	—	—	—	—	23	61
Hardy, Le. *See* L.	—	—	—	—	—	—	—	—	—	—	—	—	—	—
Hardy, Miss Margaret E.	Staplehurst	1893	Interiors	—	—	—	—	1	—	—	—	—	—	1
Hardy, Miss Nina	London	1890-1893	Domestic	—	—	1	—	—	—	—	2	4	1	8
Hardy, Norman	London	1891	Domestic	—	—	1	—	—	—	—	—	—	—	1
Hardy, Paul	Bexley Heath	1890	Historical	—	—	1	—	—	—	—	—	—	—	1
Hardy, Thomas	London	1778-1801	Portraits	—	—	35	—	—	—	—	—	—	—	35
Hardy, Thomas Bush, R.B.A. §	London	1870-1893	Sea Pieces	—	—	32	—	81	—	12	—	—	16	141
Hardy, W.	London	1785-1803	Figures	—	—	2	—	—	—	—	—	—	—	2
Hardy, W.	London	1851-1852	Landscape	—	—	2	—	—	—	—	—	—	—	2
Hardy, W. H.	London	1868-1892	Landscape	—	—	—	—	3	—	—	—	—	—	3
Hardy, W. J.	London	1854-1856	Landscape	—	—	—	—	2	—	—	—	—	—	2
Hardy, W. W.	London	1818-1856	Flowers	—	—	12	—	1	—	—	—	—	—	13
Hare, G. W.	London	1846	Figures	—	—	—	—	1	—	—	—	—	—	1
Hare, Henry T.	London	1890-1893	Architecture	—	—	3	—	—	—	—	—	—	—	3
Hare, Julius, R.C.A.	Conway	1887-1889	Landscape	—	—	2	—	1	—	—	—	—	—	3
Hare, Miss Margaret Lily	Exeter	1887	Flowers	—	—	—	—	—	—	1	—	—	—	1
Hare, R.	Bath	1819	Landscape	—	—	1	—	—	—	—	—	—	—	1
Hare, St. George, R.I. ‡ φ	London	1880-1893	Domestic	—	—	15	—	18	—	4	3	—	18	58
Hare, Hon. W. H.	—	1808	Landscape	—	—	1	—	—	—	—	—	—	—	1
Hare, Miss	London	1770	Still Life	—	4	—	—	—	—	—	—	—	—	4
Harford, Alfred	Bristol	1886	Landscape	—	—	—	—	—	—	—	—	—	1	1
Harford, W.	London	1874-1878	Landscape	—	—	—	8	—	—	—	—	—	—	8
Hargitt, Edward, R.I. ‡ φ	Edinburgh	1852-1893	Landscape	—	—	19	11	1	—	255	—	—	53	339
Hargrave —	Exeter	1780	Figures	1	—	—	—	—	—	—	—	—	—	1
Hargrave, Frank H.	Knaresborough	1885-1886	Landscape	—	—	2	—	—	—	—	—	—	—	2
Hargrave, William Wallace	York	1859	Landscape	—	—	—	—	—	—	—	—	—	2	2
Hargreaves, George §	Liverpool	1824-1834	Miniatures	—	—	—	—	7	—	—	—	—	—	7
Hargreaves, Henry	—	1883	Landscape	—	—	—	—	1	—	—	—	—	—	1
Hargreaves, Thomas §	Liverpool	1798-1831	Portraits	—	—	9	—	9	—	—	—	—	—	18
Hargreaves, T.	Woolwich	1829-1843	Portraits	—	—	3	—	1	—	—	—	—	—	4
Hargreaves, W.	Liverpool	1813-1820	Portraits	—	—	4	—	—	—	—	—	—	—	4
Harland, T. W.	London	1832-1854	Portraits	—	—	17	—	—	—	—	—	—	—	17
Harley, George	London	1817-1865	Landscape	—	—	2	—	1	13	—	—	—	1	17
Harley, Henry	London	1891	Sea Pieces	—	—	—	—	—	—	—	—	—	2	2
Harley, Herbert E.	London	1884-1893	Historical	—	—	4	—	5	—	—	—	—	13	22
Harley, J.	London	1811	Flowers	—	—	1	—	—	—	—	—	—	—	1
Harley, R.	London	1856-1865	Domestic	—	—	3	—	—	—	—	—	—	—	3
Harley, Vincent H.	London	1890-1891	Domestic	—	—	—	—	—	—	—	—	—	3	3
Harlin, Miss Kate	Birmingham	1888	Domestic	—	—	1	—	—	—	—	—	—	—	1
Harling, W. O.	Chester	1849-1878	Portraits	—	—	27	4	2	—	—	—	—	—	33

Name.	Town.	First and Last Year of Ex.	Speciality.	S. A.	F. S.	R. A.	B. I.	S. S.	O. W.	N. W.	G. G.	N. G.	V. E.	Total.
Harlowe, G.	—	1841	Figures	—	—	1	—	—	—	—	—	—	—	1
Harlow, George Henry	London	1804-1818	Portraits	—	—	45	5	—	—	—	—	—	—	50
Harman —	—	1800	Architecture	—	—	1	—	—	—	—	—	—	—	1
Harman, Miss Geraldine	London	1880-1893	Miniatures	—	—	11	—	2	—	1	—	—	—	14
Harman, Miss Harriette	London	1881-1893	Miniatures	—	—	5	—	1	—	1	—	—	—	7
Harman, Ruth	London	1887	Landscape	—	—	—	—	1	—	—	—	—	—	1
Harmsworth, J.	Greenwich	1861-1879	Landscape	—	—	—	—	4	—	—	—	—	—	4
Harnack, John	London	1884-1889	Landscape	—	—	—	—	7	—	—	—	—	—	7
Harnett, William M.	London	1885	Still Life	—	—	1	—	—	—	—	—	—	—	1
Harper, Claudius	London	1882-1893	Historical	—	—	3	—	—	—	—	—	5	3	11
Harper, Miss Cecily T.	London	1886-1891	Churches	—	—	1	—	5	—	—	—	—	—	6
Harper, E.	York	1859-1860	Landscape	—	—	—	3	—	—	—	—	—	—	3
Harper, Edward S.	Birmingham	1885-1893	Domestic	—	—	6	—	—	—	1	—	—	—	7
Harper, F. G.	London	1884	Flowers	—	—	—	—	1	—	—	—	—	—	1
Harper, Gertrude	London	1889	Flowers	—	—	—	—	1	—	—	—	—	—	1
Harper, Henry Andrew	London	1858-1893	Landscape	—	—	24	—	26	—	8	3	—	57	118
Harper, H. C.	London	1876-1881	Portraits	—	—	—	—	—	—	—	—	—	4	4
Harper, John	Wednesbury	1814-1824	Still Life	—	—	11	4	—	—	—	—	—	—	15
Harper, J. R.	London	1877	Sculpture	—	—	1	—	—	—	—	—	—	—	1
Harper, R.	London	1833	Sculpture	—	—	—	—	1	—	—	—	—	—	1
Harper, T.	London	1817-1843	Portraits	—	—	19	—	—	—	—	—	—	—	19
Harper, T.	London	1840	Landscape	—	—	2	—	—	—	—	—	—	—	2
Harper, Thomas	Newcastle	1856-1875	Sea Pieces	—	—	—	—	4	—	—	—	—	—	4
Harper, T. G.	—	1786-1787	Landscape	—	—	2	—	—	—	—	—	—	—	2
Harpignies, H.	Paris	1881-1883	Landscape	—	—	—	—	—	—	2	2	—	—	4
Harraden, R.	London	1799	Buildings	—	—	5	—	—	—	—	—	—	—	5
Harraden, R. B.§	Cambridge	1823-1830	Landscape	—	—	—	2	21	—	—	—	—	—	23
Harral, Horace	London	1862-1876	Engraving	—	—	10	—	—	—	—	—	—	13	23
Harriett, Miss	London	1853	Figures	—	—	1	—	—	—	—	—	—	—	1
Harrington, A.	London	1871-1874	Sea Pieces	—	—	—	—	11	—	—	—	—	—	11
Harrington, C.	London	1818	Landscape	—	—	1	—	—	—	—	—	—	—	1
Harrington, E.	Birnam	1876	Landscape	—	—	—	—	—	—	—	—	—	1	1
Harrington, Harry	Manchester	1890	Architecture	—	—	1	—	—	—	—	—	—	—	1
Harrington, Miss	—	1796-1797	Flowers	—	—	2	—	—	—	—	—	—	—	2
Harriott, W. H.§	London	1811-1837	Landscape	—	—	4	11	42	—	—	—	—	—	57
Harris —	—	1771	Rustic	—	1	—	—	—	—	—	—	—	—	1
Harris, Alfred, Junr.	Bingley	1865-1868	Landscape	—	—	—	—	—	—	—	—	—	5	5
Harris, Mrs. A.	Kirkby L'nsdale	1878	Domestic	—	—	—	—	—	—	—	—	—	1	1
Harris, Lady Alice	Ascot	1893	Figures	—	—	1	—	—	—	—	—	—	—	1
Harris, Arthur	Newport	1892	Landscape	—	—	1	—	—	—	—	—	—	—	1
Harris, Master Charles	—	1780	Portraits	1	—	—	—	—	—	—	—	—	—	1
Harris, Edwin	Birmingham	1882-1893	Domestic	—	—	9	—	1	—	—	1	—	2	13
Harris, Eliza	Bath	1837	Architecture	—	—	1	—	—	—	—	—	—	—	1
Harris, Frederick	London	1868	Landscape	—	—	—	—	3	—	—	—	—	—	3
Harris, Frederick	Lincoln	1881-1892	Domestic	—	—	3	—	—	—	—	—	—	—	3
Harris, George	Foots Cray	1858-1880	Domestic	—	—	5	—	4	—	—	—	—	—	9
Harris, George Walter	London	1864-1893	Fruit	—	—	20	—	14	—	—	—	—	2	36
Harris, Henry	London	1826-1878	Landscape	—	—	5	5	16	—	—	—	—	3	29
Harris, H. C.	Cardiff	1878	Churches	—	—	1	—	—	—	—	—	—	—	1
Harris, H. Hotham	Birmingham	1865	Landscape	—	—	—	—	—	—	—	—	—	2	2
Harris, J., Junr.	London	1810	Flowers	—	—	1	—	—	—	—	—	—	—	1
Harris, J.	London	1827-1829	Buildings	—	—	1	—	1	—	—	—	—	—	2
Harris, James	Swansea	1846-1876	Sea Pieces	—	—	—	3	13	—	—	—	—	1	17
Harris, John	London	1797-1814	Figures	—	—	13	—	—	—	—	—	—	—	13
Harris, John	London	1822-1852	Figures	—	—	15	4	4	—	—	—	—	4	27
Harris, James C., H.R.I.‡	Nice	1878-1893	Landscape	—	—	1	—	—	—	13	8	—	4	26
Harris, Maude E.	London	1883-1892	Flowers	—	—	—	—	2	—	1	—	—	—	3
Harris, Miss Maude M.	Lewisham	1890	Shipping	—	—	—	—	1	—	—	—	—	—	1
Harris, Moses	London	1785	Insects	—	—	1	—	—	—	—	—	—	—	1
Harris, Robert	London	1882-1887	Domestic	—	—	1	—	2	—	—	—	—	2	5
Harris, Miss Sophia	London	1889-1891	Sculpture	—	—	2	—	—	—	—	—	—	—	2
Harris, Thomas	London	1848-1853	Architecture	—	—	4	—	—	—	—	—	—	—	4
Harris, W.	London	1788-1792	Gems	—	—	5	—	—	—	—	—	—	—	5
Harris, W.	London	1815-1818	Architecture	—	—	6	—	—	—	—	—	—	—	6
Harris, W.	London	1840	Sculpture	—	—	1	—	—	—	—	—	—	—	1
Harris, William E.	Birmingham	1883-1891	Landscape	—	—	3	—	3	—	—	—	—	5	11
Harris, W. T.	London	1877	Architecture	—	—	1	—	—	—	—	—	—	—	1
Harris, Mrs.‡ *See* Miss Fanny Rosenberg	London	1847-1872	Domestic	—	—	3	—	—	—	139	—	—	—	142
Harrison. *See* Henman and Harrison	—	—	Architecture	—	—	—	—	—	—	—	—	—	—	—
Harrison, Alexander ϕ	Paris	1885-1893	Landscape	—	—	2	—	3	—	—	—	—	12	17
Harrison, Miss Annie Jane	Newcastle	1888-1893	Miniatures	—	—	5	—	2	—	—	—	—	—	7
Harrison, Miss Anna Maria	London	1846	Flowers	—	—	1	—	—	—	—	—	—	—	1

Name.	Town.	First and Last Year of Ex.	Speciality.	S. A.	F. S.	R. A.	B. I.	S. S.	O. W.	N.W.	G. G.	N. G.	V. E.	Total.
Harrison, A. P.	London	1816-1821	Landscape	—	—	2	—	—	1	—	—	—	—	3
Harrison, Birge	Paris	1888	Landscape	—	—	—	—	2	—	—	—	—	—	2
Harrison, Brook	Shoreham	1885	Landscape	—	—	—	—	1	—	—	—	—	—	1
Harrison, B. A.	London	1824	Landscape	—	—	—	—	1	—	—	—	—	—	1
Harrison, B. R.	London	1809-1818	Architecture	—	—	3	—	—	—	—	—	—	—	3
Harrison, Charles H.	Yarmouth	1886	Landscape	—	—	—	—	—	—	2	—	—	—	2
Harrison, D.	London	1818-1821	Architecture	—	—	3	—	—	—	—	—	—	—	3
Harrison, Miss Emma Florence	London	1887-1891	Domestic	—	—	3	—	—	—	—	—	—	—	3
Harrison, Miss Emily H.	London	1892-1893	Flowers	—	—	—	—	—	—	—	—	—	2	2
Harrison, Miss Emily M.	London	1870-1871	Sea Shores	—	—	—	—	—	—	—	—	—	2	2
Harrison, Miss Fanny	London	1870-1871	Fruit	—	—	—	—	1	—	—	—	—	1	2
Harrison, Frederick	London	1846-1878	Military	—	—	5	5	1	—	—	—	—	2	13
Harrison, F. E.	London	1862-1867	Flowers	—	—	3	—	—	—	—	—	—	—	3
Harrison, G.	Highgate	1832	Architecture	—	—	1	—	—	—	—	—	—	—	1
Harrison, George, R.C.A.	Bettws-y-Coed	1867-1879	Landscape	—	—	—	—	8	—	—	—	—	4	12
Harrison, Mrs. George	London	1886	Study	—	—	—	—	—	—	—	1	—	—	1
Harrison, Captain George A.	London	1884-1890	Sculpture	—	—	—	—	—	—	4	2	—	2	8
Harrison, Gerald E.	London	1890-1892	Domestic	—	—	—	—	2	—	—	—	—	1	3
Harrison, George Henry †	London	1840-1847	Figures	—	—	14	2	11	22	—	—	—	—	49
Harrison, G. J.	London	1875	Landscape	—	—	—	—	2	—	—	—	—	—	2
Harrison, George L.	London	1878-1883	Domestic	—	—	2	—	2	—	—	—	—	2	6
Harrison, H.	London	1805-1809	Landscape	—	—	6	—	—	—	—	—	—	—	6
Harrison, Henry	Plaistow	1867	Landscape	—	—	—	—	—	—	—	—	—	1	1
Harrison, Henry C.	London	1857-1877	Sculpture	—	—	13	—	—	—	—	—	—	—	13
Harrison, J.	London	1784-1793	Miniatures	—	—	5	—	—	—	—	—	—	—	5
Harrison, John	London	1801-1852	Mythological, &c.	—	—	40	16	10	—	—	—	—	—	66
Harrison, J.	London	1833	Landscape	—	—	—	—	—	—	1	—	—	—	1
Harrison, J.	London	1827-1865	Portraits	—	—	31	—	—	—	—	—	—	—	31
Harrison, J. B.	—	1867-1872	Portraits	—	—	4	—	—	—	—	—	—	—	4
Harrison, J.	York	1846-1856	Portraits	—	—	3	—	—	—	—	—	—	7	10
Harrison, J. C.	London	1882-1891	Domestic	—	—	2	—	13	—	14	—	—	—	29
Harrison, Joseph S.	London	1889-1893	Landscape	—	—	2	—	—	—	1	—	—	—	3
Harrison, L. B.	London	1882	Landscape	—	—	1	—	—	—	—	—	—	—	1
Harrison, M.	London	1858	Landscape	—	—	1	—	—	—	—	—	—	—	1
Harrison, Miss Maria, A.R.W.S. †	London	1845-1893	Flowers	—	—	7	1	9	439	—	—	—	—	456
Harrison, M. E.	London	1875	Flowers	—	—	—	—	—	—	—	—	—	1	1
Harrison, Mdlle. Pauline	Edmonton	1834-1835	Flowers	—	—	—	—	3	—	4	—	—	—	7
Harrison, R. A.	London	1844	Stained Glass	—	—	1	—	—	—	—	—	—	—	1
Harrison, S.	London	1808	Portraits	—	—	1	—	—	—	—	—	—	—	1
Harrison, Stockdale	Leicester	1881	Architecture	—	—	1	—	—	—	—	—	—	—	1
Harrison, Miss Sarah C.	London	1889-1892	Figures	—	—	4	—	—	—	—	—	1	1	6
Harrison, Miss Theodora	London	1890-1893	Landscape	—	—	1	—	3	—	—	—	—	—	4
Harrison, Thomas	Rome	1773-1814	Architecture	—	—	5	—	—	—	—	—	—	—	5
Harrison, T.	London	1838-1840	Sculpture	—	—	2	—	—	—	—	—	—	—	2
Harrison, T. Erat	London	1875-1893	Sculpture	—	—	15	—	—	—	—	10	—	3	28
Harrison, William	London	1893	Architecture	—	—	1	—	—	—	—	—	—	—	1
Harrison, Mrs., late Miss Mary P. Rossiter ‡	London	1833-1875	Flowers	—	—	20	9	20	—	322	—	—	—	371
Harriss, D.	Oxford	1799	Landscape	—	—	1	—	—	—	—	—	—	—	1
Harroway, Henry G.	Kilburn	1889	Landscape	—	—	—	—	1	—	—	—	—	—	1
Harry, J.	London	1822-1823	Landscape	—	—	2	—	—	—	—	—	—	—	2
Hart, Alfred	London	1893	Architecture	—	—	1	—	—	—	—	—	—	—	1
Hart, Mrs. Anne E	Anerley	1886-1887	Domestic	—	—	1	—	—	—	2	—	—	—	3
Hart, Conway Weston	London	1849	Figures	—	—	—	1	—	—	—	—	—	—	1
Hart, H.	London	1841-1846	Landscape	—	—	2	—	2	—	—	—	—	—	4
Hart, Herman	Folkestone	1877-1883	Landscape	—	—	—	—	3	—	—	—	—	2	5
Hart, Horace S.	London	1887-1889	Domestic	—	—	2	—	2	—	—	—	—	—	4
Hart, J. T.	Nottingham	1856-1868	Domestic	—	—	4	12	1	—	—	—	—	1	18
Hart, J. Lawrence	Rugby	1887-1890	Landscape	—	—	—	—	1	—	1	—	—	—	2
Hart, Joel T.	Florence	1858	Portraits	—	—	1	—	—	—	—	—	—	—	1
Hart, Miss L.	—	1829-1830	Still Life	—	—	—	—	2	—	—	—	—	—	2
Hart, Mrs. P.	London	1881	Figures	—	—	—	—	—	—	—	—	—	1	1
Hart, R.	London	1830-1831	Landscape	—	—	1	1	—	—	—	—	—	—	2
Hart, Solomon Alexander, R.A.	London	1826-1881	Scriptural	—	—	122	25	34	—	3	—	—	—	184
Hart, Thomas, F.S.A.	Falmouth	1865-1880	Sea Pieces	—	—	3	—	—	—	—	2	—	20	25
Hart, W.	London	1845	Historical	—	—	—	—	1	—	—	—	—	—	1
Hart-Dyke, Miss E. *See* D.	—	—	—	—	—	—	—	—	—	—	—	—	—	—
Harte, Miss Margaret K.	Blandford	1879-1889	Domestic	—	—	3	—	—	—	—	—	—	—	3
Hartland, H. Albert	Cork	1868-1889	Landscape	—	—	21	—	13	—	2	1	—	7	44
Hartley, Alfred, R.B.A., A.R.P.E. §	London	1885-1893	Domestic	—	—	8	—	18	—	3	5	6	12	52
Hartley, Edgar	Leigh	1891	Architecture	—	—	1	—	—	—	—	—	—	—	1
Hartley, Miss E. A.	Boston, Lincs.	1871	Fruit	—	—	1	—	—	—	—	—	—	—	1
Hartley, J.	Tadcaster	1835	Portraits	—	—	—	—	3	—	—	—	—	—	3

Name.	Town.	First and Last Year of Ex.	Speciality.	S. A.	F. S.	R. A.	B. I.	S. S.	O. W.	N.W.	G. G.	N. G.	V. E.	Total
Hartley, J. S.	London	1884	Sculpture	—	—	—	—	—	—	—	1	—	—	1
Hartley, Richard	Liverpool	1890-1892	Landscape	—	—	2	—	—	—	—	—	—	—	2
Hartley, Thomas	London	1820-1860	Figures	—	—	12	13	38	1	—	—	—	—	64
Hartley, Mrs.	—	1775	Landscape	3	—	—	—	—	—	—	—	—	—	3
Hartley, Miss	London	1775	Landscape	6	—	—	—	—	—	—	—	—	—	6
Hartmann, Christian	London	1847	Domestic	—	—	1	—	—	—	—	—	—	—	1
Hartmann, Karl	London	1851-1857	Figures	—	—	—	1	18	—	—	—	—	9	28
Hartmann, R.	—	1850-1857	Domestic	—	—	7	—	—	—	—	—	—	—	7
Hartmann, Rudolf Hans	Dresden	1889-1890	Sculpture	—	—	3	—	—	—	—	—	—	—	3
Hartnell, Nathaniel	London	1829-1864	Landscape	—	—	10	6	10	—	—	—	—	8	34
Hartrick, A. Standish-	Fife	1887-1892	Figures	—	—	1	—	2	—	—	—	—	2	5
Hartry, E.	Southampton	1883-1888	Figures	—	—	—	—	1	—	—	—	—	2	3
Hartshorne, A.	Pinner	1872	Architecture	—	—	2	—	—	—	—	—	—	—	2
Hartshorne (A.) and Clark (Junr.)	London	1871	Architecture	—	—	1	—	—	—	—	—	—	—	1
Harvey, Douglas S.	London	1859	Landscape	—	—	—	1	—	—	—	—	—	—	1
Harvey, E.	London	1859	Landscape	—	—	—	1	1	—	—	—	—	—	2
Harvey, F. E.	Ipswich	1833	Architecture	—	—	1	—	—	—	—	—	—	—	1
Harvey, G.	London	1819-1848	Flowers	—	—	2	—	—	—	—	—	—	—	2
Harvey, Sir George, P.R.S.A.	Edinburgh	1832-1873	Historical	—	—	22	1	2	—	—	—	—	—	25
Harvey, George	London	1848-1878	Landscape	—	—	2	—	11	—	—	—	—	20	33
Harvey, Henry	London	1879-1889	Sculpture	—	—	2	—	—	—	—	2	—	—	4
Harvey, Miss H. M.	London	1886	Still Life	—	—	—	—	1	—	—	—	—	—	1
Harvey, J.	London	1785-1810	Architecture	—	—	17	—	—	—	—	—	—	—	17
Harvey, J. K.	London	1858	Flowers	—	—	1	—	—	—	—	—	—	—	1
Harvey, Lawrence	London	1879	Architecture	—	—	1	—	—	—	—	—	—	—	1
Harvey, T., Junr.	London	1807	Architecture	—	—	1	—	—	—	—	—	—	—	1
Harvey, William	London	1867	Architecture	—	—	1	—	—	—	—	—	—	—	1
Harvey (W.) and Smith (L. B.)	London	1887-1890	Architecture	—	—	3	—	—	—	—	—	—	—	3
Harvey, Miss	—	1793	Portraits	—	—	1	—	—	—	—	—	—	—	1
Harveymore, A.	Putney	1868	Landscape	—	—	1	—	—	—	—	—	—	—	1
Harvie, J. S.	Edinburgh	1811	Portraits	—	—	1	—	—	—	—	—	—	—	1
Harvy, Ross	London	1857	Sculpture	—	—	—	1	—	—	—	—	—	—	1
Harwood, E.	Rugby	1859	Figures	—	—	1	—	—	—	—	—	—	—	1
Harwood, H.	Bradford	1892-1893	Landscape	—	—	—	—	4	—	—	—	—	—	4
Harwood, John	London	1818-1829	Landscape	—	—	10	3	1	—	—	—	—	—	14
Harwood, John (?) James	London	1839-1871	Portraits	—	—	51	18	16	—	—	—	—	6	91
Harwood, Robert	London	1855-1879	Landscape	—	—	11	7	19	—	—	—	—	7	44
Haseler, H.	London	1814-1817	Landscape	—	—	4	—	—	5	—	—	—	—	9
Haseler, W.	Bath	1859-1860	Cattle	—	—	—	—	3	—	—	—	—	—	3
Haseltine, I. P.	—	1870	Landscape	—	—	3	—	—	—	—	—	—	—	3
Hasenpflug, C.	Prussia	1850	Ruins	—	—	1	—	—	—	—	—	—	—	1
Haskew, J. T.	London	1840	Landscape	—	—	—	—	2	—	—	—	—	—	2
Haskoll, J.	London	1824-1835	Sculpture	—	—	7	—	2	—	—	—	—	—	9
Haslam, W. D.	London	1871-1881	Figures	—	—	1	—	3	—	—	—	—	4	8
Haslehurst, Ernest W.	Lee	1888	Landscape	—	—	—	—	1	—	—	—	—	—	1
Haslem, John	London	1836-1865	Enamels	—	—	37	—	14	—	—	—	—	—	51
Haslings —	London	1813	Figures	—	—	2	—	—	—	—	—	—	—	2
Hasmer, Miss H.	Rome	1857	Historical	—	—	1	—	—	—	—	—	—	—	1
Hassam, Alfred	London	1865-1868	Figures	—	—	4	—	8	—	—	—	—	4	16
Hasse, E.	—	1859	—	—	—	—	—	2	—	—	—	—	—	2
Hassell, Edward §	London	1827-1852	Landscape	—	—	13	9	135	—	—	—	—	—	157
Hassell, John	London	1789-1819	Landscape	—	—	20	—	—	—	—	—	—	1	21
Hasta —	London	1768	Landscape	1	—	—	—	—	—	—	—	—	—	1
Hastie, Miss Grace H. ‖	London	1874-1893	Flowers	—	—	14	—	18	—	18	2	2	6	60
Hastings, Edmund	London	1816-1820	Landscape	—	—	—	—	—	22	—	—	—	—	22
Hastings, Edw.	London	1804-1827	Portraits	—	—	49	11	9	—	—	—	—	—	69
Hastings, Ethel	London	1887	Domestic	—	—	—	—	1	—	—	—	—	—	1
Hastings, George	Bristol	1869-1875	Landscape	—	—	8	—	5	—	—	—	—	2	15
Hastings, Miss Kate Gardiner	London	1878-1893	Scriptural	—	—	4	—	—	—	—	11	14	10	39
Hastings, Captain Thomas	Liverpool	1816-1821	Sea Pieces	—	—	2	1	—	2	—	—	—	—	5
Hastings, W. A.	London	1829-1831	Portraits	—	—	—	—	3	—	—	—	—	—	3
Hastings, W. S.	London	1830-1831	Portraits	—	—	3	—	—	—	—	—	—	—	3
Hastling, Miss Annie E.	Sheffield	1882-1893	Domestic	—	—	1	—	—	—	4	—	—	—	5
Hatchard, J.	London	1811	Architecture	—	—	1	—	—	—	—	—	—	—	1
Hatchett, J. C.	—	1856	Landscape	—	—	—	—	1	—	—	—	—	—	1
Hatherell, William, R.I. ‡	London	1879-1893	Figures	—	—	6	—	3	—	11	—	—	6	26
Hatton, E. W.	London	1845-1882	Portraits	—	—	29	—	1	—	—	—	—	—	30
Hatton, Miss Helen Howard	London	1879-1893	Figures	—	—	6	—	6	—	3	4	2	13	34
Hatton, T.	London	1799-1809	Architecture	—	—	6	—	—	—	—	—	—	—	6
Hauck, Philip Elias	London	1761-1763	Portraits	6	1	—	—	—	—	—	—	—	—	7
Haugh, George	Doncaster	1777-1818	Landscape	—	—	11	9	—	—	—	—	—	—	20
Haughton, Benjamin	Dawlish	1893	Landscape	—	—	2	—	—	—	—	—	—	—	2

Name.	Town.	First and Last Year of Ex.	Speciality.	S. A.	F. S.	R. A.	B. I.	S. S.	O.W.	N.W.	G. G.	N. G.	V. E.	Total.
Haughton, Moses	Birmingham	1788-1804	Enamels	—	—	13	—	—	—	—	—	—	—	13
Haughton, Moses, Junr.	—	1808-1848	Portraits	—	—	86	3	—	—	—	—	—	—	89
Haürn, Mrs.	London	1775	Miniatures	3	—	—	—	—	—	—	—	—	—	3
Hausselin, H.	London	1849	—	—	—	—	2	—	—	—	—	—	—	2
Hautman, J.	Munich	1858	Sculpture	—	—	2	—	—	—	—	—	—	—	2
Havell, Alfred C.	London	1878-1884	Figures	—	—	2	—	—	—	—	—	—	—	2
Havell, Charles Richards	Reading	1858-1866	Rural	—	—	1	4	1	—	—	—	—	2	8
Havell, Edmund	Reading	1814-1847	Landscape	—	—	4	4	—	10	—	—	—	—	18
Havell, Edmund, Junr.	Reading	1835-1893	Figures	—	—	77	16	11	—	—	—	—	5	109
Havell, Ernest B.	Madras	1890-1891	Sculpture	—	—	2	—	—	—	—	—	—	—	2
Havell, Frederick James	—	1832	Engraving	—	—	—	—	1	—	—	—	—	—	1
Havell, George	Reading	1826-1833	Interiors	—	—	4	1	5	—	—	—	—	—	10
Havell, H.	Cheltenham	1849	Dramatic	—	—	1	—	—	—	—	—	—	—	1
Havell, Robert	London	1808-1822	Landscape	—	—	3	2	—	7	—	—	—	—	12
Havell, William †	London	1804-1857	Landscape	—	—	103	42	32	154	—	—	—	—	331
Havell, Mrs. *See* Miss M. A. Hale §	—	1826-1829	Portraits	—	—	6	—	3	—	—	—	—	—	9
Havenhand, James	London	1893	Metal Work	—	—	1	—	—	—	—	—	—	—	1
Haverfield, J. T.	Callander	1870-1871	Landscape	—	—	1	—	4	—	—	—	—	—	5
Haverly, J.	Dublin	1844	Figures	—	—	—	1	—	—	—	—	—	—	1
Havermaet, Van. *See* V.	—	—	—	—	—	—	—	—	—	—	—	—	—	—
Havers, Miss Alice (Mrs. Morgan) ‖	London	1872-1889	Domestic	—	—	33	—	12	—	—	4	—	9	58
Haverty, J., R.H.A.	London	1835-1858	Portraits	—	—	17	—	8	—	—	—	—	2	27
Havill, Frederick	Cheltenham	1849-1874	Portraits	—	—	11	—	4	—	—	—	—	—	15
Haviland, Miss Harriet M.	Bridgwater	1864	Flowers	—	—	—	2	—	—	—	—	—	—	2
Haward, Francis, A.R.A.	London	1783-1797	Engraving	—	—	6	—	—	—	—	—	—	—	6
Haweis, M.	London	1875	Portraits	—	—	—	—	—	—	—	—	—	1	1
Hawes, Arthur G.	London	1890-1891	Landscape	—	—	—	—	1	—	—	—	—	1	2
Hawker, Miss Florence	London	1889	Domestic	—	—	—	—	—	—	1	—	—	—	1
Hawker, Miss Margarita E.	London	1891	Flowers	—	—	—	—	—	—	1	—	—	—	1
Hawker, J.	—	1804-1808	Landscape	—	—	3	—	—	—	—	—	—	—	3
Hawker, Joseph	London	1833	Landscape	—	—	—	—	1	—	—	—	—	—	1
Hawkes, Miss Clara M.	London	1884-1886	Heads	—	—	1	—	1	—	—	—	—	—	2
Hawkes, Mrs. E. A.	London	1852-1854	Domestic	—	—	1	2	—	—	—	—	—	4	7
Hawkes, F.	Reading	1844-1845	Landscape	—	—	—	—	2	—	—	—	—	—	2
Hawkes, Joseph	London	1839	Figures	—	—	1	—	—	—	—	—	—	—	1
Hawkins, Miss Amy	London	1892	Domestic	—	—	—	—	—	—	1	—	—	—	1
Hawkins, Miss Agnes M.	London	1872-1876	Domestic	—	—	—	—	1	—	—	—	—	1	2
Hawkins, B. W.	London	1847-1849	Sculpture	—	—	4	—	—	—	—	—	—	—	4
Hawkins, George	London	1795-1810	Architecture	—	—	12	—	—	—	—	—	—	—	12
Hawkins, George, Junr.	Hackney	1830-1848	Architecture	—	—	7	—	—	—	—	—	—	—	7
Hawkins, G.	London	1832	Landscape	—	—	1	—	—	—	—	—	—	—	1
Hawkins, Henry §	—	1820-1881	Portraits	—	—	8	2	200	3	1	—	—	—	214
Hawkins, J.	London	1879	Portraits	—	—	1	—	—	—	—	—	—	—	1
Hawkins, Miss Jane	London	1871-1874	Domestic	—	—	—	—	9	—	—	—	—	2	11
Hawkins, J. B.	London	1829	Landscape	—	—	—	1	—	—	—	—	—	—	1
Hawkins, J. B.	—	1842	Sculpture	—	—	1	—	—	—	—	—	—	—	1
Hawkins, Louise	London	1880-1888	Domestic	—	—	—	—	2	—	1	—	—	3	6
Hawkins, Mayor Rohde	London	1850-1851	Architecture	—	—	2	—	—	—	—	—	—	—	2
Hawkins, Waterhouse	London	1832-1841	Sporting	—	—	5	4	16	—	1	—	—	—	26
Hawkins, Mrs. W. H. (Louisa)	London	1839-1868	Portraits	—	—	19	—	11	—	—	—	—	—	30
Hawksley, Arthur	London	1874-1885	Landscape	—	—	4	—	5	—	—	—	—	12	21
Hawksley, Miss Florence	London	1881	Domestic	—	—	1	—	—	—	—	—	—	—	1
Hawksworth, W. T. M.	London	1881-1893	Landscape	—	—	10	—	25	—	3	—	—	6	44
Haworth, Miss E. F.	London	1844-1855	Portraits	—	—	2	—	—	—	—	—	—	—	2
Haworth, W.	London	1781	Sculpture	—	—	1	—	—	—	—	—	—	—	1
Hawthorn, Charles John	London	1832	Interiors	—	—	—	—	1	—	1	—	—	—	2
Hawthorn, C. M.	London	1833-1844	Sea Pieces	—	—	—	2	5	—	—	—	—	—	7
Hawthorn, E. D.	London	1858-1862	Figures	—	—	—	2	—	—	—	—	—	1	3
Hay, E.	London	1817	Copies	—	—	2	—	—	—	—	—	—	—	2
Hay, Miss E.	London	1826-1835	Flowers	—	—	—	—	10	—	—	—	—	—	10
Hay, F. B.	London	1859-1862	Historical	—	—	7	—	—	—	—	—	—	—	7
Hay, G. H.	—	1867	Sea Pieces	—	—	1	—	—	—	—	—	—	—	1
Hay, G. J.	London	1857	Buildings	—	—	—	1	—	—	—	—	—	—	1
Hay, James	Edinburgh	1887-1892	Domestic	—	—	—	—	—	—	2	—	—	—	2
Hay, John (Pupil of Cosway)	London	1768-1800	Miniatures	6	4	7	—	—	—	—	—	—	—	17
Hay, Miss J.	London	1797-1812	Miniatures	—	—	21	2	—	—	—	—	—	—	23
Hay, J. Macpherson	London	1893	Landscape	—	—	—	—	—	—	—	—	—	1	1
Hay, P. A., R.S.W.	London	1892-1893	Domestic	—	—	2	—	2	—	1	—	1	1	7
Hay, T. Marjoribanks	Edinburgh	1885-1893	Landscape	—	—	3	—	—	—	4	—	—	2	9
Hay, Thomas Wallace	Kew	1884-1889	Architecture	—	—	3	—	—	—	—	—	—	—	3
Hay, W.	Plymouth	1787-1797	Miniatures	—	—	16	—	—	—	—	—	—	—	16
Hay, William M.	London	1852-1881	Scriptural	—	—	17	13	39	—	—	—	—	15	84

Name.	Town.	First and Last Year of Ex.	Speciality.	S. A.	F. S.	R. A.	B. I.	S. S.	O. W.	N. W.	G. G.	N. G.	V. E.	Total.
Hayard —	—	1771	Fruit	—	—	1	—	—	—	—	—	—	—	1
Haycock, Aug. Edmonds	London	1882-1885	Domestic	—	—	3	—	2	—	—	—	—	3	8
Haycock, E.	London	1808-1820	Architecture	—	—	5	—	—	—	—	—	—	—	5
Haycock, G. B.	London	1862-1868	Still Life	—	—	11	12	9	—	—	—	—	—	32
Haycock, Washington	London	1862-1864	Sporting	—	—	—	—	5	—	—	—	—	—	5
Haydon, Benjamin Robert	Plymouth	1807-1845	Historical	—	—	11	16	30	12	—	—	—	—	69
Haydon, Samuel James Bouverie	Exeter	1840-1876	Sculpture	—	—	41	1	3	—	—	—	—	1	46
Haye, E.	—	1826	Fruit	—	—	—	—	1	—	—	—	—	—	1
Hayes, Arthur	London	1880-1893	Figures	—	—	1	—	1	—	—	—	—	3	5
Hayes, Claude, R.I.‡ φ	London	1873-1893	Domestic	—	—	40	—	41	—	54	5	4	49	193
Hayes, Edwin, R.H.A., R.I.‡ § φ	Dublin	1854-1893	Sea Pieces	—	—	61	35	111	—	338	13	19	93	670
Hayes, Miss Edith C.	Paris	1889-1892	Landscape	—	—	1	—	—	—	—	—	1	2	4
Hayes, F. William, A.R.C.A.	Liverpool	1872-1892	Landscape	—	—	17	—	4	—	3	1	—	5	30
Hayes, George, R.C.A.	Manchester	1855-1875	Landscape	—	—	3	—	4	—	—	—	—	15	22
Hayes, Henry Edgar	London	1879-1886	Figures	—	—	—	—	3	—	—	—	—	—	3
Hayes, John	London	1814-1857	Portraits	—	—	77	9	1	—	—	—	—	—	87
Hayes, J. Percy	Chiswick	1890	Domestic	—	—	—	—	—	—	—	—	—	2	2
Hayes, J. W.	London	1838-1845	Figures	—	—	1	2	—	—	—	—	—	—	3
Hayes, Miss M.	Southall	1801-1809	Portraits	—	—	4	—	—	—	—	—	—	—	4
Hayes, Michael Angelo, R.H.A.‡	Dublin	1845-1877	Military	—	—	1	—	2	—	35	—	—	3	41
Hayes, S.	London	1816	Scriptural	—	—	—	1	—	—	—	—	—	—	1
Hayes, S. J.	London	1880	Landscape	—	—	—	—	1	—	—	—	—	—	1
Hayes, T.	London	1839	Architecture	—	—	1	—	—	—	—	—	—	—	1
Hayes, W. B.	Barnes	1885-1892	Landscape	—	—	1	—	—	—	—	—	—	2	3
Hayler, Henry	London	1849-1859	Sculpture	—	—	8	—	—	—	—	—	—	—	8
Hayley, G.	London	1814	Landscape	—	—	1	—	—	—	—	—	—	—	1
Hayllar, Algernon Victor	Wallingford	1889	Engraving	—	—	2	—	—	—	—	—	—	—	2
Hayllar, Miss Edith	Wallingford	1881-1893	Domestic	—	—	10	—	16	—	—	—	—	7	33
Hayllar, James, R.B.A.§	London	1851-1893	Figures	—	—	58	23	217	—	5	—	—	64	367
Hayllar, Miss Jessica	Wallingford	1879-1893	Domestic	—	—	17	—	16	—	—	—	—	16	49
Hayllar, Miss Kate	Wallingford	1883-1893	Domestic	—	—	9	—	6	—	2	—	—	—	17
Hayllar, Miss Mary	Wallingford	1880-1885	Domestic	—	—	5	—	15	—	1	—	—	5	26
Hayman, Francis, R.A.	Exeter	1760-1772	Historical	10	—	6	—	—	—	—	—	—	—	16
Haymann, G.	London	1877	Cairo	—	—	—	—	1	—	—	—	—	—	1
Haynes, Adeline	—	1879	Flowers	—	—	—	—	1	—	—	—	—	—	1
Haynes, Arthur S.	London	1887-1890	Architecture	—	—	4	—	2	—	—	—	—	1	7
Haynes, Edward Travanyon	London	1867-1885	Historical	—	—	20	1	2	—	—	—	—	9	32
Haynes, H.	London	1843	Landscape	—	—	1	—	—	—	—	—	—	—	1
Haynes, John W.	London	1852-1882	Domestic	—	—	8	12	26	—	—	—	—	17	63
Haynes-Williams. *See* W.	—	—	—	—	—	—	—	—	—	—	—	—	—	—
Hayoit —	London	1771-1783	Flowers	—	21	—	—	—	—	—	—	—	—	21
Hays, Miss Beatrice	London	1888-1893	Domestic	—	—	3	—	3	—	—	—	—	4	10
Hays, W. B.	Greenwich	1847	Architecture	—	—	1	—	—	—	—	—	—	—	1
Hays, W. Bennett	Wandsworth	1864	Portraits	—	—	1	—	—	—	—	—	—	—	1
Hayter, Miss A.	London	1814-1830	Portraits	—	—	11	—	15	2	—	—	—	—	28
Hayter, Angelo Collen	London	1848-1852	Portraits	—	—	5	4	—	—	—	—	—	—	9
Hayter, Charles	London	1786-1832	Miniatures	—	—	201	—	10	1	—	—	—	—	212
Hayter, Miss Edith C.	London	1890	Landscape	—	—	—	—	—	—	—	—	1	—	1
Hayter, Sir George, K.S.L.	London	1809-1859	Portraits	—	—	56	40	1	—	—	—	—	1	98
Hayter, John	London	1815-1879	Historical	—	—	129	26	30	2	—	—	—	—	187
Haytley, E.	—	1760-1761	Portraits	5	—	—	—	—	—	—	—	—	—	5
Hayward, A.	London	1857-1859	Sculpture	—	—	2	—	—	—	—	—	—	—	2
Hayward, Albert	London	1869-1885	Landscape	—	—	1	—	—	—	—	—	—	1	2
Hayward, A. F. W.	London	1880-1893	Portraits	—	—	18	—	1	—	—	1	9	14	43
Hayward, Charles Foster, F.S.A.	London	1855-1893	Architecture	—	—	11	—	—	—	—	—	—	—	11
Hayward, Miss Emily L.	London	1887	Portraits	—	—	1	—	—	—	—	—	—	—	1
Hayward, Gerald S.	London	1879-1883	Miniatures	—	—	7	—	—	—	—	—	—	—	7
Hayward, H.	London	1830	Architecture	—	—	1	—	—	—	—	—	—	—	1
Hayward, J.	London	1826-1855	Architecture	—	—	11	—	—	—	—	—	—	—	11
Hayward, J. M.	Sidmouth	1872	Landscape	—	—	—	—	—	—	—	—	—	1	1
Hayward, J. S.	—	1798-1816	Landscape	—	—	30	—	—	—	—	—	—	—	30
Hayward, J. W.	—	1807	Architecture	—	—	1	—	—	—	—	—	—	—	1
Hayward, Miss Mary	London	1867-1874	Flowers	—	—	—	—	8	—	—	—	—	—	8
Hayward, Richard	London	1761-1766	Sculpture	3	—	—	—	—	—	—	—	—	—	3
Haywood, A.	London	1862-1871	Landscape	—	—	5	—	—	—	—	—	—	—	5
Haywood, Miss Evelyn Corbould-. *See* C.	—	—	—	—	—	—	—	—	—	—	—	—	—	—
Haywood, John	London	1773-1794	Architecture	—	—	8	—	—	—	—	—	—	—	8
Haywood, J. J.	London	1790-1793	Architecture	—	—	4	—	—	—	—	—	—	—	4
Haywood, Miss J. M.	London	1852-1854	Portraits	—	—	11	1	—	—	—	—	—	—	12
Haywood, M.	London	1870-1872	Domestic	—	—	—	—	4	—	—	—	—	—	4
Haywood, Mrs. Mordan (Emma)	Gipsy Hill	1884-1886	Churches	—	—	—	—	—	—	2	—	—	—	2
Haywood, W.	London	1844-1867	Architecture	—	—	4	—	—	—	—	—	—	—	4

Name.	Town.	First and Last Year of Ex.	Speciality.	S. A.	F. S.	R. A.	B. I.	S. S.	O. W.	N. W.	G. G.	N. G.	V. E.	Total.
Hazard, Hortense	London	1880	Sculpture	—	—	—	—	1	—	—	—	—	—	1
Hazlehurst, J. B.	London	1817	Portraits	—	—	2	—	—	—	—	—	—	—	2
Hazlitt, John	London	1788-1819	Miniatures	—	—	126	7	—	—	—	—	—	—	133
Hazlitt, William	London	1802-1805	Portraits	—	—	2	—	—	—	—	—	—	—	2
Head —	—	1814	Sporting	—	—	—	—	—	—	—	—	—	1	1
Head, Arthur W.	London	1886-1893	Domestic	—	—	3	—	4	—	1	—	—	—	8
Head, B. G.	London	1867-1888	Domestic	—	—	9	1	31	—	—	—	—	4	45
Head, Edward J.	Scarborough	1889-1893	Landscape	—	—	7	—	2	—	—	—	—	—	9
Head, Guy	London	1779-1800	Portraits	3	3	7	—	—	—	—	—	—	—	13
Heade, Martin J.	London	1865	Landscape	—	—	1	1	—	—	—	—	—	—	2
Headford, J.	London	1838	Sculpture	—	—	—	—	1	—	—	—	—	—	1
Headland, Miss Margaret	London	1887-1891	Flowers	—	—	4	—	—	—	—	—	—	1	5
Heagen —	—	1800	Architecture	—	—	1	—	—	—	—	—	—	—	1
Healey, C. E. H.	London	1890	Sea Pieces	—	—	—	—	1	—	—	—	—	—	1
Healey, G. R.	London	1840-1852	Figures	—	—	6	3	19	—	—	—	—	2	30
Healy, George P. A.	London	1838-1883	Portraits	—	—	32	1	6	—	—	—	—	—	39
Healy, T.	London	1785-1786	Architecture	—	—	2	—	—	—	—	—	—	—	2
Heam —	London	1783	—	—	*	—	—	—	—	—	—	—	—	—
Heape, Miss M. (?) Mary Heap	London	1821-1823	Portraits	—	—	8	—	—	—	—	—	—	—	8
Heaphy, Archibald C.	Wokingham	1870-1889	Domestic	—	—	—	—	4	—	—	—	—	—	4
Heaphy, Charles	London	1835	Historical	—	—	—	1	—	—	—	—	—	—	1
Heaphy, Miss Elizabeth. *See* Mrs. Henry	—	—	—	—	—	—	—	—	—	—	—	—	—	—
John Murray	London	1834-1843	Portraits	—	—	11	—	—	—	—	—	—	—	11
Heaphy, G.	London	1874	—	—	—	—	—	1	—	—	—	—	—	1
Heaphy, Miss M. A.§ *See* Mrs. W. Musgrave	London	1821-1832	Portraits	—	—	26	—	7	—	—	—	—	—	33
Heaphy, Miss Theodosia	London	1883-1885	Domestic	—	—	—	—	4	—	—	—	—	—	4
Heaphy, Thomas † §	London	1797-1836	Portraits	—	—	60	9	14	42	8	—	—	—	133
Heaphy, Thomas Frank §	London	1831-1874	Historical	—	—	51	8	68	—	—	—	—	—	127
Heard, Miss B.	London	1858-1860	Flowers	—	—	—	2	1	—	—	—	—	—	3
Heard, W.	—	1810	Portraits	—	—	1	—	—	—	—	—	—	—	1
Hearlin —	London	1765	Game	1	—	—	—	—	—	—	—	—	—	1
Hearn, R. H.	Paris	1866-1871	Landscape	—	—	4	—	—	—	—	—	—	—	4
Hearne, Thomas, F.S.A.	London	1765-1806	Landscape	42	12	24	—	—	—	—	—	—	—	78
Heath, A. H.	Tonbridge	1854-1855	Historical	—	—	—	1	3	—	—	—	—	—	4
Heath, Charles §	London	1801-1825	Engraving	—	—	11	—	30	—	—	—	—	—	41
Heath, Miss C,	London	1803-1806	Portraits	—	—	4	—	—	—	—	—	—	—	4
Heath, Dudley	London	1886-1893	Domestic	—	—	1	—	1	—	—	—	—	3	5
Heath, Miss E. S.	Sevenoaks	1869-1870	Landscape	—	—	—	—	—	—	—	—	—	3	3
Heath, F. A.	London	1863-1874	Engraving	—	—	4	—	—	—	—	—	—	—	4
Heath, Henry Charles	London	1851-1893	Miniatures	—	—	65	—	9	—	—	—	—	—	74
Heath, James, A.R.A.	London	1780-1834	Engraving	3	—	26	—	—	—	—	—	—	—	29
Heath, Lionel	London	1892-1893	Miniatures	—	—	2	—	—	—	—	—	—	—	2
Heath, Miss Margaret A.	London	1886-1893	Domestic	—	—	2	—	—	—	7	—	—	2	11
Heath, Miss S. F.	Tonbridge	1871	Landscape	—	—	—	—	1	—	—	—	—	—	1
Heath, Thomas Edward	Cardiff	1879	Sea Pieces	—	—	—	—	1	—	—	—	—	—	1
Heath, W.	Halifax	1850-1851	Landscape	—	—	2	—	—	—	—	—	—	—	2
Heath, William H. H.	Tonbridge	1829-1847	Figures	—	—	—	1	5	—	—	—	—	—	6
Heathcote, C.	London	1828	Architecture	—	—	1	—	—	—	—	—	—	—	1
Heathcote, Mrs. Evelyn	Winchester	1883-1888	Landscape	—	—	—	—	—	—	3	—	—	—	3
Heathcote, F.	London	1879	Rustic	—	—	—	—	1	—	—	—	—	—	1
Heathcote, W. C.	London	1871-1872	Landscape	—	—	—	—	4	—	—	—	—	—	4
Heathcote, Miss M.	Borrowdale	1867-1880	Alps	—	—	—	—	—	—	—	—	—	3	3
Heathcote, Mrs., *née* Miss Grace Hussey	Salisbury	1877-1878	Landscape	—	—	—	—	—	—	—	—	—	3	3
Heathcote and Randle	—	1889	Architecture	—	—	1	—	—	—	—	—	—	—	1
Heather, John	Colchester	1763-1765	Flowers	—	7	—	—	—	—	—	—	—	—	7
Heatherley, Thomas	London	1858-1879	Domestic	—	—	1	3	2	—	—	—	—	1	7
Heatherwell, W.	London	1881	Figures	—	—	—	—	—	—	—	—	—	1	1
Heatly, Mrs.	—	1797-1805	Landscape	—	—	10	—	—	—	—	—	—	—	10
Heaton, A.	—	1867	Landscape	—	—	1	—	—	—	—	—	—	—	1
Heaton, Clement	London	1892	Stained Glass	—	—	2	—	—	—	—	—	—	—	2
Heaton, John	Datchet	1884-1889	Landscape	—	—	—	—	1	—	5	—	—	—	6
Heaton, J. A.	London	1888	Decoration	—	—	3	—	—	—	—	—	—	—	3
Heaton, Monica	London	1880-1881	Portraits	—	—	2	—	—	—	—	—	—	1	3
Heaton, Butler, and Bayne	London	1884-1893	Architecture	—	—	8	—	—	—	—	—	—	—	8
Heaviside, J.	London	1838-1839	Figures	—	—	—	1	2	—	—	—	—	—	3
Hébert, Antoine Auguste Ernest	London	1871	Figures	—	—	1	—	—	—	—	—	—	—	1
Hebert, W. J.	London	1823-1827	Fruit	—	—	2	—	4	—	—	—	—	—	6
Hecht, Henri van der	London	1885	Landscape	—	—	—	—	1	—	—	—	—	—	1
Hecht, William	Munich	1883	Etching	—	—	2	—	—	—	—	—	—	—	2
Heckstall-Smith, Miss Edith. *See* S.	—	—	—	—	—	—	—	—	—	—	—	—	—	—
Hedgeland, J.	London	1822-1823	Architecture	—	—	3	—	—	—	—	—	—	—	3
Hedger, F.	London	1853	Landscape	—	—	1	—	—	—	—	—	—	—	1

Name.	Town.	First and Last Year of Ex.	Speciality.	S. A.	F. S.	R. A.	B. I.	S. S.	O. W.	N. W.	G. G.	N. G.	V. E.	Total.
Hedger, W.	London	1827	Architecture	—	—	1	—	—	—	—	—	—	—	1
Hedland, Miss Margaret	London	1891	Domestic	—	—	—	—	—	—	—	—	—	2	2
Hedley, Ralph	Newcastle	1879-1893	Domestic	—	—	21	—	—	—	6	—	—	—	27
Hedouin, Edmond	Paris	1875	Etching	—	—	—	—	—	—	—	—	—	1	1
Heemskerck, E. van (Van Beest)	The Hague	1873-1886	Sea Pieces	—	—	—	—	1	—	1	—	—	—	2
Heffer, Edward A.	Liverpool	1862-1885	Architecture	—	—	8	—	—	—	—	—	—	—	8
Heffernan, James §	London	1816-1837	Sculpture	—	—	24	6	12	—	—	—	—	—	42
Heffner, Carl, *or* Karl	London	1880-1888	Landscape	—	—	2	—	—	—	—	1	—	—	3
Hegg, Madame Térésa, R.I. ‡. *See* Mdlle. de Lauderset	—	—	—	—	—	—	—	—	—	—	—	—	—	—
	Vevay	1872-1893	Flowers	—	—	—	—	—	—	30	—	—	2	32
Heideloff, N.	London	1810	Architecture	—	—	1	—	—	—	—	—	—	—	1
Heidemanns, H. P.	London	1845-1864	Portraits	—	—	5	—	—	—	—	—	—	—	5
Heigel, F. N.	Munich	1866	Portraits	—	—	—	—	1	—	—	—	—	1	2
Heighway, Richard	London	1787-1793	Domestic	—	—	5	—	—	—	—	—	—	—	5
Heilbuth, Ferdinand	London	1871-1878	Landscape	—	—	2	—	—	—	—	17	—	—	19
Heine, E.	—	1863	Flowers	—	—	1	—	—	—	—	—	—	—	1
Heins, D.	London	1768-1779	Miniatures	3	1	—	—	—	—	—	—	—	—	4
Heitland, Mrs. H.	Crouch Hill	1889-1893	Portraits	—	—	—	—	1	—	2	—	—	1	4
Heitland, J.	Crouch End	1873	Figures	—	—	—	—	—	—	1	—	—	—	1
Helcké, Arnold	Guernsey	1865-1893	Sea Pieces	—	—	21	—	46	—	3	8	10	21	109
Helcké, Miss Laura	Bournemouth	1890	Flowers	—	—	—	—	—	—	—	—	—	1	1
Helfricht, Emil.	London	1883	Medals	—	—	1	—	—	—	—	—	—	—	1
Helga, Baroness. *See* Cramm.	—	—	—	—	—	—	—	—	—	—	—	—	—	—
Helie, G.	London	1875	River Scenes	—	—	—	—	1	—	—	—	—	—	1
Hellicar, Evelyn	London	1891	Architecture	—	—	1	—	—	—	—	—	—	—	1
Hellyer, T.	Ryde	1846-1862	Architecture	—	—	8	—	—	—	—	—	—	—	8
Helmick, Howard §	London	1872-1887	Domestic	—	—	19	—	9	—	—	—	—	14	42
Helmore, Rev. Thomas	London	1885	Landscape	—	—	—	—	—	—	1	—	—	—	1
Hely, E. R.	London	1850	Landscape	—	—	—	1	—	—	—	—	—	—	1
Heming, Matilda	London	1847-1855	Portraits	—	—	4	—	—	—	—	—	—	—	4
Heming, Mrs.	—	1820	Portraits	—	—	1	—	—	—	—	—	—	—	1
Heming, Miss	London	1821	Portraits	—	—	1	—	—	—	—	—	—	—	1
Hemingway, A.	Roehampton	1884	Churches	—	—	1	—	—	—	—	—	—	—	1
Hemming, Alfred O.	London	1889-1891	Stained Glass	—	—	4	—	—	—	—	—	—	—	4
Hemming, Miss Fanny	London	1885	Landscape	—	—	1	—	—	—	—	—	—	—	1
Hemming, Miss S. L.	London	1851	Figures	—	—	—	—	1	—	—	—	—	—	1
Hemming, Mrs. W. B.	London	1853-1877	Landscape	—	—	5	5	8	—	—	—	—	—	18
Hemmings, Frederick	London	1888-1889	Architecture	—	—	3	—	—	—	—	—	—	—	3
Hemmings (F.) and Delissa (J.)	London	1887	Architecture	—	—	1	—	—	—	—	—	—	—	1
Hemsley, H.	London	1785-1822	Architecture	—	—	10	—	—	—	—	—	—	—	10
Hemsley, William, R.B.A. §	London	1848-1893	Domestic	—	—	20	28	163	—	1	—	—	30	242
Hemsley, Walter Howard	London	1868-1870	Fruit	—	—	—	—	2	—	—	—	—	—	2
Hemy, Bernard Benedict	North Shields	1875-1877	Sea Pieces	—	—	—	—	2	—	—	—	—	2	4
Hemy, Charles Napier, A.R.W.S., R.I. † ‡ φ	London	1863-1893	Landscape	—	—	40	1	23	27	5	28	18	54	196
Hemy, M. W., *or* W. M.	London	1868	Venice	—	—	—	—	—	—	—	—	—	1	1
Hemy, Thomas Marie Madawaska	North Shields	1873-1893	Sea Pieces	—	—	15	—	9	—	7	4	—	21	56
Henard —	London	1785-1800	Miniatures	—	—	17	—	—	—	—	—	—	—	17
Henault —	London	1797	Domestic	—	—	3	—	—	—	—	—	—	—	3
Henderson —	Edinburgh	1785	Architecture	—	—	1	—	—	—	—	—	—	—	1
Henderson, A., *or* H.	London	1888	Landscape	—	—	—	—	—	—	1	—	—	—	1
Henderson, Miss A.	London	1853-1861	Figures	—	—	—	4	1	—	—	—	—	—	5
Henderson, Miss C.	London	1850-1854	Landscape	—	—	—	3	4	—	—	—	—	—	7
Henderson, Charles Cooper	London	1840-1848	Coachings	—	—	2	—	—	—	—	—	—	—	2
Henderson, D., *or* B.	London	1832	Churches	—	—	—	—	1	—	—	—	—	—	1
Henderson, Colonel E., R.E.	London	1865	Cairo	—	—	—	—	—	—	—	—	—	1	1
Henderson, E. M.	London	1815-1816	Landscape	—	—	3	—	—	—	—	—	—	—	3
Henderson, G. J.	—	1808	Figures	—	—	1	—	—	—	—	—	—	—	1
Henderson, George L.	London	1890	Etching	—	—	1	—	—	—	—	—	—	—	1
Henderson, J.	London	1782-1795	Sculpture	2	1	14	—	—	—	—	—	—	—	17
Henderson, J.	Edinburgh	1785	Architecture	—	—	1	—	—	—	—	—	—	—	1
Henderson, J.	Lancaster	1806-1825	Landscape	—	—	11	—	3	1	—	—	—	—	15
Henderson, John Morris	Glasgow	1892-1893	Landscape	—	—	1	—	—	—	—	—	1	—	2
Henderson, Joseph, R.S.W.	Glasgow	1871-1892	Domestic	—	—	20	—	4	—	—	—	1	6	31
Henderson, P.	London	1799-1829	Portraits	—	—	62	11	2	—	—	—	—	—	75
Henderson, R.	London	1854	Domestic	—	—	—	—	1	—	—	—	—	—	1
Henderson, Robert	London	1820-1830	Sculpture	—	—	11	2	—	—	—	—	—	—	13
Henderson, Robert	London	1883-1893	Miniatures	—	—	53	—	—	—	—	—	—	—	53
Henderson, W.	London	1817-1848	Fruit, etc.	—	—	3	—	4	—	—	—	—	—	7
Henderson, W.	—	1819	Landscape	—	—	1	—	—	—	—	—	—	—	1
Henderson, William	Whitby	1874-1892	Figures	—	—	—	—	9	—	—	—	—	1	10
Henderson, William	Bushey	1886-1892	Engraving	—	—	6	—	—	—	—	—	—	—	6

Name.	Town.	First and Last Year of Ex.	Speciality.	S. A.	F. S.	R. A.	B. I.	S. S.	O. W.	N.W.	G. G.	N. G.	V. E.	Total.
Henderson, Mrs. William	London	1816-1841	Mythological	—	—	11	8	2	—	—	—	—	—	21
Henderson, W. S. P.	London	1836-1874	Domestic	—	—	30	64	55	—	—	—	—	4	153
Henderson, Miss	—	1809-1810	Landscape	—	—	2	—	—	—	—	—	—	—	2
Hendley, G. E.	London	1886	Rustic	—	—	—	—	1	—	—	—	—	—	1
Hendrie, Robert	Eynsford	1867-1868	Sporting	—	—	1	—	—	—	—	—	—	1	2
Hendrix, J. Louis	Antwerp	1870	Scriptural	—	—	—	—	—	—	—	—	—	1	1
Heneker, R. W. *See also* Lawford and Heneker	London	1846-1849	Architecture	—	—	3	—	—	—	—	—	—	—	3
Heness, A.	London	1858-1874	Sculpture	—	—	6	—	—	—	—	—	—	—	6
Henkes, Gerke	The Hague	1880-1884	Domestic	—	—	—	—	—	—	3	3	—	—	6
Henkley, Henry	London	1886	Buildings	—	—	—	—	—	—	1	—	—	—	1
Henley, A. W.	London	1880-1881	Landscape	—	—	—	—	—	—	—	1	—	2	3
Henley, J.	London	1836-1843	Landscape	—	—	1	1	2	—	—	—	—	—	4
Henley, Lionel Charles, R.B.A. §	London	1862-1893	Domestic	—	—	10	3	124	—	—	—	—	8	145
Henley, W. B.	Birmingham	1854-1856	Landscape	—	—	—	3	—	—	—	—	—	—	3
Henman, C. *See also* Alexander and Henman	Reading	1852-1853	Architecture	—	—	3	—	—	—	—	—	—	—	3
Henman, Charles, Junr. *See also* Smith and	—	—	—	—	—	—	—	—	—	—	—	—	—	—
Henman	London	1862-1892	Architecture	—	—	2	—	—	—	—	—	—	—	2
Henman, William	Stockton-on-Tees	1877-1893	Architecture	—	—	2	—	—	—	—	—	—	—	2
Henman and Harrison	London	1862	Architecture	—	—	1	—	—	—	—	—	—	—	1
Hennessy, William J., N.A.	London	1871-1893	Landscape	—	—	16	—	2	—	—	24	5	16	63
Henning. *See* Potts, Sulman and Henning, *and*	—	—	—	—	—	—	—	—	—	—	—	—	—	—
Hooker and Henning	—	—	Architecture	—	—	—	—	—	—	—	—	—	—	—
Henning, A. S.	London	1825-1834	Figures	—	—	1	3	19	—	—	—	—	—	23
Henning, John §	London	1812-1835	Sculpture	—	—	20	—	35	—	—	—	—	—	55
Henning, John, Junr. §	London	1816-1852	Sculpture	—	—	17	8	37	—	—	—	—	—	62
Henning, Samuel §	London	1824-1832	Sculpture	—	—	6	2	10	—	—	—	—	—	18
Henning, Walton G.	London	1865-1887	Portraits	—	—	6	—	—	—	—	—	—	—	6
Henning, Mrs.	London	1854	Portraits	—	—	1	—	—	—	—	—	—	—	1
Henri, Lucien	Sydney	1887	Flowers	—	—	1	—	—	—	—	—	—	—	1
Henry, Charles	Brighton	1832	Landscape	—	—	—	1	—	—	—	—	—	—	1
Henry, Edward L., N.A.	London	1875-1879	Sporting	—	—	1	—	2	—	—	—	—	—	3
Henry, Francis A.	London	1883-1887	Landscape	—	—	2	—	1	—	—	—	—	—	3
Henry, George, A.R.S.A.	Glasgow	1887-1892	Historical	—	—	—	—	1	—	—	1	—	1	3
Henry, James L.	London	1877-1893	Landscape	—	—	16	—	27	—	1	1	—	29	74
Henry, William	London	1847-1883	Venice	—	—	13	13	66	—	—	—	—	17	109
Hensel, Wilhelm	—	1839	Scriptural	—	—	—	2	—	—	—	—	—	—	2
Henshall, J.	London	1848-1863	Buildings	—	—	5	15	2	—	—	—	—	48	70
Henshall, John Henry, A.R.W.S. †	London	1878-1893	Figures	—	—	16	—	9	44	1	—	—	9	79
Henshaw, Miss Emily	—	1839	Portraits	—	—	1	—	—	—	—	—	—	—	1
Henshaw, Frederick Henry	London	1829-1864	Landscape	—	—	38	46	27	—	—	—	—	1	112
Henshaw, William	London	1775	Portraits	—	—	2	—	—	—	—	—	—	—	2
Hensman, Frank H.	Windsor	1890	Landscape	—	—	1	—	—	—	—	—	—	—	1
Hensman, Miss Rosa Fryer	London	1886-1893	Domestic	—	—	—	—	6	—	—	—	—	3	9
Hensman, Walter	London	1876-1891	Decorations	—	—	9	—	—	—	—	—	—	—	9
Henton, George Moore	Leicester	1884-1893	Churches	—	—	2	—	—	—	10	—	—	1	13
Henzell, Isaac §	London	1854-1875	Domestic	—	—	7	3	61	—	—	—	—	—	71
Hepburn, Mrs. Blanche	London	1891	Domestic	—	—	—	—	—	—	—	—	—	1	1
Hepper, G.	London	1866-1868	Animals	—	—	—	3	2	—	—	—	—	—	5
Hepworth, Walter	London	1885-1886	Landscape	—	—	1	—	2	—	1	1	—	1	6
Herbert —.	—	1783	Landscape	—	—	1	—	—	—	—	—	—	—	1
Herbert, Alfred	London	1844-1860	Sea Pieces	—	—	14	3	26	—	—	—	—	—	43
Herbert, Arthur John	London	1855-1856	Historical	—	—	2	—	—	—	—	—	—	—	2
Herbert, C.	London	1822	Architecture	—	—	1	—	—	—	—	—	—	—	1
Herbert, Cyril Wiseman	London	1870-1875	Domestic	—	—	5	—	—	—	—	—	—	—	5
Herbert, Frank	London	1857-1866	Figures	—	—	1	1	—	—	—	—	—	—	2
Herbert, J. D.	London	1832-1835	Portraits	—	—	6	—	—	—	—	—	—	—	6
Herbert, John Rogers, R.A., H.R.I. ‡	London	1830-1889	Scriptural	—	—	102	26	7	—	4	—	—	1	140
Herbert, R.	Leatherhead	1892-1893	Landscape	—	—	—	—	2	—	—	—	—	—	2
Herbert, Sydney	Cheltenham	1865-1887	Sea Pieces	—	—	—	—	1	—	4	—	—	—	5
Herbert, T.	Malvern	1868-1870	Landscape	—	—	—	—	6	—	—	—	—	—	6
Herbert, W.	London	1824	Flowers	—	—	—	1	—	—	—	—	—	—	1
Herbert, Wilfrid V.	London	1863-1891	Domestic	—	—	27	—	—	—	—	—	—	3	30
Herbst, G.	—	1800	Portraits	—	—	2	—	—	—	—	—	—	—	2
Herbst, Miss	—	1801	Portraits	—	—	1	—	—	—	—	—	—	—	1
Herbsthoffer, Charles	Manchester	1853	Domestic	—	—	1	—	—	—	—	—	—	—	1
Herdman, Duddington	Edinburgh	1888-1893	Domestic	—	—	7	—	—	—	—	—	—	—	7
Herdman, Miss Maud	Tyrone	1891-1892	Portraits	—	—	3	—	—	—	—	—	—	—	3
Herdman, Robert, R.S.A., R.S.W.	Edinburgh	1861-1887	Domestic	—	—	38	2	—	—	—	—	—	—	40
Herdman, William Gawin	Liverpool	1834-1861	Buildings	—	—	5	—	1	—	—	—	—	—	6
Hereford, E.	Greenock	1884-1888	Venice	—	—	—	—	—	—	2	—	—	—	2
Herford, Miss A. Laura	London	1861-1869	Figures	—	—	6	1	6	—	—	—	—	3	16
Hering, A. G.	London	1826	Landscape	—	—	1	—	—	—	—	—	—	—	1

Name.	Town.	First and Last Year of Ex.	Speciality.	S. A.	F. S.	R. A.	B. I.	S. S.	O. W.	N. W.	G. G.	N. G.	V. E.	Total.
Hering, F.	London	1825-1836	Architecture	—	—	5	—	—	—	—	—	—	—	5
Hering, George Edwards	London	1836-1880	Landscape	—	—	88	86	10	—	—	—	—	11	195
Hering, Mrs. G. E.	London	1853-1858	Landscape	—	—	6	3	—	—	—	—	—	—	9
Heriot, G.	London	1797	Landscape	—	—	3	—	—	—	—	—	—	—	3
Herklots, Rev. Gerard Andreas	London	1878	Landscape	—	—	—	—	2	—	—	—	—	—	2
Herkomer, Miss Bertha	Watford	1889-1890	Flowers	—	—	—	—	—	—	—	—	—	2	2
Herkomer, Herman G. φ	London	1883-1893	Portraits	—	—	12	—	5	—	—	1	9	33	60
Herkomer, Professor Hubert, R.A., A.R.W.S., R.I., R.P.E.† ‡ φ	Southampton	1868-1893	Figures	—	—	87	—	2	4	47	45	17	45	247
Herkomer, Lorenz, Senr.	Southampton	1872	Figures	—	—	—	—	—	—	—	—	—	1	1
Herman, Ludwig	London	1862-1873	Landscape	—	—	1	—	—	—	—	—	—	9	10
Herman, R. W.	London	1847	Landscape	—	—	—	1	—	—	—	—	—	—	1
Hermann, H.	London	1858-1859	Domestic	—	—	5	—	—	—	—	—	—	—	5
Hermon and Wontner	London	1841-1842	Architecture	—	—	2	—	—	—	—	—	—	—	2
Hermstin, O.	London	1880	Landscape	—	—	1	—	—	—	—	—	—	—	1
Hern, Charles E.	London	1884-1893	Landscape	—	—	5	—	6	—	8	—	—	—	19
Hernan, Van. *See* V.	—	—	—	—	—	—	—	—	—	—	—	—	—	—
Héroult, H.	London	1838	Domestic	—	—	—	—	2	—	—	—	—	—	2
Héroult, Mrs.	London	1838	Landscape	—	—	1	—	—	—	—	—	—	—	1
Herrick, William Salter	London	1852-1880	Figures	—	—	34	7	—	—	—	—	—	—	41
Herries, H.	—	1855	Eastern	—	—	1	—	—	—	—	—	—	—	1
Herries, H. C.	London	1865-1873	Landscape	—	—	—	—	1	—	—	—	—	25	26
Herring, Benjamin	Tonbridge	1861-1863	Sporting	—	—	—	4	2	—	—	—	—	—	6
Herring, C.	London	1842	Animals	—	—	—	—	1	—	—	—	—	—	1
Herring, F.	London	1826	Churches	—	—	—	—	1	—	—	—	—	—	1
Herring, John Frederick	London	1818-1868	Sporting	—	—	22	44	82	—	—	—	—	19	167
Herring, John Frederick, Junr.	London	1860-1875	Sporting	—	—	3	10	53	—	—	—	—	4	70
Herring, Mrs. J. F. (K.) ‖	London	1852-1866	Domestic	—	—	1	—	1	—	—	—	—	—	2
Herrington, Fred. W.	London	1882-1890	Still Life	—	—	—	—	1	—	1	—	—	—	2
Herron, G.	—	1810-1826	Buildings	—	—	4	—	1	—	—	—	—	—	5
Hertel, A.	London	1879	Landscape	—	—	—	—	—	—	—	3	—	—	3
Hertford, Mrs. A.	West Malvern	1863-1868	Figures	—	—	—	4	5	—	—	—	—	1	10
Hervé, A.	London	1841-1843	Portraits	—	—	3	—	—	—	—	—	—	—	3
Hervé, C. S.	London	1828-1858	Portraits	—	—	28	—	1	—	—	—	—	—	29
Hervé, E.	—	1811	—	—	—	*	—	—	—	—	—	—	—	—
Hervé, F.	London	1818-1840	Miniatures	—	—	29	—	—	—	—	—	—	—	29
Hervé, H.	London	1813-1843	Miniatures	—	—	10	—	—	—	—	—	—	—	10
Hervé, Mrs. Margaret	London	1783-1816	Miniatures	2	—	12	—	—	—	—	—	—	—	14
Hervé, P.	London	1802-1820	Miniatures	—	—	11	—	—	—	—	—	—	—	11
Hervé, Rosa	London	1837	Portraits	—	—	1	—	—	—	—	—	—	—	1
Hervieu, Aug.	London	1819-1858	Figures	—	—	31	3	13	—	—	—	—	—	47
Hervy, Leslie	Bedford	1893	Flowers	—	—	—	—	1	—	—	—	—	—	1
Heselden, W. S.	—	1800	Landscape	—	—	1	—	—	—	—	—	—	—	1
Heseltine, Arthur	London	1879-1880	Landscape	—	—	—	—	—	—	—	—	—	3	3
Heseltine, John Postle, R.P.E.	London	1869-1893	Etching	—	—	27	—	—	—	—	—	—	4	31
Heseltine, W.	London	1799-1805	Portraits	—	—	7	—	—	—	—	—	—	—	7
Hesketh, Robert	London	1841-1891	Architecture	—	—	8	—	—	—	—	—	—	—	8
Hester, Edward Gilbert	Chiswick	1882-1893	Engraving	—	—	12	—	—	—	—	—	—	—	12
Hetherington, Ivystan	London	1875-1893	Landscape	—	—	13	—	4	—	—	7	7	22	53
Hetling, M.	—	1809	Landscape	—	—	1	—	—	—	—	—	—	—	1
Heuhan, J.	Glasgow	1810-1813	Portraits	—	—	4	—	—	—	—	—	—	—	4
Heureun, L'. *See* L.	—	—	—	—	—	—	—	—	—	—	—	—	—	—
Heurteloup —, *or* Heurtelope	—	1876	Landscape	—	—	—	—	1	—	—	—	—	—	1
Heuss —	Germany	1842-1844	Portraits	—	—	3	—	—	—	—	—	—	—	3
Hewet, J.	London	1824	Portraits	—	—	—	—	1	—	—	—	—	—	1
Hewetson, Miss Edith	London	1893	Landscape	—	—	—	—	—	—	—	—	—	1	1
Hewetson, Edward	Cannes	1889	Landscape	—	—	1	—	—	—	—	—	—	—	1
Hewett, G.	London	1823-1828	Portraits	—	—	2	—	3	—	—	—	—	—	5
Hewett, Sir Prescott Gardiner, F.R.S., H.R.W.S. †	London	1877-1890	Landscape	—	—	—	—	—	16	—	4	—	—	20
Hewett, Miss Sarah F.	Leamington	1851-1883	Domestic	—	—	1	—	1	—	1	—	—	12	15
Hewett, T.	—	1813	Landscape	—	—	1	—	—	—	—	—	—	—	1
Hewins, Alfred J.	Wolv'rhampton	1891	Landscape	—	—	1	—	—	—	—	—	—	—	1
Hewitson, Christopher	Rome	1786-1790	Sculpture	—	—	2	—	—	—	—	—	—	—	2
Hewitt, Alice J.	St. Leonards	1888	Historical	—	—	—	—	1	—	—	—	—	1	2
Hewitt, Alfred E.	Guernsey	1891	Architecture	—	—	1	—	—	—	—	—	—	—	1
Hewitt, Miss Beatrice M.	London	1884-1893	Portraits	—	—	7	—	—	—	3	—	—	—	10
Hewitt, H.	Bristol	1845-1870	Landscape	—	—	2	8	4	—	—	—	—	—	14
Hewitt, Henry George, R.B.A. §	London	1884-1893	Landscape	—	—	3	—	3	—	—	—	—	1	7
Hewitt, T.	London	1836	Churches	—	—	1	—	—	—	—	—	—	—	1
Hewitt, Miss	Fowey	1834	Flowers	—	—	—	—	—	—	4	—	—	—	4
Hewkley, Henry	London	1890-1893	Landscape	—	—	1	—	2	—	—	—	—	—	3

Name.	Town.	First and Last Year of Ex.	Speciality.	S. A.	F. S.	R. A.	B. I.	S. S.	O. W.	N.W.	G. G.	N. G.	V. E.	Total.
Hewlett, Arthur L.	Bushey	1889-1893	Domestic	—	—	2	—	—	—	—	—	—	—	2
Hewlett, D.	London	1847-1860	Sculpture	—	—	3	1	9	—	—	—	—	—	13
Hewlett, James	Bath	1799-1828	Flowers	—	—	15	7	4	11	—	—	—	16	53
Hewson, Stephen	London	1775-1805	Miniatures	18	16	52	—	—	—	—	—	—	—	86
Hewson, Miss	—	1789	Portraits	—	—	1	—	—	—	—	—	—	—	1
Heydemann, Willie	London	1886-1890	Etching	—	—	6	—	—	—	—	—	—	—	6
Heyden, W.	London	1866	Domestic	—	—	1	—	—	—	—	—	—	—	1
Heydendhall, C.	London	1881	Landscape	—	—	—	—	—	—	—	—	—	1	1
Heydendhal, J.	London	1879-1881	Military	—	—	2	—	1	—	—	—	—	—	3
Heyermans, John A. (?) H.	Antwerp	1874-1883	Domestic	—	—	1	—	—	—	—	3	—	1	5
Heyes, Austin. *See* Whelan and Heyes	—	—	Architecture	—	—	—	—	—	—	—	—	—	—	—
Heywood, Tom	Oldham	1880	Domestic	—	—	—	—	—	—	—	—	—	1	1
Heyworth, R.	London	1890	Landscape	—	—	—	—	—	—	—	—	—	1	1
Hiaktake, Y.	London	1876	Landscape	—	—	1	—	—	—	—	—	—	—	1
Hibbert, Miss	London	1836-1840	Miniatures	—	—	8	—	2	—	—	—	—	—	10
Hickel, Karl Anton	London	1778-1796	Domestic	3	1	15	—	—	—	—	—	—	—	19
Hickey, John (?) Noah	London	1777-1794	Sculpture	—	—	18	—	—	—	—	—	—	—	18
Hickey, Thomas	London	1772-1792	Portraits	—	—	16	—	—	—	—	—	—	—	16
Hickin, George	Greenwich	1858-1877	Still Life	—	—	7	6	24	—	—	—	—	26	63
Hickin, G. A.	Birmingham	1880	Landscape	—	—	1	—	—	—	—	—	—	—	1
Hickman, Miss Evelyn	St. Leonards	1891	Landscape	—	—	1	—	—	—	—	—	—	—	1
Hicks, Albert S.	Sydenham	1885	Domestic	—	—	1	—	—	—	—	—	—	—	1
Hicks, George Elgar, R.B.A. §	London	1847-1892	Domestic	—	—	112	12	26	—	—	5	—	8	163
Hicks, George Matthew	Ostend	1854-1856	Landscape	—	—	3	2	1	—	—	—	—	—	6
Hicks, James	Redruth	1876-1878	Architecture	—	—	3	—	—	—	—	—	—	—	3
Hicks, Jane	London	1837-1839	Landscape	—	—	—	—	5	—	—	—	—	—	5
Hicks, Julian	London	1865	Landscape	—	—	—	1	—	—	—	—	—	—	1
Hicks, Lilburne ‡	London	1830-1860	Domestic	—	—	10	2	6	—	59	—	—	—	77
Hicks, Miss Mary	Colchester	1890	Game	—	—	—	—	1	—	—	—	—	—	1
Hicks, Miss Minnie J.	Hendon	1892	Domestic	—	—	1	—	1	—	—	—	—	—	2
Hickson, Miss Annie W.	London	1886-1891	Flowers	—	—	2	—	—	—	1	—	—	—	3
Hickson, Miss Margaret	London	1879-1892	Still Life	—	—	7	—	7	—	4	—	1	6	25
Hier, Van. *See* V.	—	—	—	—	—	—	—	—	—	—	—	—	—	—
Hiffin, E. A.	London	1855	Architecture	—	—	1	—	—	—	—	—	—	—	1
Higgin, W.	—	1786	Portraits	—	—	1	—	—	—	—	—	—	—	1
Higgins, Miss C.	Venice	1873-1882	Landscape	—	—	1	—	3	—	—	—	—	—	4
Higgins, V.	—	1838	Landscape	—	—	1	—	—	—	—	—	—	—	1
Higgins, W.	London	1811	Portraits	—	—	1	—	—	—	—	—	—	—	1
Higgins, Wayman	Bath	1862-1863	Landscape	—	—	—	1	2	—	—	—	—	—	3
Higgins, William A. A.	Birmingham	1891-1893	Landscape	—	—	2	—	—	—	—	—	—	—	2
Higginson, Miss May	Torquay	1888-1892	Flowers	—	—	2	—	2	—	—	—	—	—	4
Higgs —	London	1774	Mythological	1	—	—	—	—	—	—	—	—	—	1
Higgs, Miss Madeleine	Barnet	1886	Still Life	—	—	1	—	—	—	—	—	—	1	2
Higham, J. W.	Norwich	1821-1835	Enamels	—	—	17	—	12	—	1	—	—	—	30
Higham, Thomas	London	1824-1830	Engraving	—	—	—	—	4	—	—	—	—	—	4
Highmore, Joseph	—	1760-1761	Portraits	3	2	—	—	—	—	—	—	—	—	5
Higs, R.	London	1786-1796	Enamels	—	—	11	—	—	—	—	—	—	—	11
Higton, T.	London	1801-1815	Sporting	—	—	15	—	—	—	—	—	—	—	15
Hildebrand, A.	London	1879-1886	Sculpture	—	—	1	—	—	—	—	1	—	—	2
Hildebrandt, Edouard	London	1848	Landscape	—	—	1	1	—	—	—	—	—	—	2
Hilder, P. John	London	1829-1839	Landscape	—	—	9	14	14	—	—	—	—	—	37
Hilder, Richard	London	1830-1851	Landscape	—	—	22	29	37	—	—	—	—	—	88
Hilditch, George	London	1823-1856	Landscape	—	—	73	89	82	—	—	—	—	—	244
Hilditch, Richard H.	London	1823-1865	Landscape	—	—	44	52	51	—	—	—	—	—	147
Hiles, Bartram	London	1893	Venice	—	—	—	—	1	—	—	—	—	—	1
Hiles, George	London	1892	Landscape	—	—	1	—	—	—	—	—	—	—	1
Hiles, Henry	Liscard	1888-1889	Architecture	—	—	2	—	—	—	—	—	—	—	2
Hill, Arthur, R.B.A. §	Nottingham	1858-1893	Figures	—	—	26	2	28	—	—	—	—	17	73
Hill, Alfred	Cork	1876	Architecture	—	—	1	—	—	—	—	—	—	—	1
Hill, A. C. E.	London	1888-1893	Domestic	—	—	—	—	2	—	—	—	—	1	3
Hill, Arthur G.	London	1880-1891	Architecture	—	—	2	—	—	—	—	—	—	—	2
Hill, Charles G.	London	1836	Still Life	—	—	—	1	1	—	—	—	—	—	2
Hill, Diana	—	1785	Miniatures	—	—	3	—	—	—	—	—	—	—	3
Hill, D. H.	London	1868-1871	Landscape	—	—	1	—	4	—	—	—	—	—	5
Hill, David Octavius, R.S.A.	Edinburgh	1832-1868	Landscape	—	—	4	1	2	—	—	—	—	1	8
Hill, Mrs. David Octavius, late Miss Amelia R. Paton	Edinburgh	1863-1874	Sculpture	—	—	18	—	—	—	—	—	—	—	18
Hill, Edith	—	1883	Sculpture	—	—	—	—	1	—	—	—	—	—	1
Hill, Miss Ellen G.	London	1864-1893	Figures	—	—	12	2	1	—	8	—	—	27	50
Hill, Fanny	Leamington	1879	Flowers	—	—	—	—	1	—	—	—	—	—	1
Hill, Henry	London	1813-1814	Figures	—	—	3	—	—	—	—	—	—	—	3

Name.	Town.	First and Last Year of Ex.	Speciality.	S. A.	F. S.	R. A.	B. I.	S. S.	O. W.	N.W.	G. G.	N. G.	V. E.	Total.
Hill, Mrs. Henry	London	1847	Landscape	—	—	—	1	—	—	—	—	—	—	1
Hill, J.	London	1775-1791	Miniatures	4	—	8	—	—	—	—	—	—	—	12
Hill, J.	London	1780-1825	Landscape	—	3	6	—	—	—	—	—	—	—	9
Hill, J.	London	1818	Architecture	—	—	1	—	—	—	—	—	—	—	1
Hill, James	London	1761-1770	Sculpture	11	—	—	—	—	—	—	—	—	—	11
Hill, James	London	1875	Landscape	—	—	—	—	1	—	—	—	—	—	1
Hill, Justus	London	1879-1891	Domestic	—	—	9	—	2	—	1	—	—	1	13
Hill, J. B.	Birmingham	1839-1850	Figures	—	—	2	1	2	—	—	—	—	—	5
Hill, Mrs. J. Gray (C. E.)	Birkenhead	1888-1889	Buildings	—	—	—	—	—	—	—	4	—	—	4
Hill, J. Henry	London	1865-1879	Landscape	—	—	—	—	1	—	—	—	—	1	2
Hill, James John §	London	1842-1881	Rustic Figures	—	—	10	5	122	—	—	—	—	—	137
Hill, James S. §	London	1875-1893	Landscape	—	—	8	—	31	—	1	1	—	18	59
Hill, Miss Kate	London	1845-1873	Landscape	—	—	—	—	6	—	—	—	—	1	7
Hill, Miss L. M.	London	1852-1854	Figures	—	—	1	2	1	—	—	—	—	—	4
Hill, Leonard Raven-	London	1885-1893	Domestic	—	—	3	—	4	—	5	3	—	8	23
Hill, Nathaniel, A.R.H.A.	London	1886-1893	Figures	—	—	—	—	—	—	—	—	—	4	4
Hill, Miss Nora	Hampstead	1867	Churches	—	—	—	—	—	—	—	—	—	1	1
Hill, R.	London	1863	Figures	—	—	—	—	1	—	—	—	—	—	1
Hill, Roland	London	1889-1890	Architecture	—	—	2	—	—	—	—	—	—	—	2
Hill, Thomas	London	1800-1822	Landscape	—	—	9	3	—	—	—	—	—	—	12
Hill, Thomas	London	1871-1893	Figures	—	—	13	—	9	—	—	—	1	8	31
Hill, Thomas Joseph	London	1855	Architecture	—	—	1	—	—	—	—	—	—	—	1
Hill, W. N.	London	1856	Architecture	—	—	1	—	—	—	—	—	—	—	1
Hill, William Robert	London	1859-1884	Landscape	—	—	—	4	—	—	—	—	—	2	6
Hill, St. *See* S.	—	—	—	—	—	—	—	—	—	—	—	—	—	—
Hill-Snowe, Miss Lilly	London	1880-1885	Domestic	—	—	1	—	—	—	—	—	—	1	2
Hilliard, Constance	Uxbridge	1877	Flowers	—	—	—	—	—	—	—	—	—	1	1
Hillard, S.	London	1847	Historical	—	—	—	1	—	—	—	—	—	—	1
Hilliar, J.	London	1808	Architecture	—	—	1	—	—	—	—	—	—	—	1
Hilliard, Lawrence	Uxbridge	1876-1887	Still Life	—	—	—	—	—	—	7	—	—	15	22
Hilliard, William Henry	Boston, U.S.A.	1880	Landscape	—	—	1	—	—	—	—	—	—	—	1
Hillier, Miss Harriet C.	London	1850-1857	Portraits	—	—	—	—	7	—	—	—	—	—	7
Hillingford, Robert Alexander	London	1864-1893	Historical	—	—	20	2	1	—	—	—	—	4	27
Hills, Gordon Macdonald	London	1860	Architecture	—	—	1	—	—	—	—	—	—	—	1
Hills, John	London	1766-1779	Seals	3	3	2	—	—	—	—	—	—	—	8
Hills, Robert †	London	1791-1844	Animals	—	—	44	2	—	600	—	—	—	—	646
Hills, Mrs. W.	Leyton	1870	Figures	—	—	—	—	1	—	—	—	—	—	1
Hills, Mrs.	London	1778	Stained Glass	3	—	—	—	—	—	—	—	—	—	3
Hills, Miss	—	1799	Flowers	—	—	2	—	—	—	—	—	—	—	2
Hillyard, H.	London	1833	Ruins	—	—	—	—	1	—	—	—	—	—	1
Hillyard, J. W.	London	1833-1861	Animals	—	—	—	1	7	—	—	—	—	—	8
Hilton, Henry	Trefrew	1880-1883	Landscape	—	—	4	—	1	—	—	—	—	—	5
Hilton, Miss Marie E.	London	1889	Still Life	—	—	1	—	—	—	—	—	—	—	1
Hilton, Robert	Cricklewood	1886	Landscape	—	—	1	—	2	—	—	—	—	—	3
Hilton, William	Nottingham	1777-1783	Portraits	3	—	1	—	—	—	—	—	—	—	4
Hilton, William, R.A.	London	1803-1839	Scriptural	—	—	31	20	1	—	—	—	—	—	52
Hime, Harry	Liverpool	1887-1892	Landscape	—	—	5	—	—	—	1	—	—	—	6
Hinchliff, C. H.	Dinan	1877	Figures	—	—	—	—	1	—	—	—	—	—	1
Hinchliff, John	London	1768-1772	Sculpture	2	—	—	—	—	—	—	—	—	—	2
Hinchliff, John Elley	London	1814-1849	Sculpture	—	—	36	9	—	—	—	—	—	—	45
Hinchliff, W.	London	1872	Landscape	—	—	—	—	1	—	—	—	—	—	1
Hinchliff, Miss	—	1811	Landscape	—	—	2	—	—	—	—	—	—	—	2
Hinchliffe, Major C. H.	Instow	1889	Landscape	—	—	—	—	—	—	2	—	—	—	2
Hinckley, Thomas Hewes	Boston, U.S.A.	1858	Dogs	—	—	2	—	—	—	—	—	—	—	2
Hincks, S. C.	Bagshot	1858-1867	Sporting	—	—	—	7	2	—	—	—	—	—	9
Hincks, William	London	1781-1797	Miniatures	—	1	23	—	—	—	—	—	—	—	24
Hind, Ellen Mary	London	1887-1889	Landscape	—	—	—	—	1	—	1	—	—	—	2
Hind, Frank	Leamington	1885-1893	Spanish	—	—	13	—	17	—	—	2	—	2	34
Hind, Miss M. A.	London	1845	Fruit	—	—	—	—	1	—	—	—	—	—	1
Hind, Miss P.	London	1844-1845	Fruit	—	—	2	—	1	—	—	—	—	—	3
Hind, Miss	London	1845	Fruit	—	—	—	—	1	—	—	—	—	—	1
Hindley, Godfrey C.	London	1876-1893	Flowers	—	—	28	—	9	—	1	—	—	20	58
Hindu Artist	—	1841	Historical	—	—	1	—	—	—	—	—	—	—	1
Hine, Miss Esther	London	1885	Study	—	—	—	—	—	—	1	—	—	—	1
Hine, George Thomas	Newton Abbot	1875-1890	Architecture	—	—	1	—	—	—	—	—	—	1	2
Hine, Harry, R.I. ‡ φ	London	1873-1893	Landscape	—	—	8	—	4	—	130	—	1	30	173
Hine, Mrs. Harry, A.R.P.E. *See* Miss Victoria	—	—	—	—	—	—	—	—	—	—	—	—	—	—
S. Colkett	St. Albans	1876-1893	Landscape	—	—	—	—	2	—	12	—	—	5	19
Hine, H. G.	Brighton	1830-1851	Sea Pieces	—	—	6	—	12	—	—	—	—	—	18
Hine, Henry George, V.P.R.I. ‡	London	1856-1893	Sea Pieces	—	—	2	—	4	—	306	—	—	1	313
Hine, Mary E.	London	1873	Figures	—	—	—	—	—	—	—	—	—	1	1
Hine, William Egerton	London	1873-1892	Landscape	—	—	2	—	8	—	6	—	4	12	32

Name.	Town.	First and Last Year of Ex.	Speciality.	S. A.	F. S.	R. A.	B. I.	S. S.	O. W.	N.W.	G. G.	N. G.	V. E.	Total.
Hine, Mrs. W. E	Dorking	1889	Landscape	—	—	—	—	—	—	1	—	—	—	1
Hines, Frederick	London	1875-1893	Landscape	—	—	14	—	48	—	3	2	—	8	75
Hines, Theodore	London	1876-1889	Landscape	—	—	7	—	32	—	—	1	—	9	49
Hinley, Alfred	Birmingham	1890	Buildings	—	—	1	—	—	—	—	—	—	—	1
Hinson, Miss Ethel Brooke	Beckingham	1886-1891	Domestic	—	—	4	—	—	—	—	—	—	—	4
Hinton, G.	London	1841	Enamels	—	—	1	—	—	—	—	—	—	—	1
Hinton, Miss	London	1776	Needlework	1	—	—	—	—	—	—	—	—	—	1
Hintz, Julius	London	1840	Sea Pieces	—	—	—	1	—	—	—	—	—	—	1
Hipkins, Miss Edith	London	1879-1885	Domestic	—	—	2	—	7	—	—	1	—	5	15
Hipsley, John Henry	London	1882-1892	Flowers	—	—	—	—	2	—	1	—	—	—	3
Hipwood, Miss Sarah	London	1868-1869	Fruit	—	—	—	—	2	—	—	—	—	—	2
Hird, W.	London	1867	Flowers	—	—	—	1	—	—	—	—	—	—	1
Hirst, Norman	Bushey	1890-1893	Engraving	—	—	3	—	—	—	—	—	—	—	3
Hiscocks, Alfred James	London	1836	Architecture	—	—	1	—	—	—	—	—	—	—	1
Hiscox, George D.	Slough	1879-1893	Landscape	—	—	14	—	18	—	8	—	1	9	50
Hiscox, Laura M.	Slough	1880-1884	Rustic	—	—	—	—	6	—	—	—	—	—	6
Hislop, Andrew	Glasgow	1889	Landscape	—	—	1	—	—	—	—	—	—	—	1
Hitch, J.	—	1874	Landscape	—	—	—	—	1	—	—	—	—	—	1
Hitch, N.	London	1884	Portraits	—	—	1	—	—	—	—	—	—	—	1
Hitchcock, Arthur	Balham	1884	Domestic	—	—	—	—	1	—	—	—	—	—	1
Hitchcock, George	London	1883-1892	Domestic	—	—	5	—	1	—	2	—	—	1	9
Hitchcock, J.	London	1790-1793	Portraits	—	—	4	—	—	—	—	—	—	—	4
Hitchcock, J. J.	London	1827-1829	Architecture	—	—	3	—	—	—	—	—	—	—	3
Hitchcock, Miss Kate	London	1884-1890	Domestic	—	—	2	—	1	—	2	—	—	5	10
Hitchcock, S.	London	1882	Landscape	—	—	—	—	—	—	—	—	—	1	1
Hitchens, Alfred	London	1884-1893	Domestic	—	—	6	—	—	—	—	2	—	4	12
Hitchings, E. G.	London	1829-1833	Landscape	—	—	2	1	1	—	—	—	—	—	4
Hitchings, Miss Henrietta C.	Wargrave	1856-1858	Landscape	—	—	2	—	3	—	—	—	—	2	7
Hitchings, J.	London	1860-1870	Rustic	—	—	—	—	16	—	—	—	—	—	16
Hitchins, John	London	1865-1874	Landscape	—	—	1	—	—	—	—	—	—	9	10
Hitchins, John B.	London	1873-1876	Sea Pieces	—	—	—	—	4	—	—	—	—	2	6
Hitz, Miss Dora	London	1890	Domestic	—	—	1	—	—	—	—	—	—	—	1
Hixon, J.	London	1825	Cattle	—	—	—	—	2	—	—	—	—	—	2
Hixon, James Thompson ‡	London	1856-1867	Eastern	—	—	—	5	5	—	10	—	—	25	45
Hixon, W.	—	1824	Engraving	—	—	—	—	5	—	—	—	—	—	5
Hixon, W. J.	London	1825-1857	Cattle	—	—	4	10	13	—	—	—	—	26	53
Hoare, Rev. Arthur M.	Southampton	1871-1872	Landscape	—	—	—	—	1	—	—	—	—	1	2
Hoare, George T.	Slough	1888-1891	Landscape	—	—	2	—	—	—	—	—	—	2	4
Hoare, Prince	London	1781-1815	Historical	—	—	13	—	—	—	—	—	—	—	13
Hoare, William, R.A.	Bath	1761-1783	Portraits	2	1	22	—	—	—	—	—	—	—	25
Hoare, Mrs.	—	1766	Historical	1	—	—	—	—	—	—	—	—	—	1
Hoare, Miss	Bath	1761-1764	Historical	1	4	—	—	—	—	—	—	—	—	5
Hobbs, Miss Katie	Bourton	1889-1892	Flowers	—	—	—	—	5	—	1	—	—	1	7
Hobcroft, John	London	1773-1778	Architecture	—	—	3	—	—	—	—	—	—	—	3
Hobday, H. H.	Birmingham	1830-1832	Sporting	—	—	1	4	5	—	—	—	—	—	10
Hobday, William Armfield	London	1794-1830	Miniatures	—	—	103	2	—	—	—	—	—	—	105
Hobden, Frank	London	1879-1893	Domestic	—	—	5	—	14	—	17	—	—	27	63
Hobley, Edward G.	—	1893	Domestic	—	—	1	—	—	—	—	—	—	—	1
Hobson, Miss Alice Mary, R.I. ‡	Leicester	1879-1893	Landscape	—	—	—	—	—	—	27	—	—	2	29
Hobson, Miss Ellen M.	London	1884	Landscape	—	—	—	—	—	—	1	—	—	—	1
Hobson, F. W.	London	1891	Landscape	—	—	—	—	1	—	—	—	—	—	1
Hobson, G.	Bath	1862	Landscape	—	—	—	—	2	—	—	—	—	—	2
Hobson, Henry E.	Bath	1857-1866	Figures	—	—	1	2	—	—	—	—	—	—	3
Hobson, Miss Mabel E.	London	1889-1893	Miniatures	—	—	17	—	—	—	—	—	—	—	17
Hobson, W.	London	1801	Architecture	—	—	1	—	—	—	—	—	—	—	1
Hock, Daniel	Vienna	1890-1893	Domestic	—	—	2	—	—	—	—	—	—	—	2
Hodder, Albert	Worcester	1872-1890	Sea Pieces	—	—	8	—	1	—	2	—	—	1	12
Hodder, Mrs. Charlotte	Worcester	1883	Flowers	—	—	1	—	—	—	—	—	—	—	1
Hodge —	London	1765-1775	Miniatures	7	3	—	—	—	—	—	—	—	—	10
Hodge, Miss E. G.	London	1886-1887	Flowers	—	—	—	—	—	—	—	—	—	3	3
Hodge, H. *See also* Butler and Hodge	London	1847	Architecture	—	—	1	—	—	—	—	—	—	—	1
Hodge, Miss Ina	London	1888	Flowers	—	—	1	—	1	—	—	—	—	—	2
Hodge, R. P.	London	1769-1780	Fruit	—	12	—	—	—	—	—	—	—	—	12
Hodges, Charles Howard	London	1768-1783	Miniatures	1	1	—	—	—	—	—	—	—	—	2
Hodges, E.	London	1844-1846	Sea Pieces	—	—	—	—	6	—	—	—	—	—	6
Hodges, Ernest	Groombridge	1888-1893	Portraits	—	—	1	—	—	—	—	—	—	4	5
Hodges, Miss Florence M.	London	1890	Churches	—	—	1	—	—	—	—	—	—	—	1
Hodges, J. Sydney	Liverpool	1854-1893	Portraits	—	—	35	8	4	—	—	2	—	1	50
Hodges, Miss Mary Anne E.	London	1851-1852	Domestic	—	—	2	—	—	—	—	—	—	—	2
Hodges, William, R.A., F.S.A.	London	1766-1794	Landscape	24	7	74	—	—	—	—	—	—	—	105
Hodges, W	London	1824	Portraits	—	—	1	—	—	—	—	—	—	—	1
Hodges, W. J.	London	1853	Sketch	—	—	—	1	—	—	—	—	—	—	1

Name.	Town.	First and Last Year of Ex.	Speciality.	S. A.	F. S.	R. A.	B. I.	S. S.	O.W.	N.W.	G.G.	N. G.	V. E.	Total.
Hodgeson, E.	London	1780-1788	Flowers	—	—	7	—	—	—	—	—	—	—	7
Hodgetts, R. M.	London	1826	Domestic	—	—	—	—	1	—	—	—	—	—	1
Hodgetts T.	London	1801-1846	Landscape & Engraving	—	—	10	2	11	—	—	—	—	—	23
Hodgkin, John Eliot, F.S.A.	Liverpool	1874	Etching	—	—	—	—	—	—	—	—	—	4	4
Hodgins, Henry, F.S.A.	London	1778-1783	Landscape	4	—	—	—	—	—	—	—	—	—	4
Hodgkins, Thomas F.	London	1835-1875	Landscape	—	—	3	4	6	—	—	—	—	2	15
Hodgkins, Miss. *See* Mrs. Grace.	—	—	—	—	—	—	—	—	—	—	—	—	—	—
Hodgkinson, Edward	Chester	1885-1887	Architecture	—	—	3	—	—	—	—	—	—	—	3
Hodgskinson, J.	London	1774-1786	Architecture	—	12	3	—	—	—	—	—	—	—	15
Hodgson, Charles	Norwich	1802-1824	Buildings	—	—	4	1	—	—	—	—	—	—	5
Hodgson, David	Norwich	1818-1864	Landscape	—	—	1	27	11	—	—	—	—	—	39
Hodgson, Mrs. Dora	London	1885	Fruit	—	—	—	—	—	—	—	—	—	1	1
Hodgson, Edward, F.S.A.	London	1762-1791	Flowers	5	59	—	—	—	—	—	—	—	—	64
Hodgson, Sir George	—	1838	Landscape	—	—	1	—	—	—	—	—	—	—	1
Hodgson, George	Nottingham	1886	Fruit	—	—	1	—	—	—	—	—	—	—	1
Hodgson, J.	Bury St. Edm'ds	1874	Landscape	—	—	1	—	1	—	—	—	—	—	2
Hodgson, John Evan, R.A., H.F.R.P.E.	London	1856-1893	Domestic	—	—	90	4	1	—	—	—	—	45	140
Hodgson, W.	London	1806-1812	Scriptural	—	—	1	1	—	—	—	—	—	—	2
Hodgson, W.	London	1838-1841	Horses	—	—	3	—	—	—	—	—	—	—	3
Hodgson, William J.	Scarborough	1878-1893	"Punch"	—	—	1	—	—	—	—	—	—	1	2
Hodgson, Miss	—	1770-1775	Flowers	—	5	—	—	—	—	—	—	—	—	5
Hodson, Shirley	London	1872-1882	Domestic	—	—	—	—	—	—	—	—	—	2	2
Hodson, Samuel John, R.W.S., R.B.A., R.C.A. § †	London	1858-1893	Domestic	—	—	13	1	19	90	—	—	—	16	139
Hodson, T.	London	1865	Domestic	—	—	—	—	2	—	—	—	—	—	2
Hoeterickx, E.	Paris	1881	Domestic	—	—	—	—	—	—	—	3	—	—	3
Hoff, Karl	Düsseldorf	1877	Figures	—	—	1	—	—	—	—	—	—	—	1
Hoffcauer, F.	London	1872	Historical	—	—	2	—	—	—	—	—	—	—	2
Hoffman, H. W.	London	1878-1880	Landscape	—	—	—	—	1	—	—	—	—	3	4
Hofland, Thomas Christopher §	Kew	1798-1843	Landscape	—	—	72	141	118	—	—	—	—	8	339
Hofland, Thomas Richard	Richmond	1844-1845	Landscape	—	—	—	2	—	—	—	—	—	—	2
Hog, James	—	1773	Portraits	—	2	—	—	—	—	—	—	—	—	2
Hogan, John	London	1833-1850	Sculpture	—	—	4	—	—	—	—	—	—	—	4
Hogarth —	—	1783	Dramatic	—	1	—	—	—	—	—	—	—	—	1
Hogarth, T. C.	London	1859	Landscape	—	—	—	1	—	—	—	—	—	—	1
Hogarth, William	London	1761	Domestic	5	—	—	—	—	—	—	—	—	—	5
Hogg, Herbert W.	Derby	1883-1885	Sculpture	—	—	5	—	—	—	—	—	—	—	5
Hogg, J.	London	1841-1844	Portraits	—	—	—	—	3	—	—	—	—	—	3
Hoghton, Miss de. *See* D.	—	—	—	—	—	—	—	—	—	—	—	—	—	—
Hogley, Stephen E.	Holmforth	1874-1881	Landscape	—	—	—	—	2	—	—	—	—	—	2
Hoguet, Charles	London	1869	Landscape	—	—	1	—	—	—	—	—	—	—	1
Hohenlohe-Langenburg, Prince Victor of.	—	—	—	—	—	—	—	—	—	—	—	—	—	—
See Count Gleichen	London	1890-1892	Sculpture	—	—	1	—	—	—	—	2	—	—	3
Hoisky, T. J.	London	1833	Portraits	—	—	—	—	1	—	—	—	—	—	1
Holbech, N. P.	London	1825	Portraits	—	—	1	—	—	—	—	—	—	—	1
Hold, Abel	Barnsley	1849-1871	Game	—	—	16	1	1	—	—	—	—	—	18
Holdby —	Reigate	1777	Landscape	6	—	—	—	—	—	—	—	—	—	6
Holden, Albert William	London	1881-1893	Domestic	—	—	2	—	11	—	—	—	—	2	15
Holden, E.	London	1840-1846	Landscape	—	—	—	—	7	—	—	—	—	—	7
Holden, J.	London	1843	Flowers	—	—	1	—	—	—	—	—	—	—	1
Holden, Miss Louisa Jane	London	1840-1843	Miniatures	—	—	6	—	—	—	—	—	—	—	6
Holden, Miss Margaret. *See* Mrs. Backhouse.	—	—	—	—	—	—	—	—	—	—	—	—	—	—
Holden, S.	Greenwich	1845-1847	Flowers	—	—	4	—	—	—	—	—	—	—	4
Holder, Miss Charlotte	London	1857-1860	Domestic	—	—	—	—	1	—	—	—	—	3	4
Holder, Edwin	Isleworth	1856-1864	Landscape	—	—	—	9	2	—	—	—	—	11	22
Holder, Edward Henry	Scarborough	1864-1893	Landscape	—	—	6	1	33	—	—	—	—	10	50
Holder, H. W.	Scarborough	1876	Landscape	—	—	—	—	2	—	—	—	—	—	2
Holdich, W. Whyte-	Bexley	1878-1887	Landscape	—	—	—	—	5	—	2	—	—	—	7
Holding, Henry James G.	Manchester	1867-1870	Landscape	—	—	—	—	—	—	—	—	—	6	6
Holding, John	Manchester	1877-1880	Landscape	—	—	—	—	3	—	—	—	—	3	6
Holding, Matthew Henry, A.R.I.B.A.	Northampton	1878-1891	Architecture	—	—	3	—	—	—	—	—	—	—	3
Holditch, J.	London	1785	Fish	—	—	1	—	—	—	—	—	—	—	1
Hole, Miss Alice	Maidenhead	1886	Landscape	—	—	1	—	—	—	—	—	—	—	1
Hole, William B., R.S.A., R.S.W., R.P.E.	Edinburgh	1873-1893	Etching	—	—	13	—	—	—	—	—	—	1	14
Holfeld, Hippolyte	London	1858	Scriptural	—	—	2	—	—	—	—	—	—	—	2
Holgate, J.	London	1887	Sea Pieces	—	—	—	—	—	—	1	—	—	1	2
Holiday, Henry	London	1858-1892	Historical	—	—	35	—	—	—	—	27	—	14	76
Holiday, H. G.	London	1855-1863	Landscape	—	—	—	1	4	—	—	—	—	—	5
Holl, Charles	London	1874	Engraving	—	—	1	—	—	—	—	—	—	—	1
Holl, Francis, A.R.A.	London	1856-1883	Engraving	—	—	20	—	—	—	—	—	—	—	20
Holl, Frank, R.A., A.R.W.S.†	London	1864-1888	Domestic	—	—	87	2	5	1	—	24	2	11	132
Holl, Mrs. Frank	London	1881-1882	Flowers	—	—	—	—	6	—	—	—	—	—	6
Holl, Henry Benjamin	London	1828-1829	Engraving	—	—	—	—	3	—	—	—	—	—	3

Name.	Town.	First and Last Year of Ex.	Speciality.	S. A.	F. S.	R. A.	B. I.	S. S.	O. W.	N. W.	G. G.	N. G.	V. E.	Total.
Holl, William	London	1860-1871	Engraving	—	—	22	—	—	—	—	—	—	—	22
Hollaender, Alphons	Florence	1884	Churches	—	—	—	—	—	—	—	—	—	1	1
Hollagan, M. J.	London	1795-1809	Landscape	—	—	20	—	—	—	—	—	—	—	20
Holland, Miss Ada R.	London	1888-1893	Portraits	—	—	3	—	5	—	2	—	1	3	14
Holland, Mrs. Charlotte F.	London	1882-1885	Landscape	—	—	—	—	2	—	—	—	—	1	3
Holland, F.	London	1868	Domestic	—	—	—	—	1	—	—	—	—	—	1
Holland, G.	London	1839-1841	Sea Pieces	—	—	—	—	9	—	—	—	—	—	9
Holland, Gertrude	London	1875	Churches	—	—	—	—	—	—	—	—	—	1	1
Holland, H.	London	1831	Architecture	—	—	1	—	—	—	—	—	—	—	1
Holland, Henry	London	1878-1890	Domestic	—	—	1	—	—	—	2	—	—	3	6
Holland, H. L.	London	1810	Architecture	—	—	1	—	—	—	—	—	—	—	1
Holland, Henry T.	London	1885	Animals	—	—	—	—	1	—	—	—	—	—	1
Holland, James § †	London	1815-1869	Landscape	—	—	32	91	108	194	3	—	—	9	437
Holland, John	London	1764-1770	Portraits	4	—	—	—	—	—	—	—	—	—	4
Holland, John	Nottingham	1831-1879	Landscape	—	—	—	4	25	—	—	—	—	1	30
Holland, J.	London	1828	Flowers	—	—	1	—	—	—	—	—	—	—	1
Holland, Sir Nathaniel Dance, R.A. *See* Dance.	—	—	—	—	—	—	—	—	—	—	—	—	—	—
Holland, P.	London	1781-1793	Miniatures	—	—	7	—	—	—	—	—	—	—	7
Holland, Philip	London	1850-1886	Still Life	—	—	8	—	49	—	—	—	—	8	65
Holland, Philip Sidney	London	1877-1884	Domestic	—	—	6	—	5	—	1	—	—	5	17
Holland, Richard	London	1771-1773	Architecture	—	—	4	—	—	—	—	—	—	—	4
Holland, Sebastopol S.	Nottingham	1877-1890	Landscape	—	—	1	—	2	—	—	—	—	1	4
Holland, Thomas J. B.	London	1881	Buildings	—	—	1	—	—	—	—	—	—	—	1
Holland, W.	—	1823	Landscape	—	—	1	—	—	—	—	—	—	—	1
Holland, W. F.	London	1845	Architecture	—	—	2	—	—	—	—	—	—	—	2
Holland, W. G.	London	1830	Coast Scenes	—	—	—	—	1	—	—	—	—	—	1
Hollen —	—	1830	—	—	—	—	—	*	—	—	—	—	—	—
Holliday, Edward	Croydon	1874-1884	Fruit	—	—	5	—	33	—	—	—	—	3	41
Holliday, Lily	Croydon	1879-1884	Flowers	—	—	—	—	14	—	—	—	—	1	15
Hollidge, J., *or* T.	London	1872	Churches	—	—	—	—	—	—	—	—	—	2	2
Hollidge, William	London	1872	Woodcuts	—	—	—	—	—	—	—	—	—	1	1
Hollingdale, Horatio R., R.B.A. §	London	1881-1893	Landscape	—	—	10	—	55	—	—	—	—	11	76
Hollingdale, Richard	Strood	1850-1893	Domestic	—	—	18	6	11	—	—	—	—	—	35
Hollings, G. Seymour	London	1865-1871	Landscape	—	—	1	1	8	—	—	—	—	8	18
Hollingshead, W.	Willesden	1889	Architecture	—	—	1	—	—	—	—	—	—	—	1
Hollingsworth, R. M.	London	1824	Architecture	—	—	1	—	2	—	—	—	—	—	3
Hollingworth, Thomas	London	1857-1885	Figures	—	—	1	3	2	—	—	—	—	4	10
Hollins, H. Plant-. *See* P.	—	—	—	—	—	—	—	—	—	—	—	—	—	—
Hollins, J.	—	1800	Architecture	—	—	1	—	—	—	—	—	—	—	1
Hollins, John, A.R.A.	London	1819-1855	Historical	—	—	101	35	6	—	1	—	—	—	143
Hollins, Peter	Birmingham	1822-1871	Sculpture	—	—	44	—	1	1	—	—	—	—	46
Hollins, William	Birmingham	1821-1825	Sculpture	—	—	7	—	—	—	—	—	—	—	7
Hollis, C.	London	1801-1813	Architecture	—	—	4	—	—	—	—	—	—	—	4
Hollis, Charles T.	Windsor	1881-1882	Landscape	—	—	1	—	1	—	—	—	—	—	2
Hollis, Thomas	London	1834	Architecture	—	—	1	—	—	—	—	—	—	—	1
Hollogan, Master J.	—	1790	Heads	2	—	—	—	—	—	—	—	—	—	2
Holloway, Charles Edward, R.I. ‡	London	1866-1893	Churches	—	—	32	—	7	—	70	12	—	46	167
Holloway, G.	London	1842-1843	Portraits	—	—	1	—	4	—	—	—	—	—	5
Holloway, J.	London	1864	Landscape	—	—	—	2	—	—	—	—	—	—	2
Holloway, L.	London	1857-1865	Figures	—	—	8	2	3	—	—	—	—	—	13
Holloway, Thomas	London	1773-1792	Portraits	16	—	19	—	—	—	—	—	—	—	35
Hollway, Miss Janet	London	1887-1892	Miniatures	—	—	9	—	—	—	2	—	—	—	11
Hollyer, Christopher C.	London	1867-1872	Engraving	—	—	2	—	—	—	—	—	—	—	2
Hollyer, Miss Eva	Chester	1891-1892	Domestic	—	—	1	—	3	—	—	—	—	—	4
Hollyer, F.	London	1881	—	—	—	—	—	—	—	—	—	—	*	—
Holman, Francis	London	1767-1784	Sea Pieces	—	10	17	—	—	—	—	—	—	—	27
Holme, Lauritz, F.S.A.	London	1761-1773	Sculpture	15	—	—	—	—	—	—	—	—	—	15
Holme, William	London	1833-1849	Figures	—	—	2	3	5	—	—	—	—	—	10
Holmes, B.	Leytonstone	1876-1877	Landscape	—	—	—	—	2	—	—	—	—	—	2
Holmes, Basil	London	1844-1850	Landscape	—	—	2	6	11	—	—	—	—	—	19
Holmes, Edward, R.B.A. §	London	1841-1891	Landscape	—	—	20	11	159	—	—	2	—	2	194
Holmes, E. N.	London	1860-1871	Architecture	—	—	1	1	—	—	—	—	—	—	2
Holmes, G.	London	1799-1802	Landscape	—	—	7	—	—	—	—	—	—	—	7
Holmes, George Augustus, R.B.A. §	London	1852-1893	Domestic	—	—	24	10	110	—	—	1	—	6	151
Holmes, H.	London	1847-1852	Figures	—	—	1	2	10	—	—	—	—	2	15
Holmes, Mrs. Henry	London	1880-1882	Sculpture	—	—	—	—	—	—	—	—	—	4	4
Holmes, James § †	London	1798-1849	Miniatures and Domestic	—	—	18	3	142	32	1	—	—	29	225
Holmes, J., Junr.	London	1836-1859	Figures	—	—	3	1	20	—	—	—	—	—	24
Holmes, M.	London	1826	Domestic	—	—	—	1	—	—	—	—	—	—	1
Holmes, Marcus H.	Bristol	1826-1833	Domestic	—	—	1	—	2	—	—	—	—	—	3
Holmes, Mrs. N.	London	1830	Landscape	—	—	3	—	—	—	—	—	—	—	3
Holmes, Miss Rhoda	C. of Good Hope	1881	Figures	—	—	1	—	1	—	—	—	—	1	3

Name.	Town.	First and Last Year of Ex.	Speciality.	S. A.	F. S.	R. A.	B. I.	S. S.	O. W.	N. W.	G. G.	N. G.	V. E.	Total.
Holmes, Richard Rivington, F.S.A.	Windsor	1872-1891	Landscape	—	—	5	—	—	—	—	15	2	2	24
Holmes, Miss Sophia	Dublin	1886-1891	Flowers	—	—	1	—	1	—	6	—	—	—	8
Holmes, W.	—	1848	Domestic	—	—	—	—	1	—	—	—	—	—	1
Holmes, Mrs.	—	1799	Portraits	—	—	1	—	—	—	—	—	—	—	1
Holmes, Miss	London	1834-1843	Copies	—	—	1	—	2	—	—	—	—	—	3
Holroyd, Charles, R.P.E.	London	1883-1893	Domestic	—	—	7	—	—	—	3	1	—	4	15
Holroyd, Mrs. F. F.	London	1892	Portraits	—	—	—	—	—	—	—	—	1	—	1
Holroyd, T.	London	1860-1878	Landscape	—	—	9	3	6	—	—	—	—	—	18
Holroyd, Miss	—	1799	Landscape	—	—	1	—	—	—	—	—	—	—	1
Holst, Laurits	Scarborough	1878-1889	Sea Pieces	—	—	3	—	—	—	—	—	—	—	3
Holst, Von. *See* V.	—	—	—	—	—	—	—	—	—	—	—	—	—	—
Holt —	London	1779	Architecture	—	1	—	—	—	—	—	—	—	—	1
Holt, Miss A. H. *See* Mrs. Jackson	London	1853-1856	Still Life	—	—	—	—	6	—	—	—	—	—	6
Holt, Miss A. Julia Vesey-. *See* V.	—	—	—	—	—	—	—	—	—	—	—	—	—	—
Holt, E. F.	London	1850-1865	Historical	—	—	7	12	36	—	—	—	—	—	55
Holt, Mrs. E. F.	London	1857	Domestic	—	—	—	—	1	—	—	—	—	—	1
Holt, J.	London	1828-1863	Landscape	—	—	2	—	17	—	—	—	—	—	19
Holt, J.	London	1855	Sculpture	—	—	1	—	—	—	—	—	—	—	1
Holt, Miss Mary Ann	London	1863-1868	Flowers	—	—	—	—	2	—	—	—	—	—	2
Holte, A. B.	London	1875	Landscape	—	—	—	—	1	—	—	—	—	—	1
Holte, Frank A.	London	1867-1869	Landscape	—	—	—	—	1	—	—	—	—	4	5
Holwell, W.	—	1786-1790	Portraits	2	—	1	—	—	—	—	—	—	—	3
Holworthy, James †	London	1803-1813	Landscape	—	—	3	—	—	36	—	—	—	—	39
Holyoake, Rowland	London	1880-1893	Domestic	—	—	12	—	58	—	5	1	—	17	93
Holyoake, William, R.B.A.§	London	1858-1888	Domestic	—	—	14	6	53	—	—	—	—	7	80
Homan, Miss Gertrude	London	1886-1893	Domestic	—	—	11	—	8	—	—	—	—	2	21
Homan (W.) and Son	London	1882-1883	Architecture	—	—	3	—	—	—	—	—	—	—	3
Home, Robert	London	1770-1813	Portraits	—	—	23	—	—	—	—	—	—	—	23
Homer, Winslow, N.A.	Cullercoats	1878-1882	Figures	—	—	2	—	—	—	—	—	—	—	2
Homfray, J.	London	1824-1843	Landscape	—	—	3	—	7	—	—	—	—	—	10
Hone, Alfred	London	1836-1852	Sculpture	—	—	14	—	2	—	—	—	—	—	16
Hone, A., Junr.	London	1856	Sculpture	—	—	1	—	—	—	—	—	—	—	1
Hone, Camillus	London	1775-1780	Portraits	—	8	6	—	—	—	—	—	—	—	14
Hone, Horace, A.R.A.	London	1772-1822	Enamels	—	—	158	1	—	—	—	—	—	—	159
Hone, John	London	1778-1782	Portraits	—	3	—	—	—	—	—	—	—	—	3
Hone, Nathaniel, R.A.	London	1760-1784	Portraits	32	—	69	—	—	—	—	—	—	—	101
Hone, Nathaniel, R.H.A.	Paris	1869	Landscape	—	—	1	—	—	—	—	—	—	—	1
Honnywell-Hall, W. *See* Hall.	—	—	—	—	—	—	—	—	—	—	—	—	—	—
Honyman, John	Glasgow	1879-1880	Architecture	—	—	2	—	—	—	—	—	—	—	2
Hood, Hon. Albert	London	1874-1878	Domestic	—	—	2	—	4	—	—	—	—	—	6
Hood, Agnes J.	London	1888	Portraits	—	—	—	—	1	—	—	—	—	—	1
Hood, George Percy Jacomb-, R.P.E.§	London	1877-1893	Domestic	—	—	21	—	27	—	—	13	11	11	83
Hood, John	London	1762-1771	Sea Pieces	1	21	—	—	—	—	—	—	—	—	22
Hood, Thomas	—	1849	Landscape	—	—	1	—	—	—	—	—	—	—	1
Hook, Allan J.	Farnham	1876-1893	Landscape	—	—	26	—	—	—	—	—	—	—	26
Hook, Bryan	Silberbeck	1879-1893	Landscape	—	—	30	—	—	—	—	—	—	4	34
Hook, Mrs. Eliza	London	1773-1786	Miniatures	3	—	7	—	—	—	—	—	—	—	10
Hook, James Clarke, R.A., H.F.R.P.E.	London	1839-1893	Sea Pieces	—	—	161	8	1	—	—	1	—	3	174
Hook, Samuel	London	1882-1887	Landscape	—	—	—	—	1	—	1	—	—	—	2
Hooke, B.	—	1801-1810	Landscape	—	—	6	—	—	—	—	—	—	—	6
Hooke, Richard	Manchester	1872	Portraits	—	—	1	—	—	—	—	—	—	—	1
Hooker, W.	London	1811	Fruit	—	—	2	—	—	—	—	—	—	—	2
Hooker and Henning	London	1884	Architecture	—	—	1	—	—	—	—	—	—	—	1
Hooker and Wheeler	Brenchley	1861	Architecture	—	—	1	—	—	—	—	—	—	—	1
Hoole, William	London	1861	Landscape	—	—	—	—	—	—	—	—	—	1	1
Hooley, J. C.	London	1820	Architecture	—	—	1	—	—	—	—	—	—	—	1
Hooper, Alfred William	London	1873-1881	Churches	—	—	2	—	1	—	—	—	—	3	6
Hooper, Francis	London	1890-1892	Architecture	—	—	2	—	—	—	—	—	—	—	2
Hooper, J.	London	1877-1878	Landscape	—	—	—	—	4	—	—	—	—	—	4
Hooper, John Horace	London	1885-1892	Landscape	—	—	5	—	—	—	—	—	—	—	5
Hooper, Luther	London	1870-1891	Domestic	—	—	5	—	6	—	4	—	—	20	35
Hooper, Miss Margaret L.	London	1877-1892	Landscape	—	—	4	—	—	—	1	2	—	5	12
Hooper, W. Cuthbert	Odiham	1880	Landscape	—	—	—	—	1	—	—	—	—	—	1
Hooper, William G.	London	1870-1891	Domestic	—	—	3	—	4	—	1	—	—	12	20
Hooper, Miss	—	1762	Flowers	—	2	—	—	—	—	—	—	—	—	2
Hooper, Miss	London	1842-1843	Landscape	—	—	—	—	2	—	—	—	—	—	2
Hoorne, Mrs.	London	1776	Miniatures	5	—	—	—	—	—	—	—	—	—	5
Hooton, C.	Nottingham	1830	Scriptural	—	—	—	—	1	—	—	—	—	—	1
Hooton, Mary T.	Croydon	1874	Flowers	—	—	—	—	—	—	—	—	—	1	1
Hopcraft, John	London	1771	Architecture	1	—	—	—	—	—	—	—	—	—	1
Hope, E.	London	1868	Miniatures	—	—	—	—	—	—	—	—	—	1	1
Hope, G.	London	1854	Landscape	—	—	1	—	—	—	—	—	—	—	1

Name.	Town.	First and Last Year of Ex.	Speciality.	S. A.	F. S.	R. A.	B. I.	S. S.	O. W.	N. W.	G. G.	N. G.	V. E.	Total.
Hope, J. B.	London	1844-1845	Landscape	—	—	—	1	1	—	—	—	—	—	2
Hope, J. W.	London	1831-1832	Figures	—	—	—	—	2	—	—	—	—	—	2
Hope, William Henry	Guildford	1874-1890	Landscape	—	—	—	—	2	—	—	—	—	2	4
Hope, Mrs.	London	1892-1893	Domestic	—	—	—	—	—	—	—	—	3	—	3
Hopkin, T.	London	1854	Sculpture	—	—	1	—	—	—	—	—	—	—	1
Hopkins, Arthur, A.R.W.S. †	London	1872-1893	Domestic	—	—	15	—	2	106	—	—	—	32	155
Hopkins, Everard	London	1884-1885	Landscape	—	—	—	—	—	—	5	—	—	—	5
Hopkins, Mrs. Edward, late Miss Frances A. Beechey	London	1860-1891	Canadian Scenery	—	—	11	—	4	—	—	—	—	70	85
Hopkins, Miss Hannah H.	Odiham, Hants	1871-1879	Domestic	—	—	6	—	2	—	—	—	—	14	22
Hopkins, J.	London	1791-1809	Miniatures	—	—	30	—	—	—	—	—	—	—	30
Hopkins, J. D.	London	1831-1832	Architecture	—	—	1	—	1	—	—	—	—	—	2
Hopkins, M. R.	Oxford	1880	Pen and Ink	—	—	—	—	—	—	—	—	—	1	1
Hopkins, W.	Windsor Castle	1803-1811	Portraits	—	—	13	—	—	—	—	—	—	—	13
Hopkins, W.	London	1846-1870	Figures	—	—	—	1	24	—	—	—	—	—	25
Hopkins, W. A.	London	1844	Sculpture	—	—	1	—	—	—	—	—	—	—	1
Hopkins, William H.	Keynsham, Bath	1853-1890	Sporting	—	—	37	21	24	—	—	—	—	21	103
Hopkins, Miss	Worcester	1862-1864	Flowers	—	—	—	—	5	—	—	—	—	—	5
Hopkinson, Miss Anne E.	Forest Hill	1877-1887	Fruit	—	—	2	—	5	—	2	—	—	—	9
Hopkinson, Robert	London	1762-1788	Landscape	3	2	4	—	—	—	—	—	—	—	9
Hopley, Edward William John	London	1844-1869	Allegorical	—	—	15	26	7	—	—	—	—	—	48
Hopper, Charles W.	London	1893	Landscape	—	—	1	—	—	—	—	—	—	—	1
Hopper, Cuthbert	Odiham	1880	Landscape	—	—	1	—	—	—	—	—	—	—	1
Hopper, Humphrey	London	1799-1834	Sculpture	—	—	31	2	1	—	—	—	—	—	34
Hopper, Thomas	London	1807-1848	Architecture	—	—	15	—	—	—	—	—	—	—	15
Hopperton, W.	London	1809-1811	Architecture	—	—	3	—	—	—	—	—	—	—	3
Hoppner, C. W.	St. Albans	1827	Sea Pieces	—	—	—	—	1	—	—	—	—	—	1
Hoppner, John, R.A.	London	1780-1809	Portraits	—	—	168	—	—	—	—	—	—	—	168
Hoppner, Lascelles H.	London	1811-1815	Portraits	—	—	11	1	—	—	—	—	—	—	12
Hoppner, R. Belgrave	London	1807-1827	Sea Pieces	—	—	7	21	—	—	—	—	—	—	28
Hopton. *See* Williams and Hopton	—	—	Architecture	—	—	—	—	—	—	—	—	—	—	—
Hopwood, Miss Hannah	London	1811-1824	Landscape	—	—	6	—	1	—	—	—	—	—	7
Hopwood, H. S.	Manchester	1884-1893	Domestic	—	—	2	—	—	—	2	—	—	—	4
Hopwood, James, Junr.	London	1802-1825	Portraits	—	—	6	—	—	—	—	—	—	—	6
Hopwood, W.	London	1801-1804	Illustrations	—	—	7	—	—	—	—	—	—	—	7
Hopwood, W.	—	1824	Landscape	—	—	—	—	1	—	—	—	—	—	1
Hoguet, Charles	Berlin	1868-1869	Landscape	—	—	—	—	—	—	—	—	—	3	3
Hore, J.	London	1837	Architecture	—	—	3	—	—	—	—	—	—	—	3
Horeau, H.	Paris	1852	Architecture	—	—	1	—	—	—	—	—	—	—	1
Horlor, G. W.	Cheltenham	1849-1890	Animals	—	—	19	35	33	—	—	—	—	7	94
Horlor, Joseph	Bath	1834-1866	Landscape	—	—	—	13	11	—	—	—	—	—	24
Horman-Fisher, Maud	London	1876-1881	Landscape	—	—	—	—	—	—	—	—	—	20	20
Horn, C.	London	1819-1830	Domestic	—	—	8	—	—	—	—	—	—	—	8
Horn, J. B.	Folkestone	1858-1860	Sea Pieces	—	—	—	—	3	—	—	—	—	—	3
Horn, R.	London	1812-1815	Architecture	—	—	2	—	—	—	—	—	—	—	2
Hornbrook, T. L.	Plymouth	1836-1845	Sea Pieces	—	—	4	—	2	—	—	—	—	—	6
Horncastle, Miss Jane A.	London	1863-1869	Flowers	—	—	1	—	5	—	—	—	—	1	7
Horne, Edward Henry	London	1866-1873	Architecture	—	—	1	—	1	—	—	—	—	—	2
Hornel, E. A.	Glasgow	1890	Historical	—	—	—	—	—	—	—	2	—	—	2
Horner, G. (?) Christopher	London	1857-1867	Landscape	—	—	—	7	—	—	—	—	—	—	7
Horner, H. P.	London	1875	Architecture	—	—	1	—	—	—	—	—	—	—	1
Horner, John	London	1876-1891	Domestic	—	—	—	—	4	—	1	—	—	1	6
Horner, Rev. W.	—	1808-1820	Landscape	—	—	4	—	—	—	—	—	—	—	4
Horniman, John	London	1889	Portraits	—	—	—	—	—	—	—	—	—	1	1
Hornsby, W.	London	1821	Portraits	—	—	1	—	—	—	—	—	—	—	1
Hornung, T.	Geneva	1838-1839	Historical	—	—	3	—	—	—	—	—	—	—	3
Horrak, John	Rome	1867	Domestic	—	—	—	—	—	—	—	—	—	5	5
Horrak, T.	London	1858-1862	Figures	—	—	8	—	—	—	—	—	—	—	8
Horschelt, Theodor	Munich	1869-1870	Military	—	—	4	—	—	—	—	—	—	2	6
Horsfall, Ernest	London	1891-1893	Figures	—	—	—	—	1	—	—	—	—	1	2
Horsfall, W.	—	1796	Landscape	—	—	1	—	—	—	—	—	—	—	1
Horsford, A. H.	London	1860-1871	Domestic	—	—	—	4	18	—	—	—	—	—	22
Horsford, A. J.	London	1859	Historical	—	—	1	—	—	—	—	—	—	—	1
Horsley, Master	London	1774	Heads	—	1	—	—	—	—	—	—	—	—	1
Horsley, Charles	Lewisham	1877-1893	Landscape	—	—	—	—	—	—	—	—	—	5	5
Horsley, Gerald Callcott	London	1882-1893	Architecture	—	—	32	—	—	—	—	—	—	—	32
Horsley, Hopkins Horsley Hobday	Birmingham	1832-1866	Landscape	—	—	23	21	36	—	—	—	—	27	107
Horsley, John Callcott, R.A.	London	1837-1893	Domestic	—	—	120	11	—	—	—	—	—	—	131
Horsley, T. J.	London	1820-1833	Portraits	—	—	5	—	—	—	1	—	—	—	6
Horsley, W.	London	1798	Flowers	—	—	1	—	—	—	—	—	—	—	1
Horsley, Walter Charles	London	1875-1893	Domestic	—	—	35	—	1	—	1	—	—	11	48
Horton, C.	Nottingham	1828	Figures	—	—	—	—	2	—	—	—	—	—	2

Name.	Town.	First and Last Year of Ex.	Speciality.	S. A.	F. S.	R. A.	B. I.	S. S.	O. W.	N.W.	G. G.	N. G.	V. E.	Total.
Horton, Miss Etty	London	1892-1893	Domestic	—	—	1	—	2	—	—	—	—	—	3
Horton, Mrs. L.	London	1826-1832	Portraits	—	—	—	—	10	—	—	—	—	—	10
Horton, Miss S. E.	London	1890-1893	Churches	—	—	—	—	1	—	2	—	—	—	3
Horton, William T.	London	1890	Architecture	—	—	1	—	—	—	—	—	—	—	1
Horwell, Charles	London	1785-1805	Sculpture	—	—	28	—	—	—	—	—	—	—	28
Horwick, Emanuel Henry	—	1886-1890	Domestic	—	—	—	—	—	—	5	1	—	—	6
Horwitz, B.	London	1874-1885	Landscape	—	—	—	—	5	—	—	—	—	—	5
Horwitz, Emanuel H.	London	1888-1891	Domestic	—	—	—	—	2	—	—	—	—	3	5
Horwitz, Miss Helena	London	1889-1890	Miniatures	—	—	3	—	—	—	—	—	—	—	3
Horwitz, Herbert A.	London	1892-1893	Domestic	—	—	2	—	1	—	—	—	—	—	3
Horwitz, Miss Louise B.	London	1892	Miniatures	—	—	1	—	—	—	—	—	—	—	1
Hose, Mrs. M.	London	1827	Portraits	—	—	—	—	1	—	—	—	—	—	1
Hosking, William	Buckfastleigh	1825-1829	Architecture	—	—	1	—	9	—	—	—	—	—	10
Hoskins, G.	—	1831	Temple	—	—	—	—	1	—	—	—	—	—	1
Hoskyn, Mary G.	Kilburn	1879	Still Life	—	—	—	—	1	—	—	—	—	—	1
Hossack, J.	London	1865	Study	—	—	—	—	1	—	—	—	—	—	1
Hotman —	London	1800	Figures	—	—	1	—	—	—	—	—	—	—	1
Hough, William	Coventry	1857-1890	Flowers, etc.	—	—	28	1	14	—	3	—	—	33	79
Houghton, Arthur Boyd †	Richmond	1859-1874	Domestic	—	—	10	4	3	11	—	—	—	8	36
Houghton, John W.	London	1876-1879	Domestic	—	—	—	—	—	—	—	—	—	4	4
Houghton, M. P.	London	1875-1877	Landscape	—	—	1	—	—	—	—	—	—	2	3
Houlditch, J.	London	1784-1791	Game	—	—	2	—	—	—	—	—	—	—	2
Houliere, De la. *See* D.	—	—	—	—	—	—	—	—	—	—	—	—	—	—
Houlton, J. T.	London	1842-1863	Figures	—	—	3	—	—	—	—	—	—	11	14
Hounsom, G.	London	1796-1806	Miniatures	—	—	43	—	—	—	—	—	—	—	43
Houssoullier, W.	Paris	1845	Mythological	—	—	1	—	—	—	—	—	—	—	1
Houston, Miss Frances	Naples	1890	Heads	—	—	1	—	—	—	—	—	—	—	1
Houston, H.	London	1841-1842	Landscape	—	—	2	—	—	—	—	—	—	—	2
Houston, John Adam, R.S.A., R.I. ‡	London	1840-1885	Domestic	—	—	45	21	5	—	81	—	—	9	161
Houston, J. P.	London	1836-1838	Landscape	—	—	—	2	4	—	—	—	—	—	6
Houten, Mdme. Mesdag Van. *See* V.	—	—	—	—	—	—	—	—	—	—	—	—	—	—
Hove, Van. *See* V.	—	—	—	—	—	—	—	—	—	—	—	—	—	—
Hovenden, Thomas	Pont Avern, Finisterre	1876-1880	Landscape	—	—	—	—	1	—	—	—	—	4	5
Hovle, J.	—	1803	Landscape	—	—	1	—	—	—	—	—	—	—	1
How, F. Douglas	Wakefield	1889	Landscape	—	—	—	—	—	—	1	—	—	—	1
How, Samuel	London	1879	Architecture	—	—	1	—	—	—	—	—	—	—	1
Howard, Miss Annie	London	1859-1893	Miniatures	—	—	29	—	3	—	—	—	—	—	32
Howard, C.	London	1864	Landscape	—	—	—	—	1	—	—	—	—	—	1
Howard, Miss Catherine	London	1888-1890	Landscape	—	—	1	—	2	—	1	—	—	—	4
Howard, Miss Charlotte E.	Oakhurst	1885-1893	Miniatures	—	—	11	—	—	—	2	—	—	—	13
Howard, Miss Elizabeth H.	Hemel Hempstead	1856-1881	Fruit	—	—	—	1	1	—	—	—	—	1	3
Howard, E. S.	Sheffield	1834-1870	Landscape	—	—	2	—	3	—	—	—	—	1	6
Howard, Frank	London	1824-1846	Mythological	—	—	43	26	9	—	—	—	—	—	78
Howard, George	London	1868-1889	Landscape	—	—	—	—	—	—	—	34	4	11	49
Howard, Henry, R.A.	Rome	1794-1847	Mythological	—	—	259	72	2	—	—	—	—	—	333
Howard, Henry	Kidderminster	1880-1893	Landscape	—	—	2	—	4	—	—	—	—	—	6
Howard, H. T.	London	1889	Landscape	—	—	—	—	1	—	—	—	—	—	1
Howard, H. Wickham	Chiswick	1890-1892	Landscape	—	—	—	—	—	—	—	1	—	2	3
Howard, J.	London	1880	Landscape	—	—	—	—	—	—	—	—	—	1	1
Howard, Marion	London	1879	Domestic	—	—	—	—	—	—	—	—	—	1	1
Howard, Miss Sarah T.	London	1840-1851	Miniatures	—	—	44	—	—	—	—	—	—	—	44
Howard, Theodore A.	London	1880-1881	Architecture	—	—	4	—	—	—	—	—	—	—	4
Howard, Vernon	London	1864-1889	Landscape	—	—	1	—	11	—	11	—	—	3	26
Howard, Mrs.	—	1783	Needlework	1	—	—	—	—	—	—	—	—	—	1
Howarth, F. A.	Catford	1884	Buildings	—	—	—	—	1	—	—	—	—	—	1
Howe, B. A.	London	1844-1857	Sporting	—	—	—	—	3	—	—	—	—	—	3
Howe, F. N.	Southsea	1875	Landscape	—	—	—	—	—	—	—	—	—	1	1
Howe, James	Edinburgh	1816	Battle Pieces	—	—	—	1	—	—	—	—	—	—	1
Howe, H.	Isleworth	1862	Landscape	—	—	—	—	1	—	—	—	—	—	1
Howe, J.	London	1829-1842	Sculpture	—	—	4	—	—	—	—	—	—	—	4
Howe, M. C.	East Indies	1782	—	—	*	—	—	—	—	—	—	—	—	—
Howell, A. P.	London	1854	Sculpture	—	—	1	—	—	—	—	—	—	—	1
Howell, C.	London	1798-1807	Sculpture	—	—	2	—	—	—	—	—	—	—	2
Howell, Miss Constance E.	London	1878-1882	Flowers	—	—	—	—	3	—	—	—	—	3	6
Howell, Charles Henry	London	1850-1877	Architecture	—	—	7	—	—	—	—	—	—	—	7
Howell, Samuel	London	1829-1854	Portraits	—	—	11	4	33	—	—	—	—	—	48
Howell, Sophia H. M.	London	1781-1788	Miniatures	—	—	26	—	—	—	—	—	—	—	26
Howell, Sydney	London	1841-1851	Portraits	—	—	5	—	—	—	—	—	—	—	5
Howells, T. C. F.	London	1873-1878	Landscape	—	—	—	—	2	—	—	—	—	1	3
Howes, B.	London	1852-1853	Sculpture	—	—	2	—	—	—	—	—	—	—	2
Howes, F.	London	1850	Figures	—	—	—	1	—	—	—	—	—	—	1
Howes, John	London	1772-1793	Enamels	—	—	40	—	—	—	—	—	—	—	40

Name.	Town.	First and Last Year of Ex.	Speciality.	S. A.	F. S.	R. A.	B. I.	S. S.	O.W.	N. W.	G. G.	N. G.	V. E.	Total.
Howes, T.	London	1866	Figures	—	—	1	—	—	—	—	—	—	—	1
Howgate, William Arthur	Leeds	1884-1893	Landscape	—	—	13	—	9	—	1	—	—	—	23
Howitt, Miss Anna Mary	London	1854-1855	Figures	—	—	1	—	—	—	—	—	—	2	3
Howitt, Samuel	London	1783-1815	Sporting	3	—	10	—	—	—	—	—	—	3	16
Howlet, S. B.	—	1826	Landscape	—	—	1	—	—	—	—	—	—	—	1
Howlett, Bartholomew	London	1803	Architecture	—	—	1	—	—	—	—	—	—	—	1
Howman, Rev. G. E.	—	1827	Landscape	—	—	1	—	—	—	—	—	—	—	1
Howse, Miss C. (?) Kate	London	1881	Domestic	—	—	1	—	—	—	—	—	—	—	1
Howse, F.	London	1846-1849	Historical	—	—	4	—	—	—	—	—	—	—	4
Howse, Fred. D.	London	1884-1893	Figures	—	—	5	—	—	—	—	—	1	6	12
Howse, George ‡	London	1830-1861	Buildings	—	—	26	6	4	—	531	—	—	—	567
Hoyoll, Philip	London	1864-1875	Domestic	—	—	10	6	27	—	—	—	—	4	47
Hoyte, Mrs. Lucy	Balham	1893	Landscape	—	—	—	—	1	—	—	—	—	—	1
Huard, Frans	London	1872-1879	Domestic	—	—	4	—	12	—	—	—	—	8	24
Huard, Louis	London	1857-1872	Figures	—	—	—	2	—	—	—	—	—	1	3
Hubard, Henri	London	1867-1869	Landscape	—	—	3	—	2	—	—	—	—	1	6
Hubbard, B.	Louth	1839-1864	Sporting	—	—	7	—	—	—	—	—	—	—	7
Hubbard, G. A.	Bexley Heath	1865	Fruit, etc.	—	—	—	—	4	—	—	—	—	—	4
Hubbard, J.	London	1867	Domestic	—	—	1	—	—	—	—	—	—	—	1
Hubbard, W.	Crayford	1867	Flowers	—	—	—	1	4	—	—	—	—	—	5
Huber, J.	London	1785	Landscape	—	—	1	—	—	—	—	—	—	—	1
Hubert, H. L.	London	1878-1889	Sculpture	—	—	6	—	—	—	—	—	—	—	6
Hubert, P.	—	1828	Interiors	—	—	1	—	—	—	—	—	—	—	1
Hubert, V.	Ryde	1871	Sea Pieces	—	—	—	—	1	—	—	—	—	—	1
Hubert, Miss S.	London	1841	Scriptural	—	—	1	1	—	—	—	—	—	—	2
Hubrichs —	London	1769	Portraits	1	—	—	—	—	—	—	—	—	—	1
Huck, Johann Gerhard	London	1784-1786	Scriptural	—	—	7	—	—	—	—	—	—	—	7
Hucklebridge, Miss M.	London	1837-1852	Portraits	—	—	31	—	8	—	—	—	—	—	39
Hucks, Miss H. M.	Hereford	1880	Domestic	—	—	—	—	1	—	—	—	—	—	1
Huddesford —	London	1775	Portraits	—	—	2	—	—	—	—	—	—	—	2
Huddesford, Rev. G.	—	1786-1810	Fruit	—	—	2	1	—	—	—	—	—	—	3
Hudson. *See* Mawson and Hudson	—	—	Architecture	—	—	—	—	—	—	—	—	—	—	—
Hudson —	—	1781	Portraits	—	—	1	—	—	—	—	—	—	—	1
Hudson, Miss Anne	London	1830	Birds	—	—	—	—	2	—	—	—	—	—	2
Hudson (A.) and Barrett (G.)	Southsea	1877	Architecture	—	—	1	—	—	—	—	—	—	—	1
Hudson, Alfred A.	Southsea	1881	Architecture	—	—	2	—	—	—	—	—	—	—	2
Hudson, A. M.	London	1829-1831	Birds	—	—	—	—	4	—	—	—	—	—	4
Hudson, B.	London	1852-1853	Portraits	—	—	4	—	2	—	—	—	—	—	6
Hudson, Charles	London	1848-1874	Landscape	—	—	3	—	2	—	—	—	—	—	5
Hudson, Miss Edith H.	Bradford	1888-1889	Landscape	—	—	2	—	—	—	—	—	—	—	2
Hudson, F. H.	London	1843-1855	Portraits	—	—	5	—	3	—	—	—	—	—	8
Hudson, Henry John	London	1881-1893	Portraits	—	—	16	—	1	—	—	2	2	35	56
Hudson, John	—	1829	Architecture	—	—	1	—	—	—	—	—	—	—	1
Hudson, R.	London	1818-1829	Allegorical	—	—	5	3	2	—	—	—	—	—	10
Hudson, Robert, Junr.	Sheffield	1873-1879	Landscape	—	—	1	—	3	—	—	—	—	—	4
Hudson, Thomas	London	1761-1779	Portraits	9	1	—	—	—	—	—	—	—	—	10
Hudson, William ‡	Croydon	1803-1846	Portraits	—	—	161	—	37	—	15	—	—	—	213
Hudson, William	London	1838-1844	Architecture	—	—	6	—	—	—	—	—	—	—	6
Hudson, Mrs.	London	1764	Landscape	—	1	—	—	—	—	—	—	—	—	1
Hue, C. B.	London	1857-1863	Sea Pieces	—	—	2	5	10	—	—	—	—	—	17
Hue, Miss E.	London	1861-1871	Landscape	—	—	—	—	7	—	—	—	—	—	7
Hue, W. B.	London	1801-1819	Architecture	—	—	7	—	—	—	—	—	—	—	7
Hueffer, Mrs. Frank. *See* Miss Catherine Madox Brown.	—	—	—	—	—	—	—	—	—	—	—	—	—	—
Huet, V.	London	1804-1806	Miniatures	—	—	22	—	—	—	—	—	—	—	22
Huet-Villiers, F. *See* V.	—	—	—	—	—	—	—	—	—	—	—	—	—	—
Huey, A.	London	1814-1818	Miniatures	—	—	7	—	—	—	—	—	—	—	7
Huffam, A. M.	Edmonton	1828-1832	Engraving	—	—	—	—	3	—	—	—	—	—	3
Huffam, H.	—	1832	Figures	—	—	—	1	—	—	—	—	—	—	1
Huffam, Miss M.	Bath	1874	Copies	—	—	1	—	—	—	—	—	—	—	1
Hugard —	London	1848	Landscape	—	—	1	—	—	—	—	—	—	—	1
Hugel, E.	London	1818	Portraits	—	—	1	—	—	—	—	—	—	—	1
Huggins, Miss Anna	London	1854-1855	Game	—	—	3	—	—	—	—	—	—	—	3
Huggins, J.	London	1817-1826	Sea Pieces	—	—	5	—	—	—	—	—	—	—	5
Huggins, J. M., Junr.	London	1827-1842	Sea Pieces	—	—	—	1	4	—	—	—	—	—	5
Huggins, T. W.	London	1819	Sea Pieces	—	—	1	—	—	—	—	—	—	—	1
Huggins, W.	London	1790	Sculpture	—	—	1	—	—	—	—	—	—	—	1
Huggins, William	Liverpool	1842-1875	Animals	—	—	31	8	1	—	—	—	—	—	40
Huggins, William John	London	1820-1845	Sea Pieces	—	—	10	16	7	—	—	—	—	—	33
Hughes, A.	London	1831-1842	Cattle	—	—	1	1	—	—	—	—	—	—	2
Hughes, Alice	Widcombe	1890-1891	Domestic	—	—	—	—	2	—	—	—	—	—	2
Hughes, Miss Amy	Wallington	1881-1882	Domestic	—	—	—	—	—	—	—	1	—	1	2

Name.	Town.	First and Last Year of Ex.	Speciality.	S. A.	F. S.	R. A.	B. I.	S. S.	O. W.	N.W.	G. G.	N. G.	V. E.	Total.
Hughes, Arthur	London	1849-1893	Domestic	—	—	57	—	—	—	—	7	9	17	90
Hughes, Arthur Foord	Wallington	1878-1893	Domestic	—	—	3	—	2	—	5	1	4	6	21
Hughes, Edmund	London	1879	Landscape	—	—	—	—	—	—	—	—	—	1	1
Hughes, Edward	London	1847-1892	Historical	—	—	38	14	11	—	—	2	—	4	69
Hughes, Edwin	London	1872-1890	Domestic	—	—	15	—	—	—	—	—	—	6	21
Hughes, Edward Robert, A.R.W.S. †	London	1870-1893	Domestic	—	—	15	—	—	14	1	13	8	15	66
Hughes, F.	—	1830	Flowers	—	—	—	2	—	—	—	—	—	—	2
Hughes, Miss F. L.	London	1884	Fish	—	—	—	—	—	—	1	—	—	—	1
Hughes, George	London	1813-1858	Landscape	—	—	66	9	4	—	—	—	—	—	79
Hughes, Godfrey	Kew	1891-1893	Landscape	—	—	—	—	—	—	—	—	2	1	3
Hughes, Miss Georgina Ball-. *See* B.	—	—	—	—	—	—	—	—	—	—	—	—	—	—
Hughes, G. B.	—	1826	Sculpture	—	—	2	—	—	—	—	—	—	—	2
Hughes, George Frederick	London	1873-1879	Landscape	—	—	—	—	4	—	—	—	—	—	4
Hughes, H.	London	1827-1851	Landscape	—	—	—	4	6	—	—	—	—	—	10
Hughes, Henry. *See also* Ward and Hughes	London	1859-1883	Windows	—	—	4	—	—	—	—	—	—	—	4
Hughes, Henry Harold	Bangor	1892	Buildings	—	—	1	—	—	—	—	—	—	—	1
Hughes, John	London	1819-1838	Landscape	—	—	5	7	7	—	—	—	—	—	19
Hughes, J. J.	Birmingham	1838-1867	Landscape	—	—	2	10	22	—	—	—	—	33	67
Hughes, J. P.	—	1830	Lithography	—	—	—	—	1	—	—	—	—	—	1
Hughes, Leonard, R.C.A.	Holywell	1889	Portraits	—	—	1	—	—	—	—	—	—	—	1
Hughes, Miss Louisa M. *See* Mrs. J. T. Watts.	—	—	—	—	—	—	—	—	—	—	—	—	—	—
Hughes, Miss Mary	Brentford	1891	Figures	—	—	—	—	—	—	1	—	—	—	1
Hughes, Nathan	London	1849-1870	Historical	—	—	—	1	1	—	—	—	—	—	2
Hughes, R.	London	1794-1799	Landscape	—	—	6	—	—	—	—	—	—	—	6
Hughes, R.	London	1819-1828	Architecture	—	—	3	—	—	—	—	—	—	—	3
Hughes, Robert Ball	London	1822-1828	Sculpture	—	—	4	—	—	—	—	—	—	—	4
Hughes, R. E.	Tooting	1872	Domestic	—	—	—	—	2	—	—	—	—	—	2
Hughes, S. G.	London	1829	Landscape	—	—	—	—	2	—	—	—	—	—	2
Hughes, S. J.	London	1837	Landscape	—	—	1	—	—	—	—	—	—	—	1
Hughes, Thomas	London	1826-1836	Sculpture	—	—	6	—	3	—	—	—	—	—	9
Hughes, Talbot	London	1871-1893	Landscape	—	—	6	—	1	—	—	5	—	1	13
Hughes, T. J.	London	1851-1865	Domestic	—	—	10	1	2	—	—	—	—	3	16
Hughes, Thomas John	London	1879-1892	Domestic	—	—	—	—	7	—	3	—	—	3	13
Hughes, Vernon	London	1852-1855	Figures	—	—	5	4	—	—	—	—	—	—	9
Hughes, W.	London	1828-1829	Portraits	—	—	2	—	—	—	—	—	—	—	2
Hughes, William	London	1830-1853	Landscape	—	—	7	3	11	—	1	—	—	—	22
Hughes, William	London	1862-1888	Still Life	—	—	30	8	71	—	—	31	—	21	161
Hughes, W. C.	Scarborough	1880	Landscape	—	—	—	—	—	—	—	—	—	1	1
Hughes, W. H.	London	1877-1880	Pen and Ink	—	—	—	—	—	—	—	—	—	6	6
Hughes, W. W.	Shrewsbury	1830-1846	Landscape	—	—	—	—	3	—	—	—	—	—	3
Hughes, Mrs.	London	1843	Flowers	—	—	—	—	1	—	—	—	—	—	1
Hughes, Mrs. *See* Miss Kate Gilbert.	—	—	—	—	—	—	—	—	—	—	—	—	—	—
Hughes, Miss	London	1838	Portraits	—	—	1	—	—	—	—	—	—	—	1
Hughes, Miss	Woolpits	1860	Churches	—	—	1	—	—	—	—	—	—	—	1
Hughes-Stanton, Horace. *See* Stanton.	—	—	—	—	—	—	—	—	—	—	—	—	—	—
Huguet, C.	London	1872	Sea Pieces	—	—	—	—	1	—	—	—	—	—	1
Huiber, J. D.	—	1875	Charcoal	—	—	—	—	—	—	—	—	—	6	6
Hulk, A.	London	1875-1890	Landscape	—	—	3	—	15	—	—	—	—	1	19
Hulk, Abraham, Junr.	Dorking	1876-1893	Landscape	—	—	19	—	1	—	—	—	—	4	24
Hulk, William F.	London	1875-1893	Cattle	—	—	45	—	43	—	13	—	—	29	130
Hull, Miss Clementina M.	London	1866-1891	Landscape	—	—	2	—	4	—	4	—	—	6	16
Hull, Edward.	London	1827-1877	Domestic	—	—	7	—	18	—	—	—	—	18	43
Hull, George	Leicester	1877-1886	Landscape	—	—	—	—	—	—	1	—	—	1	2
Hull, Miss Mary A.	Leicester	1877-1887	Fruit	—	—	1	—	—	—	3	—	—	—	4
Hull, Thomas H.	London	1775-1800	Miniatures	—	—	73	—	—	—	—	—	—	—	73
Hull, T. H.	London	1827-1828	Portraits	—	—	2	—	3	—	—	—	—	—	5
Hull, William	London	1858-1877	Pastoral	—	—	8	—	3	—	—	—	—	18	29
Hullah, Miss Caroline E.	London	1863-1867	Figures	—	—	2	—	—	—	—	—	—	2	4
Hulland, William T.	Farnworth	1885	Engraving	—	—	1	—	—	—	—	—	—	—	1
Hulley, H.	Hackney	1783-1787	Landscape	—	—	10	—	—	—	—	—	—	—	10
Hullmandel, Charles Joseph	London	1816-1826	Eruptions	—	—	3	3	1	—	—	—	—	—	7
Hulme, Miss Alice L.	London	1877-1890	Still Life	—	—	3	—	2	—	—	—	—	1	6
Hulme, E.	Clapham	1840-1854	Landscape	—	—	3	2	4	—	—	—	—	—	9
Hulme, Frederick William	London	1845-1884	Landscape	—	—	40	5	5	—	—	—	—	66	116
Hulme, Robert C.	London	1862-1876	Fruit	—	—	1	—	2	—	—	—	—	1	4
Hulme, T. O.	London	1864-1867	Landscape	—	—	—	2	4	—	—	—	—	—	6
Hulton, Everard	London	1882	Landscape	—	—	1	—	—	—	—	—	—	—	1
Hulton, William	London	1882-1889	Landscape	—	—	5	—	6	—	—	—	—	1	12
Hume, Sir Abraham	London	1809-1812	Dramatic	—	—	—	2	—	—	—	—	—	—	2
Hume, Miss Amelia. *See* Mrs. Charles Long	—	—	—	—	—	—	—	—	—	—	—	—	—	—
and Lady Farnborough.	—	—	—	—	—	—	—	—	—	—	—	—	—	—
Hume, J. Henry	London	1875-1881	Landscape	—	—	11	—	11	—	—	—	—	5	27

Name.	Town.	First and Last Year of Ex.	Speciality.	S. A.	F. S.	R. A.	B. I.	S. S.	O. W.	N. W.	G. G.	N. G.	V. E.	Total.
Hume, Robert	Edinburgh	1891-1893	Landscape	—	—	2	—	5	—	1	—	—	—	8
Hume, T. H.	Sutton	1878	Landscape	—	—	—	—	—	—	—	—	—	1	1
Hume, T. O.	London	1864-1893	Landscape	—	—	24	2	20	—	—	—	—	8	54
Hume, Mrs. T. O. *See* Miss Edith Dunn	London	1870-1892	Domestic	—	—	32	—	14	—	3	2	—	22	73
Humphrey —	—	1810	Portraits	—	—	1	—	—	—	—	—	—	—	1
Humphrey, C.	London	1789-1791	Architecture	—	—	4	—	—	—	—	—	—	—	4
Humphrey, Edward J.	London	1872-1889	Domestic	—	—	13	—	7	—	4	—	—	18	42
Humphrey, Ozias, R.A.	Honiton	1765-1797	Miniatures	10	—	48	—	—	—	—	—	—	—	58
Humphreys, C.	—	1800	Landscape	—	—	1	—	—	—	—	—	—	—	1
Humphreys, F. W.	Birmingham	1858	Landscape	—	—	—	1	—	—	—	—	—	—	1
Humphreys, Miss J. K.	London	1865-1886	Scriptural	—	—	3	—	7	—	—	—	—	3	13
Humphries, W.	London	1791-1793	Landscape	2	—	2	—	—	—	—	—	—	—	4
Humphris, William H.	Falmouth	1881-1891	Domestic	—	—	1	—	6	—	—	—	—	6	13
Humphry, C.	London	1878-1880	Domestic	—	—	—	—	5	—	—	—	—	—	5
Humphry, Miss Elizabeth H.	London	1762-1771	Shell Work	—	5	—	—	—	—	—	—	—	—	5
Humphry, Miss K. Maude	London	1883-1891	Portraits	—	—	1	—	1	—	—	—	—	—	2
Humphrys —	London	1771	Portraits	—	2	—	—	—	—	—	—	—	—	2
Hundley, Philip	London	1869-1880	Domestic	—	—	—	—	16	—	—	—	—	8	24
Hunes, A. G.	London	1785	Mythological	—	—	1	—	—	—	—	—	—	—	1
Hungerford —	—	1836	Animals	—	—	—	—	1	—	—	—	—	—	1
Hunn, Thomas H.	Hackney	1878-1890	Landscape	—	—	7	—	13	—	4	—	—	7	31
Hunneman, Christopher William	London	1776-1793	Miniatures	—	—	25	—	—	—	—	—	—	—	25
Hunt. *See* Shrigley and Hunt, *and* Verity and Hunt	—	—	Architecture	—	—	—	—	—	—	—	—	—	—	—
Hunt, Alfred	Reading	1870-1874	Sea Pieces	—	—	—	—	3	—	—	—	—	—	3
Hunt, Andrew	Liverpool	1852-1856	Domestic	—	—	2	—	3	—	—	—	—	2	7
Hunt, Arthur Ackland	London	1863-1887	Figures	—	—	13	4	22	—	6	—	—	19	64
Hunt, Miss Amy Henrietta	London	1887-1891	Sculpture	—	—	5	—	5	—	—	—	—	—	10
Hunt, Alfred William, R.W.S. †	Liverpool	1846-1893	Landscape	—	—	37	—	6	334	—	2	5	11	395
Hunt, Charles	London	1846-1891	Domestic	—	—	10	5	16	—	—	—	—	—	31
Hunt, Miss Emily	Liverpool	1856-1862	Still Life	—	—	2	—	2	—	—	—	—	6	10
Hunt, E. Aubrey	London	1878-1892	Landscape	—	—	11	—	45	—	—	1	2	8	67
Hunt, Miss Eva E.	Greenwich	1885-1893	Flowers	—	—	4	—	16	—	—	3	—	—	23
Hunt, Mrs. Emma C. W.	London	1884	Flowers	—	—	4	—	—	—	—	—	—	—	4
Hunt, F. H.	London	1854	Sculpture	—	—	2	—	—	—	—	—	—	—	2
Hunt, George	London	1855	—	—	—	—	—	—	—	—	—	—	*	—
Hunt, George Henry	London	1878	Architecture	—	—	1	—	—	—	—	—	—	—	1
Hunt, George Sidney	Shacklewell	1880-1886	Engraving	—	—	3	—	1	—	—	—	—	—	4
Hunt, H. S.	Lee	1893	Domestic	—	—	—	—	1	—	—	—	—	—	1
Hunt, J. A.	—	1872	Portraits	—	—	3	—	—	—	—	—	—	—	3
Hunt, J. E.	London	1832	Architecture	—	—	1	—	—	—	—	—	—	—	1
Hunt, Miss Maria	Liverpool	1856-1866	Fruit, etc.	—	—	3	—	1	—	—	—	—	—	4
Hunt, Captain N. Augustus	—	1789-1811	Landscape	—	—	4	—	—	—	—	—	—	—	4
Hunt, R.	London	1802-1842	Portraits	—	—	13	—	—	—	—	—	—	—	13
Hunt, S. V.	Norwich	1826-1828	Landscape	—	—	—	3	1	—	—	—	—	—	4
Hunt, T.	—	1803	Miniatures	—	—	5	—	—	—	—	—	—	—	5
Hunt, Thomas, R.S.W.	Glasgow	1881-1891	Domestic	—	—	10	—	—	—	4	—	—	—	14
Hunt, Thomas F.	London	1816-1828	Architecture	—	—	6	—	—	—	—	—	—	—	6
Hunt, T. Greenwood	Chelmsford	1873-1878	Domestic	—	—	3	—	—	—	—	—	—	2	5
Hunt, Walter	Wandsworth	1881-1893	Animals	—	—	19	—	—	—	—	—	—	—	19
Hunt, William	Greenwich	1889-1893	Landscape	—	—	7	—	5	—	—	2	—	—	14
Hunt, William Henry, † (R.A. of Amsterdam)	London	1807-1864	Figures	—	—	14	6	1	796	—	—	—	—	817
Hunt, William Holman, A.R.S.A., R.W.S. †	London	1846-1893	Historical	—	—	25	1	1	38	—	15	2	1	83
Hunt, William H. Thurlow	London	1883-1885	Portraits	—	—	2	—	5	—	—	—	—	—	7
Hunt, Mrs.	Putney	1831	Landscape	—	—	1	—	—	—	—	—	—	—	1
Hunt, Steward, and Knight	London	1884	Architecture	—	—	1	—	—	—	—	—	—	—	1
Hunter. *See* Morris and Hunter	—	—	Architecture	—	—	—	—	—	—	—	—	—	—	—
Hunter, A.	London	1841	Domestic	—	—	1	—	—	—	—	—	—	—	1
Hunter, Miss Ada	London	1886-1893	Miniatures	—	—	6	—	—	—	3	—	—	—	9
Hunter, Miss Blanche F.	London	1889-1890	Domestic	—	—	1	—	—	—	2	—	—	—	3
Hunter, Colin, A.R.A., R.I, R.S.W. ‡ φ	Helensburgh	1866-1893	Sea Pieces	—	—	67	—	1	—	1	1	8	14	92
Hunter, Miss Elizabeth	London	1853-1883	Domestic	—	—	11	9	17	—	—	—	—	23	60
Hunter, G. Sherwood, R.B.A. §	Aberdeen	1882-1893	Domestic	—	—	12	—	55	—	—	—	—	8	75
Hunter, H. C.	—	1843	Sculpture	—	—	1	—	—	—	—	—	—	—	1
Hunter, James	London	1774-1777	Architecture	—	1	2	—	—	—	—	—	—	—	3
Hunter, John	London	1840	Landscape	—	—	—	—	1	—	—	—	—	—	1
Hunter, James B.	Edinburgh	1891	Engraving	—	—	1	—	—	—	—	—	—	—	1
Hunter, John Kelso	Glasgow	1847	Portraits	—	—	1	—	—	—	—	—	—	—	1
Hunter, J. P.	London	1827	Portraits	—	—	—	—	4	—	—	—	—	—	4
Hunter, Mason, R.S.W.	Edinburgh	1881-1893	Landscape	—	—	4	—	1	—	4	—	—	1	10
Hunter-Graham, James. *See* G.	—	—	—	—	—	—	—	—	—	—	—	—	—	—
Huntingdon, F. H.	Wanstead	1849-1878	Landscape	—	—	8	16	29	—	—	—	—	11	64

Name.	Town.	First and Last Year of Ex.	Speciality.	S. A.	F. S.	R. A.	B. I.	S. S.	O. W.	N. W.	G. G.	N. G.	V. E.	Total.
Huntington, Daniel, N.A.	New York	1852-1859	Scriptural	—	—	6	2	—	—	—	—	—	—	8
Huntington, G. (?) Huntinglon	London	1847	Sea Pieces	—	—	1	—	—	—	—	—	—	—	1
Huntley, W.	London	1835-1850	Figures	—	—	1	2	3	—	—	—	—	—	6
Huntley, Miss	London	1816-1825	Domestic	—	—	7	—	—	—	—	—	—	—	7
Huntley-Gordon, Herbert	London	1890-1893	Architecture	—	—	2	—	—	—	—	—	—	—	2
Hunton, Miss Charlotte	Torquay	1892-1893	Sculpture	—	—	3	—	—	—	—	—	—	—	3
Hunton, Miss Edith	Torquay	1889	Sculpture	—	—	—	—	—	—	—	—	—	1	1
Huquier, James Gabriel	London	1771-1786	Portraits	4	—	12	—	—	—	—	—	—	—	16
Hurd-Wood, J.	Leatherhead	1881	Landscape	—	—	—	—	—	—	—	—	—	2	2
Hurdle, E. H.	Topsham	1851-1855	Landscape	—	—	2	—	—	—	—	—	—	—	2
Hurlbat, F.	Newington	1798	Architecture	—	—	1	—	—	—	—	—	—	—	1
Hurlstone, F. B.	London	1857-1869	Figures	—	—	1	—	9	—	—	—	—	—	10
Hurlstone, Frederick Yeates § (President S.B.A.)	London	1821-1870	Figures	—	—	37	19	326	—	—	—	—	—	382
Hurlstone, Richard	London	1771-1780	Portraits	—	—	8	—	—	—	—	—	—	—	8
Hurlstone, Mrs.	London	1846-1856	Domestic	—	—	6	—	23	—	—	—	—	—	29
Hurst, A.	—	1778-1796	Architecture	—	—	12	—	—	—	—	—	—	—	12
Hurst, W.	Doncaster	1811	Architecture	—	—	2	—	—	—	—	—	—	—	2
Hurt, Louis B.	Ashbourne	1881-1892	Landscape	—	—	13	—	26	—	—	—	—	4	43
Hurt, Mrs. Louis B. (H. M.)	Ashbourne	1886	Landscape	—	—	—	—	1	—	—	—	—	—	1
Hurter, C.	London	1787-1789	Miniatures	—	—	2	—	—	—	—	—	—	—	2
Hurter, John Henry	London	1779-1781	Enamels	—	—	11	—	—	—	—	—	—	—	11
Hurton, C. F.	Stoke	1865	Flowers	—	—	—	—	—	—	—	—	—	1	1
Huskinson, H.	Nottingham	1832	Portraits	—	—	1	—	—	—	—	—	—	—	1
Huskinson, John	Bingham	1886-1887	Sculpture	—	—	2	—	—	—	—	—	—	—	2
Huskinson, L.	London	1839-1859	Domestic	—	—	12	5	1	—	—	—	—	—	18
Huskisson, R.	Hammersmith	1838-1847	Figures	—	—	10	2	5	—	—	—	—	—	17
Huson, Thomas, R.I., R.P.E. ‡	Liverpool	1871-1893	Landscape	—	—	13	—	20	—	59	2	—	41	135
Huson, Mrs. T.	Liverpool	1877-1878	Landscape	—	—	—	—	2	—	—	—	—	—	2
Huson, W.	—	1783	Portraits	—	—	1	—	—	—	—	—	—	—	1
Hussey, Miss Agnes	Salisbury	1877-1887	Flowers	—	—	—	—	1	—	4	—	—	3	8
Hussey, Grace	Salisbury	1876-1877	Landscape	—	—	—	—	—	—	—	—	—	3	3
Hussey, Mrs. James. *See* Miss Henrietta Grove ‖	Salisbury	1876-1877	Landscape	—	—	—	—	—	—	—	—	—	4	4
Hussey, R. C.	London	1825	Architecture	—	—	2	—	—	—	—	—	—	—	2
Hutchings, J.	Towcester	1849-1893	Historical	—	—	1	5	1	—	—	—	—	—	7
Hutchins, T.	London	1815-1819	Architecture	—	—	4	—	—	—	—	—	—	—	4
Hutchinson, A.	—	1832	Portraits	—	—	1	—	—	—	—	—	—	—	1
Hutchinson, Allen	Stoke-on-Trent	1883-1886	Sculpture	—	—	5	—	—	—	—	—	—	—	5
Hutchinson, E. L.	London	1880-1882	Figures	—	—	—	—	1	—	—	—	—	1	2
Hutchinson, F. J.	London	1837-1839	Scriptural	—	—	2	—	—	—	—	—	—	—	2
Hutchinson, George	London	1884-1887	Miniatures	—	—	2	—	—	—	—	—	—	1	3
Hutchinson, George W. C.	London	1875-1889	Domestic	—	—	3	—	4	—	—	—	—	9	16
Hutchinson, J.	London	1871	Architecture	—	—	1	—	—	—	—	—	—	—	1
Hutchinson, Mrs. Jane P.	London	1882-1883	Landscape	—	—	—	—	1	—	—	—	—	1	2
Hutchinson, M.	London	1828-1831	Portraits	—	—	4	—	—	—	—	—	—	—	4
Hutchinson, Samuel	—	1770-1802	Landscape	1	—	1	—	—	—	—	—	—	—	2
Hutchinson, W. Henry Florio	London	1843-1861	Landscape	—	—	—	—	2	—	—	—	—	7	9
Hutchison, J.	London	1792-1819	Miniatures	—	—	39	—	—	—	—	—	—	—	39
Hutchison, John, R.S.A.	Edinburgh	1861-1892	Sculpture	—	—	23	—	—	—	—	—	—	—	23
Hutchison, R. Gemmell	Edinburgh	1880-1892	Domestic	—	—	13	—	—	—	—	2	—	4	19
Hutchons, J. and W.	London	1821	Architecture	—	—	1	—	—	—	—	—	—	—	1
Huth, F.	Edinburgh	1890	Engraving	—	—	1	—	—	—	—	—	—	—	1
Hutin, G. W.	Greenwich	1827-1828	Engraving	—	—	—	—	6	—	—	—	—	—	6
Hutton, Alfred	London	1884-1886	Landscape	—	—	—	—	—	—	5	—	—	—	5
Hutton, R.	Ealing	1884	Landscape	—	—	—	—	1	—	—	—	—	—	1
Hutton, Walter C. Stritch	London	1890-1892	Portraits	—	—	1	—	—	—	—	—	—	2	3
Huttula, Richard C.	London	1866-1887	Domestic	—	—	—	—	28	—	4	—	—	21	53
Huxley. *See* Batterby and Huxley	—	—	Architecture	—	—	—	—	—	—	—	—	—	—	—
Huxley, Miss M.	London	1878-1879	Domestic	—	—	—	—	—	—	—	—	—	2	2
Huxley, Miss Marian. *See* Hon. Mrs. John Collier	—	—		—	—	—	—	—	—	—	—	—	—	—
Huxley, Miss Nellie	London	1885-1888	Domestic	—	—	2	—	—	—	—	4	1	2	9
Huybers, John	London	1887	Buildings	—	—	—	—	2	—	—	—	—	1	3
Huyter, C.	London	1788	Miniatures	—	—	5	—	—	—	—	—	—	—	5
Hyde —	—	1775	Drawing	—	1	—	—	—	—	—	—	—	—	1
Hyde. *See* Scott and Hyde	—	—	Architecture	—	—	—	—	—	—	—	—	—	—	—
Hyde, F.	London	1824	Landscape	—	—	—	—	1	—	—	—	—	—	1
Hyde, F.	—	1851	Architecture	—	—	1	—	—	—	—	—	—	—	1
Hyde, Frank	London	1872-1885	Historical	—	—	5	—	3	—	—	—	—	1	9
Hyde, Henry James	London	1883-1892	Rustic	—	—	—	—	1	—	11	—	—	6	18
Hyde, Mrs. Richard (E. L.)	London	1893	Domestic	—	—	—	—	1	—	—	—	—	—	1
Hyde, William	London	1889-1891	Landscape	—	—	4	—	—	—	—	—	—	—	4
Hyett, W.	Kettering	1816	Buildings	—	—	2	—	—	—	—	—	—	—	2
Hytche, Miss Kezia	London	1885-1893	Flowers	—	—	1	—	5	—	1	—	—	2	9

Name.	Town.	First and Last Year of Ex.	Speciality.	S. A.	F. S.	R. A.	B. I.	S. S.	O. W.	N. W.	G. G.	N. G.	V. E.	Total.
I'Anson, Charles	London	1875-1893	Landscape	—	—	13	—	17	—	9	1	—	23	63
I'Anson, Edward, P.R.I.B.A.	London	1830-1886	Architecture	—	—	8	—	—	—	—	—	—	—	8
I'Anson (Edward) and Son	London	1845-1887	Architecture	—	—	14	—	—	—	—	—	—	—	14
I'Anson, E. B.	London	1891	Architecture	—	—	1	—	—	—	—	—	—	—	1
I'Anson, F.	London	1833-1837	Portraits	—	—	2	—	2	—	—	—	—	—	4
Ibbetson, John	Down Hall	1811-1812	Landscape	—	—	—	—	—	—	—	—	—	6	6
Ibbetson, Julius Cæsar	London	1785-1818	Landscape	—	—	81	6	—	—	—	—	—	—	87
Ichenhauser, Mrs. Natalie	London	1889-1892	Figures	—	—	—	—	1	—	—	—	—	1	2
Ideson, Miss Eliz.	—	1777	Flowers	1	—	—	—	—	—	—	—	—	—	1
Ifold, Frederick	London	1846-1867	Figures	—	—	4	5	8	—	—	—	—	—	17
Illidge, Thomas Henry	Manchester	1826-1851	Portraits	—	—	14	5	13	—	—	—	—	—	32
Imhoff —	—	1846	Sculpture	—	—	1	—	—	—	—	—	—	—	1
Immanuel —	—	1783	Landscape	—	1	—	—	—	—	—	—	—	—	1
Imoff —	London	1768	Miniatures	1	—	—	—	—	—	—	—	—	—	1
Ince, J. Howard	London	1882-1893	Architecture	—	—	5	—	—	—	—	—	—	—	5
Ince, Joseph Murray	London	1826-1858	Landscape	—	—	16	23	137	—	9	—	—	12	197
Inchbold, John William	London	1849-1887	Landscape	—	—	30	1	3	—	—	2	—	6	42
Inchbold, Stanley	Bushey	1884-1892	Landscape	—	—	—	—	1	—	3	—	—	—	4
Indermaur, J. G.	London	1842-1847	Children	—	—	4	—	1	—	—	—	—	—	5
Induni, Gottardo	London	1887-1888	Sculpture	—	—	2	—	—	—	—	—	—	—	2
Ingall, J. Spence	Barnsley	1892	Sea Pieces	—	—	—	—	—	—	1	—	—	—	1
Ingalton, William	Eton	1816-1826	Landscape	—	—	9	19	5	—	—	—	—	—	33
Ingelow, B. *See* Carpenter and Ingelow	—	—	Architecture	—	—	—	—	—	—	—	—	—	—	—
Ingham, Charles Cromwell, N.A.	New York	1845	Portraits	—	—	1	—	—	—	—	—	—	—	1
Ingle, E.	London	1820	Architecture	—	—	1	—	—	—	—	—	—	—	1
Ingle, J. Lee	London	1872-1874	Sea Pieces	—	—	—	—	1	—	—	—	—	1	2
Inglefield, Commander E. A.	London	1851-1870	Sea Pieces	—	—	5	—	8	—	—	—	—	3	16
Inglis, Miss Jane	London	1859-1892	Figures	—	—	17	1	13	—	1	—	—	14	46
Inglis, Johnstone J., R.H.A.	London	1890-1893	Landscape	—	—	5	—	—	—	—	—	—	—	5
Ingpen, A. W.	Canterbury	1830-1838	Sporting	—	—	8	2	6	—	—	—	—	—	16
Ingram, Archibald B.	Norbiton	1881-1887	Landscape	—	—	—	—	1	—	—	—	—	1	2
Ingram, Miss E. J.	Frogmore	1864-1866	Landscape	—	—	—	2	—	—	—	—	—	—	2
Ingram, Margaret K.	London	1883	Venice	—	—	—	—	2	—	—	—	—	—	2
Ingram, William Ayerst, R.B.A.§	London	1880-1893	Landscape	—	—	16	—	80	—	13	—	—	11	120
Ingram, Walter Rowlands	Brussels	1862-1893	Sculpture	—	—	38	—	2	—	—	3	4	—	47
Inman, Henry	New York	1838-1845	Portraits	—	—	3	—	—	—	—	—	—	—	3
Inman, J.	London	1830	Theatrical	—	—	—	—	1	—	—	—	—	—	1
Inman, Marshall Nisbet	London	1876	Landscape	—	—	—	—	—	—	—	—	—	1	1
Inman, W. S.	London	1815-1838	Architecture	—	—	9	—	—	—	—	—	—	—	9
Innes, Miss Alice	London	1869-1870	Flowers	—	—	—	—	2	—	—	—	—	—	2
Innes, C.	London	1845-1848	Architecture	—	—	3	—	—	—	—	—	—	—	3
Innes, James Archibald	London	1866-1870	Figures	—	—	—	—	6	—	—	—	—	—	6
Inness, George, N.A.	New York	1859-1872	Landscape	—	—	3	—	—	—	—	—	—	—	3
Innocente, G.	—	1871	Figures	—	—	—	—	1	—	—	—	—	—	1
Inskip, John Henry	Scarborough	1886-1893	Landscape	—	—	10	—	5	—	—	—	—	—	15
Inskipp, James	London	1816-1864	Figures	—	—	24	83	56	—	—	—	—	1	164
Inwood, Charles Frederick	London	1814-1834	Architecture	—	—	9	—	—	—	—	—	—	—	9
Inwood, E.	London	1821-1832	Architecture	—	—	5	—	—	—	—	—	—	—	5
Inwood, Henry William	London	1809-1838	Architecture	—	—	23	—	—	—	—	—	—	—	23
Inwood, William	London	1813-1833	Architecture	—	—	6	—	—	—	—	—	—	—	6
Ireland, J.	London	1808-1830	Architecture	—	—	10	—	—	—	—	—	—	—	10
Ireland, James	Liverpool	1885-1887	Domestic	—	—	2	—	—	—	3	—	—	—	5
Ireland, Miss Jane	London	1792-1793	Miniatures	—	—	5	—	—	—	—	—	—	—	5
Ireland, Samuel	—	1782-1784	Landscape	—	—	5	—	—	—	—	—	—	—	5
Ireland, Thomas	London	1880-1893	Landscape	—	—	19	—	19	—	7	7	10	19	81
Ireland, William	London	1764-1783	Fruit	6	4	—	—	—	—	—	—	—	—	10
Ireland, Mrs.	—	1817	Flowers	—	—	1	—	—	—	—	—	—	—	1
Ireton, S.	London	1801	Architecture	—	—	1	—	—	—	—	—	—	—	1
Irvine, Hugh	London	1808-1829	Historical	—	—	27	15	—	—	—	—	—	—	42
Irvine, James	Edinburgh	1882-1884	Domestic	—	—	2	—	—	—	—	—	—	—	2
Irvine, John	London	1787-1843	Figures	—	—	29	2	3	—	—	—	—	—	34
Irvine, Miss ‖	London	1863-1871	Landscape	—	—	—	—	5	—	—	—	—	—	5
Irving, Charles M.	London	1823-1832	Landscape	—	—	3	2	4	—	—	—	—	—	9
Irving, J. Thwaite	Witley	1888-1893	Landscape	—	—	1	—	3	—	1	2	4	6	17
Irwin, Miss Annie L.	Sunderland	1886-1890	Flowers	—	—	1	—	—	—	—	—	—	2	3
Irwin, Miss Madelaine	Colchester	1888-1893	Domestic	—	—	6	—	1	—	—	—	—	—	7
Isaacs, Miss Esther S.	London	1885-1890	Domestic	—	—	1	—	—	—	—	—	—	1	2
Isaacs, Lewis Henry, M.P., C.E.	London	1872-1876	Architecture	—	—	4	—	—	—	—	—	—	—	4
Isaacs and Florence	London	1885	Architecture	—	—	1	—	—	—	—	—	—	—	1
Isaacs, Miss	London	1771-1774	Miniatures	—	12	—	—	—	—	—	—	—	—	12
Isaby, Louis Gabriel Eugène	Lägny	1883	Figures	—	—	—	—	—	—	3	—	—	—	3
Isbell, W. G. R.	St. Leonards	1886	Landscape	—	—	—	—	1	—	—	—	—	—	1

Name.	Town.	First and Last Year of Ex.	Speciality.	S. A.	F. S.	R. A.	B. I.	S. S.	O. W.	N.W.	G. G.	N. G.	V. E.	Total.
Israëls, Josef, H.R.W.S., H.R.I.†‡	The Hague	1871-1889	Domestic	—	—	7	—	—	—	21	4	—	—	32
Ival, D. J.	Paris	1855-1860	Domestic	—	—	4	—	—	—	—	—	—	—	4
Iver, R. H.	London	1871	Landscape	—	—	—	—	—	—	—	—	—	1	1
Ivey, Miss Marion Teresa	London	1884-1888	Domestic	—	—	2	—	1	—	1	—	—	—	4
Izant, Herbert	Thornt'n Heath	1880-1891	Dramatic	—	—	3	—	5	—	—	—	—	1	9
Izard, Edwin	London	1880-1885	Landscape	—	—	4	—	12	—	—	—	—	2	18
Izard, Miss Edith A.	London	1884-1890	Domestic	—	—	1	—	1	—	—	—	—	—	2
Izard, Miss Gertrude M.	London	1890-1891	Flowers	—	—	—	—	2	—	—	—	—	—	2
Jabec, La Baronne	—	1833	Portraits	—	—	1	—	—	—	—	—	—	—	1
Jack, John	London	1830-1831	Sculpture	—	—	5	—	—	—	—	—	—	—	5
Jack, Miss Patti	St. Andrews	1884	Landscape	—	—	1	—	—	—	—	—	—	—	1
Jack, Richard	Paris	1893	Portraits	—	—	1	—	—	—	—	—	—	—	1
Jacker, B.	London	1842	Dramatic	—	—	1	—	—	—	—	—	—	—	1
Jackman, Miss Kate	London	1889-1890	Domestic	—	—	—	—	—	—	—	—	—	2	2
Jackman, P.	London	1867-1870	Domestic	—	—	3	—	—	—	—	—	—	—	3
Jackman, Miss	—	1821	Landscape	—	—	1	—	—	—	—	—	—	—	1
Jackson —	London	1770	Allegorical	—	4	—	—	—	—	—	—	—	—	4
Jackson, Arthur	London	1890	Churches	—	—	—	—	—	—	1	—	—	—	1
Jackson, Miss Caroline F.	London	1847-1848	Figures	—	—	1	—	2	—	—	—	—	—	3
Jackson, E.	London	1876	Figures	—	—	—	—	1	—	—	—	—	—	1
Jackson, Emma	St. Servin	1873	Sea Pieces	—	—	—	—	2	—	—	—	—	—	2
Jackson, Miss Emily E.	London	1883-1884	Landscape	—	—	3	—	1	—	—	—	—	—	4
Jackson, Miss Emily F.	Carshalton	1875-1887	Flowers	—	—	16	—	19	—	6	2	—	17	60
Jackson, E. Jeaffreson	London	1884-1887	Buildings	—	—	3	—	—	—	—	—	—	—	3
Jackson, Miss Emily M.	Norwood	1870	Domestic	—	—	—	—	—	—	—	—	—	2	2
Jackson, Rev. Frederick C.	London	1868-1884	Sea Pieces	—	—	2	—	6	—	—	—	—	7	15
Jackson, F. Hamilton, R.B.A.§	London	1870-1893	Landscape	—	—	20	—	46	—	9	2	1	32	110
Jackson, Frederick William, R.B.A.§	Manchester	1880-1893	Landscape	—	—	19	—	13	—	—	—	—	5	37
Jackson, G.	London	1844	Game	—	—	1	—	—	—	—	—	—	—	1
Jackson, George B. W.	London	1846	Architecture	—	—	1	—	—	—	—	—	—	—	1
Jackson, G. R.	London	1872	Sculpture	—	—	1	—	—	—	—	—	—	—	1
Jackson, Miss Helen	London	1884-1893	Domestic	—	—	5	—	3	—	1	—	—	1	10
Jackson, Miss Harriet A. E. *See* Mrs. John	—	—	—	—	—	—	—	—	—	—	—	—	—	—
Browning	—	1809-1816	Scriptural	—	—	20	7	—	—	—	—	—	—	27
Jackson, Herbert P.	London	1891	Portraits	—	—	—	—	—	—	—	—	—	1	1
Jackson, John	London	1856-1871	Landscape	—	—	—	—	1	—	—	—	—	1	2
Jackson, John, R.A.	London	1804-1830	Portraits	—	—	146	20	—	—	—	—	—	—	166
Jackson, J., Junr.	Oxford	1816-1835	Portraits	—	—	16	—	—	—	—	—	—	—	16
Jackson, J.	London	1836-1837	Sculpture	—	—	4	—	—	—	—	—	—	—	4
Jackson, J. A. C.	London	1816-1825	Landscape	—	—	—	3	—	—	—	—	—	—	3
Jackson, James E.	Salford	1876-1884	Figures	—	—	4	—	4	—	—	—	—	2	10
Jackson, J. G.	London	1817-1844	Buildings	—	—	8	—	4	—	—	—	—	—	12
Jackson, John Richardson	London	1854-1876	Engraving	—	—	27	—	—	—	—	—	—	—	27
Jackson, J. W.	London	1831-1832	Portraits	—	—	2	—	—	—	—	—	—	—	2
Jackson, L.	London	1885	Landscape	—	—	—	—	2	—	—	—	—	—	2
Jackson, Louis W.	Norwood	1878-1879	Figures	—	—	1	—	—	—	—	—	—	2	3
Jackson, Mason	London	1856-1879	Landscape	—	—	2	—	—	—	—	—	—	14	16
Jackson, M.	London	1868-1869	Figures	—	—	—	—	2	—	—	—	—	—	2
Jackson, M. P. B.	London	1850-1857	Figures	—	—	3	2	5	—	—	—	—	—	10
Jackson, Robert	—	1850-1878	Sculpture	—	—	30	4	1	—	—	—	—	—	35
Jackson, Samuel†	Bristol	1823-1848	Landscape	—	—	—	1	1	49	—	—	—	—	51
Jackson, Samuel Phillips, R.W.S.†	Clifton	1851-1893	Sea Pieces	—	—	16	9	—	841	—	—	—	—	866
Jackson, Thomas Graham, A.R.A., M.A., F.SA.	London	1873-1893	Architecture	—	—	42	—	—	—	—	—	—	6	48
Jackson, T. J.	London	1843	Architecture	—	—	1	—	—	—	—	—	—	—	1
Jackson, T. J. R.	London	1791-1799	Architecture	—	—	7	—	—	—	—	—	—	—	7
Jackson, W.	London	1848-1854	Sculpture	—	—	5	—	—	—	—	—	—	—	5
Jackson, Walter	London	1874	Domestic	—	—	—	—	—	—	—	—	—	1	1
Jackson, Mrs. William	Exeter	1771	Landscape	—	—	2	—	—	—	—	—	—	—	2
Jackson, W. G. G.	Penge	1876	Heads	—	—	1	—	—	—	—	—	—	—	1
Jackson, Mrs. *See* Mrs. Holt	—	1857-1861	Still Life	—	—	—	—	3	—	—	—	—	—	3
Jacob, Miss Edith	London	1888-1893	Flowers	—	—	—	—	—	—	5	—	—	—	5
Jacob, Julius	Paris	1845-1854	Portraits	—	—	16	—	—	—	—	—	—	—	16
Jacobber —	London	1839	Fruit	—	—	—	1	—	—	—	—	—	—	1
Jacobi, E.	—	1843	Dramatic	—	—	—	—	1	—	—	—	—	—	1
Jacobs, E.	London	1859	Figures	—	—	1	—	—	—	—	—	—	—	1
Jacobs, John	London	1816-1864	Landscape	—	—	7	8	16	—	—	—	—	—	31
Jacobs, Joseph	London	1828	Portraits	—	—	—	—	1	—	—	—	—	—	1
Jacobs, John E.	London	1878-1893	Landscape	—	—	4	—	15	—	—	—	—	6	25

Name.	Town.	First and Last Year of Ex.	Speciality.	S. A.	F. S.	R. A.	B. I.	S. S.	O. W.	N. W.	G. G.	N. G.	V. E.	Total.
Jacobs, J. F.	London	1884	Flowers	—	—	—	—	1	—	—	—	—	—	1
Jacobs, Miss Louisa	London	1884-1891	Sculpture	—	—	3	—	5	—	1	—	—	2	11
Jacobson —	Denmark	1815	Sculpture	—	—	1	—	—	—	—	—	—	—	1
Jacobson, Miss S. H.	London	1875	Flowers	—	—	—	—	1	—	—	—	—	—	1
Jacoby, Professor Louis	Berlin	1884-1893	Engraving	—	—	2	—	—	—	—	—	—	—	2
Jacomb-Hood. *See* H.	—	—	—	—	—	—	—	—	—	—	—	—	—	—
Jacott, J. J.	Paris	1874	Engraving	—	—	2	—	—	—	—	—	—	—	2
Jacquand, Claudius	Paris	1844-1853	Historical	—	—	4	—	—	—	—	—	—	—	4
Jacquemart, Jules Ferdinand	Paris	1872-1877	Etching	—	—	—	—	—	—	—	—	—	35	35
Jacques, J.	London	1827-1833	Architecture	—	—	5	—	1	—	—	—	—	—	6
Jacquet, Achille	Paris	1886-1893	Etching	—	—	2	—	—	—	—	—	—	—	2
Jacquet, Miss Cecilia	London	1889-1893	Landscape	—	—	—	—	2	—	—	1	1	—	4
Jacquet, Jean Gustave	Paris	1878-1886	Figures	—	—	—	—	—	—	—	1	—	1	2
Jacquet, Jules	Paris	1884	Etching	—	—	1	—	—	—	—	—	—	—	1
Jagger, J.	London	1774-1784	Architecture	—	1	6	—	—	—	—	—	—	—	7
Jahn, C.	London	1868-1873	Sculpture	—	—	8	—	—	—	—	—	—	—	8
Jakobides, Georg	Munich	1886	Domestic	—	—	1	—	—	—	—	—	—	—	1
Jakush, M.	London	1836	Enamels	—	—	1	—	—	—	—	—	—	—	1
Jalabert, Charles François	Paris	1872	Landscape	—	—	—	—	—	—	—	—	—	1	1
Jalfon, A. J.	London	1846	Landscape	—	—	—	—	1	—	—	—	—	—	1
Jamenez —	Paris	1879	Figures	—	—	—	—	—	—	—	—	—	1	1
James —	Peterborough	1776-1783	Landscape	—	11	—	—	—	—	—	—	—	—	11
James, A.	Canterbury	1828	Sea Pieces	—	—	—	—	1	—	—	—	—	—	1
James, Miss Alice	Bath	1887-1891	Miniatures	—	—	14	—	—	—	—	—	—	—	14
James, Arthur C.	Eton	1888-1889	Landscape	—	—	—	—	—	—	4	—	—	—	4
James, C.	London	1792	Sculpture	—	—	1	—	—	—	—	—	—	—	1
James, C.	London	1828-1829	Landscape	—	—	—	—	2	—	—	—	—	—	2
James, C.	London	1881	Landscape	—	—	—	—	2	—	—	—	—	—	2
James, C. S.	London	1854-1862	Landscape	—	—	3	—	4	—	—	—	—	—	7
James, David	London	1881-1892	Sea Pieces	—	—	3	—	—	—	—	—	—	1	4
James, E.	London	1825	Portraits	—	—	2	—	—	—	—	—	—	—	2
James, Miss Edith	London	1883-1890	Landscape	—	—	3	—	2	—	—	1	—	—	6
James, Miss Emily	Edinburgh	1813	Figures	—	—	—	1	—	—	—	—	—	—	1
James, F.	London	1801	Dramatic	—	—	2	—	—	—	—	—	—	—	2
James, Francis	Florence	1832-1845	Landscape	—	—	4	1	2	—	—	—	—	—	7
James, Francis E., R.B.A.§	Hastings	1884-1888	Landscape	—	—	—	—	17	—	—	—	—	—	17
James, F. E.	London	1887	Landscape	—	—	—	—	1	—	—	—	—	—	1
James, Frank James	London	1888-1890	Landscape	—	—	1	—	6	—	—	—	—	—	7
James, George, A.R.A.	London	1762-1790	Portraits	11	5	16	—	—	—	—	—	—	—	32
James, Miss G.	Canterbury	1826-1828	Miniatures	—	—	—	—	4	—	—	—	—	—	4
James, Harry E.	London	1882-1893	Landscape	—	—	2	—	1	—	—	—	—	9	12
James, H. James	London	1889	Landscape	—	—	1	—	—	—	—	—	—	—	1
James, J.	London	1794	Portraits	—	—	1	—	—	—	—	—	—	—	1
James, J.	Barnet	1810-1816	Landscape	—	—	3	—	—	—	—	—	—	1	4
James, Joseph	London	1851-1871	Architecture	—	—	12	—	—	—	—	—	—	—	12
James, J. Dearman	London	1864	Animals	—	—	—	1	—	—	—	—	—	—	1
James, M.	Barnet	1810	Landscape	—	—	1	—	—	—	—	—	—	—	1
James, Miss M.	London	1873-1878	Flowers	—	—	—	—	4	—	—	—	—	—	4
James, Miss M. E.	London	1804	Portraits	—	—	1	—	—	—	—	—	—	—	1
James, P.	London	1874	Domestic	—	—	—	—	2	—	—	—	—	—	2
James, R.	Nottingham	1841-1851	Figures	—	—	4	1	—	—	—	—	—	—	5
James, Richard S.	London	1860-1891	Domestic	—	—	28	5	22	—	—	—	—	2	57
James, S.	London	1879-1890	Landscape	—	—	1	—	2	—	—	—	—	1	4
James, T.	Canterbury	1855	Architecture	—	—	1	—	—	—	—	—	—	—	1
James, Sir Walter Charles, Bart.	London	1849-1853	Landscape	—	—	5	2	—	—	—	—	—	—	7
James, William	London	1761-1771	Landscape	18	—	7	—	—	—	—	—	—	—	25
James, Miss (aged 14)	London	1773	Flowers	1	—	—	—	—	—	—	—	—	—	1
Jameson, Middleton	London	1877-1893	Landscape	—	—	2	—	2	—	—	—	—	5	9
Jameson, Miss Rosa	London	1886-1891	Domestic	—	—	4	—	1	—	3	—	—	3	11
Jameson, R. S.	—	1823	Landscape	—	—	1	—	—	—	—	—	—	—	1
Jameson, William	London	1871	River Scenes	—	—	—	—	—	—	—	—	—	1	1
Jameson and Wallis	London	1889	Architecture	—	—	2	—	—	—	—	—	—	—	2
Jamison, Mrs. Archer, *or* Arthur (Isabel)	St. Helens	1877-1889	Flowers	—	—	4	—	1	—	1	—	—	5	11
Jamison, Miss Sarah	Belfast	1890	Flowers	—	—	—	—	—	—	1	—	—	—	1
Jansen —, Junr.	London	1782	Mythological	—	1	—	—	—	—	—	—	—	—	1
Jansen, Fritz	London	1883-1885	Portraits	—	—	1	—	—	—	1	—	—	4	6
Jansen, P. J.	London	1882	Figures	—	—	—	—	—	—	—	—	—	1	1
J'Anson, E. (?) I'Anson	London	1794-1798	Architecture	—	—	2	—	—	—	—	—	—	—	2
Janson, E.	—	1824	Figures	—	—	1	—	—	—	—	—	—	—	1
Janvry, De. *See* D.	—	—	—	—	—	—	—	—	—	—	—	—	—	—
Japy, Louis Aimé	Paris	1881	Landscape	—	—	—	—	—	—	—	1	—	—	1
Jaques, Jules	London	1882	Landscape	—	—	—	—	1	—	—	—	—	—	1

Name.	Town.	First and Last Year of Ex.	Speciality.	S. A.	F. S.	R. A.	B. I.	S. S.	O. W.	N.W.	G. G.	N.G.	V.E.	Total.
Jaques, Miss Julia	London	1826-1836	Portraits	—	—	13	—	17	—	1	—	—	—	31
Jardine, J.	Dartford	1813	Flowers	—	—	1	—	—	—	—	—	—	—	1
Jardine, J., Junr.	Dartford	1829	Flowers	—	—	1	—	—	—	—	—	—	—	1
Jardine, Mrs. James	London	1891	Landscape	—	—	—	—	—	—	1	—	—	—	1
Jarrett, G.	London	1827-1829	Portraits	—	—	1	—	1	—	—	—	—	—	2
Jarrett, S. T.	Hackney	1826	Mythological	—	—	1	—	—	—	—	—	—	—	1
Jarvis —	London	1780	Landscape	—	1	—	—	—	—	—	—	—	—	1
Jarvis, George	London	1874-1890	Domestic	—	—	3	—	9	—	1	—	—	3	16
Jarvis (Henry) and Son	London	1870-1886	Architecture	—	—	4	—	—	—	—	—	—	—	4
Jarvis, Matthew	Liverpool	1879-1887	Landscape	—	—	1	—	2	—	3	—	—	—	6
Jay, Miss Carrie	London	1880-1883	Landscape	—	—	—	—	2	—	—	—	—	—	2
Jay, Hamilton	London	1875-1893	Domestic	—	—	7	—	21	—	—	—	1	3	32
Jay, J. A. B.	London	1878-1880	Landscape	—	—	2	—	—	—	—	—	—	—	2
Jay, J. Isabella Lee	London	1873-1881	Buildings	—	—	—	—	3	—	—	—	—	1	4
Jay, J. W.	London	1868	Figures	—	—	—	—	1	—	—	—	—	—	1
Jay, W.	London	1809-1817	Architecture	—	—	5	—	—	—	—	—	—	—	5
Jay, William Samuel, R.B.A. §	London	1868-1893	Landscape	—	—	25	—	41	—	—	10	8	13	97
Jayne, Charles	London	1838-1879	Landscape	—	—	10	12	8	—	—	—	—	—	30
Jayne, Mrs. Charles (Mary)	London	1846-1878	Landscape	—	—	13	21	19	—	—	—	—	—	53
Jazet, Paul	London	1881	Etching	—	—	—	—	—	—	—	—	—	1	1
Jeakes, J.	London	1796-1809	Landscape	—	—	11	—	—	—	—	—	—	—	11
Jean, P.	London	1787-1802	Miniatures	—	—	118	—	—	—	—	—	—	—	118
Jean, R.	London	1801-1803	Miniatures	—	—	7	—	—	—	—	—	—	—	7
Jean, St. *See* S.	—	—	—	—	—	—	—	—	—	—	—	—	—	—
Jeans —	Edinburgh	1769-1771	Sculpture	—	3	—	—	—	—	—	—	—	—	3
Jeans, T.	London	1797	Architecture	—	—	1	—	—	—	—	—	—	—	1
Jearrad, Robert William	London	1813-1838	Architecture	—	—	4	—	—	—	—	—	—	—	4
Jeauron, P. A.	—	1851	Scriptural	—	—	1	—	—	—	—	—	—	—	1
Jeayes, Miss J.	London	1872	Domestic	—	—	—	—	1	—	—	—	—	—	1
Jeens, Charles Henry	London	1860-1876	Engraving	—	—	6	—	—	—	—	—	—	—	6
Jeeves, Louie	Hitchin	1884	Animals	—	—	—	—	1	—	—	—	—	—	1•
Jefferies, J.	London	1862	Landscape	—	—	—	—	1	—	—	—	—	—	1
Jefferson, Robert	London	1853-1860	Sculpture	—	—	3	—	2	—	—	—	—	—	5
Jeffery, Miss Annie	Haywards Heath	1884-1890	Flowers	—	—	1	—	2	—	—	—	—	1	4
Jeffery, C.	New Cross	1877	Bengal	—	—	—	—	—	—	—	—	—	1	1
Jeffery, E.	Exeter	1840-1842	Landscape	—	—	3	—	—	—	—	—	—	—	3
Jefferys, Bertha	London	1890	Flowers	—	—	—	—	1	—	—	—	—	—	1
Jefferys, James	London	1773-1783	Mythological	8	—	3	—	—	—	—	—	—	—	11
Jefferys, William	Maidstone	1766-1775	Fruit	8	—	—	—	—	—	—	—	—	—	8
Jeffray, A. E.	London	1833-1848	Landscape	—	—	6	2	3	—	—	—	—	—	11
Jeffray, James	Hackney	1854-1855	Domestic	—	—	—	—	—	—	—	—	—	2	2
Jeffray, Richard	London	1835-1854	Scriptural	—	—	11	7	4	—	—	—	—	—	22
Jeffray, W.	London	1788-1789	Portraits	—	—	3	—	—	—	—	—	—	—	3
Jeffrey, Miss E. C.	Rome	1881	Figures	—	—	—	—	1	—	—	—	—	—	1
Jeffrey, James	London	1833-1852	Cattle	—	—	7	2	4	—	—	—	—	—	13
Jeffreys, Miss Edith Gwyn	London	1885-1889	Sculpture	—	—	9	—	—	—	—	—	—	—	9
Jeffroy —	London	1829	—	—	—	*	—	—	—	—	—	—	—	—
Jeffs, Mrs.	—	1807	Landscape	—	—	1	—	—	—	—	—	—	—	1
Jehly, Jacob	Austria	1891	Portraits	—	—	1	—	—	—	—	—	—	—	1
Jehner, Isaac	London	1777	Engraving	5	—	—	—	—	—	—	—	—	—	5
Jekyll, Miss	Guildford	1865	Portraits	—	—	1	—	—	—	—	—	—	—	1
Jelley, James Valentine	Birmingham	1885-1891	Landscape	—	—	12	—	—	—	1	1	—	—	14
Jellicoe, John F.	London	1865-1880	Domestic	—	—	—	—	1	—	—	—	—	4	5
Jemmett, Arthur R.	Wimbledon	1889	Architecture	—	—	1	—	—	—	—	—	—	—	1
Jenkin, William	Warrington	1870-1877	Landscape	—	—	—	—	—	—	—	—	—	4	4
Jenkins, Miss Anne	London	1876-1885	Flowers	—	—	10	—	12	—	—	—	—	11	33
Jenkins, Miss Blanche ‖	London	1872-1893	Domestic	—	—	32	—	18	—	—	4	9	26	89
Jenkins, Miss C.	—	1827-1832	Flowers	—	—	3	—	—	—	—	—	—	—	3
Jenkins, C. S.	London	1871	Landscape	—	—	—	—	—	—	—	—	—	1	1
Jenkins, David C.	Nottingham	1884-1892	Rustic	—	—	6	—	1	—	—	—	—	1	8
Jenkins, Emily Vaughan	Oxford	1890-1891	Buildings	—	—	—	—	1	—	2	—	—	—	3
Jenkins, H.	London	1854-1872	Landscape	—	—	2	—	5	—	—	—	—	—	7
Jenkins, H. E.	—	1806-1807	Landscape	—	—	2	—	—	—	—	—	—	—	2
Jenkins, J.	London	1788-1832	Buildings	—	—	11	—	2	—	—	—	—	—	13
Jenkins, Joseph John, F.S.A., R.W.S. † ‡	London	1829-1881	Figures	—	—	1	2	11	273	61	—	—	—	348
Jenkins, M.	London	1830	Portraits	—	—	1	—	—	—	—	—	—	—	1
Jenkins, T.	London	1830	Figures	—	—	—	—	1	—	—	—	—	—	1
Jenkins, W.	London	1822-1827	Ruins	—	—	4	—	—	—	—	—	—	—	4
Jenkins, W. B.	London	1827	Engraving	—	—	—	—	2	—	—	—	—	—	2
Jenkins, W. W.	London	1853-1854	Landscape	—	2	—	—	—	—	—	—	—	—	2
Jenkinson, Miss Charlotte F. A.	Farnham	1874-1889	Landscape	—	—	—	—	—	—	—	1	—	2	3
Jenks, R.	London	1823	Figures	—	—	1	—	—	—	—	—	—	—	1

Name.	Town.	First and Last Year of Ex.	Speciality.	S. A.	F. S.	R. A.	B. I.	S. S.	O. W.	N.W.	G. G.	N. G.	V. E.	Total.
Jennens, W.	London	1872	Animals	—	—	—	—	—	—	—	—	—	1	1
Jenner, G. P.	London	1834-1840	Historical	—	—	5	—	—	—	2	—	—	—	7
Jenner, G. T.	London	1834	Figures	—	—	—	—	1	—	—	—	—	—	1
Jenner, J.	London	1791	Engraving	6	—	—	—	—	—	—	—	—	—	6
Jenner, W.	—	1874	Landscape	—	—	1	—	—	—	—	—	—	—	1
Jennings, Benjamin	Rome	1849-1850	Sculpture	—	—	3	—	—	—	—	—	—	—	3
Jennings, Edward	Lee	1865-1888	Landscape	—	—	11	—	9	—	2	—	—	11	33
Jennings, Miss E.	London	1837	Animals	—	—	—	—	1	—	—	—	—	—	1
Jennings, Emma M.	Penge	1880	Buildings	—	—	—	—	1	—	—	—	—	—	1
Jennings, Edward W.	Swansea	1885	Buildings	—	—	1	—	—	—	—	—	—	—	1
Jennings, James, F.S.A.	London	1763-1793	Miniatures	40	—	1	—	—	—	—	—	—	—	41
Jennings, Joseph	London	1843	Architecture	—	—	1	—	—	—	—	—	—	—	1
Jennings, Miss Mary	Brighton	1885-1887	Miniatures	—	—	2	—	—	—	—	—	—	—	2
Jennings, S.	London	1789-1834	Scriptural	—	—	35	14	—	—	—	—	—	2	51
Jennings, W. G. §	—	1797-1830	Landscape	—	—	8	—	1	—	—	—	—	—	9
Jennons, Luke	London	1880-1881	Domestic	—	—	2	—	—	—	—	—	—	—	2
Jenour, C.	London	1825-1832	Portraits	—	—	8	—	—	—	—	—	—	—	8
Jenoure, A.	London	1847	Architecture	—	—	3	—	—	—	—	—	—	—	3
Jensen, Christian Albrecht	Copenhagen	1837-1838	Portraits	—	—	8	—	—	—	—	—	—	—	8
Jensen, E. M.	London	1864-1867	Landscape	—	—	—	3	—	—	—	—	—	—	3
Jensen, Theodor	London	1854-1864	Figures	—	—	5	7	2	—	—	—	—	—	14
Jephson, Mrs. Alfred (Harriet J.)	Cowes	1884-1889	Venice	—	—	—	—	1	—	1	3	—	—	5
Jerachau, H.	London	1874	Landscape	—	—	1	—	—	—	—	—	—	—	1
Jerichau-Baumann, Madame Elizabeth Maria	—	—	—	—	—	—	—	—	—	—	—	—	—	—
Anna (Miss Elizabeth Maria Anna Baumann)	Copenhagen	1859-1869	Domestic	—	—	22	—	—	—	—	—	—	—	22
Jerichau, F.	Copenhagen	1858-1868	Figures	—	—	3	—	—	—	—	—	—	—	3
Jermyn, G. A.	London	1833	Landscape	—	—	—	—	1	—	—	—	—	—	1
Jerningham, G.	London	1793	Architecture	—	—	1	—	—	—	—	—	—	—	1
Jerôme, Ambrosini	London	1840-1871	Historical	—	—	17	23	37	—	—	—	—	9	86
Jervis, Edward de Rosen	Sidmouth	1890	Venice	—	—	—	—	2	—	—	—	—	—	2
Jervois, W. D., R.E.	London	1847	African	—	—	—	—	1	—	—	—	—	—	1
Jervous, A.	Bridgwater	1875	Landscape	—	—	—	—	1	—	—	—	—	—	1
Jesse, George R.	Macclesfield	1872-1874	Landscape	—	—	1	—	—	—	—	—	—	1	2
Jessop, Ernest Maurice	London	1883-1890	Domestic	—	—	3	—	—	—	—	—	—	—	3
Jessop, J.	Croydon	1867-1868	Fruit	—	—	—	—	2	—	—	—	—	3	5
Jessop, W.	London	1802-1808	Figures	—	—	2	—	—	—	—	—	—	—	2
Jessup, Miss A. P.	Norwich	1787	Drawings	—	—	5	—	—	—	—	—	—	—	5
Jeune, Le. *See* L.	—	—	—	—	—	—	—	—	—	—	—	—	—	—
Jevons, Arthur	Lyndhurst	1876-1877	Landscape	—	—	—	—	—	—	—	—	—	2	2
Jevons, Mrs. Louisa E.	Durham	1893	Miniatures	—	—	1	—	—	—	—	—	—	—	1
Jevons, Miss Mary C.	London	1880-1886	Landscape	—	—	—	—	—	—	1	—	—	1	2
Jewel —	—	1793	Portraits	—	—	1	—	—	—	—	—	—	—	1
Jewitt, Clement W.	—	1893	Sculpture	—	—	—	—	1	—	—	—	—	—	1
Jewitt, Edward Holmes	Lancaster	1881	Stained Glass	—	—	1	—	—	—	—	—	—	—	1
Jex-Blake, Miss E. *See* B.	—	—	—	—	—	—	—	—	—	—	—	—	—	—
Jimenez-y-Aranda —	Seville	1877	Figures	—	—	—	—	—	—	—	—	—	2	2
Jobbins, William H.	Nottingham	1872-1886	Landscape	—	—	4	—	2	—	1	—	—	2	9
Jobling, Robert	Newcastle	1878-1892	Sea Pieces	—	—	13	—	3	—	—	—	—	—	16
Jobson, Henry	Tottenham	1873-1877	Flowers	—	—	—	—	1	—	—	—	—	6	7
John, William Goscombe	London	1886-1893	Sculpture	—	—	13	—	—	—	—	—	4	—	17
John, St. *See* S.	—	—	—	—	—	—	—	—	—	—	—	—	—	—
Johns, A.	London	1842	Figures	—	—	1	—	—	—	—	—	—	—	1
Johns, Ambrose Bowden	Plymouth	1814-1846	Landscape	—	—	13	3	4	—	—	—	—	—	20
Johns, J. W.	London	1835	Architecture	—	—	1	—	—	—	—	—	—	—	1
Johns, J. W.	London	1854	Portraits	—	—	1	—	—	—	—	—	—	—	1
Johns, Miss	Rickmansworth	1859	Still Life	—	—	—	—	1	—	—	—	—	—	1
Johnson, Lieut.-Col., C.B.	—	1829-1830	Landscape	—	—	—	—	2	—	—	—	—	—	2
Johnson, A.	—	1851	Figures	—	—	1	—	—	—	—	—	—	—	1
Johnson, Miss Adeline	London	1867-1872	Flowers	—	—	—	—	1	—	—	—	—	2	3
Johnson, A.	London	1848-1852	Sculpture	—	—	9	—	—	—	—	—	—	—	9
Johnson, A. *See also* Jones and Johnson	London	1845-1856	Architecture	—	—	6	—	—	—	—	—	—	—	6
Johnson (A.) and Pearson (J. L.)	London	1849	Architecture	—	—	2	—	—	—	—	—	—	—	2
Johnson, Alfred	London	1881-1886	Landscape	—	—	—	—	4	—	—	—	—	—	4
Johnson, A. G.	—	1812	Waterfalls	—	—	1	—	—	—	—	—	—	—	1
Johnson, Alfred J.	London	1875-1887	Domestic	—	—	6	—	7	—	2	—	—	12	27
Johnson, Mrs. A. K. (Bertha J.)	Oxford	1878-1881	Portraits	—	—	3	—	—	—	—	1	—	3	7
Johnson, Mrs. Bessie	Rugby	1893	Domestic	—	—	3	—	—	—	—	—	—	—	3
Johnson, Cyrus, R.I. ‡ φ	London	1872-1893	Domestic	—	—	35	—	8	—	25	3	2	38	111
Johnson, C.	London	1871-1874	Domestic	—	—	3	—	—	—	—	—	—	—	3
Johnson, Charles Edward, R.I. ‡ φ	London	1855-1893	Landscape	—	—	71	4	6	—	22	3	2	36	144
Johnson, C. R.	London	1880	Landscape	—	—	—	—	1	—	—	—	—	—	1
Johnson, Eastwood	Liverpool	1873-1878	Domestic	—	—	1	—	—	—	—	—	—	1	2

Name.	Town.	First and Last Year of Ex.	Speciality.	S. A.	F. S.	R. A.	B. I.	S. S.	O. W.	N. W.	G. G.	N. G.	V. E.	Total.
Johnson, Eli	London	1878-1880	Sculpture	—	—	3	—	—	—	—	—	—	—	3
Johnson, E. Borough	Basingstoke	1886-1892	Domestic	—	—	8	—	1	—	—	—	—	3	12
Johnson, Edward Killingworth, R.W.S. †	Wembly	1846-1893	Landscape	—	—	3	—	7	176	—	—	—	4	190
Johnson, F.	Croydon	1791-1797	Sporting	3	—	1	—	—	—	—	—	—	—	4
Johnson, F.	—	1867	—	—	—	*	—	—	—	—	—	—	—	—
Johnson, Miss Fanny	London	1838	Figures	—	—	1	—	—	—	—	—	—	—	1
Johnson, Mrs. F. V.	Ventnor	1855-1872	Landscape	—	—	2	—	3	—	—	—	—	—	5
Johnson, G.	Sudbury	1819	Landscape	—	—	5	—	—	—	—	—	—	—	5
Johnson, Harry, R.I.‡ φ.	London	1859-1885	Landscape	—	—	16	—	—	—	168	—	—	22	206
Johnson, Henry	London	1824-1847	Figures	—	—	12	9	12	—	—	—	—	—	33
Johnson, Herbert	London	1868-1888	Domestic	—	—	11	—	16	—	—	—	—	6	33
Johnson, Mrs. H.	London	1844-1846	Fruit	—	—	1	—	1	—	—	—	—	—	2
Johnson, Harry John	London	1845-1893	Landscape	—	—	19	39	6	—	—	—	—	1	65
Johnson, Miss Helen Mary	London	1865-1881	Landscape	—	—	—	3	8	—	—	—	—	7	18
Johnson, J.	London	1831	Sculpture	—	—	1	—	—	—	—	—	—	—	1
Johnson, James	London	1775	Buildings	—	1	—	—	—	—	—	—	—	—	1
Johnson, James	Bristol	1822-1832	Landscape	—	—	4	4	6	—	—	—	—	—	14
Johnson, John, F.S.A.	London	1773-1783	Architecture	20	—	1	—	—	—	—	—	—	—	21
Johnson, John. *See also* Newman and Johnson	London	1848-1851	Architecture	—	—	4	—	—	—	—	—	—	—	4
Johnson, John, R.C.A.	Trefrew	1876-1878	Landscape	—	—	—	—	—	—	—	—	—	3	3
Johnson, J. C.	Charlton	1870	Landscape	—	—	—	—	1	—	—	—	—	—	1
Johnson, Miss Mabel	London	1889	Landscape	—	—	—	—	—	—	1	—	—	—	1
Johnson, Mrs. Mary	London	1814-1827	Landscape	—	—	6	11	4	—	—	—	—	—	21
Johnson, Miss M. H.	London	1843-1852	Figures	—	—	5	5	34	—	—	—	—	—	44
Johnson, Nancy J.	London	1845-1848	Landscape	—	—	—	1	1	—	—	—	—	—	2
Johnson, Robin	London	1873-1880	Domestic	—	—	3	—	3	—	—	—	—	3	9
Johnson, R. H.	London	1871-1873	Landscape	—	—	—	—	4	—	—	—	—	—	4
Johnson, R. J.	London	1862-1887	Churches	—	—	6	—	—	—	—	—	—	—	6
Johnson, Samuel	London	1829	Figures	—	—	—	1	—	—	—	—	—	—	1
Johnson, Captain S.	—	1822	Horses	—	—	1	—	—	—	—	—	—	—	1
Johnson, Miss Sophia	—	1783-1809	Landscape	1	—	1	—	—	—	—	—	—	—	2
Johnson, T.	London	1798	Fruit	—	—	1	—	—	—	—	—	—	—	1
Johnson, Thomas Croshaw	London	1852-1880	Landscape	—	—	3	7	33	—	—	—	—	2	45
Johnson, V.	Nottingham	1802-1803	Portraits	—	—	4	—	—	—	—	—	—	—	4
Johnson, W.	Jersey	1864	Landscape	—	—	—	1	—	—	—	—	—	—	1
Johnson, W., Junr.	—	1800-1809	Game	—	—	2	—	—	—	—	—	—	—	2
Johnson, Will.	Bradford	1889	Landscape	—	—	1	—	—	—	—	—	—	—	1
Johnson, Captain Willes J., R.N.	—	1828-1841	Sea Pieces	—	—	3	—	—	—	—	—	—	—	3
Johnson, W. Noel	Bowdon	1892	Landscape	—	—	—	—	1	—	—	—	—	—	1
Johnson, Mrs.	—	1828	Intaglios	—	—	1	—	—	—	—	—	—	—	1
Johnson, Mrs.‖ *See* Miss Pattie Townsend.	—	—	—	—	—	—	—	—	—	—	—	—	—	—
Johnson, Miss	—	1769	Needlework	1	—	—	—	—	—	—	—	—	—	1
Johnson, Miss (?) Louisa	London	1865	Fruit	—	—	—	—	1	—	—	—	—	—	1
Johnston, Alexander	London	1836-1886	Domestic	—	—	77	49	17	—	—	—	—	4	147
Johnston, Mrs. David. *See* Miss M. A. Wheeler	London	1838-1859	Portraits	—	—	11	—	—	—	—	—	—	—	11
Johnston, Frederick	London	1855-1868	Domestic	—	—	3	10	11	—	—	—	—	3	27
Johnston, Henry ‡	London	1834-1858	Domestic	—	—	3	—	—	—	34	—	—	—	37
Johnston, Henry H.	London	1875-1882	Figures	—	—	4	—	—	—	—	—	—	15	19
Johnston, Philip Mainwaring	London	1885	Architecture	—	—	1	—	—	—	—	—	—	—	1
Johnston, R.	London	1806	Portraits	—	—	1	—	—	—	—	—	—	—	1
Johnston, R. de Grand	London	1882	Sculpture	—	—	1	—	—	—	—	—	—	—	1
Johnstone, Charles	London	1824	Sculpture	—	—	—	—	1	—	—	—	—	—	1
Johnstone, G. W., A.R.S.A., R.S.W.	Edinburgh	1885-1892	Landscape	—	—	7	—	—	—	—	—	—	—	7
Johnstone, Henry	London	1835-1853	Figures	—	—	—	4	11	—	—	—	—	—	15
Johnstone, Henry J. §	Marlow	1884-1892	Domestic	—	—	8	—	14	—	—	—	—	—	22
Johnstone, James	—	1783	Portraits	—	2	—	—	—	—	—	—	—	—	2
Johnstone, J. N.	London	1883-1885	Architecture	—	—	5	—	—	—	—	—	—	—	5
Johnstone, M. A.	London	1846-1847	Portraits	—	—	3	—	—	—	—	—	—	—	3
Johnstone, William Borthwick, R.S.A.	Edinburgh	1848-1853	Historical	—	—	—	—	—	—	—	—	—	8	8
Johnstone, Mrs.	—	1835-1839	Portraits	—	—	3	—	—	—	—	—	—	—	3
Joinet, M.	London	1804	Architecture	—	—	1	—	—	—	—	—	—	—	1
Jolley, Gwilt	London	1884-1893	Domestic	—	—	11	—	11	—	—	—	—	9	31
Jollivet, Pierre Jules	Paris	1842	—	—	—	—	—	*	—	—	—	—	—	—
Jolly, Miss Fanny C.	Bath	1856-1879	Landscape	—	—	6	1	9	—	—	—	—	19	35
Jones. *See* Salomans and Jones	—	—	Architecture	—	—	—	—	—	—	—	—	—	—	—
Jones —	Derby	1765	Fruit	—	1	—	—	—	—	—	—	—	—	1
Jones —	London	1773-1783	Architecture	3	1	—	—	—	—	—	—	—	—	4
Jones, A.	London	1839	Landscape	—	—	—	1	—	—	—	—	—	—	1
Jones, Adrian	London	1884-1893	Sculpture	—	—	9	—	—	—	1	4	—	1	15
Jones, Agnes	London	1893	Landscape	—	—	—	—	2	—	—	—	—	—	2
Jones, Anna M.	Guernsey	1868-1870	Landscape	—	—	1	—	—	—	—	—	—	1	2

Name.	Town.	First and Last Year of Ex.	Speciality.	S. A.	F. S.	R. A.	B. I.	S. S.	O.W.	N.W.	G. G.	N. G.	V. E.	Total.
Jones, A. R.	Manchester	1845	Cattle	—	—	—	1	—	—	—	—	—	—	1
Jones, Arthur S.	London	1892	Architecture	—	—	1	—	—	—	—	—	—	—	1
Jones, B.	London	1774	Miniatures	—	4	—	—	—	—	—	—	—	—	4
Jones, Champion	London	1878-1892	Sea Shores	—	—	8	—	17	—	1	1	—	1	28
Jones, Charles, R.C.A.	Barnham	1860-1891	Cattle	—	—	12	12	61	—	10	—	—	6	101
Jones, Miss Charlotte	London	1801-1823	Miniatures	—	—	41	—	—	—	—	—	—	—	41
Jones, C.	London	1824	Intaglios	—	—	1	—	—	—	—	—	—	—	1
Jones, C.	London	1827-1828	Landscape	—	—	2	—	—	—	—	—	—	—	2
Jones, Miss Constance Flood	London	1890	Domestic	—	—	—	—	—	—	—	1	—	—	1
Jones, Conway Lloyd	Wimborne	1871-1881	Landscape	—	—	—	—	8	—	—	—	—	5	13
Jones, David	Dudley	1891	Landscape	—	—	1	—	—	—	—	—	—	—	1
Jones, Mrs. D. (Viola)	Wimbledon	1893	Portraits	—	—	1	—	—	—	—	—	—	—	1
Jones, E.	London	1819-1835	Architecture	—	—	3	—	—	—	—	—	—	—	3
Jones, Edward	Shrewsbury	1833-1849	Sea Pieces	—	—	1	3	11	—	—	—	—	—	15
Jones, Edward Burne-, A.R.A. *See* B.	—	—	—	—	—	—	—	—	—	—	—	—	—	—
Jones, Miss Eliza	London	1807-1852	Miniatures	—	—	98	35	—	9	—	—	—	—	142
Jones, Miss E. C.	Harrow	1887	Figures	—	—	—	—	—	—	—	—	—	1	1
Jones, Miss Emma E. *See* Mrs. Soyer	London	1823-1837	Domestic	—	—	12	26	6	—	—	—	—	—	44
Jones, Miss E. Nora	London	1890-1893	Miniatures	—	—	7	—	—	—	—	—	—	—	7
Jones, Frederick	London	1867-1885	Landscape	—	—	1	—	—	—	—	—	—	3	4
Jones, Francis E.	London	1880	Architecture	—	—	1	—	—	—	—	—	—	—	1
Jones, Miss Frances M.	London	1882-1885	Domestic	—	—	—	—	7	—	—	—	—	—	7
Jones, George, R.A.	London	1803-1870	Landscape	—	—	221	141	1	5	—	—	—	—	368
Jones, G.	London	1832	Portraits	—	—	1	—	—	—	—	—	—	—	1
Jones, G.	London	1835	Landscape	—	—	—	—	1	—	—	—	—	—	1
Jones, G. F., F.R.I.B.A.	London	1840-1869	Architecture	—	—	10	—	—	—	—	—	—	—	10
Jones, G. H.	London	1821-1822	Architecture	—	—	2	—	—	—	—	—	—	—	2
Jones, G. Smetham-	London	1888-1893	Domestic	—	—	1	—	1	—	4	—	—	—	6
Jones, George W.	London	1885	Figures	—	—	1	—	—	—	—	—	—	—	1
Jones, Henry	London	1823-1824	Scriptural	—	—	—	2	2	—	—	—	—	—	4
Jones, Sir Horace (City Architect)	London	1856-1886	Architecture	—	—	21	—	—	—	—	—	—	—	21
Jones, Hugo	London	1848	Figures	—	—	—	1	—	—	—	—	—	—	1
Jones, H. Bolton	Finisterre	1873-1883	Landscape	—	—	3	—	2	—	—	—	—	1	6
Jones, H. C.	London	1825-1828	Figures	—	—	—	—	6	—	—	—	—	—	6
Jones, Harry C.	Epsom	1891-1893	Domestic	—	—	3	—	—	—	—	—	—	—	3
Jones, H. E.	Brentford	1882-1883	Rustic	—	—	—	—	4	—	—	—	—	2	6
Jones, H. Thaddeus. *See* Thaddeus	London	1883-1884	Portraits	—	—	3	—	—	—	—	1	—	—	4
Jones, John	London	1779-1791	Engraving	10	1	—	—	—	—	—	—	—	—	11
Jones, Miss J.	London	1828	Landscape	—	—	—	—	1	—	—	—	—	—	1
Jones, Joseph	Ashby-de-la-Zouch	1881	Landscape	—	—	—	—	—	—	—	—	—	1	1
Jones, J. Clinton, R.C.A.	Conway	1885-1889	Landscape	—	—	4	—	—	—	1	—	—	—	5
Jones, J. E. *See* Weatherley and Jones	—	—	Architecture	—	—	—	—	—	—	—	—	—	—	—
Jones, John E.	London	1842-1862	Sculpture	—	—	108	—	2	—	—	—	—	—	110
Jones, Miss J. G. E.	Gloucester	1859	Street Scenes	—	—	—	—	2	—	—	—	—	—	2
Jones, J. H.	London	1828-1833	Portraits	—	—	10	—	—	—	—	—	—	—	10
Jones, J. J.	—	1834-1835	Landscape	—	—	—	5	—	—	—	—	—	—	5
Jones, John Philpot	London	1857-1872	Architecture	—	—	16	—	—	—	—	—	—	—	16
Jones, John R.	London	1826	Portraits	—	—	—	—	1	—	—	—	—	—	1
Jones, Miss Lily	Sutton Coldfield	1891	Flowers	—	—	1	—	—	—	—	—	—	—	1
Jones, Miss Laura Edwardes	London	1882-1893	Domestic	—	—	2	—	2	—	—	—	—	2	6
Jones, Lionel J.	London	1892	Figures	—	—	—	—	—	—	1	—	—	—	1
Jones, Miss Matilda	London	1825-1859	Miniatures	—	—	27	—	—	—	—	—	—	—	27
Jones, Miss M. A.	London	1805-1809	Landscape	—	—	4	—	—	—	—	—	—	—	4
Jones, Miss M. F.	London	1885	Domestic	—	—	1	—	—	—	—	—	—	—	1
Jones, Miss Mary Helen	London	1883-1885	Heads	—	—	1	—	—	—	—	—	—	1	2
Jones, Miss Martha J.	London	1828-1861	Historical	—	—	3	1	3	—	—	—	—	—	7
Jones, Miss Martha K.	London	1845-1863	Fruit	—	—	3	4	3	—	—	—	—	—	10
Jones, Miss Maud Raphael	Bradford	1889-1893	Rustic	—	—	10	—	—	—	3	2	9	—	24
Jones, Nathaniel	London	1774	Architecture	—	1	—	—	—	—	—	—	—	—	1
Jones, Owen	London	1831-1861	Architecture	—	—	12	—	—	—	—	—	—	—	12
Jones, R.	—	1780	Heads	—	—	1	—	—	—	—	—	—	—	1
Jones, R.	Reading	1818-1820	Sporting	—	—	11	—	—	—	—	—	—	—	11
Jones, Reginald	Eltham	1880-1893	Landscape	—	—	8	—	13	—	9	2	—	—	32
Jones, Richard	London	1810-1844	Mythological	—	—	—	1	3	—	—	—	—	—	4
Jones, Rowland G.	London	1889-1893	Architecture	—	—	6	—	—	—	—	—	—	—	6
Jones, R. J. Cornewall	Ryde	1886	Churches	—	—	1	—	—	—	—	—	—	—	1
Jones, R. M.	London	1833	Portraits	—	—	1	—	—	—	—	—	—	—	1
Jones, R. P.	London	1776-1812	Cameos	1	—	10	—	—	—	—	—	—	—	11
Jones, Miss Sophia	London	1789-1796	Miniatures	—	—	4	—	—	—	—	—	—	—	4
Jones, Mrs. S.	London	1797-1812	Miniatures	—	—	37	—	—	—	—	—	—	1	38
Jones, S. J. E.	London	1820-1845	Sporting	—	—	14	14	19	—	—	—	—	—	47
Jones, Thomas, F.S.A.	London	1765-1815	Landscape	55	—	12	—	—	—	—	—	—	—	67

Name.	Town.	First and Last Year of Ex.	Speciality.	S. A.	F. S.	R. A.	B. I.	S. S.	O. W.	N.W.	G. G.	N. G.	V. E.	Total
JONES, THEODORE	London	1879-1889	Landscape	—	—	4	—	11	—	1	—	—	—	16
JONES, THOMAS	London	1806-1835	Landscape	—	—	—	8	—	—	2	—	—	—	10
JONES, SIR THOMAS ALFRED, P.R.H.A.	Dublin	1872-1879	Portraits	—	—	5	—	—	—	—	—	—	—	5
JONES, T. HAMPSON	Liverpool	1874-1892	Landscape	—	—	20	—	—	—	3	3	—	5	31
JONES, T. HARRY	Concarnean	1880-1881	Landscape	—	—	—	—	1	—	—	—	—	2	3
JONES, T. W.	London	1832-1871	Scriptural	—	—	9	5	2	—	—	—	—	—	16
JONES, VIOLA	London	1881	Crayons	—	—	—	—	—	—	—	—	—	1	1
JONES, W.	London	1853	Landscape	—	—	—	—	1	—	—	—	—	—	1
JONES, WILLIAM	Bath	1764-1771	Fruit	2	1	2	—	—	—	—	—	—	—	5
JONES, W.	London	1843-1853	Sculpture	—	—	15	—	—	—	—	—	—	—	15
JONES, W.	London	1818-1833	Scriptural	—	—	8	—	—	—	—	—	—	—	8
JONES, WILLIAM	Chester	1834-1836	Portraits	—	—	2	1	2	—	—	—	—	—	5
JONES, W. B.	London	1811	Landscape	—	—	—	1	—	—	—	—	—	—	1
JONES, WATKIN D.	London	1846-1861	Sculpture	—	—	10	2	—	—	—	—	—	—	12
JONES, WILLIAM E.	Bristol	1849-1871	Landscape	—	—	6	13	9	—	—	—	—	—	28
JONES, W. H. H.	London	1845-1878	Landscape	—	—	10	—	6	—	—	—	—	4	20
JONES, MRS. W. H. H.	London	1843	Landscape	—	—	1	—	—	—	—	—	—	—	1
JONES, W. L.	London	1852-1855	Sculpture	—	—	4	—	—	—	—	—	—	—	4
JONES, MRS.	—	1783	Gems	—	—	1	—	—	—	—	—	—	—	1
JONES, MRS.	—	1852	Landscape	—	—	—	—	1	—	—	—	—	—	1
JONES, MISS	London	1777	Flowers	1	—	—	—	—	—	—	—	—	—	1
JONES AND JOHNSON	London	1850-1851	Architecture	—	—	3	—	—	—	—	—	—	—	3
JONES-PARRY, THOMAS P.	Wrexham	1884-1888	Landscape	—	—	—	—	—	—	3	—	—	—	3
JONGHE, DE. *See* D.	—	—	—	—	—	—	—	—	—	—	—	—	—	—
JONVAUX —	London	1831	Miniatures	—	—	3	—	—	—	—	—	—	—	3
JOPLING, J.	—	1816	Architecture	—	—	1	—	—	—	—	—	—	—	1
JOPLING, JOSEPH MIDDLETON‡	London	1848-1884	Domestic	—	—	30	—	21	—	126	37	—	26	240
JOPLING, MRS. J. M.,‖ LATE MISS LOUISE GOODE.	—	—	—	—	—	—	—	—	—	—	—	—	—	—
See also Mrs. Frank Romer	London	1874-1893	Landscape	—	—	41	—	11	—	2	32	—	51	137
JORDAN, O.	London	1841-1846	Architecture	—	—	3	—	1	—	—	—	—	—	4
JORDAN, MISS	London	1849-1850	Domestic	—	—	—	1	1	—	—	—	—	—	2
JORDEN, G.	London	1835-1842	Sculpture	—	—	4	—	2	—	—	—	—	—	6
JORIS, PIO	Rome	1879	Landscape	—	—	—	—	1	—	—	—	—	—	1
JOSEPH, DELISSA	London	1889	Architecture	—	—	1	—	—	—	—	—	—	—	1
JOSEPH, F. B.	London	1873	Landscape	—	—	—	—	1	—	—	—	—	—	1
JOSEPH, GEORGE FRANCIS, A.R.A.	London	1788-1846	Historical	—	—	146	14	—	—	—	—	—	—	160
JOSEPH, MRS. LILY DELISSA	London	1891-1893	Portraits	—	—	—	—	—	—	—	—	—	6	6
JOSEPH, SAMUEL, R.S.A.	London	1811-1846	Sculpture	—	—	100	—	11	—	—	—	—	—	111
JOSEY, JOHN WILLIAM	London	1891-1892	Engraving	—	—	2	—	—	—	—	—	—	—	2
JOSEY, RICHARD	London	1867-1887	Engraving	—	—	19	—	—	—	—	—	—	2	21
JOSI, CHARLES §	London	1827-1851	Sporting	—	—	9	12	53	—	—	—	—	—	74
JOSI, HENRY	London	1832-1833	Landscape	—	—	—	—	2	—	—	—	—	—	2
JOSSELIN DE JONG, P. DE. *See* De Jong.	—	—	—	—	—	—	—	—	—	—	—	—	—	—
JOUBERT, FERDINAND JEAN	London	1855-1881	Engraving	—	—	6	—	—	—	—	—	—	—	6
JOUFFROY, P.	London	1765-1767	Stained Glass	2	2	—	—	—	—	—	—	—	—	4
JOURET, HENRY	London	1773-1774	Figures	—	2	—	—	—	—	—	—	—	—	2
JOURIER, J. P.	—	1834	Landscape	—	—	—	1	—	—	—	—	—	—	1
JOWERS, ALFRED	London	1875	Landscape	—	—	—	—	—	—	—	—	—	1	1
JOY, A., R.H.A.	London	1838	Figures	—	—	—	1	—	—	—	—	—	—	1
JOY, ALBERT BRUCE, R.H.A.	London	1866-1893	Sculpture	—	—	115	—	—	—	—	1	—	—	116
JOY, CAROLINE	London	1845-1855	Domestic	—	—	2	—	—	—	—	—	—	—	2
JOY, GEORGE WILLIAM	Bristol	1872-1893	Figures	—	—	28	—	1	—	—	—	—	8	37
JOY, JOHN CANTILOE	Yarmouth	1826-1827	Sea Pieces	—	—	—	—	6	—	—	—	—	—	6
JOY, JESSEY	Richmond, Yorkshire	1843-1869	Figures	—	—	4	2	4	—	—	—	—	—	10
JOY, MISS JESSE M.	London	1841-1868	Historical	—	—	—	5	6	—	—	—	—	14	25
JOY, MISS M. E.	London	1866-1867	Figures	—	—	1	1	—	—	—	—	—	—	2
JOY, R.	London	1864	Figures	—	—	—	—	1	—	—	—	—	—	1
JOY, THOMAS MUSGROVE	Maidstone	1831-1867	Historical	—	—	67	82	50	—	1	—	—	*	200
JOY, WILLIAM	Yarmouth	1823-1845	Sea Pieces	—	—	2	2	3	—	—	—	—	—	7
JOYCE, MISS MARY	Norwood	1880-1893	Domestic	—	—	3	—	5	—	9	—	—	—	17
JOYNER, J.	London	1825-1833	Landscape	—	—	1	1	1	—	—	—	—	—	3
JOYNER, M.	London	1837-1868	Moonlight	—	—	2	1	3	—	—	—	—	—	6
JUDD, JOHN	Chelmsford	1774-1793	Landscape	2	—	5	—	—	—	—	—	—	—	7
JUDGE, GEORGE	London	1831-1832	Architecture	—	—	2	—	—	—	—	—	—	—	2
JUDKIN, REV. THOMAS JAMES	Southgate	1823-1849	Landscape	—	—	20	4	17	—	—	—	—	—	41
JUDKINS, MISS ELIZABETH	London	1772-1775	Engraving	2	—	—	—	—	—	—	—	—	—	2
JUDLIN, ALEXIS	London	1773-1776	Miniatures	—	—	7	—	—	—	—	—	—	—	7
JUENGLING, FRED.	New York	1881	Wood Engraving	—	—	—	—	—	—	—	—	—	6	6
JUKES, H. W.	—	1831	Historical	—	—	—	—	1	—	—	—	—	—	1
JUKES, J.	London	1775-1802	Miniatures	1	—	22	—	—	—	—	—	—	—	23
JULIAN, G.	London	1820-1823	Architecture	—	—	4	—	—	—	—	—	—	—	4
JULIAN, M.	Acton	1870	Sheep	—	—	—	—	2	—	—	—	—	—	2

Name.	Town.	First and Last Year of Ex.	Speciality.	S. A.	F. S.	R. A.	B. I.	S. S.	O. W.	N. W.	G. G.	N. G.	V. E.	Total.
JULIAN, R.	Exeter	1834	Landscape	—	—	1	—	—	—	—	—	—	—	1
JULIANA, SIGNOR JOSÈ.	Rome	1881-1882	Domestic	—	—	—	—	2	—	—	—	—	3	5
JULYAN, MISS MARY E.	Dublin	1863-1866	Flowers	—	—	2	—	2	—	—	—	—	—	4
JUMP, R.	London	1842	Sea Pieces	—	—	—	2	—	—	—	—	—	—	2
JUNCK, FERDINAND	London	1858-1889	Sculpture	—	—	26	3	24	—	—	—	—	37	90
JUNCK, OSCAR ALEXANDER	London	1880-1888	Sculpture	—	—	2	—	—	—	—	1	—	2	5
JUNDT, G.	Paris	1881	Landscape	—	—	—	—	—	—	—	1	—	—	1
JUNES, C.	—	1847	Architecture	—	—	1	—	—	—	—	—	—	—	1
JUPP, RICHARD	London	1778-1798	Architecture	—	—	3	—	—	—	—	—	—	—	3
JUPP, WILLIAM	London	1762-1763	Architecture	2	—	—	—	—	—	—	—	—	—	2
JUPP, WILLIAM, JUNR.	London	1794-1804	Architecture	—	—	9	—	—	—	—	—	—	—	9
JURINE, A.	Geneva	1825	Portraits	—	—	1	—	—	—	—	—	—	—	1
JURY, JULIUS	London	1860-1864	Figures	—	—	1	4	4	—	—	—	—	—	9
JUSTYNE, P. WILLIAM	London	1837-1838	Landscape	—	—	1	—	2	—	—	—	—	—	3
JUTSUM, HENRY ‡	London	1836-1869	Landscape	—	—	68	75	19	—	34	—	—	7	203
KACHLER, T. T.	London	1775	Portraits	—	—	1	—	—	—	—	—	—	—	1
KAEHLER, H.	London	1837-1844	Sculpture	—	—	8	—	1	—	—	—	—	—	9
KALCKREUTH, STANISLAUS, COUNT OF	Weimar	1869	Landscape	—	—	1	—	—	—	—	—	—	—	1
KAMECKE, O., VON. *See* V.	—	—	—	—	—	—	—	—	—	—	—	—	—	—
KANGIESSER, W. F.	London	1814-1815	Landscape	—	—	—	—	—	1	—	—	—	5	6
KAPPARDAKI, S.	London	1887	Portraits	—	—	1	—	—	—	—	—	—	—	1
KARPEN, MISS R.	London	1868	Landscape	—	—	—	—	1	—	—	—	—	—	1
KATES, A. H.	London	1849	Churches	—	—	1	—	—	—	—	—	—	—	1
KATOWY, DE. *See* D.	—	—	—	—	—	—	—	—	—	—	—	—	—	—
KAUFFMAN, MISS ANNA ANGELICA CATHERINA, R.A.	Rome	1765-1797	Allegorical	—	5	77	—	—	—	—	—	—	—	82
KAUFFMAN, JOHN JOSEPH	London	1771-1779	Scriptural	—	—	11	—	—	—	—	—	—	—	11
KAUFFMANN, H.	Hamburgh	1836	Rustic	—	—	1	—	—	—	—	—	—	—	1
KAULBACH, E.	London	1853-1857	Portraits	—	—	4	—	—	—	—	—	—	—	4
KAVANAGH, JOSEPH W., R.H.A.	Dublin	1886-1888	Domestic	—	—	2	—	—	—	—	—	—	—	2
KAY, ARCHIBALD, R.S.W.	Glasgow	1890-1892	Landscape	—	—	4	—	—	—	—	—	—	—	4
KAY, JAMES	Glasgow	1889-1890	Shipping	—	—	2	—	—	—	—	—	—	—	2
KAY, JOSEPH	London	1793-1813	Architecture	—	—	14	—	—	—	—	—	—	—	14
KAY, RICHARD	Hastings	1883	Landscape	—	—	—	—	1	—	—	—	—	1	2
KAY, W. P.	London	1831-1841	Architecture	—	—	3	—	—	—	—	—	—	—	3
KEAN, MICHAEL	London	1765-1790	Miniatures	—	4	22	—	—	—	—	—	—	—	26
KEANE, JOHN B., F.R.I.A., F.S.C.E.	Dublin	1842	Architecture	—	—	1	—	—	—	—	—	—	—	1
KEARNAN, THOMAS ‡	London	1821-1850	Landscape	—	—	2	—	1	—	25	—	—	—	28
KEARNEY, WILLIAM HENRY, V.P.N.W.S. ‡	London	1823-1858	Landscape	—	—	9	—	6	—	170	—	—	2	187
KEARSE, T.	—	1800	Insects	—	—	1	—	—	—	—	—	—	—	1
KEARSE, MRS. *See* Miss Mary Lawrence	—	1814-1830	Flowers	—	—	20	—	—	—	—	—	—	—	20
KEARSLEY, MISS H. §	London	1824-1858	Figures	—	—	44	20	25	—	1	—	—	—	90
KEARSLEY, THOMAS	London	1792-1801	Portraits	—	—	35	—	—	—	—	—	—	—	35
KEATE, GEORGE	—	1766-1789	Landscape	6	—	30	—	—	—	—	—	—	—	36
KEATE, MISS	—	1791	Domestic	4	—	—	—	—	—	—	—	—	—	4
KEATES, HENRY T. *See also* Bateman and Keates	London	1889	Architecture	—	—	1	—	—	—	—	—	—	—	1
KEATING, GEORGE	London	1775-1776	Heads	—	3	—	—	—	—	—	—	—	—	3
KEATING, MRS. ‖	Ventnor	1863	Sporting	—	—	—	2	—	—	—	—	—	—	2
KEATINGE, MRS. R. H. (JULIA A.)	London	1884-1888	Domestic	—	—	3	—	—	—	—	—	—	—	3
KECK, MISS S.	—	1771	Portraits	—	—	1	—	—	—	—	—	—	—	1
KEEBLE, H. A.	London	1797-1806	Architecture	—	—	6	—	—	—	—	—	—	—	6
KEEFE, DANIEL, *or* O'KEEFFE	London	1769-1786	Miniatures	—	3	22	—	—	—	—	—	—	—	25
KEELEY, JOHN	Birmingham	1883-1892	Landscape	—	—	—	—	2	—	8	—	—	—	10
KEELING, MISS AGNES	Sydenham	1878	Flowers	—	—	1	—	—	—	—	—	—	1	2
KEELING, BASSETT	London	1867	Architecture	—	—	1	—	—	—	—	—	—	—	1
KEELING, MICHAEL	London	1782-1809	Portraits	—	—	8	—	—	—	—	—	—	—	8
KEELING, WILLIAM	Sheffield	1891	Landscape	—	—	1	—	—	—	—	—	—	—	1
KEELING, WILLIAM KNIGHT, R.I. ‡	Manchester	1840-1885	Figures	—	—	1	1	—	—	60	—	—	—	62
KEEN, ARTHUR	London	1883	Buildings	—	—	1	—	—	—	—	—	—	—	1
KEEN, W.	London	1804	Portraits	—	—	1	—	—	—	—	—	—	—	1
KEENAN, J.	Bath	1791-1815	Portraits	—	—	66	1	—	—	—	—	—	—	67
KEENAN, MISS L.	London	1834-1836	Portraits	—	—	3	—	4	—	—	—	—	—	7
KEENAN, MRS.	Windsor	1807-1813	Landscape	—	—	8	—	—	—	—	—	—	—	8
KEENE, ALFRED	Bath	1854-1866	Landscape	—	—	—	—	7	—	—	—	—	—	7
KEENE, A. J.	Derby	1892-1893	Landscape	—	—	—	—	2	—	—	—	—	—	2
KEENE, CHARLES	London	1876-1879	"Punch"	—	—	—	—	—	—	—	—	—	26	26
KEENE, C. S.	London	1849	Historical	—	—	—	—	—	—	—	—	—	2	2
KEENE, HENRY E.	London	1866-1876	Landscape	—	—	—	—	—	—	—	—	—	5	5
KEENE, J. B.	London	1848	Figures	—	—	—	—	1	—	—	—	—	—	1

Name.	Town.	First and Last Year of Ex.	Speciality.	S. A.	F. S.	R. A.	B. I.	S. S.	O. W.	N.W.	G. G.	N.G.	V. E.	Total.
Keene, Theodosius	London	1770-1777	Architecture	2	—	1	—	—	—	—	—	—	—	3
Keene, W. C.	London	1877-1891	Landscape	—	—	6	—	11	—	2	—	—	4	23
Keens, A. W.	London	1855-1864	Fruit	—	—	—	2	1	—	—	—	—	—	3
Keens, H. L.	London	1822-1860	Fruit	—	—	8	5	8	—	—	—	—	—	21
Keeson, A.	London	1847	Scriptural	—	—	—	1	—	—	—	—	—	—	1
Keir, Robert	Edinburgh	1814	Landscape	—	—	—	—	1	—	—	—	—	—	1
Keith, Alexander	London	1846-1862	Landscape	—	—	2	2	2	—	—	—	—	1	7
Keith, Allan	London	1880	Landscape	—	—	—	—	—	—	—	—	—	1	1
Keith, G. M.	—	1822	River Scenes	—	—	1	—	—	—	—	—	—	—	1
Keith, Mrs. L. M.	London	1889-1890	Flowers	—	—	—	—	—	—	—	—	1	1	2
Keith, Miss Mouat	—	1818	Indian Landscape	—	—	2	—	—	—	—	—	—	—	2
Kell, E. I. (?) Ellen	London	1877	Flowers	—	—	—	—	1	—	—	—	—	—	1
Kell, J. S.	London	1868	Landscape	—	—	—	—	1	—	—	—	—	—	1
Kell, Thomas	London	1880	Architecture	—	—	2	—	—	—	—	—	—	—	2
Kell, W. F.	London	1875-1877	Landscape	—	—	—	—	2	—	—	—	—	—	2
Keller, Miss B.	Spilsby	1877	Study	—	—	—	—	1	—	—	—	—	—	1
Keller, Mrs. Evelyn R.	Walton-on-Thames	1892	Miniatures	—	—	2	—	—	—	—	—	—	—	2
Keller, Miss Fanny H. M.	London	1883-1892	Miniatures	—	—	12	—	1	—	—	—	—	2	15
Kellog, M. K.	Paris	1857	Portraits	—	—	1	—	—	—	—	—	—	—	1
Kellow, Miss Kate	London	1893	Miniatures	—	—	1	—	—	—	—	—	—	—	1
Kelly, H.	Norton	1879	Flowers	—	—	—	—	1	—	—	—	—	—	1
Kelly, J.	—	1834	Sculpture	—	—	2	—	—	—	—	—	—	—	2
Kelly, John	London	1886	Architecture	—	—	1	—	—	—	—	—	—	—	1
Kelly, Nicholas	Edinburgh	1810-1831	Flowers	—	—	3	—	—	—	—	—	—	—	3
Kelly, O'. *See* O.	—	—	—	—	—	—	—	—	—	—	—	—	—	—
Kelly, Robert George	London	1853-1888	Landscape	—	—	5	3	6	—	—	—	—	2	16
Kelly, R. Talbot, R.B.A. §	Birkenhead	1885-1893	Landscape	—	—	2	—	12	—	5	—	—	2	21
Kelly, Tom	Newmarket	1888-1893	Landscape	—	—	—	—	—	—	—	—	10	—	10
Kelsey, Master Francis	—	1776	Figures	—	1	—	—	—	—	—	—	—	—	1
Kelsey, Frank	London	1887-1893	Sea Pieces	—	—	1	—	8	—	—	—	—	3	12
Kelsey, Charles J. Samuel	London	1840-1877	Sculpture	—	—	11	—	—	—	—	—	—	—	11
Keman, G. A.	London	1793-1807	Miniatures	—	—	29	—	—	—	—	—	—	—	29
Kemm, Robert	London	1874-1885	Figures	—	—	—	—	13	—	—	—	—	—	13
Kemp, A.	London	1865	Landscape	—	—	—	—	1	—	—	—	—	—	1
Kemp, Amy K. P.	London	1889-1890	Landscape	—	—	—	—	2	—	—	—	—	—	2
Kemp, Mrs. Davidson (A.)	London	1867-1870	Figures	—	—	1	—	2	—	—	—	—	4	7
Kemp, Georgie W.	—	1886	Flowers	—	—	—	—	—	—	1	—	—	—	1
Kemp, John	Gloucester	1868-1876	Landscape	—	—	—	—	4	—	—	—	—	7	11
Kemp, Miss L.	—	1803-1804	Flowers	—	—	2	—	—	—	—	—	—	—	2
Kemp, Walter M.	London	1870-1889	Sculpture	—	—	3	—	2	—	—	—	—	—	5
Kemp, Vander. *See* V.	—	—	—	—	—	—	—	—	—	—	—	—	—	—
Kempe, Miss Harriet	London	1867-1892	Domestic	—	—	31	—	17	—	1	—	—	27	76
Kemplay, Charles H.	London	1872-1874	Landscape	—	—	1	—	—	—	—	—	—	5	6
Kempson, Miss M. Freeman ‖	Croydon	1868-1884	Landscape	—	—	1	—	22	—	—	—	—	2	25
Kempson, Frederick R.	Hereford	1861-1893	Architecture	—	—	5	—	—	—	—	—	—	—	5
Kempson and Fowler	Llandaff	1890-1891	Architecture	—	—	2	—	—	—	—	—	—	—	2
Kempthorne, S.	Gloucester	1833-1840	Architecture	—	—	9	—	—	—	—	—	—	—	9
Kemshead, J.	London	1791-1825	Architecture	—	—	2	—	—	—	—	—	—	—	2
Kemshead, J. L.	London	1807	Cattle	—	—	2	—	—	—	—	—	—	—	2
Kendall, Henry E.	London	1799-1843	Architecture	—	—	29	—	—	—	—	—	—	—	29
Kendall, Henry Edward	London	1823-1862	Architecture	—	—	20	—	1	—	—	—	—	—	21
Kendall and Mew	London	1878	Architecture	—	—	1	—	—	—	—	—	—	—	1
Kendall, John	London	1781-1784	Architecture	—	—	5	—	—	—	—	—	—	—	5
Kendall, J. G.	London	1843-1862	Landscape	—	—	6	14	14	—	—	—	—	2	36
Kendrick, Miss Emma Eleanora	London	1811-1840	Miniatures	—	—	89	1	74	18	10	—	—	—	192
Kendrick, Josephus	London	1813-1830	Sculpture	—	—	28	2	15	—	—	—	—	—	45
Kendrick, Matthew, R.H.A.	London	1842-1846	Sea Pieces	—	—	1	3	5	—	—	—	—	—	9
Kenealy, Noel Byron	Watford	1886-1893	Engraving	—	—	3	—	1	—	—	—	—	—	4
Kenmore, F.	London	1890	Landscape	—	—	—	—	1	—	—	—	—	—	1
Kennard, Miss E. C	London	1866-1869	Sculpture	—	—	2	—	—	—	—	—	—	—	2
Kennaway, C. G.	London	1891	Domestic	—	—	—	—	—	—	1	—	—	—	1
Kennecott —	—	1840	Religious	—	—	—	—	1	—	—	—	—	—	1
Kennedy, Charles Napier φ	London	1872-1893	Domestic	—	—	26	—	14	—	—	4	11	46	10
Kennedy, Mrs. C. N. (Miss Lucy Marwood)	London	1886-1893	Domestic	—	—	—	—	—	—	3	—	6	—	9
Kennedy, E.	—	1842	Rustic	—	—	1	—	—	—	—	—	—	—	1
Kennedy, Edward Sherard	London	1863-1890	Historical	—	—	18	—	9	—	4	1	—	17	49
Kennedy, Mrs. E. S. (Miss Florence Laing)	London	1880-1893	Domestic	—	—	4	—	1	—	—	1	—	4	10
Kennedy, G.	London	1866	Figures	—	—	—	1	—	—	—	—	—	—	1
Kennedy, G. P.	London	1843-1851	Architecture	—	—	7	—	—	—	—	—	—	—	7
Kennedy, H. Arthur	London	1875	Mythological	—	—	—	—	—	—	—	—	—	1	1
Kennedy, J.	London	1823	Portraits	—	—	1	—	—	—	—	—	—	—	1
Kennedy, Joseph	Kidderminster	1861-1888	Domestic	—	—	4	1	9	—	—	—	—	—	14

Name.	Town.	First and Last Year of Ex.	Speciality.	S. A.	F. S.	R. A.	B. I.	S. S.	O.W.	N.W.	G. G.	N. G.	V. E.	Total.
Kennedy, S.	—	1868	Architecture	—	—	1	—	—	—	—	—	—	—	1
Kennedy, William	Glasgow	1886-1892	Domestic	—	—	1	—	—	—	—	3	—	—	4
Kennedy, William Denholm	London	1833-1865	Figures	—	—	52	22	16	—	—	—	—	—	90
Kennell, W. H.	London	1872-1880	Still Life	—	—	—	—	5	—	—	—	—	7	12
Kennerley, J.	London	1803-1828	Portraits	—	—	4	—	5	—	—	—	—	—	9
Kenney, Miss M. T.	London	1837-1840	Portraits	—	—	2	—	1	—	—	—	—	—	3
Kennington, Thomas Benjamin, R.B.A. § φ	London	1880-1893	Domestic	—	—	23	—	16	—	3	3	—	42	87
Kennion, Charles James	London	1804-1853	Landscape	—	—	26	—	5	—	—	—	—	7	38
Kennion, E., F.S.A.	London	1790-1807	Landscape	24	—	8	—	—	—	—	—	—	—	32
Kensett, John Frederick	New York	1845	Landscape	—	—	2	4	—	—	—	—	—	—	6
Kent, John	London	1771-1773	Landscape	—	—	5	—	—	—	—	—	—	—	5
Kent, J. J.	London	1809-1811	Architecture	—	—	2	—	—	—	—	—	—	—	2
Kentish, P.	—	1783	Landscape	—	1	—	—	—	—	—	—	—	—	1
Kentish, Miss	—	1815	Churches	—	—	1	—	—	—	—	—	—	—	1
Kenwell, Miss Anna Maria. *See* Mrs. Charretie.	—	—	—	—	—	—	—	—	—	—	—	—	—	—
Kenworthy, Miss Esther	Ealing	1881-1882	Flowers	—	—	2	—	1	—	—	—	—	—	3
Kenyon, Hon. E. F.	London	1879	Domestic	—	—	1	—	—	—	—	—	—	—	1
Kenyon, George	London	1892	Architecture	—	—	1	—	—	—	—	—	—	—	1
Ker, W. A.	London	1874-1878	Domestic	—	—	—	—	1	—	—	—	—	5	6
Kerk, De. *See* D.	—	—	—	—	—	—	—	—	—	—	—	—	—	—
Kerkhove, V. D.	London	1878	Domestic	—	—	—	—	1	—	—	—	—	—	1
Kerkhove, Vanden. *See* V.	—	—	—	—	—	—	—	—	—	—	—	—	—	—
Kernot, Mrs. James H.	London	1855-1856	Eastern	—	—	—	—	—	—	—	—	—	2	2
Kernott, James	London	1829	Engraving	—	—	—	—	1	—	—	—	—	—	1
Kerns, Miss Miriam	London	1874-1879	Domestic	—	—	—	—	5	—	—	—	—	2	7
Kerr, Charles H. M., R.B.A. §	London	1884-1893	Domestic	—	—	13	—	12	—	1	—	—	9	35
Kerr, Mrs. Elizabeth	London	1763	Flowers	—	1	—	—	—	—	—	—	—	—	1
Kerr, George C.	London	1873-1893	Sea Pieces	—	—	11	—	20	—	19	—	—	8	58
Kerr, Henry W., A.R.S.A., R.S.W.	Edinburgh	1890-1892	Domestic	—	—	5	—	—	—	1	—	—	—	6
Kerr, Miss Margaret	London	1877	Domestic	—	—	—	—	3	—	—	—	—	—	3
Kerr, Robert	London	1862-1873	Architecture	—	—	6	—	—	—	—	—	—	—	6
Kerr, T.	London	1850	Figures	—	—	1	—	—	—	—	—	—	—	1
Kerr-Lawson, J.	Pitteween	1890	Shipping	—	—	—	—	1	—	—	—	—	—	1
Kerry, William L.	Liverpool	1865-1881	Landscape	—	—	4	—	1	—	—	2	—	11	18
Kersey, Miss A. M.	Framlington	1830-1846	Domestic	—	—	1	—	1	—	—	—	—	—	2
Kershaw, T.	London	1803	Portraits	—	—	1	—	—	—	—	—	—	—	1
Kessisoglu, Miss Esther	London	1891-1892	Flowers	—	—	—	—	2	—	—	—	—	—	2
Keswick, William	—	1887	Landscape	—	—	—	—	—	—	—	—	—	1	1
Ketchlee, Miss Nellie M.	Wadhurst	1891-1892	Domestic	—	—	—	—	2	—	—	—	—	—	2
Kete, M. Ten. *See* Tenkate.	—	—	—	—	—	—	—	—	—	—	—	—	—	—
Ketling, M.	—	1807	Landscape	—	—	1	—	—	—	—	—	—	—	1
Kettle, Miss Clara E. F. ‖	Weymouth	1845-1866	Portraits	—	—	9	—	10	—	—	—	—	—	19
Kettle, Henry	London	1772	Figures	1	—	—	—	—	—	—	—	—	—	1
Kettle, Sir Rupert	Wolv'rhampton	1864-1884	Scriptural	—	—	—	1	—	—	1	—	—	—	2
Kettle, Tilly, F.S.A.	London	1761-1783	Portraits	26	1	11	—	—	—	—	—	—	—	38
Kettlewell, John William	Leeds	1866	Flowers	—	—	—	—	1	—	—	—	—	—	1
Keux, Le. *See* L.	—	—	—	—	—	—	—	—	—	—	—	—	—	—
Keyes, G. J., *or* T.	London	1811-1817	Architecture	—	—	5	—	—	—	—	—	—	—	5
Keyl, Friedrich Wilhelm	London	1847-1872	Animals	—	—	42	34	—	—	—	—	—	—	76
Keymer, M. H.	London	1787	Portraits	—	—	3	—	—	—	—	—	—	—	3
Keys, Miss Frances M.	Mitcham	1856-1877	Landscape	—	—	3	—	36	—	—	—	—	8	47
Keys, G. F.	London	1889-1893	Landscape	—	—	2	—	5	—	—	—	—	—	7
Keys, George Scott	Hatcham	1856-1875	Landscape	—	—	1	—	24	—	—	—	—	4	29
Keyse, Thomas	London	1761-1799	Flowers	3	35	2	—	—	—	—	—	—	—	40
Keyworth, T.	—	1819	Landscape	—	—	1	—	—	—	—	—	—	—	1
Keyworth, W. D.	Hull	1837-1844	Sculpture	—	—	7	—	1	—	—	—	—	—	8
Keyworth, William Day, Junr.	London	1863-1893	Sculpture	—	—	25	—	—	—	—	—	—	—	25
Khnopff, Fernand	Brussels	1891-1893	Portraits	—	—	—	—	—	—	—	—	5	2	7
Kibbler, W. Ambrose	Hackney	1891	Landscape	—	—	—	—	—	—	1	—	—	—	1
Kidd, John Bartholomew, R.S.A.	Edinburgh	1833	Landscape	—	—	—	1	—	—	—	—	—	—	1
Kidd, R. C.	Kew	1798	Architecture	—	—	1	—	—	—	—	—	—	—	1
Kidd, William, R.S.A.	London	1817-1853	Domestic	—	—	33	68	88	2	—	—	—	16	207
Kidner, William	London	1878-1888	Portraits	—	—	2	—	—	—	—	—	—	—	2
Kidner and Berry	London	1893	Architecture	—	—	4	—	—	—	—	—	—	—	4
Kidson, H. E.	Liverpool	1887-1888	Landscape	—	—	—	—	—	—	2	—	—	—	2
Kiesel, Professor	London	1890	Heads	—	—	—	—	—	—	—	1	—	—	1
Kilburn —.	London	1770-1775	Flowers	1	5	—	—	—	—	—	—	—	—	6
Kilburn, T.	—	1800	Still Life	—	—	2	—	—	—	—	—	—	—	2
Kilburn, W. E.	London	1848	Photographic	—	—	—	—	—	—	—	—	—	1	1
Kilburne, George G., R.I. ‡ φ	London	1862-1893	Figures	—	—	20	—	5	—	163	4	—	28	220
Kilburne, George Goodwin, R.B.A. §	London	1871-1893	Sporting	—	—	19	—	32	—	—	—	—	15	66

Name.	Town.	First and Last Year of Ex.	Speciality.	S. A.	F. S.	R. A.	B. I.	S. S.	O. W.	N.W.	G. G.	N. G.	V. E.	Total.
Kilburne, Miss S. E.	London	1871	Domestic	—	—	—	—	1	—	—	—	—	2	3
Killick, T.	Petworth	1864	Still Life	—	—	2	—	—	—	—	—	—	—	2
Killingbeck, Benjamin	London	1769-1789	Sporting	12	28	11	—	—	—	—	—	—	—	51
Killmister, C. Gordon	London	1889	Buildings	—	—	—	—	—	—	1	—	—	—	1
Killmister (C. Gordon) and Briggs (R. A.)	London	1887-1889	Architecture	—	—	2	—	—	—	—	—	—	—	2
Kilpack, Miss Sarah Louisa	London	1867	Sea Pieces	—	—	—	2	—	—	—	—	—	—	2
Kilpin, Legh M.	London	1886-1888	Domestic	—	—	1	—	—	—	—	—	—	1	2
Kilvington, Miss E.	London	1833	Landscape	—	—	—	—	1	—	—	—	—	—	1
Kimpton, W.	London	1784	Architecture	—	—	2	—	—	—	—	—	—	—	2
Kincaird, E. B.	London	1875-1876	Sea Pieces	—	—	—	—	2	—	—	—	—	—	2
Kinch, H.	Fareham	1811-1824	Sporting	—	—	17	—	—	—	—	—	—	—	17
Kindersley, Miss Fanny K.	Dorchester	1883-1885	Domestic	—	—	—	—	—	—	3	—	—	—	3
Kindon, Miss M. E.	Croydon	1874-1893	Domestic	—	—	8	—	21	—	9	—	—	6	44
King, A.	London	1804-1805	Landscape	—	—	2	—	—	—	—	—	—	—	2
King, Miss Agnes Gardner ‖	London	1882-1892	Miniatures	—	—	2	—	9	—	15	—	—	1	27
King, Berkeley	London	1814-1835	Moonlight	—	—	4	6	7	—	—	—	—	4	21
King, C.	London	1792-1800	Architecture	—	—	8	—	—	—	—	—	—	—	8
King, C.	London	1807-1834	Landscape	—	—	2	2	—	—	—	—	—	—	4
King, Charles Robert Baker	London	1885-1886	Architecture	—	—	2	—	—	—	—	—	—	—	2
King, Edward	Petersfield	1889-1893	Domestic	—	—	13	—	—	—	—	1	—	—	14
King, Emily	London	1848-1849	Portraits	—	—	2	—	—	—	—	—	—	—	2
King, Mrs. E. Brownlow	London	1868-1873	Domestic	—	—	—	—	13	—	—	—	—	—	13
King, Edward R.	Petersfield	1884-1893	Portraits	—	—	2	—	4	—	—	—	—	6	12
King, Miss Ethel Slade	London	1884-1893	Portraits	—	—	18	—	—	—	—	1	—	1	20
King, Miss Elizabeth Thomson	London	1880-1891	Domestic	—	—	2	—	4	—	2	—	—	5	13
King, Fred.	London	1889-1891	Rustic	—	—	—	—	2	—	—	—	—	—	2
King, Frank G. W.	London	1893	Landscape	—	—	—	—	1	—	—	—	—	—	1
King, F. H.	London	1873	Flowers	—	—	—	—	1	—	—	—	—	—	1
King, G.	London	1771-1778	Sculpture	1	5	—	—	—	—	—	—	—	—	6
King, Haynes, R.B.A.§	London	1855-1893	Domestic	—	—	40	10	161	—	4	—	—	41	256
King, H.	London	1828-1845	Sculpture	—	—	8	—	6	—	—	—	—	—	14
King, Henry	Edmonton	1839-1846	Landscape	—	—	—	1	5	—	—	—	—	—	6
King, H. B.	Norwich	1874	Cairo	—	—	—	—	1	—	—	—	—	—	1
King, J.	London	1796-1797	Landscape	—	—	4	—	—	—	—	—	—	—	4
King, John	Dartmouth	1817-1830	Architecture	—	—	8	—	1	—	—	—	—	—	9
King, John	London	1814-1847	Scriptural	—	—	29	36	13	2	—	—	—	1	81
King, J. Arthur	London	1876-1885	Landscape	—	—	2	—	3	—	1	—	—	7	13
King, Captain John Duncan	London	1824-1858	Landscape	—	—	18	39	2	—	—	—	—	—	59
King, John Lockwood	Surbiton	1880	Architecture	—	—	1	—	—	—	—	—	—	—	1
King, J. W.	London	1838-1853	Domestic	—	—	10	6	6	—	—	—	—	—	22
King, John W.	London	1893	Rustic	—	—	—	—	1	—	—	—	—	2	3
King, Miss Katherine	London	1869	Game	—	—	—	—	—	—	—	—	—	1	1
King, Miss Lydia B.	London	1886-1890	Domestic	—	—	2	—	3	—	2	—	—	1	8
King, Margaret	London	1779-1787	Crayons	—	—	16	—	—	—	—	—	—	—	16
King, P.	—	1827	Landscape	—	—	—	1	—	—	—	—	—	—	1
King, Thomas R.	London	1839-1846	Landscape	—	—	—	—	15	—	—	—	—	—	15
King, Mrs. Thomas R.	London	1848	Landscape	—	—	—	—	2	—	—	—	—	—	2
King, William	Totteridge	1761-1767	Flowers	1	11	—	—	—	—	—	—	—	—	12
King, William	London	1769-1782	Sculpture	—	7	—	—	—	—	—	—	—	—	7
King, Hon. Miss Wilhelmina	—	1770-1775	Still Life	7	—	1	—	—	—	—	—	—	—	8
King, W. Gunning	London	1878-1893	Figures	—	—	12	—	4	—	—	6	1	7	30
King, W. H.	Edmonton	1836	Buildings	—	—	—	—	1	—	—	—	—	—	1
King, Yeend, R.B.A., R.I.§ ‡ φ	London	1874-1893	Domestic	—	—	36	—	115	—	38	7	—	31	227
King-Salter, J., *or* P.	Rome	1877-1880	Domestic	—	—	1	—	—	—	—	1	—	—	2
Kingdon, Walter	London	1879-1887	Figures	—	—	1	—	—	—	—	1	—	—	2
Kingsbury, Henry	London	1776-1791	Landscape	2	—	4	—	—	—	—	—	—	—	6
Kingsbury, T. U.	London	1874-1878	Coast Scenes	—	—	—	—	7	—	—	—	—	—	7
Kingsley, Miss Lydia	London	1890-1893	Still Life	—	—	1	—	1	—	3	—	—	—	5
Kingston, Gertrude A.	London	1887	Figures	—	—	—	—	1	—	—	—	—	—	1
Kingston, James A.	Ealing	1890	Landscape	—	—	—	—	1	—	—	—	—	—	1
Kingston, Miss S.	London	1843-1846	Still Life	—	—	1	—	4	—	—	—	—	—	5
Kinloch, George W.	Edinburgh	1884	Sculpture	—	—	3	—	—	—	—	—	—	—	3
Kinnaird, F. B. S.	London	1865-1875	Domestic	—	—	—	2	1	—	—	—	—	—	3
Kinnaird, F. G.	London	1864-1881	Figures	—	—	1	1	12	—	—	—	—	—	14
Kinnaird, Henry J.	London	1880-1891	Landscape	—	—	7	—	7	—	—	—	—	2	16
Kinnaird, T. J.	Chiswick	1874	Landscape	—	—	2	—	—	—	—	—	—	—	2
Kinnard, W.	London	1807-1828	Architecture	—	—	25	—	—	—	—	—	—	—	25
Kinnear, James	Edinburgh	1880-1892	Landscape	—	—	4	—	—	—	1	—	—	—	5
Kinnebrook, W. A.	London	1843-1863	Figures	—	—	6	1	7	—	—	—	—	—	14
Kinsett, J.	London	1848	Landscape	—	—	1	—	—	—	—	—	—	—	1
Kinsley, Albert, R.B.A., A.R.C.A.§	London	1881-1893	Landscape	—	—	15	—	45	—	13	—	6	6	85
Kinson, Chevalier	Paris	1822	Portraits	—	—	1	—	—	—	—	—	—	—	1

Name.	Town.	First and Last Year of Ex.	Speciality.	S. A.	F. S.	R. A.	B. I.	S. S.	O. W.	N.W.	G. G.	N. G.	V. E.	Total.
Kinton, Miss Florence	Great Malvern	1884	Domestic	—	—	1	—	—	—	—	—	—	—	1
Kiörboe, Charles Frederick	Paris	1847-1848	Sporting	—	—	2	3	—	—	—	—	—	—	5
Kipling, Mary	London	1843-1848	Miniatures	—	—	9	—	—	—	—	—	—	—	9
Kirby, Edmund	Liverpool	1877-1893	Architecture	—	—	4	—	—	—	—	—	—	—	4
Kirby, Joshua, F.R.S.	London	1761-1770	Landscape	12	—	—	—	—	—	—	—	—	—	12
Kirby, J. R.	London	1877-1878	Sea Pieces	—	—	—	—	—	—	—	—	—	4	4
Kirby, Miss U.	London	1855-1857	Portraits	—	—	3	—	—	—	—	—	—	—	3
Kirchbach, E.	London	1857-1859	Scriptural	—	—	3	—	—	—	—	—	—	—	3
Kirchhoffer, H.	London	1837-1843	Portraits	—	—	10	1	3	—	—	—	—	—	14
Kirchmayr, Cherubino	London	1886-1890	Domestic	—	—	4	—	—	—	—	—	—	—	4
Kirk, C.	Sleaford	1850	Architecture	—	—	1	—	—	—	—	—	—	—	1
Kirk, J.	Birmingham	1847-1854	Sculpture	—	—	5	4	—	—	—	—	—	—	9
Kirk, John, F.S.A.	London	1760-1795	Medals	28	2	12	—	—	—	—	—	—	—	42
Kirk, Joseph R., R.H.A.	Dublin	1845-1862	Sculpture	—	—	8	—	—	—	—	—	—	—	8
Kirk, Thomas	London	1785-1794	Scriptural	—	—	11	—	—	—	—	—	—	—	11
Kirk, T.	London	1796	Figures	—	—	2	—	—	—	—	—	—	—	2
Kirk, Thomas, R.H.A.	Dublin	1825-1845	Sculpture	—	—	8	1	1	—	—	—	—	—	10
Kirk, W. B., A.R.H.A.	Worcester	1848-1857	Sculpture	—	—	6	—	—	—	—	—	—	—	6
Kirkaldy, D.	Glasgow	1861	Ships	—	—	1	—	—	—	—	—	—	—	1
Kirkby, G.	London	1828-1829	Landscape	—	—	2	—	—	—	—	—	—	—	2
Kirkby, Thomas	London	1796-1847	Portraits	—	—	43	12	—	—	—	—	—	—	55
Kirkley, Miss C.	London	1796-1797	Miniatures	—	—	3	—	—	—	—	—	—	—	3
Kirkley, Miss S.	London	1793-1797	Miniatures	—	—	4	—	—	—	—	—	—	—	4
Kirkman, Miss	London	1815-1825	Landscape	—	—	12	—	1	—	—	—	—	—	13
Kirkpatrick, Ethel	Harrow	1891-1893	Fishing Boats	—	—	—	—	2	—	2	—	—	—	4
Kirkpatrick, Miss Ida	London	1888-1893	Sea Pieces	—	—	—	—	11	—	1	—	—	—	12
Kirkpatrick, Richard	London	1812-1817	Figures	—	—	11	1	—	—	—	—	—	—	12
Kirkpatrick, W.	London	1841	Landscape	—	—	—	—	2	—	—	—	—	—	2
Kirkup, S.	Florence	1833-1836	Portraits	—	—	2	—	—	—	—	—	—	—	2
Kirtland, G.	Woodstock	1791-1798	Figures	—	—	2	—	—	—	—	—	—	—	2
Kissling, Richard	Gunnersbury	1887	Sculpture	—	—	1	—	—	—	—	—	—	—	1
Kiste, J. A.	Plymouth	1844-1846	Landscape	—	—	2	—	—	—	—	—	—	—	2
Kiste, A.	London	1840	Portraits	—	—	—	—	3	—	—	—	—	—	3
Kitchen, Miss Elizabeth	London	1832	Portraits	—	—	1	—	—	—	—	—	—	—	1
Kitchen, Miss E. M.	London	1850-1852	Flowers, etc.	—	—	—	—	4	—	—	—	—	—	4
Kitchen, H.	London	1802	Miniatures	—	—	6	—	—	—	—	—	—	—	6
Kitchen, H.	London	1810-1813	Architecture	—	—	4	—	—	—	—	—	—	—	4
Kitchen, J. D.	—	1834	Landscape	—	—	1	—	—	—	—	—	—	—	1
Kitchen, T. S.	London	1833-1852	Landscape	—	—	22	3	31	—	—	—	—	—	56
Kitchingman, John	London	1766-1781	Miniatures	—	9	31	—	—	—	—	—	—	—	40
Kite, J. Milner-. *See* M.	—	—	—	—	—	—	—	—	—	—	—	—	—	—
Kitson, Miss Catherine M.	London	1886-1892	Figures	—	—	1	—	1	—	1	—	—	—	3
Kitson, Robert L.	Huddersfield	1890-1891	Domestic	—	—	3	—	—	—	—	—	—	—	3
Kitson, S.	Rome	1877-1880	Sculpture	—	—	3	—	—	—	—	—	—	—	3
Kitton, Fred. G.	London	1879-1888	Wood Engraving	—	—	—	—	1	—	2	—	—	2	5
Kitton, R.	Norwich	1847	Architecture	—	—	3	—	—	—	—	—	—	—	3
Klein, Miss A.	London	1887	Flowers	—	—	1	—	—	—	—	—	—	—	1
Klengel, F. C.	London	1816	Landscape	—	—	—	2	—	—	—	—	—	—	2
Klimsch, Eugen	Frankfort	1890	Domestic	—	—	1	—	—	—	—	—	—	—	1
Klinkitch, Maurice	London	1877-1881	Wood Engraving	—	—	—	—	—	—	—	—	—	3	3
Kliny, J. N.	London	1880	—	—	—	—	—	—	—	—	*	—	—	—
Klotz, Herman	Vienna	1891	Wood Carving	—	—	2	—	—	—	—	—	—	—	2
Knaggs, Miss Nancy	London	1887-1893	Sea Pieces	—	—	1	—	11	—	3	—	—	—	15
Knapp, J.	London	1817	Architecture	—	—	1	—	—	—	—	—	—	—	1
Knapping, Miss Edith M.	Blackheath	1877-1878	Domestic	—	—	1	—	—	—	—	—	—	1	2
Knapping, Miss M. Helen	Blackheath	1876-1890	Flowers	—	—	2	—	13	—	3	1	—	4	23
Kneen, William	London	1891	Sea Shores	—	—	—	—	1	—	—	—	—	—	1
Knell, J. H.	London	1833-1834	Sea Pieces	—	—	4	—	—	—	—	—	—	—	4
Knell, William Adolphus	London	1825-1874	Sea Pieces	—	—	29	44	20	—	—	—	—	—	93
Knell, W. Callcott	London	1848-1871	Sea Pieces	—	—	3	3	9	—	—	—	—	2	17
Kneller, W.	Fareham	1819-1821	Portraits	—	—	2	—	—	—	—	—	—	—	2
Knewstub, W. Holmes	London	1881-1884	Landscape	—	—	—	—	—	—	—	—	—	3	3
Knewstub, W. J.	London	1865-1881	Domestic	—	—	5	—	3	—	—	—	—	7	15
Knight. *See* Hunt, Steward, and Knight	—	—	Architecture	—	—	—	—	—	—	—	—	—	—	—
Knight, Adam	Nottingham	1892	Landscape	—	—	—	—	1	—	—	—	—	—	1
Knight, Miss Adah	Gloucester	1893	Domestic	—	—	2	—	—	—	—	—	—	—	2
Knight, Alfred E.	Hackney	1879	Fruit	—	—	—	—	1	—	—	—	—	—	1
Knight, C.	London	1793-1816	Miniatures	—	—	4	—	—	—	—	—	—	—	4
Knight, C.	Chester	1892	Landscape	—	—	1	—	—	—	—	—	—	—	1
Knight, Miss Clara	London	1880-1889	Landscape	—	—	2	—	7	—	2	—	—	7	18
Knight, C. J.	London	1844	Sculpture	—	—	1	—	—	—	—	—	—	—	1
Knight, C. Neil-	London	1891-1892	Domestic	—	—	—	—	2	—	—	—	—	2	4

Name.	Town.	First and Last Year of Ex.	Speciality.	S. A.	F. S.	R. A.	B. I.	S. S.	O.W.	N.W.	G. G.	N. G.	V. E.	Total.
Knight, Charles Parsons	Bristol	1853-1893	Landscape	—	—	33	4	22	—	—	—	13	31	103
Knight, Edward	London	1824	Landscape	—	—	—	1	—	—	—	—	—	—	1
Knight, Miss Emma	Bath	1882-1893	Stained Glass	—	—	4	—	1	—	—	—	—	—	5
Knight, Frederick George	Penge	1877-1892	Architecture	—	—	5	—	—	—	—	—	—	—	5
Knight, G. J.	Hackney	1878	Landscape	—	—	—	—	—	—	—	—	—	1	1
Knight, Henry Hull	London	1863-1877	Landscape	—	—	—	—	3	—	—	—	—	6	9
Knight, John	London	1830	Domestic	—	—	1	—	—	—	—	—	—	—	1
Knight, John	London	1818-1830	Architecture	—	—	3	—	3	—	—	—	—	—	6
Knight, Joseph, R.I., R.C.A., A.R.P.E. ‡ φ	Sevenoaks	1861-1893	Landscape	—	—	61	—	1	—	60	4	—	115	241
Knight, J. B.	Dorchester	1818-1819	Architecture	—	—	4	—	—	—	—	—	—	—	4
Knight, James P.	London	1849-1867	Fruit	—	—	—	2	2	—	—	—	—	—	4
Knight, John Prescott, R.A.	London	1824-1878	Portraits	—	—	227	22	26	—	1	—	—	—	276
Knight, Mrs. J. P.	London	1832-1837	Domestic	—	—	2	3	3	—	—	—	—	—	8
Knight, John William Buxton, R.B.A., R.C.A.§	Sevenoaks	1863-1893	Landscape	—	—	46	—	71	—	1	20	8	27	173
Knight, Mary	Sevenoaks	1871-1876	Landscape	—	—	—	—	2	—	—	—	—	1	3
Knight, Miss Mary Anne (Pupil of A. Plimer)	London	1803-1831	Miniatures	—	—	30	—	—	2	—	—	—	—	32
Knight, Paul	Bettws-y-Coed	1883-1891	Domestic	—	—	3	—	1	—	—	—	—	2	6
Knight, S. J.	London	1824	Domestic	—	—	—	1	—	—	—	—	—	—	1
Knight, Valentine	Folkestone	1871	Landscape	—	—	—	—	—	—	—	—	—	1	1
Knight, W.	London	1807-1845	Architecture	—	—	13	—	—	—	—	—	—	—	13
Knight, William	Chelmsford	1829-1846	Landscape	—	—	—	—	15	—	4	—	—	—	19
Knight, W. F.	London	1841	Churches	—	—	1	—	—	—	—	—	—	—	1
Knight, William Henry	London	1844-1864	Domestic	—	—	29	17	8	—	—	—	—	2	56
Knight, W. S.	Sevenoaks	1860-1861	Landscape	—	—	—	—	2	—	—	—	—	—	2
Knight, Miss	London	1790	Mythological	—	—	1	—	—	—	—	—	—	—	1
Knightley, Thomas Edward	London	1864-1880	Architecture	—	—	2	—	—	—	—	—	—	—	2
Knothe, Alice	Dresden	1873	Figures	—	—	—	—	—	—	—	—	—	1	1
Knowles, Davidson, R.B.A.§	London	1879-1893	Landscape	—	—	10	—	33	—	—	1	1	20	65
Knowles, F. M'Gillivray	Clapton	1892-1893	Landscape	—	—	—	—	1	—	—	—	—	1	2
Knowles, G.	London	1845-1848	Ruins	—	—	3	—	—	—	—	—	—	—	3
Knowles, Geo. Sheridan, R.I., R.B.A., A.R.C.A.§‡	London	1885-1893	Domestic	—	—	9	—	27	—	12	—	—	3	51
Knowles, G. T.	Dover	1853	Landscape	—	—	—	1	—	—	—	—	—	—	1
Knowles, Miss Juliet	Manchester	1888	Fruit	—	—	1	—	—	—	1	—	—	—	2
Knowles, James Thomas	London	1843-1860	Architecture	—	—	4	—	—	—	—	—	—	—	4
Knowles, Leonora C. E.	London	1844	Portraits	—	—	1	—	—	—	—	—	—	—	1
Knowles, William Pitcairn	Christchurch	1882-1892	Landscape	—	—	2	—	5	—	5	—	2	—	14
Knowles, Mrs.	—	1803	Landscape	—	—	1	—	—	—	—	—	—	—	1
Knox, B. D.	Caversham	1873-1878	Sea Pieces	—	—	3	—	—	—	—	—	—	3	6
Knox, G. J.	London	1839-1859	Landscape	—	—	9	1	20	—	—	—	—	—	30
Knox, John	London	1829-1849	Landscape	—	—	5	6	4	—	—	—	—	—	15
Knox, T.	Keswick	1849	Landscape	—	—	1	—	—	—	—	—	—	2	3
Kobell, Kendrick (?) Hendrik	London	1770	Sea Pieces	—	1	—	—	—	—	—	—	—	—	1
Koberwein, George	London	1862-1876	Portraits	—	—	30	1	3	—	—	—	—	5	39
Koberwein, Miss Georgina F. *See* Mrs. Terrell	London	1876-1878	Figures	—	—	8	—	2	—	—	—	—	8	18
Koberwein, J.	London	1859	Figures	—	—	2	—	—	—	—	—	—	—	2
Koberwein, Miss Rosa	London	1876-1885	Domestic	—	—	10	—	1	—	1	3	—	13	28
Koch, Alexander	London	1890-1893	Architecture	—	—	3	—	—	—	—	—	—	—	3
Koch, Walter	Bushey	1893	Figures	—	—	—	—	—	—	—	—	—	1	1
Koe, Lawrence E. (?) Leonard	Brighton	1888-1892	Sculpture	—	—	1	—	2	—	1	—	—	4	8
Koe, Winifred	Blackheath	1888	Flowers	—	—	—	—	1	—	—	—	—	—	1
Koe, Mrs.	London	1840	—	—	—	—	—	*	—	—	—	—	—	—
Koekkoek, Hermanns	London	1865-1876	Sea Pieces	—	—	1	3	—	—	—	—	—	—	4
Koekkoek, Hermanns P.	London	1864-1881	Sea Pieces	—	—	—	4	2	—	—	—	—	2	8
Koekkoek, N.	London	1866	Lake Scenes	—	—	1	—	—	—	—	—	—	—	1
Koelman, J.	Rome	1858	Portraits	—	—	1	—	—	—	—	—	—	—	1
Koenig, S.	London	1818	Portraits	—	—	2	—	—	—	—	—	—	—	2
Koldewey, B. H.	Dordrecht	1889	Landscape	—	—	—	—	—	—	—	—	—	1	1
Koller, R.	—	1857	Cattle	—	—	1	—	—	—	—	—	—	—	1
Kondrup, Miss Katinka	London	1880-1886	Sculpture	—	—	2	—	—	—	—	—	—	—	2
Konig —	—	1852	Domestic	—	—	2	—	—	—	—	—	—	—	2
Koningh, De. *See* D.	—	—	—	—	—	—	—	—	—	—	—	—	—	—
Konstam, Miss Gertrude A.	London	1883-1885	Domestic	—	—	—	—	—	—	—	—	—	2	2
Kopf, R.	Stuttgart	1874	Portraits	—	—	1	—	—	—	—	—	—	—	1
Kopf, Professor T.	Rome	1869-1877	Sculpture	—	—	5	—	—	—	—	2	—	—	7
Koster, E.	London	1857-1859	Sea Pieces	—	—	1	—	1	—	—	—	—	—	2
Koster, De. *See* De Costa.	—	—	—	—	—	—	—	—	—	—	—	—	—	—
Kozanecki, L.	London	1839-1848	Game	—	—	3	—	—	—	—	—	—	—	3
Kovàschi, John	London	1854	Domestic	—	—	—	—	—	—	—	—	—	1	1
Kramer, J. H.	London	1765-1775	Portraits	2	4	2	—	—	—	—	—	—	—	8
Krausse, R.	Leipzig	1865-1866	Scriptural	—	—	2	—	—	—	—	—	—	—	2
Kray, W.	Rome	1876	Figures	—	—	—	—	2	—	—	—	—	—	2
Kreader, Charles	London	1835	Moonlight	—	—	—	—	1	—	—	—	—	—	1

Name.	Town.	First and Last Year of Ex.	Speciality.	S. A.	F. S.	R. A.	B. I.	S. S.	O. W.	N. W.	G. G.	N. G.	V. E.	Total.
Kremer, J. C.	London	1872	Sculpture	—	—	1	—	—	—	—	—	—	—	1
Kremer, P.	London	1829	Historical	—	—	—	1	—	—	—	—	—	—	1
Kretzschiner, H.	Berlin	1852	Historical	—	—	1	—	—	—	—	—	—	—	1
Kricheldorf, Carl	Tetbury	1892-1893	Domestic	—	—	5	—	2	—	—	—	—	—	7
Kuckuth. *See* Beenson and Kuckuth	—	—	Architecture	—	—	—	—	—	—	—	—	—	—	—
Kühn, Friedrich	Munich	1885	Sculpture	—	—	1	—	—	—	—	—	—	—	1
Kummer, Paul	London	1882-1890	Domestic	—	—	4	—	—	—	—	—	—	—	4
Kummings, Richard	Scarborough	1876	Pen and Ink	—	—	—	—	—	—	—	—	—	3	3
Kümpel, William	London	1855-1879	Figures	—	—	7	1	1	—	—	1	—	10	20
Kuntze, Edward J. A.	London	1860-1863	Sculpture	—	—	16	—	—	—	—	—	—	—	16
Kuytenbrouwer, M. A.	Brussels	1852	Landscape	—	—	2	—	—	—	—	—	—	—	2
Kyd, James	Worcester	1855-1875	Domestic	—	—	2	6	9	—	—	—	—	1	18
Kylberg, Regina	Ealing	1884-1885	Italy	—	—	—	—	5	—	—	—	—	—	5
Laar, Vander. *See* V.	—	—	—	—	—	—	—	—	—	—	—	—	—	—
Labar, Miss	London	1766-1783	Hair Work	—	12	—	—	—	—	—	—	—	—	12
Labruzzi, Signor	Rome	1776	Portraits	—	1	—	—	—	—	—	—	—	—	1
Laby, Alexander	London	1864-1866	Scriptural	—	—	—	—	3	—	—	—	—	—	3
Lacazette, Miss A.	London	1883	Domestic	—	—	—	—	1	—	—	—	—	—	1
Lacey, C. J. de. *See* D.	—	—	—	—	—	—	—	—	—	—	—	—	—	—
Lacey, Frederick W.	Brentford	1885-1886	Architecture	—	—	2	—	—	—	—	—	—	—	2
Lacey, W. S.	London	1827-1838	Landscape	—	—	6	—	5	—	—	—	—	—	11
Lachemoitz, S.	Düsseldorf	1849	Figures	—	—	1	—	—	—	—	—	—	—	1
Lack, J.	Preston	1855-1865	Landscape	—	—	1	1	—	—	—	—	—	—	2
Lacklan, J.	London	1806-1809	Landscape	—	—	6	—	—	—	—	—	—	—	6
Lacoste, H. B.	London	1860	Flowers	—	—	1	—	1	—	—	—	—	—	2
Lacoste, M. R.	Paris	1871	Landscape	—	—	—	—	—	—	—	—	—	1	1
Lacour, Octave L.	Teddington	1887-1891	Etching	—	—	4	—	—	—	—	—	—	—	4
Lacretelle, Jean Edouard	London	1851-1891	Portraits	—	—	25	—	1	—	—	—	—	5	31
Ladbroke, E.	London	1820	Landscape	—	—	1	—	—	—	—	—	—	—	1
Ladbrooke, F.	Bury St. Edm'ds	1860-1864	Domestic	—	—	—	—	4	—	—	—	—	—	4
Ladbrooke, Henry,	North Walsham	1834-1865	Landscape	—	—	—	3	10	—	—	—	—	—	13
Ladrooke, John Berney	Norwich	1821-1872	Landscape	—	—	3	10	35	—	—	—	—	—	48
Ladrooke, Robert	Norwich	1811-1822	Landscape	—	—	5	8	—	—	—	—	—	—	13
Ladd, Miss Anne	London	1769	Fruit	2	—	—	—	—	—	—	—	—	—	2
Ladds, John	London	1877-1886	Architecture	—	—	4	—	—	—	—	—	—	—	4
Lade —	London	1770	Fruit	2	—	—	—	—	—	—	—	—	—	2
Ladell, Edward	Colchester	1856-1886	Fruit	—	—	21	5	2	—	—	—	—	3	31
Ladeuil, Leonard Morel	London	1865-1885	Sculpture	—	—	4	—	—	—	—	—	—	—	4
Laevernz, G.	London	1882	Domestic	—	—	1	—	—	—	—	—	—	—	1
Lafage, De. *See* D.	—	—	—	—	—	—	—	—	—	—	—	—	—	—
Lafarge, John	New York	1872	Flowers	—	—	1	—	—	—	—	—	—	—	1
Lafaye, P.	London	1843	Historical	—	—	—	1	—	—	—	—	—	—	1
Lafenestre, G.	Hereford	1877	Sheep	—	—	—	—	1	—	—	—	—	—	1
Laffert, C.	London	1809-1813	Enamels	—	—	2	—	—	—	—	—	—	—	2
Lafolie, Y.	London	1868	Portraits	—	—	1	—	—	—	—	—	—	—	1
Lafollie De. *See* D.	—	—	—	—	—	—	—	—	—	—	—	—	—	—
Lafond, J. E.	Paris	1869	Historical	—	—	1	—	—	—	—	—	—	—	1
Laforest. *See* Salter and Laforest	—	—	Architecture	—	—	—	—	—	—	—	—	—	—	—
Lagier, Mdlle. E.	Geneva	1859	Figures	—	—	1	—	—	—	—	—	—	—	1
Laguillermie, Frédéric Auguste	Paris	1878-1889	Etching	—	—	2	—	—	—	—	—	—	—	2
La Haye, Alexis	Nismes	1893	Domestic	—	—	1	—	—	—	—	—	—	—	1
Lahee and Mabin	London	1845	Architecture	—	—	1	—	—	—	—	—	—	—	1
Laidlaw, H. Guiseppe	London	1885	Landscape	—	—	—	—	1	—	—	—	—	—	1
Laidlay, Miss Lucy	Wimborne	1891-1892	Flowers	—	—	—	—	—	—	—	—	—	2	2
Laidlay, William J.	London	1882-1893	Landscape	—	—	16	—	15	—	—	3	8	—	42
Laine, Francis	London	1776-1790	Miniatures	77	—	5	—	—	—	—	—	—	—	82
Laing, David	London	1795-1822	Architecture	—	—	9	—	—	—	—	—	—	—	9
Laing, Miss Florence. *See* Mrs. E. S. Kennedy.	—	—	—	—	—	—	—	—	—	—	—	—	—	—
Laing, Frank, A.R.P.E.	Kircaldy	1893	Landscape	—	—	1	—	—	—	—	—	—	—	1
Laing, Miss Isabella	Twickenham	1868-1872	Fruit	—	—	1	—	5	—	—	—	—	1	7
Laing, James G., R.S.W.	Glasgow	1883-1892	Landscape	—	—	16	—	1	—	3	2	—	—	22
Laing, William Wardlaw	Liverpool	1873-1892	Figures	—	—	16	—	1	—	2	1	—	—	20
Lains, C.	London	1857	Architecture	—	—	1	—	—	—	—	—	—	—	1
Lainson, Thomas J.	Brighton	1891	Architecture	—	—	1	—	—	—	—	—	—	—	1
Lair —	London	1776	Miniatures	—	—	1	—	—	—	—	—	—	—	1
Laird, Miss Alicia H. ‖	London	1846-1865	Miniatures	—	—	30	—	—	—	—	—	—	—	30
Lait, Edward	London	1865-1869	Landscape	—	—	—	—	4	—	—	—	—	—	4
Lajos, L. Bruck-. *See* B.	—	—	—	—	—	—	—	—	—	—	—	—	—	—
Lake, F.	Taunton	1834	Portraits	—	—	1	—	—	—	—	—	—	—	1

Name.	Town.	First and Last Year of Ex.	Speciality.	S. A.	F. S.	R. A.	B. I.	S. S.	O. W.	N.W.	G. G.	N. G.	V. E.	Total.
Lake, Miss Gertrude	Manchester	1893	Domestic	—	—	—	—	—	—	1	—	—	—	1
Lake, S.	London	1819	Architecture	—	—	1	—	—	—	—	—	—	—	1
Lalanne, F. Maxime	Paris	1872-1881	Etching	—	—	—	—	—	—	—	—	—	19	19
Lalauze, Adolphe	London	1875-1879	Etching	—	—	—	—	—	—	—	—	—	3	3
Lallemand, Jean Baptiste	London	1773	Still Life	1	—	—	—	—	—	—	—	—	—	1
Lalone, A.	London	1842	Figures	—	—	—	—	1	—	—	—	—	—	1
Lamb, Edward Buckton, F.R.I.B.A.	London	1824-1869	Architecture	—	—	58	—	5	—	—	—	—	—	63
Lamb, Edward Beckitt	Brockley	1893	Architecture	—	—	1	—	—	—	—	—	—	—	1
Lamb, Miss H.	London	1872	Figures	—	—	—	—	1	—	—	—	—	—	1
Lamb, Henry	Malvern	1834-1861	Landscape	—	—	—	1	—	—	2	—	—	16	19
Lamb, J.	London	1827-1834	Landscape	—	—	4	—	—	—	—	—	—	—	4
Lambdin, George Cochran	Philadelphia	1858	Domestic	—	—	1	—	—	—	—	—	—	—	1
Lambert, C.	—	1800	Landscape	—	—	1	—	—	—	—	—	—	—	1
Lambert, Clement	Brighton	1880-1892	Landscape	—	—	8	—	20	—	10	5	1	23	67
Lambert, E. F.	London	1823-1846	Historical	—	—	15	—	7	—	—	—	—	—	22
Lambert, Edwin J.	London	1877-1892	Landscape	—	—	1	—	3	—	—	—	—	9	13
Lambert, James	London	1761-1778	Landscape	17	30	7	—	—	—	—	—	—	—	54
Lambert, James, Junr.	Lewes	1769-1778	Flowers	—	18	5	—	—	—	—	—	—	—	23
Lambert, J. W.	Carshalton	1822-1851	Sporting	—	—	9	4	11	—	—	—	—	—	24
Lambert, Louis Eugène	Paris	1883	Domestic	—	—	—	—	—	—	1	—	—	—	1
Lambert, P.	London	1775-1783	Engraving	4	3	—	—	—	—	—	—	—	—	7
Lamborne, Peter Spendelowe, F.S.A.	Cambridge	1760-1774	Miniatures and Engraving	19	—	—	—	—	—	—	—	—	—	19
Lami, Louis Eugène	London	1850	Historical	—	—	1	—	—	—	—	—	—	—	1
Lammin, Miss	London	1886	Flowers	—	—	—	—	1	—	—	—	—	—	1
Lamond, Miss	Hampton Wick	1878	Sea Pieces	—	—	—	—	—	—	—	—	—	1	1
Lamont, Thomas R., A.R.W.S. †	Greenock	1861-1893	Domestic	—	—	4	—	—	103	—	2	—	3	112
La Monte, Miss Elish	Belfast	1856-1859	Miniatures	—	—	7	—	—	—	—	—	—	—	7
Lamoriniere, F.	Antwerp	1869	Landscape	—	—	1	—	—	—	—	—	—	—	1
Lamotte, Alphonse	Paris	1888-1893	Engraving	—	—	4	—	—	—	—	—	—	—	4
Lamqua —	Canton	1835-1845	Portraits	—	—	2	—	—	—	—	—	—	—	2
Lancaster, Alfred Dobree	London	1863-1890	Figures	—	—	12	1	1	—	—	—	—	9	23
Lancaster, Hume §	London	1836-1849	Sea Pieces	—	—	23	31	78	—	—	—	—	—	132
Lancaster, John	London	1882-1884	Landscape	—	—	—	—	3	—	—	—	—	—	3
Lancaster, Rev. R. W.	—	1800-1827	Landscape	—	—	33	—	—	—	—	—	—	—	33
Lancaster, W. C.	London	1830-1831	Portraits	—	—	2	—	—	—	—	—	—	—	2
Lancaster, Mrs.	London	1840	Landscape	—	—	—	1	—	—	—	—	—	—	1
Lance, E.	London	1810	Architecture	—	—	1	—	—	—	—	—	—	—	1
Lance, Miss E.	London	1859-1861	Fruit	—	—	3	—	—	—	—	—	—	—	3
Lance, Miss Eveline	Chiswick	1891-1893	Landscape	—	—	—	—	3	—	2	—	—	—	5
Lance, George	London	1824-1864	Fruit	—	—	38	135	48	—	14	—	—	—	235
Lance, William	London	1887	Domestic	—	—	—	—	—	—	—	—	—	1	1
Lance, Wilmot	Ipswich	1893	Flowers	—	—	—	—	2	—	—	—	—	—	2
Lance, W. B.	Chiswick	1882	Domestic	—	—	—	—	1	—	—	—	—	—	1
Lancey, T.	Greenwich	1793-1799	Landscape	—	—	5	—	—	—	—	—	—	—	5
Lançon, A.	Hastings	1880	Domestic	—	—	—	—	—	—	—	—	—	3	3
Land, Miss E.	—	1833	Landscape	—	—	—	—	—	—	1	—	—	—	1
Landells, Ebenezer	London	1833-1837	Wood Engraving	—	—	—	—	2	—	—	—	—	—	2
Landells, J.	London	1835	Seashores	—	—	1	—	—	—	—	—	—	—	1
Landells, Robert Thomas	London	1863-1876	Military	—	—	—	—	45	—	—	—	—	8	53
Lander, Alice	London	1859-1860	Figures	—	—	—	—	—	—	—	—	—	3	3
Lander, Henry Longley	London	1864-1887	Landscape	—	—	5	1	27	—	1	—	—	11	45
Lander, Mrs. Mary E.	Fareham	1854-1857	Figures	—	—	—	—	3	—	—	—	—	—	3
Lander, R.	London	1827	Mythological	—	—	—	1	—	—	—	—	—	—	1
Lander, Wills	London	1887-1891	Landscape	—	—	2	—	2	—	—	—	1	1	6
Landers, Mrs.	—	1836	Landscape	—	—	1	—	—	—	—	—	—	—	1
Landesmann, Madame	Geneva	1859	Domestic	—	—	1	—	—	—	—	—	—	—	1
Landi, Aristodemo	Florence	1881	Flowers	—	—	1	—	—	—	—	—	—	—	1
Landon, H.	London	1827	Portraits	—	—	—	—	1	—	—	—	—	—	1
Landon, John	Enfield	1798-1827	Landscape	—	—	13	1	—	—	—	—	—	—	14
Landon, T.	Cheshunt	1795-1797	Landscape	—	—	5	—	—	—	—	—	—	—	5
Landor, G. Dick	Edinburgh	1848	Landscape	—	—	—	—	—	—	—	—	—	2	2
Landseer, Charles, R.A.	London	1822-1879	Historical	—	—	73	26	11	—	—	—	—	—	110
Landseer, Sir Edwin Henry, R.A.	London	1815-1873	Animals	—	—	179	94	4	9	—	—	—	—	286
Landseer, Miss Emma. ‖ *See* Mrs. McKenzie	—	1838-1842	Animals	—	—	—	3	2	—	—	—	—	—	5
Landseer, George	London	1850-1858	Figures	—	—	21	12	1	—	—	—	—	—	34
Landseer, Henry	London	1820-1833	Landscape	—	—	—	9	14	1	—	—	—	—	24
Landseer, Miss Jessica ‖	London	1816-1866	Landscape	—	—	10	7	6	9	—	—	—	—	32
Landseer, John, A.R.A.	London	1791-1852	Engraving	1	—	17	—	2	—	—	—	—	—	20
Landseer, Thomas, A.R.A.	London	1832-1877	Engraving	—	—	35	2	2	—	4	—	—	—	43
Landsheer, E.	London	1863-1870	Sculpture	—	—	12	1	—	—	—	—	—	—	13
Lane, Albert	Barnstaple	1856-1872	Landscape	—	—	3	1	10	—	—	—	—	4	18
Lane, Anna Louisa	London	1778-1782	Miniatures	—	—	4	—	—	—	—	—	—	—	4

Name.	Town.	First and Last Year of Ex.	Speciality.	S. A.	F. S.	R. A.	B. I.	S. S.	O. W.	N. W.	G. G.	N. G.	V. E.	Total.
Lane, Rev. C. G.	Little Gaddesden	1868-1873	Landscape	—	—	—	—	3	—	—	—	—	2	5
Lane, Miss C. S.	London	1856-1859	Domestic	—	—	5	—	—	—	—	—	—	—	5
Lane, E.	London	1830-1839	Landscape	—	—	1	3	—	—	—	—	—	—	4
Lane, Miss E.	London	1865-1868	Flowers	—	—	—	—	—	—	—	—	—	6	6
Lane, Miss F.	Plymouth	1870	Portraits	—	—	1	—	—	—	—	—	—	—	1
Lane, G. A.	London	1837	Landscape	—	—	—	—	2	—	—	—	—	—	2
Lane, G. Ousley	London	1857-1859	Architecture	—	—	3	—	—	—	—	—	—	—	3
Lane, H.	London	1808-1810	Architecture	—	—	4	—	—	—	—	—	—	—	4
Lane, H.	London	1828-1830	Figures	—	—	5	—	—	—	—	—	—	—	5
Lane, H.	Bexley Heath	1868-1870	Flowers, etc.	—	—	—	—	4	—	—	—	—	—	4
Lane, H. F.	London	1831-1836	Figures	—	—	—	3	—	—	—	—	—	—	3
Lane, J.	London	1851	Scriptural	—	—	—	2	—	—	—	—	—	—	2
Lane, John Bryant	Cornwall	1808-1834	Portraits	—	—	16	3	3	—	—	—	—	—	22
Lane, Miss Louisa	London	1769-1777	Hair Work	32	—	—	—	—	—	—	—	—	—	32
Lane, Miss Mary	London	1770-1773	Hair Work	7	—	—	—	—	—	—	—	—	—	7
Lane, R.	London	1815-1826	Architecture	—	—	3	—	—	—	—	—	—	—	3
Lane, Richard James, A.R.A.	London	1824-1872	Lithography	—	—	67	—	16	—	—	—	—	—	83
Lane, Samuel	London	1804-1857	Portraits	—	—	217	1	4	—	—	—	—	—	222
Lane, Miss Sarah H.	London	1843-1872	Figures	—	—	4	4	5	—	—	—	—	—	13
Lane, Theodore	London	1816-1830	Domestic	—	—	7	7	3	—	—	—	—	—	17
Lane, Walter	London	1880-1881	Metal Work	—	—	3	—	—	—	—	—	—	—	3
Lane, William	London	1777	Gems	1	—	18	—	—	—	—	—	—	—	19
Lane, William	London	1798-1815	Portraits & Miniatures	—	—	44	1	—	—	—	—	—	—	45
Lang, A.	London	1841	Architecture	—	—	1	—	—	—	—	—	—	—	1
Lang, C. E.	London	1831-1842	Architecture	—	—	3	—	1	—	—	—	—	—	4
Lang, J.	London	1849-1852	Landscape	—	—	—	—	4	—	—	—	—	—	4
Langdale, Marmaduke A.	London	1864-1891	Landscape	—	—	15	1	19	—	—	—	—	24	59
Langdon, E.	London	1846-1848	Landscape	—	—	3	—	3	—	—	—	—	—	3
Langdon, T.	London	1785-1802	Miniatures	—	—	41	—	—	—	—	—	—	—	41
Langelaan, H	London	1865	Sheep	—	—	1	—	—	—	—	—	—	—	1
Langenhoeffel, J.	London	1788	Mythological	—	—	5	—	—	—	—	—	—	—	5
Langford —	—	1843	Drawings	—	—	—	—	1	—	—	—	—	—	1
Langham, Hon. Mrs. E., *or* G.	London	1879-1882	Landscape	—	—	—	—	—	—	—	1	—	1	2
Langham, John. *See also* Burkett and Langham	Leicester	1854-1890	Architecture	—	—	6	—	—	—	—	—	—	—	6
Langl, H.	London	1845-1850	Animals	—	—	3	—	—	—	—	—	—	—	3
Langlands, George Nasmyth-	Edinburgh	1890-1893	Landscape	—	—	5	—	—	—	—	—	—	—	5
Langley, E., *or* C.	London	1855	Enamels	—	—	—	—	—	—	—	—	—	1	1
Langley, R.	London	1834-1845	Fruit	—	—	1	2	2	—	—	—	—	—	5
Langley, Walter, R.I. ‡	Birmingham	1880-1893	Domestic	—	—	1	—	4	—	30	—	—	4	39
Langlin, Victoriano Codina-. *See also* C.	London	1878-1883	Figures	—	—	4	—	—	—	—	—	—	—	4
Langlois de Sens, C.	London	1831-1849	Portraits	—	—	12	—	5	—	—	—	—	—	17
Langlois, C., Junr.	London	1835-1847	Portraits	—	—	9	—	—	—	—	—	—	—	9
Langlois, M. E. W.	London	1867-1872	Still Life	—	—	3	—	—	—	—	—	—	—	3
Langlois, Mark W.	London	1862-1873	Sea Pieces	—	—	—	—	9	—	—	—	—	2	11
Langshaw, J.	Bristol	1865	Landscape	—	—	—	—	1	—	—	—	—	—	1
Langstone, Alfred	London	1872	Architecture	—	—	1	—	—	—	—	—	—	—	1
Lankester, Arthur	London	1858-1865	Domestic	—	—	2	2	—	—	—	—	—	—	4
Lanman, Mrs. H.	London	1836	Portraits	—	—	2	—	—	—	—	—	—	—	2
Lansdell, Elizabeth	Burwash	1847	Portraits	—	—	1	—	—	—	—	—	—	—	1
Lansdell, Mark J.	London	1884-1885	Architecture	—	—	3	—	—	—	—	—	—	—	3
Lansdown, J.	London	1817-1828	Architecture	—	—	4	—	—	—	—	—	—	—	4
Lantéri, Edouard	London	1885-1893	Sculpture	—	—	32	—	—	—	—	—	1	—	33
Lanz, Alfred	Paris	1890	Sculpture	—	—	2	—	—	—	—	—	—	—	2
Lapidge, Edward	Hampton Wick	1808-1851	Architecture	—	—	9	—	—	—	—	—	—	—	9
Laporte, George Henry ‡	London	1821-1873	Sporting	—	—	9	21	18	—	160	—	—	—	208
Laporte, John	London	1779-1835	Landscape	—	—	110	102	18	—	14	—	—	45	289
Laporte, Miss Mary Ann ‡	London	1813-1845	Portraits	—	—	4	3	—	—	15	—	—	—	22
Lapostolet, Charles	Paris	1872-1881	Seashores	—	—	1	—	—	—	—	3	—	4	8
Lapworth, William E.	London	1891	Landscape	—	—	—	—	—	—	1	—	—	—	1
Lara, G.	London	1862-1871	Rural	—	—	—	1	16	—	—	—	—	—	17
Larbalestier, P.	Jersey	1857	Landscape	—	—	1	—	—	—	—	—	—	—	1
Large, J.	London	1834	Portraits	—	—	1	—	—	—	—	—	—	—	1
Laris, F. G.	—	1883	Flowers	—	—	—	—	1	—	—	—	—	—	1
Lark, Tremayne	London	1882-1885	Domestic	—	—	2	—	1	—	—	—	—	—	3
Larkin, Miss J.	—	1827-1831	Portraits	—	—	9	—	—	—	—	—	—	—	9
Larkin, T.	—	1825	Portraits	—	—	1	—	—	—	—	—	—	—	1
Larkins, F.	London	1835-1847	Landscape	—	—	—	—	2	—	—	—	—	—	2
Larkins, W.	London	1853-1856	Portraits	—	—	—	—	3	—	—	—	—	—	3
Larson, Virginia	London	1880	Figures	—	—	—	—	1	—	—	—	—	—	1
Larsson, Carl	Nemours	1885-1886	Domestic	—	—	—	—	—	—	2	—	—	—	2
Lascelles, Thomas W.	Cookham Dene	1885-1891	Domestic	—	—	6	—	2	—	—	—	—	—	8
Lasch, E.	London	1870	Figures	—	—	—	—	—	—	—	—	—	1	1

Name.	Town.	First and Last Year of Ex.	Speciality.	S. A.	F. S.	R. A.	B. I.	S. S.	O. W.	N. W.	G. G.	N. G.	V. E.	Total.
Lasch, Professor Karl Johann	London	1879	Portraits	—	—	1	—	—	—	—	—	—	—	1
Laslett, Thomas Newnham	Charlton	1865	Architecture	—	—	1	—	—	—	—	—	—	—	1
Lassonguer, J. P.	London	1847	Portraits	—	—	2	—	—	—	—	—	—	—	2
Latham, B. M.	London	1887-1888	Sculpture	—	—	—	—	1	—	—	—	—	1	2
Latham, Miss Frances A.	London	1861	Landscape	—	—	—	—	1	—	—	—	—	—	1
Latham, Francis P.	London	1889	River Scenes	—	—	—	—	—	—	1	—	—	—	1
Latham, J.	London	1787-1791	Still Life	—	—	8	—	—	—	—	—	—	—	8
La Thangue, H. H. φ	Dulwich	1877-1893	Figures	—	—	11	—	5	—	—	8	10	5	39
Lathrop, Francis	New York	1872	Figures	—	—	1	—	—	—	—	—	—	1	2
Latilla, Eugenio H. §	London	1828-1859	Portraits	—	—	6	15	70	—	—	—	—	—	91
Latilla, F. Z.	London	1839-1840	Figures	—	—	—	—	3	—	—	—	—	—	3
Latoix, Gaspard	Leamington	1883-1887	Etching	—	—	1	—	3	—	—	—	—	—	4
La Tour —	London	1767	Figures	—	3	—	—	—	—	—	—	—	—	3
Latour, Henry Fantin-. *See* Fantin.	—	—	—	—	—	—	—	—	—	—	—	—	—	—
Latre, De. *See* D.	—	—	—	—	—	—	—	—	—	—	—	—	—	—
Latrouwer, Le. *See* Le.	—	—	—	—	—	—	—	—	—	—	—	—	—	—
Latzarus, Miss Edith M.	London	1890-1892	Flowers	—	—	1	—	3	—	—	—	—	—	4
Lauber, Adolph	London	1870-1879	Flowers	—	—	4	—	1	—	—	—	—	—	5
Laud, Miss Emma J.	—	1832-1833	Landscape	—	—	2	—	—	—	—	—	—	—	2
Lauder, Charles J., R.S.W.	Richmond	1890	Buildings	—	—	—	—	1	—	—	—	—	—	1
Lauder, James Eckford, R.S.A.	Edinburgh	1841-1858	Dramatic	—	—	6	7	1	—	—	—	—	38	52
Lauder, Robert Scott, R.S.A.	London	1827-1861	Historical	—	—	25	11	—	—	—	—	—	65	101
Lauderset, Mdlle. Teresa de. *See* Mdme. Hegg	—	—	—	—	—	—	—	—	—	—	—	—	—	—
Laugée, François Désiré	Paris	1871-1874	Miniatures	—	—	15	—	—	—	—	—	—	7	22
Laugée, Georges	Paris	1884	Figures	—	—	—	—	—	—	—	—	—	1	1
Laundy, George Albert	London	1878-1893	Landscape	—	—	1	—	—	—	1	—	—	10	12
Laune, De. *See* D.	—	—	—	—	—	—	—	—	—	—	—	—	—	—
Laupheimer, Anton	London	1882-1886	Domestic	—	—	1	—	1	—	—	—	—	—	2
Laurence, H.	London	1872-1874	Portraits	—	—	1	—	1	—	—	—	—	—	2
Laurence, O. B. (?) S. L.	London	1848	Sculpture	—	—	—	1	—	—	—	—	—	—	1
Laurence, Samuel	London	1834-1891	Portraits	—	—	91	—	14	—	—	2	—	4	111
Laurence, Sydney M.	St. Ives, C'nwall	1890	Venice	—	—	—	—	2	—	—	—	—	—	2
Laurence, Thomas, F.S.A.	London	1770-1776	Landscape	5	—	—	—	—	—	—	—	—	—	5
Laurens, Jules	Paris	1875	Landscape	—	—	—	—	—	—	—	—	—	2	2
Laurent, Madame Marie Pauline	Paris	1839-1852	Enamels	—	—	11	—	—	—	—	—	—	—	11
Laurenty, M. Jullien	London	1795-1798	Cattle	—	—	2	—	—	—	—	—	—	—	2
Laurenzy —	—	1815	Cattle	—	—	—	—	—	—	—	—	—	1	1
Laurie, R. H.	London	1796-1801	Shells	—	—	6	—	—	—	—	—	—	—	6
Laurie, W.	London	1846-1847	Architecture	—	—	2	—	—	—	—	—	—	—	2
Lavers, Arthur E.	London	1882	Landscape	—	—	—	—	1	—	—	—	—	—	1
Laverty, A., *or* G., Sorel	Ryde	1881-1886	Flowers	—	—	—	—	6	—	—	—	—	2	8
Lavery, John, A.R.S.A.	Glasgow	1886-1893	Domestic	—	—	9	—	4	—	—	4	—	4	21
Lavezzari, Andre	London	1871-1872	Figures	—	—	—	—	16	—	—	—	—	—	16
Laville, E.	Paris	1876-1877	Scriptural	—	—	—	—	—	—	—	—	—	3	3
Law, Miss Annie	London	1876-1888	Landscape	—	—	—	—	27	—	—	—	—	—	27
Law, Miss Beatrice	London	1884-1888	Landscape	—	—	—	—	6	—	—	—	—	—	6
Law, David, R.B.A., R.P.E. §	London	1869-1893	Landscape	—	—	45	—	83	—	1	—	—	25	15.
Law, E.	Sheffield	1829-1832	Sculpture	—	—	4	—	—	—	—	—	—	—	4
Law, Edward	London	1860-1883	Landscape	—	—	3	—	13	—	—	—	—	15	31
Law, Ernest	London	1891-1893	Landscape	—	—	—	—	3	—	—	—	—	—	3
Law, E. F., F.R.I.B.A.	Northampton	1850-1869	Architecture	—	—	3	—	—	—	—	—	—	—	3
Law, Henry	—	1832	Landscape	—	—	—	1	—	—	—	—	—	—	1
Law, William	London	1860-1874	Fruit	—	—	1	1	2	—	—	—	—	8	12
Law, Mrs. W.	Putney	1854-1862	Flowers	—	—	1	5	—	—	—	—	—	—	6
Lawder, R.	—	1826	Heads	—	—	—	—	1	—	—	—	—	—	1
Lawes, Charles Bennet	London	1872-1890	Sculpture	—	—	9	—	5	—	—	—	—	4	18
Lawford, Edgar C.	London	1876-1893	Domestic	—	—	2	—	—	—	—	—	—	3	5
Lawford, Mrs. Rowland	London	1866-1882	Flowers	—	—	—	—	2	—	—	—	—	17	19
Lawford and Heneker	London	1854	Architecture	—	—	2	—	—	—	—	—	—	—	2
Lawless, Matthew James	London	1857-1863	Domestic	—	—	11	—	2	—	—	—	—	6	19
Lawlor, John, A.R.H.A.	London	1848-1883	Sculpture	—	—	63	5	21	—	—	—	—	4	93
Lawlor, Michael	London	1877-1891	Sculpture	—	—	7	—	—	—	—	1	—	—	8
Lawlor, Uniacke James	London	1854-1856	Portraits	—	—	2	1	1	—	—	—	—	—	4
Lawlor, W. J.	London	1874-1875	Domestic	—	—	—	—	2	—	—	—	—	—	2
Lawrance, Bringhurst B.	London	1877-1884	Animals	—	—	—	—	1	—	—	—	—	2	3
Lawrance, T.	London	1850-1855	Figures	—	—	—	3	—	—	—	—	—	—	3
Lawranson, Thomas, F.S.A.	London	1762-1777	Portraits	24	2	—	—	—	—	—	—	—	—	26
Lawranson, William, F.S.A.	London	1760-1780	Portraits	24	2	8	—	—	—	—	—	—	—	34
Lawrence, Miss E. A.	—	1800	Shells	—	—	1	—	—	—	—	—	—	—	1
Lawrence, Miss Edith M.	London	1884-1886	Flowers	—	—	—	—	9	—	—	—	—	1	10
Lawrence, Georgina	London	1886-1888	Still Life	—	—	—	—	2	—	—	—	—	—	2
Lawrence, Henry	London	1871-1884	Figures	—	—	1	—	11	—	—	—	—	3	15

Name.	Town.	First and Last Year of Ex.	Speciality.	S. A.	F. S.	R. A.	B. I.	S. S.	O. W.	N.W.	G. G.	N. G.	V. E.	Total.
Lawrence, J.	London	1842	Portraits	—	—	—	—	2	—	—	—	—	—	2
Lawrence, John C.	London	1871-1888	Figures	—	—	7	—	10	—	—	1	—	5	23
Lawrence, Leonard E.	London	1880-1892	Figures	—	—	5	—	1	—	—	—	—	3	9
Lawrence, Miss Mary. *See* Mrs. Kearse	London	1794-1813	Flowers	—	—	32	—	—	—	—	—	—	—	32
Lawrence, P. S.	London	1826-1828	Sea Pieces	—	—	—	—	3	—	—	—	—	—	3
Lawrence, R.	Birmingham	1793-1814	Sporting	—	—	5	—	—	—	—	—	—	—	5
Lawrence, Richard	London	1815-1831	Sculpture	—	—	—	3	4	—	—	—	—	—	7
Lawrence, Sir Thomas, P.R.A.	London	1787-1831	Portraits	—	—	311	3	1	—	—	—	—	—	315
Lawrence, Miss	London	1812	Flowers	—	—	1	—	—	—	—	—	—	—	1
Lawrie, Robert	London	1775	Portraits	3	—	—	—	—	—	—	—	—	—	3
Laws, Charles	London	1855	Architecture	—	—	2	—	—	—	—	—	—	—	2
Lawson, Alexander	Wolv'rhampton	1890-1893	Landscape	—	—	6	—	—	—	—	—	—	2	8
Lawson, Cecil Gordon	London	1869-1882	Landscape	—	—	18	—	12	—	—	18	—	7	55
Lawson, Mrs. Cecil.‖ *See* Miss Constance B. Philip	Haslemere	1880-1892	Flowers	—	—	14	—	3	—	13	12	7	7	56
Lawson, David Arthur	London	1851-1864	Domestic	—	—	1	4	2	—	—	—	—	8	15
Lawson, E.	London	1877	Flowers	—	—	—	—	1	—	—	—	—	—	1
Lawson, Edith M.	London	1891	Interiors	—	—	—	—	1	—	—	—	—	—	1
Lawson, Francis Wilfred	London	1867-1887	Figures	—	—	14	—	4	—	—	1	—	31	50
Lawson, George Anderson	London	1862-1893	Sculpture	—	—	48	1	1	—	2	—	—	12	64
Lawson, John	Sheffield	1893	Landscape	—	—	—	—	—	—	1	—	—	—	1
Lawson, J. Kerr-. *See* K.	—	—	—	—	—	—	—	—	—	—	—	—	—	—
Lawson, J. S.	—	1831	Portraits	—	—	—	—	1	—	—	—	—	—	1
Lawson, Lizzie	—	1881	Domestic	—	—	—	—	—	—	—	—	—	1	1
Lawson, Miss Marion	Tooting	1886	Figures	—	—	—	—	—	—	—	—	—	1	1
Lawson, Miss M. S.	Bexley Heath	1832-1840	Portraits	—	—	—	—	4	—	—	—	—	—	4
Lawson, William	Edinburgh	1819-1864	Portraits	—	—	6	2	11	—	—	—	—	—	19
Lawson, Mrs. William. *See* Miss Elizabeth R. Stone	London	1854-1888	Flowers	—	—	—	—	3	—	—	9	3	—	15
Laxton, W. R.	London	1796-1814	Architecture	—	—	19	—	—	—	—	—	—	2	21
Layton, Mrs. E. M.	Chiswick	1872-1875	Domestic	—	—	—	—	2	—	—	—	—	—	2
Layton, F. W.	London	1873	Game	—	—	—	—	3	—	—	—	—	—	3
Layton, H. B.	Richmond	1867	River Scenes	—	—	1	—	—	—	—	—	—	—	1
Lazzarini, P.	Carrara	1875	Sculpture	—	—	3	—	—	—	—	—	—	—	3
Lea, Miss Anna M. *See* Mrs. Merritt	London	1871-1876	Portraits	—	—	10	—	—	—	—	—	—	1	11
Lea, E.	London	1829-1842	Figures	—	—	12	3	3	—	—	—	—	—	18
Lea, H.	London	1863-1877	Sea Pieces	—	—	1	1	1	—	—	—	—	—	3
Lea, J.	London	1823	Portraits	—	—	1	—	—	—	—	—	—	—	1
Lea, James T.	London	1832-1836	Sea Pieces	—	—	—	—	6	—	—	—	—	—	6
Lea, W.	London	1794	Sculpture	—	—	1	—	—	—	—	—	—	—	1
Lea, William J.	London	1831-1836	Architecture	—	—	4	—	—	—	—	—	—	—	4
Lea, Mrs.	—	1842	Flowers	—	—	—	—	1	—	—	—	—	—	1
Leach, Miss A.	Merton	1808	Domestic	—	—	1	—	—	—	—	—	—	—	1
Leach, Claude Pemberton	London	1893	Architecture	—	—	1	—	—	—	—	—	—	—	1
Leach, Miss E.	Merton	1808-1813	Flowers	—	—	4	—	—	—	—	—	—	—	4
Leach, J.	Merton	1792-1794	Flowers	—	—	6	—	—	—	—	—	—	—	6
Leachman, J.	London	1812-1834	Architecture	—	—	14	—	—	—	—	—	—	—	14
Leachman, J.	London	1848-1850	Landscape	—	—	2	—	4	—	—	—	—	—	6
Leadbetter, Thomas	Edinburgh	1890-1891	Landscape	—	—	2	—	—	—	—	—	—	—	2
Leadbitter, Miss S. M.	London	1857-1874	Portraits	—	—	—	—	6	—	—	—	—	—	6
Leader, Benjamin Williams-, A.R.A. *See* Williams	Worcester	1857-1893	Sea Pieces	—	—	93	6	6	—	—	—	—	25	130
Leader, Mrs. B. W. (Mary)	Worcester	1878-1885	Flowers	—	—	4	—	—	—	—	—	—	1	5
Leader, G.	London	1792-1804	Medals	—	—	11	—	—	—	—	—	—	—	11
Leader, P. H.	Brentford	1797	Medals	—	—	2	—	—	—	—	—	—	—	2
Leahy, Edward Daniel	London	1820-1852	Portraits	—	—	33	25	1	—	—	—	—	—	59
Leak, W.	London	1838	Portraits	—	—	1	—	—	—	—	—	—	—	1
Leake, Henry	London	1765-1766	Portraits	3	—	—	—	—	—	—	—	—	—	3
Leake, S.	London	1826-1827	Figures	—	—	3	—	3	—	—	—	—	—	6
Leake, T. B.	London	1827	Figures	—	—	—	—	1	—	—	—	—	—	1
Leake, Miss	—	1780-1785	Flowers	—	—	3	—	—	—	—	—	—	—	3
Leakey, James	Exeter	1821-1846	Landscape	—	—	12	—	—	—	—	—	—	—	12
Lear, C. H.	London	1842-1852	Figures	—	—	10	3	5	—	—	—	—	—	18
Lear, Edward	London	1836-1879	Landscape	—	—	19	5	4	—	—	3	—	6	37
Lear, J. M.	Bath	1871-1872	Domestic	—	—	—	—	—	—	—	—	—	4	4
Learmouth, Alexander	London	1858-1859	Landscape	—	—	—	2	1	—	—	—	—	—	3
Learmouth, J.	London	1836	Sculpture	—	—	2	—	—	—	—	—	—	—	2
Leathem, W. J.	Brighton	1840-1855	Sea Pieces	—	—	13	1	9	—	—	—	—	—	23
Leather, Mrs. R. K. *See* Miss Amy H. Foster	Teignmouth	1893	Landscape	—	—	—	—	—	—	—	—	1	—	1
Leather, Walter E.	London	1867-1868	Flowers	—	—	1	—	—	—	—	—	—	1	2
Leavers, Miss Lucy A.	Nottingham	1887-1889	Domestic	—	—	3	—	—	—	—	—	—	—	3
Le Bas, Miss	Guernsey	1839	Portraits	—	—	—	—	1	—	—	—	—	—	1

Name.	Town.	First and Last Year of Ex.	Speciality.	S. A.	F. S.	R. A.	B. I.	S. S.	O. W.	N.W.	G. G.	N.G.	V.E.	Total.
Lebour, A.	London	1853-1869	Figures	—	—	9	1	11	—	—	—	—	2	23
Le Bourg, A.	Paris	1881	Landscape	—	—	—	—	—	—	—	—	—	1	1
Le Breton, Miss Rosa	—	1865	Domestic	—	—	—	—	—	—	—	—	—	1	1
Le Capelain, John	Jersey	1833-1842	Sea Pieces	—	—	—	—	1	—	1	—	—	—	2
Le Cave, P.	London	1801	Landscape	—	—	2	—	—	—	—	—	—	—	2
Leche, Randal	Chester	1861-1863	Landscape	—	—	2	—	7	—	—	—	—	—	9
Leck, William	London	1888	Architecture	—	—	1	—	—	—	—	—	—	—	1
Leckie, Miss Mary Mulready. *See* Mrs. Stone	London	1840-1844	Portraits	—	—	5	—	—	—	—	—	—	—	5
Lecky, Miss S.	London	1878	Figures	—	—	—	—	—	—	—	—	—	1	1
Le Clear, Thomas	New York	1873	Portraits	—	—	2	—	—	—	—	—	—	—	2
Lecocq, Miss	Richmond	1772-1773	Miniatures	—	2	—	—	—	—	—	—	—	—	2
Lecomte, Paul	London	1887-1888	Churches	—	—	—	—	—	—	1	—	—	2	3
Lecomte-Du Nouy, Jules Jean Antoine	Paris	1871	Figures	—	—	1	—	—	—	—	—	—	—	1
Lecount, Ger. Geo.	London	1808-1813	Scriptural	—	—	5	3	—	—	—	—	—	—	8
Le Couteux, Lionel Aristide	Paris	1877-1880	Etching	—	—	—	—	—	—	—	—	—	8	8
Ledger, E.	London	1833	Landscape	—	—	1	—	—	—	—	—	—	—	1
Ledger, Mrs. E. (Marion)	London	1893	Sculpture	—	—	1	—	—	—	—	—	—	—	1
Ledger, Miss M.	London	1858	Flowers	—	—	—	—	1	—	—	—	—	—	1
Lediard, H.	London	1850	Portraits	—	—	1	—	—	—	—	—	—	—	1
Ledingham, James	Bradford	1892	Architecture	—	—	1	—	—	—	—	—	—	—	1
Ledsam, M.	Norwood	1879-1880	Sea Pieces	—	—	—	—	—	—	—	—	—	2	2
Ledward, R. A.	London	1882-1890	Sculpture	—	—	12	—	—	—	—	—	4	—	16
Lee, A.	London	1838	Architecture	—	—	1	—	—	—	—	—	—	—	1
Lee, Annie	London	1891	Flowers	—	—	—	—	1	—	—	—	—	—	1
Lee, Barnard H.	London	1865	Historical	—	—	—	1	—	—	—	—	—	—	1
Lee, B. D.	Chichester	1819-1821	Portraits	—	—	2	—	—	—	—	—	—	—	2
Lee, Charles	London	1848	Architecture	—	—	1	—	—	—	—	—	—	—	1
Lee, David T.	Birmingham	1863-1889	Figures	—	—	7	2	5	—	1	1	—	1	17
Lee, E.	—	1824	Animals	—	—	1	—	—	—	—	—	—	—	1
Lee, Emily	Leatherhead	1882-1883	Landscape	—	—	—	—	1	—	1	—	—	—	2
Lee, Ernest Claude	London	1875-1887	Architecture	—	—	16	—	—	—	—	—	—	—	16
Lee, E. F.	—	1870	Architecture	—	—	1	—	—	—	—	—	—	—	1
Lee, F. G.	London	1858	Architecture	—	—	1	—	—	—	—	—	—	—	1
Lee, Frederick Richard, R.A.	Barnstaple	1822-1870	Landscape	—	—	171	131	24	—	—	—	—	—	326
Lee, Sir George	—	1846	Landscape	—	—	1	—	—	—	—	—	—	—	1
Lee, Joseph	London	1809-1853	Enamels	—	—	27	—	2	—	—	—	—	—	29
Lee, J.	London	1840	Landscape	—	—	1	—	—	—	—	—	—	—	1
Lee, John	Rockferry	1860-1861	Domestic	—	—	—	—	2	—	—	—	—	—	2
Lee, John	London	1891	Figures	—	—	—	—	1	—	—	—	—	—	1
Lee, John Ingle	London	1868-1891	Figures	—	—	6	—	1	—	—	—	—	8	15
Lee, J. J.	Rockferry	1863-1867	Domestic	—	—	6	—	—	—	—	—	—	—	6
Lee, James N.	London	1873-1891	Animals	—	—	6	—	3	—	3	—	—	2	14
Lee, J. R.	London	1864-1872	Landscape	—	—	4	1	2	—	—	—	—	—	7
Lee, John Thomas. *See also* Ball, Lee, and	—	—	—	—	—	—	—	—	—	—	—	—	—	—
Pattinson	London	1890-1891	Architecture	—	—	3	—	—	—	—	—	—	—	3
Lee, Miss Louisa E.	London	1870-1874	Landscape	—	—	—	—	—	—	—	—	—	2	2
Lee, Miss M. L. Gwendoline	London	1892	Figures	—	—	—	—	—	—	—	—	—	1	1
Lee, Mrs. R.	London	1843	Flowers	—	—	1	—	—	—	—	—	—	—	1
Lee, Rachael	Putney	1882	Flowers	—	—	—	—	1	—	—	—	—	—	1
Lee, Sidney	Prestwich	1888	Medals	—	—	1	—	—	—	—	—	—	—	1
Lee, Sydney Williams	London	1879-1888	Domestic	—	—	9	—	4	—	—	—	—	2	15
Lee, Thomas	London	1774-1776	Architecture	—	—	3	—	—	—	—	—	—	—	3
Lee, T., Junr.	London	1814-1824	Architecture	—	—	9	—	—	—	—	—	—	—	9
Lee, Thomas Stirling	Paris	1878-1893	Sculpture	—	—	16	—	3	—	—	6	5	—	30
Lee, William ‡	London	1844-1855	Domestic	—	—	3	—	5	—	91	—	—	1	100
Lee, Miss	London	1844-1845	Flowers	—	—	2	—	—	—	—	—	—	—	2
Lee and Smith	London	1875	Architecture	—	—	2	—	—	—	—	—	—	—	2
Leeds, W. H.	London	1829-1849	Architecture	—	—	8	—	5	—	—	—	—	—	13
Leekey, G. G.	London	1847-1850	Landscape	—	—	3	4	—	—	—	—	—	—	7
Leeming, T.	London	1811-1822	Miniatures	—	—	25	—	—	—	—	—	—	—	25
Leeming and Leeming	Halifax	1885	Architecture	—	—	1	—	—	—	—	—	—	—	1
Lees, Charles, R.S.A.	Edinburgh	1832-1863	Historical	—	—	6	5	1	—	—	—	—	—	12
Lees, F. J.	London	1865-1866	Portraits	—	—	1	—	—	—	—	—	—	1	2
Lees, Miss Ida	Ryde	1891	Landscape	—	—	1	—	—	—	—	—	—	—	1
Lees, J. H.	London	1870	Landscape	—	—	—	—	2	—	—	—	—	—	2
Leese, Spencer	London	1882	Churches	—	—	—	—	1	—	—	—	—	—	1
Leesmith, Miss Mary L.	Bushey	1893	Portraits	—	—	1	—	—	—	—	—	—	—	1
Leeson. *See* Oliver and Leeson	—	—	Architecture	—	—	—	—	—	—	—	—	—	—	—
Leeuw, De. *See* D.	—	—	—	—	—	—	—	—	—	—	—	—	—	—
Le Fanu, G. B.	London	1878-1885	Landscape	—	—	4	—	7	—	1	—	—	3	15
Lefebvre, Charles	London	1891	Landscape	—	—	1	—	—	—	—	—	—	—	1
Lefebvre, Jules Joseph	—	1892-1893	Portraits	—	—	—	—	—	—	—	—	—	2	2

Name.	Town.	First and Last Year of Ex.	Speciality.	S. A.	F. S.	R. A.	B. I.	S. S.	O. W.	N.W.	G. G.	N. G.	V. E.	Total.
Le Fleming, Miss Mildred	Ambleside	1884-1891	Landscape	—	—	—	—	—	—	3	—	—	—	3
Lefroy, Miss C. E.	Thornt'n Heath	1866-1867	Landscape	—	—	—	—	2	—	—	—	—	—	2
Leftwich, G.	London	1851-1853	Landscape	—	—	2	2	1	—	—	—	—	—	5
Leftwich, G. R.	London	1875-1880	Domestic	—	—	—	—	—	—	—	—	—	2	2
Leftwich, H. T.	London	1848-1874	Landscape	—	—	2	3	2	—	—	—	—	—	7
Legat, Francis	London	1796-1800	Engraving	—	—	2	—	—	—	—	—	—	—	2
Legé, F. A.	London	1814-1825	Sculpture	—	—	10	3	—	—	—	—	—	—	13
Legg, George	London	1835-1859	Architecture	—	—	8	—	—	—	—	—	—	—	8
Legg, Henry Simpson	London	1860-1878	Architecture	—	—	11	—	—	—	—	—	—	—	11
Legg, William	London	1773-1776	Architecture	—	1	3	—	—	—	—	—	—	—	4
Legg, W. D.	Stamford	1801	Architecture	—	—	1	—	—	—	—	—	—	—	1
Legge, Arthur	Doncaster	1886-1892	Landscape	—	—	5	—	—	—	2	—	—	—	7
Legge, M. C.	London	1880	Landscape	—	—	—	—	—	—	—	—	—	1	1
Leggett, Alexander	Edinburgh	1860-1870	Sea Pieces	—	—	1	—	1	—	—	—	—	—	2
Legrand, C. F.	London	1778	Flowers	—	—	1	—	—	—	—	—	—	—	1
Legrand, Miss Louise	Plymouth	1891	Miniatures	—	—	1	—	—	—	—	—	—	—	1
Legrew, James	London	1826-1857	Sculpture	—	—	30	2	5	—	—	—	—	—	37
Legros, Professor Alphonse, R.P.E.	London	1864-1889	Figures	—	—	37	—	—	—	—	59	44	34	174
Le Hardy, F.	London	1790-1802	Miniatures	4	—	21	—	—	—	—	—	—	—	25
Lehmann, Henri	London	1863-1866	Portraits	—	—	4	—	—	—	—	—	—	—	4
Lehmann, Rudolf	London	1851-1893	Portraits	—	—	103	—	—	—	—	32	53	8	196
Leicester, G. O.	London	1833	Architecture	—	—	1	—	—	—	—	—	—	—	1
Leifchild, Henry Stormont	London	1844-1882	Sculpture	—	—	40	—	—	—	—	—	—	—	40
Leigh, Master	London	1772	Landscape	—	1	—	—	—	—	—	—	—	—	1
Leigh, Miss Clara Maria. *See* Mrs. Alexander Pope *and* Mrs. Wheatley.	—	—	—	—	—	—	—	—	—	—	—	—	—	—
Leigh, H. G.	London	1872	Landscape	—	—	1	—	—	—	—	—	—	—	1
Leigh, Jared	London	1761-1767	Sea Pieces	—	23	—	—	—	—	—	—	—	—	23
Leigh, James Mathews	London	1825-1849	Scriptural	—	—	25	23	29	—	—	—	—	—	77
Leigh, Roger	Barham Court	1868-1887	Landscape	—	—	—	—	2	—	—	—	—	2	4
Leigh, R. J.	Antwerp	1887-1893	Landscape	—	—	1	—	1	—	—	—	—	—	2
Leighton, Charles Blair	Kingsland	1843-1855	Portraits	—	—	13	3	1	—	—	—	—	—	17
Leighton, Edmund Blair φ	London	1874-1893	Figures	—	—	34	—	5	—	—	—	—	42	81
Leighton, Sir Frederick, Bart., P.R.A., R.W.S., H.R.C.A., H.R.S.W. § †	London	1855-1893	Figures	—	—	152	—	22	4	—	54	—	11	243
Leighton, John, F.S.A.	London	1858-1872	Architecture	—	—	1	—	—	—	—	—	—	1	2
Leighton, John	London	1889	Figures	—	—	—	—	2	—	—	—	—	—	2
Leighton, Miss Sarah	London	1883	Flowers	—	—	—	—	—	—	1	—	—	—	1
Leignes, Master (aged 12)	London	1776-1780	Landscape	2	7	—	—	—	—	—	—	—	—	9
Leignes, Miss (aged 13)	—	1766	Landscape	2	—	—	—	—	—	—	—	—	—	2
Leignes, Miss (aged 12)	London	1774-1780	Landscape	—	11	—	—	—	—	—	—	—	—	11
Leiper, William, A.R.S.A.	Glasgow	1874-1876	Architecture	—	—	2	—	—	—	—	—	—	1	3
Leitch, R.	London	1845-1854	Landscape	—	—	—	3	2	—	—	—	—	—	5
Leitch, Richard P.	London	1844-1862	Sea Pieces	—	—	10	—	5	—	—	—	—	—	15
Leitch, William Leighton, V.P.N.W.S.‡	London	1832-1883	Landscape	—	—	11	2	2	—	201	—	—	4	220
Leivers, William	—	1779	Sporting	—	—	3	—	—	—	—	—	—	—	3
Le Jeune, A.	London	1825	Portraits	—	—	1	—	—	—	—	—	—	—	1
Le Jeune, Elizabeth	London	1844	Portraits	—	—	1	—	—	—	—	—	—	—	1
Le Jeune, Henry L., A.R.A.	London	1840-1893	Scriptural	—	—	83	21	3	—	—	—	—	1	108
Lekegian, Gabriel	Constantinople	1883-1885	Domestic	—	—	3	—	—	—	—	—	—	—	3
Le Keux, John H.	London	1853-1865	Architecture	—	—	11	—	—	—	—	—	—	—	11
Leland, Henry	Paris	1876-1877	Landscape	—	—	—	—	—	—	—	—	—	2	2
Leland, J. B.	London	1834	Dogs	—	—	—	—	1	—	—	—	—	—	1
Le Latrouwer, A.	London	1867	Landscape	—	—	—	1	—	—	—	—	—	—	1
Leloir, Alexandre Louis	London	1874-1881	Domestic	—	—	—	—	—	—	—	—	—	3	3
Lemaire, J. A.	—	1880	—	—	—	*	—	—	—	—	—	—	—	—
Lemaire, Madame Madeleine	Paris	1881-1892	Portraits	—	—	—	—	—	—	—	1	—	1	2
Le Maistre, F. W. S.	London	1888-1892	Landscape	—	—	—	—	5	—	—	—	—	2	7
Leman, Miss Alicia J.	Putney	1891	Sporting	—	—	1	—	—	—	—	—	—	—	1
Leman, J. C.	Putney	1876	Etching	—	—	1	—	—	—	—	—	—	—	1
Lemann, Miss E. A.	Bathampton	1878	Landscape	—	—	—	—	1	—	—	—	—	—	1
Lemasle, Miss	London	1853	Ducks	—	—	—	—	—	—	—	—	—	1	1
Le Mason —	Paris	1790	Sculpture	—	—	4	—	—	—	—	—	—	—	4
Lemoine, Madame	London	1816	Figures	—	—	2	—	—	—	—	—	—	—	2
Lemon, Alfred D.	London	1838-1867	Figures	—	—	—	7	5	—	—	—	—	—	12
Lemon, Arthur	London	1878-1893	Landscape	—	—	29	—	—	—	—	11	12	7	59
Lemon, Mrs. Arthur (Blanche)	London	1880-1890	Portraits	—	—	1	—	—	—	—	—	2	2	5
Lemon, Henry	London	1855-1866	Engraving	—	—	8	—	—	—	—	—	—	—	8
Lenain, Louis	Mons	1876-1877	Etching	—	—	—	—	—	—	—	—	—	4	4
Lenbach, Professor Franz Ritter Von	Berlin	1893	Portraits	—	—	—	—	—	—	—	—	—	3	3
Lendrum, Miss Florence	Huddersfield	1893	Domestic	—	—	1	—	—	—	—	—	—	—	1
Lengo, H.	London	1872	Birds	—	—	—	—	1	—	—	—	—	—	1

Name.	Town.	First and Last Year of Ex.	Speciality.	S. A.	F. S.	R. A.	B. I.	S. S.	O. W.	N. W.	G. G.	N. G.	V. E.	Total.
LENNARD —	—	1783	Copies	—	1	—	—	—	—	—	—	—	—	1
LENOX, MISS A.	London	1877	Domestic	—	—	—	—	1	—	—	—	—	—	1
LENS, ANDREW BENJAMIN	London	1764-1779	Miniatures	6	5	—	—	—	—	—	—	—	—	11
LENTZ, J. F.	London	1825-1831	Flowers	—	—	3	2	1	—	—	—	—	—	6
LEO, ANSEL	London	1884-1885	Sculpture	—	—	1	—	—	—	—	—	—	—	1
LEON. *See* Zorn and Leon	—	—	—	—	—	—	—	—	—	—	—	—	—	—
LEONARD, JOHN HENRY	London	1865-1881	Landscape	—	—	5	—	33	—	—	—	—	61	99
LEONARD, W.	London	1821	Landscape	—	—	1	—	—	—	—	—	—	—	1
LEPAGE, JULES BASTIEN-	Paris	1878-1880	Portraits	—	—	4	—	—	—	—	9	—	2	15
LEPARD. *See* Harding and Lepard	—	—	Engraving	—	—	—	—	—	—	—	—	—	—	—
LEPEC, CHARLES	Paris	1871	Miniatures	—	—	1	—	—	—	—	—	—	—	1
LE PETIT, ALFRED	Paris	1875	Rustic	—	—	—	—	—	—	—	—	—	1	1
LE PETIT, FERDINAND	London	1882-1884	Rabbits	—	—	2	—	—	—	—	—	—	—	2
LE PETTIT, H.	London	1874-1882	Figures	—	—	—	—	3	—	—	—	—	—	3
LÉPINE, A.	Paris	1883	River Scenes	—	—	—	—	—	—	—	2	—	—	2
LE POITTEVIN, EDMOND M. E.	Paris	1840-1852	Historical	—	—	2	—	—	—	—	—	—	—	2
LE PORTE —	—	1778	Drawings	—	—	1	—	—	—	—	—	—	—	1
LE QUESNE, MISS ROSE	London	1886-1893	Sculpture	—	—	7	—	1	—	—	—	—	—	8
LEQUEUTRE A.	London	1831-1836	Dramatic	—	—	6	1	—	—	—	—	—	—	7
LE RAT, PAUL EDME	Paris	1888-1891	Etching	—	—	2	—	—	—	—	—	—	—	2
LE RESCHE, S.	London	1864	Scriptural	—	—	1	—	—	—	—	—	—	—	1
LERIUS, VAN. *See* V.	—	—	—	—	—	—	—	—	—	—	—	—	—	—
LE ROHO, H. L.	Clapham	1842-1846	Figures	—	—	6	—	1	—	—	—	—	—	7
LEROUX, J.	Southampton	1771-1784	Architecture	—	—	5	—	—	—	—	—	—	—	5
LEROY, MISS H. F.	London	1872-1883	Domestic	—	—	—	—	2	—	—	—	—	—	2
LERPINIER, DANIEL	London	1773-1783	Landscape	—	18	—	—	—	—	—	—	—	—	18
LERRY, WILLIAM	Birmingham	1863	Landscape	—	—	—	—	1	—	—	—	—	—	1
LESAGE, MISS CLARA	London	1892	Buildings	—	—	—	—	—	—	—	—	—	1	1
LESCALLIER, ANTHONY	London	1777	Interiors	—	—	1	—	—	—	—	—	—	—	1
LESCHALLAS, J.	London	1791-1823	Figures	—	—	22	3	—	—	—	—	—	15	40
LESLIE, CHARLES	Wimbledon Common	1835-1863	Landscape	—	—	5	3	16	—	—	—	—	24	48
LESLIE, CHARLES ROBERT, R.A.	London	1813-1859	Figures	—	—	76	11	—	1	—	—	—	—	88
LESLIE, G.	London	1832-1835	Game	—	—	4	—	4	—	4	—	—	—	12
LESLIE, GEORGE DUNLOP, R.A.	London	1857-1893	Domestic	—	—	77	12	2	—	—	4	1	25	121
LESLIE, HARRY	London	1871-1881	Figures	—	—	3	—	2	—	—	3	—	40	48
LESLIE, HARRY C.	London	1868-1874	Landscape	—	—	—	—	2	—	—	—	—	17	19
LESLIE, H. H.	London	1850	Figures	—	—	—	1	—	—	—	—	—	—	1
LESLIE, SIR JOHN, BART.	London	1877-1883	Portraits	—	—	—	—	—	—	—	6	—	—	6
LESLIE, JOHN	London	1853-1867	Portraits	—	—	15	2	1	—	—	—	—	—	18
LESLIE, ROBERT C.	London	1843-1887	Sea Pieces	—	—	38	5	2	—	—	—	—	28	73
LESLIE, THOMAS	London	1828	Landscape	—	—	—	—	2	—	—	—	—	—	2
LESLIE, MRS.	London	1871	Landscape	—	—	—	—	—	—	—	—	—	1	1
LESLIE, MISS	London	1824-1825	Portraits	—	—	3	—	—	—	—	—	—	—	3
LE SOUEF, MISS JESSIE	Wanstead	1866	Flowers	—	—	1	—	—	—	—	—	—	1	2
LESSEUF, A.	London	1832	Portraits	—	—	1	—	—	—	—	—	—	—	1
LESSLY —	London	1778	Flowers	2	—	—	—	—	—	—	—	—	—	2
LESSORE, JULES, R.I. ‡	Southwick	1879-1892	Landscape	—	—	9	—	21	—	29	8	—	10	77
LESTER, G.	London	1864-1865	Figures	—	—	—	—	2	—	—	—	—	—	2
LESTER, H.	London	1820-1821	Architecture	—	—	2	—	—	—	—	—	—	—	2
LESTER, T. V.	London	1866-1880	Domestic	—	—	—	—	1	—	—	—	—	1	2
LE STRANGE, W.	London	1807	Bridges	—	—	1	—	—	—	—	—	—	—	1
LESWELL, EMILY	Dublin	1855	Flowers	—	—	—	—	1	—	—	—	—	—	1
LE TALL, CHARLES, McL.	London	1883-1886	Landscape	—	—	2	—	—	—	—	—	—	2	4
LE TEXIER, MISS	—	1802	Landscape	—	—	1	—	—	—	—	—	—	—	1
LETHABY, WILLIAM RICHARD	London	1881-1890	Churches	—	—	9	—	—	—	—	—	—	—	9
LETHBRIDGE, J.	—	1815	Architecture	—	—	—	—	—	—	—	—	—	1	1
LETHBRIDGE, WALTER STEPHENS	London	1801-1829	Miniatures	—	—	58	—	4	—	—	—	—	—	62
LETHERBROW, JOHN H.	Manchester	1877-1881	Historical	—	—	—	—	—	—	—	—	—	5	5
LETT, FREDERICK	London	1843	Architecture	—	—	1	—	—	—	—	—	—	—	1
LETTERET DE MONTIGNY	London	1774	Engraving	2	—	—	—	—	—	—	—	—	—	2
LETTS, MISS E. F.	London	1878	Figures	—	—	—	—	1	—	—	—	—	—	1
LETTS, T.	London	1835	Flowers	—	—	2	—	—	—	—	—	—	—	2
LEVACK, JOHN	Airdrie	1856-1857	Figures	—	—	—	—	2	—	—	—	—	—	2
LEVENTHORP, MISS M.	London	1796	Portraits	—	—	1	—	—	—	—	—	—	—	1
L'EVEQUE, HENRY	London	1812-1820	Figures	—	—	12	1	—	—	—	—	—	15	28
LEVER, G.	Rewington	1802	Architecture	—	—	1	—	—	—	—	—	—	—	1
LEVEROTTI, G.	London	1838	Sculpture	—	—	1	—	—	—	—	—	—	—	1
LEVEROTTI, JULIAN	London	1881	Sculpture	—	—	1	—	—	—	—	—	—	—	1
LEVERTON, THOMAS	London	1771-1803	Architecture	—	—	34	—	—	—	—	—	—	—	34
LEVERTON, WILLIAM	London	1780-1807	Architecture	—	—	10	—	—	—	—	—	—	—	10
LEVIN, PHÖBUS (?) PHOLIUS §	London	1855-1878	Figures	—	—	11	4	63	—	—	—	—	—	78
LEVIN, MISS VICTORIA	London	1869-1886	Domestic	—	—	—	—	18	—	—	—	—	1	19

Name.	Town.	First and Last Year of Ex.	Speciality.	S. A.	F. S.	R. A.	B. I.	S. S.	O. W.	N. W.	G. G.	N. G.	V. E.	Total.
Levison, Miss Rachel	London	1856-1859	Sculpture	—	—	6	—	—	—	—	—	—	—	6
Levitt, L. C.	Manchester	1867	Wheat	—	—	—	—	1	—	—	—	—	—	1
Levy, Emile	Passy	1875	Figures	—	—	—	—	—	—	—	—	—	4	4
Levy, Miss Julia M.	London	1883-1888	Domestic	—	—	4	—	—	—	—	1	—	1	6
Levy, S.	—	1819	Landscape	—	—	1	—	—	—	—	—	—	—	1
Lewen, Sharp, and Arpin	London	1887-1889	Architecture	—	—	5	—	—	—	—	—	—	—	5
Lewer, W. H.	—	1817	Architecture	—	—	1	—	—	—	—	—	—	—	1
Lewes, S.	Twickenham	1785	—	—	—	*	—	—	—	—	—	—	—	—
Lewin —	London	1764-1782	Flowers	—	6	—	—	—	—	—	—	—	—	6
Lewin, F.	—	1813	Architecture	—	—	1	—	—	—	—	—	—	—	1
Lewin, S.	Boston	1852-1862	Architecture	—	—	2	—	—	—	—	—	—	—	2
Lewin, Stephen	London	1890-1893	Domestic	—	—	—	—	—	—	—	—	—	3	3
Lewis —	—	1775	Architecture	2	—	—	—	—	—	—	—	—	—	2
Lewis, A.	London	1886	Landscape	—	—	—	—	—	—	1	—	—	—	1
Lewis, Alfred C.	London	1893	Sculpture	—	—	1	—	—	—	—	—	—	—	1
Lewis, Arthur James	London	1848-1893	Landscape	—	—	38	2	—	—	—	2	3	2	47
Lewis, Miss Anne Madelaine	Sevenoaks	1880-1893	Flowers	—	—	2	—	8	—	—	—	—	4	14
Lewis, Charles	London	1772-1791	Fruit	14	—	4	—	—	—	—	—	—	—	18
Lewis, Charles George	London	1875	Engraving	—	—	1	—	—	—	—	—	—	—	1
Lewis, C. H.	London	1841-1843	Figures	—	—	—	—	3	—	—	—	—	—	3
Lewis, Charles James, R.I. ‡ φ	London	1853-1893	Domestic	—	—	49	26	43	—	72	5	1	187	383
Lewis, C. W. Mansel, R.P.E.	Llanelly	1872-1882	Domestic	—	—	9	—	—	—	—	—	—	7	16
Lewis, E.	Tunb'dge Wells	1847-1855	Miniatures	—	—	12	—	—	—	—	—	—	—	12
Lewis, Miss E.	London	1870-1893	Landscape	—	—	—	—	38	—	—	—	—	—	38
Lewis, Evelyn C.	Putney	1889	Landscape	—	—	—	—	2	—	—	—	—	—	2
Lewis, Frederick Christian	London	1802-1853	Landscape	—	—	56	51	24	29	—	—	—	—	160
Lewis, F. C.	—	1870	Oriental	—	—	—	—	1	—	—	—	—	—	1
Lewis, Miss Florence E.	London	1881	Flowers	—	—	1	—	—	—	—	—	—	—	1
Lewis, G.	London	1805-1817	Landscape	—	—	5	—	—	8	—	—	—	—	13
Lewis, George Robert	London	1817-1859	Figures	—	—	45	18	20	—	5	—	—	7	95
Lewis, H.	Düsseldorf	1866-1867	Landscape	—	—	—	—	3	—	—	—	—	—	3
Lewis, H.	London	1868	Miniatures	—	—	4	—	—	—	—	—	—	—	4
Lewis, James	London	1774-1800	Architecture	7	—	2	—	—	—	—	—	—	—	9
Lewis, Miss Janet	London	1891	Landscape	—	—	—	—	—	—	1	—	—	—	1
Lewis, John, F.S.A.	London	1762-1776	Landscape	11	—	—	—	—	—	—	—	—	—	11
Lewis, J.	London	1801-1812	Portraits	—	—	34	2	—	—	—	—	—	—	36
Lewis, J.	London	1804	Figures	—	—	1	—	—	—	—	—	—	—	1
Lewis, J.	—	1824	Buildings	—	—	—	—	1	—	—	—	—	—	1
Lewis, John	London	1842-1848	Landscape	—	—	2	—	—	—	—	—	—	—	2
Lewis, J. A.	London	1885	Portraits	—	—	1	—	—	—	—	—	—	—	1
Lewis, John Frederick, R.A., P.O.W.S., H.R.S.A. †	London	1820-1877	Animals	—	—	82	25	5	100	—	—	—	—	212
Lewis, J. Hardwick	London	1867-1890	Domestic	—	—	16	—	18	—	—	—	—	6	40
Lewis, Lennard	London	1848-1893	Landscape	—	—	32	7	26	—	7	5	6	23	106
Lewis, Mrs. Lennard	London	1878-1879	Figures	—	—	—	—	4	—	—	—	—	—	4
Lewis, Miss M. A.	London	1877-1880	Landscape	—	—	—	—	3	—	—	—	—	—	3
Lewis, R.	London	1877	Landscape	—	—	—	—	1	—	—	—	—	—	1
Lewis, Richard Jeffreys §	London	1843-1851	Figures	—	—	6	1	5	—	—	—	—	—	12
Lewis, Samuel	London	1774-1791	Still Life	2	6	—	—	—	—	—	—	—	—	8
Lewis, Shelton	Henley	1875-1880	Landscape	—	—	1	—	3	—	—	—	—	9	13
Lewis, Miss Sylvia C.	Putney	1889-1890	Landscape	—	—	—	—	5	—	—	—	—	—	5
Lewis, Thomas	London	1835-1852	Portraits	—	—	8	1	14	—	—	—	—	1	24
Lewis, Professor Thomas Hayter. *See also* Finden and Lewis	London	1839	Architecture	—	—	1	—	—	—	—	—	—	—	1
Lewis, William	London	1804-1838	Landscape	—	—	129	35	22	—	1	—	—	25	212
Lewis, William	—	1870	Domestic	—	—	—	—	1	—	—	—	—	—	1
Lewis, William George Blackmore	London	1883-1889	Architecture	—	—	4	—	—	—	—	—	—	—	4
Lewis, Mrs.	—	1783	Landscape	2	—	—	—	—	—	—	—	—	—	2
Lewis, Miss	—	1802-1803	Miniatures	—	—	3	—	—	—	—	—	—	—	3
Lewis, T. Noyes-. *See* N.	—	—	—	—	—	—	—	—	—	—	—	—	—	—
Ley, G.	Brighton	1849-1851	Figures	—	—	2	—	—	—	—	—	—	—	2
Ley, G. William	Brighton	1850	Figures	—	—	—	1	—	—	—	—	—	—	1
Leycester, R. Neville	London	1883	Fruit	—	—	—	—	2	—	—	—	—	—	2
Leyde, Otto Theodore, R.S.A., R.S.W.	Edinburgh	1877-1888	Portraits	—	—	3	—	—	—	—	—	—	2	5
Leyland, Joseph Bentley	London	1839	Sculpture	—	—	—	—	1	—	—	—	—	—	1
Leys, Baron Jean Auguste Henri	Antwerp	1845-1868	Historical	—	—	2	—	—	—	—	—	—	—	2
Lhermitte, Leon Augustin	London	1872-1881	Figures	—	—	4	—	—	—	—	—	—	73	77
Lhuillier, Victor Gustave	London	1877-1888	Etching	—	—	4	—	—	—	—	—	—	6	10
L'Heureun, Miss	—	1796	Fruit	—	—	2	—	—	—	—	—	—	—	2
Liart, Matthew	London	1766-1767	Engraving	2	—	—	—	—	—	—	—	—	—	2
Liberty, Miss Amelia	London	1854-1856	Miniatures	—	—	2	—	—	—	—	—	—	—	2
Liberty, Miss Octavia	Nottingham	1881-1882	Flowers	—	—	—	—	—	—	—	2	—	—	2

Name.	Town.	First and Last Year of Ex.	Speciality.	S. A.	F. S.	R. A.	B. I.	S. S.	O.W.	N. W.	G. G.	N. G.	V. E.	Total.
Libour, Madame Colin-. *See* C.	—	—	—	—	—	—	—	—	—	—	—	—	—	—
Liczewski —	Berlin	1780	Candlelight	1	—	—	—	—	—	—	—	—	—	1
Liddell, H.	London	1888	Landscape	—	—	—	—	—	—	—	—	—	1	1
Liddell, Tom	London	1886	Figures	—	—	—	—	—	—	—	—	—	1	1
Liddell, T. Hodgson	London	1887-1888	Landscape	—	—	2	—	—	—	—	—	—	—	2
Liddell, Miss Violet	—	1887	Portraits	—	—	—	—	—	—	—	1	—	—	1
Lidderdale, Charles Sillem §	London	1851-1893	Domestic	—	—	36	17	25	—	—	—	—	17	95
Lieb, Michael. *See* Munkacsy.	—	—	—	—	—	—	—	—	—	—	—	—	—	—
Liebreich, R.	London	1879	Sculpture	—	—	1	—	—	—	—	—	—	—	1
Lier, Adolf	London	1865	Landscape	—	—	1	—	—	—	—	—	—	—	1
Lies, J.	London	1841	Figures	—	—	1	—	—	—	—	—	—	—	1
Lieste, C.	Haerlem	1853-1854	Landscape	—	—	1	1	—	—	—	—	—	—	2
Light, T.	London	1806-1808	Miniatures	—	—	4	—	—	—	—	—	—	—	4
Lightbody, Robert	Liverpool	1888	Landscape	—	—	—	—	—	—	1	—	—	—	1
Lightfoot, Peter	London	1856	Engraving	—	—	1	—	—	—	—	—	—	—	1
Lighton, Sir Christopher Robert, Bart.	Brighton	1891	Shipping	—	—	—	—	—	—	1	—	—	—	1
Lilburne, Mrs. T.	—	1825	Miniatures	—	—	1	—	—	—	—	—	—	—	1
Liley, Henry G.	London	1878-1891	Architecture	—	—	8	—	—	—	—	—	—	—	8
Lilley, Miss Elizabeth A.	London	1885-1891	Domestic	—	—	4	—	4	—	—	—	—	—	8
Lilley, H.	—	1843	Portraits	—	—	1	—	—	—	—	—	—	—	1
Lilley, John	—	1832-1846	Portraits	—	—	13	3	15	—	—	—	—	—	31
Lillie, Charles T.	London	1882	Flowers	—	—	—	—	2	—	—	—	—	—	2
Lillie, Robert	Dulwich	1893	Seaside	—	—	—	—	—	—	—	—	—	1	1
Lillingston, G. B. P.	Cheltenham	1871-1882	Domestic	—	—	1	—	9	—	—	—	—	12	22
Lillingstone, Juliana	Torquay	1866	Landscape	—	—	—	—	—	—	—	—	—	1	1
Lilois, Louis	Paris	1872	Domestic	—	—	—	—	—	—	—	—	—	1	1
Limbrey, Miss M. D.	Barnes	1858-1859	Domestic	—	—	—	—	—	—	—	—	—	6	6
Limner, Luke	London	1854	Windows	—	—	1	—	—	—	—	—	—	—	1
Lin, Clifton	—	1884-1887	Flowers	—	—	—	—	10	—	—	3	—	—	13
Lincell, C.	London	1800	Portraits	—	—	1	—	—	—	—	—	—	—	1
Linden, E. V. D.	London	1881	Sculpture	—	—	1	—	—	—	—	—	—	—	1
Linden, G.	Chiswick	1890-1891	Sea Pieces	—	—	—	—	—	—	—	—	—	2	2
Linden, Van. *See* V.	—	—	—	—	—	—	—	—	—	—	—	—	—	—
Linder, F.	Paris	1874	Rustic	—	—	—	—	—	—	—	—	—	1	1
Linder, Miss P.	London	1885	Domestic	—	—	1	—	—	—	—	—	—	—	1
Lindgreen, N.	London	1792	Architecture	—	—	1	—	—	—	—	—	—	—	1
Lindner, G. M.	Birmingham	1869	Landscape	—	—	—	—	—	—	—	—	—	1	1
Lindner, Moffat P., R.B.A. §	London	1880-1892	Landscape	—	—	11	—	12	—	3	7	7	4	44
Lindoe, D.	London	1797-1798	Landscape	—	—	3	—	—	—	—	—	—	—	3
Lindsay, Sir Coutts, Bart., R.I. ‡	London	1862-1890	Portraits	—	—	10	—	—	—	11	43	—	3	67
Lindsay, Lady, of Balcarres, R.I., ‡ ‖	—	1876-1892	Domestic	—	—	—	—	—	—	51	53	8	2	114
Lindsay, Hon. Mrs. Lloyd, afterwards Lady Wantage	—	1878	Interiors	—	—	—	—	—	—	—	1	—	—	1
Lindsay, Mrs. Ruth	Rugeley	1882	Fruit	—	—	—	—	—	—	—	—	—	1	1
Lindsay, Thomas ‡	London	1833-1861	Landscape	—	—	—	—	4	—	347	—	—	—	351
Lindsay, Thomas M.	Rugby	1893	Landscape	—	—	—	—	—	—	1	—	—	—	1
Lindsay, Miss Violet. *See* Mrs. Manners *and* Marchioness of Granby	Wantage	1879-1882	Portraits	—	—	2	—	—	—	—	10	—	6	18
Lindsay, W. H.	London	1852	Architecture	—	—	2	—	—	—	—	—	—	—	2
Lindsay and Flower	London	1856	Architecture	—	—	1	—	—	—	—	—	—	—	1
Lindström, Arvid M.	London	1882-1887	Landscape	—	—	6	—	1	—	—	—	—	1	8
Lines, F.	London	1828-1829	Portraits	—	—	2	—	1	—	—	—	—	—	3
Lines, Henry H.	Birmingham	1818-1846	Landscape	—	—	18	2	8	—	—	—	—	—	28
Lines, Samuel	Birmingham	1817-1833	Landscape	—	—	3	—	—	—	1	—	—	—	4
Lines, Samuel Restell	Birmingham	1832-1833	Buildings	—	—	—	—	2	—	11	—	—	—	13
Lingard, Henry	Ealing	1884	Landscape	—	—	1	—	—	—	—	—	—	—	1
Lingard, Miss	Tottenham	1831-1836	Figures	—	—	4	2	3	—	—	—	—	—	9
Lingeman, J.	London	1874	Domestic	—	—	—	—	—	—	—	—	—	1	1
Lingford, T. J.	London	1843	Fruit	—	—	—	—	1	—	—	—	—	—	1
Lingham, G.	London	1840	Study	—	—	—	1	—	—	—	—	—	—	1
Lingwood, Edward J.	Needham Market	1884-1893	Landscape	—	—	10	—	4	—	—	—	—	1	15
Linley, J.	London	1786-1793	Enamels	—	—	8	—	—	—	—	—	—	—	8
Linn, David	London	1847-1862	Landscape	—	—	1	6	6	—	—	—	—	11	24
Linnell, John †	London	1807-1881	Landscape	—	—	177	92	—	53	—	—	—	—	322
Linnell, J., Junr.	Reigate	1858	Flowers	—	—	1	—	—	—	—	—	—	—	1
Linnell, James Thomas	London	1850-1888	Landscape	—	—	38	—	—	—	—	—	—	1	39
Linnell, Miss Mary	Redhill	1868-1869	Landscape	—	—	—	—	2	—	—	—	—	—	2
Linnell, Thomas G.	Redhill	1864-1884	Landscape	—	—	12	5	3	—	1	—	—	5	26
Linnell, William	London	1851-1891	Landscape	—	—	45	—	—	—	—	—	—	—	45
Linnig, W.	London	1863-1875	Domestic	—	—	2	—	—	—	—	—	—	—	2
Linning —	London	1775-1776	Sculpture	2	—	—	—	—	—	—	—	—	—	2
Linsell, C.	London	1801-1830	Portraits	—	—	28	—	—	—	—	—	—	—	28

Name.	Town.	First and Last Year of Ex.	Speciality.	S. A.	F. S.	R. A.	B. I.	S. S.	O. W.	N. W.	G. G.	N. G.	V. E.	Total.
Linsell, W. C.	London	1811	Portraits	—	—	1	—	—	—	—	—	—	—	1
Linton, Henry D.	London	1855-1876	Woodcuts	—	—	5	—	—	—	—	—	—	1	6
Linton, J.	Greenwich	1814-1854	Flowers	—	—	31	—	4	—	—	—	—	—	35
Linton, Sir James Dromgole, P.R.I., H.R.S.W. ‡ φ	London	1863-1893	Historical	—	—	8	—	4	—	104	14	3	34	167
Linton, J. Gilbert	Bristol	1872	Figures	—	—	—	—	—	—	—	—	—	1	1
Linton, James W. R.	London	1890-1893	Domestic	—	—	—	—	—	—	6	—	—	2	8
Linton, William §	London	1817-1871	Landscape	—	—	57	78	101	11	1	—	—	—	248
Linton, William James	London	1837-1876	Woodcuts	—	—	13	—	1	—	—	—	—	3	17
Lintz, Ernest	London	1875-1891	Domestic	—	—	3	—	8	—	—	3	—	7	21
Lintz, J. F.	London	1830	Fruit	—	—	—	—	1	—	—	—	—	—	1
Linwood, Mrs. Hannah	—	1776	Needlework	1	—	—	—	—	—	—	—	—	—	1
Linwood, Miss Mary	Birmingham	1776-1778	Needlework	2	—	—	—	—	—	—	—	—	—	2
Linzell, John J.	Tottenham	1881	Landscape	—	—	—	—	—	—	—	—	—	1	1
Lion —	London	1771	Portraits	3	—	—	—	—	—	—	—	—	—	3
Liotard, John Stephen	London	1773-1774	Miniatures	—	—	7	—	—	—	—	—	—	—	7
Liparini, Ludovico	Venice	1842-1843	Historical	—	—	1	1	—	—	—	—	—	—	2
Lippincott, W. H.	London	1877-1878	Figures	—	—	1	—	—	—	—	—	—	2	3
Lipscombe, Miss Jessie	Peterborough	1885-1887	Sculpture	—	—	3	—	—	—	—	—	—	—	3
Lisle, De. *See* D.	—	—	—	—	—	—	—	—	—	—	—	—	—	—
Lissmore, Charles	London	1883	Sea Pieces	—	—	—	—	—	—	—	—	—	2	2
Lister, Hon. Beatrix	—	1881	Flowers	—	—	—	—	—	—	—	1	—	—	1
Lister, E. M.	Leyton	1882	Flowers	—	—	—	—	1	—	—	—	—	—	1
Lister, George	London	1881-1882	Flowers	—	—	—	—	2	—	—	—	—	—	2
Lister, Miss	—	1784	Landscape	—	—	1	—	—	—	—	—	—	—	1
Liston, J.	London	1846-1848	Landscape	—	—	2	—	2	—	—	—	—	—	4
Litchfield, Miss E. C.	—	1796-1801	Landscape	—	—	5	—	—	—	—	—	—	—	5
Little, Miss Emily	London	1888-1891	Buildings	—	—	2	—	—	—	—	—	3	—	5
Little, G. Leon	London	1884-1888	Portraits	—	—	—	—	7	—	—	—	—	—	7
Little, J. S.	London	1843	Sculpture	—	—	1	—	—	—	—	—	—	—	1
Little, Robert, A.R.W.S., R.S.W. †	Edinburgh	1885-1893	Domestic	—	—	9	—	—	22	8	—	—	7	46
Little, Thomas	London	1832-1851	Architecture	—	—	12	—	—	—	—	—	—	—	12
Little, Walter	Bexley Heath	1864-1878	Domestic	—	—	1	—	8	—	—	—	—	3	12
Littleford —	—	1762-1763	Miniatures	4	—	—	—	—	—	—	—	—	—	4
Littler, Frank E.	London	1887	Architecture	—	—	1	—	—	—	—	—	—	—	1
Littler, Joseph	—	1885	Historical	—	—	—	—	1	—	—	—	—	—	1
Littler, William Farran	London	1887-1892	Portraits	—	—	1	—	—	—	—	—	—	1	2
Littlewood. *See* Mangnall and Littlewood	—	—	Architecture	—	—	—	—	—	—	—	—	—	—	—
Littlewood, James	London	1887	Flowers	—	—	—	—	1	—	—	—	—	—	1
Livens, Miss Dora B.	Croydon	1892-1893	Domestic	—	—	—	—	4	—	—	—	—	—	4
Livens, Horace Mann	Croydon	1883-1893	Domestic	—	—	2	—	21	—	1	—	—	9	33
Liverati, C. E.	London	1827-1828	Theatrical	—	—	3	—	1	—	—	—	—	—	4
Liverseege, Henry	Manchester	1828-1832	Domestic	—	—	5	5	8	—	—	—	—	—	18
Livesay, A.	Portsea	1839	Architecture	—	—	3	—	—	—	—	—	—	—	3
Livesay, F.	Portsmouth	1869-1881	Landscape	—	—	2	—	11	—	—	—	—	3	16
Livesay, Richard	London	1776-1821	Portraits	—	—	98	—	—	—	—	—	—	—	98
Livett, Louis Charles	Manchester	1866-1873	Figures	—	—	1	—	1	—	—	—	—	17	19
Livingston, John	London	1834	Landscape	—	—	—	—	1	—	—	—	—	—	1
Livock, J.	London	1836-1853	Architecture	—	—	7	—	—	—	—	—	—	—	7
Lizars, William Home	Edinburgh	1812	Domestic	—	—	2	—	—	—	—	—	—	—	2
Llewehlyn —	London	1780	Figures	—	1	—	—	—	—	—	—	—	—	1
Llewellyn, William	London	1891-1893	Portraits	—	—	—	—	—	—	—	—	—	9	9
Llewellyn, W. B.	—	1812-1814	Landscape	—	—	2	—	—	—	—	—	—	—	2
Llewellyn, William H. Samuel, R.B.A. §	London	1883-1893	Portraits	—	—	18	—	24	—	2	11	12	8	75
Llewelyn, Miss E.	London	1877	Flowers	—	—	1	—	—	—	—	—	—	—	1
Llewelyn, J. D.	London	1874	Flowers	—	—	—	—	1	—	—	—	—	—	1
Lloyd, Andrew	London	1881	Landscape	—	—	—	—	1	—	—	—	—	—	1
Lloyd, E.	Ellesmere	1861	Sheep	—	—	1	—	—	—	—	—	—	—	1
Lloyd, Miss Edith	London	1893	Flowers	—	—	—	—	—	—	1	—	—	—	1
Lloyd, Mrs. E. A.	—	1893	Portraits	—	—	—	—	—	—	—	—	—	1	1
Lloyd, E. G.	London	1843-1845	Landscape	—	—	3	—	—	—	—	—	—	—	3
Lloyd, G. W.	London	1870-1871	Buildings	—	—	2	—	—	—	—	—	—	—	2
Lloyd, H.	—	1838	Architecture	—	—	1	—	—	—	—	—	—	—	1
Lloyd, Mrs. H.	London	1850-1853	Flowers	—	—	—	—	4	—	—	—	—	1	5
Lloyd, Harriette	London	1862	—	—	—	—	—	1	—	—	—	—	—	1
Lloyd, J.	London	1833-1834	Landscape	—	—	—	—	—	—	2	—	—	—	2
Lloyd, John	Brighton	1860-1866	Landscape	—	—	1	10	8	—	—	—	—	—	19
Lloyd, J. Andrew	London	1888-1891	Landscape	—	—	1	—	—	—	—	1	—	1	3
Lloyd, John H.	London	1830-1845	Landscape	—	—	4	10	—	—	—	—	—	—	14
Lloyd, L. W.	London	1821-1830	Architecture	—	—	9	—	1	—	—	—	—	—	10
Lloyd, Mrs. Mary, R.A. *See* Miss Moser	London	1797-1802	Flowers	—	—	4	—	—	—	—	—	—	—	4
Lloyd, Miss M.	London	1862-1863	Flowers	—	—	1	2	—	—	—	—	—	—	3
Lloyd, M. C.	London	1865	Sculpture	—	—	1	—	—	—	—	—	—	—	1

Name.	Town.	First and Last Year of Ex.	Speciality.	S. A.	F. S.	R. A.	B. I.	S. S.	O. W.	N.W.	G. G.	N. G.	V. E.	Total.
Lloyd, R.	London	1802-1803	Architecture	—	—	2	—	—	—	—	—	—	—	2
Lloyd, R. Malcolm	Catford Bridge	1879-1892	Landscape	—	—	9	—	33	—	6	—	—	14	62
Lloyd, T.	London	1813-1817	Architecture	—	—	5	—	—	—	—	—	—	—	5
Lloyd, T.	—	1825	Sea Pieces	—	—	1	—	—	—	—	—	—	—	1
Lloyd, Thomas James, R.W.S.†	Walmer	1870-1893	Landscape	—	—	38	—	21	83	—	—	—	44	186
Lloyd, Mrs. Watkins	London	1877	Landscape	—	—	—	—	—	—	—	—	—	1	1
Lloyd, W. Stuart, R.B.A.§	—	1875-1893	Landscape	—	—	25	—	117	—	13	2	—	24	181
Lloyd-Jones, C.	Wimborne	1871-1876	Landscape	—	—	—	—	2	—	—	—	—	—	2
Lloyds, F.	London	1858-1861	Landscape	—	—	1	1	1	—	—	—	—	—	3
Lluellyn, Mrs.	London	1889	Sea Pieces	—	—	—	—	—	—	—	—	—	2	2
Loat, Samuel	London	1826-1832	Architecture	—	—	4	—	3	—	—	—	—	—	7
Lobley, James	Brighton	1865-1887	Domestic	—	—	15	—	2	—	—	—	—	12	29
Locatelli, John Baptista	—	1778-1790	Sculpture	—	—	14	—	—	—	—	—	—	—	14
Loch, Miss Alice Helen	London	1882-1888	Landscape	—	—	—	—	1	—	3	—	—	—	4
Lochée, John Charles	London	1776-1790	Sculpture	—	—	19	—	—	—	—	—	—	—	19
Lochner, William C.	London	1798-1811	Architecture	—	—	7	—	—	—	—	—	—	—	7
Lock, A. H.	London	1874-1875	Birds	—	—	—	—	—	—	—	—	—	2	2
Lock, C.	London	1828-1829	Architecture	—	—	2	—	—	—	—	—	—	—	2
Lock, Frederick	London	1843-1846	Portraits	—	—	3	—	—	—	—	—	—	—	3
Lock, Frederick William	London	1845-1871	Figures	—	—	2	—	7	—	—	—	—	—	9
Lock, Samuel Robert	Brighton	1849-1854	Portraits	—	—	19	—	8	—	—	—	—	—	27
Lock, T. Roe	Lynton	1867	Landscape	—	—	—	—	1	—	—	—	—	—	1
Locker, John	London	1862-1875	Domestic	—	—	1	4	20	—	—	—	—	—	25
Lockhart, William E., R.S.A., A.R.W.S.†	Edinburgh	1873-1893	Historical	—	—	19	—	—	39	—	5	—	—	63
Lockhead, Miss (aged 10)	London	1779	Needlework	—	2	—	—	—	—	—	—	—	—	2
Locking, E.	London	1847	Domestic	—	—	1	—	—	—	—	—	—	—	1
Locking, Kate	Chertsey	1881-1882	Domestic	—	—	—	—	3	—	—	—	—	—	3
Locking, Miss Nora	London	1882-1891	Domestic	—	—	3	—	2	—	—	—	—	3	8
Locking, R.	—	1846	Domestic	—	—	1	—	—	—	—	—	—	—	1
Lockwood, H. F., F.S.A.	Hull	1834-1842	Architecture	—	—	2	—	—	—	—	—	—	—	2
Lockwood, T. M.	Chester	1877-1893	Architecture	—	—	6	—	—	—	—	—	—	—	6
Lockwood, William Henry	London	1874-1888	Architecture	—	—	7	—	—	—	—	—	—	—	7
Lockwood and Mawson	London	1870	Architecture	—	—	3	—	—	—	—	—	—	—	3
Lockyer, Florence A.	London	1886	Landscape	—	—	—	—	1	—	—	—	—	—	1
Lockyer, J. M.	London	1849	Churches	—	—	1	—	—	—	—	—	—	—	1
Lockyer, S. B.	London	1855	Domestic	—	—	—	—	—	—	—	—	—	2	2
Lodder —	—	1813	River Scenes	—	—	1	—	—	—	—	—	—	—	1
Lodder, Captain Charles A.	Edinburgh	1874-1882	Sea Pieces	—	—	—	—	8	—	—	—	—	2	10
Lodder, W. P. J.	London	1783-1804	Portraits	—	1	14	—	—	—	—	—	—	—	15
Loder, R.	London	1801	Portraits	—	—	1	—	—	—	—	—	—	—	1
Lodge, Edward Howitt	London	1890-1893	Landscape	—	—	1	—	3	—	1	—	—	1	6
Lodge, Miss Florence F.	Lee	1889	Flowers	—	—	1	—	—	—	—	—	—	—	1
Lodge, George E.	London	1881-1891	Domestic	—	—	7	—	3	—	—	—	—	8	18
Lodge, Reginald B.	Edmonton	1881-1890	Landscape	—	—	5	—	1	—	—	—	—	1	7
Loft, James	London	1832-1863	Sculpture	—	—	18	—	3	—	—	—	—	—	21
Lofthouse, S. H. S.	London	1874	Landscape	—	—	—	—	1	—	—	—	—	3	4
Lofthouse, Mrs., A.R.W.S.† *See* Miss Mary Forster	Walton-on-Thames	1885	Landscape	—	—	—	—	—	32	—	—	—	—	32
Logan, J.	London	1821	Landscape	—	—	1	—	—	—	—	—	—	—	1
Logan, R. F.	Edinburgh	1883	Sea Pieces	—	—	—	—	—	—	1	—	—	—	1
Loggan, J.	London	1790	Miniatures	—	—	11	—	—	—	—	—	—	—	11
Logsdail, Miss Marian	Lincoln	1886-1893	Domestic	—	—	13	—	—	—	—	—	—	—	13
Logsdail, William	Lincoln	1877-1893	Domestic	—	—	37	—	7	—	—	7	6	10	67
Loison, Pierre	London	1867	Sculpture	—	—	1	—	—	—	—	—	—	—	1
Lomas, J. L.	—	1862-1874	Domestic	—	—	—	—	2	—	—	—	—	—	2
Lomas, W.	London	1817	Architecture	—	—	1	—	—	—	—	—	—	—	1
Lomas, William	London	1877-1889	Domestic	—	—	7	—	1	—	—	—	—	2	10
Lomax, Arthur	Liverpool	1875	Landscape	—	—	—	—	—	—	—	—	—	1	1
Lomax, G.	—	1823	Portraits	—	—	1	—	—	—	—	—	—	—	1
Lomax, John Arthur, R.B.A.§ ϕ	Didsbury	1879-1893	Domestic	—	—	17	—	26	—	1	—	—	12	56
Lomax, John C.	London	1889-1891	Landscape	—	—	3	—	—	—	—	—	—	—	3
Lomax, J. O'Bryen	Chichester	1853-1880	Sea Pieces	—	—	4	—	10	—	—	—	—	2	16
Lomax, L.	London	1883	Landscape	—	—	—	—	2	—	—	—	—	—	2
Lombardi, Eugenio	London	1888	Sculpture	—	—	1	—	—	—	—	—	—	—	1
Lomid, T.	Norwich	1844-1845	Landscape	—	—	3	—	—	—	—	—	—	—	3
London, J.	London	1807	Architecture	—	—	1	—	—	—	—	—	—	—	1
Londoni —, Junr.	—	1782	Rustic	—	3	—	—	—	—	—	—	—	—	3
Long, Amelia, Lady. *See* Mrs. Long.	—	—	—	—	—	—	—	—	—	—	—	—	—	—
Long, A.	Cambridge	1843-1847	Landscape	—	—	6	1	—	—	—	—	—	—	7
Long, Mrs. Charles, afterwards Amelia, Lady Long, and Lady Farnborough	—	1807-1822	Landscape	—	—	34	—	—	—	—	—	—	—	34
Long, Edwin, R.A.	Bath	1855-1891	Figures	—	—	93	13	4	—	—	—	—	3	113

Name.	Town.	First and Last Year of Ex.	Speciality.	S. A.	F. S.	R. A.	B. I.	S. S.	O. W.	N. W.	G. G.	N. G.	V. E.	Total.
Long, Miss Emily L.	London	1890-1892	Landscape	—	—	1	—	1	—	—	—	—	—	2
Long, E. W.	London	1851-1855	Figures	—	—	5	2	1	—	—	—	—	—	8
Long, F.	—	1834	Architecture	—	—	3	—	—	—	—	—	—	—	3
Long, H.	Hackney	1874	Landscape	—	—	—	—	1	—	—	—	—	—	1
Long, J.	Doneraile	1819	Game	—	—	1	—	—	—	—	—	—	—	1
Long, J.	London	1861	Sculpture	—	—	—	1	—	—	—	—	—	—	1
Long, John O., R.S.W.	London	1868-1881	Landscape	—	—	13	—	3	—	—	—	—	37	53
Long, John St. John	London	1825-1829	Scriptural	—	—	2	3	5	—	—	—	—	—	10
Long, Rose H.	London	1872	Buildings	—	—	—	—	—	—	—	—	—	1	1
Long, S. B.	London	1863-1864	Sculpture	—	—	2	1	—	—	—	—	—	—	3
Long, T.	London	1802	Architecture	—	—	1	—	—	—	—	—	—	—	1
Long, W.	—	1800	Enamels	—	—	1	—	—	—	—	—	—	—	1
Long, William	London	1821-1855	Historical	—	—	33	13	19	—	—	—	—	—	65
Longastre, De. *See* D.	—	—	—	—	—	—	—	—	—	—	—	—	—	—
Longbottom, Robert I.	London	1830-1845	Animals	—	—	10	5	14	—	3	—	—	—	32
Longfield, T. H.	Dublin	1870-1875	Churches	—	—	3	—	—	—	—	—	—	—	3
Longhurst, F. G.	London	1869-1877	Landscape	—	—	—	—	5	—	—	—	—	—	5
Longman, Charlotte	Farnboro' Hill	1879	Landscape	—	—	—	—	—	—	—	—	—	1	1
Longman, Eleanor D.	London	1879-1880	Flowers	—	—	—	—	1	—	—	—	—	2	3
Longmore, W. S.	Walthamstow	1875-1879	Buildings	—	—	3	—	1	—	—	—	—	4	8
Longmuir, A. D.	Paris	1869-1881	Landscape	—	—	1	—	—	—	—	—	—	2	3
Longsdon, David	Forest Hill	1865-1893	Landscape	—	—	4	—	4	—	—	3	—	14	25
Longshaw, Frank W., A.R.C.A.	Conway	1885	Landscape	—	—	—	—	1	—	—	—	—	—	1
Longstaffe, Edgar	Newport, Essex	1885-1889	Landscape	—	—	6	—	—	—	—	—	—	—	6
Longstaffe, John	Paris	1891	Portraits	—	—	1	—	—	—	—	—	—	—	1
Lonjew, Mrs.	—	1761	Needlework	—	1	—	—	—	—	—	—	—	—	1
Lonsdale, Horatio Walter	London	1871-1886	Architecture	—	—	7	—	—	—	—	—	—	—	7
Lonsdale, James	London	1802-1838	Portraits	—	—	138	7	87	1	—	—	—	—	233
Lonsdale, R. T.	—	1826-1849	Domestic	—	—	16	13	29	—	—	—	—	—	58
Lonza, Antonia	London	1890	Domestic	—	—	1	—	—	—	—	—	—	—	1
Loo, Van. *See* V.	—	—	—	—	—	—	—	—	—	—	—	—	—	—
Looker —	London	1764	Coat of Arms	—	1	—	—	—	—	—	—	—	—	1
Loomis, Chester	Paris	1879-1884	Historical	—	—	1	—	—	—	—	—	—	1	2
Loppé, Gustave	London	1873	Landscape	—	—	2	—	—	—	—	—	—	—	2
Loraine, Nevison Arthur, R.B.A. §	Chiswick	1889-1893	Domestic	—	—	4	—	10	—	—	—	—	5	19
Lord, John	Liverpool	1834-1855	Domestic	—	—	9	1	1	—	—	—	—	—	11
Lord, Stanhope	London	1883	—	—	—	—	—	—	—	*	—	—	—	—
Lorenz, J.	Hamburg	1880-1884	Medals	—	—	4	—	—	—	—	—	—	—	4
Lorimer, Alfred	London	1878	Landscape	—	—	—	—	—	—	—	—	—	1	1
Lorimer, John Henry, A.R.S.A., R.S.W. ϕ	Edinburgh	1878-1893	Domestic	—	—	21	—	—	—	2	2	6	15	46
Loring, Francis William	Florence	1886-1893	Landscape	—	—	4	—	—	—	—	—	—	—	4
Lormier, E.	Paris	1875	Figures	—	—	1	—	—	—	—	—	—	—	1
Lorne, H.R.H. Marchioness of. *See* Princess Louise.	—	—	—	—	—	—	—	—	—	—	—	—	—	—
Lotan, J.	London	1797	Architecture	—	—	1	—	—	—	—	—	—	—	1
Lote, H.	London	1853-1856	Architecture	—	—	2	—	—	—	—	—	—	—	2
Lothian, G.	London	1846	Landscape	—	—	—	1	—	—	—	—	—	—	1
Lott, Frederick Tully	London	1852-1879	Landscape	—	—	—	4	24	—	—	—	—	—	28
Loud, A. Bertram, R.C.A.	Balham	1884-1887	Domestic	—	—	3	—	—	—	—	—	—	—	3
Loudan, William Mouat	Dulwich	1880-1893	Domestic	—	—	9	—	17	—	—	6	3	16	51
Loudon, J. C.	London	1804-1817	Landscape	—	—	5	—	—	—	—	—	—	—	5
Lough, G.	London	1845	Sculpture	—	—	1	—	—	—	—	—	—	—	1
Lough, John Graham	London	1826-1863	Sculpture	—	—	49	16	—	—	—	—	—	—	65
Louise, H.R.H. Princess, H.R.S.W. †	—	1868-1892	Sculpture	—	—	3	—	—	21	—	6	1	—	31
Lound, Thomas	Norwich	1846-1857	Coast Scenes	—	—	18	10	—	—	—	—	—	—	28
Loup, Miss	—	1797	Portraits	—	—	1	—	—	—	—	—	—	—	1
Loutherbourgh, De. *See* D.	—	—	—	—	—	—	—	—	—	—	—	—	—	—
Lovatti, Signor Augusto	London	1888	Landscape	—	—	—	—	—	—	—	—	1	—	1
Love, George	London	1834-1835	Landscape	—	—	—	—	3	—	—	—	—	—	3
Love, H. B.	Norwich	1833-1836	Portraits	—	—	—	—	4	—	—	—	—	—	4
Lovegrove —	Great Marlow	1770	Miniatures	—	1	—	—	—	—	—	—	—	—	1
Lovegrove, H.	High Wycombe	1829-1844	Fish	—	—	1	2	10	—	—	—	—	—	13
Lovegrove, J.	London	1850	Landscape	—	—	—	—	1	—	—	—	—	—	1
Lovell, Charles Edward	London	1890-1892	Figures	—	—	—	—	—	—	—	—	1	2	3
Lovell, Miss Elizabeth M.	London	1883-1884	Flowers	—	—	—	—	1	—	1	—	—	—	2
Lovell, Richard John	London	1891-1892	Architecture	—	—	3	—	—	—	—	—	—	—	3
Lovell, Robert S.	London	1889-1890	Portraits	—	—	2	—	—	—	—	—	—	—	2
Lover, Samuel, R.H.A.	Dublin	1832-1862	Miniatures	—	—	58	—	—	—	—	—	—	—	58
Lovering, Miss Ida ‖	Norwood	1881-1893	Domestic	—	—	5	—	3	—	1	—	—	4	13
Low, Charles	London	1870-1893	Landscape	—	—	9	—	42	—	7	—	—	6	64
Low, Charlotte E.	London	1880	Flowers	—	—	—	—	1	—	—	—	—	—	1
Low, George	London	1849-1869	Architecture	—	—	4	—	—	—	—	—	—	—	4

Name.	Town.	First and Last Year of Ex.	Speciality.	S. A.	F. S.	R. A.	B. I.	S. S.	O. W.	N.W.	G. G.	N. G.	V. E.	Total.
Lowcock, Charles Frederick	Leeds	1878-1892	Domestic	—	—	16	—	10	—	—	—	—	2	28
Lowder, J.	London	1803	—	—	—	*	—	—	—	—	—	—	—	—
Lowe, Miss Ellen	Wimbledon	1889	Flowers	—	—	1	—	—	—	—	—	—	—	1
Lowe, Edward S.	Wanstead	1893	Landscape	—	—	1	—	—	—	—	—	—	1	2
Lowe, G. E.	Harlech	1885	Landscape	—	—	—	—	1	—	—	—	—	—	1
Lowe, Mauritius	London	1766-1786	Miniatures	6	—	12	—	—	—	—	—	—	—	18
Lowe, Miss Mary C.	Bromley	1888-1891	Domestic	—	—	1	—	—	—	—	—	—	1	2
Lowe, S. L.	Finchley	1849	Flowers	—	—	1	—	—	—	—	—	—	—	1
Lowe, T.	London	1845	Portraits	—	—	1	—	—	—	—	—	—	—	1
Lowe, W. D.	Llantwith	1872	Landscape	—	—	—	—	—	—	—	—	—	1	1
Lowe, Miss	London	1848	Flowers	—	—	—	—	1	—	—	—	—	—	1
Lowenstam, Leopold	London	1879-1893	Etching	—	—	17	—	—	—	2	—	—	7	26
Lowenthal, Miss Bertha	London	1888-1893	Flowers	—	—	2	—	2	—	2	—	—	1	7
Lowenthal, E.	Rome	1865-1881	Figures	—	—	6	—	—	—	—	—	—	—	6
Lower, E. W.	London	1843	Architecture	—	—	1	—	—	—	—	—	—	—	1
Lowes, J. H.	London	1861-1862	Landscape	—	—	—	2	—	—	—	—	—	—	2
Lowndes, Miss Mary	London	1884-1886	Landscape	—	—	—	—	1	—	—	—	—	1	2
Lowry, J. W.	London	1829-1831	Sea Pieces	—	—	2	2	—	—	—	—	—	—	4
Lowry, Miss M.	London	1808-1809	Portraits	—	—	4	—	—	—	—	—	—	—	4
Lowther, J. H.	—	1857-1866	Sculpture	—	—	4	—	—	—	—	—	—	—	4
Luard, John Dalbiac	London	1855-1858	Historical	—	—	4	—	—	—	—	—	—	—	4
Lübbers, H.	London	1882	Sea Coast	—	—	1	—	—	—	—	—	—	—	1
Lüben, A.	Berlin	1875	Fish	—	—	1	—	—	—	—	—	—	—	1
Lubersac, T. F. de	London	1795-1798	Miniatures	—	—	14	—	—	—	—	—	—	—	14
Lucas, Alfred	London	1867-1886	Engraving	—	—	4	—	—	—	—	—	—	—	4
Lucas, Arthur	London	1881-1893	Landscape	—	—	1	—	—	—	3	6	18	2	30
Lucas, Albert Durer	Romsey	1859-1878	Flowers, etc.	—	—	—	8	17	—	—	—	—	12	37
Lucas, Miss A. M.	Hitchin	1875	Landscape	—	—	—	—	—	—	—	—	—	1	1
Lucas, Bernard J.	Tooting	1885-1891	Landscape	—	—	—	—	—	—	—	8	2	—	10
Lucas, C.	London	1840-1841	Architecture	—	—	2	—	—	—	—	—	—	—	2
Lucas, C.	Croydon	1875	Flowers	—	—	—	—	3	—	—	—	—	—	3
Lucas, David	London	1828	Figures	—	—	—	—	1	—	—	—	—	—	1
Lucas, Miss Evelyn. *See* Miss Edith Evelyn.	—	—	—	—	—	—	—	—	—	—	—	—	—	—
Lucas, E. G Handel	Croydon	1875-1893	Domestic	—	—	12	—	17	—	—	2	—	10	41
Lucas, Miss Florence	Acton	1892	Landscape	—	—	—	—	—	—	1	—	—	—	1
Lucas, George	London	1863-1893	Landscape	—	—	25	—	29	—	12	6	—	4	76
Lucas, Miss Hannah	London	1888	Churches	—	—	—	—	—	—	1	—	—	—	1
Lucas, Horatio Joseph	London	1870-1873	Etching	—	—	9	—	—	—	—	—	—	4	13
Lucas, John	London	1828-1874	Portraits	—	—	96	13	7	—	—	—	—	1	117
Lucas, J., Junr.	London	1867	Sculpture	—	—	—	—	1	—	—	—	—	—	1
Lucas, Mrs. Jeanie	London	1873	Fruit	—	—	—	—	2	—	—	—	—	—	2
Lucas, John Seymour, A.R.A., R.I., F.S.A ‡	London	1867-1893	Historical	—	—	64	—	17	—	14	—	—	21	116
Lucas, Mrs. John Seymour. *See* Miss Marie	—	—	—	—	—	—	—	—	—	—	—	—	—	—
Cornelissen	London	1879-1893	Domestic	—	—	12	—	8	—	1	—	—	5	26
Lucas, John Templeton	London	1859-1876	Domestic	—	—	7	13	36	—	—	—	—	1	57
Lucas, Miss Lancaster	London	1890-1893	Figures	—	—	—	—	—	—	—	1	—	1	2
Lucas, Louis	Paris	1878	Etching	—	—	—	—	—	—	—	—	—	1	1
Lucas, Miss Mary	London	1877	Fruit	—	—	—	—	1	—	—	—	—	—	1
Lucas, May L.	London	1891	Portraits	—	—	1	—	—	—	—	—	—	—	1
Lucas, Richard Cockle	London	1829-1859	Sculpture	—	—	89	12	60	—	—	—	—	—	161
Lucas, Ralph W.	Blackheath	1821-1852	Landscape	—	—	44	12	19	—	2	—	—	—	77
Lucas, Mrs. R. W.	Greenwich	1846	Flowers	—	—	1	—	—	—	—	—	—	—	1
Lucas, Samuel	London	1830-1866	Landscape	—	—	7	4	2	—	—	—	—	2	15
Lucas, S. Bright	London	1883-1891	Landscape	—	—	—	—	2	—	1	—	—	—	3
Lucas, Master William (aged 10)	—	1772-1780	Heads	—	2	—	—	—	—	—	—	—	—	2
Lucas, W.	—	1828	—	—	—	*	—	—	—	—	—	—	—	—
Lucas, William ‡	London	1856-1880	Domestic	—	—	15	2	12	—	100	—	—	1	130
Lucas, Mrs.	London	1867	Fruit	—	—	—	1	—	—	—	—	—	—	1
Lucchesi, Andrea	London	1881-1893	Sculpture	—	—	23	—	2	—	—	—	—	—	25
Lucchesi, G.	—	1892	Thistles	—	—	—	—	—	—	—	—	1	—	1
Lucchesi, Professor U.	London	1882	Sculpture	—	—	1	—	—	—	—	—	—	—	1
Luchini, C.	London	1833	Portraits	—	—	2	—	—	—	—	—	—	—	2
Luck, Von. *See* V.	—	—	—	—	—	—	—	—	—	—	—	—	—	—
Luckie, A. D.	London	1874	Flowers	—	—	—	—	1	—	—	—	—	—	1
Lucy, Mrs. Anne, late Miss Anne Bishop	London	1843-1847	Domestic	—	—	2	—	—	—	—	—	—	—	2
Lucy, Charles	London	1834-1873	Historical	—	—	42	14	8	—	1	—	—	6	71
Lucy, Charles Hampden	London	1869-1891	Landscape	—	—	3	—	10	—	—	—	—	2	15
Lucy, Edward Falkland	London	1884-1893	Landscape	—	—	1	—	—	—	2	—	1	—	4
Lucy, H. A.	London	1874	Domestic	—	—	—	—	1	—	—	—	—	—	1
Ludby, Max, R.I., R.B.A.§ ‡	Cookham	1879-1893	Landscape	—	—	5	—	55	—	21	3	—	16	100
Ludlow, Henry Stephen (Hal)	London	1880-1893	Domestic	—	—	8	—	—	—	—	—	—	1	9
Ludlow, W.	—	1852	Landscape	—	—	1	—	—	—	—	—	—	—	1

Name.	Town.	First and Last Year of Ex.	Speciality.	S. A.	F. S.	R. A.	B. I.	S. S.	O. W.	N. W.	G. G.	N. G.	V. E.	Total.
Ludovici, Albert, R.B.A.§	Paris	1848-1891	Domestic	—	—	26	13	224	—	8	1	—	51	323
Ludovici, Albert, Junr., R.B.A.§	Paris	1870-1893	Domestic	—	—	9	—	147	—	1	1	—	28	186
Ludovici, Miss Marguerite	London	1876-1893	Flowers	—	—	4	—	62	—	—	—	—	10	76
Ludwig, E.	London	1847	Scriptural	—	—	—	—	1	—	—	—	—	—	1
Lugar, A.	London	1816	Architecture	—	—	1	—	—	—	—	—	—	—	1
Lugar, R.	London	1799-1841	Architecture	—	—	24	—	—	—	—	—	—	—	24
Lukeing, William J. (?) Luking	London	1840-1863	Landscape	—	—	7	7	18	—	—	—	—	53	85
Luker, A.	Merton	1885	Landscape	—	—	1	—	—	—	—	—	—	—	1
Luker, Gilham	London	1869	Landscape	—	—	—	—	—	—	—	—	—	2	2
Luker, G. Lewis	London	1876-1891	Architecture	—	—	2	—	6	—	8	—	—	—	16
Luker, William	Faringdon	1851-1889	Eastern	—	—	57	29	127	—	—	—	—	28	241
Luker, Mrs. William	London	1865-1879	Landscape	—	—	5	—	13	—	—	—	—	1	19
Luker, William, Junr.	London	1870-1893	Domestic	—	—	7	—	10	—	6	—	—	9	32
Luker, Miss	London	1868	Game	—	—	—	—	1	—	—	—	—	—	1
Lukin, G.	London	1810	Portraits	—	—	1	—	—	—	—	—	—	—	1
Luminai, E.	Paris	1878-1879	Crayons	—	—	—	—	—	—	—	—	—	4	4
Lumley, Arthur	London	1876	Domestic	—	—	2	—	—	—	—	—	—	1	3
Lumley, A. Fairfax	London	1881	Domestic	—	—	—	—	—	—	—	—	—	2	2
Lumley, Augustus Savile	London	1855-1881	Domestic	—	—	8	7	7	—	—	—	—	1	23
Lumley, Sir John Savile, K.C.B.	Brussels	1880	Etching	—	—	—	—	—	—	—	—	—	1	1
Lund, Niels M.	London	1887-1893	Landscape	—	—	12	—	—	—	—	—	—	—	12
Lundgren, Egron †	London	1862-1875	Figures	—	—	2	—	—	93	—	—	—	—	95
Luntley, James	London	1851-1858	Portraits	—	—	6	1	—	—	—	—	—	—	7
Luny, Thomas	London	1777-1837	Sea Battle Pieces	3	1	29	2	—	—	—	—	—	—	35
Luppen, Joseph Van. *See* V.	—	—	—	—	—	—	—	—	—	—	—	—	—	—
Lupton, Miss Edith	London	1871-1893	Flowers	—	—	2	—	8	—	—	—	—	4	14
Lupton, Nevil Oliver	London	1851-1877	Landscape	—	—	42	22	11	—	—	—	—	29	104
Lupton, Robert	London	1770	Still Life	—	1	—	—	—	—	—	—	—	—	1
Lupton, Thomas Goff	London	1811-1825	Engraving	—	—	4	—	7	—	—	—	—	—	11
Lürssen, Eduard	Berlin	1883	Sculpture	—	—	2	—	—	—	—	—	—	—	2
Luscombe, Henry A.	Plymouth	1845-1865	Shipping	—	—	11	—	—	—	—	—	—	—	11
Lutteroth, Professor A.	Hamburg	1891	Venice	—	—	—	—	—	—	3	—	—	—	3
Lutwidge, C. R. F.	Tunb'dge Wells	1865-1870	Ruins	—	—	—	—	—	—	—	—	—	2	2
Lutyens, Charles Augustus Henry	London	1860-1893	Sporting	—	—	41	11	1	—	—	1	—	1	55
Lutyens, Edwin L.	London	1890-1891	Landscape	—	—	3	—	—	—	—	—	—	—	3
Lutyens, F. M.	London	1889-1891	Domestic	—	—	—	—	—	—	—	1	—	1	2
Luxmoore, Arthur C. H., F.S.A.	London	1854-1886	Sculpture	—	—	17	—	4	—	—	2	—	56	79
Luxmoore, Mrs. Arthur (Kate F.)	London	1875-1880	Figures	—	—	—	—	—	—	—	—	—	5	5
Luxmoore, C. N.	Torquay	1867-1868	Pen and Ink	—	—	1	—	—	—	—	—	—	2	3
Luxmoore, D. H.	London	1880	Wood Engraving	—	—	—	—	—	—	—	—	—	2	2
Luxmoore, Miss Myra E.	London	1887-1893	Portraits	—	—	1	—	1	—	—	—	—	1	3
Luz, Julius Marsden	Streatham	1883-1890	Domestic	—	—	5	—	2	—	—	—	—	—	7
Lydon, F. A.	Great Driffield	1861	Domestic	—	—	1	—	—	—	—	—	—	—	1
Lyford, W.	London	1784-1789	Architecture	—	—	5	—	—	—	—	—	—	—	5
Lyle, Byron	London	1887	Domestic	—	—	—	—	—	—	—	—	—	1	1
Lyle, Thomas B.	London	1887	Domestic	—	—	1	—	—	—	—	—	—	—	1
Lynam and Rickman	Stoke-on-Trent	1886	Architecture	—	—	1	—	—	—	—	—	—	—	1
Lynch, Albert	—	1893	Portraits	—	—	—	—	—	—	—	—	—	1	1
Lynch, Daniel	London	1827-1833	Figures	—	—	5	—	3	—	2	—	—	—	10
Lynch, James Henry	London	1856-1865	Lithography	—	—	25	—	—	—	—	—	—	—	25
Lynden —	—	1783	Flowers	1	4	—	—	—	—	—	—	—	—	5
Lyndon —	—	1847	Architecture	—	—	1	—	—	—	—	—	—	—	1
Lyndon, Herbert	London	1879-1893	Landscape	—	—	10	—	18	—	4	1	—	13	46
Lyndon, Mrs.	London	1811	Portraits	—	—	2	—	—	—	—	—	—	—	2
Lynn, John	London	1826-1838	Sea Pieces	—	—	—	9	5	—	—	—	—	—	14
Lynn, Samuel Ferres, R.H.A.	London	1856-1875	Sculpture	—	—	26	1	—	—	—	—	—	—	27
Lyon, Miss A.	London	1885	Animals	—	—	1	—	—	—	—	—	—	—	1
Lyon, Charles E.	London	1889	Flowers	—	—	1	—	—	—	—	—	—	—	1
Lyon, Miss C. E.	Leamington	1872	Figures	—	—	—	—	—	—	—	—	—	1	1
Lyon, David	London	1774	Sporting	—	2	—	—	—	—	—	—	—	—	2
Lyon, E.	London	1827	Sculpture	—	—	—	1	—	—	—	—	—	—	1
Lyon, Miss E. F.	London	1885	Domestic	—	—	—	—	1	—	—	—	—	1	2
Lyon, George P.	Glasgow	1885	Landscape	—	—	1	—	—	—	—	—	—	—	1
Lyon, J.	London	1803-1805	Miniatures	—	—	2	—	—	—	—	—	—	—	2
Lyon, Lucy S.	London	1888	Flowers	—	—	—	—	1	—	—	—	—	—	1
Lyon, Peter	London	1772	Portraits	—	—	1	—	—	—	—	—	—	—	1
Lyon, Walter Fitzgerald	London	1877-1878	Architecture	—	—	2	—	—	—	—	—	—	—	2
Lyoncourt, Baron de. *See also* De	London	1874	Landscape	—	—	1	—	—	—	—	—	—	—	1
Lyons, Thomas	London	1867	Fruit	—	—	—	—	—	—	—	—	—	1	1
Lysons, Samuel	London	1785-1801	Architecture	—	—	16	—	—	—	—	—	—	—	16
Lyster, R.	Cork	1857	Historical	—	—	1	—	—	—	—	—	—	—	1
Lyttelton, Lady	—	1771-1780	Crayons	2	—	3	—	—	—	—	—	—	—	5

Name.	Town.	First and Last Year of Ex.	Speciality.	S. A.	F. S.	R. A.	B. I.	S. S.	O. W.	N. W.	G. G.	N. G.	V. E.	Total
Maas, Miss Edith	London	1890-1893	Miniatures	—	—	9	—	—	—	—	—	—	—	9
Mabbet, R.	London	1780-1781	Miniatures	—	—	2	—	—	—	—	—	—	—	2
Maberley. *See* Carling and Maberley	—	—	Architecture	—	—	—	—	—	—	—	—	—	—	—
Mabey, Charles H.	London	1863-1889	Sculpture	—	—	9	—	—	—	—	—	—	—	9
Mabin. *See* Lahee and Mabin	—	—	Architecture	—	—	—	—	—	—	—	—	—	—	—
Mac, Robert F.	London	1867-1870	Landscape	—	—	1	2	3	—	—	—	—	—	6
Macallister, A. D.	London	1854	Domestic	—	—	1	—	—	—	—	—	—	—	1
Macallum, Hamilton, R.I., R.S.W. ‡ ϕ	London	1866-1893	Sea Pieces	—	—	21	—	13	—	28	9	7	95	173
McArdell, James	London	1760-1765	Engraving	14	—	—	—	—	—	—	—	—	—	14
Macartan, Luke	London	1829-1830	Figures	—	—	3	3	—	—	—	—	—	—	6
MacArthur, Miss Blanche F.	London	1870-1888	Domestic	—	—	18	—	48	—	—	—	—	26	92
MacArthur, C. M.	London	1873-1876	Landscape	—	—	2	—	4	—	—	—	—	—	6
Macarthur, Lindsey G.	Oban	1890-1893	Landscape	—	—	1	—	—	—	—	—	1	1	3
MacArthur, Miss Mary	London	1872-1888	Domestic	—	—	3	—	11	—	—	—	—	3	17
Macartney, Carlile Henry Hayes	London	1874-1893	Landscape	—	—	26	—	—	—	—	1	—	5	32
Macartney, Mervyn Ed.	London	1882-1889	Architecture	—	—	9	—	—	—	—	—	—	—	9
Macaulay, Miss Kate, R.S.W. ‖	Bettws-y-Coed	1872-1884	Landscape	—	—	6	—	23	—	1	—	—	11	41
McBean, Miss M. E.	—	1856-1859	Figures	—	—	2	—	—	—	—	—	—	—	2
MacBean, Major-General W. Forbes	Dinan	1880	Landscape	—	—	—	—	—	—	—	—	—	1	1
Macbeth, James	London	1872-1889	Landscape	—	—	15	—	7	—	9	3	—	37	71
Macbeth, L.	Edinburgh	1886	Portraits	—	—	1	—	—	—	—	—	—	—	1
Macbeth, Norman, R.S.A.	Greenock	1837-1886	Portraits	—	—	26	—	—	—	—	—	—	3	29
Macbeth, Robert Walker, A.R.A., R.I., R.P.E. † ‡ ϕ	London	1870-1893	Domestic, etc.	—	—	70	—	—	42	4	23	8	76	223
Macbeth-Raeburn, Henry, A.R.P.E.	Edinburgh	1881-1893	Domestic	—	—	17	—	1	—	4	—	—	6	28
MacBride, Alexander, R.S.W.	Glasgow	1889-1891	Landscape	—	—	—	—	—	—	4	—	—	—	4
MacBride, Charles	Edinburgh	1890	Sculpture	—	—	1	—	—	—	—	—	—	—	1
McBride, John Alexander Paterson	Liverpool	1848-1853	Sculpture	—	—	3	—	—	—	—	—	—	—	3
MacBride, William	Glasgow	1890-1892	Landscape	—	—	2	—	—	—	—	—	—	—	2
McCall, Gertrude S.	Leicester	1887	Fruit	—	—	—	—	2	—	—	—	—	—	2
M'Call, William	London	1818-1837	Historical	—	—	25	19	6	—	—	—	—	—	50
McCallum, Andrew	Nottingham	1849-1889	Landscape	—	—	53	4	5	—	—	1	—	9	72
Maccallum, G.	Edinburgh	1866-1868	Sculpture	—	—	5	—	—	—	—	—	—	—	5
McCalmont, Miss Ethel E.	London	1883	Landscape	—	—	1	—	—	—	—	—	—	—	1
McCalmont, H. B.	Hampton Court	1881	Venice	—	—	—	—	1	—	—	—	—	—	1
Maccari, Cesare	Rome	1873-1880	Figures	—	—	—	—	—	—	—	—	—	3	3
Maccarthy, Amelia	London	1843	Sculpture	—	—	2	—	—	—	—	—	—	—	2
Maccarthy, Mrs. C.	London	1854	Sculpture	—	—	1	—	—	—	—	—	—	—	1
McCarthy, Carleton	London	1838-1866	Sculpture	—	—	14	9	—	—	—	—	—	—	23
McCarthy, Miss Gertrude	London	1838-1853	Sculpture	—	—	4	1	—	—	—	—	—	—	5
MacCarthy, Hamilton P.	London	1875-1884	Sculpture	—	—	9	—	—	—	—	1	—	—	10
McCarthy, Hamilton, W.	London	1838-1867	Sculpture	—	—	23	13	—	—	—	—	—	—	36
McCarthy, Hamilton, and Carlton	London	1846	Sculpture	—	—	—	2	—	—	—	—	—	—	2
Maccarthy, Mrs. H.	London	1857	Sculpture	—	—	1	—	—	—	—	—	—	—	1
McCarthy, John S.	London	1873-1885	Sculpture	—	—	1	—	1	—	—	—	—	—	2
McCarthy, Mrs. S.	London	1853-1858	Sculpture	—	—	2	3	—	—	—	—	—	—	5
McCarthy, S. J.	London	1833-1839	Sculpture	—	—	1	—	1	—	—	—	—	—	2
MacCarthy, Walter Emilius	London	1877	Architecture	—	—	1	—	—	—	—	—	—	—	1
McCarty, W. W.	London	1877	Landscape	—	—	—	—	1	—	—	—	—	—	1
McCaul, G. J.	—	1874	Landscape	—	—	—	—	1	—	—	—	—	—	1
McCaul, Miss Meta W.	Chislehurst	1884	Fishing Boats	—	—	—	—	1	—	—	—	—	—	1
McCausland, Miss Charlotte Katherine	London	1881-1892	Domestic	—	—	5	—	10	—	—	2	—	7	24
McCleery, Robert C.	London	1887-1892	Landscape	—	—	—	—	—	—	4	—	—	—	4
McClosky, A. Binford	Paris	1893	Flowers	—	—	—	—	1	—	—	—	—	—	1
M'Closky, William J.	London	1892-1893	Domestic	—	—	—	—	1	—	1	—	—	3	5
McCloy, Samuel	Waterford	1859-1891	Landscape	—	—	1	—	9	—	1	—	—	—	11
McClymont, J. I.	Edinburgh	1893	Domestic	—	—	1	—	—	—	—	—	—	—	1
Macco —	Bavaria	1826	Portraits	—	—	2	—	—	—	—	—	—	—	2
McCormick, Arthur D.	London	1889-1893	Domestic	—	—	2	—	9	—	—	—	—	—	11
McCracken, Miss Katherine	Blackheath	1877-1893	Landscape	—	—	—	—	—	—	13	—	7	3	23
McCulloch, George	London	1859-1893	Figures	—	—	25	—	7	—	—	1	—	37	70
Macculloch, Horatio, R.S.A.	Edinburgh	1843-1851	Landscape	—	—	2	1	—	—	—	—	—	4	7
Macculloch, J.	Woolwich	1798-1804	Landscape	—	—	5	—	—	—	—	—	—	—	5
Macculloch, James, R.B.A., R.S.W. §	London	1872-1893	Landscape	—	—	4	—	74	—	16	1	—	21	116
Macculloch, John, M.D., F.R.S.	London	1827-1828	Architecture	—	—	2	—	—	—	—	—	—	—	2
McCulloch, J. M.	London	1849	Architecture	—	—	1	—	—	—	—	—	—	—	1
Macdonald. *See* Read and Macdonald	—	—	Architecture	—	—	—	—	—	—	—	—	—	—	—
Macdonald, Alfred	Oxford	1868-1885	Landscape	—	—	3	—	—	—	—	—	—	—	3
Macdonald, Alexander	Rome	1868-1893	Sculpture	—	—	3	—	—	—	1	—	—	1	5
Macdonald, Miss A.	London	1870-1877	Landscape	—	—	—	—	7	—	—	—	—	—	7
Macdonald, C.	London	1857	Domestic	—	—	1	—	—	—	—	—	—	—	1
Macdonald, D.	London	1847-1853	Landscape	—	—	1	4	—	—	—	—	—	—	5

Name.	Town.	First and Last Year of Ex.	Speciality.	S. A.	F. S.	R. A.	B. I.	S. S.	O. W.	N. W.	G. G.	N. G.	V. E.	Total.
MacDonald, Miss H. M.	London	1873	Portraits	—	—	1	—	—	—	—	—	—	—	1
McDonald, John	London	1843-1848	Landscape	—	—	2	—	—	—	—	—	—	—	2
MacDonald, John B., R.S.A.	Edinburgh	1866-1876	Historical	—	—	6	—	—	—	—	—	—	—	6
Macdonald, Lawrence, R.S.A.	Edinburgh	1828-1857	Sculpture	—	—	48	1	1	—	—	—	—	—	50
Macdonald, William	London	1848	Landscape	—	—	—	—	1	—	—	—	—	—	1
Macdonald, William A.	London	1884-1893	Landscape	—	—	2	—	2	—	—	—	—	1	5
McDonnell, F.	London	1846-1852	Sculpture	—	—	2	—	—	—	—	—	—	—	2
Macdonnell, John	London	1788-1804	Architecture	1	—	13	—	—	—	—	—	—	—	14
McDonnell, Laurence, A.	Dublin	1893	Buildings	—	—	1	—	—	—	—	—	—	—	1
McDougal, John	Liverpool	1877-1893	Sea Pieces	—	—	18	—	7	—	4	1	—	7	37
Macdougall, Allan	Glasgow	1851-1853	Landscape	—	—	—	—	—	—	—	—	—	3	3
Macdougall, Norman M.	London	1874-1885	Figures	—	—	5	—	12	—	3	—	—	6	26
McDowell, G. Moore	London	1882-1885	Stained Glass	—	—	3	—	—	—	—	—	—	—	3
MacDowell, Patrick, R.A.	London	1822-1870	Sculpture	—	—	78	3	8	—	—	—	—	—	89
MacDowell, P., Junr.	London	1861	Sculpture	—	—	1	—	—	—	—	—	—	—	1
Macdowell, R. C.	London	1858-1865	Sculpture	—	—	3	—	—	—	—	—	—	—	3
Macduff, William	London	1844-1876	Domestic	—	—	9	10	1	—	—	—	—	5	25
Mace, F.	London	1820-1840	Sculpture	—	—	9	—	16	—	—	—	—	—	25
M'Emlyn, Miss	London	1861	Domestic	—	—	—	—	—	—	—	—	—	2	2
McEntee, Jervis	New York	1872-1880	Landscape	—	—	2	—	—	—	—	—	—	2	4
McEvoy, William	London	1866-1867	Landscape	—	—	—	1	6	—	—	—	—	—	7
McEwan —	London	1782-1783	Furniture	—	2	—	—	—	—	—	—	—	—	2
McEwan, Charles	Glasgow	1885-1890	Landscape	—	—	2	—	1	—	—	—	—	—	3
McEwan, Tom, R.S.W.	Helensburgh	1887	Domestic	—	—	1	—	—	—	—	—	—	—	1
McFadden, A.	Southampton	1872	Figures	—	—	—	—	1	—	—	—	—	—	1
McFadden, Frank G.	Bushey	1878-1892	Buildings	—	—	3	—	—	—	—	1	—	10	14
McFadden, Rowland	Southampton	1874-1879	Landscape	—	—	—	—	—	—	—	—	—	2	2
McFall, C. Haldane	London	1891	Domestic	—	—	1	—	—	—	—	—	—	—	1
Macfarlane, J. L. (?) John R.	London	1863-1868	Flowers	—	—	4	2	5	—	—	—	—	—	11
Macfarren, I. J.	London	1839-1846	Landscape	—	—	8	2	30	—	—	—	—	—	40
Macfee, John	London	1887	Landscape	—	—	—	—	—	—	1	—	—	—	1
McFergus —	—	1783	Landscape	—	1	—	—	—	—	—	—	—	—	1
Macgavin, J.	London	1797-1820	Miniatures	—	—	5	—	—	—	—	—	—	—	5
Macgavin, W.	London	1793-1807	Miniatures	—	—	8	—	—	—	—	—	—	—	8
McGhie, John	London	1891-1893	Domestic	—	—	3	—	—	—	—	—	—	—	3
McGibbon, Alexander	Glasgow	1891	Buildings	—	—	1	—	—	—	—	—	—	—	1
McGill, David	London	1889-1893	Sculpture	—	—	8	—	—	—	—	—	—	—	8
McGill, William Murdoch	London	1867-1877	Landscape	—	—	—	—	3	—	—	—	—	—	3
McGill, Mrs. W. M. (Fanny)	Richmond	1888	Landscape	—	—	1	—	—	—	—	—	—	—	1
Macgillivray, Pittendrigh, A.R.S.A.	Glasgow	1891-1892	Sculpture	—	—	3	—	—	—	—	—	—	—	3
Macgour, Miss H. C. Preston	Edinburgh	1893	Domestic	—	—	1	—	—	—	—	—	—	—	1
Macgregor, Archie G.	London	1884-1893	Sculpture	—	—	5	—	—	—	2	—	4	1	12
Macgregor, Miss Jessie ‖	Liverpool	1872-1893	Domestic	—	—	33	—	1	—	—	—	—	7	41
McGregor, Robert, R.S.A.	Edinburgh	1876-1889	Domestic	—	—	6	—	—	—	—	1	—	5	12
McGregor, Miss Sarah	London	1869-1885	Flowers	—	—	—	—	7	—	—	—	—	1	8
Macgregor, W. Y., R.S.W.	Glasgow	1883-1885	Fruit	—	—	2	—	—	—	—	—	—	—	2
McGuiness, Bingham, R.H.A.	Dublin	1882-1892	Landscape	—	—	—	—	—	—	10	—	—	1	11
McHeath, Charlotte D.	London	1870-1871	Domestic	—	—	—	—	—	—	—	—	—	2	2
Machell, Reginald	London	1881-1893	Domestic	—	—	5	—	8	—	1	2	—	4	20
MacIan, Ronald Robert, A.R.S.A.	London	1835-1857	Landscape	—	—	13	13	13	—	—	—	—	24	63
McIan, Mrs. R. R. (Fanny)	London	1835-1852	Historical	—	—	10	10	13	—	—	—	—	5	38
McIlwaine, J. B. L., A.R.H.A.	Dublin	1892	Landscape	—	—	—	—	2	—	—	—	—	—	2
McInnes, A.	London	1806-1808	Architecture	—	—	4	—	—	—	—	—	—	—	4
McInnes, Alexander	London	1848-1854	Landscape	—	—	1	5	2	—	—	—	—	2	10
McInnes, Miss Ellen	London	1854-1865	Flowers	—	—	—	4	2	—	—	—	—	—	6
McInnes, Robert	London	1841-1866	Historical	—	—	27	4	—	—	—	—	—	1	32
McInnes, S.	London	1849-1852	Historical	—	—	2	—	—	—	—	—	—	—	2
MacIntosh —	London	1768-1769	Miniatures	2	—	—	—	—	—	—	—	—	—	2
Macintosh, Colin M.	London	1882	Landscape	—	—	—	—	—	—	—	—	—	3	3
Macintosh, John M., R.B.A. §	London	1880-1893	Landscape	—	—	18	—	45	—	14	7	—	3	87
McIntyre, James	—	1867-1891	Sea Pieces	—	—	10	—	6	—	—	—	—	—	16
McIntyre, Joseph Wrightson	London	1866-1885	Landscape	—	—	—	3	43	—	—	—	—	—	46
McIntyre, R. Finlay	London	1879-1892	Landscape	—	—	1	—	3	—	—	—	—	1	5
McIntyre, Mrs. *See* Mrs. Denis Dighton	—	1841-1854	Fruit	—	—	3	—	—	—	—	—	—	—	3
Macirone, Miss Cecilia A.	London	1855-1859	Flowers	—	—	1	2	1	—	—	—	—	—	4
Macirone, Miss Emily	London	1846-1878	Domestic	—	—	27	—	45	—	—	—	—	14	86
Mackay, Mrs. Barbara	—	1891	Portraits	—	—	—	—	—	—	—	—	—	1	1
McKay, David B. *See* W. J. Roffe	London	1871-1877	Domestic	—	—	3	—	2	—	—	—	—	—	5
McKay, Miss G.	London	1886	—	—	—	—	—	—	—	*	—	—	—	—
Mackay, Master Richard	London	1775-1790	Figures	2	1	—	—	—	—	—	—	—	—	3
Mackay, Rose	London	1892-1893	Domestic	—	—	—	—	2	—	—	—	—	1	3
Mackay, T. W.	London	1826-1853	Domestic	—	—	6	7	12	—	—	—	—	—	25

Name.	Town.	First and Last Year of Ex.	Speciality.	S. A.	F. S.	R. A.	B. I.	S. S	O.W.	N.W.	G. G.	N. G.	V. E.	Total.
Mackay, Miss	—	1775	Flowers	—	1	—	—	—	—	—	—	—	—	1
McKechnie, G. M.	London	1824-1827	Landscape	—	—	—	1	6	—	—	—	—	—	7
Mackei, B. Jessopp	London	1889	Historical	—	—	—	—	1	—	—	—	—	—	1
Mackellar, Duncan, R.S.W.	Glasgow	1883-1892	Figures	—	—	2	—	—	—	2	1	—	—	5
Mackennal, E. Bertram	Madeley	1886	Sculpture	—	—	1	—	—	—	—	—	—	—	1
McKenny, R.	London	1843	Landscape	—	—	2	—	—	—	—	—	—	—	2
Mackenzie, Lady	London	1875	Domestic	—	—	—	—	—	—	—	—	—	1	1
McKenzie, Alexander	London	1777-1799	Sculpture	—	4	25	—	—	—	—	—	—	—	29
Mackenzie, Alexander Marshall, A.R.S.A.	Aberdeen	1885-1888	Landscape	—	—	2	—	—	—	—	—	—	—	2
Mackenzie, Miss E.	London	1857	Figures	—	—	1	—	—	—	—	—	—	—	1
Mackenzie, Mrs. E. Phillipe	Oxon	1866-1868	Domestic	—	—	—	—	6	—	—	—	—	—	6
Mackenzie, Frederick †	Romford	1804-1853	Buildings	—	—	1	—	1	92	—	—	—	11	115
Mackenzie, Frank J.	Godalming	1891-1893	Landscape	—	—	3	—	3	—	—	—	—	—	6
Mackenzie, George	London	1833-1844	Landscape	—	—	7	—	6	—	—	—	—	—	13
Mackenzie, H. A. O.	London	1891	Domestic	—	—	—	—	1	—	—	—	—	—	1
Mackenzie, Mrs. Isabella	—	1843-1846	Portraits	—	—	2	—	—	—	—	—	—	—	2
McKenzie, Miss Jane	London	1852-1858	Miniatures	—	—	13	—	—	—	—	—	—	—	13
Mackenzie, John D.	Newlyn	1886-1891	Historical	—	—	3	—	1	—	—	—	—	—	4
Mackenzie, J. M.	London	1846	Figures	—	—	1	—	—	—	—	—	—	—	1
Mackenzie, James M.	Woodside	1882	River Scenes	—	—	—	—	—	—	—	—	—	1	1
Mackenzie, James Wilson	Liverpool	1888-1890	Domestic	—	—	3	—	—	—	—	—	—	—	3
Mackenzie, Kenneth	London	1884-1893	Landscape	—	—	18	—	1	—	—	—	2	13	34
Mackenzie, Miss Muir	London	1871-1876	Figures	—	—	2	—	—	—	—	—	—	1	3
Mackenzie, M. H.	London	1877	Figures	—	—	—	—	2	—	—	—	—	—	2
Mackenzie, S. A. Muir	London	1871-1877	Domestic	—	—	2	—	1	—	—	—	—	2	5
McKenzie, Mrs. ‖ *See* Miss Emma Landseer	—	1845-1860	Animals	—	—	2	5	—	—	—	—	—	—	7
McKerrell, J.	London	1804-1811	Landscape	—	—	2	—	—	—	—	—	—	—	2
McKewan, David Hall ‡	London	1836-1873	Landscape	—	—	22	2	20	—	498	—	—	—	542
McKewen, M. W.	London	1872-1875	Domestic	—	—	—	—	18	—	—	—	—	—	18
Mackey, J.	London	1845	Heads	—	—	1	—	—	—	—	—	—	—	1
Mackie, Miss Annie	London	1887-1893	Flowers	—	—	3	—	—	—	1	—	—	—	4
Mackie, Charles H.	Portobello	1889-1893	Landscape	—	—	3	—	—	—	—	1	—	—	4
Mackie, J. B.	Deptford	1838-1839	Portraits	—	—	2	—	—	—	—	—	—	—	2
Mackie, W.	London	1810-1813	Architecture	—	—	5	—	—	—	—	—	—	—	5
Mackie, W. B.	London	1830-1831	Miniatures	—	—	4	—	—	—	—	—	—	—	4
Mackinlay, Thomas	London	1863-1870	Figures	—	—	5	1	—	—	—	—	—	—	6
McKinnon, Finlay	London	1891-1893	Landscape	—	—	—	—	—	—	2	—	—	—	2
Mackintosh, T.	London	1818-1820	Architecture	—	—	2	—	—	—	—	—	—	—	2
Macklin, Thomas Eyre	London	1889-1893	Domestic	—	—	4	—	—	—	—	—	—	—	4
Mackreth, Miss Harriet F. S.	Newcastle	1828-1842	Miniatures	—	—	23	—	1	—	—	—	—	—	24
Mackworth, Audley	London	1884-1890	Scriptural	—	—	7	—	—	—	—	—	—	1	8
Mackworth, Miss T.	Teddington	1886	Portraits	—	—	—	—	—	—	1	—	—	—	1
McLachlan, Miss Aileen M.	London	1885-1893	Landscape	—	—	—	—	—	—	—	—	—	8	8
McLachlan, H.	Ealing	1886	Figures	—	—	—	—	—	—	—	—	—	1	1
McLachlan, Miss H.	London	1881-1882	Still Life	—	—	—	—	2	—	—	—	—	—	2
McLachlan, Thomas Hope φ	Weybridge	1875-1893	Landscape	—	—	34	—	—	—	—	18	13	22	87
McLaren, C.	London	1871	Landscape	—	—	1	—	—	—	—	—	—	—	1
McLaren, James M. *See also* Coad and Maclaren	London	1887-1890	Architecture	—	—	4	—	—	—	—	—	—	—	4
Maclaren, John S.	Edinburgh	1890-1892	Landscape	—	—	2	—	2	—	—	—	—	—	4
MacLaren, Thomas	London	1885-1892	Architecture	—	—	9	—	—	—	—	—	—	—	9
Maclaren, Walter	Capri	1869-1893	Landscape	—	—	11	—	—	—	—	10	13	10	44
McLaren (J. M.), Dunn, and Watson (R.)	London	1891	Architecture	—	—	2	—	—	—	—	—	—	—	2
MacLaughlin, Frances	Tenbury	1878	Churches	—	—	—	—	—	—	—	—	—	1	1
Maclean, Alexander	London	1868-1893	Domestic	—	—	7	—	4	—	—	—	—	8	19
Maclean, Hector	Brighton	1880	Landscape	—	—	—	—	1	—	—	—	—	—	1
Maclean, Norman	London	1876-1879	Etching	—	—	—	—	—	—	—	—	—	2	2
Maclean, Thomas Nelson §	London	1870-1891	Sculpture	—	—	32	—	24	—	2	33	1	5	97
MacLeay, Kenneth, R.S.A., R.S.W.	Edinburgh	1865	Miniatures	—	—	3	—	—	—	—	—	—	—	3
Macleay, Macneil, A.R.S.A.	Edinburgh	1839	Landscape	—	—	1	—	—	—	—	—	—	—	1
Macleay, Miss	—	1824	Flowers	—	—	1	—	—	—	—	—	—	—	1
Macleod, D.	London	1793	Miniatures	—	—	1	—	—	—	—	—	—	—	1
McLeod, G.	London	1856	Domestic	—	—	1	—	—	—	—	—	—	—	1
Macleod, Miss Jessie	London	1845-1875	Historical	—	—	10	29	43	—	—	—	—	—	82
Macleod, Mrs.	—	1775	Needlework	1	1	—	—	—	—	—	—	—	—	2
Maclise, Daniel, R.A. ‡	London	1829-1871	Historical	—	—	83	20	21	—	*	—	—	—	124
Maclure, Andrew	London	1857-1881	Landscape	—	—	6	—	—	—	—	—	—	—	6
MacManus, Henry, R.H.A.	London	1839-1843	Historical	—	—	2	4	16	—	—	—	—	—	22
McMara, H.	London	1855	Domestic	—	—	—	—	1	—	—	—	—	—	1
MacMaster, James, R.B.A., R.S.W. §	Glasgow	1885-1892	Landscape	—	—	5	—	25	—	2	—	—	—	32
McMichael, Mrs. W.	Bridgenorth	1844-1849	Fruit	—	—	—	—	2	—	—	—	—	—	2
McMillan, Miss Emmeline S. A.	Wimbledon	1885-1891	Domestic	—	—	2	—	—	—	3	—	—	—	5
McMinn, J. K.	London	1871-1873	Flowers	—	—	—	—	2	—	—	—	—	—	2

Name.	Town.	First and Last Year of Ex.	Speciality.	S. A.	F. S.	R. A.	B. I.	S. S.	O. W.	N.W.	G. G.	N. G.	V. E.	Total.
MacMoreland, Patrick John	Manchester	1774-1782	Miniatures	6	—	9	—	—	—	—	—	—	—	15
Macnab, John	London	1855-1890	Landscape	—	—	1	—	—	—	—	—	—	2	3
Macnab, Peter, R.B.A. §	London	1864-1892	Landscape	—	—	17	1	58	—	2	—	—	18	96
Macnamara, F. A.	London	1840-1850	Portraits	—	—	—	—	2	—	—	—	—	—	2
Macnee, Sir Daniel, P.R.S.A.	Glasgow	1840-1881	Portraits	—	—	98	—	—	—	—	—	—	—	98
McNee, J.	Glasgow	1832	Portraits	—	—	2	—	—	—	—	—	—	—	2
Macnee, R. Russell	Edinburgh	1892	Landscape	—	—	1	—	—	—	—	—	—	—	1
MacNicol, Miss Bessie	Glasgow	1893	Domestic	—	—	1	—	—	—	—	—	—	—	1
McNiven, Lieut.-Col.	London	1846	Landscape	—	—	—	—	2	—	—	—	—	—	2
MacNiven, D P.	London	1881-1883	Domestic	—	—	—	—	2	—	—	—	—	—	2
MacNiven, John, R.S.W.	Glasgow	1889-1893	River Scenes	—	—	3	—	—	—	—	—	—	—	3
McPhearson, C.	London	1833	Coast Scenes	—	—	1	—	—	—	—	—	—	—	1
McPhearson, J.	London	1833-1839	Sea Pieces	—	—	1	3	11	—	—	—	—	—	15
Macpherson, Miss Barbara H.	Kilburn	1882-1885	Landscape	—	—	—	—	4	—	4	—	—	—	8
Macpherson, John	London	1865-1884	Landscape	—	—	1	—	12	—	1	—	—	8	22
Macpherson, M. ‡	London	1828-1834	Portraits	—	—	2	—	—	—	1	—	—	—	3
McPhirson, J. R.	—	1849	Landscape	—	—	1	—	—	—	—	—	—	—	1
McPhisk —	—	1783	Landscape	—	1	—	—	—	—	—	—	—	—	1
Macquin, Rev. A. D.	—	1801-1808	Domestic	—	—	4	—	—	—	—	—	—	—	4
McQuoid, Master Charles	—	1780-1783	Drawings	—	2	—	—	—	—	—	—	—	—	2
McQuoid, Percy T, R.I. ‡ φ	London	1866-1889	Domestic	—	—	10	—	10	—	25	3	—	79	127
Macquoid, Mrs. Percy	London	1888	Sculpture	—	—	—	—	—	—	4	—	—	—	4
McQuoid, S.	London	1774-1783	Shipping	—	18	—	—	—	—	—	—	—	—	18
McQuoid, Master Samuel	—	1780	Drawing	—	1	—	—	—	—	—	—	—	—	1
Macquoid, Thomas R., R.I. ‡ φ	London	1838-1893	Churches	—	—	23	—	15	—	66	—	—	149	253
MacRae, Mary	London	1893	Figures	—	—	—	—	1	—	—	—	—	—	1
Macreth, Robert	London	1824-1830	Landscape	—	—	—	9	1	—	—	—	—	—	10
MacTaggart, Mrs. A.	London	1824	Landscape	—	—	—	5	—	—	—	—	—	—	5
McTaggart, William, R.S.A., R.S.W.	Edinburgh	1866-1875	Domestic	—	—	11	—	—	—	—	—	—	—	11
MacVeal, R.	London	1847	Landscape	—	—	1	—	—	—	—	—	—	—	1
McWhirter, Miss Agnes Eliza	Edinburgh	1867-1879	Still Life	—	—	3	—	—	—	—	—	—	19	22
McWhirter, John, A.R.A., H.R.S.A., R.I. ‡ φ	Edinburgh	1865-1893	Landscape	—	—	78	—	—	—	11	5	2	25	121
McWilliam, R.	London	1818-1825	Architecture	—	—	3	—	—	—	—	—	—	—	3
Madden, Wyndham	London	1870-1871	Landscape	—	—	—	—	—	—	—	—	—	2	2
Maddox, George §	London	1796-1843	Ruins	—	—	4	—	42	—	—	—	—	—	46
Maddox, Mrs. G. §	London	1824-1829	Landscape	—	—	—	—	3	—	—	—	—	—	3
Maddox, Richard Willes	Southampton	1873-1892	Historical	—	—	2	—	4	—	3	—	3	8	20
Maddox, Willes	London	1844-1853	Historical	—	—	13	5	6	—	—	—	—	3	27
Madot, Miss A. E.	London	1859	Figures	—	—	1	—	—	—	—	—	—	—	1
Madot, Adolphus M.	London	1852-1864	Figures	—	—	8	4	6	—	—	—	—	3	21
Madou, M., H.R.I. ‡	Brussels	1870-1874	Domestic	—	—	—	—	—	—	5	—	—	—	5
Madrassi, L.	—	1876-1892	Sculpture	—	—	2	—	—	—	1	—	—	2	5
Madrazo, Don Frederic	Madrid	1873	Portraits	—	—	1	—	—	—	—	—	—	—	1
Maes, H.	London	1826	Figures	—	—	1	—	—	—	—	—	—	—	1
Maes, H.	Finchley	1878	Domestic	—	—	—	—	1	—	—	—	—	—	1
Maffei, Signor	Nice	1866-1868	Sculpture	—	—	2	—	—	—	—	—	—	—	2
Magenis, H.	London	1828	Portraits	—	—	—	—	1	—	—	—	—	—	1
Magill, L.	London	1891	Domestic	—	—	—	—	1	—	—	—	—	—	1
Magnes, Isidore	London	1849-1852	Portraits	—	—	2	—	—	—	—	—	—	—	2
Magniac, Hon. Mrs.	Bedford	1875	Landscape	—	—	—	—	1	—	—	—	—	—	1
Magnus, Miss Emma	Manchester	1878-1892	Domestic	—	—	4	—	8	—	—	—	—	5	17
Magnus, Miss Rose	Manchester	1884-1893	Flowers	—	—	—	—	18	—	—	—	—	6	24
Magor, M. A.	London	1878	Landscape	—	—	—	—	—	—	—	—	—	2	2
Magrath, William	London	1879-1893	Domestic	—	—	6	—	6	—	5	—	—	4	21
Maguire, Miss Adelaide A.	London	1868-1876	Landscape	—	—	4	—	2	—	—	—	—	4	10
Maguire, Miss Bertha	London	1883-1893	Flowers	—	—	—	—	—	—	7	—	—	—	7
Maguire, Miss Helena J.	London	1881-1893	Domestic	—	—	7	—	4	—	21	—	—	1	33
Maguire, J.	London	1815-1816	Flowers	—	—	2	—	—	—	—	—	—	—	2
Maguire, Sidney Calton	London	1880-1882	Enamels	—	—	5	—	2	—	—	—	—	—	7
Maguire, Thomas Herbert	London	1846-1887	Figures	—	—	40	9	8	—	—	—	—	4	61
Mahomed, H.	Brighton	1837	Domestic	—	—	1	—	—	—	—	—	—	—	1
Mahomed, Mrs. J. D. K. *See* Miss Emma L. Black	—	—	—	—	—	—	—	—	—	—	—	—	—	—
Mahon, R.	London	1788-1789	Figures	—	—	3	—	—	—	—	—	—	—	3
Mahoney, James ‡	London	1866-1878	Domestic	—	—	6	—	—	—	10	—	—	5	21
Maignan, A.	Paris	1878	Figures	—	—	—	—	—	—	—	—	—	1	1
Maiks, G.	Penge	1878	Heads	—	—	—	—	1	—	—	—	—	—	1
Maile, Alfred	Langdale	1871-1889	Churches	—	—	5	—	2	—	—	1	—	3	11
Maile, J.	—	1824	Sporting	—	—	—	—	3	—	—	—	—	—	3
Maine, S. W.	—	1844	Architecture	—	—	1	—	—	—	—	—	—	—	1
Mainwaring, Miss	London	1822-1824	Miniatures	—	—	6	—	—	—	—	—	—	—	6
Mair, George	London	1831-1846	Architecture	—	—	15	—	2	—	1	—	—	—	18
Maisey, Thomas, P.N.W.C. ‡	London	1818-1840	Landscape	—	—	5	—	6	2	28	—	—	—	41

Name.	Town.	First and Last Year of Ex.	Speciality.	S. A.	F. S.	R. A.	B. I.	S. S.	O. W.	N.W.	G. G.	N. G.	V. E.	Total.
Maistre, F. W. S. Le. *See* L.	—	—	—	—	—	—	—	—	—	—	—	—	—	—
Maitland, Captain Alex. Fuller	Belfast	1887-1893	Sea Pieces	—	—	5	—	2	—	—	—	—	2	9
Maitland, J. E.	London	1882	River Scenes	—	—	—	—	—	—	—	—	—	1	1
Maitland, Paul F.	London	1887	Landscape	—	—	—	—	2	—	—	—	—	—	2
Majoli, Luigi	Rome	1880	Portraits	—	—	1	—	—	—	—	—	—	—	1
Major, Miss Charlotte. *See* Mrs. C. Wyllie.	—	—	—	—	—	—	—	—	—	—	—	—	—	—
Major, Henry A.	London	1859-1873	Fruit	—	—	—	—	6	—	—	—	—	—	6
Major, H. L.	London	1868	Fruit	—	—	—	—	1	—	—	—	—	—	1
Major, Mrs. R. H.	London	1848	Portraits	—	—	—	—	1	—	—	—	—	—	1
Major, Thomas, A.R.A.	London	1761-1776	Engraving	—	5	1	—	—	—	—	—	—	—	6
Major, W.	East Sheen	1873	Portraits	—	—	1	—	—	—	—	—	—	—	1
Major, W. Wreford	—	1878-1879	Portraits	—	—	—	—	—	—	—	2	—	—	2
Makin, J. R.	Manchester	1878	Domestic	—	—	—	—	—	—	—	—	—	1	1
Malapeau, E.	London	1871	Poultry	—	—	—	—	4	—	—	—	—	—	4
Malbon, William	London	1834	Sporting	—	—	—	—	1	—	—	—	—	—	1
Malchair, John. *See* Melchair.	—	—	—	—	—	—	—	—	—	—	—	—	—	—
Malcolm, Miss Beatrice	London	1892	Figures	—	—	—	—	—	—	—	—	—	1	1
Malcolm, J.	London	1862	Domestic	—	—	1	—	—	—	—	—	—	—	1
Malcolm, James Peller	London	1791	Landscape	—	—	2	—	—	—	—	—	—	—	2
Malcolm, Miss L.	London	1870	Fruit	—	—	—	—	2	—	—	—	—	—	2
Malcolm, R.	Broadstairs	1874-1879	Sea Pieces	—	—	1	—	2	—	—	—	—	7	10
Maldarelli, F.	Naples	1867	Historical	—	—	1	—	—	—	—	—	—	—	1
Malempré, L.	London	1887-1891	Domestic	—	—	7	—	—	—	—	—	—	7	14
Malempré, Louis Auguste	London	1848-1879	Sculpture	—	—	20	4	—	—	—	—	—	2	26
Malgo, S.	London	1788	Portraits	—	—	1	—	—	—	—	—	—	—	1
Maliphant, George §	London	1806-1833	Architecture	—	—	11	—	11	—	—	—	—	—	22
Maliphant, William	London	1887-1893	Domestic	—	—	2	—	5	—	3	—	—	1	11
Malkin, A. C.	London	1843-1855	Rivers	—	—	—	3	8	—	—	—	—	—	11
Malkin, S.	London	1821-1829	Landscape	—	—	3	9	4	—	—	—	—	—	16
Malkin, Miss	London	1846-1849	Landscape	—	—	—	—	2	—	—	—	—	—	2
Malleson, Katherine	Croydon	1870-1873	Landscape	—	—	—	—	—	—	—	—	—	8	8
Mallet, Harriette	London	1882	Flowers	—	—	—	—	—	—	—	—	—	3	3
Mallet, Pierre	Brighton	1887-1893	Etching	—	—	6	—	—	—	—	—	—	—	6
Mallison, F.	London	1802	Architecture	—	—	1	—	—	—	—	—	—	—	1
Mallock, G.	London	1838	Monuments	—	—	1	—	—	—	—	—	—	—	1
Mallock, M. J.	—	1876	Etching	—	—	—	—	—	—	—	—	—	1	1
Mallows, Charles Edward	London	1888-1892	Architecture	—	—	10	—	—	—	—	—	—	—	10
Malpas, Edward	London	1773-1780	Engraving	4	3	—	—	—	—	—	—	—	—	7
Malpas, T.	London	1796-1806	Architecture	—	—	5	—	—	—	—	—	—	—	5
Malroy, D. Florence	London	1857-1860	Figures	—	—	1	1	—	—	—	—	—	—	2
Maltby, Charles Frederick	London	1843	Architecture	—	—	1	—	—	—	—	—	—	—	1
Malton, C.	London	1807-1810	Architecture	—	—	3	—	—	—	—	—	—	—	3
Malton, James	London	1761-1803	Buildings	7	2	50	—	—	—	—	—	—	—	59
Malton, Thomas	London	1772-1785	Architecture	—	—	5	—	—	—	—	—	—	—	5
Malton, Thomas, Junr.	London	1768-1803	Buildings	—	2	128	—	—	—	—	—	—	—	130
Maminger, A.	London	1856	Domestic	—	—	—	1	—	—	—	—	—	—	1
Manara, O. (?) Horace de M.	London	1847-1849	Portraits	—	—	5	—	—	—	—	—	—	—	5
Mancini, A.	—	1893	Portraits	—	—	—	—	—	—	—	—	—	1	1
Mandy, J. C.	London	1811-1833	Portraits	—	—	24	—	—	2	—	—	—	—	26
Manet, Edward	Paris	1873-1874	Etching	—	—	—	—	—	—	—	—	—	4	4
Manfred, H.	London	1855	London	—	—	—	—	2	—	—	—	—	—	2
Manfredi, B.	London	1807-1811	Scriptural	—	—	2	2	—	—	—	—	—	—	4
Mangiarelli, N.	London	1878	Landscape	—	—	—	—	—	—	—	—	—	1	1
Mangil —. (?) Mangin	London	1763-1764	Sculpture	2	—	—	—	—	—	—	—	—	—	2
Mangles, Alice	Tongham	1881	Heather	—	—	—	—	—	—	—	—	—	1	1
Mangnall and Littlewood	Manchester	1890	Architecture	—	—	1	—	—	—	—	—	—	—	1
Manini, Chevalier Gaetano	London	1761-1775	Historical	7	19	—	—	—	—	—	—	—	—	26
Manley, C. Macdonald	London	1884-1889	Landscape	—	—	—	—	2	—	2	—	—	—	4
Manley, George P.	—	1848-1859	Landscape	—	—	10	—	2	—	—	—	—	2	14
Manley, Henry	London	1769-1771	Metal Work	6	—	—	—	—	—	—	—	—	—	6
Manley, H. B.	London	1863-1868	Fruit	—	—	1	—	2	—	—	—	—	—	3
Manly, Miss Alice Elfrida	London	1872-1893	Landscape	—	—	14	—	14	—	3	—	—	13	44
Manly, Miss Eleanor E.	London	1875-1893	Domestic	—	—	8	—	6	—	6	—	—	9	29
Manly, Mrs. Sarah	London	1887-1892	Flowers	—	—	1	—	—	—	3	—	—	—	4
Mann, Alexander ϕ	Glasgow	1883-1893	Domestic	—	—	10	—	17	—	—	—	—	13	40
Mann, Edward	London	1857-1870	Domestic	—	—	1	—	9	—	—	—	—	1	11
Mann, Miss Eliza, afterwards Mrs. Archibald Allan.	—	—	—	—	—	—	—	—	—	—	—	—	—	—
Mann, Miss Florence	Edinburgh	1883-1886	Portraits	—	—	3	—	4	—	—	—	—	1	8
Mann, Frank W.	London	1888-1893	Domestic	—	—	3	—	—	—	—	—	—	—	3
Mann, Harrington	London	1882-1892	Domestic	—	—	9	—	1	—	—	—	—	—	10
Mann, Joshua Hargrave Sams, R.B.A. §	London	1849-1884	Domestic	—	—	34	29	128	—	2	—	—	25	218

Name.	Town.	First and Last Year of Ex.	Speciality.	S. A.	F. S.	R. A.	B. I.	S. S.	O. W.	N. W.	G. G.	N. G.	V. E.	Total.
Mann, Mabel M.	London	1885	Flowers	—	—	—	—	1	—	—	—	—	—	1
Mann, W. H.	London	1881	Landscape	—	—	—	—	—	—	—	1	—	—	1
Manners, Miss E. F.	—	1806-1808	Landscape	—	—	6	—	—	—	—	—	—	—	6
Manners, Mrs. Henry. *See* Miss Violet Lindsay,	—	—	—	—	—	—	—	—	—	—	—	—	—	—
and Marchioness of Granby	London	1883-1886	Portraits	—	—	1	—	—	—	—	8	—	—	9
Manners, R.	—	1807-1808	Landscape	—	—	5	—	—	—	—	—	—	—	5
Manners, William, R.B.A. §	Bradford	1889-1893	Landscape	—	—	2	—	9	—	—	—	—	—	11
Manners, W. H.	London	1830	Portraits	—	—	1	—	—	—	—	—	—	—	1
Mannfeld, Conrad	London	1878-1893	Landscape	—	—	2	—	5	—	—	2	—	5	14
Mannin, Mrs. *See* Miss Millington	London	1833-1857	Miniatures	—	—	43	13	—	—	—	—	—	—	56
Manning, Charles	London	1801-1812	Sculpture	—	—	8	2	—	—	—	—	—	—	10
Manning, Miss Eliza F.	Surbiton	1879-1889	Domestic	—	—	2	—	—	—	1	—	—	4	7
Manning, J.	London	1832	Sculpture	—	—	1	—	—	—	—	—	—	—	1
Manning, Michael P.	—	1862	Landscape	—	—	1	—	—	—	—	—	—	—	1
Manning, M. R.	Dublin	1892	Flowers	—	—	—	—	1	—	—	—	—	—	1
Manning, R. H.	London	1841-1842	Landscape	—	—	2	—	—	—	—	—	—	—	2
Manning, Samuel	London	1806-1858	Sculpture	—	—	38	—	—	—	—	—	—	—	38
Manning, William Westley	London	1890-1893	Landscape	—	—	—	—	2	—	1	—	—	2	5
Manning and Mew	London	1856	Architecture	—	—	1	—	—	—	—	—	—	—	1
Mannskersch, J. C.	London	1799-1800	Landscape	—	—	4	—	—	—	—	—	—	—	4
Mansell, Major	—	1802	Portraits	—	—	1	—	—	—	—	—	—	—	1
Mansell, Miss Marianne	London	1876-1893	Miniatures	—	—	4	—	5	—	—	—	—	—	9
Mansell, W.	London	1786-1801	Illustrations	—	—	2	—	—	—	—	—	—	—	2
Mansell, Mrs.	Windsor	1822	Flowers	—	—	—	1	—	—	—	—	—	—	1
Mansfield, G.	London	1799-1803	Architecture	—	—	5	—	—	—	—	—	—	—	5
Mansfield, R. J.	London	1837	Architecture	—	—	1	—	—	—	—	—	—	—	1
Mansion, L.	London	1829-1835	Historical	—	—	3	—	1	—	—	—	—	—	4
Mans-Kirch, F. J.	London	1793-1819	Battle Pieces	—	—	10	2	—	—	—	—	—	—	12
Manson, George	Edinburgh	1873-1875	Figures	—	—	1	—	—	—	—	—	—	6	7
Mant, Captain C.	London	1872	Architecture	—	—	1	—	—	—	—	—	—	—	1
Mantell, Edward Walter	Swindon	1858-1860	Architecture	—	—	3	—	—	—	—	—	—	—	3
Manton, Miss Elizabeth	London	1868-1878	Domestic	—	—	—	—	5	—	—	—	—	12	17
Manton, G.	London	1818-1831	Portraits	—	—	15	—	—	—	—	—	—	—	15
Manton, G. Grenville	London	1878-1891	Portraits	—	—	23	—	5	—	—	—	—	8	36
Manuel —	London	1771-1783	Cattle	—	2	—	—	—	—	—	—	—	—	2
Manvele, G.	London	1795	Architecture	—	—	1	—	—	—	—	—	—	—	1
Manwaring, G. R.	London	1844-1845	Figures	—	—	1	—	3	—	—	—	—	—	4
Manzini, C.	London	1842	Portraits	—	—	3	—	—	—	—	—	—	—	3
Manzini, G.	London	1885	Sculpture	—	—	1	—	—	—	—	—	—	—	1
Maplestone, Miss Florence E.	London	1868-1885	Historical	—	—	—	—	19	—	2	—	—	—	21
Maplestone, Henry ‡	London	1841-1884	Landscape	—	—	—	—	11	—	349	—	—	2	362
Maraino, Innocenzo	London	1770	Architecture	—	—	1	—	—	—	—	—	—	—	1
Marais, Adolph	Arundel	1885	Landscape	—	—	1	—	—	—	—	—	—	—	1
Marak, Julius	Paris	1876	Charcoal	—	—	—	—	—	—	—	—	—	2	2
Marcello. *See also* Colonna-Castiglione	Paris	1865	Sculpture	—	—	1	—	—	—	—	—	—	—	1
Marcette, H.	Spa, Belgium	1854	Landscape	—	—	1	—	—	—	—	—	—	—	1
March, Edward	Leeds	1862-1867	Landscape	—	—	3	1	—	—	—	—	—	—	4
Marchant, Nathaniel, R.A., F.S.A.	London	1765-1811	Sculpture	17	—	40	4	—	—	—	—	—	—	61
Marchi, Guiseppe Filippo Liberati, F.S.A.	London	1766-1775	Engraving	18	—	—	—	—	—	—	—	—	—	18
Marcilly, Millet De. *See* D.	—	—	—	—	—	—	—	—	—	—	—	—	—	—
Marco —	—	1761	Flowers	—	1	—	—	—	—	—	—	—	—	1
Marcuard, C.	London	1810-1819	Portraits	—	—	3	—	—	—	—	—	—	—	3
Mare, De la. *See* D.	—	—	—	—	—	—	—	—	—	—	—	—	—	—
Mares, Miss E. J.	London	1854	Landscape	—	—	1	—	—	—	—	—	—	—	1
Mares, Henry	London	1833-1851	Sculpture	—	—	7	—	3	—	—	—	—	—	10
Mareshal, P.	London	1850	Enamels	—	—	2	—	—	—	—	—	—	—	2
Margetson, H. T.	London	1893	Sculpture	—	—	1	—	—	—	—	—	—	—	1
Margetson, William Henry	London	1881-1893	Portraits	—	—	16	—	2	—	3	6	*	6	33
Margetts, Miss Ada	Oxford	1861-1863	Flowers	—	—	3	3	2	—	—	—	—	—	8
Margetts, Mrs. Mary ‡	London	1841-1877	Flowers	—	—	1	—	—	—	124	—	—	—	125
Margitson, Mrs. Maria	Norwich	1857-1864	Fruit	—	—	—	1	9	—	—	—	—	—	10
Maria, De. *See* D.	—	—	—	—	—	—	—	—	—	—	—	—	—	—
Marichal, Peter	London	1870	Figures	—	—	—	—	—	—	—	—	—	1	1
Marie, Adrien	Paris	1875-1880	Figures	—	—	—	—	—	—	—	—	—	16	16
Maris, Jacobus	The Hague	1874-1881	Landscape	—	—	1	—	—	—	—	5	—	—	6
Maris, Willem	Paris	1878-1880	Animals	—	—	—	—	—	—	—	2	—	1	3
Marius de Maria	Rome	1887	Landscape	—	—	—	—	—	—	—	2	—	—	2
Mark, E. W.	London	1843	Portraits	—	—	2	—	—	—	—	—	—	—	2
Markes, A.	London	1833-1834	Architecture	—	—	2	—	—	—	—	—	—	—	2
Markes, Richmond W.	London	1824	Figures	—	—	—	1	—	—	—	—	—	—	1
Markham, W.	—	1796	Architecture	—	—	1	—	—	—	—	—	—	—	1
Markham, R.	—	1798-1808	Sea Pieces	—	—	3	—	—	—	—	—	—	—	3

Name.	Town.	First and Last Year of Ex.	Speciality.	S. A.	F. S.	R. A.	B. I.	S. S.	O. W.	N.W.	G. G.	N. G.	V. E.	Total.
Marks —	London	1791	Architecture	2	—	—	—	—	—	—	—	—	—	2
Marks, Miss Anne	London	1893	Figures	—	—	1	—	—	—	—	—	—	—	1
Marks, Barnett Samuel, R.C.A.	Cardiff	1859-1891	Figures	—	—	39	—	1	—	—	1	—	3	44
Marks, Edmund	London	1841-1869	Landscape	—	—	7	2	9	—	—	—	—	—	18
Marks, Miss Florence	London	1889-1892	Study	—	—	1	—	—	—	—	—	—	2	3
Marks, George	Penge	1876-1893	Landscape	—	—	45	—	29	—	16	—	—	32	122
Marks, Henry Stacy, R.A., R.W.S., H.R.C.A.,	—	—	—	—	—	—	—	—	—	—	—	—	—	—
H.F.R.P.E. †	London	1853-1893	Historical	—	—	84	4	3	150	—	15	—	105	361
Marks, J.	London	1790-1799	Architecture	—	—	8	—	—	—	—	—	—	—	8
Marks, J. G.	Mitcham	1866-1874	Domestic	—	—	—	—	—	—	—	—	—	9	9
Marlow, William	London	1762-1807	Landscape	125	2	25	—	—	—	—	—	—	—	152
Marlowe, Miss Florence	Sutton	1873-1888	Figures	—	—	1	—	5	—	—	—	—	1	7
Marny, Paul	Birmingham	1866-1890	Landscape	—	—	1	—	—	—	—	—	—	1	2
Marochetti, Baron Carlo, R.A.	London	1851-1867	Sculpture	—	—	35	—	—	—	—	—	—	—	35
Marolda, Emilio	London	1882	Sea Pieces	—	—	—	—	2	—	—	—	—	—	2
Marquis, J. Richard, R.H.A.	Dublin	1862-1884	Landscape	—	—	2	—	1	—	—	—	—	3	6
Marr, C. W.	London	1832	Landscape	—	—	—	—	1	—	—	—	—	—	1
Marr, J. W. Hamilton, A.R.C.A.	Kingswood	1885-1888	Landscape	—	—	—	—	—	—	—	1	—	2	3
Marr, Mrs. J. W. Hamilton (Sophie)	Kingswood	1892	Flowers	—	—	—	—	—	—	—	—	—	2	2
Marrable, Miss Edith. *See* Mrs. A. Ferguson ‖	London	1878-1882	Flowers	—	—	—	—	—	—	—	—	—	4	4
Marrable, Frederick	London	1843-1870	Architecture	—	—	12	—	—	—	—	—	—	—	12
Marrable, Mrs. ‖ late Miss Madeline Cockburn	London	1864-1892	Landscape	—	—	6	—	7	—	2	6	—	17	38
Marrian, J.	Birmingham	1818	Medals	—	—	1	—	—	—	—	—	—	—	1
Marriott. *See* Hambly and Marriott	—	—	Architecture	—	—	—	—	—	—	—	—	—	—	—
Marriott, Frederick	London	1891	Heads	—	—	1	—	—	—	—	—	—	—	1
Marris, R.	London	1770-1784	Landscape	—	4	10	—	—	—	—	—	—	—	14
Marrs, Mrs.	London	1871	Flowers	—	—	—	—	2	—	—	—	—	—	2
Marsden, Richard	London	1820-1824	Landscape	—	—	1	2	—	—	—	—	—	—	3
Marsden, T.	London	1824	Heads	—	—	—	1	—	—	—	—	—	—	1
Marsh, Arthur H., A.R.W.S., R.B.A. † §	London	1865-1893	Domestic	—	—	16	—	3	108	—	1	—	11	139
Marsh, Mrs. Arthur. *See* Mrs. M. R. Corbett.	—	—	—	—	—	—	—	—	—	—	—	—	—	—
Marsh, Charles F.	East Grinstead	1892-1893	Domestic	—	—	1	—	1	—	—	—	—	—	2
Marsh, Miss Emily F.	London	1893	Flowers	—	—	—	—	1	—	—	—	—	—	1
Marsh, J.	Woodside, Epping	1828-1830	Landscape	—	—	—	1	11	—	—	—	—	—	12
Marsh, Miss J.	London	1875	Flowers	—	—	—	—	1	—	—	—	—	—	1
Marsh, R.	London	1791	Miniatures	2	—	—	—	—	—	—	—	—	—	2
Marsh, Richard Brewster	London	1875	Architecture	—	—	1	—	—	—	—	—	—	—	1
Marsh, S.	London	1845	Architecture	—	—	1	—	—	—	—	—	—	—	1
Marshall, Benjamin	London	1800-1819	Sporting	—	—	13	—	—	—	—	—	—	—	13
Marshall, Charles	London	1828-1884	Landscape	—	—	54	52	149	—	19	—	—	38	312
Marshall, Charles, Junr.	London	1864-1886	Landscape	—	—	2	2	4	—	2	—	—	11	21
Marshall, Miss C.	London	1876	Buildings	—	—	1	—	—	—	—	—	—	—	1
Marshall, Charles Edward, R.B.A. §	London	1872-1893	Figures	—	—	13	—	31	—	—	—	—	14	58
Marshall, D.	London	1836-1837	Landscape	—	—	—	—	3	—	—	—	—	—	3
Marshall, F.	London	1824-1828	Landscape	—	—	3	—	2	—	—	—	—	—	5
Marshall, F.	Croydon	1876	Still Life	—	—	—	—	1	—	—	—	—	—	1
Marshall, F. J.	—	1848	Domestic	—	—	—	—	1	—	—	—	—	—	1
Marshall, G.	York	1822-1825	Portraits	—	—	4	—	—	—	—	—	—	—	4
Marshall, G. M. B.	London	1858	Domestic	—	—	—	—	1	—	—	—	—	—	1
Marshall, Henry J.	London	1880	Figures	—	—	—	—	1	—	—	—	—	—	1
Marshall, Herbert M., R.W.S., R.P.E. †	London	1871-1893	Landscape	—	—	2	—	8	277	—	—	1	43	331
Marshall, J.	London	1830	Sea Pieces	—	—	—	3	—	—	—	—	—	—	3
Marshall, John	London	1840-1879	Sporting	—	—	8	—	17	—	—	—	—	—	25
Marshall, John	Croydon	1881-1893	Fruit	—	—	10	—	—	—	—	—	1	10	21
Marshall, J. D.	London	1846-1860	Historical	—	—	5	3	1	—	—	—	—	—	9
Marshall, J. Fitz	Croydon	1876-1893	Still Life	—	—	16	—	13	—	—	6	17	20	72
Marshall, J. Miller	Norwich	1886-1890	Landscape	—	—	2	—	1	—	3	—	—	—	6
Marshall, Lambert	London	1828-1829	Sporting	—	—	—	1	1	—	—	—	—	—	2
Marshall, Mary	London	1829	Portraits	—	—	1	—	—	—	—	—	—	—	1
Marshall, Mrs. Philippa	Exeter	1868-1880	Flowers	—	—	—	—	2	—	—	—	—	3	5
Marshall, Peter Paul	Tottenham	1863-1877	Landscape	—	—	1	1	—	—	—	—	—	3	5
Marshall, R.	Oxford	1877	Game	—	—	—	—	1	—	—	—	—	—	1
Marshall, Mrs. Rose	Leeds	1879-1890	Flowers	—	—	10	—	16	—	—	2	—	6	34
Marshall, Roberto Angelo Kittermaster	London	1864-1890	Landscape	—	—	11	—	14	—	10	—	—	9	44
Marshall, T.	London	1827-1831	Engraving	—	—	3	—	5	—	—	—	—	—	8
Marshall, Thomas Falcon	Liverpool	1839-1878	Domestic	—	—	60	40	43	—	—	—	—	3	146
Marshall, Thomas Mervyn Bouchier	London	1855-1858	Figures	—	—	9	1	—	—	—	—	—	—	10
Marshall, W.	London	1870-1883	Sculpture	—	—	6	—	—	—	—	—	—	—	6
Marshall, Miss Wilhelmina	London	1890-1891	Domestic	—	—	2	—	—	—	—	—	—	1	3
Marshall, William Calder, R.A.	Edinburgh	1835-1891	Sculpture	—	—	141	18	13	—	—	—	—	—	172
Marshall, William Elstob	London	1859-1881	Sporting	—	—	8	5	18	—	—	—	—	9	40
Marsham, Miss	London	1852	Flowers	—	—	—	—	2	—	—	—	—	—	2

Name.	Town.	First and Last Year of Ex.	Speciality.	S. A.	F. S.	R. A.	B. I.	S. S.	O. W.	N. W.	G. G.	N. G.	V. E.	Total.
Marshman, J.	Bangor	1876	Bull-fight	—	—	—	—	—	—	—	—	—	1	1
Marston —	—	1825	Portraits	—	—	1	—	—	—	—	—	—	—	1
Marston, Colonel	—	1818	Landscape	—	—	1	—	—	—	—	—	—	—	1
Marston, F. R. W.	—	1891	Historical	—	—	—	—	—	—	—	—	—	1	1
Marston, Miss Mabel G.	London	1885-1893	Flowers	—	—	4	—	10	—	—	1	—	4	19
Mart, F. Griffiths	London	1892	Figures	—	—	—	—	—	—	1	—	—	—	1
Martell, J.	London	1780-1788	Still Life	7	—	9	—	—	—	—	—	—	—	16
Marten, Elliot H.	Hawick, N. B.	1886	Landscape	—	—	1	—	—	—	—	—	—	—	1
Marten, J.	Canterbury	1822-1834	Architecture	—	—	2	—	—	—	2	—	—	—	4
Marten, W. J.	Rome	1876	Domestic	—	—	—	—	—	—	—	—	—	2	2
Martens, Conrad	London	1833-1837	Moonlight	—	—	7	—	—	—	—	—	—	—	7
Martens, Henry	London	1828-1854	Battle Pieces	—	—	—	6	36	—	1	—	—	—	43
Martens, W. T. (?) J.	Rome	1874-1887	Venice	—	—	1	—	—	—	—	1	—	—	2
Martial, A. P.	Paris	1874-1881	Etching	—	—	—	—	—	—	—	—	—	6	6
Martial, R.	London	1881	Etching	—	—	—	—	—	—	—	—	—	1	1
Martin —	London	1821	Portraits	—	—	1	—	—	—	—	—	—	—	1
Martin, A.	London	1809-1817	Architecture	—	—	2	—	—	—	—	—	—	—	2
Martin, Ambrose ‡	London	1830-1844	Landscape	—	—	3	2	7	—	3	—	—	—	15
Martin, A. A.	London	1857-1861	Domestic	—	—	—	1	3	—	—	—	—	—	4
Martin, Carolus	London	1771-1772	Furniture	—	2	—	—	—	—	—	—	—	—	2
Martin, Charles	London	1834-1891	Portraits	—	—	53	2	9	—	3	—	—	9	76
Martin, C. H.	London	1838-1858	Landscape	—	—	12	—	11	—	—	—	—	—	23
Martin, David, F.S.A.	London	1765-1790	Portraits	—	—	73	—	2	—	—	—	—	—	75
Martin, David	Glasgow	1892	Landscape	—	—	—	—	—	—	1	—	—	—	1
Martin, D. W.	London	1867-1872	Oriental	—	—	—	—	—	—	—	—	—	3	3
Martin, Edward	Worthing	1845-1861	Landscape	—	—	—	4	10	—	—	—	—	11	25
Martin, Miss Elizabeth	London	1761-1783	Flowers	2	4	—	—	—	—	—	—	—	—	6
Martin, Elias, A.R.A.	London	1769-1790	Landscape	—	1	47	—	—	—	—	—	—	—	48
Martin, Mrs. E.	London	1876	Sculpture	—	—	1	—	—	—	—	—	—	—	1
Martin, Miss Eliza	London	1863-1868	Figures	—	—	5	—	2	—	—	—	—	11	18
Martin, Mrs. Florence	London	1876-1892	Figures	—	—	4	—	15	—	—	—	1	6	26
Martin, G.	London	1771-1772	Hair Work	—	2	—	—	—	—	—	—	—	—	2
Martin, Henry	Newlyn	1870-1892	Domestic	—	—	19	—	2	—	1	—	—	16	38
Martin, H. D.	—	1883-1885	Landscape	—	—	—	—	1	—	—	1	—	—	2
Martin, Henry Harrison	London	1847-1882	Figures	—	—	10	20	56	—	—	—	—	—	86
Martin, J.	Canterbury	1782-1802	Landscape	—	—	4	—	—	—	—	—	—	—	4
Martin, John, K.L. ‡	London	1811-1852	Scriptural	—	—	83	37	62	—	18	—	—	12	212
Martin, J.	—	1845	Landscape	—	—	1	—	—	—	—	—	—	—	1
Martin, Johann Friedrich	London	1771-1780	Engraving	9	4	—	—	—	—	—	—	—	—	13
Martin, John F.	London	1837-1851	Figures	—	—	—	2	19	—	—	—	—	—	21
Martin, John H.	London	1871-1889	Landscape	—	—	2	—	2	—	—	—	—	—	4
Martin, J. W.	London	1847	Game	—	—	—	—	2	—	—	—	—	—	2
Martin, L.	London	1851-1859	River Scenes	—	—	4	1	1	—	—	—	—	—	6
Martin, L.	London	1865	Sculpture	—	—	1	—	—	—	—	—	—	—	1
Martin, Miss Mary D.	London	1875-1882	Landscape	—	—	2	—	1	—	—	—	—	7	10
Martin, P.	London	1869	Alps	—	—	—	—	—	—	—	—	—	1	1
Martin, R.	London	1826-1838	Figures	—	—	2	1	21	—	—	—	—	—	24
Martin, R. T.	London	1844-1846	Figures	—	—	—	2	3	—	—	—	—	—	5
Martin, Robert Wallace	London	1863-1888	Sculpture	—	—	8	—	—	—	—	—	—	—	8
Martin, T.	London	1839	Historical	—	—	1	—	—	—	—	—	—	—	1
Martin, T. W.	—	1822	Portraits	—	—	1	—	—	—	—	—	—	—	1
Martin, William	London	1775-1831	Allegorical	—	—	22	4	1	—	—	—	—	—	27
Martin, W. R.	London	1847	Domestic	—	—	—	—	1	—	—	—	—	—	1
Martin, Y. F.	London	1845	Portraits	—	—	—	—	2	—	—	—	—	—	2
Martin, Miss	—	1824	Churches	—	—	1	—	—	—	—	—	—	—	1
Martin, St. *See* S.	—	—	—	—	—	—	—	—	—	—	—	—	—	—
Martindale —	—	1782	Landscape	—	2	—	—	—	—	—	—	—	—	2
Martineau, Mrs. Basil (Clara)	London	1873-1890	Flowers	—	—	3	—	4	—	—	—	—	3	10
Martineau, Miss Edith, A.R.W.S. †	London	1862-1893	Landscape	—	—	25	—	6	74	9	6	—	46	166
Martineau, Edward Henry	London	1853-1891	Architecture	—	—	3	—	—	—	—	—	—	—	3
Martineau, Miss Gertrude	London	1862-1891	Figures	—	—	12	—	9	—	5	1	—	40	67
Martineau, Robert Braithwaite	London	1852-1872	Historical	—	—	11	—	—	—	—	—	—	2	13
Martinetti, A.	London	1880	Domestic	—	—	—	—	1	—	—	—	—	—	1
Martino, Mrs. Francis Richard. *See* Miss Anna Blunden.	—	—	—	—	—	—	—	—	—	—	—	—	—	—
Martino, Cavalier Edward de	London	1879	Shipping	—	—	—	—	—	—	—	4	—	—	4
Martino, Del Don	London	1874-1879	Venice	—	—	2	—	—	—	—	—	—	3	5
Martyn, Dora	Kimbolton	1884-1886	Domestic	—	—	—	—	2	—	—	—	—	—	2
Martyn, Miss Ethel K., A.R.P.E.	London	1886-1893	Portraits	—	—	7	—	2	—	—	—	—	—	9
Martyn, Greville	Norwood	1886	Rustic	—	—	—	—	1	—	—	—	—	—	1
Martyn, T.	London	1808	Portraits	—	—	1	—	—	—	—	—	—	—	1
Martyr, J. Greville	Norwood	1887	Domestic	—	—	1	—	—	—	—	—	—	—	1
Martyr, T.	London	1794-1799	Architecture	—	—	8	—	—	—	—	—	—	—	8

Name.	Town.	First and Last Year of Ex.	Speciality.	S. A.	F. S.	R. A.	B. I.	S. S.	O. W.	N.W.	G. G.	N. G.	V. E.	Total.
MARVIN, J.	London	1815-1819	Architecture	—	—	5	—	—	—	—	—	—	—	5
MARVIN, PHILIP J.	Ryde	1875-1888	Architecture	—	—	12	—	—	—	—	—	—	—	12
MARVOLUTTI, B.	London	1850	Sculpture	—	—	2	—	—	—	—	—	—	—	2
MARWOOD, D.	Richmond	1888-1891	Landscape	—	—	—	—	—	—	2	—	—	4	6
MARWOOD, MISS LUCY. *See* Mrs. C. N. Kennedy.	—	—	—	—	—	—	—	—	—	—	—	—	—	—
MASARET —	—	1774	Sculpture	2	—	—	—	—	—	—	—	—	—	2
MASE, H.	London	1878	Figures	—	—	—	—	3	—	—	—	—	—	3
MASEY —	London	1769	Shipping	—	1	—	—	—	—	—	—	—	—	1
MASEY. *See* Norton and Masey	—	—	Architecture	—	—	—	—	—	—	—	—	—	—	—
MASEY, FRANCIS	London	1887-1889	Architecture	—	—	3	—	—	—	—	—	—	—	3
MASEY, PHILIP EDWARD	London	1858-1889	Architecture	—	—	8	2	—	—	—	—	—	—	10
MASKALL, MISS	London	1807-1823	Portraits	—	—	5	—	—	—	—	—	—	—	5
MASKALL, MISS ELIZA	London	1802-1833	Landscape	—	—	19	20	—	—	—	—	—	—	39
MASKALL, MISS MARY	London	1803-1832	Figures	—	—	17	2	1	—	—	—	—	—	20
MASKELL —	—	1825	Sculpture	—	—	1	—	—	—	—	—	—	—	1
MASON —	London	1807	Architecture	—	—	1	—	—	—	—	—	—	—	1
MASON, ABRAHAM JOHN	London	1829	Wood Engraving	—	—	—	—	1	—	—	—	—	—	1
MASON, ALFRED WILLIAM	London	1876-1882	Figures	—	—	—	—	2	—	—	—	—	4	6
MASON, BENJAMIN	London	1802-1807	Landscape	—	—	2	1	—	—	—	—	—	—	3
MASON, BLOSSOM	London	1881-1885	Flowers	—	—	—	—	2	—	—	—	—	—	2
MASON, CHARLES	London	1884	Figures	—	—	1	—	—	—	—	—	—	—	1
MASON, DAVID	London	1866	Sea Pieces	—	—	—	—	2	—	—	—	—	—	2
MASON, EDITH	London	1879-1880	Domestic	—	—	—	—	—	—	—	—	—	2	2
MASON, MISS ELEANOR	Denmark Hill	1864-1865	Figures	—	—	1	2	—	—	—	—	—	—	3
MASON, MRS. EVELYN	London	1884-1887	Flowers	—	—	2	—	2	—	—	—	—	—	4
MASON, ERNOLD A.	London	1883	Domestic	—	—	1	—	—	—	—	—	—	—	1
MASON, E. F.	London	1848	Figures	—	—	—	—	2	—	—	—	—	—	2
MASON, G. FINCH	London	1874-1876	Domestic	—	—	—	—	—	—	—	—	—	5	5
MASON, GEORGE HEMMING, A.R.A.	Rome	1857-1872	Landscape	—	—	25	—	—	—	—	—	—	12	37
MASON, JAMES	London	1761-1783	Engraving	17	19	—	—	—	—	—	—	—	—	36
MASON, JAMES	Twickenham	1826-1833	Sculpture	—	—	4	—	5	—	—	—	—	—	9
MASON, MISS MARY	Putney	1869-1891	Landscape	—	—	—	—	7	—	1	—	—	1	9
MASON, MILES B.	London	1877-1886	Landscape	—	—	1	—	12	—	—	—	—	1	14
MASON, MISS M. WATTS	London	1893	Figures	—	—	—	—	—	—	—	—	—	1	1
MASON, R. H.	Barnes	1857-1859	Still Life	—	—	—	—	—	—	—	—	—	8	8
MASON, S.	Kingston	1843	Architecture	—	—	1	—	—	—	—	—	—	—	1
MASON, S.	London	1872-1875	Landscape	—	—	1	—	6	—	—	—	—	—	7
MASON, T.	—	1829	Wood Engraving	—	—	—	—	2	—	—	—	—	—	2
MASON, WILLIAM	—	1782-1786	Figures	—	—	3	—	—	—	—	—	—	—	3
MASON, W.	London	1832	Architecture	—	—	1	—	—	—	—	—	—	—	1
MASON, W. H.	Chichester	1860-1888	Sea Pieces	—	—	6	8	19	—	1	—	—	43	77
MASON, WILLIAM HENRY	London	1858-1880	Landscape	—	—	2	7	1	—	—	—	—	2	12
MASON, M. MORTON	East Retford	1875-1877	Landscape	—	—	—	—	—	—	—	—	—	3	3
MASON, MRS.	Denmark Hill	1855-1865	Fruit	—	—	—	1	3	—	—	—	—	—	4
MASON, LE. *See* L.	—	—	—	—	—	—	—	—	—	—	—	—	—	—
MASQUERIER, JOHN JAMES	London	1795-1844	Portraits	—	—	71	18	—	—	—	—	—	—	89
MASSALOFF, N.	Paris	1872	Etching	—	—	—	—	—	—	—	—	—	1	1
MASSART, JOHN	London	1773-1774	Sculpture	—	—	2	—	—	—	—	—	—	—	2
MASSÉ, PIERRE AUGUSTIN	London	1888-1892	Etching	—	—	2	—	—	—	—	—	—	—	2
MASSES, W. J.	London	1881	Engraving	—	—	—	—	—	—	—	—	—	1	1
MASSET, ERNEST	London	1879-1880	Sea Pieces	—	—	—	—	—	—	—	—	—	3	3
MASSEY, FREDERICK	Penrhyn	1893	Sea Pieces	—	—	—	—	1	—	1	—	—	—	2
MASSEY, HENRY G., A.R.P.E.	London	1884-1891	Domestic	—	—	4	—	2	—	10	—	—	—	16
MASSINI, PROFESSOR	Rome	1877	Sculpture	—	—	—	—	—	—	—	1	—	—	1
MASSON, A.	London	1881	Engraving	—	—	—	—	—	—	—	—	—	1	1
MASSOT —	Geneva	1830-1836	Domestic	—	—	1	1	1	—	—	—	—	—	3
MASSY, E. MARTIN	Derby	1888-1890	Landscape	—	—	—	—	5	—	—	—	—	—	5
MASSY-BAKER, G. H.	London	1891	Portraits	—	—	—	—	—	—	—	—	—	1	1
MASTERS, E.	Woking	1869	Landscape	—	—	—	—	1	—	—	—	—	—	1
MASTERS, H.	Southampton	1876-1879	Landscape	—	—	—	—	5	—	—	—	—	—	5
MASTERS, W.	London	1866	Landscape	—	—	—	—	1	—	—	—	—	—	1
MATCAR, HUON ARTHUR	Liverpool	1883	Architecture	—	—	1	—	—	—	—	—	—	—	1
MATESDORF, T.	London	1886	Portraits	—	—	2	—	—	—	—	—	—	—	2
MATHER, A.	London	1834	Architecture	—	—	1	—	—	—	—	—	—	—	1
MATHER, JOHN ROBERT	Newcastle	1862-1873	Sea Pieces	—	—	—	—	13	—	—	—	—	4	17
MATHEWES, MISS BLANCHE	Sutton	1888-1893	Domestic	—	—	5	—	—	—	—	—	—	—	5
MATHEWS, MISS A.	London	1864-1868	Figures	—	—	—	—	6	—	—	—	—	—	6
MATHEWS, CHARLES J. (the actor)	London	1835	Landscape	—	—	1	—	—	—	—	—	—	—	1
MATHEWS, MRS. F. C.	London	1880-1892	Landscape	—	—	—	—	1	—	4	—	—	1	6
MATHEWS, JOHN CHESTER	London	1884-1888	Horses	—	—	—	—	—	—	—	1	—	1	2
MATHEWS, MISS MINNIE	London	1886-1887	Churches	—	—	2	—	—	—	—	—	—	—	2
MATHEWS, M. A. A.	Oxford	1857-1862	Still Life	—	—	1	5	—	—	—	—	—	—	6

Name.	Town.	First and Last Year of Ex.	Speciality.	S. A.	F. S.	R. A.	B. I.	S. S.	O. W.	N. W.	G. G.	N. G.	V. E.	Total.
Mathias, Gabriel	—	1761-1762	Portraits	—	7	—	—	—	—	—	—	—	—	7
Mathieu —	London	1881	Figures	—	—	—	—	—	—	—	—	—	1	1
Mathison, Andrea	London	1771-1775	Landscape	—	1	3	—	—	—	—	—	—	—	4
Matkin, Miss Susanna	Stamford	1884	Landscape	—	—	—	—	—	—	1	—	—	—	1
Matson, C.	London	1816-1819	Architecture	—	—	3	—	—	—	—	—	—	—	3
Mattalia, James	London	1862-1866	Domestic	—	—	—	4	—	—	—	—	—	—	4
Matthes, L.	London	1873-1879	Sculpture	—	—	2	—	—	—	—	—	—	—	2
Mattheson, Von. *See* V.	—	—	—	—	—	—	—	—	—	—	—	—	—	—
Matthew, T.	London	1840	Architecture	—	—	1	—	—	—	—	—	—	—	1
Matthews, A.	—	1801	Architecture	—	—	1	—	—	—	—	—	—	—	1
Matthews, C.	Highgate	1825	Ruins	—	—	2	—	—	—	—	—	—	—	2
Matthews, C. J.	London	1835	Lakes	—	—	1	—	—	—	—	—	—	—	1
Matthews, E.	London	1878	Landscape	—	—	—	—	—	—	—	—	—	2	2
Matthews, H.	London	1798-1808	Historical	—	—	12	—	—	—	—	—	—	—	12
Matthews, Mrs. H.	—	1801-1803	Landscape	—	—	2	—	—	—	—	—	—	—	2
Matthews, John	London	1772	Architecture	—	—	1	—	—	—	—	—	—	—	1
Matthews, John	Windsor	1822-1826	Landscape	—	—	1	1	—	—	—	—	—	—	2
Matthews, Joseph	London	1869-1881	Landscape	—	—	—	—	5	—	—	—	—	5	10
Matthews, Miss Julia B.	Richmond	1893	Historical	—	—	—	—	1	—	1	—	—	—	2
Matthews, J. C.	London	1886-1887	Domestic	—	—	—	—	2	—	—	—	—	—	2
Matthews, P. §	London	1828	Landscape	—	—	—	—	1	—	—	—	—	—	1
Matthews, R. A.	Earls Colne	1891	Landscape	—	—	—	—	1	—	—	—	—	—	1
Matthews, T.	—	1811	Portraits	—	—	1	—	—	—	—	—	—	—	1
Matthews, William	London	1876	Pencil	—	—	—	—	—	—	—	—	—	1	1
Matthews, W. L.	Birmingham	1822-1826	Architecture	—	—	3	—	1	—	—	—	—	—	4
Matthison, William	Banbury	1885-1893	Landscape	—	—	—	—	17	—	4	—	—	—	21
Matton, Miss Ida	Paris	1891	Sculpture	—	—	1	—	—	—	—	—	—	—	1
Mattos, Henry T. De. *See* D.	—	—	—	—	—	—	—	—	—	—	—	—	—	—
Matzura, P. J.	London	1816	Sculpture	—	—	1	—	—	—	—	—	—	—	1
Maucourt, Charles	London	1761-1767	Portraits	17	—	—	—	—	—	—	—	—	—	17
Maud, W. T.	London	1890	Portraits	—	—	—	—	—	—	—	—	—	1	1
Maugham, J.	—	1862	Waterfalls	—	—	1	—	—	—	—	—	—	—	1
Maugham, S. M.	London	1862	Domestic	—	—	—	—	1	—	—	—	—	—	1
Maughan, Miss	—	1861	Landscape	—	—	1	—	—	—	—	—	—	—	1
Maule, Henry	London	1849-1860	Landscape	—	—	3	4	4	—	—	—	—	—	11
Maule, James	Lewisham	1835-1863	Sea Pieces	—	—	10	5	9	—	—	—	—	1	25
Mauley, J.	London	1844	Sea Pieces	—	—	—	—	2	—	—	—	—	—	2
Maull, C.	—	1839	Sea Pieces	—	—	1	—	—	—	—	—	—	—	1
Maund, George C.	London	1853-1871	Landscape	—	—	3	—	8	—	—	—	—	—	11
Maundrell, Charles Gilder	Paris	1884-1891	Domestic	—	—	5	—	3	—	8	—	—	3	19
Mauqué, A. R.	London	1831	Cattle	—	—	1	—	—	—	—	—	—	—	1
Maur, W. C.	London	1881	Landscape	—	—	—	—	2	—	—	—	—	—	2
Maurer, Jacob	London	1872	Landscape	—	—	—	—	1	—	—	—	—	—	1
Maurier, Du. *See* D.	—	—	—	—	—	—	—	—	—	—	—	—	—	—
Mauris, J.	London	1774-1775	Enamels	—	—	9	—	—	—	—	—	—	—	9
Mauve, Anton	—	1880	Rustic	—	—	—	—	—	—	—	3	—	—	3
Mavrogordato, A. J.	London	1892-1893	Buildings	—	—	2	—	—	—	—	—	—	—	2
Maw, John Hornby	Hastings	1840-1848	Architecture	—	—	6	—	—	—	—	—	—	—	6
Mawbrye, E.	London	1782	Portraits	—	—	1	—	—	—	—	—	—	—	1
Mawe, Miss Annie L.	Chislehurst	1891-1893	Churches	—	—	—	—	1	—	1	—	—	—	2
Mawe, G.	—	1843	Portraits	—	—	1	—	—	—	—	—	—	—	1
Mawe, S.	—	1838	Sculpture	—	—	1	—	—	—	—	—	—	—	1
Mawley, E.	London	1807	Architecture	—	—	1	—	—	—	—	—	—	—	1
Mawley, George	London	1858-1872	Landscape	—	—	24	—	26	—	—	—	—	56	106
Mawley, Henry	London	1817-1841	Architecture	—	—	8	—	—	—	—	—	—	—	8
Mawson. *See* Lockwood and Mawson	—	—	Architecture	—	—	—	—	—	—	—	—	—	—	—
Mawson, Miss Elizabeth Cameron	Gateshead	1877-1892	Flowers	—	—	2	—	4	—	7	—	—	2	15
Mawson and Hudson	Bedford	1891	Architecture	—	—	1	—	—	—	—	—	—	—	1
Maxie, Paul	London	1869	Animals	—	—	—	—	—	—	—	—	—	1	1
Maximos, Mrs.	London	1887	Pastels	—	—	1	—	—	—	—	—	—	—	1
Maxse, Mrs.	London	1890	Malaga	—	—	—	—	—	—	—	—	—	2	2
Maxwell, George	London	1787-1789	Landscape	—	—	4	—	—	—	—	—	—	—	4
Maxwell, Hamilton, R.S.W.	Glasgow	1883-1887	Landscape	—	—	1	—	1	—	2	—	—	—	4
Maxwell, Miss H. C.	London	1837-1839	Landscape	—	—	2	—	1	—	—	—	—	—	3
Maxwell, R.	London	1840-1841	Figures	—	—	2	—	2	—	—	—	—	—	4
May, A.	London	1813	Portraits	—	—	1	—	—	—	—	—	—	—	1
May, Arthur Dampier	Lee	1872-1893	Landscape	—	—	23	—	9	—	3	3	—	15	53
May, Arthur Powell	Lee	1875-1893	Landscape	—	—	1	—	22	—	9	—	—	16	48
May, Mrs. A. S.	London	1887-1892	Landscape	—	—	—	—	1	—	—	2	5	—	8
May, A. W.	London	1875-1891	Landscape	—	—	6	—	—	—	—	—	—	4	10
May, B.	London	1819	Architecture	—	—	1	—	—	—	—	—	—	—	1
May, Charles	London	1771-1783	Portraits	—	27	1	—	—	—	—	—	—	—	28

Name.	Town.	First and Last Year of Ex.	Speciality.	S. A.	F. S.	R. A.	B. I.	S. S.	O.W.	N.W.	G. G.	N. G.	V. E.	Total.
May, Edward John	Turnham Green	1881-1892	Architecture	—	—	22	—	—	—	—	—	—	—	22
May, Mrs. Frank (Clementina)	Elstree	1884-1892	Domestic	—	—	—	—	2	—	—	—	—	2	4
May, Miss Gertrude Brooke	London	1887-1893	Landscape	—	—	2	—	3	—	—	3	5	—	13
May, Mrs. Gisborne	London	1845-1848	Landscape	—	—	9	—	—	—	—	—	—	—	9
May, Henry G.	Twickenham	1867-1868	Sculpture	—	—	2	—	—	—	—	—	—	—	2
May, H. Goulton	Highgate	1886-1887	Domestic	—	—	—	—	1	—	2	—	—	—	3
May, James	London	1860-1866	Domestic	—	—	1	—	9	—	—	—	—	—	10
May, Miss Kate	London	1877-1883	Figures	—	—	4	—	2	—	—	—	—	2	8
May, Miss Margery	London	1879-1885	Rustic	—	—	1	—	—	—	—	—	—	4	5
May, R.	London	1852	Domestic	—	—	1	—	—	—	—	—	—	—	1
May, Thomas	Romsey	1766	Sculpture	—	1	—	—	—	—	—	—	—	—	1
May, William Charles	London	1875-1888	Sculpture	—	—	17	—	1	—	—	—	—	—	18
May, W. Holmes, R.P.E.	Merton	1880	Landscape	—	—	—	—	1	—	—	—	—	—	1
May, Walter William, R.I. ‡ φ	London	1859-1893	Sea Pieces	—	—	5	1	12	—	281	—	—	45	344
Mayaud, J. B.	London	1821-1826	Portraits	—	—	16	—	—	—	—	—	—	—	16
Maye, Henry Thomas	London	1854-1867	Domestic	—	—	3	—	2	—	—	—	—	—	5
Mayer, A.	London	1825-1841	Figures	—	—	8	—	5	—	—	—	—	—	13
Mayer, A.	London	1865	River Scenes	—	—	1	—	—	—	—	—	—	—	1
Mayer, Mrs. (Millicent Phelps)	London	1893	Figures	—	—	—	—	—	—	—	—	—	1	1
Mayer, Miss	—	1805	Landscape	—	—	1	—	—	—	—	—	—	—	1
Mayhew, C. and G.	London	1837	Architecture	—	—	1	—	—	—	—	—	—	—	1
Mayhew, G. W.	London	1839	Buildings	—	—	1	—	—	—	—	—	—	—	1
Mayhew, J.	London	1792-1796	Architecture	—	—	6	—	—	—	—	—	—	—	6
Maynard, Master	London	1764-1775	Still Life	—	6	—	—	—	—	—	—	—	—	6
Maynard, Harriette	London	1885	Domestic	—	—	—	—	1	—	—	—	—	—	1
Maynard, Thomas	London	1777-1812	Portraits	—	—	36	—	—	—	—	—	—	—	36
Maynard, Miss	—	1813-1814	Still Life	—	—	2	—	—	—	—	—	—	—	2
Mayo, Miss M.	Winchester	1873	Buildings	—	—	—	—	—	—	—	—	—	1	1
Mayor, Barnaby, F.S.A.	London	1767-1774	Landscape	15	—	—	—	—	—	—	—	—	—	15
Mayor, Fred.	London	1888-1892	Domestic	—	—	4	—	2	—	—	—	—	—	6
Mazell, Peter, F.S.A.	London	1761-1797	Engraving	46	—	2	—	—	—	—	—	—	—	48
Mazzoni, A.	London	1875	Flowers	—	—	—	—	—	—	—	—	—	1	1
Mead, C.	London	1794	Figures	—	—	2	—	—	—	—	—	—	—	2
Mead, J. C.	London	1819-1827	Architecture	—	—	8	—	—	—	—	—	—	—	8
Mead, Larkin G.	Florence	1891	Sculpture	—	—	1	—	—	—	—	—	—	—	1
Mead, Miss Mary P.	London	1877-1883	Landscape	—	—	—	—	6	—	—	—	—	1	7
Mead, T.	London	1867-1868	Landscape	—	—	—	—	4	—	—	—	—	—	4
Mead, Miss	—	1778	Crayons	—	—	1	—	—	—	—	—	—	—	1
Meade, Arthur	St. Ives, Cornw'l	1888-1893	Figures	—	—	7	—	2	—	—	—	1	1	11
Meadows, Arthur Joseph	London	1862-1885	Sea Pieces	—	—	4	10	22	—	—	—	—	—	36
Meadows, Edwin L.	London	1854-1872	Landscape	—	—	5	4	24	—	—	—	—	—	33
Meadows, J.	London	1812-1845	Figures	—	—	8	1	8	—	—	—	—	—	17
Meadows, J.	London	1816-1823	Landscape	—	—	3	—	—	—	—	—	—	—	3
Meadows, James	London	1854-1863	Sea Pieces	—	—	21	14	18	—	—	—	—	35	88
Meadows, James Edwin	London	1853-1875	Landscape	—	—	26	17	55	—	—	—	—	42	140
Meadows, Joseph Kenny	London	1830-1838	Portraits	—	—	1	—	4	—	—	—	—	—	5
Meadows, J. M.	London	1849	Landscape	—	—	—	—	1	—	—	—	—	—	1
Meadows, K.	London	1845-1853	Dramatic	—	—	2	—	—	—	—	—	—	—	2
Meadows, W.	London	1830-1832	Portraits	—	—	3	—	—	—	—	—	—	—	3
Meakin, Miss M. L.	London	1843-1862	Portraits	—	—	11	—	—	—	—	—	—	—	11
Mearns, A.	Lewisham	1855-1864	Sporting	—	—	—	4	2	—	—	—	—	—	6
Mearns, Miss Fanny	London	1870-1881	Landscape	—	—	5	—	13	—	—	—	—	—	18
Mearns, Miss Lois	Faversham	1864-1880	Domestic	—	—	2	—	14	—	—	—	—	—	16
Mears, P.	—	1825	Landscape	—	—	1	—	—	—	—	—	—	—	1
Mease, J.	London	1797-1798	Sporting	—	—	2	—	—	—	—	—	—	—	2
Measham, Henry	Manchester	1867-1883	Portraits	—	—	18	—	—	—	1	—	—	9	28
Measor, W.	Exeter	1837-1864	Scriptural	—	—	11	1	8	—	—	—	—	—	20
Measor, W. B. M.	London	1854-1872	Portraits	—	—	8	—	—	—	—	—	—	—	8
Medallists, Society of	—	1888-1889	Medals	—	—	—	—	—	—	—	—	4	—	4
Medina, John	London	1772-1774	Portraits	6	—	—	—	—	—	—	—	—	—	6
Medland, J.	London	1789-1828	Architecture	—	—	14	—	1	—	—	—	—	—	15
Medland, John	London	1875-1892	Churches	—	—	2	—	1	—	3	—	—	3	9
Medland, J. G.	London	1875-1877	Flowers	—	—	—	—	6	—	—	—	—	—	6
Medland, Thomas	Hertford	1777-1822	Landscape	—	—	30	5	—	—	—	—	—	—	35
Medland, W.	London	1808-1814	Portraits	—	—	3	—	—	—	—	—	—	—	3
Medland, Miss	Hertford	1808	Heads	—	—	1	—	—	—	—	—	—	—	1
Medley, Samuel	London	1792-1805	Domestic	—	—	28	—	—	—	—	—	—	—	28
Medlycott, Hubert J.	Somerset	1878-1893	River Scenes	—	—	—	—	24	—	15	3	—	11	53
Medwin, Leslie	London	1892	Landscape	—	—	—	—	—	—	—	—	—	1	1
Mee, A. P.	London	1824-1837	Architecture	—	—	8	—	—	—	—	—	—	—	8
Mee, Frank W.	Manchester	1892	Architecture	—	—	1	—	—	—	—	—	—	—	1
Mee, Mrs., late Miss Anne Foldstone	London	1804-1837	Miniatures	—	—	39	3	—	—	—	—	—	—	42

Name.	Town.	First and Last Year of Ex.	Speciality.	S. A.	F. S.	R. A.	B. I.	S. S.	O. W.	N.W.	G. G.	N. G.	V. E.	Total.
Meek, Mrs. M. A.	London	1832-1837	Landscape	—	—	1	3	8	—	—	—	—	—	12
Meen, Margaret	London	1775-1810	Flowers	—	—	6	—	—	—	—	—	—	3	9
Meers, Mrs. *See* Miss Dujardin	London	1835-1836	Landscape	—	—	—	1	1	—	—	—	—	—	2
Meeson, Frederick R.	London	1876	Architecture	—	—	1	—	—	—	—	—	—	—	1
Meggison, J. T.	Durham	1869	Figures	—	—	—	—	1	—	—	—	—	—	1
Mégret, A.	London	1863-1866	Sculpture	—	—	8	—	—	—	—	—	—	—	8
Megson, A.	London	1865-1867	Landscape	—	—	1	—	—	—	—	—	—	2	3
Mein, Miss Margaret J.	Edinburgh	1885-1891	Study	—	—	1	—	1	—	1	—	—	—	3
Meissonier, Jean Louis Ernest, Hon. R.A.	Paris	1841-1877	Historical	—	—	2	—	—	—	—	—	—	1	3
Mejanel, P.	London	1834	Portraits	—	—	1	—	—	—	—	—	—	—	1
Mekel, Ferté	London	1809-1810	Flowers	—	—	—	3	—	—	—	—	—	—	3
Melby, Wilhelm	London	1853-1868	Sea Pieces	—	—	11	15	4	—	—	—	—	5	35
Melchair, John	Oxford	1773	Landscape	—	—	1	—	—	—	—	—	—	—	1
Melchior, Wilhelm	London	1850-1851	Sporting	—	—	3	1	—	—	—	—	—	—	4
Meldrum, Thomas	Nottingham	1886-1891	Rustic	—	—	5	—	—	—	—	—	—	—	5
Melingue, Gaston	London	1879	Etching	—	—	—	—	—	—	—	—	—	1	1
Melle, Francesco	London	1773-1775	Historical	1	6	—	—	—	—	—	—	—	—	7
Mellian, C. F. Maximilian	London	1763-1764	Sculpture	—	2	—	—	—	—	—	—	—	—	2
Melling, Henry	London	1829-1853	Battle Pieces	—	—	2	3	5	—	—	—	—	—	10
Mellish, Thomas	London	1761-1766	Sea Pieces	5	—	—	—	—	—	—	—	—	—	5
Melville, Alexander	London	1846-1878	Battle Pieces	—	—	4	4	8	—	—	—	—	—	16
Melville, Mrs. Alexander. ‖ *See* Miss Eliza Anne Smallbone	London	1856-1883	Scriptural	—	—	6	11	24	—	—	—	—	—	41
Melville, Arthur, A.R.W.S., H.R.S.A., R.S.W.†	London	1878-1893	Figures	—	—	13	—	—	19	8	5	1	5	51
Melville, Henry	London	1826-1841	Figures	—	—	1	—	19	—	—	—	—	—	20
Melville, Harden S.	London	1837-1879	Domestic	—	—	6	10	17	—	—	—	—	—	33
Melville, Miss Pattie	—	1868-1869	Figures	—	—	—	—	3	—	—	—	—	—	3
Melville, W.	London	1851-1861	Figures	—	—	—	1	—	—	—	—	—	1	2
Mencie, M.	Preston	1873	Birds	—	—	—	—	1	—	—	—	—	—	1
Mencks, Chevalier	London	1766	Figures	—	1	—	—	—	—	—	—	—	—	1
Mendham, Miss Edith	Clifton	1888	Historical	—	—	—	—	—	—	1	—	—	—	1
Mendham, Robert	Eye	1821-1858	Domestic	—	—	2	4	—	—	—	—	—	—	6
Mendoza, A. M.	London	1878-1887	Mythological	—	—	1	—	1	—	—	—	—	—	2
Menpes, Mortimer L., F.R.G.S., R.B.A., R.P.E.§	London	1880-1892	Domestic	—	—	30	—	30	—	6	20	—	5	91
Menta, Edouard	Nice	1882-1891	Lakes	—	—	3	—	—	—	—	—	—	—	3
Menzel, Professor Adolph Frederic Erdman Hon. R.W.S.†	Berlin	1882-1888	Buildings	—	—	—	—	—	3	—	1	—	—	4
Menzies, John	London	1864-1892	Landscape	—	—	4	—	2	—	1	—	—	3	10
Menzies, Mrs. John (Maria)	Hull	1880-1885	Landscape	—	—	3	—	—	—	3	—	—	—	6
Menzies, Miss Maria	Hull	1886	Landscape	—	—	—	—	—	—	1	—	—	—	1
Menzies, William A.	London	1886-1890	Domestic	—	—	4	—	1	—	1	—	—	—	7
Meo, Gaetana	London	1875-1893	Landscape	—	—	1	—	4	—	—	17	18	2	42
Mequignon, P.	London	1791-1826	Portraits	—	—	7	—	—	—	—	—	—	—	7
Mercati —	—	1767-1769	Landscape	—	11	—	—	—	—	—	—	—	—	11
Mercer, Frederick	Birmingham	1872-1893	Landscape	—	—	—	—	6	—	4	—	—	4	14
Mercier —	London	1777-1778	Flowers	2	—	1	—	—	—	—	—	—	—	3
Mercier, Major Charles	Manchester	1863	Portraits	—	—	1	—	—	—	—	—	—	—	1
Mercier, Philip	London	1760-1779	Figures	3	—	1	—	—	—	—	—	—	—	4
Mercier, Miss Ruth	Cannes	1885	Landscape	—	—	1	—	—	—	1	2	—	—	4
Mercier, Mrs.	—	1761	Miniatures	5	—	—	—	—	—	—	—	—	—	5
Meredith, G.	London	1772-1799	Architecture	—	—	13	—	—	—	—	—	—	—	13
Meredith, M.	London	1810-1811	Architecture	—	—	2	—	—	—	—	—	—	—	2
Meredith, William	Manchester	1873-1874	Landscape	—	—	—	—	—	—	—	—	—	2	2
Meredith, Miss	London	1766-1777	Needlework	4	—	—	—	—	—	—	—	—	—	4
Meredyth, C.	—	1833	Ruins	—	—	1	—	—	—	—	—	—	—	1
Merignan, Miss A.	London	1866	Figures	—	—	—	—	—	—	—	—	—	1	1
Merle, Hugues	Paris	1869	Figures	—	—	2	—	—	—	—	—	—	—	2
Merlin, C. E. P.	Athens	1880	Figures	—	—	1	—	—	—	—	—	—	—	1
Merrett, T. H.	Romford	1844	Sculpture	—	—	1	—	—	—	—	—	—	—	1
Merrett, Walter	London	1873-1893	Sculpture	—	—	21	—	6	—	—	—	—	—	27
Merrick, Mrs. Emily M.	London	1879-1893	Domestic	—	—	9	—	13	—	—	3	—	4	29
Merrifield, T.	London	1815-1823	Sculpture	—	—	16	1	—	—	—	—	—	—	17
Merrifield, Mrs.	London	1875	Buildings	—	—	—	—	1	—	—	—	—	—	1
Merrifield, Mrs.	Brighton	1851	Portraits	—	—	—	—	2	—	—	—	—	—	2
Merrin. *See* Collins and Merrin	—	—	Architecture	—	—	—	—	—	—	—	—	—	—	—
Merritt, Mrs. Henry. ‖ *See* Miss Anna Lea	London	1878-1893	Portraits	—	—	26	—	—	—	—	4	3	19	52
Merritt, T. L.	Maidstone	1847	Flowers	—	—	1	—	—	—	—	—	—	—	1
Merritt, William J.	London	1886-1890	Sea Pieces	—	—	5	—	3	—	1	—	—	6	15
Merry, Godfrey	London	1883-1891	Domestic	—	—	2	—	8	—	—	—	—	5	15
Mertz, J. C.	Amsterdam	1848-1850	Domestic	—	—	3	—	—	—	—	—	—	—	3
Mesdag, Hendrik Willem	The Hague	1871-1890	Sea Pieces	—	—	10	—	—	—	—	2	2	5	19

Name.	Town.	First and Last Year of Ex.	Speciality.	S. A.	F. S.	R. A.	B. I.	S. S.	O. W.	N.W.	G. G.	N.G.	V.E.	Total.
Mesgrigny, F. de	Paris	1881	Landscape	—	—	—	—	—	—	—	2	—	—	2
Mess, N.	Scheveningen	1891	Sculpture	—	—	1	—	—	—	—	—	—	—	1
Messing, John	London	1773-1774	Landscape	2	—	1	—	—	—	—	—	—	—	3
Metcalfe, Mrs. A.	London	1845-1849	Scriptural	—	—	1	—	1	—	—	—	—	—	2
Metcalfe, W.	London	1861	Landscape	—	—	1	—	3	—	—	—	—	—	4
Metcalfe, Miss	London	1830	Copies	—	—	—	—	3	—	—	—	—	—	3
Metheun, Cathcart W.	—	1884	Landscape	—	—	—	—	—	—	1	—	—	—	1
Metz, Conrad Martin	London	1774-1794	Portraits	2	3	30	—	—	—	—	—	—	—	35
Metz, Miss Gertrude	London	1772-1774	Fruit	5	—	5	—	—	—	—	—	—	—	10
Metz, S.	London	1791	Mythological	—	—	1	—	—	—	—	—	—	—	1
Metzmacher, Emile Pierre	London	1883	Figures	—	—	1	—	—	—	—	—	—	—	1
Meulen, F. P. J.	—	1880	Domestic	—	—	—	—	—	—	—	1	—	—	1
Meulen, Vander. *See* V.	—	—	—	—	—	—	—	—	—	—	—	—	—	—
Meunier, Madame	London	1836	Study	—	—	—	1	2	—	—	—	—	—	3
Meuron, De. *See* D.	—	—	—	—	—	—	—	—	—	—	—	—	—	—
Meute, C.	London	1881	Figures	—	—	—	—	—	—	—	—	—	1	1
Mew, Frederick. *See also* Kendall and Mew, *and* Manning and Mew	London	1858-1874	Architecture	—	—	4	—	—	—	—	—	—	—	4
Meyden, Van. *See* V.	—	—	—	—	—	—	—	—	—	—	—	—	—	—
Meyer, Miss Beatrice	London	1873-1893	Historical	—	—	1	—	48	—	4	—	—	18	71
Meÿer, Miss Constance	London	1866-1882	Flowers	—	—	—	—	—	—	—	—	—	23	23
Meyer, F.	London	1792-1794	Architecture	—	—	3	—	—	—	—	—	—	—	3
Meyer, Frederick John	London	1826-1844	Portraits	—	—	21	3	42	—	—	—	—	—	66
Meyer, F. W.	Putney	1869-1892	Sea Pieces	—	—	21	—	41	—	—	—	—	8	70
Meyer, Hendrick	London	1790-1804	Landscape	—	—	13	—	—	—	—	—	—	—	13
Meyer, Hans	Berlin	1876	Engraving	—	—	—	—	—	—	—	—	—	1	1
Meyer, Henry §	London	1821-1833	Engraving	—	—	12	1	105	—	—	—	—	—	118
Meyer, H. B. F.	—	1829-1830	Portraits	—	—	—	—	4	—	—	—	—	—	4
Meyer, J.	London	1791	Landscape	—	—	4	—	—	—	—	—	—	—	4
Meyer, Jeremiah, R.A.	London	1760-1783	Miniatures	13	—	18	—	—	—	—	—	—	—	31
Meÿer, Miss Julia	London	1893	Flowers	—	—	—	—	—	—	—	—	—	1	1
Meyer, Jean Georges	Berlin	1863	Domestic	—	—	1	—	—	—	—	—	—	—	1
Meyer, M.	Esher	1834	Game	—	—	2	—	—	—	—	—	—	—	2
Meÿer, Miss Margaret	London	1872-1886	Flowers	—	—	1	—	2	—	—	—	—	5	8
Meÿer, Mary H.	London	1868-1885	Flowers	—	—	—	—	—	—	—	—	—	16	16
Meyer, T.	London	1843-1852	Architecture	—	—	4	—	—	—	—	—	—	—	4
Meyerheim, Franz	Berlin	1879	Pencil	—	—	—	—	—	—	—	—	—	4	4
Meyerheim, Paul	Berlin	1877-1883	Rustic	—	—	—	—	—	—	2	1	—	14	17
Meyerheim, Robert	London	1875-1893	Landscape	—	—	30	—	14	—	2	—	—	16	62
Meyers, Adolph C.	New Brighton	1891-1893	Landscape	—	—	2	—	—	—	—	—	—	—	2
Meymott, W.	London	1784-1788	Architecture	—	—	2	—	—	—	—	—	—	—	2
Meyrick, Miss Myra	Aylsham	1889-1891	Algiers	—	—	1	—	—	—	3	—	—	—	4
Meyrick, Miss	Barnes	1837	Landscape	—	—	—	—	6	—	—	—	—	—	6
Mezzara, Charles.	Paris	1890	Portraits	—	—	1	—	—	—	—	—	—	—	1
Mezzora, M.	London	1815	Figures	—	—	—	1	—	—	—	—	—	—	1
Michael, Frederick Howard	London	1892-1893	Domestic	—	—	1	—	1	—	—	—	—	1	3
Michael, L. H.	London	1845-1874	Landscape	—	—	8	—	12	—	—	—	—	—	20
Michael, Max	London	1839-1869	Domestic	—	—	4	—	—	—	—	—	—	2	6
Michael, W. A.	London	1853-1892	Landscape	—	—	—	—	1	—	—	—	—	4	5
Michel, St. *See* S.	—	—	—	—	—	—	—	—	—	—	—	—	—	—
Michele, De. *See* D.	—	—	—	—	—	—	—	—	—	—	—	—	—	—
Michelin, M. J.	Paris	1850-1851	Figures	—	—	2	—	—	—	—	—	—	—	2
Michelli, Cavaliere M.	London	1825	Landscape	—	—	—	1	—	—	—	—	—	—	1
Michetti, Carlo	—	1878-1880	Figures	—	—	—	—	—	—	—	—	—	2	2
Michie, J.	Acton	1870-1875	Domestic	—	—	3	—	12	—	—	—	—	—	15
Michie, John Coutts-, A.R.S.A.	Aberdeen	1889-1893	Landscape	—	—	6	—	3	—	—	3	—	4	16
Michie, Miss M. Coutts-	Aberdeen	1892	Flowers	—	—	1	—	—	—	—	—	—	—	1
Michie, John D.	Edinburgh	1864	Landscape	—	—	1	—	—	—	—	—	—	—	1
Michold, E.	London	1860	Domestic	—	—	—	—	1	—	—	—	—	—	1
Micholls, Miss A.	Manchester	1872-1877	Figures	—	—	2	—	2	—	—	—	—	—	4
Mickleham, R.	London	1812	Architecture	—	—	1	—	—	—	—	—	—	—	1
Micklethwaite, John Thomas	London	1877-1881	Architecture	—	—	2	—	—	—	—	—	—	—	2
Micklethwaite (J. T.) and Clarke (Somers)	London	1890	Architecture	—	—	1	—	—	—	—	—	—	—	1
Micocci, Guiseppe	London	1887	Mountains	—	—	—	—	—	—	—	1	—	—	1
Middiman, Samuel	London	1772-1824	Landscape	6	1	11	3	—	—	—	—	—	—	21
Middleton —	Manchester	1838	Architecture	—	—	1	—	—	—	—	—	—	—	1
Middleton, Charles, F.S.A.	London	1762-1772	Sculpture	6	—	—	—	—	—	—	—	—	—	6
Middleton, Charles	Salisbury	1778-1793	Architecture	4	—	11	—	—	—	—	—	—	—	15
Middleton, Miss Fanny	York	1884-1887	Landscape	—	—	—	—	1	—	1	—	—	—	2
Middleton, J.	London	1781	Architecture	—	—	1	—	—	—	—	—	—	—	1
Middleton, John	Norwich	1847-1855	Landscape	—	—	14	15	—	—	—	—	—	—	29
Middleton, James Godsell	London	1826-1872	Portraits	—	—	78	30	50	—	—	—	—	38	196

Name.	Town.	First and Last Year of Ex.	Speciality.	S. A.	F. S.	R. A.	B. I.	S. S.	O. W.	N.W.	G. G.	N. G.	V. E.	Total.
Middleton, J. H.	London	1882	Architecture	—	—	1	—	—	—	—	—	—	—	1
Middleton, James R.	Glasgow	1891-1893	Domestic	—	—	2	—	1	—	—	—	—	—	3
Middleton, J. T.	London	1855-1856	Domestic	—	—	—	—	—	—	—	—	—	3	3
Middleton, Miss Katherine	London	1890-1891	Landscape	—	—	—	—	2	—	—	—	—	—	2
Middleton, M.	—	1835	Portraits	—	—	—	—	1	—	—	—	—	—	1
Middleton, Miss Mary E.	York	1884-1892	Landscape	—	—	1	—	2	—	—	—	—	—	3
Midforth, Charles Henry	London	1884-1891	Architecture	—	—	5	—	1	—	—	—	—	3	9
Midgley, J. H.	Surbiton	1880	Landscape	—	—	—	—	—	—	—	—	—	1	1
Midwood, W. H.	London	1867-1871	Domestic	—	—	—	—	2	—	—	—	—	—	2
Mielich, Alphonse	Paris	1891-1893	Domestic	—	—	2	—	1	—	—	—	—	—	3
Miglioretti, Pascal	Milan	1865-1866	Sculpture	—	—	3	—	—	—	—	—	—	—	3
Mignot, Louis Remy	New York	1863-1871	Landscape	—	—	8	10	2	—	—	—	—	—	20
Mijn, Vander. *See* V.	—	—	—	—	—	—	—	—	—	—	—	—	—	—
Mikel, F.	London	1809-1818	Flowers	—	—	3	—	—	—	—	—	—	1	4
Milanese, Il	London	1777-1779	Mythological	—	—	3	—	—	—	—	—	—	—	3
Milbourn, John (Pupil of F. Cotes, R.A.)	London	1772-1774	Portraits	—	—	4	—	—	—	—	—	—	—	4
Milbourne, C.	London	1790	Drawings	1	—	—	—	—	—	—	—	—	—	1
Milbourne, Henry	London	1797-1826	Landscape	—	—	20	15	—	—	—	—	—	—	35
Milburn, George	London	1869	Sculpture	—	—	1	—	—	—	—	—	—	—	1
Milburn, R.	—	1815	Portraits	—	—	1	—	—	—	—	—	—	—	1
Mildmay, C. St. John	London	1880	Venice	—	—	—	—	2	—	—	—	—	—	2
Mileham, Charles Henry Money	London	1882-1888	Architecture	—	—	5	—	—	—	—	—	—	—	5
Miles, Arthur	London	1851-1880	Figures	—	—	13	2	77	—	—	—	—	—	92
Miles, Miss Annie Stewart	London	1888-1893	Flowers	—	—	4	—	3	—	—	—	—	—	7
Miles, C.	London	1838-1843	Architecture	—	—	2	—	—	—	—	—	—	—	2
Miles, Edward	London	1775-1797	Miniatures	—	—	53	—	—	—	—	—	—	—	53
Miles, F. L.	—	1825	Battle Pieces	—	—	1	—	—	—	—	—	—	—	1
Miles, G.	—	1822-1824	Still Life	—	—	—	8	—	—	—	—	—	—	8
Miles, G. Frank	London	1874-1887	Figures	—	—	21	—	—	—	—	4	—	—	25
Miles, G. H.	London	1824-1829	Portraits	—	—	5	—	1	—	—	—	—	—	6
Miles, Miss Helen Jane Arundel	London	1861-1878	Rustic	—	—	—	—	11	—	—	—	—	9	20
Miles, J.	—	1834	Religious	—	—	—	1	—	—	—	—	—	—	1
Miles, J. L.	—	1825	—	—	—	—	—	1	—	—	—	—	—	1
Miles, Leonidas Clint	London	1858-1883	Landscape	—	—	4	5	77	—	—	—	—	—	86
Miles, Thomas	London	1767-1768	Landscape	2	—	—	—	—	—	—	—	—	—	2
Miles, T. G. H.	London	1874-1881	Landscape	—	—	—	—	11	—	—	—	—	—	11
Miles, Thomas Rose	London	1869-1888	Sea Pieces	—	—	6	—	14	—	—	—	—	1	21
Miles, W.	Exeter	1841	Animals	—	—	—	1	—	—	—	—	—	—	1
Miles, Mrs.	London	1860	Figures	—	—	—	—	1	—	—	—	—	—	1
Miles, Master	Tottenham	1766	Animals	—	1	—	—	—	—	—	—	—	—	1
Milesi, Alessandro	Venice	1890	Figures	—	—	1	—	—	—	—	—	—	—	1
Milesi, Miss Bianca	London	1824	Portraits	—	—	4	—	—	—	—	—	—	—	4
Milford, H.	—	1808-1811	Portraits	—	—	3	—	—	—	—	—	—	—	3
Mill, J.	London	1800-1803	Architecture	—	—	2	—	—	—	—	—	—	—	2
Mill, J.	Bath	1855	Landscape	—	—	—	1	—	—	—	—	—	—	1
Millais, Everett	London	1888-1889	Sculpture	—	—	—	—	—	—	—	—	2	—	2
Millais, Sir John Everett, Bart., R.A., H.R.I.,	—	—	—	—	—	—	—	—	—	—	—	—	—	—
H.R.C.A. ‡	London	1846-1893	Figures	—	—	180	2	—	—	1	34	5	5	227
Millais, William Henry	London	1853-1892	Landscape	—	—	7	—	—	—	10	1	—	1	19
Millar, J. H. C.	London	1884-1886	Landscape	—	—	3	—	—	—	—	—	—	1	4
Millar, Harold R.	Tooting	1892	Fables	—	—	1	—	—	—	—	—	—	—	1
Millar, James	Birmingham	1771-1790	Figures	1	—	6	—	—	—	—	—	—	—	7
Millard, Charles S.	London	1866-1889	Landscape	—	—	—	—	2	—	3	—	—	2	7
Millard, Miss E.	London	1893	Monuments	—	—	—	—	1	—	—	—	—	—	1
Millard, Fred.	Newlyn	1882-1893	Domestic	—	—	3	—	15	—	—	—	—	6	24
Millard, Walter J. N.	London	1881-1889	Landscape	—	—	4	—	—	—	—	—	—	1	5
Miller, Miss Alice	London	1884-1886	Landscape	—	—	—	—	3	—	—	—	—	2	5
Miller, C.	London	1833	Illustrations	—	—	—	1	2	—	—	—	—	—	3
Miller, Charles S.	London	1883-1891	Coast Scenes	—	—	7	—	16	—	—	—	—	3	26
Miller, E. J.	London	1891	Landscape	—	—	—	—	—	—	1	—	—	—	1
Miller, Francis	London	1886	Landscape	—	—	—	—	—	—	—	—	—	1	1
Miller, Frederick	Brighton	1880-1892	Sea Pieces	—	—	1	—	—	—	3	—	—	1	5
Miller, Fred.	London	1886-1893	Engraving	—	—	4	—	—	—	—	—	—	—	4
Miller, Felix Martin	London	1842-1880	Sculpture	—	—	92	10	7	—	—	—	—	12	121
Miller, George	Bath	1827-1853	Landscape	—	—	—	—	2	—	—	—	—	—	2
Miller, George	Chislehurst	1890-1891	Flowers	—	—	1	—	5	—	—	—	—	—	6
Miller, George James Somerton	London	1857-1877	Sculpture	—	—	24	1	—	—	—	—	—	—	25
Miller, Harrison	Abingdon	1891-1892	Domestic	—	—	2	—	4	—	—	—	—	—	6
Miller, Miss Henrietta ‖	London	1884-1889	Flowers	—	—	2	—	5	—	2	1	—	—	10
Miller, J.	London	1846-1864	Figures	—	—	4	3	2	—	—	—	—	1	10
Miller, James, F.S.A.	London	1773-1791	Landscape	41	—	11	—	—	—	—	—	—	—	52
Miller, James	London	1768-1782	Portraits	1	3	6	—	—	—	—	—	—	—	10

Name.	Town.	First and Last Year of Ex.	Speciality.	S. A.	F. S.	R. A.	B. I.	S. S.	O. W.	N. W.	G. G.	N. G.	V. E.	Total.
Miller, John	London	1819-1823	Flowers	—	—	4	—	—	—	—	—	—	—	4
Miller, John	London	1828-1829	Architecture	—	—	3	—	—	—	—	—	—	—	3
Miller, John	London	1761-1769	Engraving	21	2	—	—	—	—	—	—	—	—	23
Miller, John, F.S.A.	London	1767-1788	Landscape	41	—	6	—	—	—	—	—	—	—	47
Miller, John	Glasgow	1876-1890	Landscape	—	—	3	—	—	—	—	1	—	—	4
Miller, John D.	London	1882-1893	Engraving	—	—	10	—	—	—	—	—	—	1	11
Miller, John Douglas	London	1869-1877	Fruit	—	—	3	—	8	—	—	—	—	—	11
Miller, John Frederick, F.S.A.	London	1768-1780	Landscape	19	—	—	—	—	—	—	—	—	—	19
Miller, J. H.	London	1803-1829	Landscape	—	—	6	—	1	1	—	—	—	3	11
Miller, Miss Jessie J. A. I.	London	1882-1888	Miniatures	—	—	6	—	—	—	—	—	—	—	6
Miller, J. S.	London	1767	Landscape	3	—	—	—	—	—	—	—	—	—	3
Miller, Mary	Tottenham	1869	Landscape	—	—	—	—	—	—	—	—	—	1	1
Miller, Philip Homan, A.R.H.A.	London	1877-1892	Figures	—	—	6	—	11	—	—	—	—	3	20
Miller, Mrs. Sophia	London	1892-1893	Flowers	—	—	2	—	—	—	2	—	—	—	4
Miller, Miss Sarah Alice	Bishop's Stortford	1880-1888	Domestic	—	—	—	—	12	—	—	—	—	—	12
Miller, Tobias, F.S.A.	London	1765-1790	Engraving	10	—	—	—	—	—	—	—	—	—	10
Miller, T. Harrison	Abingdon	1889-1891	Rustic	—	—	—	—	—	—	—	—	—	3	3
Miller, William, F.S.A.	London	1780-1803	Historical	29	—	18	—	—	—	—	—	—	—	47
Miller, W.	London	1837-1838	Landscape	—	—	2	—	—	—	—	—	—	—	2
Miller, William E.	London	1871-1893	Portraits	—	—	26	—	13	—	—	1	1	8	49
Miller, Mrs. W. E. *See* Miss Mary Backhouse	London	1883-1893	Domestic	—	—	4	—	4	—	—	—	—	8	16
Miller, William G.	Glasgow	1892-1893	Domestic	—	—	2	—	—	—	1	—	—	—	3
Miller, W. H.	London	1836-1851	Landscape	—	—	—	—	10	—	—	—	—	—	10
Millet, Francis David φ	New York	1879-1892	Figures	—	—	7	—	—	—	—	—	1	12	20
Millet, G.	London	1872	Sculpture	—	—	—	—	1	—	—	—	—	—	1
Millet, Jean Francois	Paris	1872-1876	Figures	—	—	—	—	—	—	—	—	—	4	4
Millett, H.	Bath	1809-1817	Miniatures	—	—	9	—	—	—	—	—	—	—	9
Millett, J., *or* F.	—	1837-1838	Portraits	—	—	3	—	—	—	—	—	—	—	3
Millichap, G. T.	London	1845-1846	Landscape	—	—	1	—	1	—	—	—	—	—	2
Millichap, Thomas	London	1813-1821	Portraits	—	—	11	7	—	—	—	—	—	—	18
Milligan, J.	London	1817-1824	Sculpture	—	—	7	—	—	—	—	—	—	—	7
Milling, H.	London	1832	Historical	—	—	2	—	—	—	—	—	—	—	2
Millington, Henry	London	1761-1811	Miniatures	—	16	1	—	—	—	—	—	—	—	17
Millington, James Heath	London	1831-1870	Portraits	—	—	27	8	22	—	—	—	—	—	57
Millington, T. J.	Greenwich	1831	Sea Pieces	—	—	1	1	2	—	—	—	—	—	4
Millington, Miss. *See* Mrs. Mannin	—	1829-1832	Portraits	—	—	9	—	4	—	—	—	—	—	13
Millner, William	Gainsborough	1845-1891	Figures	—	—	11	2	11	—	—	—	—	—	24
Mills —.	—	1783	Landscape	—	1	—	—	—	—	—	—	—	—	1
Mills, A.	London	1807	Figures	—	—	3	—	—	—	—	—	—	—	3
Mills, A. W.	London	1834	Buildings	—	—	—	—	2	—	—	—	—	—	2
Mills, C.	—	1827-1833	Landscape	—	—	2	—	—	—	—	—	—	—	2
Mills, Miss E. ‖	London	1875	Landscape	—	—	1	—	—	—	—	—	—	—	1
Mills, Edward	London	1890-1893	Landscape	—	—	1	—	—	—	—	—	—	1	2
Mills, Fred. C.	London	1884-1891	Portraits	—	—	2	—	—	—	—	—	—	—	2
Mills, George	London	1816-1823	Medals	—	—	14	—	—	—	—	—	—	—	14
Mills, H.	London	1833-1835	Landscape	—	—	1	2	—	—	—	—	—	—	3
Mills, J.	London	1799	Architecture	—	—	1	—	—	—	—	—	—	—	1
Mills, John	London	1801-1837	Portraits	—	—	6	5	11	—	—	—	—	—	22
Mills, J.	Bath	1850	Sculpture	—	—	1	—	—	—	—	—	—	—	1
Mills, Miss Louie	Blackheath	1889	Moonlight	—	—	—	—	—	—	1	—	—	—	1
Mills, Michael	—	1834-1844	Sculpture	—	—	1	1	—	—	—	—	—	—	2
Mills, R.	—	1818	Still Life	—	—	1	—	—	—	—	—	—	—	1
Mills, S. F.	London	1858-1882	Domestic	—	—	10	—	13	—	—	—	—	24	47
Mills, T. F.	London	1867	Domestic	—	—	—	1	—	—	—	—	—	—	1
Mills, William	Birmingham	1883-1888	Landscape	—	—	2	—	2	—	—	—	—	2	6
Mills, Mrs.	—	1816	Portraits	—	—	1	—	—	—	—	—	—	—	1
Millson, Frederick	Teddington	1885-1888	Figures	—	—	1	—	2	—	—	—	—	—	3
Millyar, W.	London	1853	Sculpture	—	—	1	—	—	—	—	—	—	—	1
Milne, Ada E.	London	1879-1882	Landscape	—	—	—	—	1	—	—	—	—	6	7
Milne, H. D.	Crayford	1875-1881	Still Life	—	—	—	—	4	—	—	—	—	—	4
Milne, Joseph	Edinburgh	1887-1892	Landscape	—	—	5	—	—	—	—	—	—	—	5
Milne, William Oswald	London	1874-1887	Architecture	—	—	2	—	—	—	—	—	—	—	2
Milner, C. B.	London	1832-1834	Landscape	—	—	—	4	2	—	—	—	—	—	6
Milner, Miss Elizabeth Eleanor	Balham	1887-1892	Still Life	—	—	6	—	—	—	—	—	—	2	8
Milner, Fred.	Cheltenham	1887-1892	Landscape	—	—	3	—	—	—	—	—	—	1	4
Milner-Kite, J.	Paris	1884-1892	Figures	—	—	—	—	4	—	—	—	—	2	6
Milnes, Miss Annie	Bradford	1892-1893	Domestic	—	—	1	—	—	—	—	—	—	2	3
Milnes, Thomas	London	1842-1866	Sculpture	—	—	26	—	—	—	—	—	—	—	26
Milo, T.	London	1842	Portraits	—	—	—	—	1	—	—	—	—	—	1
Milton, John	Peckham	1767-1776	Sea Pieces	3	30	—	—	—	—	—	—	—	—	33
Milton, J.	London	1785-1803	Medals	—	—	10	—	—	—	—	—	—	—	10
Milton, J.	London	1825-1836	Portraits	—	—	2	—	—	—	—	—	—	—	2

Name.	Town.	First and Last Year of Ex.	Speciality.	S. A.	F. S.	R. A.	B. I.	S. S.	O. W.	N.W.	G. G.	N. G.	V. E.	Total.
Miltonberg, J. Jacob	London	1776-1786	Enamels	—	—	2	—	—	—	—	—	—	—	2
Milward, Miss Clementina	London	1893	Landscape	—	—	—	—	—	—	—	—	—	1	1
Milward, Mary	Farnham	1879-1880	Landscape	—	—	—	—	1	—	—	—	—	1	2
Minardi, C. Tommaso	London	1865	Scriptural	—	—	—	—	1	—	—	—	—	—	1
Minasi, James	London	1802-1847	Portraits	—	—	17	—	1	—	—	—	—	—	18
Minchin, Hamilton	London	1882	Still Life	—	—	—	—	1	—	—	—	—	—	1
Minguet, A.	Antwerp	1851	Churches	—	—	—	1	—	—	—	—	—	—	1
Minnett, J.	London	1812	Landscape	—	—	1	—	—	—	—	—	—	—	1
Minns, Miss Fanny M.	Newport I. of W.	1890	Flowers	—	—	—	—	1	—	—	—	—	—	1
Minor, Robert C.	London	1879-1881	Landscape	—	—	4	—	—	—	—	2	—	2	8
Minôt, Edwin, *or* Edward	London	1864-1875	Still Life	—	—	—	3	5	—	—	—	—	2	10
Mins, C.	London	1833-1840	Sea Pieces	—	—	4	5	10	—	—	—	—	—	19
Minshall, Miss M. W.	Oswestry	1886	Landscape	—	—	—	—	—	—	1	—	—	—	1
Minshul, Captain	—	1772-1773	Domestic	2	—	—	—	—	—	—	—	—	—	2
Minshull, Miss Georgina	Birmingham	1874-1877	Portraits	—	—	3	—	—	—	—	—	—	—	3
Minshull, R. T.	Liverpool	1866-1885	Figures	—	—	11	—	8	—	—	—	—	2	21
Minton, H.	London	1825	Landscape	—	—	1	—	—	—	—	—	—	—	1
Minton, Miss J. F.	Bristol	1832	Flowers	—	—	—	—	1	—	—	—	—	—	1
Minton, John W.	London	1866-1891	Medals	—	—	9	—	—	—	—	—	—	—	9
Minton, T. J.	London	1868	Medals	—	—	1	—	—	—	—	—	—	—	1
Minx —	Spain	1770	Figures	—	1	—	—	—	—	—	—	—	—	1
Mitan, Miss A.	London	1840-1842	Landscape	—	—	—	1	4	—	—	—	—	—	5
Mitan, James	London	1773-1818	Sculpture	—	1	6	—	—	—	—	—	—	*	7
Mitan, Samuel	London	1840	Historical	—	—	—	—	1	—	—	—	—	—	1
Mitchell, Arnold Bidlake	Clapton	1885-1893	Architecture	—	—	24	—	—	—	—	—	—	—	24
Mitchell (A. B.) and Butler	London	1888-1890	Architecture	—	—	6	—	—	—	—	—	—	—	6
Mitchell, Charles William	Newcastle	1876-1893	Figures	—	—	7	—	—	—	—	3	2	—	12
Mitchell, E.	London	1852	Landscape	—	—	3	2	4	—	—	—	—	—	9
Mitchell, Edward	London	1854-1871	Sculpture	—	—	5	—	5	—	—	—	—	—	10
Mitchell, Miss Emily	London	1872-1892	Figures	—	—	1	—	5	—	—	—	—	1	7
Mitchell, F.	London	1819-1829	Landscape	—	—	2	—	1	—	—	—	—	—	3
Mitchell, G.	London	1836	Sculpture	—	—	1	—	—	—	—	—	—	—	1
Mitchell, James (?) John	London	1824-1831	Engraving	—	—	—	—	6	—	—	—	—	—	6
Mitchell, James	London	1850-1852	Sculpture	—	—	3	—	—	—	—	—	—	—	3
Mitchell, John	Aberdeen	1884-1885	Landscape	—	—	2	—	—	—	—	—	—	—	2
Mitchell, J. A.	London	1832	Historical	—	—	1	—	—	—	—	—	—	—	1
Mitchell, James B.	London	1883	Portraits	—	—	—	—	—	—	1	—	—	—	1
Mitchell, Mrs. James B.	London	1879-1887	Flowers	—	—	2	—	—	—	—	7	—	4	13
Mitchell, J. T.	London	1798-1830	Enamels	—	—	64	2	11	—	—	—	—	4	81
Mitchell, Mrs. Mary	Bickley	1889-1893	Miniatures	—	—	8	—	—	—	—	—	—	—	8
Mitchell, Miss M. D.	London	1876-1882	Flowers	—	—	—	—	2	—	—	2	—	2	6
Mitchell, M. L.	London	1870	Domestic	—	—	1	—	—	—	—	—	—	—	1
Mitchell, Percy	London	1886	Landscape	—	—	—	—	—	—	—	—	—	1	1
Mitchell, Philip, R.I. ‡	Plymouth	1854-1893	Landscape	—	—	—	—	—	—	338	—	—	—	338
Mitchell, Robert	London	1782-1798	Architecture	—	—	6	—	—	—	—	—	—	—	6
Mitchell, Robert	Bromley	1858	Engraving	—	—	1	—	—	—	—	—	—	—	1
Mitchell, Sidney	Edinburgh	1884-1887	Architecture	—	—	3	—	—	—	—	—	—	—	3
Mitchell (Sydney) and Wilson	Edinburgh	1890	Architecture	—	—	1	—	—	—	—	—	—	—	1
Mitchell, Tom	Bradford	1888	Landscape	—	—	—	—	—	—	—	1	—	—	1
Mitchell, Thomas	London	1763-1789	Sea Pieces	—	20	16	—	—	—	—	—	—	—	36
Mitchell, Thomas, Junr.	London	1780	Engraving	—	3	—	—	—	—	—	—	—	—	3
Mitchell, Miss	London	1810-1812	Miniatures	—	—	3	—	—	—	—	—	—	—	3
Mniszech, Count André	—	1880	Portraits	—	—	—	—	—	—	—	1	—	—	1
Moberly, Alfred	Hythe	1882	Flowers	—	—	—	—	—	—	—	—	—	1	1
Moberley, Mrs. H. G. (Mariqueta, J.)	London	1884-1893	Domestic	—	—	8	—	5	—	8	—	2	10	33
Mocatta, D.	London	1831-1847	Architecture	—	—	14	—	—	—	—	—	—	—	14
Mocatta, Miss L.	London	1889	Flowers	—	—	—	—	—	—	1	—	—	—	1
Mocatta, Maria	London	1883	Domestic	—	—	—	—	—	—	—	—	—	1	1
Mocatta, Rebecca	London	1882-1883	Domestic	—	—	—	—	2	—	—	—	—	—	2
Moes, Wally P. C.	Amsterdam	1885-1886	Domestic	—	—	—	—	3	—	—	—	—	—	3
Moffat, Arthur Elwell	Edinburgh	1886-1890	Landscape	—	—	3	—	—	—	3	—	—	—	6
Moffatt, W. B. *See also* Scott and Moffatt	London	1856	Architecture	—	—	1	—	—	—	—	—	—	—	1
Mogford, Henry	London	1837-1846	Churches	—	—	4	—	5	—	—	—	—	—	9
Mogford, John, R.I. ‡ φ	London	1846-1885	Landscape	—	—	33	28	20	—	292	4	—	15	392
Mogford, Thomas	Exeter	1838-1866	Landscape	—	—	43	11	23	—	—	—	—	2	79
Mohn, Ernest	Greenwich	1870-1873	Engraving	—	—	2	—	—	—	—	—	—	—	2
Mohr, J. M.	London	1872-1881	Sculpture	—	—	4	—	—	—	—	—	—	—	4
Moir, Ellen	Edinburgh	1871-1881	Animals	—	—	—	—	—	—	—	—	—	2	2
Moira, Edward Lobo	London	1848-1887	Miniatures	—	—	122	—	—	—	3	—	—	—	125
Moira, Gerald E.	London	1891-1893	Miniatures	—	—	6	—	—	—	—	—	—	1	7
Mole, Miss Clara	London	1886-1887	Birds	—	—	—	—	—	—	3	—	—	—	3
Mole, John Henry, V.P.R.I. ‡	London	1845-1887	Figures	—	—	11	1	5	—	679	4	—	12	712

Name.	Town.	First and Last Year of Ex.	Speciality.	S. A.	F. S.	R. A.	B. I.	S. S.	O. W.	N.W.	G. G.	N. G.	V. E.	Total.
Molesworth, J.	London	1819	Scriptural	—	—	—	1	—	—	—	—	—	—	1
Molinari, G.	London	1876	Portraits	—	—	1	—	—	—	—	—	—	—	1
Molineux, E.	London	1874	Flowers	—	—	—	—	1	—	—	—	—	—	1
Molineux, M.	London	1888	Landscape	—	—	1	—	—	—	—	—	—	—	1
Möllea, J. F.	London	1847-1873	Portraits	—	—	15	—	—	—	—	—	—	—	15
Moller, F.	Paris	1876	Wood Engraving	—	—	—	—	—	—	—	—	—	2	2
Molony, C.	London	1870	Figures	—	—	—	—	3	—	—	—	—	—	3
Molroy, F.	London	1853	Figures	—	—	—	1	—	—	—	—	—	—	1
Mols, Robert	Paris	1879	Sea Shores	—	—	1	—	—	—	—	—	—	—	1
Moltino, Francis	London	1847-1867	Sea Pieces	—	—	8	13	9	—	—	—	—	—	30
Monarchy —	London	1783	Landscape	—	1	—	—	—	—	—	—	—	—	1
Moncrieff, Col. Alexander	London	1883	Landscape	—	—	—	—	—	—	1	—	—	1	2
Monet, Claude	London	1871-1887	Landscape	—	—	—	—	4	—	—	—	—	2	6
Monge, De. *See* D.	—	—	—	—	—	—	—	—	—	—	—	—	—	—
Monger, Arthur P.	Ewell	1889-1890	Sculpture	—	—	2	—	—	—	—	—	—	—	2
Monger, J.	London	1832-1845	Game	—	—	—	—	7	—	—	—	—	—	7
Mongin, Augustin	Paris	1874-1881	Etching	—	—	2	—	—	—	—	—	—	7	9
Mongrèdien, Miss J.	London	1887	Heads	—	—	—	—	—	—	—	—	—	1	1
Monies, A. H.	London	1797-1809	Portraits	—	—	5	—	—	—	—	—	—	—	5
Monk, E. V. H.	London	1829	Figures	—	—	1	—	—	—	—	—	—	—	1
Monk, M. C.	—	1780	Miniatures	—	—	1	—	—	—	—	—	—	—	1
Monk, Van. *See* V.	—	—	—	—	—	—	—	—	—	—	—	—	—	—
Monkhouse, Miss Mary F.	Manchester	1884-1891	Figures	—	—	2	—	—	—	—	—	1	—	3
Monkswell, Lord. § *See also* Rt. Hon. Sir R. P. Collier	London	1886	Landscape	—	—	—	—	—	—	—	2	—	—	2
Monque, A. *See* Mouque.	—	—	—	—	—	—	—	—	—	—	—	—	—	—
Monro, A. B.	Edinburgh	1842-1847	Landscape	—	—	2	—	—	—	—	—	—	—	2
Monro, C. C.	London	1872-1885	Landscape	—	—	1	—	1	—	—	—	—	2	4
Monro, Charles C. Binning	London	1874-1890	Sea Pieces	—	—	10	—	—	—	—	—	—	—	10
Monro, Henry	London	1811-1814	Historical	—	—	15	2	—	—	—	—	—	—	17
Monro, J. C.	London	1866-1873	Figures	—	—	5	1	12	—	—	—	—	—	18
Monro, R.	London	1826	Portraits	—	—	—	—	1	—	—	—	—	—	1
Montagu, Miss Ellen	London	1888	Figures	—	—	1	—	—	—	—	—	—	—	1
Montague —	London	1806	Portraits	—	—	1	—	—	—	—	—	—	—	1
Montague, Alfred §	London	1832-1883	Landscape	—	—	23	51	156	—	—	—	—	93	323
Montague, Arthur	—	1872-1875	Landscape	—	—	—	—	5	—	—	—	—	—	5
Montague, Alice L.	Dover	1869	Flowers	—	—	—	—	—	—	—	—	—	2	2
Montague, Miss Ellen	Windsor	1837-1849	Figures	—	—	1	—	5	—	—	—	—	—	6
Montague, H.	London	1806-1861	Figures	—	—	8	12	9	—	4	—	—	—	33
Montague, H. Irving	London	1873-1883	Figures	—	—	1	—	9	—	—	—	—	19	29
Montague, H. J.	London	1873-1876	Street Scenes	—	—	1	—	—	—	—	—	—	4	5
Montague, J.	London	1797	Miniatures	—	—	5	—	—	—	—	—	—	—	5
Montague, M.	—	1832	Portraits	—	—	1	—	—	—	—	—	—	—	1
Montague, Mrs.	London	1871	Still Life	—	—	—	—	—	—	—	—	—	1	1
Montaigne, William John	Upper Clapton	1839-1889	Historical	—	—	30	23	30	—	—	—	—	8	91
Montalba, Anthony	London	1875-1881	Landscape	—	—	3	—	—	—	—	—	—	1	4
Montalba, A. R.	London	1847-1884	Figures	—	—	1	2	1	—	—	—	—	—	4
Montalba, Miss Clara, R.W.S.†	London	1866-1893	Buildings	—	—	17	1	12	86	—	9	9	14	148
Montalba, Miss Ellen	London	1868-1891	Dramatic	—	—	13	—	2	—	—	—	—	1	16
Montalba, Miss Henrietta Skerrett	London	1876-1893	Sculpture	—	—	16	—	—	—	—	19	3	1	39
Montalba, Miss Hilda	London	1873-1893	Figures	—	—	19	—	20	—	—	12	9	21	81
Montalba, R.	London	1848	Figures	—	—	2	—	—	—	—	—	—	—	2
Montbard, Georges	London	1874-1886	Landscape	—	—	2	—	6	—	4	—	—	35	47
Monte, La. *See* L.	—	—	—	—	—	—	—	—	—	—	—	—	—	—
Montefiore, E. B. Stanley	London	1872-1890	Domestic	—	—	10	—	—	—	—	—	—	5	15
Montefiore, E. L.	Paris	1872-1877	Etching	—	—	—	—	—	—	—	—	—	10	10
Monteverde, Giulio	Milan	1875	Figures	—	—	1	—	—	—	—	—	—	—	1
Montford, Horace	London	1870-1893	Sculpture	—	—	44	—	1	—	—	—	—	—	45
Montford, Paul R.	London	1892-1893	Sculpture	—	—	4	—	2	—	—	—	—	—	6
Montfort, H.	Paris	1845	Figures	—	—	1	—	—	—	—	—	—	—	1
Montgaant —	London	1783	Sporting	—	1	—	—	—	—	—	—	—	—	1
Montgomery, J.	Richmond	1878	Landscape	—	—	—	—	—	—	—	—	—	1	1
Montgomery, R. E. M.	Antwerp	1870-1892	Landscape	—	—	4	—	—	—	—	—	—	—	4
Monti, Raffaelle	London	1853-1860	Sculpture	—	—	6	—	—	—	—	—	—	—	6
Montpezat, De. *See* D.	—	—	—	—	—	—	—	—	—	—	—	—	—	—
Montrose, R. F.	London	1871-1872	Landscape	—	—	1	—	3	—	—	—	—	—	4
Monvel, Boutet de. *See* D.	—	—	—	—	—	—	—	—	—	—	—	—	—	—
Monzies, Louis, A.R.P.E.	Paris	1875-1890	Etchings	—	—	1	—	—	—	—	—	—	2	3
Moody, Edward G.	London	1876-1890	Landscape	—	—	1	—	1	—	—	—	—	2	4
Moody, Miss Fannie ‖	London	1885-1893	Animals	—	—	8	—	7	—	—	—	—	4	19
Moody, Francis Wollaston (?) Thomas	London	1850-1877	Figures	—	—	10	5	3	—	—	—	—	—	18
Moody, Miss Mary	London	1877-1878	Fruit	—	—	—	—	2	—	—	—	—	3	5

Name.	Town.	First and Last Year of Ex.	Speciality.	S. A.	F. S.	R. A.	B. I.	S. S.	O. W.	N. W.	G. G.	N. G.	V. E.	Total.
Moody, R.	London	1836-1844	Sculpture	—	—	6	—	—	—	—	—	—	—	6
Moon, C. T.	London	1837-1849	Landscape	—	—	16	5	6	—	—	—	—	—	27
Moon, Miss Emmeline M.	Horsham	1888	Flowers	—	—	—	—	1	—	—	—	—	—	1
Moon, Henry George	London	1880-1893	Landscape	—	—	5	—	8	—	3	—	—	1	17
Moon, James	London	1842	Architecture	—	—	1	—	—	—	—	—	—	—	1
Moon, William H. B.	Scarborough	1889	Fruit	—	—	1	—	—	—	—	—	—	—	1
Moorat, E. S.	London	1876	Landscape	—	—	—	—	1	—	—	—	—	—	1
Moore, Albert Joseph, A.R.W.S. †	London	1857-1893	Figures	—	—	42	—	2	16	1	31	2	10	104
Moore, Miss Agnes E. C.	London	1881-1885	Flowers	—	—	—	—	—	—	1	1	—	4	6
Moore, A. Harvey	Putney	1874-1893	Landscape	—	—	26	—	17	—	—	—	2	12	57
Moore, Miss Annie Osborne	London	1889-1890	Flowers	—	—	1	—	—	—	—	—	—	1	2
Moore, Alexander Poole	London	1793-1806	Architecture	—	—	15	—	—	—	—	—	—	—	15
Moore, Barlow	Erith	1863-1870	River Scenes	—	—	1	2	2	—	—	—	—	1	6
Moore, Bertha	London	1890	Flowers	—	—	—	—	1	—	—	—	—	—	1
Moore, Charles	—	1768-1773	Portraits	—	38	—	—	—	—	—	—	—	—	38
Moore, Charles †	London	1822-1828	Churches	—	—	—	—	—	8	—	—	—	—	8
Moore, Christopher, R.H.A. †	London	1821-1860	Sculpture	—	—	132	17	40	—	—	—	—	—	189
Moore, C. H.	London	1884	Mountains	—	—	1	—	—	—	—	—	—	—	1
Moore, Claude T. Stanfield	London	1882	Sea Pieces	—	—	—	—	1	—	—	—	—	—	1
Moore, Edwin	York	1855-1885	Landscape	—	—	11	—	—	—	3	—	—	26	40
Moore, Ernest	Barnsley	1888	Interiors	—	—	—	—	1	—	—	—	—	—	1
Moore, Miss Ethel M. (?) Esther	Chiswick	1890-1893	Sculpture	—	—	5	—	—	—	—	—	1	—	6
Moore, F.	London	1841	Landscape	—	—	—	—	1	—	—	—	—	—	1
Moore, Francis John	London	1783-1795	Landscape	3	1	3	—	—	—	—	—	—	—	7
Moore, Fred. W.	Thames Ditton	1882	Sculpture	—	—	1	—	—	—	—	—	—	—	1
Moore, G.	London	1797-1840	Architecture	—	—	20	—	—	—	—	—	—	—	20
Moore, George Belton	London	1830-1870	Landscape	—	—	32	31	29	—	—	—	—	48	140
Moore, Henry	Guildford	1828	Architecture	—	—	—	—	1	—	—	—	—	—	1
Moore, Henry, A.R.A., R.W.S. † § φ	York	1853-1893	Landscape	—	—	107	15	174	55	—	23	10	166	550
Moore, H. Humphrey	Paris	1891	Domestic	—	—	1	—	—	—	—	—	—	—	1
Moore, H. Wilkinson	Oxford	1882-1890	Architecture	—	—	7	—	—	—	—	—	—	—	7
Moore, James (?)	London	1766-1776	Sculpture	—	55	—	—	—	—	—	—	—	—	55
Moore, James, Junr.	—	1771-1775	Sculpture	—	13	—	—	—	—	—	—	—	—	13
Moore, James	Sheffield	1890	Figures	—	—	1	—	—	—	—	—	—	—	1
Moore, J.	Sheffield	1827-1837	Portraits	—	—	7	—	—	—	—	—	—	—	7
Moore, J.	London	1853	Landscape	—	—	—	—	3	—	—	—	—	—	3
Moore, Miss J.	London	1856	Sculpture	—	—	1	—	—	—	—	—	—	—	1
Moore, Miss Jennie	London	1877-1893	Domestic	—	—	9	—	4	—	4	—	3	19	39
Moore, John	London	1767-1777	Sculpture	—	22	2	—	—	—	—	—	—	—	24
Moore, John	London	1827-1831	Portraits	—	—	1	—	7	—	—	—	—	—	8
Moore, John	London	1828	Engraving	—	—	—	—	1	—	—	—	—	—	1
Moore, John Collingham	London	1853-1881	Figures	—	—	60	1	—	—	—	14	—	79	154
Moore, J. G.	London	1856	Portraits	—	—	1	—	—	—	—	—	—	—	1
Moore, J. Marchmont	London	1832-1835	Domestic	—	—	6	—	9	—	3	—	—	—	18
Moore, Miss Madeleine	Eastbourne	1887	Flowers	—	—	—	—	—	—	1	—	—	—	1
Moore, Miss Madena	London	1879-1881	Portraits	—	—	4	—	2	—	—	—	—	—	6
Moore, Morris	London	1843-1844	Scriptural	—	—	7	3	2	—	—	—	—	—	12
Moore, Miss M. A.	—	1811	Portraits	—	—	1	—	—	—	—	—	—	—	1
Moore, R. H.	Highgate	1885-1889	Sculpture	—	—	—	—	1	—	1	—	—	—	2
Moore, Sidney	London	1879-1893	Landscape	—	—	3	—	41	—	—	—	—	9	53
Moore, Thomas	London	1761-1796	Architecture	—	2	2	—	—	—	—	—	—	—	4
Moore (T.) and White (W. H.)	London	1891	Architecture	—	—	1	—	—	—	—	—	—	—	1
Moore, W.	London	1830-1856	Sporting	—	—	—	1	5	—	—	—	—	—	6
Moore, William	London	1764-1772	Hair Work	2	5	—	—	—	—	—	—	—	—	7
Moore, William	York	1855-1888	Landscape	—	—	9	—	—	—	8	—	—	54	71
Moore, William J.	London	1885-1892	Domestic	—	—	3	—	—	—	—	—	—	—	3
Moore, Miss	London	1771-1777	Needlework	5	—	—	—	—	—	—	—	—	—	5
Moore, Miss	London	1859	—	—	—	—	—	1	—	—	—	—	—	1
Moormans, Frans	London	1876-1879	Domestic	—	—	—	—	2	—	—	—	—	1	3
Moran, Thomas	New York	1879	Landscape	—	—	1	—	—	—	—	—	—	—	1
Morand, E. E.	Paris	1881	Flowers	—	—	—	—	—	—	—	3	—	—	3
Morani, A.	London	1889	Rustic	—	—	—	—	—	—	—	—	1	—	1
Morant, Charles Harbord	London	1886-1893	Domestic	—	—	1	—	—	—	—	—	—	2	3
Morby, Kate	London	1871	Flowers	—	—	—	—	—	—	—	—	—	1	1
Morby, Walter J.	London	1875-1889	Landscape	—	—	2	—	16	—	1	—	—	2	21
Mordaunt, F.	London	1842-1845	Figures	—	—	1	1	1	—	—	—	—	—	3
Mordecai, Joseph	London	1873-1893	Domestic	—	—	15	—	1	—	—	—	—	4	20
More, Jacob, F.S.A.	London	1771-1789	Landscape	11	—	11	—	—	—	—	—	—	—	22
Moreau, Adrien	Paris	1877	Domestic	—	—	1	—	—	—	—	—	—	—	1
Moreau, C.	Paris	1869	Domestic	—	—	1	—	—	—	—	—	—	—	1
Moreau, Gustave	Paris	1877	Figures	—	—	—	—	—	—	—	1	—	—	1
Moreau, J.	Paris	1783-1811	Figures	2	—	5	—	—	—	—	—	—	—	7

Name.	Town.	First and Last Year of Ex.	Speciality.	S. A.	F. S.	R. A.	B. I.	S. S.	O. W.	N.W.	G. G.	N. G.	V. E.	Total.
MOREING, CHARLES	London	1832-1845	Architecture	—	—	4	—	—	—	—	—	—	—	4
MOREL-LADEUIL, LEONARD. *See* L.	—	—	—	—	—	—	—	—	—	—	—	—	—	—
MORELL, D'ARCY	Calais	1877-1880	Sea Pieces	—	—	1	—	1	—	—	1	—	1	4
MORELL, L.	—	1840	Landscape	—	—	—	—	2	—	—	—	—	—	2
MORELLE, JOHN P.	Chiswick	1884-1886	Figures	—	—	1	—	1	—	1	—	—	—	3
MORELLI, MARIANO	—	1872	Copies	—	—	—	—	—	—	—	—	—	1	1
MORENO, MATIAS	Paris	1881	Figures	—	—	1	—	—	—	—	—	—	—	1
MORESBY, MISS	—	1778	Portraits	—	1	—	—	—	—	—	—	—	—	1
MORGAN, ALFRED	London	1862-1890	Domestic	—	—	22	7	35	—	—	22	—	6	92
MORGAN, ALFRED GEORGE	Highgate	1879	Landscape	—	—	—	—	1	—	—	—	—	—	1
MORGAN, CHARLES	Birmingham	1885-1889	Coast Scenes	—	—	—	—	3	—	—	—	—	—	3
MORGAN, CHARLES W.	Evesham	1872-1879	Figures	—	—	—	—	—	—	—	—	—	5	5
MORGAN, E.	—	1834	Landscape	—	—	—	1	—	—	—	—	—	—	1
MORGAN, E. P.	London	1883	Landscape	—	—	—	—	1	—	—	—	—	—	1
MORGAN, FREDERICK φ	Aylesbury	1865-1893	Domestic	—	—	46	4	23	—	3	2	—	25	103
MORGAN, FRANK SOMERVILLE	London	1883-1888	Domestic	—	—	—	—	2	—	5	—	—	—	7
MORGAN, GEORGE	London	1859-1860	Architecture	—	—	2	—	—	—	—	—	—	—	2
MORGAN, GEORGE W.	London	1868-1881	Medals	—	—	14	—	—	—	—	—	—	—	14
MORGAN, H.	Guildford	1877	Domestic	—	—	1	—	—	—	—	—	—	—	1
MORGAN, J.	London	1801-1821	Architecture	—	—	5	—	—	—	—	—	—	—	5
MORGAN, J.	London	1803	Portraits	—	—	1	—	—	—	—	—	—	—	1
MORGAN, J.	Bath	1807	Landscape	—	—	1	—	—	—	—	—	—	—	1
MORGAN, JOHN, R.B.A. §	London	1852-1886	Domestic	—	—	66	26	114	—	—	—	—	17	223
MORGAN, JOHN	Paris	1854-1866	Historical	—	—	2	2	3	—	—	—	—	—	7
MORGAN, MISS J.	Rome	1869	Sculpture	—	—	1	—	—	—	—	—	—	—	1
MORGAN, J. D.	London	1830-1831	Architecture	—	—	2	—	—	—	—	—	—	—	2
MORGAN, J. W.	Greenwich	1819-1833	Landscape	—	—	6	1	7	—	—	—	—	—	14
MORGAN, MISS KATE	London	1884-1890	Figures	—	—	6	—	—	—	—	1	—	—	7
MORGAN, M. L.	London	1888	Landscape	—	—	—	—	—	—	1	—	—	—	1
MORGAN, M. S.	London	1856-1861	Sea Pieces	—	—	—	2	5	—	—	—	—	—	7
MORGAN, MRS. MARY VERNON	Birmingham	1880-1893	Flowers	—	—	6	—	16	—	—	—	—	3	25
MORGAN, MRS. S. LOUISA	Manchester	1883	Portraits	—	—	1	—	—	—	—	—	—	—	1
MORGAN, T. H.	Salterton	1877	Landscape	—	—	—	—	1	—	—	—	—	—	1
MORGAN, WALTER J., R.B.A. §	London	1876-1893	Domestic	—	—	5	—	70	—	1	—	—	14	90
MORGAN, MRS. *See* Miss Alice Havers.	—	—	—	—	—	—	—	—	—	—	—	—	—	—
MORGAN, MISS	—	1791	Portraits	1	—	—	—	—	—	—	—	—	—	1
MORGAN AND PHIPSON	London	1856	Architecture	—	—	1	—	—	—	—	—	—	—	1
MORGAN DE. *See* D.	—	—	—	—	—	—	—	—	—	—	—	—	—	—
MORGE, J. S.	London	1858	Architecture	—	—	1	—	—	—	—	—	—	—	1
MORICE, MISS A. A.	Brenchley	1871-1885	Landscape	—	—	2	—	8	—	—	—	—	2	12
MORIER, DAVID	London	1760-1768	Portraits	4	—	—	—	—	—	—	—	—	—	4
MORIN, EDWARD ‡ (?) EDMOND	Paris	1858-1878	Domestic	—	—	—	—	—	—	23	—	—	2	25
MORINIERE, DE LA. *See* D.	—	—	—	—	—	—	—	—	—	—	—	—	—	—
MORING, J.	London	1840-1846	Medals	—	—	5	—	—	—	—	—	—	—	5
MORISON, D.	London	1821-1850	Sculpture	—	—	34	—	—	—	—	—	—	—	34
MORISON, DOUGLAS † ‡	Datchet	1836-1846	Landscape	—	—	6	—	—	17	13	—	—	—	36
MORISON, J. A.	London	1879	Domestic	—	—	—	—	—	—	—	—	—	1	1
MORISON, R.	London	1791	Architecture	—	—	2	—	—	—	—	—	—	—	2
MORITZ, C.	London	1778-1783	Portraits	—	—	4	—	—	—	—	—	—	—	4
MORLAND, GEORGE	London	1773-1804	Animals, etc.	34	33	38	—	—	—	—	—	—	—	105
MORLAND, HENRY ROBERT	London	1760-1792	Domestic	17	93	8	—	—	—	—	—	—	—	118
MORLAND, JAMES S.	Liverpool	1877-1893	Domestic	—	—	4	—	—	—	1	2	—	1	8
MORLAND, MISS MARIA, AFTERWARDS MRS. WILLIAM WARD	London	1785-1786	Domestic	—	—	2	—	—	—	—	—	—	—	2
MORLAND, MC. *See* MAC.	—	—	—	—	—	—	—	—	—	—	—	—	—	—
MORLEY, E.	Salisbury	1832	Animals	—	—	—	1	—	—	—	—	—	—	1
MORLEY, GEORGE	London	1832-1860	Sporting	—	—	40	2	—	—	—	—	—	—	42
MORLEY, H.	London	1837-1853	Cattle	—	—	1	—	7	—	—	—	—	—	8
MORLEY, ROBERT, R.B.A. §	London	1879-1893	Animals	—	—	5	—	30	—	—	—	—	14	49
MORLEY, W. S.	—	1845	Sporting	—	—	1	—	—	—	—	—	—	—	1
MORLON, ANTOINE P. E.	London	1891-1892	Domestic	—	—	2	—	—	—	—	—	—	—	2
MORNER, J.	—	1835	Figures	—	—	—	1	—	—	—	—	—	—	1
MORNEWICK, CHARLES AUGUSTUS	Dover	1826-1875	Sea Pieces	—	—	2	15	23	—	—	—	—	4	44
MORNEWICK, CHARLES AUGUSTUS, JUNR.	London	1845-1874	Sea Pieces	—	—	20	12	9	—	—	—	—	—	41
MORNEWICK, HENRY CLAUDE	Dover	1827-1846	Sea Pieces	—	—	1	1	1	—	—	—	—	—	3
MORRELL, R. J.	London	1839	Animals	—	—	1	—	1	—	—	—	—	—	2
MORRELL, MISS	Malden	1855-1874	Domestic	—	—	14	—	—	—	—	—	—	—	14
MORRIS, A.	London	1788-1794	Portraits	—	—	9	—	—	—	—	—	—	—	9
MORRIS, ALFRED	Deptford	1853-1873	Sporting	—	—	2	17	14	—	—	—	—	1	34
MORRIS, MISS ALICE	Manchester	1886	Flowers	—	—	—	—	—	—	2	—	—	—	2
MORRIS, ANDREW	Southampton	1887	Landscape	—	—	2	—	—	—	—	—	—	—	2
MORRIS, MRS. BEST, LATE MISS SHARPE	—	1822-1841	Portraits	—	—	12	—	—	—	—	—	—	—	12

Name.	Town.	First and Last Year of Ex.	Speciality.	S. A.	F. S.	R. A.	B. I.	S. S.	O. W.	N.W.	G. G.	N. G.	V. E.	Total.
Morris, Miss C. B.	London	1855-1867	Miniatures	—	—	7	—	—	—	—	—	—	—	7
Morris, Charles Greville	Manchester	1886-1893	Landscape	—	—	16	—	—	—	—	—	—	2	18
Morris, D.	—	1798	Portraits	—	—	1	—	—	—	—	—	—	—	1
Morris, Ebenezer Butler	London	1833-1863	Historical	—	—	17	19	10	—	—	—	—	—	46
Morris, George Llewelyn	London	1891	Architecture	—	—	1	—	—	—	—	—	—	—	1
Morris, Miss Helena	London	1890	Churches	—	—	—	—	—	—	1	—	—	—	1
Morris, Henry	London	1838-1844	Landscape	—	—	—	—	2	—	—	—	—	—	2
Morris, J.	London	1813-1816	Portraits	—	—	5	—	—	—	—	—	—	—	5
Morris, J.	London	1873-1877	Fruit	—	—	—	—	2	—	—	—	—	—	2
Morris (James A.) and De Boinville (C. A. C.)	London	1891	Architecture	—	—	1	—	—	—	—	—	—	—	1
Morris (James A.) and Hunter	—	1889-1893	Architecture	—	—	6	—	—	—	—	—	—	—	6
Morris, J. C.	Greenwich	1851-1863	Sheep, etc.	—	—	9	19	16	—	—	—	—	4	48
Morris, J. W.	London	1866-1867	Sporting	—	—	—	3	—	—	—	—	—	—	3
Morris, M.	London	1845	Cattle	—	—	—	1	—	—	—	—	—	—	1
Morris, Mittie	Kilburn	1883	Buildings	—	—	—	—	1	—	—	—	—	—	1
Morris, Oliver	London	1866-1892	Landscape	—	—	1	—	1	—	2	—	—	5	9
Morris, Philip Richard, A.R.A.	London	1857-1893	Scriptural	—	—	83	11	19	—	—	31	—	34	178
Morris, Robert	London	1768-1809	Landscape	4	—	1	1	—	—	—	—	—	—	6
Morris, Robert	—	1780-1781	Architecture	—	—	4	—	—	—	—	—	—	—	4
Morris, R.	London	1833-1844	Landscape	—	—	2	3	8	—	—	—	—	—	13
Morris, R.	London	1863	Game	—	—	—	—	1	—	—	—	—	—	1
Morris, Thomas	Oxford	1826-1831	Architecture	—	—	1	—	2	—	—	—	—	—	3
Morris, Thomas	London	1766-1794	Portraits	—	5	5	—	—	—	—	—	—	—	10
Morris, T. A. D.	London	1838-1843	Architecture	—	—	2	—	—	—	—	—	—	—	2
Morris, Mrs. T. Wilson	London	1885-1890	Etching	—	—	4	—	—	—	—	—	—	—	4
Morris, W.	Hornsey	1866	Study	—	—	—	—	—	—	—	—	—	1	1
Morris, William Bright φ	London	1869-1893	Landscape	—	—	32	—	—	—	—	3	4	19	58
Morris, W. Walker	Greenwich	1850-1867	Sporting	—	—	7	14	12	—	—	—	—	—	33
Morris, Mrs.	London	1780	Landscape	1	—	—	—	—	—	—	—	—	—	1
Morrish, Sydney S.	London	1852-1893	Landscape	—	—	35	2	9	—	—	—	—	—	46
Morrish, W. S.	Changford	1866-1886	Landscape	—	—	4	—	12	—	—	—	—	10	26
Morrison, Colin	Rome	1778	Sculpture	—	—	1	—	—	—	—	—	—	—	1
Morrison, J.	London	1825	Sculpture	—	—	—	—	3	—	—	—	—	—	3
Morrison, R.	London	1844-1857	Sculpture	—	—	10	2	5	—	—	—	—	—	17
Morrison, Robert E.	Liverpool	1883-1890	Domestic	—	—	10	—	2	—	2	—	—	5	19
Morrison, W.	Dublin	1823	Landscape	—	—	2	—	—	—	—	—	—	—	2
Morrison, W.	London	1827	Engraving	—	—	—	—	1	—	—	—	—	—	1
Morrison, W.	Dublin	1828-1835	Architecture	—	—	6	—	—	—	—	—	—	—	6
Morrison, W. W.	Hanwell	1877-1885	Historical	—	—	—	—	1	—	—	—	—	1	2
Morrison, Miss	London	1858	Landscape	—	—	—	—	1	—	—	—	—	—	1
Morrow, Albert G.	London	1890-1893	Domestic	—	—	4	—	—	—	—	—	—	—	4
Morse, Captain	—	1779-1787	Figures	—	—	11	—	—	—	—	—	—	—	11
Morse, J.	—	1786-1804	Domestic	—	—	9	—	—	—	—	—	—	—	9
Morse, Samuel F. B.	London	1813-1815	Figures	—	—	3	1	—	—	—	—	—	—	4
Morten, Mrs. J. Wells	London	1887	Landscape	—	—	—	—	—	—	1	—	—	—	1
Morten, Thomas	London	1855-1866	Historical	—	—	5	2	5	—	—	—	—	13	25
Mortimer —	London	1778-1782	Figures	—	5	—	—	—	—	—	—	—	—	5
Mortimer, G.	Hendon	1848	Landscape	—	—	1	—	—	—	—	—	—	—	1
Mortimer, G. A.	London	1847	Figures	—	—	—	—	1	—	—	—	—	—	1
Mortimer, John Hamilton, A.R.A., Pres. F.S.A.	London	1762-1779	Portraits	89	3	13	—	—	—	—	—	—	—	105
Mortimer, John Hamilton	London	1806	Historical	—	—	—	4	—	—	—	—	—	—	4
Mortimer, Robert	London	1891	Architecture	—	—	1	—	—	—	—	—	—	—	1
Mortlock, Miss Ethel	London	1878-1893	Portraits	—	—	21	—	—	—	—	2	—	—	23
Morton, Andrew	London	1821-1845	Figures	—	—	58	35	4	—	—	—	—	—	97
Morton, Lieut. C., R.N.	—	1819	Monuments	—	—	1	—	—	—	—	—	—	—	1
Morton, Edgar	London	1885-1886	Landscape	—	—	—	—	2	—	—	—	—	1	3
Morton, George	London	1879-1893	Domestic	—	—	13	—	9	—	7	1	—	24	54
Morton, Henry	London	1807-1825	Flowers	—	—	11	—	—	3	—	—	—	6	20
Morton, J.	London	1791-1807	Landscape	—	—	16	—	—	—	—	—	—	—	16
Morton, J., Junr.	London	1808-1817	Churches	—	—	9	—	—	—	—	—	—	—	9
Morton, Maria	London	1839-1851	Miniatures	—	—	2	—	—	—	—	—	—	—	2
Morton, R.	London	1794	Architecture	—	—	1	—	—	—	—	—	—	—	1
Morton, T. Corson	Glasgow	1887-1890	Landscape	—	—	—	—	1	—	—	1	—	—	2
Morton, William	Manchester	1869-1876	Landscape	—	—	—	—	—	—	—	—	—	2	2
Morton, W. S.	London	1864	Architecture	—	—	1	—	—	—	—	—	—	—	1
Moscheles, Felix	London	1862-1889	Figures	—	—	22	2	1	—	—	18	1	4	48
Moseley, Henry	London	1842-1866	Portraits	—	—	24	1	6	—	—	—	—	—	31
Moseley, Mrs. Henry. ‖ *See* Miss M. A. Chalon	London	1841-1866	Miniatures	—	—	78	1	—	—	—	—	—	—	79
Moseley, R. S.	London	1862-1893	Domestic	—	—	15	13	37	—	—	—	—	5	70
Moseley, William	Ealing	1821-1861	Architecture	—	—	16	—	—	—	—	—	—	—	16
Moseley, Messrs.	London	1856	Architecture	—	—	1	—	—	—	—	—	—	—	1
Moser, George Michael, R.A.	London	1760-1770	Metal Work	13	—	3	—	—	—	—	—	—	—	16

Name.	Town.	First and Last Year of Ex.	Speciality.	S. A.	F. S.	R. A.	B. I.	S. S.	O. W.	N.W.	G. G.	N. G.	V. E.	Total
Moser, Joseph	London	1774-1787	Enamels	—	—	12	—	—	—	—	—	—	—	12
Moser, Miss Mary, R.A. *See* Mrs. Lloyd	London	1760-1792	Flowers	10	—	32	—	—	—	—	—	—	—	42
Moser, Robert James	London	1871-1893	Landscape	—	—	5	—	1	—	8	—	—	1	15
Moses, Henry	London	1828	Sea Pieces	—	—	—	—	2	—	—	—	—	—	2
Mosler, Henry	Paris	1892	Domestic	—	—	2	—	—	—	—	—	—	—	2
Mosley, L.	Burton-on-Trent	1859	Domestic	—	—	—	—	—	—	—	—	—	2	2
Mosley, R.	Dublin	1840-1841	Gems	—	—	5	—	—	—	—	—	—	—	5
Mosnier, Jean Laurent	Paris	1791-1796	Portraits	—	—	32	—	—	—	—	—	—	—	32
Moss, John H. B.	Gloucester	1892	Study	—	—	1	—	—	—	—	—	—	—	1
Moss, S.	Bristol	1828-1829	Portraits	—	—	1	—	2	—	—	—	—	—	3
Moss, William	London	1775-1782	Architecture	—	—	7	—	—	—	—	—	—	—	7
Moss, W. G.	London	1814-1827	Landscape	—	—	19	3	3	—	—	—	—	—	25
Mossa, Alexis	Nice	1876	Landscape	—	—	—	—	—	—	—	—	—	1	1
Mosses, Alexander	Liverpool	1820	Figures	—	—	1	—	—	—	—	—	—	—	1
Mosses, W. J.	London	1876	Sea Pieces	—	—	—	—	1	—	—	—	—	—	1
Mossman, David	Newcastle	1853-1888	Miniatures, etc.	—	—	10	—	9	—	8	—	—	—	27
Mossman, George	London	1846	Sculpture	—	—	2	—	—	—	—	—	—	—	2
Mossman, John, R.S.A.	Glasgow	1868-1879	Sculpture	—	—	6	—	—	—	—	—	—	—	6
Mossman, W. H.	London	1838-1840	Figures	—	—	—	—	2	—	—	—	—	—	2
Mostyn, Tom E.	Stockport	1891	Landscape	—	—	1	—	—	—	—	—	—	—	1
Mote, G. W.	London	1857-1877	Figures	—	—	15	5	18	—	—	—	—	14	52
Mote, W. H., Junr.	London	1855	Figures	—	—	—	—	1	—	—	—	—	—	1
Motelli, G.	London	1846	Sculpture	—	—	1	—	—	—	—	—	—	—	1
Motelli, M.	London	1855	Sculpture	—	—	1	—	—	—	—	—	—	—	1
Mothans, Alfred	London	1883	Landscape	—	—	—	—	—	—	1	—	—	—	1
Mott, Miss Alice M.	Walton-on-Thames	1877-1892	Miniatures	—	—	12	—	3	—	—	—	—	5	20
Mott, Edwin	London	1872-1877	Domestic	—	—	—	—	4	—	—	—	—	1	5
Mott, J.	London	1854	Game	—	—	1	—	1	—	—	—	—	—	2
Mott, J. N.	London	1845	Portraits	—	—	1	—	—	—	—	—	—	—	1
Mott, Miss Laura	London	1892	Portraits	—	—	1	—	—	—	—	—	—	—	1
Mott, R. S.	London	1871-1872	Cattle, etc.	—	—	—	—	2	—	—	—	—	—	2
Motte, Henri	Neuilly	1882	Historical	—	—	1	—	—	—	—	—	—	—	1
Motte, De la. *See* D.	—	—	—	—	—	—	—	—	—	—	—	—	—	—
Mottez, V.	Bievres	1849-1877	Portraits	—	—	8	—	—	—	—	2	—	—	10
Mottram, A.	London	1886	Landscape	—	—	—	—	—	—	1	—	—	—	1
Mottram, Charles	London	1861-1877	Engraving	—	—	7	—	—	—	—	—	—	—	7
Mottram, Charles Sim, R.B.A. §	London	1876-1893	Sea Pieces	—	—	28	—	68	—	16	—	—	6	118
Mottram, J. M.	London	1888	Birds	—	—	—	—	—	—	1	—	—	—	1
Mouchet, A.	London	1816	Portraits	—	—	2	—	—	—	—	—	—	—	2
Mould, J. W.	London	1848	Landscape	—	—	1	—	—	—	—	—	—	—	1
Moulting, George	London	1847-1857	Portraits	—	—	2	—	15	—	—	—	—	—	17
Moultray, J. Douglas	Edinburgh	1870-1872	Landscape	—	—	2	—	—	—	—	—	—	—	2
Mounsey, R. K.	London	1887	Domestic	—	—	—	—	—	—	—	—	—	2	2
Mountague, F. William	London	1831	Architecture	—	—	1	—	—	—	—	—	—	—	1
Mountain, William	London	1881-1883	Landscape	—	—	—	—	2	—	—	—	—	2	4
Mountford, Edward William	London	1885-1893	Architecture	—	—	22	—	—	—	—	—	—	—	22
Mountstephen, Eley George	London	1782-1791	Sculpture	—	1	21	—	—	—	—	—	—	—	22
Mouque, A.	London	1838-1844	Cattle	—	—	—	1	5	—	—	—	—	—	6
Mourant, E.	London	1883	Landscape	—	—	—	—	—	—	1	—	—	—	1
Mouvell, M. Boulet De *See* D.	—	—	—	—	—	—	—	—	—	—	—	—	—	—
Mowbray, A. Mardon	Eastbourne	1882-1890	Architecture	—	—	2	—	—	—	—	—	—	—	2
Mowson, J.	London	1797-1808	Mythological	—	—	16	—	—	—	—	—	—	—	16
Moxon, J.	Edinburgh	1880	Rustic	—	—	—	—	2	—	—	—	—	—	2
Moye, J. J.	London	1859	Architecture	—	—	1	—	—	—	—	—	—	—	1
Moye, Joseph Staines	London	1865-1880	Architecture	—	—	3	—	—	—	—	—	—	—	3
Moyes, F.	London	1881	Landscape	—	—	—	—	1	—	—	—	—	—	1
Moysey, Rev. C. A.	—	1806-1809	Sea Pieces	—	—	3	—	—	—	—	—	—	—	3
Mücke, Heinrich Karl Anton	London	1883	Domestic	—	—	1	—	—	—	—	—	—	—	1
Muckley, Arthur Fairfax	—	1886-1891	Landscape	—	—	2	—	1	—	—	1	—	2	6
Muckley, Louis F.	Stourbridge	1887-1891	Landscape	—	—	2	—	—	—	—	2	—	—	4
Muckley, William J., R.B.A. §	Wolverhampt'n	1858-1893	Flowers	—	—	52	2	21	—	5	26	—	8	114
Mudge —	London	1783	Landscape	—	1	—	—	—	—	—	—	—	—	1
Mudge, Alfred	Richmond	1862-1877	Figures	—	—	1	3	—	—	—	—	—	—	4
Muheim, J.	Altorf	1859	Landscape	—	—	1	—	—	—	—	—	—	—	1
Mühlenfeldt, Mrs. Louisa S.	London	1846-1865	Flowers	—	—	4	11	11	—	—	—	—	1	27
Muhrman, Henry	London	1884-1890	Rustic	—	—	—	—	8	—	1	7	—	—	16
Muir, Miss Agnes	London	1879	Domestic	—	—	1	—	—	—	—	—	—	—	1
Muir, David	London	1884-1888	Landscape	—	—	1	—	1	—	—	—	—	—	2
Muir, H.	London	1857	Landscape	—	—	—	—	1	—	—	—	—	—	1
Muir, Miss Jessie	London	1884	Churches	—	—	—	—	—	—	1	—	—	—	1
Muir, W. Temple	Burnham	1887-1891	Landscape	—	—	2	—	—	—	—	—	—	1	3
Muirhead, Charles	Liverpool	1886-1891	Landscape	—	—	5	—	—	—	1	—	—	1	7

Name.	Town.	First and Last Year of Ex.	Speciality.	S. A.	F. S.	R. A.	B. I.	S. S.	O. W.	N. W.	G. G.	N. G.	V. E.	Total.
Muirhead, John, R.S.W.	London	1889-1893	Landscape	—	—	4	—	—	—	—	—	—	—	4
Muirhead, L.	Tetsworth	1877-1884	Florence	—	—	1	—	—	—	2	—	—	—	3
Mulcahy, J. H., A.R.H.A.	Limerick	1852	Landscape	—	—	—	—	1	—	—	—	—	—	1
Mulholland, R.	London	1831	Buildings	—	—	—	—	1	—	—	—	—	—	1
Muller, Professor Carl	Düsseldorf	1872-1889	Scriptural	—	—	7	—	—	—	—	3	—	—	10
Müller, Daniel	Putney	1863-1878	Sporting	—	—	4	4	16	—	—	—	—	—	24
Müller, E.	Rome	1875	Sculpture	—	—	2	—	—	—	—	—	—	—	2
Müller, Edmund Gustavus	Bristol	1836-1871	Landscape	—	—	—	1	12	—	—	—	—	—	13
Muller, Mrs. E. G., late Miss Rosa Branwhite.	Bristol	1861-1867	Landscape	—	—	—	—	3	—	—	—	—	—	3
Muller, Frans	London	1872-1877	Mountains	—	—	1	—	1	—	—	—	—	—	2
Muller, G. de Coburg	Rome	1870	Domestic	—	—	1	—	—	—	—	—	—	—	1
Muller, Paul	London	1881	Landscape	—	—	1	—	—	—	—	—	—	—	1
Muller, R.	London	1789-1800	Portraits	—	—	28	—	—	—	—	—	—	—	28
Müller Robert Antoine	London	1872-1881	Portraits	—	—	7	—	3	—	—	—	—	—	10
Muller, W.	Windsor	1797	Portraits	—	—	1	—	—	—	—	—	—	—	1
Müller, William James	Bristol	1833-1845	Landscape	—	—	17	14	9	—	—	—	—	—	40
Mullholland, J.	London	1793-1805	Architecture	—	—	4	—	—	—	—	—	—	—	4
Mullins, Edwin Roscoe	London	1873-1893	Sculpture	—	—	36	—	14	—	—	21	20	17	108
Mullins, George	London	1770-1775	Landscape	—	—	16	—	—	—	—	—	—	—	16
Mullins, J.	London	1814-1827	Architecture	—	—	6	—	—	—	—	—	—	—	6
Mullins, T. P.	London	1881	Landscape	—	—	—	—	2	—	—	—	—	—	2
Mulock, Frederick C.	London	1888-1893	Landscape	—	—	4	—	—	—	—	1	—	1	6
Mulready, Aug. E.	London	1863-1886	Domestic	—	—	12	—	—	—	—	—	—	1	13
Mulready, Eliza R.	London	1828	Landscape	—	—	1	—	—	—	—	—	—	—	1
Mulready, J.	London	1831-1843	Domestic	—	—	7	3	1	—	—	—	—	—	11
Mulready, Michael	London	1830-1851	Portraits	—	—	21	—	1	—	—	—	—	—	22
Mulready, P. A.	London	1827-1855	Domestic	—	—	13	1	3	—	—	—	—	—	17
Mulready, William, R.A.	London	1804-1862	Figures	—	—	77	5	1	—	—	—	—	—	83
Mulready, William Junr.	London	1831-1842	Game	—	—	6	7	5	—	—	—	—	—	18
Mulready, Mrs., late Miss Elizabeth Varley.	London	1811-1819	Landscape	—	—	13	5	—	11	—	—	—	1	30
Mulrenin, B., R.H.A.	Dublin	1851	Portraits	—	—	2	—	—	—	—	—	—	—	2
Mulvany, George F., A.R.H.A.	Dublin	1836-1839	Figures	—	—	2	—	—	—	—	—	—	—	2
Mummery, Horace	London	1888-1893	Landscape	—	—	1	—	11	—	1	—	—	—	13
Mummery, J. Howard	London	1875-1878	Landscape	—	—	—	—	3	—	—	—	—	3	6
Mummery, S.	Dover	1877	Landscape	—	—	—	—	2	—	—	—	—	—	2
Munby, H. R.	London	1846-1847	Landscape	—	—	4	—	—	—	—	—	—	—	4
Mundy, C.	London	1832-1834	River Scenes	—	—	1	—	3	—	1	—	—	—	5
Mundy, H.	London	1831	Figures	—	—	—	1	—	—	—	—	—	—	1
Munger, Gilbert	London	1879-1885	Landscape	—	—	7	—	1	—	—	—	—	1	9
Munkacsy, Michael de (Michael Lieb)	Paris	1880-1882	Domestic	—	—	2	—	—	—	—	—	—	—	2
Munn, G.	Northfleet	1859	Landscape	—	—	1	—	—	—	—	—	—	—	1
Munn, George Frederick, R.B.A. §	London	1875-1886	Figures	—	—	13	—	19	—	—	5	—	12	49
Munn, James	London	1764-1774	Landscape	2	4	—	—	—	—	—	—	—	—	6
Munn, N. P.	Greenwich	1798	Landscape	—	—	3	—	—	—	—	—	—	—	3
Munn, Paul Sandby	Greenwich	1799-1815	Landscape	—	—	29	—	—	40	—	—	—	—	69
Munn, W. A.	—	1852	Coast Scenes	—	—	1	—	—	—	—	—	—	—	1
Munns, Henry Turner	Birmingham	1866-1891	Domestic	—	—	8	2	10	—	—	—	—	—	20
Munro, Alexander	London	1849-1870	Sculpture	—	—	97	14	—	1	—	—	—	2	114
Munro, Mrs. Campbell (Henrietta M.)	London	1878-1888	Portraits	—	—	2	—	—	—	—	2	—	—	4
Munro, Charlotte	—	1870	Heads	—	—	—	—	1	—	—	—	—	—	1
Munro, Ensign John	—	1775	Landscape	1	—	—	—	—	—	—	—	—	—	1
Munro, J. Calder	Cheltenham	1860-1861	Domestic	—	—	—	—	—	—	—	—	—	2	2
Munthe, L.	London	1877-1881	Landscape	—	—	4	—	—	—	—	—	—	—	4
Muntz, J. H.	—	1762	Landscape	5	—	—	—	—	—	—	—	—	—	5
Muraton, Madame	Paris	1873	Flowers	—	—	1	—	—	—	—	—	—	—	1
Murch, Mrs. Arthur	Rome	1880-1890	Figures	—	—	—	—	—	—	—	22	6	1	29
Murch, Edith	Rome	1878	Landscape	—	—	—	—	—	—	—	—	—	2	2
Murch, Henry	Bath	1850-1851	Landscape	—	—	1	3	—	—	—	—	—	—	4
Murdoch, W. G. Burn-	Edinburgh	1891	Portraits	—	—	1	—	—	—	—	—	—	—	1
Murphy, D. B., father of Mrs. Jameson	London	1800-1827	Portraits	—	—	27	1	—	—	—	—	—	—	28
Murphy, Michael	London	1890-1893	Sculpture	—	—	2	—	—	—	—	—	—	—	2
Murphy, Miss	—	1783	Mythological	—	1	—	—	—	—	—	—	—	—	1
Murray —	London	1763-1770	Miniatures	2	13	—	—	—	—	—	—	—	—	15
Murray, Alexander Henry Hallam	London	1881-1892	Buildings	—	—	7	—	2	—	4	—	—	3	16
Murray, Charles Fairfax	London	1867-1890	Domestic	—	—	2	—	—	—	—	17	5	4	28
Murray, Charles Oliver, R.P.E.	London	1872-1893	Etching	—	—	30	—	—	—	—	—	—	25	55
Murray, C. S.	London	1855	River Scenes	—	—	—	—	—	—	—	—	—	1	1
Murray, David, A.R.A., A.R.W.S., A.R.S.A. R.S.W. † φ	Glasgow	1875-1893	Landscape	—	—	42	—	—	46	2	41	16	28	175
Murray, E.	London	1880	Domestic	—	—	1	—	—	—	—	—	—	—	1
Murray, Hon. Lady Edith	London	1880	Buildings	—	—	—	—	1	—	—	—	—	2	3
Murray, Ethel	London	1883	Figures	—	—	—	—	1	—	—	—	—	—	1

Name.	Town.	First and Last Year of Ex.	Speciality.	S. A.	F. S.	R. A.	B. I.	S. S.	O. W.	N.W.	G. G.	N. G.	V. E.	Total.
Murray, Miss Elizabeth Emily	London	1888-1890	Domestic	—	—	—	—	—	—	2	—	—	—	2
Murray, Mrs. Eliza Dundas	London	1859-1861	Sea Pieces	—	—	1	—	1	—	—	—	—	—	2
Murray, Frank	London	1876-1892	Landscape	—	—	16	—	8	—	5	—	—	27	56
Murray, Miss Florence E.	London	1890	Buildings	—	—	—	—	1	—	—	—	—	—	1
Murray, G.	London	1791-1793	Architecture	2	—	2	—	—	—	—	—	—	—	4
Murray, H.	London	1850-1860	Historical	—	—	—	2	1	—	—	—	—	—	3
Murray, Mrs. Henry John. ‡ *See* Miss Elizabeth	—	—	—	—	—	—	—	—	—	—	—	—	—	—
Heaphy	London	1846-1882	Figures	—	—	7	—	2	—	52	1	—	8	70
Murray, James	London	1858-1865	Architecture	—	—	8	—	—	—	—	—	—	—	8
Murray, J. Reid	Glasgow	1892	Landscape	—	—	1	—	—	—	—	—	—	—	1
Murray, Miss Maria	Dulwich	1852-1881	Figures	—	—	4	—	2	—	—	—	—	1	7
Murray, Mungo	London	1768	Shipping	—	2	—	—	—	—	—	—	—	—	2
Murray, Robert Cuninghame	London	1893	Architecture	—	—	1	—	—	—	—	—	—	—	1
Murray, W.	London	1866	Sculpture	—	—	1	—	—	—	—	—	—	—	1
Murray, W. Bazett	London	1871-1875	Figures	—	—	1	—	—	—	—	—	—	6	7
Murray, W. Hay	Hastings	1880-1884	Landscape	—	—	3	—	—	—	—	—	—	—	3
Murray-Cookesley, Mrs. Margaret. *See* C.	—	—	—	—	—	—	—	—	—	—	—	—	—	—
Mus, Boniface	London	1790	Landscape	1	—	—	—	—	—	—	—	—	—	1
Muschamp, Francis	London	1865-1881	Landscape	—	—	—	3	17	—	—	—	—	—	20
Muschamp, F. Sydney	London	1870-1893	Figures	—	—	5	—	38	—	—	—	—	12	55
Musgrave, G. A.	London	1877	Pen and Ink	—	—	—	—	—	—	—	—	—	1	1
Musgrave, Rev. G. M. §	—	1816-1826	Ruins	—	—	3	—	11	—	—	—	—	—	14
Musgrave, Harry	London	1884-1893	Sea Pieces	—	—	8	—	—	—	—	—	—	2	10
Musgrave, Thomas M.	London	1844-1862	Still Life	—	—	2	8	10	—	—	—	—	—	20
Musgrave, Mrs. W. *See* Miss M. A. Heaphy	—	1833-1847	Portraits	—	—	10	—	—	—	—	—	—	—	10
Musgrave, W. T.	Edinburgh	1841-1847	Portraits	—	—	2	—	—	—	—	—	—	—	2
Musgrave, Miss	Sidmouth	1891	Flowers	—	—	—	—	1	—	—	—	—	—	1
Muspratt, R. F. L.	Flint	1872	Buildings	—	—	1	—	—	—	—	—	—	—	1
Muss, Charles	London	1800-1823	Enamels	—	—	21	—	—	—	—	—	—	—	21
Mussard, J.	London	1763-1768	Miniatures	3	—	—	—	—	—	—	—	—	—	3
Mussini, Professor, Luigi	Siena	1866	Landscape	—	—	1	—	—	—	—	—	—	—	1
Musurus, P.	London	1858	Portraits	—	—	—	—	1	—	—	—	—	—	1
Mutrie, Miss Annie Feray	Manchester	1851-1882	Flowers	—	—	47	6	—	—	—	—	—	4	57
Mutrie, Miss Martha Darley	Manchester	1853-1884	Flowers	—	—	43	1	—	—	3	—	—	2	49
Myall, H. A.	—	1835-1838	Figures	—	—	—	—	3	—	—	—	—	—	3
Myddleton, J.	—	1803	Miniatures	—	—	3	—	—	—	—	—	—	—	3
Myers, G.	London	1853	Buildings	—	—	1	—	—	—	—	—	—	—	1
Myers, Miss Hannah	London	1893	Miniatures	—	—	1	—	—	—	—	—	—	—	1
Myers, John	London	1883-1886	Domestic	—	—	3	—	—	—	—	—	—	—	3
Myers, Simeon	London	1874-1875	Etching	—	—	—	—	—	—	—	—	—	3	3
Mylne, H.	London	1866	Heads	—	—	1	—	—	—	—	—	—	—	1
Mylne, Robert	London	1845	Architecture	—	—	1	—	—	—	—	—	—	—	1
Mylne, Mrs. Robert William	London	1867	Portraits	—	—	1	—	—	—	—	—	—	—	1
Mylne, W. C.	London	1797-1802	Landscape	—	—	2	—	—	—	—	—	—	—	2
Myres, T. H.	Preston	1877	Architecture	—	—	1	—	—	—	—	—	—	—	1
Nacciarone, Gustave	London	1884	Figures	—	—	—	—	1	—	—	—	—	—	1
Naden, T.	—	1862	Architecture	—	—	1	—	—	—	—	—	—	—	1
Naegely, Henry	London	1879-1893	Landscape	—	—	2	—	—	—	—	—	—	—	2
Naftel, Miss Isabel	Guernsey	1870-1873	Portraits	—	—	4	—	—	—	—	—	—	—	4
Naftel, Miss Maude, A.R.W.S. † ‖	London	1875-1889	Flowers	—	—	9	—	—	16	5	11	2	10	53
Naftel, Paul Jacob, R.W.S. †	Guernsey	1850-1891	Landscape	—	—	—	—	—	689	—	2	—	—	691
Naftel, Mrs. Paul J. ‖ *See* Miss Isabel	—	—	—	—	—	—	—	—	—	—	—	—	—	—
Oakley	Guernsey	1857-1891	Domestic	—	—	10	—	13	—	9	10	5	7	54
Nailor, Miss	—	1819	Portraits	—	—	2	—	—	—	—	—	—	—	2
Naish, John	London	1790-1795	Miniatures	—	—	9	—	—	—	—	—	—	—	9
Naish, J.	—	1872	Architecture	—	—	1	—	—	—	—	—	—	—	1
Naish, John George	Midhurst	1843-1893	Nymphs, etc.	—	—	39	20	2	—	—	—	—	34	95
Naish, William	London	1786-1800	Miniatures	—	—	42	—	—	—	—	—	—	—	42
Nalder, James H.	London	1853-1881	Figures	—	—	3	8	16	—	—	—	—	7	34
Nankivell, Miss Helen L.	London	1892-1893	Buildings	—	—	—	—	3	—	—	—	—	—	3
Napier, Lady, of Magdala	London	1892-1893	Landscape	—	—	—	—	—	—	—	—	—	2	2
Napier, Mrs. Eva	London	1885-1889	Landscape	—	—	1	—	1	—	—	—	—	1	3
Napier, John J.	London	1856-1876	Portraits	—	—	32	5	—	—	—	—	—	—	37
Napier, J. Macvicar	Ganrock	1889-1890	Seashores	—	—	2	—	—	—	—	—	—	—	2
Napier, General Sir William	Bath	1821-1858	Sculpture	—	—	2	—	—	—	—	—	—	—	2
Napper, Harry, *or* Nipper.	London	1890-1891	Seashores	—	—	—	—	2	—	—	—	—	—	2
Naril, C.	—	1876	Battles	—	—	1	—	—	—	—	—	—	—	1
Narrien, J.	—	1810	Architecture	—	—	1	—	—	—	—	—	—	—	1
Nash, Edward	London	1800-1820	Miniatures	—	—	17	—	—	—	—	—	—	—	17

Name.	Town.	First and Last Year of Ex.	Speciality.	S. A.	F. S.	R. A.	B. I.	S. S.	O. W.	N.W.	G. G.	N. G.	V. E.	Total.
Nash, Edwin	London	1832-1848	Architecture	—	—	7	—	1	—	—	—	—	—	8
Nash, Miss Elizabeth F.	Cambridge	1830-1836	Portraits	—	—	3	—	—	—	—	—	—	—	3
Nash, Frederick †	London	1799-1856	Landscape	—	—	51	63	7	472	—	—	—	23	616
Nash, G. V.§	London	1827-1830	Portraits	—	—	—	—	4	—	—	—	—	—	4
Nash, John	London	1796-1805	Architecture	—	—	24	—	—	—	—	—	—	—	24
Nash, Joseph †	Dulwich	1831-1879	Historical	—	—	3	11	—	276	6	—	—	—	296
Nash, Joseph, Junr., R.I.‡	London	1859-1893	Sea Pieces	—	—	4	—	4	—	18	—	—	16	42
Nash, J. E.	London	1845-1847	Architecture	—	—	2	—	—	—	—	—	—	—	2
Nash, Mrs. J. N. (Laura E.)	Guernsey	1872-1874	Domestic	—	—	—	—	—	—	—	—	—	3	3
Nash, J. O.	Plymouth	1891-1893	Sea Pieces	—	—	—	—	—	—	2	—	—	—	2
Nash, Walter Hilton	London	1889	Architecture	—	—	2	—	—	—	—	—	—	—	2
Nasmyth, Alexander §	Edinburgh	1807-1839	Landscape	—	—	9	18	3	—	—	—	—	—	30
Nasmyth, Miss A. G.	Edinburgh	1829-1838	Landscape	—	—	1	4	11	—	—	—	—	—	16
Nasmyth, Barbara	London	1854-1866	Landscape	—	—	—	—	7	—	—	—	—	—	7
Nasmyth, Miss Charlotte	Manchester	1837-1866	Landscape	—	—	6	2	31	—	—	—	—	—	39
Nasmyth, Miss E.	London	1838-1866	Landscape	—	—	—	1	1	—	—	—	—	—	2
Nasmyth, Miss Jane	Edinburgh	1826-1866	Landscape	—	—	—	5	11	—	—	—	—	—	16
Nasmyth, Miss Margaret	Manchester	1841-1865	Landscape	—	—	—	—	11	—	—	—	—	—	11
Nasmyth, Miss. *See* Mrs. E. Terry.	—	—	—	—	—	—	—	—	—	—	—	—	—	—
Nasmyth, Patrick §	London	1811-1832	Landscape	—	—	20	78	23	—	—	—	—	—	121
Nasmyth-Langlands, George. *See* L.	—	—	—	—	—	—	—	—	—	—	—	—	—	—
Nathan, Adelaide A. Burnett	London	1883-1886	Domestic	—	—	—	—	4	—	—	—	—	—	4
Nathan, Annette M.	London	1881-1886	Domestic	—	—	—	—	4	—	—	—	—	—	4
Nathan, Miss Fanny	Richmond	1892	Landscape	—	—	—	—	—	—	—	—	—	1	1
Nathusius, Madame Susanne Von	Madsburg	1880-1885	Portraits	—	—	—	—	—	—	—	1	—	1	2
Natorp, Gustav	London	1884-1893	Sculpture	—	—	6	—	—	—	—	—	—	—	6
Nattes, John Claude †	London	1781-1814	Landscape	—	—	50	—	—	34	—	—	—	—	84
Nattress, George	London	1866-1888	Buildings	—	—	22	—	—	—	3	—	1	5	31
Naughten, Miss Elizabeth	London	1867-1882	Landscape	—	—	—	—	2	—	—	—	—	11	13
Navier, G.	Paris	1872	Domestic	—	—	—	—	2	—	—	—	—	—	2
Navlet, V.	Paris	1869	Buildings	—	—	1	—	—	—	—	—	—	—	1
Navone, Edoardo	Surbiton	1891	Domestic	—	—	1	—	—	—	—	—	—	—	1
Nayler, Miss S. E.	—	1812-1819	Portraits	—	—	2	—	—	—	—	—	—	—	2
Naylor, Mrs. Francis Hare. *See* Miss Georgina Shipley.	—	—	—	—	—	—	—	—	—	—	—	—	—	—
Naylor, Miss Marie J.	Barnes	1883-1892	Portraits	—	—	3	—	10	—	—	—	—	1	14
Naylor, T.	London	1788	Shipping	—	—	2	—	—	—	—	—	—	—	2
Neal, David	Munich	1874	Historical	—	—	1	—	—	—	—	—	—	—	1
Neale, Edward	London	1858-1881	Landscape	—	—	1	6	9	—	—	—	—	9	25
Neale, Edward J.	Dulwich	1886-1889	Landscape	—	—	—	—	2	—	—	—	—	—	2
Neale, Rev. Edward Pate	—	1817-1833	Landscape	—	—	3	—	—	—	—	—	—	—	3
Neale, G. Hall	Liverpool	1891-1892	Domestic	—	—	2	—	—	—	—	—	—	—	2
Neale, J.	London	1801	Landscape	—	—	1	—	—	—	—	—	—	—	1
Neale, J.	London	1846	Domestic	—	—	1	—	—	—	—	—	—	—	1
Neale, James, F.S.A., F.R.I.B.A.	London	1877-1893	Architecture	—	—	19	—	—	—	—	—	—	—	19
Neale, John Preston	London	1797-1844	Landscape	—	—	47	14	6	7	—	—	—	—	74
Neale, Dr. M. R.	—	1801-1828	Landscape	—	—	1	1	—	—	—	—	—	—	2
Neale, Miss	London	1797-1800	Miniatures	—	—	5	—	—	—	—	—	—	—	5
Neave, Sir Digby	—	1836-1864	Landscape	—	—	1	1	—	—	—	—	—	—	2
Needham, Lieut.-Col.	London	1880	Landscape	—	—	—	—	—	—	—	1	—	—	1
Needham, E.	London	1786-1790	Portraits	—	—	5	—	—	—	—	—	—	—	5
Needham, Jonathan	London	1858-1870	Landscape	—	—	—	—	—	—	—	—	—	29	29
Needham, Joseph G.	London	1860-1874	Landscape	—	—	—	2	7	—	—	—	—	—	9
Negelen —	London	1837-1839	Portraits	—	—	11	—	—	—	—	—	—	—	11
Neil, H.	—	1800-1804	Landscape	—	—	4	—	—	—	—	—	—	—	4
Neil-Knight, C. *See* K.	—	—	—	—	—	—	—	—	—	—	—	—	—	—
Neille —	London	1790	Architecture	1	—	—	—	—	—	—	—	—	—	1
Neilson, E.	London	1883	Still Life	—	—	—	—	1	—	—	—	—	—	1
Nelson, A.	London	1766-1790	Landscape	13	—	2	—	—	—	—	—	—	—	15
Nelson, Mrs. D.	—	1856	Portraits	—	—	1	—	—	—	—	—	—	—	1
Nelson, George	London	1837-1869	Sculpture	—	—	14	—	—	—	—	—	—	—	14
Nelson, S.	London	1790-1800	Architecture	—	—	6	—	—	—	—	—	—	—	6
Nelson, Miss S. R.	Twickenham	1846-1847	Figures	—	—	—	—	2	—	—	—	—	—	2
Nelson, Thomas Marsh	London	1830-1837	Architecture	—	—	6	—	—	—	—	—	—	—	6
Nelson, William J.	London	1879-1883	Domestic	—	—	1	—	1	—	—	—	—	—	2
Nepean, Evan	—	1820	Landscape	—	—	2	—	—	—	—	—	—	—	2
Neret, Adrien Moreau	Paris	1886-1889	Figures	—	—	—	—	2	—	1	—	—	—	3
Nerly, F.	Venice	1843	Venice	—	—	1	—	—	—	—	—	—	—	1
Neruda, L. Norman	—	1886	Figures	—	—	—	—	—	—	—	1	—	—	1
Nesbit, John, F.S.A.	—	1768	Historical	1	—	—	—	—	—	—	—	—	—	1
Nesbitt, Miss Fannie M.	London	1881-1885	Landscape	—	—	—	—	1	—	—	—	—	1	2
Nesbitt, Miss Frances E.	London	1888-1893	Rustic	—	—	—	—	16	—	2	—	—	—	18

Name.	Town.	First and Last Year of Ex.	Speciality.	S. A.	F. S.	R. A.	B. I.	S. S.	O. W.	N.W.	G. G.	N. G.	V. E.	Total.
Nesbitt, John	Edinburgh	1870-1888	Landscape	—	—	16	—	—	—	—	—	—	—	16
Nesbitt, Sidney	London	1872-1878	Landscape	—	—	1	—	2	—	—	—	—	5	8
Nesfield, William Andrews †	London	1823-1851	Landscape	—	—	—	—	—	91	—	—	—	—	91
Netscher, W. A.	London	1829-1830	Domestic	—	—	—	4	—	—	—	—	—	—	4
Nettleship, John Trivett	London	1871-1893	Animals	—	—	20	—	1	—	3	9	7	20	60
Neuhuys, Albert	—	1880-1883	Domestic	—	—	—	—	—	—	—	3	—	1	4
Neuhuys, Joseph	—	1880	Landscape	—	—	—	—	—	—	—	1	—	—	1
Neümans, Alphonse	Scarborough	1873-1889	Figures	—	—	3	—	2	—	—	—	—	—	5
Neustein, A. S.	London	1848	Landscape	—	—	2	—	—	—	—	—	—	—	2
Neuville, Alphonse de. *See* D.	—	—	—	—	—	—	—	—	—	—	—	—	—	—
Nevay, James	Rome	1773-1791	Historical	3	—	2	—	—	—	—	—	—	—	5
Neve, A. Aug.	London	1888-1889	Domestic	—	—	1	—	—	—	—	—	—	1	2
Neve, William West	London	1877-1881	Architecture	—	—	6	—	—	—	—	—	—	—	6
Neve (W. W.) and Newton (Ernest)	—	1882-1893	Architecture	—	—	2	—	—	—	—	—	—	—	2
Nevill, Ralph, F.S.A.	London	1870-1889	Architecture	—	—	9	—	—	—	—	—	—	—	9
Nevin, D. M.	London	1783	Miniatures	—	1	—	—	—	—	—	—	—	—	1
Nevins, W. Probyn-	London	1885	Domestic	—	—	—	—	—	—	—	—	—	1	1
New, Miss E.	Munster	1864	Portraits	—	—	1	—	—	—	—	—	—	—	1
New, G. R.	London	1810-1814	Architecture	—	—	2	—	—	—	—	—	—	—	2
Newbery, Francis H.	Glasgow	1884-1891	Domestic	—	—	2	—	1	—	—	—	—	1	4
Newbery, Miss Maud	Blackheath	1892	Fruit	—	—	1	—	—	—	—	—	—	—	1
Newberry, John E.	London	1889-1891	Architecture	—	—	2	—	—	—	—	—	—	—	2
Newberry, W. M.	London	1836-1845	Portraits	—	—	2	—	3	—	—	—	—	—	5
Newbold, Miss Annie	London	1892	Landscape	—	—	—	—	—	—	—	—	—	1	1
Newbolt, J.	London	1868	Landscape	—	—	1	—	—	—	—	—	—	—	1
Newby, Alfred T.	Leicester	1885-1890	Landscape	—	—	—	—	—	—	2	—	—	—	2
Newcombe, Miss Bertha ‖	Croydon	1876-1893	Landscape	—	—	9	—	8	—	1	—	—	16	34
Newcombe, Frederick Clive (Suker)	Liverpool	1875-1887	Landscape	—	—	9	—	—	—	—	—	—	—	9
Newcombe, G.	London	1825-1828	Engraving	—	—	4	—	5	—	—	—	—	—	9
Newcomen, Mrs. Olive (?) Miss	London	1862-1872	Animals	—	—	8	2	4	—	—	—	—	1	15
Newell, Hugh	Hollywood, Ireland	1861	Figures	—	—	1	—	3	—	—	—	—	2	6
Newell, J.	London	1817-1827	Portraits	—	—	2	—	—	—	—	—	—	—	2
Newell, Miss S.	London	1819-1838	Miniatures	—	—	40	—	4	—	—	—	—	—	44
Newenham, Frederick	London	1838-1855	Historical	—	—	19	17	—	—	—	—	—	3	39
Newenham, Miss Kate. *See* Mrs. Curwen Gray	—	—	—	—	—	—	—	—	—	—	—	—	—	—
Newham, W.	London	1797	Architecture	—	—	1	—	—	—	—	—	—	—	1
Newman, Miss Catherine M.	London	1886-1892	Flowers	—	—	1	—	1	—	4	—	—	—	6
Newman, Mrs. Charlotte J.	London	1873-1882	Decorations	—	—	2	—	—	—	—	—	—	—	2
Newman, Dudley	London	1892	Architecture	—	—	1	—	—	—	—	—	—	—	1
Newman, Miss E.	London	1862-1863	Fruit	—	—	2	—	—	—	—	—	—	—	2
Newman, E. E.	London	1871	Flowers	—	—	—	—	—	—	—	—	—	1	1
Newman, Miss Florence	London	1890-1893	Sculpture	—	—	7	—	—	—	—	—	2	—	9
Newman, F.	London	1793-1817	Architecture	—	—	3	—	—	—	—	—	—	—	3
Newman (F. B.) and Johnson (J.)	London	1852	Architecture	—	—	1	—	—	—	—	—	—	—	1
Newman, Henry R.	Florence	1879-1885	Buildings	—	—	1	—	—	—	—	4	—	—	5
Newman, John, F.S.A.	London	1807-1838	Architecture	—	—	6	—	—	—	—	—	—	—	6
Newman, Paul	Blackheath	1891-1892	Sculpture	—	—	2	—	—	—	—	—	—	—	2
Newman, Philip Harry	London	1872-1891	Designs	—	—	27	—	9	—	—	—	—	—	36
Newman, Samuel J.	Southampton	1876-1886	Architecture	—	—	4	—	—	—	—	—	—	—	4
Newman, T. H.	London	1841	Miniatures	—	—	1	—	—	—	—	—	—	—	1
Newman, W. S.	London	1780-1798	Architecture	—	—	6	—	—	—	—	—	—	—	6
Newman, Miss	—	1826	Flowers	—	—	1	—	—	—	—	—	—	—	1
Newmarch, Strafford	London	1866-1874	Landscape	—	—	1	1	4	—	—	—	—	—	6
Newmegen, Florence A.	London	1893	Landscape	—	—	—	—	1	—	—	—	—	—	1
Newnham, Simon Viscount	—	1762-1763	Etching	3	—	—	—	—	—	—	—	—	—	3
Newnham, Miss Margaret	London	1864-1865	Fruit	—	—	1	1	—	—	—	—	—	—	2
Newnham, W. H.	London	1822-1830	Architecture	—	—	2	—	—	—	—	—	—	—	2
Newnum, T. E.	York	1846	Landscape	—	—	—	—	1	—	—	—	—	—	1
Newsham, R.	London	1798	Architecture	—	—	1	—	—	—	—	—	—	—	1
Newton, A. H.	London	1851-1856	Landscape	—	—	1	—	3	—	—	—	—	—	4
Newton, Alfred Pizzey, R.W.S. †	London	1855-1883	Landscape	—	—	5	—	1	249	—	—	—	—	255
Newton, C. F.	London	1826	Sporting	—	—	1	—	—	—	—	—	—	—	1
Newton, Charles M.	London	1889-1892	Domestic	—	—	4	—	—	—	—	—	—	—	4
Newton, Mrs. Charles J., late Miss Mary Severn	London	1863-1866	Portraits	—	—	7	—	—	—	—	—	—	4	11
Newton, Ernest. *See also* Neve and Newton	London	1882-1892	Architecture	—	—	18	—	—	—	—	—	—	—	18
Newton, Francis Milner, R.A.	London	1760-1774	Portraits	7	—	8	—	—	—	—	—	—	—	15
Newton, Miss F. M.	Bath	1802	Flowers	—	—	1	—	—	—	—	—	—	—	1
Newton, G.	London	1850-1859	Figures	—	—	2	1	8	—	—	—	—	—	11
Newton, G. H.	London	1858-1871	Landscape	—	—	—	—	14	—	—	—	—	—	14
Newton, Gilbert Stuart, R.A.	London	1818-1833	Domestic	—	—	27	22	—	—	—	—	—	—	49

Name.	Town.	First and Last Year of Ex.	Speciality.	S. A.	F. S.	R. A.	B. I.	S. S.	O. W.	N.W.	G. G.	N.G.	V.E.	Total.
Newton, H. ‡	London	1837-1839	Figures	—	—	—	—	—	—	22	—	—	—	22
Newton, H. J.	—	1833	Portraits	—	—	1	—	—	—	—	—	—	—	1
Newton, Harry Robert	London	1856-1862	Architecture	—	—	8	—	—	—	—	—	—	—	8
Newton, James	London	1776-1777	Engraving	4	—	—	—	—	—	—	—	—	—	4
Newton, John	London	1871-1873	Architecture	—	—	3	—	—	—	—	—	—	—	3
Newton, John Edward	Liverpool	1858-1883	Fruit	—	—	18	2	11	—	1	—	—	5	37
Newton, Miss M. E.	London	1793-1802	Still Life	—	—	3	—	—	—	—	—	—	—	3
Newton, Robert	London	1824-1829	Engraving	—	—	—	—	6	—	—	—	—	—	6
Newton, William, F.S.A.	London	1760-1784	Architecture	10	3	7	—	—	—	—	—	—	—	20
Newton, Sir William John	London	1808-1863	Miniatures	—	—	379	1	—	—	—	—	—	—	380
Newton, Mrs.	London	1815-1820	Flowers	—	—	2	—	—	—	—	—	—	—	2
Ney, Miss E.	Berlin	1866-1868	Sculpture	—	—	3	—	—	—	—	—	—	—	3
Nias, J. M.	Brighton	1878-1879	Landscape	—	—	—	—	2	—	—	—	—	1	3
Niavi, H.	London	1856	Sculpture	—	—	1	—	—	—	—	—	—	—	1
Nibbs, Richard Henry	London	1841-1889	Sea Pieces	—	—	42	38	96	—	—	—	—	29	205
Nichol, Miss Bessie	London	1888-1892	Landscape	—	—	1	—	1	—	—	—	—	4	6
Nichol, Edwin	London	1876-1891	Landscape	—	—	16	—	13	—	—	—	—	4	33
Nichol, H. W.	London	1848	Portraits	—	—	1	—	—	—	—	—	—	—	1
Nicholas, Miss F.	Norwood	1841-1855	Landscape	—	—	—	—	5	—	—	—	—	—	5
Nicholas, P.	—	1783-1788	Sea Pieces	—	—	5	—	—	—	—	—	—	—	5
Nicholl, Andrew, R.H.A.	Belfast	1832-1867	Landscape	—	—	10	4	3	—	3	—	—	2	22
Nicholl, Samuel Joseph. *See also* Willson and Nicholl	— London	— 1856-1888	— Architecture	—	—	16	—	—	—	—	—	—	—	16
Nicholl, Mrs. Samuel Joseph. *See* Miss Agnes Rose Bouvier	— London	— 1874-1892	— Domestic	—	—	8	—	26	—	14	—	—	2	50
Nicholl, W. G.	London	1822-1861	Sculpture	—	—	8	—	2	—	—	—	—	—	10
Nicholls —	Farnham	1838	Fish	—	—	1	—	—	—	—	—	—	—	1
Nicholls, Miss A.	London	1877	Landscape	—	—	—	—	—	—	—	—	—	1	1
Nicholls, Burr H.	Finisterre	1879-1880	Domestic	—	—	—	—	—	—	—	—	—	3	3
Nicholls, Charles	London	1857-1862	Figures	—	—	2	3	—	—	—	—	—	—	5
Nicholls, Charles Wynne, R.H.A.	London	1855-1886	Domestic	—	—	9	7	39	—	—	—	—	17	72
Nicholls, Edward	London	1885-1889	Sculpture	—	—	2	—	—	—	—	—	—	—	2
Nicholls, G. P.	London	1870-1873	Engraving	—	—	3	—	—	—	—	—	—	—	3
Nicholls, H.	Leamington	1857-1858	Fruit	—	—	—	1	1	—	—	—	—	—	2
Nicholls, J. J.	London	1848-1859	Architecture	—	—	7	—	—	—	—	—	—	—	7
Nicholls, Mrs. Rhoda H.	London	1884	Buildings	—	—	1	—	—	—	—	—	—	—	1
Nicholls, Thomas	London	1810-1837	Architecture	—	—	4	—	2	—	—	—	—	—	6
Nicholls, Thomas	London	1864	Sculpture	—	—	2	—	—	—	—	—	—	—	2
Nichols, Alfred	London	1866	Landscape	—	—	—	—	—	—	—	—	—	1	1
Nichols, C.	London	1838	Architecture	—	—	—	—	1	—	—	—	—	—	1
Nichols, Miss Catherine Maude, R.P.E.	Norwich	1877-1891	Etching	—	—	13	—	5	—	—	—	1	16	35
Nichols, Daniell Cubitt	London	1851-1860	Architecture	—	—	2	—	—	—	—	—	—	—	2
Nichols, G. A.	London	1840	Animals	—	—	—	—	1	—	—	—	—	—	1
Nichols, W. P.	Devizes	1885	Landscape	—	—	—	—	—	—	2	—	—	—	2
Nichols, Miss Mary Anne	London	1839-1850	Miniatures	—	—	12	—	37	—	—	—	—	5	54
Nichols, Miss	London	1865	Domestic	—	—	—	—	1	—	—	—	—	—	1
Nicholson, Alexander	Caterham	1871-1884	Landscape	—	—	—	—	6	—	1	—	—	—	7
Nicholson, Miss Alice M.	Newcastle	1884-1888	Still Life	—	—	2	—	1	—	1	—	—	—	4
Nicholson, Miss Emily	London	1842-1869	Landscape	—	—	12	—	19	—	—	—	—	—	31
Nicholson, Ellen M.	London	1847	Scriptural	—	—	—	1	—	—	—	—	—	—	1
Nicholson, Francis †	Whitby	1789-1833	Landscape	6	—	11	—	1	279	—	—	—	21	318
Nicholson, George	London	1831-1832	Landscape	—	—	4	3	3	—	—	—	—	—	10
Nicholson, H.	London	1842-1843	Sculpture	—	—	2	—	—	—	—	—	—	—	2
Nicholson, Hugh	Balham	1893	Miniatures	—	—	1	—	—	—	—	—	—	—	1
Nicholson, J.	Dorking	1848-1850	Cameos	—	—	7	—	—	—	—	—	—	—	7
Nicholson, John M.	Douglas	1880-1885	Landscape	—	—	—	—	—	—	1	7	—	—	8
Nicholson, Michael Angelo	London	1812-1828	Architecture	—	—	5	—	—	—	—	—	—	—	5
Nicholson, Miss M. A.	London	1803-1815	Landscape	—	—	2	—	—	2	—	—	—	6	10
Nicholson, Richard E.	Halifax	1882-1888	Birds	—	—	2	—	—	—	1	—	—	—	3
Nicholson, Lady Sarah Elizabeth	Totteridge	1880	Figures	—	—	1	—	—	—	—	—	—	—	1
Nicholson, Thomas Henry	London	1838	Sculpture	—	—	3	—	—	—	—	—	—	—	3
Nicholson, T. H.	London	1869	Figures	—	—	—	—	—	—	—	—	—	1	1
Nicholson, William, R.S.A.	Newcastle	1808-1822	Portraits	—	—	7	—	—	2	—	—	—	—	9
Nicholson, William Adams	London	1822-1823	Architecture	—	—	2	—	—	—	—	—	—	—	2
Nickson, Miss F. K.	Balham	1886	Rustic	—	—	—	—	1	—	—	—	—	—	1
Nicol, Erskine, R.S.A., A.R.A.	Edinburgh	1851-1893	Domestic	—	—	53	6	—	—	—	—	—	—	59
Nicol, Erskine E.	Colinton, N.B.	1890-1892	Landscape	—	—	2	—	—	—	—	—	—	—	2
Nicol, John Watson φ	London	1876-1893	Historical	—	—	22	—	—	—	—	—	—	13	35
Nicol, William W.	Cheltenham	1848-1864	Domestic	—	—	9	6	—	—	—	—	—	4	19
Nicolas, J. H.	London	1834	Sea Pieces	—	—	1	—	—	—	1	—	—	—	2
Nicolet, Gabriel	London	1884-1893	Domestic	—	—	6	—	—	—	1	—	—	2	9
Nicoli, C.	London	1881	Sculpture	—	—	—	—	1	—	—	—	—	—	1

Name.	Town.	First and Last Year of Ex.	Speciality.	S. A.	F. S.	R. A.	B. I.	S. S.	O. W.	N. W.	G. G.	N. G.	V. E.	Total
Nicoli, F.	London	1818-1819	Sculpture	—	—	4	—	—	—	—	—	—	—	4
Nicolson, John P.	Leith	1891-1893	Landscape	—	—	5	—	2	—	—	—	—	2	9
Niel, Mdlle. Gabrielle	London	1875	Etching	—	—	—	—	—	—	—	—	—	2	2
Nield, W.	London	1839-1844	Architecture	—	—	3	—	—	—	—	—	—	—	3
Niemann, Edward H.	London	1863-1867	Landscape	—	—	—	2	—	—	—	—	—	—	2
Nietnann, Edmund John	Beaconsfield	1844-1872	Landscape	—	—	29	45	40	—	—	—	—	63	177
Nieuwerhuys, E.	London	1868	Figures	—	—	2	—	—	—	—	—	—	—	2
Nightingale, Frederick C.	Wimbledon	1865-1885	Landscape	—	—	—	—	—	—	—	—	—	74	74
Nightingale, John Slaper	London	1873	Architecture	—	—	1	—	—	—	—	—	—	—	1
Nightingale, Leonard Charles	London	1877-1893	Domestic	—	—	10	—	8	—	1	—	—	4	23
Nightingale, Mrs. L. C. (Agnes)	London	1881-1885	Landscape	—	—	2	—	1	—	—	—	—	—	3
Nightingale, R.	Maldon	1847-1874	Sporting	—	—	4	—	25	—	—	—	—	—	29
Nihill, Miss A.	—	1825-1829	Portraits	—	—	2	—	—	—	—	—	—	—	2
Nillett, W.	Lewisham	1867	Churches	—	—	—	—	1	—	—	—	—	—	1
Ninham, W.	London	1797	Portraits	—	—	1	—	—	—	—	—	—	—	1
Nisbet —	—	1763	Landscape	2	—	—	—	—	—	—	—	—	—	2
Nisbet, Miss Frances E.	London	1886	Domestic	—	—	—	—	—	—	—	—	—	1	1
Nisbet, H.	London	1885	Sea Pieces	—	—	—	—	1	—	—	—	—	—	1
Nisbet, Pollok S., R.S.W.	Edinburgh	1884	Coast Scenes	—	—	1	—	—	—	—	—	—	—	1
Nisbet, Robert B., A.R.S.A., R.B.A., R.S.W., R.I. ‡ §	Edinburgh	1888-1893	Landscape	—	—	14	—	18	—	11	2	—	—	45
Nisbett, Miss Ethel C.	London	1884-1893	Flowers	—	—	4	—	5	—	6	—	—	1	16
Nisbett, J. S.	Edinburgh	1871	Landscape	—	—	1	—	—	—	—	—	—	—	1
Nisbett, M.	London	1843	Landscape	—	—	2	1	—	—	—	—	—	—	3
Nittis, J. de. *See* De.	—	—	—	—	—	—	—	—	—	—	—	—	—	—
Niven, David P. M.	London	1880	Landscape	—	—	—	—	1	—	—	—	—	—	1
Niven, William, F.S.A., A.R.P.E.	London	1877-1885	Architecture	—	—	2	—	—	—	—	—	—	1	3
Nixon, Rev. John	—	1784-1815	Landscape	—	—	41	—	—	—	—	—	—	—	41
Nixon, James, A.R.A.	London	1765-1807	Miniatures	11	—	127	13	—	—	—	—	—	—	151
Nixon, J. F.	Tonbridge	1864	Fruit	—	—	—	—	1	—	—	—	—	—	1
Nixon, James Henry	London	1830-1847	Scriptural	—	—	16	5	1	—	—	—	—	—	22
Nixon, Marian	London	1876-1877	Domestic	—	—	—	—	—	—	—	—	—	3	3
Nixon, Rev. Robert	Foots Cray	1790-1808	Landscape	4	—	18	—	—	—	—	—	—	—	22
Nixon, Samuel	London	1826-1846	Sculpture	—	—	13	2	2	—	—	—	—	—	17
Nixon, W. J.	London	1819-1822	Architecture	—	—	2	—	—	—	—	—	—	—	2
Nixon, W. J.	—	1834	Animals	—	—	—	1	—	—	—	—	—	—	1
Nixon, Mrs.	Tonbridge	1865	Fruit	—	—	2	—	—	—	—	—	—	—	2
Noa, Madame Jessie	London	1858-1866	Portraits	—	—	2	—	7	—	—	—	—	—	9
Noakes, C.	London	1828-1829	Figures	—	—	2	1	—	—	—	—	—	—	3
Noakes, Charles G.	Sydenham	1885-1888	Flowers	—	—	—	—	—	—	2	—	—	—	2
Noakes, James	London	1871-1872	Landscape	—	—	—	—	1	—	—	—	—	2	3
Noble, Miss Charlotte M.	London	1871-1892	Domestic	—	—	—	—	41	—	—	—	—	—	41
Noble, F. W.	London	1880	River Scenes	—	—	—	—	1	—	—	—	—	—	1
Noble, G. J. L.	London	1825-1840	Figures	—	—	9	2	13	—	—	—	—	—	24
Noble, James §	London	1829-1878	Domestic	—	—	25	14	156	—	—	—	—	—	195
Noble, J., F.I.B.A.	London	1838	Architecture	—	—	1	—	—	—	—	—	—	—	1
Noble, J. Campbell, R.S.A.	Edinburgh	1880-1893	Landscape	—	—	9	—	1	—	—	1	—	—	11
Noble, John Sargeant, R.B.A. §	London	1866-1893	Sporting	—	—	46	—	96	—	—	—	—	1	143
Noble, Miss Marion	Willesden	1884	Domestic	—	—	1	—	—	—	—	—	—	1	2
Noble, Matthew	London	1845-1876	Sculpture	—	—	100	—	—	—	—	—	—	—	100
Noble, R.	London	1841-1842	Figures	—	—	2	—	—	—	—	—	—	—	2
Noble, Robert, A.R.S.A.	Edinburgh	1889-1893	Figures	—	—	11	—	—	—	—	2	1	4	18
Noble, Robert Heysham §	London	1821-1861	Landscape	—	—	5	5	27	—	—	—	—	—	37
Noble, R. P.	London	1836-1861	Landscape	—	—	35	1	38	—	—	—	—	4	78
Noble, R. S.	London	1852	Landscape	—	—	1	—	—	—	—	—	—	—	1
Noble, William Bonneau	London	1809-1811	Landscape	—	—	5	—	—	—	—	—	—	—	5
Noblett, H. John ‡	London	1832-1835	Landscape	—	—	1	—	6	—	8	—	—	—	15
Nodder, F. P.	London	1773-1788	Hair Work	15	3	5	—	—	—	—	—	—	—	23
Nodder, R. P.	London	1793-1820	Sporting	—	—	27	—	—	—	—	—	—	—	27
Noel, Mrs. A.	London	1795-1804	Allegorical	—	—	25	—	—	—	—	—	—	—	25
Noel, Miss F.	London	1800-1805	Landscape	—	—	6	—	—	—	—	—	—	—	6
Noel, J.	London	1804	Historical	—	—	1	—	—	—	—	—	—	—	1
Noel, Jules	Paris	1880	Landscape	—	—	—	—	—	—	—	—	—	2	2
Noel, Louis	Finisterre	1877	Rustic	—	—	—	—	2	—	—	—	—	—	2
Nogues, T.	London	1840-1843	Miniatures	—	—	7	—	—	—	—	—	—	—	7
Nollekens, Joseph, R.A.	London	1761-1816	Sculpture	—	10	138	7	—	—	—	—	—	—	155
Nonnen, Annie	Gottenburgh	1861-1864	Landscape	—	—	1	—	1	—	—	—	—	—	2
Nooth, W. Wright-	London	1887-1892	Etching	—	—	7	—	—	—	—	—	—	—	7
Norbury —	London	1783	Landscape	—	2	—	—	—	—	—	—	—	—	2
Norbury, Edwin A., R.C.A.	Rhyl	1885-1892	Domestic	—	—	1	—	—	—	1	—	—	2	4
Norbury, Miss M. A.	London	1889-1890	Domestic	—	—	—	—	2	—	1	—	—	—	3
Norbury, Richard, R.C.A.	Liverpool	1852-1878	Domestic	—	—	10	—	2	—	—	—	—	1	13

Name.	Town.	First and Last Year of Ex.	Speciality.	S. A.	F. S.	R. A.	B. I.	S. S.	O. W.	N. W.	G. G.	N. G.	V. E.	Total.
NORDGREN, MISS ANNA	London	1885-1893	Rustic	—	—	9	—	2	—	—	1	4	5	21
NORDLING, A.	London	1886	Coast Scenes	—	—	—	—	2	—	—	—	—	—	2
NORIE, ORLANDO	London	1876-1889	Battles	—	—	2	—	—	—	2	—	—	1	5
NORIE, R.	Edinburgh	1846	Landscape	—	—	1	—	—	—	—	—	—	—	1
NORIS, R.	Edinburgh	1844	Landscape	—	—	—	1	—	—	—	—	—	—	1
NORMA, N.	—	1849	Architecture	—	—	1	—	—	—	—	—	—	—	1
NORMAN, A. F.	London	1848-1849	Landscape	—	—	—	3	2	—	—	—	—	—	5
NORMAN, MRS. CAROLINE H.	Devonport	1874-1891	Flowers	—	—	9	—	2	—	8	—	—	5	24
NORMAN, MISS G.	London	1887	Domestic	—	—	—	—	—	—	—	—	—	1	1
NORMAN, GEORGE PARSONS	London	1873-1874	Seashores	—	—	—	—	3	—	—	—	—	—	3
NORMAN, H. T.	London	1874	Landscape	—	—	—	—	1	—	—	—	—	—	1
NORMAN, PARSONS	London	1874-1892	Sea Pieces	—	—	3	—	11	—	—	—	—	—	14
NORMAN, PHILIP	London	1876-1893	Landscape	—	—	15	—	6	—	22	17	15	28	103
NORMAN, W. T.	Devonport	1834-1843	Landscape	—	—	2	5	2	—	—	—	—	—	9
NORMAND, ERNEST	Norwood	1881-1893	Figures	—	—	18	—	—	—	—	—	1	1	20
NORMAND, MRS. ERNEST. *See* Miss Henrietta Rae	—	1885-1893	Figures	—	—	11	—	—	—	—	3	5	3	22
NORMANN, A.	Düsseldorf	1885-1891	Norway	—	—	6	—	—	—	—	—	—	—	6
NORRIS, MISS HELEN BRAMWELL	Dulwich	1893	Flowers	—	—	—	—	—	—	—	—	—	1	1
NORRIS, HUGH L.	London	1888-1892	Domestic	—	—	2	—	—	—	4	—	—	1	7
NORRIS, RICHARD, *or* PHILIP	London	1766	Architecture	—	1	—	—	—	—	—	—	—	—	1
NORRIS, T.	—	1838	Buildings	—	—	1	—	—	—	—	—	—	—	1
NORRIS, WILLIAM	London	1885-1893	Rustic	—	—	4	—	7	—	4	—	—	5	20
NORRIS, WILLIAM FOXLEY	Eton	1884-1887	Landscape	—	—	1	—	1	—	—	—	—	—	2
NORRIS, MISS	London	1841-1842	Figures	—	—	—	—	2	—	—	—	—	—	2
NORSWORTHY, W.	London	1839	Architecture	—	—	1	—	—	—	—	—	—	—	1
NORTH. *See* Saul and North	—	—	Metal Work	—	—	—	—	—	—	—	—	—	—	—
NORTH, ARTHUR WILLIAM	Newlyn	1882-1887	Domestic	—	—	2	—	5	—	—	—	—	1	8
NORTH, G.	—	1824	Architecture	—	—	1	—	—	—	—	—	—	—	1
NORTH, JOHN W., A.R.A., R.W.S.†	Taunton	1865-1893	Domestic	—	—	9	—	—	99	—	11	10	12	141
NORTH, MISS L.	—	1810	Wax	—	—	1	—	—	—	—	—	—	—	1
NORTH, LUCY E.	London	1870-1871	Landscape	—	—	—	—	1	—	—	—	—	2	3
NORTH, M.	—	1874	Figures	—	—	1	—	—	—	—	—	—	—	1
NORTH, R. P.	London	1856-1858	Fruit	—	—	—	3	—	—	—	—	—	—	3
NORTH, MRS. S. W. (JANE A.)	London	1873-1891	Miniatures	—	—	31	—	—	—	—	—	—	—	31
NORTH, MISS	—	1790	Landscape	—	—	1	—	—	—	—	—	—	—	1
NORTHCOTE, JAMES, R.A. (PUPIL OF REYNOLDS)	Plymouth	1773-1831	Historical	—	—	229	22	15	—	—	—	—	—	266
NORTON —	—	1760	Sea Pieces	1	—	—	—	—	—	—	—	—	—	1
NORTON, BENJAMIN CAM	Sheffield	1862	Landscape	—	—	—	2	—	—	—	—	—	—	2
NORTON, H.	London	1853-1858	Figures	—	—	8	2	1	—	—	—	—	—	11
NORTON, JOHN, F.R.I.B.A. *See also* Clarke and	—	—	—	—	—	—	—	—	—	—	—	—	—	—
Norton	London	1851-1871	Architecture	—	—	19	—	—	—	—	—	—	—	19
NORTON (J.) AND MASEY	London	1867	Architecture	—	—	1	—	—	—	—	—	—	—	1
NORTON, MISS S.	London	1853-1854	Figures	—	—	—	1	2	—	—	—	—	—	3
NORTON, WILLIAM EDWARD	Boston, U.S.A.	1878-1893	Sea Pieces	—	—	20	—	3	—	4	3	—	6	36
NORWOOD, ARTHUR HARDING	London	1889-1893	Landscape	—	—	—	—	5	—	—	—	—	1	6
NOST, ADAM	London	1779	Sculpture	—	—	1	—	—	—	—	—	—	—	1
NOST, VAN. *See* V.	—	—	—	—	—	—	—	—	—	—	—	—	—	—
NOTLEY AND TROLLOPE	London	1883-1885	Architecture	—	—	3	—	—	—	—	—	—	—	3
NOTT, MISS EVELYN E. C. PYKE-	London	1891-1893	Miniatures	—	—	3	—	—	—	—	—	—	1	4
NOTT, ISABEL C. PYKE-	London	1893	Figures	—	—	—	—	1	—	—	—	—	—	1
NOTTIDGE, (?) MISS CAROLINE. *See* Mrs. Nottidge-	—	—	—	—	—	—	—	—	—	—	—	—	—	—
Fry	Stetham	1867-1879	Sculpture	—	—	18	—	—	—	—	—	—	4	22
NOTTINGHAM, MISS E.	London	1856-1861	Landscape	—	—	2	—	—	—	—	—	—	—	2
NOTTINGHAM, R.	London	1853-1875	Landscape	—	—	12	1	29	—	—	—	—	3	45
NOTZ, J.	London	1831-1840	Miniatures	—	—	15	—	—	—	—	—	—	—	15
NOTZ, M.	London	1827	Portraits	—	—	1	—	—	—	—	—	—	—	1
NOURSE, MISS ELIZABETH	London	1891-1893	Domestic	—	—	3	—	1	—	1	—	—	1	6
NOVELLO, A.	—	1840	Sculpture	—	—	1	—	—	—	—	—	—	—	1
NOVELLO, E. P.	London	1833-1834	Figures	—	—	2	—	—	—	—	—	—	—	2
NOVELLO, J.	—	1833	Scriptural	—	—	—	1	—	—	—	—	—	—	1
NOVICE, GEORGE W.	London	1824-1833	Still Life	—	—	3	4	5	—	—	—	—	—	12
NOVICE, WILLIAM	London	1809-1833	Domestic	—	—	5	20	3	—	—	—	—	—	28
NOVICE, W. F.	London	1828-1829	Animals	—	—	2	—	—	—	—	—	—	—	2
NOVO, STEFANO	London	1892	Domestic	—	—	1	—	—	—	—	—	—	—	1
NOVOSIELSKI —	London	1772-1794	Architecture	—	—	5	—	—	—	—	—	—	—	5
NOVRA, B.	London	1859-1860	Sculpture	—	—	2	—	—	—	—	—	—	—	2
NOVRA, HENRY	London	1870-1876	Figures	—	—	—	—	4	—	—	—	—	4	8
NOWELL, ARTHUR T.	Runcorn	1881-1893	Domestic	—	—	16	—	—	—	1	—	1	—	18
NOWLAN, MISS CARLOTTA	London	1885-1891	Flowers	—	—	3	—	—	—	2	—	—	—	5
NOWLAN, FRANK	London	1866-1886	Domestic	—	—	5	—	5	—	—	—	—	18	28
NOY, MRS. R.	Norwich	1871	Fruit	—	—	—	—	1	—	—	—	—	—	1
NOYES, MISS DORA	London	1883-1893	Figures	—	—	14	—	12	—	1	1	1	5	34

Name.	Town.	First and Last Year of Ex.	Speciality.	S. A.	F. S.	R. A.	B. I.	S. S.	O. W.	N. W.	G. G.	N. G.	V. E.	Total.
Noyes, H. J.	Shrewsbury	1873-1874	Flowers	—	—	1	—	2	—	—	—	—	—	3
Noyes, Miss Mary	Southfields	1883-1888	Domestic	—	—	—	—	4	—	1	—	—	1	6
Noyes, Miss Theodora	London	1887	Landscape	—	—	1	—	—	—	—	—	—	—	1
Noyes, W. P.	Southampton	1796-1797	Landscape	—	—	3	—	—	—	—	—	—	—	3
Noyes-Lewis, T.	Barnet	1892-1893	Figures	—	—	—	—	—	—	—	—	—	2	2
Nozal, Alexandre	Paris	1879	Crayons	—	—	—	—	—	—	—	—	—	3	3
Nugent, M. A.	—	1790	Architecture	—	—	4	—	—	—	—	—	—	—	4
Nugent, Thomas	London	1791-1829	Portraits	—	—	18	—	—	—	—	—	—	—	18
Nuitz, A.	London	1847	Figures	—	—	1	—	—	—	—	—	—	—	1
Nunes, A. J.	—	1778-1797	Portraits	—	—	2	—	—	—	—	—	—	—	2
Nunn, J. W.	London	1865	Fruit	—	—	—	—	1	—	—	—	—	—	1
Nurse, W. M.	London	1807-1809	Architecture	—	—	2	—	—	—	—	—	—	—	2
Nursey, C. L.	Ipswich	1844-1871	Sea Pieces	—	—	—	1	4	—	—	—	—	—	5
Nursey, P.	London	1799-1801	Landscape	—	—	4	—	—	—	—	—	—	—	4
Nursey, Rev. Perry	Woodbridge	1801-1829	Battle Pieces	—	—	4	1	—	—	—	—	—	—	5
Nuthall, W. H.	—	1826	Cattle	—	—	1	—	—	—	—	—	—	—	1
Nutter, J.	Bristol	1864-1865	Domestic	—	—	1	—	3	—	—	—	—	—	4
Nutter, Miss Katherine M.	London	1883-1890	Flowers	—	—	5	—	1	—	2	—	—	—	8
Nutter, William	London	1782-1783	Allegorical	—	—	3	—	—	—	—	—	—	—	3
Nuyen, W. F. T.	The Hague	1838	Landscape	—	—	1	—	—	—	—	—	—	—	1
Nye, George F.	London	1839-1843	Portraits	—	—	—	—	10	—	—	—	—	—	10
Nye, Herbert	London	1885-1891	Sculpture	—	—	9	—	—	—	2	—	—	2	13
Oakes, A.	Matlock	1872	Landscape	—	—	—	—	1	—	—	—	—	—	1
Oakes, Frederick G.	London	1866-1869	Figures	—	—	—	1	3	—	—	—	—	—	4
Oakes, H. F.	London	1841-1847	Figures	—	—	—	2	—	—	—	—	—	—	2
Oakes, John Wright, A.R.A.‡	Liverpool	1847-1888	Landscape	—	—	90	28	11	—	3	—	—	23	155
Oakeshott, George J.	Ealing	1887	Churches	—	—	2	—	—	—	—	—	—	—	2
Oakley, A.	London	1893	Domestic	—	—	—	—	1	—	—	—	—	—	1
Oakley, Miss Agnes	London	1854-1856	Flowers	—	—	—	—	5	—	—	—	—	—	5
Oakley, B.	London	1859	Domestic	—	—	—	—	3	—	—	—	—	—	3
Oakley, Miss Isabel. *See* Mrs. P. J. Naftel.	—	—	—	—	—	—	—	—	—	—	—	—	—	—
Oakley, Miss L.	London	1850	Portraits	—	—	1	—	—	—	—	—	—	—	1
Oakley, Miss Maria L.	London	1854-1865	Fruit, etc.	—	—	—	—	4	—	—	—	—	—	4
Oakley, Octavius †	Derby	1826-1867	Portraits	—	—	30	—	1	221	—	—	—	1	253
Oakley, William Harold	London	1881-1888	Architecture	—	—	4	—	1	—	1	—	—	—	6
Oakley, Mrs. *See* Miss Beatson, afterwards	—	—	—	—	—	—	—	—	—	—	—	—	—	—
Lady Oakley.	—	—	—	—	—	—	—	—	—	—	—	—	—	—
Oates, Captain Mark	London	1789-1811	Portraits	—	—	2	—	—	—	—	—	—	—	2
Obbard, Miss C.	Blackheath	1867	Fruit	—	—	1	—	—	—	—	—	—	—	1
Oben, J. George	London	1810-1816	Landscape	—	—	21	—	—	—	—	—	—	18	39
Obici, G.	Rome	1846	Sculpture	—	—	1	—	—	—	—	—	—	—	1
O'Brien, L. R., P.R.C.A.	London	1887-1890	Sea Coasts	—	—	1	—	2	—	3	1	—	—	7
O'Brien, T., *or* O'Brine	London	1864-1866	Landscape	—	—	—	2	5	—	—	—	—	—	7
O'Connor, A.	London	1846-1871	Landscape	—	—	5	—	1	—	—	—	—	—	6
O'Connor, John, R.I., R.H.A.‡	London	1853-1888	Landscape	—	—	28	6	26	—	12	29	—	42	143
O'Connor, James A.§	London	1822-1840	Landscape	—	—	21	39	18	—	—	—	—	—	78
O'Connor, M.	London	1846-1848	Architecture	—	—	2	—	—	—	—	—	—	—	2
O'Connor, W. H.	London	1859-1865	Figures	—	—	4	—	1	—	—	—	—	—	5
Oddie, Arthur C.	London	1875	Figures	—	—	—	—	—	—	—	—	—	1	1
Oddy, Henry Raphael	Halifax	1883-1892	Landscape	—	—	2	—	—	—	1	—	—	—	3
O'Doherty, W. J.	London	1857-1864	Sculpture	—	—	6	3	—	—	—	—	—	—	9
Odolfredi, Count	Richmond	1875	Sculpture	—	—	—	—	—	—	—	—	—	2	2
O'Donoghue, J.	London	1846	Flowers	—	—	—	—	1	—	—	—	—	—	1
Oeionomo, A.	Manchester	1867	Landscape	—	—	1	—	—	—	—	—	—	—	1
O'Fagen —	London	1778	Landscape	—	3	—	—	—	—	—	—	—	—	3
Offor, Miss Beatrice	Sydenham	1887-1893	Figures	—	—	4	—	—	—	—	—	—	—	4
Offord, John J.	London	1886	Domestic	—	—	1	—	—	—	—	—	—	—	1
Offord, Miss Mary H.	London	1886	Landscape	—	—	1	—	—	—	—	—	—	—	1
Ogborne, John	—	1783	Engraving	—	—	1	—	—	—	—	—	—	—	1
Ogborne, John	London	1828-1834	Historical	—	—	—	1	1	—	—	—	—	—	2
Ogden, H. H.	London	1862-1867	Sculpture	—	—	2	—	—	—	—	—	—	—	2
Ogden, Miss Jane	London	1879-1882	Flowers	—	—	5	—	2	—	—	—	—	5	12
Ogé, P.	—	1880	Sculpture	—	—	1	—	—	—	—	—	—	—	1
Ogg, C. H.	Putney	1842-1843	Miniatures	—	—	2	—	3	—	—	—	—	—	5
Ogg, H. A.	Putney	1844-1846	Landscape	—	—	—	—	3	—	—	—	—	—	3
Ogier, P.	London	1793-1800	Miniatures	—	—	4	—	—	—	—	—	—	—	4
Ogilvie, Frederick D.	North Shields	1875-1886	Sea Pieces	—	—	-	—	2	—	—	—	—	4	8
Ogilvie, Frank S.	Bushey	1888-1893	Domestic	—	—	6	—	6	—	1	—	—	1	14
Ogilvie, J. D.	Edinburgh	1885	Landscape	—	—	1	—	—	—	—	—	—	—	1

Name.	Town.	First and Last Year of Ex.	Speciality.	S. A.	F. S.	R. A.	B. I.	S. S.	O.W.	N. W.	G. G.	N. G.	V. E.	Total.
Ogilvy, James S.	London	1893	Landscape	—	—	—	—	—	—	—	—	1	1	2
Ogle, Rev. G.	—	1801	Landscape	—	—	1	—	—	—	—	—	—	—	1
Ogle, John Connell	London	1844-1864	Sea Pieces	—	—	5	7	7	—	—	—	—	—	19
O'Grady, Miss A. B.	London	1851-1852	Historical	—	—	—	—	2	—	—	—	—	—	2
O'Hagan, Mrs. H.	London	1854	Portraits	—	—	1	—	—	—	—	—	—	—	1
O'Hara, Miss Helen ‖	Portstewart	1884-1893	Domestic	—	—	—	—	—	—	13	—	—	—	13
O'Keeffe, Daniel. *See* Keefe.	—	—		—	—	—	—	—	—	—	—	—	—	—
O'Kelly, Aloysius C.	London	1876-1892	Figures	—	—	20	—	17	—	3	—	—	10	50
Okey, Samuel	London	1767-1768	Engraving	2	—	—	—	—	—	—	—	—	—	2
Olafson, B.	London	1882	Landscape	—	—	—	—	1	—	—	—	—	—	1
Oldaker, Francis A.	Epsom	1882	Landscape	—	—	—	—	1	—	—	—	—	—	1
Oldfield, C. F.	London	1838-1841	Architecture	—	—	4	—	—	—	—	—	—	—	4
Oldfield, H. G.	London	1787-1790	Architecture	3	—	2	—	—	—	—	—	—	—	5
Oldfield, J.	London	1825-1854	Landscape	—	—	2	—	1	—	—	—	—	—	3
Oldfield, J. Reffitt-	London	1891-1892	Landscape	—	—	—	—	—	—	—	—	5	—	5
Oldham, Miss Emma	Chesterfield	1890-1892	Miniatures	—	—	3	—	—	—	—	—	—	—	3
Oldham, F. H.	Manchester	1882-1884	Architecture	—	—	3	—	—	—	—	—	—	—	3
Oldham, G. R.	Chipping Norton	1854-1857	Landscape	—	—	—	—	6	—	—	—	—	—	6
Olding, L.	London	1852-1863	Domestic	—	—	—	1	4	—	—	—	—	—	5
Oldmeadow, F. A.	Bushey	1840-1851	Sporting	—	—	6	—	—	—	—	—	—	—	6
Oldmeadow, J. C.	Bushey	1841-1849	Landscape	—	—	1	2	—	—	—	—	—	3	6
Oldofredi, Count S.	—	1880	Sculpture	—	—	2	—	—	—	—	—	—	—	2
Oliphant. *See* Wilmshurst and Oliphant.	—	—	—	—	—	—	—	—	—	—	—	—	—	—
Oliphant, F. W.	London	1849-1855	Historical	—	—	5	—	—	—	—	—	—	—	5
Oliphant, Kingsley	London	1890	Architecture	—	—	1	—	—	—	—	—	—	—	1
Olive —	London	1772-1773	Portraits	4	—	—	—	—	—	—	—	—	—	4
Olive, Miss Fanny	London	1889	Miniatures	—	—	1	—	—	—	—	—	—	—	1
Oliver —	London	1791	Portraits	—	—	1	—	—	—	—	—	—	—	1
Oliver, Rev. A.	London	1880	Landscape	—	—	—	—	—	—	—	—	—	1	1
Oliver, Archer James, A.R.A.	London	1791-1842	Portraits and Fruit	—	—	210	62	—	—	—	—	—	—	272
Oliver, C. F.	London	1868	Figures	—	—	—	—	1	—	—	—	—	—	1
Oliver, Mrs. C. N.	London	1866-1868	Flowers	—	—	—	—	3	—	—	—	—	—	3
Oliver, F.	London	1853-1856	Buildings	—	—	4	—	—	—	—	—	—	—	4
Oliver, George D.	Carlisle	1885-1887	Architecture	—	—	3	—	—	—	—	—	—	—	3
Oliver, Harry. *See also* Wigg, Son, and Oliver	London	1837-1849	Architecture	—	—	4	—	1	—	—	—	—	—	5
Oliver, Isaac	London	1824-1853	Game	—	—	—	—	15	—	—	—	—	—	15
Oliver, John	London	1790	Landscape	1	—	—	—	—	—	—	—	—	—	1
Oliver, R.	London	1817-1825	Landscape	—	—	7	4	—	—	—	—	—	—	11
Oliver, Robert Dudley	London	1883-1892	Portraits	—	—	14	—	—	—	—	—	—	—	14
Oliver, Samuel Euclid	London	1769	Sculpture	—	2	1	—	—	—	—	—	—	—	3
Oliver, T.	London	1868-1869	Landscape	—	—	—	—	3	—	—	—	—	—	3
Oliver, William ‡	London	1829-1854	Landscape	—	—	29	54	36	—	257	—	—	68	444
Oliver, William	London	1867-1882	Figures	—	—	14	1	1	—	—	—	—	2	18
Oliver, Mrs. William, R.I., ‡ late Miss Emma Eburne (afterwards Mrs. John Sedgwick)	London	1842-1886	Landscape	—	—	34	19	39	—	366	—	—	84	542
Oliver, W. Redivivus	Watford	1861-1862	Landscape	—	—	—	—	2	—	—	—	—	—	2
Oliver, Miss	Watford	1867	Still Life	—	—	—	—	3	—	—	—	—	—	3
Oliver and Leeson	Newcastle	1892	Architecture	—	—	1	—	—	—	—	—	—	—	1
Olivier, Herbert A.	London	1883-1893	Portraits	—	—	26	—	—	—	7	1	10	4	48
Olivier, M.	Paris	1772-1773	Figures	4	—	6	—	—	—	—	—	—	—	10
Olivieri, D. A., *or* J. O.	—	1833-1835	Sculpture	—	—	—	—	5	—	—	—	—	—	5
Olivieri, E. A.	London	1852-1866	Sculpture	—	—	10	—	—	—	—	—	—	—	10
Olrik, H.	Copenhagen	1873	Portraits	—	—	1	—	—	—	—	—	—	—	1
Olsson, Julius, R.B.A. §	Purley	1888-1893	Landscape	—	—	3	—	20	—	—	2	—	8	33
Olst, Van. *See* V.	—	—		—	—	—	—	—	—	—	—	—	—	—
O'Mahoney, Miss Florence	London	1877-1885	Monks	—	—	1	—	1	—	—	—	—	—	2
O'Meara, Frank	Nemours	1877-1887	Landscape	—	—	—	—	—	—	—	2	—	2	4
O'Neal, Jeffery Hamet, F.S.A.	London	1763-1772	Miniatures	13	—	—	—	—	—	—	—	—	—	13
O'Neil, C.	London	1821	Sculpture	—	—	1	—	—	—	—	—	—	—	1
O'Neil, Miss C. S.	London	1859-1864	Flowers	—	—	4	—	—	—	—	—	—	—	4
O'Neil, F.	—	1839	Landscape	—	—	1	—	—	—	—	—	—	—	1
O'Neil, Henry Nelson, A.R.A.	London	1838-1879	Historical	—	—	94	34	14	—	—	—	—	—	142
O'Neill, George Bernard	Woolwich	1847-1893	Domestic	—	—	72	—	—	—	—	—	—	—	72
O'Neill, Hugh	Oxford	1812	Landscape	—	—	—	—	—	—	—	—	—	4	4
O'Neill, J. G.	London	1874	Sea Coasts	—	—	—	—	1	—	—	—	—	—	1
Onion, E. J.	London	1825-1859	Domestic	—	—	3	10	8	—	—	—	—	1	22
Opie, Edward	St. Agnes, Cornwall	1839-1886	Domestic	—	—	49	—	1	—	—	—	—	—	50
Opie, John, R.A.	London	1782-1807	Historical	—	—	143	8	—	—	—	—	—	—	151
Oppenoorth, Willem J.	London	1880-1893	Landscape	—	—	—	—	2	—	—	—	—	2	4
Oppey, Master	Penrhyn, Cornwall	1780	Heads	1	—	—	—	—	—	—	—	—	—	1
Oram, Edward	London	1766-1799	Landscape	3	—	29	—	—	—	—	—	—	—	32
Oram, Miss	London	1836-1839	Domestic	—	—	—	—	8	—	—	—	—	—	8

Name.	Town.	First and Last Year of Ex.	Speciality.	S. A.	F. S.	R. A.	B. I.	S. S.	O. W.	N. W.	G. G.	N. G.	V. E.	Total.
Orchard, Miss A. G.	London	1892	Heads	—	—	—	—	—	—	—	—	—	1	1
Orchard, J.	Greenwich	1847-1848	Historical	—	—	2	—	2	—	—	—	—	—	4
Orchardson, William Quiller, R.A.	London	1863-1893	Historical	—	—	67	1	—	—	—	3	2	1	74
Orczy, Baroness Emmuska	London	1888-1892	Domestic	—	—	3	—	2	—	—	—	—	—	5
Orderson, Mrs. T. E.	Brighton	1825-1835	Flowers	—	—	1	—	8	—	—	—	—	—	9
Ordersworth, Miss	London	1828	Portraits	—	—	—	—	2	—	—	—	—	—	2
Ordish, F. W.	London	1848-1870	Architecture	—	—	6	—	—	—	—	—	—	—	6
Ordish, R. W.	London	1868	Architecture	—	—	1	—	—	—	—	—	—	—	1
Orme, Alfred	Liverpool	1881-1887	Miniatures	—	—	9	—	—	—	—	—	—	—	9
Orme, Daniel	London	1797-1801	Miniatures	—	—	39	—	—	—	—	—	—	—	39
Orme, E.	London	1801-1803	Architecture	—	—	3	—	—	—	—	—	—	—	3
Orme, William	London	1797-1819	Landscape	—	—	20	—	—	—	—	—	—	—	20
Ormsby, V.	London	1870-1886	Domestic	—	—	12	—	1	—	—	—	—	11	24
Orpheus, V.	London	1892	Buildings	—	—	—	—	1	—	—	—	—	—	1
Orr, J. N. J.	London	1843	Figures	—	—	2	—	1	—	—	—	—	—	3
Orr, Patrick W.	Glasgow	1893	Portraits	—	—	1	—	—	—	—	—	—	—	1
Orridge, Miss Caroline	London	1890	Domestic	—	—	—	—	1	—	—	—	—	—	1
Orrock, James, R.I. ‡ φ	London	1858-1893	Landscape	—	—	13	—	6	—	196	18	7	34	274
Orsi, C.	Toscano	1881	Sculpture	—	—	1	—	—	—	—	—	—	—	1
Ortmanns, Auguste	Fontainebleau	1865-1871	Landscape	—	—	1	—	1	—	—	—	—	1	3
Ortner, E.	London	1858-1861	Medals	—	—	6	—	—	—	—	—	—	—	6
Os, Van. *See* V.	—	—	—	—	—	—	—	—	—	—	—	—	—	—
Osborn, Miss Emily Mary ‖	London	1851-1893	Domestic	—	—	43	4	11	—	—	7	9	7	81
Osborne, C.	Norwich	1821-1825	Portraits	—	—	6	—	1	—	—	—	—	—	7
Osborne, R.	London	1792-1822	Architecture	—	—	6	—	—	—	—	—	—	—	6
Osborne, Walter F., R.H.A. φ	Dublin	1884-1893	Landscape	—	—	17	—	—	—	—	1	1	19	38
Oscroft, Samuel William	Nottingham	1866-1893	Landscape	—	—	3	—	1	—	14	—	—	18	36
Osgood, C.	London	1842	Portraits	—	—	1	—	—	—	—	—	—	—	1
Osgood, J.	Newbury	1834-1845	Domestic	—	—	—	—	20	—	—	—	—	—	20
Osgood, S. S.	London	1836-1839	Portraits	—	—	5	2	2	—	—	—	—	—	9
Osmond, Arthur James	London	1886	Sculpture	—	—	—	—	1	—	—	—	—	—	1
Osmond, John	Lee	1881	Landscape	—	—	—	—	1	—	—	—	—	—	1
Ossani, Alexander (?) Alessandro	Edinburgh	1857-1888	Portraits	—	—	24	—	15	—	—	2	—	1	42
Ostell, Miss Mary M.	London	1893	Game	—	—	—	—	—	—	1	—	—	—	1
Ostrehan, George W.	London	1893	Stained Glass	—	—	1	—	1	—	—	—	—	—	2
Oswald, Frank	Croydon	1857-1874	Sea Pieces	—	—	—	—	15	—	—	—	—	*	15
Oswald, John H.	Edinburgh	1871-1890	Landscape	—	—	7	—	—	—	2	—	—	4	13
Otley, Rev. C. B.	—	1808-1821	Landscape	—	—	4	—	—	—	—	—	—	—	4
Ott, A.	London	1790	Historical	—	—	2	—	—	—	—	—	—	—	2
Ottewel, B. J.	Wimbledon	1885-1892	Landscape	—	—	4	—	1	—	—	—	—	—	5
Ottley, William Young	—	1823	Scriptural	—	—	1	—	—	—	—	—	—	—	1
Ottewell, B. J.	Wimbledon	1884-1893	Landscape	—	—	—	—	—	—	1	3	9	—	13
Otway, J.	Waterford	1888	Figures	—	—	—	—	—	—	—	1	—	—	1
Ouchterlony, Miss	London	1812-1813	Landscape	—	—	1	1	—	—	—	—	—	—	2
Ought, Master	London	1768-1778	Portraits	—	11	—	—	—	—	—	—	—	—	11
Ould, E. A. *See also* Grayson and Ould	Chester	1883	Architecture	—	—	1	—	—	—	—	—	—	—	1
Ouless, Walter William, R.A.	London	1869-1893	Portraits	—	—	126	—	—	—	—	—	—	1	127
Oulett, Jesse J.	Willesden	1887	Domestic	—	—	—	—	—	—	—	—	—	1	1
Ousey, Buckley	Conway	1887-1889	Sea Shores	—	—	1	—	1	—	—	—	—	1	3
Outrim, John	London	1846-1874	Engraving	—	—	4	—	—	—	—	—	—	—	4
Ovenden, F. W.	London	1834-1843	Sea Pieces	—	—	1	—	6	—	—	—	—	—	7
Ovenden, T.	London	1817-1832	Fish	—	—	4	—	—	—	—	—	—	—	4
Overbeck, Friedrich	Rome	1853	Scriptural	—	—	1	—	—	—	—	—	—	—	1
Overbury, Miss L.	London	1874	Flowers	—	—	—	—	1	—	—	—	—	—	1
Overend, William Heysham φ	London	1872-1893	Sea Pieces	—	—	4	—	3	—	—	—	—	16	23
Overton —	London	1764-1766	Architecture	—	4	—	—	—	—	—	—	—	—	4
Overton, Thomas	London	1818-1838	Miniatures	—	—	33	—	1	—	2	—	—	—	36
Owen, A. C.	Oxford	1868	Landscape	—	—	—	—	1	—	—	—	—	—	1
Owen, Rev. Edward Price	London	1839-1853	Scriptural	—	—	—	8	4	—	—	—	—	2	14
Owen, T. E.	—	1843	Architecture	—	—	1	—	—	—	—	—	—	—	1
Owen, Samuel	London	1794-1810	Sea Pieces	—	—	8	—	—	—	—	—	—	29	37
Owen, William, R.A.	London	1792-1824	Portraits	—	—	203	7	—	—	—	—	—	—	210
Owen, William	Warrington	1891	Architecture	—	—	1	—	—	—	—	—	—	—	1
Owtram, Robert L.	Beckenham	1892	Portraits	—	—	2	—	—	—	—	—	—	—	2
Oyston, George	London	1891	Landscape	—	—	—	—	—	—	1	—	—	—	1
Pace, Ion	London	1880-1892	Windows	—	—	10	—	—	—	—	—	—	—	10
Pack, F. C.	London	1822-1840	Landscape	—	—	3	11	—	—	—	—	—	—	14
Packard, E.	Ipswich	1877-1880	Domestic	—	—	—	—	—	—	—	—	—	2	2
Packe, Christopher	London	1786-1796	Portraits	—	—	7	—	—	—	—	—	—	—	7

Name.	Town.	First and Last Year of Ex.	Speciality.	S. A.	F. S.	R. A.	B. I.	S. S.	O. W.	N.W.	G. G.	N. G.	V. E.	Total.
Padday, Charles M.	London	1889-1893	Landscape	—	—	5	—	8	—	—	—	—	1	14
Padgett, John	London	1828-1839	Landscape	—	—	—	—	4	—	—	—	—	—	4
Padgett, William	Twickenham	1879-1893	Figures	—	—	9	—	8	—	—	10	24	17	68
Padley, J. W.	Swansea	1842	Sea Pieces	—	—	—	—	3	—	—	—	—	—	3
Padley, R. W.	Nottingham	1815	Domestic	—	—	—	2	—	—	—	—	—	—	2
Padmore, William Pinder	London	1843	Architecture	—	—	2	—	—	—	—	—	—	—	2
Padwick, H. C.	London	1889	Landscape	—	—	—	—	1	—	—	—	—	—	1
Pagani, Luigi	Milan	1870-1880	Sculpture	—	—	7	—	—	—	—	—	—	—	7
Page —	London	1799	Portraits	—	—	1	—	—	—	—	—	—	—	1
Page, Flood	London	1861-1864	Domestic	—	—	3	—	—	—	—	—	—	4	7
Page, G.	London	1833-1851	Figures	—	—	2	1	7	—	—	—	—	—	10
Page, George Gordon	London	1864-1880	Architecture	—	—	2	—	—	—	—	—	—	—	2
Page, G. R.	London	1834-1838	Historical	—	—	—	—	3	—	—	—	—	—	3
Page, Henry	London	1878-1892	Sculpture	—	—	11	—	4	—	—	—	—	9	24
Page, H. F.	London	1858-1865	Figures	—	—	3	17	3	—	—	—	—	—	23
Page, Henry Maurice	London	1878-1890	Animals	—	—	11	—	54	—	—	—	—	3	68
Page, H. R.	London	1875-1878	Figures	—	—	—	—	—	—	—	—	—	4	4
Page, Miss P.	—	1815-1819	Flowers	—	—	4	—	—	—	—	—	—	—	4
Page, P. F.	London	1814-1819	Architecture	—	—	4	—	—	—	—	—	—	—	4
Page, Robert	Great Claxton	1880-1890	Domestic	—	—	11	—	4	—	—	—	—	6	21
Page, Richard Charles	London	1880	Architecture	—	—	1	—	—	—	—	—	—	—	1
Page, S.	—	1803	Architecture	—	—	1	—	—	—	—	—	—	—	1
Page, Miss Sarah	Paris	1892-1893	Portraits	—	—	2	—	—	—	—	—	—	—	2
Page, S. H.	London	1851	Sculpture	—	—	1	—	—	—	—	—	—	—	1
Page, T., F.G.S.	London	1851-1863	Architecture	—	—	7	—	—	—	—	—	—	—	7
Page, W.	London	1816-1860	Ruins	—	—	19	—	—	—	—	—	—	—	19
Paget. *See* Goddard and Paget	—	—	Architecture	—	—	—	—	—	—	—	—	—	—	—
Paget, Lord C.	London	1871	Sculpture	—	—	1	—	—	—	—	—	—	—	1
Paget, Miss Elise	Pinner	1877-1888	Domestic	—	—	2	—	10	—	6	1	—	2	21
Paget, H. M., R.B.A. §	London	1874-1892	Sporting	—	—	18	—	4	—	—	3	*	7	32
Paget, Mrs. H. M.	Bedford Park	1883-1884	Figures	—	—	—	—	—	—	—	2	—	—	2
Paget, Sidney	London	1878-1891	Figures	—	—	13	—	6	—	—	—	1	10	30
Paget, Walter	London	1878-1888	Figures	—	—	3	—	2	—	—	1	—	1	7
Pagliano, M.	London	1880	Landscape	—	—	—	—	—	—	—	—	—	1	1
Paice, Bowes A.	London	1883	Architecture	—	—	1	—	—	—	—	—	—	—	1
Paice, George	Croydon	1878-1889	Landscape	—	—	6	—	4	—	—	—	—	2	12
Paillou, Peter	London	1763-1800	Miniatures	1	1	68	—	—	—	—	—	—	—	70
Pain, G. R.	London	1810-1814	Architecture	—	—	5	—	—	—	—	—	—	—	5
Pain, J.	London	1803-1805	Architecture	—	—	3	—	—	—	—	—	—	—	3
Pain, Robert Tucker	Frimley	1863-1877	Landscape	—	—	6	3	6	—	—	—	—	29	44
Pain, W.	London	1798-1809	Architecture	—	—	6	—	—	—	—	—	—	—	6
Paine, Miss Edith A.	London	1883-1885	Landscape	—	—	—	—	—	—	—	2	—	—	2
Paine, James	London	1761-1794	Architecture	47	—	5	—	—	—	—	—	—	—	52
Paine, James, Junr.	London	1761-1764	Landscape	6	5	—	—	—	—	—	—	—	—	11
Paine, James, Junr., F.S.A.	Rome	1769-1788	Architecture and Sculpture	17	—	3	—	—	—	—	—	—	—	20
Paine, J. D.	London	1828-1843	Architecture	—	—	22	—	—	—	—	—	—	—	22
Pairpoint, T. J.	London	1857-1869	Sculpture	—	—	6	—	—	—	—	—	—	—	6
Pakington, Hon. H. P. M.	London	1888-1892	Landscape	—	—	3	—	—	—	—	—	—	—	3
Paley. *See* Sharp and Paley	—	—	Architecture	—	—	—	—	—	—	—	—	—	—	—
Paley and Austin	Lancaster	1874-1891	Architecture	—	—	6	—	—	—	—	—	—	—	6
Palgrave, Robert	London	1865	Architecture	—	—	1	—	—	—	—	—	—	—	1
Palin, W. Long	Stifford	1881	Figures	—	—	—	—	—	—	—	—	—	1	1
Palin, William Mainwaring	London	1887-1893	Domestic	—	—	8	—	5	—	2	—	—	1	16
Palisades, W. L. G.	London	1863	Figures	—	—	—	2	—	—	—	—	—	—	2
Pallier, L.	London	1818	Portraits	—	—	1	—	—	—	—	—	—	—	1
Palmer. *See* Turner and Palmer	—	—	Architecture	—	—	—	—	—	—	—	—	—	—	—
Palmer, Miss Ada M.	Claremont	1884-1887	Sculpture	—	—	4	—	1	—	—	—	—	—	5
Palmer, Miss Charity	London	1852-1859	Still Life	—	—	4	—	8	—	—	—	—	9	21
Palmer, Miss Charlotte E.	Odiham	1877	Landscape	—	—	1	—	1	—	—	—	—	—	2
Palmer, Miss E.	Bath	1813-1815	Landscape	—	—	—	7	—	—	—	—	—	—	7
Palmer, Miss Gertrude	Wolverhampt'n	1884	Landscape	—	—	—	—	1	—	—	—	—	—	1
Palmer, G. H.	London	1832-1835	Architecture	—	—	2	—	—	—	—	—	—	—	2
Palmer, G. H.	London	1876-1888	Landscape	—	—	—	—	1	—	1	—	—	2	4
Palmer, H.	Reading	1828-1877	Architecture	—	—	3	—	1	—	—	—	—	—	4
Palmer, Miss H.	—	1801	Landscape	—	—	1	—	—	—	—	—	—	—	1
Palmer, Harry Sutton, R.B.A. §	London	1870-1893	Landscape	—	—	6	—	11	—	—	—	—	16	33
Palmer, John	London	1877-1887	Still Life	—	—	1	—	1	—	—	—	—	—	2
Palmer, Miss M.	—	1821	Figures	—	—	1	—	—	—	—	—	—	—	1
Palmer, N.	London	1829-1844	Sculpture	—	—	13	—	4	—	—	—	—	—	17
Palmer, Samuel, R.W.S. †	London	1819-1882	Rustic	—	—	57	20	10	178	—	—	—	1	266
Palmer, Mrs. S.	London	1840-1842	Landscape	—	—	5	3	—	—	—	—	—	—	8
Palmer, T., Junr.	London	1798-1804	Architecture	—	—	4	—	—	—	—	—	—	—	4

Name.	Town.	First and Last Year of Ex.	Speciality.	S. A.	F. S.	R. A.	B. I.	S. S.	O. W.	N. W.	G. G.	N. G.	V. E.	Total
Palmer, W.	London	1784-1796	Figures	—	—	9	—	—	—	—	—	—	—	9
Palmer, W.	—	1803	Architecture	—	—	1	—	—	—	—	—	—	—	1
Palmer, William	London	1869-1889	Landscape	—	—	2	—	1	—	—	—	—	—	3
Palmer, William James	London	1858-1888	Landscape	—	—	4	—	9	—	3	—	—	18	34
Palmer, Mrs. W. J.	London	1872-1879	Flowers	—	—	—	—	9	—	—	—	—	—	9
Palmer, Miss	Bath	1800-1819	Landscape	—	—	1	14	—	—	—	—	—	—	15
Palmer, Miss	—	1833	Flowers	—	—	—	—	—	—	1	—	—	—	1
Panati, Carlo	London	1887	Sculpture	—	—	1	—	—	—	—	—	—	—	1
Panchard, R.	Bath	1804	Architecture	—	—	1	—	—	—	—	—	—	—	1
Pane, J.	—	1797	Miniatures	—	—	1	—	—	—	—	—	—	—	1
Pannett, P. S.	—	1839	Architecture	—	—	1	—	—	—	—	—	—	—	1
Pannini, N.	Rome	1858	Scriptural	—	—	1	—	—	—	—	—	—	—	1
Panormo, C.	London	1833-1834	Sculpture	—	—	5	—	—	—	—	—	—	—	5
Pantin —	London	1783	Architecture	1	—	—	—	—	—	—	—	—	—	1
Panton, Alexander	London	1861-1888	Landscape	—	—	9	8	69	—	—	—	—	—	86
Panton, L.	—	1761	Architecture	—	1	—	—	—	—	—	—	—	—	1
Panzetta, J.	London	1789-1810	Sculpture	—	—	9	—	—	—	—	—	—	—	9
Paoletti, Antonio Silvio	London	1881-1891	Domestic	—	—	4	—	1	—	2	—	—	6	13
Pape, William	Leeds	1892	Stained Glass	—	—	4	—	—	—	—	—	—	—	4
Papendick, C.	London	1823-1831	Architecture	—	—	5	—	1	—	—	—	—	—	6
Papendrecht, J. H. Van	Rotterdam	1888-1889	Domestic	—	—	2	—	—	—	—	—	—	—	2
Papera, J. P.	London	1829-1830	Sculpture	—	—	2	—	—	—	—	—	—	—	2
Papperitz, Georg	Munich	1886-1888	Portraits	—	—	2	—	—	—	—	—	—	—	2
Papworth, C.	London	1802-1844	Landscape	—	—	3	1	—	—	—	—	—	—	4
Papworth, Edgar George, Senr.	London	1832-1866	Sculpture	—	—	62	1	25	—	—	—	—	—	88
Papworth, Edgar George, Junr.	London	1852-1882	Sculpture	—	—	79	—	8	—	—	1	—	—	88
Papworth, F.	London	1845	Vesuvius	—	—	—	1	—	—	—	—	—	—	1
Papworth, George, R.H.A.	London	1796-1803	Architecture	—	—	4	—	—	—	—	—	—	—	4
Papworth, John	London	1791-1827	Architecture	—	—	23	—	—	—	—	—	—	11	34
Papworth, John Buonarotti	London	1839-1841	Architecture	—	—	3	—	—	—	—	—	—	—	3
Papworth, John Woody, F.R.I.B.A.	London	1837-1851	Architecture	—	—	11	—	—	—	—	—	—	—	11
Papworth, R.	London	1811-1816	Architecture	—	—	3	—	—	—	—	—	—	—	3
Papworth, T.	London	1794-1815	Sculpture	—	—	27	—	—	—	—	—	—	—	27
Papworth, Wyatt A., F.R.I.B.A.	London	1836-1851	Architecture	—	—	16	—	—	—	—	—	—	—	16
Paraire, E. L.	London	1854-1859	Architecture	—	—	3	—	—	—	—	—	—	—	3
Paralta, Francisco	London	1881	Figures	—	—	—	—	—	—	—	—	—	1	1
Paravey, Mdlle.	Grosville	1850	Flowers	—	—	1	—	—	—	—	—	—	—	1
Parbury, George	London	1764-1791	Sculpture	7	—	11	—	—	—	—	—	—	—	18
Parc, Du. *See* D.				—	—	—	—	—	—	—	—	—	—	—
Pardon, James	Canterbury	1811-1848	Portraits	—	—	13	—	5	—	—	—	—	—	18
Parez, C.	London	1826-1835	Landscape	—	—	—	—	2	—	—	—	—	—	2
Parez, Joseph	London	1820-1835	Historical	—	—	4	2	6	1	—	—	—	—	13
Parez, Lewis §	London	1821-1831	Copies or Eng'ving	—	—	12	—	32	—	—	—	—	—	44
Paris, T. C.	London	1855-1856	Landscape	—	—	2	—	—	—	—	—	—	—	2
Paris, Walter	London	1849-1891	Landscape	—	—	2	—	7	—	7	1	1	9	27
Paris, Miss	—	1850	Buildings	—	—	1	—	—	—	—	—	—	—	1
Parisani, Count Napoleone	Rome	1890-1893	Landscape	—	—	—	—	—	—	—	—	5	—	5
Pariset, D. P.	London	1768-1769	Engraving	2	—	—	—	—	—	—	—	—	—	2
Parish, C.	London	1832-1840	Sculpture	—	—	2	—	—	—	—	—	—	—	2
Park. *See* Garlick, Park, and Sykes	—	—	Architecture	—	—	—	—	—	—	—	—	—	—	—
Park, G. H.	London	1876	Landscape	—	—	—	—	—	—	—	—	—	1	1
Park, Henry	Bristol	1847-1864	Cattle	—	—	4	1	4	—	—	—	—	—	9
Park, John	London	1875-1885	Etching	—	—	1	—	—	—	—	—	—	9	10
Park, Patrick, R.S.A.	London	1836-1855	Sculpture	—	—	54	8	29	—	—	—	—	—	91
Park, Miss R.	Greenwich	1834	Miniatures	—	—	4	—	—	—	—	—	—	—	4
Park, T.	London	1780-1781	Architecture	—	—	5	—	—	—	—	—	—	—	5
Parke, Benjamin	London	1794-1808	Landscape	—	—	9	1	—	—	—	—	—	—	10
Parke, Henry	London	1815-1835	Architecture	—	—	33	—	—	—	7	—	—	—	40
Parke, R.	London	1876	Still Life	—	—	—	—	—	—	—	—	—	1	1
Parker, Master	—	1775	Heads	—	1	—	—	—	—	—	—	—	—	1
Parker, A. M.	Nottingham	1839-1840	Cattle	—	—	1	—	1	—	—	—	—	—	2
Parker, C. R.	London	1828-1829	Portraits	—	—	—	2	5	—	—	—	—	—	7
Parker, Edward	London	1830	Figures	—	—	—	1	—	—	—	—	—	—	1
Parker, Esther	Gillingham	1834	Flowers, etc.	—	—	—	—	3	—	—	—	—	—	3
Parker, Miss Ellen Grace	London	1875-1893	Flowers	—	—	6	—	18	—	—	—	—	16	40
Parker, Frederick	London	1833-1847	Castles	—	—	4	3	36	—	4	—	—	—	47
Parker, Miss F.	London	1849-1859	Domestic	—	—	—	—	1	—	—	—	—	4	5
Parker, Frederick H. A., R.B.A. §	London	1881-1893	Domestic	—	—	7	—	38	—	—	—	—	6	51
Parker, Henry Perlee, H.R.S.A.	Newcastle	1817-1863	Historical	—	—	23	40	23	—	4	—	—	61	151
Parker, James	London	1783	Engraving	1	1	—	—	—	—	—	—	—	—	2
Parker, John	London	1763	Historical	—	2	—	—	—	—	—	—	—	—	2
Parker, John	London	1765-1785	Landscape	—	7	9	—	—	—	—	—	—	—	16

Name.	Town.	First and Last Year of Ex.	Speciality.	S. A.	F. S.	R. A.	B. I.	S. S.	O. W.	N. W.	G. G.	N. G.	V. E.	Total.
Parker, John, R.W.S.† φ	London	1867-1893	Domestic	—	—	9	—	4	185	—	9	12	52	271
Parker, Joseph	London	1762-1777	Landscape	1	19	1	—	—	—	—	—	—	—	21
Parker, J. B.	London	1867	Figures	—	—	—	—	3	—	—	—	—	—	3
Parker, J. C.	Folkestone	1868	Landscape	—	—	—	—	2	—	—	—	—	—	2
Parker, J. G.	London	1820-1822	Flowers	—	—	3	—	—	—	—	—	—	—	3
Parker, Miss Louise	London	1892-1893	Domestic	—	—	—	—	2	—	—	—	—	—	2
Parker, Miss Nevillia	Bedford Park	1881-1888	Domestic	—	—	1	—	2	—	—	—	—	1	4
Parker, Miss Phœbe	Clitheroe	1885-1886	Domestic	—	—	2	—	—	—	—	—	—	—	2
Parker, R.	London	1832-1834	Architecture	—	—	4	—	—	—	—	—	—	—	4
Parker, R. H.	London	1848-1858	Domestic	—	—	1	—	3	—	—	—	—	—	4
Parker, Miss Sybil C.	Clitheroe	1872-1893	Domestic	—	—	7	—	1	—	—	—	—	—	8
Parker, T.	London	1867-1868	Domestic	—	—	2	—	1	—	—	—	—	—	3
Parker, Mrs. T.	—	1824	Fruit	—	—	1	—	—	—	—	—	—	—	1
Parker, Miss V.	London	1875	Figures	—	—	—	—	1	—	—	—	—	—	1
Parkes, Miss C.	London	1806	Flowers	—	—	1	—	—	—	—	—	—	—	1
Parkes, Robert Bowyer	London	1867-1883	Engraving	—	—	2	—	—	—	—	—	—	2	4
Parkes, Miss S.	London	1876	Landscape	—	—	1	—	—	—	—	—	—	—	1
Parkins, J. B.	London	1835	Domestic	—	—	—	—	1	—	—	—	—	—	1
Parkinson, Miss Amelia	London	1872-1873	Flowers	—	—	—	—	2	—	—	—	—	—	2
Parkinson, Miss Florence	London	1893	Miniatures	—	—	1	—	—	—	—	—	—	—	1
Parkinson, Frederick Claudius J.	London	1846-1849	Architecture	—	—	4	—	—	—	—	—	—	—	4
Parkinson, J. T.	London	1806-1831	Architecture	—	—	12	—	—	—	—	—	—	—	12
Parkinson, John W.	Portsmouth	1880	Domestic	—	—	1	—	—	—	—	—	—	—	1
Parkinson, Rawlinson	London	1840-1853	Architecture	—	—	4	—	—	—	—	—	—	—	4
Parkinson, Sydney	London	1765-1766	Flowers	—	4	—	—	—	—	—	—	—	—	4
Parkinson, Thomas	London	1769-1789	Portraits	4	6	16	—	—	—	—	—	—	—	26
Parkinson, William	London	1883-1891	Domestic	—	—	4	—	5	—	—	—	—	—	9
Parkinson, William H.	Bradford	1892-1893	Landscape	—	—	4	—	1	—	—	—	—	—	5
Parkinson, Miss	—	1815-1828	Landscape	—	—	11	—	—	—	—	—	—	—	11
Parkman, Henry S.	Bristol	1847-1856	Portraits	—	—	8	—	1	—	—	—	—	—	9
Parkyn, J. H.	Bristol	1884-1889	Flowers	—	—	4	—	—	—	1	—	—	—	5
Parkyns —.	Nottingham	1791	Engraving	2	—	—	—	—	—	—	—	—	—	2
Parkyns, G.	—	1772-1813	Landscape	5	—	3	—	—	—	—	—	—	—	8
Parkyns, L. B.	—	1808-1817	Castles	—	—	4	—	—	—	—	—	—	—	4
Parkyns, Major	—	1804	Fruit	—	—	1	—	—	—	—	—	—	—	1
Parlby, George	London	1884-1892	Stained Glass	—	—	7	—	—	—	—	—	—	—	7
Parlby, J.	—	1870-1873	Landscape	—	—	—	—	5	—	—	—	—	2	7
Parlby, James	London	1777	Architecture	—	—	1	—	—	—	—	—	—	—	1
Parlby, Major S.	London	1845	Figures	—	—	—	—	1	—	—	—	—	—	1
Parmentier, De. *See* D.	—	—	—	—	—	—	—	—	—	—	—	—	—	—
Parminter, G.	London	1848	Buildings	—	—	1	—	—	—	—	—	—	—	1
Parnall, J., *or* G.	—	1845	Portraits	—	—	1	—	—	—	—	—	—	—	1
Parnell, A. M.	Dublin	1874	Domestic	—	—	—	—	2	—	—	—	—	—	2
Parnell, Mrs. A.	Dublin	1874	Figures	—	—	—	—	1	—	—	—	—	—	1
Parnell, Charles Jocelyn	London	1868	Architecture	—	—	1	—	—	—	—	—	—	—	1
Parnell (C. O.) and Smith (A.)	London	1848	Architecture	—	—	1	—	—	—	—	—	—	—	1
Parnell, Miss G.	London	1846-1857	Miniatures	—	—	10	—	15	—	—	—	—	—	25
Parr, A. H.	London	1876	Domestic	—	—	1	—	—	—	—	—	—	—	1
Parr, Miss Agnes R.	Gravesend	1885-1893	Miniatures	—	—	4	—	—	—	1	—	—	—	5
Parr, C.	London	1785	Rustic	—	—	1	—	—	—	—	—	—	—	1
Parr, Sam.	Nottingham	1890	Landscape	—	—	1	—	—	—	—	—	—	—	1
Parris, Edmund Thomas	London	1816-1874	Historical	—	—	26	36	18	—	5	—	—	1	86
Parris, J.	London	1826	Architecture	—	—	1	—	—	—	—	—	—	—	1
Parris, Miss Mary Ann	London	1845-1869	Flowers	—	—	4	2	1	—	—	—	—	1	8
Parris, Robert	London	1828	Architecture	—	—	1	—	—	—	—	—	—	—	1
Parris, W. A.	London	1845	Architecture	—	—	1	—	—	—	—	—	—	—	1
Parrish, Charles	London	1885	Architecture	—	—	1	—	—	—	—	—	—	—	1
Parrish, J.	London	1815	Architecture	—	—	1	—	—	—	—	—	—	—	1
Parrish, Stephen	Philadelphia	1881	Etching	—	—	—	—	—	—	—	—	—	14	14
Parrott, G.	London	1844	Portraits	—	—	1	—	—	—	—	—	—	—	1
Parrott, H.	Nottingham	1852	Landscape	—	—	1	—	—	—	—	—	—	—	1
Parrott, S.	Nottingham	1841-1853	Landscape	—	—	4	—	3	—	—	—	—	—	7
Parrott, William	London	1835-1875	Landscape	—	—	25	19	25	—	—	—	—	34	103
Parry, A.	London	1850-1865	Domestic	—	—	1	—	1	—	—	—	—	—	2
Parry, C.	St. Albans	1843	Churches	—	—	—	—	1	—	—	—	—	—	1
Parry, Charles James	London	1881-1891	Landscape	—	—	4	—	1	—	—	—	—	2	7
Parry, David H.	London	1891-1893	Landscape	—	—	1	—	—	—	—	—	—	1	2
Parry, G.	London	1834	Still Life	—	—	—	—	1	—	1	—	—	—	2
Parry, H.	London	1825	Dead Game	—	—	—	—	2	—	—	—	—	—	2
Parry, H. B.	London	1827	Architecture	—	—	1	—	—	—	—	—	—	—	1
Parry, J.	Manchester	1803	Rustic	—	—	1	—	—	—	—	—	—	—	1
Parry, J.	London	1802-1839	Sculpture	—	—	7	—	—	—	—	—	—	—	7

Name.	Town.	First and Last Year of Ex.	Speciality.	S. A.	F. S.	R. A.	B. I.	S. S.	O. W.	N.W.	G. G.	N.G.	V.E.	Total
Parry, J., Junr.	London	1828-1841	Intaglios	—	—	7	—	—	—	—	—	—	—	7
Parry, John	Surbiton	1867-1868	Landscape	—	—	—	—	—	—	—	—	—	3	3
Parry, T., *or* J.	London	1833-1834	Landscape	—	—	—	—	—	—	3	—	—	—	3
Parry, Thomas P. Jones-. *See* J.	—	—	—	—	—	—	—	—	—	—	—	—	—	—
Parry, William, A.R.A.	London	1762-1788	Portraits	4	3	22	—	—	—	—	—	—	—	29
Pars, William, A.R.A.	London	1760-1776	Portraits	2	11	27	—	—	—	—	—	—	—	40
Pars, Miss	—	1786	Portraits	—	—	1	—	—	—	—	—	—	—	1
Parsey, A.	London	1828-1843	Historical	—	—	14	—	9	—	—	—	—	—	23
Parsons, Alfred, R.I. ‡ ϕ	Frome	1868-1893	Still Life	—	—	39	—	9	—	20	15	14	104	201
Parsons, Arthur Wilde	London	1867-1893	Sea Pieces	—	—	1	—	6	—	6	—	—	—	13
Parsons, Miss Beatrice E.	London	1889-1893	Figures	—	—	4	—	—	—	—	—	—	1	5
Parsons, Miss Charlotte M.	Blackheath	1891	Sculpture	—	—	1	—	—	—	—	—	—	—	1
Parsons, Miss E.	Frome	1886	—	—	—	—	—	—	—	—	*	—	—	—
Parsons, Francis, F.S.A.	London	1763-1783	Portraits	15	—	—	—	—	—	—	—	—	—	15
Parsons, Mrs. G.	Poltesco	1869	Landscape	—	—	—	—	1	—	—	—	—	1	2
Parsons, G. W.	Woolwich	1828-1829	Portraits	—	—	—	—	2	—	—	—	—	—	2
Parsons, Herbert	Lewisham	1874	Domestic	—	—	—	—	—	—	—	—	—	1	1
Parsons, Miss H.	London	1853-1854	Landscape	—	—	—	—	2	—	—	—	—	—	2
Parsons, J. R.	London	1850-1888	Figures	—	—	7	—	—	—	—	1	1	—	9
Parsons, Miss Letitia Margaret	Frome	1877-1887	Flowers	—	—	9	—	1	—	6	2	—	25	43
Parsons, William	London	1763-1773	Fruit	1	2	—	—	—	—	—	—	—	—	3
Parsons, Miss	London	1857	Heads	—	—	1	—	—	—	—	—	—	—	1
Parting, Miss Florence	Ealing	1883	Domestic	—	—	—	—	—	—	—	—	—	1	1
Partington, J. H. E. (?) S.	Stockport	1873-1888	Figures	—	—	16	—	—	—	1	4	—	—	21
Parton, Ernest ϕ	London	1874-1893	Landscape	—	—	46	—	20	—	24	16	11	37	154
Parton, H. Woodbridge	London	1885	Flowers	—	—	1	—	—	—	—	—	—	—	1
Partridge, Miss Annie St. John	London	1888	Figures	—	—	—	—	—	—	1	—	—	—	1
Partridge, Miss Charlotte	London	1847-1853	Miniatures	—	—	8	—	—	—	—	—	—	—	8
Partridge, Miss Ellen ‖	London	1844-1893	Miniatures	—	—	23	1	—	—	—	—	—	11	35
Partridge, J.	London	1781-1792	Still Life	—	—	5	—	—	—	—	—	—	—	5
Partridge, John	London	1815-1861	Portraits	—	—	72	58	—	—	—	—	—	—	130
Partridge, William O.	Paris	1891-1892	Sculpture	—	—	2	—	—	—	—	—	—	—	2
Pascoe, William	Plymouth	1842-1844	Landscape	—	—	3	3	3	—	—	—	—	—	9
Pash, Miss Florence	London	1885-1892	Domestic	—	—	1	—	12	—	—	—	—	—	13
Pasini, A.	London	1879	Etching	—	—	—	—	—	—	—	—	—	1	1
Pasley, Miss Louisa M.	Southampton	1880-1884	Sculpture	—	—	2	—	—	—	—	—	—	—	2
Pasley, M.	London	1868	Landscape	—	—	—	—	1	—	—	—	—	—	1
Pasley, Miss Nancy A. Sabine	London	1886-1892	Domestic	—	—	—	—	1	—	—	—	—	10	11
Pasmore, Daniel	London	1829-1865	Domestic	—	—	16	—	—	—	—	—	—	47	63
Pasmore, Daniel, Junr. §	London	1829-1891	Domestic	—	—	9	7	86	—	2	—	—	—	104
Pasmore, Emily	London	1881-1884	Flowers	—	—	—	—	4	—	—	—	—	—	4
Pasmore, F. G., Junr.	London	1875-1884	Domestic	—	—	—	—	15	—	—	—	—	—	15
Pasmore, John	London	1830-1845	Domestic	—	—	11	3	3	—	—	—	—	—	17
Pasmore, John F.	London	1841-1866	Domestic	—	—	30	23	11	—	—	—	—	26	90
Pasmore, Mrs. J. F.	London	1861-1878	Domestic	—	—	2	4	41	—	—	—	—	—	47
Pasquier —	Paris	1772	Enamels	—	—	9	—	—	—	—	—	—	—	9
Pasquier, E. J. ‡ §	Colchester	1828-1832	Landscape	—	—	—	—	5	—	7	—	—	—	12
Pasquier, Jonathan *or* James Abbott	London	1851-1872	Figures	—	—	6	—	3	—	—	—	—	7	16
Pasquin, Anthony. *See* John Williams	—	1802	Figures	—	—	1	—	—	—	—	—	—	—	1
Passall —	—	1783	Landscape	—	1	—	—	—	—	—	—	—	—	1
Passavant, John	London	1769-1776	Hair Work	4	6	—	—	—	—	—	—	—	—	10
Passavant, Philip, F.S.A.	London	1771-1778	Hair Work	9	—	—	—	—	—	—	—	—	—	9
Passavant, P.	—	1801	Rustic	—	—	2	—	—	—	—	—	—	—	2
Passavant, Mrs.	London	1771-1772	Hair Work	2	—	—	—	—	—	—	—	—	—	2
Passey, Charles H.	London	1870-1885	Landscape	—	—	—	—	3	—	—	—	—	1	4
Passini, Ludwig, H.R.I. ‡	Venice	1883-1891	Portraits	—	—	1	—	—	—	2	—	—	—	3
Pastorini, Benedict	—	1775-1776	Decoration	—	—	2	—	—	—	—	—	—	—	2
Pastorini, F. E.	London	1812-1833	Miniatures	—	—	14	—	—	3	—	—	—	—	17
Pastorini, J.	London	1812-1834	Miniatures	—	—	19	—	—	—	—	—	—	—	19
Pastorini, W. V.	London	1825-1826	Portraits	—	—	2	—	—	—	—	—	—	—	2
Patalano, Enrico	London	1890	Portraits	—	—	1	—	—	—	—	—	—	—	1
Paterson, Alexander N.	London	1890	Churches	—	—	1	—	—	—	1	—	—	—	2
Paterson, Miss Caroline, afterwards Mrs. S. Sharpe	London	1878-1892	Domestic	—	—	—	—	—	—	3	—	—	11	14
Paterson, Miss Eglington Margaret. *See* Mrs. James Pearson.	—	—	—	—	—	—	—	—	—	—	—	—	—	—
Paterson, Emily M.	Edinburgh	1891	Landscape	—	—	—	—	2	—	—	—	—	—	2
Paterson, George M.	Edinburgh	1881-1886	Historical	—	—	2	—	—	—	—	—	—	—	2
Paterson, Miss Helen. *See* Mrs. Allingham	London	1870-1874	Domestic	—	—	2	—	—	—	—	—	—	15	17
Paterson, James, R.S.W.	Paris	1879-1892	Landscape	—	—	5	—	5	—	—	3	—	1	14
Paterson, Robert	Edinburgh	1870-1889	Engraving	—	—	7	—	—	—	—	—	—	6	13
Paterson, S.	London	1809-1824	Architecture	—	—	8	—	—	—	—	—	—	—	8

Name.	Town.	First and Last Year of Ex.	Speciality.	S. A.	F. S.	R. A.	B. I.	S. S.	O. W.	N. W.	G. G.	N. G.	V. E.	Total.
Paterson, W. R.	London	1823-1841	Landscape	—	—	7	6	4	—	—	—	—	—	17
Patey, Miss Ethel J.	Bexley	1891-1892	Portraits	—	—	—	—	3	—	—	—	—	1	4
Patience, J.	London	1786-1808	Architecture	—	—	12	—	—	—	—	—	—	—	12
Patience, T.	London	1796-1797	Architecture	—	—	2	—	—	—	—	—	—	—	2
Patience, T.	London	1798-1800	Sculpture	—	—	4	—	—	—	—	—	—	—	4
Patmore, Miss Bertha G.	London	1876-1882	Domestic	—	—	9	—	—	—	—	—	—	—	9
Paton, Miss Amelia R. *See* Mrs. D. O. Hill.	—	—	—	—	—	—	—	—	—	—	—	—	—	—
Paton, Frank	Gravesend	1872-1890	Animals	—	—	20	—	4	—	—	—	—	6	30
Paton, Hugh, A.R.P.E.	Manchester	1885	Landscape	—	—	—	—	1	—	—	—	—	—	1
Paton, Sir Joseph Noel, R.S.A.	Dunfermline	1856-1883	Allegorical	—	—	14	1	—	—	—	3	—	—	18
Paton, Richard	London	1762-1780	Sea Pieces	18	—	15	—	—	—	—	—	—	—	33
Paton, Waller Hugh, R.S.A., R.S.W.	Edinburgh	1860-1885	Landscape	—	—	15	—	—	—	4	—	—	17	36
Patrick, J.	—	1808-1813	Portraits	—	—	3	—	—	—	—	—	—	—	3
Patrick, J. Rutherford	Preston Kirk	1891	Landscape	—	—	1	—	—	—	—	—	—	—	1
Patrickson, Miss	London	1815	Domestic	—	—	—	1	—	—	—	—	—	—	1
Patry, Edward	Sydenham	1880-1893	Domestic	—	—	16	—	4	—	—	—	—	2	22
Patten, Alfred Fowler, R.B.A. §	London	1850-1888	Domestic	—	—	18	22	118	—	—	—	—	1	159
Patten, C.	London	1825-1827	Portraits	—	—	4	—	—	—	—	—	—	—	4
Patten, E.	London	1794-1808	Miniatures	—	—	10	—	—	—	—	—	—	—	10
Patten, Edmund	London	1838-1842	Sea Pieces	—	—	2	—	11	—	—	—	—	—	13
Patten, George, A.R.A.	London	1819-1864	Portraits	—	—	131	16	—	—	—	—	—	—	147
Patten, G. B.	London	1836	Landscape	—	—	—	1	—	—	—	—	—	—	1
Patten, Leonard	London	1889	Landscape	—	—	1	—	—	—	—	—	—	—	1
Patten, William	London	1791-1844	Portraits	—	—	90	3	5	—	8	—	—	—	106
Patten, William Vandyke	London	1844-1871	Cameos	—	—	37	—	19	—	—	—	—	—	56
Patten, Miss	London	1826-1836	Miniatures	—	—	16	—	—	—	—	—	—	—	16
Patterson, A. D.	London	1879	Architecture	—	—	—	—	—	—	—	—	—	1	1
Patterson, Miss Catherine P.	London	1887-1890	Flowers	—	—	—	—	—	—	3	—	—	—	3
Patterson, G.	Birmingham	1877	Landscape	—	—	—	—	1	—	—	—	—	—	1
Patterson, H.	London	1840-1851	Portraits	—	—	2	—	—	—	—	—	—	—	2
Patterson, S.	London	1789	Portraits	—	—	1	—	—	—	—	—	—	—	1
Patterson, Stirling	Edinburgh	1893	Domestic	—	—	1	—	—	—	—	—	—	—	1
Pattinson. *See* Ball, Lee, and Pattinson	—	—	Architecture	—	—	—	—	—	—	—	—	—	—	—
Pattison, Anne R.	Hastings	1876	Churches	—	—	—	—	—	—	—	—	—	1	1
Pattison, Carl	Düsseldorf	1880-1884	Sea Pieces	—	—	1	—	3	—	—	—	—	—	4
Pattison, Charles T., *or* J.	London	1883	Landscape	—	—	—	—	—	—	—	—	—	2	2
Pattison, J.	London	1854	Landscape	—	—	1	—	—	—	—	—	—	—	1
Pattison, Robert T.	London	1855-1864	Domestic	—	—	3	2	1	—	—	—	—	—	6
Pattison, W. R. S.	London	1854-1857	Landscape	—	—	1	—	—	—	—	—	—	10	11
Patton —	—	1762	Architecture	2	—	—	—	—	—	—	—	—	—	2
Paul —	London	1815	Landscape	—	—	—	2	—	—	—	—	—	—	2
Paul, A. L.	London	1882-1885	River Scenes	—	—	—	—	6	—	—	—	—	—	6
Paul, Bernard	London	1766-1769	Portraits	2	—	—	—	—	—	—	—	—	—	2
Paul, Clara	Leicester	1880	Harbours	—	—	—	—	1	—	—	—	—	—	1
Paul, Miss Florence	Waltham Cross	1886-1889	Landscape	—	—	—	—	1	—	—	—	—	2	3
Paul, Sir John Dean, Bart.	—	1802-1837	Landscape	—	—	20	—	—	—	—	—	—	—	20
Paul, J. G.	London	1880-1884	Landscape	—	—	—	—	3	—	—	—	—	—	3
Paul, L.	London	1766-1767	Portraits	2	—	—	—	—	—	—	—	—	—	2
Paul, Maclean	London	1889	Domestic	—	—	—	—	—	—	1	—	—	—	1
Paul, Peter	London	1859	Domestic	—	—	1	—	—	—	—	—	—	—	1
Paul, Robert Boyd	London	1857-1876	Figures	—	—	2	1	10	—	—	—	—	1	14
Paull, Miss Edith C.	London	1889-1890	Landscape	—	—	—	—	3	—	—	—	—	—	3
Paull, H. J.	London	1856	Architecture	—	—	1	—	—	—	—	—	—	—	1
Paull, Roland W.	London	1887-1890	Architecture	—	—	5	—	—	—	—	—	—	—	5
Paull and Bickerdike (B.)	Manchester	1873-1875	Architecture	—	—	2	—	—	—	—	—	—	—	2
Paull and Bonella	London	1880-1886	Architecture	—	—	2	—	—	—	—	—	—	—	2
Paulson, Mrs. Anna	Mansfield	1838-1857	Fruit, etc.	—	—	—	1	8	—	—	—	—	31	40
Paulson, F.	London	1877-1878	Portraits	—	—	2	—	—	—	—	—	—	—	2
Pavillon —	Edinburgh	1768-1770	Mythological	2	—	—	—	—	—	—	—	—	—	2
Pavy, Eugène	London	1878-1884	Figures	—	—	4	—	8	—	—	1	—	3	16
Pavy, Philip	London	1874-1883	Figures	—	—	4	—	23	—	—	—	—	2	29
Pawle, F.	Reigate	1858-1862	Landscape	—	—	—	—	6	—	—	—	—	—	6
Pawley, James	London	1854-1869	Animals	—	—	1	1	1	—	—	—	—	—	3
Pawsey, Miss	—	1800-1803	Flowers	—	—	3	—	—	—	—	—	—	—	3
Paxton, John, F.S.A.	Rome	1766-1807	Portraits	30	—	13	—	—	—	—	—	—	—	43
Paxton, Sir Joseph	London	1854-1856	Architecture	—	—	5	—	—	—	—	—	—	—	5
Paxton, T.	Hoxton	1800-1802	Landscape	—	—	4	—	—	—	—	—	—	—	4
Paxton, W. A.	Hoxton	1789-1791	Landscape	—	—	3	—	—	—	—	—	—	—	3
Paye, C. W.	—	1806-1808	Miniatures	—	—	6	—	—	—	—	—	—	—	6
Paye, Richard Morton	London	1773-1808	Historical	12	1	66	3	—	—	—	—	—	—	82
Paye, Miss	London	1798-1807	Miniatures	—	—	32	—	—	—	—	—	—	—	32
Payne. *See* Tyerman and Payne	—	—	Architecture	—	—	—	—	—	—	—	—	—	—	—

Name.	Town.	First and Last Year of Ex.	Speciality.	S. A.	F. S.	R. A.	B. I.	S. S.	O.W.	N.W.	G. G.	N. G.	V. E.	Total.
Payne, A.	Newark	1858	Historical	—	—	1	—	—	—	—	—	—	—	1
Payne, Arthur Charles	London	1881	Pen and Ink	—	—	—	—	—	—	—	—	—	1	1
Payne, Arthur Frederick	Lynn	1866-1884	Etching	—	—	5	—	—	—	1	13	—	1	20
Payne, A. H.	Southampton	1830-1833	Landscape	—	—	3	—	—	—	—	—	—	—	3
Payne, B.	London	1875	Domestic	—	—	—	—	1	—	—	—	—	—	1
Payne, Miss C.	Leipsic	1864	Portraits	—	—	1	—	—	—	—	—	—	—	1
Payne, Edward	Cardiff	1877-1879	Pen and Ink	—	—	—	—	—	—	—	—	—	3	3
Payne, E. J.	London	1845-1848	Landscape	—	—	3	—	—	—	—	—	—	—	3
Payne, Miss Florence	Oxford	1885-1886	Flowers	—	—	1	—	—	—	1	—	—	—	2
Payne, H.	London	1823	Portraits	—	—	1	—	—	—	—	—	—	—	1
Payne, Mrs. H.	London	1835	Portraits	—	—	1	—	—	—	—	—	—	—	1
Payne, H. Ada	London	1881-1885	Landscape	—	—	—	—	3	—	—	—	—	—	3
Payne, J.	London	1827	Landscape	—	—	1	—	—	—	—	—	—	—	1
Payne, Thomas	London	1762-1767	Landscape	3	6	—	—	—	—	—	—	—	—	9
Payne, William	Plymouth	1776-1830	Landscape	17	—	22	50	2	17	—	—	—	—	108
Payne, W.	London	1850	Portraits	—	—	1	—	—	—	—	—	—	—	1
Payne, W. R.	London	1802-1845	Landscape	—	—	1	—	1	—	—	—	—	—	2
Paytherus, Miss	—	1803	Portraits	—	—	1	—	—	—	—	—	—	—	1
Payton, Joseph	Warwick	1861-1870	Domestic	—	—	10	2	—	—	—	—	—	2	14
Peacan, John Philip	London	1880-1891	Landscape	—	—	1	—	3	—	—	—	—	3	7
Peace, C. S.	London	1876	Landscape	—	—	1	—	—	—	—	—	—	—	1
Peach, H. F.	London	1820-1835	Landscape	—	—	2	3	1	—	—	—	—	—	6
Peachy, J.	London	1786-1787	Canada	—	—	5	—	—	—	—	—	—	—	5
Peacock, Miss Emma	Brighton	1845-1846	Churches	—	—	3	—	—	—	—	—	—	—	3
Peacock, H.	Bath	1827	Landscape	—	—	—	1	—	—	—	—	—	—	1
Peacock, J.	Dublin	1817-1818	Scriptural	—	—	1	1	—	—	—	—	—	—	2
Peacock, M.	London	1810-1830	Landscape	—	—	9	14	—	—	—	—	—	—	23
Peacock, Ralph	London	1888-1893	Figures	—	—	5	—	5	—	—	1	—	7	18
Peake, Miss Emma	London	1855-1858	Portraits	—	—	4	—	1	—	—	—	—	—	5
Peake, F.	London	1844-1846	Figures	—	—	2	—	1	—	—	—	—	—	3
Peake, J.	London	1761-1771	Engraving	8	—	—	—	—	—	—	—	—	—	8
Peake, John N.	London	1853-1861	Domestic	—	—	2	2	6	—	—	—	—	—	10
Peake, R. B.	London	1816	Domestic	—	—	1	—	—	—	—	—	—	—	1
Peale, R.	London	1768-1803	Miniatures	6	—	2	—	—	—	—	—	—	—	8
Peale, Rembrandt	London	1833	Portraits	—	—	4	—	—	—	—	—	—	—	4
Pearce, Arthur E.	London	1882-1886	Landscape	—	—	—	—	1	—	2	—	—	—	3
Pearce, Miss Blanche D.	London	1888	Flowers	—	—	1	—	—	—	—	—	—	—	1
Pearce, Christina	Cheltenham	1889	Domestic	—	—	—	—	—	—	—	—	—	1	1
Pearce, Charles Sprague	London	1875-1882	Domestic	—	—	—	—	1	—	—	—	—	4	5
Pearce, Elizabeth	London	1889	Domestic	—	—	—	—	1	—	—	—	—	—	1
Pearce, Maresco	London	1858-1860	Historical	—	—	2	1	—	—	—	—	—	—	3
Pearce, Stephen	London	1837-1885	Portraits	—	—	92	3	3	—	—	1	—	—	99
Pearce, S. Tring	London	1878-1881	Historical	—	—	—	—	1	—	—	—	—	5	6
Pearce, William	London	1798-1799	Miniatures	—	—	2	—	—	—	—	—	—	—	2
Pearce, William	Brighton	1884	Domestic	—	—	—	—	—	—	—	—	—	1	1
Peard, Miss Frances M.	Torquay	1888-1891	Landscape	—	—	—	—	—	—	3	—	—	—	3
Pearman, H.	—	1831	Landscape	—	—	—	—	1	—	—	—	—	—	1
Pears, Miss Augusta	—	1893	Flowers	—	—	—	—	—	—	—	—	1	—	1
Pearsall, Henry W.	Bath	1824-1861	Landscape	—	—	12	12	12	—	4	—	—	1	41
Pearsall, S. J.	London	1826-1827	Flowers, etc.	—	—	—	—	2	—	—	—	—	—	2
Pearse, Alfred	London	1877-1880	Figures	—	—	—	—	1	—	—	—	—	3	4
Pearse, F. M.	London	1892	Flowers	—	—	—	—	1	—	—	—	—	—	1
Pearson, Blanche A.	Anerley	1892	Landscape	—	—	—	—	1	—	—	—	—	—	1
Pearson, Mrs. Charles, § late Miss Mary Martha Dutton	London	1821-1842	Portraits	—	—	31	15	37	—	—	—	—	—	83
Pearson, Cornelius	London	1843-1891	Landscape	—	—	4	—	145	—	5	—	—	17	171
Pearson, Frank L.	London	1891-1893	Architecture	—	—	3	—	—	—	—	—	—	—	3
Pearson, George	London	1869-1872	Wood Engraving	—	—	1	—	—	—	—	—	—	1	2
Pearson, H. J. S.	Greenwich	1844	Landscape	—	—	2	—	—	—	—	—	—	—	2
Pearson, James	London	1775-1777	Stained Glass	10	—	—	—	—	—	—	—	—	—	10
Pearson, Mrs. James, late Miss Eglington Margaret Paterson	London	1775-1777	Birds	10	—	—	—	—	—	—	—	—	—	10
Pearson, John	Huddersfield	1876-1890	Landscape	—	—	2	—	8	—	—	—	—	—	10
Pearson, John Loughborough, R.A., F.S.A. *See* Johnson and Pearson	London	1851-1892	Architecture	—	—	48	—	—	—	—	—	—	—	48
Pearson, William	London	1798-1809	Landscape	—	—	18	—	—	—	—	—	—	18	36
Pearson, Miss	London	1824-1826	Portraits	—	—	1	—	1	—	—	—	—	—	2
Peart, Charles	London	1778-1798	Sculpture	—	—	32	—	—	—	—	—	—	—	32
Peart, W.	—	1815	Flowers	—	—	1	—	—	—	—	—	—	—	1
Pease, Miss E. R. E.	Woolwich	1846	Flowers	—	—	—	1	—	—	—	—	—	—	1
Pease, William	Woolwich	1823-1832	Portraits	—	—	3	—	5	—	—	—	—	—	8

Name.	Town.	First and Last Year of Ex.	Speciality.	S. A.	F. S.	R. A.	B. I.	S. S.	O. W.	N. W.	G. G.	N. G.	V. E.	Total.
Peat, Miss M.	London	1796-1797	Miniatures	—	—	2	—	—	—	—	—	—	—	2
Peat, Thomas	London	1791-1805	Enamels	—	—	23	—	—	—	—	—	—	—	23
Peck, Frederick	Maidstone	1859-1872	Architecture	—	—	7	—	—	—	—	—	—	—	7
Peck, H. W.	London	1817-1821	Sculpture	—	—	4	3	—	—	—	—	—	—	7
Peck, Robert	Dulwich	1874	Landscape	—	—	—	—	—	—	—	—	—	1	1
Peckham, R. F.	Paris	1877	Domestic	—	—	—	—	—	—	—	—	—	2	2
Peckitt, T.	Deptford	1881-1888	Churches	—	—	2	—	2	—	—	—	—	—	4
Peckitt, William	York	1761	Stained Glass	—	1	—	—	—	—	—	—	—	—	1
Pedder, John	Liverpool	1875-1893	Landscape	—	—	19	—	5	—	15	3	—	8	50
Pedley, J. L.	Southampton	1845-1875	Architecture	—	—	16	—	2	—	—	—	—	—	18
Peebles, Alexander M. (City Architect)	London	1874-1882	Architecture	—	—	7	—	—	—	—	—	—	—	7
Peel, Miss Amy	Walthamstow	1876-1884	Landscape	—	—	—	—	22	—	—	—	—	—	22
Peel, Annie	Clitheroe	1882	Flowers	—	—	—	—	—	—	—	—	—	1	1
Peel, Archibald R.	London	1864-1866	Landscape	—	—	—	4	1	—	—	—	—	—	5
Peel, Miss C. Bertha	Clitheroe	1883-1884	Landscape	—	—	—	—	—	—	2	—	—	—	2
Peel, Miss Florence ‖	Cork	1857-1869	Figures	—	—	3	1	3	—	—	—	—	8	15
Peel, James, R.B.A. §	London	1842-1893	Landscape	—	—	69	37	248	—	—	—	—	149	503
Peel, Miss J.	London	1867	Miniatures	—	—	1	—	—	—	—	—	—	—	1
Peel, Miss J. Maud	Clitheroe	1878-1885	Flowers	—	—	2	—	3	—	1	—	—	1	7
Peele, John Thomas, R.B.A. §	London	1852-1891	Domestic	—	—	28	13	161	—	—	—	—	—	202
Peers, Miss Jane Miller	Torquay	1865-1866	Buildings	—	—	—	—	—	—	—	—	—	2	2
Peggs, Wallace	London	1889	Fungi	—	—	—	—	—	—	1	—	—	—	1
Pegler, Charles William	London	1823-1833	Portraits	—	—	15	—	10	—	—	—	—	—	25
Pegram, Frederick	London	1889-1892	Domestic	—	—	2	—	—	—	—	—	—	3	5
Pegram, Henry A.	London	1884-1893	Sculpture	—	—	13	—	—	—	—	—	9	—	22
Pegsworth, J.	London	1781	Miniatures	—	—	1	—	—	—	—	—	—	—	1
Peill, Mrs. H.	London	1830-1836	Flowers	—	—	4	—	—	—	1	—	—	—	5
Peirane, L.	—	1856	Architecture	—	—	1	—	—	—	—	—	—	—	1
Peirce, C. J.	London	1838-1848	Architecture	—	—	4	—	—	—	—	—	—	—	4
Peirson, Miss Nellie	Gravesend	1890	Figures	—	—	1	—	—	—	—	—	—	—	1
Pelez, F.	Paris	1869	Venice	—	—	1	—	—	—	—	—	—	—	1
Pelham, Emily	Liverpool	1867-1879	Fruit	—	—	—	—	4	—	—	—	—	—	4
Pelham, Henry	London	1777-1778	Miniatures	—	—	5	—	—	—	—	—	—	—	5
Pelham, James	Bath	1832-1868	Portraits	—	—	8	—	3	—	—	—	—	6	17
Pelham, James, Junr.	Liverpool	1865-1881	Landscape	—	—	1	—	—	—	—	1	—	3	5
Pelham, O.	London	1848	Figures	—	—	—	—	2	—	—	—	—	—	2
Pelham, Miss R.	London	1852	Armour	—	—	—	1	—	—	—	—	—	—	1
Pelham, Thomas Kent	London	1860-1891	Domestic	—	—	25	16	54	—	—	—	—	7	102
Pelissier, F. S.	London	1886-1889	Landscape	—	—	1	—	3	—	1	1	—	—	6
Pellegrin, Louis Antoine Victor	London	1872-1873	Figures	—	—	1	—	3	—	—	—	—	—	4
Pellegrini, Carlo ("Ape")	London	1878-1883	Portraits	—	—	1	—	—	—	—	10	—	—	11
Pellegrini, D.	London	1793-1815	Historical	—	—	35	1	—	2	—	—	—	—	38
Pellegrini, R.	London	1893	Buildings	—	—	—	—	1	—	—	—	—	—	1
Pelletier, A.	London	1816-1847	Still Life	—	—	32	—	—	2	—	—	—	—	34
Pellicini —	London	1779	Landscape	—	2	—	—	—	—	—	—	—	—	2
Pells, Mrs.	London	1774	Flowers	1	—	—	—	—	—	—	—	—	—	1
Peltro, John	London	1779	Engraving	—	4	—	—	—	—	—	—	—	—	4
Pember, A.	—	1855	Landscape	—	—	—	—	—	—	—	—	—	1	1
Pemberton, Mrs. Wykeham Leigh	London	1885	Figures	—	—	—	—	—	—	—	1	—	—	1
Pemel, J.	London	1838-1851	Figures	—	—	13	5	1	—	—	—	—	—	19
Pendini, Ugo	London	1890	Domestic	—	—	—	—	—	—	—	—	—	1	1
Penfold, Frank C.	Finisterre	1880-1883	Domestic	—	—	—	—	1	—	—	—	—	2	3
Penley, Aaron Edwin ‡	Southampton	1835-1870	Landscape	—	—	18	1	20	—	309	—	—	—	348
Penley, Edwin A.	London	1853-1872	Landscape	—	—	—	—	11	—	—	—	—	7	18
Pennacchini, O. P.	London	1885	Sculpture	—	—	1	—	—	—	—	—	—	—	1
Pennachini, R.	London	1863	Sculpture	—	—	1	—	—	—	—	—	—	—	1
Pennell, Eugene H.	London	1882-1890	Landscape	—	—	3	—	1	—	—	—	—	—	4
Penniall, Arthur	London	1874-1876	Domestic	—	—	—	—	4	—	—	—	—	1	5
Pennington —	London	1764	Figures	—	2	—	—	—	—	—	—	—	—	2
Pennington, R. G. Harper	London	1885-1886	Figures	—	—	1	—	12	—	—	—	—	—	13
Pennington, E. G.	London	1854-1858	Architecture	—	—	3	—	—	—	—	—	—	—	3
Pennington, Frederick	Bedford Park	1893	Architecture	—	—	1	—	—	—	—	—	—	—	1
Pennington, Miss S.	London	1840	Portraits	—	—	1	—	—	—	—	—	—	—	1
Pennithorne, Sir James	London	1823-1840	Architecture	—	—	4	—	—	—	—	—	—	—	4
Pennoyer, Mrs. C. Ellen	London	1893	Miniatures	—	—	2	—	—	—	—	—	—	—	2
Penny, C.	London	1816-1825	Miniatures	—	—	7	—	1	—	—	—	—	—	8
Penny, Edward, R.A.	London	1762-1782	Portraits	10	—	21	—	—	—	—	—	—	—	31
Penny, G.	London	1851	Landscape	—	—	—	—	1	—	—	—	—	—	1
Penny, J.	London	1788	Domestic	—	—	2	—	—	—	—	—	—	—	2
Penny, J. S.	London	1793-1813	Flowers	—	—	9	—	—	—	—	—	—	—	9
Penny and Hanson	—	1874	Architecture	—	—	1	—	—	—	—	—	—	—	1

Name.	Town.	First and Last Year of Ex.	Speciality.	S. A.	F. S.	R. A.	B. I.	S. S.	O. W.	N. W.	G. G.	N. G.	V. E.	Total.
PENNYMAN, J.	London	1807-1808	Landscape	—	—	2	1	—	—	—	—	—	—	3
PENROSE, FRANCIS CRANMER, M.A.	London	1838-1881	Architecture	—	—	14	—	—	—	—	—	—	—	14
PENROSE, JAMES DOYLE	London	1889-1891	Portraits	—	—	2	—	—	—	—	1	—	—	3
PENSON, A. R.	London	1838	Architecture	—	—	2	—	—	—	—	—	—	—	2
PENSON, FREDERICK T.	Stoke-on-Trent	1891-1892	Mythological	—	—	2	—	—	—	—	—	—	—	2
PENSON, JAMES	London	1850	Architecture	—	—	1	—	—	—	—	—	—	—	1
PENSON, R. KYRKE, F.S.A., R.I. ‡	London	1836-1872	Sea Pieces	—	—	9	—	1	—	134	—	—	1	145
PENSON, T. M.	Oswestry	1836-1857	Landscape	—	—	5	—	—	—	—	—	—	—	5
PENSON, W.	—	1820	Landscape	—	—	1	—	—	—	—	—	—	—	1
PENSTONE, EDWARD	London	1871-1889	Domestic	—	—	1	—	25	—	—	—	—	19	45
PENSTONE, JOHN JEWELL	London	1835-1887	Figures	—	—	4	—	3	—	1	—	—	2	10
PENSTONE, WILLIAM	London	1880	Architecture	—	—	1	—	—	—	—	—	—	—	1
PENTREATH, R. T.	London	1844-1861	Sea Pieces	—	—	19	—	2	—	—	—	—	—	21
PENWARNE, J.	—	1807	Landscape	—	—	1	—	—	—	—	—	—	—	1
PEPLOE, FITZGERALD C.	Weobly	1887-1889	Sculpture	—	—	3	—	—	—	—	—	—	—	3
PEPPER, C.	London	1819-1827	Architecture	—	—	3	—	—	—	—	—	—	—	3
PEPPER, JOSEPH	London	1864-1873	Sculpture	—	—	9	—	—	—	—	—	—	—	9
PEPPER, W.	London	1808	Architecture	—	—	1	—	—	—	—	—	—	—	1
PEPPER, W.	Brighton	1846-1854	Sculpture	—	—	5	—	—	—	—	—	—	—	5
PEPPER, WM., JUNR.	London	1852-1868	Sculpture	—	—	5	—	—	—	—	—	—	—	5
PEPPERCORN, ARTHUR D.	London	1869-1893	Landscape	—	—	11	—	26	—	—	2	9	15	63
PERCIVAL, MISS BESSIE	Oxford	1885-1891	Domestic	—	—	5	—	—	—	—	—	—	2	7
PERCIVAL, HONBLE. CHARLES	—	1770	Landscape	1	—	—	—	—	—	—	—	—	—	1
PERCIVAL, WALTER	Longton	1892	Architecture	—	—	1	—	—	—	—	—	—	—	1
PERCY, MISS AMY DORA	Sutton	1883-1886	Landscape	—	—	1	—	3	—	—	—	—	—	4
PERCY, MISS EMILY	London	1868-1872	Figures	—	—	—	—	4	—	—	—	—	3	7
PERCY, H.	London	1828-1830	Architecture	—	—	—	—	2	—	—	—	—	—	2
PERCY, HERBERT S.	Sutton	1880-1885	Domestic	—	—	—	—	8	—	—	—	—	4	12
PERCY, J.	London	1793-1795	Architecture	—	—	2	—	—	—	—	—	—	—	2
PERCY, J. C.	London	1855	River Scenes	—	—	2	—	—	—	—	—	—	—	2
PERCY, J. F.	London	1828-1839	Sculpture	—	—	5	1	1	—	—	—	—	—	7
PERCY, MRS. LILIAN SNOW	Twickenham	1886-1888	Still Life	—	—	—	—	2	—	—	—	—	—	2
PERCY, S.	London	1786-1804	Miniatures	—	—	9	—	—	—	—	—	—	—	9
PERCY, SIDNEY R. (WILLIAMS FAMILY)	London	1842-1886	Landscape	—	—	73	48	73	—	—	—	—	78	272
PERCY, THOMAS	London	1829-1834	Architecture	—	—	5	—	—	—	—	—	—	—	5
PERCY, WILLIAM	Manchester	1854-1879	Portraits	—	—	15	—	—	—	—	—	—	2	17
PERCY-ROBERTSON. *See* R.	—	—	—	—	—	—	—	—	—	—	—	—	—	—
PERDRAU, MDLLE.	Paris	1839	Figures	—	—	1	—	—	—	—	—	—	—	1
PEREDA, RAIMONDO	Rome	1880	Sculpture	—	—	1	—	—	—	—	—	—	—	1
PEREIRA, FERDINAND	London	1874	Landscape	—	—	—	—	—	—	—	—	—	1	1
PERIGAL, ARTHUR	London	1810-1828	Historical	—	—	9	12	—	—	—	—	—	—	21
PERIGAL, ARTHUR, R.S.W., R.S.A	Edinburgh	1858-1884	Landscape	—	—	11	2	1	—	1	—	—	18	33
PERIGNON, ALEXIS	Paris	1841	Portraits	—	—	1	—	—	—	—	—	—	—	1
PERKIN, MISS ISABELL L.	Tiverton	1892-1893	Flowers	—	—	2	—	—	—	—	—	—	—	2
PERKIN, JOSEPH C. *See* Cheston and Perkin.		—	Architecture	—	—	—	—	—	—	—	—	—	—	—
PERKIN AND BULMER	Leeds	1881	Architecture	—	—	1	—	—	—	—	—	—	—	1
PERKINS —	—	1782	Landscape	—	2	—	—	—	—	—	—	—	—	2
PERKINS, ARTHUR E.	Finchley	1889-1892	Buildings	—	—	4	—	—	—	—	—	—	—	4
PERKINS, CHARLES P.	London	1874-1887	Miniatures	—	—	8	—	—	—	—	—	—	—	8
PERKINS, GEORGE	Manchester	1880-1885	Sea Pieces	—	—	1	—	1	—	—	—	—	1	3
PERKINS, J.	Oxford	1850-1852	Rustic	—	—	—	1	3	—	—	—	—	—	4
PERKINS, L.	Hants	1812	Landscape	—	—	—	—	—	—	—	—	—	1	1
PERLOTTO, T.	London	1854	Portraits	—	—	—	—	3	—	—	—	—	—	3
PERMAN, W. A.	Greenwich	1836-1837	Flowers	—	—	2	—	—	—	—	—	—	—	2
PERNOTIN, B.	London	1786-1797	Historical	—	—	11	—	—	—	—	—	—	—	11
PERO, W.	London	1869	Harbours	—	—	—	—	—	—	—	—	—	1	1
PERRACHE, J. P.	London	1784-1785	Enamels	—	—	14	—	—	—	—	—	—	—	14
PERRAULT, LEON BAZILE	London	1871	Domestic	—	—	1	—	—	—	—	—	—	—	1
PERRAULT, MISS	London	1780	Landscape	—	13	—	—	—	—	—	—	—	—	13
PERRIER, E. SANCHEZ-. *See* S.	—	—	—	—	—	—	—	—	—	—	—	—	—	—
PERRIN, ALFRED FEYEN-, R.C.A.	Birmingham	1870-1891	Landscape	—	—	1	—	3	—	—	—	—	1	5
PERRIN, MISS IDA S.	London	1888-1892	Landscape	—	—	2	—	2	—	—	—	—	2	6
PERRIN, JOHN W. ROSS	London	1884-1893	Miniatures	—	—	9	—	6	—	2	—	—	3	20
PERRING, RICHARD	—	1776	Landscape	—	1	—	—	—	—	—	—	—	—	1
PERRING, W.	London	1852-1853	Portraits	—	—	3	—	—	—	—	—	—	—	3
PERRONNEAU, J. B.	—	1761	Portraits	1	—	—	—	—	—	—	—	—	—	1
PERROTI, ANGELICA	London	1772-1775	Crayons	—	—	6	—	—	—	—	—	—	—	6
PEROTTI, PIETRO	London	1775	Historical	—	—	2	—	—	—	—	—	—	—	2
PERROW. *See* Salter and Perrow	—	—	Architecture	—	—	—	—	—	—	—	—	—	—	—
PERRY —	London	1764-1783	Flowers & Engraving	—	6	—	—	—	—	—	—	—	—	6
PERRY, ALFRED	London	1847-1881	Landscape	—	—	30	7	20	—	—	—	—	27	84
PERRY, MISS ALICE B.	Gunnersbury	1890	Landscape	—	—	1	—	—	—	—	—	—	—	1

Name.	Town.	First and Last Year of Ex.	Speciality.	S. A.	F. S.	R. A.	B. I.	S. S.	O. W.	N.W.	G. G.	N.G.	V.E.	Total.
Perry, H.	London	1810-1848	Portraits	—	—	8	—	*	—	—	—	—	1	9
Perry, John	London	1791-1809	Figures	—	—	2	—	—	—	—	—	—	—	2
Perry, J. C. §	London	1824-1843	Landscape	—	—	10	3	19	—	—	—	—	—	32
Perry, John Tavenor	London	1879-1891	Architecture	—	—	5	—	—	—	—	—	—	—	5
Perry (J. T.) and Reed	London	1890	Architecture	—	—	1	—	—	—	—	—	—	—	1
Perry, William J.	London	1870-1871	Domestic	—	—	—	—	2	—	—	—	—	6	8
Pertz, Miss Anna J.	Florence	1880-1889	Figures	—	—	7	—	—	—	—	2	—	1	10
Perugini, Charles Edward	London	1863-1893	Figures	—	—	53	2	2	—	—	—	5	7	69
Perugini, Mrs. Charles Edward, ‖ late Miss Kate Dickens, and Mrs. Charles Collins	— London	— 1875-1893	— Domestic	— —	— —	— 23	— —	— 2	— —	— 3	— 3	— 11	— 5	— 47
Pesenti, D.	London	1882	Interiors	—	—	1	—	—	—	—	—	—	—	1
Pessina, G. D.	London	1848-1866	Portraits	—	—	3	—	—	—	—	—	—	—	3
Peters, Rev. Matthew William, R.A.	London	1766-1807	Historical	14	2	25	1	—	—	—	—	—	—	42
Peters, Miss	—	1780	Miniatures	—	—	1	—	—	—	—	—	—	—	1
Pether, Abraham, F.S.A.	London	1773-1811	Landscape	24	39	61	1	—	—	—	—	—	—	125
Pether, A., Junr.	Southampton	1810-1811	Landscape	—	—	3	—	—	—	—	—	—	—	3
Pether, Henry	Greenwich	1828-1865	Landscape	—	—	7	1	3	—	—	—	—	—	11
Pether, Sebastian	London	1812-1832	Moonlight	—	—	5	2	1	—	—	—	—	—	8
Pether, Rev. Thomas	London	1772-1783	Sculpture	—	25	1	—	—	—	—	—	—	—	26
Pether, William, F.S.A.	London	1764-1794	Engraving and Portraits	20	10	11	—	—	—	—	—	—	—	41
Petherick, Edith M.	London	1889	Landscape	—	—	—	—	1	—	—	—	—	—	1
Petherick, Horace W.	London	1859-1891	Scriptural	—	—	2	—	3	—	—	—	—	1	6
Pethybridge, J. Ley	Launceston	1885-1893	Landscape	—	—	2	—	4	—	—	—	—	—	6
Peto, Morton K.	Pinner	1881-1884	Domestic	—	—	1	—	—	—	—	—	—	1	2
Peto, Sir Samuel Morton	London	1830	Architecture	—	—	1	—	1	—	—	—	—	—	2
Peto. *See* George and Peto	—	—	Architecture	—	—	—	—	—	—	—	—	—	—	—
Petrie, Miss Elizabeth C.	London	1879-1890	Landscape	—	—	—	—	11	—	4	—	—	1	16
Petrie, George, R.H.A.	Dublin	1818	Landscape	—	—	2	—	—	—	—	—	—	—	2
Petrie, S. Graham	London	1886-1893	Landscape	—	—	1	—	5	—	3	1	—	3	13
Pettafor, Charles R.	Greenwich	1862-1893	Landscape	—	—	12	1	17	—	2	—	—	18	50
Pettie, John, R.A.	Edinburgh	1860-1893	Historical	—	—	119	3	2	—	—	7	—	10	141
Pettie, Marion	London	1874	Flowers	—	—	—	—	—	—	—	—	—	1	1
Pettit, C. A.	London	1771-1814	Architecture	—	1	1	—	—	—	—	—	—	—	2
Pettit, Le. *See* L.	—	—	—	—	—	—	—	—	—	—	—	—	—	—
Pettitt, Alfred	Birmingham	1850-1871	Landscape	—	—	—	2	3	—	—	—	—	4	9
Pettitt, Charles	London	1855-1859	Landscape	—	—	—	2	4	—	—	—	—	6	12
Pettitt, Edwin Alfred	London	1858-1880	Landscape	—	—	13	9	42	—	—	—	—	18	82
Pettitt, Mrs. E. A.	—	1870	Landscape	—	—	—	—	1	—	—	—	—	—	1
Pettitt, George	Hastings	1857-1862	Landscape	—	—	2	10	—	—	—	—	—	27	39
Pettitt, Joseph Paul, § (?) Pane	Birmingham	1845-1880	Landscape	—	—	6	12	104	—	—	—	—	—	123
Pettitt, Miss Jenny	London	1869	Landscape	—	—	—	—	1	—	—	—	—	—	1
Pettitt, P.	London	1862-1864	Domestic	—	—	—	—	4	—	—	—	—	—	4
Pettittson, C. J.	London	1852	Landscape	—	—	—	—	2	—	—	—	—	—	2
Petty, W. R.	London	1886-1893	Domestic	—	—	1	—	1	—	5	—	—	2	9
Peuckert, Edward A.	London	1893	Sea Shores	—	—	2	—	—	—	—	—	—	—	2
Pfachler, Emil H.	London	1853-1856	Landscape	—	—	—	—	5	—	—	—	—	1	6
Pfander, Charles	London	1859-1860	Architecture	—	—	1	—	2	—	—	—	—	—	3
Pfeiffer, Mrs. J. Emily	Putney	1876-1882	Flowers	—	—	3	—	—	—	—	2	—	3	8
Pforr, J. G.	London	1787	Landscape	—	—	2	—	—	—	—	—	—	—	2
Phalipon —	—	1832	Sculpture	—	—	1	—	—	—	—	—	—	—	1
Phelps —	—	1764	Heads	1	—	—	—	—	—	—	—	—	—	1
Phelps, Eliza H.	London	1778-1780	Miniatures	—	—	2	—	—	—	—	—	—	—	2
Phelps, J.	London	1808-1826	Engraving	—	—	4	—	4	—	—	—	—	—	8
Phelps, Miss Millicent	London	1890-1892	Figures	—	—	5	—	1	—	—	—	—	1	7
Pheney, Richard	London	1855-1858	Landscape	—	—	—	—	1	—	—	—	—	5	6
Philip, Miss Constance B. *See* Mrs. Cecil Lawson	London	1874-1879	Flowers, etc.	—	—	10	—	11	—	—	—	—	7	28
Philip, John Birnie	London	1858-1875	Sculpture	—	—	22	—	—	—	—	—	—	—	22
Philippoteaux, Felix Emmanuel Henri	Paris	1875-1879	Battle Pieces	—	—	4	—	—	—	—	—	—	—	4
Philips, C.	London	1766-1783	Engraving	—	17	—	—	—	—	—	—	—	—	17
Philips, N. G.	Liverpool	1819-1829	Landscape	—	—	3	—	—	—	—	—	—	—	3
Philips, R. E.	London	1833-1841	Architecture	—	—	3	—	1	—	1	—	—	—	5
Phillan, R. P.	Sydenham	1854	Architecture	—	—	1	—	—	—	—	—	—	—	1
Phillimore, Lady	London	1881	River Scenes	—	—	—	—	—	—	—	—	—	1	1
Phillimore, C.	—	1796	Animals	—	—	1	—	—	—	—	—	—	—	1
Phillimore, G., *or* B. J.	Woburn	1855-1865	Fruit	—	—	—	5	1	—	—	—	—	—	6
Phillimore, Reginald P.	Bedford Park	1889-1891	Buildings	—	—	1	—	—	—	1	—	—	—	2
Phillip, Colin Bent, A.R.W.S., R.S.W. †	London	1882-1893	Landscape	—	—	12	—	—	59	9	—	—	—	80
Phillip, F. W.	London	1833	Domestic	—	—	—	—	1	—	—	—	—	—	1
Phillip, John, R.A.	London	1836-1867	Spanish	—	—	55	12	6	—	—	—	—	—	73
Phillipon, A.	—	1830	Historical	—	—	—	1	—	—	—	—	—	—	1
Phillipp, J. P.	London	1842-1845	Historical	—	—	5	2	4	—	—	—	—	—	11
Phillips —.	Brussels	1782	Portraits	—	—	1	—	—	—	—	—	—	—	1

Name.	Town.	First and Last Year of Ex.	Speciality.	S. A.	F. S.	R. A.	B. I.	S. S.	O.W.	N.W.	G. G.	N.G.	V. E.	Total.
Phillips, Alfred P.	London	1872-1893	Landscape	—	—	9	—	6	—	—	—	—	12	27
Phillips, Arthur	Nottingham	1889	Flowers	—	—	1	—	—	—	—	—	—	—	1
Phillips, A. M.	Denmark Hill	1873-1880	Landscape	—	—	—	—	16	—	—	—	—	—	16
Phillips, Blackburne	London	1872	Billingsgate	—	—	—	—	—	—	—	—	—	1	1
Phillips, C.	—	1832	Historical	—	—	1	—	—	—	—	—	—	—	1
Phillips, Miss Emily R.	London	1855-1866	Domestic	—	—	—	—	2	—	—	—	—	—	2
Phillips, F. A.	Dewsbury	1869-1877	Portraits	—	—	4	—	—	—	—	—	—	—	4
Phillips, G.	—	1815	Architecture	—	—	—	—	—	—	—	—	—	1	1
Phillips, G.	London	1865	Allegorical	—	—	—	—	—	—	—	—	—	1	1
Phillips, Giles Firman ‡	London	1830-1866	Sea Pieces	—	—	17	10	50	—	16	—	—	10	103
Phillips, George H.	London	1819-1827	Landscape	—	—	8	1	13	1	—	—	—	—	23
Phillips, H.	London	1794-1800	Landscape	—	—	3	—	—	—	—	—	—	—	3
Phillips, Henry	London	1820	Architecture	—	—	1	—	—	—	—	—	—	—	1
Phillips, Miss Harriet	London	1854-1855	Figures	—	—	1	—	1	—	—	—	—	—	2
Phillips, Helen	Putney	1890-1891	Landscape	—	—	—	—	2	—	—	—	—	—	2
Phillips, H. S.	—	1874	Figures	—	—	—	—	1	—	—	—	—	—	1
Phillips, Henry Wyndham. (Sec. to A.G.B.I.)	London	1838-1868	Portraits	—	—	76	13	—	—	—	—	—	2	91
Phillips, J.	London	1784-1799	Landscape	—	—	8	—	—	—	—	—	—	—	8
Phillips, J.	London	1790-1832	Architecture	—	—	18	—	—	—	—	—	—	—	18
Phillips, James	London	1807-1836	Landscape	—	—	2	2	1	—	—	—	—	—	5
Phillips, John	London	1832-1837	Domestic	—	—	—	—	5	—	2	—	—	—	7
Phillips, J. H.	London	1858-1867	Landscape	—	—	—	2	5	—	—	—	—	—	7
Phillips, J. S.	London	1822-1842	Sculpture	—	—	16	2	8	—	—	—	—	—	26
Phillips, J. W.	London	1857-1865	Figures	—	—	3	—	—	—	—	—	—	—	3
Phillips, Lawrence Barnett, A.R.P.E.	London	1874-1893	Etching	—	—	16	—	2	—	—	1	1	5	25
Phillips, Miss Mary	London	1789-1819	Landscape	—	—	4	—	—	—	—	—	—	—	4
Phillips, Miss M. A.	London	1872	Flowers	—	—	—	—	1	—	—	—	—	—	1
Phillips, Mariquita J.	Epsom	1881-1882	Domestic	—	—	—	—	—	—	—	—	—	3	3
Phillips, Peregrine	London	1771-1778	Historical	—	8	1	—	—	—	—	—	—	—	9
Phillips, Philip	London	1826-1865	Landscape	—	—	17	24	41	—	—	—	—	—	82
Phillips, Mrs. Philip, formerly Miss Elizabeth Rous	London	1832-1878	Churches	—	—	7	4	27	—	—	—	—	15	53
Phillips, S.	London	1802-1806	Portraits	—	—	3	—	—	—	—	—	—	—	3
Phillips, Thomas, R.A.	London	1792-1846	Portraits	—	—	341	1	—	—	—	—	—	—	342
Phillips, T. W.	London	1821-1826	Landscape	—	—	3	2	1	—	—	—	—	—	6
Phillips, William	Highbury	1890-1891	Landscape	—	—	—	—	4	—	—	—	—	3	7
Phillott, Miss Constance, A.R.W.S. †	London	1864-1893	Domestic	—	—	15	—	5	57	—	1	3	38	119
Philp, James George, R.I. ‡	London	1848-1885	Landscape	—	—	9	—	5	—	347	—	—	3	364
Phinney, Miss Emma E.	London	1880	Sculpture	—	—	—	—	—	—	—	1	—	—	1
Phipps, Charles John, F.S.A.	Bath	1863-1876	Architecture	—	—	6	—	—	—	—	—	—	—	6
Phipps, Edmund	Liverpool	1886	Landscape	—	—	—	—	—	—	1	—	—	—	1
Phipps, J.	London	1838	Buildings	—	—	1	—	1	—	—	—	—	—	2
Phipson, R. M. *See also* Morgan and Phipson	Ipswich	1848-1865	Architecture	—	—	18	—	—	—	—	—	—	—	18
Phipson, W. B., *or* P.	London	1860-1869	Landscape	—	—	—	—	4	—	—	—	—	—	4
Phiz. *See* Hablot K. Browne.	—	—	—	—	—	—	—	—	—	—	—	—	—	—
Phœnix, George	Bournemouth	1889-1891	Domestic	—	—	2	—	—	—	—	—	—	—	2
Phyffers, J. B.	London	1848	Sculpture	—	—	—	1	—	—	—	—	—	—	1
Phyffers, Theodore	London	1850-1864	Sculpture	—	—	13	1	3	—	—	—	—	—	17
Physick, Charles	London	1832-1834	Sculpture	—	—	1	1	2	—	—	—	—	—	4
Physick, Edward	London	1810-1842	Sculpture	—	—	31	9	15	—	—	—	—	—	55
Physick, Edward Gustavus	London	1822-1868	Sculpture	—	—	55	19	28	—	—	—	—	—	102
Physick, Edward James	London	1849-1857	Sculpture	—	—	—	2	1	—	—	—	—	—	3
Physick, E. W.	London	1836-1871	Sculpture	—	—	17	—	1	—	—	—	—	—	18
Physick, Robert	London	1836-1880	Sculpture	—	—	8	5	60	—	—	—	—	—	73
Physick, Robert §	London	1859-1866	Animals	—	—	5	4	18	—	—	—	—	—	27
Physick, Mrs. R.	London	1856	Sculpture	—	—	1	—	—	—	—	—	—	—	1
Physick, Sidney H.	London	1890	Portraits	—	—	1	—	—	—	—	—	—	—	1
Physick, T.	Manchester	1847-1872	Landscape	—	—	3	2	—	—	—	—	—	—	5
Physick, Thomas	London	1867-1881	Sculpture	—	—	—	—	7	—	—	—	—	—	7
Physick, W.	London	1849	Sea Pieces	—	—	—	1	—	—	—	—	—	—	1
Physick, William	London	1864-1890	Sculpture	—	—	1	6	8	—	—	—	—	—	15
Picard —	London	1766	Carving	—	1	—	—	—	—	—	—	—	—	1
Picart, Charles	London	1798-1802	Portraits	—	—	3	—	—	—	—	—	—	—	3
Picard, F.	London	1844	Landscape	—	—	1	—	—	—	—	—	—	—	1
Piccini, Antonio	London	1879	Etching	—	—	—	—	—	—	—	—	—	3	3
Picken, Andrew	London	1835	Churches	—	—	1	—	—	—	—	—	—	—	1
Picken, Miss Eleanor E.	London	1842	Portraits	—	—	1	—	1	—	—	—	—	—	2
Picken, J.	London	1844	Buildings	—	—	1	—	—	—	—	—	—	—	1
Picken, Thomas	London	1846-1875	Landscape	—	—	1	—	10	—	—	—	—	—	11
Pickering, Charles	London	1886	Military	—	—	—	—	—	—	1	—	—	—	1
Pickering, Miss Evelyn	London	1876-1889	Figures	—	—	—	—	—	—	1	21	3	7	32
Pickering, Ferdinand	London	1831-1882	Historical	—	—	32	9	6	—	—	—	—	—	47

Name.	Town.	First and Last Year of Ex.	Speciality.	S. A.	F. S.	R. A.	B. I.	S. S.	O. W.	N. W.	G. G.	N. G.	V. E.	Total.
Pickering, George	Chester	1815-1828	Landscape	—	—	—	—	4	11	—	—	—	—	15
Pickering, J.	London	1831-1832	Animals	—	—	—	4	—	—	—	—	—	—	4
Pickering, J. L., R.B.A. § ϕ	Abinger	1872-1893	Landscape	—	—	34	—	29	—	—	—	2	31	96
Pickersgill, Frederick Richard, R.A.	London	1839-1875	Historical	—	—	50	6	—	—	—	—	—	—	56
Pickersgill, Henry Hall	London	1834-1862	Figures	—	—	44	8	—	—	—	—	—	—	52
Pickersgill, Henry William, R.A.	London	1806-1872	Portraits	—	—	384	26	—	—	—	—	—	—	410
Pickersgill, Mrs. H. (Jane)	London	1848-1863	Domestic	—	—	7	1	—	—	—	—	—	—	8
Pickersgill, Miss M. A.	London	1832-1838	Copies	—	—	8	—	4	—	—	—	—	—	12
Pickersgill, Richard	London	1826-1853	Sea Pieces	—	—	26	7	8	—	3	—	—	—	44
Pickersgill, Mrs. Rose M.	Hayes	1889	Heads	—	—	1	—	—	—	—	—	—	—	1
Pickett, Miss Mary S.	Dulwich	1892-1893	Domestic	—	—	2	—	—	—	2	—	—	—	4
Pickett, W.	London	1792-1820	Landscape	—	—	44	—	—	—	—	—	—	—	44
Pickett, W. V.	London	1852-1864	Architecture	—	—	4	—	—	—	—	—	—	—	4
Pickler, Adolph	Munich	1881	Scriptural	—	—	—	—	—	—	—	—	—	1	1
Pickman, J. T.	—	1826	Architecture	—	—	—	—	1	—	—	—	—	—	1
Pickman, W.	London	1825-1844	Sculpture	—	—	23	—	6	—	—	—	—	—	29
Picknell, William L., R.B.A. §	Pontaven	1877-1890	Domestic	—	—	10	—	6	—	—	—	—	2	18
Picot, Victor Marie, F.S.A.	London	1769-1774	Engraving	17	—	—	—	—	—	—	—	—	—	17
Picot, Mrs. Angelique	London	1770-1783	Engraving	5	—	—	—	—	—	—	—	—	—	5
Pidding, Henry James §	Greenwich	1818-1864	Figures	—	—	26	42	177	—	—	—	—	—	245
Pidgeon, G. F.	London	1804-1819	Medals	—	—	15	—	—	—	—	—	—	—	15
Pidgeon, Henry Clark ‡	London	1838-1880	Landscape	—	—	4	2	15	—	258	—	—	—	279
Pienne, Georges	Finchley	1891-1892	Landscape	—	—	3	—	—	—	—	—	—	—	3
Pierce, R.	London	1827	Ruins	—	—	1	—	—	—	—	—	—	—	1
Pierce, Sarah	London	1785-1790	Miniatures	—	—	7	—	—	—	—	—	—	—	7
Pierce, Mrs. W. *See* Miss Beaumont	London	1833-1836	Domestic	—	—	—	3	4	—	—	—	—	—	7
Piercy, Frederick	London	1850-1882	Portraits	—	—	12	—	9	—	—	—	—	—	21
Piercy, Mrs. Frederick. *See* Miss Catherine Agnes Wornum.	—	—	—	—	—	—	—	—	—	—	—	—	—	—
Piercy, Frederick Hawkins	London	1880-1883	Sculpture	—	—	1	—	3	—	—	—	—	—	4
Pierie, Captain	—	1775	Landscape	1	—	—	—	—	—	—	—	—	—	1
Pierrepont, Miss C. Constance	London	1877-1879	Flowers	—	—	—	—	2	—	—	—	—	1	3
Pigeon, Mrs.	London	1772	Birds	1	—	—	—	—	—	—	—	—	—	1
Piggott, John	Coventry	1859-1882	Landscape	—	—	1	1	—	—	—	—	—	—	2
Pigot, R. St. Ledger	London	1864-1871	Domestic	—	—	1	—	7	—	—	—	—	—	8
Pigott, Charles	Eltham	1888-1893	Landscape	—	—	—	—	4	—	1	—	—	—	5
Pigott, F. T	London	1880	Architecture	—	—	1	—	—	—	—	—	—	—	1
Pigott, W. H.	Sheffield	1869-1893	Domestic	—	—	4	—	2	—	7	—	—	—	13
Pigott, Miss	—	1802	Portraits	—	—	3	—	—	—	—	—	—	—	3
Pike, Miss A. G.	Highgate	1889	Landscape	—	—	—	—	3	—	—	—	—	—	3
Pike, Clement E.	Loughborough	1880-1884	Rustic	—	—	—	—	1	—	—	—	—	2	3
Pike, Joseph	London	1888-1890	Landscape	—	—	1	—	3	—	—	—	—	—	4
Pike, N. H.	London	1889	Landscape	—	—	1	—	—	—	—	—	—	—	1
Pike, Sidney	Taplow	1880-1892	Landscape	—	—	16	—	13	—	—	—	—	12	41
Pike, W. H., R.B.A. § ϕ	Plymouth	1874-1893	Landscape	—	—	2	—	60	—	8	—	—	15	85
Pilchard, J.	London	1873	Horses	—	—	—	—	2	—	—	—	—	—	2
Pilkington, F. M. M.	London	1891	Landscape	—	—	—	—	—	—	1	—	—	—	1
Pilkington, H.	London	1839-1856	Cattle	—	—	10	8	—	—	—	—	—	—	18
Pilkington, Miss Maud E.	London	1888-1893	Figures	—	—	1	—	9	—	1	—	—	—	11
Pilkington, R. W.	—	1808-1827	Architecture	—	—	2	—	—	—	—	—	—	—	2
Pilkington, Sir William, Bart.	London	1780-1790	Architecture	—	—	4	—	—	—	—	—	—	—	4
Pill, Martha	Lewisham	1884-1885	Landscape	—	—	—	—	2	—	—	—	—	—	2
Pillé, Henri	Paris	1876	Figures	—	—	—	—	—	—	—	—	—	1	1
Pillé, William	London	1875-1880	Landscape	—	—	—	—	1	—	—	—	—	14	15
Pilleau, F. Startin	London	1882-1892	Churches	—	—	—	—	—	—	9	—	—	1	10
Pilleau, Henry, R.I. ‡ ϕ	London	1850-1893	Landscape	—	—	25	10	30	—	76	—	—	172	313
Pilleau, Lt.-Col. H. E., *or* G.	Brighton	1892-1893	Landscape	—	—	—	—	—	—	2	—	—	—	2
Pillement, Jean	London	1760-1780	Landscape	8	4	—	—	—	—	—	—	—	—	12
Piloteil, George	London	1876	Etching	—	—	3	—	—	—	—	—	—	3	6
Pilsbury, E.	—	1810	Miniatures	—	—	1	—	—	—	—	—	—	—	1
Pilsbury, Miss Elizabeth	Leicester	1879-1881	Landscape	—	—	4	—	—	—	—	—	—	—	4
Pilsbury, Wilmot, A.R.W.S. †	London	1866-1893	Domestic	—	—	26	—	6	230	—	2	—	47	311
Pimm, William E.	London	1890-1892	Domestic	—	—	1	—	4	—	—	—	—	—	5
Pincat, Daniel, *or* Pincot	—	1767-1771	Stone Work	1	7	—	—	—	—	—	—	—	—	8
Pinches, Frederick	London	1886	Architecture	—	—	1	—	—	—	—	—	—	—	1
Pinches, John	London	1847-1860	Medals	—	—	3	—	—	—	—	—	—	—	3
Pinches, Thomas Ryan	London	1836-1854	Medals	—	—	7	—	—	—	—	—	—	—	7
Pincott, W. H.	London	1856	Figures	—	—	1	—	—	—	—	—	—	—	1
Pine, Miss J.	London	1797-1808	Domestic	—	—	3	2	—	—	—	—	—	—	5
Pine, Robert Edge	London	1760-1784	Portraits	29	11	10	—	—	—	—	—	—	—	50
Pine, Simon	Bath	1765-1771	Miniatures	15	—	3	—	—	—	—	—	—	—	18
Pingel, Gustav	London	1884	Sculpture	—	—	1	—	—	—	—	—	—	—	1

Name.	Town.	First and Last Year of Ex.	Speciality.	S. A.	F. S.	R. A.	B. I.	S. S.	O.W.	N.W.	G. G.	N. G.	V. E.	Total.
Pingo, Henry	London	1772-1773	Flowers	—	15	—	—	—	—	—	—	—	—	15
Pingo, John	London	1765-1774	Seals, etc.	—	10	—	—	—	—	—	—	—	—	10
Pingo, Lewis	London	1760-1782	Medals	4	35	—	—	—	—	—	—	—	—	39
Pingo, Thomas	London	1763-1774	Medals	—	16	—	—	—	—	—	—	—	—	16
Pingret, Edouard Henri Théophile	London	1819	Portraits	—	—	4	—	—	—	—	—	—	—	4
Pinhorn-Wood, L. *See* W.	—	—		—	—	—	—	—	—	—	—	—	—	—
Pink, W.	London	1828-1844	Sculpture	—	—	8	—	1	—	—	—	—	—	9
Pinker, Henry Richard	London	1875-1893	Sculpture	—	—	33	—	—	—	—	—	—	—	33
Pinkerton, W. E.	London	1885	Buildings	—	—	2	—	—	—	—	—	—	—	2
Pinsley, A.	London	1859	Sea Pieces	—	—	—	1	—	—	—	—	—	—	1
Pinto, J. J. de Sonza-	Paris	1882	Portraits	—	—	1	—	—	—	—	—	—	—	1
Pinwell, George John †	London	1865-1875	Domestic	—	—	—	—	—	60	—	—	—	8	68
Pio, A.	London	1860	Figures	—	—	1	—	—	—	—	—	—	—	1
Piper, F. M.	London	1780	Architecture	—	—	1	—	—	—	—	—	—	—	1
Piper, Herbert William	London	1871-1889	Landscape	—	—	4	—	10	—	—	—	—	19	33
Pirie, George	Glasgow	1888-1891	Figures	—	—	3	—	—	—	—	1	—	—	4
Pisa, Alberto	London	1892-1893	Portraits	—	—	1	—	—	—	—	—	—	—	1
Pissarro, C.	Seine-et-Oise	1878	Rustic	—	—	—	—	—	—	—	—	—	1	1
Pistrucci, Benedetto	London	1830-1840	Medals	—	—	7	—	—	—	—	—	—	—	7
Pistrucci, Miss M. Eliza	—	1847-1848	Gems	—	—	—	4	—	—	—	—	—	—	4
Pistrucci, Miss Ellen	—	1847-1848	Gems	—	—	—	3	—	—	—	—	—	—	3
Pitcairn, Miss Constance	London	1881-1886	Flowers	—	—	2	—	1	—	—	—	—	1	4
Pitcher, W. H.	London	1880	Domestic	—	—	—	—	—	—	—	—	—	1	1
Pite, Arthur Beresford	London	1882-1892	Architecture	—	—	5	—	—	—	—	—	—	—	5
Pite, William Alfred	London	1887-1893	Architecture	—	—	5	—	—	—	—	—	—	—	5
Pithou —	London	1768-1773	Mythological	1	4	—	—	—	—	—	—	—	—	5
Pitman, C.	Worcester	1828	Horses	—	—	—	—	1	—	—	—	—	—	1
Pitman, Miss Edith H.	Solihull	1887	Landscape	—	—	—	—	—	—	—	—	—	1	1
Pitman, Miss Janetta R. A.	Nottingham	1880-1890	Still Life	—	—	16	—	2	—	9	1	—	2	30
Pitman, John	Worcester	1820-1827	Game	—	—	1	1	1	—	—	—	—	—	3
Pitman, Miss Sarah Bennard	London	1839-1840	Miniatures	—	—	3	—	—	—	—	—	—	—	3
Pitt, Douglas	London	1893	Landscape	—	—	—	—	—	—	1	—	—	—	1
Pitt, R.	London	1795	Birds	—	—	1	—	—	—	—	—	—	—	1
Pitt, Thomas Henry	London	1827-1852	Landscape	—	—	4	11	24	—	—	—	—	—	39
Pitt, William	Birmingham	1853-1890	Landscape	—	—	4	10	55	—	1	—	—	17	87
Pitt, Mrs. W.	London	1848-1851	Miniatures	—	—	7	—	—	—	—	—	—	—	7
Pitt, W. H.	London	1825	Buildings	—	—	—	—	1	—	—	—	—	—	1
Pittar, I. J.	London	1845-1856	Domestic	—	—	7	2	—	—	—	—	—	7	16
Pittard, Charles William	London	1878-1891	Still Life	—	—	8	—	7	—	—	—	—	—	15
Pittaro, Charles	London	1881	Sporting	—	—	—	—	—	—	—	—	—	1	1
Pittatore, M.	London	1869	Portraits	—	—	1	—	—	—	—	—	—	—	1
Pitts, Frederick	London	1856-1882	Sporting	—	—	3	2	6	—	—	—	—	—	11
Pitts, J.	London	1842-1870	Sculpture	—	—	6	—	—	—	—	—	—	—	6
Pitts, Marcus W.	London	1887	Domestic	—	—	—	—	—	—	—	—	—	1	1
Pitts, Thomas	London	1834	Portraits	—	—	—	—	1	—	—	—	—	—	1
Pitts, William	London	1823-1840	Sculpture	—	—	18	5	10	—	—	—	—	—	33
Pitts, Mrs.	London	1864	Flowers	—	—	—	—	1	—	—	—	—	—	1
Pixell, Miss Maria	Wargrave	1793-1811	Landscape	—	—	31	3	—	—	—	—	—	—	34
Pizzetta, U.	London	1813	Portraits	—	—	2	—	—	—	—	—	—	—	2
Place, George	London	1791-1797	Miniatures	—	—	43	—	—	—	—	—	—	—	43
Place, Miss Rosa	London	1859-1868	Fruit	—	—	6	—	3	—	—	—	—	—	9
Plant, W.	London	1819-1828	Enamels	—	—	4	—	—	2	—	—	—	—	6
Plant-Hollins, H.	Milford	1891	Rustic	—	—	—	—	2	—	—	—	—	—	2
Plass, A. F.	London	1850	Figures	—	—	1	—	—	—	—	—	—	—	1
Plastow, A. B., *or* C. B.	London	1844-1848	Landscape	—	—	2	—	—	—	—	—	—	—	2
Platt —	London	1780	Graining	2	—	—	—	—	—	—	—	—	—	2
Platt, Miss Emily	London	1832-1838	Domestic	—	—	5	—	6	—	—	—	—	—	11
Platt, G.	London	1798-1800	Landscape	—	—	2	—	—	—	—	—	—	—	2
Platt, Henry	London	1825-1865	Rustic	—	—	7	22	26	—	9	—	—	—	64
Platt, J.	—	1814	Portraits	—	—	1	—	—	—	—	—	—	—	1
Platt, Samuel	London	1803-1837	Fruit	—	—	20	16	6	—	—	—	—	—	42
Platt, S., Junr.	—	1823-1825	Fruit	—	—	2	—	—	—	—	—	—	—	2
Platt, T.	London	1799	Landscape	—	—	1	—	—	—	—	—	—	—	1
Platt, William	London	1793-1796	Poetical	—	—	2	—	—	—	—	—	—	—	2
Plaw, John, F.S.A.	London	1773-1800	Architecture	12	—	20	—	—	—	—	—	—	—	32
Plaw, Miss P.	London	1790	Landscape	5	—	—	—	—	—	—	—	—	—	5
Player, F. da Ponte	Ventnor	1873-1881	Sea Pieces	—	—	1	—	11	—	—	—	—	10	22
Player, William H.	Ventnor	1858-1884	Landscape	—	—	2	5	2	—	1	—	—	19	29
Playfair, J.	London	1783-1793	Architecture	—	—	14	—	—	—	—	—	—	—	14
Playfair, James Charles	London	1865-1876	Domestic	—	—	4	—	7	—	—	—	—	9	20
Playfair, William Henry, R.S.A.	Edinburgh	1838	Architecture	—	—	1	—	—	—	—	—	—	—	1

Name.	Town.	First and Last Year of Ex.	Speciality.	S. A.	F. S.	R. A.	B. I.	S. S.	O. W.	N.W.	G. G.	N. G.	V. E.	Total.
Plews, Miss Helen M.	London	1887-1893	Figures	—	—	—	—	—	—	2	—	—	4	6
Plimer, Andrew	London	1786-1830	Miniatures	—	—	50	3	2	—	—	—	—	—	55
Plimer, Nathaniel	London	1787-1815	Miniatures	5	—	28	—	—	—	—	—	—	—	33
Plimpton, Miss Constance E.	London	1882-1893	Domestic	—	—	17	—	12	—	2	—	—	5	36
Plimpton, G. R.	London	1834-1838	Landscape	—	—	1	—	3	—	1	—	—	—	5
Plochhorst, B.	Berlin	1881	Scriptural	—	—	1	—	—	—	—	—	—	—	1
Ploszezynski, N.	London	1850	Portraits	—	—	1	—	—	—	—	—	—	—	1
Plott, John, F.S.A.	London	1764-1803	Miniatures	23	—	17	—	—	—	—	—	—	—	40
Plowden, Miss Edith R.	London	1885-1889	Domestic	—	—	1	—	1	—	—	—	—	—	2
Plowman, Elise	London	1843	Figures	—	—	1	—	—	—	—	—	—	—	1
Plowman, T.	Oxford	1826-1839	Architecture	—	—	6	—	—	—	—	—	—	—	6
Plum, R. B.	Worcester	1874-1886	Landscape	—	—	1	—	—	—	—	—	—	1	2
Plumbe, Rowland	London	1872-1890	Architecture	—	—	13	—	—	—	—	—	—	—	13
Plumley, Thomas P.	London	1865	Sculpture	—	—	1	—	—	—	—	—	—	—	1
Plummer, H. L.	London	1837-1845	Domestic	—	—	11	—	3	—	—	—	—	—	14
Plumpton, A. W.	Merton	1874	Pen and Ink	—	—	—	—	—	—	—	—	—	1	1
Plumridge, W.	London	1778-1779	Architecture	—	1	1	—	—	—	—	—	—	—	2
Plura, J.	London	1782-1786	Sculpture	—	—	4	—	—	—	—	—	—	—	4
Poate, R.	Portsmouth	1845-1869	Figures	—	—	—	1	3	—	—	—	—	—	4
Pockels, Miss C.	London	1869	Figures	—	—	1	—	—	—	—	—	—	—	1
Pocklington, F. C.	London	1879-1884	Landscape	—	—	—	—	—	—	—	2	—	—	2
Pocock, A.	—	1841	Landscape	—	—	1	—	—	—	—	—	—	—	1
Pocock, H.	London	1875	Landscape	—	—	—	—	1	—	—	—	—	—	1
Pocock, H. Childe	London	1880-1892	Domestic	—	—	2	—	5	—	8	—	—	1	16
Pocock, Innes	London	1852	Sporting	—	—	—	1	—	—	—	—	—	—	1
Pocock, Isaac	London	1803-1818	Domestic	—	—	73	47	—	—	—	—	—	—	120
Pocock, J.	London	1850-1860	Domestic	—	—	—	1	3	—	—	—	—	—	4
Pocock, Miss Julia	London	1871-1888	Portraits	—	—	7	—	2	—	—	—	—	6	15
Pocock, J. W.	Layton	1799-1802	Landscape	—	—	3	—	—	—	—	—	—	—	3
Pocock, Lexden L.	London	1872-1893	Landscape	—	—	19	—	19	—	8	—	—	27	73
Pocock, Miss Margaret	London	1883	Miniatures	—	—	1	—	—	—	—	—	—	—	1
Pocock, Maurice A.	London	1878-1881	Architecture	—	—	4	—	—	—	—	—	—	—	4
Pocock, Nicholas †	London	1782-1817	Sea Pieces	—	—	113	25	—	184	—	—	—	—	322
Pocock, W. F.	London	1799-1841	Architecture	—	—	21	—	—	—	—	—	—	—	21
Pocock, W. T.	London	1817	Naval Battles	—	—	—	—	—	3	—	—	—	—	3
Pocock, W. W., A.I.B.A.	London	1837-1859	Architecture	—	—	5	—	—	—	—	—	—	—	5
Poddard, J.	—	1847	Portraits	—	—	1	—	—	—	—	—	—	—	1
Podmore, R.	—	1809-1813	Landscape	—	—	3	—	—	—	—	—	—	—	3
Poggi, Anthony	Rome	1776-1781	Portraits	—	—	3	—	—	—	—	—	—	—	3
Pohlmann, Miss Charlotte	Nottingham	1888-1893	Figures	—	—	1	—	—	—	—	—	—	1	2
Poingdestre, Charles H.	London	1849-1890	Sporting	—	—	24	2	2	—	9	1	2	10	50
Poingdestre, W. W.	London	1856	Animals	—	—	—	1	—	—	—	—	—	—	1
Pointer, R. M.	London	1851	Figures	—	—	—	1	—	—	—	—	—	—	1
Poittevin, Le. *See* L.	—	—	—	—	—	—	—	—	—	—	—	—	—	—
Poix-Tydel, De. *See* D.	—	—	—	—	—	—	—	—	—	—	—	—	—	—
Polack, J.	London	1823	Portraits	—	—	1	—	—	—	—	—	—	—	1
Poland, Charles	London	1846	Architecture	—	—	1	—	—	—	—	—	—	—	1
Pole, T. G.	London	1839-1843	Sea Pieces	—	—	1	—	4	—	—	—	—	—	5
Polehalt, Emily	London	1872	River Scenes	—	—	—	—	—	—	—	—	—	1	1
Poley, Edward William	London	1876-1884	Architecture	—	—	5	—	—	—	—	—	—	—	5
Pollack, Solomon	London	1790-1835	Miniatures	—	—	67	—	5	—	—	—	—	—	72
Pollak, J.	—	1861-1878	Sculpture	—	—	2	1	—	—	—	—	—	—	3
Pollard, A. Read	Worthing	1884-1885	Domestic	—	—	—	—	—	—	—	—	—	2	2
Pollard, F.	Brighton	1837-1839	Landscape	—	—	—	—	3	—	—	—	—	—	3
Pollard, James	London	1821-1846	Sporting	—	—	5	3	4	—	—	—	—	—	12
Pollard, Miss Kattern	Hitchin	1892-1893	Domestic	—	—	—	—	5	—	1	—	—	—	6
Pollard, Miss Renira	London	1887-1893	Flowers	—	—	1	—	1	—	3	—	—	1	6
Pollard, Robert	—	1783	Landscape	—	2	—	—	—	—	—	—	—	—	2
Pollard, S. G.	London	1864-1877	Domestic	—	—	7	4	11	—	—	—	—	9	31
Pollden, R.	Christchurch	1793	Architecture	—	—	1	—	—	—	—	—	—	—	1
Pollen, J. H.	London	1866-1883	Domestic	—	—	—	—	—	—	—	13	—	1	14
Pollen, John Hungerford, F.S.A.	London	1861-1887	Architecture	—	—	5	—	—	—	—	—	—	—	5
Pollentine, Alfred	London	1861-1880	Venice	—	—	—	2	23	—	—	—	—	—	25
Pollentine, R. J.	London	1852-1862	Landscape	—	—	3	2	4	—	—	—	—	—	9
Pollentine, W. H.	London	1847-1850	Sea Pieces	—	—	2	1	—	—	—	—	—	—	3
Pollet, J.	Paris	1865	Sculpture	—	—	1	—	—	—	—	—	—	—	1
Pollexfen, J.	London	1882	Flowers	—	—	—	—	1	—	—	—	—	—	1
Pollock, Frederick	London	1866	Landscape	—	—	—	—	—	—	—	—	—	1	1
Pollock, Maurice	London	1882-1889	Landscape	—	—	1	—	1	—	—	3	3	—	8
Polter, Miss E.	London	1860	Figures	—	—	—	1	—	—	—	—	—	—	1
Pomeroy, Frederick W.	London	1885-1893	Sculpture	—	—	17	—	1	—	—	—	2	—	20
Poncia, W.	London	1844	Scriptural	—	—	1	—	—	—	—	—	—	—	1

Name.	Town.	First and Last Year of Ex.	Speciality.	S. A.	F. S.	R. A.	B. I.	S. S.	O. W.	N. W.	G. G.	N. G.	V. E.	Total
Poncy, Alfred Vevier De	London	1871-1890	Domestic	—	—	5	—	13	—	—	—	—	22	40
Ponder, James R.	London	1881-1884	Domestic	—	—	1	—	1	—	—	—	—	—	2
Ponder, S.	London	1794-1796	Architecture	—	—	3	—	—	—	—	—	—	—	3
Ponsan, Edouard Bernard Debat-. *See* D.	—	—	—	—	—	—	—	—	—	—	—	—	—	—
Ponsford, John	London	1820-1821	Architecture	—	—	2	—	—	—	—	—	—	—	2
Ponsford, John	Plymouth	1823-1857	Portraits	—	—	4	1	5	—	—	—	—	—	10
Ponsonby, Hon. Gerald	London	1867	Landscape	—	—	—	—	—	—	—	—	—	1	1
Ponthon, A.	London	1798-1800	Miniatures	—	—	5	—	—	—	—	—	—	—	5
Ponting, Charles E.	Marlborough	1892-1893	Architecture	—	—	6	—	—	—	—	—	—	—	6
Ponton and Gough	Bristol	1871	Architecture	—	—	1	—	—	—	—	—	—	—	1
Pool, J. L.	London	1802-1817	Architecture	—	—	5	—	—	—	—	—	—	—	5
Poole, Chris.	Poole	1882-1891	Landscape	—	—	5	—	25	—	9	—	—	1	40
Poole, Frederick Victor	Southampton	1890-1891	Domestic	—	—	2	—	—	—	—	—	—	—	2
Poole, Paul Falconer, R.A. ‡	London	1830-1879	Historical	—	—	65	13	13	—	4	—	—	—	95
Poole, Samuel	London	1892-1893	Domestic	—	—	2	—	3	—	—	—	—	—	5
Poole, T. R.	London	1799-1800	Sculpture	—	—	3	—	—	—	—	—	—	—	3
Poole, William	London	1826-1838	Portraits	—	—	—	—	12	—	—	—	—	—	12
Poole, William	Sheffield	1854	Interiors	—	—	—	—	—	—	—	—	—	4	4
Poole, W. J.	London	1816	Architecture	—	—	1	—	—	—	—	—	—	—	1
Pope, Alexander	London	1787-1821	Miniatures	—	—	67	—	—	—	—	—	—	—	67
Pope, Mrs. Alexander, formerly Miss Clara	—	—	—	—	—	—	—	—	—	—	—	—	—	—
Maria Leigh and Mrs. Francis Wheatley	London	1808-1838	Fruit	—	—	41	2	2	—	—	—	—	—	45
Pope, Arthur Edward	London	1884-1885	British Museum	—	—	—	—	—	—	—	—	—	2	2
Pope, F. George	—	1856	Domestic	—	—	—	—	1	—	—	—	—	—	1
Pope, Gustav	London	1852-1892	Domestic	—	—	43	14	27	—	—	—	—	20	104
Pope, Henry	Birmingham	1872-1886	Landscape	—	—	—	—	5	—	2	—	—	—	7
Pope, Robert Philip	London	1859-1862	Architecture	—	—	4	—	—	—	—	—	—	—	4
Pope, S.	—	1876	Sculpture	—	—	1	—	—	—	—	—	—	—	1
Popert, Miss Charlotte	London	1883-1889	Domestic	—	—	—	—	1	—	4	—	—	—	5
Popkin, G. P.	Llanwrst	1850-1859	Landscape	—	—	6	—	15	—	—	—	—	—	21
Popplewell, Isaac	London	1773	Drawing	—	1	—	—	—	—	—	—	—	—	1
Porden, C.	London	1782-1784	Architecture	—	—	2	—	—	—	—	—	—	—	2
Porden, C. F.	London	1810-1825	Architecture	—	—	5	—	—	—	—	—	—	—	5
Porden, William	London	1778-1813	Architecture	—	—	47	—	—	—	—	—	—	—	47
Portaels, E.	London	1870	Historical	—	—	1	—	—	—	—	—	—	—	1
Portaels, J.	—	1893	Portraits	—	—	—	—	—	—	—	—	—	1	1
Portaels, T.	London	1869	Scriptural	—	—	1	—	—	—	—	—	—	—	1
Porte, Le. *See* L.	—	—	—	—	—	—	—	—	—	—	—	—	—	—
Porter, Alfred T.	London	1882-1888	Historical	—	—	3	—	—	—	—	—	—	3	6
Porter, Daniel	London	1888-1893	Domestic	—	—	8	—	8	—	—	—	—	4	20
Porter, Edward P.	London	1892	Coaching	—	—	—	—	—	—	—	—	—	1	1
Porter, Frank	Twickenham	1893	Landscape	—	—	1	—	—	—	—	—	—	—	1
Porter, F. W.	London	1866-1874	Architecture	—	—	3	—	—	—	—	—	—	—	3
Porter (F. W.) and Boulnois (W. A.)	London	1849	Architecture	—	—	1	—	—	—	—	—	—	—	1
Porter, G.	London	1815-1837	Architecture	—	—	5	—	—	—	—	—	—	—	5
Porter, Miss Ida	London	1885-1886	Flowers	—	—	—	—	1	—	1	—	—	—	2
Porter, J.	Titchfield	1784-1824	Scriptural	—	—	2	—	—	—	—	—	—	—	2
Porter, John	London	1826-1870	Historical	—	—	4	2	11	—	—	—	—	—	17
Porter, Miss Maud	London	1888-1893	Portraits	—	—	9	—	—	—	2	—	1	9	21
Porter, Miss M. C.	London	1859	Churches	—	—	1	—	—	—	—	—	—	—	1
Porter, Percy C.	London	1880-1887	Landscape	—	—	—	—	6	—	1	—	—	1	8
Porter, Sir Robert Kerr	London	1792-1832	Historical	—	—	38	—	1	—	—	—	—	—	39
Porter, Thomas	London	1860-1875	Architecture	—	—	4	—	—	—	—	—	—	—	4
Porter, W.	London	1788-1802	Portraits	—	—	18	—	—	—	—	—	—	—	18
Porterler, J.	—	1830	Dramatic	—	—	—	2	—	—	—	—	—	—	2
Porteus, Edgar	London	1868-1878	Domestic	—	—	2	—	18	—	—	—	—	1	21
Portevin —	Paris	1864	Figures	—	—	1	—	—	—	—	—	—	—	1
Portielie, Gerard	Antwerp	1883	Domestic	—	—	—	—	—	—	—	—	—	1	1
Posselwhite, James	London	1870	Engraving	—	—	2	—	—	—	—	—	—	—	2
Postlethwaite, Miss Elinor	Kilburn	1889-1891	Flowers	—	—	1	—	1	—	—	—	—	—	2
Postlethwaite, Miss Mary E.	Kilburn	1891-1892	Domestic	—	—	—	—	3	—	—	—	—	—	3
Postma —	London	1860	Landscape	—	—	2	—	—	—	—	—	—	—	2
Potchett, Miss Caroline H.	Great Ponton	1862-1881	Landscape	—	—	—	—	23	—	—	—	—	—	23
Potchett, Miss Emily	London	1869-1880	Landscape	—	—	—	—	15	—	—	—	—	—	15
Potelet, H.	London	1832	Domestic	—	—	—	—	1	—	—	—	—	—	1
Pott, Charles L.	London	1888-1890	Landscape	—	—	—	—	3	—	—	—	—	1	4
Pott, Laslett John, R.B.A. §	London	1860-1893	Historical	—	—	40	—	3	—	—	—	—	—	43
Potten, Christopher	London	1875-1880	Landscape	—	—	1	—	4	—	—	—	—	—	5
Potten, Miss	London	1875	Fruit	—	—	—	—	1	—	—	—	—	—	1
Potter, Arthur	Chiswick	1882-1892	Domestic	—	—	3	—	3	—	—	—	—	3	9
Potter, Charles, R.C.A.	Oldham	1867-1892	Landscape	—	—	10	—	—	—	2	2	—	8	22
Potter, Miss Emily	London	1854-1861	Domestic	—	—	1	2	—	—	—	—	—	—	3

Name.	Town.	First and Last Year of Ex.	Speciality.	S. A.	F. S.	R. A.	B. I.	S. S.	O. W.	N. W.	G. G.	N. G.	V. E.	Total.
Potter, Frank H., R.B.A. §	London	1870-1887	Domestic	—	—	3	—	45	—	—	1	—	8	57
Potter, F. S.	London	1862-1874	Sculpture	—	—	9	—	—	—	—	—	—	—	9
Potter, Percy C.	—	1885	Sea Shores	—	—	—	—	1	—	—	—	—	—	1
Potter, R. H.	London	1845-1865	Architecture	—	—	25	—	—	—	—	—	—	—	25
Potter, R. S. H.	London	1812-1814	Portraits	—	—	6	—	—	—	—	—	—	4	10
Potter, Sydney	Chiswick	1883-1890	Landscape	—	—	3	—	3	—	—	—	—	4	10
Pottinger, H.	London	1872	Sea Pieces	—	—	—	—	2	—	—	—	—	—	2
Potts, George B.	London	1833-1860	Landscape	—	—	28	14	28	—	—	—	—	—	70
Potts, Sulman, and Hennings	London	1886	Architecture	—	—	1	—	—	—	—	—	—	—	1
Pouget, F.	London	1820-1849	Architecture	—	—	7	—	—	—	—	—	—	—	7
Poulson —	—	1846	Flowers	—	—	1	—	—	—	—	—	—	—	1
Poulter, Harry	London	1887-1893	Domestic	—	—	5	—	—	—	—	—	—	—	5
Poulter, J. A.	London	1850-1860	Landscape	—	—	3	4	4	—	—	—	—	—	11
Poulter, Marian	Dover	1862	Landscape	—	—	—	—	1	—	—	—	—	—	1
Poultney, J.	London	1788	Architecture	—	—	1	—	—	—	—	—	—	—	1
Poulton, Miss A.	London	1868-1869	Fruit	—	—	—	—	2	—	—	—	—	—	2
Poulton, Elizabeth	Homerton	1847	—	—	—	—	—	*	—	—	—	—	—	—
Poulton, George	Homerton	1846-1856	Landscape	—	—	—	4	12	—	—	—	—	—	16
Poulton, James	Homerton	1844-1859	Still Life	—	—	5	3	14	—	—	—	—	—	22
Poulton, W. F.	Reading	1847	Architecture	—	—	1	—	—	—	—	—	—	—	1
Pouncett, R.	—	1840	Landscape	—	—	1	—	—	—	—	—	—	—	1
Pouncy, B. T.	London	1772-1789	Engraving	10	—	3	—	—	—	—	—	—	—	13
Pound, D. J.	London	1855	Engraving	—	—	—	—	1	—	—	—	—	—	1
Powell, Alfred	London	1866-1892	Landscape	—	—	17	—	52	—	20	—	—	26	115
Powell, Mrs. Alfred	London	1883-1889	Landscape	—	—	—	—	2	—	—	—	—	—	2
Powell, Alfred H.	London	1890-1891	Churches	—	—	3	—	—	—	—	—	—	—	3
Powell, C.	Monmouth	1883	Landscape	—	—	—	—	1	—	—	—	—	—	1
Powell, Cordall, F.S.A.	London	1768-1780	Landscape	14	—	—	—	—	—	—	—	—	—	14
Powell, Charles Edward	London	1882	Architecture	—	—	1	—	—	—	—	—	—	—	1
Powell, C. F.	London	1831-1835	Landscape	—	—	5	—	16	—	8	—	—	—	29
Powell, Miss C. J.	Charlton	1874-1877	Flowers	—	—	2	—	—	—	—	—	—	—	2
Powell, C. M.	London	1783-1821	Sea Pieces	—	—	29	11	—	—	—	—	—	—	40
Powell, David	London	1866-1867	Landscape	—	—	—	—	—	—	—	—	—	2	2
Powell, Miss E. Folliott	London	1887-1893	Domestic	—	—	3	—	—	—	—	—	—	1	4
Powell, Edward Turner	London	1892	Architecture	—	—	1	—	—	—	—	—	—	—	1
Powell, E. W.	London	1857-1860	Domestic	—	—	—	—	—	—	—	—	—	7	7
Powell, F.	London	1814	Enamels	—	—	—	1	—	—	—	—	—	—	1
Powell, Sir Francis, R.W.S., P.R.S.W. †	Dunoon	1856-1893	Sea Pieces	—	—	—	—	—	190	—	—	—	16	206
Powell, Frank	London	1855-1864	Landscape	—	—	3	2	5	—	—	—	—	—	10
Powell, Frederick Atkinson	London	1882-1884	Buildings	—	—	—	—	4	—	—	—	—	—	4
Powell, F. S. B.	London	1872-1876	Landscape	—	—	2	—	—	—	—	—	—	—	2
Powell, Hugh Peter	London	1856-1870	Landscape	—	—	2	4	5	—	—	—	—	7	18
Powell (James) and Sons	London	1892	Stained Glass	—	—	2	—	—	—	—	—	—	—	2
Powell, John	London	1796-1833	Landscape	—	—	75	—	—	5	—	—	—	—	80
Powell, John (Pupil of Reynolds)	London	1778-1785	Portraits	—	—	9	—	—	—	—	—	—	—	9
Powell, Joseph, P.N.W.S. ‡	London	1808-1834	Enamels	—	—	2	9	31	—	29	—	—	49	120
Powell, Mrs. J.	London	1875-1876	Landscape	—	—	—	—	2	—	—	—	—	—	2
Powell, James C.	London	1882	Landscape	—	—	—	—	—	—	—	—	—	1	1
Powell, J. H.	Birmingham	1850-1857	Windows	—	—	3	—	—	—	—	—	—	—	3
Powell, Joseph Rubens	London	1835-1871	Domestic	—	—	10	5	17	—	—	—	—	1	33
Powell, Leonard M.	Hertford	1882-1893	Landscape	—	—	5	—	2	—	5	—	1	2	15
Powell, P.	London	1826-1854	Sea Pieces	—	—	10	6	9	—	5	—	—	—	30
Powell, Richard	London	1853	Domestic	—	—	—	1	—	—	—	—	—	—	1
Powell, S.	London	1799	Landscape	—	—	4	—	—	—	—	—	—	—	4
Powell, Samuel K.	London	1884	Figures	—	—	—	—	1	—	—	—	—	—	1
Powell, T.	London	1812-1830	Enamels	—	—	9	—	—	—	—	—	—	—	9
Powell, William Henry	London	1878-1889	Architecture	—	—	5	—	—	—	—	—	—	—	5
Powell, Captain W. W.	London	1861	Landscape	—	—	—	1	—	—	—	—	—	—	1
Power, A.	Maidstone	1800	Flowers	—	—	2	—	—	—	—	—	—	—	2
Power, J., M.D.	London	1841-1842	Landscape	—	—	—	—	2	—	—	—	—	—	2
Power, Miss Lucy	London	1892-1893	Portraits	—	—	1	—	1	—	—	—	—	—	2
Power, R.	London	1839	Historical	—	—	—	—	1	—	—	—	—	—	1
Powers, Hiram	Florence	1841-1867	Sculpture	—	—	6	—	—	—	—	—	—	—	6
Powers, Longworth	Florence	1886	Sculpture	—	—	1	—	—	—	—	—	—	—	1
Powers, Preston	London	1882	Figures	—	—	1	—	—	—	—	—	—	—	1
Powle, George	London	1764-1770	Miniatures	4	6	—	—	—	—	—	—	—	—	10
Pownall, Miss Ellen Louise	London	1888-1890	Miniatures	—	—	3	—	—	—	—	—	—	—	3
Pownall, Frederick Hyde	London	1852-1867	Architecture	—	—	6	—	—	—	—	—	—	—	6
Pownall, George. *See* Wigg and Pownall	—	1841	Architecture	—	—	1	—	—	—	—	—	—	—	1
Pownall, Miss	London	1874	Figures	—	—	1	—	—	—	—	—	—	—	1
Poyet, L.	London	1845-1848	Figures	—	—	1	1	—	—	—	—	—	—	2
Poynder, T.	London	1798	Architecture	—	—	1	—	—	—	—	—	—	—	1

Name.	Town.	First and Last Year of Ex.	Speciality.	S. A.	F. S.	R. A.	B. I.	S. S.	O. W.	N.W.	G. G.	N. G.	V. E.	Total.
Poyner, William, H.	London	1852-1878	Domestic	—	—	5	5	4	—	—	—	—	1	15
Poynter, Ambrose	London	1817-1852	Architecture	—	—	9	—	—	—	—	—	—	—	9
Poynter, Ambrose M.	London	1893	Book-plates	—	—	—	—	—	—	—	—	1	—	1
Poynter, Edward James, R.A., R.W.S., H.F.R.P.E. †	London	1859-1893	Historical	—	—	70	1	—	35	—	63	15	71	255
Poynter, James	London	1880	Still Life	—	—	—	—	—	—	—	—	—	2	2
Poyser, T. J.	Liverpool	1862	Figures	—	—	1	—	—	—	—	—	—	—	1
Pozzo, G. da. *See* D.	—	—	—	—	—	—	—	—	—	—	—	—	—	—
Prades, De. *See* D.	—	—	—	—	—	—	—	—	—	—	—	—	—	—
Pradez, Edith	Liege	1882	Buildings	—	—	—	—	2	—	—	—	—	—	2
Pradilla, J.	—	1877	Landscape	—	—	—	—	3	—	—	—	—	—	3
Praeger, Miss S. Rosamond	Holywood	1891	Sculpture	—	—	1	—	—	—	—	—	—	—	1
Praetorius, Charles	London	1888	Flowers	—	—	1	—	—	—	—	—	—	—	1
Prager, Alfred	London	1887-1889	Domestic	—	—	—	—	—	—	3	—	—	—	3
Pranker, Robert	London	1761-1767	Engraving	—	12	—	—	—	—	—	—	—	—	12
Prater, T.	London	1855	Landscape	—	—	—	—	2	—	—	—	—	—	2
Prater, William	London	1873	Domestic	—	—	—	—	1	—	—	—	—	—	1
Pratt —	London	1765-1766	Fruit	2	—	—	—	—	—	—	—	—	—	2
Pratt, A. J. Epps	Haslemere	1874-1879	Landscape	—	—	1	—	3	—	—	—	—	—	4
Pratt, Claude	Birmingham	1887-1892	Domestic	—	—	—	—	—	—	2	—	—	4	6
Pratt, Edward	Edinburgh	1880	Domestic	—	—	1	—	—	—	—	—	—	—	1
Pratt, G.	London	1798	Architecture	—	—	1	—	—	—	—	—	—	—	1
Pratt, Hilton L.	Stoke-on-Trent	1867-1873	Landscape	—	—	1	—	1	—	—	—	—	—	2
Pratt, J.	London	1791-1793	Architecture	—	—	5	—	—	—	—	—	—	—	5
Pratt, John	Leeds	1882-1889	Flowers	—	—	9	—	—	—	—	—	—	—	9
Pratt, Jonathan	Birmingham	1871-1893	Domestic	—	—	4	—	6	—	—	—	—	8	18
Pratt, Joseph Bishop	London	1874-1893	Engraving	—	—	21	—	—	—	—	—	—	1	22
Pratt, Mrs. J. Burnett	Aberdeen	1843-1848	Landscape	—	—	—	1	3	—	—	—	—	2	6
Pratt, Ralph	Leeds	1881-1893	Fruit	—	—	9	—	—	—	—	—	—	—	9
Pratt, William	Glasgow	1880-1893	Landscape	—	—	3	—	—	—	—	—	—	—	3
Pratt, William B.	Clapton	1883	Iron Work	—	—	1	—	—	—	—	—	—	—	1
Pratten, Mrs.	Haslemere	1875	Flowers	—	—	—	—	—	—	—	—	—	1	1
Precorbin, Mrs. De	London	1806	Flowers	—	—	1	—	—	—	—	—	—	—	1
Predl, Madame	London	1826	Scriptural	—	—	2	—	—	—	—	—	—	—	2
Prehn, William	London	1862-1890	Sculpture	—	—	7	—	—	—	—	2	—	—	9
Preindlsberger, Miss Marianne	London	1883-1884	Figures	—	—	1	—	—	—	—	—	—	1	2
Prell, Hermann	Berlin	1889	Figures	—	—	1	—	—	—	—	—	—	—	1
Prendergast, George	Kilburn	1872-1876	Domestic	—	—	—	—	2	—	—	—	—	3	5
Prentice, Andrew N.	London	1892	Architecture	—	—	3	—	—	—	—	—	—	—	3
Prentice, Miss Kate	London	1880-1884	Landscape	—	—	—	—	—	—	2	1	—	2	5
Prentis, Edward §	London	1823-1850	Domestic	—	—	2	4	52	—	—	—	—	—	58
Prescott, H. P.	London	1847-1848	Heads	—	—	1	2	—	—	—	—	—	—	3
Prescott-Davies, N. *See* D.	—	—	—	—	—	—	—	—	—	—	—	—	—	—
Pressland, E. C.	London	1854	Architecture	—	—	2	—	—	—	—	—	—	—	2
Preston, A. C.	Chester	1888	Landscape	—	—	—	—	—	—	1	—	—	—	1
Preston, E.	London	1824-1843	Portraits	—	—	17	—	6	—	1	—	—	—	24
Preston, Miss Eliza	—	1773	Landscape	—	2	—	—	—	—	—	—	—	—	2
Preston, Mrs. H. J.	London	1855-1867	Landscape	—	—	6	8	—	—	—	—	—	—	14
Preston, Josephine	London	1888	Birds	—	—	—	—	1	—	—	—	—	—	1
Preston, R.	London	1842	Moonlight	—	—	1	—	1	—	—	—	—	—	2
Preston, Thomas	London	1764-1773	Miniatures	—	3	—	—	—	—	—	—	—	—	3
Preston, Thomas	London	1826-1850	Portraits	—	—	9	—	20	—	—	—	—	—	29
Preston and Vaughan	Manchester	1891-1892	Architecture	—	—	2	—	—	—	—	—	—	—	2
Pretty, C. E.	Rugby	1810	Flowers	—	—	1	—	—	—	—	—	—	—	1
Pretty, E.	Rugby	1811-1837	Architecture	—	—	4	—	—	—	—	—	—	—	4
Pretty, Edward	Northampton	1852-1856	Landscape	—	—	—	—	2	—	—	—	—	1	3
Pretty, J.	Northampton	1836	Domestic	—	—	—	—	1	—	—	—	—	—	1
Preuschen, Baroness Hermine Von		1885	Still Life	—	—	1	—	—	—	—	—	—	—	1
Preziosi —	London	1863	Landscape	—	—	1	—	—	—	—	—	—	—	1
Price, Alice	StokeNewingt'n	1881	Domestic	—	—	—	—	1	—	—	—	—	—	1
Price, Miss Annabella	Southampton	1823	Flowers	—	—	1	—	—	—	—	—	—	—	1
Price, Miss Blackwood	—	1890	Portraits	—	—	—	—	—	—	—	1	—	—	1
Price, Edward	Lichfield	1823-1854	Landscape	—	—	3	7	7	—	—	—	—	—	17
Price, Edmund N.	London	1888-1889	Stained Glass	—	—	2	—	—	—	—	—	—	—	2
Price, Frank Corbyn	London	1888-1893	Landscape	—	—	8	—	7	—	2	—	—	—	17
Price, Mrs. Frank Corbyn (Lydia J.)	London	1890-1893	Domestic	—	—	3	—	—	—	5	—	—	—	8
Price, Frederick G.	Romford	1862-1863	Rustic	—	—	—	1	4	—	—	—	—	—	5
Price, G.	London	1842	Architecture	—	—	1	—	—	—	—	—	—	—	1
Price, Miss Grace	Old Charlton	1861-1862	Fruit	—	—	—	—	2	—	—	—	—	—	2
Price, Miss Isabella	London	1885-1886	Miniatures	—	—	—	—	—	—	—	6	—	—	6
Price, James	London	1842-1876	Landscape	—	—	26	7	38	—	—	—	—	4	75

Name.	Town.	First and Last Year of Ex.	Speciality.	S. A.	F. S.	R. A.	B. I.	S. S.	O.W.	N.W.	G. G.	N.G.	V. E.	Total.
Price, Julius Mendès	London	1884-1890	Domestic	—	—	3	—	4	—	—	3	—	7	17
Price, T. E.	Cheltenham	1847-1859	Domestic	—	—	—	1	2	—	—	—	—	—	3
Price, W. Frederick	Liverpool	1878-1881	Landscape	—	—	1	—	1	—	—	2	—	—	4
Price, William Lake †	London	1828-1852	Buildings	—	—	7	—	—	49	5	—	—	2	63
Price, William Leike	Corbetts Tey, Essex	1841	Architecture	—	—	1	—	—	—	—	—	—	—	1
Price, Miss	—	1845	Sculpture	—	—	1	—	—	—	—	—	—	—	1
Prichard, J.	Llandaff	1864	Architecture	—	—	1	—	—	—	—	—	—	—	1
Prichard, W. S.	London	1874-1882	Landscape	—	—	—	—	3	—	—	—	—	3	6
Prichard and Seddon	London	1859-1862	Architecture	—	—	7	—	—	—	—	—	—	—	7
Prideaux-Brune, Miss Gertrude R.	Padstow	1878-1893	Sea Pieces	—	—	1	—	7	—	—	—	—	20	28
Priest, Alfred	London	1833-1847	Sea Pieces	—	—	17	23	49	—	—	—	—	—	89
Priest, Miss E. A.	London	1848	Landscape	—	—	—	—	1	—	—	—	—	—	1
Priestman, Arnold, R.B.A. §	Bradford	1883-1893	Landscape	—	—	9	—	21	—	—	7	7	—	44
Priestman, Bertram	London	1889-1893	Domestic	—	—	2	—	9	—	—	4	—	2	17
Prince, L.	—	1783	Landscape	—	2	—	—	—	—	—	—	—	—	2
Pringle, Miss Agnes	London	1884-1893	Figures	—	—	5	—	2	—	2	—	—	—	9
Pringle, J.	Deptford	1800-1818	Sea Pieces	—	—	5	—	—	—	—	—	—	—	5
Pringle, John William Graham	London	1867-1879	Landscape	—	—	—	1	46	—	—	—	—	5	52
Pringle, Miss Lydia	London	1893	Portraits	—	—	—	—	1	—	—	—	—	—	1
Pringle, W. J.	London	1826-1827	Dramatic	—	—	—	1	3	—	—	—	—	—	4
Prinsep, Valentine Cameron, R.A.	London	1862-1893	Domestic	—	—	100	—	2	—	—	22	4	12	140
Prinsep, William	—	1850	India	—	—	1	—	—	—	—	—	—	—	1
Prinsep, William Haldimand	London	1856	Landscape	—	—	1	—	—	—	—	—	—	—	1
Printer, J.	Emsworth	1807-1808	Architecture	—	—	3	—	—	—	—	—	—	—	3
Priolo, Paolo	London	1857-1880	Historical	—	—	7	—	35	—	—	—	—	1	43
Prior, Edward S.	London	1882-1890	Architecture	—	—	7	—	—	—	—	—	—	—	7
Prior, Thomas Abiel	London	1864-1874	Engraving	—	—	2	—	—	—	—	—	—	—	2
Prior, William Henry	London	1833-1857	Landscape	—	—	2	1	14	—	4	—	—	—	21
Pritchard, Edward F. D.	Bristol	1852-1873	Sea Pieces	—	—	7	18	8	—	—	—	—	1	34
Pritchard, Miss Mary E.	London	1893	Flowers	—	—	1	—	1	—	—	—	—	—	2
Pritchard, Thomas	Tunb'dge Wells	1866-1877	Landscape	—	—	8	—	1	—	—	—	—	9	18
Pritchett, Edward	London	1828-1864	Venice	—	—	3	17	3	—	—	—	—	—	23
Pritchett, James Pigott	London	1808-1809	Architecture	—	—	2	—	—	—	—	—	—	—	2
Pritchett, Robert T., F.S.A.	London	1851-1877	Landscape	—	—	4	—	1	—	—	—	—	13	18
Pritchett, S.	—	1858	Landscape	—	—	2	—	—	—	—	—	—	—	2
Pritchett, Miss	London	1871	Landscape	—	—	—	—	1	—	—	—	—	—	1
Pritt, Henry	Preston	1888	Landscape	—	—	—	—	—	—	1	—	—	—	1
Pritt, Thomas	London	1861-1864	Cattle	—	—	—	4	7	—	—	—	—	1	12
Prittie, Edward, R.H.A.	—	1883	Historical	—	—	1	—	—	—	—	—	—	—	1
Probyn-Nevins, W. *See* N.	—	—	—	—	—	—	—	—	—	—	—	—	—	—
Proctor, Adam Edwin, R.B.A. §	London	1882-1893	Landscape	—	—	6	—	50	—	—	—	—	17	73
Proctor, J.	London	1833	Architecture	—	—	1	—	—	—	—	—	—	—	1
Proctor, Jessy	London	1869	Still Life	—	—	—	—	—	—	—	—	—	1	1
Proctor, John	London	1879-1883	Landscape	—	—	—	—	4	—	—	—	—	—	4
Proctor, Miss M. A.	London	1858-1859	Landscape	—	—	1	—	—	—	—	—	—	2	3
Proctor, Thomas	London	1780-1794	Portraits	2	2	16	—	—	—	—	—	—	—	20
Proctor, William	London	1836-1854	Portraits	—	—	3	1	6	—	—	—	—	—	10
Profaze, Mrs. Annie	London	1870-1872	Figures	—	—	—	—	3	—	—	—	—	—	3
Propert, John Lumsden	London	1870-1882	Etching	—	—	15	—	—	—	—	—	—	15	30
Prosalindi, Cavalier Paul §	—	1826	Sculpture	—	—	1	—	—	—	—	—	—	—	1
Proschwitzky, Frank	London	1883-1889	Still Life	—	—	2	—	—	—	—	—	—	—	2
Prosperi, Christopher	London	1810-1816	Sculpture	—	—	22	2	—	—	—	—	—	—	24
Prosser, G. F.	London	1826-1828	Architecture	—	—	2	—	—	—	—	—	—	—	2
Prosser, H.	Croydon	1828	Architecture	—	—	2	—	—	—	—	—	—	—	2
Prosser, T.	London	1819	Architecture	—	—	1	—	—	—	—	—	—	—	1
Prosser, William Henry	London	1887-1892	Sculpture	—	—	8	—	2	—	—	—	—	—	10
Prothero, Rev. Canon G.	London	1888	Landscape	—	—	—	—	1	—	—	—	—	—	1
Prothero, Henry A.	Cheltenham	1891	Reredos	—	—	1	—	—	—	—	—	—	—	1
Prout, Agnes	London	1869	Sea Shores	—	—	—	—	1	—	—	—	—	—	1
Prout, J. Skinner ‡	London	1839-1876	Landscape	—	—	—	—	—	—	278	—	—	3	281
Prout, Mary	London	1869	Still Life	—	—	—	—	1	—	—	—	—	1	2
Prout, Samuel †	Plymouth	1803-1851	Landscape	—	—	28	8	—	560	—	—	—	60	656
Provan, Miss Elizabeth G.	Glasgow	1884-1892	Flowers	—	—	4	—	—	—	—	—	—	—	4
Provis, Alfred	Chippenham	1843-1886	Domestic	—	—	49	35	31	—	—	—	—	34	149
Provis, Ann Jemima	London	1787	Miniatures	—	—	2	—	—	—	—	—	—	—	2
Provis, W. A.	London	1810	Architecture	—	—	1	—	—	—	—	—	—	—	1
Prowse-Reilly, N. *See* R.	—	—	—	—	—	—	—	—	—	—	—	—	—	—
Prynne, Edward A. Fellowes-	London	1886-1893	Portraits	—	—	2	—	—	—	—	1	—	—	3
Prynne, George H. Fellowes-	London	1880-1893	Architecture	—	—	9	—	—	—	—	—	—	—	9
Pryce, Thomas Edward	London	1882-1892	Architecture	—	—	6	—	—	—	—	—	—	—	6
Pryse, J. E.	London	1828	Architecture	—	—	—	—	1	—	—	—	—	—	1
Puckle, Miss Ethel M.	Sutton	1885	Flowers	—	—	1	—	—	—	—	—	—	—	1

Name.	Town.	First and Last Year of Ex.	Speciality.	S. A.	F. S.	R. A.	B. I.	S. S.	O. W.	N. W.	G. G.	N. G.	V. E.	Total.
Puddick, J. E.	London	1851	Landscape	—	—	—	1	—	—	—	—	—	—	1
Pugh, Charles J.	London	1795-1828	Landscape	—	—	19	—	—	—	—	—	—	—	19
Pugh, Edward	London	1793-1821	Miniatures	—	—	25	1	—	—	—	—	—	—	26
Pugh, Herbert, F.S.A.	London	1760-1776	Cattle	40	—	—	—	—	—	—	—	—	—	40
Pugh, J.	London	1800-1808	Dramatic	—	—	5	—	—	—	—	—	—	—	5
Pughe, Miss Buddig A.	Liverpool	1886-1888	Miniatures	—	—	3	—	—	—	1	—	—	—	4
Pugin, Augustus †	London	1799-1831	Churches	—	—	18	3	—	77	—	—	—	—	98
Pugin, Augustus Northmore Welby	Ramsgate	1849-1862	Architecture	—	—	8	—	—	—	—	—	—	—	8
Pugin, Edward Welby Northmore	Birmingham	1854-1879	Architecture	—	—	16	—	—	—	—	—	—	—	16
Pugin (P.) and Welby (C.)	London	1876	Architecture	—	—	1	—	—	—	—	—	—	—	1
Pugin and Pugin	London	1880-1890	Architecture	—	—	5	—	—	—	—	—	—	—	5
Pugin, Peter Paul	London	1871-1879	Landscape	—	—	1	—	7	—	—	—	—	8	16
Pulham, Mrs. James	London	1814	Figures	—	—	—	—	—	—	—	—	—	1	1
Pullan, Richard Popplewell	London	1856-1882	Sculpture	—	—	2	—	—	—	—	—	—	—	2
Pullen, T. W.	London	1832-1842	Churches	—	—	6	—	1	—	—	—	—	—	7
Puller, J.	London	1827	Landscape	—	—	1	—	—	—	—	—	—	—	1
Puller, John Anthony	London	1821-1867	Domestic	—	—	43	53	82	—	—	—	—	—	178
Puller, T.	London	1828-1835	Cattle	—	—	—	—	7	—	—	—	—	—	7
Pulvermacher, Miss Anna	London	1882-1887	Still Life	—	—	2	—	3	—	—	—	—	4	9
Punnett, P. S.	London	1835	Architecture	—	—	2	—	—	—	—	—	—	—	2
Puntita, Madame	London	1859	Portraits	—	—	1	—	—	—	—	—	—	—	1
Purcell, Mrs. M. C.	London	1880	Landscape	—	—	—	—	1	—	—	—	—	—	1
Purcell, P. V.	Merton	1846-1850	Landscape	—	—	5	—	1	—	—	—	—	—	6
Purchas, Thomas J.	Guildford	1879-1891	Landscape	—	—	4	—	1	—	—	—	—	9	14
Purchase, Alfred	Fishguard	1874-1889	Rocks	—	—	1	—	1	—	—	—	—	—	2
Purchase, E. Keynes	London	1884	Organ Case	—	—	1	—	—	—	—	—	—	—	1
Purday, Miss Sarah T.	London	1845-1847	Portraits	—	—	2	—	1	—	—	—	—	—	3
Purdon, George	London	1772-1777	Landscape	1	6	—	—	—	—	—	—	—	—	7
Purkis, Miss A. B.	London	1875	Figures	—	—	—	—	1	—	—	—	—	—	1
Purser, C.	London	1821-1824	Architecture	—	—	2	—	—	—	—	—	—	—	2
Purser, Miss Sarah	Dublin	1885-1892	Portraits	—	—	2	—	—	—	—	1	1	—	4
Purser, W.	London	1805-1834	Architecture	—	—	22	—	1	—	—	—	—	—	23
Purton, Cecil P.	Bridgnorth	1871-1876	Landscape	—	—	—	—	1	—	—	—	—	6	7
Purton, W.	—	1849	Architecture	—	—	1	—	—	—	—	—	—	—	1
Purves, Miss C. J.	London	1881-1885	Flowers	—	—	—	—	—	—	—	2	—	—	2
Purves, R.	London	1864	Sculpture	—	—	1	—	—	—	—	—	—	—	1
Putland —	London	1772	Hair Work	3	—	—	—	—	—	—	—	—	—	3
Puttinalli —	Rome	1843	Sculpture	—	—	1	—	—	—	—	—	—	—	1
Puyenbrock. G.	London	1852	Sculpture	—	—	—	1	—	—	—	—	—	—	1
Pybus, H.	London	1839	Game	—	—	—	—	4	—	—	—	—	—	4
Pybus, W.	London	1836-1839	Figures	—	—	—	5	2	—	—	—	—	—	7
Pye, Miss A.	London	1859	Domestic	—	—	—	1	—	—	—	—	—	—	1
Pye, Charles	London	1769-1826	Engraving	7	—	—	—	3	—	—	—	—	—	10
Pye, C.	London	1802	Portraits	—	—	2	—	—	—	—	—	—	—	2
Pye, James	London	1780-1803	Landscape	—	—	12	—	—	—	—	—	—	—	12
Pye, John	Birmingham	1824-1829	Engraving	—	—	—	—	4	—	—	—	—	—	4
Pye, Thomas	London	1776	Portraits	—	—	1	—	—	—	—	—	—	—	1
Pye, William	Hadleigh	1881-1890	Landscape	—	—	1	—	13	—	4	—	—	12	30
Pyke, C.	—	1799	Architecture	—	—	1	—	—	—	—	—	—	—	1
Pyke, Mary	London	1888	Courtyard	—	—	—	—	—	—	—	1	—	—	1
Pyke-Nott. *See* N.	—	—	—	—	—	—	—	—	—	—	—	—	—	—
Pyle, Robert	London	1761-1766	Portraits	3	8	—	—	—	—	—	—	—	—	11
Pym, B.	London	1793-1805	Miniatures	—	—	39	—	—	—	—	—	—	—	39
Pyne, Miss Annie C.	London	1886-1892	Landscape	—	—	—	—	6	—	8	—	—	—	14
Pyne, Charles	London	1861-1880	Landscape	—	—	1	—	54	—	—	—	—	7	62
Pyne, C. C.	London	1836-1839	Buildings	—	—	2	1	—	—	—	—	—	—	3
Pyne, Miss Eva E.	London	1886-1893	Landscape	—	—	—	—	8	—	8	—	—	—	16
Pyne, George †	London	1826-1843	Landscape	—	—	—	—	2	39	—	—	—	—	41
Pyne, James Baker §	Bristol	1828-1870	Landscape	—	—	7	28	206	—	11	—	—	—	252
Pyne, Thomas, R.I., R.B.A. § ‡	London	1863-1893	Landscape	—	—	14	—	110	—	64	—	—	44	232
Pyne, William Henry †	London	1790-1815	Portraits	—	—	22	—	—	58	—	—	—	—	80
Pyne, W. B.	London	1878-1879	Landscape	—	—	—	—	3	—	—	—	—	—	3
Pyuyl, Van der. *See* V.	—	—	—	—	—	—	—	—	—	—	—	—	—	—
Quadal, M. F.	Moravia	1772-1793	Figures	4	—	11	—	—	—	—	—	—	—	15
Quadrone, Jean B.	London	1888	Sporting	—	—	1	—	—	—	—	—	—	—	1
Quartley, Arthur	London	1884-1885	Landscape	—	—	—	—	2	—	—	—	—	1	3
Quartremaine, G. W.	Stratford-on-Avon	1881-1882	Game	—	—	—	—	—	—	—	—	—	2	2
Quelin, De. *See* D.	—	—	—	—	—	—	—	—	—	—	—	—	—	—
Querangal, Mdlle. Y. de	London	1876	Horses	—	—	—	—	1	—	—	—	—	—	1

Name.	Town.	First and Last Year of Ex.	Speciality.	S. A.	F. S.	R. A.	B. I.	S. S.	O. W.	.W.	G. .	N. G.	V. E.	Total.
Quezroy, Louis A.	Moulins-sur-Allier	1872	Rustic	—	—	—	—	—	—	—	—	—	3	3
Quick, Richard	London	1884-1886	Domestic	—	—	—	—	2	—	—	—	—	—	2
Quilly, John P.	London	1824-1832	Engraving	—	—	—	—	8	—	—	—	—	—	8
Quilter, Harry	London	1884-1892	Landscape	—	—	—	—	—	—	—	—	—	11	11
Quinsac, Charles	Liverpool	1878	Charcoal	—	—	—	—	—	—	—	—	—	3	3
Quinton, Alfred Robert	London	1874-1893	Landscape	—	—	7	—	18	—	9	1	—	9	44
Raalte, Mrs. C. Van. *See* V.	—	—	—	—	—	—	—	—	—	—	—	—	—	—
Rabeuf, Hippolyte	London	1893	Domestic	—	—	1	—	—	—	—	—	—	—	1
Rachel, Madame	Milan	1886	Figures	—	—	—	—	—	—	1	—	—	—	1
Rackham, Arthur	Wandsworth	1888-1890	Landscape	—	—	2	—	4	—	2	—	—	—	8
Rackstrow, Benjamin	London	1763	Sculpture	—	4	—	—	—	—	—	—	—	—	4
Radcliff, Miss Anne	Dover	1841-1842	Landscape	—	—	1	—	4	—	—	—	—	—	5
Radcliffe, Radcliffe W.	Guildford	1875-1891	Domestic	—	—	27	—	28	—	9	1	—	37	102
Radclyffe, Charles Walter	London	1847-1887	Landscape	—	—	3	5	3	—	5	—	—	18	34
Radclyffe, Edward	Birmingham	1859-1863	Engraving	—	—	7	—	—	—	—	—	—	—	7
Radclyffe, William	Birmingham	1831	Engraving	—	—	—	—	4	—	—	—	—	—	4
Radclyffe, William, Junr.	Birmingham	1834-1843	Portraits	—	—	2	—	2	—	—	—	—	—	4
Raddon, William	London	1829-1831	Engraving	—	—	—	—	2	—	—	—	—	—	2
Radford, Edward, A.R.W.S. †	London	1865-1893	Figures	—	—	9	—	16	62	—	—	—	13	100
Radford, James	London	1841-1859	Landscape	—	—	15	5	7	—	—	—	—	1	28
Rae, Cecil W.	London	1889-1893	Portraits	—	—	2	—	—	—	—	—	—	7	9
Rae, Miss Henrietta R. *See* Mrs. Ernest	—	—	—	—	—	—	—	—	—	—	—	—	—	—
Normand	London	1879-1884	Landscape	—	—	5	—	8	—	—	—	—	4	17
Rae, Miss Iso	London	1891-1893	Figures	—	—	—	—	1	—	—	—	—	1	2
Rae, Miss Mary	London	1879-1887	Portraits	—	—	1	—	—	—	1	—	—	1	3
Raeburn, Sir Henry, R.A.	Edinburgh	1792-1823	Portraits	—	—	53	—	—	—	—	—	—	—	53
Raeburn, H. Macbeth. *See* M.	—	—	—	—	—	—	—	—	—	—	—	—	—	—
Raemackers, John Adrien	London	1864-1892	Sculpture	—	—	43	2	13	—	—	—	—	1	59
Raemaekers, Mary	—	1883	Sculpture	—	—	—	—	1	—	—	—	—	—	1
Raffel, Charles	London	1872	Landscape	—	—	—	—	—	—	—	—	—	1	1
Raffel, E.	London	1874	Domestic	—	—	2	—	—	—	—	—	—	—	2
Raffield, J.	London	1797-1825	Architecture	—	—	14	—	—	—	—	—	—	—	14
Rafter, H.	Coventry	1856	Sporting	—	—	—	—	—	—	—	—	—	1	1
Raggi, Mario	London	1854-1892	Sculpture	—	—	16	—	—	—	—	—	—	—	16
Raggin, Miss E.	London	1858	Landscape	—	—	1	—	—	—	—	—	—	—	1
Raggio, Guiseppe	Rome	1877-1878	Figures	—	—	—	—	1	—	—	—	—	1	2
Ragon, Adolphe	London	1872-1893	Landscape	—	—	11	—	21	—	9	—	—	39	80
Rahe, Charles T.	London	1867	Landscape	—	—	—	—	—	—	—	—	—	1	1
Raigersfield, Captain	—	1798-1811	Sea Pieces	—	—	5	—	—	—	—	—	—	—	5
Railton, F. J.	London	1846-1866	Landscape	—	—	17	23	11	—	—	—	—	—	51
Railton, William	London	1829-1851	Architecture	—	—	22	—	1	—	—	—	—	—	23
Raimbach, Abraham	London	1797-1805	Portraits	—	—	13	—	—	—	—	—	—	—	13
Raimbach, D.	—	1860-1868	Sea Pieces	—	—	1	1	—	—	—	—	—	—	2
Raimbach, David L.	Birmingham	1887	Heads	—	—	—	—	—	—	1	—	—	—	1
Raimbach, D. W.	Greenwich	1843-1855	Portraits	—	—	16	—	6	—	—	—	—	—	22
Raimbach, Louis	London	1882-1883	Miniatures	—	—	2	—	—	—	—	—	—	—	2
Raimbach, Miss	Greenwich	1835-1855	Miniatures	—	—	55	—	1	—	—	—	—	—	56
Rainbow, W. C.	London	1883	Landscape	—	—	—	—	—	—	1	—	—	—	1
Raincock, Miss Sophia	London	1847-1873	Domestic	—	—	2	—	5	—	—	—	—	—	7
Rainey, William, R.I. ‡ φ	London	1876-1893	Landscape	—	—	13	—	6	—	12	—	—	9	40
Rainford, E.	London	1850-1864	Historical	—	—	3	3	—	—	—	—	—	—	6
Rainger, Gus	London	1871	Domestic	—	—	—	—	1	—	—	—	—	—	1
Rainger, William Augustus	London	1866	Landscape	—	—	—	—	2	—	—	—	—	—	2
Rajon, A.	Willesden	1890	Shipping	—	—	1	—	—	—	—	—	—	—	1
Rajon, Paul Adolphe	Paris	1872-1887	Etching	—	—	11	—	—	—	—	—	—	19	30
Ralfe, Mrs. E.	London	1892	Landscape	—	—	—	—	2	—	—	—	—	—	2
Ralfs, W.	Tonbridge	1832-1834	Lakes Scenes	—	—	—	—	1	—	2	—	—	—	3
Ralli, H.	London	1882-1883	Domestic	—	—	—	—	—	—	—	2	—	—	2
Ralli, Theodore J.	London	1879-1883	Domestic	—	—	5	—	—	—	—	—	—	—	5
Ralph, Benjamin.	London	1763-1775	Moonlight	10	2	—	—	—	—	—	—	—	—	12
Ralph, G. Keith	London	1778-1811	Portraits	9	—	35	1	—	—	—	—	—	—	45
Ralston, William	London	1875-1881	"Punch"	—	—	—	—	—	—	—	—	—	4	4
Ram, Miss Jane A.	Norwood	1892-1893	Sculpture	—	—	1	—	2	—	—	—	—	2	5
Ramberg, John Henry	London	1782-1788	Historical	—	—	12	—	—	—	—	—	—	—	12
Ramie, C. W.	New Malden	1885-1888	Landscape	—	—	3	—	3	—	—	—	—	—	6
Ramie, Marian	New Malden	1886	Flowers	—	—	—	—	2	—	—	—	—	—	2
Rampling, C.	London	1815	Architecture	—	—	7	—	—	—	—	—	—	—	7
Ramsay, Miss F. L.	Beaumaris	1890-1893	Flowers	—	—	—	—	—	—	—	—	—	2	2
Ramsay, James	London	1803-1854	Portraits	—	—	144	18	7	—	—	—	—	—	169

Name.	Town.	First and Last Year of Ex.	Speciality.	S. A.	F. S.	R. A.	B. I.	S. S.	O. W.	N.W.	G. G.	N. G.	V. E.	Total.
Ramsay, Sir J. H.	Banff	1875	Architecture	—	—	2	—	—	—	—	—	—	—	2
Ramsden, Richard H.	London	1883-1884	Miniatures	—	—	3	—	—	—	—	—	—	—	3
Ramsden, Thomas	Leeds	1883-1893	Flowers	—	—	1	—	7	—	—	—	—	—	8
Ramsey, J.	London	1887	Landscape	—	—	—	—	1	—	—	—	—	—	1
Ramus, C. A.	London	1827-1833	Landscape	—	—	4	—	—	—	—	—	—	—	4
Rand, J.	London	1840	Portraits	—	—	1	—	—	—	—	—	—	—	1
Rand, R.	London	1774-1785	Seals	3	—	1	—	—	—	—	—	—	—	4
Randal, Charles	London	1892	Miniatures	—	—	2	—	—	—	—	—	—	—	2
Randal, Frank	London	1887-1893	Landscape	—	—	2	—	—	—	—	—	—	—	2
Randall, G.	Manchester	1836	Venice	—	—	—	1	—	—	—	—	—	—	1
Randall, James	London	1798-1814	Architecture	—	—	21	—	—	—	—	—	—	—	21
Randall, John	London	1864-1874	Domestic	—	—	—	—	3	—	—	—	—	3	6
Randall, Nathaniel Thomas	London	1837-1857	Architecture	—	—	6	—	—	—	—	—	—	—	6
Randall, William Frederick	London	1879-1891	Architecture	—	—	5	—	—	—	—	—	—	—	5
Randall, W. R.	Slough	1830-1836	Landscape	—	—	—	—	8	—	1	—	—	—	9
Randanini, Carlo	Rome	1883	Figures	—	—	1	—	—	—	—	—	—	—	1
Randell, James	Buckingham	1849-1864	Landscape	—	—	7	5	—	—	—	—	—	10	22
Randle. *See* Heathcote and Randle	—	—	Architecture	—	—	—	—	—	—	—	—	—	—	—
Randle, Florence	Plymouth	1879-1880	Birds	—	—	—	—	—	—	—	—	—	2	2
Randolph, Edmund	London	1875	Landscape	—	—	—	—	—	—	—	—	—	1	1
Ranger, Miss	London	1847	Scriptural	—	—	—	2	—	—	—	—	—	—	2
Rankin, A. Scott	Edinburgh	1892	Animals	—	—	1	—	—	—	—	—	—	—	1
Rankin, Mary	London	1880	Figures	—	—	—	—	—	—	—	—	—	2	2
Rankley, Alfred	London	1841-1871	Domestic	—	—	38	4	4	—	—	—	—	—	46
Ranwell, W.	Woolwich	1830-1843	Landscape	—	—	2	—	1	—	—	—	—	—	3
Raper, Miss A.	London	1838	Landscape	—	—	1	1	1	—	—	—	—	—	3
Raper, H.	H.M.S. Tyne	1820	Landscape	—	—	1	—	—	—	—	—	—	—	1
Raphael, Mrs. Arthur (Mary F.)	London	1889-1893	Portraits	—	—	—	—	—	—	—	—	—	7	7
Raphael, W.	Manchester	1877	Still Life	—	—	—	—	1	—	—	—	—	—	1
Rapisardi, Signor	Florence	1868	Dramatic	—	—	2	—	—	—	—	—	—	—	2
Rappard, Miss Clara (C. von Rappard)	London	1880-1887	Figures	—	—	3	—	—	—	—	—	—	—	3
Rappard, Miss Josine	Wandsworth	1886-1893	Miniatures	—	—	5	—	—	—	2	—	—	1	8
Rascovich, Roberto	London	1883	Figures	—	—	—	—	—	—	1	—	—	—	1
Rasell, Robert	Chichester	1868-1880	Landscape	—	—	—	—	3	—	—	1	—	1	5
Rasinelli, Robert	Rome	1881	Landscape	—	—	—	—	—	—	—	—	—	1	1
Rassano, C.	Paris	1878	Landscape	—	—	—	—	—	—	—	—	—	1	1
Rastrick, J. U.	London	1817	Landscape	—	—	1	—	—	—	—	—	—	—	1
Rath, B.	—	1862	Landscape	—	—	—	—	1	—	—	—	—	—	1
Rathbone, Harold S.	Liverpool	1884-1890	Portraits	—	—	—	—	—	—	—	6	—	3	9
Rathbone, John	London	1785-1806	Landscape	2	—	48	—	—	—	—	—	—	—	50
Rathbone, Mrs.	London	1802	Landscape	—	—	1	—	—	—	—	—	—	—	1
Rathjens, William	Withington	1879-1881	Flowers	—	—	2	—	—	—	—	—	—	—	2
Rattray, Wellwood, R.S.W.	Glasgow	1883-1892	Landscape	—	—	17	—	—	—	—	5	—	—	22
Rauch, Christian Daniel	Berlin	1833	Sculpture	—	—	1	—	—	—	—	—	—	—	1
Raudnitz, Albert	London	1883	Portraits	—	—	1	—	1	—	—	—	—	—	2
Rauh, W.	London	1839	Domestic	—	—	1	1	—	—	—	—	—	—	2
Rausseaux, E.	Paris	1879	Engraving	—	—	—	—	—	—	—	—	—	1	1
Ravel, Jules	Paris	1879-1880	Figures	—	—	1	—	5	—	—	—	—	—	6
Raven, Jane A.	—	1868-1878	Landscape	—	—	—	—	—	—	—	—	—	5	5
Raven, John Samuel	St. Leonards	1849-1877	Landscape	—	—	40	13	1	—	—	—	—	27	81
Ravenet, Simon Francois, A.R.A.	London	1760-1771	Engraving	19	2	1	—	—	—	—	—	—	—	22
Ravenhill, Miss Anna	London	1878-1884	Churches	—	—	—	—	3	—	—	—	—	1	4
Ravenhill, Miss Margaret F.	London	1880-1882	Ruins	—	—	—	—	2	—	—	1	—	—	3
Raven-Hill, Leonard. *See* H.	—	—	—	—	—	—	—	—	—	—	—	—	—	—
Ravenscroft, P.	London	1871	Landscape	—	—	—	—	—	—	—	—	—	1	1
Ravenscroft, William	Reading	1892	Architecture	—	—	1	—	—	—	—	—	—	—	1
Ravenscroft, Miss	—	1824	Landscape	—	—	1	—	—	—	—	—	—	—	1
Rawdon, J. Dawson	—	1842	Landscape	—	—	1	—	—	—	—	—	—	—	1
Rawle, John S.	Nottingham	1870-1887	Religious	—	—	14	—	2	—	3	—	—	5	24
Rawle, Samuel	London	1801-1806	Landscape	—	—	2	—	—	—	—	—	—	—	2
Rawlence, Fred. A.	Salisbury	1886	Study	—	—	—	—	—	—	—	—	—	1	1
Rawlings, Ada	Sydenham	1881	Landscape	—	—	—	—	1	—	—	—	—	—	1
Rawlings, J.	London	1855-1861	Domestic	—	—	1	—	—	—	—	—	—	3	4
Rawlings, W.	London	1863	Figures	—	—	—	—	1	—	—	—	—	—	1
Rawlins, E. S.	Turnham Green	1867	Landscape	—	—	—	1	—	—	—	—	—	—	1
Rawlins, Miss Sophia	—	1783	Landscape	—	2	—	—	—	—	—	—	—	—	2
Rawlins, Thomas	Norwich	1767-1770	Landscape	5	—	5	—	—	—	—	—	—	—	10
Rawlins, T. J.	London	1840	Architecture	—	—	1	—	—	—	—	—	—	—	1
Rawlinson, Miss E.	Matlock	1831-1832	Landscape	—	—	—	3	1	—	—	—	—	—	4
Rawlinson, J.	Doncaster	1798	Architecture	—	—	1	—	—	—	—	—	—	—	1
Rawlinson, James (Pupil of Romney)	Derby	1798	Domestic	—	—	1	—	—	—	—	—	—	—	1
Rawlinson, Sir Robert, K.C.B., C.E.	London	1853-1859	Architecture	—	—	3	—	—	—	—	—	—	—	3

Name.	Town.	First and Last Year of Ex.	Speciality.	S. A.	F. S.	R. A.	B. I.	S. S.	O. W.	N. W.	G. G.	N. G.	V. E.	Total.
Rawnsley, Mrs. H. D. (Edith)	Ambleside	1882-1884	Landscape	—	—	1	—	—	—	2	—	—	—	3
Rawse, S.	Richmond	1827	Engraving	—	—	—	—	1	—	—	—	—	—	1
Rawstane, J.	London	1787-1788	Architecture	—	—	3	—	—	—	—	—	—	—	3
Rawstone, E.	London	1865-1876	Domestic	—	—	1	—	4	—	—	—	—	—	5
Rawstorne, John	Birmingham	1793-1800	Architecture	—	—	4	—	—	—	—	—	—	—	4
Ray, W. David	London	1883-1885	Landscape	—	—	—	—	3	—	—	—	—	—	3
Rayment, Robert	London	1875-1885	Landscape	—	—	—	—	3	—	1	—	—	3	7
Raymond, Francis	Tooting	1778	Miniatures	—	1	—	—	—	—	—	—	—	—	1
Raymond, G.	Edinburgh	1828	Figures	—	—	—	—	1	—	—	—	—	—	1
Raymond, John	London	1772	Portraits	—	1	—	—	—	—	—	—	—	—	1
Raymond, Miss Maud	Blackheath	1890	Sculpture	—	—	1	—	—	—	—	—	—	—	1
Raymont, F.	—	1829	Portraits	—	—	1	—	—	—	—	—	—	—	1
Rayne, Maria	—	1783-1784	Landscape	—	—	2	—	—	—	—	—	—	—	2
Rayner, Miss Frances, afterwards Mrs. Coppinger	Brighton	1861	Churches	—	—	—	—	1	—	—	—	—	—	1
Rayner, Miss Louise J.	London	1852-1893	Landscape	—	—	31	1	12	—	17	—	—	30	91
Rayner, L. R.	London	1855	Churches	—	—	4	—	—	—	—	—	—	—	4
Rayner, Miss Margaret ‖	St. Leonards	1866-1890	Landscape	—	—	—	—	3	—	1	—	—	3	7
Rayner, Miss Nancy †	London	1848-1855	Portraits	—	—	3	—	—	15	—	—	—	6	24
Rayner, Robert	—	1774	Figures	—	1	—	—	—	—	—	—	—	—	1
Rayner, Mrs. Rosa	Hanwell	1885	Flowers	—	—	1	—	—	—	—	—	—	—	1
Rayner, Miss Rose	London	1854-1866	Portraits	—	—	3	—	2	—	—	—	—	—	5
Rayner, Richard M.	Brighton	1861-1869	Landscape	—	—	—	—	4	—	—	—	—	2	6
Rayner, Samuel A. †	London	1821-1872	Churches	—	—	20	4	22	30	—	—	—	17	93
Rayner, Thomas	—	1773-1774	Figures	—	2	—	—	—	—	—	—	—	—	2
Rayner, Mrs.	London	1842	Sculpture	—	—	—	—	1	—	—	—	—	—	1
Raze, E.	London	1855	Flowers	—	—	—	—	—	—	—	—	—	1	1
Read, Alexander	—	1770	Portraits	1	—	—	—	—	—	—	—	—	—	1
Read, Miss Catherine	London	1760-1779	Portraits	14	16	6	—	—	—	—	—	—	—	36
Read, Charles Carter	Birmingham	1890-1893	Landscape	—	—	2	—	4	—	—	—	1	—	7
Read, David Charles	Sarum	1823-1840	Landscape	—	—	1	7	6	—	—	—	—	—	14
Read, Edward H.	London	1890-1893	Landscape	—	—	—	—	4	—	—	—	—	—	4
Read, F. §	London	1817-1852	Portraits	—	—	27	—	31	—	—	—	—	—	58
Read, F. Junr.	London	1855-1857	Miniatures	—	—	3	—	—	—	—	—	—	—	3
Read, G. A.	Nottingham	1876	Fruit	—	—	1	—	—	—	—	—	—	—	1
Read, Henry	Twickenham	1875-1877	Figures	—	—	—	—	2	—	—	—	—	—	2
Read, Herbert	London	1886	Architecture	—	—	1	—	—	—	—	—	—	—	1
Read, J.	London	1856-1863	Domestic	—	—	4	1	5	—	—	—	—	—	10
Read, John	Bedford	1773-1783	Game	31	—	2	—	—	—	—	—	—	—	33
Read, J. C.	London	1847-1849	Portraits	—	—	2	—	—	—	—	—	—	—	2
Read, Miss Mary	London	1849-1850	Domestic	—	—	4	3	—	—	—	—	—	—	7
Read, Nicholas	London	1764-1780	Sculpture	1	2	—	—	—	—	—	—	—	—	3
Read, Richard	Birmingham	1777	Engraving	1	—	—	—	—	—	—	—	—	—	1
Read, Samuel, R.W.S. †	Greenwich	1843-1883	Churches	—	—	18	—	13	212	—	—	—	16	259
Read, William	London	1778-1808	Miniatures	1	—	3	—	—	—	—	—	—	—	4
Read, Mrs.	London	1805-1814	Portraits	—	—	7	—	—	—	—	—	—	—	7
Read, Miss, Junr.	London	1769-1800	Figures	—	2	2	—	—	—	—	—	—	—	4
Read and Macdonald	London	1892	Architecture	—	—	2	—	—	—	—	—	—	—	2
Reade-Westhead, G. *See* W.	—	—	—	—	—	—	—	—	—	—	—	—	—	—
Reading, Miss C. R.	London	1874	Fruit	—	—	—	—	2	—	—	—	—	—	2
Reading, Mrs. E. C.	—	1874	Heads	—	—	—	—	1	—	—	—	—	—	1
Readshaw, Miss Emily S.	Düsseldorf	1883	Flowers	—	—	1	—	—	—	—	—	—	—	1
Ready, A.	London	1874-1876	Sea Pieces	—	—	5	—	—	—	—	—	—	—	5
Ready, H. J.	London	1845	Landscape	—	—	2	—	—	—	—	—	—	—	2
Ready, William James Durant (signed W. F. R.)	London	1861-1867	Sea Pieces	—	—	2	3	1	—	—	—	—	—	6
Ream, C. P.	Balham	1892	Fruit	—	—	1	—	—	—	—	—	—	—	1
Reason, Miss Florence	London	1883-1893	Domestic	—	—	7	—	1	—	2	—	—	—	10
Rebecca, Biagio, A.R.A.	London	1770-1772	Scriptural	—	—	3	—	—	—	—	—	—	—	3
Rebecca, J. B.	London	1818-1827	Architecture	—	—	4	—	—	—	—	—	—	—	4
Record, James	London	1768-1780	Portraits	7	2	—	—	—	—	—	—	—	—	9
Redaway, James C.	London	1824-1832	Engraving	—	—	—	—	14	—	—	—	—	—	14
Reddie, Arthur W. L.	London	1876-1885	Portraits	—	—	4	—	1	—	—	—	—	2	7
Redfarn, W. B.	Cambridge	1869-1870	Sporting	—	—	—	—	1	—	—	—	—	3	4
Redfern, James Frank	London	1859-1876	Sculpture	—	—	18	—	2	—	—	—	—	—	20
Redfern, Richard	Manchester	1873-1889	Landscape	—	—	6	—	—	—	1	—	—	1	8
Redford, George	Worcester	1850-1885	Portraits	—	—	—	1	1	—	—	5	—	3	10
Redgate, A. W.	Castle Donington	1886-1893	Landscape	—	—	13	—	2	—	—	—	—	—	15
Redgrave, Evelyn Leslie	London	1872-1888	Landscape	—	—	12	—	8	—	7	—	—	12	39
Redgrave, Miss Frances M.	London	1864-1882	Domestic	—	—	14	1	2	—	—	—	—	—	17
Redgrave, Gilbert Richard	London	1879	Architecture	—	—	1	—	—	—	—	—	—	—	1
Redgrave, J.	London	1820	—	—	—	*	—	—	—	—	—	—	—	—

Name.	Town.	First and Last Year of Ex.	Speciality.	S. A.	F. S.	R. A.	B. I.	S. S.	O. W.	N.W.	G. G.	N. G.	V. E.	Total.
Redgrave, J. Fraser	London	1843-1849	Rustic	—	—	—	1	2	—	—	—	—	9	12
Redgrave, Richard, C.B., R.A.	London	1825-1883	Domestic	—	—	141	18	18	—	—	—	—	11	188
Redgrave, Mrs. Richard	London	1865	Landscape	—	—	—	—	—	—	—	—	—	1	1
Redmond, Thomas	London *or* Bath	1762-1783	Miniatures	6	13	11	—	—	—	—	—	—	—	30
Redmore, Henry	Hull	1868	Sea Pieces	—	—	2	—	—	—	—	—	—	1	3
Redrup, Sidney	Windsor	1887	Domestic	—	—	1	—	—	—	—	—	—	—	1
Reed —	—	1776-1783	Sea Pieces	—	6	—	—	—	—	—	—	—	—	6
Reed, Miss Annie L.	Gipsey Hill	1888	Miniatures	—	—	2	—	—	—	—	—	—	—	2
Reed, C. T.	London	1874-1880	Landscape	—	—	—	—	1	—	—	—	—	2	3
Reed, E.	Walthamstow	1774-1801	Landscape	1	—	2	—	—	—	—	—	—	—	3
Reed, Edward	London	1890	Historical	—	—	—	—	—	—	—	—	1	—	1
Reed, Edward Tennyson	London	1885-1892	Historical	—	—	—	—	—	—	—	—	9	1	10
Reed, F.	—	1828	Buildings	—	—	1	—	—	—	—	—	—	—	1
Reed, F. E.	London	1830	Landscape	—	—	1	—	—	—	—	—	—	—	1
Reed, Fred. H. *See also* Perry and Reed	London	1884	Architecture	—	—	1	—	—	—	—	—	—	—	1
Reed, J.	London	1839-1861	Figures	—	—	6	1	—	—	—	—	—	—	7
Reed, Joseph Charles ‡	London	1860-1877	Landscape	—	—	1	—	3	—	186	—	—	—	190
Reed, Miss Kate	Tunb'dge Wells	1873-1882	Still Life	—	—	—	—	9	—	—	—	—	1	10
Reed, L. E.	Tiverton	1819-1823	Landscape	—	—	3	—	—	—	—	—	—	—	3
Reed, Miss Mary	London	1879-1892	Landscape	—	—	—	—	9	—	1	—	—	4	14
Reed, Robert	Edinburgh	1818-1820	Architecture	—	—	4	—	—	—	—	—	—	—	4
Reed, W. T.	Bakewell	1875-1881	Landscape	—	—	—	—	25	—	—	—	—	—	25
Reekers, H.	London	1847	Fruit	—	—	—	1	—	—	—	—	—	—	1
Reekes, Richard	London	1810	Miniatures	—	—	5	—	—	—	—	—	—	—	5
Rees, John	London	1852-1879	Landscape	—	—	2	5	36	—	—	—	—	34	77
Rees, Miss M. R.	London	1865-1872	Fruit	—	—	1	—	2	—	—	—	—	—	3
Reeve, Miss Alice	Chiswick	1878-1881	Domestic	—	—	—	—	1	—	—	—	—	2	3
Reeve, A. W.	London	1831-1848	Engraving	—	—	2	—	4	—	—	—	—	—	6
Reeve, G.	London	1830-1842	Sculpture	—	—	2	—	1	—	—	—	—	—	3
Reeve, Hope	London	1879	Landscape	—	—	—	—	1	—	—	—	—	—	1
Reeve, H. G.	—	1829	Landscape	—	—	—	—	4	—	—	—	—	—	4
Reeve, J.	London	1857	Cattle	—	—	—	—	—	—	—	—	—	1	1
Reeve, J. Arthur	London	1887-1891	Architecture	—	—	3	—	—	—	—	—	—	—	3
Reeve, J. F.	London	1824	Landscape	—	—	1	—	—	—	—	—	—	—	1
Reeve, R. G.	Dorking	1844-1848	Flowers	—	—	1	—	8	—	—	—	—	—	9
Reeve, Miss	—	1856	Dogs	—	—	1	—	—	—	—	—	—	—	1
Reeves, E.	London	1843	Portraits	—	—	—	—	1	—	—	—	—	—	1
Reeves, Miss Eliza	—	1822-1824	Domestic	—	—	3	—	—	—	—	—	—	—	3
Reeves, E. B.	London	1846	Domestic	—	—	1	—	—	—	—	—	—	—	1
Reeves, George H.	Chester	1882-1884	Trees	—	—	2	—	1	—	—	—	—	—	3
Reeves, Miss Mary	Cork	1871-1887	Landscape	—	—	—	—	2	—	3	—	—	2	7
Reffitt-Oldfield, J. *See* O.	—	—	—	—	—	—	—	—	—	—	—	—	—	—
Regamey, Felix	London	1872	Domestic	—	—	—	—	—	—	—	—	—	5	5
Regamey, Guillaume	Paris	1869-1874	Figures	—	—	5	—	—	—	—	—	—	9	14
Regemonte, Van. *See* V.	—	—	—	—	—	—	—	—	—	—	—	—	—	—
Regemorter, Van. *See* V.	—	—	—	—	—	—	—	—	—	—	—	—	—	—
Regnart, C.	London	1806	Sculpture	—	—	1	—	—	—	—	—	—	—	1
Rehberg, F.	Berlin	1815	Mythological	—	—	6	—	—	—	—	—	—	—	6
Reichenbach, Count Waldemar. *See* V.	—	—	—	—	—	—	—	—	—	—	—	—	—	—
Reid, Archibald D., A.R.S.A., R.S.W.	Aberdeen	1872-1891	Landscape	—	—	6	—	—	—	—	1	—	—	7
Reid, Edith M.	Croydon	1873-1880	Landscape	—	—	1	—	2	—	—	—	—	6	9
Reid, Miss Flora M.	London	1879-1893	Animals	—	—	8	—	47	—	—	9	5	4	73
Reid, Sir George, P.R.S.A., H.R.S.W., LL.D.	Aberdeen	1865-1893	Landscape	—	—	18	—	1	—	—	—	—	—	19
Reid, George Ogilvy, A.R.S.A.	Edinburgh	1887-1893	Domestic	—	—	12	—	—	—	—	1	—	—	13
Reid, John R. § φ	London	1876-1893	Domestic	—	—	29	—	52	—	1	23	5	30	140
Reid, Miss Lizzie	London	1882-1893	Domestic	—	—	2	—	19	—	—	9	1	4	35
Reid, Miss Marion	London	1889-1891	Landscape	—	—	2	—	—	—	—	—	—	—	2
Reid, Samuel	Glasgow	1883-1892	Landscape	—	—	3	—	—	—	1	—	—	—	4
Reid, W.	London	1865-1875	Coast Scenes	—	—	—	—	4	—	—	—	—	—	4
Reigersfeld, J.	—	1807	Architecture	—	—	1	—	—	—	—	—	—	—	1
Reilly, Fred.	London	1890	Landscape	—	—	—	—	—	—	—	—	—	1	1
Reilly, John L.	London	1857-1866	Portraits	—	—	7	1	4	—	—	—	—	—	12
Reilly, Nora Trouse	London	1889-1891	Domestic	—	—	—	—	2	—	1	—	—	—	3
Reilly, S.	—	1836	Architecture	—	—	1	—	—	—	—	—	—	—	1
Reinagle, Miss Charlotte	London	1798-1821	Landscape	—	—	12	15	—	—	—	—	—	—	27
Reinagle, Mrs. C.	London	1811	Landscape	—	—	—	1	—	—	—	—	—	—	1
Reinagle, F.	London	1806	Landscape	—	—	1	—	—	—	—	—	—	—	1
Reinagle, Miss Fanny	London	1800-1812	Landscape	—	—	6	11	—	—	—	—	—	—	17
Reinagle, George Philip	London	1822-1835	Sea Pieces	—	—	37	30	5	—	—	—	—	—	72
Reinagle, Miss H.	London	1824-1862	Landscape	—	—	—	10	3	—	—	—	—	—	13
Reinagle, H.	London	1848	Landscape	—	—	—	2	—	—	—	—	—	—	2
Reinagle, J.	London	1832	Landscape	—	—	—	7	—	—	—	—	—	—	7

Name.	Town.	First and Last Year of Ex.	Speciality.	S. A.	F. S.	R. A.	B. I.	S. S.	O. W	N.W.	G. G.	N.G.	V. E.	Total.
Reinagle, Miss O. G.	London	1824-1832	Landscape	—	—	11	7	—	—	—	—	—	—	18
Reinagle, Philip, R.A.	London	1773-1832	Landscape	—	—	114	138	1	—	—	—	—	—	253
Reinagle, P. A.	London	1804-1811	Sporting	—	—	6	4	—	—	—	—	—	—	10
Reinagle, Baron von	London	1854	Portraits	—	—	—	—	3	—	—	—	—	—	3
Reinagle, R. N.	London	1798	Figures	—	—	5	—	—	—	—	—	—	—	5
Reinagle, Ramsey Richard, R.A. †	London	1788-1857	Landscape	—	—	244	51	2	67	—	—	—	—	364
Reinhart, Benjamin Franklin	London	1863-1867	Scriptural	—	—	1	6	1	—	—	—	—	—	8
Reinhart, Charles S.	Paris	1883	Domestic	—	—	—	—	—	—	1	—	—	—	1
Reinhart, H.	Austria	1881	Domestic	—	—	1	—	—	—	—	—	—	1	2
Reitz, S. C. Bosch-. *See* B.	—	—	—	—	—	—	—	—	—	—	—	—	—	—
Rejlander, Oscar Gustave	London	1848-1873	Portraits	—	—	4	—	—	—	—	—	—	—	4
Rémandas, Madame Lily	London	1889-1893	Miniatures	—	—	6	—	—	—	—	—	—	—	6
Remdé, F.	Saxe-Weimar	1854	Figures	—	—	1	—	—	—	—	—	—	—	1
Renard, Edward	London	1879-1893	Landscape	—	—	2	—	5	—	—	—	—	—	7
Renaldi, Francesco	London	1777-1798	Portraits	1	—	12	—	—	—	—	—	—	—	13
Rendall, Arthur D.	London	1889-1892	Domestic	—	—	4	—	1	—	—	—	—	—	5
Rennell, W.	—	1805-1806	Portraits	—	—	2	—	—	—	—	—	—	—	2
Rennell, Mrs.	—	1805	Dramatic	—	—	1	—	—	—	—	—	—	—	1
Rennet, C.	London	1805-1806	Portraits	—	—	2	—	—	—	—	—	—	—	2
Rennett, Miss	London	1778	Landscape	—	1	—	—	—	—	—	—	—	—	1
Rennie, George	London	1828-1838	Sculpture	—	—	14	—	3	—	—	—	—	—	17
Rennie, G. B.	London	1859	Architecture	—	—	1	—	—	—	—	—	—	—	1
Renny, Miss M.	London	1872-1873	Landscape	—	—	—	—	—	—	—	—	—	3	3
Renouard, Paul	Paris	1879-1891	Figures	—	—	—	—	—	—	—	—	—	7	7
Renouf, Mrs.	London	1883	Still Life	—	—	—	—	2	—	—	—	—	—	2
Renoux, M.	London	1841	Figures	—	—	2	—	—	—	—	—	—	—	2
Renshaw, Alice	London	1881	Figures	—	—	—	—	1	—	—	—	—	—	1
Renshaw, Ellen	Clapton	1840-1842	Miniatures	—	—	2	—	—	—	—	—	—	—	2
Renton, John	Hoxton	1799-1841	Landscape	—	—	40	10	1	—	—	—	—	—	51
Renton, Miss Lizzie	London	1875-1879	Dramatic	—	—	—	—	4	—	—	—	—	1	5
Renwick, G. R.	London	1859	Sculpture	—	—	1	—	—	—	—	—	—	—	1
Repton, G. Stanley	London	1801-1802	Landscape	—	—	3	—	—	—	—	—	—	—	3
Repton, Humphrey	Bury St. Edm'ds	1787-1802	Landscape	—	—	15	—	—	—	—	—	—	—	15
Repton, John Adey	London	1798-1804	Architecture	—	—	14	—	—	—	—	—	—	—	14
Resch, E. L.	London	1863	Sculpture	—	—	1	—	—	—	—	—	—	—	1
Resche, Le. *See* L.	—	—	—	—	—	—	—	—	—	—	—	—	—	—
Restall, W.	London	1824-1828	Architecture	—	—	1	—	2	—	—	—	—	—	3
Reuss, Miss Lilly	Manchester	1890	Miniatures	—	—	1	—	—	—	—	—	—	—	1
Reütte, A.	—	1807	Architecture	—	—	1	—	—	—	—	—	—	—	1
Reve, R. G.	—	1831	Engraving	—	—	—	—	1	—	—	—	—	—	1
Reveley, Willey	London	1781-1793	Architecture	—	—	12	—	—	—	—	—	—	—	12
Revill, W. H.	London	1868-1870	Poultry	—	—	—	—	5	—	—	—	—	—	5
Reville, H. Whitaker	Ealing	1881-1885	Domestic	—	—	—	—	2	—	—	—	—	—	2
Rew, Charles Henry. *See also* Driver and Rew	London	1878-1884	Buildings	—	—	4	—	—	—	—	—	—	—	4
Rew, E.	—	1865	Figures	—	—	1	—	—	—	—	—	—	—	1
Rey —	—	1763-1764	Sea Pieces	5	—	—	—	—	—	—	—	—	—	5
Réyé, H.	Paris	1874-1878	Landscape	—	—	—	—	—	—	—	—	—	9	9
Reymann, Teodoro	London	1872-1874	Domestic	—	—	—	—	4	—	—	—	—	—	4
Reynard, F.	Paris	1869	Domestic	—	—	1	—	—	—	—	—	—	—	1
Reyners, Joseph F.	London	1890	Sculpture	—	—	1	—	—	—	—	—	—	—	1
Reynolds, Apollonia	Guildford	1882	Still Life	—	—	—	—	1	—	—	—	—	1	2
Reynolds, Miss A. G.	—	1854	Sculpture	—	—	1	—	—	—	—	—	—	—	1
Reynolds, Miss Clara	London	1892	Domestic	—	—	—	—	1	—	—	—	—	—	1
Reynolds, E.	London	1822	Portraits	—	—	1	—	—	—	—	—	—	—	1
Reynolds, Miss Elizabeth. *See* Mrs. William	—	—	—	—	—	—	—	—	—	—	—	—	—	—
Walker	London	1818-1835	Miniatures	—	—	47	—	3	—	—	—	—	—	50
Reynolds, Miss Fanny	London	1828-1830	Miniatures	—	—	4	—	—	—	—	—	—	—	4
Reynolds, Frank	London	1850-1856	Figures	—	—	—	2	2	—	—	—	—	—	4
Reynolds, Frederick George	London	1859-1887	Landscape	—	—	32	—	8	—	—	—	—	18	58
Reynolds, G. S.	London	1836-1848	Figures	—	—	—	4	9	—	—	—	—	—	13
Reynolds, Mrs. G. S.	London	1835-1848	Figures	—	—	5	—	—	—	—	—	—	—	5
Reynolds, Sir Joshua, P.R.A.	Plympton	1760-1790	Portraits	25	—	247	—	—	—	—	—	—	—	272
Reynolds, J.	London	1830-1860	Landscape	—	—	1	—	10	—	—	—	—	—	11
Reynolds, Miss M. E.	Ambleside	1852	Animals	—	—	1	—	—	—	—	—	—	—	1
Reynolds, R.	London	1854-1855	Scriptural	—	—	—	2	—	—	—	—	—	—	2
Reynolds, R. W.	West Ham	1832	Flowers	—	—	1	—	—	—	—	—	—	—	1
Reynolds, Samuel William	London	1797-1834	Landscape	—	—	65	56	10	—	—	—	—	—	131
Reynolds, Samuel William, Junr.	London	1820-1845	Portraits	—	—	39	6	—	—	—	—	—	—	45
Reynolds, Walter	London	1859-1885	Landscape	—	—	7	—	41	—	2	—	—	1	51
Reynolds, Miss	Chelmsford	1778	Flowers	1	—	—	—	—	—	—	—	—	—	1
Reynolds-Stephens, William	London	1884-1893	Domestic	—	—	12	—	2	—	4	1	1	—	20
Rezia, Felice A.	London	1866-1876	Landscape	—	—	3	3	—	—	—	—	—	4	10

Name.	Town.	First and Last Year of Ex.	Speciality.	S. A.	F. S.	R. A.	B. I.	S. S.	O. W.	N. W.	G. G.	N. G.	V. E.	Total.
Rhead, George Wooliscroft, R.P.E.	London	1873-1892	Domestic	—	—	6	—	3	—	1	—	—	8	18
Rheam, Henry R., R.I.‡	Birkenhead	1887-1893	Domestic	—	—	6	—	1	—	3	—	—	—	10
Rhind, John, R.S.A.	Edinburgh	1885-1888	Sculpture	—	—	4	—	—	—	—	—	—	—	4
Rhodes, Mrs. E. J.	London	1882-1887	Sculpture	—	—	1	—	2	—	—	—	—	—	3
Rhodes, F. R.	Birmingham	1841-1843	Landscape	—	—	5	1	—	—	—	—	—	—	6
Rhodes, H.	London	1795-1826	Architecture	—	—	9	—	—	—	—	—	—	—	9
Rhodes, H.	London	1869-1871	Flowers	—	—	1	—	1	—	—	—	—	—	2
Rhodes, Miss H.	Sheffield	1811-1813	Landscape	—	—	5	—	—	—	—	—	—	—	5
Rhodes, H. Douglas	London	1885	Landscape	—	—	—	—	1	—	—	—	—	—	1
Rhodes, Henry J.	London	1869-1882	Flowers	—	—	4	—	2	—	—	—	—	4	10
Rhodes, John	London	1832-1843	Domestic	—	—	9	4	—	—	—	—	—	—	13
Rhodes, Joseph	Leeds	1811	Landscape	—	—	—	2	—	—	—	—	—	—	2
Rhodes, John N.	Leeds	1839-1842	Rustic	—	—	2	4	2	—	—	—	—	—	8
Rhodes, Rowland	Preston	1886-1889	Sculpture	—	—	3	—	—	—	—	—	—	—	3
Rhodes, W.	London	1834-1836	Landscape	—	—	—	7	—	—	—	—	—	—	7
Rhodes, W. P.	London	1871-1878	Enamels	—	—	2	—	—	—	—	—	—	2	4
Rhys, Oliver	London	1876-1893	Landscape	—	—	8	—	3	—	—	2	—	4	17
Ribbing, Miss S.	London	1873-1875	Portraits	—	—	6	—	—	—	—	—	—	—	6
Ribbing, De. *See* D.	—	—		—	—	—	—	—	—	—	—	—	—	—
Ribblesdale, Thomas, 4th Baron	London	1892	Sporting	—	—	—	—	—	—	—	—	1	—	1
Ribot, E.	Paris	1865	Figures	—	—	1	—	—	—	—	—	—	—	1
Ricard, Gustave	London	1871	Portraits	—	—	1	—	—	—	—	—	—	—	1
Ricardo, Halsey Ralph	London	1883-1892	Architecture	—	—	6	—	—	—	—	—	—	—	6
Ricci, Alfred	London	1889	Rustic	—	—	—	—	—	—	—	—	1	—	1
Ricci, H.	—	1878	Portraits	—	—	—	—	—	—	—	1	—	—	1
Ricci, Paolo	London	1884	Sculpture	—	—	—	—	—	—	—	1	—	—	1
Rice, Frederick A.	London	1893	Heads	—	—	1	—	—	—	—	—	—	—	1
Rich, Anthony	London	1854	Landscape	—	—	—	—	—	—	—	—	—	3	3
Rich, Edmund	London	1765	Architecture	—	1	—	—	—	—	—	—	—	—	1
Rich, Frederick W.	London	1866-1867	Landscape	—	—	—	—	—	—	—	—	—	2	2
Rich, William George	London	1876-1884	Landscape	—	—	1	—	8	—	—	—	—	—	9
Richard, E.	—	1854	Sculpture	—	—	1	—	—	—	—	—	—	—	1
Richard, R.	Warwick	1865	Durham	—	—	—	—	—	—	—	—	—	1	1
Richard, Miss Aimee G.	London	1893	Flowers	—	—	1	—	—	—	—	—	—	—	1
Richards, Miss Alice S.	London	1892-1893	Domestic	—	—	—	—	2	—	—	—	—	—	2
Richards, Charles	Keynsham	1854-1857	Sporting	—	—	4	4	7	—	—	—	—	6	21
Richards, Edmund	Charlton	1771-1775	Landscape	—	15	—	—	—	—	—	—	—	—	15
Richards, Miss Emma G.	London	1850-1854	Portraits	—	—	8	1	—	—	—	—	—	—	9
Richards, Frank	Newlyn	1892	Churches	—	—	1	—	—	—	—	—	—	—	1
Richards, George	London	1855-1883	Figures	—	—	1	1	—	—	—	—	—	1	3
Richards, H.	London	1858	Landscape	—	—	—	1	—	—	—	—	—	—	1
Richards, Miss Helena	London	1892	Landscape	—	—	—	—	1	—	—	—	—	—	1
Richards, Henry	London	1857-1858	Sea Pieces	—	—	—	2	—	—	—	—	—	—	2
Richards, John Inigo, R.A., F.S.A.	London	1769-1809	Landscape	5	—	39	—	—	—	—	—	—	—	44
Richards, J.	London	1762-1800	Landscape	29	18	14	—	—	—	—	—	—	—	61
Richards, J.	London	1837	Domestic	—	—	—	—	3	—	—	—	—	—	3
Richards, R. P.	Liverpool	1860-1877	Sea Pieces	—	—	11	1	3	—	—	—	—	2	17
Richards, Thomas Robert	London	1878-1884	Architecture	—	—	2	—	—	—	—	—	—	—	2
Richards, W.	London	1838-1841	Game	—	—	—	—	3	—	—	—	—	—	3
Richards, W. S.	—	1871	Landscape	—	—	1	—	—	—	—	—	—	—	1
Richards, William T.	Philadelphia	1860-1892	Landscape	—	—	11	—	1	—	—	2	—	11	25
Richards, Miss	—	1778	Needlework	1	—	—	—	—	—	—	—	—	—	1
Richardson, Alice	London	1776	Crayons	—	—	3	—	—	—	—	—	—	—	3
Richardson, Arthur	London	1876-1890	Architecture	—	—	2	—	—	—	—	—	—	1	3
Richardson, Charles	Newcastle	1855-1891	Landscape	—	—	26	—	6	—	2	—	—	60	94
Richardson, Mrs. Charles	—	1846	Landscape	—	—	1	—	—	—	—	—	—	—	1
Richardson, C. Douglas	London	1884-1888	Sculpture	—	—	3	—	1	—	—	—	—	1	5
Richardson, Charles James	London	1837-1862	Architecture	—	—	17	—	—	—	—	—	—	—	17
Richardson, D.	London	1783-1830	Still Life	—	—	12	—	14	—	—	—	—	—	26
Richardson, Edward ‡	London	1856-1875	Landscape	—	—	2	—	—	—	187	—	—	—	189
Richardson, Ellen	London	1891	Figures	—	—	—	—	1	—	—	—	—	—	1
Richardson, Esdaile	Lewes	1884	Sea Pieces	—	—	—	—	—	—	—	—	—	1	1
Richardson, Edward M.	London	1829-1866	Sculpture	—	—	28	5	12	—	—	—	—	—	45
Richardson, Frederick Stuart, R.S.W.	Sandy	1884-1893	Domestic	—	—	20	—	5	—	13	—	1	14	53
Richardson, F. W.	London	1877-1883	Landscape	—	—	3	—	—	—	—	—	—	—	3
Richardson, George, F.S.A.	London	1766-1793	Architecture	14	1	9	—	—	—	—	—	—	—	24
Richardson, George	Newcastle	1828-1833	Landscape	—	—	—	6	—	—	2	—	—	—	8
Richardson, G. C.	London	1877	Architecture	—	—	1	—	—	—	—	—	—	—	1
Richardson, Henry Burdon	London	1828-1872	Landscape	—	—	6	—	7	—	—	—	—	5	18
Richardson, John J., R.I.‡ φ	London	1846-1893	Landscape	—	—	26	4	7	—	37	—	—	81	155
Richardson, J. V.	Oxford	1846	Churches	—	—	2	—	—	—	—	—	—	—	2
Richardson, R.	Sidmouth	1890	Landscape	—	—	—	—	—	—	1	—	—	—	1

Name.	Town.	First and Last Year of Ex.	Speciality.	S. A.	F. S.	R. A.	B. I.	S. S.	O. W.	N.W.	G. G.	N. G.	V. E.	Total.
Richardson, Thomas Miles ‡	Newcastle	1818-1847	Landscape	—	—	13	24	19	11	23	—	—	—	90
Richardson, Thomas Miles, Junr., R.S.A., R.W.S. †	Newcastle	1832-1889	Landscape	—	—	6	3	5	702	1	—	—	2	719
Richardson, W.	London	1783-1794	Architecture	—	—	5	—	—	—	—	—	—	—	5
Richardson, William	London	1842-1877	Landscape	—	—	16	3	18	—	—	—	—	6	43
Richardson, W. H.	London	1802-1810	Architecture	—	—	2	—	—	—	—	—	—	—	2
Richardson, Mrs.	London	1769-1775	Portraits	15	—	—	—	—	—	—	—	—	—	15
Richbell, T.	Chatham	1792-1825	Sea Pieces	—	—	9	—	—	—	—	—	—	—	9
Riches, J.	London	1832-1833	Ruins	—	—	2	—	—	—	—	—	—	—	2
Richeton, Leon	London	1875-1888	Etching	—	—	9	—	—	—	—	—	—	16	25
Richley, R.	London	1821-1827	Architecture	—	—	2	—	—	—	—	—	—	—	2
Richman, F.	London	1813	Landscape	—	—	2	—	—	—	—	—	—	—	2
Richmond, George, R.A., D.C.L., F.S.A., LL.D.	London	1825-1888	Portraits	—	—	196	3	5	—	—	—	—	1	205
Richmond, Julia	London	1866	Flowers	—	—	—	—	—	—	—	—	—	2	2
Richmond, James C.	London	1856-1878	Landscape	—	—	1	—	—	—	—	—	—	5	6
Richmond, Thomas	London	1795-1825	Miniatures	—	—	46	—	—	—	—	—	—	—	46
Richmond, Thomas, Junr.	London	1822-1860	Portraits	—	—	45	—	6	—	—	—	—	—	51
Richmond, William Blake, A.R.A., F.S.A., M.A.	London	1861-1893	Portraits	—	—	37	2	—	—	—	119	26	3	187
Richter, Adrien Louis	London	1848	Domestic	—	—	1	—	—	—	—	—	—	—	1
Richter, Professor Gustav	Berlin	1874	Portraits	—	—	1	—	—	—	—	—	—	—	1
Richter, H.	—	1878	Study	—	—	—	—	—	—	—	1	—	—	1
Richter, Henry J. †	London	1788-1856	Portraits	—	—	37	4	3	88	—	—	—	18	150
Richter, Miss Henrietta S.	London	1842-1849	Miniatures	—	—	6	—	—	—	—	—	—	—	6
Richter, John Augustus	London	1782-1783	Sculpture	—	8	—	—	—	—	—	—	—	—	8
Richter, M.	Paris	1851	Game	—	—	2	—	—	—	—	—	—	—	2
Rickards, R.	—	1794	Landscape	—	—	1	—	—	—	—	—	—	—	1
Rickards, R. F.	London	1822-1827	Landscape	—	—	—	2	—	—	—	—	—	—	2
Rickards, Samuel, F.S.A.	London	1768-1781	Miniatures	10	1	4	—	—	—	—	—	—	—	15
Rickards, T.	London	1819	Architecture	—	—	1	—	—	—	—	—	—	—	1
Rickards, T. W.	London	1876	Landscape	—	—	—	—	1	—	—	—	—	—	1
Rickatson, Octavius, R.B.A §	London	1877-1893	Landscape	—	—	25	—	35	—	8	2	2	15	87
Rickerby, Miss Eliza G.	—	1840-1843	Miniatures	—	—	3	—	—	—	—	—	—	—	3
Rickerby, Elizabeth	—	1844	Portraits	—	—	1	—	—	—	—	—	—	—	1
Rickets, John	Gloucester	1771	Sculpture	—	1	—	—	—	—	—	—	—	—	1
Ricketts, Miss Amy	Bath	1889-1890	Miniatures	—	—	3	—	—	—	—	—	—	—	3
Ricketts, Charles	London	1886-1887	Historical	—	—	—	—	—	—	2	—	—	—	2
Ricketts, Miss C.	London	1866-1867	Domestic	—	—	—	2	—	—	—	—	—	—	2
Ricketts, Charles Robert	London	1868-1879	Sea Pieces	—	—	7	—	3	—	—	—	—	2	12
Ricketts, C. S.	London	1887	Scriptural	—	—	—	—	1	—	—	—	—	—	1
Ricketts, R.	London	1792	Architecture	—	—	1	—	—	—	—	—	—	—	1
Rickman, Thomas Miller, F.S.A. *See* Lynam and Rickman	—	—	Architecture	—	—	—	—	—	—	—	—	—	—	—
Ricks, James	London	1868-1885	Domestic	—	—	8	—	11	—	—	—	—	3	22
Ricozzi, A.	Milan	1846	Figures	—	—	1	—	—	—	—	—	—	—	1
Riddell, Lady Buchanan	London	1885	Coast Scenes	—	—	—	—	—	—	1	—	—	—	1
Riddell, R. A.	—	1793	Landscape	—	—	1	—	—	—	—	—	—	—	1
Riddell, Wdem	Lynmouth	1878	Rustic	—	—	—	—	1	—	—	—	—	—	1
Riddett, Leonard Charles	London	1893	Landscape	—	—	—	—	1	—	—	—	—	—	1
Ride, John	London	1773-1781	Architecture	—	—	3	—	—	—	—	—	—	—	3
Rider —	London	1782	Engraving	—	1	—	—	—	—	—	—	—	—	1
Rider, J.	London	1842-1849	Landscape	—	—	8	2	10	—	—	—	—	—	20
Rider, Urban	Dover	1883-1886	Landscape	—	—	—	—	—	—	4	—	—	—	4
Rider, William	Leamington	1824-1842	Landscape	—	—	6	16	—	—	—	—	—	—	22
Ridge, Alfred Monday	London	1866-1883	Architecture	—	—	5	—	—	—	—	—	—	—	5
Ridgeway, Miss E.	Penmaenmawr	1874	Flowers	—	—	—	—	1	—	—	—	—	—	1
Ridgway, William	London	1863-1885	Engraving	—	—	9	—	—	—	—	—	—	1	10
Ridley, Miss Annie	London	1864-1870	Flowers	—	—	—	1	1	—	—	—	—	1	3
Ridley, Edward	London	1831-1834	Figures	—	—	1	—	1	—	—	—	—	—	2
Ridley, Henry Stephen	London	1852-1859	Architecture	—	—	7	—	—	—	—	—	—	—	7
Ridley, Matthew White	London	1857-1888	Figures	—	—	19	3	6	—	1	1	—	7	37
Ridley, S. H.	London	1831-1832	Landscape	—	—	1	—	1	—	—	—	—	—	2
Ridley, W.	London	1844	Landscape	—	—	1	—	—	—	—	—	—	—	1
Ridley, W. J.	London	1829	Architecture	—	—	2	—	—	—	—	—	—	—	2
Ridley-Corbet, M. *See* C.	—	—		—	—	—	—	—	—	—	—	—	—	—
Rieck, E.	London	1858	Sea Pieces	—	—	—	—	2	—	—	—	—	—	2
Riésener, Louis Antoine Léon	Paris	1870	Figures	—	—	—	—	1	—	—	—	—	—	1
Rigaud, Miss E. A.	London	1797-1800	Portraits	—	—	8	—	—	—	—	—	—	—	8
Rigaud, John Francis, R.A.	London	1772-1815	Historical	—	—	155	21	—	—	—	—	—	—	176
Rigaud, Stephen Francis †	London	1797-1852	Scriptural	—	—	38	24	6	50	—	—	—	9	127
Rigby, Cuthbert, A.R.W.S. †	Southport	1874-1893	Landscape	—	—	7	—	—	223	—	—	—	13	243
Rigby, Mrs. Eliza	London	1771-1773	Needlework	3	—	—	—	—	—	—	—	—	—	3
Rigby, Mrs. Honora M. (?) Miss	Chester	1891-1893	Sculpture	—	—	1	—	—	—	—	—	1	—	2
Rigby, Mrs.	Esher	1867	Landscape	—	—	—	—	1	—	—	—	—	—	1

Name.	Town.	First and Last Year of Ex.	Speciality.	S. A.	F. S.	R. A.	B. I.	S. S.	O. W.	N.W.	G. G.	N. G.	V. E.	Total.
RIGBYE, HARRIETTE	Ambleside	1879	Landscape	—	—	—	—	—	—	—	—	—	1	1
RIGG, ARTHUR H.	Bradford	1888-1891	Landscape	—	—	1	—	1	—	—	3	3	—	8
RIGG, JANE	—	1853	Landscape	—	—	—	—	1	—	—	—	—	—	1
RIGNY, LE CHEVALIER DE	London	1795-1799	Landscape	—	—	9	—	—	—	—	—	—	—	9
RILEY, THOMAS	London	1878-1892	Figures	—	—	19	—	1	—	4	3	4	12	43
RILEY, W.	London	1844-1850	Figures	—	—	1	1	7	—	—	—	—	—	9
RIMER, MRS. LOUISA SERENA	London	1855-1875	Flowers	—	—	11	21	34	—	—	—	—	6	72
RIMER, WILLIAM	London	1845-1888	Historical	—	—	6	6	12	—	—	—	—	1	25
RIMINGTON, ALEX. WALLACE, A.R.P.E.	Weston-super-Mare	1880-1893	Landscape	—	—	14	—	—	—	2	1	—	2	19
RIMMER, ALFRED	Chester	1878	Woodcuts	—	—	—	—	—	—	—	—	—	3	3
RIMMER, HEBER	Chester	1892	Architecture	—	—	1	—	—	—	—	—	—	—	1
RINEHART, WILLIAM HENRY	Rome	1872	Sculpture	—	—	1	—	—	—	—	—	—	—	1
RING, A. T. N.	—	1852	Architecture	—	—	1	—	—	—	—	—	—	—	1
RINGEL, DANIEL	Paris	1886	Sculpture	—	—	1	—	—	—	—	—	—	—	1
RINGWOOD, R.	London	1835-1843	Sculpture	—	—	3	—	—	—	—	—	—	—	3
RINNING, J.	London	1785	Landscape	—	—	1	—	—	—	—	—	—	—	1
RINTOUL, WILLIAM	London	1791	Sea Pieces	1	—	—	—	—	—	—	—	—	—	1
RINZI, ERNEST	London	1886-1893	Miniatures	—	—	18	—	—	—	—	—	—	—	18
RIOS, R. DE LOS	London	1878-1888	Domestic	—	—	1	—	—	—	—	—	—	8	9
RIOV, CAPTAIN	London	1769	Architecture	—	5	—	—	—	—	—	—	—	—	5
RIPLEY, RICHARD, JUNR.	London	1779	Architecture	—	—	1	—	—	—	—	—	—	—	1
RIPLEY, R. R.	London	1856-1879	Landscape	—	—	—	2	3	—	—	—	—	—	5
RIPPINGILLE, ALEX.	Clifton	1824-1835	Domestic	—	—	1	—	5	—	—	—	—	—	6
RIPPINGILLE, EDWARD VILLIERS	Bristol	1813-1857	Figures	—	—	41	19	12	—	—	—	—	—	72
RIPPINGILLE, R.	—	1822	Figures	—	—	2	—	—	—	—	—	—	—	2
RIPPINGILLE, T.	London	1849	Figures	—	—	—	—	1	—	—	—	—	—	1
RISCHGITZ, ALICE	London	1880-1881	Landscape	—	—	—	—	—	—	—	—	—	2	2
RISCHGITZ, EDWARD	London	1878-1881	Landscape	—	—	—	—	—	—	—	1	—	29	30
RISCHGITZ, MISS MARY	London	1882-1892	Flowers	—	—	6	—	8	—	—	—	—	3	17
RISHWORTH, R.	London	1830	Figures	—	—	1	—	—	—	—	—	—	—	1
RISING, JOHN	London	1785-1815	Portraits	13	—	91	12	—	—	—	—	—	—	116
RISING, W. H.	London	1818	Landscape	—	—	2	—	—	—	—	—	—	—	2
RISLEY, J. *See* Smith (A.) and Risley (J.)	—	—	Architecture	—	—	—	—	—	—	—	—	—	—	—
RITCHIE. *See* Brandon and Ritchie	—	—	Architecture	—	—	—	—	—	—	—	—	—	—	—
RITCHIE, A.	London	1842-1845	Architecture	—	—	3	—	—	—	—	—	—	—	3
RITCHIE, ALEXANDER HENDYSIDE, A.R.S.A.	Edinburgh	1830-1868	Sculpture	—	—	11	—	—	—	—	—	—	—	11
RITCHIE, ELEANORA	London	1880	Domestic	—	—	—	—	1	—	—	—	—	—	1
RITCHIE, JOHN	Musselburgh	1840	Sculpture	—	—	1	1	—	—	—	—	—	—	2
RITCHIE, JOHN	London	1858-1875	Figures	—	—	18	9	12	—	—	—	—	—	39
RITCHIE, ROBERT	London	1847	Architecture	—	—	1	—	—	—	—	—	—	—	1
RITSON, J.	London	1855-1859	Landscape	—	—	—	2	—	—	—	—	—	—	2
RITTER, LORENZ	Nürnberg	1881-1886	Castles	—	—	1	—	—	—	—	2	—	2	5
RITTER, LOUIS	London	1881-1884	Figures	—	—	1	—	—	—	—	—	—	1	2
RIVERS, C.	London	1799-1804	Historical	—	—	10	—	—	—	—	—	—	—	10
RIVERS, C. A.	London	1831-1851	Sculpture	—	—	54	2	7	—	—	—	—	—	63
RIVERS, GEORGE	London	1817	Buildings	—	—	—	1	—	—	—	—	—	—	1
RIVERS, LEOPOLD, R.B.A. §	London	1873-1893	Landscape	—	—	32	—	151	—	18	—	—	18	219
RIVERS, MISS M. A.	London	1842-1844	Sculpture	—	—	3	—	—	—	—	—	—	—	3
RIVERS, R. GODFREY	Brighton	1879-1884	Landscape	—	—	1	—	1	—	—	—	—	1	3
RIVERS, WILLIAM JOSEPH	London	1843-1855	Still Life and Sculpture	—	—	1	5	—	—	—	—	—	—	6
RIVIERE, MISS ANNETTE L.	Oxford	1870-1887	Figures	—	—	6	—	—	—	1	—	—	11	18
RIVIERE, BRITON, R.A.	Cheltenham	1851-1893	Animals	—	—	82	3	6	—	—	4	—	30	125
RIVIERE, MRS. BRITON (ALICE)	Bromley	1868-1872	Flowers	—	—	3	—	—	—	—	—	—	7	10
RIVIERE, D.	London	1799	Figures	—	—	1	—	—	—	—	—	—	—	1
RIVIERE, DANIEL VALENTINE	London	1823-1840	Domestic	—	—	13	—	—	—	—	—	—	—	13
RIVIERE, MISS F.	London	1831-1834	Miniatures	—	—	9	—	—	—	—	—	—	—	9
RIVIERE, HUGH G.	London	1893	Portraits	—	—	1	—	—	—	—	—	—	—	1
RIVIERE, HENRY PARSONS, A.R.W.S. † ‡	London	1832-1888	Figures	—	—	6	7	19	299	101	—	—	—	432
RIVIERE, WILLIAM	London	1826-1860	Domestic	—	—	20	17	7	—	—	—	—	—	44
RIVIERE, MRS. W.	London	1871	Fruit	—	—	—	—	3	—	—	—	—	—	3
RIVOIRE, F.	Paris	1881	Flowers	—	—	—	—	—	—	—	2	—	—	2
RIX, MISS MARY ANNE ‡	London	1833-1835	Landscape	—	—	2	—	—	—	4	—	—	—	6
RIXON, MISS LAURA	London	1886	Fruit	—	—	—	—	1	—	—	—	—	1	2
RIXON, WILLIAM AUGUSTUS, R.B.A. §	Staines	1880-1891	Rustic	—	—	6	—	18	—	—	1	—	5	30
RIZAS, W. A.	London	1878-1889	Domestic	—	—	—	—	1	—	5	—	—	—	6
ROACH, A.	—	1830	Historical	—	—	1	—	—	—	—	—	—	—	1
ROBART, M.	Haverhill	1849	Figures	—	—	—	—	1	—	—	—	—	—	1
ROBART, V.	Paris	1851	Portraits	—	—	1	—	—	—	—	—	—	—	1
ROBB, G. M.	London	1860-1881	Landscape	—	—	14	2	12	—	—	—	—	5	33
ROBBINS, MISS ANNA	Thetford	1867	Still Life	—	—	—	—	1	—	—	—	—	—	1
ROBBINSON, MRS. MARGARET	London	1854-1870	Dramatic	—	—	13	—	6	—	—	—	—	—	19

Name.	Town.	First and Last Year of Ex.	Speciality.	S. A.	F. S.	R. A.	B. I.	S. S.	O.W.	N.W.	G. G.	N. G.	V. E.	Total.
ROBERT —	London	1849	Portraits	—	—	1	—	—	—	—	—	—	—	1
ROBERT, B.	London	1813	Landscape	—	—	1	—	—	—	—	—	—	—	1
ROBERT, MDLLE. CAROLINE	Sutton	1886	Landscape	—	—	1	—	—	—	—	—	—	—	1
ROBERT, W. VICTOR DU PUY	London	1848-1850	Figures	—	—	—	3	4	—	—	—	—	—	7
ROBERTON, ALFRED J.	London	1884-1886	Landscape	—	—	—	—	5	—	—	—	—	—	5
ROBERTS —	Dublin	1771-1777	Sporting	1	2	—	—	—	—	—	—	—	—	3
ROBERTS —	—	1836	Landscape	—	—	1	—	—	—	—	—	—	—	1
ROBERTS, A.	London	1793	Sporting	—	—	1	—	—	—	—	—	—	—	1
ROBERTS, A.	London	1854	Scriptural	—	—	1	—	—	—	—	—	—	—	1
ROBERTS, MISS ALICE	London	1777	Portraits	1	—	—	—	—	—	—	—	—	—	1
ROBERTS, ANNIE	London	1874-1881	Landscape	—	—	—	—	10	—	—	—	—	—	10
ROBERTS, BENJAMIN	Chislehurst	1847-1872	Fruit	—	—	9	24	29	—	—	—	—	—	62
ROBERTS, C.	—	1815	Architecture	—	—	—	—	—	—	—	—	—	1	1
ROBERTS, CHARLES	London	1868-1874	Engraving	—	—	—	—	—	—	—	—	—	2	2
ROBERTS, MRS. CHANDLER	London	1855-1885	Flowers	—	—	—	—	3	—	1	—	—	—	4
ROBERTS, C. F.	London	1780-1791	Domestic	1	9	—	—	—	—	—	—	—	—	10
ROBERTS, DAVID, R.A. §	London	1824-1864	Landscape	—	—	101	32	46	—	—	—	—	—	179
ROBERTS, E.	King's Walden	1812	Architecture	—	—	1	—	—	—	—	—	—	—	1
ROBERTS, EDWARD, F.S.A.	London	1852-1862	Architecture	—	—	4	—	—	—	—	—	—	—	4
ROBERTS, E.	London	1867	Landscape	—	—	—	—	1	—	—	—	—	—	1
ROBERTS, MRS. ETIENNE	Norwood	1892-1893	Flowers	—	—	—	—	1	—	—	—	—	1	2
ROBERTS, EDWIN	London	1862-1886	Domestic	—	—	3	—	46	—	—	—	—	1	50
ROBERTS, ELLIS	London	1886-1893	Miniatures	—	—	9	—	—	—	—	1	—	8	18
ROBERTS, ELSIE	Sheffield	1882	Flowers	—	—	—	—	—	—	—	—	—	1	1
ROBERTS, F. A.	London	1859-1866	Domestic	—	—	—	—	7	—	—	—	—	—	7
ROBERTS, F. M.	London	1878	Figures	—	—	—	—	—	—	—	—	—	1	1
ROBERTS, F. W. B.	Haverhill	1848-1870	Landscape	—	—	—	1	9	—	—	—	—	—	10
ROBERTS, GEORGE	Dublin	1775	Landscape	2	—	—	—	—	—	—	—	—	—	2
ROBERTS, G.	London	1843-1853	Buildings	—	—	4	—	—	—	—	—	—	—	4
ROBERTS, MISS G.	—	1813-1814	Still Life	—	—	2	—	—	—	—	—	—	—	2
ROBERTS, H.	London	1838-1843	Architecture	—	—	5	—	—	—	—	—	—	—	5
ROBERTS, HENRY BENJAMIN, R.I. ‡ §	London	1859-1880	Domestic	—	—	15	10	8	—	64	—	—	6	103
ROBERTS, HERBERT H.	Norwich	1869-1887	Domestic	—	—	3	—	—	—	—	—	—	—	3
ROBERTS, H. LARPENT	London	1863-1873	Landscape	—	—	6	3	5	—	—	—	—	—	14
ROBERTS, HENRY WILLIAM	Leicester	1885-1886	Landscape	—	—	—	—	—	—	2	—	—	—	2
ROBERTS, JAMES	London	1773-1799	Portraits	—	—	31	—	—	—	—	—	—	—	31
ROBERTS, JAMES	Leeds	1858-1876	Landscape	—	—	1	1	8	—	—	—	—	1	11
ROBERTS, JOHN	London	1774-1825	Miniatures	6	—	69	—	—	—	—	—	—	—	75
ROBERTS, J. A.	London	1813	Historical	—	—	—	—	—	1	—	—	—	—	1
ROBERTS, JOHN L.	London	1771-1825	Engraving	—	11	—	—	14	—	—	—	—	—	25
ROBERTS, J. L.	London	1828	Domestic	—	—	—	—	1	—	—	—	—	—	1
ROBERTS, LAVINIA	London	1864-1867	Rustic	—	—	—	—	4	—	—	—	—	—	4
ROBERTS, MISS LOUISA	London	1851-1869	Portraits	—	—	2	—	9	—	—	—	—	4	15
ROBERTS, MISS MARION	London	1885-1886	Churches	—	—	—	—	1	—	2	—	—	—	3
ROBERTS, PERCY	London	1878	Woodcut	—	—	—	—	—	—	—	—	—	1	1
ROBERTS, SIR R., BART.	—	1865	Sea Pieces	—	—	1	—	—	—	—	—	—	—	1
ROBERTS, ROBERT	London	1843	Landscape	—	—	1	—	—	—	—	—	—	—	1
ROBERTS, R. R.	Denmark Hill	1850-1857	Landscape	—	—	—	—	22	—	—	—	—	—	22
ROBERTS, R. S.	London	1812	Landscape	—	—	—	1	—	—	—	—	—	—	1
ROBERTS, SAMUEL	London	1778-1782	Still Life	—	—	4	—	—	—	—	—	—	—	4
ROBERTS, SAMUEL	London	1824	Landscape	—	—	—	1	—	—	—	—	—	—	1
ROBERTS, MISS S.	Haverhill	1851	Landscape	—	—	—	—	1	—	—	—	—	—	1
ROBERTS, THOMAS E., R.B.A. §	London	1850-1893	Domestic	—	—	12	—	127	—	—	—	—	5	144
ROBERTS, THOMAS SOTELLE, R.H.A.	London	1789-1818	Landscape	—	—	59	14	—	2	—	—	—	9	84
ROBERTS, W.	—	1828	Landscape	—	—	1	—	—	—	—	—	—	—	1
ROBERTS, W.	London	1877	Landscape	—	—	—	—	1	—	—	—	—	—	1
ROBERTS, WINIFRED RUSSELL	London	1893	Landscape	—	—	—	—	2	—	—	—	—	—	2
ROBERTS, W. T.	London	1872	Etching	—	—	—	—	—	—	—	—	—	3	3
ROBERTS, W. T. B, A.R.P.E.	Winchester	1880	Landscape	—	—	1	—	—	—	—	—	—	—	1
ROBERTS, MRS.	London	1851	Flowers	—	—	1	—	—	—	—	—	—	—	1
ROBERTS-CROMPTON, MISS MILDRED. *See* C.	—	—	—	—	—	—	—	—	—	—	—	—	—	—
ROBERTSON, CAPTAIN	—	1778	Landscape	—	—	5	—	—	—	—	—	—	—	5
ROBERTSON —	—	1836	Landscape	—	—	1	—	—	—	—	—	—	—	1
ROBERTSON, A.	London	1765-1796	Landscape	1	—	7	—	—	—	—	—	—	—	8
ROBERTSON, ANDREW, A.R.H.A.	London	1802-1842	Miniatures	—	—	292	4	1	37	—	—	—	21	355
ROBERTSON, MRS. ANNA	London	1783	Flowers	1	1	—	—	—	—	—	—	—	—	2
ROBERTSON, ARCHIBALD	—	1772-1775	Landscape	—	—	3	—	—	—	—	—	—	—	3
ROBERTSON, ARTHUR, A.R.P.E.	London	1876-1891	Domestic	—	—	8	—	21	—	9	—	—	1	39
ROBERTSON, ALFRED J.	London	1883	Landscape	—	—	—	—	1	—	—	—	—	—	1
ROBERTSON, CHARLES	Dublin	1790-1810	Miniatures	—	—	8	—	—	—	—	—	—	4	12
ROBERTSON, CHARLES, A.R.W.S., R.P.E. †	Aix en Provence	1863-1892	Figures	—	—	14	—	2	103	1	—	—	27	147
ROBERTSON, MISS CHRISTIANA	London	1822	Domestic	—	—	—	1	—	—	—	—	—	—	1

Name.	Town.	First and Last Year of Ex.	Speciality.	S. A.	F. S.	R. A.	B. I.	S. S.	O. W.	N. W.	G. G.	N. G.	V. E.	Total.
Robertson, Charles John	Gainsborough	1798-1830	Portraits	—	—	23	—	—	21	—	—	—	1	45
Robertson, D.	London	1812-1827	Architecture	—	—	7	—	—	—	—	—	—	—	7
Robertson, David M., A.R.S.A.	Douglas	1892	Domestic	—	—	1	—	—	—	—	—	—	—	1
Robertson, E.	London	1830-1837	Miniatures	—	—	11	—	—	—	—	—	—	—	11
Robertson, Eric J. Forbes	London	1885-1891	Landscape	—	—	2	—	5	—	—	1	—	—	8
Robertson, George, F.S.A.	London	1772-1790	Landscape	84	—	3	—	—	—	—	—	—	—	87
Robertson, George Edward	London	1883-1893	Domestic	—	—	10	—	3	—	—	—	—	3	16
Robertson, G. J.	London	1827-1836	Portraits	—	—	3	—	2	—	—	—	—	—	5
Robertson, Henry	Ipswich	1888-1892	Figures	—	—	2	—	—	—	—	—	—	—	2
Robertson, Henry Robert, R.P.E.	Slough	1861-1893	Domestic	—	—	47	1	17	—	8	1	—	29	103
Robertson, J.	London	1815-1836	Landscape	—	—	13	—	4	2	6	—	—	4	29
Robertson, J.	London	1833-1840	Medals	—	—	4	—	—	—	—	—	—	—	4
Robertson, John	Liverpool	1844-1867	Figures	—	—	13	4	—	—	—	—	—	—	17
Robertson, Mrs. James, late Miss Saunders	—	1823-1849	Miniatures	—	—	128	6	131	—	—	—	—	4	269
Robertson, Johnston Forbes-	London	1873-1892	Portraits	—	—	8	—	—	—	—	12	1	11	32
Robertson, J. R.	London	1866	Figures	—	—	1	—	—	—	—	—	—	—	1
Robertson, Kay	Edinburgh	1892	Figures	—	—	1	—	—	—	—	—	—	—	1
Robertson, L. Roy	London	1866	Figures	—	—	—	2	—	—	—	—	—	—	2
Robertson, Miss Margaret Forbes-	London	1892-1893	Miniatures	—	—	4	—	—	—	—	—	—	1	5
Robertson, Percy, A.R.P.E.	Godalming	1887-1893	Etching	—	—	4	—	—	—	1	—	—	—	5
Robertson, S.	London	1855-1856	Domestic	—	—	—	—	—	—	—	—	—	2	2
Robertson, T.	Derby	1799	Landscape	—	—	1	—	—	—	—	—	—	—	1
Robertson, Tom	Glasgow	1889-1892	Landscape	—	—	3	—	6	—	—	—	—	1	10
Robertson, Victor J.	London	1892	Illustrations	—	—	1	—	—	—	—	—	—	—	1
Robertson, W.	London	1797-1798	Architecture	—	—	3	—	—	—	—	—	—	—	3
Robertson, W.	London	1820-1823	Portraits	—	—	4	—	—	—	—	—	—	—	4
Robertson, William ‡	London	1829-1835	Sea Pieces	—	—	—	—	4	—	116	—	—	—	120
Robertson, Walford Graham-	London	1889-1893	Portraits	—	—	—	—	—	—	—	—	12	3	15
Robertson, W. S.	London	1851-1855	Rustic	—	—	5	—	—	—	—	—	—	—	5
Robertson, Miss	—	1809	Portraits	—	—	1	—	—	—	—	—	—	—	1
Robertson, Miss	London	1843	Miniatures	—	—	15	—	—	—	—	—	—	—	15
Robie, Jean Baptiste	Tulse Hill	1848-1875	Flowers	—	—	1	—	—	—	—	—	—	1	2
Robin, Madame Eline	London	1826-1829	Flowers	—	—	6	—	—	—	—	—	—	—	6
Robineau, A.	London	1785-1788	Portraits	—	—	7	—	—	—	—	—	—	—	7
Robinet, Paul	London	1883	Domestic	—	—	—	—	1	—	—	—	—	—	1
Robins, Mrs. A.	London	1879	Portraits	—	—	1	—	—	—	—	—	—	—	1
Robins, B.	London	1871	Domestic	—	—	—	—	1	—	—	—	—	—	1
Robins, Miss D. E.	Brighton	1856-1858	Figures	—	—	—	—	—	—	—	—	—	6	6
Robins, Edward C., F.S.A.	London	1854-1890	Architecture	—	—	11	—	—	—	—	—	—	—	11
Robins, G.	London	1827	Architecture	—	—	1	—	—	—	—	—	—	—	1
Robins, Miss Gertrude M.	London	1887	Figures	—	—	1	—	—	—	—	—	—	—	1
Robins, Miss Ida S.	London	1884-1886	Figures	—	—	5	—	—	—	—	—	—	—	5
Robins, J. E.	London	1861-1863	Portraits	—	—	3	—	—	—	—	—	—	—	3
Robins, Luke	—	1763	Flowers	1	—	—	—	—	—	—	—	—	—	1
Robins, Matthew	London	1858	—	—	—	—	—	—	—	—	—	—	*	—
Robins, Thomas Sewell ‡	London	1829-1879	Sea Pieces	—	—	7	39	21	—	317	—	—	28	412
Robinson. *See* Coe and Robinson	—	—	Architecture	—	—	—	—	—	—	—	—	—	—	—
Robinson, Miss A.	London	1871	Flowers	—	—	—	—	1	—	—	—	—	—	1
Robinson, Miss Annie Louisa. *See* Mrs. J. W. Swynnerton	Manchester	1879-1886	Portraits	—	—	8	—	—	—	—	6	—	—	14
Robinson, Archibald	—	1767	Landscape	1	—	—	—	—	—	—	—	—	—	1
Robinson, Arthur	London	1878-1879	Landscape	—	—	1	—	1	—	—	—	—	2	4
Robinson, Arthur P.	London	1890	Landscape	—	—	1	—	—	—	—	—	—	—	1
Robinson, C.	London	1869-1884	Heads	—	—	1	—	—	—	—	—	—	1	2
Robinson, Charles F., A.R.P.E.	London	1874-1890	Landscape	—	—	4	—	12	—	1	—	—	5	22
Robinson, Douglas F.	Paris	1890-1893	Landscape	—	—	2	—	1	—	—	—	—	1	4
Robinson, Edward	London	1826-1838	Landscape	—	—	1	8	6	—	—	—	—	—	15
Robinson, E.	London	1852	Architecture	—	—	1	—	—	—	—	—	—	—	1
Robinson, E.	London	1890	Landscape	—	—	1	—	—	—	—	—	—	—	1
Robinson, Miss Edith Brearey	Scarborough	1889-1893	Landscape	—	—	2	—	3	—	4	—	—	—	9
Robinson, Miss E. Julia	Dorking	1869-1893	Landscape	—	—	—	—	—	—	10	2	—	2	14
Robinson, Edward W.	London	1859-1876	Landscape	—	—	5	—	27	—	—	—	—	12	44
Robinson, F.	London	1819	Sea Pieces	—	—	1	—	—	—	—	—	—	—	1
Robinson, Frederic Caley, R.B.A. §	London	1877-1893	Figures	—	—	—	—	28	—	—	—	—	2	30
Robinson, G.	London	1827	Portraits	—	—	1	—	—	—	—	—	—	—	1
Robinson, Miss G.	Chichester	1879	Birds	—	—	1	—	—	—	—	—	—	1	2
Robinson, George Crosland	London	1882-1893	Figures	—	—	7	—	2	—	—	—	1	5	15
Robinson, G. J.	London	1825-1831	Architecture	—	—	7	—	—	—	—	—	—	—	7
Robinson, Gerald Philip, A.R.P.E.	London	1878-1893	Engraving	—	—	7	—	—	—	—	1	—	2	10
Robinson, George Thomas, F.S.A.	Wolverhampt'n	1850-1878	Architecture	—	—	8	—	—	—	—	—	—	—	8
Robinson, Hugh	London	1780-1782	Portraits	—	—	3	—	—	—	—	—	—	—	3
Robinson, H.	London	1819-1822	Flowers	—	—	3	—	—	—	—	—	—	—	3

Name.	Town.	First and Last Year of Ex.	Speciality.	S. A.	F. S.	R. A.	B. I.	S. S.	O. W.	N.W.	G. G.	N. G.	V. E.	Total.
ROBINSON, HENRY HAREWOOD	Finisterre	1884-1891	Domestic	—	—	9	—	7	—	—	1	—	4	21
ROBINSON, MRS. H. H. (M. D. WEBB)	St. Ives	1888-1893	Domestic	—	—	6	—	—	—	—	—	—	—	6
ROBINSON, H. P.	London	1852	Landscape	—	—	1	—	—	—	—	—	—	—	1
ROBINSON, H. WALTER	London	1889	Landscape	—	—	—	—	—	—	1	—	—	—	1
ROBINSON, J.	Newcastle	1845	Landscape	—	—	—	1	—	—	—	—	—	—	1
ROBINSON, JOHN	Norwood	1867-1880	Flowers	—	—	—	—	—	—	—	—	—	12	12
ROBINSON, JOHN	London	1848-1885	Architecture	—	—	10	—	—	—	—	—	—	—	10
ROBINSON, JOSEPH	London	1790-1816	Miniatures	2	—	25	—	—	—	—	—	—	—	27
ROBINSON, JOSEPH	Norwood	1862-1872	Fruit	—	—	3	2	2	—	—	—	—	—	7
ROBINSON, JOSEPH	London	1882-1883	Landscape	—	—	—	—	—	—	1	—	—	2	3
ROBINSON, J. CARLETON	Clifton, Yorks.	1865	Landscape	—	—	—	—	—	—	—	—	—	3	3
ROBINSON, SIR JOHN CHARLES, C.B., F.S.A., R.P.E.	Hanley	1847-1881	Landscape	—	—	8	—	—	—	—	2	—	2	12
ROBINSON, J. E. H.	London	1805-1841	Sea Pieces	—	—	46	12	11	—	—	—	—	—	69
ROBINSON, JOHN HENRY, R.A.	London	1824-1864	Engraving	—	—	5	—	6	—	—	—	—	—	11
ROBINSON, J. H.	Godalming	1875-1876	Landscape	—	—	—	—	2	—	—	—	—	1	3
ROBINSON, J. S.	London	1789	Portraits	—	—	1	—	—	—	—	—	—	—	1
ROBINSON, MATTHIAS	London	1856-1884	Domestic	—	—	3	10	37	—	—	—	—	8	58
ROBINSON, MRS. M. D. WEBB	London	1889-1891	Domestic	—	—	—	—	—	—	—	—	—	3	3
ROBINSON, MISS NELLIE	Scarborough	1889	Landscape	—	—	1	—	—	—	—	—	—	—	1
ROBINSON, PETER FREDERICK, F.S.A., F.G.S.	London	1795-1833	Architecture	—	—	67	—	—	—	—	—	—	—	67
ROBINSON, R.	London	1797-1802	Portraits	—	—	2	—	—	—	—	—	—	—	2
ROBINSON, SAMUEL	London	1775-1821	Architecture	—	—	15	—	—	—	—	—	—	—	15
ROBINSON, WILLIAM	London	1770	Architecture	—	1	—	—	—	—	—	—	—	—	1
ROBINSON, WILLIAM	Leeds	1822-1854	Portraits and Landscape	—	—	19	6	12	—	—	—	—	9	46
ROBINSON, WILLIAM	Manchester	1884-1889	Landscape	—	—	1	—	—	—	4	—	—	—	5
ROBINSON, W. A.	London	1842-1863	Rustic	—	—	14	1	10	—	—	—	—	—	25
ROBJOHNS, F.	Tavistock	1865	Landscape	—	—	—	—	—	—	—	—	—	1	1
ROBLES, J.	—	1871	Figures	—	—	1	—	—	—	—	—	—	—	1
ROBOTHAM, MISS FRANCES C.	London	1893	Figures	—	—	1	—	—	—	—	—	—	—	1
ROBSON. *See* Walton and Robson	—	—	Architecture	—	—	—	—	—	—	—	—	—	—	—
ROBSON, E. F.	—	1835	Landscape	—	—	—	—	1	—	—	—	—	—	1
ROBSON, EDWARD ROBERT, F.S.A. *See also* Flockton and Robson, *and* Stevenson and Robson	London	1873-1893	Architecture	—	—	18	—	—	—	—	—	7	—	25
ROBSON (E. R.) AND STEVENSON (S. J.)	London	1875	Architecture	—	—	1	—	—	—	—	—	—	—	1
ROBSON, MISS GERTRUDE	London	1893	Churches	—	—	—	—	3	—	—	—	—	—	3
ROBSON, GEORGE FENNEL †	Durham	1807-1833	Landscape	—	—	8	—	—	651	—	—	—	41	700
ROBSON, MISS HENRIETTA	New Brighton	1872-1881	Flowers	—	—	2	—	—	—	—	—	—	3	5
ROBSON, J.	London	1797-1833	Architecture	—	—	33	—	—	—	—	—	—	—	33
ROBSON, J.	London	1824	Portraits	—	—	—	—	1	—	—	—	—	—	1
ROBSON, MISS J. S.	Ripon	1873	Flowers	—	—	—	—	1	—	—	—	—	—	1
ROBSON, R.	—	1832-1834	Figures	—	—	—	2	2	—	—	—	—	—	4
ROBSON, THOMAS	London	1803-1844	Figures	—	—	21	4	2	—	—	—	—	—	27
ROBSON, W. F.	London	1876	Landscape	—	—	—	—	—	—	—	—	—	1	1
ROBY, J.	—	1838	Landscape	—	—	1	—	—	—	—	—	—	—	1
ROCCA, ANDREA	London	1771-1772	Crayons	—	—	4	—	—	—	—	—	—	—	4
ROCHARD, FRANCOIS T. ‡	London	1820-1857	Miniatures	—	—	148	—	22	—	70	—	—	—	240
ROCHARD, SIMON JAMES	London	1816-1845	Miniatures	—	—	191	13	21	—	5	—	—	—	230
ROCHDALE, A.	London	1888	Flowers	—	—	—	—	—	—	—	—	—	1	1
ROCHE, ALEXANDER, A.R.S.A.	Glasgow	1889-1892	Figures	—	—	2	—	—	—	—	3	—	—	5
ROCHE, MARK	St. Albans	1876-1887	Sculpture	—	—	12	—	—	—	—	—	—	—	12
ROCHE, SAMPSON TOWGOOD	London	1817	Portraits	—	—	2	—	—	—	—	—	—	—	2
ROCHE, THOMAS S.	London	1861-1869	Sea Pieces	—	—	—	—	8	—	—	—	—	—	8
ROCHE, WALTER	London	1878-1888	Sculpture	—	—	23	—	—	—	—	—	—	—	23
ROCHEFORT COUNTESS OF	—	1851	Portraits	—	—	1	—	—	—	—	—	—	—	1
ROCHUSSEN, C.	—	1880	Historical	—	—	—	—	—	—	—	2	—	—	2
ROCKSTRO, DE. *See* D.	—	—	—	—	—	—	—	—	—	—	—	—	—	—
ROCQUEPLANT, C.	Paris	1834	Landscape	—	—	1	—	—	—	—	—	—	—	1
RODD, J. R.	London	1833	Landscape	—	—	—	—	—	—	1	—	—	—	1
RODECK, CARL	Hamburg	1878-1881	Landscape	—	—	3	—	—	—	—	—	—	—	3
RODEN, W. T.	Birmingham	1856-1879	Scriptural	—	—	6	2	4	—	—	—	—	—	12
RODIN, AUGUSTE	Paris	1882-1884	Sculpture	—	—	2	—	—	—	—	1	—	1	4
RODGERS, JOSEPH	Newark	1889	Landscape	—	—	1	—	—	—	—	—	—	—	1
RODGERS, ROBERT	Wandsworth	1890	Sculpture	—	—	2	—	—	—	—	—	—	—	2
RODWELL, T.	London	1814-1816	Rustic	—	—	3	—	—	—	—	—	—	—	3
ROE, FRED.	London	1885-1893	Domestic	—	—	7	—	—	—	—	—	—	15	22
ROE, MISS HENRIETTA A.	—	1880	Figures	—	—	1	—	—	—	—	—	—	—	1
ROE, J.	—	1771-1790	Landscape	3	—	2	—	—	—	—	—	—	—	5
ROE, ROBERT ERNEST	Cambridge	1868-1875	Sea Pieces	—	—	—	—	4	—	—	—	—	—	4
ROE, ROBERT HENRY	Cambridge	1846-1868	Animals	—	—	10	11	16	—	—	—	—	—	37
ROE, RICHARD MAULEVERER	London	1880-1881	Landscape	—	—	—	—	3	—	—	—	—	—	3
ROE, WALTER HERBERT	London	1882-1893	Domestic	—	—	4	—	16	—	2	—	—	13	35

Name.	Town.	First and Last Year of Ex.	Speciality.	S. A.	F. S.	R. A.	B. I.	S. S.	O. W.	N.W.	G. G.	N. G.	V. E.	Total.
Roe, W. J.	London	1853	Landscape	—	—	—	1	—	—	—	—	—	—	1
Roe, Miss	London	1820	Domestic	—	—	—	—	—	1	—	—	—	—	1
Roegels, Franz	Barmen	1879	Portraits	—	—	1	—	—	—	—	—	—	—	1
Roëhn, A.	London	1844	Historical	—	—	—	1	—	—	—	—	—	—	1
Roehn, M.	London	1803	Figures	—	—	3	—	—	—	—	—	—	—	3
Roeloss, W.	—	1880	Rustic	—	—	—	—	—	—	—	3	—	—	3
Roffe, Alfred F.	London	1872-1883	Landscape	—	—	—	—	—	—	—	—	—	6	6
Roffe, Alfred T.	London	1822-1829	Figures	—	—	1	—	2	—	—	—	—	—	3
Roffe, William John. *See* D. McKay	London	1845-1889	Landscape	—	—	14	10	12	—	—	4	—	2	42
Rogatewier, B. A.	London	1853	Cattle	—	—	—	—	1	—	—	—	—	—	1
Rogers —	London	1765	Metal Work	—	1	—	—	—	—	—	—	—	—	1
Rogers, A.	London	1856-1860	Enamels	—	—	—	—	4	—	—	—	—	—	4
Rogers, Arthur Lee	Liverpool	1885-1888	Landscape	—	—	8	—	1	—	1	—	—	1	11
Rogers, B.	Stafford	1800-1803	Landscape	—	—	6	—	—	—	—	—	—	—	6
Rogers, Miss Evelyn E.	Kingston	1889-1893	Miniatures	—	—	4	—	1	—	1	—	—	—	6
Rogers, Miss E. F.	London	1859	Landscape	—	—	—	—	—	—	—	—	—	1	1
Rogers, Frederick	London	1870-1877	Architecture	—	—	3	—	—	—	—	—	—	—	3
Rogers, Frederick	London	1889-1890	Sculpture	—	—	2	—	—	—	—	—	—	—	2
Rogers, George	—	1761-1793	Landscape	2	—	2	—	—	—	—	—	—	—	4
Rogers, Miss Gina J.	London	1886-1888	Landscape	—	—	—	—	—	—	2	—	—	—	2
Rogers, H.	London	1835-1837	Portraits	—	—	2	—	—	—	—	—	—	—	2
Rogers, Henry P.	London	1829-1832	Domestic	—	—	—	2	—	—	—	—	—	—	2
Rogers, J.	London	1838-1864	Figures	—	—	3	1	6	—	—	—	—	—	10
Rogers, James Edward, A.R.H.A.	London	1876-1893	Landscape	—	—	4	—	—	—	20	—	—	26	50
Rogers, Mrs. Jane Masters	London	1850-1870	Portraits	—	—	16	1	2	—	—	—	—	—	19
Rogers, Miss Jane M.	London	1849-1861	Enamels	—	—	—	2	4	—	—	—	—	—	6
Rogers, Miss Kate	London	1884-1885	Flowers	—	—	—	—	1	—	1	—	—	—	2
Rogers, Miss M.	Acton	1876-1879	Flowers	—	—	2	—	2	—	—	—	—	—	4
Rogers, Mark	London	1880-1891	Sculpture	—	—	17	—	—	—	—	—	—	—	17
Rogers, M. J.	Thame	1872	Fruit	—	—	—	—	—	—	—	—	—	1	1
Rogers, Philip Hutchins	Plymouth	1808-1851	Landscape	—	—	24	47	14	—	3	—	—	3	91
Rogers, R.	—	1788	Landscape	—	—	1	—	—	—	—	—	—	—	1
Rogers, Thomas, F.S.A.	London	1766-1790	Architecture	13	—	3	—	—	—	—	—	—	—	16
Rogers, W.	London	1810	Architecture	—	—	1	—	—	—	—	—	—	—	1
Rogers, W. P.	London	1825-1867	Rustic	—	—	1	5	2	—	—	—	—	—	8
Roget, John Lewis	London	1867-1877	Landscape	—	—	—	—	—	—	—	—	—	30	30
Rogier, John M.	Hastings	1884-1891	Domestic	—	—	7	—	—	—	—	—	—	—	7
Rohden, T.	—	1854	Scriptural	—	—	1	—	—	—	—	—	—	—	1
Roho, Le. *See* L.	—	—		—	—	—	—	—	—	—	—	—	—	—
Rola —	London	1843	Miniatures	—	—	2	—	—	—	—	—	—	—	2
Roldan, Don José	Seville	1860	Figures	—	—	1	—	—	—	—	—	—	—	1
Rolfe, Alexander F.	London	1839-1871	Fish	—	—	—	6	52	—	—	—	—	40	98
Rolfe, Mrs. A. F.	London	1866	Sporting	—	—	—	—	1	—	—	—	—	—	1
Rolfe, Edmund	London	1830-1847	Still Life	—	—	1	6	5	—	—	—	—	—	12
Rolfe, F.	London	1849-1853	Fish	—	—	—	2	4	—	—	—	—	—	6
Rolfe, Henry Leonidas	London	1847-1881	Fish	—	—	16	23	92	—	—	—	—	40	171
Rolfe, Miss Julia L.	Maidstone	1875	Coast Scenes	—	—	—	—	1	—	—	—	—	1	2
Rolfe, W. E.	London	1802-1853	Architecture	—	—	33	—	5	—	—	—	—	1	39
Roll —	—	1893	Portraits	—	—	—	—	—	—	—	—	—	2	2
Rollaston, W. A.	Birmingham	1884-1887	Landscape	—	—	—	—	—	—	—	—	—	2	2
Rolle, E.	London	1830	Game	—	—	1	—	—	—	—	—	—	—	1
Roller, George R., R.P.E.	Basingstoke	1887-1892	Domestic	—	—	2	—	5	—	—	—	—	2	9
Roller, Mrs. Nettie Huxley	London	1891-1893	Domestic	—	—	—	—	—	—	—	—	2	—	2
Rolleston, Miss Lucy	London	1888	Domestic	—	—	—	—	—	—	—	—	—	1	1
Rollins, John Wenlock	London	1887-1893	Sculpture	—	—	7	—	—	—	—	—	1	—	8
Rolls, Charles	London	1855-1857	Fruit	—	—	—	4	—	—	—	—	—	—	4
Rolls, Miss Florence	Caterham	1888-1889	Domestic	—	—	1	—	1	—	—	—	—	—	2
Rolls, Miss F. A. Dudley-. *See* D.	—	—		—	—	—	—	—	—	—	—	—	—	—
Rolls, M. S.	—	1839	Historical	—	—	1	—	2	—	—	—	—	—	3
Rolph, J. A.	—	1820	Architecture	—	—	1	—	—	—	—	—	—	—	1
Rolshoven, J.	London	1892	Flowers	—	—	—	—	1	—	—	—	—	—	1
Rolt, Charles	Merton	1845-1867	Figures	—	—	19	9	33	—	—	—	—	—	61
Rolt, J.	London	1833	Flowers	—	—	2	—	—	—	—	—	—	—	2
Rolt, V., *or* B. C.	London	1893	Landscape	—	—	—	—	1	—	—	—	—	—	1
Roma, Spiridone	London	1774-1778	Portraits	—	—	4	—	—	—	—	—	—	—	4
Romaine-Walker and Tanner	London	1884-1891	Architecture	—	—	6	—	—	—	—	—	—	—	6
Romako, A.	London	1873	Figures	—	—	1	—	—	—	—	—	—	—	1
Romer, Mrs. *See* Mrs. J. M. Jopling, late Miss Louisa Goode	—	1870-1873	Figures	—	—	9	—	7	—	—	—	—	9	25
Romer, T.	London	1853	Sea Pieces	—	—	—	1	—	—	—	—	—	—	1
Romer, William	London	1855	Domestic	—	—	1	—	—	—	—	—	—	—	1
Romilly, Madame D'Ausse	London	1828-1837	Portraits	—	—	3	—	—	—	—	—	—	—	3

Name.	Town.	First and Last Year of Ex.	Speciality.	S. A.	F. S.	R. A.	B. I.	S. S.	O. W.	N. W.	G. G.	N. G.	V. E.	Total.
Romilly, G. T.	London	1852-1875	Landscape	—	—	1	—	10	—	—	—	—	1	12
Romilly, W.	London	1849	Landscape	—	—	2	—	—	—	—	—	—	—	2
Romney, George, F.S.A.	London	1763-1772	Portraits	10	15	—	—	—	—	—	—	—	—	25
Romney, John	London	1807-1846	Engraving	—	—	2	—	24	—	—	—	—	—	26
Ronca, J.	London	1865-1871	Sculpture	—	—	18	—	—	—	—	—	—	—	18
Rondel, H.	—	1893	Portraits	—	—	—	—	—	—	—	—	—	1	1
Rondi, E.	London	1853-1873	Portraits	—	—	11	—	—	—	—	—	—	—	11
Ronner, Mdlle. Henriette	Brussels	1891-1893	Domestic	—	—	1	—	—	—	2	—	—	2	5
Roods, Thomas	London	1833-1867	Rustic	—	—	20	21	18	—	—	—	—	6	65
Rooff, W. A.	London	1879	Flowers	—	—	—	—	1	—	—	—	—	—	1
Rook, O.	London	1867	Landscape	—	—	—	2	—	—	—	—	—	—	2
Rooke, Bernard	Sittingbourne	1879-1888	Domestic	—	—	4	—	1	—	—	—	—	—	5
Rooke, Thomas Matthews, A.R.W.S. †	London	1871-1893	Scriptural	—	—	25	—	—	48	3	12	15	5	108
Rooker, Edward	London	1760-1768	Buildings	11	—	—	—	—	—	—	—	—	—	11
Rooker, Edward, Junr.	—	1763-1768	Engraving	5	—	—	—	—	—	—	—	—	—	5
Rooker, Michael Angelo, A.R.A.	London	1767-1800	Buildings	1	—	98	—	—	—	—	—	—	—	99
Roole, Miss	—	1802	Buildings	—	—	1	—	—	—	—	—	—	—	1
Room, Henry	London	1826-1848	Portraits	—	—	15	9	15	—	—	—	—	—	39
Roonkin, J.	London	1792	Miniatures	—	—	1	—	—	—	—	—	—	—	1
Rope, Miss Ellen M.	London	1885-1893	Sculpture	—	—	18	—	—	—	—	—	1	—	19
Rope, G. T.	Wickham	1876-1885	Sporting	—	—	2	—	1	—	—	—	—	—	3
Roper. *See* Bell and Roper	—	—	Architecture	—	—	—	—	—	—	—	—	—	—	—
Roper, A. F.	London	1841-1846	Portraits	—	—	3	—	—	—	—	—	—	—	3
Roper, Cecil B.	Halifax	1888-1890	Architecture	—	—	5	—	—	—	—	—	—	—	5
Roper, D.	London	1797-1822	Architecture	—	—	8	—	—	—	—	—	—	—	8
Roper, Frederick William	London	1881	Architecture	—	—	1	—	—	—	—	—	—	—	1
Roper, G. F. *See* Smith and Roper	—	—	Architecture	—	—	—	—	—	—	—	—	—	—	—
Roper, J.	London	1815-1817	Architecture	—	—	2	—	—	—	—	—	—	—	2
Roper, Richard	London	1761-1765	Portraits	3	9	—	—	—	—	—	—	—	—	12
Roper, W.	London	1804	Architecture	—	—	1	—	—	—	—	—	—	—	1
Rorke, Miss E.	London	1874	Domestic	—	—	—	—	—	—	—	—	—	1	1
Rosa, Joseph	Dresden	1772	Cattle	2	—	—	—	—	—	—	—	—	—	2
Rosarius. *See* Miss R. Brett	Dublin	1858-1862	Flowers	—	—	3	—	—	—	—	—	—	—	3
Roscoe, S. G. W.	London	1874-1888	Landscape	—	—	3	—	27	—	10	—	—	4	44
Rose, G.	—	1807	Architecture	—	—	1	—	—	—	—	—	—	—	1
Rose, H.	London	1836	Architecture	—	—	1	—	—	—	—	—	—	—	1
Rose, Henry	London	1893	Architecture	—	—	2	—	—	—	—	—	—	—	2
Rose, Miss H. Ethel	Peckham	1877-1890	Figures	—	—	5	—	9	—	5	—	—	11	30
Rose, H. Randolph	London	1880-1893	Figures	—	—	3	—	11	—	13	1	2	15	45
Rose, Joseph	Rome	1770-1798	Sculpture	—	—	4	—	—	—	—	—	—	—	4
Rose, Mrs. Lily	London	1885-1886	Sculpture	—	—	2	—	—	—	—	—	—	—	2
Rose, Richard H.	London	1869-1889	Domestic	—	—	—	—	10	—	6	—	—	8	24
Rose, W.	London	1791-1799	Architecture	—	—	9	—	—	—	—	—	—	—	9
Rose, W.	—	1831	Domestic	—	—	1	—	—	—	—	—	—	—	1
Rose, William S.	Wargrave	1845-1875	Landscape	—	—	25	37	50	—	—	—	—	28	140
Rosen, Count George von	Sweden	1868-1869	Figures	—	—	3	—	—	—	—	—	—	—	3
Rosenberg, C.	London	1818	Flowers	—	—	2	—	—	—	—	—	—	—	2
Rosenberg, Charles, Junr.	London	1844-1848	Domestic	—	—	3	2	5	—	—	—	—	—	10
Rosenberg, Miss Ethel J.	London	1883-1893	Miniatures	—	—	21	—	—	—	—	—	—	5	26
Rosenberg, Mrs. F.	Leamington	1857	Portraits	—	—	1	—	—	—	—	—	—	—	1
Rosenberg, Miss Fanny. *See* Mrs. Harris	Bath	1845	Flowers	—	—	1	—	—	—	—	—	—	—	1
Rosenberg, George F. †	Bath	1846-1869	Landscape	—	—	1	—	—	230	—	—	—	—	231
Rosenberg, Miss H. B.	London	1836-1837	Flowers	—	—	1	—	1	—	—	—	—	—	2
Rosenberg, Miss Mary Ann. *See* Mrs. William Duffield	Bath	1848-1849	Flowers	—	—	—	—	4	—	—	—	—	—	4
Rosenberg, T.	London	1829-1844	Portraits	—	—	—	1	1	—	—	—	—	—	2
Rosenberg, William George Home	London	1871-1884	Miniatures	—	—	2	—	—	—	—	—	—	1	3
Rosenthal, S.	London	1865-1868	Portraits	—	—	2	—	—	—	—	—	—	—	2
Rosenthal, T. Edward	Munich	1881	Portraits	—	—	1	—	—	—	—	—	—	—	1
Rosher, Mrs. G. B.	London	1881-1893	Domestic	—	—	6	—	5	—	—	—	—	4	15
Roskell, Nicholas R.	London	1861-1872	Domestic	—	—	8	—	—	—	—	—	—	1	9
Ross, A.	—	1809	Landscape	—	—	1	—	—	—	—	—	—	—	1
Ross, A.	Inverness	1870	Architecture	—	—	1	—	—	—	—	—	—	—	1
Ross, A. H.	London	1884	Landscape	—	—	1	—	—	—	—	—	—	—	1
Ross, C. M.	—	1885	Portraits	—	—	—	—	—	—	—	1	—	—	1
Ross, Miss Christina P., R.S.W.	Edinburgh	1878-1890	Figures	—	—	1	—	3	—	5	—	—	—	9
Ross, F.	London	1828-1849	Engraving	—	—	—	—	2	—	—	—	—	—	2
Ross, G.	—	1807-1810	Landscape	—	—	3	—	—	—	—	—	—	—	3
Ross, H. (Father of Sir W. C. Ross, R.A.)	London	1814	Miniatures	—	—	1	—	—	—	—	—	—	—	1
Ross, H., Junr.	London	1815-1845	Miniatures	—	—	34	—	—	—	—	—	—	—	34
Ross, Henry	London	1854-1867	Sculpture	—	—	4	—	2	—	—	—	—	—	6
Ross, Henry	Accrington	1886	Architecture	—	—	1	—	—	—	—	—	—	—	1

Name.	Town.	First and Last Year of Ex.	Speciality.	S. A.	F. S.	R. A.	B. I.	S. S.	O. W.	N. W.	G. G.	N. G.	V. E.	Total.
Ross, Mrs. H. *See* Miss Maria Smith (Mother of Sir W. C. Ross, R.A.)	London	1808-1814	Portraits	—	—	3	—	—	—	—	—	—	—	3
Ross, James	Worcester	1791	Architecture	—	—	1	—	—	—	—	—	—	—	1
Ross, J.	London	1833	Landscape	—	—	1	—	—	—	—	—	—	—	1
Ross, J.	London	1878-1883	Study	—	—	1	—	1	—	—	—	—	—	2
Ross, Mrs. Jane	London	1880-1892	Landscape	—	—	1	—	5	—	—	—	—	—	6
Ross, Miss Janet	London	1817-1828	Portraits	—	—	9	—	10	—	—	—	—	—	19
Ross, J. Thorburn	Edinburgh	1885-1892	Landscape	—	—	4	—	—	—	1	—	—	—	5
Ross, Miss Madge	London	1891-1892	Portraits	—	—	2	—	—	—	—	—	—	—	2
Ross, Miss Magdalene. *See* Mrs. Edwin Dalton	—	1820-1841	Miniatures	—	—	33	—	2	—	—	—	—	—	35
Ross, Miss Maria	London	1833	Miniatures	—	—	1	—	—	—	—	—	—	—	1
Ross, Mary	Highbury	1840	Flowers	—	—	1	—	—	—	—	—	—	—	1
Ross, Robert Thorburn, R.S.A.	Edinburgh	1871-1879	Domestic	—	—	6	—	2	—	—	—	—	—	8
Ross, W.	—	1801	Landscape	—	—	1	—	—	—	—	—	—	—	1
Ross, William, Senr.	London	1809-1825	Historical	—	—	5	—	—	—	—	—	—	—	5
Ross, W.	London	1816-1854	Portraits	—	—	15	11	5	—	—	—	—	—	31
Ross, Sir William Charles, R.A.	London	1809-1859	Miniatures	—	—	304	5	—	—	—	—	—	—	309
Rosser, F.	London	1865	Sculpture	—	—	1	—	—	—	—	—	—	—	1
Rossetti, Dante Gabriel Charles	London	1849-1850	Scriptural	—	—	—	—	—	—	—	—	—	2	2
Rossetti, Mrs. W. M. *See* Miss Lucy Madox Brown.	—	—	—	—	—	—	—	—	—	—	—	—	—	—
Rossi, Alexander M.	Preston	1870-1893	Domestic	—	—	49	—	47	—	16	—	—	15	127
Rossi, Ellenor O.	London	1836	Landscape	—	—	1	—	—	—	—	—	—	—	1
Rossi, F. O.	London	1830-1848	Sculpture	—	—	3	—	2	—	—	—	—	—	5
Rossi, Henry §	London	1817-1847	Sculpture	—	—	12	5	21	—	—	—	—	—	38
Rossi, John Charles Felix, R.A.	London	1782-1834	Sculpture	—	—	73	11	11	—	—	—	—	—	95
Rossi, Mrs. S. A.	London	1874-1875	Domestic	—	—	—	—	2	—	—	—	—	1	3
Rossi-Scotti, Count Lemmi	Rome	1890	Figures	—	—	—	—	—	—	—	—	1	—	1
Rossiter, Miss A. M.	London	1845	Flowers	—	—	1	—	—	—	—	—	—	—	1
Rossiter, Charles	London	1852-1890	Figures	—	—	39	20	37	—	—	—	—	58	154
Rossiter, Mrs. Charles, late Miss Frances Fripp Seares	London	1862-1892	Domestic	—	—	12	3	10	—	5	—	—	18	48
Rossiter, Frances A.	London	1888	Birds	—	—	—	—	1	—	—	—	—	—	1
Rossiter, Henry	London	1885	Landscape	—	—	—	—	—	—	1	—	—	—	1
Rossiter, Miss Mary P. *See* Mrs. Harrison.	—	—	—	—	—	—	—	—	—	—	—	—	—	—
Rost, Adolph E. L.	London	1892-1893	Sculpture	—	—	2	—	—	—	—	—	—	—	2
Rotch, Arthur	London	1880	Florence	—	—	—	—	—	—	—	—	—	1	1
Rotch, B.	London	1820	Landscape	—	—	1	—	—	—	—	—	—	—	1
Roth, George, F.S.A.	London	1771-1815	Miniatures and Fish	8	3	5	—	—	—	—	—	—	5	21
Roth, Thomas	London	1803-1828	Enamels	—	—	43	1	3	—	—	—	—	—	47
Roth, William	London	1768-1777	Portraits	13	2	—	—	—	—	—	—	—	—	15
Rothschild, Baroness Nathaniel de	Paris	1879	Landscape	—	—	—	—	—	—	—	2	—	—	2
Rothwell, Richard, R.H.A.	London	1830-1863	Figures	—	—	72	28	1	—	—	—	—	1	102
Rothwell, Selim Botton	Manchester	1874-1881	Etching	—	—	4	—	—	—	—	—	—	7	11
Rothwell, S. R.	Manchester	1871	Buildings	—	—	1	—	—	—	—	—	—	—	1
Rothwell, T.	Torquay	1875-1877	Landscape	—	—	—	—	—	—	—	—	—	3	3
Rotowsky, L.	—	1806	Flowers	—	—	1	—	—	—	—	—	—	—	1
Rotta, Silvio G.	—	1881	Domestic	—	—	1	—	—	—	—	—	—	—	1
Rotting, H.	Düsseldorf	1857	Portraits	—	—	1	—	—	—	—	—	—	—	1
Roubiliac, Louis François	London	1760-1761	Sculpture	6	—	—	—	—	—	—	—	—	—	6
Rouch, A.	London	1818-1833	Sculpture	—	—	8	3	—	—	—	—	—	—	11
Roudebush, J. Heywood	—	1891	Sculpture	—	—	—	—	1	—	—	—	—	—	1
Rougeron, E.	London	1880	Figures	—	—	—	—	—	—	—	—	—	1	1
Roughton, Mrs. E. M.	London	1889-1893	Buildings	—	—	—	—	4	—	—	—	—	—	4
Roukin, J.	London	1785	Miniatures	—	—	3	—	—	—	—	—	—	—	3
Roullier, J.	London	1788	Landscape	—	—	1	—	—	—	—	—	—	—	1
Roumieu, Robert Lewis. *See also* Gough and Roumieu	London	1849-1854	Architecture	—	—	4	—	—	—	—	—	—	—	4
Round, Cecil M.	Blackheath	1884-1890	Landscape	—	—	7	—	4	—	—	1	2	3	17
Rous, Bart.	London	1869-1879	Domestic	—	—	1	—	1	—	—	—	—	1	3
Rous, Miss Elizabeth. *See* Mrs. Philip Phillips.	—	—	—	—	—	—	—	—	—	—	—	—	—	—
Rouse, C.	Birmingham	1877	Landscape	—	—	—	—	1	—	—	—	—	—	1
Rouse, F. B.	Peckham	1874-1884	Landscape	—	—	—	—	4	—	—	—	—	1	5
Rouse, Fred. J. C. V.	London	1888-1893	Landscape	—	—	8	—	6	—	—	—	—	—	14
Rouse, J.	London	1817	Architecture	—	—	1	—	—	—	—	—	—	—	1
Rouse, Robert William Arthur, R.B.A. §	London	1882-1893	Landscape	—	—	39	—	56	—	8	—	—	14	117
Rousseau, Theodore	—	1872	Etching	—	—	—	—	—	—	—	—	—	1	1
Roussel, Theodore, R.B.A. §	London	1886-1893	Portraits	—	—	—	—	6	—	—	1	—	2	9
Roussoff, Alexandre N.	Venice	1880-1888	Venice	—	—	5	—	—	—	1	—	—	4	10
Routh, Mrs. R. S. Arden	Linton	1870	Landscape	—	—	1	—	2	—	—	—	—	—	3
Routledge, Miss Emily	London	1870-1874	Figures	—	—	—	—	3	—	—	—	—	1	4
Rouvier, Madame. *See* Vignon.	—	—	—	—	—	—	—	—	—	—	—	—	—	—

Name.	Town.	First and Last Year of Ex.	Speciality.	S. A.	F. S.	R. A.	B. I.	S. S.	O. W.	N.W.	G. G.	N.G.	V. E.	Total.
ROUVIERE, M.	London	1785-1786	Architecture	—	—	2	—	—	—	—	—	—	—	2
ROUW, H.	London	1796-1821	Portraits	—	—	9	—	—	—	—	—	—	—	9
ROUW, PETER	London	1787-1840	Sculpture	—	—	146	—	—	28	—	—	—	—	174
ROUW, R.	—	1799	Sculpture	—	—	1	—	—	—	—	—	—	—	1
ROVERAY, DE. *See* D.	—	—	—	—	—	—	—	—	—	—	—	—	—	—
ROVRAY, DE. *See* D.	—	—	—	—	—	—	—	—	—	—	—	—	—	—
ROWAN, ALEXANDER	London	1852-1859	Scriptural	—	—	2	9	—	—	—	—	—	7	18
ROWAN, WILLIAM G.	Glasgow	1891-1892	Architecture	—	—	2	—	—	—	—	—	—	—	2
ROWAT, JAMES	Glasgow	1892	Architecture	—	—	1	—	—	—	—	—	—	—	1
ROWBOTHAM, CHARLES	London	1877-1888	Landscape	—	—	—	—	3	—	4	—	—	1	8
ROWBOTHAM, MISS E.	London	1852-1855	Portraits	—	—	—	—	5	—	—	—	—	—	5
ROWBOTHAM, T.	London	1834	Interiors	—	—	—	—	1	—	—	—	—	—	1
ROWBOTHAM, THOMAS LEESON ‡	London	1840-1875	Landscape	—	—	4	—	16	—	464	—	—	1	485
ROWDEN, MISS JESSIE	Oxford	1891	Landscape	—	—	—	—	—	—	1	—	—	—	1
ROWE, MISS A. M.	London	1855	Landscape	—	—	1	—	—	—	—	—	—	—	1
ROWE, E. ARTHUR	London	1885-1893	Domestic	—	—	17	—	21	—	11	—	6	3	58
ROWE, MISS EDITH D'OYLEY	London	1889-1892	Churches	—	—	—	—	2	—	3	—	—	—	5
ROWE, GEORGE	London	1872	Etching	—	—	—	—	—	—	—	—	—	2	2
ROWE, GEORGE JAMES	Woodbridge	1830-1862	Landscape	—	—	21	11	10	—	—	—	—	—	42
ROWE, H.	London	1799	—	—	—	*	—	—	—	—	—	—	—	—
ROWE, SUSAN	Tunb'dge Wells	1853	Miniatures	—	—	4	—	—	—	—	—	—	—	4
ROWE, SIDNEY GRANT	London	1877-1893	Landscape	—	—	9	—	30	—	2	—	—	17	58
ROWE, TRYTHALL TOM	London	1882-1893	Landscape	—	—	15	—	24	—	4	—	—	13	56
ROWE, THOMAS WILLIAM	South Shields	1862-1878	Sculpture	—	—	11	—	—	—	—	—	—	—	11
ROWE, WILLIAM J. MONKHOUSE	London	1882-1891	Domestic	—	—	3	—	—	—	—	—	—	—	3
ROWLAND, A. G.	London	1823	Architecture	—	—	1	—	—	—	—	—	—	—	1
ROWLANDSON, THOMAS	London	1775-1787	Caricatures	4	—	20	—	—	—	—	—	—	—	24
ROWLETT, G.	London	1847	Dramatic	—	—	—	1	—	—	—	—	—	—	1
ROWLEY, MISS A. M.	London	1872	Miniatures	—	—	1	—	—	—	—	—	—	—	1
ROWLEY, MISS ELIZABETH	Edmonton	1852-1859	Domestic	—	—	8	1	5	—	—	—	—	6	20
ROWLEY, E. S.	London	1859-1875	Landscape	—	—	9	3	13	—	—	—	—	—	25
ROWLEY, MRS. FRANCIS	London	1893	Portraits	—	—	—	—	—	—	—	—	1	—	1
ROWLEY, HON. H.	London	1866	Flowers	—	—	1	—	—	—	—	—	—	—	1
ROWLEY, H.	London	1861-1862	Scriptural	—	—	—	2	1	—	—	—	—	—	3
ROWLEY, WILLIAM	Bilston	1829	Ruins	—	—	—	1	—	—	—	—	—	—	1
ROWLSTONE, F.	London	1824-1841	Candlelight	—	—	1	7	20	—	—	—	—	—	28
ROWSE, SAMUEL W.	New York	1873	Portraits	—	—	1	—	—	—	—	—	—	—	1
ROWSELL, REV. T. NORMAN	Eltham	1889-1890	Landscape	—	—	—	—	—	—	2	—	—	—	2
ROWSTORNE, EDWIN	Southgate	1891	Domestic	—	—	1	—	—	—	—	—	—	—	1
ROXBY, C. W.	London	1875-1890	Still Life	—	—	—	—	19	—	—	—	—	2	21
ROY, EUGENE ARMAND	London	1848-1859	Sea Pieces	—	—	1	—	1	—	—	—	—	—	2
ROY, J. §	London	1826-1828	Churches	—	—	1	—	3	—	—	—	—	—	4
ROY, L.	London	1809	Landscape	—	—	2	—	—	—	—	—	—	—	2
ROYAL, H.R.H. PRINCESS, H.R.I. ‡	—	1880-1881	Figures	—	—	—	—	—	—	2	—	—	—	2
ROYAL, MISS ELIZABETH	London	1865-1871	Domestic	—	—	—	—	2	—	—	—	—	7	9
ROYAL, THOMAS	London	1770-1776	Sculpture	4	—	—	—	—	—	—	—	—	—	4
ROYBET, FERDINAND VICTOR LEON	London	1875-1892	Portraits	—	—	—	—	—	—	—	—	—	3	3
ROYER, PETER	London	1774-1778	Landscape	9	—	8	—	—	—	—	—	—	—	17
ROYLE, H.	Southport	1893	Landscape	—	—	—	—	—	—	—	—	—	1	1
ROYNON, J.	Norwich	1799	Architecture	—	—	1	—	—	—	—	—	—	—	1
ROYNON, R.	London	1800	Architecture	—	—	1	—	—	—	—	—	—	—	1
RUBBIGLIARD, VINCENZO	London	1776-1777	Portraits	—	—	3	—	—	—	—	—	—	—	3
RUBENS, FRANZ	London	1884-1885	Landscape	—	—	2	—	—	—	—	—	—	—	2
RUBENSTEIN —.	—	1760-1761	Game	5	—	—	—	—	—	—	—	—	—	5
RUBIDGE, J. W.	London	1823-1824	Portraits	—	—	3	—	1	—	—	—	—	—	4
RUBIO, G. G.	Geneva	1861	Figures	—	—	1	—	—	—	—	—	—	—	1
RUCK, T.	London	1809-1821	Architecture	—	—	8	—	—	—	—	—	—	—	8
RUCKLE, T. C.	London	1839-1840	Domestic	—	—	2	2	—	—	—	—	—	—	4
RUDD, MISS AGNES J.	Bournemouth	1888-1893	Landscape	—	—	5	—	1	—	1	—	—	—	7
RUDD, JOHN	London	1774	Architecture	—	—	1	—	—	—	—	—	—	—	1
RUDDLE, DANIEL	London	1875	Architecture	—	—	1	—	—	—	—	—	—	—	1
RUDDOCK, SAMUEL	London	1856-1892	Sculpture	—	—	37	—	—	—	—	—	—	—	37
RUDEAUX E.	London	1879-1881	Etching	—	—	—	—	—	—	—	—	—	4	4
RUDGE, BRADFORD	Bedford	1840-1883	Landscape	—	—	7	—	43	—	—	—	—	37	87
RUDGE, E.	Coventry	1820-1823	Landscape	—	—	3	—	—	—	—	—	—	—	3
RUDGE, MRS.	Witley	1872-1873	Domestic	—	—	—	—	1	—	—	—	—	1	2
RUDYERD, HENRY	—	1769-1773	Landscape	4	—	—	—	—	—	—	—	—	—	4
RUFF, GEORGE, SENR.	Brighton	1877-1886	Landscape	—	—	2	—	7	—	2	—	—	2	13
RUFF, GEORGE, JUNR.	London	1879-1880	Still Life	—	—	—	—	3	—	—	—	—	—	3
RUFFO, MADAME	London	1875-1876	Domestic	—	—	—	—	—	—	—	—	—	2	2
RUFFORD, MRS.	Blackheath	1881	Pen and Ink	—	—	—	—	—	—	—	—	—	2	2
RUGGLES, W. H.	Lewisham	1833-1846	Sporting	—	—	2	—	—	—	—	—	—	—	2

Name.	Town.	First and Last Year of Ex.	Speciality.	S. A.	F. S.	R. A.	B. I.	S. S.	O. W.	N.W.	G. G.	N. G.	V. E.	Total.
RUINART, JULES	Hastings	1871	Naples	—	—	—	—	—	—	—	—	—	1	1
RUITH, VAN. *See* V.	—	—		—	—	—	—	—	—	—	—	—	—	—
RUL, HENRY	Antwerp	1888-1890	Landscape	—	—	3	—	—	—	—	—	—	—	3
RUMBALL, T.	London	1871	Architecture	—	—	1	—	—	—	—	—	—	—	1
RUMBLE, FREDERICK	London	1850-1879	Churches	—	—	—	—	—	—	—	—	—	10	10
RUMBLE, T.	London	1831	Architecture	—	—	1	—	—	—	—	—	—	—	1
RUMLEY, MISS ELIZABETH. *See* Mrs. B. Dawson	London	1851-1858	Fruit	—	—	9	12	9	—	—	—	—	2	32
RUMPH, G.	London	1775	Sculpture	—	—	1	—	—	—	—	—	—	—	1
RUMPH, G. C.	London	1775-1781	Eastern	1	—	2	—	—	—	—	—	—	—	3
RUMSEY, E. *See also* Simmons and Rumsey	—	1848	Architecture	—	—	3	—	—	—	—	—	—	—	3
RUNCIMAN, ALEXANDER	London	1762-1782	Landscape	—	7	10	—	—	—	—	—	—	—	17
RUNCIMAN, CHARLES	London	1825-1867	Historical	—	—	16	25	16	—	3	—	—	14	74
RUNCIMAN, M.	London	1772	Mythological	—	—	1	—	—	—	—	—	—	—	1
RÜNTZ, ERNEST	London	1891-1893	Architecture	—	—	4	—	—	—	—	—	—	—	4
RUSHER, R. EATON	London	1886-1889	Chairs	—	—	—	—	1	—	—	—	—	1	2
RUSHTON, MISS KATE A.	London	1892	Flowers	—	—	—	—	1	—	—	—	—	—	1
RUSHFORTH, THOMAS HENRY	London	1849-1853	Architecture	—	—	2	—	—	—	—	—	—	—	2
RUSHTON, JOSIAH	Worcester	1875-1881	Landscape	—	—	1	—	10	—	—	—	—	—	11
RUSHWORTH, W.	London	1872-1874	Ruins	—	—	3	—	—	—	—	—	—	—	3
RUSKIN, JOHN, LL.D., D.C.L., H.R.W.S. †	Ambleside	1873-1884	Landscape	—	—	—	—	—	17	—	—	—	5	22
RUSSELL, MISS BERTHA A.	London	1888-1893	Domestic	—	—	2	—	—	—	—	—	—	1	3
RUSSELL, SIR B. F.	—	1848	Landscape	—	—	1	—	—	—	—	—	—	—	1
RUSSELL, C.	London	1811-1814	Landscape	—	—	2	—	—	—	—	—	—	1	3
RUSSELL, CHARLES, R.H.A.	Dublin	1889	Domestic	—	—	1	—	—	—	—	—	—	—	1
RUSSELL, C. J. W.	Ipswich	1848	Architecture	—	—	1	—	—	—	—	—	—	—	1
RUSSELL, E.	London	1878	Domestic	—	—	—	—	—	—	—	—	—	1	1
RUSSELL, MISS ELIZABETH M.	Guildford	1849-1850	Flowers	—	—	—	—	4	—	—	—	—	—	4
RUSSELL, EDWIN WENSLEY	London	1855-1878	Figures	—	—	11	3	16	—	—	—	—	19	49
RUSSELL, FREDERICK	Ipswich	1847	Architecture	—	—	1	—	—	—	—	—	—	—	1
RUSSELL, F. B.	London	1830-1833	Architecture	—	—	3	—	—	—	—	—	—	—	3
RUSSELL, G.	London	1810	Architecture	—	—	1	—	—	—	—	—	—	—	1
RUSSELL, H. A.	Woolwich	1851-1852	Figures	—	—	2	—	—	—	—	—	—	—	2
RUSSELL, H. H.	London	1829-1845	Architecture	—	—	2	—	—	—	—	—	—	—	2
RUSSELL, JAMES	Bath	1878-1887	Flowers	—	—	—	—	—	—	—	—	—	2	2
RUSSELL, JOHN, R.A.	London	1768-1806	Crayons	3	2	330	2	—	—	—	—	—	—	337
RUSSELL, MISS JULIANA	Surbiton	1865-1877	Domestic	—	—	—	—	—	—	—	—	—	15	15
RUSSELL, MISS JANET C.	Surbiton	1868-1893	Domestic	—	—	5	—	5	—	—	—	—	8	18
RUSSELL, J. J.	Dublin	1818-1823	Portraits	—	—	4	—	—	—	—	—	—	—	4
RUSSELL, J. W.	—	1870	Buildings	—	—	—	—	1	—	—	—	—	—	1
RUSSELL, NORMAN SCOTT	London	1869	Portraits	—	—	—	—	—	—	—	—	—	1	1
RUSSELL, S.	London	1840	Portraits	—	—	1	—	—	—	—	—	—	—	1
RUSSELL, S.	London	1874	Portraits	—	—	1	—	—	—	—	—	—	—	1
RUSSELL, SAMUEL B.	London	1889	Architecture	—	—	1	—	—	—	—	—	—	—	1
RUSSELL, THOMAS	Dorking	1830	Figures	—	—	1	—	—	—	—	—	—	—	1
RUSSELL, T. H.	London	1832	Figures	—	—	1	—	—	—	—	—	—	—	1
RUSSELL, W.	London	1834-1843	Landscape	—	—	2	—	11	—	—	—	—	—	13
RUSSELL, WALLACE	Glasgow	1889	Domestic	—	—	1	—	—	—	—	—	—	—	1
RUSSELL, WILLIAM	London	1805-1809	Portraits	—	—	8	3	—	—	—	—	—	—	11
RUSSELL, W. W.	—	1891	Portraits	—	—	—	—	—	—	—	—	—	3	3
RUSSELL, MISS	—	1805-1813	Figures	—	—	7	—	—	—	—	—	—	—	7
RUSSELL AND GIBSON	London	1892	Landscape	—	—	1	—	—	—	—	—	—	—	1
RUST, MISS BEATRICE AGNES	London	1883-1893	Portraits	—	—	10	—	5	—	3	—	—	1	19
RUSTON, GEORGE	London	1891	Landscape	—	—	—	—	—	—	1	—	—	—	1
RUTER, FRANZ	—	1886	Venice	—	—	—	—	—	—	—	1	—	—	1
RUTLAND, CHARLES 6TH DUKE OF	Belvoir Castle	1872	Landscape	—	—	1	—	—	—	—	—	—	—	1
RUTLEDGE, WILLIAM	Sunderland	1881-1892	Rustic	—	—	—	—	2	—	—	—	—	1	3
RUTLEY, T.	London	1823	Landscape	—	—	1	—	—	—	—	—	—	—	1
RUTSON, J.	Thirsk	1868-1875	Landscape	—	—	—	—	16	—	—	—	—	—	16
RUTTER, EDWARD	London	1877-1882	Buildings	—	—	—	—	3	—	—	—	—	5	8
RUTTY, J.	London	1839	Architecture	—	—	1	—	—	—	—	—	—	—	1
RYAL —	—	1777	Sculpture	1	—	—	—	—	—	—	—	—	—	1
RYALL, HENRY THOMAS	London	1846-1859	Engraving	—	—	2	—	1	—	—	—	—	—	3
RYAN, CLAUDE	London	1874-1883	Flowers	—	—	—	—	8	—	—	—	—	—	8
RYAN, CHARLES J.	Ventnor	1885-1891	Landscape	—	—	2	—	—	—	1	—	—	—	3
RYAN, F., *or* T. E.	Blackheath	1879	Venice	—	—	—	—	1	—	—	—	—	—	1
RYAN, H.	Kingstown	1869	Figures	—	—	1	—	—	—	—	—	—	—	1
RYAN, H. S.	London	1854	Figures	—	—	1	—	—	—	—	—	—	—	1
RYDER, MISS EMILY S.	London	1866-1874	Figures	—	—	—	2	8	—	—	—	—	2	12
RYDER, MISS HARRIET E.	Lee	1892-1893	Domestic	—	—	—	—	—	—	—	—	—	2	2
RYDER, MISS LETITIA	London	1771	Needlework	—	1	—	—	—	—	—	—	—	—	1
RYDER, THOMAS	London	1766-1767	Engraving	—	2	—	—	—	—	—	—	—	—	2
RYLAND, HENRY	London	1883-1893	Figures	—	—	5	—	—	—	18	3	9	3	38

Name.	Town.	First and Last Year of Ex.	Speciality.	S. A.	F. S.	R. A.	B. I.	S. S.	O. W.	N.W.	G. G.	N. G.	V. E.	Total.
Ryland, Joseph	London	1775-1787	Wax Models	2	—	1	—	—	—	—	—	—	—	3
Ryland, William	Sheffield	1884	Landscape	—	—	—	—	1	—	—	—	—	—	1
Ryland, William Wynne	London	1761-1775	Engraving	4	—	7	—	—	—	—	—	—	—	11
Ryle, Arthur J., R.B.A. §	London	1889-1893	Landscape	—	—	1	—	12	—	—	—	11	—	24
Ryley, Charles Reuben	London	1778-1798	Domestic	—	1	54	—	—	—	—	—	—	—	55
Ryley, E.	London	1833-1837	Sculpture	—	—	14	—	—	—	—	—	—	—	14
Ryley, J.	London	1854-1865	Fruit	—	—	1	4	3	—	—	—	—	—	8
Ryley, Jane	London	1857	Rustic	—	—	—	—	1	—	—	—	—	—	1
Rymer, Chadwick Francis	London	1843-1848	Cattle	—	—	2	—	3	—	—	—	—	—	5
Rymer, C. W.	London	1875	Domestic	—	—	—	—	—	—	—	—	—	1	1
Rymer, J. W.	Ealing	1854-1855	Sea Shores	—	—	—	2	—	—	—	—	—	—	2
Rymsdyk, A. V.	London	1769-1775	Portraits	9	—	3	—	—	—	—	—	—	—	12
Rymsdyk —, Junr.	London	1778	Enamels	—	—	2	—	—	—	—	—	—	—	2
Rynd, Miss Edith	Oxford	1892-1893	Churches	—	—	—	—	—	—	3	—	—	—	3
Rysbrack, John Michael	London	1763-1769	Sculpture	8	15	—	—	—	—	—	—	—	—	23
Ryves, Thomas	—	1762	Heads	1	—	—	—	—	—	—	—	—	—	1
Sacco, G.	London	1852-1857	Miniatures	—	—	10	—	—	—	—	—	—	—	10
Sache, F.	London	1869-1872	Landscape	—	—	1	—	1	—	—	—	—	—	2
Sacheverel-Coke, Alfred. *See* C.	—	—	—	—	—	—	—	—	—	—	—	—	—	—
Sachse, Edward J.	Norwood	1884-1893	Landscape	—	—	7	—	3	—	2	—	—	—	12
Sadd, H. S.	London	1832	Engraving	—	—	—	—	1	—	—	—	—	—	1
Saddler, John	London	1855-1883	Engraving	—	—	21	—	5	—	—	—	—	18	44
Sadée, Philip	London	1874-1880	Domestic	—	—	1	—	—	—	—	1	—	—	2
Sadler, George	London	1878-1883	Landscape	—	—	—	—	6	—	—	—	—	4	10
Sadler, Miss Kate	Horsham	1878-1893	Flowers	—	—	10	—	6	—	26	—	—	10	52
Sadler, Thomas	London	1878-1886	Flowers	—	—	1	—	3	—	—	—	—	4	8
Sadler, William	Barnes	1889	Heads	—	—	1	—	—	—	—	—	—	—	1
Sadler, Walter Dendy § φ	London	1872-1893	Domestic	—	—	35	—	24	—	—	2	—	26	87
Saffrey, Henry	London	1875	Etching	—	—	—	—	—	—	—	—	—	1	1
Sain, Edouard Alexandre	Paris	1874	Figures	—	—	1	—	—	—	—	—	—	—	1
Sainsbury, Everton	London	1877-1885	Domestic	—	—	15	—	8	—	—	1	—	8	32
Sainsbury, Miss Grace E.	London	1889-1893	Domestic	—	—	2	—	5	—	—	—	—	1	8
Sainsbury, Mrs. Maria Tuke	London	1889-1892	Flowers	—	—	1	—	2	—	2	—	—	—	5
Sainsbury, S. Fox	London	1888-1892	Domestic	—	—	—	—	3	—	—	—	—	—	3
St. Aubin, De	London	1795-1802	Miniatures	—	—	7	—	—	—	—	—	—	—	7
St. Aubyn, James Piers	London	1850-1886	Architecture	—	—	3	—	—	—	—	—	—	—	3
St. Clair, A.	London	1873	Domestic	—	—	—	—	1	—	—	—	—	—	1
St. Dalmas, De. *See* D.	—	—	—	—	—	—	—	—	—	—	—	—	—	—
St. Evre, G.	Paris	1828-1829	Historical	—	—	5	—	—	—	—	—	—	—	5
Saint-Francois, L.	—	1876	Military	—	—	—	—	—	—	—	—	—	5	5
St. Gaudens, A.	—	1880	Sculpture	—	—	—	—	—	—	—	3	—	—	3
St. George, J.	London	1843-1847	Landscape	—	—	2	2	3	—	—	—	—	—	7
St. Hill, H.	—	1834	Architecture	—	—	1	—	—	—	—	—	—	—	1
St. Jean, Simon	Lyons	1848-1860	Flowers	—	—	2	2	—	—	—	—	—	—	4
St. John, Georgina	Torquay	1873	Sea Pieces	—	—	—	—	1	—	—	—	—	—	1
St. John, R.	Oxford	1855-1856	Landscape	—	—	—	—	3	—	—	—	—	—	3
St. Martin, Yves Grenier de	London	1858	Figures	—	—	—	1	—	—	—	—	—	—	1
St. Maur, John	London	1880	Domestic	—	—	—	—	—	—	—	—	—	1	1
St. Michel, Chevalier de	London	1785	Portraits	—	—	6	—	—	—	—	—	—	—	6
Sainton, Charles P.	London	1886-1888	Landscape	—	—	5	—	—	—	—	3	—	1	9
St. Pierre, Gaston	Paris	1885	Figures	—	—	1	—	—	—	—	—	—	—	1
Salabert, F.	London	1836-1845	Portraits	—	—	16	—	—	—	—	—	—	—	16
Salaman, Miss Isabella J.	London	1889	Portraits	—	—	1	—	—	—	—	—	—	—	1
Salaman, Miss Julia. *See* Mrs. L. Goodman	—	—	—	—	—	—	—	—	—	—	—	—	—	—
Salaman, Miss Kate	London	1834-1856	Miniatures	—	—	18	2	3	—	—	—	—	—	23
Salanson, Miss Eugenie	London	1892	Figures	—	—	1	—	—	—	—	—	—	—	1
Salisbury, J.	Westbury	1783-1784	Portraits	—	1	1	—	—	—	—	—	—	—	2
Sallitt, Miss Lily	Ickley	1891	Flowers	—	—	1	—	—	—	—	—	—	—	1
Salmon, E.	London	1866	Sculpture, etc.	—	—	—	—	3	—	—	—	—	—	3
Salmon, Miss H.	London	1827-1828	Historical	—	—	—	—	2	—	—	—	—	—	2
Salmon, Miss Helen R.	Glasgow	1884-1890	Flowers	—	—	6	—	—	—	—	—	—	—	6
Salmon, J.	London	1868	Sea Pieces	—	—	—	—	—	—	—	—	—	1	1
Salmon (J.) and Son	Glasgow	1880	Architecture	—	—	1	—	—	—	—	—	—	—	1
Salmon, John Cuthbert, R.C.A.	Liverpool	1878-1892	Landscape	—	—	11	—	—	—	1	—	—	2	14
Salmon, J. E.	London	1865-1876	Landscape	—	—	—	6	9	—	—	—	—	—	15
Salmon, J. F.	London	1838-1873	Landscape	—	—	2	1	7	—	—	—	—	—	10
Salmon, W. R. D.	Glamorgan	1851-1857	Cattle	—	—	5	—	4	—	—	—	—	—	9
Salomans, F., F.S.B.A.	—	1880	Venice	—	—	—	—	—	—	—	1	—	—	1

Name.	Town.	First and Last Year of Ex.	Speciality.	S. A.	F. S.	R. A.	B. I.	S. S.	O. W.	N. W.	G. G.	N. G.	V. E.	Total.
Salomans, M.	London	1871	Rome	—	—	—	—	—	—	—	—	—	1	1
Salome, De. *See* D.	—	—	—	—	—	—	—	—	—	—	—	—	—	—
Salomon, Adam	Paris	1880	Sculpture	—	—	1	—	—	—	—	—	—	—	1
Salomon, R.	London	1802-1827	Sea Pieces	—	—	1	2	—	—	—	—	—	—	3
Salomons, Edward	London	1874-1893	Churches	—	—	4	—	—	—	—	6	13	—	23
Salomons (Edward) and Ely (John)	Manchester	1881-1886	Architecture	—	—	2	—	—	—	—	—	—	—	2
Salomons, Miss J. R.	London	1867	Flowers	—	—	1	2	—	—	—	—	—	—	3
Salomons and Jones	London	1870-1871	Architecture	—	—	3	—	—	—	—	—	—	—	3
Salomons and Wornum	London	1878-1886	Architecture	—	—	6	—	—	—	—	—	—	—	6
Salsbury, Robert	London	1878-1890	Landscape	—	—	1	—	9	—	—	—	—	9	19
Salt, S. A.	London	1879	Landscape	—	—	—	—	1	—	—	—	—	—	1
Salter, Miss Anne G.	Leamington	1869-1885	Still Life	—	—	—	—	2	—	—	—	—	11	13
Salter, J.	Torquay	1848-1875	Landscape	—	—	2	—	21	—	—	—	—	—	23
Salter, P.	Edinburgh	1849	Sculpture	—	—	1	—	—	—	—	—	—	—	1
Salter, P. King-. *See* K.	—	—	—	—	—	—	—	—	—	—	—	—	—	—
Salter, S. *See also* Spurr and Salter	London	1845	Architecture	—	—	1	—	—	—	—	—	—	—	1
Salter, Stephen, Junr.	London	1872	Architecture	—	—	1	—	—	—	—	—	—	—	1
Salter, William, M.A.F. §	Honiton	1822-1875	Mythological	—	—	6	28	101	—	—	—	—	—	135
Salter, William Philip	London	1847-1851	Figures	—	—	4	1	1	—	—	—	—	3	9
Salter, Mrs. M. F.	London	1842-1857	Figures	—	—	3	2	1	—	—	—	—	—	6
Salter, Mrs.	London	1879	Flowers	—	—	—	—	1	—	—	—	—	—	1
Salter and Adams	London	1893	Architecture	—	—	1	—	—	—	—	—	—	—	1
Salter and Laforest	London	1855	Architecture	—	—	1	—	—	—	—	—	—	—	1
Salter and Perrow	London	1862	Sculpture	—	—	1	—	—	—	—	—	—	—	1
Saltfleet, Frank	Sheffield	1892	Landscape	—	—	—	—	—	—	1	—	—	—	1
Saltmer, Miss Florence A.	Redhill	1882-1893	Landscape	—	—	11	—	2	—	1	2	—	10	26
Salvenda —	—	1778	Landscape	—	2	—	—	—	—	—	—	—	—	2
Salviati, Dr. A.	Venice	1865	Enamels	—	—	1	—	—	—	—	—	—	—	1
Salvin, Anthony, F.S.A.	London	1823-1838	Architecture	—	—	8	—	—	—	—	—	—	—	8
Salvin, Miss	Haslemere	1869	Landscape	—	—	1	—	—	—	—	—	—	—	1
Salway, J.	London	1785-1789	Architecture	—	—	3	—	—	—	—	—	—	—	3
Sambourne, E. Linley	London	1875-1892	"Punch"	—	—	19	—	—	—	—	—	—	24	43
Sambourne, Miss	—	1831	Drawing	—	—	—	—	1	—	—	—	—	—	1
Sammons, J. E.	Wisbeach	1843	Landscape	—	—	1	1	1	—	—	—	—	—	3
Sampson, Herbert	London	1879	Still Life	—	—	—	—	2	—	—	—	—	—	2
Sampson, James Henry	London	1869-1879	Sea Pieces	—	—	12	—	21	—	—	—	—	11	44
Sampson, L.	London	1889-1890	Landscape	—	—	—	—	—	—	—	—	—	2	2
Sampson, Robert W.	London	1889	Architecture	—	—	1	—	—	—	—	—	—	—	1
Sampson, Thomas	London	1838-1856	Historical	—	—	13	1	4	—	—	—	—	4	22
Samson —	—	1783	Drawing	—	1	—	—	—	—	—	—	—	—	1
Samson, Miss E. Alice	Upwey	1876-1877	Etching	—	—	—	—	—	—	—	—	—	2	2
Samuel, George	London	1785-1823	Landscape	—	—	94	54	—	—	—	—	—	—	148
Samuel, Richard	London	1768-1785	Historical	5	—	16	—	—	—	—	—	—	—	21
Samwell, Mrs. *See* Miss Augusta Cole	London	1864-1869	Miniatures	—	—	7	—	—	—	—	—	—	—	7
Samworth, Miss Joanna	Hastings	1867-1881	Pen and Ink	—	—	8	—	—	—	—	—	—	24	32
Sanchez-Perrier, E.	London	1880	Figures	—	—	1	—	—	—	—	—	—	—	1
Sancroft, D. A.	London	1869	Sea Pieces	—	—	—	—	2	—	—	—	—	—	2
Sandby, Paul, R.A.	London	1760-1809	Landscape	39	2	125	14	—	—	—	—	—	—	180
Sandby, Thomas, R.A.	Windsor	1767-1782	Architecture	2	—	9	—	—	—	—	—	—	—	11
Sandby, Thomas Paul	London	1791-1811	Landscape	—	—	3	1	—	—	—	—	—	—	4
Sandeman, Mrs. B. (Mary)	London	1884-1886	Domestic	—	—	3	—	—	—	—	—	—	—	3
Sandercock, Henry Ardmore	Moulsey	1867-1883	Landscape	—	—	9	—	7	—	1	—	—	8	25
Sanders —	London	1773-1780	Engraving	14	—	—	—	—	—	—	—	—	—	14
Sanders, Arthur N.	Lewisham	1865-1871	Engraving	—	—	3	—	—	—	—	—	—	—	3
Sanders, A. T.	Bath	1825	Landscape	—	—	—	—	1	—	—	—	—	—	1
Sanders, Miss Ellen	London	1866-1868	Domestic	—	—	1	2	—	—	—	—	—	—	3
Sanders, George	London	1844-1866	Engraving	—	—	7	—	—	—	—	—	—	—	7
Sanders, G. S.	London	1834-1835	Landscape	—	—	1	—	2	—	—	—	—	—	3
Sanders, H.	London	1812-1855	Landscape	—	—	—	1	1	—	—	—	—	—	2
Sanders, John	London	1771-1824	Scriptural	8	4	48	—	—	—	—	—	—	—	60
Sanders, John	London	1787-1828	Architecture	—	—	16	—	—	—	—	—	—	—	16
Sanders, J. A.	London	1810-1827	Landscape	—	—	10	9	1	—	—	—	—	—	20
Sanders, R., Junr.	London	1790	—	—	—	*	—	—	—	—	—	—	—	—
Sanders, T. H.	Worcester	1855-1862	Historical	—	—	2	4	—	—	—	—	—	4	10
Sanders, T. Hale-	Balham	1874-1892	River Scenes	—	—	8	—	9	—	2	—	—	—	19
Sanders, W.	London	1826-1838	Still Life	—	—	—	—	23	—	9	—	—	—	32
Sanders, William Bliss	Nottingham	1875	Architecture	—	—	1	—	—	—	—	—	—	—	1
Sanders, Walter G.	London	1882-1892	Flowers	—	—	13	—	6	—	—	—	—	3	22
Sanders, Mrs.	—	1838	Scriptural	—	—	1	—	—	—	—	—	—	—	1
Sanderson —	—	1770	Miniatures	1	—	—	—	—	—	—	—	—	—	1
Sanderson, John	London	1817-1828	Architecture	—	—	7	—	—	—	—	—	—	—	7
Sanderson, John	Lincoln	1890	Landscape	—	—	—	—	1	—	—	—	—	—	1

Name.	Town.	First and Last Year of Ex.	Speciality.	S. A.	F. S.	R. A.	B. I.	S. S.	O.W.	N.W.	G. G.	N.G.	V. E.	Total.
Sanderson, Julia J.	London	1881-1882	Domestic	—	—	—	—	4	—	—	—	—	—	4
Sanderson, J. W.	London	1790-1816	Architecture	—	—	14	—	—	—	—	—	—	—	14
Sanderson, Miss S. M.	London	1891	Landscape	—	—	1	—	—	—	—	—	—	—	1
Sandoz, A.	Paris	1879	Figures	—	—	—	—	—	—	—	—	—	1	1
Sands, A.	Norwich	1859	Domestic	—	—	—	1	—	—	—	—	—	—	1
Sands, D.	London	1765	Scriptural	—	1	—	—	—	—	—	—	—	—	1
Sands, J. *See also* Winterbottom and Sands	London	1813-1820	Architecture	—	—	4	—	—	—	—	—	—	—	4
Sandys, Miss E.	Norwich	1868-1874	Portraits	—	—	5	—	—	—	—	—	—	—	5
Sandys, F.	Bury St. Edm'ds	1797-1809	Architecture	—	—	15	—	—	—	—	—	—	—	15
Sandys, Frederick K.	Norwich	1851-1886	Portraits	—	—	47	2	—	—	—	9	—	1	59
Sandys, S.	—	1835-1839	Landscape	—	—	3	—	—	—	—	—	—	—	3
Sanford, Miss S. Ellen	London	1887-1892	Domestic	—	—	—	—	—	—	5	—	—	—	5
Sang, Frederick	London	1846-1884	Architecture	—	—	15	—	—	—	—	—	—	—	15
Sang, Frederick J.	London	1877-1893	Landscape	—	—	4	—	5	—	—	—	—	9	18
Sanger, John, F.S.A.	London	1763-1773	Landscape	8	—	—	—	—	—	—	—	—	—	8
Sangiovanni, Benedetto	London	1830-1848	Sculpture	—	—	12	10	30	—	—	—	—	—	52
Sanguinetti, Edgarde	Florence	1880-1889	Figures	—	—	2	—	5	—	2	1	—	1	11
Sani, A.	—	1873	Domestic	—	—	—	—	1	—	—	—	—	—	1
Sansom, A.	London	1876	Wood Engraving	—	—	—	—	—	—	—	—	—	1	1
Sansom, L. Charles	London	1870-1871	Figures	—	—	—	—	3	—	—	—	—	—	3
Sant, George §	London	1856-1877	Landscape	—	—	28	12	7	—	—	—	—	5	52
Sant, H. R.	London	1891	River Scenes	—	—	—	—	—	—	—	—	—	1	1
Sant, James, R.A.	London	1840-1893	Portraits	—	—	247	22	2	—	—	4	—	7	282
Santer, W. S.	London	1845-1849	Sea Pieces	—	—	—	—	4	—	—	—	—	—	4
Santler, G.	London	1810	Architecture	—	—	1	—	—	—	—	—	—	—	1
Santler, R.	London	1785-1787	Wax	—	—	8	—	—	—	—	—	—	—	8
Santler, W.	Surrey	1815	Architecture	—	—	1	—	—	—	—	—	—	—	1
Santley, Edith	London	1879	Sketch	—	—	—	—	1	—	—	—	—	—	1
Santoro, R.	Rome	1876	Landscape	—	—	—	—	—	—	—	—	—	2	2
Saquez, A. G.	London	1832-1836	Historical	—	—	3	—	3	—	—	—	—	—	6
Sargeant, John	London	1824-1839	Rustic	—	—	6	5	9	—	2	—	—	—	22
Sargeant, Alfred	London	1874	Wood Engraving	—	—	—	—	—	—	—	—	—	1	1
Sargent, Frederick	London	1854-1874	Portraits	—	—	10	—	—	—	—	—	—	—	10
Sargent, H.	London	1795-1797	Portraits	—	—	2	—	—	—	—	—	—	—	2
Sargent, H. Garton	London	1889-1890	Landscape	—	—	2	—	—	—	—	—	—	—	2
Sargent, John Singer	Paris	1882-1893	Portraits	—	—	19	—	—	—	—	6	7	—	32
Sargent, Mrs. W. K.	London	1855	Miniatures	—	—	1	—	—	—	—	—	—	—	1
Sarjeant, G. R.	London	1811-1849	Churches	—	—	16	4	2	—	2	—	—	5	29
Sarjent, C. S.	London	1812	Landscape	—	—	1	—	—	—	—	—	—	—	1
Sarjent, Emily	London	1845-1864	Scriptural	—	—	9	—	7	—	—	—	—	—	16
Sarjent, F. J.	London	1802-1803	Landscape	—	—	2	—	—	—	—	—	—	—	2
Sarney —	London	1766-1767	Miniatures	—	2	—	—	—	—	—	—	—	—	2
Sartain, T.	—	1830	Portraits	—	—	—	—	1	—	—	—	—	—	1
Sartain, William	Paris	1876-1877	Algiers	—	—	—	—	—	—	—	—	—	2	2
Sarto, Del. *See* D.	—	—	—	—	—	—	—	—	—	—	—	—	—	—
Sartoris, E. J.	London	1879	Portraits	—	—	—	—	—	—	—	1	—	—	1
Sartorius, C. J.	London	1810-1821	Sea Pieces	—	—	6	—	—	—	—	—	—	—	6
Sartorius, Francis	London	1773-1791	Sporting	7	20	12	—	—	—	—	—	—	—	39
Sartorius, F.	London	1799-1808	Sea Pieces	—	—	12	—	—	—	—	—	—	—	12
Sartorius, G. W.	London	1773-1779	Cattle	—	9	—	—	—	—	—	—	—	—	9
Sartorius, John	London	1768-1777	Sporting	1	62	—	—	—	—	—	—	—	—	63
Sartorius, J. F.	London	1793-1831	Sporting	—	—	20	—	4	—	—	—	—	—	24
Sartorius, John N.	London	1778-1824	Sporting	1	31	78	—	—	—	—	—	—	—	110
Sartorius, Miss M.	London	1813	Still Life	—	—	—	1	—	—	—	—	—	—	1
Sass, Miss E.	London	1798-1808	Flowers	—	—	13	—	—	—	—	—	—	—	13
Sass, Henry	London	1807-1839	Mythological	—	—	84	8	3	—	—	—	—	—	95
Sass, Miss Henrietta	London	1797-1813	Landscape	—	—	15	6	—	—	—	—	—	—	21
Sass, H. W.	London	1852	Architecture	—	—	1	—	—	—	—	—	—	—	1
Sass, Richard	London	1791-1813	Landscape	—	—	77	38	—	—	—	—	—	16	131
Sass, Mrs. R.	—	1798-1812	Flowers	—	—	6	—	—	—	—	—	—	—	6
Sass, Miss	—	1805	Flowers	—	—	1	—	—	—	—	—	—	—	1
Sassoon, Alfred	London	1890	Domestic	—	—	—	—	—	—	—	—	—	1	1
Sassoon, Mrs. A. (Theresa)	Brenchley	1889	Domestic	—	—	1	—	—	—	—	—	—	—	1
Satchell, Theodore	Putney	1883-1890	Sea Shores	—	—	2	—	5	—	2	—	—	1	10
Satchwell, R. W.	London	1793-1818	Miniatures	—	—	71	—	—	—	—	—	—	—	71
Satt, W.	Brighton	1835	Coast Scenes	—	—	—	—	1	—	—	—	—	—	1
Satterlee, Walter	London	1892	Flowers	—	—	1	—	—	—	—	—	—	—	1
Satterley, J. T.	Sevenoaks	1848	Still Life	—	—	2	—	—	—	—	—	—	—	2
Satur, De. *See* D.	—	—	—	—	—	—	—	—	—	—	—	—	—	—
Sauber, Robert, R.B.A. §	London	1888-1893	Domestic	—	—	5	—	12	—	1	—	—	10	28
Saubergue, John	London	1827-1830	Portraits	—	—	1	1	2	—	—	—	—	—	4
Sauerweide, Alexander	London	1815-1816	Historical	—	—	1	3	—	1	—	—	—	—	5

Name.	Town.	First and Last Year of Ex.	Speciality.	S. A.	F. S.	R. A.	B. I.	S. S.	O. W.	N. W.	G. G.	N. G.	V. E.	Total.
Saul, G. H.	Florence	1876-1887	Sculpture	—	—	4	—	—	—	—	1	—	—	5
Saul, George P. D.	London	1891	Metal Work	—	—	1	—	—	—	—	—	—	—	1
Saul and North	London	1890	Metal Work	—	—	1	—	—	—	—	—	—	—	1
Saule, P. Graves	Plymouth	1872	Landscape	—	—	—	—	—	—	—	—	—	2	2
Saulson, Madame	London	1873	Figures	—	—	—	—	1	—	—	—	—	—	1
Saunders. *See* Francis and Saunders *and* Gotch	—	—	—	—	—	—	—	—	—	—	—	—	—	—
and Saunders	—	—	Architecture	—	—	—	—	—	—	—	—	—	—	—
Saunders, Alick Boyd	London	1887-1893	Sculpture	—	—	3	—	—	—	—	—	3	—	6
Saunders, Charles L.	Conway	1881-1885	Landscape	—	—	6	—	—	—	—	—	—	—	6
Saunders, George, F.R.S.	London	1781-1789	Architecture	—	—	3	—	—	—	—	—	—	—	3
Saunders, G.	London	1846	Illustrations	—	—	1	—	—	—	—	—	—	—	1
Saunders, George L.	London	1829-1853	Miniatures	—	—	30	—	11	—	—	—	—	—	41
Saunders, Henry	London	1881	Sculpture	—	—	—	—	1	—	—	—	—	1	2
Saunders, J.	London	1830	Portraits	—	—	1	—	—	—	—	—	—	—	1
Saunders, Joseph	London	1772-1808	Miniatures	—	1	41	1	—	—	—	—	—	—	43
Saunders, J. K.	London	1870	Miniatures	—	—	2	—	—	—	—	—	—	—	2
Saunders, Paul	London	1763	Tapestry	—	1	—	—	—	—	—	—	—	—	1
Saunders, R.	London	1801-1828	Miniatures	—	—	31	—	—	—	—	—	—	—	31
Saunders, W. A.	—	1848	Architecture	—	—	3	—	—	—	—	—	—	—	3
Saunders, Miss. *See* Mrs. James Robertson	—	—	—	—	—	—	—	—	—	—	—	—	—	—
Sauveur —	London	1772	Portraits	3	—	—	—	—	—	—	—	—	—	3
Savage, James	London	1799-1832	Architecture	—	—	14	—	—	—	—	—	—	—	14
Savage, J. H.	London	1840-1853	Figures	—	—	1	5	4	—	—	—	—	—	10
Savage, Reginald	London	1886-1890	Portraits	—	—	1	—	2	—	6	—	2	1	12
Savill, Miss Edith	London	1880-1883	Portraits	—	—	4	—	4	—	1	—	—	2	11
Savill, Miss Gertrude May	Brighton	1891-1893	Portraits	—	—	2	—	—	—	—	—	—	—	2
Saville, Miss Josephine	Colchester	1863-1885	Domestic	—	—	3	—	6	—	—	1	—	2	12
Saville, W.	Dover	1862-1867	Landscape	—	—	—	6	—	—	—	—	—	—	6
Savry, H.	London	1876	Cattle	—	—	1	—	—	—	—	—	—	—	1
Sawney, A.	—	1814-1815	Landscape	—	—	1	—	—	—	—	—	—	—	1
Saword, Mrs.	Blackheath	1808-1811	Miniatures	—	—	1	1	—	—	—	—	—	—	2
Sawyer, Miss Amy	Croydon	1887-1893	Domestic	—	—	6	—	—	—	—	—	—	1	7
Sawyer, F.	Bristol	1841	Historical	—	—	1	—	—	—	—	—	—	—	1
Sawyer, R. D.	Paris	1886	River Scenes	—	—	1	—	—	—	—	—	—	—	1
Sax, Bernhard	Rome	1856-1877	Sculpture	—	—	5	—	—	—	—	—	—	—	5
Saxon, George	Bruton	1875-1885	Figures	—	—	1	—	1	—	—	—	—	5	7
Saxon, James	London	1795-1817	Portraits	—	—	17	—	—	—	—	—	—	—	17
Saxon, Samuel	London	1778-1782	Architecture	—	—	5	—	—	—	—	—	—	—	5
Saxoni, C.	London	1846	Buildings	—	—	4	—	—	—	—	—	—	—	4
Say —	—	1774	Drawing	1	—	—	—	—	—	—	—	—	—	1
Say, Fred. R.	London	1825-1854	Portraits	—	—	78	8	1	—	—	—	—	—	87
Say, William	London	1825-1833	Engraving	—	—	—	—	5	—	—	—	—	—	5
Sayer —	—	1783	Fruit	—	3	—	—	—	—	—	—	—	—	3
Sayer, George	London	1835-1848	Portraits	—	—	3	—	1	—	—	—	—	—	4
Sayer, Miss Jessie C.	Brockley	1887-1892	Flowers	—	—	1	—	—	—	1	—	—	—	2
Sayer, Lawrence	London	1878	Churches	—	—	—	—	—	—	—	—	—	1	1
Sayers, E. C.	London	1845-1853	Churches	—	—	3	2	1	—	—	—	—	—	6
Sayers, Reuben T. W.	London	1841-1867	Domestic	—	—	13	16	9	—	—	—	—	20	58
Scace, J.	London	1815	Architecture	—	—	1	—	—	—	—	—	—	—	1
Scale, Bernard	Mangrove	1775	Landscape	—	3	—	—	—	—	—	—	—	—	3
Scales, James	London	1808-1827	Landscape	—	—	6	2	2	—	—	—	—	—	10
Scampton, Miss Mary	Coventry	1879-1882	Flowers	—	—	—	—	4	—	—	—	—	—	4
Scandrett, Thomas	London	1824-1870	Churches	—	—	13	4	25	—	—	—	—	—	42
Scanes, Miss Agnes	London	1880-1892	Portraits	—	—	2	—	5	—	4	—	—	7	18
Scanes, Edwin L.	London	1885-1893	Domestic	—	—	2	—	3	—	—	—	—	1	6
Scanes, Mrs. *See* Miss Maude Goodman.	—	—	—	—	—	—	—	—	—	—	—	—	—	—
Scanlan, Robert R.	Plymouth	1832-1876	Domestic	—	—	17	3	3	—	—	—	—	9	32
Scannell, Miss Edith M. S.	—	1870-1893	Domestic	—	—	11	—	2	—	—	—	—	4	17
Scappa, E. C.	London	1872-1880	Landscape	—	—	—	—	2	—	—	—	—	10	12
Scappa, G. A.	London	1867-1886	Landscape	—	—	5	—	15	—	—	—	—	48	68
Scappa, Miss	Hastings	1874-1875	Landscape	—	—	—	—	—	—	—	—	—	4	4
Scarfe, F.	London	1825	Figures	—	—	1	—	—	—	—	—	—	—	1
Scarlet, James	—	1769-1770	Domestic	—	5	—	—	—	—	—	—	—	—	5
Scarrow, Thomas	London	1831	Portraits	—	—	1	—	—	—	—	—	—	—	1
Schaak, J. S. C.	London	1761-1769	Portraits	7	17	—	—	—	—	—	—	—	—	24
Schacht, C.	—	1831	Landscape	—	—	1	—	—	—	—	—	—	—	1
Schaefels, Hendrick	London	1860	Town	—	—	—	1	—	—	—	—	—	—	1
Schäfer, Henry Thomas, R.B.A. §	London	1873-1893	Domestic	—	—	29	—	53	—	1	3	—	12	98
Schalander, F. W.	London	1868	Churches	—	—	—	—	2	—	—	—	—	—	2
Schalk —	—	1761	Landscape	3	—	—	—	—	—	—	—	—	—	3
Schampheleer, De. *See* D.	—	—	—	—	—	—	—	—	—	—	—	—	—	—

Name.	Town.	First and Last Year of Ex.	Speciality.	S. A.	F. S.	R. A.	B. I.	S. S.	O. W.	N. W.	G. G.	N. G.	V. E.	Total.
Scharf, George ‡	London	1817-1850	Landscape	—	—	28	—	4	—	14	—	—	—	46
Scharf, Sir George, K.C.B., F.S.A.	London	1845-1846	Ruins	—	—	6	2	—	—	—	—	—	—	8
Scharpf, Joseph	Broadstairs	1892-1893	Sea Pieces	—	—	—	—	10	—	—	—	—	—	10
Scheemakers, Peter	London	1765-1780	Sculpture	7	8	—	—	—	—	—	—	—	—	15
Scheemakers, Thomas	London	1765-1804	Sculpture	—	46	16	—	—	—	—	—	—	—	62
Scheffer, Ary. *See* Schyfer	Paris	1851-1856	Scriptural	—	—	2	—	—	—	—	—	—	—	2
Scheffer, Henri	London	1839	Figures	—	—	2	—	—	—	—	—	—	—	2
Scheffer, J. G.	London	1848	Figures	—	—	6	—	—	—	—	—	—	—	6
Schelfhout, Andrew	London	1847	Winter Scenes	—	—	—	1	—	—	—	—	—	—	1
Schell, Miss Lily	Brighton	1880-1885	Domestic	—	—	1	—	5	—	—	—	—	1	7
Schenck, Auguste Frederic Albrecht	Ecouen	1872-1876	Landscape	—	—	2	—	—	—	—	—	—	1	3
Schenck, J.	London	1859	Landscape	—	—	1	—	—	—	—	—	—	—	1
Schendel, Van. *See* V.	—	—	—	—	—	—	—	—	—	—	—	—	—	—
Schenk, Mrs. Agnes	London	1880-1884	Domestic	—	—	1	—	5	—	—	—	—	4	10
Schenk, Frederick E. E.	Stoke-on-Trent	1886-1893	Sculpture	—	—	8	—	—	—	—	—	—	—	8
Schenley, Hermione	London	1885	Still Life	—	—	—	—	1	—	—	—	—	—	1
Scheppelen —	London	1768	Portraits	1	—	—	—	—	—	—	—	—	—	1
Schetky, John Alexander	London	1816-1817	Landscape	—	—	—	—	—	4	—	—	—	—	4
Schetky, John Christian	Oxford	1808-1872	Sea Pieces	—	—	66	6	15	7	—	—	—	36	130
Schetky, J. T.	Oxford	1805-1825	Sea Pieces	—	—	9	—	—	—	—	—	—	6	15
Scheurenberg, J.	Düsseldorf	1878-1879	Domestic	—	—	2	—	—	—	—	—	—	—	2
Schiavone, Felice	Florence	1832-1844	Scriptural	—	—	2	1	—	—	—	—	—	—	3
Schick, P.	Hastings	1853-1854	Miniatures	—	—	4	—	—	—	—	—	—	—	4
Schiller, H. Carl	London	1844-1867	Portraits	—	—	2	—	2	—	—	—	—	—	4
Schirmacher, Miss M. Dora	Liverpool	1885-1889	Landscape	—	—	2	—	—	—	—	—	—	—	2
Schjerfbeck, Miss H.	St. Ives, Cornw'l	1887-1889	Domestic	—	—	—	—	—	—	—	—	—	3	3
Schlesinger, Henri Guillaume	Vienna	1851-1873	Portraits	—	—	2	—	—	—	—	—	—	1	3
Schloesser, Carl	Paris	1858-1892	Domestic	—	—	25	—	—	—	—	10	—	—	35
Schmäck, Miss Emily	London	1837-1845	Domestic	—	—	20	8	1	—	—	—	—	—	29
Schmalz, Herbert Gustave	London	1879-1893	Domestic	—	—	28	—	—	—	—	24	2	5	59
Schmid, Louis	London	1834-1843	Portraits	—	—	3	1	—	—	—	—	—	—	4
Schmidt, Emil	London	1892-1893	Domestic	—	—	—	—	2	—	—	—	—	—	2
Schmidt, Edward Allan-	London	1868-1877	Domestic	—	—	3	—	—	—	—	—	—	2	5
Schmidt, Guido	Aix-la-Chapelle	1846-1884	Figures	—	—	15	3	3	—	—	—	—	1	22
Schmidt, Henry	—	1834	Figures	—	—	—	1	—	—	—	—	—	—	1
Schmiechen, Hermann	London	1884-1893	Portraits	—	—	6	—	—	—	—	1	—	—	7
Schmitt, G. P.	London	1862-1863	Domestic	—	—	3	—	—	—	—	—	—	—	3
Schmitt, S.	London	1872	Enamels	—	—	1	—	—	—	—	—	—	—	1
Schnabel, Marie	London	1888-1889	Figures	—	—	—	—	2	—	—	—	—	—	2
Schnebbelie, Jacob C.	London	1786-1791	Buildings	—	—	7	—	—	—	—	—	—	—	7
Schnebbelie, Robert Bremmel	London	1803-1821	Buildings	—	—	9	—	—	—	—	—	—	—	9
Schnitzspahn, C.	London	1857	Sculpture	—	—	3	—	—	—	—	—	—	—	3
Schobinger, Madame de, late Miss Burdon	London	1859	Domestic	—	—	—	—	—	—	—	—	—	4	4
Schoefft, A.	London	1859-1860	Portraits	—	—	2	—	—	—	—	—	—	—	2
Schoenberger, M.	London	1816	Mythological	—	—	—	2	—	2	—	—	—	—	4
Schofield, J.	London	1802	Architecture	—	—	1	—	—	—	—	—	—	—	1
Schofield, Miss J.	Streatham	1833	Rustic	—	—	1	—	—	—	—	—	—	—	1
Schofield, John W.	Halifax	1889-1893	Landscape	—	—	3	—	—	—	—	—	—	—	3
Scholander, F. W.	London	1868	Venice	—	—	1	—	—	—	—	—	—	—	1
Scholderer, Otto	Putney	1871-1893	Game	—	—	40	—	7	—	—	2	—	18	67
Schoojans, Adolphe	London	1871-1884	Sculpture	—	—	11	—	—	—	—	—	—	—	11
Schopin, M.	London	1877	Mythological	—	—	—	—	1	—	—	—	—	—	1
Schotel, P. T.	Taunton	1844	Sea Pieces	—	—	—	—	1	—	—	—	—	—	1
Schots, Charles Louis	London	1872-1891	Sculpture	—	—	6	—	—	—	—	—	—	—	6
Schott, Cecil	London	1887	Figures	—	—	1	—	—	—	—	—	—	—	1
Schrader, Jules	Berlin	1849-1880	Portraits	—	—	2	—	—	—	—	—	—	—	2
Schroder, H.	London	1793	Portraits	—	—	3	—	—	—	—	—	—	—	3
Schröder, Walter G.	Chester	1890-1893	Landscape	—	—	2	—	7	—	—	—	—	—	9
Schroester, Adeline	—	1877	Flowers	—	—	1	—	—	—	—	—	—	—	1
Schrowder, B.	London	1781	Sculpture	—	—	4	—	—	—	—	—	—	—	4
Schulhof, Miss S. Edith	London	1891-1892	Study	—	—	—	—	1	—	—	—	—	1	2
Schultz, Robert Weir	London	1885-1892	Architecture	—	—	6	—	—	—	—	—	—	—	6
Schurig, Felix	Dresden	1876	Figures	—	—	—	—	—	—	—	—	—	1	1
Schutze, A.	Southampton	1884	Domestic	—	—	—	—	1	—	—	—	—	—	1
Schwanfelder, Charles Henry	Leeds	1809-1826	Sporting	—	—	10	6	—	—	—	—	—	—	16
Schwartz —	London	1768	Portraits	1	—	—	—	—	—	—	—	—	—	1
Schwartze, Miss Theresa	Amsterdam	1880-1885	Figures	—	—	1	—	1	—	—	—	—	1	3
Schweickhardt, Heinrich Wilhelm	London	1788-1796	Landscape	6	—	22	—	—	—	—	—	—	—	28
Schweickhardt, J. W.	London	1786	Landscape	—	—	2	—	—	—	—	—	—	—	2
Schweiger, Hans	London	1884	Domestic	—	—	—	—	—	—	—	2	—	—	2
Schweinfurth, Dr. G.	London	1877	Africa	—	—	—	—	—	—	—	—	—	2	2

Name.	Town.	First and Last Year of Ex.	Speciality.	S. A.	F. S.	R. A.	B. I.	S. S.	O. W.	N. W.	G. G.	N. G.	V. E.	Total.
Schwiter, Baron L.	Paris	1833-1836	Portraits	—	—	4	—	—	—	—	—	—	—	4
Schwiter, De. *See* D.	—	—	—	—	—	—	—	—	—	—	—	—	—	—
Schyfer, A. (?) Scheffer	Paris	1854	Portraits	—	—	1	—	—	—	—	—	—	—	1
Scifoni, Anatolio	London	1879	Figures	—	—	1	—	—	—	—	—	—	—	1
Sciptius, George	London	1768-1780	Enamels	3	—	9	—	—	—	—	—	—	—	12
Sclater, E.	Dover	1865-1871	Sea Pieces	—	—	—	—	2	—	—	—	—	—	2
Sclater-Booth, Miss	London	1881-1884	Portraits	—	—	—	—	—	—	—	3	—	—	3
Scobie, A. J.	Esher	1867	Sculpture	—	—	1	—	—	—	—	—	—	—	1
Scoles, J. J.	London	1820-1854	Architecture	—	—	10	—	—	—	—	—	—	—	10
Scollay, Miss	Boston, U.S.A.	1769	Needlework	1	—	—	—	—	—	—	—	—	—	1
Score, William (Pupil of Reynolds)	London	1781-1794	Portraits	—	—	14	—	—	—	—	—	—	—	14
Scorgoni, T.	London	1883	Animals	—	—	1	—	—	—	—	—	—	—	1
Scorzoni, Alessandro	London	1884	Domestic	—	—	—	—	—	—	—	—	—	1	1
Scotney, Francis	London	1811-1833	Sea Pieces & Enamels	—	—	28	10	5	1	—	—	—	—	44
Scott —	London	1770	Sculpture	—	1	—	—	—	—	—	—	—	—	1
Scott —	—	1786	Sea Pieces	—	—	2	—	—	—	—	—	—	—	2
Scott, A.	London	1807-1808	Portraits	—	—	2	—	—	—	—	—	—	—	2
Scott, A.	London	1856	River Scenes	—	—	—	—	1	—	—	—	—	—	1
Scott, Alexander	London	1870-1879	Engraving	—	—	3	—	—	—	—	—	—	1	4
Scott, Mrs. Alma	London	1888	Flowers	—	—	1	—	—	—	—	—	—	—	1
Scott, Miss Amy	London	1860-1891	Fruit	—	—	2	—	5	—	3	—	—	4	14
Scott, Miss Alice M.	London	1880-1889	Portraits	—	—	7	—	—	—	—	—	—	1	8
Scott, Bessie D.	London	1879-1881	Landscape	—	—	—	—	—	—	—	—	—	2	2
Scott, B. F.	London	1790-1792	Miniatures	2	—	1	—	—	—	—	—	—	—	3
Scott, B. F.	London	1833-1849	Mountains	—	—	1	—	1	—	—	—	—	—	2
Scott, Miss Catherine	London	1867-1888	Landscape	—	—	—	—	1	—	1	—	—	2	4
Scott, Charles James §	Brighton	1819-1834	Landscape	—	—	2	12	38	—	—	—	—	—	52
Scott, David, R.S.A.	Edinburgh	1840-1848	Historical	—	—	2	—	—	—	—	—	—	3	5
Scott, E.	Dover	1839	Sea Pieces	—	—	—	—	1	—	—	—	—	—	1
Scott, Miss Edith	London	1882	Figures	—	—	—	—	1	—	—	—	—	—	1
Scott, Master Edmund	London	1774-1796	Portraits	—	5	1	—	—	—	—	—	—	—	6
Scott, Miss Emily	Brighton	1826-1855	Portraits	—	—	14	—	24	—	—	—	—	—	38
Scott, Miss Emily Anne, afterwards Mrs. Seymour	Brighton	1825-1855	Portraits	—	—	19	—	38	—	—	—	—	—	57
Scott, Elizabeth Dundas	London	1877-1878	Landscape	—	—	—	—	—	—	—	—	—	4	4
Scott, E. E.	London	1869-1870	Architecture	—	—	2	—	—	—	—	—	—	—	2
Scott (E. E.) and Hyde	Brighton	1875-1876	Architecture	—	—	2	—	—	—	—	—	—	—	2
Scott, Esther P.	London	1893	Sea Pieces	—	—	—	—	1	—	—	—	—	—	1
Scott, F.	London	1822	Portraits	—	—	1	—	—	—	—	—	—	—	1
Scott, Miss Fanny C.	London	1868-1871	Fruit	—	—	1	—	2	—	—	—	—	—	3
Scott, F. J.	Chatham	1849	Portraits	—	—	1	—	—	—	—	—	—	—	1
Scott, G.	London	1802-1832	Architecture	—	—	2	—	—	—	—	—	—	—	2
Scott, G.	London	1835-1847	Landscape	—	—	—	5	13	—	—	—	—	—	18
Scott, G.	London	1860	Mythological	—	—	—	1	—	—	—	—	—	—	1
Scott, Sir George Gilbert, R.A.	London	1847-1878	Architecture	—	—	45	—	—	—	—	—	—	—	45
Scott (G. G.) and Moffatt (W. B.)	London	1842	Architecture	—	—	2	—	—	—	—	—	—	—	2
Scott, George Gilbert, M.A., F.S.A.	London	1871-1884	Architecture	—	—	13	—	—	—	—	—	—	—	13
Scott, H. L.	Paris	1881	Streets	—	—	—	—	—	—	—	4	—	—	4
Scott, Henrietta S.	London	1891	Landscape	—	—	—	—	1	—	—	—	—	—	1
Scott, H. T.	London	1863	Figures	—	—	—	1	—	—	—	—	—	—	1
Scott, H. Y. D.	London	1867	Architecture	—	—	1	—	—	—	—	—	—	—	1
Scott, J.	—	1761-1762	Sculpture	—	2	—	—	—	—	—	—	—	—	2
Scott, J.	London	1790	Flowers	—	—	1	—	—	—	—	—	—	—	1
Scott, J.	London	1863	Flowers	—	—	1	—	—	—	—	—	—	—	1
Scott, James	London	1773	Landscape	—	1	—	—	—	—	—	—	—	—	1
Scott, James	London	1821-1844	Portraits	—	—	18	3	11	—	—	—	—	—	32
Scott, James	London	1857-1889	Engraving	—	—	12	—	—	—	—	—	—	—	12
Scott, John	—	1831	Engraving	—	—	—	—	2	—	—	—	—	—	2
Scott, John, R.I., R.B.A., ‡ § φ	London	1837-1893	Domestic	—	—	13	4	50	—	28	1	1	37	134
Scott, J. B.	London	1871	Landscape	—	—	—	—	1	—	—	—	—	—	1
Scott, John Douglas	London	1871-1881	Landscape	—	—	3	—	4	—	—	—	—	—	7
Scott, Miss J. E.	London	1863-1867	Portraits	—	—	5	—	—	—	—	—	—	—	5
Scott, John H.	Brighton	1849-1886	Landscape	—	—	3	—	4	—	3	—	—	13	23
Scott, J. J.	London	1863-1864	Figures	—	—	—	2	—	—	—	—	—	—	2
Scott, John Oldrid, F.S.A.	London	1869-1893	Architecture	—	—	41	—	—	—	—	—	—	—	41
Scott, J. R.	London	1827	Engraving	—	—	—	—	1	—	—	—	—	—	1
Scott, James R.	London	1854-1871	Sea Pieces	—	—	1	3	3	—	—	—	—	—	7
Scott, James V.	Edinburgh	1877-1889	Landscape	—	—	3	—	—	—	10	—	—	9	22
Scott, Miss Katherine	Streatham	1872-1892	Flowers	—	—	4	—	6	—	15	—	—	16	41
Scott, Laurence	Cheltenham	1883-1893	Domestic	—	—	9	—	1	—	—	—	—	7	17
Scott, M.	London	1792	Historical	—	—	1	—	—	—	—	—	—	—	1
Scott, M.	London	1854	Portraits	—	—	1	—	—	—	—	—	—	—	1

Name.	Town.	First and Last Year of Ex.	Speciality.	S. A.	F. S.	R. A.	B. I.	S. S.	O. W.	N.W.	G. G.	N. G.	V. E.	Total.
Scott, Miss M. † *See* Mrs. Brookbank	Brighton	1823-1833	Fruit	—	—	—	—	1	21	—	—	—	—	22
Scott, Mrs. Nora	London	1876	Camels	—	—	—	—	—	—	—	—	—	1	1
Scott, R.	London	1827	Domestic	—	—	—	—	1	—	—	—	—	—	1
Scott, Richard	Beulah Hill	1883	Landscape	—	—	—	—	—	—	1	—	—	—	1
Scott, Robert Bagge	London	1886-1891	Landscape	—	—	6	—	—	—	—	—	—	—	6
Scott, Miss R. C.	London	1871-1875	Domestic	—	—	—	—	4	—	—	—	—	—	4
Scott, Samuel	Twickenham	1761-1771	Landscape	3	1	1	—	—	—	—	—	—	—	5
Scott, Tom, A.R.S.A., R.S.W.	Edinburgh	1887	Military	—	—	—	—	—	—	1	—	—	—	1
Scott, Thomas D.	London	1889-1893	Miniatures	—	—	7	—	—	—	—	—	—	—	7
Scott, Walter	London	1831-1850	Domestic	—	—	11	—	1	—	—	—	—	—	12
Scott, Walter	London	1877-1878	Landscape	—	—	—	—	—	—	—	—	—	3	3
Scott, William †	Brighton	1810-1855	Landscape	—	—	10	4	1	229	—	—	—	—	244
Scott, William, R.P.E.	London	1876-1893	Architecture	—	—	8	—	3	—	—	—	—	7	18
Scott, William Bell, LL.D.	Newcastle	1840-1873	Domestic	—	—	7	9	4	—	—	—	—	11	31
Scott, W. C.	Brighton	1818	Landscape	—	—	—	2	—	—	—	—	—	—	2
Scott, William Wallace	London	1841-1859	Portraits	—	—	35	1	1	—	—	—	—	—	37
Scott, Miss	London	1802-1804	Miniatures	—	—	5	—	—	—	—	—	—	—	5
Scott-Smith, Miss Jessie	Balham	1883-1893	Miniatures	—	—	11	—	—	—	3	—	—	—	14
Scotti, Count Lemmi Rossi-. *See* R.	—	—	—	—	—	—	—	—	—	—	—	—	—	—
Scoular, James	London	1761-1787	Miniatures	7	1	32	—	—	—	—	—	—	—	40
Scoular, William	London	1815-1846	Sculpture	—	—	59	10	15	—	—	—	—	—	84
Scratchley —	London	1770-1772	Engraving	1	2	—	—	—	—	—	—	—	—	3
Scratton, G.	—	1842	Architecture	—	—	1	—	—	—	—	—	—	—	1
Scriven, Edward	London	1824-1828	Engraving	—	—	—	—	13	—	—	—	—	—	13
Scriven, H.	London	1845-1849	Landscape	—	—	2	—	—	—	—	—	—	—	2
Scriven, J. W.	London	1890-1893	Sculpture	—	—	2	—	—	—	—	—	—	—	2
Scrivener, A.	London	1821	Architecture	—	—	1	—	—	—	—	—	—	—	1
Scrope, William	London	1808-1851	Landscape	—	—	6	19	—	—	—	—	—	—	25
Scrymgeour, J. M.	London	1832-1836	Scriptural	—	—	3	2	3	—	—	—	—	—	8
Scull, W. D.	London	1886	Insects	—	—	—	—	1	—	—	—	—	—	1
Scully, Harry	Cork	1887-1893	Landscape	—	—	—	—	—	—	3	—	—	—	3
Scurry, J.	London	1850-1852	Sculpture	—	—	8	—	—	—	—	—	—	—	8
Seabrook, Grace	London	1872-1874	Figures	—	—	—	—	2	—	—	—	—	1	3
Seabrook, S. S.	London	1824	Portraits	—	—	2	—	—	—	—	—	—	—	2
Seaforth, C. H.	London	1825-1853	Sea Pieces	—	—	49	25	5	—	—	—	—	—	79
Seager, Mrs.	London	1827	Portraits	—	—	1	—	—	—	—	—	—	—	1
Seagrave, H. W.	London	1819-1827	Figures	—	—	2	—	—	—	—	—	—	—	2
Sealy, Allen Culpeper	London	1873-1886	Landscape	—	—	19	—	21	—	—	—	—	12	52
Sealy, J.	London	1809-1816	Sculpture	—	—	5	1	—	—	—	—	—	—	6
Search, R. D.	London	1875-1877	Architecture	—	—	1	—	—	—	—	—	—	2	3
Seare, S.	London	1852	Landscape	—	—	1	—	—	—	—	—	—	—	1
Seares, Miss Frances Fripp. *See* Mrs. Charles Rossiter.	—	—	—	—	—	—	—	—	—	—	—	—	—	—
Seares, G. S.	—	1808-1810	Landscape	—	—	4	—	—	—	—	—	—	—	4
Searle —	London	1772	Landscape	2	—	—	—	—	—	—	—	—	—	2
Searle, A. H.	London	1888	Landscape	—	—	—	—	1	—	—	—	—	—	1
Searle, Charles Gray	London	1862	Architecture	—	—	1	—	—	—	—	—	—	—	1
Searle, F.	Redhill	1877	Fruit	—	—	—	—	1	—	—	—	—	—	1
Searle, R.	London	1798	Architecture	—	—	1	—	—	—	—	—	—	—	1
Searle, W. H.	London	1819	Architecture	—	—	1	—	—	—	—	—	—	—	1
Searle, Son, and Yelf	London	1865	Architecture	—	—	1	—	—	—	—	—	—	—	1
Sears, L.	—	1854	Landscape	—	—	1	—	—	—	—	—	—	—	1
Season, R.	—	1806	Architecture	—	—	1	—	—	—	—	—	—	—	1
Seaton, Miss A. E.	Sheffield	1886	Shells	—	—	—	—	—	—	—	1	—	—	1
Seaton, Christopher, F.S.A.	London	1760-1772	Seals	15	—	—	—	—	—	—	—	—	—	15
Seaton, C.	London	1858	Sketch	—	—	—	—	1	—	—	—	—	—	1
Seaton, John Thomas. (?) Seton	Bath	1761-1777	Portraits	13	—	3	—	—	—	—	—	—	—	16
Seawell, S.	London	1847-1851	Landscape	—	—	2	—	2	—	—	—	—	—	4
Sebastian de Brocilla	London	1833	Figures	—	—	1	—	—	—	—	—	—	—	1
Sebbers, L. H.	London	1849-1854	Scriptural	—	—	8	—	—	—	—	—	—	—	8
Sebbon, R.	Liverpool	1845	Landscape	—	—	—	—	1	—	—	—	—	—	1
Seben, Van. *See* V.	—	—	—	—	—	—	—	—	—	—	—	—	—	—
Seccombe, Colonel F. S., R.A.	Tilbury	1876-1885	Military	—	—	—	—	11	—	2	—	—	1	14
Seccombe, Miss	—	1776-1778	Needlework	3	—	—	—	—	—	—	—	—	—	3
Seckendorff, Count, H.R.I. ‡	Berlin	1887-1893	Venice	—	—	—	—	—	—	16	—	—	—	16
Secombe —	London	1774	Portraits	1	—	—	—	—	—	—	—	—	—	1
Sedcole, Herbert	London	1889	Engraving	—	—	1	—	—	—	—	—	—	—	1
Sedding, Edmund H.	London	1886-1892	Architecture	—	—	4	—	—	—	—	—	—	—	4
Sedding, John D.	London	1875-1891	Architecture	—	—	40	—	—	—	—	—	—	—	40
Seddon, Fanny	London	1869-1874	Landscape	—	—	—	—	—	—	—	—	—	4	4
Seddon, John Pollard. *See* Pritchard and Seddon	London	1862-1878	Architecture	—	—	27	—	—	—	—	—	—	—	27

Name.	Town.	First and Last Year of Ex.	Speciality.	S. A.	F. S.	R. A.	B. I.	S. S.	O.W.	N.W.	G. G.	N.G.	V. E.	Total.
Seddon, Thomas B.	London	1852-1856	Landscape	—	—	6	—	—	—	—	—	—	—	6
Seddon and Carter	Cardiff	1890-1892	Architecture	—	—	4	—	—	—	—	—	—	—	4
Sedgefield, Miss Isabel M.	London	1889-1891	Flowers	—	—	1	—	5	—	—	—	—	—	6
Sedger, George	London	1886-1892	Architecture	—	—	4	—	—	—	—	—	—	—	4
Sedgwick, William	London	1786-1787	Landscape	—	—	4	—	—	—	—	—	—	—	4
Sedgwick, Mrs. *See* Mrs. William Oliver, *and* Miss Emma Eburne.	—	—	—	—	—	—	—	—	—	—	—	—	—	—
Seeley, Miss Ellen	Richmond	1880-1888	Miniatures	—	—	6	—	—	—	—	—	—	—	6
Seeley, Miss E. L.	London	1873-1875	Domestic	—	—	3	—	—	—	—	—	—	—	3
Seeley, Josh.	London	1827-1828	Cattle	—	—	—	2	3	—	—	—	—	—	5
Seeley, R.	Kingston	1876-1877	Landscape	—	—	1	—	2	—	—	—	—	—	3
Seeley, Miss	—	1828	—	—	—	—	—	*	—	—	—	—	—	—
Seghars, Van. *See* V.	—	—	—	—	—	—	—	—	—	—	—	—	—	—
Seguier, John	London	1811-1822	Landscape	—	—	12	—	—	—	—	—	—	—	12
Seguin, G.	Paris	1831	Scriptural	—	—	1	—	—	—	—	—	—	—	1
Sein, Mangul	—	1859	Portraits	—	—	—	—	1	—	—	—	—	—	1
Selb, Victor	London	1889	Sea Shores	—	—	—	—	1	—	—	—	—	—	1
Selby, Edgar H.	London	1890	Architecture	—	—	1	—	—	—	—	—	—	—	1
Selby, T.	Canterbury	1853	Buildings	—	—	—	1	—	—	—	—	—	—	1
Sell, Charles	London	1880	Battles	—	—	1	—	—	—	—	—	—	—	1
Sellar, Charles A., R.S.W.	Edinburgh	1888	Portraits	—	—	1	—	—	—	—	—	—	—	1
Sellers, James H. *See* Douglas and Sellers	Heworth	1891-1892	Architecture	—	—	2	—	—	—	—	—	—	—	2
Sellett, J.	London	1797	Game	—	—	2	—	—	—	—	—	—	—	2
Sellon, William	Twyford	1876-1877	Domestic	—	—	2	—	—	—	—	—	—	—	2
Sells, V. P.	London	1851-1865	Churches	—	—	12	—	15	—	—	—	—	—	27
Selous, Henry Courtney. *See* Slous	London	1838-1885	Historical	—	—	26	21	—	—	—	—	—	—	47
Selous, Miss J.	London	1861	Domestic	—	—	—	—	1	—	—	—	—	—	1
Sembach, A.	London	1876-1878	Landscape	—	—	1	—	3	—	—	—	—	—	4
Sénéchal, A.	London	1795	Portraits	—	—	1	—	—	—	—	—	—	—	1
Senga —	Starcross	1872	Portraits	—	—	—	—	1	—	—	—	—	—	1
Senior, E. N.	London	1848	Domestic	—	—	—	—	1	—	—	—	—	—	1
Senior, Mark	Ossett	1892	Landscape	—	—	1	—	—	—	—	—	—	—	1
Senties, T.	London	1852-1858	Portraits	—	—	18	—	7	—	—	—	—	—	25
Senyard, Christopher	London	1829	Domestic	—	—	—	—	1	—	—	—	—	—	1
Sephton, George Harcourt	Sevenoaks	1885-1892	Rustic	—	—	3	—	2	—	—	—	—	3	8
Sephyel, Professor	London	1876	Domestic	—	—	—	—	1	—	—	—	—	—	1
Serle, Miss H.	London	1874	Fruit	—	—	—	—	1	—	—	—	—	—	1
Sermon, E.	—	1833	Engraving	—	—	—	—	1	—	—	—	—	—	1
Serres, Miss A. E.	—	1789-1800	Landscape	—	—	3	—	—	—	—	—	—	—	3
Serres, Dominic, R.A.	London	1761-1793	Sea Pieces	8	21	105	—	—	—	—	—	—	—	134
Serres, Dominic M.	London	1778-1804	Landscape	—	—	9	—	—	—	—	—	—	—	9
Serres, Miss H.	—	1790-1800	Flowers	—	—	7	—	—	—	—	—	—	—	7
Serres, John	—	1776-1779	Landscape	—	—	3	—	—	—	—	—	—	—	3
Serres, Miss Joanna	London	1788-1803	Landscape	—	—	9	—	—	—	—	—	—	—	9
Serres, John Thomas	London	1780-1825	Sea Pieces	—	—	67	10	1	—	—	—	—	—	78
Serres, Mrs. John Thomas (Olivia). (Princess Olive of Cumberland?)	London	1793-1811	Landscape	—	—	14	13	—	—	—	—	—	—	27
Serres, Miss S.	—	1800	Flowers	—	—	1	—	—	—	—	—	—	—	1
Serres, Miss	—	1783	Landscape	—	—	1	—	—	—	—	—	—	—	1
Servandoni —	London	1774-1778	Buildings	16	4	—	—	—	—	—	—	—	—	20
Servant —	London	1764	Landscape	—	2	—	—	—	—	—	—	—	—	2
Setchel, Miss Elizabeth	London	1832-1844	Domestic	—	—	6	1	2	—	—	—	—	—	9
Setchel, H.	London	1835	Domestic	—	—	—	—	1	—	—	—	—	—	1
Setchel, Miss Sarah ‡	London	1831-1867	Domestic	—	—	9	—	15	—	34	—	—	—	58
Seth-Smith, William H.	London	1885-1892	Architecture	—	—	6	—	—	—	—	—	—	—	6
Seton, Charles C.	London	1881-1892	Domestic	—	—	11	—	3	—	—	2	—	2	18
Seton, John Thomas. *See* Seaton.	—	—	—	—	—	—	—	—	—	—	—	—	—	—
Settle, W. F.	London	1867	Sea Pieces	—	—	—	1	—	—	—	—	—	—	1
Severdoneck, Van. *See* V.	—	—	—	—	—	—	—	—	—	—	—	—	—	—
Severn, Arthur, R.I. ‡ ϕ	London	1863-1893	Landscape	—	—	1	—	—	—	44	9	—	109	163
Severn, Miss A. M.	London	1852-1856	Domestic	—	—	3	—	—	—	—	—	—	—	3
Severn, Benjamin	London	1766-1772	Portraits	1	—	1	—	—	—	—	—	—	—	2
Severn, James	London	1825	Figures	—	—	—	1	—	—	—	—	—	—	1
Severn, Joseph	Rome	1817-1868	Figures	—	—	53	8	—	1	—	—	—	1	63
Severn, Miss Mary. *See* Mrs. Charles J. Newton	—	—	—	—	—	—	—	—	—	—	—	—	—	—
Severn, Walter, R.C.A.	London	1853-1889	Deer	—	—	2	—	1	—	—	7	—	34	44
Seward, Edwin, R.C.A., F.R.I.B.A.	Cardiff	1890	Buildings	—	—	1	—	—	—	—	—	—	—	1
Seward, Mrs. Edwin (Edith Jessie)	Cardiff	1889-1891	Landscape	—	—	2	—	—	—	—	—	—	—	2
Seward, H. H.	London	1797-1823	Architecture	—	—	29	—	—	—	—	—	—	—	29
Seward, W.	London	1813-1815	Architecture	—	—	5	—	—	—	—	—	—	—	5
Sewell, B.	Norwich	1797-1799	Churches	—	—	3	—	—	—	—	—	—	—	3
Sewell, G. H.	Rome	1875	Venice	—	—	—	—	—	—	—	—	—	1	1
Sextie, William A.	Marlborough	1848	Sporting	—	—	1	—	—	—	—	—	—	—	1

Name.	Town.	First and Last Year of Ex.	Speciality.	S. A.	F. S.	R. A.	B. I.	S. S.	O. W.	N.W.	G. G.	N. G.	V. E.	Total.
Seydel, E.	London	1860	Figures	—	—	—	1	—	—	—	—	—	—	1
Seyffarth, Miss Agnes E.	London	1850-1859	Historical	—	—	3	—	4	—	—	—	—	—	7
Seyffarth, Mrs. Woldemar.† *See* Miss Louisa Sharpe	London	1835-1842	Domestic	—	—	—	—	—	25	—	—	—	—	25
Seymour, George L.	London	1876-1888	Animals	—	—	—	—	1	—	1	—	—	16	18
Seymour, Miss Harriette Anne ‖	London	1866	Landscape	—	—	1	—	—	—	—	—	—	—	1
Seymour, J. Sydney	London	1877-1878	River Scenes	—	—	—	—	2	—	—	—	—	1	3
Seymour, Robert	London	1822	Historical	—	—	1	—	—	—	—	—	—	—	1
Seymour, Miss T. D.	London	1867	Moonlight	—	—	—	—	—	—	—	—	—	1	1
Seymour, Walter	London	1873-1892	Domestic	—	—	3	—	4	—	—	—	—	1	8
Seymour, Mrs.	—	1765-1776	Paper Work	—	49	—	—	—	—	—	—	—	—	49
Seymour, Mrs. *See* Miss Emily Anne Scott.	—	—	—	—	—	—	—	—	—	—	—	—	—	—
Seymour, Miss	—	1773-1776	Paper Work	—	3	—	—	—	—	—	—	—	—	3
Shackleton, John	London	1763-1766	Portraits	—	6	—	—	—	—	—	—	—	—	6
Shade, William	London	1875-1887	Domestic	—	—	3	—	—	—	—	1	—	—	4
Shakespear, J.	—	1807	Portraits	—	—	1	—	—	—	—	—	—	—	1
Shalders, George ‡	London	1848-1873	Landscape	—	—	15	4	41	—	77	—	—	—	137
Shand, J.	London	1818-1820	Portraits	—	—	5	—	—	—	—	—	—	—	5
Shand, W.	London	1807	Architecture	—	—	1	—	—	—	—	—	—	—	1
Shannan, A. McF.	Glasgow	1893	Sculpture	—	—	1	—	—	—	—	—	—	—	1
Shannon, Charles Haslewood, A.R.P.E.	London	1885-1889	Figures	—	—	2	—	3	—	5	3	—	3	16
Shannon, James Jebusa, R.B.A. § φ	London	1881-1893	Portraits	—	—	29	—	9	—	—	9	18	27	92
Shannon, M.	London	1800-1808	Architecture	—	—	5	—	—	—	—	—	—	—	5
Sharland, Miss L. A.	London	1876	Domestic	—	—	—	—	1	—	—	—	—	—	1
Sharp. *See* Lewen, Sharp, and Arpin	—	—	Architecture	—	—	—	—	—	—	—	—	—	—	—
Sharp, Arthur William	London	1875	Landscape	—	—	1	—	—	—	—	—	—	—	1
Sharp, Edward	London	1857-1859	Landscape	—	—	1	—	—	—	—	—	—	2	3
Sharp, Joseph	London	1772	Landscape	—	1	—	—	—	—	—	—	—	—	1
Sharp, Miss M. A.	Reading	1883-1885	Buildings	—	—	—	—	—	—	—	5	—	—	5
Sharp, Michael W.	London	1801-1836	Domestic	—	—	46	31	4	—	—	—	—	—	81
Sharp, R. H.	York	1819	Ruins	—	—	2	—	—	—	—	—	—	—	2
Sharp, Thomas	Paris	1830-1869	Sculpture	—	—	44	7	9	—	—	—	—	4	64
Sharp, William	London	1819-1831	Engraving	—	—	3	*	8	—	—	—	—	—	11
Sharp, Miss	London	1869	Churches	—	—	—	—	—	—	—	—	—	1	1
Sharpe, Miss Charlotte B.	London	1838-1842	Portraits	—	—	7	—	—	—	—	—	—	—	7
Sharpe, Charles W.	Birmingham	1858-1883	Engraving	—	—	5	—	—	—	—	—	—	—	5
Sharpe, Edmund, M.A., F.R.I.B.A.	Lancaster	1875	Architecture	—	—	1	—	—	—	—	—	—	—	1
Sharpe (E.) and Paley	Lancaster	1846	Architecture	—	—	4	—	—	—	—	—	—	—	4
Sharpe, Miss Eliza †	London	1817-1869	Portraits	—	—	33	—	—	87	—	—	—	—	120
Sharpe, Miss E. A.	Dover	1889	Flowers	—	—	—	—	—	—	1	—	—	—	1
Sharpe, Miss F.	London	1867	Domestic	—	—	2	—	—	—	—	—	—	—	2
Sharpe, G. W.	London	1865-1868	Landscape	—	—	3	3	3	—	—	—	—	2	11
Sharpe, J.	London	1822-1833	Landscape	—	—	2	—	—	—	—	—	—	—	2
Sharpe, J. B.	London	1861-1876	Sea Pieces	—	—	8	—	—	—	—	—	—	1	9
Sharpe, J. C.	London	1842	Architecture	—	—	2	—	—	—	—	—	—	—	2
Sharpe, J. F.	Hackney	1826-1838	Portraits	—	—	30	—	19	—	—	—	—	—	49
Sharpe, J. T.	—	1830	Portraits	—	—	1	—	—	—	—	—	—	—	1
Sharpe, Miss Louisa, † afterwards Mrs. Woldemar Seyffarth	London	1817-1833	Portraits	—	—	29	—	—	14	—	—	—	—	43
Sharpe, M.	London	1830	Flowers	—	—	1	—	—	—	—	—	—	—	1
Sharpe, Miss Mary	London	1865-1880	Figures	—	—	1	—	—	—	—	—	—	2	3
Sharpe, Miss Mary Anne §	London	1819-1879	Domestic	—	—	23	—	27	—	—	—	—	—	50
Sharpe, R. G.	—	1829	Portraits	—	—	—	—	1	—	—	—	—	—	1
Sharpe, Mrs. S. *See* Miss Caroline Paterson.	—	—	—	—	—	—	—	—	—	—	—	—	—	—
Sharpe, Sutton	London	1878-1881	Etching	—	—	—	—	—	—	—	—	—	8	8
Sharpe, William	London	1861-1879	Domestic	—	—	—	—	16	—	—	—	—	1	17
Sharpe, Miss. *See* Mrs. Best Morris.	—	—	—	—	—	—	—	—	—	—	—	—	—	—
Sharpe, Miss	London	1817-1828	Portraits	—	—	22	—	—	—	—	—	—	—	22
Sharpland, Mrs. A. F. Terrell (Ellen)	Brighton	1883-1890	Still Life	—	—	4	—	—	—	—	—	—	—	4
Sharples, G.	London	1815-1823	Portraits	—	—	6	—	—	—	—	—	—	—	6
Sharples, James	Cambridge	1779-1785	Portraits	—	—	14	—	—	—	—	—	—	—	14
Sharples, Miss Rolinda §	Bristol	1820-1836	Domestic	—	—	8	—	11	—	—	—	—	—	19
Sharples, Mrs.	London	1783-1807	Miniatures	1	—	5	—	—	—	—	—	—	—	6
Shaw, A.	London	1826-1839	Churches	—	—	5	8	2	—	—	—	—	—	15
Shaw, A. Winter	London	1891-1892	Landscape	—	—	1	—	2	—	—	—	—	—	3
Shaw, Byam	London	1893	Domestic	—	—	1	—	—	—	—	—	—	—	1
Shaw, Charles E.	Preston	1884-1892	Landscape	—	—	2	—	1	—	2	—	—	10	15
Shaw, Frederick	Liverpool	1876-1891	Landscape	—	—	4	—	—	—	1	—	—	2	7
Shaw, G.	London	1859-1862	Still Life	—	—	—	—	3	—	—	—	—	—	3
Shaw, H.	London	1821-1848	Architecture	—	—	4	—	—	—	—	—	—	—	4
Shaw, Henry, F.S.A.	London	1878-1881	Architecture	—	—	3	—	—	—	—	—	—	—	3
Shaw, Hugh George	Stratford-on-Avon	1873-1889	Domestic	—	—	2	—	26	—	—	—	—	2	30

Name.	Town.	First and Last Year of Ex.	Speciality.	S. A.	F. S.	R. A.	B. I.	S. S.	O. W.	N. W.	G. G.	N. G.	V. E.	Total.
Shaw, James	London	1776-1787	Portraits	—	—	5	—	—	—	—	—	—	—	5
Shaw, John, F.R.S.	London	1799-1846	Architecture	—	—	26	—	—	—	—	—	—	—	26
Shaw, Joshua	Bath	1802-1841	Cattle	—	—	9	22	2	—	—	—	—	—	33
Shaw, J.	London	1851-1853	Sporting	—	—	—	—	2	—	—	—	—	—	2
Shaw, John J.	Tottenham	1885-1892	Architecture	—	—	7	—	—	—	—	—	—	—	7
Shaw, Miss Kathleen	Totteridge	1886-1889	Rustic	—	—	1	—	7	—	—	—	—	—	8
Shaw, Miss Kathleen T.	Blackheath	1889-1893	Sculpture	—	—	2	—	—	—	—	—	3	—	5
Shaw, Richard Norman, R.A.	London	1870-1892	Architecture	—	—	34	—	—	—	—	—	—	—	34
Shaw, T.	London	1819	Architecture	—	—	2	—	—	—	—	—	—	—	2
Shaw, William, F.S.A.	London	1760-1772	Sporting	27	—	—	—	—	—	—	—	—	—	27
Shaw, William F.	London	1875	Landscape	—	—	—	—	—	—	—	—	—	1	1
Shaw, Walter J.	London	1878-1893	Landscape	—	—	20	—	—	—	—	—	—	1	21
Shaw, W. R. B.	London	1839-1846	Landscape	—	—	4	1	—	—	—	—	—	—	5
Shaw, Miss	London	1829-1830	Flowers	—	—	1	2	—	—	—	—	—	—	3
Shayer, C.	Southampton	1879	Sporting	—	—	—	—	1	—	—	—	—	—	1
Shayer, William §	Southampton	1825-1870	Landscape	—	—	6	82	338	—	—	—	—	—	426
Shayer, William J.	Southampton	1829-1885	Sporting	—	—	2	1	19	—	—	—	—	2	24
Sheaf, H. S.	London	1847	Portraits	—	—	1	—	—	—	—	—	—	—	1
Sheard, Thomas F. M.	Paris	1891-1893	Domestic	—	—	2	—	1	—	3	—	—	1	7
Shee, J. A.	London	1833	Portraits	—	—	—	—	1	—	—	—	—	—	1
Shee, Sir Martin Archer, P.R.A.	London	1789-1845	Portraits	—	—	324	19	—	—	—	—	—	—	343
Shee, Martin Archer, Junr.	London	1827-1833	Historical	—	—	6	4	—	—	—	—	—	—	10
Sheels —	—	1783	Landscape	—	1	—	—	—	—	—	—	—	—	1
Sheerer, William	—	1773	Drawings	—	2	—	—	—	—	—	—	—	—	2
Sheffield, George	London	1825-1835	Portraits	—	—	6	—	2	—	—	—	—	—	8
Sheffield, George	Wilmslow	1872-1890	Landscape	—	—	6	—	1	—	—	—	—	10	17
Sheffield, Margaret A.	Blackheath	1887-1890	Landscape	—	—	2	—	7	—	—	—	—	—	9
Sheffield, Mrs. Mary	—	1806-1813	Flowers	—	—	7	—	—	—	—	—	—	—	7
Sheffield, Miss Mary J.	Blackheath	1887-1893	Flowers	—	—	4	—	14	—	—	—	—	1	19
Sheffield, T. Percy	Farnham	1883	Landscape	—	—	1	—	—	—	—	—	—	—	1
Sheffield, W. E.	London	1789-1792	Still Life	—	—	3	—	—	—	—	—	—	—	3
Sheil, E., R.H.A.	Cork	1866-1868	Figures	—	—	1	—	1	—	—	—	—	—	2
Sheldon —	London	1774-1775	Portraits	—	6	—	—	—	—	—	—	—	—	6
Sheldon, Alfred	London	1844-1865	Fruit	—	—	—	2	3	—	—	—	—	—	5
Sheldon, Frederick S.	London	1885-1886	Sculpture	—	—	1	—	2	—	—	—	—	—	3
Sheldrake, J.	London	1780	Figures	—	—	1	—	—	—	—	—	—	—	1
Shelley, Frederick	London	1890	Sculpture	—	—	1	—	—	—	—	—	—	—	1
Shelley, Henry	Dunkerque	1853-1862	Historical	—	—	1	2	—	—	—	—	—	—	3
Shelley, Samuel †	London	1773-1808	Miniatures	5	—	245	15	—	63	—	—	—	—	328
Shellshear, Miss Alicia J.	London	1873-1887	Figures	—	—	4	—	3	—	—	—	—	3	10
Shelly, Arthur	Plymouth	1875-1888	Landscape	—	—	5	—	11	—	2	—	—	12	30
Shelly, Miss Jane	—	1762	Needlework	—	1	—	—	—	—	—	—	—	—	1
Shelston, J.	London	1810	Architecture	—	—	3	—	—	—	—	—	—	—	3
Shelton, Sidney	London	1881-1889	Landscape	—	—	2	—	2	—	—	—	—	—	4
Shenton, Miss Ellen	London	1850-1859	Sculpture	—	—	7	—	—	—	—	—	—	—	7
Shenton, F. C.	London	1825-1832	Engraving	—	—	—	—	9	—	—	—	—	—	9
Shenton, Henry Chawner	London	1846-1860	Engraving	—	—	5	—	—	—	—	—	—	—	5
Shenton, J.	London	1845	Sculpture	—	—	1	—	—	—	—	—	—	—	1
Shenton, William Kernot	London	1857-1871	Sculpture	—	—	16	—	—	—	—	—	—	—	16
Shepard, Henry Dunkin	London	1885-1891	Domestic	—	—	5	—	1	—	16	3	—	—	25
Shepard, Mrs. H. D. (Jessie)	—	1888	Still Life	—	—	1	—	—	—	—	—	—	—	1
Shepard, T.	London	1831	Architecture	—	—	1	—	—	—	—	—	—	—	1
Shephard, Eric A.	Torquay	1886	Landscape	—	—	1	—	—	—	—	—	—	—	1
Shepheard, George	London	1800-1842	Landscape	—	—	50	3	25	1	—	—	—	17	96
Shepheard, G.	London	1830	River Scenes	—	—	—	—	2	—	—	—	—	—	2
Shepheard, George Wallwyn	London	1837-1851	Landscape	—	—	19	—	—	—	—	—	—	—	19
Shepheard, Lewis Henry	London	1844-1875	Landscape	—	—	5	—	8	—	—	—	—	—	13
Shepherd, Fanny	Manchester	1863	Fruit	—	—	—	—	1	—	—	—	—	—	1
Shepherd, George Sidney ‡	London	1831-1858	Still Life	—	—	17	—	43	—	223	—	—	—	283
Shepherd, Herbert C.	Bridgend	1890	Figures	—	—	1	—	—	—	—	—	—	—	1
Shepherd, J.	London	1823	Domestic	—	—	1	—	—	—	—	—	—	—	1
Shepherd, Miss Julia C.	Manchester	1868-1870	Flowers	—	—	—	—	3	—	—	—	—	—	3
Shepherd, S.	London	1875	Landscape	—	—	—	—	1	—	—	—	—	—	1
Shepherd, Thomas Hosmer	London	1831-1832	Landscape	—	—	—	—	4	—	—	—	—	—	4
Shepherd, W. A.	Hoddesdon	1847-1852	Landscape	—	—	—	—	5	—	—	—	—	—	5
Sheppard, Miss Charlotte Lillian	London	1884-1886	Animals	—	—	—	—	1	—	—	—	—	2	3
Sheppard, G.	London	1797-1802	Miniatures	—	—	4	—	—	—	—	—	—	—	4
Sheppard, Miss M. R.	Bridgenorth	1842-1843	Scriptural	—	—	—	—	4	—	—	—	—	—	4
Sheppard, Oliver	London	1891-1893	Sculpture	—	—	2	—	—	—	—	—	—	—	2
Sheppard, Philip	Bath	1861-1866	Landscape	—	—	3	—	3	—	—	—	—	3	9
Sheppard, W.	London	1810-1811	Architecture	—	—	2	—	—	—	—	—	—	—	2
Sheppard, Miss	—	1818	Flowers	—	—	1	—	—	—	—	—	—	—	1

Name.	Town.	First and Last Year of Ex.	Speciality.	S. A.	F. S.	R. A.	B. I.	S. S.	O. W.	N. W.	G. G.	N. G.	V. E.	Total
SHEPPERDSON, A. M.	London	1831	Landscape	—	—	—	—	1	—	—	—	—	—	1
SHEPPERSON, J.	London	1820	Still Life	—	—	—	1	—	—	—	—	—	—	1
SHEPPERSON, MATTHEW	London	1811-1821	Portraits	—	—	4	—	—	—	—	—	—	10	14
SHERARD-KENNEDY, EDWARD. *See* K.	—	—	—	—	—	—	—	—	—	—	—	—	—	—
SHERATON, J. RITSON	Bangor	1860-1862	Sea Pieces	—	—	—	2	—	—	—	—	—	—	2
SHERATON, T.	London	1840-1846	Domestic	—	—	3	1	1	—	—	—	—	—	5
SHERBORN, CHARLES WILLIAM, R.P.E.	London	1863-1893	Etching	—	—	36	—	—	—	—	—	—	9	45
SHERBORN, G. F.	Brentford	1853-1855	Landscape	—	—	—	2	1	—	—	—	—	—	3
SHERBORNE —	London	1776	Miniatures	1	—	—	—	—	—	—	—	—	—	1
SHERIDAN, HARRY	Whitehaven	1857	Landscape	—	—	1	—	—	—	—	—	—	—	1
SHERIDAN, J.	London	1786-1790	Portraits	2	—	4	—	—	—	—	—	—	—	6
SHERIDAN, R.	London	1785	Figures	—	—	1	—	—	—	—	—	—	—	1
SHERIFF, JAMES	London	1776	Landscape	1	—	—	—	—	—	—	—	—	—	1
SHERLEY, MISS C.	London	1842-1849	Domestic	—	—	1	—	16	—	—	—	—	—	17
SHERLING, J.	London	1849	Portraits	—	—	1	—	—	—	—	—	—	—	1
SHERLOCK —	London	1775	Wood Carving	—	1	—	—	—	—	—	—	—	—	1
SHERLOCK, JOHN A.	London	1892	Domestic	—	—	—	—	1	—	—	—	—	—	1
SHERLOCK, WILLIAM, F.S.A.	London	1764-1806	Portraits	44	—	22	—	—	—	—	—	—	—	66
SHERLOCK, WILLIAM P.	London	1801-1810	Landscape	—	—	9	—	—	—	—	—	—	—	9
SHERMAN, W.	London	1830	Scriptural	—	—	1	—	—	—	—	—	—	—	1
SHERRARD, MISS FLORENCE E.	London	1884-1893	Domestic	—	—	7	—	7	—	—	—	—	1	15
SHERRARD, JAMES	London	1829-1833	Landscape	—	—	1	2	—	—	—	—	—	—	3
SHERRATT, E.	London	1787-1792	Miniatures	—	—	2	—	—	—	—	—	—	—	2
SHERRATT, THOMAS	London	1861-1880	Engraving	—	—	7	—	—	—	—	—	—	—	7
SHERRIFF, MISS ANNIE	London	1886	Flowers	—	—	—	—	1	—	—	—	—	—	1
SHERRIFF, CHARLES	London	1770-1831	Miniatures	—	6	89	3	8	—	—	—	—	—	106
SHERRIFF, G. VINCENT	Liverpool	1875-1877	Landscape	—	—	1	—	—	—	—	—	—	3	4
SHERRIFF, J.	Birmingham	1827	Seals	—	—	1	—	—	—	—	—	—	—	1
SHERRIFFE, MRS. ANNIE	London	1885-1888	Domestic	—	—	4	—	—	—	—	—	—	2	6
SHERRIN, GEORGE CAMPBELL	London	1880-1889	Architecture	—	—	14	—	—	—	—	—	—	—	14
SHERRIN, JOHN, R.I. ‡	London	1859-1893	Fruit	—	—	41	—	7	—	151	—	—	7	206
SHERWIN, ENOCH	Shelton	1819-1824	Fruit	—	—	1	2	—	—	—	—	—	—	3
SHERWIN, JOHN KEYSE	London	1774-1784	Engraving	1	—	8	—	—	—	—	—	—	—	9
SHETKEY, ALEXANDER	London	1822	Landscape	—	—	—	2	—	—	—	—	—	—	2
SHIELDS, ADA WENTWORTH. *See* W.	—	—	—	—	—	—	—	—	—	—	—	—	—	—
SHIELDS, FREDERICK J., A.R.W.S. †	Manchester	1865-1893	Scriptural	—	—	—	—	—	106	—	—	—	—	106
SHIELDS, HENRY	Glasgow	1890-1891	Sea Coasts	—	—	—	—	2	—	—	—	—	—	2
SHIELDS, HARRY G.	East Barnet	1889-1893	Landscape	—	—	3	—	16	—	—	—	—	6	25
SHIELDS, THOMAS W.	Paris	1880	Figures	—	—	1	—	—	—	—	—	—	—	1
SHIELLS, MISS MARY	—	1783	Portraits	1	—	—	—	—	—	—	—	—	—	1
SHIELLS, MISS SARAH	London	1783-1790	Portraits	4	1	6	—	—	—	—	—	—	—	11
SHIELS, WILLIAM, R.S.A.	London	1808-1852	Domestic	—	—	8	17	12	—	—	—	—	—	37
SHINDLER, MISS FLORENCE A.	Clapton	1888	Architecture	—	—	1	—	—	—	—	—	—	—	1
SHINER, CHRISTOPHER M.	London	1892	Architecture	—	—	1	—	—	—	—	—	—	—	1
SHIPHAM, B.	Nottingham	1852-1872	Landscape	—	—	9	11	15	—	—	—	—	29	64
SHIPLEY, MISS GEORGIANA, AFTERWARDS MRS.	—	—	—	—	—	—	—	—	—	—	—	—	—	—
FRANCIS HARE NAYLOR	—	1781	Portraits	—	—	1	—	—	—	—	—	—	—	1
SHIPWAY, J.	Worcester	1857	Architecture	—	—	2	—	—	—	—	—	—	—	2
SHIPWRIGHT, EMILY A.	London	1893	Still Life	—	—	—	—	1	—	—	—	—	—	1
SHIRLAW, WALTER	London	1881-1891	Domestic	—	—	3	—	—	—	—	—	—	—	3
SHIRLEY, MRS. ARTHUR	—	1859-1866	Horses	—	—	—	1	—	—	—	—	—	1	2
SHIRLEY, MISS ELIZABETH	London	1890-1891	Flowers	—	—	—	—	—	—	3	—	—	—	3
SHIRLEY, HENRY	London	1843-1870	Domestic	—	—	16	40	36	—	—	—	—	—	92
SHIRLEY, J.	London	1830-1832	Landscape	—	—	3	—	—	—	—	—	—	—	3
SHIRREFF, JOHN	Aberdeen	1890	Domestic	—	—	1	—	—	—	—	—	—	—	1
SHIRVING, ARCHIBALD	London	1778-1799	Miniatures	—	—	4	—	—	—	—	—	—	—	4
SHOOSMITH, T. L.	Northampton	1893	Landscape	—	—	—	—	—	—	1	—	—	—	1
SHOPPEE, CHARLES HERBERT	London	1890	Architecture	—	—	1	—	—	—	—	—	—	—	1
SHOPPEE, CHARLES JOHN	London	1860-1876	Architecture	—	—	2	—	—	—	—	—	—	—	2
SHORE, B. E.	London	1893	Landscape	—	—	—	—	1	—	—	—	—	—	1
SHORE, CAPTAIN HON. F. W. J.	Clonmel	1883-1888	Oriental	—	—	2	—	1	—	—	—	—	8	11
SHORE, HON. HENRY W., R.N.	London	1883-1884	Landscape	—	—	—	—	—	—	2	—	—	—	2
SHORSMITH —	London	1819	Portraits	—	—	2	—	—	—	—	—	—	—	2
SHORT, FRANK, R.P.E.	London	1874-1893	Engraving	—	—	26	—	4	—	—	—	—	—	30
SHORT, F. J.	Ramsgate	1871-1876	Sea Pieces	—	—	—	—	1	—	—	—	—	3	4
SHORT, FRED. GOLDEN	Lyndhurst	1885-1892	Landscape	—	—	4	—	6	—	1	—	—	12	23
SHORT, PERCY	Hackney	1888-1892	Figures	—	—	3	—	1	—	—	—	—	2	6
SHORT, RICHARD, R.C.A	Cardiff	1882-1889	Sea Pieces	—	—	9	—	2	—	—	2	—	4	17
SHORT, W. J.	London	1836-1845	Architecture	—	—	9	—	2	—	—	—	—	—	11
SHORTHOUSE, MISS STELLA H.	Croydon	1887-1888	Flowers	—	—	2	—	—	—	—	—	—	—	2
SHORTO, H. H.	Salisbury	1823-1826	Landscape	—	—	2	3	1	—	—	—	—	—	6
SHOTTEN, J.	—	1863	Portraits	—	—	1	—	—	—	—	—	—	—	1

Name.	Town.	First and Last Year of Ex.	Speciality.	S. A.	F. S.	R. A.	B. I.	S. S.	O. W.	N.W.	G. G.	N. G.	V. E.	Total.
Shoubridge, W.	London	1831-1853	Buildings	—	—	6	3	1	—	2	—	—	—	12
Shoubridge, William	Teddington	1875-1877	Domestic	—	—	—	—	—	—	—	—	—	7	7
Shoubridge, Mrs. W.	London	1870	Landscape	—	—	1	—	—	—	—	—	—	—	1
Shout, Robert Howard	London	1845-1849	Architecture	—	—	5	—	—	—	—	—	—	—	5
Shovers, E.	—	1847	Architecture	—	—	1	—	—	—	—	—	—	—	1
Shrapnel, N. H. S.	Gosport	1849-1850	Sporting	—	—	—	2	3	—	—	—	—	—	5
Shrapnell, E. S.	Shirley	1860	Game	—	—	—	—	1	—	—	—	—	—	1
Shrigley and Hunt	Lancaster	1882-1893	Architecture	—	—	16	—	—	—	—	—	—	—	16
Shrimpton, Miss Ada M.	London	1889-1893	Domestic	—	—	3	—	7	—	5	—	—	—	15
Shring, Margaret S.	Uppingham	1880	Landscape	—	—	—	—	—	—	—	—	—	1	1
Shrubsole, W. G.	Maidstone	1881-1886	Landscape	—	—	5	—	—	—	—	—	—	—	5
Shubrook, Miss Emma L.	London	1887	Landscape	—	—	—	—	1	—	1	—	—	—	2
Shubrook, Miss Laura A.	London	1889-1893	Flowers	—	—	2	—	10	—	—	—	—	5	17
Shubrook, Miss Minnie J.	London	1885-1893	Flowers	—	—	15	—	14	—	3	—	—	5	37
Shuckard, Frederick P.	London	1868-1888	Domestic	—	—	13	—	3	—	—	—	—	2	18
Shuffrey, Leonard A.	London	1889	Architecture	—	—	1	—	—	—	—	—	—	—	1
Shuldham, E. B.	London	1864-1889	Landscape	—	—	—	1	5	—	—	—	—	—	6
Shury, George Salisbury	London	1859-1876	Engraving	—	—	8	—	—	—	—	—	—	—	8
Shury, G. W.	Ealing	1833-1838	Landscape	—	—	—	—	1	—	4	—	—	—	5
Shute, Mrs.	London	1886-1888	Portraits	—	—	—	—	—	—	2	1	—	—	3
Shuter, Miss Agnes	London	1881-1884	Sculpture	—	—	3	—	—	—	—	—	—	—	3
Shuter, William	London	1771-1791	Fruit	11	15	4	—	—	—	—	—	—	—	30
Shwab —	London	1768	Engraving	1	—	—	—	—	—	—	—	—	—	1
Shÿffers. *See* Beernaert and Shÿffers	—	—	Carvings	—	—	—	—	—	—	—	—	—	—	—
Sibley, Charles	London	1826-1847	Still Life	—	—	10	6	8	—	—	—	—	—	24
Sibley, Frederick T., R.C.A.	London	1879-1893	River Scenes	—	—	1	—	—	—	—	—	1	4	6
Sibley, G.	London	1844	Architecture	—	—	1	—	—	—	—	—	—	—	1
Sibley, R. S.	London	1838-1839	Architecture	—	—	2	—	—	—	—	—	—	—	2
Sibson, H.	London	1826-1863	Sculpture	—	—	4	—	4	—	—	—	—	—	8
Siccama, R. R.	London	1856	River Scenes	—	—	1	—	—	—	—	—	—	—	1
Sichell, Ernest	Bradford	1885-1893	Sculpture	—	—	1	—	—	—	—	—	2	—	3
Sickert, Bernhard	London	1885-1889	Domestic	—	—	1	—	9	—	—	2	—	—	12
Sickert, Oswald	London	1857-1883	Dramatic	—	—	2	1	—	—	—	2	—	4	9
Sickert, Walter	London	1883-1888	Domestic	—	—	1	—	21	—	1	—	—	3	26
Siddons, Mrs. Sarah (the Actress)	—	1802	Sculpture	—	—	1	—	—	—	—	—	—	—	1
Sidebottom, A.	London	1851	Portraits	—	—	1	—	2	—	—	—	—	—	3
Sidley, Albert	London	1881	Landscape	—	—	—	—	1	—	—	—	—	—	1
Sidley, Samuel, R.B.A., A.R.C.A. §	Manchester	1855-1890	Figures	—	—	30	1	11	—	—	5	—	8	55
Sidney, Herbert	Paris	1876-1883	Historical	—	—	2	—	1	—	—	—	—	1	4
Siervant, Sam.	London	1765	Metal Work	—	1	—	—	—	—	—	—	—	—	1
Sievier, R. M.	London	1846	Sculpture	—	—	1	—	—	—	—	—	—	—	1
Sievier, Robert William	London	1822-1844	Sculpture	—	—	48	7	16	—	—	—	—	—	71
Sigmund, Benjamin D.	London	1880-1893	Domestic	—	—	25	—	28	—	25	—	—	7	85
Signol, Emile	Paris	1853-1866	Scriptural	—	—	3	—	—	—	—	—	—	—	3
Signorini, Telemaco	London	1882-1885	Landscape	—	—	1	—	—	—	—	4	—	—	5
Sigurta, Luigi	London	1774	Portraits	—	—	1	—	—	—	—	—	—	—	1
Silburn, A.	London	1873-1885	Landscape	—	—	3	—	1	—	—	—	—	—	4
Silk, W.	London	1823-1825	Landscape	—	—	1	—	5	—	—	—	—	—	6
Sillavan, George	Manchester	1872	Pen and Ink	—	—	—	—	—	—	—	—	—	1	1
Sillem, Charles	London	1883-1889	Sporting	—	—	3	—	3	—	—	—	—	—	6
Sillett, James	Norwich	1796-1837	Game	—	—	43	—	2	—	—	—	—	4	49
Silverthorne, J.	—	1849	Portraits	—	—	1	—	—	—	—	—	—	—	1
Silvester —	London	1782-1788	Sculpture	—	6	4	—	—	—	—	—	—	—	10
Silvester, Miss H. H.	Windsor	1839	Sketch	—	—	—	—	1	—	—	—	—	—	1
Sim, James	London	1870-1893	Rustic	—	—	12	—	1	—	2	—	—	—	15
Sim, William	London	1855	Architecture	—	—	2	—	—	—	—	—	—	—	2
Simcock, T.	London	1779-1791	Enamels	1	—	3	—	—	—	—	—	—	—	4
Simering, R.	Berlin	1871	Sculpture	—	—	4	—	—	—	—	—	—	—	4
Simkin, J.	Lambeth	1875	Fruit	—	—	—	—	2	—	—	—	—	—	2
Simkin, Miss L.	London	1877	Landscape	—	—	—	—	1	—	—	—	—	—	1
Simkinson, Francis G.	London	1865-1868	Landscape	—	—	—	—	—	—	—	—	—	5	5
Simmonds, Thomas C.	Derby	1881	Landscape	—	—	1	—	—	—	—	—	—	—	1
Simmons, A.	London	1830-1832	Architecture	—	—	5	—	—	—	—	—	—	—	5
Simmons, A. J.	London	1853-1860	Figures	—	—	7	2	5	—	—	—	—	—	14
Simmons, C.	London	1857	Domestic	—	—	—	—	1	—	—	—	—	—	1
Simmons, Edward E.	Paris	1881-1890	Figures	—	—	5	—	3	—	—	1	—	2	11
Simmons, Mrs. E. E. (Vesta S.)	St. Ives, Cornw'l	1889-1890	Figures	—	—	—	—	—	—	—	1	—	1	2
Simmons, H. P.	London	1861-1865	Domestic	—	—	4	—	—	—	—	—	—	—	4
Simmons, John	Bristol	1772-1776	Portraits	—	—	3	—	—	—	—	—	—	—	3
Simmons, J. Deane	Dorking	1882-1889	Rustic	—	—	7	—	14	—	13	—	—	15	49
Simmons, William Henry	London	1857-1882	Engraving	—	—	21	—	—	—	—	—	—	—	21
Simmons, W. St. Clair	London	1878-1893	Landscape	—	—	7	—	4	—	11	—	5	20	47

Name.	Town.	First and Last Year of Ex.	Speciality.	S. A.	F. S.	R. A.	B. I.	S. S.	O. W.	N. W.	G. G.	N. G.	V. E.	Total.
Simmons and Rumsey	—	1850	Architecture	—	—	1	—	—	—	—	—	—	—	1
Simms, A. G.	London	1859-1873	Sporting	—	—	5	9	20	—	—	—	—	7	41
Simms, C. Nares	—	1878	Landscape	—	—	—	—	—	—	—	1	—	—	1
Simms, G. H.	Bath	1864-1865	Landscape	—	—	—	1	1	—	—	—	—	—	2
Simon, Miss Eva	London	1892	British Museum	—	—	—	—	—	—	—	—	—	1	1
Simon, J. P.	London	1785-1786	Miniatures	—	—	7	—	—	—	—	—	—	—	7
Simonau, George ‡	Brussels	1859-1870	Landscape	—	—	—	—	—	—	21	—	—	—	21
Simonds, George	Rome	1866-1893	Sculpture	—	—	36	—	—	—	—	1	4	5	46
Simoneau, F.	London	1818-1860	Portraits	—	—	18	4	1	—	—	—	—	—	23
Simonetti, Cavaliere Attilio	—	1876	Portraits	—	—	1	—	—	—	—	—	—	—	1
Simoni, G.	London	1884	Algeria	—	—	1	—	—	—	—	—	—	—	1
Simons, E.	Liverpool	1798	Flowers	—	—	1	—	—	—	—	—	—	—	1
Simons, Marcius	Northampton	1891	Domestic	—	—	1	—	—	—	—	—	—	—	1
Simonson, D.	London	1858-1859	Historical	—	—	5	—	—	—	—	—	—	—	5
Simpkin, T.	London	1786-1794	Architecture	—	—	2	—	—	—	—	—	—	—	2
Simpkins —	London	1783	Copies	—	3	—	—	—	—	—	—	—	—	3
Simpson, Miss Agnes	London	1827-1848	Portraits	—	—	24	—	10	—	—	—	—	—	34
Simpson, Alice M.	London	1885	Flowers	—	—	—	—	1	—	—	—	—	—	1
Simpson, C.	London	1811	Figures	—	—	1	—	—	—	—	—	—	—	1
Simpson, Charles	London	1833-1847	Landscape	—	—	4	8	7	—	1	—	—	—	20
Simpson, C. N.	Stamford	1828-1831	Buildings	—	—	3	—	—	—	—	—	—	—	3
Simpson, Miss Eugenie	Hackney	1883-1888	Flowers	—	—	7	—	2	—	—	—	—	4	13
Simpson, Francis	London	1827-1833	Landscape	—	—	1	—	2	—	—	—	—	—	3
Simpson, F., Junr.	—	1828-1832	Landscape	—	—	3	—	—	—	—	—	—	—	3
Simpson, F.	Wakefield	1878	Architecture	—	—	2	—	—	—	—	—	—	—	2
Simpson, Mrs. F.	Derby	1831	Sporting	—	—	1	—	—	—	—	—	—	—	1
Simpson, Frederick Moore	London	1885-1892	Architecture	—	—	5	—	—	—	—	—	—	—	5
Simpson, G.	London	1799	Miniatures	—	—	1	—	—	—	—	—	—	—	1
Simpson, G.	—	1807	Landscape	—	—	1	—	—	—	—	—	—	—	1
Simpson, G., Junr.	—	1807	Portraits	—	—	1	—	—	—	—	—	—	—	1
Simpson, G.	London	1812-1827	Landscape	—	—	4	—	6	—	—	—	—	—	10
Simpson, George G.	London	1883-1885	Studies	—	—	2	—	—	—	—	—	—	—	2
Simpson, Henry	London	1875-1891	Figures	—	—	4	—	10	—	6	4	—	5	29
Simpson, Harry B.	London	1886-1888	Domestic	—	—	2	—	—	—	2	—	—	—	4
Simpson, H. Hardey	Bowden	1885-1888	Sporting	—	—	2	—	2	—	—	—	—	—	4
Simpson, John	London	1807-1847	Portraits	—	—	126	15	12	—	—	—	—	—	153
Simpson, John	London	1831-1871	Enamels	—	—	28	—	2	—	—	—	—	—	30
Simpson, J. H.	—	1877	Sporting	—	—	1	—	—	—	—	—	—	—	1
Simpson, John W.	London	1878-1881	Architecture	—	—	2	—	—	—	—	—	—	—	2
Simpson (J. W.) and Allen (E. M. J.)	London	1893	Architecture	—	—	1	—	—	—	—	—	—	—	1
Simpson, Mrs. Katharine	Whitby	1892-1893	Fishing Boats	—	—	—	—	3	—	—	—	—	—	3
Simpson, Miss Mary	London	1849-1858	Miniatures	—	—	12	—	—	—	—	—	—	—	12
Simpson, Miss Margaret H. A.	London	1881-1890	Domestic	—	—	2	—	7	—	—	—	—	2	11
Simpson, O. N.	—	1829	Landscape	—	—	—	—	1	—	—	—	—	—	1
Simpson, Philip	London	1824-1837	Domestic	—	—	14	9	9	—	—	—	—	—	32
Simpson, Miss R.	London	1875	Domestic	—	—	—	—	1	—	—	—	—	—	1
Simpson, Miss Sophia	London	1862-1863	Figures	—	—	1	1	1	—	—	—	—	—	3
Simpson, Thomas	London	1765-1778	Engraving	1	6	1	—	—	—	—	—	—	—	8
Simpson, Thomas	London	1887-1891	Landscape	—	—	2	—	4	—	—	—	—	—	6
Simpson, T. M.	London	1804-1821	Historical	—	—	18	—	—	—	—	—	—	—	18
Simpson, T. Penkhule	Newcastle-under-Lyne	1847	Enamels	—	—	—	1	—	—	—	—	—	—	1
Simpson, William, R.I. ‡	London	1874-1893	Eastern	—	—	—	—	1	—	43	—	—	—	44
Simpson, W. B.	London	1820	Portraits	—	—	1	—	—	—	—	—	—	—	1
Simpson, W. B.	London	1838-1840	Ship Cabins	—	—	2	—	—	—	—	—	—	—	2
Simpson, W. Graham	London	1878-1889	Miniatures	—	—	6	—	1	—	—	—	—	—	7
Simpson, W. H. φ	London	1866-1886	Landscape	—	—	3	—	18	—	—	—	—	15	36
Simpson, William Page	London	1859-1877	Enamels	—	—	8	—	3	—	—	—	—	—	11
Simpson, Mrs. *See* Miss Maria E. Burt	Willesden	1882-1883	Miniatures	—	—	5	—	—	—	2	—	—	—	7
Simpson, Miss	—	1799	Landscape	—	—	1	—	—	—	—	—	—	—	1
Sims —	London	1782	Drawings	—	2	—	—	—	—	—	—	—	—	2
Sims, Charles	London	1840-1875	Landscape	—	—	13	15	32	—	—	—	—	3	63
Sims, Charles H.	London	1893	Animals	—	—	1	—	—	—	—	—	—	—	1
Sims, Frederick	Stockwell	1859	Figures	—	—	1	—	—	—	—	—	—	—	1
Sims, Frederick Thomas	London	1859-1860	Landscape	—	—	—	2	—	—	—	—	—	—	2
Sims, G. ‡	London	1829-1840	Landscape	—	—	11	15	31	—	61	—	—	—	118
Sims, William	London	1821-1867	Portraits	—	—	25	7	3	—	—	—	—	—	35
Sims, William Percy	London	1848	Architecture	—	—	1	—	—	—	—	—	—	—	1
Simson, J.	—	1845	Study	—	—	—	1	—	—	—	—	—	—	1
Simson, William, R.S.A.	Edinburgh	1826-1848	Domestic	—	—	25	30	1	—	—	—	—	—	56
Sinclair, John	Liverpool	1872-1890	Landscape	—	—	3	—	8	—	2	—	—	4	17
Sindici, Mrs. Francesca Stuart	London	1892-1893	Military	—	—	2	—	—	—	—	—	—	—	2
Sinding, Otto	Edinburgh	1890	Figures	—	—	—	—	—	—	1	—	—	—	1

Name.	Town.	First and Last Year of Ex.	Speciality.	S. A.	F. S.	R. A.	B. I.	S. S.	O. W.	N.W.	G. G.	N. G.	V. E.	Total.
SINGER, MISS AMY M.	Frome	1882-1889	Sculpture	—	—	9	—	—	—	—	—	—	—	9
SINGER, MISS MARY ANNE	Frome	1889	Sculpture	—	—	—	—	—	—	—	—	1	—	1
SINGER, W. H.	Frome	1875	Street Scenes	—	—	—	—	—	—	—	—	—	2	2
SINGLETON —	—	1807	Portraits	—	—	1	—	—	—	—	—	—	—	1
SINGLETON, HENRY	London	1780-1839	Scriptural	2	—	285	157	5	—	—	—	—	—	449
SINGLETON, MRS. H.	London	1808-1822	Miniatures	—	—	9	6	—	—	—	—	—	—	15
SINGLETON, JOSEPH	London	1773-1788	Miniatures	—	—	30	—	—	—	—	—	—	—	30
SINGLETON, MISS MARIA	London	1815-1822	Portraits	—	—	6	—	—	—	—	—	—	—	6
SINGLETON, MISS SARAH MACKLARINAN	London	1787-1813	Miniatures	—	—	74	—	—	—	—	—	—	—	74
SINGLETON, WILLIAM	London	1770-1790	Enamels	6	—	4	—	—	—	—	—	—	—	10
SINKEL, H. Y.	Düsseldorf	1875	Scriptural	—	—	—	—	1	—	—	—	—	2	3
SINNETT, MISS SOPHIA	Southampton	1853-1858	Domestic	—	—	4	2	5	—	—	—	—	—	11
SINTRAM, H. S. R.	London	1880	Rustic	—	—	—	—	—	—	—	1	—	—	1
SINTZENICH, GUSTAV	London	1809-1838	Still Life	—	—	8	—	10	—	—	—	—	—	18
SINTZENICH, GUSTAVUS ELLINTHORPE	London	1844-1866	Historical	—	—	16	11	13	—	—	—	—	3	43
SISSMORE, CHARLES	London	1885-1887	Landscape	—	—	1	—	—	—	—	—	—	3	4
SITWELL, CAPTAIN H.	London	1868	Sea Pieces	—	—	—	—	1	—	—	—	—	—	1
SIVED, G.	London	1780	Domestic	—	2	—	—	—	—	—	—	—	—	2
SIVIER, G.	London	1852-1865	Fruit	—	—	5	4	—	—	—	—	—	—	9
SKAIFE, T.	Liverpool	1846-1852	Miniatures	—	—	6	—	—	—	—	—	—	—	6
SKEAF, D.	London	1807-1819	Landscape	—	—	9	3	—	—	—	—	—	—	12
SKEAT, EDMUND	London	1790	Landscape	1	—	—	—	—	—	—	—	—	—	1
SKEATS, FRANK G.	Southampton	1876-1887	Landscape	—	—	—	—	3	—	2	—	—	1	6
SKEATS, THOMAS	Southampton	1875-1882	Flowers	—	—	—	—	13	—	—	—	—	6	19
SKEEMAKERS, T.	London	1782-1788	Sculpture	—	—	7	—	—	—	—	—	—	—	7
SKELLY, COLONEL	—	1792-1794	Landscape	—	—	5	—	—	—	—	—	—	—	5
SKELTON, MISS CATHERINE	London	1822-1830	Fruit	—	—	1	—	1	—	—	—	—	—	2
SKELTON, JOSEPH	Hinckley	1888-1893	Domestic	—	—	1	—	—	—	1	—	—	5	7
SKELTON, PERCIVAL	Norwood	1850-1861	Landscape	—	—	3	—	1	—	—	—	—	—	4
SKETCHLEY —	London	1783	Flowers	—	1	—	—	—	—	—	—	—	—	1
SKIDMORE, MISS HARRIET	London	1875-1890	Domestic	—	—	1	—	5	—	—	—	—	—	6
SKILBECK, CLEMENT O.	London	1884-1892	Scriptural	—	—	1	—	1	—	1	—	4	2	9
SKILL, FREDERICK JOHN ‡	London	1858-1881	Landscape	—	—	11	—	17	—	176	3	—	43	250
SKILLETT, S. D.	London	1845-1856	Sea Pieces	—	—	8	4	3	—	—	—	—	3	18
SKILLINGTON, G.	London	1838-1841	Cattle	—	—	1	—	4	—	—	—	—	—	5
SKINNER, EDWARD F.	London	1888-1891	Landscape	—	—	2	—	2	—	—	—	—	—	4
SKINNER, JOHN	London	1776-1787	Miniatures	—	—	2	—	—	—	—	—	—	—	2
SKINNER, MISS V. M.	Saxmundham	1870	Still Life	—	—	—	—	1	—	—	—	—	—	1
SKIPWORTH, ARTHUR HENRY	London	1889-1893	Reredos	—	—	6	—	—	—	—	—	—	—	6
SKIPWORTH, FRANK MARKHAM	London	1882-1893	Figures	—	—	25	—	12	—	4	13	10	33	97
SKIRVING, ALEXANDER	Glasgow	1874-1876	Architecture	—	—	3	—	—	—	—	—	—	—	3
SKOTTOWE, CHARLES	London	1834-1842	Figures	—	—	6	5	1	—	—	—	—	—	12
SKURRY, MISS E.	London	1800	Miniatures	—	—	1	—	—	—	—	—	—	—	1
SLACK, MISS M. E.	London	1871-1875	Figures	—	—	1	—	5	—	—	—	—	1	7
SLADE. *See* Williams, West, and Slade	—	—	Architecture	—	—	—	—	—	—	—	—	—	—	—
SLADE SCHOOL	—	1882	Medals	—	—	—	—	—	—	—	1	—	—	1
SLADER, SAMUEL ERNEST	London	1876-1879	Fruit	—	—	1	—	1	—	—	—	—	5	7
SLATER, C. H.	Manchester	1867	Fruit	—	—	—	—	1	—	—	—	—	—	1
SLATER, GEORGE. *See also* Barkentin	London	1861-1863	Sculpture	—	—	3	—	—	—	—	—	—	—	3
SLATER, JOSEPH	London	1772-1787	Portraits	—	5	4	—	—	—	—	—	—	—	9
SLATER, JOSIAH	London	1806-1833	Miniatures	—	—	130	—	—	—	—	—	—	—	130
SLATER, JOSIAH, JUNR.	London	1808-1818	Portraits	—	—	6	—	—	—	—	—	—	—	6
SLATER, J. ATWOOD	London	1883-1893	Churches	—	—	11	—	—	—	1	—	—	—	12
SLATER, JOHN F.	Forest Hall, Northumberland	1889-1892	Rustic	—	—	3	—	—	—	—	—	—	—	3
SLATER, J. R.	London	1836	Sculpture	—	—	1	—	—	—	—	—	—	—	1
SLATER, J. T.	London	1873	Landscape	—	—	—	—	2	—	—	—	—	—	2
SLATER, J. W. (?) ISAAC W.	London	1803-1836	Miniatures	—	—	67	—	—	—	—	—	—	—	67
SLATER, PETER	London	1846-1870	Sculpture	—	—	30	—	—	—	—	—	—	—	30
SLATER, WILLIAM	London	1856-1859	Architecture	—	—	4	—	—	—	—	—	—	—	4
SLATER (W.) AND CARPENTER (R. H.)	London	1865-1868	Architecture	—	—	3	—	—	—	—	—	—	—	3
SLATER, WALTER JAMES, R.C.A.	Manchester	1877-1890	Landscape	—	—	11	—	—	—	1	—	—	—	12
SLEAP, J. A.	London	1858-1859	River Scenes	—	—	—	—	—	—	—	—	—	6	6
SLEIGH, JOHN	London	1841-1872	Landscape	—	—	1	—	3	—	—	—	—	12	16
SLEIGH, MRS. WARNER (PHILL)	London	1881-1883	Sculpture	—	—	4	—	—	—	—	—	—	—	4
SLINGER, F. J.	London	1858-1867	Domestic	—	—	3	4	—	—	—	—	—	1	8
SLINGSBY, JOSEPH	London	1787-1799	Architecture	2	—	8	—	—	—	—	—	—	—	10
SLOANE, MISS MARY A.	London	1889-1893	Landscape	—	—	—	—	3	—	7	—	—	1	11
SLOCOMBE, ALFRED, R.C A.	London	1862-1887	Flowers	—	—	6	2	4	—	1	—	—	5	18
SLOCOMBE, CHARLES PHILIP	London	1850-1882	Etching	—	—	30	4	17	—	—	—	—	23	74
SLOCOMBE, EDWARD C., R.P.E.	London	1868-1893	Etching	—	—	29	—	2	—	—	—	—	11	42
SLOCOMBE, FREDERICK ALBERT, R.P.E. ‡	London	1866-1892	Etching	—	—	40	—	64	—	4	—	—	42	150
SLOCOMBE, SHIRLEY CHARLES LLEWELLYN	London	1887-1893	Heads	—	—	1	—	—	—	4	—	—	1	6

Name.	Town.	First and Last Year of Ex.	Speciality.	S. A.	F. S.	R. A.	B. I.	S. S.	O. W.	N.W.	G. G.	N. G.	V. E.	Total.
Slous, George	Deptford	1791-1839	Miniatures	—	—	65	9	1	—	—	—	—	—	75
Slous, Henry Courtney. *See* Selous	London	1818-1831	Portraits	—	—	8	4	6	—	—	—	—	—	18
Slous, Mrs.	—	1812	Landscape	—	—	1	—	—	—	—	—	—	—	1
Sluce, J. A.	London	1833-1837	Portraits	—	—	5	—	2	—	—	—	—	—	7
Small, Miss Florence	Nottingham	1881-1893	Domestic	—	—	11	—	1	—	—	—	—	8	20
Small, William, R.I. ‡	London	1869-1893	Landscape	—	—	30	—	—	—	61	1	—	54	146
Smallbone, Miss Eliza Anne. *See* Mrs. Alexander	—	—	—	—	—	—	—	—	—	—	—	—	—	—
Melville	Blackheath	1854-1855	Landscape	—	—	1	2	1	—	—	—	—	—	4
Smallfield, Frederick, A.R.W.S. †	London	1849-1893	Figures	—	—	39	6	11	425	2	11	—	38	532
Smallfield, Philip C.	London	1882-1887	Domestic	—	—	5	—	2	—	1	—	—	2	10
Smallwood, C.	London	1873	Landscape	—	—	—	—	1	—	—	—	—	—	1
Smallwood, William Frome	London	1826-1834	Landscape	—	—	17	—	8	—	—	—	—	—	25
Smart, Charles J.	London	1867-1891	Still Life	—	—	—	—	2	—	2	—	—	—	4
Smart, John, F.S.A.	London	1762-1813	Miniatures	107	—	41	—	—	—	—	—	—	—	148
Smart, John, Junr.	London	1770-1811	Miniatures	2	2	23	—	—	—	—	—	—	—	27
Smart, John	Ipswich	1791-1850	Historical	1	—	2	14	6	—	—	—	—	—	23
Smart, John, R.S.A., R.S.W., R.B.A. §	Edinburgh	1870-1892	Landscape	—	—	24	—	8	—	4	8	—	2	46
Smart, R.	London	1855-1856	Landscape	—	—	—	3	—	—	—	—	—	—	3
Smart, R. K.	London	1832-1833	Sea Pieces	—	—	1	—	13	—	—	—	—	—	14
Smart, Samuel Paul	London	1774-1797	Miniatures	2	—	24	—	—	—	—	—	—	—	26
Smart, T.	London	1835-1855	Historical	—	—	9	8	19	—	—	—	—	—	36
Smartley, H.	St. Heliers	1839-1845	Figures	—	—	—	—	2	—	—	—	—	—	2
Smeasters —	London	1767	Landscape	—	1	—	—	—	—	—	—	—	—	1
Smeeton, A. Williams	London	1855-1860	Sea Pieces	—	—	—	—	7	—	—	—	—	4	11
Smeeton, G.	Kibworth	1832-1834	Portraits	—	—	2	—	1	—	—	—	—	—	3
Smeeton, J.	Leamington	1838-1856	Figures	—	—	—	1	7	—	—	—	—	—	8
Smetham, James	London	1851-1876	Domestic	—	—	18	2	17	—	—	—	—	1	38
Smetham-Jones, G. *See* J.	—	—	—	—	—	—	—	—	—	—	—	—	—	—
Smirke, Miss Mary	London	1809-1814	Landscape	—	—	6	—	—	—	—	—	—	—	6
Smirke, Robert, R.A., F.S.A.	London	1775-1834	Historical	7	—	25	1	5	—	—	—	—	—	38
Smirke, Sir Robert, R.A.	London	1801-1810	Architecture, etc.	—	—	5	—	—	—	—	—	—	—	5
Smirke, Sydney, R.A., F.R.I.B.A.	London	1820-1869	Architecture	—	—	14	—	—	—	—	—	—	—	14
Smith. *See* Campbell and Smith, *and* Lee and Smith	—	—	Architecture	—	—	—	—	—	—	—	—	—	—	—
Smith —	Bristol	1780	Figures	—	2	—	—	—	—	—	—	—	—	2
Smith —	London	1790-1817	Medals	—	—	2	—	—	—	—	—	—	—	2
Smith —	London	1840	Sporting	—	—	2	—	—	—	—	—	—	—	2
Smith, Captain	—	1791	Portraits	—	—	1	—	—	—	—	—	—	—	1
Smith, A.	Stourhead	1837-1838	Domestic	—	—	—	1	3	—	—	—	—	—	4
Smith, Adam	London	1768-1770	Engraving	—	7	—	—	—	—	—	—	—	—	7
Smith, Alfred. *See also* Parnell and Smith	London	1843-1872	Architecture	—	—	13	—	—	—	—	—	—	—	13
Smith (A.) and Henman	London	1872	Architecture	—	—	1	—	—	—	—	—	—	—	1
Smith (A.) and Risley (T.)	London	1865	Architecture	—	—	2	—	—	—	—	—	—	—	2
Smith (A.) and Thurston	London	1851-1853	Architecture	—	—	3	—	—	—	—	—	—	—	3
Smith, Anker, A.R.A.	London	1794-1818	Engraving	—	—	31	—	1	—	—	—	—	—	32
Smith, Miss Annie	Royston	1874-1880	Landscape	—	—	1	—	1	—	—	—	—	—	2
Smith, Arthur	London	1874-1885	Landscape	—	—	2	—	13	—	—	—	—	—	15
Smith, Mrs. A.	—	1837	Flowers	—	—	1	—	—	—	—	—	—	—	1
Smith, A. B.	Devonport	1870-1872	Landscape	—	—	—	—	3	—	—	—	—	—	3
Smith, Albert D.	London	1888-1891	Architecture	—	—	5	—	—	—	—	—	—	—	5
Smith, Albert G.	London	1889	Landscape	—	—	2	—	—	—	—	—	—	—	2
Smith, Arthur John	London	1873-1891	Sculpture	—	—	9	—	6	—	—	—	2	2	19
Smith, Miss Anna Leigh	Algiers	1876-1886	Oriental	—	—	—	—	—	—	1	1	—	5	7
Smith, Mrs. Beatrice	London	1890	Domestic	—	—	—	—	—	—	—	—	—	1	1
Smith, B.	London	1842-1851	Sculpture	—	—	19	—	—	—	—	—	—	—	19
Smith, Bernard	London	1875-1893	Architecture	—	—	4	—	—	—	—	—	—	—	4
Smith, Bryce	London	1843-1861	Miniatures	—	—	13	—	2	—	—	—	—	—	15
Smith, Bernard E.	London	1878-1886	Architecture	—	—	7	—	—	—	—	—	—	—	7
Smith, Miss Barbara Leigh. *See* Madame	—	—	—	—	—	—	—	—	—	—	—	—	—	—
Eugène Bodichon	London	1850-1856	Landscape	—	—	8	1	2	—	—	—	—	10	21
Smith, Miss C.	Dulwich	1875	Landscape	—	—	—	—	1	—	—	—	—	—	1
Smith, Mrs. Caroline	London	1832-1869	Figures	—	—	4	10	18	—	—	—	—	—	32
Smith, Chadwell	Rye	1886-1892	Domestic	—	—	1	—	2	—	—	—	—	7	10
Smith, Charles	London	1776-1797	Historical	3	—	13	—	—	—	—	—	—	—	16
Smith, Charles	London	1815-1827	Allegorical	—	—	20	2	—	—	—	—	—	—	22
Smith, Charles	London	1820-1841	Sculpture	—	—	25	2	10	—	—	—	—	—	37
Smith, Charles	Greenwich	1857-1893	Landscape	—	—	52	30	145	—	3	—	—	72	302
Smith (Charles) and Son	Reading	1885-1887	Architecture	—	—	3	—	—	—	—	—	—	—	3
Smith, Miss Clifford	London	1823-1855	Miniatures	—	—	5	—	—	—	—	—	—	7	12
Smith, Coke	—	1881	Historical	—	—	—	—	—	—	—	2	—	—	2
Smith, Colvin, R.S.A.	Edinburgh	1830-1871	Portraits	—	—	13	2	1	—	—	—	—	—	16
Smith, Carlton Alfred, R.I., R.B.A. § ‡ φ	London	1871-1893	Domestic	—	—	17	—	158	—	23	—	—	45	243
Smith, Mrs. Carlton A.	London	1883-1893	Sea Shores	—	—	—	—	15	—	—	—	—	1	16

Name.	Town.	First and Last Year of Ex.	Speciality.	S. A.	F. S.	R. A.	B. I.	S. S.	O. W.	N. W.	G. G.	N. G.	V. E.	Total.
Smith, C. Christopher	Brockley	1888	Landscape	—	—	1	—	—	—	—	—	—	—	1
Smith, C. Dowton	London	1842-1854	Sea Pieces	—	—	9	5	17	—	—	—	—	—	31
Smith, Charles Edward	London	1860-1868	Sculpture	—	—	3	—	—	—	—	—	—	—	3
Smith, C. Frithjof	Munich	1889	Domestic	—	—	1	—	—	—	—	—	—	—	1
Smith, Charles Harriot	London	1809-1824	Sculpture, etc.	—	—	9	—	—	—	—	—	—	—	9
Smith, Mrs. C. H.	London	1837-1875	Miniatures	—	—	13	—	—	—	—	—	—	—	13
Smith, Miss Constance J.	Bath	1890-1893	Miniatures	—	—	2	—	—	—	—	—	—	—	2
Smith, C. L.	—	1795-1806	Sporting	—	—	6	—	—	—	—	—	—	—	6
Smith, C. M.	London	1847	Landscape	—	—	—	—	2	—	—	—	—	—	2
Smith, C. M.	Watford	1881	Birds	—	—	—	—	—	—	—	—	—	1	1
Smith, Charles Raymond	London	1842-1876	Sculpture	—	—	7	—	—	—	—	—	—	—	7
Smith, C. S.	London	1808-1828	Architecture	—	—	6	—	—	—	—	—	—	—	6
Smith, Charles S.	Reading	1885	Buildings	—	—	1	—	—	—	—	—	—	—	1
Smith, Miss Clifford S.	London	1832-1851	Domestic	—	—	3	—	12	—	—	—	—	—	15
Smith, C. Welby	London	1839-1885	Sea Pieces	—	—	4	—	7	—	—	—	—	—	11
Smith, C. William	London	1861	Sea Pieces	—	—	—	—	—	—	—	—	—	3	3
Smith, D.	London	1813	Animals	—	—	1	—	—	—	—	—	—	—	1
Smith, D. Murray	London	1893	Landscape	—	—	—	—	2	—	—	—	—	1	3
Smith, E.	London	1827-1875	Scriptural	—	—	3	1	13	—	—	—	—	—	17
Smith, E.	Sheffield	1843	Sculpture	—	—	1	—	—	—	—	—	—	—	1
Smith, Edward	Capri	1875-1876	Landscape	—	—	—	—	—	—	—	—	—	3	3
Smith, Miss Emma	London	1799-1808	Miniatures	—	—	35	—	—	—	—	—	—	5	40
Smith, Miss Emily	Dublin	1856-1861	Domestic	—	—	2	—	3	—	—	—	—	—	5
Smith, Ernest	London	1869-1889	Landscape	—	—	6	—	2	—	—	—	—	—	8
Smith, Miss Eliza A.	London	1865-1867	Fruit	—	—	—	1	—	—	—	—	—	3	4
Smith, Edward Blount	London	1877-1893	Landscape	—	—	4	—	13	—	3	6	3	15	44
Smith, E. Cleave-. *See* Cleavesmith.	—	—	—	—	—	—	—	—	—	—	—	—	—	—
Smith, Edwin D.	London	1816-1847	Miniatures	—	—	66	—	13	—	3	—	—	—	82
Smith, Miss E. D.	—	1838	Miniatures	—	—	1	—	—	—	—	—	—	—	1
Smith, Miss Edith Heckstall	Beckenham	1884-1890	Rustic	—	—	4	—	6	—	3	—	—	2	15
Smith, Mrs. E. S.	London	1860	Still Life	—	—	—	—	1	—	—	—	—	—	1
Smith, Miss E. Toulmin	London	1868-1872	Domestic	—	—	—	—	6	—	—	—	—	2	8
Smith, Francesco	London	1768-1802	Vesuvius, etc.	1	—	11	—	—	—	—	—	—	—	12
Smith, F.	—	1800-1804	Landscape	—	—	8	—	—	—	—	—	—	—	8
Smith, Frederick	London	1873-1876	Figures	—	—	2	—	—	—	—	—	—	2	4
Smith, F. A.	London	1832-1833	Intaglios	—	—	2	—	—	—	—	—	—	—	2
Smith, Frederick G.	Stroud Green	1889	Stained Glass	—	—	1	—	—	—	—	—	—	—	1
Smith, Mrs. F. G.	London	1869	Figures	—	—	—	—	—	—	—	—	—	1	1
Smith, F. H.	London	1820-1831	Scriptural	—	—	—	2	—	—	—	—	—	—	2
Smith, Miss Frederica J.	London	1862-1863	Fruit	—	—	—	—	3	—	—	—	—	—	3
Smith, F. M. Bell-	London	1888	Landscape	—	—	1	—	1	—	—	—	—	—	2
Smith, F. R.	London	1881	Landscape	—	—	—	—	—	—	—	—	—	1	1
Smith, F. S.	London	1847	Figures	—	—	2	—	—	—	—	—	—	—	2
Smith, Frederick William	London	1818-1828	Sculpture	—	—	14	—	—	—	—	—	—	—	14
Smith, G.	London	1789-1805	Miniatures	1	—	37	—	—	—	—	—	—	—	38
Smith, George	Chichester	1760-1774	Landscape	2	103	4	—	—	—	—	—	—	—	109
Smith, George	London	1801-1829	Architecture	—	—	19	—	—	—	—	—	—	—	19
Smith, G., Junr.	London	1803-1849	Architecture	—	—	15	—	—	—	—	—	—	—	15
Smith, George	—	1887	Architecture	—	—	1	—	—	—	—	—	—	—	1
Smith (G.) and Barnes (W.)	London	1837-1838	Architecture	—	—	4	—	—	—	—	—	—	—	4
Smith, George	London	1828-1836	Mythological	—	—	5	2	2	—	—	—	—	—	9
Smith, George	London	1847-1887	Domestic	—	—	78	26	15	—	5	—	—	10	134
Smith, Mrs. Graham	London	1891-1892	Portraits	—	—	—	—	—	—	—	—	3	—	3
Smith, George Armfield. *See* Armfield	London	1836-1839	Sporting	—	—	5	2	1	—	—	—	—	—	8
Smith, George E.	London	1874-1880	Sea Shores	—	—	—	—	1	—	—	—	—	3	4
Smith, G. F.	London	1871	Figures	—	—	2	—	—	—	—	—	—	—	2
Smith, Garden G., R.S.W.	Edinburgh	1891	Landscape	—	—	—	—	4	—	—	—	—	—	4
Smith, G. H.	London	1825-1837	Architecture	—	—	14	—	—	—	—	—	—	—	14
Smith, G. J.	Turnham Green	1839-1841	Still Life	—	—	—	2	2	—	—	—	—	—	4
Smith, G. J.	Derby	1866	Scriptural	—	—	1	—	—	—	—	—	—	—	1
Smith, G. R.	London	1847-1873	Figures	—	—	3	—	—	—	—	—	—	—	3
Smith, Miss G. S.	London	1808-1809	Flowers	—	—	2	—	—	—	—	—	—	—	2
Smith, G. W.	Lichfield	1814-1825	Landscape	—	—	—	1	2	11	—	—	—	2	16
Smith, H.	—	1800	—	—	—	*	—	—	—	—	—	—	—	—
Smith, H.	London	1838-1850	Architecture	—	—	2	—	—	—	—	—	—	—	2
Smith, H.	London	1838-1864	Domestic	—	—	1	3	2	—	—	—	—	—	6
Smith, H.	London	1832	Portraits	—	—	—	—	1	—	—	—	—	—	1
Smith, H.	Blackheath	1844	Sculpture	—	—	1	—	—	—	—	—	—	—	1
Smith, Harry	Greenhithe	1869	Landscape	—	—	—	—	1	—	—	—	—	—	1
Smith, Hely	Market Rasen	1890-1891	Figures	—	—	1	—	1	—	—	—	—	—	2
Smith, H. A.	London	1827-1844	Sculpture	—	—	4	—	—	—	—	—	—	—	4
Smith, Hugh Bellingham	Lee	1891-1893	Figures	—	—	2	—	6	—	—	—	—	—	8

Name.	Town.	First and Last Year of Ex.	Speciality.	S. A.	F. S.	R. A.	B. I.	S. S.	O. W.	N. W.	G. G.	N. G.	V. E.	Total.
Smith, Henry Bain-. *See* B.	—	—	—	—	—	—	—	—	—	—	—	—	—	—
Smith, H. C.	London	1820-1833	Sporting	—	—	6	5	7	—	—	—	—	—	18
Smith, Mrs. H. Clarendon ‡	London	1858-1877	Domestic	—	—	—	—	—	—	29	—	—	—	29
Smith, Miss Helen Donald-. *See* D.	—	—	—	—	—	—	—	—	—	—	—	—	—	—
Smith, Mrs. Hannah E.	London	1888-1889	Miniatures	—	—	2	—	—	—	—	—	—	—	2
Smith, Harry F.	London	1886	Sea Pieces	—	—	—	—	1	—	—	—	—	—	1
Smith, H. G.	London	1839-1856	Portraits	—	—	19	—	—	—	—	—	—	—	19
Smith, H. J.	London	1838	Landscape	—	—	—	—	1	—	—	—	—	—	1
Smith, Herbert Luther	London	1830-1854	Scriptural	—	—	27	10	6	—	—	—	—	—	43
Smith, Henry Smith	London	1825-1844	Domestic	—	—	30	4	13	—	—	—	—	—	47
Smith, J.	London	1819	Domestic	—	—	—	1	—	—	—	—	—	—	1
Smith, James	London	1773-1789	Miniatures	1	1	24	—	—	—	—	—	—	—	26
Smith, James	London	1822-1847	Sculpture	—	—	—	3	—	—	—	—	—	—	3
Smith, Joachim, F.S.A.	Bath	1760-1814	Sculpture	51	2	15	—	—	—	—	—	—	—	68
Smith, John	Chichester	1760-1764	Landscape	2	14	—	—	—	—	—	—	—	—	16
Smith, John † (Warwick Smith)	London	1807-1823	Landscape	—	—	—	—	—	159	—	—	—	3	162
Smith, John	London	1854-1876	Landscape	—	—	—	3	2	—	—	—	—	—	5
Smith, Miss J.	London	1802-1809	Miniatures	—	—	13	—	—	—	—	—	—	—	13
Smith, Miss J.	London	1824-1839	Landscape	—	—	1	1	1	—	—	—	—	—	3
Smith, J. Bell	London	1830-1865	Domestic	—	—	20	10	10	—	—	—	—	66	106
Smith, John Brandon	London	1859-1884	Landscape	—	—	22	16	41	—	—	—	—	—	79
Smith, James Burrell	Alnwick	1850-1881	Landscape	—	—	—	—	53	—	—	—	—	12	65
Smith, James Bennett H.	London	1842-1846	Portraits	—	—	6	—	—	—	—	—	—	—	6
Smith, Joseph Clarendon	London	1806-1812	Landscape	—	—	9	1	—	—	—	—	—	27	37
Smith, J. C.	London	1838-1840	Portraits	—	—	3	—	—	—	—	—	—	—	3
Smith, J. Clifford	London	1868-1872	Landscape	—	—	2	—	—	—	—	—	—	—	2
Smith, Miss Julia Cecilia	London	1872-1880	Figures	—	—	—	—	12	—	—	—	—	3	15
Smith, John Henry	London	1852-1893	Domestic	—	—	14	4	17	—	—	—	—	13	48
Smith, J. John	London	1813-1833	Sea Pieces	—	—	6	3	7	—	—	—	—	—	16
Smith, J. L.	—	1832	Horses	—	—	—	—	1	—	—	—	—	—	1
Smith, James MacLaren	London	1873-1876	Illustrations	—	—	7	—	3	—	—	—	—	—	10
Smith, J. Moyr	London	1874-1889	Decorations	—	—	3	—	—	—	—	—	—	3	6
Smith, J. P.	Canterbury	1878	Churches	—	—	—	—	—	—	—	—	—	1	1
Smith, John Raphael	London	1773-1805	Crayons & Engravings	48	8	73	—	—	—	—	—	—	—	129
Smith, John Rubens	London	1796-1811	Portraits	—	—	48	—	—	—	—	—	—	—	48
Smith, J. S.	London	1851	Landscape	—	—	3	—	—	—	—	—	—	—	3
Smith, Miss Jessie Scott-. *See* Scott.	—	—	—	—	—	—	—	—	—	—	—	—	—	—
Smith, John Thomas (Antiquity Smith)	London	1787-1788	Landscape	—	—	2	—	—	—	—	—	—	—	2
Smith, James Whittet	London	1859-1886	Landscape	—	—	6	—	26	—	5	—	—	24	61
Smith, James William	London	1864-1867	Animals	—	—	—	—	2	—	—	—	—	—	2
Smith, James William Garrett	London	1878-1887	Landscape	—	—	10	—	6	—	1	1	—	—	18
Smith, K.	London	1824	Landscape	—	—	1	—	—	—	—	—	—	—	1
Smith, Kate Alice	London	1879	Flowers	—	—	—	—	1	—	—	—	—	—	1
Smith, L.	London	1849	Figures	—	—	3	—	—	—	—	—	—	—	3
Smith, L. B. *See* Harvey and Smith	—	—	Architecture	—	—	—	—	—	—	—	—	—	—	—
Smith, Miss Lucy Bentley, afterwards Mrs. Bentley	Devonport	1879-1893	Domestic	—	—	5	—	3	—	4	—	—	—	12
Smith, Miss Maria. *See* Mrs. H. Ross	London	1791-1808	Miniatures	1	—	—	1	—	—	—	—	—	—	2
Smith, Miss Matilda	London	1823-1824	Miniatures	—	—	2	—	—	—	—	—	—	—	2
Smith, M.	London	1848-1849	Landscape	—	—	—	3	—	—	—	—	—	—	3
Smith, Lieut. M.	—	1805	Landscape	—	—	2	—	—	—	—	—	—	—	2
Smith, Miller	Norwich	1885-1893	Domestic	—	—	2	—	2	—	4	—	—	1	9
Smith, Miss M. A.	London	1804-1810	Miniatures	—	—	6	—	—	—	—	—	—	—	6
Smith, Maxwell M.	London	1892	Architecture	—	—	1	—	—	—	—	—	—	—	1
Smith, Nathaniel	London	1761-1773	Sculpture	6	3	2	—	—	—	—	—	—	—	11
Smith, Noel	London	1889-1891	Landscape	—	—	2	—	—	—	1	—	—	—	3
Smith, Miss Olive Wheeler	Addiscombe	1878-1883	Flowers	—	—	2	—	2	—	—	—	—	2	6
Smith, P.	London	1844	Landscape	—	—	1	—	—	—	—	—	—	—	1
Smith, Mrs. Percy	London	1869	Pen and Ink	—	—	—	—	—	—	—	—	—	3	3
Smith, R.	London	1837-1855	Sculpture	—	—	21	—	2	—	—	—	—	—	23
Smith, R.	London	1774-1790	Architecture	4	—	2	—	—	—	—	—	—	—	6
Smith, R.	—	1811	Flowers	—	—	1	—	—	—	—	—	—	—	1
Smith, Reginald	Sheffield	1872-1893	Landscape	—	—	4	—	2	—	2	—	—	—	8
Smith, Richard	London	1825	Landscape	—	—	—	1	—	—	—	—	—	—	1
Smith, Rosa	Croydon	1893	Still Life	—	—	—	—	1	—	—	—	—	—	1
Smith, Robert Catterson	London	1880-1890	Landscape	—	—	7	—	6	—	—	—	—	6	19
Smith, Mrs. R. Catterson	London	1882	Flowers	—	—	—	—	—	—	—	—	—	1	1
Smith, R. Chipchase-	Streatham	1866-1888	Landscape	—	—	—	—	—	—	3	—	—	11	14
Smith, R. M.	London	1832	Sculpture	—	—	1	—	—	—	—	—	—	—	1
Smith, Miss Rosa M.	London	1883-1893	Flowers	—	—	1	—	5	—	—	—	—	—	6
Smith, Robert Ormerod	Rome	1855	Sculpture	—	—	1	—	—	—	—	—	—	—	1
Smith, Miss Rosina R.	London	1860-1871	Sculpture	—	—	—	—	3	—	—	—	—	—	3
Smith, S.	Worcester	1811-1828	Landscape	—	—	—	—	3	—	—	—	—	11	14

Name.	Town.	First and Last Year of Ex.	Speciality.	S. A.	F. S.	R. A.	B. I.	S. S.	O. W.	N.W.	G. G.	N. G.	V. E.	Total.
Smith, S.	London	1823	Landscape	—	—	—	1	—	—	—	—	—	—	1
Smith, S.	London	1807-1829	Architecture	—	—	2	—	—	—	—	—	—	—	2
Smith, Samuel	London	1768-1776	Landscape	5	1	—	—	—	—	—	—	—	—	6
Smith, Miss Sophia	Bath	1766-1804	Miniatures	4	—	8	—	—	—	—	—	—	—	12
Smith, Stephen	Blackheath	1882	Landscape	—	—	—	—	—	—	1	—	—	—	1
Smith, Stuart	London	1858	Landscape	—	—	—	1	—	—	—	—	—	—	1
Smith, Sydney	London	1852-1867	Rustic	—	—	5	—	3	—	—	—	—	—	8
Smith, Miss Sarah Burrell	—	1873-1877	Landscape	—	—	—	—	3	—	—	—	—	—	3
Smith, Stephen Catterson, R.H.A.	Dublin	1828-1858	Portraits	—	—	8	2	—	—	—	—	—	—	10
Smith (S. E.) and Tweedale (J.)	Leeds	1887	Architecture	—	—	1	—	—	—	—	—	—	—	1
Smith, S. G.	London	1846	Mythological	—	—	—	1	—	—	—	—	—	—	1
Smith, Samuel Mountjoy	London	1823-1859	Sea Pieces	—	—	4	8	5	—	—	—	—	12	29
Smith, Sidney R. James	London	1888-1893	Architecture	—	—	6	—	—	—	—	—	—	—	6
Smith, S. S.	London	1870-1877	Engraving	—	—	2	—	—	—	—	—	—	—	2
Smith, S. Theobald	London	1863-1891	Landscape	—	—	—	1	3	—	1	—	—	—	5
Smith, Thomas	London	1773-1788	Miniatures	4	—	6	—	—	—	—	—	—	—	10
Smith, Thomas	Derby	1760-1801	Landscape	3	1	1	—	—	—	—	—	—	—	5
Smith, Rev. T.	—	1797-1812	Landscape	—	—	3	—	—	—	—	—	—	—	3
Smith, Thomas	Lewisham	1821-1877	Sculpture	—	—	45	2	32	—	—	—	—	—	79
Smith, Thomas	—	1823-1836	Landscape	—	—	—	13	—	—	—	—	—	—	13
Smith, Tom	London	1882-1885	Landscape	—	—	—	—	1	—	—	—	—	1	2
Smith, Thomas	London	1852	Architecture	—	—	2	—	—	—	—	—	—	—	2
Smith (T.) and Son	Hertford	1861-1867	Architecture	—	—	3	—	—	—	—	—	—	—	3
Smith, T. B.	Bath	1833	Portraits	—	—	1	—	—	—	—	—	—	—	1
Smith, T. B.	London	1859	Landscape	—	—	—	—	2	—	—	—	—	—	2
Smith, Thomas Correggio	London	1767-1769	Miniatures	3	—	—	—	—	—	—	—	—	—	3
Smith, T. C.	London	1835	Landscape	—	—	—	—	1	—	—	—	—	—	1
Smith, Thomas Henry	London	1888-1891	Architecture	—	—	4	—	—	—	—	—	—	—	4
Smith, T. L.	London	1850	Ruins	—	—	3	—	—	—	—	—	—	—	3
Smith, Thomas Roger	London	1860-1881	Architecture	—	—	10	—	—	—	—	—	—	—	10
Smith (T. Roger) and Gale (Arthur J.)	London	1886-1893	Architecture	—	—	7	—	—	—	—	—	—	—	7
Smith, T. S.	London	1869	Figures	—	—	1	—	—	—	—	—	—	—	1
Smith, T. Strethill	London	1892	Architecture	—	—	1	—	—	—	—	—	—	—	1
Smith, Thomas Tayler	London	1868-1874	Architecture	—	—	2	—	—	—	—	—	—	—	2
Smith (T. T.) and Roper (G. F.)	London	1877	Architecture	—	—	1	—	—	—	—	—	—	—	1
Smith, Miss T. W.	London	1865	Flowers	—	—	1	—	—	—	—	—	—	—	1
Smith, U. T.	London	1826-1827	Landscape	—	—	1	—	1	—	—	—	—	—	2
Smith, W.	London	1843	Cattle	—	—	1	—	—	—	—	—	—	—	1
Smith, W.	London	1830-1831	Portraits	—	—	3	—	1	—	—	—	—	—	4
Smith, W.	London	1834-1851	Figures	—	—	5	—	—	—	—	—	—	—	5
Smith, W.	Leeds	1860	Portraits	—	—	2	—	—	—	—	—	—	—	2
Smith, W.	Newport	1841-1859	Animals	—	—	15	—	—	—	—	—	—	—	15
Smith, Mrs. W.	Edmonton	1858-1860	Domestic	—	—	1	1	2	—	—	—	—	—	4
Smith, Mrs. W.	London	1859	Landscape	—	—	—	—	—	—	—	—	—	1	1
Smith, Wells	London	1870-1875	Domestic	—	—	—	—	16	—	—	—	—	—	16
Smith, William	Chichester	1761-1776	Fruit	6	10	—	—	—	—	—	—	—	—	16
Smith, William	London	1774-1802	Portraits	—	—	4	—	—	—	—	—	—	—	4
Smith, William	London	1813-1847	Sporting	—	—	17	15	7	9	—	—	—	—	48
Smith, William	London	1860	Architecture	—	—	1	—	—	—	—	—	—	—	1
Smith, W. A.	London	1821-1826	Architecture	—	—	2	—	—	—	—	—	—	—	2
Smith, W. Armfield	London	1832-1861	Portraits	—	—	8	—	3	—	—	—	—	33	44
Smith, W. A.	London	1885-1892	Landscape	—	—	—	—	1	—	—	3	4	—	8
Smith, W. B.	Sudbury	1833	Fish	—	—	1	—	—	—	—	—	—	—	1
Smith, William Bassett-	London	1880-1887	Landscape	—	—	1	—	—	—	—	4	—	—	5
Smith, William Collingwood, R.W.S. †	London	1836-1887	Landscape	—	—	32	15	21	1064	—	—	—	—	1132
Smith, William H.	London	1863-1880	Fruit	—	—	6	8	17	—	—	—	—	3	34
Smith, W. Harding C., R.B.A. §	London	1868-1893	Domestic	—	—	7	—	29	—	8	—	—	19	63
Smith, William H. Seth-. *See* Seth.	—	—	—	—	—	—	—	—	—	—	—	—	—	—
Smith, William J.	London	1837-1855	Landscape	—	—	9	5	3	—	—	—	—	—	17
Smith, W. P.	London	1843-1858	Landscape	—	—	8	—	10	—	—	—	—	—	18
Smith, William Richard	London	1824-1839	Engraving	—	—	—	—	4	—	—	—	—	—	4
Smith, W. J.	Brighton	1857	Figures	—	—	—	—	1	—	—	—	—	—	1
Smith, Mrs. *See* Miss Stone	London	1791	Still Life	2	—	—	—	—	—	—	—	—	—	2
Smith, Mrs. (?) Clarendon	London	1836	Portraits	—	—	1	—	—	—	—	—	—	—	1
Smith, Miss	London	1799-1804	Landscape	—	—	7	—	—	—	—	—	—	—	7
Smith, Miss	London	1823	Fruit	—	—	1	—	—	—	—	—	—	—	1
Smith, Miss	London	1823-1824	Landscape	—	—	2	—	—	—	—	—	—	—	2
Smith, Miss	Sheffield	1842	Fruit	—	—	—	1	—	—	—	—	—	—	1
Smithers, Collier	London	1892	Portraits	—	—	1	—	—	—	—	—	—	—	1
Smithers, H.	Eton	1849	Still Life	—	—	—	1	—	—	—	—	—	—	1
Smithett, Agnes L., *or* J.	London	1893	Buildings	—	—	—	—	1	—	—	—	—	—	1
Smithson —	—	1830	Miniatures	—	—	—	—	1	—	—	—	—	—	1

Name.	Town.	First and Last Year of Ex.	Speciality.	S. A.	F. S.	R. A.	B. I.	S. S.	O.W.	N.W.	G. G.	N. G.	V. E.	Total.
SMITHYES, ARTHUR W., *or* U.	London	1883	Landscape	—	—	—	—	—	—	—	—	—	1	1
SMYTH —	—	1777	Animals	—	—	1	—	—	—	—	—	—	—	1
SMYTH, C.	Brighton	1874	Historical	—	—	1	—	—	—	—	—	—	—	1
SMYTH, COKE	London	1842-1867	Domestic	—	—	4	9	3	—	—	—	—	—	16
SMYTH, EDWARD	London	1819-1844	Fruit	—	—	17	—	7	—	—	—	—	—	24
SMYTH, EMILY R.	Ipswich	1850-1861	Domestic	—	—	5	4	4	—	—	—	—	1	14
SMYTH, H.	Sneinton, Notts	1845	Landscape	—	—	1	—	1	—	—	—	—	—	2
SMYTH, MRS. ISABELLA	London	1780	Still Life	1	—	—	—	—	—	—	—	—	—	1
SMYTH, M.	Brighton	1874	Domestic	—	—	—	—	1	—	—	—	—	—	1
SMYTH, S.	—	1800	Landscape	—	—	1	—	—	—	—	—	—	—	1
SMYTH, T.	Ipswich	1854-1862	Sporting	—	—	3	—	17	—	—	—	—	—	20
SMYTH, W.	London	1825	Fruit	—	—	—	—	1	—	—	—	—	—	1
SMYTH, WALTER MONTAGUE	London	1890-1893	Landscape	—	—	—	—	11	—	6	—	—	2	19
SMYTHE, D.	London	1863	Domestic	—	—	—	—	1	—	—	—	—	—	1
SMYTHE, LESLIE E. B.	London	1863-1867	Landscape	—	—	—	—	4	—	—	—	—	—	4
SMYTHE, LIONEL P., A.R.W.S., R.I. † ‡ φ.	London	1860-1893	Figures	—	—	35	6	31	6	36	—	—	23	137
SMYTHE, RICHARD	London	1888-1889	Engraving	—	—	2	—	—	—	—	—	—	—	2
SMYTHE, W. H.	London	1830	Portraits	—	—	—	—	1	—	—	—	—	—	1
SMYTHIES —	—	1782	Poker Pictures	—	1	—	—	—	—	—	—	—	—	1
SMYTHIES, MRS.	—	1782	Poker Pictures	—	1	—	—	—	—	—	—	—	—	1
SMYTHSON, MARCUS H.	London	1877-1884	Domestic	—	—	1	—	—	—	—	—	—	5	6
SNAPE, MARTIN	Gosport	1875-1890	Figures	—	—	17	—	1	—	—	2	—	8	28
SNAPE, WILLIAM H.	Gosport	1885-1892	Etching	—	—	4	—	—	—	—	—	—	—	4
SNARD, MRS. T. G.	Bishop's Stortford	1849	Landscape	—	—	1	—	—	—	—	—	—	—	1
SNELL, G.	London	1844	Churches	—	—	1	—	—	—	—	—	—	—	1
SNELL, HENRY SAXON	London	1865-1883	Architecture	—	—	4	—	—	—	—	—	—	—	4
SNELL, JAMES HERBERT, R.B.A. §	London	1879-1893	Landscape	—	—	20	—	42	—	2	5	7	17	93
SNELLGROVE, T.	London	1800-1827	Miniatures	—	—	14	—	—	—	—	—	—	—	14
SNEYD, MRS. ELEANOR F.	London	1892-1893	Miniatures	—	—	5	—	—	—	—	—	—	—	5
SNOOKE, W. *See also* Allen, Snooke, and Stock	London	1836	Architecture	—	—	1	—	—	—	—	—	—	—	1
SNOOKE AND STOCK	London	1876	Architecture	—	—	1	—	—	—	—	—	—	—	1
SNOSWELL, W. T.	—	1846	Architecture	—	—	1	—	—	—	—	—	—	—	1
SNOW, HELENA	Dalston	1879	Fruit	—	—	—	—	1	—	—	—	—	—	1
SNOW, J. W.	London	1832	Sporting	—	—	—	—	2	—	—	—	—	—	2
SNOWE, MISS LILLY HILL-. *See* H.	—	—	—	—	—	—	—	—	—	—	—	—	—	—
SNOWMAN, ISAAC	London	1892-1893	Domestic	—	—	1	—	—	—	—	—	—	1	2
SOADY, B.	—	1840	Landscape	—	—	1	—	—	—	—	—	—	—	1
SOANE, SIR JOHN, R.A.	London	1772-1836	Architecture	—	—	168	—	—	—	—	—	—	—	168
SOANE, J., JUNR.	London	1811	Architecture	—	—	2	—	—	—	—	—	—	—	2
SODEN, JOHN E.	London	1861-1887	Domestic	—	—	6	7	64	—	—	—	—	1	78
SODEN, MISS SUSANNAH	London	1866-1890	Flowers	—	—	4	—	4	—	1	—	—	7	16
SOHN, CARL	—	1883	Portraits	—	—	1	—	—	—	—	—	—	—	1
SOILLEUX, FREDERICK	London	1870-1871	Fruit	—	—	—	—	2	—	—	—	—	—	2
SOILLEUX, MISS	—	1810-1816	Fruit	—	—	4	—	—	—	—	—	—	—	4
SOLDI, ANDREA	London	1761-1769	Portraits	4	1	—	—	—	—	—	—	—	—	5
SOLLY, N. NEAL	London	1883	Landscape	—	—	—	—	—	—	1	—	—	—	1
SOLLY, SAMUEL	London	1869-1871	Landscape	—	—	2	—	—	—	—	—	—	1	3
SOLOMON, ABRAHAM	London	1840-1862	Domestic	—	—	33	7	5	—	—	—	—	—	45
SOLOMON, JOSEPH	London	1864	Portraits	—	—	—	—	1	—	—	—	—	—	1
SOLOMON, J. L.	London	1854-1856	Buildings	—	—	1	3	—	—	—	—	—	—	4
SOLOMON, J. W.	London	1827-1849	Domestic	—	—	16	6	5	—	—	—	—	—	27
SOLOMON, MISS REBECCA	London	1851-1875	Domestic	—	—	17	3	2	—	—	—	—	17	39
SOLOMON, SIMEON	London	1858-1872	Domestic	—	—	15	—	—	—	—	—	—	38	53
SOLOMON, SOLOMON J. φ	London	1881-1893	Figures	—	—	25	—	7	—	—	3	1	22	58
SOLOMONS —	London	1782	Portraits	—	1	—	—	—	—	—	—	—	—	1
SOLOMONS, RICHARD	Liverpool	1823	Ships	—	—	1	—	—	—	—	—	—	—	1
SOMERSCALES, JOHN	Hull	1893	Architecture	—	—	1	—	—	—	—	—	—	—	1
SOMERSCALES, THOMAS	Hull	1893	Sea Pieces	—	—	1	—	—	—	—	—	—	2	3
SOMERSET, FRANK	Paris	1878-1883	Figures	—	—	2	—	1	—	—	—	—	3	6
SOMERSET, MISS J.	London	1888	Landscape	—	—	1	—	1	—	—	—	—	2	4
SOMERSET, RICHARD GAY	Manchester	1871-1893	Landscape	—	—	20	—	10	—	—	2	6	14	52
SOMMERS, OTTO	London	1875-1877	Landscape	—	—	—	—	8	—	—	—	—	—	8
SONZA-PINTO, J. J. *See* P.	—	—	—	—	—	—	—	—	—	—	—	—	—	—
SOORD, ALFRED U.	Bushey	1893	Figures	—	—	1	—	—	—	—	—	—	—	1
SOPER, GEORGE	London	1890-1893	Landscape	—	—	1	—	3	—	—	—	—	—	4
SOPER, THOMAS JAMES	Edmonton	1836-1890	Landscape	—	—	47	48	57	—	15	—	—	76	243
SOPER, WILLIAM	London	1882-1883	Enamels	—	—	2	—	—	—	—	—	—	—	2
SORBY, THOMAS CHARLES, F.R.G.S.	London	1856-1864	Architecture	—	—	3	—	—	—	—	—	—	—	3
SORENJEN, C. F.	Paris	1855	Sea Pieces	—	—	1	—	—	—	—	—	—	—	1
SORESBY, J.	London	1821	Portraits	—	—	1	—	—	—	—	—	—	—	1
SORRELL, T.	London	1854	Landscape	—	—	—	—	1	—	—	—	—	—	1
SOTHEBY, HANS W.	London	1873	Landscape	—	—	—	—	2	—	—	—	—	1	3

Name.	Town.	First and Last Year of Ex.	Speciality.	S. A.	F. S.	R. A.	B. I.	S. S.	O. W.	N.W.	G. G.	N. G.	V. E.	Total.
Sothern, Miss Fanny	London	1871-1875	Portraits	—	—	2	—	5	—	—	—	—	6	13
Souef, Le. *See* L.	—	—	—	—	—	—	—	—	—	—	—	—	—	—
Soulten, A. C.	London	1871-1873	Domestic	—	—	—	—	2	—	—	—	—	—	2
Sounes, W.	London	1820-1847	Medals	—	—	4	—	—	—	—	—	—	—	4
Sounes, William Henry	London	1846	Medals	—	—	1	—	—	—	—	—	—	—	1
South —	—	1852	Animals	—	—	—	1	—	—	—	—	—	—	1
South, R. S.	London	1825	Architecture	—	—	1	—	—	—	—	—	—	—	1
Southby, Claudia	London	1869-1874	Flowers	—	—	—	—	1	—	—	—	—	2	3
Southerden, J. E.	London	1827-1835	Still Life	—	—	2	6	23	—	—	—	—	—	31
Southerden, Walker J.	—	1832	Landscape	—	—	—	1	—	—	—	—	—	—	1
Southern, J. M.	Liverpool	1879-1892	Landscape	—	—	9	—	—	—	—	1	—	—	10
Southgate, Miss Elsie	London	1878-1887	Landscape	—	—	3	—	5	—	—	—	—	5	13
Southwell, W. H.	London	1870	Domestic	—	—	1	—	—	—	—	—	—	—	1
Soutten, A. Camille	London	1873-1874	Domestic	—	—	—	—	2	—	—	—	—	1	3
Soutterant, De. *See* D.	—	—	—	—	—	—	—	—	—	—	—	—	—	—
Soward, J.	London	1809	Architecture	—	—	2	—	—	—	—	—	—	—	2
Sowden, John	Bradford	1863-1892	Flowers, etc.	—	—	5	—	—	—	1	2	1	—	9
Sowerby, James	London	1774-1790	Still Life	5	—	6	—	—	—	—	—	—	—	11
Sowerby, J. G.	Gateshead	1876-1885	Landscape	—	—	5	—	—	—	—	—	—	9	14
Sowerby, Miss Kate	London	1883-1893	Sculpture	—	—	4	—	1	—	—	—	—	—	5
Soyer, Madame. *See* Miss Emma Jones	London	1838-1843	Figures	—	—	2	12	8	—	—	—	—	—	22
Spackman, Miss Mary A.	London	1892	Flowers	—	—	1	—	—	—	—	—	—	—	1
Spain, John Henry	London	1889-1892	Churches	—	—	1	—	2	—	—	—	—	1	4
Spalding, G.	London	1821-1832	Miniatures	—	—	12	—	—	—	—	—	—	—	12
Spalding, G. B.	Reading	1840-1849	Sporting	—	—	5	—	—	—	—	—	—	—	5
Spalding and Cross	London	1891-1893	Architecture	—	—	2	—	—	—	—	—	—	—	2
Spang, Michael Henry	—	1760-1762	Sculpture	9	—	—	—	—	—	—	—	—	—	9
Spanton, W. S.	Bury St. Edm'ds	1867-1868	Portraits	—	—	2	—	—	—	—	—	—	—	2
Sparkes, Mrs. J. *See* Miss Catherine Adelaide	—	—	—	—	—	—	—	—	—	—	—	—	—	—
Edwards	London	1869-1891	Domestic	—	—	11	—	—	—	6	1	—	17	35
Sparks, Herbert B.	London	1893	Miniatures	—	—	1	—	—	—	—	—	—	—	1
Spartali, Miss Marie. *See* Mrs. W. J. Stillman	London	1867-1871	Figures	—	—	2	—	—	—	—	—	—	12	14
Spear, E. F.	—	1873	Domestic	—	—	—	—	—	—	—	—	—	1	1
Speare, G.	London	1810-1826	Landscape	—	—	5	—	—	—	—	—	—	—	5
Speare, R.	London	1799-1812	Landscape	—	—	17	—	—	—	—	—	—	—	17
Spearman, F. A., *or* H.	London	1828	Portraits	—	—	1	—	—	—	—	—	—	—	1
Speed, Harold	London	1892-1893	Landscape	—	—	2	—	2	—	—	—	—	1	5
Speed, Miss Katharine G.	London	1888	Domestic	—	—	—	—	—	—	—	1	—	—	1
Spence, Benjamin Edward	Rome	1849-1866	Sculpture	—	—	5	—	—	—	—	—	—	—	5
Spence, Ernest	London	1884-1891	Domestic	—	—	4	—	—	—	1	—	—	2	7
Spence, F.	London	1891	Fruit	—	—	—	—	—	—	1	—	—	—	1
Spence, Henry	Bushey	1884	Landscape	—	—	—	—	1	—	—	—	—	—	1
Spence, J. M.	London	1848	Figures	—	—	1	—	—	—	—	—	—	—	1
Spence, R.	Leeds	1858	—	—	—	—	—	—	—	—	—	—	*	—
Spence, Thomas Ralph	Newcastle	1876-1893	Landscape	—	—	7	—	—	—	—	1	5	—	13
Spence, William	Liverpool	1821-1844	Sculpture	—	—	8	—	—	—	—	—	—	—	8
Spence, W. B.	Florence	1856-1869	Figures	—	—	1	1	—	—	—	—	—	—	2
Spencelayh, Charles	Chatham	1887-1892	Miniatures	—	—	2	—	—	—	—	—	—	2	4
Spencer, Miss Blanche	London	1879-1888	Domestic	—	—	—	—	6	—	1	—	—	1	8
Spencer, C.	—	1836	—	—	—	—	—	1	—	—	—	—	—	1
Spencer, Gervase	London	1761-1774	Enamels	5	—	—	—	—	—	—	—	—	—	5
Spencer, H.	—	1827	Landscape	—	—	—	—	1	—	—	—	—	—	1
Spencer, Harry	London	1882	Landscape	—	—	—	—	—	—	—	—	—	1	1
Spencer, J.	London	1804-1822	Architecture	—	—	3	—	—	—	—	—	—	—	3
Spencer, John S.	London	1835-1863	Dramatic	—	—	1	6	6	—	—	—	—	—	13
Spencer, T.	—	1834	Figures	—	—	—	1	—	—	—	—	—	—	1
Spencer, William Ball	London	1843	Portraits	—	—	2	—	—	—	—	—	—	—	2
Spencer, William Frederick	London	1868-1869	Sculpture	—	—	3	—	—	—	—	—	—	—	3
Spencer, Mrs.	—	1783	Portraits	—	1	—	—	—	—	—	—	—	—	1
Spencer, Mrs. *See* Miss Celia Gandy	London	1836	Flowers	—	—	3	—	—	—	—	—	—	—	3
Spender, Miss C.	London	1862-1864	Domestic	—	—	—	2	1	—	—	—	—	—	3
Spender, Mrs.	London	1861	Flowers	—	—	—	—	—	—	—	—	—	1	1
Spenlove, Frank Spenlove-	Shortlands	1885-1893	Figures	—	—	16	—	23	—	8	—	1	9	57
Sperling, J. W.	London	1845-1848	Sporting	—	—	3	—	—	—	—	—	—	—	3
Spicer, Charles	London	1888	Domestic	—	—	1	—	—	—	—	—	—	—	1
Spicer, Henry, F.S.A.	London	1765-1804	Enamels	12	—	47	—	—	—	—	—	—	—	59
Spicer, Miss J.	London	1801-1802	Enamels	—	—	2	—	—	—	—	—	—	—	2
Spicer, Miss M. A.	London	1799-1803	Enamels	—	—	6	—	—	—	—	—	—	—	6
Spiers, Miss Bessie J. ‖	London	1884-1893	Landscape	—	—	2	—	3	—	12	—	—	—	17
Spiers, Benjamin Walter	London	1875-1893	Domestic	—	—	17	—	31	—	19	—	—	8	75
Spiers, Miss Charlotte H. ‖	London	1873-1893	Landscape	—	—	1	—	8	—	12	2	—	5	28
Spiers, E. J.	—	1852-1853	Landscape	—	—	—	—	—	—	—	—	—	2	2

Name.	Town.	First and Last Year of Ex.	Speciality.	S. A.	F. S.	R. A.	B. I.	S. S.	O. W.	N. W.	G. G.	N. G.	V. E.	Total.
Spiers, Richard Phène, F.S.A. *See also* Wyatt	—	—	—	—	—	—	—	—	—	—	—	—	—	—
and Spiers	London	1862-1893	Buildings	—	—	98	—	21	—	27	8	1	46	201
Spiller, John	London	1778-1786	Sculpture	—	—	4	—	—	—	—	—	—	—	4
Spiller, John	London	1780-1805	Architecture	—	—	8	—	—	—	—	—	—	—	8
Spiller, W. H.	London	1884-1886	Still Life	—	—	—	—	—	—	—	—	—	3	3
Spillman, William	London	1853-1861	Domestic	—	—	—	1	5	—	—	—	—	2	8
Spilsbury, Edgar Ashe	London	1800-1828	Animals	—	—	21	10	—	—	—	—	—	—	31
Spilsbury, John	London	1763-1771	Engraving	3	—	—	—	—	—	—	—	—	—	3
Spilsbury, Jonathan	London	1776-1807	Portraits	—	—	13	1	—	—	—	—	—	—	14
Spilsbury, Miss Mary. *See* Mrs. John Taylor	London	1792-1808	Domestic	—	—	47	20	—	—	—	—	—	—	67
Spindler —	London	1834-1836	Figures	—	—	9	—	2	—	—	—	—	—	11
Spindler, Walter E.	Paris	1892-1893	Scriptural	—	—	2	—	—	—	—	—	1	2	5
Spinks, Thomas	London	1872-1880	Landscape	—	—	1	—	6	—	—	—	—	—	7
Spiridon, G. S.	London	1871	Animals	—	—	1	—	—	—	—	—	—	—	1
Spong, Walter Brookes	London	1881-1885	Landscape	—	—	3	—	—	—	3	—	—	—	6
Spooner, Charles	London	1891	Architecture	—	—	1	—	—	—	—	—	—	—	1
Spooner, J. S.	Llanwrst	1854-1874	Landscape	—	—	2	1	—	—	—	—	—	—	3
Spooner, Rev. —	Chesham	1766-1774	Scriptural	—	16	—	—	—	—	—	—	—	—	16
Sprague, Miss Edith	London	1883-1893	Domestic	—	—	5	—	2	—	—	—	—	20	27
Spread, William, R.P.E.	London	1880-1889	Buildings	—	—	12	—	2	—	2	—	—	3	19
Spreat, W.	Exeter	1841-1848	Landscape	—	—	—	8	3	—	—	—	—	—	11
Spreck, Miss B. A.	London	1860	Figures	—	—	—	—	1	—	—	—	—	—	1
Sprinck, Leon	London	1893	Portraits	—	—	1	—	—	—	—	—	—	—	1
Springer, C.	Amsterdam	1854-1855	Buildings	—	—	2	—	—	—	—	—	—	—	2
Springett, Louis C.	—	1879	River Scenes	—	—	—	—	—	—	—	—	—	1	1
Sprosse, Carl	London	1852-1853	Venice	—	—	2	—	3	—	—	—	—	—	5
Spry, Rev. H.	Oxford	1800-1801	Landscape	—	—	2	—	—	—	—	—	—	—	2
Spry, William	London	1832-1847	Still Life	—	—	15	1	21	—	6	—	—	—	43
Spurling, Miss Alys	Kelvedon	1891	Figures	—	—	—	—	—	—	1	—	—	—	1
Spurr, E. A.	—	1853	Architecture	—	—	1	—	—	—	—	—	—	—	1
Spurr (E. A.) and Arnold	—	1853	Architecture	—	—	1	—	—	—	—	—	—	—	1
Spurr and Salter	—	1849	Architecture	—	—	2	—	—	—	—	—	—	—	2
Spurr, Gertrude E.	London	1888-1889	Flowers	—	—	—	—	3	—	—	—	—	—	3
Spurrell, B.	London	1822-1824	Architecture	—	—	2	—	—	—	—	—	—	—	2
Spyers, James	Hampton Court	1780-1790	Architecture	—	—	3	—	—	—	—	—	—	—	3
Squim —	London	1783	—	—	*	—	—	—	—	—	—	—	—	—
Squire, Miss Alice, R.I. ‡ ‖	London	1864-1893	Landscape	—	—	29	—	5	—	26	4	—	39	103
Squire, Miss Emma	London	1862-1891	Still Life	—	—	9	—	11	—	—	—	—	14	34
Squire, Miss Helen	London	1891-1893	Domestic	—	—	2	—	—	—	2	—	—	2	6
Squire, John	Ross, Hereford	1867-1886	Landscape	—	—	3	—	50	—	1	—	—	15	69
Squire, Josiah	London	1829-1834	Figures	—	—	3	5	4	—	—	—	—	—	12
Squires, H.	Stratford	1864-1875	Flowers	—	—	2	7	18	—	—	—	—	1	28
Squirhill, D. G.	London	1828	Architecture	—	—	1	—	—	—	—	—	—	—	1
Srieve, A. R.	London	1837	Landscape	—	—	1	—	—	—	—	—	—	—	1
Stabb, Mrs. H. Sparke	Liphook	1893	Landscape	—	—	—	—	—	—	1	—	—	—	1
Stable —	London	1767-1775	Portraits	1	1	—	—	—	—	—	—	—	—	2
Stable, Miss Fanny	London	1877-1890	Landscape	—	—	4	—	4	—	2	—	—	7	17
Stables —	London	1783	Landscape	—	5	—	—	—	—	—	—	—	—	5
Stables, T. G.	Ambleside	1884	Landscape	—	—	—	—	—	—	1	—	—	—	1
Stables, Miss T. J.	Lancaster	1880-1884	Landscape	—	—	2	—	4	—	—	—	—	—	6
Stacey, H. E.	Weston-super-Mare	1872	Landscape	—	—	—	—	1	—	—	—	—	—	1
Stacey, Walter S. § ϕ	London	1871-1891	Domestic	—	—	12	—	19	—	1	—	—	26	58
Stacey, Miss	—	1817	Flowers	—	—	1	—	—	—	—	—	—	—	1
Stacke, E. G.	—	1849	Portraits	—	—	1	—	—	—	—	—	—	—	1
Stackpoole, Miss Mary Constance	London	1887-1893	Figures	—	—	5	—	—	—	2	1	—	2	10
Stacpoole, Frederick, A.R.A.	London	1841-1893	Engraving	—	—	43	1	12	—	—	—	—	—	56
Stade, Miss H.	Finchley	1868	Flowers	—	—	1	—	—	—	—	—	—	—	1
Stadler, Joseph Constantine	London	1787	Landscape	—	—	4	—	—	—	—	—	—	—	4
Stafford, John Phillips	London	1877-1886	Domestic	—	—	3	—	—	—	—	—	—	4	7
Stafford, T. W.	London	1840-1841	Landscape	—	—	2	1	—	—	—	—	—	—	3
Staigg, Richard M.	Boston, U.S.A.	1847-1864	Portraits	—	—	4	—	—	—	—	—	—	—	4
Staines, E., Junr.	London	1844-1847	Landscape	—	—	—	—	4	—	—	—	—	—	4
Staines, F. W.	London	1828-1846	Landscape	—	—	11	—	—	—	—	—	—	—	11
Staines, P. H.	London	1869	Animals	—	—	—	—	—	—	—	—	—	1	1
Stakeman, A.	London	1883	Landscape	—	—	—	—	—	—	1	—	—	—	1
Stakes, W.	London	1788	Architecture	—	—	1	—	—	—	—	—	—	—	1
Stalker, Ebenezer	—	1825	Engraving	—	—	—	—	3	—	—	—	—	—	3
Stalker, George Frederick	London	1874	Architecture	—	—	1	—	—	—	—	—	—	—	1
Stallwood, N.	London	1797-1798	Architecture	—	—	2	—	—	—	—	—	—	—	2
Stamford, A.	London	1851-1863	Landscape	—	—	—	5	12	—	—	—	—	—	17
Stamford, G.	London	1838	Landscape	—	—	1	—	—	—	—	—	—	—	1
Stamp, Ernest	Bushey	1892	Landscape	—	—	1	—	—	—	—	—	—	—	1

Name.	Town.	First and Last Year of Ex.	Speciality.	S. A.	F. S.	R. A.	B. I.	S. S.	O. W.	N.W.	G. G.	N. G.	V. E.	Total.
Standfust, G. B.	London	1844	Sporting	—	—	1	—	—	—	—	—	—	—	1
Standish, W.	London	1859	Sporting	—	—	—	1	—	—	—	—	—	—	1
Standish-Hartrick, A. *See* H.	—	—		—	—	—	—	—	—	—	—	—	—	—
Standley —	London	1764	Portraits	—	2	—	—	—	—	—	—	—	—	2
Standley, C. P.	London	1844	Portraits	—	—	—	—	1	—	—	—	—	—	1
Standring, Arthur	Manchester	1885	Landscape	—	—	1	—	—	—	—	—	—	—	1
Stanesby, Alexander	London	1848-1854	Portraits	—	—	8	—	3	—	—	—	—	—	11
Stanesby, Joshua	London	1821-1854	Portraits	—	—	11	3	1	—	—	—	—	1	16
Stanesby, John Tatham	London	1833-1834	Pen and Ink	—	—	—	—	5	—	—	—	—	—	5
Stanesby, Samuel	London	1850-1853	Portraits	—	—	2	—	2	—	—	—	—	—	4
Stanfield, C.	Leeds	1890-1892	Landscape	—	—	2	—	—	—	—	—	—	1	3
Stanfield, George Clarkson	London	1844-1876	Landscape	—	—	73	49	—	—	—	—	—	5	127
Stanfield, William Clarkson, R.A. §	London	1820-1867	Sea Pieces	—	—	135	22	21	—	—	—	—	—	178
Stanford, R.	London	1817-1819	Architecture	—	—	3	—	—	—	—	—	—	—	3
Stanhope, G.	Turnham Green	1861	Historical	—	—	—	1	—	—	—	—	—	—	1
Stanhope, J. R. Spencer ‡	London	1859-1892	Historical	—	—	12	—	—	—	6	18	7	11	54
Stanhope, Miss Spencer	—	1885-1889	Sculpture	—	—	—	—	1	—	—	1	—	—	2
Stanier, Henry	Birmingham	1860-1864	Domestic	—	—	—	—	12	—	—	—	—	2	14
Stanier, R.	London	1776	Scriptural	1	—	—	—	—	—	—	—	—	—	1
Staniland, A. J.	London	1865	Figures	—	—	—	1	—	—	—	—	—	—	1
Staniland, Charles Joseph, R.I. ‡ φ	London	1861-1893	Domestic	—	—	6	2	7	—	62	—	—	10	87
Staniland, G. S.	Liverpool	1858	Landscape	—	—	—	1	—	—	—	—	—	—	1
Stanley —	London	1768-1769	Portraits	4	—	—	—	—	—	—	—	—	—	4
Stanley, Archer	London	1847-1877	Landscape	—	—	16	—	18	—	—	—	—	5	39
Stanley, Charles H.	London	1824-1860	Landscape	—	—	7	15	4	—	—	—	—	—	26
Stanley, C. P.	London	1844	Buildings	—	—	2	—	—	—	—	—	—	—	2
Stanley, Caleb Robert	London	1812-1867	Landscape	—	—	32	87	23	3	10	—	—	4	159
Stanley, C. W.	London	1848	Portraits	—	—	1	—	—	—	—	—	—	—	1
Stanley, G.	London	1800	Landscape	—	—	1	—	—	—	—	—	—	—	1
Stanley, Harold J.	Munich	1860-1864	Figures	—	—	3	1	1	—	—	—	—	—	5
Stanley, Mrs. H. M. *See* Miss Dorothy Tennant	London	1892-1893	Domestic	—	—	1	—	—	—	—	—	4	—	5
Stanley, Miss Kate	London	1879-1893	Landscape	—	—	—	—	4	—	—	—	—	15	19
Stanley, Montague, A.R.S.A.	Rothsay	1833-1834	Landscape	—	—	1	4	5	—	1	—	—	—	11
Stanley, Miss M.	London	1875-1877	Figures	—	—	—	—	1	—	—	—	—	1	2
Stanmore, H.	London	1864-1868	Landscape	—	—	2	—	3	—	—	—	—	2	7
Stannard, Alfred	Norwich	1826-1860	Landscape	—	—	—	8	7	—	—	—	—	—	15
Stannard, Miss A.	Norwich	1859	Still Life	—	—	1	1	—	—	—	—	—	—	2
Stannard, Alfred George	Norwich	1851-1864	Landscape	—	—	4	8	6	—	—	—	—	—	18
Stannard, Mrs. A. G.	Norwich	1855	Landscape	—	—	—	—	1	—	—	—	—	—	1
Stannard, Miss Eloise Harriet ‖	Norwich	1852-1893	Fruit	—	—	30	29	1	—	—	—	—	1	61
Stannard, Harry	Bedford	1892-1893	Landscape	—	—	—	—	3	—	—	—	—	—	3
Stannard, Henry J.	Bedford	1890-1893	Landscape	—	—	—	—	7	—	—	—	—	—	7
Stannard, Joseph	Norwich	1820-1829	Sea Pieces	—	—	—	9	4	—	—	—	—	—	13
Stannard, Mrs. J. (Anna)	Norwich	1832-1833	Still Life	—	—	—	4	1	—	—	—	—	—	5
Stannard, William John	—	1848	Landscape	—	—	—	—	1	—	—	—	—	—	1
Stannus, Anthony Carey	London	1862-1880	Figures	—	—	5	5	13	—	—	1	—	16	40
Stannus, Caroline	London	1883	Flowers	—	—	—	—	1	—	—	—	—	—	1
Stannus, Hugh	London	1886	Architecture	—	—	1	—	—	—	—	—	—	—	1
Stanton, Elizabeth	Gravesend	1879	Figures	—	—	—	—	1	—	—	—	—	—	1
Stanton, Emily R.	Stroud	1872-1893	Flowers	—	—	3	—	—	—	—	—	—	12	15
Stanton, G. Clark, A.R.S.A.	Edinburgh	1875	Rustic	—	—	—	—	1	—	—	—	—	—	1
Stanton, Horace Hughes-	London	1873-1893	Domestic	—	—	5	—	—	—	2	4	1	9	21
Stanton, Miss Rose Emily	Stroud	1872-1892	Still Life	—	—	7	—	—	—	4	—	—	9	20
Stanton, Miss Sandys	Leicester	1893	Flowers	—	—	—	—	—	—	1	—	—	—	1
Stanton, Miss Sarah	London	1843-1848	Landscape	—	—	3	1	3	—	—	—	—	—	7
Staple, J.	Chatham	1839	Fruit	—	—	—	—	1	—	—	—	—	—	1
Staples, John C.	Sible Hedingham	1876-1880	Landscape	—	—	—	—	—	—	—	—	—	6	6
Staples, Mrs. John C. *See* Miss Mary Ellen Edwards, *and* Mrs. Freer	Hedingham	1874-1888	Domestic	—	—	10	—	—	—	—	—	—	22	32
Staples, Robert Ponsonby	London	1875-1893	Figures	—	—	11	—	12	—	—	15	—	24	62
Staples, S.	London	1824-1837	Architecture	—	—	6	—	2	—	—	—	—	—	8
Stapleton, Mrs. George	London	1880-1885	Still Life	—	—	—	—	—	—	1	—	—	2	3
Stapleton, W.	London	1845-1857	Landscape	—	—	—	—	4	—	—	—	—	—	4
Stapylton, H. E. E.	—	1856	Landscape	—	—	1	—	—	—	—	—	—	—	1
Stark, Arthur James	Windsor	1848-1887	Landscape	—	—	35	33	51	—	3	—	—	57	179
Stark, Mrs. A. J. (R. Isabella)	London	1880-1889	Still Life	—	—	—	—	—	—	1	—	—	1	2
Stark, F. M.	Chagford	1892-1893	Domestic	—	—	—	—	2	—	—	—	—	—	2
Stark, James	Norwich	1812-1859	Landscape	—	—	66	136	54	10	4	—	—	4	274
Stark, Mrs. James	London	1832-1834	Fruit	—	—	—	1	5	—	—	—	—	—	6
Stark, Robert	London	1883-1893	Sculpture	—	—	13	—	1	—	—	—	—	—	14
Starkey, J.	London	1799-1818	Architecture	—	—	2	—	—	—	—	—	—	—	2
Starkie Edyth	—	1893	Portraits	—	—	—	—	—	—	—	—	—	1	1

Name.	Town.	First and Last Year of Ex.	Speciality.	S. A.	F. S.	R. A.	B. I.	S. S.	O. W.	N. W.	G. G.	N. G.	V. E.	Total.
Starling, Albert	Sutton	1878-1893	Domestic	—	—	12	—	9	—	1	—	—	3	25
Starling, Miss Marion A.	Brighton	1883	Flowers	—	—	1	—	—	—	—	—	—	—	1
Starr, Miss Louisa. *See* Madame Canziani	London	1863-1884	Figures	—	—	36	—	2	—	—	6	—	16	60
Starr, Sidney, R.B.A. §	London	1872-1889	Domestic	—	—	6	—	42	—	1	1	—	16	66
Statham, Henry Heathcote	Liverpool	1872-1893	Architecture	—	—	6	—	—	—	—	—	—	—	6
Stavely, W.	London	1785-1805	Portraits	—	—	54	—	—	—	—	—	—	—	54
Stead, Fred.	Bradford	1892-1893	Portraits	—	—	2	—	—	—	—	—	—	—	2
Stead, T.	London	1797-1801	Architecture	—	—	2	—	—	—	—	—	—	—	2
Steadman, J. T.	Liverpool	1887-1891	Domestic	—	—	—	—	3	—	—	—	—	—	3
Steadman, W.	London	1857	Sculpture	—	—	2	—	—	—	—	—	—	—	2
Stebbing, Mrs. G.	London	1861	Figures	—	—	1	—	—	—	—	—	—	—	1
Stebbing, J. L.	London	1809-1813	Architecture	—	—	4	—	—	—	—	—	—	—	4
Stecchi, Fabio	London	1891	Sculpture	—	—	1	—	—	—	—	—	—	—	1
Stedman, W.	London	1858	Figures	—	—	—	—	2	—	—	—	—	—	2
Steeden, O.	London	1823	Portraits	—	—	1	—	—	—	—	—	—	—	1
Steedman, Amy	London	1856	Fruit	—	—	—	—	2	—	—	—	—	—	2
Steedman, Charles	London	1826-1858	Landscape	—	—	25	44	53	—	—	—	—	—	122
Steedman, G.	—	1824	Domestic	—	—	1	—	—	—	—	—	—	—	1
Steel, John Sydney	London	1889-1893	Sporting	—	—	4	—	5	—	—	3	—	2	14
Steele, Adeline	St. Louis, U.S.A	1847	Figures	—	—	1	—	—	—	—	—	—	—	1
Steele, Miss Jane	London	1810-1812	Landscape	—	—	5	—	—	—	—	—	—	10	15
Steele, Jeremiah	Nottingham	1801-1826	Miniatures	—	—	27	3	—	—	—	—	—	—	30
Steele, J. S.	Reigate	1858	Landscape	—	—	—	—	1	—	—	—	—	—	1
Steele, Madame Louise	London	1875-1877	Enamels	—	—	4	—	—	—	—	—	—	—	4
Steele, Louis John	London	1871-1886	Etching	—	—	11	—	—	—	—	—	—	9	20
Steele, Miss Mary E.	Reigate	1868-1874	Domestic	—	—	—	—	1	—	—	—	—	2	3
Steell, David G., A.R.S.A.	Edinburgh	1891	Sporting	—	—	1	—	—	—	—	—	—	—	1
Steell, Gourlay, R.S.A.	Edinburgh	1865-1880	Animals	—	—	10	—	—	—	—	—	—	—	10
Steell, Sir John, R.S.A.	Edinburgh	1837-1876	Sculpture	—	—	9	—	—	—	—	—	—	—	9
Steeple, John	Birmingham	1852-1886	Landscape	—	—	7	—	31	—	7	—	—	15	60
Steer, Miss Fanny	London	1833-1842	Landscape	—	—	—	—	26	—	—	—	—	—	26
Steer, Henry R., R.I. ‡	London	1880-1893	Domestic	—	—	3	—	23	—	54	—	—	10	90
Steer, P.	—	1854	Landscape	—	—	—	—	—	—	—	—	—	1	1
Steer, Philip Wilson	Gloucester	1883-1888	Figures	—	—	3	—	4	—	—	4	—	1	12
Steers, A.	High Wycombe	1837	Portraits	—	—	1	—	—	—	—	—	—	—	1
Steers, Miss Fanny ‡	London	1846-1860	Landscape	—	—	—	—	—	—	59	—	—	—	59
Steers, W.	London	1823-1831	Portraits	—	—	7	—	1	—	—	—	—	—	8
Steffeck, Karl Constantin Heinrich	Berlin	1863	Sporting	—	—	1	—	—	—	—	—	—	—	1
Steffelaar, Nico	London	1885	Domestic	—	—	—	—	3	—	—	—	—	—	3
Steiger, Isabel de. *See* D.	—	—	—	—	—	—	—	—	—	—	—	—	—	—
Steil, Henry	London	1836-1838	Historical	—	—	—	3	2	—	—	—	—	—	5
Stein, John T.	Walworth	1833-1835	Landscape	—	—	—	1	—	—	4	—	—	—	5
Stein, Robert	London	1813-1843	Landscape	—	—	3	5	5	3	—	—	—	—	16
Steinhäusser, C.	London	1870	Sculpture	—	—	2	—	2	—	—	—	—	—	4
Steinheil, A.	Paris	1877	Figures	—	—	—	—	—	—	—	—	—	1	1
Steinmetz, John Henry	Homerton	1840-1884	Buildings	—	—	2	—	—	—	1	—	—	1	4
Steinthal, Mrs. Emmeline P.	Ilkley	1890-1893	Sculpture	—	—	3	—	—	—	—	—	—	—	3
Stenhouse, J. Armstrong	London	1888-1892	Architecture	—	—	6	—	—	—	—	—	—	—	6
Stennet, R.	Bath	1803	Game	—	—	1	—	—	—	—	—	—	—	1
Stenning, Alexander Rose	London	1873-1892	Architecture	—	—	6	—	—	—	—	—	—	—	6
Stent, Frederick Warburton	London	1846	Churches	—	—	1	—	—	—	—	—	—	—	1
Stephanoff, Fileter N.	London	1778-1781	Historical	—	—	6	—	—	—	—	—	—	—	6
Stephanoff, Francis Philip	London	1807-1845	Historical	—	—	49	54	1	11	—	—	—	9	124
Stephanoff, Mrs. F. P. (Gertrude)	London	1783-1808	Flowers	—	—	6	1	—	—	—	—	—	—	7
Stephanoff, James †	London	1810-1859	Historical	—	—	20	33	5	245	—	—	—	15	318
Stephany, G.	London	1791-1803	Ivory Carving	—	—	13	—	—	—	—	—	—	—	13
Stephany, L.	London	1861-1862	Landscape	—	—	—	2	—	—	—	—	—	—	2
Stephenoff —	—	1782	Landscape	—	4	—	—	—	—	—	—	—	—	4
Stephens —	London	1765	Architecture	1	—	—	—	—	—	—	—	—	—	1
Stephens, A.	London	1812-1839	Miniatures	—	—	30	—	—	—	—	—	—	—	30
Stephens, C.	London	1859	Landscape	—	—	—	1	—	—	—	—	—	—	1
Stephens, C. V.	London	1840-1879	Landscape	—	—	—	3	4	—	—	—	—	—	7
Stephens, Charles William. *See also* Williams and Stephens	London	1886	Architecture	—	—	2	—	—	—	—	—	—	—	2
Stephens, Miss E.	London	1839-1844	Landscape	—	—	—	—	8	—	—	—	—	—	8
Stephens, Edward Bowring, A.R.A.	Exeter	1838-1883	Sculpture	—	—	100	7	1	—	—	—	—	—	108
Stephens, Miss Emily H.	London	1880-1893	Rustic	—	—	—	—	—	—	—	2	1	—	3
Stephens, Frederic George	London	1852-1854	Portraits	—	—	2	—	—	—	—	—	—	—	2
Stephens, Miss Helen E.	London	1892	Portraits	—	—	—	—	1	—	—	—	—	—	1
Stephens, J.	Worcester	1830-1852	Sculpture	—	—	3	—	4	—	—	—	—	—	7
Stephens, L.	London	1824-1829	Miniatures	—	—	10	—	—	—	—	—	—	—	10
Stephens, Miss L.	Beckenham	1892	Figures	—	—	—	—	1	—	—	—	—	—	1

Name.	Town.	First and Last Year of Ex.	Speciality.	S. A.	F. S.	R. A.	B. I.	S. S.	O.W.	N.W.	G. G.	N. G.	V. E.	Total.
Stephens, O. L.	London	1872	Domestic	—	—	—	—	2	—	—	—	—	—	2
Stephens, R.	—	1888	Sculpture	—	—	—	—	—	—	—	—	1	—	1
Stephens, W.	London	1840	Portraits	—	—	1	—	—	—	—	—	—	—	1
Stephens, W. Reynolds. *See* R.	—	—	—	—	—	—	—	—	—	—	—	—	—	—
Stephenson, C. J.	—	1815	Architecture	—	—	1	—	—	—	—	—	—	—	1
Stephenson, G.	London	1845	Landscape	—	—	—	—	1	—	—	—	—	—	1
Stephenson, Miss Isabel H.	London	1883-1887	Flowers	—	—	—	—	6	—	—	—	—	1	7
Stephenson, J.	London	1785	Portraits	—	—	2	—	—	—	—	—	—	—	2
Stephenson, James	London	1856-1884	Engraving	—	—	15	—	—	—	—	—	—	1	16
Stephenson, W.	London	1792-1802	Architecture	—	—	4	—	—	—	—	—	—	—	4
Stephenson, W.	London	1844	Architecture	—	—	1	—	—	—	—	—	—	—	1
Stephenson and Hunt	London	1859	Architecture	—	—	1	—	—	—	—	—	—	—	1
Sterling, E. C.	London	1867-1877	Portraits	—	—	3	—	—	—	—	—	—	7	10
Sterling, Miss Helen	London	1870-1882	Figures	—	—	1	—	3	—	—	—	—	26	30
Stern, Marcus	London	1865	Historical	—	—	—	—	1	—	—	—	—	1	2
Sternberg, Frank, A.R.P.E.	Leeds	1885-1891	Engraving	—	—	10	—	—	—	—	—	—	—	10
Sterndale, O. J.	Bakewell	1875-1881	Landscape	—	—	—	—	4	—	—	—	—	—	4
Sterry, Ida S.	Croydon	1892	Buildings	—	—	—	—	1	—	—	—	—	—	1
Sterry, John Ashby-	London	1858-1892	Sea Pieces	—	—	—	1	—	—	—	—	—	1	2
Steuart, Miss Alice M. Gow	London	1887	Figures	—	—	1	—	—	—	—	—	—	—	1
Stevens, Albert	London	1872-1893	Landscape	—	—	7	—	71	—	6	2	—	18	104
Stevens, Mrs. Albert. *See* Miss Mary Draper	London	1889-1891	Animals	—	—	4	—	1	—	1	—	—	—	6
Stevens, Alfred	London	1874-1876	Sculpture	—	—	2	—	—	—	—	—	—	1	3
Stevens, Alfred, R.B.A. §	Paris	1887-1893	Domestic	—	—	—	—	5	—	—	—	—	1	6
Stevens, Edward, A.R.A.	London	1762-1773	Architecture	7	5	16	—	—	—	—	—	—	—	28
Stevens, E. N.	—	1848-1849	Architecture	—	—	2	—	—	—	—	—	—	—	2
Stevens, Francis †	Exeter	1804-1823	Landscape	—	—	12	2	—	78	—	—	—	—	92
Stevens, Frederick	London	1878	Sepia	—	—	—	—	—	—	—	—	—	1	1
Stevens, Frederick W.	Bombay	1880	Architecture	—	—	1	—	—	—	—	—	—	—	1
Stevens, George §	London	1810-1864	Fruit	—	—	22	75	246	—	—	—	—	—	343
Stevens, John, R.S.A.	London	1815-1864	Scriptural	—	—	16	29	12	—	—	—	—	—	57
Stevens, John Hargrave	London	1847	Architecture	—	—	1	—	—	—	—	—	—	—	1
Stevens, Miss Kate	Derby	1891	Flowers	—	—	1	—	—	—	—	—	—	—	1
Stevens, L.	London	1827-1829	Figures	—	—	—	—	3	—	—	—	—	—	3
Stevens, P. H.	Eton	1849	Historical	—	—	—	1	—	—	—	—	—	—	1
Stevens, Miss Susanna	—	1887	Portraits	—	—	—	—	—	—	—	1	—	—	1
Stevens, T.	London	1831-1844	Miniatures	—	—	5	—	—	—	—	—	—	—	5
Stevens, Thomas	Thames Ditton	1891-1893	Landscape	—	—	1	—	1	—	1	—	—	—	3
Stevens, W. K.	London	1877-1889	Domestic	—	—	6	—	8	—	6	—	—	—	20
Stevens, Walter Rupert	London	1874-1891	Landscape	—	—	4	—	24	—	4	—	1	13	46
Stevens and Alexander	London	1844-1845	Architecture	—	—	4	—	—	—	—	—	—	—	4
Stevenson, David W., R.S.A.	Edinburgh	1868-1892	Sculpture	—	—	12	—	—	—	—	—	1	—	13
Stevenson, George	London	1881	Etching	—	—	—	—	—	—	—	—	—	2	2
Stevenson, Ida	London	1891	Landscape	—	—	—	—	1	—	—	—	—	—	1
Stevenson, J. C.	—	1810	Landscape	—	—	1	—	—	—	—	—	—	—	1
Stevenson, J. H.	London	1776-1833	Miniatures	2	2	43	—	—	—	—	—	—	—	47
Stevenson, John James	London	1874-1893	Architecture	—	—	20	—	—	—	—	—	—	—	20
Stevenson, Miss R.	London	1801-1802	Miniatures	—	—	2	—	—	—	—	—	—	—	2
Stevenson, Robert A. M.	London	1879-1888	Landscape	—	—	5	—	1	—	—	—	—	3	9
Stevenson, R. Macaulay	Glasgow	1884-1892	Landscape	—	—	2	—	—	—	—	—	—	—	2
Stevenson, S. J. *See* Robson and Stevenson	—	—	Architecture	—	—	—	—	—	—	—	—	—	—	—
Stevenson, T. *or* F., W.	Iver	1880	Domestic	—	—	—	—	—	—	—	—	—	1	1
Stevenson, W.	London	1777-1778	Miniatures	—	—	5	—	—	—	—	—	—	—	5
Stevenson, W.	London	1805	Landscape	—	—	1	—	—	—	—	—	—	—	1
Stevenson, W.	London	1848	Portraits	—	—	1	—	—	—	—	—	—	—	1
Stevenson, Walter	London	1876-1883	Domestic	—	—	5	—	12	—	—	—	—	1	18
Stevenson, W. Grant, A.R.S.A.	Edinburgh	1874-1892	Domestic	—	—	8	—	5	—	—	—	—	3	16
Stevenson (S. J.) and Robson (E. R.)	London	1873-1875	Architecture	—	—	2	—	—	—	—	—	—	—	2
Steward. *See* Hunt, Steward, and Knight	—	—	Architecture	—	—	—	—	—	—	—	—	—	—	—
Steward, H. S. R.	London	1881	Figures	—	—	—	—	—	—	—	2	—	—	2
Stewardson, Thomas	London	1803-1826	Domestic	—	—	83	26	—	—	—	—	—	—	109
Stewart, Allan	Edinburgh	1892-1893	Portraits	—	—	2	—	—	—	—	—	—	—	2
Stewart, Miss Amy	London	1889-1890	Figures	—	—	1	—	1	—	—	—	—	—	2
Stewart, Anthony	London	1807-1820	Miniatures	—	—	12	—	—	—	—	—	—	—	12
Stewart, Charles, F.S.A.	London	1762-1790	Landscape	36	4	—	—	—	—	—	—	—	—	40
Stewart, Charles E.	London	1890-1893	Domestic	—	—	2	—	—	—	—	—	—	—	2
Stewart, Miss Dora M.	London	1882-1887	Flowers	—	—	—	—	5	—	5	—	—	—	10
Stewart, Miss Elizabeth	London	1778	Portraits	1	—	—	—	—	—	—	—	—	—	1
Stewart, Miss Eunice	London	1884	Landscape	—	—	—	—	1	—	—	—	—	—	1
Stewart, F. A.	London	1828-1832	Landscape	—	—	3	7	14	—	—	—	—	—	24
Stewart, Miss Florence	London	1884-1886	Flowers	—	—	1	—	—	—	—	2	—	—	3
Stewart, G.	London	1791-1792	Architecture	—	—	2	—	—	—	—	—	—	—	2

Name.	Town.	First and Last Year of Ex.	Speciality.	S. A.	F. S.	R. A.	B. I.	S. S.	O. W.	N. W.	G. G.	N. G.	V. E.	Total.
Stewart, Gabriel	London	1783-1793	Portraits	9	—	1	—	—	—	—	—	—	—	10
Stewart, George	London	1790	Landscape	1	—	—	—	—	—	—	—	—	—	1
Stewart, George	London	1851-1885	Landscape	—	—	17	—	6	—	—	—	—	3	26
Stewart, George A.	—	1874	Landscape	—	—	1	—	1	—	—	—	—	1	3
Stewart, Miss Grace Campbell	London	1843-1856	Miniatures	—	—	13	—	—	—	—	—	—	—	13
Stewart, H.	—	1826	Portraits	—	—	1	—	—	—	—	—	—	—	1
Stewart, Hope J.	London	1859-1865	Portraits	—	—	—	5	8	—	—	—	—	—	13
Stewart, H. W.	—	1847	Landscape	—	—	1	—	—	—	—	—	—	—	1
Stewart, Sir James	—	1823-1833	Horses	—	—	3	—	2	—	—	—	—	—	5
Stewart, James, R.S.A. §	Edinburgh	1825-1861	Figures	—	—	21	16	148	—	—	—	—	—	185
Stewart, John §	London	1828-1865	Landscape	—	—	4	3	20	—	—	—	—	5	32
Stewart, J. A.	Dundee	1864	Rustic	—	—	—	1	—	—	—	—	—	—	1
Stewart, J. E.	London	1846-1849	Landscape	—	—	2	—	1	—	—	—	—	—	3
Stewart, J. G.	London	1844	Flowers	—	—	1	—	—	—	—	—	—	—	1
Stewart, James Lawson	London	1883-1889	Landscape	—	—	2	—	2	—	3	—	—	1	8
Stewart, J. Malcolm	Witley	1866-1889	Rustic	—	—	1	—	2	—	—	—	—	10	13
Stewart, Miss Katherine	London	1887-1893	Figures	—	—	3	—	5	—	—	—	2	—	10
Stewart, Mrs. Mary	London	1888-1890	Miniatures	—	—	5	—	—	—	—	—	—	—	5
Stewart, Miss M.	London	1791-1819	Domestic	—	—	12	—	—	2	—	—	—	—	14
Stewart, Robert	London	1777-1783	Sculpture	11	—	—	—	—	—	—	—	—	—	11
Stewart, R.	—	1813	Architecture	—	—	1	—	—	—	—	—	—	—	1
Stewart, T.	London	1784-1801	Portraits	—	—	23	—	—	—	—	—	—	—	23
Stewart, Mrs.	London	1803	Portraits	—	—	1	—	—	—	—	—	—	—	1
Stewert, James	London	1767	Sculpture	—	1	—	—	—	—	—	—	—	—	1
Stiffe, C. E.	London	1882-1890	Landscape	—	—	3	—	—	—	—	—	—	—	3
Stiffe, John Gillbee	London	1872-1888	Landscape	—	—	1	—	2	—	—	—	—	—	3
Stigand, Miss Helen M.	London	1868-1882	Landscape	—	—	5	—	10	—	—	—	—	5	20
Stikeman, Miss Annie	Blackheath	1882-1884	Flowers	—	—	—	—	2	—	1	—	—	—	3
Stillman, Miss Effie	Rome	1892-1893	Sculpture	—	—	—	—	—	—	—	—	13	—	13
Stillman, Miss Lisa R.	London	1888-1893	Portraits	—	—	—	—	—	—	—	—	19	—	19
Stillman, William J.	London	1860	Landscape	—	—	—	—	1	—	—	—	—	—	1
Stillman, Mrs. W. J. *See* Miss Marie Spartali	London	1872-1893	Figures	—	—	5	—	1	—	2	21	18	12	59
Stilwell, J.	Tooting	1849-1855	Cattle	—	—	1	4	2	—	—	—	—	—	7
Stinton, H.	London	1830-1831	Flowers	—	—	3	—	—	—	—	—	—	—	3
Stirling, Miss Evangeline	London	1880-1888	Sculpture	—	—	3	—	—	—	—	—	—	—	3
Stirling, John	Aberdeen	1855-1871	Domestic	—	—	24	4	—	—	—	—	—	—	28
Stirling, Miss Nina	London	1885-1888	Flowers	—	—	2	—	2	—	—	—	—	1	5
Stirling, William	London	1885-1892	Architecture	—	—	7	—	—	—	—	—	—	—	7
Stiven, John	London	1824	Game	—	—	—	—	2	—	—	—	—	—	2
Stjernstedts, Madame S.	London	1882	Sweden	—	—	1	—	—	—	—	—	—	—	1
Stobbarts, Jan	London	1867	Buildings	—	—	—	1	—	—	—	—	—	—	1
Stock, Edward	London	1834-1842	Landscape	—	—	—	—	14	—	—	—	—	—	14
Stock, Miss Edith A.	Richmond	1880-1889	Flowers	—	—	3	—	3	—	2	—	—	3	11
Stock, Francis R.	London	1875-1884	Domestic	—	—	17	—	17	—	—	—	—	37	71
Stock, Henry. *See also* Allen, Snooke, and Stock,	—	—	—	—	—	—	—	—	—	—	—	—	—	—
and Snooke and Stock	London	1886-1887	Architecture	—	—	3	—	—	—	—	—	—	—	3
Stock, Henry J., R.I. ‡ φ	London	1874-1893	Figures	—	—	16	—	—	—	39	4	—	21	80
Stock, Miss Mary	Hereford	1816	Figures	—	—	—	1	—	—	—	—	—	—	1
Stockdale, C. W. (?) W. Colebrooke	London	1860-1867	Churches	—	—	2	—	—	—	—	—	—	—	2
Stockdale, F. C.	Torquay	1852-1854	Architecture	—	—	2	—	—	—	—	—	—	—	2
Stockdale, F. W. L.	—	1808-1821	Landscape	—	—	22	—	—	—	—	—	—	—	22
Stocker, Miss Florence A.	Maidenhead	1885-1886	Landscape	—	—	—	—	—	—	2	—	—	—	2
Stocks, Arthur, R.I. ‡	London	1866-1890	Domestic	—	—	59	4	2	—	16	—	—	34	115
Stocks, Bernard O.	London	1881-1890	Still Life	—	—	3	—	—	—	3	—	—	1	7
Stocks, G. B.	Newcastle	1885	Sea Coasts	—	—	1	—	—	—	—	—	—	—	1
Stocks, Miss Katherine M.	London	1877-1889	Flowers	—	—	6	—	—	—	10	—	—	14	30
Stocks, Lumb, R.A.	London	1832-1892	Engraving	—	—	42	—	2	—	—	—	—	—	44
Stocks, R. Bremner	—	1885	Portraits	—	—	—	—	—	—	—	1	—	—	1
Stocks, S. C.	—	1833	Figures	—	—	1	—	—	—	—	—	—	—	1
Stocks, Walter Fryer	London	1862-1893	Landscape	—	—	95	6	33	—	21	—	—	120	275
Stodart, George J.	Godstone	1880-1891	Engraving	—	—	4	—	—	—	—	—	—	2	6
Stoddart, Miss Frances	Edinburgh	1837-1840	Landscape	—	—	3	—	—	—	—	—	—	—	3
Stohl, M.	—	1858	Domestic	—	—	3	—	—	—	—	—	—	—	3
Stohwasser, Miss Rosina	London	1882-1884	Buildings	—	—	—	—	—	—	1	—	—	1	2
Stokeld, J.	Sunderland	1862-1865	Domestic	—	—	1	—	4	—	—	—	—	—	5
Stokes, Adrian S. φ	London	1871-1893	Domestic	—	—	28	—	11	—	2	9	8	38	96
Stokes, Mrs. Adrian (Marianne) ‖	London	1884-1893	Figures	—	—	9	—	3	—	—	2	1	9	24
Stokes, E.	—	1831	Landscape	—	—	1	—	—	—	—	—	—	—	1
Stokes, Folliott	St. Ives, Cornw'l	1892-1893	Landscape	—	—	—	—	3	—	—	—	—	—	3
Stokes, G.	London	1827-1851	Architecture	—	—	11	—	—	—	—	—	—	—	11
Stokes, G. H.	London	1854-1864	Architecture	—	—	3	—	—	—	—	—	—	—	3
Stokes, H.	London	1876	Landscape	—	—	—	—	1	—	—	—	—	—	1

Name.	Town.	First and Last Year of Ex.	Speciality.	S. A.	F. S.	R. A.	B. I.	S. S.	O. W.	N.W.	G. G.	N.G.	V.E.	Total.
Stokes, J.	Hounslow	1846-1863	Landscape	—	—	2	21	2	—	—	—	—	—	25
Stokes, Leonard Aloysius Scott	London	1882-1893	Architecture	—	—	23	—	—	—	—	—	—	—	23
Stokes (Leonard) and Ware (Charles E.)	London	1883	Architecture	—	—	1	—	—	—	—	—	—	—	1
Stokes, R.	—	1828-1831	Architecture	—	—	3	—	2	—	—	—	—	—	5
Stokes, W. P.	Hook	1855	Domestic	—	—	—	1	—	—	—	—	—	—	1
Stokes, Miss	London	1838	Landscape	—	—	—	—	1	—	—	—	—	—	1
Stokoe —	—	1808	Architecture	—	—	2	—	—	—	—	—	—	—	2
Stone, Ada	London	1879-1888	Still Life	—	—	—	—	3	—	—	—	—	1	4
Stone, Coutts	London	1843-1881	Architecture	—	—	7	—	—	—	—	—	—	—	7
Stone, Mrs. Coward	Bath	1812-1822	Landscape	—	—	—	4	—	—	—	—	—	—	4
Stone, Miss Elizabeth. *See* Mrs. William	—	—	—	—	—	—	—	—	—	—	—	—	—	—
Lawson	Brighton	1852-1853	Flowers	—	—	—	—	2	—	—	—	—	—	2
Stone, Eleanor	London	1866	Landscape	—	—	—	—	—	—	—	—	—	1	1
Stone, Miss Ellen	London	1870-1878	Domestic	—	—	2	—	—	—	—	—	—	13	15
Stone, Frank, A.R.A. †	London	1833-1860	Domestic	—	—	42	24	10	26	—	—	—	—	102
Stone, F. H.	Norwich	1821	Architecture	—	—	1	—	—	—	—	—	—	—	1
Stone, George	London	1832	Moonlight	—	—	—	1	—	—	—	—	—	—	1
Stone, Henry	London	1838-1886	Architecture	—	—	9	—	—	—	—	—	—	—	9
Stone, Marcus C., R.A. φ	London	1858-1893	Historical	—	—	51	—	—	—	—	—	—	10	61
Stone, Mary Mulready. *See* Mrs. Leckie	—	1845-1846	Portraits	—	—	2	—	—	—	—	—	—	—	2
Stone, Percy Goddard	London	1883	Architecture	—	—	1	—	—	—	—	—	—	—	1
Stone, T.	London	1797	Military	—	—	1	—	—	—	—	—	—	—	1
Stone, W.	London	1867-1869	Domestic	—	—	1	—	1	—	—	—	—	—	2
Stone, W. Henry	Coventry	1867	Domestic	—	—	—	—	—	—	—	—	—	1	1
Stone, Miss. *See* Mrs. Smith	—	1780-1786	Still Life	1	—	5	—	—	—	—	—	—	—	6
Stonehouse, C.	London	1833-1865	Domestic	—	—	35	19	4	—	—	—	—	—	58
Stones, Miss Emily R.	London	1882-1889	Flowers	—	—	1	—	12	—	6	—	—	1	20
Stoney, Charles B.	London	1879-1893	Flowers	—	—	25	—	3	—	—	—	2	12	42
Stop, Vander. *See* V.	—	—	—	—	—	—	—	—	—	—	—	—	—	—
Stopford, W. H.	London	1867-1880	Landscape	—	—	1	—	2	—	—	—	—	—	3
Stoppelear, Herbert	—	1761-1771	Portraits	6	—	—	—	—	—	—	—	—	—	6
Stoppoloni, Auguste	London	1893	Domestic	—	—	2	—	—	—	—	—	—	—	2
Storck, W. B.	London	1858	Dramatic	—	—	—	—	1	—	—	—	—	—	1
Stordy, J.	London	1786-1788	Miniatures	—	—	3	—	—	—	—	—	—	—	3
Storer, Miss	—	1783	Landscape	1	—	—	—	—	—	—	—	—	—	1
Storer, Henry Sargant	London	1814-1836	Churches	—	—	20	—	—	—	—	—	—	—	20
Storer, Louisa	London	1816-1843	Flowers	—	—	10	—	—	—	—	—	—	—	10
Storey, George Adolphus, A.R.A.	London	1852-1893	Domestic	—	—	86	2	10	—	1	—	—	20	119
Storey, John	Newcastle	1849-1851	Landscape	—	—	—	—	3	—	—	—	—	—	3
Storm, G. F.	London	1828	Portraits	—	—	—	—	1	—	—	—	—	—	1
Stormont, Howard Gull	Brighton	1884-1892	Landscape	—	—	—	—	4	—	1	—	—	—	5
Storr, George	London	1826-1829	Landscape	—	—	—	5	—	—	—	—	—	—	5
Storr, J.	London	1824	Landscape	—	—	1	—	—	—	—	—	—	—	1
Storr, Milton	Haslemere	1890-1891	Landscape	—	—	1	—	1	—	—	—	—	—	2
Stortenbeker, P.	—	1880	Landscape	—	—	—	—	—	—	—	1	—	—	1
Stortz, C.	London	1856	Figures	—	—	—	—	—	—	—	—	—	1	1
Story, Miss Blanche	—	1881-1888	Flowers	—	—	—	—	—	—	—	9	—	—	9
Story, J.	Plymouth	1793	Sea Pieces	—	—	1	—	—	—	—	—	—	—	1
Story, Julian	Rome	1882-1893	Portraits	—	—	3	—	—	—	—	13	2	3	21
Story, Miss Mary L. (?) S.	Nottingham	1880-1886	Flowers	—	—	2	—	—	—	—	5	—	—	7
Story, Waldo W., R.B.A. §	Rome	1882-1890	Sculpture	—	—	1	—	1	—	—	13	—	—	15
Stothard, Alfred Joseph	London	1821-1845	Sculpture	—	—	26	—	—	—	—	—	—	—	26
Stothard, Charles Alfred	London	1811	Historical	—	—	1	—	—	—	—	—	—	—	1
Stothard, James	London	1777	Landscape	3	—	—	—	—	—	—	—	—	—	3
Stothard, Robert T., F.S.A.	London	1821-1857	Historical	—	—	18	2	—	—	—	—	—	—	20
Stothard, Thomas, R.A.	London	1778-1834	Historical	—	—	90	8	13	—	—	—	—	—	111
Stott, Edward	Paris	1883-1893	Landscape	—	—	8	—	—	—	—	4	20	3	35
Stott, J.	London	1829-1830	Sporting	—	—	7	—	—	—	—	—	—	—	7
Stott, John	Paris	1881	Figures	—	—	—	—	—	—	—	1	—	—	1
Stott, William (of Oldham), R.B.A. §	Paris	1881-1893	Landscape	—	—	3	—	21	—	—	3	1	4	32
Stourton, Everard	London	1891-1893	Sculpture	—	—	1	—	—	—	—	—	3	—	4
Stow, Edward	London	1832-1833	Landscape	—	—	1	—	1	—	5	—	—	—	7
Stow, W. C.	London	1829-1843	Architecture	—	—	4	—	—	—	—	—	—	—	4
Stowers, C.	London	1811-1821	Sculpture	—	—	3	—	—	—	—	—	—	—	3
Stowers, Thomas	London	1778-1814	Landscape	—	—	38	6	—	5	—	—	—	—	49
Stowers, T., Junr.	London	1805-1808	Landscape	—	—	3	—	—	—	—	—	—	—	3
Stowers, T. Gordon	London	1873-1882	Portraits	—	—	2	—	3	—	—	—	—	—	5
Stowey, P.	Exeter	1775	Architecture	2	—	—	—	—	—	—	—	—	—	2
Stowley —	London	1775	Portraits	—	1	—	—	—	—	—	—	—	—	1
Strachan, A. Claude	Liverpool	1891-1892	Landscape	—	—	2	—	—	—	1	—	—	—	3
Strachey, Henry	London	1888-1893	Landscape	—	—	6	—	—	—	—	1	—	—	7
Strafford, Miss Anne	—	1811	Landscape	—	—	1	—	—	—	—	—	—	—	1

Name.	Town.	First and Last Year of Ex.	Speciality.	S. A.	F. S.	R. A.	B. I.	S. S.	O. W.	N. W.	G. G.	N. G.	V. E.	Total.
Strafford, G.	London	1842-1845	Landscape	—	—	3	1	—	—	—	—	—	—	4
Strahan, Bland	London	1879	Heads	—	—	—	—	—	—	—	—	—	1	1
Strang, William, R.P.E.	Glasgow	1879-1893	Etching	—	—	9	—	—	—	—	1	—	3	13
Strange, Albert	Liverpool	1878-1891	Landscape	—	—	9	—	3	—	6	—	—	2	20
Strange, Sir Robert, F.S.A.	London	1760-1775	Engraving	17	—	—	—	—	—	—	—	—	—	17
Strange, Le. *See* L.	—	—	—	—	—	—	—	—	—	—	—	—	—	—
Strapp, M. George	London	1886	Domestic	—	—	—	—	1	—	—	—	—	—	1
Straszynski, L.	London	1867	Domestic	—	—	1	—	—	—	—	—	—	—	1
Strath, B.	London	1866	Landscape	—	—	—	—	1	—	—	—	—	—	1
Stratham, Miss	—	1837-1838	Landscape	—	—	2	—	—	—	—	—	—	—	2
Stratten, Miss Lucy A.	Hessle	1890	Heads	—	—	1	—	—	—	—	—	—	—	1
Stratton, Miss Helen	London	1892-1893	Domestic	—	—	—	—	2	—	1	—	—	—	3
Streater, Henry William	Henley	1851-1858	Landscape	—	—	—	10	3	—	—	—	—	6	19
Streatfield, Rev. Thomas	—	1800	Historical	—	—	1	—	—	—	—	—	—	—	1
Streatfield, Thomas Edw. Champion	London	1874	Architecture	—	—	2	—	—	—	—	—	—	—	2
Strecker, J.	London	1880	Domestic	—	—	1	—	—	—	—	—	—	—	1
Street, Arthur Edmund, M.A.	London	1885-1892	Architecture	—	—	13	—	—	—	—	—	—	—	13
Street, George Edmund, R.A., F.S.A.	London	1848-1881	Architecture	—	—	72	—	—	—	—	—	—	—	72
Street, Georgina A.	London	1858-1861	Flowers	—	—	1	—	5	—	—	—	—	—	6
Street, Miss Kate	London	1880-1893	Domestic	—	—	13	—	4	—	4	—	—	3	24
Streeter, Miss Rosalie Ethel	Brighton	1893	Still Life	—	—	—	—	—	—	—	—	—	1	1
Streeton, Arthur	London	1891	Australia	—	—	1	—	—	—	—	—	—	—	1
Stretch, Matt	London	1872-1874	Domestic	—	—	—	—	—	—	—	—	—	3	3
Stretton, H.	London	1834	Landscape	—	—	1	—	—	—	—	—	—	—	1
Stretton, Miss Hesba D.	Lee	1884-1886	Flowers	—	—	1	—	1	—	—	—	—	—	2
Stretton, Philip Eustace	London	1884-1893	Animals	—	—	18	—	3	—	—	—	—	8	29
Strickland, Miss Frances	Cracombe	1830-1852	Still Life	—	—	1	—	2	—	—	—	—	—	3
Stride, P.	London	1872-1877	Domestic	—	—	—	—	4	—	—	—	—	—	4
Stringer, James	London	1802-1803	Architecture	—	—	2	—	—	—	—	—	—	—	2
Stroëhling, P. E.	London	1803-1826	Historical	—	—	23	3	2	—	—	—	—	—	28
Strong, C. E.	Gravesend	1851-1856	Sea Pieces	—	—	4	4	1	—	—	—	—	1	10
Strong, H.	Ilfracombe	1840	Landscape	—	—	—	—	2	—	—	—	—	—	2
Strong, J.	Balham	1888	River Scenes	—	—	—	—	—	—	1	—	—	—	1
Stroud, Miss H. M.	Bushey	1892	Landscape	—	—	—	—	1	—	—	—	—	—	1
Strudwick, John Melhuish	London	1865-1893	Scriptural	—	—	1	—	3	—	—	14	6	1	25
Strudwick, William	London	1863-1879	Landscape	—	—	—	—	1	—	—	1	—	—	2
Struthers, Miss	London	1832	Landscape	—	—	—	—	1	—	—	—	—	—	1
Strutt, Arthur Edw.	Gravesend	1886-1889	Landscape	—	—	—	—	—	—	3	—	—	—	3
Strutt, Arthur J.	Rome	1855	Landscape	—	—	1	—	—	—	—	—	—	—	1
Strutt, Alfred W., R.B.A., F.R.G.S., A.R.P.E. §	Croydon	1877-1893	Domestic	—	—	35	—	49	—	9	—	—	9	102
Strutt, Joseph	London	1779-1784	Historical	—	—	9	—	—	—	—	—	—	—	9
Strutt, Jacob George	London	1819-1858	Landscape	—	—	21	24	2	—	—	—	—	—	47
Strutt, Miss Rosa J.	—	1884	Landscape	—	—	—	—	—	—	—	—	—	1	1
Strutt, W.	London	1819-1821	Architecture	—	—	4	—	—	—	—	—	—	—	4
Strutt, William, R.B.A. §	Writtle	1865-1893	Domestic	—	—	23	1	27	—	—	—	—	1	52
Strutt, W. T.	London	1795-1822	Miniatures	—	—	30	—	—	—	—	—	—	—	30
Stuart, A.	London	1827-1841	Portraits	—	—	4	1	—	—	—	—	—	—	5
Stuart, Amy	London	1893	Domestic	—	—	—	—	1	—	—	—	—	—	1
Stuart, A. T. Burnett-	Wells	1884-1885	Buildings	—	—	—	—	—	—	2	—	—	—	2
Stuart, Charles, F.S.A.	London	1854-1893	Fruit	—	—	34	22	87	—	3	1	1	11	159
Stuart, Mrs. Charles. *See* Miss J. M. Bowkett.	—	—	—	—	—	—	—	—	—	—	—	—	—	—
Stuart, C. E. Gordon	London	1888-1890	Domestic	—	—	—	—	3	—	—	—	—	1	4
Stuart, Ernest	London	1889	Landscape	—	—	—	—	1	—	—	—	—	—	1
Stuart, F.	London	1843	Architecture	—	—	1	—	—	—	—	—	—	—	1
Stuart, Miss F.	London	1851-1856	Fruit	—	—	2	—	—	—	—	—	—	—	2
Stuart, Gilbert Charles (American)	London	1777-1785	Portraits	—	—	13	—	—	—	—	—	—	—	13
Stuart, Miss G. E.	London	1848	Fruit	—	—	1	—	—	—	—	—	—	—	1
Stuart, James (Athenian)	London	1765-1783	Antiquities	—	121	—	—	—	—	—	—	—	—	121
Stuart, J. A.	—	1869	Landscape	—	—	—	—	1	—	—	—	—	—	1
Stuart, J. E.	Greenwich	1876	Fruit	—	—	—	—	1	—	—	—	—	—	1
Stuart, L.	Catford Bridge	1876-1878	River Scenes	—	—	—	—	4	—	—	—	—	2	6
Stuart, Hon. Miss Louisa. *See* Marchioness of	—	—	—	—	—	—	—	—	—	—	—	—	—	—
Waterford.	—	—	—	—	—	—	—	—	—	—	—	—	—	—
Stuart, William	London	1848-1867	Sea Pieces	—	—	2	16	4	—	—	—	—	—	22
Stuart, Mrs. William	London	1853-1863	Landscape	—	—	—	1	2	—	—	—	—	—	3
Stuart, W. E. D.	London	1846-1858	Fruit	—	—	16	25	26	—	—	—	—	4	71
Stuart, Miss	London	1849-1855	Fruit	—	—	—	6	2	—	—	—	—	—	8
Stuart-Wortley. *See* W.	—	—	—	—	—	—	—	—	—	—	—	—	—	—
Stubbing —	—	1802	Architecture	—	—	1	—	—	—	—	—	—	—	1
Stubble, H.	London	1785-1791	Miniatures	—	—	6	—	—	—	—	—	—	—	6
Stubbs, George, F.S.A., A.R.A.	London	1761-1806	Animals	60	—	53	8	—	—	—	—	—	—	121
Stubbs, George	Boulogne	1837-1860	Figures	—	—	8	3	24	—	—	—	—	—	35

Name.	Town.	First and Last Year of Ex.	Speciality.	S. A.	F. S.	R. A.	B. I.	S. S.	O. W.	N.W.	G. G.	N. G.	V. E.	Total.
Stubbs, George Townley	London	1771-1782	Engraving	5	—	1	—	—	—	—	—	—	—	6
Stubbs, R.	London	1773-1774	Landscape	2	—	—	—	—	—	—	—	—	—	2
Stubbs, Ralph R.	Hull	1856-1873	Landscape	—	—	3	2	10	—	—	—	—	2	17
Stubbs, Samuel	London	1867-1870	Sea Pieces	—	—	—	1	1	—	—	—	—	—	2
Stubbs, T.	London	1774	Portraits	1	—	—	—	—	—	—	—	—	—	1
Stubbs, Woodhouse	Sunderland	1893	Flowers	—	—	1	—	—	—	—	—	—	—	1
Stuchlik, Camill	Prague	1890	Domestic	—	—	1	—	—	—	—	—	—	—	1
Stuckey, G.	London	1849-1855	Portraits	—	—	1	—	2	—	—	—	—	—	3
Studdert, Rev. G.	Colchester	1891-1893	Landscape	—	—	—	—	—	—	—	—	—	3	3
Stulpner, J. H.	London	1785	Indian	—	—	2	—	—	—	—	—	—	—	2
Stump, S. John	London	1802-1849	Miniatures	—	—	236	55	47	21	—	—	—	8	367
Sturdee, Percy	London	1885-1889	Domestic	—	—	2	—	1	—	—	—	—	—	3
Sturgeon, Miss Kate	London	1882-1892	Domestic	—	—	4	—	7	—	9	—	—	—	20
Sturgess, John	London	1875-1884	Sporting	—	—	—	—	1	—	—	—	—	3	4
Stürmer, Von. *See* V.	—	—	—	—	—	—	—	—	—	—	—	—	—	—
Sturt, Captain	—	1775	Landscape	2	—	—	—	—	—	—	—	—	—	2
Sturtevant, Charles T.	Taunton	1866	Fruit	—	—	—	2	—	—	—	—	—	—	2
Stutely, Charles	London	1843-1857	Architecture	—	—	2	—	—	—	—	—	—	—	2
Stutely, Martin Joseph	London	1829-1835	Architecture	—	—	3	—	2	—	—	—	—	—	5
Style, Jane M.	Liverpool	1879	Figures	—	—	—	—	1	—	—	—	—	—	1
Such, W. T.	Sutton Coldfield	1855-1857	Landscape	—	—	1	2	—	—	—	—	—	6	9
Suchemont, De. *See* D.	—	—	—	—	—	—	—	—	—	—	—	—	—	—
Suchment, Mdlle. A. A. de. *See* D.	—	—	—	—	—	—	—	—	—	—	—	—	—	—
Suchlowski, I.	London	1866	Military	—	—	—	—	1	—	—	—	—	—	1
Suddards, Frank	Bournemouth	1884	Flowers	—	—	—	—	—	—	1	—	—	—	1
Suddenwood, Mrs. H.	London	1798-1800	Fruit	—	—	6	—	—	—	—	—	—	—	6
Suffield, J. P.	London	1824-1825	Landscape	—	—	2	—	—	—	—	—	—	—	2
Suffrein, De. *See* D.	—	—	—	—	—	—	—	—	—	—	—	—	—	—
Sugars, Miss Fanny	Manchester	1889	Flowers	—	—	1	—	—	—	—	—	—	—	1
Sugden (W.) and Son	Stafford	1893	Architecture	—	—	1	—	—	—	—	—	—	—	1
Suggate, F. W.	London	1878-1882	Flowers	—	—	1	—	2	—	—	—	—	2	5
Suhrlandt, C.	London	1884	Sporting	—	—	—	—	1	—	—	—	—	—	1
Suhrlandt, R.	London	1840-1854	Scriptural	—	—	3	—	—	—	—	—	—	—	3
Suker. *See* F. C. Newcombe.	—	—	—	—	—	—	—	—	—	—	—	—	—	—
Suker, Arthur	Merton	1886	Sea Pieces	—	—	1	—	—	—	—	—	—	—	1
Sullivan, Frederick	London	1858	Architecture	—	—	1	—	—	—	—	—	—	—	1
Sullivan, James F.	Putney	1875-1877	Caricatures	—	—	—	—	—	—	—	—	—	5	5
Sullivan, Luke	London	1764-1770	Miniatures	14	—	—	—	—	—	—	—	—	—	14
Sullivan, M.	Putney	1870	Landscape	—	—	1	—	—	—	—	—	—	—	1
Sullivan, William Holmes, R.C.A.	Liverpool	1870-1876	Figures	—	—	1	—	—	—	—	—	—	4	5
Sully, R. M.	London	1825-1827	Portraits	—	—	3	1	3	—	—	—	—	—	7
Sully, Thomas	Philadelphia	1820-1840	Figures	—	—	2	3	—	—	—	—	—	—	5
Sulman, John. *See also* Potts, Sulman, and Henman	London	1875-1885	Architecture	—	—	14	—	—	—	—	—	—	—	14
Summerbell, L.	London	1879	Portraits	—	—	1	—	—	—	—	—	—	—	1
Summers, Charles	London	1849-1876	Sculpture	—	—	44	—	—	—	—	—	—	—	44
Summers, S. N.	London	1764-1806	Portraits	—	1	6	—	—	—	—	—	—	—	7
Sumner, G. Heywood Maunoir	London	1878-1881	Etching	—	—	2	—	—	—	—	—	—	13	15
Sumner, Margaret L.	London	1882	Landscape	—	—	—	—	—	—	—	—	—	1	1
Sumpter, H.	London	1816-1847	Still Life	—	—	10	19	16	2	—	—	—	—	47
Surgey, J. B.	London	1851-1883	Landscape	—	—	11	3	18	—	—	—	—	6	38
Surrey, J.	London	1852-1858	Portraits	—	—	2	—	—	—	—	—	—	—	2
Surtees, John	Newcastle	1846-1892	Landscape	—	—	32	10	7	—	—	—	—	67	116
Surtees, Mrs.	London	1873-1888	Landscape	—	—	1	—	12	—	—	—	—	20	33
Surtevant, C. T.	London	1853	Scriptural	—	—	—	1	—	—	—	—	—	—	1
Sutcliffe, Miss B.	London	1871-1875	Landscape	—	—	—	—	2	—	—	—	—	—	2
Sutcliffe, Miss Harriette	London	1881-1893	Domestic	—	—	14	—	—	—	—	—	—	2	16
Sutcliffe, John	London	1853-1856	Domestic	—	—	2	—	—	—	—	—	—	4	6
Sutcliffe, Lester	Leeds	1880-1886	Landscape	—	—	3	—	7	—	—	—	—	2	12
Sutcliffe, Mrs. L. T.	Whitby	1893	Flowers	—	—	1	—	—	—	—	—	—	—	1
Sutcliffe, Thomas ‡	Leeds	1856-1871	Landscape	—	—	1	—	—	—	109	—	—	—	110
Suter, R.	London	1827-1854	Architecture	—	—	5	—	—	—	—	—	—	—	5
Sutherland, Miss Fanny	London	1876-1886	Domestic	—	—	10	—	—	—	1	—	—	5	16
Sutherland, George Mowbray	London	1861-1866	Domestic	—	—	1	—	—	—	—	—	—	2	3
Sutherland, Miss G. M.	London	1827-1833	Landscape	—	—	—	—	7	—	—	—	—	—	7
Sutherland, Miss J.	London	1847-1852	Historical	—	—	—	2	2	—	—	—	—	3	7
Suthers, Leghe	Southport	1885-1893	Domestic	—	—	7	—	—	—	—	—	—	—	7
Suthers, W.	London	1878-1887	Flowers	—	—	5	—	12	—	1	—	—	6	24
Suttill, Miss Ada P.	Bridport	1889-1890	Flowers	—	—	2	—	—	—	—	—	—	—	2
Sutton, B.	Greenwich	1831-1832	Landscape	—	—	—	—	4	—	—	—	—	—	4
Sutton, G. M.	Worcester	1875	Still Life	—	—	—	—	1	—	—	—	—	—	1
Sutton, J.	Cockermouth	1798-1801	Portraits	—	—	6	—	—	—	—	—	—	—	6

Name.	Town.	First and Last Year of Ex.	Speciality.	S. A.	F. S.	R. A.	B. I.	S. S.	O. W.	N. W.	G. G.	N. G.	V. E.	Total.
Sutton, J.	Edinburgh	1876-1890	Landscape	—	—	8	—	—	—	—	—	—	—	8
Sutton, T	London	1771-1773	Architecture	3	—	—	—	—	—	—	—	—	—	3
Sutton, T.	—	1868	Fish	—	—	1	—	—	—	—	—	—	—	1
Svoboda, Alexander	London	1870-1871	Cities	—	—	—	—	4	—	—	—	—	—	4
Swaffield, Helena M.	Sevenoaks	1891-1893	Figures	—	—	—	—	3	—	—	—	—	1	4
Swain, Joseph	London	1872-1877	Wood Engraving	—	—	—	—	—	—	—	—	—	7	7
Swain, Ned, R.P.E.	London	1876-1885	Etching	—	—	4	—	10	—	—	—	—	7	21
Swaine, Francis	London	1762-1783	Sea Pieces	48	76	—	—	—	—	—	—	—	—	124
Swaine, John	London	1863-1869	Engraving	—	—	10	—	—	—	—	—	—	—	10
Swaine, John Barak	London	1837	Figures	—	—	—	1	—	—	—	—	—	—	1
Swaine, Monamy	London	1769-1774	Sea Pieces	—	6	—	—	—	—	—	—	—	—	6
Swaine, T.	London	1805	Architecture	—	—	1	—	—	—	—	—	—	—	1
Swainson, Miss Mary	London	1884-1892	Sculpture	—	—	1	—	—	—	—	3	1	—	5
Swainson, William	London	1884-1888	Miniatures	—	—	3	—	—	—	1	—	—	—	4
Swainston, Miss Laura	Sunderland	1890-1892	Domestic	—	—	2	—	—	—	—	—	—	—	2
Swallow, Miss Jane F.	London	1864-1869	Fruit	—	—	1	—	5	—	—	—	—	9	15
Swallow, John Charles	London	1858-1876	Landscape	—	—	3	—	4	—	—	—	—	3	10
Swan, Miss Alice Macallan	Cork	1882-1890	Flowers	—	—	8	—	—	—	2	—	—	—	10
Swan, C. E.	London	1893	Lion	—	—	1	—	—	—	—	—	—	—	1
Swan, Miss Emily R.	London	1893	Flowers	—	—	1	—	2	—	—	—	—	—	3
Swan, John Macallan, A.R.A.	Paris	1878-1892	Historical	—	—	13	—	—	—	—	2	3	8	26
Swan, Miss Mary E.	Bromley	1890-1893	Portraits	—	—	1	—	—	—	—	—	—	3	4
Swan, Mrs.	London	1888-1891	Domestic	—	—	—	—	—	—	—	1	2	—	3
Swandale, G.	London	1824-1844	Dramatic	—	—	4	—	4	—	—	—	—	—	8
Swanwick, Harold, A.R.C.A.	Winsford	1889-1893	Rustic	—	—	6	—	5	—	1	—	—	1	13
Swarbreck, Samuel Dukinfield	London	1852-1863	Abbeys	—	—	8	14	4	—	—	—	—	30	56
Sweet, Ada M.	Clapham	1889-1891	Domestic	—	—	—	—	3	—	—	—	—	1	4
Sweeting, John	Worthing	1879	Figures	—	—	—	—	1	—	—	—	—	—	1
Sweeting, R. G.	London	1845-1865	Landscape	—	—	4	3	—	—	—	—	—	—	7
Swift, Clement N.	Pontaven	1878-1880	Domestic	—	—	—	—	—	—	—	—	—	5	5
Swift, Edmund	Liverpool	1866-1868	Domestic	—	—	—	1	4	—	—	—	—	—	5
Swift, Miss Georgina ‖	Blackheath	1855-1874	Figures	—	—	4	1	13	—	—	—	—	—	18
Swift, Miss Catherine Seaton Forman (Kate).‖	—	—	—	—	—	—	—	—	—	—	—	—	—	—
See Mrs. Christopher Bisschop	Blackheath	1855-1868	Domestic	—	—	5	8	11	—	—	—	—	—	24
Swift, Miss Louise B.	London	1868-1873	Portraits	—	—	1	—	—	—	—	—	—	1	2
Swift, Mrs. W. B. (E. H.) ‖	London	1833-1859	Figures	—	—	12	—	2	—	—	—	—	—	14
Swinburne, T. H.	London	1855-1856	Still Life	—	—	1	—	2	—	—	—	—	—	3
Swingler, John Frank	London	1886-1893	Still Life	—	—	13	—	5	—	—	—	—	7	25
Swinnerton, J.	London	1839-1851	Landscape	—	—	—	—	3	—	—	—	—	—	3
Swinson, Edward S.	London	1893	Figures	—	—	1	—	—	—	—	—	—	—	1
Swinstead, Alfred H.	London	1874-1888	Domestic	—	—	4	—	1	—	—	—	—	—	5
Swinstead, Charles Hillyard	London	1863-1891	Landscape	—	—	1	2	6	—	—	—	—	3	12
Swinstead, Eliza L. (?) J.	Dalston	1881	Flowers	—	—	—	—	1	—	—	—	—	—	1
Swinstead, George Hillyard, R.B.A. §	London	1877-1893	Domestic	—	—	17	—	25	—	—	—	—	14	56
Swinton, James Rannie	London	1844-1874	Portraits	—	—	85	2	15	—	—	—	—	—	102
Swire, John	Wakefield	1883-1887	Domestic	—	—	—	—	1	—	1	—	—	—	2
Swoboda, Rudolf	London	1885-1892	Oriental	—	—	3	—	8	—	—	—	—	1	12
Swynnerton, Joseph William	Rome	1873-1892	Sculpture	—	—	4	—	—	—	—	1	7	—	12
Swynnerton, Mrs. Joseph William, ‖ late Miss	—	—	—	—	—	—	—	—	—	—	—	—	—	—
Anna Louisa Robinson	London	1887-1893	Portraits	—	—	—	—	—	—	—	3	15	1	19
Sydnas, A.	Norwich	1868	Figures	—	—	1	—	—	—	—	—	—	—	1
Sydney, John	Chiswick	1893	Domestic	—	—	—	—	—	—	—	—	—	1	1
Syer, H. R.	London	1874-1879	Landscape	—	—	—	—	13	—	—	—	—	—	13
Syer, John, R.I. ‡ §	Bristol	1832-1885	Landscape	—	—	19	11	68	—	81	4	—	7	190
Syer, James	Clifton	1867-1878	Sea Pieces	—	—	3	—	14	—	—	—	—	—	17
Syer, K. S.	London	1798	Figures	—	—	1	—	—	—	—	—	—	—	1
Sykes, Arthur. *See also* Garlick, Park, and Sykes	London	1889	Architecture	—	—	1	—	—	—	—	—	—	—	1
Sykes, A. Bernard	Catford	1893	Allegorical	—	—	—	—	1	—	—	—	—	—	1
Sykes, Sir Francis §	—	1832	Sketch	—	—	—	—	1	—	—	—	—	—	1
Sykes, F., F.S.A.	York	1776	Portraits	1	—	—	—	—	—	—	—	—	—	1
Sykes, George	London	1761-1774	Enamels	6	—	—	—	—	—	—	—	—	—	6
Sykes, Godfrey	London	1862-1864	Mosaics	—	—	3	—	—	—	—	—	—	—	3
Sykes, Henry, R.B.A. §	London	1877-1893	Landscape	—	—	7	—	11	—	4	—	1	3	26
Sykes, Miss Lilian	Croydon	1888-1889	Landscape	—	—	—	—	—	—	2	—	—	—	2
Sykes, Miss Marianne	London	1876-1891	Miniatures	—	—	19	—	2	—	—	—	—	—	21
Sykes, Peace	Huddersfield	1872-1890	Landscape	—	—	4	—	2	—	4	—	—	—	10
Sykes, Mrs.	London	1840-1859	Miniatures	—	—	7	—	—	—	—	—	—	—	7
Sylva, Van Damme-	London	1885	Landscape	—	—	—	—	2	—	—	—	—	—	2
Sylvester, C. J	London	1846-1849	Landscape	—	—	7	—	—	—	—	—	—	5	12
Sylvester, John Henry	London	1876-1891	Domestic	—	—	3	—	8	—	—	—	—	5	16
Sylvester, W.	London	1814	Flowers	—	—	1	—	—	—	—	—	—	—	1
Syme, John S., R.S.A.	Edinburgh	1819-1820	Portraits	—	—	2	—	—	—	—	—	—	—	2

Name.	Town.	First and Last Year of Ex.	Speciality.	S. A.	F. S.	R. A.	B. I.	S. S.	O. W.	N.W.	G. G.	N. G.	V. E.	Total.
Syme, Patrick, R.S.A.	Edinburgh	1817	Fruit	—	—	2	—	—	—	—	—	—	—	2
Symes, Mrs.	—	1847	Fruit	—	—	1	—	—	—	—	—	—	—	1
Symington, D. L.	London	1891	Landscape	—	—	—	—	1	—	—	—	—	—	1
Symon, Elizabeth	Surbiton	1864-1866	Landscape	—	—	—	—	1	—	—	—	—	1	2
Symonds, E.	Dover	1836	Portraits	—	—	1	—	—	—	—	—	—	—	1
Symonds, William Robert	Ipswich	1876-1893	Domestic	—	—	35	—	—	—	—	3	1	16	55
Symons, William Christian §	London	1865-1891	Domestic	—	—	25	—	58	—	1	2	—	14	100
Tabatier, V.	Nice	1877	Landscape	—	—	—	—	—	—	—	—	—	2	2
Taber, F.	London	1803	Architecture	—	—	1	—	—	—	—	—	—	—	1
Tachetti, Padre	—	1768	Miniatures	—	5	—	—	—	—	—	—	—	—	5
Taconet, Charles	London	1790-1792	Medals	—	—	4	—	—	—	—	—	—	—	4
Tadolini, Adam Scipione	Rome	1830-1853	Sculpture	—	—	2	—	—	—	—	—	—	—	2
Tafe, W. A.	London	1877	Landscape	—	—	—	—	2	—	—	—	—	1	3
Taggart, Mrs. A. M.	London	1828	Landscape	—	—	—	—	1	—	—	—	—	—	1
Tagore, Miss B. B.	London	1874	Figures	—	—	—	—	1	—	—	—	—	—	1
Taiee, A.	London	1875	Etching	—	—	—	—	—	—	—	—	—	2	2
Tait, J.	London	1862	Churches	—	—	1	—	—	—	—	—	—	—	1
Tait, Mrs. M. A.	London	1839-1846	Landscape	—	—	3	3	—	—	—	—	—	—	6
Tait, Robert S.	London	1845-1875	Portraits	—	—	24	1	—	—	—	—	—	—	25
Taitt, G. W.	London	1797-1810	Portraits	—	—	3	—	—	—	—	—	—	—	3
Takush, M.	London	1834-1837	Enamels	—	—	3	—	—	—	—	—	—	—	3
Talbert, Bruce James	London	1870-1876	Architecture	—	—	8	—	—	—	—	—	—	—	8
Talbot, George Q. P.	Venice	1881-1888	Figures	—	—	4	—	—	—	6	2	—	—	12
Talfourd, Field	London	1845-1874	Portraits	—	—	34	1	—	—	—	—	—	73	108
Tallemache, Richard	London	1808-1818	Landscape	—	—	7	8	—	—	—	—	—	—	15
Tallemache, William	London	1812-1816	Sculpture	—	—	3	4	—	—	—	—	—	—	7
Tallent, J.	London	1797	Miniatures	—	—	1	—	—	—	—	—	—	—	1
Talmage, A. M.	St. Ives, Cornw'l	1893	Landscape	—	—	—	—	1	—	—	—	—	1	2
Tamburini —	Chichester	1882	Figures	—	—	—	—	—	—	—	—	—	1	1
Tamerlain —	—	1780	Drawings	—	4	—	—	—	—	—	—	—	—	4
Tamlin, J.	London	1883	Study	—	—	—	—	1	—	—	—	—	—	1
Tancredi, R.	London	1870	Historical	—	—	1	—	—	—	—	—	—	—	1
Taning, J.	London	1834	Architecture	—	—	1	—	—	—	—	—	—	—	1
Tanner. *See* Romaine-Walker and Tanner	—	—	Architecture	—	—	—	—	—	—	—	—	—	—	—
Tanner, A.	London	1844-1850	Landscape	—	—	—	—	6	—	—	—	—	—	6
Tanneur P.	Paris	1841	Sea Pieces	—	—	4	—	—	—	—	—	—	—	4
Tannock, F.	London	1834	Portraits	—	—	1	—	—	—	—	—	—	—	1
Tannock, James	London	1813-1841	Portraits	—	—	44	—	1	—	—	—	—	—	45
Tannock, W.	London	1818-1831	Domestic	—	—	15	—	1	—	—	—	—	—	16
Tanqueray, Alice F.	London	1886	Domestic	—	—	—	—	1	—	—	—	—	—	1
Tantardini, Antonio	Milan	1875	Sculpture	—	—	1	—	—	—	—	—	—	—	1
Tapiro, Jose	Rome	1865-1889	Interiors	—	—	—	—	—	—	—	1	—	1	2
Tapp, Miss C.	Shortlands	1889	Churches	—	—	—	—	—	—	1	—	—	—	1
Tappen, G.	Christchurch	1802-1827	Architecture	—	—	9	—	—	—	—	—	—	—	9
Tapper, Walter J.	London	1892-1893	Architecture	—	—	2	—	—	—	—	—	—	—	2
Tapping, M. G.	—	1797-1799	Sporting	—	—	3	—	—	—	—	—	—	—	3
Tapson, Mary Alice,	London	1876-1880	Domestic	—	—	—	—	—	—	—	—	—	4	4
Tapster, R.	Barnet	1803	Architecture	—	—	1	—	—	—	—	—	—	—	1
Taragnola, Chevalier G.	London	1815-1820	Sculpture	—	—	4	—	—	—	—	—	—	—	4
Tarbuck, E. L.	London	1848-1854	Architecture	—	—	2	—	—	—	—	—	—	—	2
Target, F.	London	1836	Animals	—	—	1	—	—	—	—	—	—	—	1
Targett, Thomas G.	Salisbury	1869	Game	—	—	—	—	—	—	—	—	—	1	1
Tarlton, John	London	1872-1875	Wood Engraving	—	—	—	—	—	—	—	—	—	3	3
Tarran, Thomas	Surbiton	1888	Sculpture	—	—	—	—	1	—	—	—	—	—	1
Tarrant, J.	London	1777	Stained Glass	1	—	—	—	—	—	—	—	—	—	1
Tarrant, J.	London	1823	Landscape	—	—	1	—	—	—	—	—	—	—	1
Tarrant, Percy	London	1879-1891	Domestic	—	—	9	—	1	—	1	—	—	6	17
Tarring, John	London	1838-1878	Architecture	—	—	9	—	—	—	—	—	—	—	9
Tarring, S. C.	London	1846-1854	Architecture	—	—	4	—	—	—	—	—	—	—	4
Tarry, Miss Alice (Mrs. Frederick Goodall)	London	1890-1893	Domestic	—	—	4	—	—	—	—	—	—	—	4
Tarte, J.	London	1819-1821	Architecture	—	—	2	—	—	—	—	—	—	—	2
Tarver, Edward John	London	1874-1878	Architecture	—	—	6	—	—	—	—	—	—	—	6
Tasker, Francis William	London	1875-1886	Architecture	—	—	6	—	—	—	—	—	—	—	6
Tasker, Miss Helen	—	1840-1843	Flowers	—	—	1	—	1	—	—	—	—	—	2
Tasker, J.	London	1782-1814	Architecture	—	—	4	—	—	—	—	—	—	—	4
Tasker, T.	London	1812-1813	Architecture	—	—	2	—	—	—	—	—	—	—	2
Tasker, William	London	1857-1859	Architecture	—	—	2	—	—	—	—	—	—	—	2
Tassaert, Philip J., F.S.A.	—	1769-1785	Landscape	38	1	2	—	—	—	—	—	—	—	41
Tassaert —, Junr.	Munich	1783	Scriptural	4	—	—	—	—	—	—	—	—	—	4

Name.	Town.	First and Last Year of Ex.	Speciality.	S. A.	F. S.	R. A.	B. I.	S. S.	O. W.	N.W.	G. G.	N. G.	V. E.	Total.
Tassie, James	London	1767-1791	Cameo Portraits	2	—	50	—	—	—	—	—	—	—	52
Tassie, William	London	1798-1804	Gems	—	—	5	—	—	—	—	—	—	—	5
Tate, T. F.	London	1850	Landscape	—	—	1	—	—	—	—	—	—	—	1
Tate, W. Christopher	London	1828-1833	Sculpture	—	—	7	—	2	—	—	—	—	—	9
Tate, William, F.S.A. (Pupil of Wright, of Derby)	Manchester	1771-1804	Portraits	12	—	12	—	—	—	—	—	—	—	24
Tatebey, John	London	1827	Landscape	—	—	—	2	—	—	—	—	—	—	2
Tatham, Charles Heathcote	London	1797-1836	Architecture	—	—	53	—	—	—	—	—	—	—	53
Tatham, Fred.	London	1825-1854	Miniatures and Sculpture	—	—	66	3	7	—	—	—	—	—	76
Tatham, Miss Helen S.	Shanklin	1878-1891	Landscape	—	—	1	—	3	—	—	—	—	2	6
Tattam, R.	London	1786	Landscape	—	—	1	—	—	—	—	—	—	—	1
Tattersall, George	London	1840-1848	Architecture	—	—	6	—	—	—	—	—	—	—	6
Taunce de Laune, C. de L.	London	1872	Karnac	—	—	—	—	—	—	—	—	—	1	1
Taunton, William	London	1855-1875	Landscape	—	—	1	—	7	—	—	—	—	3	11
Taxe, Theobald	London	1865-1867	Domestic	—	—	1	6	—	—	—	—	—	—	7
Tayler, A. Chevallier- φ	London	1879-1893	Domestic	—	—	10	—	2	—	—	—	—	16	28
Tayler, Charles Foot	Isle of Wight	1820-1853	Miniatures	—	—	39	—	—	—	—	—	—	—	39
Tayler, E.	London	1802-1830	Miniatures	—	—	24	—	—	—	—	—	—	—	24
Tayler, Edward	London	1849-1893	Miniatures	—	—	265	—	10	—	2	1	1	32	311
Tayler, Harry	London	1882-1883	Miniatures	—	—	2	—	—	—	—	—	—	—	2
Tayler, Miss Ida R.	London	1884-1893	Domestic	—	—	9	—	18	—	1	1	—	11	40
Tayler, J. Frederick, P.R.W.S. †	London	1830-1889	Figures	—	—	5	5	—	528	—	—	—	18	556
Tayler, Miss Kate	London	1872-1893	Flowers	—	—	2	—	—	—	2	—	—	3	7
Tayler, Miss Minna	London	1884-1893	Domestic	—	—	10	—	6	—	—	—	—	7	23
Tayler, Miss Nina	London	1890	Landscape	—	—	—	—	—	—	—	1	—	—	1
Tayler, Norman E., A.R.W.S. †	London	1863-1893	Flowers	—	—	13	1	1	90	—	—	—	1	106
Tayler, T.	London	1840	Portraits	—	—	1	—	—	—	—	—	—	—	1
Tayler, T.	London	1792-1821	Architecture	—	—	11	—	—	—	—	—	—	—	11
Taylerson, John E.	London	1884-1893	Sculpture	—	—	17	—	—	—	—	—	—	—	17
Taylor —	—	1765	Fruit	1	—	—	—	—	—	—	—	—	—	1
Taylor, Alexander	London	1774-1796	Miniatures	12	—	22	—	—	—	—	—	—	—	34
Taylor, Alfred	London	1879-1886	Domestic	—	—	7	—	6	—	—	—	—	2	15
Taylor, Miss Ada E.	London	1876-1881	Fruit	—	—	1	—	1	—	—	—	—	5	7
Taylor, Alfred Henry ‡	London	1832-1867	Domestic	—	—	26	4	38	—	107	—	—	25	200
Taylor, Andrew Thomas	London	1875-1881	Architecture	—	—	5	—	—	—	—	—	—	—	5
Taylor, Charles	London	1776-1782	Engraving	12	—	—	—	—	—	—	—	—	—	12
Taylor, Charles	London	1836-1871	Historical	—	—	17	—	4	—	—	—	—	—	21
Taylor, Charles, Junr.	—	1841-1883	Sea Pieces	—	—	4	8	51	—	1	—	—	11	75
Taylor, Miss Charlotte	London	1874-1884	Still Life	—	—	—	—	—	—	2	—	—	1	3
Taylor, C. A.	London	1844	Historical	—	—	2	—	—	—	—	—	—	—	2
Taylor, E.	London	1818-1824	Architecture	—	—	4	—	—	—	—	—	—	—	4
Taylor, E.	London	1825	Miniatures	—	—	2	—	—	—	—	—	—	—	2
Taylor, Edward	London	1773	Hair Work	1	—	—	—	—	—	—	—	—	—	1
Taylor, Edwin	Birmingham	1860-1872	Landscape	—	—	—	—	—	—	—	—	—	4	4
Taylor, Emma	Ipswich	1865	Figures	—	—	—	—	1	—	—	—	—	—	1
Taylor, Miss Etty	Birmingham	1888	Landscape	—	—	2	—	—	—	—	1	—	—	3
Taylor, Ernest E.	London	1882-1893	Flowers	—	—	—	—	1	—	—	—	—	1	2
Taylor, Edward Ingram	London	1881-1893	Stained Glass	—	—	2	—	—	—	1	—	—	8	11
Taylor, Edward J.	London	1881-1891	Landscape	—	—	4	—	7	—	—	—	—	—	11
Taylor, Edward R.	Birmingham	1861-1893	Landscape	—	—	30	3	23	—	3	3	2	16	80
Taylor, G.	London	1790	Portraits	—	—	1	—	—	—	—	—	—	—	1
Taylor, G. Hart	Devoran	1879-1880	Landscape	—	—	—	—	1	—	—	2	—	—	3
Taylor, G. L.	London	1820-1822	Ruins	—	—	10	—	—	—	—	—	—	—	10
Taylor, H.	London	1843	Sculpture	—	—	1	—	—	—	—	—	—	—	1
Taylor, Harry	London	1839-1870	Figures	—	—	—	—	12	—	—	—	—	—	12
Taylor, Mrs. Herbert (Annie)	London	1854-1856	Figures	—	—	—	—	1	—	—	—	—	2	3
Taylor, H. J.	London	1832-1834	Still Life	—	—	—	—	3	—	—	—	—	—	3
Taylor, Henry King	London	1857-1869	Sea Pieces	—	—	6	24	31	—	—	—	—	15	76
Taylor, Isaac, F.S.A.	London	1765-1780	Engraving	31	—	—	—	—	—	—	—	—	—	31
Taylor, J.	Southampton	1798-1842	Architecture	—	—	20	—	—	—	1	—	—	—	21
Taylor, J.	Plumstead	1863-1865	Fruit	—	—	2	—	—	—	—	—	—	—	2
Taylor, James	London	1770-1776	Engraving	10	—	—	—	—	—	—	—	—	—	10
Taylor, Miss Jane	Rye	1872-1874	Flowers	—	—	—	—	3	—	—	—	—	—	3
Taylor, John, F.S.A.	London	1764-1786	Miniatures	69	2	11	—	—	—	—	—	—	—	82
Taylor, John, Junr.	London	1777-1790	Landscape	10	—	—	—	—	—	—	—	—	—	10
Taylor, John (called "Old Taylor")	London	1778-1838	Historical	—	—	42	27	1	—	—	—	—	—	70
Taylor, John	London	1861-1864	Architecture	—	—	3	—	—	—	—	—	—	—	3
Taylor, John	London	1867-1876	Landscape	—	—	3	—	—	—	—	—	—	3	6
Taylor, John	London	1879-1881	Sculpture	—	—	6	—	—	—	—	2	—	—	8
Taylor, Mrs. John. *See* Miss Mary Spilsbury	—	1810-1813	Domestic	—	—	—	12	—	—	—	—	—	—	12
Taylor, Joseph	Oxford	1847-1867	Landscape	—	—	3	4	—	—	—	—	—	—	7
Taylor, Joshua	London	1846-1877	Landscape	—	—	1	13	6	—	—	—	—	—	20

Name.	Town.	First and Last Year of Ex.	Speciality.	S. A.	F. S.	R. A.	B. I.	S. S.	O. W.	N.W.	G. G.	N. G.	V. E.	Total.
Taylor, John D.	Glasgow	1884-1888	Landscape	—	—	4	—	—	—	—	—	—	—	4
Taylor, J. F.	London	1826-1840	Figures	—	—	2	—	2	—	—	—	—	—	4
Taylor, J. Fraser	—	1884	Rustic	—	—	—	—	—	—	—	2	—	—	2
Taylor, Joseph H.	London	1827-1841	Architecture	—	—	6	—	—	—	—	—	—	—	6
Taylor, Miss J. T.	Hertford	1860	Architecture	—	—	1	—	—	—	—	—	—	—	1
Taylor, J. Wyckliffe	Surbiton	1880-1886	Animals	—	—	1	—	—	—	—	8	—	3	12
Taylor, Miss Lizzie	Birmingham	1883-1889	Buildings	—	—	3	—	—	—	—	—	—	—	3
Taylor, L. *See* Wright and Taylor.	—	—	—	—	—	—	—	—	—	—	—	—	—	—
Taylor, Martha	—	1787	Flowers	—	—	1	—	—	—	—	—	—	—	1
Taylor, Medland	—	1893	Stained Glass	—	—	1	—	—	—	—	—	—	—	1
Taylor, Nora	London	1881	Landscape	—	—	—	—	1	—	—	—	—	—	1
Taylor, P.	—	1819	Sculpture	—	—	1	—	—	—	—	—	—	—	1
Taylor, Miss Pauline	Southport	1868-1869	Still Life	—	—	—	—	4	—	—	—	—	5	9
Taylor, Richard	London	1763-1791	Landscape	—	2	20	—	—	—	—	—	—	—	22
Taylor, S.	London	1807-1849	Figures	—	—	1	4	4	—	—	—	—	—	9
Taylor, Stephen	Winchester	1817-1849	Sporting	—	—	48	29	42	—	—	—	—	—	119
Taylor, Miss S.	—	1780	Needlework	1	—	—	—	—	—	—	—	—	—	1
Taylor, Miss S. M. Louisa	Oxford	1867-1884	Domestic	—	—	1	—	3	—	—	1	—	3	8
Taylor, T.	London	1792-1809	Landscape	—	—	57	—	—	—	—	—	—	—	57
Taylor, Thomas	London	1843-1852	Architecture	—	—	2	—	—	—	—	—	—	—	2
Taylor, Tom	London	1883-1893	Domestic	—	—	3	—	11	—	11	—	—	2	27
Taylor, William	London	1766	Architecture	1	—	—	—	—	—	—	—	—	—	1
Taylor, W.	—	1811	Domestic	—	—	1	—	—	—	—	—	—	—	1
Taylor, William	London	1812-1852	Figures	—	—	19	7	7	—	—	—	—	—	33
Taylor, W.	Hitchin	1859	Game	—	—	1	—	—	—	—	—	—	—	1
Taylor, Mrs. W.	—	1822	Portraits	—	—	1	—	—	—	—	—	—	—	1
Taylor, W. A.	London	1838	Architecture	—	—	1	—	—	—	—	—	—	—	1
Taylor, W. B.	London	1820-1855	Landscape	—	—	4	—	1	—	—	—	—	—	5
Taylor, William B. Sarsfield ‡	London	1829-1847	Battle Pieces	—	—	22	16	1	—	5	—	—	—	44
Taylor, William George	London	1882-1883	Stained Glass	—	—	3	—	—	—	—	—	—	—	3
Taylor (W. G.) and Griffiths (W. J.)	London	1881-1891	Stained Glass	—	—	9	—	—	—	—	—	—	—	9
Taylor, W. S.	—	1813-1816	Rustic	—	—	3	—	—	—	—	—	—	—	3
Taylor, William W.	Kirkaldy	1880	Sculpture	—	—	1	—	—	—	—	—	—	—	1
Taylor, Mrs.	London	1775	Flowers	—	1	—	—	—	—	—	—	—	—	1
Taylor, Miss	London	1827-1831	Landscape	—	—	2	—	2	—	—	—	—	—	4
Taylor, Gordon, and Bousfield	London	1886	Architecture	—	—	1	—	—	—	—	—	—	—	1
Teasdale, John	London	1877-1878	Landscape	—	—	—	—	—	—	—	—	—	3	3
Tebbitt, Miss Gertrude	London	1890	Animals	—	—	—	—	—	—	—	—	—	1	1
Tebbitt, Henri	East Molesey	1882-1884	Landscape	—	—	1	—	1	—	—	—	—	—	2
Tebby, Arthur Kemp	London	1883-1892	Domestic	—	—	1	—	5	—	—	—	—	2	8
Tebby, Leighton	London	1885-1888	Landscape	—	—	1	—	3	—	—	—	—	—	4
Tedder, M.	Woking	1885-1891	Landscape	—	—	—	—	—	—	3	—	—	—	3
Teed, Mrs. Frank L.	London	1893	Flowers	—	—	—	—	—	—	1	—	—	—	1
Teering, Sir R. F., Bart.	Chichester	1876	Landscape	—	—	—	—	—	—	—	—	—	3	3
Teesdale, C.	London	1883-1886	Landscape	—	—	—	—	—	—	4	—	—	—	4
Teesdale, Miss Emma	—	1851	Portraits	—	—	1	—	—	—	—	—	—	—	1
Teixeira-de-Mattos, H.	London	1893	Sculpture	—	—	1	—	—	—	—	—	—	—	1
Tekusch, Miss Margaret ‖	London	1845-1888	Miniatures	—	—	85	—	11	—	—	—	—	—	96
Telbin, Henry	London	1866	Landscape	—	—	—	—	3	—	—	—	—	—	3
Telbin, Miss Mary	London	1884	Figures	—	—	—	—	—	—	—	—	—	1	1
Telbin, William ‡	London	1839-1874	Landscape	—	—	1	6	3	—	12	—	—	1	23
Telbin, W. L.	London	1875	Landscape	—	—	—	—	1	—	—	—	—	1	2
Telbin, W. T., Junr.	London	1866-1881	Sea Pieces	—	—	—	—	5	—	—	—	—	—	5
Telfer, Mrs. C. (C.)	London	1892	Flowers	—	—	—	—	1	—	—	—	—	—	1
Telfer, W. D.	London	1845-1847	Domestic	—	—	3	—	—	—	—	—	—	—	3
Temple, Captain	Guernsey	1867	Landscape	—	—	—	—	—	—	—	—	—	1	1
Temple, Alfred G.	Norwood	1881-1890	Landscape	—	—	2	—	1	—	—	—	—	—	3
Temple, Charles H.	Ironbridge	1893	Architecture	—	—	1	—	—	—	—	—	—	—	1
Temple, E.	London	1862-1874	Domestic	—	—	—	—	12	—	—	—	—	—	12
Temple, J.	London	1795-1802	Architecture	—	—	3	—	—	—	—	—	—	—	3
Temple, Robert Scott	Edinburgh	1874-1889	Landscape	—	—	12	—	1	—	—	—	—	—	13
Templeton, J. S.	London	1830-1857	Portraits	—	—	34	2	2	—	—	—	—	—	38
Templeton, P. A.	London	1847	Sculpture	—	—	1	—	—	—	—	—	—	—	1
Tempra, Quirino	London	1884	Sculpture	—	—	1	—	—	—	—	—	—	—	1
Tendi, A.	London	1793-1797	Figures	—	—	2	—	—	—	—	—	—	—	2
Tenerani, Chevalier Pietro	Rome	1846-1854	Sculpture	—	—	2	—	—	—	—	—	—	—	2
Tenison, Miss N.	London	1893	Flowers	—	—	—	—	1	—	—	—	—	—	1
Tenison, William	London	1873	Sorrento	—	—	—	—	—	—	—	—	—	1	1
Teniswood, G. F.	Barnes	1856-1876	Landscape	—	—	12	7	20	—	—	—	—	6	45
Tenkate, Herman	London	1872-1876	Domestic	—	—	—	—	1	—	—	—	—	1	2
Tennant, Miss Dorothy. *See* Mrs. H. M. Stanley	London	1879-1890	Domestic	—	—	4	—	—	—	—	18	6	10	38

Name.	Town.	First and Last Year of Ex.	Speciality.	S. A.	F. S.	R. A.	B. I.	S. S.	O. W.	N. W.	G. G.	N. G.	V. E.	Total.
Tennant, John F. §	London	1820-1873	Landscape	—	—	18	54	340	—	4	—	—	—	416
Tennant, Mrs. R. N.	—	1852	Heads	—	—	2	—	—	—	—	—	—	—	2
Tennick, W. G.	London	1877	Landscape	—	—	—	—	—	—	—	—	—	2	2
Tenniel, Sir John, R.I. ‡	London	1835-1880	Historical	—	—	14	—	16	—	27	—	—	8	65
Tennison, W.	—	1873	Italy	—	—	—	—	2	—	—	—	—	—	2
Tennyson, J.	London	1865	Landscape	—	—	—	1	—	—	—	—	—	—	1
Ternbat, R.	Maidstone	1818	Landscape	—	—	1	—	—	—	—	—	—	—	1
Ternouth, John	London	1819-1849	Sculpture	—	—	46	1	25	—	—	—	—	—	72
Terrell, Mrs. *See* Georgina F. Koberwein	London	1879-1887	Domestic	—	—	15	—	3	—	2	—	—	6	26
Terrell, R. H.	—	1855	Figures	—	—	1	—	—	—	—	—	—	—	1
Terris, John, R.S.W.	Glasgow	1890-1892	Landscape	—	—	2	—	—	—	1	—	—	—	3
Territt, J.	Taunton	1845	Domestic	—	—	—	—	1	—	—	—	—	—	1
Terry, C.	London	1819-1820	Landscape	—	—	3	—	—	—	—	—	—	—	3
Terry, D.	London	1798-1803	Architecture	—	—	4	—	—	—	—	—	—	—	4
Terry, Mrs. E., *née* Nasmyth	London	1816-1833	Landscape	—	—	—	19	2	—	—	—	—	—	21
Terry, Elizabeth	London	1846-1853	Landscape	—	—	2	—	—	—	—	—	—	—	2
Terry, Henry	London	1879-1893	Domestic	—	—	13	—	19	—	12	—	1	19	64
Terry, J.	—	1865	—	—	—	—	—	1	—	—	—	—	—	1
Terry, Miss Jane	London	1856	Landscape	—	—	1	—	—	—	—	—	—	—	1
Terry, Robert	London	1762-1770	Landscape	2	2	2	—	—	—	—	—	—	—	6
Terry, Miss Sarah	Aylesbury	1862-1879	Sculpture	—	—	11	—	—	—	—	—	—	1	12
Terry, W. F.	London	1864-1873	Landscape	—	—	—	1	6	—	—	—	—	—	7
Tesson, L.	London	1866	Figures	—	—	—	—	2	—	—	—	—	—	2
Testelin, A. J.	London	1867-1874	Domestic	—	—	—	—	4	—	—	—	—	1	5
Tetlow —	—	1767-1775	Miniatures	7	—	1	—	—	—	—	—	—	—	8
Teulon, Samuel Saunders	London	1835-1864	Architecture	—	—	38	—	—	—	—	—	—	—	38
Teulon, William Milford	London	1854-1875	Architecture	—	—	8	—	—	—	—	—	—	—	8
Texier, Le. *See* L.	—	—	—	—	—	—	—	—	—	—	—	—	—	—
Teyssonnieres, Pierre	Bordeaux	1874	Etching	—	—	—	—	—	—	—	—	—	2	2
Thacker, Samuel T.	London	1886-1888	Sea Pieces	—	—	—	—	2	—	—	—	—	1	3
Thaddeus, H. Jones, A.R.H.A. *See* Jones	London	1885-1889	Portraits	—	—	—	—	3	—	—	4	—	—	7
Thagardh, P.	London	1892	Landscape	—	—	—	—	—	—	—	—	—	1	1
Thane, W.	London	1807-1818	Landscape	—	—	9	—	—	—	—	—	—	—	9
Thangue, La. *See* L.	—	—	—	—	—	—	—	—	—	—	—	—	—	—
Thannberg, De. *See* D.	—	—	—	—	—	—	—	—	—	—	—	—	—	—
Thannenberg, L. D.	London	1852	Portraits	—	—	—	—	1	—	—	—	—	—	1
Thatcher, C. F.	London	1816-1846	Scriptural	—	—	40	15	1	—	—	—	—	—	56
Thayer, Abbot H.	Paris	1877	Domestic	—	—	—	—	—	—	—	—	—	1	1
Theakston, C.	London	1825-1831	Sculpture	—	—	2	—	—	—	—	—	—	—	2
Theakston, Joseph	London	1809-1837	Sculpture	—	—	14	3	1	—	—	—	—	—	18
Theakston, J. H.	London	1832	Sculpture	—	—	1	—	—	—	—	—	—	—	1
Theed, E. Frank	London	1873-1888	Sculpture	—	—	19	—	—	—	—	—	—	—	19
Theed, William, R.A.	London	1789-1818	Sculpture	—	—	18	5	—	—	—	—	—	—	13
Theed, William	London	1824-1885	Sculpture	—	—	88	3	—	—	—	—	—	—	91
Thelwall, J. A.	London	1883-1886	Domestic	—	—	4	—	1	—	—	—	—	—	5
Thelwall, Weymouth Birkbeck	London	1867-1868	Landscape	—	—	—	—	1	—	—	—	—	2	3
Theobald, H. ‡	London	1845-1851	Domestic	—	—	2	—	—	—	23	—	—	—	25
Theobald, S S.	Putney	1885-1886	Landscape	—	—	—	—	—	—	3	—	—	—	3
Theobald, W.	London	1817	Sporting	—	—	2	—	—	—	—	—	—	—	2
Theweneti, J.	London	1860-1876	Landscape	—	—	—	—	2	—	—	—	—	1	3
Theweneti, L.	London	1824-1831	Miniatures	—	—	8	—	—	—	—	—	—	—	8
Thick, Miss C.	London	1802-1844	Miniatures	—	—	44	—	—	—	—	—	—	—	44
Thick, Miss Eliza	London	1801-1836	Miniatures	—	—	28	—	—	—	—	—	—	—	28
Thick, W.	London	1787-1815	Miniatures	—	—	29	—	—	—	—	—	—	—	29
Thicknesse (Philip) and Willink (W. E.)	Liverpool	1886	Architecture	—	—	1	—	—	—	—	—	—	—	1
Thiede, Edwin Adolf	Lewisham	1882-1889	Miniatures	—	—	6	—	—	—	—	—	—	1	7
Thielcke, H.	London	1805-1816	Scriptural	—	—	9	3	—	—	—	—	—	—	12
Thienon, L.	—	1852	Ruins	—	—	1	—	—	—	—	—	—	—	1
Thieron, L.	London	1837	River Scenes	—	—	1	—	—	—	—	—	—	—	1
Thimm, Franz	London	1850-1852	Landscape	—	—	2	—	—	—	—	—	—	—	2
Thirion, Eugene Romain	Paris	1874	Portraits	—	—	1	—	—	—	—	—	—	—	1
Thirsby, J.	—	1798	Portraits	—	—	2	—	—	—	—	—	—	—	2
Thirtle, John	Norwich	1808	Figures	—	—	1	—	—	—	—	—	—	—	1
Thiselton, A. U.	—	1831	Pen and Ink	—	—	1	—	—	—	—	—	—	—	1
Tholen, W. B.	London	1883-1887	Landscape	—	—	1	—	1	—	—	—	—	—	2
Tholson, W.	London	1810	Miniatures	—	—	1	—	—	—	—	—	—	—	1
Thom, James	London	1815	Domestic	—	—	—	2	—	—	—	—	—	—	2
Thom, James Crawford	Brentford	1864-1873	Domestic	—	—	7	3	23	—	—	—	—	5	38
Thomas —	—	1770	Miniatures	1	—	—	—	—	—	—	—	—	—	1
Thomas —	—	1797	Landscape	—	—	1	—	—	—	—	—	—	—	1
Thomas, A.	London	1783	Fruit	3	20	—	—	—	—	—	—	—	—	23
Thomas, Annie H.	London	1883-1889	Sea Shores	—	—	—	—	2	—	—	—	—	—	2

Name.	Town.	First and Last Year of Ex.	Speciality.	S. A.	F. S.	R. A.	B. I.	S. S.	O. W.	N.W.	G. G.	N. G.	V. E.	Total.
Thomas, B.	London	1836	Sea Shores	—	—	1	—	—	—	—	—	—	—	1
Thomas, Clifton	Salisbury	1884	Landscape	—	—	1	—	—	—	—	—	—	—	1
Thomas, Dudley	London	1881	Landscape	—	—	—	—	2	—	—	—	—	—	2
Thomas, Miss D. H.	Llandudno	1878-1892	Game	—	—	—	—	—	—	1	—	—	1	2
Thomas, Miss E.	London	1869	Rustic	—	—	—	—	1	—	—	—	—	—	1
Thomas, Edgar Herbert	Cardiff	1888	Portraits	—	—	—	—	—	—	—	—	—	1	1
Thomas, Frederick	London	1892-1893	Sculpture	—	—	1	—	—	—	—	—	—	—	1
Thomas, F. D.	London	1882	Landscape	—	—	—	—	—	—	—	—	—	2	2
Thomas, Miss Fanny E.	Shortland	1880	Landscape	—	—	—	—	1	—	—	2	—	—	3
Thomas, Miss Florence Elizabeth, afterwards Mrs. Alfred Williams	London	1852-1868	Fruit	—	—	2	7	11	—	—	—	—	—	20
Thomas, F. Inigo, A.R.P.E.	London	1893	Landscape	—	—	1	—	—	—	—	—	—	—	1
Thomas, F. G.	—	1828	Landscape	—	—	1	—	—	—	—	—	—	—	1
Thomas, G.	—	1816	Landscape	—	—	1	—	—	—	—	—	—	—	1
Thomas, Grosvenor, R.S.W.	Glasgow	1892	Landscape	—	—	1	—	—	—	—	—	—	—	1
Thomas, George A.	Hildenborough	1885	Landscape	—	—	1	—	—	—	—	—	—	—	1
Thomas, George Housman	London	1851-1868	Figures	—	—	19	1	—	—	—	—	—	9	29
Thomas, H.	London	1800	Figures	—	—	1	—	—	—	—	—	—	—	1
Thomas, John	London	1842-1861	Sculpture	—	—	44	1	—	—	—	—	—	—	45
Thomas, J. A. *See* Whitfield and Thomas	—	—	Architecture	—	—	—	—	—	—	—	—	—	—	—
Thomas, John Evan	London	1838-1870	Sculpture	—	—	53	—	2	—	—	—	—	—	55
Thomas, James Havard	Bristol	1872-1890	Sculpture	—	—	21	—	1	—	—	4	2	—	28
Thomas, J. L.	London	1855-1869	Landscape	—	—	4	—	7	—	—	—	—	—	11
Thomas, M.	Canterbury	1801-1811	Architecture	—	—	10	—	—	—	—	—	—	—	10
Thomas, Miss Margaret	Croydon	1868-1880	Domestic	—	—	11	—	17	—	—	—	—	5	33
Thomas, Mary	London	1878	Landscape	—	—	—	—	—	—	—	—	—	1	1
Thomas, Matthew Edward	London	1816-1853	Architecture	—	—	6	6	5	—	—	—	—	—	17
Thomas, M. F.	London	1872	Landscape	—	—	—	—	—	—	—	—	—	1	1
Thomas, Percy, R.P.E.	London	1866-1893	Figures	—	—	31	—	31	—	—	—	—	19	81
Thomas, Robert Kent	London	1864-1881	Etching	—	—	6	1	—	—	—	—	—	10	17
Thomas, R. S.	Portsea	1839-1842	Sea Pieces	—	—	3	—	—	—	—	—	—	—	3
Thomas, Sidney	London	1867-1868	Landscape	—	—	—	—	—	—	—	—	—	2	2
Thomas, S. Seymour	Paris	1890-1892	Portraits	—	—	1	—	—	—	—	—	—	1	2
Thomas, William	London	1780-1799	Architecture	—	—	7	—	—	—	—	—	—	—	7
Thomas, William	London	1806-1837	Figures	—	—	30	8	8	—	—	—	—	—	46
Thomas, William	London	1839-1846	Sculpture	—	—	4	—	2	—	—	—	—	—	6
Thomas, W.	Hampton	1838-1862	Landscape	—	—	1	1	1	—	—	—	—	—	3
Thomas, William Cave	London	1843-1884	Historical	—	—	20	3	—	—	1	—	—	27	51
Thomas, William Luson, R.I. ‡ φ	London	1860-1889	Domestic	—	—	—	—	7	—	173	—	—	4	184
Thomas, W. M.	London	1848-1871	Sculpture	—	—	23	—	—	—	—	—	—	—	23
Thomas, W. Murray	Cobham	1891	Sea Pieces	—	—	—	—	2	—	—	—	—	—	2
Thomas, Mrs.	—	1775	Scriptural	—	2	—	—	—	—	—	—	—	—	2
Thomas, Mrs.	London	1858-1861	Fruit	—	—	4	—	—	—	—	—	—	—	4
Thomas, Miss	—	1841-1842	Landscape	—	—	2	—	—	—	—	—	—	—	2
Thomason, T.	London	1834	Still Life	—	—	—	—	2	—	—	—	—	—	2
Thomason, Yeoville	London	1886	Architecture	—	—	1	—	—	—	—	—	—	—	1
Thompson —	York	1776-1782	Landscape	3	2	—	—	—	—	—	—	—	—	5
Thompson, Alfred	Paris	1863-1876	Domestic	—	—	5	—	4	—	—	—	—	4	13
Thompson, Baylis	London	1855-1856	Landscape	—	—	—	—	—	—	—	—	—	4	4
Thompson, Mrs. Christiana	London	1879	Landscape	—	—	1	—	—	—	—	—	—	—	1
Thompson, C. Mary	London	1877	Etching	—	—	—	—	—	—	—	—	—	1	1
Thompson, E.	London	1845	Portraits	—	—	1	—	—	—	—	—	—	—	1
Thompson, E.	London	1877	Domestic	—	—	—	—	1	—	—	—	—	—	1
Thompson, Miss Elizabeth. ‡ ‖ *See* Mrs. Butler *and* Lady Butler	—	1867-1875	Military	—	—	3	—	—	—	9	—	—	15	27
Thompson, Miss E.	Teignmouth	1869	Flowers	—	—	—	—	1	—	—	—	—	—	1
Thompson, Ernest E.	London	1881	Pen and Ink	—	—	—	—	—	—	—	—	—	2	2
Thompson, E. H.	Putney	1871-1872	Landscape	—	—	—	—	4	—	—	—	—	—	4
Thompson, E. W.	Paris	1832-1839	Miniatures	—	—	9	—	—	—	—	—	—	—	9
Thompson, F.	—	1852	Architecture	—	—	2	—	—	—	—	—	—	—	2
Thompson, Frank	Durham	1875-1890	Landscape	—	—	—	—	2	—	—	—	—	—	2
Thompson, G.	London	1810-1839	Architecture	—	—	3	—	—	—	—	—	—	—	3
Thompson, Gabrielle	Munich	1889-1891	Flowers	—	—	2	—	—	—	—	—	—	—	2
Thompson, George	London	1892	Portraits	—	—	—	—	—	—	—	—	1	—	1
Thompson, G. A.	Albury	1851	Landscape	—	—	1	—	—	—	—	—	—	—	1
Thompson, G. B.	London	1873	Landscape	—	—	—	—	1	—	—	—	—	—	1
Thompson, George Douglas	London	1836-1838	Study	—	—	—	1	3	—	—	—	—	—	4
Thompson, G. H.	Southampton	1879-1885	Landscape	—	—	2	—	—	—	—	—	—	1	3
Thompson, G. Ivan	London	1876	Landscape	—	—	—	—	—	—	—	—	—	3	3
Thompson, H.	Walth'm Abbey	1846	Flowers	—	—	1	—	1	—	—	—	—	—	2
Thompson, Sir Henry	London	1865-1886	Domestic	—	—	12	—	—	—	—	1	—	9	22
Thompson, H. Raymond	London	1892	Portraits	—	—	1	—	—	—	—	—	—	—	1

Name.	Town.	First and Last Year of Ex.	Speciality.	S. A.	F. S.	R. A.	B. I.	S. S.	O. W.	N.W.	G. G.	N. G.	V. E.	Total.
Thompson, Harry S.	Birmingham	1880	Landscape	—	—	—	—	1	—	—	—	—	—	1
Thompson, Miss Isa	Cullercoats	1885-1893	Domestic	—	—	2	—	8	—	—	—	—	—	10
Thompson, J.	London	1791	Architecture	—	—	1	—	—	—	—	—	—	—	1
Thompson, Josh.	—	1838	Sculpture	—	—	1	—	—	—	—	—	—	—	1
Thompson, Jacob (of Penrith)	London	1824-1866	Figures	—	—	27	4	11	—	—	—	—	—	42
Thompson, James	London	1855	Athens	—	—	—	—	—	—	—	—	—	2	2
Thompson, John	—	1831	Engraving	—	—	—	—	1	—	—	—	—	—	1
Thompson, J. J.	London	1857-1863	Architecture	—	—	3	—	—	—	—	—	—	—	3
Thompson, James Robert	London	1808-1843	Architecture	—	—	27	—	—	—	—	—	—	4	31
Thompson, Miss Kate	—	1874-1883	Domestic	—	—	4	—	—	—	—	1	—	8	13
Thompson, Miss Margaret	Hitchin	1871-1893	Domestic	—	—	—	—	3	—	3	—	—	2	8
Thompson, Mark	Sunderland	1865-1866	Landscape	—	—	—	2	—	—	—	—	—	—	2
Thompson, Matt. Raine	London	1881	Landscape	—	—	1	—	—	—	—	—	—	—	1
Thompson, N.	London	1809	Miniatures	—	—	5	—	—	—	—	—	—	—	5
Thompson, Nelly	London	1888	Figures	—	—	—	—	1	—	—	—	—	—	1
Thompson, R.	London	1807	Dramatic	—	—	1	—	—	—	—	—	—	—	1
Thompson, R. A.	London	1848-1852	Landscape	—	—	—	3	—	—	—	—	—	—	3
Thompson, T.	London	1793-1796	Miniatures	—	—	7	—	—	—	—	—	—	—	7
Thompson, Thomas, Junr.	Walworth	1783	Heads	—	2	—	—	—	—	—	—	—	—	2
Thompson, Thomas	London	1797-1810	Sea Pieces	—	—	28	6	—	—	—	—	—	—	34
Thompson, Thomas Clement, R.H.A.	Dublin	1816-1857	Portraits	—	—	96	27	24	—	—	—	—	—	147
Thompson, T. F.	—	1825	Portraits	—	—	—	—	2	—	—	—	—	—	2
Thompson, Thomas H.	—	1783	Enamels	—	7	—	—	—	—	—	—	—	—	7
Thompson, T. W.	London	1857-1864	Landscape	—	—	—	—	2	—	—	—	—	—	2
Thompson, William, F.S.A. (called "Blarney")	London	1760-1782	Portraits	43	1	—	—	—	—	—	—	—	—	44
Thompson, W.	London	1781-1784	Landscape	—	—	9	—	—	—	—	—	—	—	9
Thompson, William	—	1891	Portraits	—	—	—	—	—	—	—	—	—	2	2
Thompson, Wilfred H.	London	1884-1893	Historical	—	—	3	—	1	—	10	—	—	7	21
Thompson, W. J.	London	1795	Architecture	—	—	1	—	—	—	—	—	—	—	1
Thomson, Mrs. A.	London	1850	Historical	—	—	1	—	—	—	—	—	—	—	1
Thomson, Miss A. E.	Newstead	1884-1886	Flowers	—	—	—	—	2	—	—	—	—	—	2
Thomson, Miss Bessie	London	1884-1886	Flowers	—	—	—	—	3	—	—	—	—	—	3
Thomson, Miss C.	London	1827	Portraits	—	—	—	—	1	—	—	—	—	—	1
Thomson, David	Edinburgh	1807-1813	Landscape	—	—	1	1	—	—	—	—	—	3	5
Thomson, E.	London	1801	Portraits	—	—	1	—	—	—	—	—	—	—	1
Thomson, Emile	Paris	1872	Wood Engraving	—	—	—	—	—	—	—	—	—	2	2
Thomson, E. Gertrude	Manchester	1875-1881	Figures	—	—	—	—	—	—	—	—	—	9	9
Thomson, George	London	1886-1892	Domestic	—	—	2	—	2	—	1	—	—	—	5
Thomson, Gordon	London	1878	Domestic	—	—	2	—	—	—	—	—	—	—	2
Thomson, Henry, R.A.	London	1792-1834	Mythological	—	—	83	3	1	—	—	—	—	—	87
Thomson, H.	—	1818	Miniatures	—	—	2	—	—	—	—	—	—	—	2
Thomson, James	London	1822-1853	Architecture	—	—	28	—	—	—	—	—	—	—	28
Thomson, Rev. John (of Duddingston)	Edinburgh	1813-1831	Landscape	—	—	1	2	3	—	—	—	—	—	6
Thomson, John	Manchester	1866-1872	Landscape	—	—	9	—	—	—	—	—	—	—	9
Thomson, J.	London	1891-1893	Landscape	—	—	—	—	4	—	—	—	—	—	4
Thomson, John Knighton	London	1849-1883	Figures	—	—	25	3	46	—	—	—	—	36	110
Thomson, J. Leslie, R.B.A., R.I. ‡ § φ	London	1872-1893	Landscape	—	—	49	—	57	—	1	12	6	32	157
Thomson, Mrs. Mary	London	1843-1852	Sculpture	—	—	4	3	4	—	—	—	—	—	11
Thomson, William	London	1880-1890	Landscape	—	—	—	—	2	—	—	—	—	—	2
Thomson, William	Bolton	1893	Portraits	—	—	1	—	—	—	—	—	—	—	1
Thomson, Miss Winifred Hope	London	1890-1893	Miniatures	—	—	6	—	—	—	—	—	2	—	8
Thomson, William John, R.S.A.	London	1796-1843	Domestic	—	—	68	9	2	5	—	—	—	20	104
Thorburn, Archibald	Kelso	1880-1893	Sporting	—	—	16	—	1	—	—	—	—	—	17
Thorburn, Robert, A.R.A.	London	1837-1884	Miniatures	—	—	265	—	—	—	—	—	—	1	266
Thorn, Miss Sarah Elizabeth	London	1838-1846	Domestic	—	—	7	5	27	—	—	—	—	—	39
Thorn, T.	London	1887	Domestic	—	—	1	—	—	—	—	—	—	—	1
Thornbold —	—	1783	Cattle	—	1	—	—	—	—	—	—	—	—	1
Thornbury, W. A.	London	1883-1886	Landscape	—	—	—	—	3	—	—	—	—	—	3
Thornbury, Miss H. L.	Barnes	1875	Domestic	—	—	—	—	1	—	—	—	—	—	1
Thorne, J.	London	1815	Figures	—	—	2	—	—	—	—	—	—	—	2
Thorne, J.	Lewisham	1838-1864	Rustic	—	—	—	—	17	—	—	—	—	—	17
Thorne, R.	London	1788-1802	Landscape	—	—	4	—	—	—	—	—	—	—	4
Thorne, R. S.	London	1835	River Scenes	—	—	—	—	1	—	—	—	—	—	1
Thornely, Charles, R.B.A. §	London	1858-1893	Sea Pieces	—	—	49	4	50	—	8	5	3	82	201
Thorneley, Mrs.	London	1835	Flowers	—	—	—	—	1	—	—	—	—	—	1
Thornewaite, R.	London	1880	Rustic	—	—	1	—	—	—	—	—	—	—	1
Thornthwaite —, Junr.	London	1770-1776	Sculpture	7	—	—	—	—	—	—	—	—	—	7
Thornthwaite, Andrew	London	1771	Architecture	1	—	—	—	—	—	—	—	—	—	1
Thornton, Miss Catherine	Ickley	1874-1889	Buildings	—	—	—	—	—	—	2	—	—	5	7
Thornton, M. J.	London	1887	Figures	—	—	—	—	—	—	2	—	—	—	2
Thornton, Thomas	London	1778-1785	Landscape	1	—	11	—	—	—	—	—	—	—	12
Thornton, W.	Reigate	1837-1865	Landscape	—	—	7	—	11	—	—	—	—	1	19

Name.	Town.	First and Last Year of Ex.	Speciality.	S. A.	F. S.	R. A.	B. I.	S. S.	O. W.	N.W.	G. G.	N. G.	V. E.	Total.
Thornycroft, Miss Alyn M.	London	1864-1892	Sculpture	—	—	14	2	1	—	—	—	—	14	31
Thornycroft, Miss Helen ‖	London	1864-1892	Scriptural	—	—	20	—	4	—	3	—	3	60	90
Thornycroft, Thomas	London	1836-1874	Sculpture	—	—	42	5	—	—	—	—	—	—	47
Thornycroft, Mrs. Thomas. ‖ *See* Miss Mary Francis	London	1840-1888	Sculpture	—	—	43	9	1	—	—	—	2	6	61
Thornycroft, Miss Theresa G.	London	1874-1883	Scriptural	—	—	6	—	—	—	—	—	—	4	10
Thornycroft, William Hamo, R.A.	London	1872-1893	Sculpture	—	—	60	—	—	—	1	7	1	3	72
Thorp, Miss Adelaide C.	Northcourt	1893	Portraits	—	—	1	—	—	—	—	—	—	—	1
Thorp, William Henry	Leeds	1884-1893	Architecture	—	--	4	—	—	—	—	—	—	—	4
Thorpe, Mrs. Elizabeth	Brussels	1869	Sea Pieces	—	—	—	—	—	—	—	—	—	2	2
Thorpe, John	London	1834-1873	Coast Scenes	—	—	39	13	26	—	2	—	—	92	172
Thors, Joseph	London	1863-1884	Landscape	—	—	6	2	15	—	—	—	—	1	24
Thors, S.	London	1880	Still Life	—	—	—	—	1	—	—	—	—	—	1
Threlfall, R.	London	1838-1840	Landscape	—	—	1	—	4	—	—	—	—	—	5
Thring, G.	—	1864	Landscape	—	—	—	—	1	—	—	—	—	—	1
Throp, John	Leeds	1857-1880	Sculpture	—	—	9	—	—	—	—	—	—	—	9
Thrupp, Frederick	London	1832-1880	Sculpture	—	—	71	9	6	—	—	—	—	4	90
Thrupp, J.	London	1821-1832	Architecture	—	—	4	—	—	—	—	—	—	—	4
Thuillay, Du. *See* D.	—	—	—	—	—	—	—	—	—	—	—	—	—	—
Thumann, P.	Weimar	1867-1892	Domestic	—	—	2	—	—	—	—	—	—	—	2
Thurgar, Miss Lucy	London	1783	Domestic	—	2	—	—	—	—	—	—	—	—	2
Thurlow, Miss Margaret C. T. G.	Wimbledon	1892	Sculpture	—	—	1	—	—	—	—	—	—	—	1
Thurlow, T.	Saxmundham	1841-1872	Sculpture	—	—	5	1	—	—	—	—	—	—	6
Thurnall, Harry J.	Royston	1875-1893	Flowers	—	—	4	—	7	—	1	—	—	3	15
Thursby, Miss	—	1793	Landscape	—	—	1	—	—	—	—	—	—	—	1
Thurstle, F.	—	1799	Landscape	—	—	1	—	—	—	—	—	—	—	1
Thurstle, S.	—	1799	Landscape	—	—	1	—	—	—	—	—	—	—	1
Thurston. *See* Smith and Thurston	—	—	Architecture	—	—	—	—	—	—	—	—	—	—	—
Thurston, G.	London	1818-1831	Scriptural	—	—	6	—	1	—	—	—	—	—	7
Thurston, John	London	1794-1829	Illustrations	—	—	16	—	—	5	—	—	—	—	21
Thurston, J. C.	London	1818-1827	Domestic	—	—	5	—	5	—	—	—	—	—	10
Thurston, Mrs.	London	1845	Snow Piece	—	—	—	—	1	—	—	—	—	—	1
Thurstun, Mrs. Ray (Charlotte)	Headcorn	1888-1893	Landscape	—	—	2	—	5	—	—	—	—	8	15
Thurzan, Miss Mary	—	1783	Portraits	1	—	—	—	—	—	—	—	—	—	1
Thwaites, Lieut.-Colonel	London	1833	Figures	—	—	—	—	—	—	1	—	—	—	1
Thwaites, W. W.	London	1819-1826	Figures	—	—	1	—	1	—	—	—	—	—	2
Tibbatts, J.	London	1801-1820	Portraits	—	—	12	—	—	—	—	—	—	—	12
Tichbourne, Mrs. Mary	Isleworth	1763-1766	Portraits	3	—	—	—	—	—	—	—	—	—	3
Tickell, H.	London	1842	Portraits	—	—	1	—	—	—	—	—	—	—	1
Tidd, Julius	London	1773-1779	Landscape	1	4	—	—	—	—	—	—	—	—	5
Tiddeman, Miss Florence	London	1871-1881	Figures	—	—	11	—	9	—	—	—	—	4	24
Tiddeman, Miss Letitia E. H.	Stokenchurch	1870-1890	Domestic	—	—	—	—	—	—	4	—	—	3	7
Tidemand, Adolphe	Düsseldorf	1864-1874	Domestic	—	—	2	—	—	—	—	—	—	—	2
Tidey, Alfred	Twickenham	1875-1887	Domestic	—	—	2	—	—	—	1	—	—	6	9
Tidey, Arthur	London	1831-1877	Miniatures	—	—	116	1	17	—	—	—	—	—	134
Tidey, A. W.	London	1856	Landscape	—	—	1	—	—	—	—	—	—	—	1
Tidey, Henry F. ‡	London	1839-1872	Miniatures	—	—	67	1	10	—	103	—	—	—	181
Tidmarsh, H. E.	London	1880-1889	Buildings	—	—	3	—	3	—	1	—	—	6	13
Tiffin, Miss Alice Elizabeth	Salisbury	1873	Landscape	—	—	—	—	1	—	—	—	—	—	1
Tiffin, Henry	London	1845-1874	Landscape	—	—	20	24	21	—	—	—	—	1	66
Tiffin, James Benjamin	London	1847-1849	Landscape	—	—	2	3	—	—	—	—	—	—	5
Tiffin, Miss Lydia Emily	London	1863	Fruit	—	—	—	—	2	—	—	—	—	—	2
Tiffin, Walter Francis. *See* Francis	Salisbury	1845-1867	Miniatures	—	—	39	12	17	—	—	—	—	—	68
Tilleard, Miss E.	Tooting	1844	Figures	—	—	—	—	1	—	—	—	—	—	1
Tiller, Mrs.	London	1819-1821	Miniatures	—	—	3	—	—	—	—	—	—	—	3
Tillidge, T. H.	London	1833	Figures	—	—	—	—	1	—	—	—	—	—	1
Tillotson, J.	London	1821-1856	Portraits	—	—	8	—	—	—	—	—	—	—	8
Tillotson, Mary	London	1839-1844	Portraits	—	—	6	—	—	—	—	—	—	—	6
Tilstone, J. R.	London	1827-1829	Miniatures	—	—	2	—	—	—	—	—	—	—	2
Tilt, Archibald	Sutton	1875-1877	Figures	—	—	1	—	1	—	—	—	—	1	3
Tilt, E. P.	Epsom	1868	Figures	—	—	1	—	—	—	—	—	—	—	1
Tilt, F. A.	Epsom	1866-1868	Enamels	—	—	10	—	—	—	—	—	—	—	10
Tiltman, Alfred Hessell. *See also* Deane and Tiltman	London	1883-1893	Architecture	—	—	5	—	—	—	—	—	—	—	5
Tilton, John Rollin	Rome	1873-1878	Landscape	—	—	1	—	—	—	—	1	—	—	2
Timbrell, Henry	London	1833-1843	Sculpture	—	—	12	1	1	—	—	—	—	—	14
Timbrell, James C.	—	1830-1848	Domestic	--	—	3	5	1	—	—	—	—	—	9
Timings, Samuel	Birmingham	1865-1869	Landscape	—	—	2	—	6	—	—	—	—	—	8
Tindall, Robert Edwin	Monmouth	1857-1863	Landscape	—	—	7	—	—	—	—	—	—	12	19
Tindall, William Edwin, R.B.A. §	Leeds	1888-1893	Landscape	—	—	10	—	6	—	—	—	—	—	16
Tingecombe, John	Greenwich	1827-1844	Landscape	—	—	2	23	1	—	—	—	—	—	26
Tinkler, T. C.	London	1841-1854	Architecture	—	—	2	—	—	—	—	—	—	—	2

Name.	Town.	First and Last Year of Ex.	Speciality.	S. A.	F. S.	R. A.	B. I.	S. S.	O. W.	N. W.	G. G.	N. G.	V. E.	Total.
Tinkler, W. A.	Putney	1839	Landscape	—	—	1	—	—	—	—	—	—	—	1
Tinlin, G. D.	London	1880	Buildings	—	—	—	—	—	—	—	—	—	1	1
Tinworth, George, R.B.A. §	London	1866-1893	Sculpture	—	—	18	—	6	—	—	5	—	—	29
Tippet, W. V.	Bristol	1866	Rustic	—	—	—	—	2	—	—	—	—	—	2
Tisley, Samuel	London	1818	Landscape	—	—	1	—	—	—	—	—	—	—	1
Tissot, James	London	1864-1881	Domestic	—	—	17	—	2	—	—	31	—	27	77
Titcombe, William H. Y., R.B.A. §	London	1881-1893	Domestic	—	—	8	—	12	—	—	—	—	4	24
Tite, W.	London	1817-1826	Architecture	—	—	7	—	—	—	—	—	—	—	7
Tite, Sir William, C.B., F.S.A., F.R.S.	London	1854-1860	Architecture	—	—	2	—	—	—	—	—	—	—	2
Titford, R. D.	Bromley	1845-1860	Landscape	—	—	—	1	1	—	—	—	—	4	6
Titian —, Junr.	London	1782	Venus	—	1	—	—	—	—	—	—	—	—	1
Tito, Ettore	Venice	1892	Domestic	—	—	2	—	—	—	—	—	—	—	2
Tivoli, De. *See* D.	—	—	—	—	—	—	—	—	—	—	—	—	—	—
Tizard, Miss Kate	London	1890-1892	Sculpture	—	—	2	—	—	—	—	1	—	—	3
Toberentz, Mrs. Catherine	—	1890-1892	Figures	—	—	1	—	—	—	—	—	1	—	2
Tobin, Mrs. Clare	Manchester	1889-1890	Portraits	—	—	—	—	—	—	—	2	—	—	2
Tobin, J.	—	1776	Landscape	—	—	1	—	—	—	—	—	—	—	1
Tod, A.	London	1800-1805	Architecture	—	—	4	—	—	—	—	—	—	—	4
Tod, David A.	London	1885	Sculpture	—	—	1	—	—	—	—	—	—	—	1
Todd —	—	1783	Shipping	—	1	—	—	—	—	—	—	—	—	1
Todd, A.	Scarborough	1820-1821	Portraits	—	—	2	—	—	—	—	—	—	—	2
Todd, Miss Elizabeth M.	London	1890	Landscape	—	—	—	—	—	—	1	—	—	—	1
Todd, Miss Helen	London	1857-1870	Fruit	—	—	2	—	3	—	—	—	—	—	5
Todd, Charles T.	Tunb'dge Wells	1852-1892	Domestic	—	—	2	—	—	—	—	—	—	—	2
Todd, Henry G.	Ipswich	1888	Still Life	—	—	1	—	2	—	—	—	—	—	3
Todd, H. W.	London	1848	Architecture	—	—	1	—	—	—	—	—	—	—	1
Todd, John George	Ecouen	1861-1892	Flowers	—	—	10	—	—	—	—	—	—	—	10
Todd, Manly	Belvedere	1887	Landscape	—	—	—	—	—	—	1	—	—	—	1
Todd, Ralph	Tooting	1880-1893	Landscape	—	—	3	—	10	—	4	—	—	1	18
Todd, Richard	London	1807-1823	Domestic	—	—	8	3	—	—	—	—	—	—	11
Todd, T.	Ulverstone	1874	Fruit	—	—	—	—	1	—	—	—	—	—	1
Todderick, Miss	London	1762-1774	Miniatures	12	4	—	—	—	—	—	—	—	—	16
Tofano, Eduardo	London	1888-1889	Portraits	—	—	2	—	—	—	—	—	2	—	4
Toft, Albert A.	London	1885-1893	Sculpture	—	—	21	—	3	—	1	—	—	3	28
Toft, Peter	London	1872-1893	Landscape	—	—	6	—	30	—	4	2	7	10	59
Toldervy, W. F.	London	1842-1847	Landscape	—	—	5	7	6	—	—	—	—	—	18
Toldervy, Mrs.	Croydon	1842	Landscape	—	—	—	—	1	—	—	—	—	—	1
Tolhurst, Miss Edith, afterwards Mrs. Fred. J. Gordon	Highbury	1888-1891	Figures	—	—	2	—	—	—	—	—	—	2	4
Tollemache, Hon. Duff	London	1883-1892	Portraits	—	—	2	—	1	—	—	—	—	3	6
Tollock, B. L. Montague	London	1890	Landscape	—	—	—	—	—	—	1	—	—	—	1
Tolly, Edward	London	1848-1867	Sporting	—	—	9	3	1	—	—	—	—	9	22
Tolstoy, Count	—	1815	Portraits	—	—	1	—	—	—	—	—	—	—	1
Tomalin, Miss	London	1838-1859	Miniatures	—	—	8	—	—	—	—	—	—	—	8
Tomasich, A.	London	1872-1876	Sculpture	—	—	12	—	—	—	—	—	—	—	12
Tomber, G.	London	1824-1828	Landscape	—	—	1	3	—	—	—	—	—	—	4
Tomkins, Charles	London	1773-1779	Landscape	—	—	15	—	—	—	—	—	—	—	15
Tomkins, Charley	London	1828	Landscape	—	—	2	—	—	—	—	—	—	—	2
Tomkins, Charles Algernon	London	1872-1893	Engraving	—	—	13	—	—	—	—	—	—	—	13
Tomkins, C. F. §	London	1825-1844	Landscape	—	—	—	28	114	—	—	—	—	—	142
Tomkins, Charles John	London	1869-1892	Figures	—	—	10	—	5	—	—	—	—	—	15
Tomkins, Miss E.	London	1823-1840	Still Life	—	—	12	—	11	—	—	—	—	—	23
Tomkins, Miss Isabella A.	London	1860-1873	Domestic	—	—	1	2	1	—	—	—	—	1	5
Tomkins, M.	London	1796	Domestic	—	—	1	—	—	—	—	—	—	—	1
Tomkins, Miss M.	London	1824-1825	Miniatures	—	—	4	—	—	—	—	—	—	—	4
Tomkins, Peltro William	London	1799-1832	Engraving	—	—	7	—	—	—	—	—	—	—	7
Tomkins, W.	London	1799-1812	Medals	—	—	10	—	—	—	—	—	—	—	10
Tomkins, William, A.R.A.	London	1761-1790	Landscape	14	15	78	—	—	—	—	—	—	—	107
Tomlin, G. M.	—	1848	Figures	—	—	1	—	—	—	—	—	—	—	1
Tomlinson, George Dodgson	Huddersfield	1848-1872	Portraits	—	—	3	—	—	—	—	—	—	—	3
Tomlinson, J.	Woolwich	1788	Landscape	—	—	1	—	—	—	—	—	—	—	1
Tomlinson, J.	London	1824-1853	Portraits	—	—	31	—	2	—	—	—	—	—	33
Tomlinson, R.	—	1806-1810	Sculpture	—	—	3	—	—	—	—	—	—	—	3
Tomlinson, W.	Redditch	1858-1859	Domestic	—	—	2	—	—	—	—	—	—	—	2
Tompkins, Miss Clementina	London	1877	Domestic	—	—	2	—	—	—	—	—	—	—	2
Toms, Peter, R.A.	London	1769-1772	Portraits	—	—	4	—	—	—	—	—	—	—	4
Tomson, Arthur	London	1882-1893	Landscape	—	—	14	—	6	—	—	5	10	—	35
Tonelli, Signora Anna	London	1794-1797	Portraits	—	—	9	—	—	—	—	—	—	—	9
Tonelli, Domenico A.	Croydon	1889-1890	Sculpture	—	—	2	—	—	—	—	—	—	—	2
Tonge, C.	London	1892	Landscape	—	—	—	—	—	—	—	—	1	—	1
Tonge, Robert	London	1840-1853	Landscape	—	—	1	—	1	—	—	—	—	—	2
Tonkowsky, Paul N.	Venice	1884	Figures	—	—	1	—	—	—	—	—	—	—	1

Name.	Town.	First and Last Year of Ex.	Speciality.	S. A.	F. S.	R. A.	B. I.	S. S.	O.W.	N.W.	G. G.	N.G.	V. E.	Total.
Tonlin, W.	London	1830	Flowers	—	—	1	—	—	—	—	—	—	—	1
Tonneau, F.	Kilburn	1877	Figures	—	—	—	—	—	—	—	—	—	1	1
Tonneau, Jos.	London	1864-1891	Domestic	—	—	5	4	5	—	—	—	—	—	14
Tonneau, Miss J.	London	1878	Domestic	—	—	—	—	1	—	—	—	—	—	1
Tonvaux. *See* Jonvaux.	—	—	—	—	—	—	—	—	—	—	—	—	—	—
Toogood, Mrs. H. *See* Miss F. A. Curtis	London	1851	Sculpture	—	—	1	—	—	—	—	—	—	—	1
Took, William	London	1857-1892	Landscape	—	—	6	1	—	21	—	—	—	4	32
Tootal, J. Batty	Wakefield	1846	Landscape	—	—	—	—	1	—	—	—	—	—	1
Toovey, Edwin	Leamington	1865-1867	Landscape	—	—	—	—	1	—	—	—	—	2	3
Toovey, Richard G. H., R.P.E.	Leamington	1879-1887	Coast Scenes	—	—	13	—	23	—	3	1	—	9	49
Topffer, A.	London	1816	Figures	—	—	1	—	—	—	—	—	—	—	1
Topham, Francis William. † ‡	London	1832-1877	Domestic	—	—	7	3	3	119	38	—	—	—	170
Topham, Frank William Warwick, R.I. ‡ ϕ	London	1860-1893	Figures	—	—	60	4	4	—	20	13	14	47	162
Topham, W.	London	1870	Figures	—	—	1	—	—	—	—	—	—	—	1
Topham, Miss	London	1868	Fruit	—	—	—	—	—	—	—	—	—	3	3
Toplin, J. M.	—	1852	Portraits	—	—	1	—	—	—	—	—	—	—	1
Toplis, C.	—	1808-1817	Landscape	—	—	2	—	—	—	—	—	—	—	2
Toplis, Charles H.	London	1842-1872	Portraits	—	—	6	—	3	—	—	—	—	—	9
Toplis, William A.	Sheffield	1875-1893	Landscape	—	—	9	—	3	—	—	—	—	1	13
Topping, F.	—	1774-1786	Landscape	—	1	7	—	—	—	—	—	—	—	8
Topping, M.	—	1783	Landscape	—	—	1	—	—	—	—	—	—	—	1
Toragnola, Chev. J.	London	1816-1817	Sculpture	—	—	—	2	—	—	—	—	—	—	2
Tormer, B.	Rome	1852	Domestic	—	—	1	—	—	—	—	—	—	—	1
Torrelli, Lot	Florence	1876-1886	Sculpture	—	—	5	—	2	—	—	—	—	—	7
Torromé, Francisco J.	Tulse Hill	1890-1893	Landscape	—	—	—	—	5	—	1	—	—	—	6
Torry, John T.	London	1886	Landscape	—	—	—	—	2	—	2	—	—	—	4
Tothill, Miss Mary D.	Bristol	1881-1885	Landscape	—	—	—	—	—	—	3	—	—	1	4
Tott, De. *See* D.	—	—	—	—	—	—	—	—	—	—	—	—	—	—
Tottie, C.	London	1839-1842	Architecture	—	—	3	—	—	—	—	—	—	—	3
Touisant, R.	London	1876	Domestic	—	—	—	—	1	—	—	—	—	—	1
Toulmin, E. O.	London	1844-1854	Landscape	—	—	3	1	7	—	—	—	—	—	11
Tour, J. B.	Paris	1876	Landscape	—	—	—	—	—	—	—	—	—	1	1
Tour, La. *See* L.	—	—	—	—	—	—	—	—	—	—	—	—	—	—
Tourneur, Miss Louise	Paris	1890	Portraits	—	—	1	—	—	—	—	—	—	—	1
Tournier, Gaspard	London	1878	Architecture	—	—	1	—	—	—	—	—	—	—	1
Tourrier, Alfred Holst	London	1854-1889	Historical	—	—	17	5	22	—	—	—	—	8	52
Tourrier, G. L.	London	1870-1876	Domestic	—	—	3	—	6	—	—	—	—	—	9
Tourrier, J.	London	1834-1848	River Scenes	—	—	14	4	5	—	—	—	—	—	23
Toussaint, Augustus	London	1775-1788	Miniatures	—	—	26	—	—	—	—	—	—	—	26
Tovey, J.	Bristol	1843	Scriptural	—	—	—	1	—	—	—	—	—	—	1
Tovey, Miss Mary S.	London	1872-1876	Figures	—	—	7	—	11	—	—	—	—	1	19
Tovey, Samuel Griffiths	Bristol	1847-1865	Venice	—	—	5	17	11	—	—	—	—	—	33
Towers, James, A.R.C.A.	Liverpool	1878-1889	Landscape	—	—	9	—	3	—	2	2	—	1	17
Towers, Samuel	Bolton	1884-1892	Landscape	—	—	3	—	—	—	—	—	—	—	3
Towne, Charles	London	1799-1823	Landscape	—	—	12	4	—	—	—	—	—	1	17
Towne, E.	London	1806-1809	Landscape	—	—	4	—	—	—	—	—	—	—	4
Towne, Francis, F.S.A.	London	1762-1815	Landscape	16	3	27	10	—	—	—	—	—	—	56
Towne, J.	London	1784	Portraits	—	—	1	—	—	—	—	—	—	—	1
Towne, J.	London	1834-1866	Sculpture	—	—	14	—	—	—	—	—	—	—	14
Towne, T.	Walth'm Abbey	1787-1791	Portraits	—	—	7	—	—	—	—	—	—	—	7
Townley, Miss Annie B.	Birmingham	1883-1884	Buildings	—	—	—	—	1	—	2	—	—	—	3
Townley, Charles	London	1778-1795	Engraving, etc.	2	21	16	—	—	—	—	—	—	—	39
Townley, J.	London	1783	Flowers	—	—	1	—	—	—	—	—	—	—	1
Townley, Miss Minnie	Birmingham	1876-1887	Landscape	—	—	1	—	4	—	—	—	—	1	6
Townroe, Reuben	London	1874-1880	Sculpture	—	—	2	—	—	—	—	—	—	4	6
Townsend. *See* Banks and Townsend	—	—	Architecture	—	—	—	—	—	—	—	—	—	—	—
Townsend, Alfred O.	Bristol	1888-1893	Landscape	—	—	2	—	1	—	2	1	2	2	10
Townsend, Frederick	Leamington	1861-1866	Landscape	—	—	6	—	—	—	—	—	—	5	11
Townsend, Mrs. Frederick	Fareham	1866	Landscape	—	—	—	—	—	—	—	—	—	2	2
Townsend, Miss F.	Nuneaton	1884	Landscape	—	—	—	—	—	—	—	1	—	—	1
Townsend, Frederick H.	London	1888	Military	—	—	2	—	—	—	—	—	—	—	2
Townsend, F. J.	Chertsey	1872	Landscape	—	—	1	—	—	—	—	—	—	—	1
Townsend, Henry James	London	1839-1866	Figures	—	—	17	2	1	—	—	—	—	1	21
Townsend, John	London	1776-1778	Portraits	6	—	—	—	—	—	—	—	—	—	6
Townsend, J.	London	1841-1842	Landscape	—	—	2	1	—	—	—	—	—	—	3
Townsend, Miss Mary	London	1843-1849	Domestic	—	—	5	1	4	—	—	—	—	—	10
Townsend, Miss S. E.	London	1848-1861	Domestic	—	—	—	—	9	—	—	—	—	—	9
Townsend, Miss Pattie. ‖ *See* Mrs. Johnson	Nuneaton	1877-1892	Landscape	—	—	3	—	2	—	17	—	—	18	40
Townshend, Alice	Wimbledon	1879	Landscape	—	—	—	—	—	—	—	—	—	1	1
Townshend, Arthur Louis	London	1880-1886	Sporting	—	—	5	—	—	—	—	—	—	3	8
Townshend, James	London	1883-1891	Landscape	—	—	4	—	4	—	5	—	—	2	15
Tozer, Henry E.	Cape Cornwall	1892	Sea Shores	—	—	1	—	—	—	—	—	—	—	1

Name.	Town.	First and Last Year of Ex.	Speciality.	S. A.	F. S.	R. A.	B. I.	S. S.	O. W.	N. W.	G. G.	N. G.	V. E.	Total.
Tracey, O.	—	1870	Landscape	—	—	—	—	1	—	—	—	—	—	1
Trafford, Major	London	1893	Egypt	—	—	—	—	1	—	—	—	—	—	1
Traies, Frank D.	London	1849-1854	Landscape	—	—	—	—	5	—	—	—	—	—	5
Traies, William	Exeter	1817-1845	Landscape	—	—	4	—	—	—	—	—	—	—	4
Trail, Miss A. A.	London	1823-1833	Miniatures	—	—	14	—	7	—	—	—	—	—	21
Trail, Cecil G.	Malden	1892	Domestic	—	—	—	—	—	—	—	—	—	1	1
Trant, Miss	—	1766	Miniatures	2	—	—	—	—	—	—	—	—	—	2
Trantschold, Manfred	London	1893	Domestic	—	—	—	—	—	—	—	—	—	1	1
Trappes, Francis M.	Manchester	1868-1885	Landscape	—	—	7	—	7	—	—	—	—	1	15
Trautschold, William	London	1849-1875	Figures	—	—	6	1	1	—	—	—	—	4	12
Travers, Mrs. Florence	Weybridge	1889-1893	Rustic	—	—	—	—	8	—	4	—	—	—	12
Travers, George	London	1851-1859	Landscape	—	—	6	11	9	—	—	—	—	14	40
Travis, Henry	London	1824-1832	Portraits	—	—	3	—	2	—	—	—	—	—	5
Travis, H.	Sydenham	1873	Ruins	—	—	1	—	—	—	—	—	—	—	1
Trayer, Jules Baptiste Jules	London	1869-1882	Domestic	—	—	3	—	—	—	—	—	—	—	3
Treadwell, Miss M.	London	1872-1875	Flowers	—	—	—	—	7	—	—	—	—	—	7
Treaves, E.	London	1815	Architecture	—	—	1	—	—	—	—	—	—	—	1
Tredray, John	London	1832	Sketch	—	—	—	1	—	—	—	—	—	—	1
Tree, Philip H.	St. Leonard's	1887-1893	Architecture	—	—	4	—	—	—	—	—	—	—	4
Treeby, J. W.	London	1869-1875	Domestic	—	—	4	—	1	—	—	—	—	—	5
Treen, W.	London	1833-1877	Portraits	—	—	1	—	3	—	—	—	—	—	4
Trego, J. J. William	Balham	1883	Landscape	—	—	—	—	1	—	—	—	—	—	1
Trego, W.	London	1862-1875	Historical	—	—	—	3	8	—	—	—	—	1	12
Tremewan, M.	Lewisham	1886	Landscape	—	—	—	—	1	—	—	—	—	—	1
Trench, John A.	Birkenhead	1893	Landscape	—	—	—	—	1	—	—	—	—	—	1
Trendall, E. W.	London	1815-1838	Architecture	—	—	20	—	3	—	1	—	—	1	25
Trent, S.	London	1783	Landscape	1	—	—	—	—	—	—	—	—	—	1
Trentacoste, Domenico	London	1891-1893	Sculpture	—	—	5	—	—	—	—	—	—	—	5
Trentanove, A.	London	1860-1868	Sculpture	—	—	13	—	—	—	—	—	—	—	13
Trentham, Fanny	London	1885	Landscape	—	—	—	—	1	—	—	—	—	—	1
Trery, H. C.	London	1849-1854	Cattle	—	—	5	1	—	—	—	—	—	—	6
Tresham, Henry, R.A.	London	1789-1806	Historical	—	—	33	—	—	—	—	—	—	—	33
Tress, Richard	London	1848-1850	Architecture	—	—	2	—	—	—	—	—	—	—	2
Trevinnard, A.	London	1797-1806	Miniatures	—	—	14	—	—	—	—	—	—	—	14
Trevinnard, W. J.	London	1799	Portraits	—	—	1	—	—	—	—	—	—	—	1
Trevor, Edward	London	1841-1846	Domestic	—	—	2	—	—	—	—	—	—	—	2
Trevor, Edward	Manchester	1885	Landscape	—	—	1	—	—	—	—	—	—	—	1
Trevor, Miss Helen Mabel	London	1881-1885	Figures	—	—	1	—	3	—	—	—	—	—	4
Triaud, L.	London	1811-1819	Portraits	—	—	4	—	—	—	—	—	—	—	4
Trier, Mrs. Adeline	London	1879-1893	Flowers	—	—	5	—	4	—	—	—	—	2	11
Trimen, A.	London	1842-1854	Architecture	—	—	5	—	—	—	—	—	—	—	5
Trimmings, Miss	London	1860	Flowers	—	—	1	—	2	—	—	—	—	—	3
Tringham, Holland	Streatham	1891-1893	Rustic	—	—	1	—	5	—	—	—	—	—	6
Tringham, Mrs. W.	—	1839	Landscape	—	—	1	—	—	—	—	—	—	—	1
Tripp, Capel N.	Gloucester	1881	Architecture	—	—	1	—	—	—	—	—	—	—	1
Triqueti, Baron Henri De. *See* D.	—	—	—	—	—	—	—	—	—	—	—	—	—	—
Trobridge, George	Belfast	1884-1889	Landscape	—	—	—	—	2	—	—	—	—	—	2
Trobridge, L.	London	1880	Landscape	—	—	—	—	—	—	—	—	—	1	1
Trokes (?) Troakes —, Junr.	—	1773	Animals	—	1	—	—	—	—	—	—	—	—	1
Trollope, G.	—	1839	Architecture	—	—	1	—	—	—	—	—	—	—	1
Trollope, John E. *See also* Giles, Gough, and Trollope, *and* Notley and Trollope	Streatham	1881-1891	Architecture	—	—	4	—	—	—	—	—	—	—	4
Trood, William Henry Hamilton	London	1879-1893	Animals	—	—	21	—	22	—	1	1	—	5	50
Trossarelli, J.	London	1773-1825	Miniatures	—	—	61	2	—	—	—	—	—	—	63
Trotman, Miss Lillias	London	1881-1893	Domestic	—	—	2	—	9	—	3	—	—	—	14
Trotman, Samuel H.	London	1866-1870	Sea Pieces	—	—	—	—	7	—	—	—	—	5	12
Trott, John S.	London	1890-1892	Landscape	—	—	3	—	—	—	—	—	—	—	3
Trotter, Miss Eliza H.	London	1811-1814	Figures	—	—	1	4	—	—	—	—	—	—	5
Trotter, Thomas	London	1771-1801	Figures	1	—	6	—	—	—	—	—	—	—	7
Trotter, Miss	London	1809-1815	Domestic	—	—	5	—	—	—	—	—	—	—	5
Troubetzkoy, Prince Pierre	London	1892-1893	Figures	—	—	1	—	—	—	—	—	1	4	6
Trought, Joseph	London	1765-1769	Architecture	—	8	—	—	—	—	—	—	—	—	8
Troughton, R. Zouch S.	London	1831-1865	Domestic	—	—	—	1	1	—	—	—	—	—	2
Troup, Francis W.	London	1889-1891	Architecture	—	—	4	—	—	—	—	—	—	—	4
Troup, J.	Aberdeen	1832	Landscape	—	—	—	—	1	—	—	—	—	—	1
Trouville, Henri	Chantilly	1881	Landscape	—	—	—	—	—	—	—	—	—	2	2
Troye, J. M. C.	London	1829	Figures	—	—	1	—	—	—	—	—	—	—	1
Truefitt, Miss F.	Edinburgh	1873	Portraits	—	—	1	—	—	—	—	—	—	—	1
Truefitt, George	London	1842-1886	Architecture	—	—	11	—	—	—	1	—	—	1	13
Truit —	St. Omer	1778	Domestic	1	—	—	—	—	—	—	—	—	—	1
Trumbull, John	London	1784-1824	Historical	—	—	16	7	1	—	—	—	—	—	24
Trump, Van. *See* V.	—	—	—	—	—	—	—	—	—	—	—	—	—	—

Name.	Town.	First and Last Year of Ex.	Speciality.	S. A.	F. S.	R. A.	B. I.	S. S.	O. W.	N. W.	G. G.	N. G.	V. E.	Total.
Truscott, Walter	Falmouth	1882-1889	Sea Pieces	—	—	—	—	10	—	—	—	—	—	10
T'Schaggeny, Edmund	London	1847-1850	Historical	—	—	2	2	—	—	—	—	—	—	4
Tschan, J. Rudolf	Teddington	1884-1887	Heads	—	—	1	—	—	—	—	—	—	1	2
Tuck, Albert	London	1877-1890	Domestic	—	—	—	—	—	—	5	—	—	6	11
Tuck, E. H.	London	1870	Domestic	—	—	—	—	1	—	—	—	—	—	1
Tuck, Harry	London	1870-1893	Domestic	—	—	2	—	29	—	15	—	—	14	60
Tuck, Miss Lucy J.	London	1879-1888	Figures	—	—	—	—	—	—	2	—	—	5	7
Tuck, S.	London	1878	Caricatures	—	—	—	—	—	—	—	—	—	1	1
Tuck, William Henry	London	1874	Portraits	—	—	1	—	—	—	—	—	—	—	1
Tucker —	London	1837	Domestic	—	—	—	—	1	—	—	—	—	—	1
Tucker, Miss Ada Eliza ‖	Bristol	1879-1884	Domestic	—	—	—	—	4	—	—	—	—	3	7
Tucker, Arthur	Windermere	1883-1892	Landscape	—	—	3	—	2	—	9	—	—	—	14
Tucker, Barff	London	1845-1850	Domestic	—	—	3	1	—	—	—	—	—	1	5
Tucker, Charles E.	London	1880-1891	Landscape	—	—	—	—	2	—	—	—	—	3	5
Tucker, Edward	Woolwich	1849-1873	Coast Scenes	—	—	2	2	13	—	—	—	—	—	17
Tucker, Frank	Bracknell	1866-1882	Landscape	—	—	—	—	—	—	—	—	—	5	5
Tucker, Frederick	Ambleside	1873-1889	Landscape	—	—	9	—	2	—	—	1	1	—	13
Tucker, H.	Ambleside	1871	Landscape	—	—	—	—	1	—	—	—	—	—	1
Tucker, Rev. James J.	India	1835-1841	Historical	—	—	—	—	10	—	—	—	—	—	10
Tucker, John Scott	London	1836	Landscape	—	—	—	—	1	—	—	—	—	—	1
Tucker, Raymond	Bristol	1852-1886	Rustic	—	—	21	—	14	—	1	—	—	10	46
Tucker, Mrs.	India	1838	Figures	—	—	—	—	1	—	—	—	—	—	1
Tuckerman, S. Salisbury	Stourbridge	1874-1885	Sea Pieces	—	—	2	—	4	—	—	—	—	1	7
Tudor, J. O.	London	1809-1822	Landscape	—	—	17	7	—	—	—	—	—	—	24
Tudor, T.	Monmouth	1809-1819	Landscape	—	—	15	—	—	—	—	—	—	—	15
Tudor, Miss	Monmouth	1774	Needlework	1	—	—	—	—	—	—	—	—	—	1
Tugwell, Miss Emma S.	Greenwich	1888	Domestic	—	—	—	—	1	—	—	—	—	—	1
Tuite, T.	Boulogne	1818-1839	Landscape	—	—	3	2	—	—	—	—	—	—	5
Tuke, Henry Sydney §	London	1879-1893	Figures	—	—	17	—	10	—	7	5	5	8	52
Tuke, Miss Maria	Hanwell	1885-1887	Landscape	—	—	1	—	—	—	1	1	—	—	3
Tulk, Augustus	Norwood	1877-1892	Still Life	—	—	3	—	11	—	—	—	—	6	20
Tull —	—	1761	Landscape	2	—	—	—	—	—	—	—	—	—	2
Tull, N.	London	1829-1852	Landscape	—	—	—	5	25	—	—	—	—	—	30
Tulloch, Frederick H.	London	1891-1892	Architecture	—	—	3	—	—	—	—	—	—	—	3
Tulloch, Miss M.	—	1806	Flowers	—	—	1	—	—	—	—	—	—	—	1
Tullock, Mrs.	Blackheath	1809	Flowers	—	—	—	—	—	—	—	—	—	1	1
Tunbridge, Miss A.	London	1858-1861	Fruit	—	—	—	3	1	—	—	—	—	—	4
Tunbridge, Miss E.	London	1856-1861	Still Life	—	—	—	4	—	—	—	—	—	—	4
Tunck, Ferdinand (should be Junck)	London	1863-1870	Sculpture	—	—	—	1	1	—	—	—	—	—	2
Tumner, J. H.	London	1873	Landscape	—	—	1	—	—	—	—	—	—	—	1
Tupper, J.	—	1788	Landscape	—	—	1	—	—	—	—	—	—	—	1
Tupper, John L.	Rugby	1854-1868	Sculpture	—	—	11	—	—	—	—	—	—	—	11
Tupper, Miss	London	1855	Fruit	—	—	—	—	2	—	—	—	—	—	2
Türck, Miss Eliza	London	1851-1886	Domestic	—	—	20	3	28	—	—	—	—	4	55
Tureni, A.	—	1815	Landscape	—	—	—	—	—	—	—	—	—	1	1
Turmeau, John	London	1772-1836	Portraits	—	3	7	—	—	—	—	—	—	1	11
Turminger, T. A. *See* Firminger	—	1839	Landscape	—	—	1	—	—	—	—	—	—	—	1
Turnbull —	—	1857	Sea Pieces	—	—	—	1	—	—	—	—	—	—	1
Turnbull, T.	London	1827	Buildings	—	—	1	—	—	—	—	—	—	—	1
Turnbull, Walter	London	1892	Sculpture	—	—	1	—	—	—	—	—	—	—	1
Turnbull, Mrs. *See* Miss Anna Charlotte Fayermann *and* Mrs. Bartholomew	London	1829-1844	Miniatures	—	—	21	—	1	—	—	—	—	—	22
Turner. *See* Baker and Turner	—	—	Stained Glass	—	—	—	—	—	—	—	—	—	—	—
Turner —	London	1774	Fruit	—	3	—	—	—	—	—	—	—	—	3
Turner, Master	—	1834	Animals	—	—	—	—	2	—	—	—	—	—	2
Turner, A.	London	1868	Indian Work	—	—	—	—	2	—	—	—	—	—	2
Turner, Agnes	Saltburn	1882	Switzerland	—	—	—	—	—	—	—	—	—	1	1
Turner, Anselm	London	1867-1871	Fruit	—	—	—	—	—	—	—	—	—	7	7
Turner, Arthur	Betchworth	1893	Landscape	—	—	—	—	—	—	—	—	—	1	1
Turner, Charles, A.R.A.	London	1810-1857	Engraving	—	—	51	—	—	—	—	—	—	—	51
Turner, Rev. C.	—	1799-1800	Portraits	—	—	2	—	—	—	—	—	—	—	2
Turner, Claridge,	London	1882-1883	Landscape	—	—	—	—	1	—	1	—	—	1	3
Turner, C. T.	Paris	1879-1880	Domestic	—	—	—	—	—	—	—	—	—	2	2
Turner, Daniel	London	1782-1801	Bridges	—	7	10	—	—	—	—	—	—	—	17
Turner, E.	London	1779-1791	Architecture	1	2	—	—	—	—	—	—	—	—	3
Turner, Edw.	London	1858-1862	Domestic	—	—	—	1	2	—	—	—	—	—	3
Turner, Ernest	London	1869-1890	Architecture	—	—	2	—	—	—	—	—	—	—	2
Turner, Elizabeth	London	1841	Portraits	—	—	1	—	—	—	—	—	—	—	1
Turner, Edwin Page	London	1880-1884	Decorations	—	—	7	—	—	—	—	—	—	—	7
Turner, Francis	London	1838-1871	Landscape	—	—	35	38	24	—	—	—	—	—	97
Turner, Frank.	Warfield	1866-1874	Churches	—	—	—	1	—	—	—	—	—	2	3
Turner, F. C. §	London	1810-1846	Sporting	—	—	11	23	36	—	—	—	—	6	76

Name.	Town.	First and Last Year of Ex.	Speciality.	S. A.	F. S.	R. A.	B. I.	S. S.	O. W.	N. W.	G. G.	N. G.	V. E.	Total.
Turner, Frank James	London	1863-1875	Domestic	—	—	—	3	3	—	—	—	—	—	6
Turner, F. M.	—	1842	Sea Pieces	—	—	—	—	1	—	—	—	—	—	1
Turner, George	London	1782-1820	Scriptural	—	—	30	17	—	—	—	—	—	—	47
Turner, George	Bristol	1865-1882	Landscape	—	—	—	—	19	—	—	—	—	—	19
Turner, G. A.	London	1836-1841	Sporting	—	—	3	1	2	—	—	—	—	—	6
Turner, Mrs. George Gordon. *See* Miss Adelaide Claxton.	—	—	—	—	—	—	—	—	—	—	—	—	—	—
Turner, H.	—	1831	Sporting	—	—	—	—	2	—	—	—	—	—	2
Turner, Hawes	London	1884-1893	Domestic	—	—	2	—	4	—	1	—	—	—	7
Turner, Henry	London	1877	Cottages	—	—	—	—	1	—	—	—	—	—	1
Turner, H. D.	Croydon	1885	Domestic	—	—	1	—	—	—	—	—	—	—	1
Turner, Master J.	London	1772-1773	Drawings	—	7	—	—	—	—	—	—	—	—	7
Turner, James, F.S.A.	London	1761-1806	Portraits	18	1	—	1	—	—	—	—	—	—	20
Turner, J.	London	1822	Portraits	—	—	1	—	—	—	—	—	—	—	1
Turner, John	London	1826-1855	Architecture	—	—	23	—	1	—	—	—	—	—	24
Turner, J.	—	1872	Sporting	—	—	1	—	—	—	—	—	—	—	1
Turner, Miss J.	London	1893	Landscape	—	—	—	—	1	—	—	—	—	—	1
Turner, Miss Jessie	Catford	1886	Flowers	—	—	—	—	—	—	—	—	—	1	1
Turner, Joseph Mallord William, R.A.	London	1790-1850	Landscape	—	—	259	17	7	—	—	—	—	—	283
Turner, Miss M.	Liverpool	1773-1798	Still Life	1	—	1	—	—	—	—	—	—	—	2
Turner, Miss M.	London	1862	Domestic	—	—	—	1	—	—	—	—	—	—	1
Turner, Mrs. Meta P. W.	London	1889-1891	Flowers	—	—	—	—	1	—	—	—	—	1	2
Turner, Miss Peggy	—	1773	Still Life	1	—	—	—	—	—	—	—	—	—	1
Turner, P.	West Ham	1781-1785	Portraits	—	—	3	—	—	—	—	—	—	—	3
Turner, P.	London	1826	Sporting	—	—	—	1	—	—	—	—	—	—	1
Turner, Master Raphael, aged 7½	London	1791	Landscape	1	—	—	—	—	—	—	—	—	—	1
Turner, Robert	London	1825-1848	Still Life	—	—	7	5	3	—	—	—	—	—	15
Turner, Sophia	London	1791-1793	Dramatic	—	—	3	—	—	—	—	—	—	—	3
Turner, T.	London	1808-1839	Landscape	—	—	18	—	—	—	—	—	—	—	18
Turner, Thackeray	London	1836-1859	Architecture	—	—	5	—	—	—	—	—	—	—	5
Turner, W.	Walthamstow	1787-1792	Landscape	—	—	4	—	—	—	—	—	—	—	4
Turner, W.	London	1804-1819	Sculpture	—	—	6	—	—	—	—	—	—	—	6
Turner, William † (of Oxford)	Oxford	1807-1862	Landscape	—	—	17	18	3	464	—	—	—	—	502
Turner, W.	London	1857	Landscape	—	—	1	—	—	—	—	—	—	—	1
Turner, W. A.	London	1844	Birds	—	—	1	—	—	—	—	—	—	—	1
Turner, William B.	Trefriw	1887-1888	Rustic	—	—	1	—	1	—	—	—	—	—	2
Turner, W. Eddowes	Nottingham	1858-1862	Cattle	—	—	—	3	4	—	—	—	—	—	7
Turner, W. H. M.	Bath	1860	Cattle	—	—	—	—	1	—	—	—	—	—	1
Turner, William L.	Derby	1886-1893	Landscape	—	—	4	—	1	—	—	—	—	—	5
Turner, Mrs.	London	1860	Landscape	—	—	—	—	1	—	—	—	—	—	1
Turner and Palmer	London	1891	Architecture	—	—	1	—	—	—	—	—	—	—	1
Turnerelli, Peter	London	1802-1838	Sculpture	—	—	108	—	—	—	—	—	—	—	108
Turning, H.	Twickenham	1839	Landscape	—	—	—	—	1	—	—	—	—	—	1
Turpin —	London	1765	Flowers	1	—	—	—	—	—	—	—	—	—	1
Turpin de Cresse, Count	Paris	1832	Landscape	—	—	4	—	—	—	—	—	—	—	4
Turquand, Miss E.	London	1802-1806	Landscape	—	—	2	—	—	—	—	—	—	—	2
Turquand, Captain G.	London	1873-1874	Figures	—	—	—	—	2	—	—	—	—	—	2
Turrell, Arthur	London	1877-1890	Engraving	—	—	6	—	—	—	—	—	—	—	6
Turrell, Alfred E.	Windsor	1879	Portraits	—	—	1	—	—	—	—	—	—	—	1
Turrell, Charles James	London	1873-1892	Miniatures	—	—	85	—	—	—	—	—	—	—	85
Turtle, Edward	Ryde	1830-1874	Coast Scenes	—	—	1	—	7	—	—	—	—	—	8
Turton, W.	Whitchurch	1830	Game	—	—	1	—	—	—	—	—	—	—	1
Tuson, G. E.	London	1853-1865	Scriptural	—	—	6	11	14	—	—	—	—	—	31
Tussaud, Francis Babington	London	1855-1856	Sculpture	—	—	4	—	1	—	—	—	—	—	5
Tussaud, Joseph Randell	London	1855-1857	Sculpture	—	—	4	—	—	—	—	—	—	2	6
Tussaud, John T.	London	1891-1892	Sculpture	—	—	2	—	—	—	—	—	—	—	2
Tuthill, G.	London	1846-1858	Landscape	—	—	1	5	2	—	—	—	—	3	11
Tuthill, George L.	London	1825-1826	Sea Pieces	—	—	—	4	4	—	—	—	—	—	8
Tuthill, Captain J. V.	London	1847	Still Life	—	—	1	1	1	—	—	—	—	—	3
Tutop, C.	London	1782	Churches	—	—	1	—	—	—	—	—	—	—	1
Tuttle, C. Franklin	London	1882-1883	Domestic	—	—	1	—	2	—	—	—	—	1	4
Tuttle, Mrs. J. B.	Glasgow	1889	Landscape	—	—	1	—	—	—	—	—	—	—	1
Tuvin, John	London	1776-1792	Miniatures	3	—	14	—	—	—	—	—	—	—	17
Tweedale, J. *See* Smith and Tweedale	—	—	Architecture	—	—	—	—	—	—	—	—	—	—	—
Tweedie, William Menzies	Liverpool	1847-1874	Portraits	—	—	33	4	1	—	—	—	—	—	38
Twigg, Mrs. Alvine Klein	London	1888-1889	Portraits	—	—	1	—	1	—	—	—	—	—	2
Twigg, Andrew R.	London	1807-1810	Domestic	—	—	2	6	—	—	—	—	—	—	8
Twigg, Joseph	London	1879-1888	Buildings	—	—	3	—	—	—	1	—	—	—	4
Twigg, J. H.	London	1839	Portraits	—	—	1	—	—	—	—	—	—	—	1
Twigg, Miss	London	1821-1840	Portraits	—	—	4	—	—	—	—	—	—	—	4
Twining, H.	London	1855	Landscape	—	—	—	1	—	—	—	—	—	—	1
Twining, Miss Eliz.	—	1831-1835	Miniatures	—	—	2	—	—	—	—	—	—	—	2

Name.	Town.	First and Last Year of Ex.	Speciality.	S. A.	F. S.	R. A.	B. I.	S. S.	O.W.	N.W.	G. G.	N. G.	V. E.	Total.
Twoart, G. C.	London	1866-1871	Sculpture	—	—	8	—	—	—	—	—	—	—	8
Twyman, E.	London	1886	Still Life	—	—	—	—	1	—	—	—	—	—	1
Twyman, Miss Miriam	London	1891-1892	Miniatures	—	—	2	—	—	—	—	—	—	—	2
Tydel, E. De Poix-. *See* D.	—	—	—	—	—	—	—	—	—	—	—	—	—	—
Tye, Miss Edith A.	London	1892-1893	Flowers	—	—	2	—	1	—	—	—	—	—	3
Tyerman, T.	London	1821	Architecture	—	—	1	—	—	—	—	—	—	—	1
Tyerman and Payne	London	1832	Architecture	—	—	1	—	—	—	—	—	—	—	1
Tyler, C. L.	Bishop's Stortford	1827-1832	Flowers	—	—	14	—	1	—	—	—	—	—	15
Tyler, Robert Emeric	London	1875	Architecture	—	—	1	—	—	—	—	—	—	—	1
Tyler, William, R.A.	London	1760-1800	Sculpture	9	—	21	—	—	—	—	—	—	—	30
Tyler, William Henry	London	1878-1893	Sculpture	—	—	25	—	1	—	3	21	3	—	53
Tylor, J. M.	Carshalton	1874	Domestic	—	—	—	—	—	—	—	—	—	1	1
Tyndale, Walter	Bath	1880-1893	Domestic	—	—	9	—	5	—	5	2	—	7	28
Tyrrell, C.	London	1820	Architecture	—	—	1	—	—	—	—	—	—	—	1
Tyrrell, Thomas	London	1884-1889	Sculpture	—	—	3	—	—	—	—	—	—	—	3
Tyrrell, W. A.	London	1854-1857	Portraits	—	—	1	—	—	—	—	—	—	1	2
Tyrwhitt, Rev. R. St. John	Oxford	1864-1887	Landscape	—	—	2	—	2	—	—	2	—	—	6
Tyson, Miss Alice	Chester	1889-1892	Flowers	—	—	2	—	—	—	—	—	—	—	2
Tytler, George	London	1819-1825	Portraits	—	—	3	—	*	1	—	—	—	—	4
Tytler, K. A. Fraser	Rosslyn	1889	Sculpture	—	—	—	—	—	—	—	1	—	—	1
Ubsdell, R. H. C.	Portsmouth	1833-1849	Historical	—	—	5	—	1	—	—	—	—	—	6
Uhlrich, H. S.	Chelsfield	1889	Engraving	—	—	1	—	—	—	—	—	—	—	1
Ulcoq, Andrew	London	1889-1893	Landscape	—	—	1	—	—	—	1	—	—	1	3
Ullmann, W. M.	London	1882	Figures	—	—	2	—	—	—	—	—	—	—	2
Ullmer, Frederic	Barnsbury	1885	Domestic	—	—	—	—	1	—	—	—	—	—	1
Ulrich, Charles F.	Venice	1889-1890	Domestic	—	—	5	—	—	—	—	—	—	—	5
Underdown, J.	London	1819-1823	Landscape	—	—	2	—	—	—	—	—	—	—	2
Underhill, Frederick Charles	London	1851-1875	Domestic	—	—	19	28	25	—	—	—	—	28	100
Underhill, Frederick Thomas	London	1868-1890	Fruit	—	—	3	—	5	—	—	—	—	1	9
Underhill, William	London	1848-1870	Domestic	—	—	13	30	19	—	—	—	—	23	85
Underwood, A. S.	London	1885	Landscape	—	—	—	—	—	—	1	—	—	—	1
Underwood, G. A.	—	1812	Architecture	—	—	1	—	—	—	—	—	—	—	1
Underwood, H. J.	London	1822-1823	Architecture	—	—	2	—	—	—	—	—	—	—	2
Underwood, Thomas Richard	London	1789-1801	Landscape	—	—	23	—	—	—	—	—	—	—	23
Undley, Maria A.	London	1873	Domestic	—	—	—	—	1	—	—	—	—	—	1
Unna, Ada	London	1890	Flowers	—	—	—	—	1	—	—	—	—	—	1
Unsworth, William Frederick. *See also*	—	—	—	—	—	—	—	—	—	—	—	—	—	—
Dodgshun and Unsworth	London	1882-1893	Architecture	—	—	8	—	1	—	—	—	—	—	9
Unwin, G. A.	London	1871	Landscape	—	—	—	—	—	—	—	—	—	1	1
Unwin, Miss Ida M.	Chilworth	1892	Domestic	—	—	—	—	—	—	—	—	—	1	1
Unwin, J.	—	1832	Figures	—	—	—	—	5	—	—	—	—	—	5
Unwin, Miss Mary L. H.	Shipley	1892	Heads	—	—	1	—	—	—	—	—	—	—	1
Unwin, R.	London	1785-1812	Historical	—	—	32	—	—	—	—	—	—	—	32
Unwin, Thomas	London	1799-1800	Portraits	—	—	2	—	—	—	—	—	—	—	2
Upham, John Witham (?) William	Offwell	1801-1812	Landscape	—	—	12	—	—	—	—	—	—	1	13
Upsdell, P.	London	1791-1792	Architecture	1	—	1	—	—	—	—	—	—	—	2
Upton, E. §	—	1838-1874	Miniatures	—	—	54	—	1	—	—	—	—	—	55
Upton, John A.	London	1881	Heads	—	—	1	—	—	—	—	—	—	—	1
Upward, J. W.	London	1803-1808	Architecture	—	—	6	—	—	—	—	—	—	—	6
U'Ren, John C.	Penzance	1885-1890	Sea Pieces	—	—	1	—	—	—	3	—	—	—	4
Urland, G.	—	1883	Military	—	—	1	—	—	—	—	—	—	—	1
Urquhart, Gregor	London	1853-1854	Historical	—	—	1	2	—	—	—	—	—	—	3
Urwick, Walter	London	1887-1893	Domestic	—	—	8	—	—	—	1	—	—	1	10
Urwick, William H., R.P.E.	London	1867-1881	Landscape	—	—	8	—	1	—	—	—	—	12	21
Ussel, (?) Nasel, Manuel	Seville	1880	Historical	—	—	—	—	—	—	—	—	—	1	1
Ussher, Arland A.	Dublin	1885-1893	Sea Pieces	—	—	1	—	—	—	3	—	—	7	11
Utchison —	London	1791	Miniatures	—	—	1	—	—	—	—	—	—	—	1
Utterson, Emily	Winchester	1875	Domestic	—	—	—	—	—	—	—	—	—	1	1
Utterson, Edward Vernon	—	1815-1828	Landscape	—	—	30	—	—	—	—	—	—	—	30
Uvedale, S.	London	1845-1847	Flowers	—	—	—	3	4	—	—	—	—	—	7
Uwins, James	London	1836-1871	Landscape	—	—	20	8	2	—	—	—	—	—	30
Uwins, Thomas, R.A. †	London	1809-1857	Figures	—	—	103	37	13	91	3	—	—	—	247
Vacher, Charles ‡	London	1838-1881	Landscape	—	—	20	1	5	—	324	—	—	—	350
Vacher, Sydney	London	1882-1893	Architecture	—	—	11	—	—	—	—	—	—	—	11
Vaere, De. *See* D.	—	—	—	—	—	—	—	—	—	—	—	—	—	—
Vaillant, V. J.	Boulogne	1874-1876	Etching	—	—	—	—	—	—	—	—	—	3	3

Name.	Town.	First and Last Year of Ex.	Speciality.	S. A.	F. S.	R. A.	B. I.	S. S.	O. W.	N.W.	G. G.	N. G.	V. E.	Total.
Valentine, J.	London	1884	Landscape	—	—	—	—	—	—	—	—	—	1	1
Valintine, G. E.	London	1819-1821	Churches	—	—	3	—	—	—	—	—	—	—	3
Valintine, N.	London	1828	Intaglios	—	—	1	—	—	—	—	—	—	—	1
Valkenberg, H.	Paris	1877	Study	—	—	—	—	—	—	—	—	—	1	1
Vallance, Aymer	London	1880	Flowers	—	—	—	—	2	—	—	—	—	—	2
Vallence, Miss Fanny	London	1876-1885	Fruit	—	—	1	—	1	—	—	—	—	1	3
Vallence, William F., R.S.A.	Edinburgh	1861-1873	Sea Pieces	—	—	5	—	—	—	—	—	—	—	5
Vallentine, Miss Emmeline	Norwood	1864-1870	Domestic	—	—	—	1	7	—	—	—	—	—	8
Valmon, Mdlle. Léonie	London	1886-1888	Etching	—	—	2	—	—	—	—	—	—	—	2
Valsecchi, Bagatti	London	1837	Enamels	—	—	2	—	—	—	—	—	—	—	2
Valter, Eugene	—	1880	Domestic	—	—	—	—	—	—	—	—	—	1	1
Valter, Miss E. M.	Birmingham	1889	Still Life	—	—	—	—	—	—	—	—	—	2	2
Valter, Frederick E.	Birmingham	1890	Rustic	—	—	—	—	2	—	—	—	—	—	2
Valter, Henry	Birmingham	1854-1864	Landscape	—	—	—	3	7	—	—	—	—	13	23
Van Assen, Benedictus Antonio	London	1788-1804	Domestic	—	—	29	—	—	—	—	—	—	—	29
Van Basse, Mdlle. M.	—	1880	Landscape	—	—	—	—	—	—	—	1	—	—	1
Van Beers, Jan	London	1882-1891	Figures	—	—	7	—	—	—	—	1	—	—	8
Van Beest, E. Van Heemskerck. *See* H.	—	—	—	—	—	—	—	—	—	—	—	—	—	—
Van Beurden, Alphonse. *See* B.	—	—	—	—	—	—	—	—	—	—	—	—	—	—
Van Bever, A.	London	1845-1873	Figures	—	—	6	3	5	—	—	—	—	—	14
Van Biesbroeck, Julius J.	London	1879-1889	Domestic	—	—	2	—	—	—	—	—	—	—	2
Van Bleeck, Pieter. *See* B.	—	—	—	—	—	—	—	—	—	—	—	—	—	—
Van Borselen, J. W.	—	1880	Landscape	—	—	—	—	—	—	—	1	—	—	1
Van Brakel, Louisa Hoyer	London	1844	Flowers	—	—	2	2	—	—	—	—	—	—	4
Van Brown, A.	—	1849	Portraits	—	—	—	—	1	—	—	—	—	—	1
Van Damme-Sylva. *See* S.	—	—	—	—	—	—	—	—	—	—	—	—	—	—
Van den Auber, H.	Finisterre	1880	Domestic	—	—	—	—	4	—	—	—	—	—	4
Van den Bos, G.	Paris	1881	Figures	—	—	—	—	—	—	—	1	—	—	1
Vanden, Bosch A.	London	1863-1865	Sculpture	—	—	4	—	—	—	—	—	—	—	4
Vandenbosch, Charles Edward	London	1866-1871	Sculpture	—	—	10	2	*	—	—	—	—	—	12
Vanden Kerkhove, A.	London	1855	Sculpture	—	—	2	—	—	—	—	—	—	—	2
Vander, Abraham B.	—	1836	Landscape	—	—	—	1	—	—	—	—	—	—	1
Van der Berghe, J. J.	London	1796-1797	Allegorical	—	—	2	—	—	—	—	—	—	—	2
Van der boeck —	—	1856	Figures	—	—	1	—	—	—	—	—	—	—	1
Vanderbush —	London	1780	Battle Pieces	—	1	—	—	—	—	—	—	—	—	1
Vander Gucht, Benjamin	London	1767-1787	Portraits	—	9	49	—	—	—	—	—	—	—	58
Vander Hagen —	—	1766-1779	Sculpture	—	8	—	—	—	—	—	—	—	—	8
Vander Hecht, Henri. *See* H.	—	—	—	—	—	—	—	—	—	—	—	—	—	—
Vanderhoof, Charles A.	Paris	1880-1881	Etching	—	—	2	—	—	—	—	—	—	3	5
Van der Kemp, S. M.	Paris	1879	Sculpture	—	—	1	—	—	—	—	—	—	—	1
Van der Laar, J. H.	The Hague	1838-1851	Domestic	—	—	5	—	—	—	—	—	—	—	5
Vandermeulen, J. F.	London	1767-1780	Sculpture	9	47	—	—	—	—	—	—	—	—	56
Vandermeulen —, Junr.	London	1772-1780	Sculpture	3	14	—	—	—	—	—	—	—	—	17
Vander Mijn, Agatha	London	1764-1768	Fruit	—	3	—	—	—	—	—	—	—	—	3
Vander Mijn, Frank	London	1761-1772	Portraits	—	40	—	—	—	—	—	—	—	—	40
Vander Mijn, Robert	London	1762-1764	Portraits	—	8	—	—	—	—	—	—	—	—	8
Vander Mijn, Mrs.	London	1764-1772	Portraits	—	16	—	—	—	—	—	—	—	—	16
Vander Pyuyl, L. F. G.	London	1785-1788	Portraits	—	—	10	—	—	—	—	—	—	—	10
Vanderstop —	—	1766	Drawing	1	—	—	—	—	—	—	—	—	—	1
Van der Velden, P.	—	1880	Domestic	—	—	—	—	—	—	—	2	—	—	2
Vandervell, W. F.	—	1829-1832	Moonlight	—	—	1	—	3	—	—	—	—	—	4
Vandervell, Miss	—	1832	Landscape	—	—	—	—	2	—	—	—	—	—	2
Van der Waay, N.	Amsterdam	1889	Figures	—	—	—	—	4	—	—	—	—	—	4
Van der Weyde, Henry	Norwood	1875-1880	Miniatures	—	—	3	—	—	—	—	—	—	1	4
Vander Weyde, Harry F.	London	1885-1892	Landscape	—	—	—	—	6	—	2	—	—	6	14
Van de Weld, W.	London	1867	Mountains	—	—	—	—	—	—	—	—	—	1	1
Vandyke, Peter	London	1762-1772	Portraits	2	17	—	—	—	—	—	—	—	—	19
Van Elven, P. T.	Paris	1865	Landscape	—	—	1	—	—	—	—	—	—	—	1
Van Everdingen, A.	Utrecht	1881	Landscape	—	—	1	—	—	—	—	—	—	—	1
Van Eycken, Jean Baptiste	Brussels	1850	Figures	—	—	2	—	—	—	—	—	—	—	2
Van Gangalen, J.	—	1850	Sea Coasts	—	—	2	—	—	—	—	—	—	—	2
Van Gelder —	London	1768	Flowers	—	1	—	—	—	—	—	—	—	—	1
Van Haanen, Cecil C. ϕ	Antwerp	1871-1890	Figures	—	—	10	—	—	—	—	2	1	4	17
Van Havermaet, P.	London	1879-1882	Portraits	—	—	2	—	—	—	—	—	—	—	2
Vanhernan, T.	London	1819	Fruit	—	—	1	—	—	—	—	—	—	—	1
Van Heyden, A.	Berlin	1881	Figures	—	—	—	—	—	—	—	—	—	2	2
Van Hier —	London	1880-1881	Landscape	—	—	—	—	2	—	—	—	—	—	2
Van Hoorn, Mdlle. C.	Arnheim	1882	Flowers	—	—	—	—	—	—	—	—	—	1	1
Van Houten, Mdme. Mesdag	—	1880	Flowers	—	—	—	—	—	—	—	2	—	—	2
Van Hove, Hubertus	—	1847	Buildings	—	—	—	2	—	—	—	—	—	—	2
Vanini, Francesco	Rome	1780	Scriptural	—	1	—	—	—	—	—	—	—	—	1
Van Lerius, Joseph Henri François	Antwerp	1864-1870	Domestic	—	—	2	—	—	—	—	—	—	2	4

Name.	Town.	First and Last Year of Ex.	Speciality.	S. A.	F. S.	R. A.	B. I.	S. S.	O. W.	N. W.	G. G.	N. G.	V. E.	Total.
Vanlinden, Pierre	London	1852-1875	Sculpture	—	—	10	6	—	—	—	—	—	—	16
Vanloo, Louis Michel	London	1765	Portraits	4	—	—	—	—	—	—	—	—	—	4
Van Luppen, Joseph (?) Von	London	1874	Landscape	—	—	1	—	—	—	—	—	—	—	1
Van Marcke, Emile	Paris	1878-1879	Cattle	—	—	—	—	—	—	—	—	—	4	4
Van Meyden, A.	Rome	1855	Domestic	—	—	1	—	—	—	—	—	—	—	1
Van Moer, F. B.	London	1872	Venice	—	—	—	—	—	—	—	—	—	1	1
Van Monk, E.	London	1832-1840	Domestic	—	—	8	1	2	—	—	—	—	—	11
Vannicola, Gaetano	Rome	1887	Landscape	—	—	—	—	—	—	—	1	—	—	1
Van Nost, John	—	1762	Sculpture	—	1	—	—	—	—	—	—	—	—	1
Vannutelli, S.	Rome	1882-1886	Portraits	—	—	—	—	—	—	—	2	—	—	2
Van Olst, J.	Flanders	1790	Flowers	2	—	—	—	—	—	—	—	—	—	2
Van Os, Gerhard J.	London	1827-1828	Landscape	—	—	2	1	—	—	—	—	—	—	3
Van Os, Jan	Flanders	1773-1791	Flowers, etc.	12	—	—	—	—	—	—	—	—	—	12
Van Papendrecht, J. H. *See* P.	—	—	—	—	—	—	—	—	—	—	—	—	—	—
Van Raalte, Mrs. C.	London	1888	Domestic	—	—	1	—	—	—	—	—	—	—	1
Van Rappard, C. *See* R.	—	—	—	—	—	—	—	—	—	—	—	—	—	—
Van Regemonte —	—	1792	Historical	—	—	1	—	—	—	—	—	—	—	1
Van Regemorter, J.	Antwerp	1828-1846	Figures	—	—	2	—	2	—	—	—	—	—	4
Van Ruith, Horace	Capri	1888-1893	Figures	—	—	5	—	1	—	2	—	1	1	10
Vans Agnew, Miss C.	London	1867-1868	Sculpture	—	—	2	—	—	—	—	—	—	—	2
Van Schendel, Petrus	Brussels	1838-1858	Candlelight	—	—	6	1	2	—	—	—	—	—	9
Van Seben, Henri	London	1857-1858	Domestic	—	—	—	4	—	—	—	—	—	2	6
Van Seghars —	Antwerp	1780	Domestic	—	1	—	—	—	—	—	—	—	—	1
Vanseverdoneck, F.	London	1862	Landscape	—	—	—	—	1	—	—	—	—	—	1
Vans Gravesande, Carel Nicolaas Storm	London	1880-1883	Etching	—	—	4	—	—	—	1	—	—	3	8
Van Trump, Minheer	—	—	Landscape	—	3	—	—	—	—	—	—	—	—	3
Van Weyde, H. F.	Paris	1891	Sea Shores	—	—	1	—	—	—	—	—	—	—	1
Van Worrell, A. B.	London	1819-1849	Cattle	—	—	8	21	28	5	—	—	—	—	62
Van Wurt, Ames	London	1877-1890	Sculpture	—	—	1	—	—	—	—	—	1	—	2
Vapi, M.	Rome	1825	Landscape	—	—	—	1	—	—	—	—	—	—	1
Varden, R.	Worcester	1843	Landscape	—	—	1	—	—	—	—	—	—	—	1
Vardon, Miss C.	—	1792	Landscape	—	—	1	—	—	—	—	—	—	—	1
Vardon, S.	London	1772-1803	Domestic	—	—	9	—	—	—	—	—	—	—	9
Vardy, John	London	1761-1818	Architecture	15	—	2	—	—	—	—	—	—	—	17
Varillat, Madame	London	1816-1820	Portraits	—	—	12	—	—	—	—	—	—	—	12
Varley, A.	London	1838	Landscape	—	—	1	—	—	—	—	—	—	—	1
Varley, Cornelius †	London	1803-1869	Landscape	—	—	29	4	29	59	—	—	—	8	129
Varley, Charles Smith	London	1839-1869	Landscape	—	—	38	4	12	—	—	—	—	—	54
Varley, Edgar John	London	1861-1887	Landscape	—	—	8	—	59	—	7	2	—	2	78
Varley, Miss Eliza C.	London	1840-1851	Landscape	—	—	3	—	1	—	—	—	—	—	4
Varley, Miss Elizabeth. *See* Mrs. Mulready.	—	—	—	—	—	—	—	—	—	—	—	—	—	—
Varley, H. G.	London	1827	Landscape	—	—	1	—	—	—	—	—	—	—	1
Varley, John †	London	1798-1843	Landscape	—	—	41	2	4	739	—	—	—	—	786
Varley, John	London	1870-1892	Landscape	—	—	15	—	11	—	16	8	—	20	70
Varley, Mrs. John	London	1883-1886	Domestic	—	—	—	—	3	—	1	—	—	—	4
Varley, Miss Lucy	London	1886-1890	Flowers	—	—	2	—	1	—	5	—	—	1	9
Varley, William Fleetwood	London	1804-1818	Landscape	—	—	21	—	—	—	—	—	—	—	21
Varolli —	Bologna	1774	Landscape	2	—	—	—	—	—	—	—	—	—	2
Varrall, J. C.	London	1825-1827	Engraving	—	—	—	—	5	—	—	—	—	—	5
Varroe, De. *See* D.	—	—	—	—	—	—	—	—	—	—	—	—	—	—
Vasey, Miss Clary	London	1891	Flowers	—	—	1	—	—	—	—	—	—	—	1
Vaslet, Lewis	London	1770-1782	Miniatures	—	—	10	—	—	—	—	—	—	—	10
Vassar, Miss L.	London	1823-1829	Portraits	—	—	1	—	5	—	—	—	—	—	6
Vasselot, Anatole Marquet De. *See* D.	—	—	—	—	—	—	—	—	—	—	—	—	—	—
Vaughan *See* Preston and Vaughan	—	—	Architecture	—	—	—	—	—	—	—	—	—	—	—
Vaughan, E.	London	1772-1814	Miniatures	8	5	13	—	—	—	—	—	—	—	26
Vaughan, Miss Letitia	London	1867	Heads	—	—	1	—	1	—	—	—	—	—	2
Vaughan, T.	London	1812-1821	Portraits	—	—	16	—	—	—	—	—	—	—	16
Vaughan, T.	London	1856-1862	Architecture	—	—	2	—	—	—	—	—	—	—	2
Vaughan, W. J.	London	1855-1858	Landscape	—	—	—	—	—	—	—	—	—	4	4
Vaux, J.	Croydon	1797-1798	Landscape	—	—	3	—	—	—	—	—	—	—	3
Vaux, De. *See* D.	—	—	—	—	—	—	—	—	—	—	—	—	—	—
Vawser, Miss Charlotte	Matlock	1837-1875	Landscape	—	—	13	1	6	—	—	—	—	—	20
Vawser, G. R.	London	1818-1847	Landscape	—	—	19	—	5	—	—	—	—	—	24
Vawser, G. R., Junr.	London	1836-1874	Landscape	—	—	39	4	3	—	—	—	—	—	46
Veal, R. M.	London	1839-1847	Landscape	—	—	1	1	1	—	—	—	—	—	3
Veck, Le De. *See* D.	—	—	—	—	—	—	—	—	—	—	—	—	—	—
Vedder, Elihu	Rome	1870-1871	Domestic	—	—	—	—	3	—	—	—	—	3	6
Vega, De la. *See* D.	—	—	—	—	—	—	—	—	—	—	—	—	—	—
Vega, Pedro De. *See* D.	—	—	—	—	—	—	—	—	—	—	—	—	—	—
Velden, P. Van der. *See* Van.	—	—	—	—	—	—	—	—	—	—	—	—	—	—
Vemaux, V.	London	1853	Landscape	—	—	1	—	—	—	—	—	—	—	1

Name.	Town.	First and Last Year of Ex.	Speciality.	S. A.	F. S.	R. A.	B. I.	S. S.	O. W.	N.W.	G. G.	N. G.	V. E.	Total.
Venables, Miss Alice	Lincoln	1884	Flowers	—	—	—	—	1	—	—	—	—	—	1
Venables, Adolphus Robert	London	1833-1873	Portraits	—	—	21	—	—	—	—	—	—	—	21
Venables, Miss Emilia Rose	London	1844-1846	Historical	—	—	2	2	—	—	—	—	—	—	4
Venables, Spencer	London	1876-1879	Figures	—	—	—	—	3	—	—	—	—	—	3
Venner, W. H. T.	London	1886	Sculpture	—	—	1	—	—	—	—	—	—	—	1
Venning, R.	London	1818-1834	Portraits	—	—	6	—	—	—	—	—	—	—	6
Verbœckhoven, Eugene Joseph	Brussels	1845-1878	Animals	—	—	3	—	1	—	—	—	—	—	4
Verbruggen —	Woolwich	1772	Landscape	1	—	—	—	—	—	—	—	—	—	1
Verey, Arthur	London	1873-1893	Rustic	—	—	10	—	63	—	2	—	—	15	90
Verfloet, Joseph	Florence	1888	Landscape	—	—	—	—	—	—	1	—	—	—	1
Verheart, Paul	London	1879-1880	Domestic	—	—	2	—	—	—	—	—	—	—	2
Verheyden, François	London	1878-1893	Sculpture	—	—	14	—	—	—	—	—	—	—	14
Verini, P. A.	London	1833	Flowers	—	—	1	—	—	—	—	—	—	—	1
Verity, Thomas and Frank T.	London	1892	Architecture	—	—	1	—	—	—	—	—	—	—	1
Verity and Hunt	London	1881	Architecture	—	—	1	—	—	—	—	—	—	—	1
Verlat, Professor Charles	Antwerp	1869-1886	Domestic	—	—	2	—	—	—	—	—	—	—	2
Vernède, Camille	London	1869-1893	Landscape	—	—	4	—	4	—	—	7	3	16	34
Vernede, H. T.	London	1876-1880	Landscape	—	—	—	—	—	—	—	—	—	2	2
Verner, Fred. Arthur	Ottawa	1881-1893	Animals	—	—	6	—	2	—	1	1	—	—	10
Verner, Miss Ida	London	1885-1893	Portraits	—	—	8	—	—	—	—	2	1	2	13
Vernet, Joseph Claude	Paris	1777	Sea Pieces	1	—	—	—	—	—	—	—	—	—	1
Vernet, T.	London	1812	Domestic	—	—	—	1	—	—	—	—	—	—	1
Vernier, Emile	Paris	1872	Lithographs	—	—	—	—	—	—	—	—	—	1	1
Vernon —	London	1772-1783	Landscape	1	1	—	—	—	—	—	—	—	—	2
Vernon, Hon. Mrs.	—	1771-1780	Landscape	2	—	1	—	—	—	—	—	—	—	3
Vernon, Arthur	High Wycombe	1874-1877	Architecture	—	—	3	—	—	—	—	—	—	—	3
Vernon, Arthur Longley	London	1871-1893	Domestic	—	—	24	—	21	—	—	—	1	29	75
Vernon, Cyrus	Manchester	1870	Historical	—	—	—	—	1	—	—	—	—	1	2
Vernon, H.	London	1874	Architecture	—	—	1	—	—	—	—	—	—	—	1
Vernon, I. R.	London	1855-1858	Fruit	—	—	3	1	1	—	—	—	—	—	5
Vernon, J. Arthur	London	1888	Landscape	—	—	1	—	—	—	—	—	—	—	1
Vernon, Miss Mary	Birmingham	1871-1873	Flowers	—	—	—	—	5	—	—	—	—	—	5
Vernon, R. Warren	London	1886-1893	Landscape	—	—	1	—	9	—	1	—	—	—	11
Vernon, Thomas	London	1857-1867	Engraving	—	—	8	—	—	—	—	—	—	—	8
Vernon, W.	London	1816	Portraits	—	—	1	—	—	—	—	—	—	—	1
Vernon, William H.	Birmingham	1858-1892	Landscape	—	—	3	5	10	—	—	—	—	1	19
Vernon, Walter Liberty	London	1879	Architecture	—	—	1	—	—	—	—	—	—	—	1
Verotti —	—	1775	Landscape	1	—	—	—	—	—	—	—	—	—	1
Verrall, Frederick	London	1884	Sea Pieces	—	—	—	—	—	—	—	—	—	1	1
Verraus, L.	London	1850	Domestic	—	—	1	—	—	—	—	—	—	—	1
Verreaux, L.	London	1857	Landscape	—	—	—	1	—	—	—	—	—	—	1
Verschaffelt —	Germany	1765	Sculpture	—	1	—	—	—	—	—	—	—	—	1
Verschaur, W.	—	1869	Domestic	—	—	—	—	—	—	—	—	—	1	1
Verstappen, M.	Rome	1825	Landscape	—	—	—	3	—	—	—	—	—	—	3
Vertue, Julia	London	1848	Landscape	—	—	1	—	—	—	—	—	—	—	1
Vertue, Rosamond	—	1847	Landscape	—	—	1	—	—	—	—	—	—	—	1
Vertunni, Achille	Rome	1869	Landscape	—	—	3	—	—	—	—	—	—	—	3
Verveer, S. L.	Scheveningen	1874	Charcoal	—	—	—	—	—	—	—	—	—	1	1
Verwee, C. L.	London	1864-1865	Domestic	—	—	1	—	1	—	—	—	—	—	2
Vesey, J. A.	London	1858-1860	Domestic	—	—	—	2	—	—	—	—	—	—	2
Vesey-Holt, Miss A. Julia	London	1884	Flowers	—	—	1	—	—	—	—	—	—	—	1
Veth, Jan	—	1891	Portraits	—	—	—	—	—	—	—	—	—	1	1
Veussell, Emma	London	1853	Portraits	—	—	1	—	—	—	—	—	—	—	1
Veyrassat, Jules	London	1874-1881	Etching	—	—	—	—	—	—	—	—	—	3	3
Vezin, Frederick	London	1884-1885	Figures	—	—	3	—	—	—	—	1	—	1	5
Vialls, Frederick Jos.	London	1884-1885	Landscape	—	—	—	—	—	—	2	—	—	—	2
Vialls, George	London	1868-1889	Architecture	—	—	3	—	—	—	—	—	—	—	3
Vibert, Jehan Georges	Paris	1872-1874	Figures	—	—	—	—	—	—	—	—	—	2	2
Vickers, Alfred	London	1828-1868	Landscape	—	—	61	125	81	—	—	—	—	—	267
Vickers, Alfred Gomersal	London	1827-1837	Sea Pieces	—	—	16	42	30	—	16	—	—	—	104
Vickers, A. H.	London	1853-1868	Landscape	—	—	5	3	6	—	—	—	—	—	14
Vickers, C.	Hertford	1838-1852	Architecture	—	—	7	—	—	—	—	—	—	—	7
Victor, J.	London	1852	Landscape	—	—	—	1	—	—	—	—	—	—	1
Vidal, E.	London	1888	Domestic	—	—	3	—	—	—	—	—	—	—	3
Vidal, L.	London	1790-1792	Flowers	—	—	4	—	—	—	—	—	—	—	4
Vidal, Paul	London	1875	Etching	—	—	—	—	—	—	—	—	—	1	1
Vieira, F.	London	1798-1799	Figures	—	—	5	—	—	—	—	—	—	—	5
Viennot, Le Chevalier	London	1826-1827	Portraits	—	—	2	—	3	—	—	—	—	—	5
Vierpyl, W.	London	1792-1795	Architecture	—	—	4	—	—	—	—	—	—	—	4
Vieusseux, E.	London	1859	Portraits	—	—	1	—	—	—	—	—	—	—	1
Vigers, Frederick	Horsham	1884-1892	Domestic	—	—	6	—	1	—	—	—	—	1	8
Vigers, George	London	1881-1890	Architecture	—	—	7	—	—	—	—	—	—	—	7

Name.	Town.	First and Last Year of Ex.	Speciality.	S. A.	F. S.	R. A.	B. I.	S. S.	O. W.	N. W.	G. G.	N. G.	V. E.	Total.
VIGERS (GEORGE) AND WAGSTAFFE (T. R.)	London	1880-1881	Architecture	—	—	3	—	—	—	—	—	—	—	3
VIGNE, G. T.	Woodford	1842	Figures	—	—	1	—	—	—	—	—	—	—	1
VIGNE, H. G.	London	1785-1787	Miniatures	—	—	2	—	—	—	—	—	—	—	2
VIGNON, CLAUDE (MADAME ROUVIER)	Paris	1883	Sculpture	—	—	1	—	—	—	—	—	—	—	1
VIGOR, CHARLES	London	1881-1893	Domestic	—	—	9	—	—	—	—	4	—	4	17
VILLAINE, H.	Paris	1846	Historical	—	—	1	—	—	—	—	—	—	—	1
VILLALOBOS, DE. *See* D.	—	—	—	—	—	—	—	—	—	—	—	—	—	—
VILLAMIL, P.	Paris	1838-1870	Figures	—	—	7	6	10	—	—	—	—	—	23
VILLE, C.	London	1831	Sculpture	—	—	1	—	—	—	—	—	—	—	1
VILLE, DE. *See* D.	—	—	—	—	—	—	—	—	—	—	—	—	—	—
VILLEBRUNE, MISS MARY DE. (After 1775 she had seven at the R.A., when Mrs. Du Noblet)	London	1771-1782	Portraits	7	8	11	—	—	—	—	—	—	—	26
VILLIERES, F.	London	1880-1886	Domestic	—	—	—	—	—	—	—	—	—	4	4
VILLIERS, FRANÇOIS HÜET	London	1803-1813	Animals	—	—	28	9	—	5	—	—	—	88	130
VILLIERS, FREDERICK	London	1882-1883	Military	—	—	2	—	—	—	—	—	—	—	2
VINALL, C.	London	1872	Landscape	—	—	1	—	—	—	—	—	—	—	1
VINCENT, MISS D.	Addlestone	1893	Flowers	—	—	—	—	1	—	—	—	—	—	1
VINCENT, MISS E. M.	London	1893	Landscape	—	—	—	—	—	—	1	—	—	—	1
VINCENT, GEORGE	Norwich	1814-1831	Landscape	—	—	9	41	12	5	—	—	—	—	67
VINCENT, HENRY	London	1879-1892	Domestic	—	—	5	—	5	—	—	—	—	1	11
VINCENT, J.	London	1831	Landscape	—	—	1	—	—	—	—	—	—	—	1
VINCENT, P.	London	1829	Coast Scene	—	—	—	—	1	—	—	—	—	—	1
VINCENT, S.	London	1865-1882	Landscape	—	—	—	—	—	—	—	—	—	40	40
VINCENT, MISS	—	1816	Shells	—	—	1	—	—	—	—	—	—	—	1
VINCENTIO —	London	1769-1772	Landscape	3	—	—	—	—	—	—	—	—	—	3
VINCK, FRANZ	Antwerp	1874	Domestic	—	—	—	—	—	—	—	—	—	1	1
VINCOTTE, THOMAS JULES	Brussels	1881	Sculpture	—	—	2	—	—	—	—	—	—	—	2
VINE, J.	London	1844	Farmyards	—	—	—	—	1	—	—	—	—	—	1
VINE, R.	London	1846-1849	Fruit	—	—	2	—	3	—	—	—	—	—	5
VINEA, FRANCESCO	London	1877-1882	Figures	—	—	7	—	—	—	—	—	—	—	7
VINER, C.	Bath	1838	Architecture	—	—	1	—	—	—	—	—	—	—	1
VINER, J. TICKELL	London	1821-1854	Domestic	—	—	13	2	5	—	—	—	—	—	20
VINOELST, EMANUEL CONSTANT	London	1868-1890	Sculpture	—	—	17	—	—	—	—	—	—	—	17
VINTER, MRS. C.	Walton-on-Thames	1874	Flowers	—	—	—	—	1	—	—	—	—	—	1
VINTER, FREDERICK ARMSTRONG	London	1874-1883	Historical	—	—	4	—	13	—	—	—	—	1	18
VINTER, MISS HARRIET EMILY	London	1879-1880	Still Life	—	—	1	—	1	—	—	—	—	—	2
VINTER, JOHN ALFRED	London	1847-1893	Domestic	—	—	68	8	30	—	—	—	—	8	114
VINTER, MRS.	London	1853-1874	Domestic	—	—	—	—	6	—	—	—	—	—	6
VIOLET, MISS M.	London	1808-1810	Domestic	—	—	4	—	—	—	—	—	—	—	4
VIOLET, PIERRE	London	1790-1819	Miniatures	1	—	114	—	—	—	—	—	—	2	117
VIOLLET-LE-DUC	Paris	1881	Mountains	—	—	—	—	—	—	—	4	—	—	4
VIPAN, MISS E. M.	Brighton	1884-1885	Flowers	—	—	—	—	1	—	—	—	—	1	2
VIRGIN, A. F. G.	Stockholm	1866	Figures	—	—	—	—	2	—	—	—	—	—	2
VISPRE, FRANCIS XAVIER, F.S.A.	London	1760-1789	Miniatures	53	—	9	—	—	—	—	—	—	—	62
VISPRE, VICTOR	London	1763-1778	Glass Painting	22	5	7	—	—	—	—	—	—	—	34
VITALBA, GIOVANNI	London	1771-1798	Landscape	—	—	10	—	—	—	—	—	—	—	10
VIVARES FRANCIS	—	1766-1768	Engraving	2	—	—	—	—	—	—	—	—	—	2
VIVARES, THOMAS	London	1764-1788	Engraving	3	3	4	—	—	—	—	—	—	—	10
VIVARES, MISS	London	1764	Flowers	—	1	—	—	—	—	—	—	—	—	1
VIVIAN, COMLEY	London	1874-1892	Portraits	—	—	10	—	2	—	—	—	—	—	12
VIVIAN, MRS. COMLEY (LIZZIE)	—	1886-1892	Miniatures	—	—	9	—	—	—	—	—	—	—	9
VIVIAN, MISS J.	Acton	1869-1877	Landscape	—	—	—	—	6	—	—	—	—	—	6
VOGET, H. C.	London	1838	Architecture	—	—	1	—	—	—	—	—	—	—	1
VOLAIRE —	—	1778	Sea Pieces	1	—	—	—	—	—	—	—	—	—	1
VOLCK, FRITZ	—	1874-1881	Domestic	—	—	—	—	3	—	—	—	—	2	5
VOLLON, ANTOINE	London	1871	Domestic	—	—	1	—	—	—	—	—	—	—	1
VOLMAR —	London	1804	Domestic	—	—	4	—	—	—	—	—	—	—	4
VOLMERSTEIN, COUNT VON DER R.	London	1861	Figures	—	—	2	—	—	—	—	—	—	—	2
VON ANGELI. *See* A.	—	—	—	—	—	—	—	—	—	—	—	—	—	—
VON BARTELS, PROFESSOR HANS	Munich	1892	Sea Shores	—	—	—	—	—	—	1	—	—	—	1
VON BORWITZ, MISS R. E.	London	1891-1892	Landscape	—	—	1	—	1	—	—	—	—	—	2
VON CHELMINSKI, JAN. *See* C.	—	—	—	—	—	—	—	—	—	—	—	—	—	—
VON CRAMM, BARONESS HELGA. *See* Cramm.	—	—	—	—	—	—	—	—	—	—	—	—	—	—
VON DER EMBE, K.	London	1853	Domestic	—	—	2	—	—	—	—	—	—	—	2
VON FOWINKEL, MISS MAGDALEN	London	1831-1846	Portraits	—	—	5	—	—	—	—	—	—	—	5
VON GLEHN, A.	Brighton	1881	Landscape	—	—	—	—	—	—	—	—	—	2	2
VON GLEHN, OSWALD	London	1879-1880	Mythological	—	—	2	—	—	—	—	—	—	—	2
VON HANNON, R.	Vienna	1849	Snow Scenes	—	—	1	—	—	—	—	—	—	—	1
VON HOLST, THEODORE M.	London	1827-1845	Historical	—	—	24	20	6	—	—	—	—	—	50
VON KAMECKE, O.	Berlin	1875	Landscape	—	—	—	—	1	—	—	—	—	—	1
VON LENBACH. *See* L.	—	—	—	—	—	—	—	—	—	—	—	—	—	—
VON LÜCK, LUD	—	1761	Sculpture	—	1	—	—	—	—	—	—	—	—	1

Name.	Town.	First and Last Year of Ex.	Speciality.	S. A.	F. S.	R. A.	B. I.	S. S.	O. W.	N. W.	G. G.	N. G.	V. E.	Total.
Von Mattheson —	—	1830	Figures	—	—	1	—	—	—	—	—	—	—	1
Von Nathusius. *See* N.	—	—	—	—	—	—	—	—	—	—	—	—	—	—
Vonner, Madame A. B. N.	London	1892	Figures	—	—	1	—	—	—	—	—	—	—	1
Von Preuschen, Baroness H. *See* P.	—	—	—	—	—	—	—	—	—	—	—	—	—	—
Von Reichenbach, Count Waldemar	Weimar	1881	Figures	—	—	1	—	—	—	—	—	—	—	1
Von Stürmer, Miss Frances	Gainsborough	1863-1874	Landscape	—	—	—	—	6	—	—	—	—	2	8
Von Weber, Ada	London	1880	Buildings	—	—	—	—	1	—	—	—	—	—	1
Vornz, E.	Paris	1878	Etching	—	—	—	—	—	—	—	—	—	2	2
Vos, Hubert, R.B.A. §	London	1888-1892	Domestic	—	—	6	—	23	—	1	2	1	19	52
Vos, H. M	Paris	1877	Landscape	—	—	—	—	—	—	—	—	—	1	1
Vose, Mrs.	Liverpool	1819	Sculpture	—	—	1	—	—	—	—	—	—	—	1
Votieri, J.	London	1869	Sculpture	—	—	1	—	—	—	—	—	—	—	1
Voyer, John	London	1767-1791	Sculpture	2	1	—	—	—	—	—	—	—	—	3
Voyez —	Newcastle	1772	Sculpture	—	6	—	—	—	—	—	—	—	—	6
Voysey, A.	London	1811	Architecture	—	—	1	—	—	—	—	—	—	—	1
Vrüntze, E. F.	London	1862	Sculpture	—	—	—	—	1	—	—	—	—	—	1
Vulliamy, G.	London	1838-1845	Architecture	—	—	2	—	—	—	—	—	—	—	2
Vulliamy, Lewis	London	1822-1838	Architecture	—	—	15	—	—	—	—	—	—	—	15
Vychan, J. L.	London	1873-1877	Landscape	—	—	2	—	10	—	—	—	—	—	12
Vyvyan, J.	London	1818-1820	Architecture	—	—	2	—	—	—	—	—	—	—	2
Vyvyan, Miss M. Caroline	London	1868-1891	Landscape	—	—	2	—	4	—	2	—	—	5	13
Waay, N. Van der. *See* V.	—	—	—	—	—	—	—	—	—	—	—	—	—	—
Waddell, D. Henderson	London	1882	Landscape	—	—	1	—	—	—	—	—	—	—	1
Waddington, Miss Maud	Whitby	1888	Landscape	—	—	—	—	—	—	1	—	—	—	1
Waddy, Frederick	London	1878	Pencil	—	—	—	—	—	—	—	—	—	1	1
Wade, Edward W.	Deptford	1862-1865	Landscape	—	—	—	3	1	—	—	—	—	—	4
Wade, Fairfax Blomfield	London	1889-1893	Architecture	—	—	4	—	—	—	—	—	—	—	4
Wade, George E.	London	1887-1893	Sculpture	—	—	10	—	—	—	—	5	1	—	16
Wade, Thomas	Preston	1864-1890	Domestic	—	—	36	4	—	—	—	—	—	3	43
Wade, W. R. §	London	1824-1828	Engraving	—	—	1	—	1	—	—	—	—	—	2
Wadham, B. B.	Liverpool	1871-1883	Landscape	—	—	1	—	3	—	—	—	—	1	5
Wadham, H. B.	London	1838-1839	Portraits	—	—	2	—	—	—	—	—	—	—	2
Wadham, Sarah	London	1880-1881	Figures	—	—	—	—	2	—	—	—	—	2	4
Wadmore, T. F.	London	1847-1877	Architecture	—	—	8	—	—	—	—	—	—	—	8
Wadsworth, Mrs.	London	1802	Portraits	—	—	2	—	—	—	—	—	—	—	2
Wadsworth, Mrs.	Nottingham	1875	Landscape	—	—	—	—	1	—	—	—	—	—	1
Waeigen, A.	London	1858	Sculpture	—	—	1	—	—	—	—	—	—	—	1
Wageman, Miss D. E.	—	1860	Churches	—	—	—	—	1	—	—	—	—	—	1
Wageman, M., Junr.	London	1866	Still Life	—	—	—	1	—	—	—	—	—	—	1
Wageman, Michael Angelo	London	1837-1879	Domestic	—	—	23	4	17	—	—	—	—	—	44
Wageman, Thomas Charles ‡	London	1816-1857	Portraits	—	—	56	1	16	—	9	—	—	—	82
Wagg —	—	1783	Still Life	—	1	—	—	—	—	—	—	—	—	1
Waggner —	London	1783	Landscape	—	2	—	—	—	—	—	—	—	—	2
Waghorn, Fred.	London	1880-1888	Architecture	—	—	3	—	1	—	3	—	—	—	7
Wagmüller, M.	Richmond	1870-1874	Sculpture	—	—	16	—	—	—	—	—	—	—	16
Wagner, Anna Sophia	London	1811	Figures	—	—	1	—	—	—	—	—	—	—	1
Wagner, Cecilia	London	1814	Portraits	—	—	1	—	—	—	—	—	—	—	1
Wagner, Edward	London	1862-1870	Landscape	—	—	—	1	1	—	—	—	—	7	9
Wagrez, E.	Paris	1856-1867	Figures	—	—	—	1	—	—	—	—	—	3	4
Wagstaffe, Thomas Rogers. *See* Vigers and Wagstaffe.	—	—	—	—	—	—	—	—	—	—	—	—	—	—
Wagstaffe, S.	Leeds	1876	Landscape	—	—	—	—	1	—	—	—	—	1	2
Wain, Louis	London	1889	Animals	—	—	—	—	1	—	—	—	—	—	1
Wainewright, F. W.	London	1838-1857	Portraits	—	—	—	—	5	—	—	—	—	—	5
Wainewright, John	—	1860-1869	Flowers	—	—	—	4	2	—	—	—	—	—	6
Wainewright, J. F.	London	1855	Sea Shores	—	—	—	1	—	—	—	—	—	—	1
Wainewright, Thomas Francis §	London	1831-1883	Landscape	—	—	26	3	222	—	—	—	—	7	258
Wainewright, Thomas Griffith	London	1821-1825	Cattle	—	—	6	1	—	—	—	—	—	—	7
Wainwright, Mary E.	London	1831-1832	Landscape	—	—	2	—	—	—	—	—	—	—	2
Wainwright, W. F.	London	1835-1850	Miniatures	—	—	9	—	—	—	—	—	—	—	9
Wainwright, William J., A.R.W.S. †	Birmingham	1882-1893	Domestic	—	—	1	—	2	14	—	—	—	—	17
Waite, Charles D.	Addiscombe	1882	Landscape	—	—	—	—	1	—	—	—	—	—	1
Waite, E.	Croydon	1868	Landscape	—	—	—	—	1	—	—	—	—	—	1
Waite, Edward W., R.B.A. §	Blackheath	1878-1893	Landscape	—	—	19	—	31	—	—	—	12	38	100
Waite, Harold	Blackheath	1893	Landscape	—	—	—	—	3	—	—	—	—	—	3
Waite, J.	London	1854-1860	Domestic	—	—	3	1	4	—	—	—	—	—	8
Waite, James Clarke, R.B.A. §	London	1863-1885	Domestic	—	—	26	4	117	—	3	—	—	6	156
Waite, Robert Thorne, R.W.S. † φ	London	1863-1893	Domestic	—	—	15	—	5	315	3	1	7	35	381
Waite, W.	London	1800-1821	Portraits	—	—	4	—	—	—	—	—	—	—	4

Name.	Town.	First and Last Year of Ex.	Speciality.	S. A.	F. S.	R. A.	B. I.	S. S.	O. W.	N. W.	G. G.	N. G.	V. E.	Total.
WAITE, WILLIAM A.	Birmingham	1884-1887	Landscape	—	—	—	—	1	—	6	—	—	—	7
WAKE, LADY	—	1774	Figures	1	—	—	—	—	—	—	—	—	—	1
WAKE, JOSEPH	Manchester	1870	Domestic	—	—	1	—	—	—	—	—	—	—	1
WAKE, JOHN CHELTENHAM	London	1858-1875	Sea Pieces	—	—	—	3	7	—	—	—	—	3	13
WAKE, MISS MARGARET	Crouch Hill	1893	Still Life	—	—	—	—	—	—	—	—	—	1	1
WALBANK, WILLIAM	London	1828-1829	Waterfalls	—	—	—	1	1	—	—	—	—	—	2
WALDECK, JEAN FREDERIC COUNT DE. *See* D.	—	—	—	—	—	—	—	—	—	—	—	—	—	—
WALDEGRAVE, C.	London	1769-1781	Landscape	—	27	3	—	—	—	—	—	—	—	30
WALDEN, E. H.	London	1855-1865	Landscape	—	—	2	—	—	—	—	—	—	1	3
WALDIE, MISS JANE, AFTERWARDS MRS. WATTS	London	1817-1820	Landscape	—	—	1	3	—	—	—	—	—	—	4
WALDO, SAMUEL L.	Brunswick	1808	Portraits	—	—	1	—	—	—	—	—	—	—	1
WALDRE, VINCENT	London	1774	Mythological	—	1	—	—	—	—	—	—	—	—	1
WALDROP, ANTOINE	Netherlands	1846-1849	Sea Pieces	—	—	1	1	—	—	—	—	—	—	2
WALE, CHARLES	London	1780	Landscape	—	6	—	—	—	—	—	—	—	—	6
WALE, SAMUEL, R.A.	London	1760-1778	Historical	14	—	14	—	—	—	—	—	—	—	28
WALENCOURT —	Paris	1827	Picture Gallery	—	—	1	—	—	—	—	—	—	—	1
WALES, H.R.H. PRINCESS OF. H.R.W.S. †	London	1881-1890	—	—	—	—	—	—	*	—	—	—	2	2
WALES, G. R.	London	1835-1836	Architecture	—	—	—	—	2	—	—	—	—	—	2
WALES, JAMES	London	1783-1791	Portraits	3	—	3	—	—	—	—	—	—	—	6
WALFORD, MISS AMY J.	London	1883-1892	Domestic	—	—	—	—	1	—	3	—	—	—	4
WALFORD, E.	London	1859	Landscape	—	—	—	—	1	—	—	—	—	—	1
WALFORD, MISS H. L.	Bushey	1891	Flowers	—	—	—	—	—	—	1	—	—	—	1
WALING, C.	London	1799-1800	Landscape	—	—	3	—	—	—	—	—	—	—	3
WALKER, MISS ALICE	London	1862	Domestic	—	—	1	1	—	—	—	—	—	—	2
WALKER, MISS AMY	London	1885-1893	Landscape	—	—	—	—	5	—	6	—	—	3	14
WALKER, ANTHONY	London	1760-1765	Engraving	6	—	—	—	—	—	—	—	—	—	6
WALKER, A. E.	London	1830	Sculpture	—	—	1	—	—	—	—	—	—	—	1
WALKER, MISS AGNES E.	London	1887-1893	Portraits	—	—	3	—	6	—	—	—	—	1	10
WALKER, ARTHUR GEORGE	London	1884-1893	Sculpture	—	—	10	—	—	—	—	—	—	1	11
WALKER, MISS BREDA	Cheltenham	1871	Figures	—	—	—	—	—	—	—	—	—	1	1
WALKER, B. W.	London	1887	Landscape	—	—	—	—	—	—	1	—	—	—	1
WALKER, MISS CORDELIA	London	1859-1868	Domestic	—	—	1	3	3	—	—	—	—	1	8
WALKER, CHARLES J.	Liverpool	1864	Landscape	—	—	1	—	—	—	—	—	—	—	1
WALKER, EDMUND	London	1836-1849	Flowers	—	—	9	—	—	—	—	—	—	—	9
WALKER, MISS ELIZA	London	1860	Domestic	—	—	—	—	1	—	—	—	—	—	1
WALKER, MISS ELIZABETH	London	1877-1882	Flowers	—	—	3	—	—	—	—	—	—	2	5
WALKER, EDWIN B.	Stockport	1892	Domestic	—	—	1	—	—	—	—	—	—	—	1
WALKER, EDWARD J.	Liverpool	1878-1879	Domestic	—	—	—	—	—	—	—	—	—	3	3
WALKER, FREDERICK, A.R.A. †	London	1863-1875	Landscape	—	—	8	—	—	38	—	—	—	4	50
WALKER, FREDERICK F.	London	1824-1826	Engraving	—	—	—	—	2	—	—	—	—	—	2
WALKER, FRANK H.	London	1878-1893	Landscape	—	—	5	—	6	—	2	—	—	2	15
WALKER, FRANCIS S., R.H.A., A.R.P.E.	London	1868-1893	Domestic	—	—	31	—	5	—	2	1	—	24	63
WALKER, GEORGE	—	1792-1795	Landscape	—	—	4	—	—	—	—	—	—	—	4
WALKER, G.	—	1797-1798	Scriptural	—	—	4	—	—	—	—	—	—	—	4
WALKER, G.	Edinburgh	1800-1815	Landscape	—	—	16	—	—	—	—	—	—	—	16
WALKER, G.	London	1835-1836	Portraits	—	—	3	—	—	—	—	—	—	—	3
WALKER, G.	London	1847	Still Life	—	—	—	1	—	—	—	—	—	—	1
WALKER, G. D. K.	London	1838	Birds	—	—	2	—	—	—	—	—	—	—	2
WALKER, HENRY	Leeds	1876-1879	Architecture	—	—	4	—	—	—	—	—	—	—	4
WALKER, HENRY	Worcester	1886	Landscape	—	—	—	—	—	—	—	—	—	1	1
WALKER, HUGH	London	1867-1875	Figures	—	—	—	—	9	—	—	—	—	—	9
WALKER, J.	London	1796-1800	Architecture	—	—	4	—	—	—	—	—	—	—	4
WALKER, J.	London	1825-1832	Landscape	—	—	6	—	—	—	1	—	—	—	7
WALKER, J.	London	1834-1847	Architecture	—	—	2	—	—	—	1	—	—	—	3
WALKER, JAMES	London	1770-1783	Domestic	4	1	—	—	—	—	—	—	—	—	5
WALKER, JOHN	London	1819	Landscape	—	—	—	1	—	—	—	—	—	—	1
WALKER, JOHN EATON	Birmingham	1855-1866	Domestic	—	—	3	4	4	—	—	—	—	6	17
WALKER, J. G.	London	1824-1826	Engraving	—	—	—	—	13	—	—	—	—	—	13
WALKER, J. G.	London	1830-1842	Sea Pieces	—	—	—	2	10	—	—	—	—	—	12
WALKER, J. H.	London	1846	Landscape	—	—	1	—	—	—	—	—	—	—	1
WALKER, JOHN HANSON	London	1869-1893	Domestic	—	—	61	—	39	—	—	10	—	24	134
WALKER, JOHN RAWSON	Nottingham	1817-1865	Landscape	—	—	15	11	6	—	—	—	—	—	32
WALKER, J. W.	Bolton	1862-1893	Domestic	—	—	16	—	3	—	8	8	8	23	66
WALKER, MISS MARION	London	1854-1877	Miniatures	—	—	7	—	—	—	—	—	—	3	10
WALKER, MRS. MARY	London	1886	Fruit	—	—	—	—	1	—	—	—	—	—	1
WALKER, MISS MAUDE	London	1887-1892	Domestic	—	—	2	—	2	—	—	—	—	2	6
WALKER, MISS MARY A.	London	1892	Landscape	—	—	—	—	1	—	—	—	—	—	1
WALKER, MISS M. C.	Willesden	1892-1893	Domestic	—	—	—	—	3	—	—	—	—	—	3
WALKER, MISS MARCELLA M.	Lee	1872-1893	Figures	—	—	19	—	1	—	—	—	—	—	20
WALKER, MISS PAULINE	Southport	1870-1882	Still Life	—	—	1	—	2	—	—	2	—	24	29
WALKER, PHILIP F.	London	1883-1890	Sea Pieces	—	—	1	—	9	—	—	—	—	—	10
WALKER, R.	London	1793-1812	Architecture	—	—	11	—	—	—	—	—	—	—	11

Name.	Town.	First and Last Year of Ex.	Speciality.	S. A.	F. S.	R. A.	B. I.	S. S.	O. W.	N.W.	G. G.	N. G.	V. E.	Total.
Walker, Robert	Manchester	1861	Illustrations	—	—	1	—	—	—	—	—	—	—	1
Walker, Samuel	London	1850-1852	Figures	—	—	2	1	—	—	—	—	—	—	3
Walker, Seymour	Hartlepool	1887	Sea Pieces	—	—	—	—	3	—	—	—	—	—	3
Walker, T.	London	1864	Landscape	—	—	—	1	—	—	—	—	—	—	1
Walker, Thomas	London	1801-1808	Portraits	—	—	13	3	—	—	—	—	—	—	16
Walker, Thomas Larkins	London	1837-1841	Architecture	—	—	12	—	—	—	—	—	—	—	12
Walker, Mrs. Theresa Snell	—	1841	Sculpture	—	—	2	—	—	—	—	—	—	—	2
Walker, W.	London	1782-1808	Portraits	—	5	22	—	—	—	—	—	—	—	27
Walker, W.	London	1805-1812	Greece	—	—	12	—	—	—	—	—	—	40	52
Walker, William †	London	1813-1849	Landscape	—	—	6	—	—	67	—	—	—	—	73
Walker, William	London	1861-1888	Portraits	—	—	2	—	5	—	—	—	—	1	8
Walker, Miss Wilhelmina Augusta	London	1870-1876	Domestic	—	—	1	—	9	—	—	—	—	2	12
Walker, William Eyre, A.R.W.S. †	Westholme	1875-1893	Landscape	—	—	3	—	1	197	—	—	2	11	214
Walker, William Henry Romaine-	London	1877-1881	Figures	—	—	2	—	2	—	—	—	—	—	4
Walker, William T. Mynors	London	1893	Architecture	—	—	1	—	—	—	—	—	—	—	1
Walker, Y. N.	London	1832	Figures	—	—	2	—	—	—	—	—	—	—	2
Walker, Mrs. William. *See* Miss Elizabeth Reynolds	—	1846-1850	Miniatures	—	—	7	—	—	—	—	—	—	—	7
Walkerson —	—	1783	Shipping	—	1	—	—	—	—	—	—	—	—	1
Wall, Miss Emily W.	London	1890-1891	Domestic	—	—	1	—	2	—	—	—	—	—	3
Wall, John, M.D.	Worcester	1773-1774	Figures	—	—	3	—	—	—	—	—	—	—	3
Wall, J.	Stroud	1868	Sculpture	—	—	3	—	—	—	—	—	—	—	3
Wall, Mrs. S.	—	1823	Flowers	—	—	1	—	—	—	—	—	—	—	1
Wall, William Archibald	London	1857-1872	Landscape	—	—	5	3	3	—	—	—	—	6	17
Wall, W. G.	—	1853	Landscape	—	—	1	—	—	—	—	—	—	—	1
Wallace, Miss Ellen	Carshalton	1838-1843	Figures	—	—	—	—	5	—	—	—	—	—	5
Wallace, Harry	Derby	1886-1891	Domestic	—	—	5	—	—	—	—	—	—	—	5
Wallace, J.	London	1844	Landscape	—	—	2	—	—	—	—	—	—	—	2
Wallace, John	London	1874-1892	Landscape	—	—	1	—	6	—	—	—	—	—	7
Wallace, R.	London	1809-1838	Architecture	—	—	15	—	—	—	—	—	—	—	15
Wallace, Robert Bruce	Manchester	1867-1881	Domestic	—	—	—	—	2	—	—	—	—	11	13
Wallace, W.	Edinburgh	1873	Sculpture	—	—	1	—	—	—	—	—	—	—	1
Wallace, William	London	1880-1892	Architecture	—	—	5	—	—	—	—	—	—	—	5
Wallander, T. W.	London	1869	Domestic	—	—	1	—	—	—	—	—	—	—	1
Wallen, Frederick	London	1867-1869	Architecture	—	—	3	—	—	—	—	—	—	—	3
Wallen, J. *See also* Ferry and Wallen	London	1801-1817	Architecture	—	—	3	—	—	—	—	—	—	—	3
Wallen, William	London	1828-1833	Churches	—	—	8	—	—	—	—	—	—	—	8
Waller, Annie E.	Gloucester	1876-1878	Domestic	—	—	—	—	—	—	—	—	—	3	3
Waller, A. Honeywood	Godalming	1884-1891	Landscape	—	—	3	—	5	—	6	—	—	—	14
Waller, C.	—	1788	Landscape	—	—	2	—	—	—	—	—	—	—	2
Waller, C.	London	1863-1865	Flowers	—	—	—	2	2	—	—	—	—	—	4
Waller, Miss E.	Greenwich	1828-1838	Sporting	—	—	5	—	1	—	—	—	—	—	6
Waller, F. S.	Gloucester	1873-1892	Architecture	—	—	3	—	—	—	—	—	—	—	3
Waller, John Green	London	1835-1853	Domestic	—	—	5	—	1	—	—	—	—	3	9
Waller, Lucy	Bletchley	1891	Flowers	—	—	—	—	1	—	—	—	—	—	1
Waller, Miss M. M.	Greenwich	1830-1832	Fruit, etc.	—	—	—	—	2	—	—	—	—	—	2
Waller, Richard	London	1857-1873	Domestic	—	—	2	—	6	—	—	—	—	1	9
Waller, Samuel Edmund φ	Gloucester	1870-1893	Domestic	—	—	26	—	2	—	—	—	—	23	51
Waller, Mrs. S. E. ‖ *See* Miss Mary L. Fowler	London	1877-1893	Domestic	—	—	20	—	—	—	—	3	—	14	37
Waller, T. J.	Chertsey	1860-1865	Rustic	—	—	—	7	3	—	—	—	—	—	10
Waller, W.	Oxford	1831-1832	London	—	—	2	—	—	—	—	—	—	—	2
Walley, E.	Bruges	1851	Historical	—	—	1	—	—	—	—	—	—	—	1
Wallin, T.	London	1888	—	—	—	—	—	—	—	—	—	—	*	—
Walling, C.	London	1807-1827	Landscape	—	—	7	—	—	—	—	—	—	—	7
Wallington, Miss	—	1773	Flowers	1	—	—	—	—	—	—	—	—	—	1
Wallis. *See* Jameson and Wallis	—	—	Architecture	—	—	—	—	—	—	—	—	—	—	—
Wallis, G.	London	1842	Historical	—	—	1	1	—	—	—	—	—	—	2
Wallis, George	London	1866-1872	Landscape	—	—	1	—	—	—	—	—	—	1	2
Wallis, G. A.	London	1785-1836	Landscape	—	—	16	8	—	—	—	—	—	—	24
Wallis, George Herbert	Chiswick	1885-1888	Landscape	—	—	—	—	—	—	—	3	—	—	3
Wallis, Henry, R.S.W. †	London	1854-1893	Historical	—	—	35	1	5	81	—	—	1	9	132
Wallis, J.	London	1808-1825	Architecture	—	—	6	—	—	—	—	—	—	—	6
Wallis, Joshua	Peckham	1809-1820	Landscape	—	—	7	—	—	—	—	—	—	—	7
Wallis, J.	London	1826-1849	Landscape	—	—	—	2	1	—	—	—	—	30	33
Wallis, Joseph H.	Cardiff	1861-1890	Sporting	—	—	6	—	—	—	—	7	1	12	26
Wallis, J. S. B.	London	1854-1865	Figures	—	—	—	2	2	—	—	—	—	—	4
Wallis, Robert	London	1824-1859	Engraving	—	—	1	—	5	—	—	—	—	—	6
Wallis, Miss Rosa	London	1878-1893	Flowers	—	—	5	—	19	—	18	—	—	10	52
Wallis, Walter	London	1851-1891	Studies	—	—	5	1	7	—	—	—	—	4	17
Wallis, Whitworth, F.S.A.	London	1884	Sea Pieces	—	—	—	—	—	—	—	—	—	1	1
Walls, William	Dunfermline	1887-1893	Animals	—	—	4	—	—	—	—	—	—	—	4
Walmisley, Frederick	London	1838-1872	Figures	—	—	21	18	17	—	—	—	—	—	56

Name.	Town.	First and Last Year of Ex.	Speciality.	S. A.	F. S.	R. A.	B. I.	S. S.	O. W.	N. W.	G. G.	N. G.	V. F.	Total.
Walmsley, Thomas	London	1750-1796	Landscape	1	—	18	—	—	—	—	—	—	—	19
Walpole, Mary	Hampton Court	1885	Landscape	—	—	—	—	—	—	1	—	—	—	1
Walpole, Miss	—	1782	Portraits	—	—	1	—	—	—	—	—	—	—	1
Walrond, Sir John W., Bart.	London	1879-1888	Landscape	—	—	1	—	—	—	4	—	—	—	5
Walsh, J.	London	1832-1851	Historical	—	—	6	—	—	—	—	—	—	—	6
Walsh, J. B.	London	1838-1841	Historical	—	—	4	—	1	—	—	—	—	—	5
Walsh, J. W.	London	1865	Figures	—	—	—	1	—	—	—	—	—	—	1
Walsh, N.	London	1872-1877	Venice	—	—	1	—	1	—	—	—	—	4	6
Walsh, Tudor E. G.	London	1885	Landscape	—	—	—	—	1	—	—	—	—	1	2
Walsh, William	London	1823-1834	Landscape	—	—	4	14	13	—	—	—	—	—	31
Walter, A.	London	1842	Sea Pieces	—	—	—	1	—	—	—	—	—	—	1
Walter, Mrs. Arthur	—	1885	Landscape	—	—	—	—	—	—	—	1	—	—	1
Walter, Mrs. Busse	Putney	1885	Portraits	—	—	—	—	1	—	—	—	—	—	1
Walter, Edward	Manchester	1848	Architecture	—	—	2	—	—	—	—	—	—	—	2
Walter, Miss Emma ‖	London	1855-1891	Flowers, etc.	—	—	7	—	65	—	7	—	—	31	110
Walter, Henry	London	1820-1846	Sporting	—	—	6	6	2	—	3	—	—	—	17
Walter, J.	Bristol	1834-1849	Sea Pieces	—	—	2	—	7	—	—	—	—	—	9
Walter, John William	London	1879	Architecture	—	—	1	—	—	—	—	—	—	—	1
Walter, Louis	London	1853-1869	Landscape	—	—	7	20	22	—	—	—	—	12	61
Walter, M. Alice	Sittingbourne	1880-1882	Flowers	—	—	—	—	—	—	—	—	—	4	4
Walter, T.	London	1849	Cattle	—	—	—	—	2	—	—	—	—	—	2
Walter, W. C.	London	1804	Portraits	—	—	1	—	—	—	—	—	—	—	1
Walters, Miss Amelia J.	London	1880-1892	Sculpture	—	—	6	—	1	—	—	—	—	3	10
Walters, Edward	London	1826-1831	Architecture	—	—	4	—	—	—	—	—	—	—	4
Walters, Frederick Arthur	London	1890-1892	Architecture	—	—	3	—	—	—	—	—	—	—	3
Walters, George Stanfield, R.B.A. §	Liverpool	1860-1893	Sea Pieces	—	—	31	5	340	—	29	2	—	67	474
Walters, L.	London	1881	Figures	—	—	—	—	—	—	—	—	—	1	1
Walters, Miss Maude	London	1889	Figures	—	—	—	—	—	—	—	1	—	—	1
Walters, Samuel	Liverpool	1834-1880	Sea Pieces	—	—	14	3	39	—	—	—	—	7	63
Walters, Thomas	London	1856-1865	Domestic	—	—	2	5	6	—	—	—	—	—	13
Walters, Mrs.	Croydon	1893	Landscape	—	—	—	—	—	—	1	—	—	—	1
Waltner, Charles Albert	London	1875-1891	Etching	—	—	11	—	—	—	—	—	—	7	18
Walton, Miss Constance, R.S.W.	Glasgow	1886-1887	Flowers	—	—	2	—	—	—	—	—	—	—	2
Walton, Miss D. S.	Dorking	1890-1892	Flowers	—	—	—	—	—	—	6	—	—	—	6
Walton, Elijah, F.G.S.	Birmingham	1851-1866	Landscape	—	—	8	10	4	—	—	—	—	13	35
Walton, E. A., A.R.S.A., R.S.W.	Glasgow	1883-1893	Landscape	—	—	7	—	—	—	—	1	—	2	10
Walton, Frank, R.I., V.P.I.O. ‡ φ	Harrow	1862-1893	Landscape	—	—	75	2	9	—	82	11	10	182	371
Walton, George	London	1882-1888	Portraits	—	—	11	—	1	—	—	—	—	1	13
Walton, Henry, F.S.A.	London	1771-1779	Portraits	9	—	4	—	—	—	—	—	—	—	13
Walton, J.	London	1821-1829	Landscape	—	—	3	—	—	—	—	—	—	—	3
Walton, Joseph	York	1855-1872	Landscape	—	—	2	15	36	—	—	—	—	22	75
Walton, James Trout	York	1851-1867	Landscape	—	—	10	14	24	—	—	—	—	26	74
Walton, John Whitehead	London	1834-1865	Historical	—	—	18	2	3	—	—	—	—	—	23
Walton, Miss Mary Ann. *See* Mrs. T. H.	—	—	—	—	—	—	—	—	—	—	—	—	—	—
Fielding	Manchester	1815-1819	Flowers	—	—	—	—	—	14	—	—	—	—	14
Walton, W.	Leicester	1814	Portraits	—	—	2	—	—	—	—	—	—	—	2
Walton, William	Bath	1861-1866	Landscape	—	—	1	—	3	—	—	—	—	2	6
Walton, W. L.	London	1834-1855	Landscape	—	—	1	—	3	—	1	—	—	—	5
Walton, W. S.	London	1853	Landscape	—	—	—	1	—	—	—	—	—	—	1
Walton, Mrs.	—	1789	Miniatures	—	—	1	—	—	—	—	—	—	—	1
Walton, Miss	London	1812	Flowers	—	—	—	2	—	—	—	—	—	—	2
Walton and Robson	Durham	1860-1862	Architecture	—	—	2	—	—	—	—	—	—	—	2
Walton, De. *See* D.	—	—	—	—	—	—	—	—	—	—	—	—	—	—
Wandby, A. J.	London	1842-1848	Domestic	—	—	—	—	6	—	—	—	—	—	6
Wane, Richard	Conway	1884-1893	Landscape	—	—	13	—	8	—	3	5	—	9	38
Wane, Mrs.	London	1779	Needlework	—	2	—	—	—	—	—	—	—	—	2
Wantage, Lady. *See* Hon. Mrs. Lloyd Lindsay	—	—	—	—	—	—	—	—	—	—	—	—	—	—
Wanter —	London	1783	Mythological	—	1	—	—	—	—	—	—	—	—	1
Wappers, Egide Charles Gustave, Baron	London	1831	Historical	—	—	—	2	—	—	—	—	—	—	2
War, De. *See* D.	—	—	—	—	—	—	—	—	—	—	—	—	—	—
Warburg, Miss Blanche	London	1890-1892	Still Life	—	—	—	—	2	—	—	—	—	—	2
Warburton, F.	London	1795-1802	Sea Pieces	—	—	8	—	—	—	—	—	—	—	8
Ward, Alfred	London	1873-1893	Figures	—	—	28	—	4	—	—	9	—	27	68
Ward, Miss Annie	Croydon	1886-1889	Domestic	—	—	3	—	—	—	—	—	—	—	3
Ward, Bernard Evans	London	1879-1893	Figures	—	—	7	—	6	—	—	—	—	2	15
Ward, C.	London	1820-1822	Architecture	—	—	3	—	—	—	—	—	—	—	3
Ward, Charles	London	1826-1869	Landscape	—	—	58	2	23	—	15	—	—	8	106
Ward, Cyril	Manchester	1890-1893	Landscape	—	—	1	—	6	—	—	—	—	—	7
Ward, Edwin Arthur	London	1883-1892	Portraits	—	—	8	—	10	—	—	12	20	19	69
Ward, Edgar M.	London	1878	Landscape	—	—	—	—	—	—	—	—	—	2	2
Ward, Edward Matthew, R.A. ‡	London	1834-1878	Historical	—	—	86	16	11	—	4	—	—	4	121
Ward, Mrs. E.M., ‖ formerly Miss Henrietta Ward	London	1849-1893	Historical	—	—	40	—	—	—	—	—	—	4	44

Name.	Town.	First and Last Year of Ex.	Speciality.	. A.	F. S.	R A.	B. I.	S. S.	.W.	N. W.	G. G.	N. G.	V. E.	Total.
Ward, Miss Eva M.	London	1873-1880	Domestic	—	—	6	—	—	—	—	—	—	—	6
Ward, Miss Flora	London	1872-1876	Domestic	—	—	3	—	—	—	—	—	—	3	6
Ward, F. E.	Belfast	1893	Architecture	—	—	1	—	—	—	—	—	—	—	1
Ward, Frederick Jabez	London	1874	Architecture	—	—	1	—	—	—	—	—	—	—	1
Ward, Captain Francis Swain, F.S.A.	London	1765-1773	Indian Views	21	—	—	—	—	—	—	—	—	—	21
Ward, G.	London	1824	Architecture	—	—	1	—	1	—	—	—	—	—	2
Ward, George Raphael	London	1821-1864	Portraits and Engraving	—	—	40	—	11	—	1	—	—	—	52
Ward, Mrs. George Raphael	London	1829-1849	Miniatures	—	—	31	—	15	—	2	—	—	—	48
Ward, George W.	Harlesden	1884-1887	Architecture	—	—	4	—	—	—	—	—	—	—	4
Ward, H.	Hanley	1851	Architecture	—	—	1	—	—	—	—	—	—	—	1
Ward, Henry	London	1834	Landscape	—	—	—	—	1	—	—	—	—	—	1
Ward, James, R.A.	London	1790-1855	Animals	2	—	298	91	9	—	—	—	—	—	400
Ward, James	London	1817-1862	Portraits and Sea Pieces	—	—	16	—	28	1	—	—	—	—	45
Ward, James	Barnes	1888-1893	Architecture	—	—	4	—	—	—	—	—	—	—	4
Ward, John	London	1808-1847	Sea Pieces	—	—	50	95	31	—	6	—	—	—	182
Ward, James Charles §	London	1830-1875	Landscape	—	—	1	13	178	—	—	—	—	—	192
Ward, Leslie	London	1868-1893	Portraits	—	—	11	—	—	—	—	3	—	21	35
Ward, Mrs. Katharine M.	London	1893	Flowers	—	—	1	—	—	—	—	—	—	—	1
Ward, Martin Theodore	London	1819-1858	Sporting	—	—	16	18	5	—	—	—	—	—	39
Ward, Orlando	London	1890	Landscape	—	—	—	—	—	—	—	—	1	—	1
Ward, R.	London	1877-1887	Sculpture	—	—	—	—	3	—	—	—	—	—	3
Ward, T.	London	1819-1840	Figures	—	—	9	—	—	—	—	—	—	—	9
Ward, Thomas	London	1884	Landscape	—	—	1	—	—	—	—	—	—	—	1
Ward, Thomas C.	London	1827-1834	Fruit	—	—	—	2	5	—	—	—	—	—	7
Ward, T. L.	Twickenham	1872	Domestic	—	—	—	—	—	—	—	—	—	1	1
Ward, William, A.R.A.	London	1785-1826	Engraving	—	—	30	—	—	—	—	—	—	—	30
Ward, William	London	1853-1860	Architecture	—	—	3	—	—	—	—	—	—	—	3
Ward, William	London	1860-1876	Landscape	—	—	16	—	5	—	—	—	—	15	36
Ward, Mrs. W. *See* Miss Maria Morland.	—	—		—	—	—	—	—	—	—	—	—	—	—
Ward, William H.	Birmingham	1850-1872	Fruit	—	—	2	14	25	—	—	—	—	—	41
Ward, William James	London	1824-1831	Engraving	—	—	—	—	19	—	—	—	—	—	19
Ward and Hughes	London	1885-1892	Stained Glass	—	—	18	—	—	—	—	—	—	—	18
Wardell, H. S.	London	1851-1852	Sculpture	—	—	2	—	—	—	—	—	—	—	2
Warden, Miss Dorothy	London	1888	Landscape	—	—	—	—	1	—	—	—	—	—	1
Wardle, Arthur	London	1880-1893	Cattle	—	—	21	—	29	—	20	—	—	27	97
Wardle, F.	London	1882-1888	Landscape	—	—	—	—	2	—	—	—	—	2	4
Wardlow, Miss Annie	Acton	1887-1892	Miniatures	—	—	5	—	—	—	2	—	—	—	7
Wardlow, Alexander Hamilton	London	1870-1893	Miniatures	—	—	12	—	5	—	3	—	—	—	20
Wardlow, Miss Eleanor Frances	London	1893	Miniatures	—	—	—	—	—	—	1	—	—	—	1
Wardlow, Miss Mary Alexandra	Acton	1885-1892	Miniatures	—	—	7	—	2	—	3	—	—	—	12
Wardman, Thomas	Potter's Bar	1886	Landscape	—	—	—	—	—	—	—	—	—	1	1
Ware, Charles E. *See* Stokes and Ware	—	—	Architecture	—	—	—	—	—	—	—	—	—	—	—
Ware (C. E.) and Stokes (Leonard)	London	1881	Architecture	—	—	3	—	—	—	—	—	—	—	3
Ware, J. P.	Southampton	1827	Architecture	—	—	—	—	1	—	—	—	—	—	1
Ware, Samuel	London	1799-1814	Architecture	—	—	9	—	—	—	—	—	—	—	9
Ware, Miss	—	1773	Flowers	—	1	—	—	—	—	—	—	—	—	1
Waring, Charles H.	Neath	1869-1872	Sea Pieces	—	—	—	—	3	—	—	—	—	3	6
Waring, F.	London	1826	Architecture	—	—	1	—	—	—	—	—	—	—	1
Waring, J.	London	1836-1837	Landscape	—	—	—	—	3	—	—	—	—	—	3
Waring, John Burley	London	1846-1859	Architecture	—	—	5	—	—	—	—	—	—	—	5
Waring (S. J.) and Sons	Liverpool	1889	Architecture	—	—	1	—	—	—	—	—	—	—	1
Warman, W.	London	1826	Portraits	—	—	1	—	—	—	—	—	—	—	1
Warne-Browne, A. J. *See* B.	—	—	—	—	—	—	—	—	—	—	—	—	—	—
Warner —	London	1775-1788	Miniatures	2	1	1	—	—	—	—	—	—	—	4
Warner, Mrs. A.	Milford	1876	Flowers	—	—	—	—	—	—	—	—	—	1	1
Warner, Miss A.	Hoddesdon	1874	Figures	—	—	—	—	1	—	—	—	—	—	1
Warner, Compton	Woodford	1865-1880	Landscape	—	—	—	—	3	—	—	—	—	7	10
Warner, G. E.	London	1843-1847	Intaglios	—	—	3	—	—	—	—	—	—	—	3
Warner, J.	—	1829	Gems	—	—	—	—	1	—	—	—	—	—	1
Warner, L.	Aldershot	1878	Flowers	—	—	—	—	—	—	—	—	—	1	1
Warner, Thomas	London	1790-1828	Intaglios	—	—	19	—	—	—	—	—	—	—	19
Warner, W.	London	1822-1846	Cameos	—	—	24	—	4	—	—	—	—	—	28
Warre, Miss M.	Wellington	1868	Portraits	—	—	1	—	—	—	—	—	—	—	1
Warren, Albert	London	1887	Flowers	—	—	—	—	—	—	1	—	—	—	1
Warren, Albert Henry	London	1860-1870	Rustic	—	—	1	—	4	—	—	—	—	—	5
Warren, B.	—	1883	Cloisters	—	—	—	—	—	—	—	1	—	—	1
Warren, B. Edward	London	1860-1872	Landscape	—	—	2	—	20	—	—	—	—	—	22
Warren, Charles	London	1833-1835	Landscape	—	—	1	—	2	—	2	—	—	—	5
Warren, Claude	London	1887	Landscape	—	—	1	—	—	—	—	—	—	—	1
Warren, C. Knighton, R.C.A.	London	1876-1892	Figures	—	—	20	—	15	—	—	—	—	2	37
Warren, Mrs. C. Knighton (Gertrude M.)	London	1881-1892	Domestic	—	—	9	—	1	—	—	—	—	—	10
Warren, Edmund George, R.I. ‡ φ	London	1852-1893	Landscape	—	—	1	—	—	—	197	2	—	19	219

Name.	Town.	First and Last Year of Ex.	Speciality.	S. A.	F. S.	R. A.	B. I.	S. S.	O. W.	N. W.	G. G.	N. G.	V. E.	Total.
Warren, Edward Prioleau	London	1888-1893	Architecture	—	—	2	—	—	—	—	—	—	—	2
Warren, Frances Bramley (Mrs. Burroughs)	London	1889	Domestic	—	—	1	—	—	—	—	—	—	—	1
Warren, Miss Fanny C.	Isleworth	1865-1866	Landscape	—	—	—	—	3	—	—	—	—	—	3
Warren, G.	London	1814	Cattle	—	—	1	—	—	—	—	—	—	—	1
Warren, Henry, K.L., P.N.W.S. ‡	London	1823-1872	Domestic	—	—	7	3	9	—	244	—	—	—	263
Warren, H. Broadhurst	Boston, U.S.A.	1887	Landscape	—	—	1	—	—	—	—	—	—	—	1
Warren, H. Clifford	London	1860-1885	Landscape	—	—	—	—	17	—	1	—	—	5	23
Warren, J.	Bath	1777	Portraits	—	—	1	—	—	—	—	—	—	—	1
Warren, R. W.	London	1827-1830	Figures	—	—	3	1	—	—	—	—	—	—	4
Warren, Slatter	London	1866-1868	Landscape	—	—	—	—	4	—	—	—	—	—	4
Warren, Miss Sarah M.	Basingstoke	1889	Interiors	—	—	1	—	—	—	—	—	—	—	1
Warren, Miss Sophy S. ‖	London	1865-1878	Landscape	—	—	6	—	38	—	—	—	—	6	50
Warren, W.	London	1796-1813	Still Life	—	—	1	1	—	—	—	—	—	—	2
Warren, William W.	London	1865-1888	Landscape	—	—	—	7	—	—	3	—	—	—	10
Warrener, William T.	Lincoln	1887-1892	Domestic	—	—	6	—	1	—	—	—	—	—	7
Warrington, Thomas	London	1829-1831	Figures	—	—	2	4	1	—	—	—	—	—	7
Warrington, W.	London	1844	Windows	—	—	2	—	—	—	—	—	—	—	2
Warry, Daniel Robert	London	1855	Architecture	—	—	1	—	—	—	—	—	—	—	1
Wart, Van. *See* V.	—	—	—	—	—	—	—	—	—	—	—	—	—	—
Warton —	London	1809	Architecture	—	—	1	—	—	—	—	—	—	—	1
Warville, F. Brissot de. *See* D.	—	—	—	—	—	—	—	—	—	—	—	—	—	—
Warwick, Anne, Countess of	London	1870-1877	Portraits	—	—	1	—	—	—	—	2	—	—	3
Warwick, Miss Edith C.	London	1868	Flowers	—	—	—	—	1	—	—	—	—	—	1
Warwick, H.	London	1854	Buildings	—	—	1	—	—	—	—	—	—	—	1
Warwick, J.	London	1808-1823	Gems	—	—	4	—	—	—	—	—	—	—	4
Warwick, J.	London	1852-1859	Architecture	—	—	5	—	—	—	—	—	—	—	5
Warwick, R. W.	London	1876-1877	Fruit	—	—	—	—	2	—	—	—	—	—	2
Warwick, Mrs.	—	1823	Portraits	—	—	1	—	—	—	—	—	—	—	1
Wasse, Arthur	Manchester	1879-1893	Domestic	—	—	12	—	1	—	—	—	—	—	13
Wassermann, J. C.	London	1880-1882	Landscape	—	—	2	—	1	—	—	—	—	1	4
Wassie, Arthur	Manchester	1881	Domestic	—	—	—	—	—	—	—	—	—	1	1
Wate, William	London	1815-1832	Landscape	—	—	24	31	14	—	2	—	—	—	71
Waterfield, Miss Margaret	Canterbury	1889-1893	Landscape	—	—	—	—	2	—	1	—	—	—	3
Waterford, Louisa, Marchioness of, formerly	—	—	—	—	—	—	—	—	—	—	—	—	—	—
Hon. Miss Stuart ‖	Ford	1877-1882	Figures	—	—	—	—	—	—	—	17	—	1	18
Waterhouse, Alfred, R.A.	Manchester	1857-1893	Architecture	—	—	64	—	—	—	—	—	—	—	64
Waterhouse, Esther	London	1884	Flowers	—	—	—	—	1	—	—	—	—	—	1
Waterhouse, John William, A.R.A., R.I. ‡	London	1872-1893	Figures	—	—	27	—	12	—	2	2	3	28	74
Waterhouse, Mrs. J. W. (Esther)	London	1884-1890	Flowers	—	—	6	—	—	—	6	—	1	—	13
Waterhouse, M.	Manchester	1861	Architecture	—	—	1	—	—	—	—	—	—	—	1
Waterhouse, Paul, M.A.	London	1891	Architecture	—	—	1	—	—	—	—	—	—	—	1
Waterhouse, W.	London	1840-1861	Domestic	—	—	6	7	13	—	—	—	—	—	26
Waterlow, Ernest Albert, A.R.A., A.R.W.S. † φ	London	1871-1893	Landscape	—	—	45	—	11	99	—	14	4	82	255
Waterman, J.	London	1827-1829	Architecture	—	—	3	—	—	—	—	—	—	—	3
Waters, Edward	London	1775-1797	Buildings	—	—	9	—	—	—	—	—	—	—	9
Waters, Miss P.	London	1799-1816	Flowers	—	—	9	—	—	—	—	—	—	—	9
Waters, R.	Newcastle	1785	Ruins	—	—	1	—	—	—	—	—	—	—	1
Waters, R., Junr.	Newcastle	1784-1785	Landscape	—	—	8	—	—	—	—	—	—	—	8
Waters, W.	London	1792-1800	Miniatures	—	—	14	—	—	—	—	—	—	—	14
Waters, W.	—	1811	Flowers	—	—	1	—	—	—	—	—	—	—	1
Waters, W. R.	Dover	1838-1867	Domestic	—	—	8	11	6	—	—	—	—	—	25
Wathen —	—	1783	Landscape	—	1	—	—	—	—	—	—	—	—	1
Wathen, G. H.	London	1845	Sea Pieces	—	—	1	—	—	—	—	—	—	—	1
Watkeys, W.	London	1822-1823	Landscape	—	—	2	—	—	—	—	—	—	—	2
Watkins, B. Colles, R.H.A.	Dublin	1857-1875	Landscape	—	—	3	1	3	—	—	—	—	7	14
Watkins, Frank	Feltham	1875-1876	Domestic	—	—	2	—	1	—	—	—	—	—	3
Watkins, J.	—	1806	Figures	—	—	1	—	—	—	—	—	—	—	1
Watkins, John	London	1855	Landscape	—	—	—	1	—	—	—	—	—	—	1
Watkins, John, R.P.E.	London	1876-1893	Etching	—	—	6	—	3	—	—	—	—	2	11
Watkins, John	London	1876-1893	Figures	—	—	5	—	16	—	11	2	—	5	39
Watkins, Joseph, R.H.A.	Dublin	1867-1871	Sculpture	—	—	3	—	1	—	—	—	—	—	4
Watkins, Mrs. W. (Kate)	Durham	1850-1888	Interiors	—	—	3	—	—	—	—	2	—	—	5
Watkins, W. H.	London	1843-1849	Miniatures	—	—	16	—	—	—	—	—	—	—	16
Watkins, William Wynne	London	1854-1861	Domestic	—	—	1	5	5	—	—	—	—	—	11
Watlington, Miss	London	1774	Portraits	—	3	—	—	—	—	—	—	—	—	3
Watson, Annie Gordon	Ryde	1888	Flowers	—	—	—	—	1	—	—	—	—	—	1
Watson, Albemarle P.	Kingsbridge	1884	Coast Scenes	—	—	—	—	1	—	—	—	—	—	1
Watson, Miss Caroline	London	1829-1843	Figures	—	—	6	—	9	—	3	—	—	—	18
Watson, Charles J., R.P.E.	Norwich	1872-1893	Sea Pieces	—	—	53	—	26	—	13	3	1	30	126
Watson, Dawson, A.R.C.A.	Llanwrst	1883-1891	Landscape	—	—	—	—	4	—	—	—	—	1	5
Watson, Edward Façon	London	1839-1870	Landscape, etc.	—	—	4	—	8	—	—	—	—	—	12
Watson, F.	Bristol	1857	Domestic	—	—	1	—	—	—	—	—	—	—	1

Name.	Town.	First and Last Year of Ex.	Speciality.	S. A.	F. S.	R. A.	B. I.	S. S.	O. W.	N.W.	G. G.	N. G.	V. E.	Total.
Watson, F. G.	Witley	1882	Fruit	—	—	—	—	2	—	—	—	—	—	2
Watson, George, P.R.S.A.	Edinburgh	1808-1828	Domestic	—	—	21	24	—	—	—	—	—	—	45
Watson, Miss Grace I.	London	1892-1893	Domestic	—	—	1	—	1	—	—	—	—	2	4
Watson, George S.	London	1891-1893	Portraits	—	—	6	—	—	—	—	—	—	1	7
Watson, Harry	London	1893	Landscape	—	—	—	—	3	—	—	—	—	—	3
Watson, Homer, R.C.A.	Pittenweem	1888-1890	Landscape	—	—	1	—	2	—	—	2	—	1	6
Watson, J.	Kilmarnock	1890	—	—	—	*	—	—	—	—	—	—	—	—
Watson, James, F.S.A.	London	1762-1775	Engraving	14	—	—	—	—	—	—	—	—	—	14
Watson, John. *See* Sir J. Watson Gordon	Edinburgh	1814-1825	Historical	—	—	3	3	—	—	—	—	—	—	6
Watson, John	London	1847-1852	Portraits	—	—	3	—	7	—	—	—	—	—	10
Watson, Miss J.	Tottenham	1863	Figures	—	—	1	—	—	—	—	—	—	—	1
Watson, John Burges	Kingston	1819-1838	Architecture	—	—	12	—	—	—	—	—	—	—	12
Watson, John Dawson, R.W.S. § †	Manchester	1853-1893	Domestic	—	—	41	2	26	267	—	3	—	33	372
Watson, J. Tom	Tynemouth	1872	Domestic	—	—	—	—	3	—	—	—	—	—	3
Watson, Mrs. Leila	Croydon	1874	Pen and Ink	—	—	—	—	—	—	—	—	—	1	1
Watson, Musgrave Lewthwaite	London	1829-1847	Sculpture	—	—	19	—	2	—	—	—	—	—	21
Watson, R. *See* Dunn and Watson *and* Maclaren, Dunn, and Watson	—	—	Architecture	—	—	—	—	—	—	—	—	—	—	—
Watson, Robert	London	1778	Domestic	—	—	6	—	—	—	—	—	—	—	6
Watson, Robert F.	London	1845-1866	Sea Pieces	—	—	14	11	10	—	—	—	—	5	40
Watson, Miss Rosalie M. ‖	London	1877-1887	Domestic	—	—	8	—	4	—	6	8	—	17	43
Watson, S.	London	1776-1795	Landscape	—	11	3	—	—	—	—	—	—	—	14
Watson, Stewart	London	1843-1847	Figures	—	—	4	1	2	—	—	—	—	—	7
Watson, Miss S. J.	Reading	1879	Etching	—	—	—	—	—	—	—	—	—	1	1
Watson, Thomas	London	1769-1776	Engraving	11	—	1	—	—	—	—	—	—	—	12
Watson, T.	Edinburgh	1819	Figures	—	—	—	—	—	2	—	—	—	—	2
Watson, T.	London	1811	Architecture	—	—	1	—	—	—	—	—	—	—	1
Watson, Thomas Henry	London	1862-1891	Architecture	—	—	18	—	—	—	—	—	—	—	18
Watson, Thomas J., A.R.W.S. § †	Tynemouth	1869-1893	Landscape	—	—	21	—	23	122	—	—	—	36	202
Watson, Thomas L.	Glasgow	1890-1893	Architecture	—	—	4	—	—	—	—	—	—	—	4
Watson, William	London	1828-1866	Portraits	—	—	43	—	3	—	—	—	—	—	46
Watson, W., Junr.	Liverpool	1866-1872	Cattle	—	—	1	—	1	—	—	—	—	—	2
Watson, William Peter, R.B.A. §	London	1883-1893	Domestic	—	—	9	—	13	—	—	—	—	8	30
Watson, Mrs. William Peter (Lizzie May)	London	1884-1893	Domestic	—	—	3	—	7	—	—	—	—	—	10
Watson, William Smellie, R.S.A.	London	1816-1823	Domestic	—	—	5	17	—	—	—	—	—	—	22
Watson, Mrs.	—	1771	Fruit	—	4	—	—	—	—	—	—	—	—	4
Watson, Mrs.	Witley	1881	Flowers	—	—	—	—	2	—	—	—	—	—	2
Watson, Miss	London	1844	Figures	—	—	1	—	—	—	—	—	—	—	1
Watt, H.	London	1861-1863	Sculpture	—	—	1	—	1	—	—	—	—	—	2
Watt, James C.	London	1893	Buildings	—	—	1	—	—	—	—	—	—	—	1
Watt, James Henry	Norwood	1856-1859	Engraving	—	—	3	—	—	—	—	—	—	—	3
Watt, Leonard	London	1893	Domestic	—	—	2	—	—	—	—	—	—	—	2
Watt, Miss Linnie ‖	Dulwich	1875-1891	Domestic	—	—	9	—	33	—	2	—	—	31	75
Watt, W. H.	London	1854-1857	Domestic	—	—	2	1	—	—	—	—	—	3	6
Watté, R. A.	London	1797-1816	Domestic	—	—	37	—	—	—	—	—	—	—	37
Watton —	—	1783	Cattle	—	2	—	—	—	—	—	—	—	—	2
Watts —	London	1775	Landscape	3	—	—	—	—	—	—	—	—	—	3
Watts, Alice J.	London	1889	Landscape	—	—	—	—	1	—	—	—	—	—	1
Watts, Frederick W.	London	1821-1862	Landscape	—	—	76	108	65	—	8	—	—	1	258
Watts, G.	London	1798	Architecture	—	—	1	—	—	—	—	—	—	—	1
Watts, George Frederick, R.A., D.C.L., H.R.C.A. *See* F. W. George	London	1837-1893	Historical	—	—	126	6	3	—	—	84	20	29	268
Watts, Henry	London	1831-1832	Landscape	—	—	1	—	1	—	1	—	—	—	3
Watts, H.	London	1860	Sculpture	—	—	1	—	—	—	—	—	—	—	1
Watts, H. H.	Oxford	1818-1841	Figures	—	—	5	8	15	—	—	—	—	—	28
Watts, J.	London	1794-1796	Enamels	—	—	2	—	—	—	—	—	—	—	2
Watts, John	London	1766-1776	Engraving	3	—	—	—	—	—	—	—	—	—	3
Watts, James T., R.C.A.	Birmingham	1873-1893	Landscape	—	—	25	—	4	—	17	2	—	5	53
Watts, Mrs. J. T., ‖ late Miss Louisa M. Hughes	Liverpool	1884-1892	Landscape	—	—	5	—	1	—	11	—	—	2	19
Watts, Leonard T., R.B.A. §	London	1892-1893	Domestic	—	—	—	—	5	—	—	—	—	3	8
Watts, S.	—	1780-1783	Landscape	—	—	5	—	—	—	—	—	—	—	5
Watts, T. E.	London	1816-1818	Landscape	—	—	3	—	—	—	—	—	—	—	3
Watts, W.	Manchester	1801-1817	Landscape	—	—	3	—	—	—	—	—	—	—	3
Watts, William	London	1821-1825	Figures	—	—	3	3	—	—	—	—	—	—	6
Watts, Walter Henry	London	1803-1830	Miniatures	—	—	67	9	—	6	—	—	—	11	93
Watts, Mrs. *See* Miss Jane Waldie.	—	—	—	—	—	—	—	—	—	—	—	—	—	—
Waudby, A. J.	London	1844-1847	Domestic	—	—	3	—	—	—	—	—	—	—	3
Waugh, Miss Elizabeth J.	Winchester	1879-1885	Miniatures	—	—	1	—	1	—	—	—	—	—	2
Waugh, Miss Nora	London	1884-1887	Flowers	—	—	—	—	2	—	1	—	—	3	6
Waugh, S. B.	Philadelphia	1841-1842	Scriptural	—	—	2	1	—	—	—	—	—	—	3
Wauters, Émile	Brussels	1884-1892	Figures	—	—	7	—	—	—	—	—	—	—	7

Name.	Town.	First and Last Year of Ex.	Speciality.	S. A.	F. S.	R. A.	B. I.	S. S.	O. W.	N.W.	G. G.	N. G.	V. E.	Total.
WAUTHIER, JOHN M.	London	1803-1823	Landscape	—	—	9	2	—	—	—	—	—	—	11
WAVERS, G.	London	1858	—	—	—	—	—	—	—	—	—	—	*	—
WAY, C.	Torquay	1861	Moonlight	—	—	—	—	1	—	—	—	—	—	1
WAY, C. JONES, R.C.A.	London	1865-1888	Landscape	—	—	5	—	11	—	2	—	—	27	45
WAY, MISS FANNY	London	1893	Miniatures	—	—	3	—	—	—	—	—	—	—	3
WAY, J.	London	1855	Landscape	—	—	1	—	—	—	—	—	—	—	1
WAY, MRS. JOHN L. (EMILY C.)	London	1886-1893	Portraits	—	—	7	—	—	—	—	—	—	—	7
WAY, THOMAS	London	1872	Lithographs	—	—	—	—	—	—	—	—	—	1	1
WAY, THOMAS R.	London	1883-1893	Landscape	—	—	6	—	8	—	13	—	—	12	39
WAY, W. COSENS	Newcastle	1867-1886	Landscape	—	—	5	—	9	—	5	2	—	5	26
WAYLEN, JAMES	London	1834-1838	Historical	—	—	3	—	—	—	—	—	—	—	3
WAYNE, R. S.	Llanbedr	1879-1882	Landscape	—	—	—	—	7	—	—	—	—	—	7
WEALL, SYDNEY F.	Pinner	1876-1877	Landscape	—	—	—	—	—	—	—	—	—	2	2
WEARNE, H.	London	1851-1856	Figures	—	—	—	3	—	—	—	—	—	—	3
WEATHERBY, J.	Newmarket	1823-1824	Still Life	—	—	2	1	—	—	—	—	—	—	3
WEATHERHEAD, G.	London	1839	Intaglios	—	—	1	—	—	—	—	—	—	—	1
WEATHERHEAD, WILLIAM HARRIS, R.I. ‡	London	1862-1893	Domestic	—	—	21	18	154	—	52	—	—	15	260
WEATHERHILL, GEORGE	Whitby	1868-1873	Sea Pieces	—	—	—	—	3	—	—	—	—	3	6
WEATHERHILL, MISS MARY	Whitby	1858-1880	Sea Pieces	—	—	—	—	3	—	—	—	—	3	6
WEATHERHILL, MISS SARAH ELLEN	Whitby	1858-1868	Domestic	—	—	—	—	3	—	—	—	—	1	4
WEATHERLEY, WILLIAM SAMUEL	London	1877-1890	Architecture	—	—	6	—	—	—	—	—	—	—	6
WEATHERLEY (W. S.) AND JONES (F. E.)	London	1880-1886	Architecture	—	—	4	—	—	—	—	—	—	—	4
WEATHERSTONE, ALFRED	London	1888-1893	Figures	—	—	3	—	—	—	—	—	—	—	3
WEAVER, J.	London	1801-1809	Sporting	—	—	4	—	—	—	—	—	—	—	4
WEAVER, MISS L.	London	1860	Cattle	—	—	1	—	—	—	—	—	—	—	1
WEBB —	Melton Mowbray	1844	Sporting	—	—	1	—	—	—	—	—	—	—	1
WEBB, MISS AMY	London	1886	Landscape	—	—	—	—	1	—	—	—	—	1	2
WEBB, ARCHIBALD	London	1825-1866	Sea Pieces	—	—	1	28	30	—	—	—	—	—	59
WEBB, ARCHIBALD, R.B.A. §	London	1886-1892	Landscape	—	—	6	—	26	—	8	—	—	5	45
WEBB, ASTON	London	1873-1893	Architecture	—	—	36	—	—	—	—	—	—	—	36
WEBB (ASTON) AND BELL (E. INGRESS)	London	1885-1893	Architecture	—	—	7	—	—	—	—	—	—	—	7
WEBB, BYRON	London	1846-1866	Animals	—	—	11	16	8	—	—	—	—	—	35
WEBB, MISS C.	Worcester	1888	Flowers	—	—	—	—	1	—	—	—	—	—	1
WEBB, CHARLES M.	London	1829	Portraits	—	—	—	—	1	—	—	—	—	—	1
WEBB, E.	London	1835	Architecture	—	—	1	—	—	—	—	—	—	—	1
WEBB, MISS ELIZA	London	1820-1827	Miniatures	—	—	11	—	—	—	—	—	—	—	11
WEBB, MRS. ELIZA	Old Charlton	1890-1893	Flowers	—	—	2	—	—	—	—	—	—	—	2
WEBB, E. W.	London	1850	Sporting	—	—	1	1	—	—	—	—	—	1	3
WEBB, G. W.	Reading	1890	Architecture	—	—	1	—	—	—	—	—	—	—	1
WEBB, HENRY	Worcester	1862-1869	Domestic	—	—	2	—	8	—	—	—	—	1	11
WEBB, HARRY GEORGE	London	1882-1893	Landscape	—	—	4	—	11	—	—	—	—	1	16
WEBB, J.	Deptford	1816	Landscape	—	—	1	—	—	—	—	—	—	—	1
WEBB, J.	London	1820	Architecture	—	—	1	—	—	—	—	—	—	—	1
WEBB, J.	—	1824	Engraving	—	—	—	—	1	—	—	—	—	—	1
WEBB, J.	Dublin	1892	Domestic	—	—	—	—	1	—	—	—	—	—	1
WEBB, JAMES	London	1850-1888	Sea Pieces	—	—	29	37	38	—	6	1	—	18	129
WEBB, JOHN COTHER	London	1875-1892	Engraving	—	—	16	—	—	—	—	—	—	3	19
WEBB, J. R.	Deptford	1828	Architecture	—	—	1	—	—	—	—	—	—	—	1
WEBB, K. S.	Henley	1880	River Scenes	—	—	—	—	1	—	—	—	—	—	1
WEBB, MISS M. D.	Dublin	1874-1885	Landscape	—	—	1	—	3	—	—	—	—	2	6
WEBB, OCTAVIUS	Guildford	1880-1889	Sporting	—	—	5	—	12	—	—	1	—	4	22
WEBB, PHILIP	London	1858	Architecture	—	—	1	—	—	—	—	—	—	—	1
WEBB, T.	London	1824	Landscape	—	—	—	1	—	—	—	—	—	—	1
WEBB, WESTFIELD, F.S.A.	London	1762-1772	Portraits	12	—	—	—	—	—	—	—	—	—	12
WEBB, WILLIAM	London	1766	Still Life	3	—	—	—	—	—	—	—	—	—	3
WEBB, W.	Tamworth	1819-1850	Sporting	—	—	7	1	—	—	—	—	—	—	8
WEBB, W.	London	1855-1857	Architecture	—	—	4	—	—	—	—	—	—	—	4
WEBBE, W.	London	1843-1861	Architecture	—	—	8	—	—	—	—	—	—	—	8
WEBBE, WILLIAM J.	Hemel Hempstead	1853-1878	Rustic	—	—	20	8	18	—	—	—	—	11	57
WEBBER —	London	1771	Miniatures	1	—	—	—	—	—	—	—	—	—	1
WEBBER, B.	Bath	1822	Flowers	—	—	1	—	—	—	—	—	—	—	1
WEBBER, HENRY	London	1773-1779	Sculpture	1	—	4	—	—	—	—	—	—	—	5
WEBBER, HENRY	London	1830	Scriptural	—	—	—	1	—	—	—	—	—	—	1
WEBBER, JOHN, R.A.	London	1776-1792	Landscape	—	—	49	—	—	—	—	—	—	—	49
WEBBER, WILLIAM JOHN SEWARD	Exeter	1870-1891	Sculpture	—	—	14	—	—	—	—	—	—	—	14
WEBER, A.	Dartmouth	1872	Landscape	—	—	—	—	—	—	—	—	—	3	3
WEBER, OTTO, A.R.W.S. † φ	London	1874-1888	Animals	—	—	27	—	—	82	—	8	—	13	130
WEBER, THEODOR	London	1871-1873	Sea Coast	—	—	5	—	—	—	—	—	—	—	5
WEBER, VON. *See* V.	—	—	—	—	—	—	—	—	—	—	—	—	—	—
WEBLING, MISS ETHEL	London	1880-1893	Miniatures	—	—	30	—	—	—	—	—	—	1	31
WEBSTER, ALFRED GEORGE	Lincoln	1876-1893	Domestic	—	—	13	—	1	—	—	—	—	3	17
WEBSTER, MISS E. A.	Bucks	1857-1863	Landscape	—	—	2	—	—	—	—	—	—	—	2

Name.	Town.	First and Last Year of Ex.	Speciality.	S. A.	F. S.	R. A.	B. I.	S. S.	O. W.	N. W.	G. G.	N. G.	V. E.	Total.
Webster, George	London	1797-1832	Sea Pieces	—	—	14	11	4	—	—	—	—	—	29
Webster, George	London	1879	Portraits	—	—	1	—	—	—	—	—	—	—	1
Webster, G. R.	Slough	1878-1879	Landscape	—	—	2	—	—	—	—	—	—	—	2
Webster, J.	—	1799	Portraits	—	—	1	—	—	—	—	—	—	—	1
Webster, John Dodsley	Sheffield	1877-1886	Architecture	—	—	3	—	—	—	—	—	—	—	3
Webster, M.	London	1818	Flowers	—	—	—	—	—	3	—	—	—	—	3
Webster, R.	London	1816-1818	Portraits	—	—	2	—	—	—	—	—	—	—	2
Webster, R. Wellesley	Manchester	1889-1892	Landscape	—	—	3	—	—	—	—	—	—	—	3
Webster, Simon, F.S.A.	London	1762-1780	Miniatures	16	1	—	—	—	—	—	—	—	—	17
Webster, Thomas, R.A.	Windsor	1823-1879	Domestic	—	—	83	39	9	—	—	—	—	—	131
Webster, T.	—	1844	Domestic	—	—	1	—	—	—	—	—	—	—	1
Webster, William	Lee	1885	Landscape	—	—	1	—	—	—	—	—	—	—	1
Wedd, Ada	London	1885-1887	Flowers	—	—	—	—	5	—	—	—	—	—	5
Wedderburn, Miss Jemima. *See* Mrs. Hugh	—	—	—	—	—	—	—	—	—	—	—	—	—	—
Blackburn	London	1848-1849	Animals	—	—	2	—	—	—	—	—	—	—	2
Weeding, N.	London	1843	Figures	—	—	—	—	1	—	—	—	—	—	1
Weedon, Augustus Walford, R.I., R.B.A. ‡ §	London	1859-1893	Landscape	—	—	23	—	109	—	57	—	—	80	269
Weedon, Edwin	London	1850	Sea Pieces	—	—	1	—	—	—	—	—	—	—	1
Weekes, Miss Charlotte J.	London	1876-1890	Figures	—	—	10	—	3	—	—	2	1	8	24
Weekes, Frederick	London	1854-1893	Battle Scenes	—	—	15	21	34	—	5	—	—	39	114
Weekes, Henry, R.A.	London	1828-1877	Sculpture	—	—	124	5	4	—	—	—	—	—	133
Weekes, Henry	London	1849-1888	Animals	—	—	26	17	21	—	—	—	—	10	74
Weekes, H. T.	London	1864	Domestic	—	—	—	—	1	—	—	—	—	—	1
Weekes, Percy	London	1879	Animals	—	—	—	—	1	—	—	—	—	—	1
Weekes, William	London	1856-1893	Animals	—	—	49	11	10	—	—	1	—	13	84
Weeks, E. L.	Tangiers	1878	Figures	—	—	2	—	—	—	—	—	—	—	2
Wegman, R. *or* B.	Copenhagen	1891	Portraits	—	—	1	—	—	—	—	—	—	—	1
Weguelin, John Reinhard φ	London	1877-1893	Figures	—	—	12	—	2	—	—	16	9	16	55
Wehnert, A.	London	1832-1836	Churches	—	—	—	—	3	—	—	—	—	—	3
Wehnert, E.	London	1832-1836	Landscape	—	—	—	—	3	—	—	—	—	—	3
Wehnert, Edward Henry ‡	London	1833-1869	Historical	—	—	3	4	3	—	147	—	—	—	157
Wehnert, F.	London	1822-1871	Architecture	—	—	24	—	2	—	—	—	—	—	26
Wehrschmidt, Daniel Albert	Bushey	1886-1893	Engraving	—	—	10	—	—	—	—	—	—	—	10
Weigall, Alfred	London	1855-1866	Miniatures	—	—	28	—	—	—	—	—	—	—	28
Weigall, Arthur Howes	London	1856-1892	Domestic	—	—	16	7	1	—	—	—	—	17	41
Weigall, Charles Harvey ‡	London	1810-1876	Domestic	—	—	20	—	2	—	419	—	—	—	441
Weigall, Miss E.	London	1853-1860	Miniatures	—	—	14	—	—	—	—	—	—	—	14
Weigall, Henry	London	1832-1855	Sculpture	—	—	17	2	4	—	—	—	—	—	23
Weigall, Henry, Junr.	London	1846-1893	Figures	—	—	147	16	—	—	—	2	2	4	171
Weigall, Miss Julia, afterwards Mrs. Capes	London	1848-1864	Miniatures	—	—	19	—	—	—	—	—	—	—	19
Weightman, J.	London	1817-1830	Architecture	—	—	3	—	—	—	—	—	—	—	3
Weighton, J., *or* Wighton	London	1863	Domestic	—	—	1	—	—	—	—	—	—	—	1
Weippert, E.	—	1800-1801	Sea Pieces	—	—	2	—	—	—	—	—	—	—	2
Weir, Mrs. Archibald (Anne)	Enfield	1884-1888	Domestic	—	—	1	—	2	—	1	—	—	6	10
Weir, Harrison William ‡	London	1843-1880	Animals	—	—	6	3	5	—	100	—	—	2	116
Weir, J. Alden	Leatherhead	1881	Figures	—	—	—	—	—	—	—	—	—	1	1
Weir, J. W.	London	1869	Domestic	—	—	—	—	1	—	—	—	—	—	1
Weir, P. J.	Edinburgh	1888	Landscape	—	—	—	—	—	—	1	—	—	—	1
Weir, W.	Edinburgh	1809	Domestic	—	—	2	—	—	—	—	—	—	—	2
Weir, William	London	1855-1865	Domestic	—	—	20	13	31	—	—	—	—	—	64
Weiss, José	Roubaix	1887-1893	Landscape	—	—	1	—	3	—	—	—	—	—	4
Weissenbruch, J. H.	—	1880	Landscape	—	—	—	—	—	—	—	2	—	—	2
Weisz, Adolphe, *or* Weiss	Paris	1872-1878	Domestic	—	—	3	—	—	—	—	1	—	—	4
Weizenberg, G.	Rome	1880-1882	Sculpture	—	—	2	—	—	—	—	—	—	—	2
Welborne, J. W.	London	1837-1839	Landscape	—	—	4	1	—	—	—	—	—	—	5
Welbourn, Master	London	1773	Drawings	—	1	—	—	—	—	—	—	—	—	1
Welby, C. *See* Pugin and Welby	—	—	Architecture	—	—	—	—	—	—	—	—	—	—	—
Welby, Miss Rose Ellen	London	1879-1893	Flowers	—	—	3	—	6	—	6	1	2	12	30
Welch, F. A. *See* Welsch.	—	—	—	—	—	—	—	—	—	—	—	—	—	—
Welch, Harry J.	London	1881-1892	Sea Shores	—	—	8	—	10	—	—	—	—	2	20
Welch, John	—	1779	Architecture	—	1	—	—	—	—	—	—	—	—	1
Welch, J.	London	1807-1813	Figures	—	—	4	—	—	—	—	—	—	—	4
Welch, Miss	London	1821	Landscape	—	—	2	—	—	—	—	—	—	—	2
Welchman, J. W.	London	1822-1824	Landscape	—	—	4	—	3	—	—	—	—	—	7
Weld, Miss Alice K. H.	London	1881-1888	Buildings	—	—	1	—	1	—	—	—	—	—	2
Weld, Mary Izod	London	1881	Landscape	—	—	—	—	—	—	—	—	—	1	1
Welfert, W.	Geneva	1841	Landscape	—	—	—	2	2	—	—	—	—	—	4
Welland, Mary J. B.	London	1876	Portraits	—	—	—	—	—	—	—	—	—	1	1
Weller, Miss Augusta	Chichester	1836-1839	Figures	—	—	3	1	3	—	—	—	—	—	7
Welles, E. F.	Worcester	1826-1856	Cattle	—	—	9	10	39	—	—	—	—	1	59
Welles, G. W.	London	1849	Landscape	—	—	—	1	—	—	—	—	—	—	1
Welles, J.	—	1784	Figures	—	—	1	—	—	—	—	—	—	—	1

Name.	Town.	First and Last Year of Ex.	Speciality.	S. A.	F. S.	R. A.	B. I.	S. S.	O. W.	N.W.	G. G.	N. G.	V. E.	Total.
Wellesley, G. E.	—	1893	Portraits	—	—	—	—	—	—	—	—	—	1	1
Wellesley, Lady Priscilla Jane. *See* Countess of Westmorland.	—	—	—	—	—	—	—	—	—	—	—	—	—	—
Wellings, W.	London	1793	Miniatures	—	—	2	—	—	—	—	—	—	—	2
Wells, Miss Augusta	London	1864-1879	Domestic	—	—	9	—	—	—	—	—	—	3	12
Wells, George, R.C.A.	Stroud Green	1842-1888	Domestic	—	—	39	18	62	—	3	—	—	22	144
Wells, Henry Tanworth, R.A.	London	1846-1893	Portraits	—	—	239	3	2	—	—	—	—	2	246
Wells, Mrs. H. T. *See* Miss Johanna Mary Boyce	London	1859-1862	Domestic	—	—	6	—	—	—	—	—	—	—	6
Wells, Mrs. H. W. (Mary)	Wallingford	1886	Domestic	—	—	1	—	—	—	—	—	—	—	1
Wells, J.	London	1783	Sea Pieces	—	—	1	—	—	—	—	—	—	—	1
Wells, J.	London	1828	Architecture	—	—	1	—	—	—	—	—	—	—	1
Wells, J.	London	1869-1871	Sea Pieces	—	—	—	—	2	—	—	—	—	—	2
Wells, Miss J.	London	1875	Landscape	—	—	—	—	1	—	—	—	—	—	1
Wells, Josiah Robert (?) Joseph	Bromley	1872-1893	Sea Pieces	—	—	5	—	10	—	14	—	—	22	51
Wells, J. S.	London	1824-1829	Architecture	—	—	1	—	4	—	—	—	—	—	5
Wells, J. Sanderson	London	1892-1893	Fishing Boats	—	—	—	—	4	—	—	—	—	—	4
Wells, L. Jennens	London	1865-1868	Birds	—	—	—	—	—	—	—	—	—	3	3
Wells, P.	London	1839	Landscape	—	—	1	—	—	—	—	—	—	—	1
Wells, Thomas	London	1786-1791	Medals	—	—	5	—	—	—	—	—	—	—	5
Wells, T.	—	1854	Figures	—	—	1	—	—	—	—	—	—	—	1
Wells, William Frederick K. †	London	1795-1813	Landscape	—	—	38	—	—	90	—	—	—	—	128
Wells, W. J.	—	1854	Sculpture	—	—	1	—	—	—	—	—	—	—	1
Wells, W. P. A.	Richmond	1893	Landscape	—	—	—	—	—	—	—	—	—	2	2
Wells, Mrs.	London	1806	Miniatures	—	—	2	—	—	—	—	—	—	—	2
Wells, Miss	London	1805-1813	Flowers	—	—	6	—	—	—	—	—	—	—	6
Welsch, F. C.	Rome	1871-1879	Venice	—	—	2	—	—	—	—	—	—	1	3
Welsh, E.	London	1771	Portraits	1	—	—	—	—	—	—	—	—	—	1
Welsh, John	London	1761-1764	Sculpture	—	3	—	—	—	—	—	—	—	—	3
Wenley, H.	London	1858	Landscape	—	—	—	—	1	—	—	—	—	—	1
Wensel, T. L.	London	1857	Historical	—	—	1	—	—	—	—	—	—	—	1
Went, Alfred	Ilkley	1893	Domestic	—	—	—	—	2	—	—	—	—	—	2
Wentworth, Lady. *See* Miss M. E. Stuart-Wortley.	—	—	—	—	—	—	—	—	—	—	—	—	—	—
Wentworth-Shields, Ada	Blackheath	1889-1892	Flowers	—	—	—	—	3	—	—	—	—	—	3
Were, T. K.	Sidmouth	1876-1877	Landscape	—	—	—	—	—	—	—	—	—	2	2
Werge, Thomas	London	1821-1824	Sea Pieces	—	—	2	2	—	—	—	—	—	—	4
Werner, Carl ‡	London	1860-1878	Churches	—	—	1	—	—	—	139	—	—	—	140
Werner, Carl	—	1884	Landscape	—	—	—	—	—	—	1	—	—	—	1
Werner, Rinaldo	Rome	1884-1890	Fountains	—	—	—	—	3	—	8	1	—	—	12
Werninck, Miss Blanche	Winslow	1893	Landscape	—	—	1	—	—	—	—	—	—	—	1
Weslake, Miss Charlotte	London	1836-1870	Fruit	—	—	6	6	4	—	—	—	—	—	16
Weslake, Miss Mary	London	1866	Figures	—	—	1	—	—	—	—	—	—	—	1
Wessell, G. G.	London	1781-1787	Sculpture	—	—	11	—	—	—	—	—	—	—	11
West. *See* Williams, West, and Slade	—	—	Architecture	—	—	—	—	—	—	—	—	—	—	—
West, Colonel	—	1773-1777	Landscape	—	—	4	—	—	—	—	—	—	—	4
West, Alexander	Manchester	1880-1884	Landscape	—	—	1	—	4	—	—	—	—	1	6
West, A.	Leatherhead	1880	Domestic	—	—	—	—	—	—	—	—	—	1	1
West, Alice	London	1853	Fruit	—	—	1	—	—	—	—	—	—	—	1
West, Miss Alice L.	Bedford Park	1889-1892	Domestic	—	—	3	—	2	—	2	—	—	—	7
West, Benjamin, P.R.A.	London	1764-1819	Historical	21	—	258	32	—	—	—	—	—	—	311
West, Benjamin, Junr.	London	1791	Drawing	—	—	1	—	—	—	—	—	—	—	1
West, Miss Blanche C.	London	1876-1882	Figures	—	—	1	—	2	—	—	—	—	1	4
West, Charles	London	1787	Landscape	—	—	1	—	—	—	—	—	—	—	1
West, C.	Portsea	1821	Portraits	—	—	1	—	—	—	—	—	—	—	1
West, Charles W.	London	1880-1882	Figures	—	—	1	—	4	—	—	—	—	—	5
West, David	Aberdeen	1890-1893	Landscape	—	—	7	—	—	—	—	—	—	—	7
West, E.	London	1858	Landscape	—	—	—	—	4	—	—	—	—	—	4
West, Miss Edith de Lancy	—	1877	Sculpture	—	—	1	—	1	—	—	—	—	—	2
West, E. E.	Bedford Park	1881	Landscape	—	—	1	—	—	—	—	—	—	—	1
West, Miss F. B.	London	1845	Domestic	—	—	—	—	1	—	—	—	—	—	1
West, Frederick E.	Acton	1877-1882	Landscape	—	—	—	—	5	—	—	—	—	—	5
West, Francis Robert	London	1790	Portraits	—	—	2	—	—	—	—	—	—	—	2
West, H. T.	London	1831-1836	Landscape	—	—	9	—	2	—	2	—	—	—	13
West, Joseph	Bath	1824-1834	Historical	—	—	—	4	—	—	—	—	—	—	4
West, J.	London	1856	Portraits	—	—	1	—	—	—	—	—	—	—	1
West, James	London	1883	Stained Glass	—	—	1	—	—	—	—	—	—	—	1
West, J. B.	London	1827-1828	Landscape	—	—	—	2	1	—	—	—	—	—	3
West, J. H.	London	1825-1827	Architecture	—	—	—	*	5	—	—	—	—	—	5
West, Joseph Walter	Harrow	1885-1893	Domestic	—	—	7	—	4	—	—	—	—	2	13
West, Miss Maud A.	Bedford Park	1880-1890	Flowers	—	—	—	—	—	—	2	—	—	1	3
West, Miss M. P.	London	1837-1839	Portraits	—	—	1	—	2	—	—	—	—	—	3

Name.	Town.	First and Last Year of Ex.	Speciality.	S. A.	F. S.	R. A.	B. I.	S. S.	O. W.	N.W.	G. G.	N. G.	V. E.	Total.
West, R.	Hackney	1805	Architecture	—	—	1	—	—	—	—	—	—	—	1
West, Robert Lucius, R.H.A.	Dublin	1771-1822	Scriptural	—	3	9	—	—	—	—	—	—	—	12
West, Richard Whately	London	1878-1888	Landscape	—	—	8	—	31	—	1	—	—	12	52
West, S.	London	1827-1830	Architecture	—	—	3	—	—	—	—	—	—	—	3
West, Samuel	London	1840-1867	Historical	—	—	23	7	1	—	—	—	—	—	31
West, Temple	London	1778-1811	Landscape	—	—	3	—	—	—	—	—	—	—	3
West, Walter, R.B.A. §	London	1893	Domestic	—	—	1	—	—	—	—	—	1	—	2
West, William §	Clifton	1824-1871	Landscape	—	—	13	14	103	—	—	—	—	—	130
West, William D.	London	1852-1877	Figures	—	—	10	3	—	—	—	—	—	1	14
West, William E.	Bristol	1824-1837	Domestic	—	—	18	15	7	—	—	—	—	—	40
Westall, J.	Birmingham	1873	Landscape	—	—	—	—	1	—	—	—	—	—	1
Westall, Richard, R.A.	London	1784-1836	Historical	—	—	313	70	1	—	—	—	—	—	384
Westall, R.	London	1848-1889	Landscape	—	—	6	—	7	—	—	—	—	—	13
Westall, William, A.R.A. †	London	1801-1849	Landscape	—	—	70	30	7	13	—	—	—	25	145
Westaway, W.	London	1853	Architecture	—	—	1	—	—	—	—	—	—	—	1
Westbrook, Miss Elizabeth W.	London	1861-1886	Figures	—	—	7	—	14	—	—	—	—	9	30
Westcott, Philip	Liverpool	1844-1861	Portraits	—	—	25	2	4	—	—	—	—	—	31
Westell, Hubert	London	1887	Architecture	—	—	1	—	—	—	—	—	—	—	1
Western, Charles	Highbury	1885-1893	Domestic	—	—	1	—	4	—	—	—	—	—	5
Westhead, G. Reade-	London	1883	Landscape	—	—	—	—	—	—	—	—	—	1	1
Westhoven, W.	London	1878	Landscape	—	—	—	—	1	—	—	—	—	—	1
Westlake, Mrs. Alice	London	1875-1878	Etching	—	—	3	—	—	—	—	—	—	7	10
Westlake, Mary	London	1872	Domestic	—	—	—	—	—	—	—	—	—	1	1
Westlake, Nathaniel Hubert John	Hendon	1872-1893	Figures	—	—	21	—	—	—	—	—	—	7	28
Westlake, Miss	—	1864	Sea Pieces	—	—	—	—	1	—	—	—	—	—	1
Westmacott, C. M.	London	1822	Sculpture	—	—	1	—	—	—	—	—	—	—	1
Westmacott, George	London	1775-1820	Sculpture	1	—	13	1	—	—	—	—	—	—	15
Westmacott, H.	Edinburgh	1833-1835	Sculpture	—	—	3	—	—	—	—	—	—	—	3
Westmacott, Mrs. H.	Durham	1866	Landscape	—	—	—	—	—	—	—	—	—	1	1
Westmacott, J.	London	1800-1806	Architecture	—	—	7	—	—	—	—	—	—	—	7
Westmacott, James Sherwin	London	1846-1886	Sculpture	—	—	67	12	2	—	2	—	—	—	83
Westmacott, Sir Richard, R.A.	London	1797-1839	Sculpture	—	—	65	—	—	—	—	—	—	—	65
Westmacott, Richard, R.A.	London	1827-1855	Sculpture	—	—	82	4	—	—	—	—	—	—	86
Westmacott, Stewart	London	1841-1869	Figures	—	—	6	3	6	—	—	—	—	—	15
Westmacott, T.	London	1796-1798	Architecture	—	—	4	—	—	—	—	—	—	—	4
Westmacott, W.	London	1816-1848	Architecture	—	—	11	—	—	—	—	—	—	—	11
Westmorland, Priscilla Anne, Countess of,	—	—	—	—	—	—	—	—	—	—	—	—	—	—
formerly Lady Priscilla Wellesley-Pole.	—	—	—	—	—	—	—	—	—	—	—	—	—	—
See Lady Burgherst	—	1842-1857	Scriptural	—	—	—	2	—	—	—	—	—	—	2
Westobey, E.	London	1806-1823	Portraits	—	—	17	—	—	—	—	—	—	—	17
Weston, Ernest	Woolwich	1884	Still Life	—	—	—	—	—	—	1	—	—	—	1
Weston, G. F.	London	1840	Landscape	—	—	—	—	1	—	—	—	—	—	1
Weston, L.	Dover	1844-1845	Landscape	—	—	1	—	1	—	—	—	—	—	2
Weston, Miss M.	Brighton	1830	Illustrations	—	—	—	—	1	—	—	—	—	—	1
Weston, T.	London	1816-1828	Landscape	—	—	9	—	—	—	—	—	—	—	9
Westphal, Miss F.	London	1864-1867	Figures	—	—	2	—	4	—	—	—	—	—	6
Westwood, Eliza	Hammersmith	1835-1837	Flowers	—	—	2	—	—	—	—	—	—	—	2
Wetherbee, George Faulkner, R.I. ‡ φ	London	1873-1893	Domestic	—	—	9	—	23	—	26	2	3	36	99
Wetherill —	London	1773-1783	Miniatures	1	—	1	—	—	—	—	—	—	—	2
Wetherill —	Ipswich	1779	Landscape	—	—	2	—	—	—	—	—	—	—	2
Wetherill, Mrs.	London	1773-1783	Portraits	5	1	—	—	—	—	—	—	—	—	6
Wetten, R.	London	1852	Architecture	—	—	1	—	—	—	—	—	—	—	1
Wetten, Robert	London	1828	Historical	—	—	—	—	1	—	—	—	—	—	1
Wetten, R. G.	London	1822-1828	Architecture	—	—	4	—	—	—	—	—	—	—	4
Weyde, Van der. *See* V.	—	—	—	—	—	—	—	—	—	—	—	—	—	—
Weyns, Jules	London	1887	Sculpture	—	—	1	—	—	—	—	—	—	—	1
Wezet —		1782	Cattle	—	1	—	—	—	—	—	—	—	—	1
Whaite, Henry Clarence, R.W.S., P.R.C.A. †	Manchester	1851-1893	Landscape	—	—	23	7	6	148	—	1	—	6	191
Whaite, James	Manchester	1867-1881	Landscape	—	—	3	—	1	—	—	2	—	5	11
Whall, Christopher W.	Edmonton	1873-1888	Portraits	—	—	3	—	2	—	—	—	—	3	8
Whalley, Adolphus Jacob	London	1875-1886	Domestic	—	—	2	—	—	—	—	—	—	1	3
Whalley, J. K.	Liverpool	1874	Domestic	—	—	—	—	—	—	—	—	—	1	1
Wharam, M.	London	1795-1797	Sporting	—	—	2	—	—	—	—	—	—	—	2
Wharton, Miss Amy C.	Old Charlton	1892	Sculpture	—	—	—	—	1	—	—	—	—	—	1
Wharton, J.	Newmarket	1864	Landscape	—	—	—	—	1	—	—	—	—	—	1
Wharton, S.	—	1810-1814	Architecture	—	—	5	—	—	—	—	—	—	—	5
Whately, Mrs. M. Alice H.	London	1892	Animals	—	—	1	—	—	—	—	—	—	—	1
Whatley, Henry	Clifton	1886-1888	Landscape	—	—	—	—	—	—	4	—	—	—	4
Wheatley, Francis, F.S.A., R.A.	London	1765-1783	Domestic	45	1	87	—	—	—	—	—	—	—	133
Wheatley, Mrs. Francis, late Miss Clara	—	—	—	—	—	—	—	—	—	—	—	—	—	—
Maria Leigh. *See* Mrs. Alexander Pope	London	1796-1807	Rustic	—	—	28	1	—	—	—	—	—	—	29
Wheatley, Oliver	London	1892-1893	Sculpture	—	—	2	—	—	—	—	—	—	—	2

Name.	Town.	First and Last Year of Ex.	Speciality.	S. A.	F. S.	R. A.	B. I.	S. S.	O. W.	N. W.	G. G.	N. G.	V. E.	Total.
Wheeler. *See* Hooker and Wheeler	—	—	Architecture	—	—	—	—	—	—	—	—	—	—	—
Wheeler, Miss Annie	London	1868-1885	Flowers	—	—	—	—	6	—	1	—	—	2	9
Wheeler, Mrs. Amy E.	London	1890-1893	Miniatures	—	—	4	—	—	—	—	—	—	—	4
Wheeler, C.	—	1834	Landscape	—	—	—	1	—	—	—	—	—	—	1
Wheeler, C. W.	London	1835	Sea Pieces	—	—	1	—	—	—	—	—	—	—	1
Wheeler, Edward J.	London	1872	Domestic	—	—	—	—	—	—	—	—	—	1	1
Wheeler, J.	Bath	1875	Sporting	—	—	—	—	1	—	—	—	—	—	2
Wheeler, Miss M. A. *See* Mrs. David Johnston	London	1834-1836	Portraits	—	—	2	—	—	—	—	—	—	—	1
Wheeler, N.	London	1812	Portraits	—	—	1	—	—	—	—	—	—	—	1
Wheeler, Miss S. A.	London	1863-1879	Fruit	—	—	1	1	8	—	1	—	—	—	11
Wheeler, T.	London	1817-1845	Miniatures	—	—	49	—	—	—	—	—	—	—	49
Wheeler, W. H.	Richmond	1881-1887	Landscape	—	—	1	—	11	—	12	—	—	2	26
Wheeler, Mrs. W. H. (Anne)	Reigate	1885-1887	Flowers	—	—	—	—	—	—	5	—	—	—	5
Wheeler, Miss	London	1889	Sea Shores	—	—	1	—	—	—	—	—	—	—	1
Wheelersmith, Olive	Addiscombe	1884-1886	Landscape	—	—	—	—	3	—	—	—	—	—	3
Wheelwright, Anna	London	1884	Flowers	—	—	—	—	1	—	—	—	—	—	1
Wheelwright, Miss Hené P.	East Grinstead	1871-1885	Landscape	—	—	1	—	5	—	—	—	—	10	16
Wheelwright, J. Hadwen	London	1834-1849	Sporting	—	—	12	6	7	—	—	—	—	—	25
Wheelwright, R.	Watford	1893	Animals	—	—	—	—	—	—	—	—	—	1	1
Wheelwright, W. H.	London	1878-1880	Interiors	—	—	—	—	—	—	—	—	—	2	2
Wheen, Miss Helen	—	1870-1872	Domestic	—	—	—	—	3	—	—	—	—	—	3
Whelan, Miss K. A.	Ryde	1874	Landscape	—	—	—	—	1	—	—	—	—	—	1
Whelan and Heyes	London	1871-1872	Architecture	—	—	2	—	—	—	—	—	—	—	2
Whessell, J.	London	1802-1823	Domestic	—	—	14	—	—	—	—	—	—	—	14
Whessel, W.	Wolverhampt'n	1803	Figures	—	—	1	—	—	—	—	—	—	—	1
Whetton, Thomas	London	1774-1786	Architecture	—	—	11	—	—	—	—	—	—	—	11
Whichcord, John, F.S.A.	Maidstone	1845-1874	Architecture	—	—	8	—	—	—	—	—	—	—	8
Whichell, J.	London	1805	Ruins	—	—	1	—	—	—	—	—	—	—	1
Whichelo, H. M.	London	1817-1842	Sea Pieces	—	—	7	11	4	—	—	—	—	—	22
Whichelo, H. W.	London	1844	Buildings	—	—	1	—	—	—	—	—	—	—	1
Whichelo, John M. †	London	1810-1865	Sea Pieces	—	—	15	13	—	210	—	—	—	—	238
Whichelo, William J.	Leatherhead	1866	Landscape	—	—	—	—	2	—	—	—	—	—	2
Whiffen, Charles E.	Cheltenham	1889-1890	Sculpture	—	—	2	—	1	—	—	—	—	—	3
Whinney, Thomas B.	London	1881-1889	Domestic	—	—	4	—	1	—	2	—	—	—	7
Whipple, John	London	1873-1893	Landscape	—	—	20	—	60	—	14	12	8	32	146
Whipple, Mrs. John (Agnes)	London	1881-1888	Flowers	—	—	5	—	1	—	—	—	—	1	7
Whistler, James Abbott McNeil, R.B.A. §	London	1859-1893	Etchings, etc.	—	—	33	—	52	—	—	40	—	30	155
Whitaker, C. H.	Rotherham	1854	Sculpture	—	—	1	—	—	—	—	—	—	—	1
Whitaker, D.	Amersham	1892-1893	Landscape	—	—	—	—	—	—	—	—	—	2	2
Whitaker, Frank	London	1844-1880	Sea Pieces	—	—	—	—	8	—	—	—	—	—	8
Whitaker, George	Exeter	1859-1873	Sea Pieces	—	—	—	1	15	—	—	—	—	10	26
Whitaker, G. G.	London	1873	Landscape	—	—	1	—	—	—	—	—	—	—	1
Whitaker, H.	London	1825	Domestic	—	—	1	—	—	—	—	—	—	—	1
Whitaker, H.	London	1838	Architecture	—	—	1	—	—	—	—	—	—	—	1
Whitaker, Marston	London	1883	Figures	—	—	—	—	2	—	—	—	—	—	2
Whitaker, W.	London	1828	Historical	—	—	1	—	4	—	—	—	—	—	5
Whitaker, William M.	London	1877	Domestic	—	—	—	—	—	—	—	—	—	1	1
Whitaker, Miss	—	1891	Portraits	—	—	—	—	—	—	—	—	—	1	1
Whitbread, W. E.	London	1870	Landscape	—	—	—	—	—	—	—	—	—	1	1
Whitburn, Thomas	Guildford	1853-1875	Figures	—	—	—	1	3	—	—	—	—	6	10
Whitby, William	London	1772-1791	Portraits	8	—	5	—	—	—	—	—	—	—	13
Whitby, W.	Mumbles	1886	Landscape	—	—	—	—	—	—	1	—	—	—	1
Whitcombe, J.	London	1821	Sea Pieces	—	—	1	—	—	—	—	—	—	—	1
Whitcombe, Thomas	London	1783-1834	Sea Pieces	—	—	56	1	1	—	—	—	—	—	58
White. *See* Christopher and White	—	—	Architecture	—	—	—	—	—	—	—	—	—	—	—
White —	—	1765	Buildings	1	—	—	—	—	—	—	—	—	—	1
White —	London	1774-1783	Buildings	—	4	—	—	—	—	—	—	—	—	4
White, A.	London	1817	Portraits	—	—	1	—	—	—	—	—	—	—	1
White, Miss Agnes	London	1885-1890	Landscape	—	—	—	—	4	—	—	—	—	—	4
White, Miss Alice	London	1873-1886	Landscape	—	—	1	—	4	—	1	—	—	1	7
White, Mrs. A. C.	London	1867-1868	Figures	—	—	—	—	2	—	—	—	—	—	2
White, Charles	London	1768-1771	Architecture	—	6	—	—	—	—	—	—	—	—	6
White, C.	Lincoln	1851-1855	Churches	—	—	2	—	—	—	—	—	—	—	2
White, Clement	London	1889	Landscape	—	—	1	—	—	—	—	—	—	—	1
White, Mrs. C.	London	1809-1844	Landscape	—	—	3	15	4	3	—	—	—	—	25
White, C. G.	London	1831-1841	Sea Pieces	—	—	1	—	1	—	—	—	—	—	2
White, C. P.	London	1865-1866	Sea Coasts	—	—	—	—	4	—	—	—	—	—	4
White D.	London	1864-1869	Figures	—	—	3	—	—	—	—	—	—	—	3
White, Dan	—	1889	Portraits	—	—	—	—	—	—	—	1	—	—	1
White, Miss Dora	London	1888	Bridges	—	—	—	—	—	—	—	1	—	—	1
White, Daniel Thomas	London	1861-1890	Domestic	—	—	15	1	9	—	—	1	—	4	30
White, Mrs. E. A.	London	1867	Figures	—	—	1	—	—	—	—	—	—	—	1

Name.	Town.	First and Last Year of Ex.	Speciality.	S. A.	F. S.	R. A.	B. I.	S. S.	O. W.	N. W.	G. G.	N. G.	V. E.	Total.
White, Eley Emlyn	London	1877	Architecture	—	—	1	—	—	—	—	—	—	—	1
White, E. Fox	London	1883	Landscape	—	—	—	—	—	—	1	—	—	—	1
White, Edmund Richard	London	1864-1893	Domestic	—	—	16	—	12	—	6	—	—	9	43
White, Miss Florence ‖	London	1881-1893	Domestic	—	—	6	—	5	—	—	1	—	8	20
White, F. G.	Taunton	1843-1858	Landscape	—	—	3	—	3	—	—	—	—	2	8
White, Frances J.	Dublin	1870	Landscape	—	—	—	—	1	—	—	—	—	—	1
White, George	Hesswell, Chester	1885-1890	Landscape	—	—	6	—	—	—	—	—	—	5	11
White, George Harlow	London	1839-1883	Landscape	—	—	24	17	43	—	—	—	—	6	90
White, G. H. P.	London	1849-1861	Landscape	—	—	—	2	—	—	—	—	—	1	3
White, H.	London	1839-1843	Portraits	—	—	2	—	—	—	—	—	—	—	2
White, Henry	London	1881	Landscape	—	—	—	—	1	—	—	—	—	—	1
White, H. Hopley	London	1805-1867	Landscape	—	—	18	—	3	—	—	—	—	—	21
White, Miss Isabel G.	Bushey	1892-1893	Figures	—	—	—	—	—	—	2	—	—	2	4
White, J.	London	1819-1828	Landscape	—	—	3	—	—	—	—	—	—	—	3
White, John, R.I. ‡ § φ	Guildford	1877-1893	Domestic	—	—	30	—	49	—	30	1	—	47	157
White, Mrs. John	London	1809-1844	Landscape	—	—	3	15	3	—	—	—	—	—	21
White, J. H.	London	1849	Landscape	—	—	—	—	1	—	—	—	—	—	1
White, Miss Josephine M.	London	1893	Figures	—	—	1	—	—	—	—	—	—	—	1
White, J. S.	London	1829-1830	Coast Scenes	—	—	3	—	1	—	—	—	—	—	4
White, J. Talmage	Ealing	1853-1893	Buildings	—	—	15	5	2	—	—	5	—	18	45
White, P. G.	—	1834	Landscape	—	—	1	—	—	—	—	—	—	—	1
White, R.	London	1808	Domestic	—	—	1	—	—	—	—	—	—	—	1
White, S.	London	1765-1814	Architecture	13	6	2	—	—	—	—	—	—	—	21
White, S.	—	1829	Study	—	—	—	1	—	—	—	—	—	—	1
White, Sydney W.	Grimsby	1892	Landscape	—	—	1	—	—	—	—	—	—	—	1
White, W.	London	1819-1821	Landscape	—	—	4	—	—	1	—	—	—	—	5
White, W.	London	1824-1838	Portraits	—	—	4	—	3	—	—	—	—	—	7
White, William, F.S.A.	London	1852-1874	Architecture	—	—	5	—	—	—	—	—	—	—	5
White, W.	Esher	1863-1886	Domestic	—	—	23	—	—	—	—	—	—	—	23
White, William	Brighton	1871	Landscape	—	—	—	—	—	—	—	—	—	1	1
White, William Henry. *See also* Moore and White	London	1870-1875	Architecture	—	—	2	—	—	—	—	—	—	—	2
White, William Johnstone	London	1804-1810	Illustrations	—	—	3	—	—	—	—	—	—	—	3
Whiteford, Sidney Trefusis	Plymouth	1860-1881	Still Life	—	—	11	—	29	—	—	—	—	13	53
Whitehead, Miss Elizabeth	Leamington	1880-1893	Flowers	—	—	6	—	3	—	—	—	—	1	10
Whitehead, Frederick	Leamington	1870-1893	Still Life	—	—	12	—	17	—	—	—	—	6	35
Whitehead, G.	London	1834	Architecture	—	—	1	—	—	—	—	—	—	—	1
Whitehead, J.	London	1807-1820	Portraits	—	—	1	—	—	1	—	—	—	—	2
Whitehead, Joseph	London	1889-1893	Sculpture	—	2	—	—	—	—	—	—	—	—	2
Whitehead, T.	London	1814-1821	Architecture	—	—	2	—	—	—	—	—	—	—	2
Whitehouse, Arthur E.	London	1880-1888	Landscape	—	—	2	—	1	—	—	—	—	3	6
Whitehouse, Miss Sarah E.	Leamington	1881-1893	Domestic	—	—	1	—	—	—	—	—	—	1	2
Whitelaw, Frederick William	London	1881	Domestic	—	—	1	—	—	—	—	—	—	—	1
Whitelaw, S. Frances	Taplow	1882	Landscape	—	—	—	—	1	—	—	—	—	—	1
Whiteley, John William	Leeds	1882-1886	Landscape	—	—	3	—	—	—	5	—	—	—	8
Whiteside, Miss R. Cordelia	London	1892	Miniatures	—	—	1	—	—	—	—	—	—	—	1
Whitfield, Mrs. Florence W.	Birmingham	1888	Flowers	—	—	1	—	—	—	—	—	—	—	1
Whitfield, Miss Helen	Wimbledon	1890-1893	Landscape	—	—	1	—	—	—	4	—	—	—	5
Whitfield (R. O.) and Thomas (J. A.)	London	1889	Architecture	—	—	1	—	—	—	—	—	—	—	1
Whiting, Fred.	London	1893	Domestic	—	—	1	—	—	—	—	—	—	—	1
Whitley, G.	London	1868-1869	Landscape	—	—	2	—	2	—	—	—	—	1	5
Whitley, Miss Kate Mary, R.I. ‡	Leicester	1884-1893	Still Life	—	—	5	—	—	—	26	—	—	—	31
Whitley, W.	London	1784-1790	Cameos, etc.	—	—	8	—	—	—	—	—	—	—	8
Whitley, William T.	London	1884-1893	Domestic	—	—	8	—	5	—	—	—	—	3	16
Whitlock, Mrs.	London	1773	Needlework	1	—	—	—	—	—	—	—	—	—	1
Whitmarsh, Mrs. T. H. (Eliza)	Blackheath	1840-1851	Figures	—	—	8	1	1	—	—	—	—	—	10
Whitmore, Bryan	Chertsey	1871-1892	Landscape	—	—	10	—	26	—	7	2	—	—	45
Whitney, Miss Blanche M.	London	1885-1893	Miniatures	—	—	2	—	—	—	1	—	—	—	3
Whitney, Miss E.	London	1884	Portraits	—	—	—	—	—	—	—	1	—	—	1
Whittaker, James W. †	Llanwrst	1862-1876	Landscape	—	—	3	—	—	162	—	—	—	1	166
Whittaker, T. L.	—	1831	Portraits	—	—	1	—	—	—	—	—	—	—	1
Whittaker W.	London	1827	Miniatures	—	—	2	—	—	—	—	—	—	—	2
Whitting, H. J.	London	1835	Architecture	—	—	1	—	—	—	—	—	—	—	1
Whitting, T.	London	1818	Portraits	—	—	1	—	—	—	—	—	—	—	1
Whittle, E.	London	1834	Portraits	—	—	—	—	—	—	1	—	—	—	1
Whittle, Miss Elizabeth	Croydon	1875-1879	Fruit	—	—	—	—	2	—	—	—	—	—	2
Whittle, Thomas, Senr.	London	1854-1868	Fruit	—	—	2	20	51	—	—	—	—	6	79
Whittle, Thomas, Junr.	Bexley	1865-1885	Landscape	—	—	5	15	52	—	—	—	—	5	77
Whittle, T. S.	Lewisham	1862	Fruit	—	—	—	1	1	—	—	—	—	—	2
Whitton, E.	London	1775-1777	Gems	—	—	3	—	—	—	—	—	—	—	3
Whitton, F.	Jamaica	1780	Gems	—	—	1	—	—	—	—	—	—	—	1
Whitwell, T. Stedman	Hackney	1806-1822	Architecture	—	—	10	—	—	—	—	—	—	—	10

Name.	Town.	First and Last Year of Ex.	Speciality.	S. A.	F. S.	R. A.	B. I.	S. S.	O. W.	N. W.	G. G.	N. G.	V. E.	Total.
Whitwell, Miss	London	1815-1820	Portraits	—	—	2	—	—	—	—	—	—	—	2
Whitworth, Charles H.	Birmingham	1879-1888	Landscape	—	—	1	—	1	—	—	—	—	5	7
Whitworth, Miss M.	—	1814	Insects	—	—	2	—	—	—	—	—	—	—	2
Whymper, Charles	London	1876-1893	Landscape	—	—	5	—	1	—	2	1	—	3	12
Whymper, F.	London	1857-1861	Landscape	—	—	3	—	3	—	—	—	—	—	6
Whymper, Josiah Wood, R.I. ‡	—	1844-1893	Landscape	—	—	11	—	14	—	414	3	—	3	445
Wymper, Mrs. J. W. (Emily)	Haslemere	1870-1885	Landscape	—	—	3	—	11	—	4	—	—	4	22
Whyte, Edward Towry, M.A.	London	1886-1889	Architecture	—	—	2	—	—	—	—	—	—	—	2
Whyte, John G.	Helensburgh	1877-1886	Flowers	—	—	5	—	—	—	—	—	—	—	5
Whyte, William Patrick	London	1883-1888	Figures	—	—	3	—	—	—	2	1	—	—	6
Whyte-Holdich, W. *See* H.	—	—	—	—	—	—	—	—	—	—	—	—	—	—
Whytell, Ann	Liverpool	1776	Shells	—	—	2	—	—	—	—	—	—	—	2
Wiche, J.	London	1811-1827	Portraits	—	—	16	—	5	—	—	—	—	—	21
Wickens, Miss	—	1813	Churches	—	—	1	—	—	—	—	—	—	—	1
Wickham, William	London	1772-1787	Architecture	—	—	8	—	—	—	—	—	—	—	8
Wickson, Paul G.	London	1882	Domestic	—	—	1	—	—	—	—	—	—	—	1
Wickstead, Philip	Jamaica	1777-1780	Figures	4	—	—	—	—	—	—	—	—	—	4
Wicksteed, C. F.	London	1802-1847	Landscape	—	—	55	37	9	—	—	—	—	—	101
Wicksteed, James	London	1779-1824	Gems	—	—	19	—	1	—	—	—	—	—	20
Widgery, Julia C.	Exeter	1872-1879	Landscape	—	—	—	—	4	—	—	—	—	—	4
Widgery, William	Exeter	1866	Landscape	—	—	—	—	1	—	—	—	—	—	1
Wiegand, N. J.	London	1869	Coast Scenes	—	—	—	—	—	—	—	—	—	1	1
Wiegand, W. Paul	London	1854-1866	Still Life	—	—	1	—	3	—	—	—	—	—	4
Wiegand, W. J.	London	1882	Figures	—	—	—	—	—	—	—	—	—	1	1
Wiener, C.	London	1863-1874	Medals	—	—	14	—	—	—	—	—	—	—	14
Wiener, Leopold	London	1864	Sculpture	—	—	1	—	—	—	—	—	—	—	1
Wiens, Siegfried M.	Sutton	1893	Rivers	—	—	1	—	—	—	—	—	—	—	1
Wiffin, H. H.	Reigate	1869	Flowers	—	—	—	—	—	—	—	—	—	2	2
Wigan, Miss Bessie	London	1888	Domestic	—	—	1	—	—	—	—	—	—	—	1
Wigan, Miss E. D.	—	1883	Sculpture	—	—	—	—	2	—	—	—	—	—	2
Wigand, F. H.	London	1846	Figures	—	—	2	—	—	—	—	—	—	—	2
Wigg (F.) and Pownall (G.)	London	1840-1845	Architecture	—	—	7	—	—	—	—	—	—	—	7
Wigg, Son, and Oliver	London	1859	Architecture	—	—	1	—	—	—	—	—	—	—	1
Wiggins, F.	London	1790-1791	Miniatures	3	—	—	—	—	—	—	—	—	—	3
Wiggoni —	London	1783	Portraits	—	1	—	—	—	—	—	—	—	—	1
Wighton, J.	London	1866	Landscape	—	—	2	—	—	—	—	—	—	—	2
Wightwick, George W.	London	1828	Buildings	—	—	1	—	—	—	—	—	—	—	1
Wigley, Miss J. N.	London	1845	Landscape	—	—	—	1	—	—	—	—	—	—	1
Wignell, Miss P. E.	Southsea	1872-1875	Fruit	—	—	—	—	7	—	—	—	—	—	7
Wigstead, H.	London	1784-1798	Landscape	—	—	11	—	—	—	—	—	—	—	11
Wilberfoss, T. C.	London	1873-1877	Churches	—	—	4	—	—	—	—	—	—	—	4
Wilcox, James	Harmead	1834	Landscape	—	—	—	—	—	—	4	—	—	—	4
Wild, Charles †	London	1803-1833	Churches	—	—	9	1	—	164	—	—	—	4	178
Wild, F. Percy	Leeds	1889-1893	Domestic	—	—	7	—	2	—	—	—	—	—	9
Wild, J. W.	London	1838-1870	Architecture	—	—	6	—	—	—	—	—	—	—	6
Wild, Mrs. *See* Miss Eliza Goodall	—	1855	Domestic	—	—	1	—	—	—	—	—	—	—	1
Wild, Miss	London	1840	Flowers	—	—	—	—	1	—	—	—	—	—	1
Wildash, Frederick	London	1892	Landscape	—	—	—	—	1	—	—	—	—	—	1
Wilday, Charles	London	1855-1865	Domestic	—	—	1	—	1	—	—	—	—	1	3
Wilde, Mrs. Amy	Liverpool	1891	Miniatures	—	—	1	—	—	—	—	—	—	—	1
Wilde, Charles, Junr.	Nottingham	1879	Landscape	—	—	—	—	1	—	—	—	—	—	1
Wilde, William	Nottingham	1864-1880	Landscape	—	—	—	—	6	—	—	—	—	2	8
Wilde, De. *See* D.	—	—	—	—	—	—	—	—	—	—	—	—	—	—
Wilding —	London	1762-1769	Miniatures	10	2	—	—	—	—	—	—	—	—	12
Wildman, Edmund	London	1829-1847	Domestic	—	—	—	—	12	—	—	—	—	—	12
Wildman, John R.	London	1823-1839	Figures	—	—	8	4	9	—	—	—	—	—	21
Wilds, A. H.	Brighton	1830-1831	Architecture	—	—	4	—	—	—	—	—	—	—	4
Wilds and Busby. *See* Busby and Wilds	Brighton	1825	Architecture	—	—	1	—	—	—	—	—	—	—	1
Wiles, Henry	Cambridge	1866-1882	Sculpture	—	—	17	—	—	—	—	—	—	—	17
Wilfred, G.	—	1878	Historical	—	—	—	—	1	—	—	—	—	—	1
Wilke, Charles Augustus William	London	1857-1876	Sculpture	—	—	15	2	5	—	—	—	—	—	22
Wilkes, Samuel	London	1857-1859	Landscape	—	—	2	—	—	—	—	—	—	3	5
Wilkes, Mrs. Sarah	London	1859-1870	Landscape	—	—	—	—	6	—	—	—	—	4	10
Wilkes, Miss Sarah	London	1869	Landscape	—	—	3	—	—	—	—	—	—	—	3
Wilkes, Miss	—	1799	Flowers	—	—	1	—	—	—	—	—	—	—	1
Wilkie, Sir David, R.A.	London	1806-1842	Historical	—	—	100	12	—	—	—	—	—	—	112
Wilkie, Miss H.	London	1874-1876	Landscape	—	—	—	—	3	—	—	—	—	—	3
Wilkin, Charles	London	1783-1808	Miniatures	—	—	24	—	—	—	—	—	—	—	24
Wilkin, Frank W.	London	1806-1837	Portraits	—	—	25	2	—	—	—	—	—	—	27
Wilkin, Henry	London	1831-1847	Miniatures	—	—	57	—	17	—	—	—	—	—	74
Wilkin, Miss	London	1856-1859	Landscape	—	—	1	—	2	—	—	—	—	—	3
Wilkins —	—	1796	Buildings	—	—	1	—	—	—	—	—	—	—	1

Name.	Town.	First and Last Year of Ex.	Speciality.	S. A.	F. S.	R. A.	B. I.	S. S.	O. W.	N. W.	G. G.	N. G.	V. E.	Total.
Wilkins, George	Derby	1880-1884	Landscape	—	—	1	—	4	—	—	—	—	—	5
Wilkins, Master James, aged 8	—	1776-1779	Heads	—	4	—	—	—	—	—	—	—	—	4
Wilkins, Master John, aged 9	—	1776-1779	Figures	—	4	—	—	—	—	—	—	—	—	4
Wilkins, J.	London	1765-1800	Sea Pieces	—	80	5	—	—	—	—	—	—	—	85
Wilkins, J. F. *or* G. F.	London	1835-1836	Portraits	—	—	2	—	2	—	—	—	—	—	4
Wilkins, J. H.	London	1815-1821	Landscape	—	—	7	—	—	—	—	—	—	—	7
Wilkins, Miss Mary A.	Dorchester	1887	Miniatures	—	—	1	—	—	—	—	—	—	—	1
Wilkins, Robert	London	1772-1788	Sea Pieces	—	—	6	—	—	—	—	—	—	—	6
Wilkins, W.	Norwich	1780-1787	Churches	—	—	10	—	—	—	—	—	—	—	10
Wilkins, William, R.A.	London	1799-1838	Architecture	—	—	52	—	—	—	—	—	—	—	52
Wilkins, W.	London	1852	Landscape	—	—	1	—	—	—	—	—	—	—	1
Wilkins, W. Noy	Dublin	1852-1864	Landscape	—	—	1	10	3	—	—	—	—	—	14
Wilkins, Mrs.	—	1773-1813	Figures	—	7	1	—	—	—	—	—	—	—	8
Wilkinson —		1783	Landscape	—	—	1	—	—	—	—	—	—	—	1
Wilkinson, Alfred Ayscough	London	1875-1881	Venice	—	—	—	—	13	—	—	—	—	—	13
Wilkinson, Charles A.	London	1881-1892	Landscape	—	—	9	—	21	—	1	1	—	11	43
Wilkinson, Miss Ellen	London	1853-1879	Flowers, etc.	—	—	2	—	18	—	—	—	—	8	28
Wilkinson, Edward Clegg	London	1882-1892	Domestic	—	—	5	—	6	—	1	—	1	8	21
Wilkinson, E. W.	London	1881	Sea Pieces	—	—	—	—	1	—	—	—	—	—	1
Wilkinson, General Fred. Green	London	1884	Military	—	—	—	—	1	—	—	—	—	—	1
Wilkinson, G.	—	1843	Architecture	—	—	1	—	—	—	—	—	—	—	1
Wilkinson, Miss Georgiana	London	1855-1876	Buildings	—	—	8	—	—	—	—	—	—	3	11
Wilkinson, Hugh	London	1870-1893	Landscape	—	—	23	—	12	—	—	14	7	25	81
Wilkinson, Henry D.	London	1887-1892	Architecture	—	—	4	—	—	—	—	—	—	—	4
Wilkinson, Miss Laura	London	1856	Fruit	—	—	1	—	—	—	—	—	—	—	1
Wilkinson, L. M.	London	1881	Flowers	—	—	—	—	—	—	—	—	—	1	1
Wilkinson, M. R.	—	1843	Portraits	—	—	1	—	—	—	—	—	—	—	1
Wilkinson, Robert	London	1773-1778	Landscape	7	—	7	—	—	—	—	—	—	—	14
Wilkinson, R.	London	1788-1789	Miniatures	—	—	2	—	—	—	—	—	—	—	2
Wilkinson, R. Ellis	Harrow	1874-1890	Rustic	—	—	10	—	1	—	3	—	—	19	33
Wilkinson, R. H.	London	1872-1874	Sea Pieces	—	—	—	—	2	—	—	—	—	1	3
Wilkinson, Robert Stark	London	1877-1881	Landscape	—	—	1	—	2	—	—	—	—	3	6
Wilkinson, W.	Oxford	1862-1865	Architecture	—	—	3	—	—	—	—	—	—	—	3
Wilkinson, W. F.	London	1858	Churches	—	—	—	—	2	—	—	—	—	—	2
Willard, Frank	London	1886	Figures	—	—	—	—	—	—	—	—	—	1	1
Willats, Mrs.	London	1881	Venice	—	—	—	—	1	—	—	—	—	—	1
Willcock, George Barrell	London	1839-1852	Landscape	—	—	12	7	31	—	—	—	—	38	88
Willcoxen, Thomas	—	1834-1835	Landscape	—	—	—	—	2	—	—	—	—	—	2
Willèms, Florente	Paris	1867-1880	Portraits	—	—	1	—	—	—	—	2	—	1	4
Willenich, Michel	London	1879	River Scenes	—	—	2	—	—	—	—	—	—	—	2
Willes, Edith A.	London	1882	Churches	—	—	—	—	1	—	—	—	—	—	1
Willes, J.	London	1838	Architecture	—	—	2	—	—	—	—	—	—	—	2
Willes, William	London	1820-1865	Landscape	—	—	10	17	—	—	—	—	—	—	27
Willett, Arthur	Brighton	1883-1892	Landscape	—	—	7	—	4	—	9	—	—	5	25
Willett, Mrs.	Chiswick	1849-1850	Flowers	—	—	—	—	3	—	—	—	—	—	3
Willey, Miss H.	Bristol	1874	Flowers	—	—	—	—	1	—	—	—	—	—	1
Willgohs, G.	Berlin	1858	Portraits	—	—	1	—	—	—	—	—	—	—	1
William-Stott. *See* S.	—	—	—	—	—	—	—	—	—	—	—	—	—	—
Williams. *See* Boddington.	—	—	—	—	—	—	—	—	—	—	—	—	—	—
Williams —	Bath	1785-1792	Portraits	—	—	2	—	—	—	—	—	—	—	2
Williams —	London	1764-1766	Sculpture	4	—	—	—	—	—	—	—	—	—	4
Williams —	London	1773	Miniatures	1	—	—	—	—	—	—	—	—	—	1
Williams —	London	1775	Portraits	2	—	—	—	—	—	—	—	—	—	2
Williams, Hon. Captain	—	1840	Figures	—	—	1	—	—	—	—	—	—	—	1
Williams, Albert	London	1882-1886	Landscape	—	—	—	—	4	—	1	—	—	—	5
Williams, Alfred	Salisbury	1880-1890	Landscape	—	—	4	—	1	—	—	—	1	—	6
Williams, Mrs. Alfred. *See* Miss Florence Elizabeth Thomas.	—	—	—	—	—	—	—	—	—	—	—	—	—	—
Williams, Alyn	London	1890-1893	Miniatures	—	—	5	—	—	—	4	—	—	—	9
Williams, Miss Anne	London	1768-1783	Portraits	1	28	3	—	—	—	—	—	—	—	32
Williams, Miss Annie	London	1892	Buildings	—	—	1	—	—	—	—	—	—	—	1
Williams (A.) and Stephens (C. W.)	London	1887	Architecture	—	—	1	—	—	—	—	—	—	—	1
Williams, Miss A. Florence	London	1877-1891	Landscape	—	—	3	—	6	—	4	—	—	4	17
Williams, Alfred M.	Tottenham	1881-1882	Domestic	—	—	—	—	1	—	—	—	—	1	2
Williams, A. Sheldon	Winchfield	1867-1881	Domestic	—	—	4	—	6	—	—	—	—	23	33
Williams, Alfred Walter (Williams Family)	London	1843-1891	Landscape	—	—	76	42	79	—	4	—	—	108	309
Williams, Benjamin. *See* Leader	Worcester	1854-1856	Landscape	—	—	4	4	—	—	—	—	—	4	12
Williams, C.	London	1825-1826	Portraits	—	—	5	—	—	—	—	—	—	—	5
Williams, C. F.	London	1827-1841	Rustic	—	—	—	3	3	—	—	—	—	—	6
Williams, Charles Frederick	Exeter	1841-1880	Landscape	—	—	7	—	14	—	—	—	—	19	40
Williams, Miss Carolina F.	Barnes	1859-1885	Landscape	—	—	12	9	64	—	—	—	—	12	97
Williams, Lieut. C. P.	London	1864-1873	Sea Pieces	—	—	—	—	6	—	—	—	—	—	6

Name.	Town.	First and Last Year of Ex.	Speciality.	S. A.	F. S.	R. A.	B. I.	S. S.	O. W.	N. W.	G. G.	N. G.	V. E.	Total.
Williams, C. R.	Birmingham	1851	Landscape	—	—	—	1	—	—	—	—	—	—	1
Williams, C. W.	London	1818-1819	Ruins	—	—	3	—	—	—	—	—	—	—	3
Williams, E.	London	1826	Domestic	—	—	—	—	1	—	—	—	—	—	1
Williams, Edward (father of Williams	—	—	—	—	—	—	—	—	—	—	—	—	—	—
Family)	London	1814-1855	Landscape	—	—	36	21	38	—	—	—	—	49	144
Williams, Edwin	Cheltenham	1844-1875	Figures	—	—	31	1	7	—	—	—	—	—	39
Williams, Mrs. Emily	London	1883-1890	Figures	—	—	—	—	—	—	—	9	4	—	13
Williams, Miss Emily	London	1869-1889	Flowers	—	—	5	—	1	—	—	—	—	6	12
Williams, Edward Charles (Williams Family)	London	1839-1865	Sea Pieces	—	—	19	23	10	—	—	—	—	84	136
Williams, Miss E. Edgington	London	1890	Domestic	—	—	1	—	—	—	—	—	—	—	1
Williams, E. H.	London	1876-1878	Architecture	—	—	2	—	—	—	—	—	—	—	2
Williams, Miss Ethel Haynes-	London	1886-1893	Flowers	—	—	1	—	—	—	1	6	—	10	18
Williams, F.	London	1850	Historical	—	—	2	—	—	—	—	—	—	—	2
Williams, Frank	London	1835-1874	Figures	—	—	30	12	20	—	—	—	—	13	75
Williams, F. D.	Paris	1877-1878	Domestic	—	—	—	—	—	—	—	—	—	2	2
Williams, Francis H.	London	1870-1891	Figures	—	—	3	—	26	—	—	—	—	4	33
Williams, F. P.	London	1851	River Scenes	—	—	—	—	2	—	—	—	—	—	2
Williams, G.	London	1801	—	—	—	*	—	—	—	—	—	—	—	—
Williams, George Augustus (Williams Family)	London	1841-1885	Landscape	—	—	72	65	140	—	—	—	—	163	440
Williams, G. B.	—	1851	Landscape	—	—	—	—	—	—	—	—	—	1	1
Williams, Gertrude M.	London	1880	Domestic	—	—	—	—	1	—	—	—	—	1	2
Williams, H.	London	1779-1792	Shipping	—	8	1	—	—	—	—	—	—	—	9
Williams, H.	London	1782-1822	Dramatic	—	—	5	—	—	—	—	—	—	—	5
Williams, H.	London	1833	Landscape	—	—	—	—	—	—	1	—	—	—	1
Williams, Harry, *or* Henry	Liverpool	1854-1877	Landscape	—	—	2	3	18	—	—	—	—	22	45
Williams, Henry	London	1832-1839	Landscape	—	—	8	—	13	—	6	—	—	—	27
Williams, Henry	Penzance	1874	Landscape	—	—	—	—	—	—	—	—	—	2	2
Williams, Herbert	London	1837-1857	Architecture	—	—	9	—	—	—	—	—	—	—	9
Williams, H. J.	London	1828-1877	Landscape	—	—	4	19	16	—	—	—	—	—	39
Williams, H. L.	Croydon	1892	Domestic	—	—	—	—	1	—	—	—	—	—	1
Williams, H. P.	London	1841-1857	Landscape	—	—	17	11	17	—	—	—	—	—	45
Williams, Hugh William (Grecian Williams)	Edinburgh	1808-1809	Landscape	—	—	—	—	—	—	—	—	—	26	26
Williams, Ida	Manchester	1876-1880	Figures	—	—	—	—	—	—	—	—	—	2	2
Williams, J.	London	1799-1810	Architecture	—	—	16	—	—	—	—	—	—	—	16
Williams, J.	London	1807	Architecture	—	—	1	—	—	—	—	—	—	—	1
Williams, J.	London	1808	Domestic	—	—	2	—	—	—	—	—	—	—	2
Williams, J.	London	1831-1835	Intaglios	—	—	4	—	—	—	—	—	—	—	4
Williams, J.	London	1831-1876	Landscape	—	—	29	43	71	—	—	—	—	—	143
Williams, James	London	1763-1776	Portraits	—	58	—	—	—	—	—	—	—	—	58
Williams, James	London	1842	Architecture	—	—	1	—	—	—	—	—	—	—	1
Williams, John. *See* Anthony Pasquin	London	1770-1775	Engraving	2	—	1	—	—	—	—	—	—	—	3
Williams, J. D.	London	1824	Heads	—	—	—	1	—	—	—	—	—	—	1
Williams, John Edgar	London	1846-1883	Domestic	—	—	26	4	24	—	—	—	—	—	54
Williams, James Francis, R.S.A.	Edinburgh	1800-1840	Sea Pieces	—	—	5	6	6	—	—	—	—	—	17
Williams, J. G.	London	1824-1858	Portraits	—	—	7	—	3	—	—	—	—	5	15
Williams, J. Godwin	Portsmouth	1825	Sea Pieces	—	—	—	1	—	—	—	—	—	—	1
Williams, J. Haynes-	Birmingham	1861-1893	Domestic	—	—	23	3	4	—	1	14	3	25	73
Williams, John Henry	Liverpool	1852-1866	Sea Pieces, etc.	—	—	—	1	3	—	—	—	—	—	4
Williams, J. J.	—	1840	Portraits	—	—	1	—	—	—	—	—	—	—	1
Williams, J. L. *See* Ebden and Williams	—	—	Architecture	—	—	—	—	—	—	—	—	—	—	—
Williams, Joseph Lionel	London	1834-1874	Domestic	—	—	13	9	36	—	—	—	—	8	66
Williams, John Michael	London	1760-1773	Portraits	3	18	—	—	—	—	—	—	—	—	21
Williams, J. M.	London	1834-1849	Sporting	—	—	8	8	9	—	1	—	—	—	26
Williams, Mrs. J. S.	Glasgow	1881	Rivers	—	—	—	—	—	—	—	1	—	—	1
Williams, James T.	London	1828-1840	Landscape	—	—	9	—	10	—	—	—	—	—	19
Williams, K. E.	London	1890	Domestic	—	—	—	—	—	—	1	—	—	—	1
Williams, L.	—	1825	Landscape	—	—	—	—	2	—	—	—	—	—	2
Williams, Miss L. Gwendolen	Wimbledon	1893	Heads	—	—	1	—	—	—	—	—	—	—	1
Williams, L. L.	Paris	1884	Landscape	—	—	—	—	1	—	—	—	—	—	1
Williams, Miss M.	London	1793	Figures	—	—	1	—	—	—	—	—	—	—	1
Williams, M. Joanna	Merton	1872	Etching	—	—	—	—	—	—	—	—	—	1	1
Williams, Miss M. Josephine	London	1892	Military	—	—	—	—	1	—	1	—	—	—	2
Williams, Miss Nina Haynes-	London	1888	Fruit	—	—	—	—	—	—	1	—	—	—	1
Williams, Penry †	London	1822-1869	Figures	—	—	34	9	2	11	—	—	—	—	56
Williams, Pownoll T.	Hastings	1872-1893	Landscape	—	—	6	—	13	—	1	3	—	31	54
Williams, R.	London	1795-1817	Portraits	—	—	8	—	—	—	—	—	—	—	8
Williams, R.	London	1822-1832	Sculpture	—	—	7	—	—	—	—	—	—	—	7
Williams, Richard A.	Chiswick	1878-1891	Landscape	—	—	1	—	4	—	—	—	—	1	6
Williams, R. P.	London	1854-1867	Miniatures	—	—	5	—	—	—	—	—	—	—	5
Williams, S.	London	1760-1791	Sculpture	10	—	2	—	—	—	—	—	—	—	12
Williams, S.	London	1807	Portraits	—	—	7	—	—	—	—	—	—	—	7
Williams, Samuel	London	1831-1845	Domestic	—	—	1	3	—	—	—	—	—	—	4

Name.	Town.	First and Last Year of Ex.	Speciality.	S. A.	F. S.	R. A.	B. I.	S. S.	O.W.	N.W.	G. G.	N. G.	V. E.	Total.
Williams, S.	London	1834-1844	Landscape	—	—	2	—	—	—	1	—	—	—	3
Williams, Solomon, R.H.A.	London	1791-1836	Historical	—	—	19	13	—	—	—	—	—	—	32
Williams, Mrs. Sydney	Balham	1871	Flowers	—	—	—	—	—	—	—	—	—	1	1
Williams, Terrick	Lewisham	1884-1893	Domestic	—	—	9	—	8	—	—	—	—	6	23
Williams, Thomas	London	1831-1850	Figures	—	—	2	3	2	—	—	—	—	—	7
Williams, T. H.	Exeter	1801-1830	Sea Pieces	—	—	7	15	1	—	—	—	—	—	23
Williams, Walter	Barnes	1853-1884	Landscape	—	—	10	14	47	—	—	—	—	37	108
Williams, William	Manchester	1763-1780	Landscape	13	1	—	—	—	—	—	—	—	—	14
Williams, William	Norwich	1770-1792	Landscape	—	—	31	—	—	—	—	—	—	—	31
Williams, W.	Edinburgh	1815	Landscape	—	—	1	—	—	—	—	—	—	—	1
Williams, W.	Bath	1841-1876	Landscape	—	—	34	40	55	—	—	—	—	—	129
Williams, William	London	1824-1839	Sculpture	—	—	14	—	7	—	—	—	—	—	21
Williams, Mrs. Walter (E.)	Barnes	1858	Miniatures	—	—	1	—	—	—	—	—	—	—	1
Williams (W. A.) and Hopton	London	1890	Architecture	—	—	1	—	—	—	—	—	—	—	1
Williams, William Charles	London	1891	Flowers	—	—	—	—	1	—	—	—	—	—	1
Williams, W. M.	—	1832	Architecture	—	—	—	—	1	—	—	—	—	—	1
Williams, William Oliver	Birmingham	1851-1863	Domestic	—	—	6	2	—	—	—	—	—	—	8
Williams, W. R.	—	1854-1855	Architecture	—	—	2	—	—	—	—	—	—	—	2
Williams, Mrs.	London	1769-1774	Shell Work	6	—	—	—	—	—	—	—	—	—	6
Williams, Mrs.	Barnes	1871-1872	Landscape	—	—	—	—	2	—	—	—	—	—	2
Williams, Miss	London	1771	Shell Work	1	—	—	—	—	—	—	—	—	—	1
Williams, Miss	Winchester	1869-1874	Landscape	—	—	—	—	1	—	—	—	—	2	3
Williams, West, and Slade	London	1892	Architecture	—	—	1	—	—	—	—	—	—	—	1
Williamshurst, J. H.	London	1876	Landscape	—	—	—	—	1	—	—	—	—	—	1
Williamson —	—	1814	Battles	—	—	—	—	—	—	—	—	—	1	1
Williamson, Daniel Alexander	London	1849-1871	Portraits	—	—	8	—	2	—	—	—	—	12	22
Williamson, D. A.	Broughton in Furness	1883	Landscape	—	—	—	—	—	—	1	—	—	—	1
Williamson, Frederick	London	1856-1893	Landscape	—	—	37	4	27	—	13	3	—	31	115
Williamson, Francis John	Esher	1853-1893	Sculpture	—	—	75	1	3	—	—	—	—	—	79
Williamson, H.	London	1836	Landscape	—	—	—	—	1	—	—	—	—	—	1
Williamson, H. H.	London	1866-1876	Sea Pieces	—	—	1	2	—	—	—	—	—	—	3
Williamson, John	London	1783	Portraits	—	—	1	—	—	—	—	—	—	—	1
Williamson, J.	London	1816	Landscape	—	—	—	1	—	—	—	—	—	—	1
Williamson, John	Edinburgh	1891-1893	Domestic	—	—	2	—	1	—	—	—	—	—	3
Williamson, J. B.	London	1855-1868	Sculpture	—	—	9	—	—	—	—	—	—	—	9
Williamson, J. B.	London	1868-1871	Sea Shores	—	—	1	—	—	—	—	—	—	3	4
Williamson, John Smith	London	1866-1880	Sea Pieces	—	—	5	—	9	—	—	—	—	12	26
Williamson, J. T.	London	1876	Sea Pieces	—	—	—	—	—	—	—	—	—	2	2
Williamson, Samuel	Liverpool	1811	Landscape	—	—	1	—	—	—	—	—	—	—	1
Williamson, Thomas	London	1825	Engraving	—	—	—	—	3	—	—	—	—	—	3
Williamson, W.	Herefordshire	1803	Portraits	—	—	1	—	—	—	—	—	—	—	1
Williamson, W.	London	1852	Sea Pieces	—	—	1	—	—	—	—	—	—	—	1
Williamson, W. H.	London	1853-1875	Sea Pieces	—	—	3	5	14	—	—	—	—	1	23
Williamson, W. M.	London	1868-1873	Landscape	—	—	6	—	3	—	—	—	—	8	17
Williamson, Mrs.	London	1802-1805	Portraits	—	—	4	—	—	—	—	—	—	—	4
Willinck (W. E.) and Thicknesse (Philip)	—	—	—	—	—	—	—	—	—	—	—	—	—	—
See Thicknesse and Willinck	Liverpool	1893	Architecture	—	—	1	—	—	—	—	—	—	—	1
Willing, T.	—	1816	Portraits	—	—	1	—	—	—	—	—	—	—	1
Willink, H. G.	London	1877-1888	Landscape	—	—	—	—	—	—	2	—	—	1	3
Willis, Edmund R.	London	1847-1851	Cattle	—	—	4	4	4	—	—	—	—	1	13
Willis, Frank	Windsor	1892	Figures	—	—	1	—	—	—	—	—	—	—	1
Willis, George William	London	1845-1869	Landscape	—	—	1	—	11	—	—	—	—	3	15
Willis, Henry Brittan, R.W.S. †	London	1844-1883	Cattle	—	—	27	18	14	366	—	—	—	70	495
Willis, Mrs. Henry Brittan	London	1855	Landscape	—	—	1	—	—	—	—	—	—	—	1
Willis, John	London	1828-1852	Churches	—	—	6	—	4	—	—	—	—	—	10
Willis, J. Cole	London	1866-1867	Domestic	—	—	—	3	1	—	—	—	—	—	4
Willis, Miss Katharina	Hendon	1893	Portraits	—	—	1	—	—	—	—	—	—	1	2
Willis, P.	London	1800-1825	Still Life	—	—	23	2	—	—	—	—	—	—	25
Willis, Richard H. A.	London	1879-1891	Sculpture	—	—	6	—	—	—	—	—	—	1	7
Willis, W.	Reading	1845-1857	Allegorical	—	—	2	—	—	—	—	—	—	—	2
Willis, Miss	London	1797-1803	Landscape	—	—	7	—	—	—	—	—	—	—	7
Willis, Miss	Twickenham	1818	Landscape	—	—	—	1	—	—	—	—	—	—	1
Willis, Miss	London	1839-1843	Portraits	—	—	2	—	—	—	—	—	—	—	2
Willison, George	London	1767-1777	Portraits	19	—	7	—	—	—	—	—	—	—	26
Willmore, Arthur	London	1858-1885	Engraving	—	—	17	—	—	—	—	—	—	1	18
Willmore, James Tibbitts, A.R.A.	London	1843-1860	Engraving	—	—	22	1	—	—	—	—	—	—	23
Willock, Richard	London	1889-1893	Architecture	—	—	3	—	—	—	—	—	—	—	3
Willott, S.	London	1872-1874	Landscape	—	—	—	—	6	—	—	—	—	—	6
Willoughby, J.	London	1808	Architecture	—	—	1	—	—	—	—	—	—	—	1
Wills, Edgar W.	London	1874-1893	Figures	—	—	8	—	10	—	—	10	2	3	33
Wills, F.	Exeter	1842-1845	Architecture	—	—	3	—	—	—	—	—	—	—	3
Wills, Henry	Cambridge	1885	Sculpture	—	—	1	—	—	—	—	—	—	—	1

Name.	Town.	First and Last Year of Ex.	Speciality.	S. A.	F. S.	R. A.	B. I.	S. S.	O. W.	N. W.	G. G.	N. G.	V. E.	Total.
Wills, Rev. James	—	1760-1766	Historical	2	1	—	—	—	—	—	—	—	—	3
Wills, T.	London	1856-1866	Sculpture	—	—	—	7	2	—	—	—	—	—	9
Wills, W. G.	London	1872-1889	Figures	—	—	2	—	—	—	—	8	1	—	11
Wills, W. J.	London	1856-1870	Sculpture	—	—	9	—	—	—	—	—	—	—	9
Wills, W. and T.	London	1884	Sculpture	—	—	1	—	—	—	—	—	—	—	1
Wills, Miss	London	1774	Flowers	—	5	—	—	—	—	—	—	—	—	5
Willshaw, J.	Newcastle-under-Lyne	1864-1866	Fruit	—	—	—	4	—	—	—	—	—	—	4
Willshire, R.	London	1802-1805	Architecture	—	—	5	—	—	—	—	—	—	—	5
Willson, Harry	London	1813-1852	Landscape	—	—	25	25	30	—	11	—	—	—	91
Willson, John J.	Leeds	1880	Sporting	—	—	—	—	—	—	—	—	—	2	2
Willson, Miss Margaret	Leeds	1888-1889	Flowers	—	—	2	—	—	—	—	—	—	—	2
Willson, Thomas	London	1799-1831	Architecture	—	—	10	—	—	—	—	—	—	—	10
Willyams, Humphry J.	Truro	1886-1887	Sea Pieces	—	—	—	—	—	—	2	—	—	—	2
Wilmot —	London	1773-1778	Still Life	4	—	2	—	—	—	—	—	—	—	6
Wilmot, Captain	—	1814	Military	—	—	—	—	—	—	—	—	—	1	1
Wilmshurst, T.	London	1848	Figures	—	—	1	—	—	—	—	—	—	—	1
Wilmshurst and Oliphant	London	1853	Architecture	—	—	1	—	—	—	—	—	—	—	1
Wilsher, T.	London	1816	Birds	—	—	1	—	—	—	—	—	—	—	1
Wilson. *See* Figgis and Wilson *and* Mitchell and Wilson	—	—	Architecture	—	—	—	—	—	—	—	—	—	—	—
Wilson —	London	1772-1783	Hair Work	3	3	—	—	—	—	—	—	—	—	6
Wilson —	London	1779	Miniatures	—	2	—	—	—	—	—	—	—	—	2
Wilson, Acton	London	1856	Sculpture	—	—	—	1	—	—	—	—	—	—	1
Wilson, Alexander	Bagshot	1803-1814	Landscape	—	—	19	2	—	—	—	—	—	—	21
Wilson, Andrew, A.R.S.A.	Great Marlow	1808-1834	Landscape	—	—	—	14	—	—	—	—	—	50	64
Wilson, Annie	Eastbourne	1878	Landscape	—	—	—	—	—	—	—	—	—	2	2
Wilson, Arthur	London	1873-1878	Churches	—	—	2	—	—	—	—	—	—	—	2
Wilson, Miss Alice C.	Weybridge	1892-1893	Flowers	—	—	1	—	—	—	1	—	—	—	2
Wilson, Miss Annie Heath	Genoa	1885-1889	Venice	—	—	—	—	3	—	—	—	—	2	5
Wilson, Miss Alice M.	London	1873-1876	Domestic	—	—	—	—	7	—	—	—	—	1	8
Wilson, A. Needham	Snaresbrook	1886-1892	Churches	—	—	6	—	—	—	—	—	—	—	6
Wilson, Miss A. S.	London	1825	Flowers	—	—	—	—	1	—	—	—	—	—	1
Wilson, Benjamin	London	1760-1783	Portraits	5	—	1	—	—	—	—	—	—	—	6
Wilson, Charles	Twickenham	1832-1855	Landscape	—	—	4	4	—	—	—	—	—	—	8
Wilson, Chester	London	1846-1855	Domestic	—	—	7	13	4	—	—	—	—	—	24
Wilson, Miss Catherine A.	London	1856-1857	Still Life	—	—	—	—	3	—	—	—	—	—	3
Wilson, Charles E.	Sheffield	1891-1893	Domestic	—	—	5	—	—	—	13	—	—	—	18
Wilson, D. R.	Bushey	1884-1886	Domestic	—	—	—	—	2	—	—	—	—	1	3
Wilson, E.	—	1800-1801	Landscape	—	—	2	—	—	—	—	—	—	—	2
Wilson, E.	London	1848	Landscape	—	—	2	—	—	—	—	—	—	—	2
Wilson, Ernest	Snaresbrook	1885-1889	Landscape	—	—	7	—	—	—	4	—	—	—	11
Wilson, E. J.	London	1864	Landscape	—	—	—	—	1	—	—	—	—	—	1
Wilson, Edgar W.	London	1886-1890	Domestic	—	—	2	—	—	—	1	—	—	—	3
Wilson, F.	London	1879	Landscape	—	—	—	—	—	—	—	—	—	1	1
Wilson, Miss Florence E.	London	1882-1890	Flowers	—	—	2	—	3	—	2	—	—	—	7
Wilson, F. R.	London	1844-1848	Architecture	—	—	2	—	—	—	—	—	—	—	2
Wilson, F. S.	London	1892-1893	Sea Shores	—	—	—	—	1	—	—	—	—	3	4
Wilson, George	London	1785-1820	Domestic	—	—	52	19	—	—	—	—	—	4	75
Wilson, George	London	1877-1885	Figures	—	—	2	—	—	—	2	1	—	2	7
Wilson, G. T.	Hastings	1875	Landscape	—	—	1	—	—	—	—	—	—	—	1
Wilson, George W.	London	1888-1893	Sculpture	—	—	2	—	—	—	1	—	1	1	5
Wilson, H.	London	1813-1824	Architecture	—	—	4	—	—	—	—	—	—	—	4
Wilson, Harry	London	1827	Venice	—	—	—	—	3	—	—	—	—	—	3
Wilson, H.	London	1843	Portraits	—	—	1	—	—	—	—	—	—	—	1
Wilson, Harry	London	1888-1893	Architecture	—	—	12	—	—	—	—	—	—	—	12
Wilson, Miss Helena	London	1857-1861	Flowers	—	—	—	—	7	—	—	—	—	—	7
Wilson, Herbert	London	1858-1880	Figures	—	—	3	3	10	—	—	3	—	—	19
Wilson, H. H.	London	1877	Landscape	—	—	—	—	1	—	—	—	—	—	1
Wilson, J.	London	1783	Portraits	—	—	2	—	—	—	—	—	—	—	2
Wilson, J.	London	1794-1796	Architecture	—	—	4	—	—	—	—	—	—	—	4
Wilson, John	London	1824-1857	Medals	—	—	39	—	4	—	—	—	—	—	43
Wilson, J.	London	1835	Architecture	—	—	1	—	—	—	—	—	—	—	1
Wilson, J.	Glasgow	1855	Landscape	—	—	1	—	—	—	—	—	—	—	1
Wilson, John	London	1884-1892	Sculpture	—	—	1	—	—	—	2	5	—	1	9
Wilson, Joseph	Putney	1873-1874	Portraits	—	—	3	—	—	—	—	—	—	—	3
Wilson, J. F.	London	1825	Portraits	—	—	—	—	1	—	—	—	—	—	1
Wilson, John H., R.S.A. §	London	1807-1856	Sea Pieces	—	—	74	149	301	5	—	—	—	—	529
Wilson, J. Harrington	London	1886	Domestic	—	—	—	—	—	—	—	—	—	1	1
Wilson, John James §	London	1831-1875	Sea Pieces	—	—	55	61	384	—	—	—	—	—	500
Wilson, J. K.	London	1837-1838	Sculpture	—	—	3	—	—	—	—	—	—	—	3
Wilson, J. T.	London	1833-1853	Portraits	—	—	13	—	*	—	—	—	—	—	13
Wilson, J. T.	London	1856-1882	Landscape	—	—	14	1	10	—	—	—	—	10	35

Name.	Town.	First and Last Year of Ex.	Speciality.	S. A.	F. S.	R. A.	B. I.	S. S.	O. W.	N.W.	G. G.	N. G.	V. E.	Total.
Wilson, James Watney	London	1871-1884	Domestic	—	—	3	—	12	—	—	—	—	1	16
Wilson, Miss Kate	London	1858-1861	Flowers	—	—	—	—	2	—	—	—	—	—	2
Wilson, Montagu	London	1889	Sculpture	—	—	1	—	—	—	—	—	—	—	1
Wilson, Miss M. *See* Mrs. A. G. Dawbarn	Folkestone	1875-1878	Sea Pieces	—	—	—	—	3	—	—	—	—	—	3
Wilson, Marie	London	1879	Landscape	—	—	—	—	1	—	—	—	—	—	1
Wilson, Miss Maria G.	London	1888	Flowers	—	—	—	—	1	—	—	—	—	—	1
Wilson, Miss Margaret O.	Windsor	1893	Etching	—	—	1	—	—	—	—	—	—	—	1
Wilson, Oscar	Blackheath	1886-1893	Domestic	—	—	2	—	11	—	1	—	—	9	23
Wilson, Paton	London	1883-1893	Sculpture	—	—	1	—	—	—	—	1	—	—	2
Wilson, P. A.	—	1850	Sculpture	—	—	2	—	—	—	—	—	—	—	2
Wilson, P. Macgregor, R.S.W.	Glasgow	1890	Sea Pieces	—	—	1	—	—	—	—	1	—	—	2
Wilson, Richard, R.A.	London	1760-1780	Landscape	33	—	30	—	—	—	—	—	—	—	63
Wilson, R.	London	1848-1864	Domestic	—	—	1	—	1	—	—	—	—	—	2
Wilson, R.	London	1850	Architecture	—	—	1	—	—	—	—	—	—	—	1
Wilson, Rosa	London	1853	Figures	—	—	1	—	—	—	—	—	—	—	1
Wilson, R. A.	London	1851-1857	Sculpture	—	—	3	5	—	—	—	—	—	—	8
Wilson, Stanley	London	1878-1883	Still Life	—	—	—	—	1	—	—	—	—	4	5
Wilson, S. H.	London	1870	Sea Pieces	—	—	1	—	—	—	—	—	—	—	1
Wilson, T.	London	1801-1804	Architecture	—	—	2	—	—	—	—	—	—	—	2
Wilson, Thomas	London	1834-1839	Landscape	—	—	8	11	14	—	—	—	—	—	33
Wilson, T. Butler	Leeds	1891	Architecture	—	—	1	—	—	—	—	—	—	—	1
Wilson, T. F.	London	1852-1854	Figures	—	—	—	—	2	—	—	—	—	—	2
Wilson, Thomas Harrington	London	1842-1886	Domestic	—	—	22	1	—	—	1	—	—	—	24
Wilson, T. J.	London	1862	Architecture	—	—	1	—	—	—	—	—	—	—	1
Wilson, Thomas Walter, R.I. ‡ φ	London	1870-1892	Landscape	—	—	4	—	7	—	58	—	—	34	103
Wilson, W	London	1798	Portraits	—	—	1	—	—	—	—	—	—	—	1
Wilson, William	London	1801-1836	Sea Pieces	—	—	37	6	18	—	—	—	—	—	61
Wilson, W.	London	1827-1866	Medals	—	—	17	—	—	—	—	—	—	—	17
Wilson, W., Junr.	London	1849-1854	Sea Pieces	—	—	2	—	10	—	—	—	—	—	12
Wilson, W.	London	1871-1875	Domestic	—	—	1	—	2	—	—	—	—	—	3
Wilson, W.	Dundee	1885-1892	Sea Shores	—	—	4	—	—	—	—	—	—	—	4
Wilson, William A.	London	1834-1865	Landscape	—	—	13	14	34	—	—	—	—	—	61
Wilson, W. Dower	London	1872-1874	Figures	—	—	1	—	—	—	—	—	—	3	4
Wilson, William Heath	London	1883-1893	Landscape	—	—	10	—	14	—	—	1	—	5	30
Wilson, W. J.	London	1853	Sea Pieces	—	—	1	—	—	—	—	—	—	—	1
Wilson, Mrs. W. R.	Wakefield	1871-1875	Figures	—	—	3	—	—	—	—	—	—	—	3
Wilson, Son, and Aldwinckle	London	1885	Architecture	—	—	1	—	—	—	—	—	—	—	1
Wilson and Dyer	London	1884	Architecture	—	—	1	—	—	—	—	—	—	—	1
Wilson and Fuller	London	1852	Architecture	—	—	1	—	—	—	—	—	—	—	1
Wilthew, L.	London	1781-1785	Miniatures	—	—	11	—	—	—	—	—	—	—	11
Wilton, A. A.	—	1837	Landscape	—	—	1	—	—	—	—	—	—	—	1
Wilton, Charles	London	1837-1847	Domestic	—	—	13	—	7	—	—	—	—	—	20
Wilton, Joseph, R.A.	London	1760-1783	Sculpture	15	—	11	—	—	—	—	—	—	—	26
Wimbush, Henry B.	Finchley	1881-1893	Landscape	—	—	3	—	—	—	—	—	—	3	6
Wimbush, John L.	London	1873-1889	Landscape	—	—	1	—	6	—	—	—	—	2	9
Wimbush, Miss Ruth	Finchley	1891	Figures	—	—	1	—	—	—	1	—	—	—	2
Wimperis, Miss A. J.	Chester	1868-1875	Landscape	—	—	—	—	6	—	—	—	—	—	6
Wimperis, Miss D.	Streatham	1893	Landscape	—	—	—	—	1	—	—	—	—	—	1
Wimperis, Edward Monson, R.I. ‡ § φ	London	1859-1893	Landscape	—	—	1	—	49	—	172	4	7	54	287
Wimperis, Miss F. M.	Chester	1875	Figures	—	—	—	—	1	—	—	—	—	—	1
Wimperis, John T.	London	1882-1887	Architecture	—	—	5	—	—	—	—	—	—	—	5
Wimperis (J. T.) and Arber	London	1889-1893	Architecture	—	—	5	—	—	—	—	—	—	—	5
Wimperis, Susan	London	1867	Domestic	—	—	—	—	1	—	—	—	—	—	1
Wimperis, Miss S. W.	Chester	1868-1871	Flowers	—	—	—	—	5	—	—	—	—	—	5
Wimpy, Charles	London	1893	Miniatures	—	—	1	—	—	—	—	—	—	—	1
Winchester, G.	Hastings	1853-1866	Landscape	—	—	1	7	36	—	—	—	—	—	44
Windass, John	York	1884-1893	Sea Pieces	—	—	3	—	2	—	—	—	—	—	5
Winde, Robert	—	1776	Figures	—	1	—	—	—	—	—	—	—	—	1
Winder, J. T.	Preston	1875	Birds	—	—	1	—	—	—	—	—	—	—	1
Winder, W. C.	London	1885	Landscape	—	—	—	—	—	—	—	—	—	1	1
Windham —, Esq.	—	1833	Portraits	—	—	—	—	—	—	1	—	—	—	1
Windham, C.	—	1807	Historical	—	—	2	—	—	—	—	—	—	—	2
Windsor, F. J.	London	1839	Portraits	—	—	1	—	—	—	—	—	—	—	1
Windsor-Fry, Harry	London	1884-1893	Domestic	—	—	2	—	3	—	3	—	—	4	12
Windus, William Lindsay	Liverpool	1847-1859	Historical	—	—	2	1	2	—	—	—	—	—	5
Wing, Adolphus H. A.	London	1848	Portraits	—	—	1	—	—	—	—	—	—	—	1
Wing, Eliza	London	1848	Flowers	—	—	1	—	—	—	—	—	—	—	1
Wing, Mary Louisa	London	1871	Flowers	—	—	—	—	1	—	—	—	—	—	1
Wing, R.	Fordingbridge	1826-1832	Landscape	—	—	1	1	1	—	—	—	—	—	3
Wing W.	London	1844-1847	Insects	—	—	2	—	—	—	—	—	—	—	2
Wingate, J. Lawton, R.S.A.	Edinburgh	1880-1889	Domestic	—	—	11	—	—	—	—	—	—	—	11
Wingfield, J.	London	1791-1798	Game	—	—	8	—	—	—	—	—	—	—	8

Name.	Town.	First and Last Year of Ex.	Speciality.	S. A.	F. S.	R. A.	B. I.	S. S.	O. W.	N. W.	G. G.	N. G.	V. E.	Total.
Wingfield, James Digman	London	1832-1872	Historical	—	—	38	94	41	—	—	—	—	45	218
Wingfield, Hon. Lewis, R.H.A.	—	1869-1875	Domestic	—	—	4	—	—	—	—	—	—	1	5
Wingfield, Peter	London	1767-1775	Enamels	4	—	4	—	—	—	—	—	—	—	8
Wingrave, F. C.	London	1793-1798	Portraits	—	—	3	—	—	—	—	—	—	—	3
Wingrove, Annette	London	1864	Figures	—	—	—	—	1	—	—	—	—	—	1
Winkfield, Frederic A.	Manchester	1873-1893	Sea Pieces	—	—	17	—	27	—	6	—	—	22	72
Winkles, Henry	London	1819-1833	Landscape	—	—	8	—	1	—	—	—	—	—	9
Winkworth, John	London	1807-1811	Architecture	—	—	4	—	—	—	—	—	—	—	4
Winmill, Charles G.	Stratford	1891	Architecture	—	—	1	—	—	—	—	—	—	—	1
Winney, Harry	Walthamstow	1881	Churches	—	—	—	—	—	—	—	—	—	1	1
Wins, M. A. H.	London	1843	Portraits	—	—	1	—	—	—	—	—	—	—	1
Winser, Charles	London	1830-1841	Portraits	—	—	2	—	—	—	—	—	—	—	2
Winser, T.	London	1870	Landscape	—	—	—	—	1	—	—	—	—	—	1
Winsor, W.	London	1846	Landscape	—	—	—	—	1	—	—	—	—	—	1
Winstanley, W.	London	1806	Landscape	—	—	—	5	—	—	—	—	—	—	5
Winston, Anne	London	1847	Figures	—	—	1	—	—	—	—	—	—	—	1
Winston, J.	—	1797	Architecture	—	—	1	—	—	—	—	—	—	—	1
Winter, Miss A.	Tulse Hill	1893	Flowers	—	—	—	—	1	—	—	—	—	—	1
Winter, C.	—	1807	Figures	—	—	2	—	—	—	—	—	—	—	2
Winter, Frederick	London	1872-1893	Sculpture	—	—	22	—	7	—	—	—	—	2	31
Winter, J. Greenwood	London	1891-1893	Figures	—	—	—	—	1	—	1	—	—	1	3
Winter, Richard Davidson	London	1890-1892	Etching	—	—	2	—	—	—	—	—	—	—	2
Winter, W. Tatton	Carshalton	1884-1893	Figures	—	—	4	—	21	—	3	—	1	3	32
Winterbottom, Austin	Sheffield	1890	Landscape	—	—	—	—	1	—	—	—	—	—	1
Winterbottom and Sands	London	1841	Architecture	—	—	1	—	—	—	—	—	—	—	1
Winterhalter, François Xavier	Paris	1852-1867	Portraits	—	—	4	—	—	—	—	—	—	—	4
Wintle, Mrs. R. P.	London	1872	Portraits	—	—	—	—	1	—	—	—	—	—	1
Winton, J. C. *See* Cave, J.	—	—	—	—	—	—	—	—	—	—	—	—	—	—
Wirgman, Charles	London	1870-1876	Japanese	—	—	—	—	—	—	—	—	—	2	2
Wirgman, Helen	London	1879-1882	Flowers	—	—	—	—	—	—	—	—	—	4	4
Wirgman, Theodore Blake	London	1867-1893	Portraits	—	—	67	—	2	—	6	1	4	59	139
Wise, William	London	1823-1876	Portraits	—	—	2	—	8	—	—	—	—	13	23
Wishart, J.	London	1798-1808	Architecture	—	—	15	—	—	—	—	—	—	—	15
Witchell, Miss Lucy	Stroud	1883-1891	Still Life	—	—	3	—	—	—	—	—	—	—	3
Witchell, Thomas	London	1778-1780	Miniatures	—	—	3	—	—	—	—	—	—	—	3
Witcombe, Miss Margaret	Guildford	1855-1871	Landscape	—	—	9	1	20	—	—	—	—	—	30
Withall, Richard Augustus. *See* Brangwyn and Withall	—	—	Architecture	—	—	—	—	—	—	—	—	—	—	—
Witherby, Henry Forbes	London	1854-1864	Landscape	—	—	7	12	10	—	—	—	—	—	29
Witherington, William Frederick, R.A.	London	1808-1863	Domestic	—	—	138	62	1	—	—	—	—	—	201
Witherington, Walter Seckham	London	1878	Architecture	—	—	1	—	—	—	—	—	—	—	1
Withers, Alfred	London	1881-1893	Landscape	—	—	11	—	2	—	—	3	—	24	40
Withers, Miss Annie	London	1893	Figures	—	—	—	—	—	—	—	—	1	—	1
Withers, Mrs. Augusta Innes ‖ §	London	1829-1865	Flowers	—	—	8	—	68	—	6	—	—	38	120
Withers, E. R.	London	1850-1852	Portraits	—	—	5	—	—	—	—	—	—	—	5
Withers, Miss Maud	London	1878-1880	Flowers	—	—	—	—	1	—	—	—	—	3	4
Withers, Robert Jewell	London	1850-1883	Architecture	—	—	6	—	—	—	—	—	—	—	6
Witkamp, E. S.	Amsterdam	1889	Domestic	—	—	—	—	1	—	—	—	—	—	1
Witter, Arthur R.	Liverpool	1884-1890	Landscape	—	—	3	—	1	—	1	—	—	—	5
Witter, W. G.	Liverpool	1885-1889	Landscape	—	—	2	—	—	—	—	—	—	—	2
Wivell, Abraham	London	1822-1859	Portraits	—	—	10	3	5	—	—	—	—	16	34
Wivell, A., Junr.	Birmingham	1848-1865	Domestic	—	—	2	4	2	—	—	—	—	—	8
Woakes, W. E.	London	1866	Figures	—	—	1	2	—	—	—	—	—	—	3
Wodehouse, Mrs. E. H.	Bath	1885	Miniatures	—	—	1	—	—	—	—	—	—	—	1
Wogan, Thomas	London	1776-1778	Miniatures	—	—	9	—	—	—	—	—	—	—	9
Woledge, F. W.	Brighton	1846	Landscape	—	—	1	—	—	—	—	—	—	—	1
Wolf, Joseph, R.I. ‡	London	1849-1881	Animals	—	—	14	7	—	—	20	—	—	8	49
Wolfe, George	Clifton	1855-1873	Sea Pieces	—	—	8	8	74	—	—	—	—	17	107
Wolfe, J. L.	London	1818	Architecture	—	—	1	—	—	—	—	—	—	—	1
Wolfe, Maynard	Shoeburyness	1870-1871	Churches	—	—	—	—	1	—	—	—	—	2	3
Wolfensberger, J.	London	1841-1842	Ruins	—	—	3	—	—	—	—	—	—	—	3
Wolff —	Rome	1839-1841	Sculpture	—	—	2	—	—	—	—	—	—	—	2
Wollen, William Barns, R.I. ‡	London	1879-1893	Domestic	—	—	8	—	—	—	14	—	—	15	37
Wolsey, Florence	London	1893	Figures	—	—	—	—	1	—	—	—	—	—	1
Wolstenholme, D.	Turnford	1803-1824	Sporting	—	—	26	—	—	—	—	—	—	—	26
Wolstenholme, D., Junr.	London	1819-1859	Sporting	—	—	13	10	13	—	—	—	—	—	36
Woltze, B.	Huddersfield	1881	Domestic	—	—	1	—	—	—	—	—	—	—	1
Wombile, T. W.	London	1834-1837	Sporting	—	—	—	—	4	—	—	—	—	—	4
Wonder, P. C.	London	1824-1831	Domestic	—	—	2	18	—	—	—	—	—	—	20
Wontner. *See* Hermon and Wontner	—	—	Architecture	—	—	—	—	—	—	—	—	—	—	—
Wontner, William Clarke	London	1879-1893	Figures	—	—	23	—	3	—	1	1	6	10	44
Wood, Mrs. Annetta T. H.	Kingston	1890	Miniatures	—	—	1	—	—	—	—	—	—	—	1

Name.	Town.	First and Last Year of Ex.	Speciality.	S. A.	F. S.	R. A.	B. I.	S. S.	O. W.	N.W.	G. G.	N.G.	V. E.	Total.
Wood, C. Haigh-	London	1874-1893	Domestic	—	—	17	—	5	—	1	—	—	8	31
Wood, Miss Catherine M. ‖ *See* Mrs. R. H.	—	—	—	—	—	—	—	—	—	—	—	—	—	—
Wright	London	1880-1891	Flowers	—	—	24	—	26	—	—	1	—	23	74
Wood, Mrs. C. W.	London	1835	Portraits	—	—	1	—	—	—	—	—	—	—	1
Wood, Daniel	Birmingham	1847-1859	Landscape	—	—	—	2	3	—	—	—	—	—	5
Wood, Daniel	Cambridge	1866	Fruit	—	—	—	1	—	—	—	—	—	—	1
Wood, Eliza A.	Hackney	1888-1889	Domestic	—	—	—	—	1	—	—	—	—	1	2
Wood, E. C.	London	1830-1831	Figures	—	—	2	—	3	—	—	—	—	—	5
Wood, Mrs. Eleanora C. ‡	London	1832-1856	Animals	—	—	—	1	13	—	11	—	—	—	25
Wood, Miss Eleanor Stuart ‖	Manchester	1876-1893	Fruit	—	—	11	—	—	—	1	11	10	—	33
Wood, Miss Emmie Stewart	London	1886-1893	Landscape	—	—	6	—	3	—	9	—	—	12	30
Wood, Edgar Thomas	Dalston	1885-1893	Buildings	—	—	—	—	5	—	—	—	—	—	5
Wood, F.	London	1817-1839	Architecture	—	—	6	—	—	—	—	—	—	—	6
Wood, G.	London	1800-1805	Architecture	—	—	2	—	—	—	—	—	—	—	2
Wood, George	London	1844-1854	Domestic	—	—	10	4	1	—	—	—	—	—	15
Wood, G. J.	London	1860	Animals	—	—	1	—	—	—	—	—	—	—	1
Wood, G. Swinford, R.C.A.	Birkenhead	1861-1889	Figures	—	—	—	3	—	—	—	2	—	—	5
Wood, Herbert	London	1875-1881	Landscape	—	—	—	—	6	—	—	—	—	2	8
Wood, Miss Hortense	Munich	1870-1880	Landscape	—	—	1	—	—	—	—	—	—	1	2
Wood, J.	London	1801-1815	Landscape	—	—	2	—	—	—	—	—	—	—	2
Wood, James	—	1828	Sculpture	—	—	—	—	1	—	—	—	—	—	1
Wood, J.	London	1846-1847	Buildings	—	—	3	—	—	—	—	—	—	—	3
Wood, John	London	1823-1862	Historical	—	—	118	68	30	—	—	—	—	—	216
Wood, Joseph	—	1761	Copies	1	—	—	—	—	—	—	—	—	—	1
Wood, John George	London	1793-1811	Landscape	—	—	11	—	—	—	—	—	—	—	11
Wood, J. Hurd-. *See* H.	—	—	—	—	—	—	—	—	—	—	—	—	—	—
Wood, J. T.	London	1798-1805	Architecture	—	—	5	—	—	—	—	—	—	—	5
Wood, J. T.	London	1853-1857	Buildings	—	—	3	—	—	—	—	—	—	—	3
Wood, J. W.	—	1838	Portraits	—	—	1	—	—	—	—	—	—	—	1
Wood, John Warrington	Rome	1868-1884	Sculpture	—	—	27	—	—	—	—	—	—	—	27
Wood, Lewis John, R.I. ‡	London	1831-1891	Churches	—	—	40	52	101	—	205	—	—	98	496
Wood, Miss L. Martina	London	1892	Study	—	—	1	—	—	—	—	—	—	—	1
Wood, Lewis Pinhorn	London	1870-1891	Landscape	—	—	4	—	43	—	5	—	—	2	54
Wood, Mrs. M.	London	1805	Landscape	—	—	1	—	—	—	—	—	—	—	1
Wood, Marshall	London	1854-1875	Sculpture	—	—	24	2	—	—	—	—	—	—	26
Wood, Lady Mary	London	1885-1888	Flowers	—	—	—	—	—	—	—	5	—	—	5
Wood, Matthew	London	1841-1855	Domestic	—	—	17	5	8	—	—	—	—	16	46
Wood, Miss Meynella	Charlton	1878-1881	Landscape	—	—	—	—	1	—	—	—	—	6	7
Wood, Robert	Newcastle	1886-1889	Landscape	—	—	—	—	—	—	1	1	—	—	2
Wood, R. H.	London	1865-1876	Landscape	—	—	13	9	31	—	—	—	—	6	59
Wood, Sancton	London	1841-1856	Architecture	—	—	5	—	—	—	—	—	—	—	5
Wood, Shakspere	Rome	1868-1871	Sculpture	—	—	5	—	—	—	—	—	—	—	5
Wood, Stanley L.	London	1885-1893	Military	—	—	1	—	—	—	3	—	—	3	7
Wood, Thomas ‡	London	1828-1853	Landscape	—	—	18	—	—	—	20	—	—	—	38
Wood, Thomas P.	London	1829-1844	Landscape	—	—	1	1	19	—	—	—	—	—	21
Wood, Thomas W.	London	1855-1872	Animals	—	—	5	—	3	—	—	—	—	2	10
Wood, T. W., Junr.	Chatham	1867	Landscape	—	—	1	—	—	—	—	—	—	—	1
Wood, Miss Ursula	London	1890-1893	Landscape	—	—	5	—	—	—	—	—	—	2	7
Wood, William	London	1788-1808	Miniatures	—	—	102	3	—	—	—	—	—	9	114
Wood, William Henry	London	1878-1881	Architecture	—	—	2	—	—	—	—	—	—	—	2
Wood, Walter James	—	1833-1861	Architecture	—	—	—	3	3	—	—	—	—	—	6
Wood, William R.	Lowestoft	1889-1893	Landscape	—	—	2	—	—	—	—	—	—	—	2
Wood, Miss	—	1775	Flowers	1	—	—	—	—	—	—	—	—	—	1
Woodall —	Halstead	1773-1776	Landscape	11	5	—	—	—	—	—	—	—	—	16
Woodbridge, T.	London	1829	Metal Work	—	—	1	—	—	—	—	—	—	—	1
Woodbridge, T. W.	Kingston	1839	Sculpture	—	—	1	—	—	—	—	—	—	—	1
Wood-Carving, National School of	—	1885	Carvings	—	—	—	—	—	—	—	1	—	—	1
Woodcock, Miss L.	Llandudno	1892	Landscape	—	—	—	—	1	—	—	—	—	—	1
Woodd (J. H. T.) and Ainslie (W.)	London	1891	Architecture	—	—	2	—	—	—	—	—	—	—	2
Woodfall, William	Halstead	1778-1787	Landscape	—	—	5	—	—	—	—	—	—	—	5
Woodford, E. B.	Putney	1878	Figures	—	—	1	—	—	—	—	—	—	—	1
Woodforde, Samuel, R.A.	London	1784-1815	Domestic	—	—	133	39	—	—	—	—	—	—	172
Woodgate, W.	London	1827	Historical	—	—	—	—	1	—	—	—	—	—	1
Woodham, W.	London	1841	Landscape	—	—	—	—	2	—	—	—	—	—	2
Woodhouse, Col. Harvey	London	1888-1889	Historical	—	—	—	—	—	—	2	—	—	—	2
Woodhouse, J. H.	Windsor	1888	Figures	—	—	—	—	—	—	1	—	—	—	1
Woodhouse, John Thomas, M.D.	London	1801-1834	Domestic	—	—	5	—	—	—	—	—	—	—	5
Woodhouse, William	Morecambe	1889	Domestic	—	—	1	—	—	—	—	—	—	—	1
Woodin, J., Junr.	London	1799-1811	Landscape	—	—	1	1	—	—	—	—	—	—	2
Woodin, Samuel, Junr.	London	1798-1843	Domestic	—	—	39	19	8	—	—	—	—	—	66
Wooding, R.	Margate	1858-1874	Landscape	—	—	—	—	13	—	—	—	—	—	13
Woodington —	London	1765	Portraits	1	—	—	—	—	—	—	—	—	—	1

Name.	Town.	First and Last Year of Ex.	Speciality.	S. A.	F. S.	R. A.	B. I.	S. S.	O.W.	N.W.	G. G.	N.G.	V. E.	Total.
Woodington, William Frederick, A.R.A.	London	1825-1881	Sculpture	—	—	47	3	2	—	—	—	—	—	52
Woodley, C.	London	1819-1839	Portraits	—	—	9	—	5	—	—	—	—	—	14
Woodley, G.	London	1836-1843	Miniatures	—	—	5	—	—	—	—	—	—	—	5
Woodley, W.	London	1821	Portraits	—	—	1	—	—	—	—	—	—	—	1
Woodlock, David	Manchester	1880-1891	Domestic	—	—	5	—	1	—	—	—	—	3	9
Woodman, Charles Horwell	London	1842-1885	Landscape	—	—	1	6	5	—	2	—	—	15	29
Woodman, M.	London	1819	Landscape	—	—	1	—	—	—	—	—	—	—	1
Woodman, Richard	London	1820-1850	Portraits	—	—	12	1	5	3	—	—	—	—	21
Woodman, Richard Horwell	London	1835-1868	Landscape	—	—	5	11	13	—	—	—	—	1	30
Woodrouffe, R.	London	1835-1854	Sporting	—	—	4	4	—	—	—	—	—	—	8
Woodrow, Miss	London	1773	Needlework	1	—	—	—	—	—	—	—	—	—	1
Woodruffe, Miss	London	1884	Figures	—	—	—	—	—	—	1	—	—	—	1
Woods, Miss Ellen M.	Bristol	1874-1881	Flowers	—	—	1	—	—	—	—	—	—	6	7
Woods, Miss Fanny. *See* Mrs. Luke Fildes.	—	—	—	—	—	—	—	—	—	—	—	—	—	—
Woods, Henry, A.R.A. φ	London	1868-1893	Venice	—	—	57	—	1	—	—	—	—	11	69
Woods, Joseph	London	1801-1815	Architecture	—	—	9	—	—	—	—	—	—	—	9
Woods, J.	London	1828	Figures	—	—	—	—	1	—	—	—	—	—	1
Woods, J. G. W.	Newbury	1889-1890	River Scenes	—	—	2	—	—	—	—	—	—	—	2
Woods, W. H.	Bristol	1854-1859	Landscape	—	—	1	2	1	—	—	—	—	—	4
Woods, Mrs.	London	1804	Landscape	—	—	1	—	—	—	—	—	—	—	1
Woodthorpe, Edmund, M.A.	London	1841-1844	Architecture	—	—	3	—	—	—	—	—	—	—	3
Woodthorpe, R. G.	London	1881	Landscape	—	—	—	—	—	—	—	—	—	2	2
Woodville, Richard Caton, R.I. ‡	Baltimore	1852-1892	Battles	—	—	11	1	—	—	1	—	1	5	19
Woodward, Miss Alice B.	London	1886-1892	Domestic	—	—	2	—	6	—	3	—	—	—	11
Woodward, J.	London	1820-1832	Enamels	—	—	19	—	2	—	—	—	—	—	21
Woodward, Miss Mary	London	1893	Domestic	—	—	—	—	1	—	—	—	—	—	1
Woodward, R.	London	1799	Architecture	—	—	1	—	—	—	—	—	—	—	1
Woodward, Thomas	London	1821-1852	Sporting	—	—	85	60	15	—	—	—	—	—	160
Woodward, William	London	1771	Miniatures	—	—	1	—	—	—	—	—	—	—	1
Woodyear —	London	1768	Sculpture	—	2	—	—	—	—	—	—	—	—	2
Woodzell and Colcutt	London	1872-1873	Architecture	—	—	2	—	—	—	—	—	—	—	2
Woolams, John	London	1836-1839	Figures	—	—	—	1	5	—	—	—	—	—	6
Woolcott, C.	London	1808-1826	Portraits	—	—	21	—	1	—	—	—	—	—	22
Woolcott, D.	—	1828	Sporting	—	—	1	—	—	—	—	—	—	—	1
Woolcott, D. E.	—	1821	Architecture	—	—	1	—	—	—	—	—	—	—	1
Wooldridge, H. Ellis	London	1867-1879	Figures	—	—	3	—	1	—	—	—	—	7	11
Wooles, W. E.	London	1828-1834	Sculpture	—	—	7	—	11	—	—	—	—	—	18
Woolett, E. J.	Tulse Hill	1835-1855	Landscape	—	—	3	—	3	—	—	—	—	—	6
Woolfe, John	London	1781	Architecture	—	—	1	—	—	—	—	—	—	—	1
Woolford, Charles H.	Musselburgh	1892	Landscape	—	—	1	—	—	—	—	—	—	—	1
Woolford, J. E. H.	London	1815	Landscape	—	—	2	—	—	—	—	—	—	—	2
Woollams, J.	London	1837	Landscape	—	—	2	—	—	—	—	—	—	—	2
Woolland, Benjamin, *or* Woollard	London	1890-1891	Architecture	—	—	2	—	—	—	—	—	—	—	2
Woollett, Henry A.	London	1857-1873	Landscape	—	—	—	—	8	—	—	—	—	5	13
Woollett, J.	—	1805-1810	Landscape	—	—	7	—	—	—	—	—	—	—	7
Woollet, William, F.S.A.	London	1760-1783	Engraving	17	5	—	—	—	—	—	—	—	—	22
Woolley, Miss Alice Mary	Sheffield	1883-1892	Flowers	—	—	4	—	5	—	—	—	—	—	9
Woolley, John	London	1778	Sculpture	1	—	—	—	—	—	—	—	—	—	1
Woolley, J.	London	1829-1834	Architecture	—	—	3	—	—	—	1	—	—	—	4
Woolley, S.	London	1791-1802	Architecture	—	—	12	—	—	—	—	—	—	—	12
Woolley, W.	London	1773-1791	Landscape	4	4	—	—	—	—	—	—	—	—	8
Woolmer, Alfred Joseph §	London	1827-1886	Domestic	—	—	12	45	355	—	—	—	—	—	412
Woolmer, Miss Ethel	London	1888-1893	Domestic	—	—	1	—	—	—	3	—	—	—	4
Woolmer, Miss M.	London	1871-1874	Domestic	—	—	—	—	6	—	—	—	—	—	6
Woolner, Miss Dorothy	London	1891	Animals	—	—	—	—	—	—	1	—	—	—	1
Woolner, Thomas, R.A.	London	1843-1893	Sculpture	—	—	119	3	—	—	4	—	—	2	128
Woolnoth, A.	Edinburgh	1872-1889	Landscape	—	—	2	—	1	—	—	—	—	—	3
Woolnoth, Charles N., R.S.W.	London	1833-1875	Landscape	—	—	—	—	—	—	3	—	—	15	18
Woolnoth, Thomas	London	1828-1857	Historical	—	—	9	4	6	—	2	—	—	—	21
Woolnoth, W.	London	1814-1831	Engraving	—	—	—	—	3	—	—	—	—	1	4
Woolnough, H.	Ipswich	1848	Architecture	—	—	1	—	—	—	—	—	—	—	1
Woon, Miss R.	London	1873	Flowers	—	—	1	—	—	—	—	—	—	—	1
Woons, J.	London	1778	Miniatures	—	—	2	—	—	—	—	—	—	—	2
Worboys, W. H.	London	1861-1862	Landscape	—	—	—	—	2	—	—	—	—	—	2
Worden, Miss Dorothy	London	1887-1893	River Scenes	—	—	2	—	6	—	—	—	—	—	8
Wores, Theodore	London	1889-1890	Japanese	—	—	2	—	2	—	—	1	2	4	11
Worlidge, Thomas	London	1761-1766	Portraits	4	7	—	—	—	—	—	—	—	—	11
Worlidge, Mrs.	London	1765-1767	Needlework	2	6	—	—	—	—	—	—	—	—	8
Worlock, S.	London	1873	Animals	—	—	—	—	1	—	—	—	—	—	1
Wormald, Ada S.	Sheffield	1879	Interiors	—	—	—	—	—	—	—	—	—	1	1
Wormald, Fanny	Hertford	1879	Flowers	—	—	—	—	—	—	—	—	—	1	1
Wormald, Lizzie	Hertford	1865	Figures	—	—	—	—	—	—	—	—	—	1	1

Name.	Town.	First and Last Year of Ex.	Speciality.	S. A.	F. S.	R. A.	B. I.	S. S.	O. W.	N.W.	G. G.	N. G.	V. E.	Total.
Wormleighton, Francis	London	1867-1885	Figures	—	—	2	—	12	—	1	—	—	4	19
Worms, Jules	Paris	1877-1883	Landscape	—	—	—	—	—	—	1	—	—	2	3
Wornum, Miss Catherine Agnes, now Mrs. Frederick Piercy	London	1872-1877	Fruit	—	—	1	—	1	—	—	—	—	1	3
Wornum, Ralph Selden. *See also* Solomons and Wornum	London	1872-1893	Buildings	—	—	12	—	—	—	—	—	—	—	12
Worrall, C.	London	1857-1870	Sculpture	—	—	14	—	—	—	—	—	—	—	14
Worrall, H.	London	1846	Architecture	—	—	1	—	—	—	—	—	—	—	1
Worrall, J. E.	Liverpool	1862-1868	Domestic	—	—	5	—	4	—	—	—	—	—	9
Worrall, Miss Kate	London	1892	Landscape	—	—	—	—	—	—	—	—	—	1	1
Worrell, J., *or* Wornell	London	1844	Sculpture	—	—	1	—	—	—	—	—	—	—	1
Worrell, Van. *See* V.	—	—	—	—	—	—	—	—	—	—	—	—	—	—
Worsdell, Miss Clara J.	Lancaster	1884-1887	Flowers	—	—	2	—	—	—	—	—	—	—	2
Worsey, Thomas	Birmingham	1856-1874	Flowers	—	—	17	19	51	—	—	—	—	12	99
Worsley, Charles N.	London	1886-1893	Landscape	—	—	3	—	10	—	1	—	—	4	18
Worsley, D. Edmund	London	1833-1854	Landscape	—	—	1	8	15	—	—	—	—	—	24
Worsley, E.	London	1846-1851	Landscape	—	—	2	—	—	—	—	—	—	—	2
Worsley, E. Maria	London	1874	Fruit	—	—	—	—	—	—	—	—	—	1	1
Worsley, H. F.	Bath	1828-1843	Landscape	—	—	3	14	7	—	—	—	—	—	24
Worsley, R. E.	London	1877	Landscape	—	—	—	—	2	—	—	—	—	—	2
Worthington, J. G.	—	1795-1804	Landscape	—	—	11	—	—	—	—	—	—	—	11
Worthington, Thomas Locke	Manchester	1885-1890	Architecture	—	—	5	—	—	—	—	—	—	—	5
Worthington, William Henry	London	1819-1839	Domestic	—	—	19	2	—	—	—	—	—	—	21
Wortley, Archibald J. Stuart-	London	1874-1893	Sporting	—	—	29	—	—	—	—	41	2	16	88
Wortley, Miss Mary Stuart, afterwards Lady Wentworth	London	1875-1893	Portraits	—	—	3	—	—	—	—	7	1	2	13
Wrathall, John J.	London	1885-1890	Stained Glass	—	—	3	—	—	—	—	—	—	—	3
Wratislaw, Miss Matilda E. ‖	Rome	1871-1884	Architecture	—	—	3	—	—	—	1	—	—	11	15
Wray, Christopher George	London	1856-1873	Architecture	—	—	4	—	—	—	—	—	—	—	4
Wray, J. M.	—	1874	Landscape	—	—	—	—	1	—	—	—	—	—	1
Wray, L.	London	1875-1879	Domestic	—	—	—	—	—	—	—	—	—	2	2
Wray, Robert Bateman	Salisbury	1770-1771	Gems	—	—	2	—	—	—	—	—	—	—	2
Wreford, Major W.	East Sheen	1874	Portraits	—	—	1	—	—	—	—	—	—	—	1
Wren, Miss Emma. *See* Mrs. Cooper.	—	—	—	—	—	—	—	—	—	—	—	—	—	—
Wren, John C.	Penzance	1874-1883	Sea Pieces	—	—	—	—	2	—	1	—	—	1	4
Wren, Miss Louisa	London	1882-1893	Portraits	—	—	3	—	—	—	5	—	—	5	13
Wright. *See* Branston and White	—	—	Domestic	—	—	—	—	—	—	—	—	—	—	—
Wright —	London	1780	Portraits	1	—	—	—	—	—	—	—	—	—	1
Wright, Alan	London	1889-1891	Architecture	—	—	3	—	—	—	—	—	—	2	5
Wright, Miss Alice M.	London	1892	Landscape	—	—	—	—	1	—	—	—	—	—	1
Wright, C.	London	1820	Sculpture	—	—	1	—	—	—	—	—	—	—	1
Wright, C.	London	1853-1871	Portraits	—	—	3	1	1	—	—	—	—	—	5
Wright, Miss Caroline	Manchester	1879	Landscape	—	—	—	—	—	—	—	—	—	2	2
Wright, Miss Carrie E.	London	1885-1886	Domestic	—	—	—	—	2	—	—	—	—	—	2
Wright, Miss Catherine M. ‖	London	1886-1890	Figures	—	—	3	—	1	—	—	2	2	4	12
Wright, Mrs. D.	London	1861-1865	Figures	—	—	2	4	3	—	—	—	—	—	9
Wright, Edward	London	1769-1782	Sea Pieces	9	1	—	—	—	—	—	—	—	—	10
Wright, Edward	London	1878-1883	Landscape	—	—	—	—	1	—	—	—	—	1	2
Wright, Eliza	Woolwich	1810-1813	Flowers	—	—	3	—	—	—	—	—	—	—	3
Wright, Miss Elizabeth	London	1773-1783	Landscape	8	—	—	—	—	—	—	—	—	—	8
Wright, Miss Elizabeth	London	1825-1830	Landscape	—	—	3	—	2	—	—	—	—	—	5
Wright, Miss Ethel	London	1887-1893	Domestic	—	—	9	—	1	—	—	—	—	13	23
Wright, Edward C. J.	London	1887	Sea Pieces	—	—	1	—	—	—	—	—	—	—	1
Wright (E. W.) and Taylor (L.)	London	1877	Architecture	—	—	2	—	—	—	—	—	—	—	2
Wright, F. P.	London	1877-1883	Fruit	—	—	—	—	3	—	—	—	—	1	4
Wright, F. T.	London	1825	Landscape	—	—	—	1	—	—	—	—	—	—	1
Wright, George	Annan	1892	Landscape	—	—	1	—	—	—	—	—	—	—	1
Wright, Miss Grace M.	London	1890	Landscape	—	—	—	—	—	—	—	—	—	1	1
Wright, H.	—	1819-1821	Landscape	—	—	2	—	—	—	—	—	—	—	2
Wright, Helena A.	Nottingham	1883	Game	—	—	—	—	1	—	—	—	—	—	1
Wright, H. C. Stepping	Norwood	1883-1888	Landscape	—	—	—	—	6	—	1	—	—	—	7
Wright, H. T.	London	1830-1844	Architecture	—	—	3	—	—	—	—	—	—	—	3
Wright, Henry William, F.S.A.	London	1867	Landscape	—	—	—	—	1	—	—	—	—	—	1
Wright, J.	London	1791	Shipping	—	—	2	—	—	—	—	—	—	—	2
Wright, J.	London	1809-1832	Landscape	—	—	2	—	1	—	—	—	—	—	3
Wright, J.	London	1831-1832	Landscape	—	—	2	—	—	—	—	—	—	—	2
Wright, J.	London	1870-1875	Sea Pieces	—	—	—	—	4	—	—	—	—	—	4
Wright, John	London	1770	Engraving	1	—	—	—	—	—	—	—	—	—	1
Wright, John	London	1795-1819	Miniatures	—	—	57	—	—	—	—	—	—	—	57
Wright, Joseph, A.R.A.	Derby	1765-1794	Domestic	43	2	40	—	—	—	—	—	—	—	85
Wright, Joseph	London	1780	Wax Model	—	—	1	—	—	—	—	—	—	—	1
Wright, J. A.	London	1859	Sculpture	—	—	1	—	—	—	—	—	—	—	1

Name.	Town.	First and Last Year of Ex.	Speciality.	S. A.	F. S.	R. A.	B. I.	S. S.	O. W.	N. W.	G. G.	N. G.	V. E.	Total.
Wright, J. H.	London	1808	Landscape	—	—	1	—	—	—	—	—	—	—	1
Wright, John Masey †	London	1808-1866	Historical	—	—	9	8	29	134	—	—	—	—	180
Wright, John William †	London	1823-1848	Portraits	—	—	35	—	—	82	—	—	—	—	117
Wright, Miss Lilian	London	1893	Still Life	—	—	—	—	2	—	—	—	—	—	2
Wright, Madame Lois	Honfleur	1880	Figures	—	—	1	—	—	—	—	—	—	—	1
Wright, Mrs. Louisa	London	1770-1777	Fruit	13	—	—	—	—	—	—	—	—	—	13
Wright, Miss Meg	Edinburgh	1891-1892	Landscape	—	—	2	—	3	—	—	—	—	—	5
Wright, Marian L.	Paris	1877	Figures	—	—	—	—	—	—	—	—	—	1	1
Wright, Mrs. Mary M.	Cambridge	1887-1891	Landscape	—	—	2	—	—	—	—	—	—	1	3
Wright, Nevill	London	1885-1889	Algiers	—	—	4	—	1	—	—	—	—	—	5
Wright, Richard, F.S.A.	London	1762-1773	Sea Pieces	25	1	—	—	—	—	—	—	—	—	26
Wright, Richard Henry	Hornsey	1885-1889	Landscape	—	—	1	—	—	—	2	—	—	3	6
Wright, Mrs. R. H. *See* Miss Catherine M. Wood	London	1892-1893	Flowers	—	—	10	—	3	—	—	—	—	2	15
Wright, R. L.	London	1824-1832	Churches	—	—	—	—	10	—	—	—	—	—	10
Wright, Robert Murdoch	Wimbledon	1889-1892	Landscape	—	—	1	—	1	—	—	—	—	—	2
Wright, Robert W.	London	1871-1889	Domestic	—	—	8	—	37	—	—	—	—	4	49
Wright, S.	London	1842	Architecture	—	—	1	—	—	—	—	—	—	—	1
Wright, T.	Newark	1801-1842	Landscape	—	—	31	3	—	—	—	—	—	—	34
Wright, Thomas	London	1815-1848	Miniatures	—	—	14	—	—	—	—	—	—	6	20
Wright, T. T.	London	1815-1830	Domestic	—	—	11	—	10	—	—	—	—	—	21
Wright, W.	—	1844	Landscape	—	—	1	—	—	—	—	—	—	—	1
Wright, W.	—	1854	Architecture	—	—	1	—	—	—	—	—	—	—	1
Wright, W.	London	1834	Coast Scenes	—	—	—	—	2	—	—	—	—	—	2
Wright, William	London	1885-1893	Domestic	—	—	2	—	13	—	—	—	—	—	15
Wright, William	London	1893	Medals	—	—	2	—	—	—	—	—	—	—	2
Wright, William F.	London	1874-1879	Landscape	—	—	1	—	3	—	—	—	—	2	6
Wright, W. J.	London	1824-1825	Domestic	—	—	3	—	2	—	—	—	—	—	5
Wright, William P.	London	1882	Birds	—	—	—	—	1	—	—	—	—	—	1
Wright, William T.	Kettering	1890-1891	Landscape	—	—	—	—	—	—	2	—	—	—	2
Wright, Mrs.	London	1770	Needlework	1	—	—	—	—	—	—	—	—	—	1
Wright, Mrs.	London	1829	Landscape	—	—	1	—	—	—	—	—	—	—	1
Wright, Mrs.	London	1831-1832	Miniatures	—	—	4	—	—	—	—	—	—	—	4
Wright, Miss	London	1772-1773	Landscape	2	—	—	—	—	—	—	—	—	—	2
Wright-Nooth, W. *See* N.	—	—	—	—	—	—	—	—	—	—	—	—	—	—
Wrightman, Hatfield, and Goldie	Sheffield	1855	Architecture	—	—	1	—	—	—	—	—	—	—	1
Wroe, Mary McNicoll	Manchester	1881-1891	Flowers	—	—	—	—	1	—	—	—	—	1	2
Wroughton, Miss	London	1825-1829	Domestic	—	—	—	7	9	—	—	—	—	—	16
Wünnenberg, Carl	Rome	1878-1883	Figures	—	—	2	—	—	—	—	—	—	—	2
Würt, Van. *See* V.	—	—	—	—	—	—	—	—	—	—	—	—	—	—
Würt, Alen	London	1870	Landscape	—	—	—	—	—	—	—	—	—	1	1
Wurth, J. W.	London	1777	Sculpture	—	—	4	—	—	—	—	—	—	—	4
Wüst, A.	Antwerp	1874-1876	Moonlight	—	—	2	—	—	—	—	—	—	—	2
Wyatt, A. C.	London	1883-1892	Landscape	—	—	5	—	13	—	6	—	3	—	27
Wyatt, Benjamin Dean	London	1811-1812	Architecture	—	—	5	—	—	—	—	—	—	—	5
Wyatt, D.	London	1846-1850	Architecture	—	—	5	—	—	—	—	—	—	—	5
Wyatt, F.	London	1877	Rustic	—	—	—	—	2	—	—	—	—	—	2
Wyatt, G.	London	1798-1812	Architecture	—	—	10	—	—	—	—	—	—	—	10
Wyatt, G. P.	London	1808-1809	Architecture	—	—	2	—	—	—	—	—	—	—	2
Wyatt, H.	London	1806-1852	Architecture	—	—	11	—	—	—	—	—	—	—	11
Wyatt, Henry	London	1817-1838	Domestic	—	—	35	28	17	—	—	—	—	—	80
Wyatt, James, R.A.	London	1770-1799	Architecture	—	—	35	—	—	—	—	—	—	—	35
Wyatt, Jeffery, R.A. *See* Sir Jeffery Wyatville, R.A.	London	1786-1824	Architecture	—	—	82	—	—	—	—	—	—	—	82
Wyatt, J.	London	1838-1844	Sculpture	—	—	3	—	—	—	—	—	—	—	3
Wyatt, J.	London	1873	Miniatures	—	—	2	—	—	—	—	—	—	—	2
Wyatt, John Drayton	London	1852-1876	Architecture	—	—	29	—	1	—	—	—	—	—	30
Wyatt, Miss Katharine Montagu	London	1889-1893	Landscape	—	—	2	—	5	—	2	—	—	—	9
Wyatt, Matthew Cotes	Windsor	1800-1832	Sculpture	—	—	25	7	1	—	—	—	—	—	33
Wyatt, Sir Matthew Digby	London	1853-1874	Architecture	—	—	40	—	—	—	—	—	—	—	40
Wyatt, Philip W.	London	1814	Architecture	—	—	1	—	—	—	—	—	—	—	1
Wyatt, Richard James	London	1818-1850	Sculpture	—	—	24	—	—	—	—	—	—	—	24
Wyatt, T.	London	1797-1804	Landscape	—	—	3	—	—	—	—	—	—	—	3
Wyatt, Thomas Henry, F.S.A.	—	1835-1879	Architecture	—	—	31	—	—	—	—	—	—	—	31
Wyatt, William Lewis	London	1795-1827	Architecture	—	—	25	—	—	—	—	—	—	—	25
Wyatt, Miss	—	1791	Needlework	2	—	—	—	—	—	—	—	—	—	2
Wyatt and Brandon. *See also* Brandon and Wyatt	London	1840-1850	Architecture	—	—	23	—	—	—	—	—	—	—	23
Wyatt and Spiers	London	1886	Architecture	—	—	1	—	—	—	—	—	—	—	1
Wyatville, G. G.	—	1832	Architecture	—	—	1	—	—	—	—	—	—	—	1
Wyatville, Sir Jeffery, R.A. *See* Jeffery Wyatt, R.A.	London	1829-1839	Architecture	—	—	13	—	—	—	—	—	—	—	13
Wyburd, Francis John, R.B.A. §	London	1846-1893	Domestic	—	—	34	31	36	—	—	—	—	12	113
Wyburd, Mrs. Francis John	London	1883	Figures	—	—	—	—	—	—	1	—	—	—	1

Name.	Town.	First and Last Year of Ex.	Speciality.	S. A.	F. S.	R. A.	B. I.	S. S.	O. W.	N. W.	G. G.	N. G.	V. E.	Total.
Wyburd, Leonard	London	1879-1893	Domestic	—	—	5	—	8	—	9	—	—	3	25
Wyburd, Miss M.	London	1878	Figures	—	—	—	—	—	—	1	—	—	—	1
Wyld, William ‡	Paris	1849-1882	Landscape	—	—	3	5	—	—	206	—	—	—	214
Wyllie, Charlie William, R.B.A. § φ	London	1871-1893	Sea Pieces	—	—	32	—	68	—	5	2	7	27	141
Wyllie, Mrs. C., late Miss Charlotte Major	London	1872-1888	Figures	—	—	—	—	—	—	—	10	1	1	12
Wyllie, M. A.	London	1885	Domestic	—	—	—	—	1	—	—	—	—	—	1
Wyllie, William Lionel, A.R.A. R.I., ‡ § φ	London	1868-1893	Sea Pieces	—	—	54	—	71	—	35	6	—	44	210
Wyllie, William Morison	London	1852-1890	Domestic	—	—	22	8	28	—	—	1	1	37	97
Wyman, Miss Florence	London	1886-1889	Flowers	—	—	—	—	7	—	1	—	—	—	8
Wyman, Miss Violet H.	London	1888-1890	Domestic	—	—	—	—	8	—	—	—	—	1	9
Wymer, R. W.	London	1786	Landscape	—	—	2	—	—	—	—	—	—	—	2
Wyndham —	London	1775	Sculpture	1	—	—	—	—	—	—	—	—	—	1
Wyndham, Captain C.	London	1858-1874	Sculpture	—	—	—	—	3	—	—	—	—	2	5
Wyndham, M. E.	—	1830	Portraits	—	—	—	—	2	—	—	—	—	—	2
Wynfield, David Wilkie	London	1859-1887	Domestic	—	—	43	11	—	—	—	—	—	27	81
Wynn, M.	London	1811	Architecture	—	—	1	—	—	—	—	—	—	—	1
Wynne, J.	London	1812-1813	Architecture	—	—	2	—	—	—	—	—	—	—	2
Wynne, Richard	—	1775	Heads	1	—	—	—	—	—	—	—	—	—	1
Wynne, R. W.	London	1801-1814	Landscape	—	—	6	—	—	—	—	—	—	—	6
Wyon, Allan	London	1886-1891	Medals	—	—	5	—	—	—	—	—	—	—	5
Wyon, Alfred Benjamin	London	1857-1886	Medals	—	—	87	2	1	—	—	—	—	1	91
Wyon, Benjamin	London	1819-1860	Medals	—	—	54	—	—	—	—	—	—	—	54
Wyon, Edward William	London	1831-1876	Sculpture	—	—	94	—	8	—	—	—	—	—	102
Wyon, George W.	London	1856-1858	Medals	—	—	2	—	—	—	—	—	—	—	2
Wyon, H.	London	1855-1856	Medals	—	—	3	—	—	—	—	—	—	—	3
Wyon, Joseph Shepherd	London	1855-1886	Medals	—	—	72	—	—	—	—	—	—	—	72
Wyon, John W.	London	1862	Domestic	—	—	1	—	—	—	—	—	—	—	1
Wyon, Leonard Charles	London	1843-1860	Medals	—	—	23	—	—	—	—	—	—	—	23
Wyon, Thomas	London	1809-1812	Medals	—	—	6	—	—	—	—	—	—	—	6
Wyon, Thomas, Junr.	London	1809-1818	Medals	—	—	20	—	—	—	—	—	—	—	20
Wyon, William, R.A.	Birmingham	1812-1848	Medals	—	—	84	—	—	1	—	—	—	—	85
Wyon, Mrs. W. H.	London	1846	Miniatures	—	—	1	—	—	—	—	—	—	—	1
Wysmüller, J. H.	London	1879-1880	Landscape	—	—	2	—	1	—	—	—	—	—	3
Xavery, J.	Holland	1772-1789	Cattle	—	2	2	—	—	—	—	—	—	—	4
Yard, C.	Dublin	1848-1857	Sea Pieces	—	—	—	—	19	—	—	—	—	—	19
Yarnold, George B.	London	1874-1876	Landscape	—	—	2	—	3	—	—	—	—	—	5
Yarnold, J. W.	London	1839-1854	Sea Pieces	—	—	15	11	24	—	—	—	—	—	50
Yates, Miss Caroline Burland. *See* Mrs. T.	—	—	—	—	—	—	—	—	—	—	—	—	—	—
C. Gotch	London	1879-1887	Landscape	—	—	1	—	6	—	—	—	—	3	10
Yates, Fred.	London	1890-1893	Landscape	—	—	3	—	—	—	—	—	5	6	14
Yates, H.	Pembroke	1877	Landscape	—	—	1	—	—	—	—	—	—	—	1
Yates, Lieut. Thomas, R.N.	London	1788-1794	Sea Pieces	—	—	9	—	—	—	—	—	—	—	9
Yatman —	—	1762	Copies	2	—	—	—	—	—	—	—	—	—	2
Yeames, William Frederick, R.A.	London	1859-1893	Historical	—	—	75	6	1	—	—	1	—	20	103
Yeates, Mrs. A.	London	1857	Flowers	—	—	—	—	1	—	—	—	—	—	1
Yeates, Mrs. J. L.	—	1824-1825	Landscape	—	—	3	—	—	—	—	—	—	—	3
Yeatherd —	London	1795	Portraits	—	—	1	—	—	—	—	—	—	—	1
Yeats, John Butler, R.H.A.	London	1879-1887	Figures	—	—	2	—	1	—	—	—	—	8	11
Yeats, Miss Nelly H.	Malvern	1887	Flowers	—	—	1	—	—	—	—	—	—	—	1
Yelf. *See* Searle, Son, and Yelf.	—	—	—	—	—	—	—	—	—	—	—	—	—	—
Yellowlees, W.	London	1829-1845	Portraits	—	—	20	—	—	—	—	—	—	—	20
Yenn, John, R.A.	London	1771-1797	Architecture	—	—	34	—	—	—	—	—	—	—	34
Yeo, Richard, R.A.	London	1760-1770	Medals	17	—	3	—	—	—	—	—	—	—	20
Yeoville, H. R.	Birmingham	1856	Architecture	—	—	1	—	—	—	—	—	—	—	1
Yetts, Miss E. M.	Homerton	1857	Landscape	—	—	—	1	1	—	—	—	—	—	2
Yetts, W.	Grt. Yarmouth	1845	Landscape	—	—	—	—	2	—	—	—	—	—	2
Yewell, G. H.	Rome	1877	Cairo	—	—	—	—	—	—	—	—	—	1	1
Yglesaias, Vincent Philip, R.B.A. §	London	1873-1893	River Scenes	—	—	23	—	127	—	—	1	—	14	165
Yglesias, Mrs. V. P. (Edith)	London	1890	Flowers	—	—	—	—	1	—	—	—	—	—	1
Ylasse, E.	London	1868	Figures	—	—	1	—	—	—	—	—	—	—	1
Yon, E.	Paris	1881	Landscape	—	—	—	—	—	—	—	2	—	—	2
Yonge, Arthur D.	Hastings	1876-1890	Landscape	—	—	3	—	—	—	—	—	—	5	8
Yorke, Hon. Mrs.	—	1771-1774	Cattle	4	—	—	—	—	—	—	—	—	—	4
Young —	Bristol	1767-1783	Miniatures	5	1	—	—	—	—	—	—	—	—	6
Young, Alexander	London	1889-1893	Landscape	—	—	5	—	—	—	—	—	—	—	5
Young, Arthur	London	1891-1893	Architecture	—	—	3	—	—	—	—	—	—	—	3
Young, A. D.	London	1891	Landscape	—	—	—	—	1	—	—	—	—	—	1
Young, B.	London	1850	Buildings	—	—	—	—	3	—	—	—	—	—	3

Name.	Town.	First and Last Year of Ex.	Speciality.	S. A.	F. S.	R. A.	B. I.	S. S.	O. W.	N.W.	G. G.	N. G.	V. E.	Total.
YOUNG, COLONEL C. B.	London	1870	Interiors	—	—	—	—	1	—	—	—	—	—	1
YOUNG, C. E.	London	1877	Landscape	—	—	—	—	—	—	—	—	—	1	1
YOUNG, MISS EMMELINE	Huddersfield	1874-1889	Figures	—	—	3	—	3	—	—	—	—	—	6
YOUNG, MISS FRANCES	London	1855-1874	Domestic	—	—	2	4	9	—	—	—	—	1	16
YOUNG, GEORGE	London	1861	Landscape	—	—	—	—	—	—	—	—	—	1	1
YOUNG, GODFREY	London	1872-1885	Sea Pieces	—	—	1	—	—	—	1	—	—	—	2
YOUNG, G. A.	London	1849	Architecture	—	—	2	—	—	—	—	—	—	—	2
YOUNG, H.	—	1832	Buildings	—	—	—	—	—	—	1	—	—	—	1
YOUNG, H. H.	Horsham	1885	Landscape	—	—	1	—	—	—	—	—	—	—	1
YOUNG, JOHN	London	1794	Engraving	—	—	2	—	—	—	—	—	—	—	2
YOUNG, J.	London	1851-1852	Figures	—	—	—	3	—	—	—	—	—	—	3
YOUNG, J. T.	London	1811-1822	Landscape	—	—	3	—	—	—	—	—	—	—	3
YOUNG, KEITH DOWNES. *See also* Hall and Young	London	1877-1892	Architecture	—	—	2	—	—	—	—	—	—	—	2
YOUNG, MISS LILIAN	London	1884-1890	Domestic	—	—	5	—	4	—	3	—	—	—	12
YOUNG, MISS MAGGIE F.	London	1889-1890	Flowers	—	—	—	—	4	—	—	—	—	4	8
YOUNG, MISS M. J.	London	1888-1892	Domestic	—	—	—	—	4	—	—	—	—	—	4
YOUNG, O. A.	London	1890	Domestic	—	—	—	—	—	—	—	—	1	—	1
YOUNG, R.	London	1816	Portraits	—	—	1	—	—	—	—	—	—	—	1
YOUNG, R. H.	London	1885	Landscape	—	—	—	—	1	—	—	—	—	—	1
YOUNG, STANLEY S.	London	1890	Domestic	—	—	1	—	—	—	—	—	—	—	1
YOUNG, TOBIAS	London	1821	Landscape	—	—	—	2	—	—	—	—	—	—	2
YOUNG, WILLIAM §	London	1828	Architecture	—	—	—	—	1	—	—	—	—	—	1
YOUNG, WILLIAM	London	1833-1893	Architecture	—	—	27	—	—	—	—	—	—	—	27
YOUNG, WILLIAM, R.S.W.	Glasgow	1874-1884	Landscape	—	—	3	—	1	—	—	—	—	—	4
YOUNG, MISS	—	1773	Flowers	—	1	—	—	—	—	—	—	—	—	1
YOUNG AND HALL. *See also* Hall and Young	London	1893	Architecture	—	—	1	—	—	—	—	—	—	—	1
YOUNGE, H.	London	1832	Buildings	—	—	1	—	1	—	—	—	—	—	2
YOUNGMAN, MISS ANNIE M., R.I. ‡ ‖	London	1877-1893	Landscape	—	—	6	—	8	—	35	1	—	7	57
YOUNGMAN, JOHN M. ‡	Saffron Walden	1834-1882	Landscape	—	—	24	1	—	—	110	—	—	3	138
YOUNGS, LAURENCE	London	1888	Architecture	—	—	1	—	1	—	—	—	—	—	2
YSENBURG, COUNT C.	London	1892	Domestic	—	—	—	—	3	—	—	—	—	—	3
YUNGE, G.	London	1855	Figures	—	—	1	—	—	—	—	—	—	—	1
YVON, ADOLPHE	Paris	1851-1874	Figures	—	—	6	—	—	—	—	—	—	—	6
ZACHO, CHRISTIAN	Copenhagen	1892	Landscape	—	—	1	—	—	—	—	—	—	—	1
ZAHNER, RUDOLF	London	1860	Landscape	—	—	2	—	—	—	—	—	—	—	2
ZAHNER, S.	London	1855	Landscape	—	—	1	—	—	—	—	—	—	—	1
ZAMBACO, MADAME M. T.	London	1886-1888	Sculpture	—	—	5	—	—	—	—	—	—	—	5
ZAMBONI, COUNT G.	Florence	1869	Landscape	—	—	1	—	—	—	—	—	—	—	1
ZANNONI, U.	Milan	1872-1875	Sculpture	—	—	3	—	—	—	—	—	—	—	3
ZEEBROS —	London	1783	Domestic	—	1	—	—	—	—	—	—	—	—	1
ZEER —	—	1783	Landscape	—	1	—	—	—	—	—	—	—	—	1
ZEIGLER —	—	1768	Miniatures	—	1	—	—	—	—	—	—	—	—	1
ZEITTER, JOHN CHRISTIAN §	London	1824-1862	Domestic	—	—	7	38	291	—	—	—	—	—	336
ZELENSKI, A.	London	1852	Domestic	—	—	2	—	—	—	—	—	—	—	2
ZELL, BEATRICE	Manchester	1880	Fruit	—	—	—	—	1	—	—	—	—	—	1
ZEUNER —	London	1778	Glass Painting	2	—	—	—	—	—	—	—	—	—	2
ZEZZOS, A.	Edinburgh	1889-1890	Figures	—	—	1	—	—	—	2	—	—	—	3
ZICHY, M.	St. Petersburg	1873	Deer Stalking	—	—	10	—	—	—	—	—	—	—	10
ZIEGLER, E.	London	1843-1852	Figures	—	—	6	4	6	—	—	—	—	—	16
ZIEGLER, HENRY BRYAN	London	1814-1874	Domestic	—	—	69	70	60	26	—	—	—	—	225
ZIEGLER, MISS	London	1844-1863	Figures	—	—	13	—	11	—	—	—	—	—	24
ZILERI, MISS S.	London	1887-1888	Fruit	—	—	1	—	—	—	—	—	—	1	2
ZIMMERMANN, ERNEST	Munich	1881-1887	Domestic	—	—	2	—	—	—	—	—	—	—	2
ZIMMERMAN, HENRY, R.B.A. §	Blackheath	1871-1889	Landscape	—	—	4	—	49	—	—	1	—	8	62
ZINK, GEORGE FREDERICK	Kilburn	1882-1893	Miniatures	—	—	23	—	5	—	6	—	—	—	34
ZO, ACHILLE	Bayonne	1882	Portraits	—	—	1	—	—	—	—	—	—	—	1
ZOBEL, GEORGE J.	London	1833-1879	Engraving	—	—	35	—	3	—	3	—	—	—	41
ZOBLE, B.	London	1798	Cattle	—	—	2	—	—	—	—	—	—	—	2
ZOFFANI, JOHANN, R.A.	London	1762-1800	Portraits	29	1	42	—	—	—	—	—	—	—	72
ZONA, A.	London	1874	Figures	—	—	1	—	—	—	—	—	—	—	1
ZORN, ANDREW LEON	London	1883-1893	Domestic	—	—	12	—	—	—	7	—	—	1	20
ZORNLIN, MISS G. M.	London	1825-1847	Landscape	—	—	1	—	2	—	—	—	—	—	3
ZUBER, JEAN HENRI	London	1884	Landscape	—	—	2	—	—	—	—	—	—	—	2
ZUCCARELLI, FRANCESCO, R.A.	Woolwich	1765-1782	Landscape	3	4	9	—	—	—	—	—	—	—	16
ZUCCHI, ANTONIO, A.R.A.	—	1770-1783	Mythological	—	1	6	—	—	—	—	—	—	—	7
ZUCCOLI, LUIGI	London	1864-1871	Domestic	—	—	5	—	—	—	—	—	—	—	5
ZULOAGA, IGNACIO	—	1893	Portraits	—	—	—	—	—	—	—	—	—	1	1
ZWECKER, T. B.	London	1853-1872	Figures	—	—	2	4	1	—	—	—	—	3	10
ZWESCHERI, GUISI	London	1880	Figures	—	—	—	—	—	—	—	—	—	2	2